Settlement and Economy in Italy
1500 BC – AD 1500

Papers of the Fifth Conference of Italian Archaeology

Edited by Neil Christie

Oxbow Monograph 41
1995

Published by
Oxbow Books, Park End Place, Oxford, OX1 1HN

© Oxbow Books and the individual authors 1995

ISBN 0 946897 89 1

This book is available direct from
Oxbow Books, Park End Place, Oxford, OX1 1HN
(Phone: 01865-241249; Fax: 01865-794449)

or

The David Brown Book Company
PO Box 511, Oakville, CT 06779
(Phone: 860-945-9329; Fax: 860-945-9468)

Printed in Great Britain by
The Short Run Press, Exeter

Contents

Introduction vii

PART I: FIELD SURVEYS – METHODOLOGIES AND RESULTS

1. Landscape archaeology in Italy – Goals for the 1990s *Graeme Barker* 1
2. Alto-Medio Polesine – Basso Veronese Project: From 'Landscape Archaeology' to 'Archaeology of the Mind' *Armando De Guio* 13
3. All or nothing at all? Criteria for the analysis of pottery from surface survey *Alison Macdonald* 25
4. Survey methodology and the site: a Roman villa from the Rieti survey *D. J. Mattingly & S. Coccia* 31
5. Attività del Centro di Documentazione della Regione Lazio *L. Ramelli di Celle* 45
6. Preliminary results of the Malafede Survey *A. Arnoldus-Huyzendveld, P. Gioia, M. Mineo & P. Pascucci* 47
7. Ricognizioni nelle valli del Tevere del Farfa: indagini sulle evidenze pre-protostoriche e arcaiche *Clarissa Belardelli* 57
8. Ricognizioni archeologiche nell'Ager Caeretanus (1990–92) *Flavio Enei* 63

PART 2: RELIGION AND RITUAL

9. From secret society to state religion: ritual and social organisation in pre- and protohistoric Italy *Ruth D. Whitehouse* 83
10. Analisi delle strutture tombali in Etruria nel bronzo finale *Laura Domanico* 89
11. Analisi delle strutture tombali in Etruria nell'età del ferro: le tombe ad incinerazione *Massimo Cardosa* 99
12. Ricerca e tesaurizzazione delle offerte negli edifici cultuali della Sardegna nuragica: nota preliminare *Maria Ausilia Fadda* 111
13. Evidence of households or of ritual meals? *M. Maaskant-Kleibrink* 123
14. Emblems of identity. An examination of the use of matt-painted pottery in the native tombs of the Salento peninsula in the 5th and 4th centuries BC *Edward Herring* 135
15. Il Santuario di Diana a Nemi (RM): nuove ricerche *Giuseppina Ghini* 143
16. I luoghi della penitenza: strategie di insediamenti dei complessi menidicanti femminili *Monica G. Sorti* 155

PART 3: SETTLEMENT AND ECONOMY

17. Economie di allevamento in Italia centrale dalla media età del bronzo alla fine dell'età del ferro *Jacopo De Grossi Mazzorin* 167

18. Le attività agricole delle comunità nuragiche nel centro Sardegna: dati archeologici e considerazioni socio-economici   *Mario Asole, Alba Foschi Nieddu & Francesco Nieddu* 179

19. The economy of an early Latin settlement, Borgo Le Ferriere-*Satricum*, 800–200 BC
   J. W. Bouma, P.A.J. Attema, A. J. Beijer, A. J. Nijboer & R.A. Olde Dubbelink 183

20. Storia di un trattruo   *Emanuella Fabbricotti* 197

21. Evoluzione dell'insediamento e dell'economia nella Sabina in età romana   *Giovanna Alvino & Tersilio Leggio* 201

22. Paesaggio agrario e produzioni artigianali nell'Etruria settentrionale costiera (ager Pisanus e Volaterranus)   *Marianella Pasquinucci & Simonetta Menchelli* 209

23. L'area del Soratte: un essempio di modellamento territoriale monastico   *Stefania Fidanza* 219

PART 4: SETTLEMENT AND SOCIETY

24. L'abitato di Torre Mordillo nel quadro dello sviluppo dell'insediamento protostorico nell'alto Ionio (Sibartide)   *L. Arancio, V. Buffa, I. Damiani, F. Trucco, A. Tagliacozzo & L. Vagnetti* 227

25. Siti costieri dal bronzo medio al bronzo finale nella Calabria centro-orientale
   Domenico Marino & Silvia Festuccia 241

26. Note sulla società della Sardegna nuragica e sulla funzione dei nuraghi   *Alessandro Usai* 253

27. Grave dimensions as a diagnostic tool for palaeodemography and social ranking. The example of Veio-Quattro Fontanili   *Wolf-Rüdiger Teegen* 261

28. Human skeletal remains from the pre-colonial Greek emporium of Pithekoussai on Ischia: Culture contact in the early VIII to the II century BC   *Marshall J. Becker* 273

29. Gentes romane dei Monti della Tolfa   *Enrico Benelli* 283

30. La villa romana di Marina di S. Nicola a Ladispoli   *Ida Caruso* 291

31. La villa romana in località Selvicciola (Ischia di Castro)   *Gianfranco Gazzetti* 297

32. The evolution of rural settlement in *regiones* V and VI from the Roman to the early medieval period   *Umberto Moscatelli* 303

33. Late antique cavemen in northern and central Italy   *Neil Christie* 311

34. L'Abruzzo fra la tarda antichità e l'altomedioevo   *Andrea Staffa* 317

35. Considerazioni intorno alle valutazioni demografiche di Paolo Diacono sul *Samnium*
   G. De Benedittis 331

PART 5: NEW RESEARCH IN SOUTH ETRURIA

36. Nuove acquisizioni sulla protostoria dell'Etruria Meridionale   *V. D'Ercole & F. Trucco* 341

37. The role of interregional contact in the development of Latial society in the Early Iron Age
   Anna Maria Bietti Sestieri 353

38. Contatti fra Etruria e Lazio antico alla fine dell'VIII secolo a.C.: la tomba di guerriero di Osteria dell'Osa   *Anna De Santis* 365

39. Nuovi elementi nello studio del ponte romano sul Fosso di Tre Ponti   *Vincenzo Antonelli* 377

40. Considerazioni sugli insediamenti in area falisca   *G. Cifani & M. Munzi* 387

41. Ricognizioni nell'Ager Faliscus meridionale   *A. Camilli, L. Carta, T. Conti, A. De Laurenzi & M. De Simone* 395

42. Nuove ricerche nell'agro capenate   *A. Camilli & B. Vitali Rosati* 403

43. Notizie preliminare sulle ricognizioni nel territorio di Capena   *Rita Turchetti & Fabio Bartolini* 413

44. La necropoli della Via Amerina a *Falerii Novi*   *L. Caretta, G. Innocenti, A. Prisco & P. Rossi* 421

45. Reconstructing a gateway city: the place of Nepi in the study of south-eastern Etruria
   C. Edwards, C. Malone & S. Stoddart 431

46. I possedimenti del monastero di S. Paolo f.l.m. (Roma) in Etruria Meridionale: indagine preliminare
    L. De Maria, F. Fei, R. Martorelli & A. Toro 441

PART 6: URBANISM

47. L'area sud occidentale del Palatino dai primi insediamenti all'età media repubblicana
    P. Pensabene, O. Colazingari, L. Borrello, P. Battistelli & S. Falzone 455
48. *Mediolanum* dall'*oppidum* celtico alla città romana   *Anna Ceresa Mori* 465
49. Staties/Statonia   *Gilda Bartolini* 477
50. Modelli d'insediamento della romanizzazione nell'Ager Gallicus e Picenus   *Mario Luni* 483
51. La nascita della città in Abruzzo: tradizioni, insediamenti e nuovi modelli (IV–I sec. a.C.)
    Adele Campanelli 493
52. Incastellamento urbano a Roma: il caso degli Orsini   *Francesca Bosman* 499

PART 7: TECHNOLOGY AND TRADE

53. Aspetti della metallurgia nell'Italia continentale tra XVI e XI secolo a.C.: produzione e relazioni
    interregionali tra area centrale tirrenica e area settentrionale   *Enrico Pellegrini* 511
54. La ricostruzione grafica di alcune strutture residenziali e di servizio in Etruria: problemi e metodi
    M. Miari 521
55. Industry and technology at Borgo Le Ferriere-*Satricum*, 700–300 BC   *Albert Nijboer* 531
56. Archeologia delle miniere: note sul rapporto tra insediamenti e mineralizzazioni in Italia centrale
    Andrea Zifferero 541
57. The supply of building materials to the city of Rome   *Janet DeLaine* 555
58. Un impianto per la produzione della calce presso *Lucus Feroniae* (Roma)   *Sergio Fontana* 563
59. La sigillata adriatica in Italia   *Gina Martella* 571
60. La ceramica a pareti sottili grigie in Italia   *Oliva Menozzi* 579
61. La ceramica comune nei siti dell'Italia settentrionale dall'età tardo antica al medioevo:
    variazioni tipologiche e funzionali del corredo domestico   *L. Maffeis & M.M. Negro Ponzi Mancini* 591
62. Produzione e distribuzione dei denari suevi e angioini nel regno di Sicilia alla luce dei rinvenimenti
    Lucia Travaini 603

Introduction

Neil Christie

These two volumes contain the majority of those papers and posters presented at the *Fifth Conference of Italian Archaeology* held in Oxford from 11–13 December, 1992. This was the latest in a series of occasional conferences held in England dedicated to the results of recent archaeological and related research on the development of pre-industrial Italy. The first of these conferences was held in Lancaster in 1977; the fourth took place in London with the Accordia Research Centre at Queen Mary and Westfield College in January 1990.

The Fifth Conference was hosted by the Department for Continuing Education at Rewley House in the University of Oxford, with alternative sessions held also at the Institute of Archaeology on Beaumont Street. Each of these institutions and their staff assisted enormously in the preparation and functioning of what was a very smooth running conference. Over one hundred and thirty people attended the *Fifth Conference of Italian Archaeology*, and out of these seventy people presented papers or posters. A high proportion of participants was of course Italian, but it was pleasing to see a strong contingent of British academics plus a number of scholars from Holland, Germany, Scandinavia and America. Space in fact prevented an even higher attendance. The busy bar and coffee lounges and the difficulty of jostling people back into lecture rooms indicated clearly the very healthy interaction and debate between participants! Despite this timetables functioned very well and most speakers commendably kept to time – due of course in no small part to the efficiency of the Chairpeople at the various sessions. The Chairpeople comprised the members of the Conference Committee, plus Dr Bryan Ward-Perkins, who kindly assisted at short notice. Members of the Committee also performed in the Plenary Overview Session at the end of the conference, with special mention to go to Dr Tim Potter who provided a typically buoyant contribution.

Within the board theme of the Oxford conference – *Settlement and Economy, 1500 BC–AD 1500* – the seventy papers presented covered a very wide range of topics, ranging from urbanism to rural settlement, to ritual activity and monastic strategies, to cemetery studies and ceramic manufacture, to Roman lime production and medieval mints. As far as possible the conference sessions have been maintained as sections within these volumes. The headings cannot of course be rigid, as many contributors have since sought to fit more fully into the overall theme of the conference. Taken as a whole, the papers can be seen to reflect the very healthy state of Italian archaeology, with research branching out on various fronts, and in all periods, with particular new emphasis on economic and industrial issues. At the same time, field survey retains its strength as the prime contributor of data, perpetually overturning previous concepts of land-use and of the scale and range of settlement activity. It is hoped of course that the *Fifth Conference of Italian Archaeology* and the publication of its many papers will help further stimulate this research activity.

All contributors to this publication are to be praised for their patience in the production of these proceedings and in accepting (on occasions) heavy editing of their papers; likewise all participants at the conference in Oxford are thanked for their support, encouragement and satisfaction. On the organisational side, extensive thanks go to Maggie Herdman and Rosemary Cottis of the Department of Continuing Education at Oxford University for their efficient administration of the conference bookings, publicity, accommodation, etc.; and to the brave group of volunteers of undergraduates and graduates from the Institute of Archaeology for ushering and projecting duties. Dr Stefano Coccia assisted admirably in acting as the chief co-ordinator in Italy.

Full acknowledgement is here given for grants for the conference generously provided by the British Academy (providing funds for travel grants for three Italian academics), the British Council (providing a grant for the conference fees of three young Italian speakers), the Dr M. Aylwin Cotton Foundation and the Hulme University Fund (both providing grants towards the costs of the reception at the Ashmolean Museum). In addition, the British Academy very generously contributed a grant to assist in meeting the costs of this substantial publication.

Finally, thanks are extended to Gabriela Canseco at Oxbow Books for coping so admirably with the production of the conference proceedings, and to my wife Jane for enduring my late-night editing sessions.

Bibliography

Blake, H. Mk., Potter, T.W. & Whitehouse, D.B. (eds.) 1978. *Papers in Italian Archaeology I. The Lancaster Seminar*. British Archeological Reports, Supplementary Series 41, 2 vols., Oxford.

Barker, G. & Hodges, R. (eds.) 1981. *Archaeology and Italian Society. Prehistoric, Roman and Medieval Studies (Papers in Italian Archaeology II)*, British Archaeological Reports, International Series 102, Oxford.

Malone, C. & Stoddart, S. (eds.) 1985. *Papers in Italian Archaeology IV. The Cambridge Conference*, British Archaeological Reports, International Series 243, 244, 245, 246, 4 vols., Oxford.

Herring, E., Whitehouse, R. & Wilkins, J. (eds.) 1991. *Papers of the Fourth Conference of Italian Archaeology. The Archaeology of Power, Parts 1 and 2*, Accordia Research Centre, 2 vols., London.

Herring, E., Whitehouse, R. & Wilkins, J. (eds.) 1992. *Papers of the Fourth Conference of Italian Archaeology. New Developments in Italian Archaeology, Parts 1 and 2,* Accordia Research Centre, 2 vols., London.

Conference Committee

Prof. Graeme Barker
Amanda Claridge
Dr John Lloyd
Dr Paul Roberts

Dr Neil Christie
Dr Stefano Coccia
Philip Perkins
Dr Ruth Whitehouse

PART 1

Field Surveys – Methodologies and Results

1

Landscape Archaeology in Italy – Goals for the 1990s

GRAEME BARKER

(School of Archaeological Studies, University of Leicester)

Summary: *This paper summarises the principal achievements of landscape archaeology in Italy over the past two decades, discusses the strengths and weaknesses of current methodologies and highlights some of the more significant issues needing clarification. Field survey methodologies are steadily improving, but are still failing to fulfil their potential in measuring human settlement history and its relationship to landscape. Appropriate methodologies need to be developed for those parts of the landscape unsuitable for fieldwalking. Integrated methodologies applied at the regional scale will be essential to make significant progress on one of the most critical problems, as first identified by Vita-Finzi, namely the alternative roles of climate and people in shaping the landscape.*

INTRODUCTION

The purpose of this paper is to review the principal achievements of landscape archaeology in Italy over the past two decades, discuss the strengths and weaknesses of current methodologies, and highlight some of the more significant issues needing clarification in the coming years. The most important of the archaeological methodologies of landscape analysis in Italy as elsewhere in the Mediterranean has been systematic field-walking. As I describe in the following section, recent results are impressive; however, although analytical techniques are steadily improving, many regional survey projects are still failing to fulfil their potential in measuring human settlement history. Appropriate methodologies also need to be developed for those parts of the landscape unsuitable for field-walking. Integrated methodologies applied at the regional scale will be essential if we are to make significant progress on perhaps the most critical problem of all, the role of human settlement and land use in shaping the Mediterranean landscape.

THE ACHIEVEMENTS OF FIELD SURVEY

Until recently many ancient historians tended to emphasise the nucleated settlement as the dominant feature of the classical landscape: as Finley (1977: 305) commented, "the Graeco-Roman world was a world of cities". Over the past three decades, however, archaeology has provided spectacular evidence for a wealth and diversity of rural settlement in classical times that were entirely unsuspected from the written sources – what John Lloyd (1991a: 238) describes as "the busy countryside". The evidence for this has been provided by systematic 'field survey' or 'field walking' (Barker & Lloyd 1991).

In Italy, where large areas of the landscape are under the plough today, field survey has provided critical information on the nature and density of rural settlement in Roman times, not simply for the 'heartland' areas of the western lowlands of central Italy north and south of Rome which are quite extensively described by the ancient writers, but also for many other regions for which the documentary record is minimal or rudimentary (Fig. 1). The density of Roman settlement on the lowlands indicated by field surveys such as in Tuscany (Albegna valley: Attolini *et al.* 1991; Dyson 1978), Lazio (Tuscania: Barker *et al.* 1993; Barker & Rasmussen 1988; Rasmussen 1991; Ager Veientanus: Potter, 1979; Ward-Perkins *et al.* 1968; Liri valley: Wightman 1981), Campania (Ager Falernus: Arthur 1991) and Molise (lower Biferno valley: Barker *et al.* 1978; Lloyd & Barker 1981; Lloyd, forthcoming a and b) is everywhere remarkable, ranging between 1.5 and 3+ sites per square kilometre (Table 1). Conditions for survey are generally less favourable away from the coastal lowlands as topography gets more rugged and areas of woodland and pasture increase, but survey at intermediate altitudes in Liguria (Luni: Ward-Perkins *et al.* 1986), inland Tuscany (Montarrenti: Barker *et al.* 1986) and Sabina (Farfa: Moreland 1986, 1987;

	Sites per km²
LOWLANDS	
Tuscania	3
Albegna valley	3
South Etruria	2
Rieti basin	2
Farfa (Tiber terraces)	1.5
Liri valley	1.5
Ager Falernus	1.5
Lower Biferno valley	1.5
INTERMEDIATE	
Montarrenti	1
Farfa (Sabine hills)	.3
Luni	.3
UPLAND	
Cicolano mountains	.2 to .1
Upper Biferno valley	.3 to .1
San Giovanni	.3 to .1

Table 1. Roman Italy: settlement densities indicated by archaeological surveys. (References to the projects are given in the text)

Rieti: Coccia & Mattingly 1992) has produced densities of .5–2 sites per square kilometre and in the mountain zone in Lazio (Cicolano mountains: Barker & Grant 1991), Molise (upper Biferno valley: Lloyd 1991b) and Basilicata (San Giovanni: Small 1991) of 1 site per 3/10 square kilometres. In terms of site morphology, these surveys indicate an extraordinary diversity of rural settlement forms in Roman Italy including villages, hamlets, sanctuaries, industrial sites, farms of different size and wealth, cottages and huts.

Some historians have argued that the archaeological surveys simply confirm known historical trends, pointing in particular to evidence produced by many lowland surveys for the growth of villa estates at the expense of smaller agricultural enterprises. However, the settlement systems and trends being revealed by these surveys, particularly where they have been part of integrated programmes of landscape analysis which have included excavation of different kinds of sites, can be shown to reflect a complex interplay between factors operating at the local, regional and Mediterranean-wide scale,

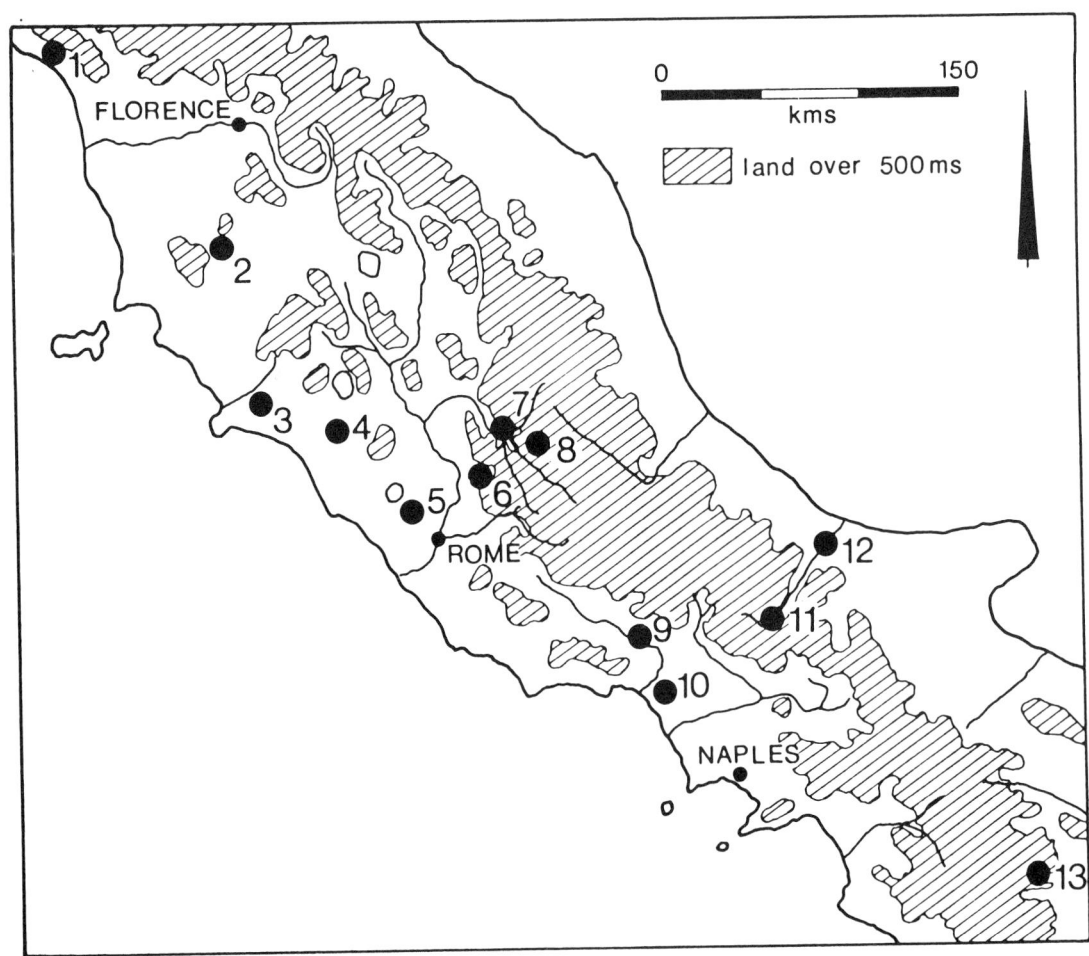

Fig. 1. Central and southern Italy, showing the archaeological surveys mentioned in the text (see also Table 1): 1. Luni; 2. Montarrenti; 3. Albegna valley/Ager Cosanus; 4. Tuscania; 5. south Etruria/Ager Veientanus; 6. Farfa; 7. Rieti basin; 8. Cicolano mountains; 9. Liri valley; 10. Ager Falernus; 11. upper Biferno valley; 12. lower Biferno valley; 13. San Giovanni.

many of which cannot be discerned from the historical sources (Lloyd 1991a). At one level they were adaptations to different environments, just as farming varies today between South Etruria and the Cicolano mountains. At the second level, they also reflect social and economic structures operating at the regional scale: the settlement patterns of South Etruria in many ways mirror the changing fortunes of Rome (Potter 1979), whilst in the upper Biferno valley the agricultural economy reflected above all the ambitions of the local elite (Lloyd 1991b). However, they also mirror the changing fortunes of the Italian economy within the empire, with consistent evidence for drastic changes to the landscape as cities such as Rome were supplied by cheaper foodstuffs produced outside Italy.

Field survey:
problems and further potential

Whilst the achievements of field survey in documenting the classical landscape in Italy are impressive, to some extent they are the predictable outcome of a number of positive advantages in the database (Barker 1991). The classical rural population was abundant, and tended to live in dispersed rather than nucleated settlements, especially in the lowland areas extensively cultivated today. For the most part farmers lived in substantial buildings made of materials such as brick and tile which survive today. They used pottery which was mass-produced and of high quality which is durable and, in the case of fine wares at least, capable of quite precise dating.

The failure of field survey to locate Italian early medieval settlement effectively is in turn the predictable outcome of a combination of negative factors. The population was much less abundant, tended to live in nucleated settlements, and particularly in hilltop locations which are frequently forested today. Many of their habitations were of wood, much of their pottery was poorly made, and is difficult to date. The principal way early medieval settlements have been investigated successfully by recent landscape surveys, for example in the Cicolano (Beavitt & Christie 1992), Farfa (Moreland 1986, 1987), Rieti (Coccia & Mattingly 1992), San Vincenzo (Hodges 1981) and Tuscania (Barker *et al.* 1993) projects, has been by first pin-pointing locations – usually densely forested hills – on the basis of documentary research and then excavating a series of test pits in the search for habitation evidence. Regional studies investigating prehistoric settlement have also had to define particular 'geomorphological windows' within the landscape offering the best potential for exposing occupation debris of the period or periods of interest, in recognition of the likelihood that most of this archaeology has been deeply buried by alluviation or carried away by erosion (Ammerman 1985; Balista & Leonardi, 1985; Cremaschi & Christopher 1985; Cremaschi *et al.* 1980).

In addition to these problems of differential 'archaeological visibility', survey archaeologists are also having to deal with factors of bias produced by the kind of regional sampling system adopted. In almost all cases resources do not permit the whole of the region to be investigated, so it has to be sampled. In Italy as elsewhere in recent years, a variety of regional sampling strategies has been employed in surveys, mostly involving random or systematic samples of quadrats or transects designed to provide a representative sample of the total surface material.

The experience of the Tuscania Survey, however, provides a cautionary tale for those arguing for a single 'correct' sampling strategy. We deliberately employed three different strategies in order to compare results: a transect sample of 40 kms^2, a random sample of 40 kms^2, and a judgemental sample of 20 kms^2 (Fig. 2). According to the first, the Etruscan landscape consisted of a cluster of small farms forming an agricultural enclave extending from the Etruscan town for some 5–6 kilometres (Barker 1988). According to the second, the landscape appeared more as a series of enclaves both round the town and elsewhere in the surrounding countryside, with indications of a rural hierarchy of hamlets and small farms. The third sample, and the composite sample, confirmed the importance of the main cluster around Tuscania and the existence of outlying clusters with local centres. It is to be hoped that other regional surveys likewise adopt flexible systems of sampling to interpret the landscape interactively as theory and data develop through the project.

The field recording sheets used by surveys increasingly reflect our awareness of the potential biases caused by changing conditions of light, weather, vegetation, team ability and so on. However, there is little evidence yet available that we are proceeding beyond qualitative awareness to the ability to measure potential bias quantitatively. Survey archaeologists frequently cite the repeatability of survey as a major advantage of this approach compared with excavation, yet there are very few examples of survey archaeologists actually repeating survey at the regional scale to test the validity of their data. One example is the Montarrenti survey near Siena, where in the Val di Rosia we used the same techniques of survey with different teams each year for five years (Barker *et al.* 1986). In this experiment most individual 'sites' and 'off-site' scatters were found each year but there were also some significant absences: one Etruscan site, for example, was only found in the first year, but the field then reverted to fallow for the rest of the study period and the site stayed invisible. However, the most significant result of the experiment was that, whilst individual sites came and went, the landscape models that could be constructed from each year's survey data for the prehistoric, Etruscan, Roman and medieval periods stayed essentially the same. But it was a small experiment and it needs to be repeated, especially in one of the lowland areas which have been the focus for most major surveys in Italy.

In recent years, survey archaeologists have become increasingly aware that an ancient landscape, no more than a modern one, does not consist of 'islands' of habitation surrounded by empty spaces (Foley 1981; Haselgrove *et al.* 1985). As well as 'sites' (the concentrations of artifacts assumed to be settlements) we have to recognise the importance of 'off-site' archaeology (distributions of sporadic or thinly scattered material across the landscape), not only for understanding the prehistoric periods – when many activities such as hunting and herding created such material – but also for the classical and later periods (Bintliff & Snodgrass 1988; Cherry *et al.* 1992). It has been better recorded and studied in temperate regions such as Britain, where surveys are generally smaller and more intensive, and the surface artifact record less abundant, than in the Mediterranean. In the Boeotia Survey in Greece, however, the density of occupation within urban sites and the intensity of land use around rural sites was mapped, the latter on the assumption that the 'off-site' spreads around the assumed focus of habitation represent ancient manuring practices and are thus an indication of the extent of cultivated land (Bintliff 1991). In the Tuscania Survey, the changing distributions and quantities of off-site data provide clear evidence for the expansion of rural settlement and land use from the Etruscan to the Roman periods (Barker *et al.* 1993). In the Montarrenti survey, changing spreads of material round two farms of medieval origin provided useful evidence for changing intensities of land use, particularly the transformation in the extent and intensity of cultivation in the seventeenth and eighteenth centuries (Fig. 3).

However, it remains true that the importance of this kind of material as a sensitive indicator of landscape

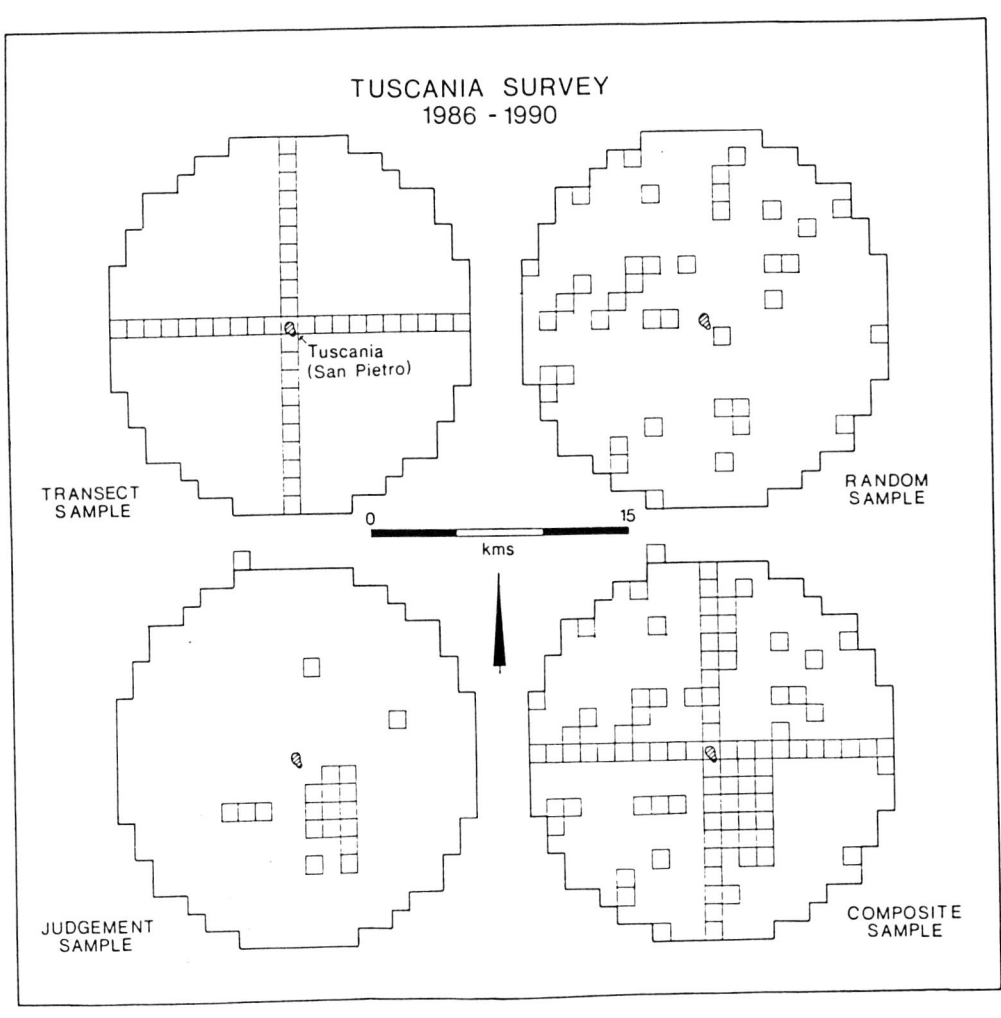

Fig. 2. The territory investigated by the Tuscania Survey, showing the three systems of regional sampling used (transect, random, judgemental) and the composite sample.

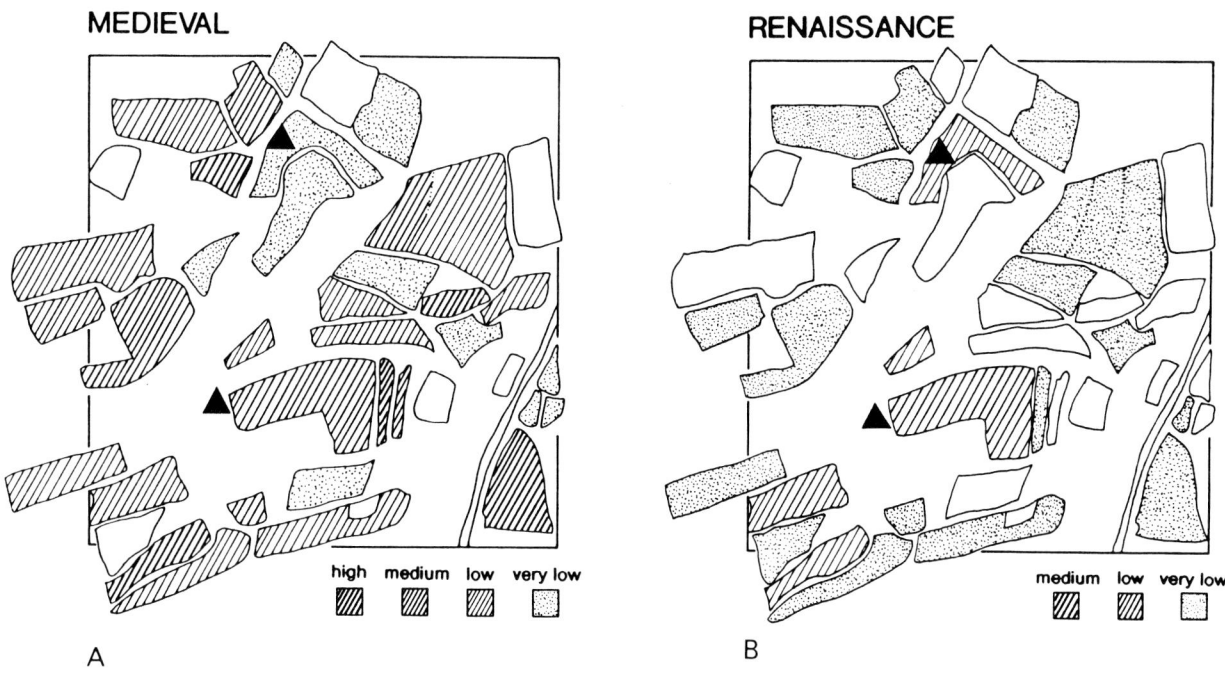

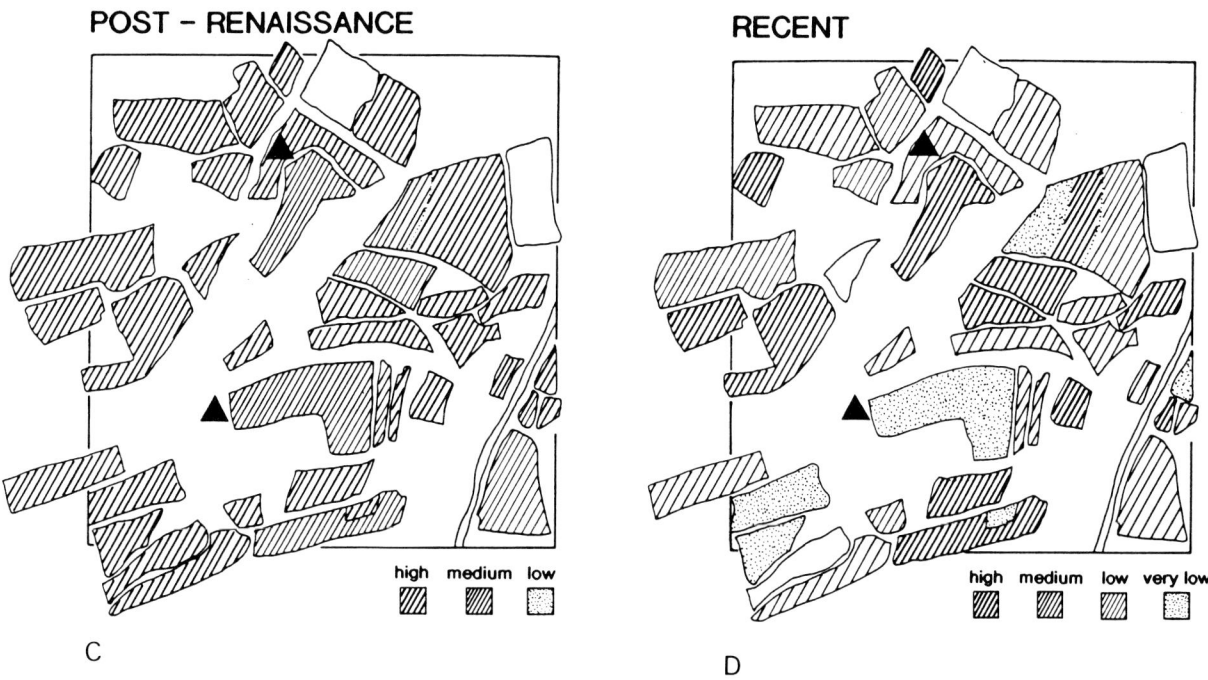

Fig. 3. Off-site pottery data in a kilometre square of the Montarrenti survey: a. 12th, 13th centuries; b. 14th century; c. 15th, 16th centuries; d. 17th, 18th, 19th centuries. The two sites marked by triangles are modern farms identified from documents as the successors of farms probably founded in the 12th century.

change has yet to be exploited properly in Italian survey projects. A powerful example of its potential has been provided by Peter Hayes' survey of Roman settlement in part of Lincolnshire in eastern England (Hayes & Lane 1992; Fig.4). All surface pottery was collected in four adjacent transects across a block of terrain. The study area consists of higher, better drained, ground on the west, and marsh to the east, but palaeoenvironmental studies indicate that during the Roman period it was undergoing small-scale but extremely significant landscape changes, with marsh spreading both northwards through the centre of the study area and eastwards from the fen margin. Changes in the total pottery distributions across the study area between the 2nd century (Samian pottery) and 3rd and 4th centuries (colour-coated wares) indicated settlement shifts reflecting these environmental changes. The southernmost block (D) suffered the greatest decline, the northernmost block (A) the least change, whereas conditions in Block B improved and in C declined, as the inner marshes declined in population and/or prosperity during the Roman period relative to the outer or silt-edge marshes. The potential of this kind of approach in Italy as a sensitive indicator of land use change is obvious, but the corollary is that the survey region as well as methodology have to be selected so that the results can be compared rigorously with other indicators of landscape change, a point to which I shall return in my conclusion.

The forested and uncultivated landscape

Conditions for both crop cultivation and field survey invariably deteriorate steadily with altitude in Italy, and a further priority for the coming years is to develop more sophisticated methodologies for investigating the archaeology of forest and pasture, as well as for investigating archaeology in forests and pastures.

In the case of forest history, documentary studies are of course an invaluable aid to reconstruction, as Rackham (1990) has shown for Britain, though he also points out how many students of ecological history "have a consistent tendency to exaggerate the woodland of the past – where the original source said 'trees', this is quoted as 'forest' and re-quoted as 'vast forest' – and to underestimate the woodland of the present" (Rackham 1992: 262). Trees form part of the landscape in different ways, not simply an amorphous forest – in managed woodland, wood-pasture, plantations, hedges, and orchards. As well as maps, documents, pictorial records, place-names and the like, the potential archaeology of woodland includes boundary walls and charcoal hearths, the indirect evidence of different kinds of timber found on excavated sites, and pollen and other microscopic botanical remains in sediments.

Pollen inevitably survives rather poorly in many Mediterranean conditions, published pollen diagrams from Italy are still very few (especially in the peninsula), and most of them provide only rather general indications of regional vegetation histories (e.g. Alessio *et al.* 1986; Bonatti 1970; Follieri *et al.* 1988; Frank 1969; Grüger 1977; Hunt & Eisner 1991; Kelly & Huntley 1991; Watts 1985). However, recent work by Jenny Harding (1992) in the Salento peninsula has demonstrated from a detailed comparison between modern core samples and vegetation surveys, that pollen and non-pollen microflora can be used as subtle indicators not only of widely different kinds of vegetation such as closed woodland and pasture but also of the intermediate mixed forms such as macchia and garrigue. As her own studies of palaeobotanical material demonstrated, the application of these methodologies offers very considerable potential for a far more sophisticated vegetation history in Italy than has been available hitherto.

Another source of information about landscape history that has hardly been studied in Italy is that of boundary walls and terraces. In the bare upland landscapes of Britain, stone walls and other boundaries survive in abundance and have been the source of detailed regional studies for many years. On Dartmoor, for example, Andrew Fleming has been able to map an entire bronze age landscape of field boundaries or 'reaves', by which land was divided up between different communities, parts of it sub-divided for arable land, and parts of it maintained as communal land presumably for animal grazing (Fleming 1988). At Roystone Grange in the Peak District of Derbyshire, Richard Hodges has demonstrated how a modern pastoral landscape divided up by dry-stone walls conceals a remarkable succession of prehistoric, Roman, medieval and post-medieval landscapes marked by stone walls of subtly different constructions, many of them incorporated within the modern field walls (Hodges 1991).

Traces of terrace walling have been found associated with late prehistoric settlements in a number of Mediterranean countries including Spain, Italy, Greece, and Cyprus. Most of these seem to be Bronze Age in date, though in Crete there is evidence for terrace wall construction for settlement reinforcement in neolithic times. There are frequent references to Mediterranean terracing from the classical period onwards, one of the earliest being Homer's comment that Odysseus was too lazy to build a dry stone wall on a slope (*Odyssey* 1.357-9). An archaeology of Mediterranean terracing is urgently required, with methodologies as refined as those developed for field system study in temperate regions. In Cyprus Peter Hayes is currently showing that the mapping of surface artifacts by normal field-walking can provide one useful indicator of antiquity, and Moody and Grove (1990) in Crete and Wagstaff (1992) in Cyprus have been attempting to describe terrace characteristics systematically in terms of construction, land use and geomorphology. Again, Italy is surely fertile ground for similar fieldwork, as initial studies in the Cicolano (Barker & Grant 1991) and Liguria (Moreno 1990) suggest.

Theoretically, different kinds of subsistence activity in the past should leave a recognisable imprint or signature on the archaeological record, enabling us to distinguish one activity from another. However, archaeologists are increasingly aware that many of our reconstructions of prehistoric, classical and medieval farming systems have been based on untested assumptions about such relationships between behaviour and material culture: for example, that farmers use particular kinds of artifacts and structures and shepherds other kinds, or that sedentary farming creates one set of distinct zoological and botanical residues and mobile pastoralism another. In recent years, therefore, many archaeologists have turned to studying the 'ethnoarchaeology' of modern societies, to refine our understanding of the link between present-day behaviour and the archaeological 'signatures' created by that behaviour.

Annie Grant and I have recently published the results of one such study in the Cicolano mountains (Barker & Grant 1991). There is no permanent settlement in these mountains today. People come from villages in the nearby Salto valley in the summer, some to farm, others to graze their sheep. The shepherds divide into those who keep their sheep in their villages in the winter (*stanziali*) and those who take their sheep to the plains around Rome for the winter (*transumanti*). These different economic groups used similar settlement units, though some small differences were observed: for example, the farmers and *stanziali* shepherds grow crops and hay, so use fields bounded by walls, and the transhumant shepherds use high altitude camps that the others do not use, creating tent footings. The material culture of the three groups was fundamentally the same, though again differed in detail. The sheep mortality profiles modelled from present-day flock dynamics were fundamentally the same whether for the 100 sheep of a *stanziale* or the 1000-plus of a transhumant shepherd. The archaeobotanical profiles modelled from the present-day cropping systems would be as difficult to distinguish. A critical part of the next phase of landscape archaeology in Italy has to be further work in ethnoarchaeology and ethnohistory to improve our methodologies for identifying land use in the archaeological record.

AGRICULTURE, CLIMATE
AND LANDSCAPE CHANGE

Ever since the publication of Vita-Finzi's classic study of Mediterranean valley alluviation (Vita-Finzi 1969), the possible roles of climatic change and human action in shaping the Holocene Mediterranean environment have been strongly debated. Vita-Finzi's original model concluded that climatic change was the primary factor responsible for the major phase of Holocene alluviation, the Younger Fill, which he dated broadly to late Roman times. Since then, a variety of earlier and later alluviation episodes have been identified by geomorphologists in various parts of the Mediterranean basin, and, like the classical Younger Fill itself, mostly been ascribed by the fieldworkers to human impact on the environment (in terms of deliberate deforestation for cultivation, or as a result of overgrazing), rather than to climatic change (e.g. Bell 1982; Chester & James 1991; Davidson 1980; Hunt *et al.* 1992; Pope & Van Andel 1984; Van Andel & Zangger 1990; Van Andel *et al.* 1985; Wagstaff 1981). In the Argolid peninsula of Greece, for example, Van Andel and Runnels (1987) have identified four major phases of Holocene alluviation between the Bronze Age and the present day, all of which they ascribed to changes in settlement and land use. Proponents of the original thesis, however, point out that aggradation episodes dated generally to classical times are significantly different in their scale and characteristics from earlier and later aggradations, suggesting that, whilst land use systems may well have been a contributory factor in their genesis, climatic change was probably still the prime mover (Bintliff 1976; Potter 1976).

To advance this debate, in order to evaluate the respective roles of climate and people in shaping the Mediterranean landscape, we need to investigate Mediterranean valleys with integrated methodologies linking geomorphology and archaeology. One example of an integrated methodology applied to the same region has been the Biferno valley survey (Barker, 1995). Seven phases of sediment formation have been identified by Chris Hunt, all of which correlate closely with archaeological and historical evidence for settlement expansion and agricultural intensification (Barker and Hunt, 1995; Table 2). The first is dated to the late prehistoric period and correlates with a significant expansion of settlement throughout the valley. The second is by far the largest prior to those of the past twenty years and correlates with a dramatic expansion of Samnite rural settlement and intensification in land use between the 3rd century BC and the 1st/2nd centuries AD. The next phase correlates with the establishment of the modern system of hilltop villages and satellite villages between the 10th and 13th centuries, the next with a second phase of village expansion between the 16th and 18th centuries, another with the last major expansion of settlement in the late 19th century, another with postwar intensification, and the last – as dramatic in its effects as that of the Samnite period – the change to deep ploughing and monoculture since the early 1970s. In the Montarrenti survey region of central Tuscany, likewise, Hunt *et al.* (1992) have identified three phases of aggradation in the Farma,

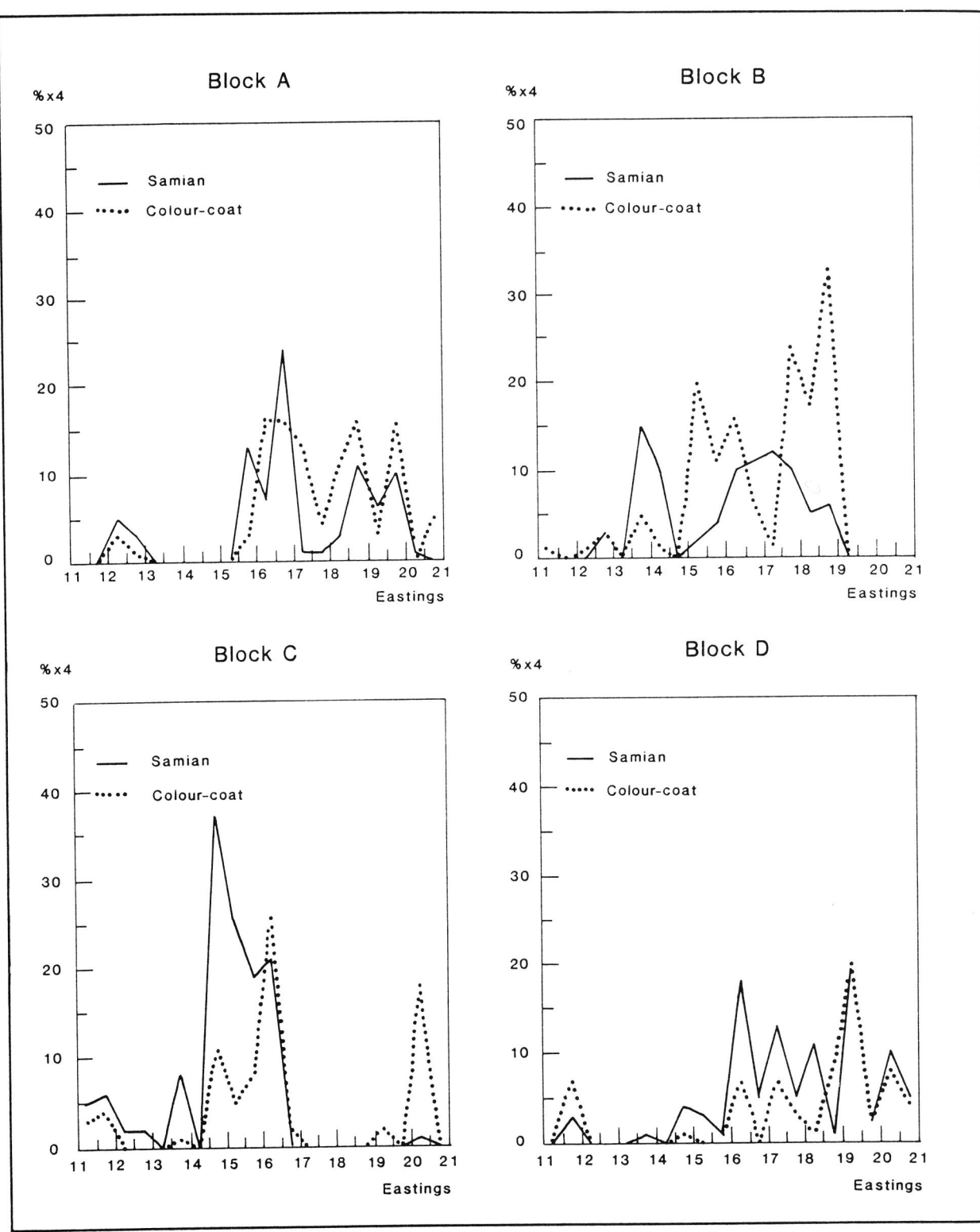

Fig. 4 Off-site survey data in part of the Lincolnshire fens in eastern England: distributions of Samian pottery (2nd century AD) and Colour-coated pottery (3rd, 4th centuries AD) across the four transects of the study area (numbered A to D from north to south). The changing distributions are subtle indicators of settlement and land use shifts in response to the expansion of marshlands (see text). (After Hayes & Lane 1992: 244).

SETTLEMENT RECORD	RIVER SEDIMENT RECORD
Mesolithic: lower valley settlement	No evidence
Neolithic: main settlements lower valley, arable-based farming	*Phase 1*: small-scale clearances
Bronze Age: settlements throughout valley, mixed cereal/stock farming	*Phase 1*: small-scale clearance
Iron Age: settlements throughout valley, first villages, wine cultivation lower valley?	*?Phase 1*: small-scale clearances
Samnite: very high rural settlement, polyculture, surplus production, proto-urban economic structure	*Phase 2*: massive clearance, predominantly open landscape
Roman: declining rural population, estate growth, market economies	*Phase 2*: continuation of predominantly open landscape
Early medieval: drastically reduced population, small expansion AD 1000–1300, small-scale farming	*Phase 3*: small-scale clearances, as Phase 1
15th-17th centuries: second phase of village expansion	*Phase 4*: increased scale of impact
19th century: dramatic population rise, marginal land cultivated, etc.	*Phase 5*: significantly increased amount of open land and erosion
1920s, 1930s: marginal land taken into cultivation, Mussolini's 'Battle for Wheat'	*Phase 6*: open landscape, very active erosion
1960s, 1970s: change to mechanisation, deep ploughing, construction of dam	*Phase 7*: dramatically increased erosion rates
1980s, 1990s: expansion of cultivated area, increasing monoculture	*Phase 8*: massive erosion, dam lake rapidly filling with sediment, etc.

Table 2. Comparison between the Holocene settlement record and river sediment record (both greatly simplified) in the Biferno valley, Molise, in central-southern Italy.

Rosia and Feccia valleys, provisionally dated to the 11th-12th, 16th-early 17th and late 19th centuries AD, and have similarly been able to ascribe them convincingly to the intensification of human activity and expansion of farming in the area.

Over the past two decades we have learned that in regional landscape analysis in Italy we have to select areas that can be studied both archaeologically and historically on more or less equal terms if we are to reconstruct diachronic settlement trends effectively. However, we also need to select areas in which the palaeoenvironmental data can also be brought into the equation on equal terms. A priority in the next phase of landscape investigation in Italy must be the definition of regional study areas that will produce sets of archaeological, palaeoenvironmental and historical data that can be compared with each other rigorously and fairly, allowing us to investigate long-term landscape histories more systematically than hitherto.

Bibliography

Alessio, M., Allegri, L., Bella, F., Calderoni, G., Cortesi, C., Dai Pra, G., De Rita, D., Esu, D., Follieri, M., Improta, S., Magri, D., Narcisi, B., Petrone, V., & Sadori, L. 1986. '14C dating, geochemical features, faunistic and palynological analyses of the upper 10m core from Valle di Castiglione (Rome, Italy)', *Geologica Romana* 26, 287–308.

Ammerman, A. J. 1985. *The Acconia Survey: Neolithic Settlement and the Obsidian Trade*, Institute of Archaeology Occasional Publication 10, London.

Arthur, P. 1991. *Romans in Northern Campania*. (British School at Rome, Archaeological Monographs 1), London.

Attolini, I., Cambi, F., Castagna, M., Celuzza, M., Fentress, E., Perkins, P. & Regoli, E. 1991. 'Political geography and productive geography between the valleys of the Albegna and the Fiora in northern Etruria', in Barker & Lloyd (eds.) 1991, 142–152.

Balista, C. & Leonardi G. 1985. 'Hill slope evolution: pre- and protohistoric occupation in the Veneto', in Malone & Stoddart (eds.) 1985, 135–152.

Barker, G. 1988. 'Archaeology and the Etruscan countryside', *Antiquity*, 62 (237), 772–785.

Barker, G. 1991. 'Approaches to archaeological survey', in Barker & Lloyd (eds.) 1991, 1–9.

Barker, G. (ed.) 1995. *A Mediterranean Valley: Landscape Archaeology and* Annales *History in the Biferno Valley*, Leicester.

Barker, G. & Grant, A. (eds.), 1991. 'Ancient and modern pastoralism in central Italy: an interdisciplinary study in the Cicolano mountains', *Papers of the British School at Rome*, 59, 15–88.

Barker, G. & Hodges, R. (eds.), 1981. *Archaeology and Italian Society*, British Archaeological Reports, International Series 102, Oxford.

Barker, G. & Hunt, C.O. 1995. 'Quaternary floor erosion and alluviation in the Biferno valley, Molise, Italy: the role of tectonics, climate, sea level change and human activity', in J.Lewin & J. Woodward (eds.), *Mediterranean Quaternary River Environments*, Rotterdam, 145–157.

Barker, G. & Lloyd, J. A, (eds.) 1991. *Roman Landscapes: Archaeological Survey in the Mediterranean Region*, (British School at Rome, Archaeological Monographs 2), London.

Barker, G. & Rasmussen, T. 1988. 'The archaeology of an Etruscan *polis*: a preliminary report on the Tuscania Project (1986 and 1987 seasons)', *Papers of the British School at Rome* 57, 25–42.

Barker, G., Grant, A. & Rasmussen, T. 1993. 'Approaches to the Etruscan landscape: the development of the Tuscania Survey', in P. Bogucki (ed.) *Case Studies in European Prehistory*, CRC Press, Florida, 229–257.

Barker, G., Lloyd, J. A., & Webley, D.P. 1978. 'A classical landscape in Molise', *Papers of the British School at Rome* 46, 35–51.

Barker, G., Coccia, S., Jones, D. A., & Sitzia, J. 1986. 'The Montarrenti survey, 1985: problems of integrating archaeological, environmental and historical data', *Archeologia Medievale* 13, 291–320.

Beavitt, P., & Christie, N. 1992. 'The Cicolano Castles project: preliminary excavation report, 1991', *Archeologia Medievale* 19, 491–506.

Bell, M. 1982. 'The effects of land-use and climate on valley sedimentation', in A. F. Harding (ed.) *Climatic Change in Later Prehistory*, Edinburgh, 127–142.

Bell, M. & J. Boardman (eds.) 1992. *Past and Present Soil Erosion: Archaeological and Geographical Perspectives*, Oxbow Monographs 22, Oxford.

Bintliff, J. 1976. 'Sediments and settlement in southern Greece', in D. A. Davidson & M. Shackley (eds.), *Geoarchaeology*, London, 267–275.

Bintliff, J. 1991. 'The Roman countryside in central Greece: observations and theories from the Boeotia Survey (1978–1987)', in Barker & Lloyd (eds.) 1991, 122–132.

Bintliff, J. & Snodgrass, A. M. 1988. 'Off-site pottery distributions: a regional and interregional perspective', *Current Anthropology* 29, 506–513.

Bonatti, E. 1970. 'Pollen sequence in the lake sediments', 26–31, in G. E. Hutchinson (ed.), 'Ianula: an account of the history and development of the Lago di Monterosi, Latium, Italy', *Transactions of the American Philosophical Society* 64, 5–175.

Bottema, S., Entjes-Nieborg G. & Van Zeist, W. (eds.) 1990. *Man's Role in the Shaping of the Eastern Mediterranean Landscape*, Rotterdam.

Cherry, J. F., Davis, J. L. & Mantzourani, E. 1992. *Landscape Archaeology as Long Term History: Northern Kheos in the Cycladic Islands*, UCLA Institute of Archaeology, Monumenta Archeologica 16, Los Angeles.

Chester, D. & James, P. 1991. 'Holocene alluviation in the Algarve, southern Portugal: the case for an anthropogenic cause', *Journal of Archaeological Science* 18, 73–87.

Coccia, S. & Mattingly, D. (eds.) 1992. 'Settlement history, environment and human exploitation of an intermontane basin in the central Apennines: the Rieti survey, 1988–1991, part 1', *Papers of the British School at Rome* 60, 213–289.

Cremaschi, M. & Christopher, C. 1985. 'Environment and palaeolithic settlement in northern Italy during the Middle Pleistocene: the Ghiardo site', in Malone & Stoddart (eds.) 1985, 105–134.

Cremaschi, M., Bernabo Brea, M., Titabassi, J., D'Agostini, A., Dall' Aglio, P.L., Magri, S., Baricchi, W., Marchesini, A., & Nepoti, S. 1980. *L'Evoluzione della Pianura Emiliana durante l'Età del Bronzo, l'Età Romana e l'Alto Medioevo: Geomorfologia ed Insediamenti*, Bollettino del Centro Polesano di Studi Storici Archeologici ed Etnografici, Rovigo.

Davidson, D.A. 1980. 'Erosion in Greece during the first and second millennia B.C.', in R. A. Cullingford, D. A. Davidson & J. Lewin (eds.), *Timescales in Geomorphology*, New York, 143–158.

Dyson, S. L. 1978. 'Settlement patterns in the Ager Cosanus: the Wesleyan University survey, 1974–76', *Journal of Field Archaeology* 5, 251–268.

Finley, M. 1977. 'The ancient city: from Fustel de Coulanges to Max Weber and beyond', *Comparative Studies in Society and History* 19, 305–327.

Fleming, A. M. 1988. *The Dartmoor Reaves*, London.

Foley, R. 1981. 'Off-site archaeology: an alternative approach for the short-sited', in I. Hodder, G. Isaac & N. Hammond (eds.), *Pattern of the Past: Studies in Honour of David Clarke*, Cambridge, 157–183.

Follieri, M., Magri, M. & Sadori, L. 1988. '250,000–year pollen record from the valle di Castiglione (Roma)', *Pollen et Spores* 30 (3–4), 329–356.

Frank, A. H. E. 1969. 'Pollen stratigraphy from the Lake of Vico (central Italy)', *Palaeogeography, Palaeoclimatology and Palaeoecology* 6, 67–85.

Grüger, E. 1977 'Pollenanalytische Untersuchung zur würmzeitlichen Vegetationsgeschichte von Kalabrien (Suditalien)', *Flora* 166 475–489.

Harding, J. L. 1992. *Holocene Environmental Change through Natural Processes and Human Influence in Salento, Southeast Italy: an Integrated Geomorphological and Palynological Investigation*, Sheffield University, unpublished PhD thesis.

Haselgrove, C., Millett, M. & Smith, I. (eds.) 1985. *Archaeology from the Ploughsoil*, Sheffield.

Hayes, P. P. & Lane, T.W. 1992. *The Fenland Project, Number 5: Lincolnshire Survey, the South-West Fens*, East Anglian Archaeology 55.

Hodges, R. 1981. 'Excavations and survey at San Vincenzo al Volturno, Molise, 1980', *Archeologia Medievale* 8, 483–502.

Hodges, R. 1991. *Wall to Wall History*, London.

Hunt, C. O. & Eisner, W. R. 1991. 'Palynology of the Mezzaluna core', in A. Voorrips, S. Loving & H. Kamermans (eds.) *The Agro Pontino Survey Project*, (Studies in Prae- und Protohistorie 6), Amsterdam, 49–59.

Hunt, C.O., Gilbertson, D. D. & Donahue, R. E. 1992. 'Palaeoenvironmental evidence for agricultural soil erosion from late Holocene deposits in the Montagnola Senese, Italy', in Bell & Boardman (eds.), 163–174.

Kelly, M. G. & Huntley, B. 1991. 'An 11000–year record of vegetation and environment from Lago di Martignano, Latium, Italy', *Journal of Quaternary Science* 6 (3), 209–224.

Lloyd, J. A. 1991a. 'Forms of rural settlement in the early Roman empire', in Barker & Lloyd (eds.), 180–193.

Lloyd, J. A. 1991b. 'Farming the highlands: Samnium and Arcadia in the Hellenistic and early Roman Imperial periods', in Barker & Lloyd (eds.), 180–193.

Lloyd, J. A. & Barker, G. 1981. 'Rural settlement in Roman Molise: problems of archaeological survey', in Barker & Hodges (eds.), 289–304.

Malone, C. & Stoddart, S. (eds.) 1985. *Papers in Italian Archaeology, IV. The Cambridge Conference*, 4 vols., BAR International Series, Oxford.

Moody, J. & Grove, A. T. 1990. 'Terraces and enclosure walls in the Cretan landscape', in Bottema, Entjes-Nieborg & Van Zeist (eds.), 83–191.

Moreland, J. 1986. 'Ricognizione intorno Farfa, 1985: resoconto preliminare', *Archeologia Medievale* 13, 333–343.

Moreland, J. 1987. 'The Farfa survey: second preliminary report', *Archeologia Medievale* 14, 409–418.

Moreno, D. 1990. *Dal Documento al Terreno: Storia e Archeologia dei Sistemi Agro-Silvo-Pastorali*, Bologna.

Pope, K. O. & Van Andel, Tj. H. 1984. 'Late Quaternary alluviation and soil formation in the southern Argolid: its history, causes and archaeological significance', *Journal of Archaeological Science* 11, 281–306.

Potter, T. W. 1976. 'Valleys and sediment: some new evidence', *World Archaeology* 8, 207–219.

Potter, T. W. 1979. *The Changing Landscape of South Etruria*, London.

Rackham, O. 1990. *Trees and Woodland in the British Landscape*, London.

Rackham, O. 1992. 'Trees and woodland in the history and archaeology of the landscape', in M. Bernardi (ed.), *Archeologia del Paesaggio*, Florence, 249–264.

Rasmussen, T. 1991. 'Tuscania and its territory', in Barker & Lloyd (eds.), 106–114.

Small, A. 1991. 'Late Roman settlement in Basilicata and western Apulia', in Barker & Lloyd (eds.), 204–222.

Van Andel, Tj. H. & Runnels, C. 1987. *Beyond the Acropolis: The Archaeology of the Greek Countryside*, Stanford.

Van Andel, Tj. H. & Zangger, W. 1990. 'Landscape stability and destabilisation in the prehistory of Greece', in Bottema, Entjes-Nieborg & Van Zeist (eds.), 139–157.

Van Andel, Tj. H., Runnels, C. N. & Pope, K. O. 1985. 'Five thousand years of land use and abuse in the southern Argolid, Greece', *Hesperia* 55, 103–128.

Vita-Finzi, C. 1969. *The Mediterranean Valleys*, Cambridge.

Wagstaff, M. 1981. 'Buried assumptions: some problems in the interpretation of the "Younger Fill" raised by recent data from Greece', *Journal of Archaeological Science* 8, 247–264.

Wagstaff, M. 1992. 'Agricultural terraces: the Vasilikos valley, Cyprus', in Bell & Boardman (eds.), 155–161.

Ward-Perkins, B., Delano-Smith, C., Gadd, D. & Mills, N.T. W. 1986. 'Luni and the *Ager Lunensis*: the rise and fall of a Roman town and its territory', *Papers of the British School at Rome* 54, 81–146.

Ward-Perkins, J. B., Kahane, A. & Murray Threipland, L. 1968. 'The Ager Veientanus survey north and east of Veii', *Papers of the British School at Rome* 36, 1–318.

Watts, W. A. 1985. 'A long pollen record from Laghi di Monticchio, southern Italy: a preliminary account', *Journal of the Geological Society*, 142, 491–499.

Wightman, E. 1981. 'The lower Liri valley: problems, trends and peculiarities', in Barker & Hodges (eds.), 275–287.

2

'Alto-Medio Polesine – Basso Veronese' Project: From a 'Landscape Archaeology' to an 'Archaeology of the Mind'

ARMANDO DE GUIO

(Dipartimento di Scienze dell'Antichità, Università di Padova)

Summary: The paper presents a number of relevant issues underlying the 'Alto- Medio Polesine - Basso Veronese' Project, a pilot Anglo-Italian field survey (1985- ongoing) in the eastern Po Plain (Verona and Rovigo districts). The evolutionary instability affecting some key-scenarios (geomorphology, demography, 'landscape of power', and 'landscape of the mind') is evaluated in the light of actual field data and in relation to the morphogenetic theories of our emerging 'Archaeology of Complexity'. Various suggestions are also discussed for the implementation of a new approach to the specific 'complexity' of the surface archaeological record.

1. PREMISE

According to Cherry (1983), we are frogs carrying out field-surveys around the Mediterranean pond, which has gradually become an important forum for surface archaeology. The Mediterranean 'world' is characterised by marked polycentrism and there are signs that our frogs are beginning to engage, just 'under the surface', in a competition for theoretical supremacy. This contest is fortunately far from the epic and bloody confrontations of some American conflicts, and is played out with gentler, more European, fair-play: perhaps the Mediterranean has given the right 'temperature' to the theoretical debate, and none of today's frogs, knowing Aesop's fable, wants too much anarchy which might cause the arrival of a watersnake-king...

The subject of this paper is a rather peculiar mixed tribe of frogs (the 'Rana italica' subspecies from the University of Padua, and the 'Rana britannica' of the University of London – Queen Mary and Westfield College), operating in the 'Alto-Medio Polesine-Basso Veronese' field-survey project (AMPBV: cf. fig. 1), directed by R. Whitehouse, J. Wilkins and myself (Balista *et al.* 1986, 1988, 1990, 1991; Balista & De Guio 1990-91; De Guio, Whitehouse & Wilkins 1989, 1990, 1992; De Guio 1991a,b, 1992; Malgarise 1989-90).

2. THE 'ALTO-MEDIO POLESINE – BASSO VERONESE' PROJECT

The project area, part of the eastern Po Plain, was selected as our survey 'Universe', firstly because of its proximity to our University and secondly because it constitutes an extraordinary reservoir of research interests. In fact this palaeo-geographic unit is an area of central interest for understanding some major morphogenetic processes which took place especially in the late prehistory and proto-history of the whole Veneto region. From a diachronic perspective the most general trait is that of an almost endemic status of 'metastable equilibrium' with an 'exposure to risk' (in formal 'Survival Analysis' terms: De Guio 1985a) involving the structural basis of the society. The general developmental pattern through time was in fact paroxystic. This manifests itself in the form of cyclical processes of 'anastrophic' integration and catastrophic disaggregation operating in what seems to be a classic chaos-theory scenario with its pulsatory spinning around 'strange attractors' (Gleick 1988; Schuster 1989). This affects a variety of spheres of interaction, or 'landscapes', involving human-human, human-nature and nature-nature relational networks, from a geomorphological landscape, to a 'landscape of power', and 'landscape of the mind' (De Guio 1991a,b, 1992).

Various key scenarios can be discussed. The geomorphology, for instance, dominated by hydrographic dynamics, is characterised by a cyclical shift from a basically lacustrine-marshy situation (Early to Middle Bronze Age, Early Iron Age, Late Roman up to last century reclamation) to a dry landscape, as the result of the senile-extinction phases of generally 'catastrophic' alluvial phenomena. The cumulative compound result

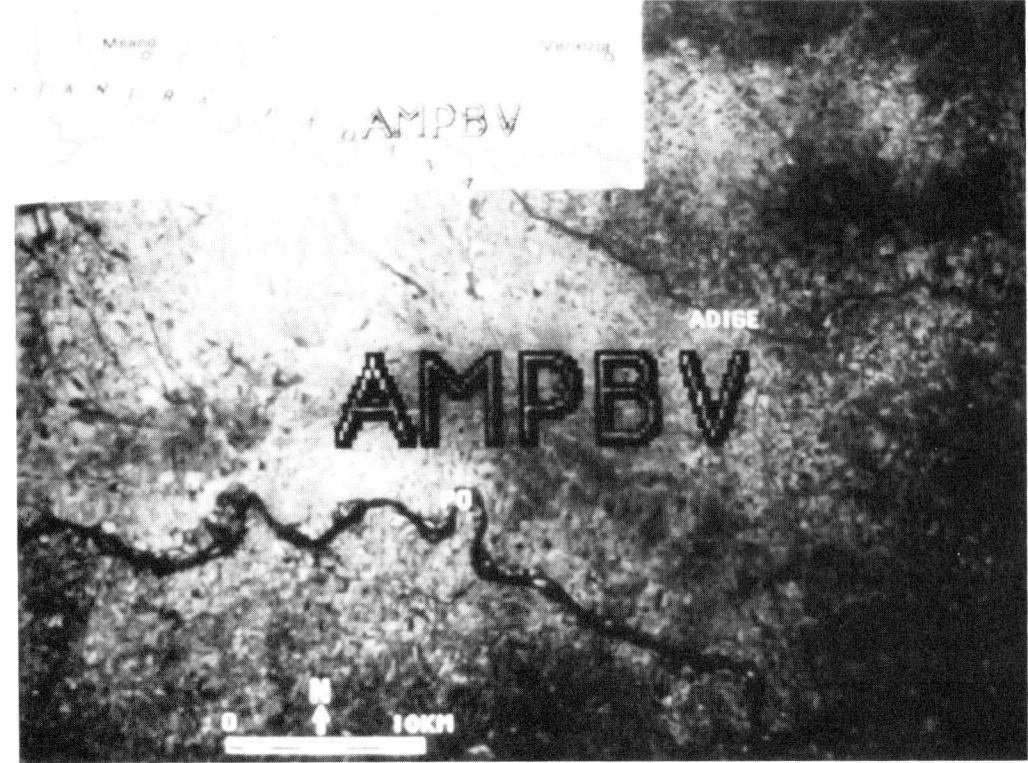

Fig. 1. The Alto-Medio Polesine – Basso Veronese (AMPBV) project area in the eastern Po Plain between Lake Garda and the Venetian Lagoon. Outer rectangle: general area of interest; inner rectangle: present field-work area highlighted by a satellite photograph (Sojuz KFA1000, 28th May 1989).

Fig. 2. The AMPBV geomorphological palimpsest (palaeohydrographic map of the area north of the River Tartaro by R. Ferri in Balista et al. 1992)

is the 'plain', which has always been an intricate morphological palimpsest (fig. 2) with a number of highly constraining morphological 'traps' for a variety of human and non-human behavioural and processual spheres.

A major and composite climax took place during the Middle Bronze Age, after a period of low population density and wetland oriented cultural ecology (with classic wetland dwelling types). A newly-emerged landscape, with a widespread network of high-ground former river banks (or 'paleo-dossi'), relics of a preceding alluvial catastrophe, offered the most suitable locational support for an incredible burst in the demographic, economical and political 'landscapes', centred on a network of new banked settlements and a massive 'logistical' control of the open countryside.

The major banked settlements (fig. 3) of Fondo Paviani (c.16 ha), Castello del Tartaro (c.11 ha) and Fabbrica dei Soci (6 ha) seem now to constitute the central focus of a polity (a newborn 'landscape of power': De Guio 1991a), the spatial rules of which we are now trying to simulate. The critical interference with other spatial and organisational spheres (e.g. the 'landscape of death') suggests other rules, governing interlandscape relationships concerning interdistances and micro and macro locating strategies. These may illuminate a composite cognitive map of the landscape, or a 'landscape of the mind', very far from our analytical reach (De Guio 1991a,b, 1992). This core-polity possibly acted as a critical creodic funnel in a 'world system' exchange network (Wallernstein 1974) extending from northern Europe to the eastern Mediterranean. The main role of the area, involved in specialised production of metals, amber, vitreous paste, bone and antler, was probably that of draining a number of key resources in a complex 'gateway dendritic system' (Smith 1987) focussed on gateway communities in Southern Italy, as demonstrated for example by repeated finds of 'Mycenaean' potsherds over the last fifteen years.

The whole scenario was in turn involved in a collapse stage lasting between the end of Late Bronze Age and the advanced phase of the Final Bronze Age; there also seems to be an interesting relation between 'survival' and rank-size, in that the larger the settlements, the later they appear to be abandoned: De Guio 1991a).

3. Method and Theory: the Critical Path

Retrospectively, our project's evolution can be seen as a trial and error trajectory through three major stages of development:

1) a 'Sampling Archaeology' stage, strongly influenced by research design issues and cookery-book sampling recipes, which trapped us in what we have called a 'Pie Archaeology' scenario;

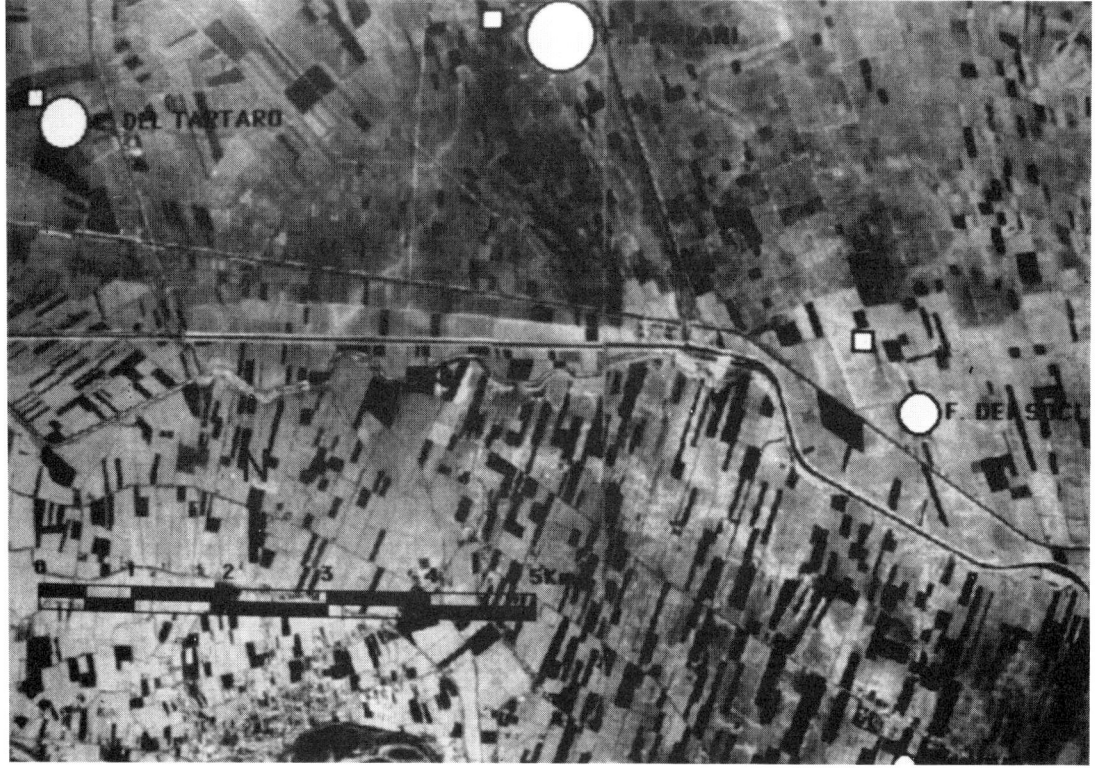

Fig. 3. Major Bronze-Age banked settlements (circles) and cemeteries (squares) of the AMPBV field-work area (cf. De Guio 1992).

2) a more advanced 'Landscape Archaeology' stage, which took account of all 'surface formation processes' within the human landscape (from intrasite to near-site, off-site and intersite);

3) the present 'Archaeology of Landscapes' stage, where a variety of 'Landscapes' (from a geomorphological landscape to a 'landscape of power' and a 'landscape of the mind') are considered for their ability to imprint the superficial archaeological record.

On the general theory side we have over the last few years made suggestions for implementing a so-called 'Archaeology of Complexity'. Some ingredients are already at hand for a very decisive shift in this direction, and they can be combined in our superficial 'minestrone'. There are in fact a lot of separate bodies of theory, research directions and more simple suggestions critically pointing to an emerging large consensus base: for instance, the new syntheses of Bintliff (1988) and of Renfrew and Bahn (1991: 'cognitive-processual' archaeology), Trigger's (1989) 'historical compromise', which just precedes the more recent and specific Annales new-wave (cf. Knapp 1992), an upgraded version of Doran's (1982, 1986) 'Multi Actor/Multi-Contract' model, that we have recently proposed (De Guio 1992).

The common denominator seems to be the 'return of the Indian' (that is of the social actors, in opposition to Flannery's (1967) search for systems behind both the arrow and the Indian). After the recovery from the 'Wounded Knee' processual offence (De Guio 1992), the rediscovery of this Indian opens the present, post-modern phase in archaeology with a mixture of ephemeral experimentalism and epocal/new-millennium expectations. The emerging panorama goes far beyond an opportunistic consensus based on a formal acceptance of the Indians (the cognitive component) and their stories (the historical component).

Perhaps the most fascinating convergence concerns holistic and non-holistic transformation-theory. I refer specifically to such domains as the thermodynamic theory on 'dissipative systems' (Nikolis & Prigogine 1991), Chaos theory (Gleik 1988; Schuster 1989; Casati 1991), and its multi-branching sub-domains and related areas, such as 'self-organized crititicality' (Back & Chen 1991) and 'anti-chaos theory' (Kauffmann 1991).

As far as the specific theory on surface archaeology is concerned, we should probably recognise that by and large the whole 'surfacies', as we call the superficial aspect of the archaeological record, is still seen as an alien in the 'twilight zone' of archaeological thought (De Guio, forthcoming). That is, despite the long trek from the Viru Valley Eden, where the first apple was bitten (Willey 1953), to Schofield's *Artifact Scatters* (1991) and Barker and Lloyd's *Roman Landscapes* (1991), we still lack an integrated approach that coherently and consistently covers all the relevant nodes of complexity of the archaeological record: surfacies, ploughzone and buried stratigraphy.

This twilight zone is in fact still a peculiar topological surface where a strange and sometimes paradoxical 'syndrome of dissociation' occurs, not only between different schools of thought, but even in the mind and analytical behaviour of a single scientist operating according to different scripts (i.e. excavation and field survey).

The key consideration is that a surfacies is not an isotropic plain to cope with at face value and with a *terra incognita* approach by using seasonal and renewable human resources (holiday-students with bags, labels and pace-rate walkman music): normally surfacies is highly patterned, although 'pattern', or, better, 'object' does not imply a direct and straight equivalence to information relevant to our problem-domains. Our surfacies, instead of offering a '*tabula absentiae*' in the form of a false isotropic plain for simple sampling games, becomes an inviting '*tabula praesentiae*' (fig. 4) with much food for thought.

It is not, however, a well ordered table: surfacies are palimpsestic, overwritten surfaces where a potentially wide variety of human and non human actors (such as worms, wind and plough), have played out their morphogenetic scripts at different resolutions of time and space, and along completely distinct functional circuits. Through time the 'surfacies formation processes' can in fact be seen as normally operating in a palimpsest to palimpsest cumulative accretion of 'complexity': the (logically) last one being the agrarian-impact palimpsest,

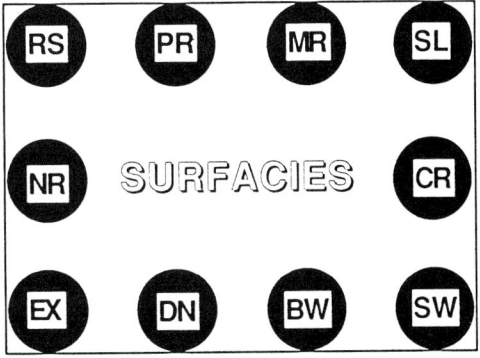

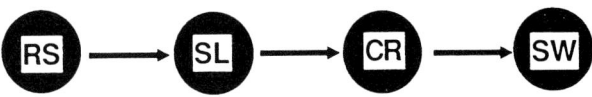

Fig. 4. Above: 'Surfacies' as a 'tabula praesentiae': different kinds of objects for pattern recognition (see text). Below: 'minimum path' strategy for surfacies objects.

that is the 'plough scenario' due to the 'plough actor'. To put order on the table we must make a number of stepwise decisions:

1) decide what kind of objects to look for;

2) search for them;

3) 'operate' on them with a variety of analytical 'operators' in order to pursue specific problem oriented targets, within a deliberately designed minimum effort strategy.

In general, ten kinds of objects may be relevant (fig. 4): some are self-evident, and need brief mention, while basic comments can be made for the others:

Remote Sensing Objects (RSs);
Prospection Objects (PRs);
Morpho-Objects (MRs), represented by positive or negative morphologies preserved on the surfacies as anomalies in a more uniform background;
Soil Objects (SLs), i.e. three dimensional units within the body of the ploughzone, characterised by a specific homogeneity in their soil properties (colour, texture, structure, macro- and micro-morphology, skeleton, inclusions, chemico-physical/pedogenic features);
Core Objects (CRs), recognised from coring mechanically or manually as 'isopach' 3d approximate models of a stratigraphic unit, interpolating a number of samples (Stein 1986);
Stratigraphic Windows Objects (SWs): these are stratigraphic units as recognised by inspection of stratigraphic sections found already 'open' onto the buried stratigraphy: e.g. drainage channels;.
Broken Window Objects (BWs), in accordance with our window analogy, they represent small but intact pieces of buried stratigraphy freshly exhumated as clods by the plough. This is valuable, often short lived, evidence which may enhance that supplied by cores and larger stratigraphic windows, with a wider spatial coverage;
Density Objects (DNs) are spatially closed units which may be defined as discriminate entities on the basis of density values of relevant arte- or ecofactual items.
Expert Objects (EXs) correspond to any configuration in the surfacies we recognise as a transformation of a specific source sociocultural or ecocultural entity, by means of an 'expertise'. The relevant expert knowledge can be the unwritten, unformalised experience of a field archaeologist, or the Artificial Intelligence of an expert system (e.g. Hugget 1985; Baker 1988; Shutt 1988);
Neuro-Objects (NRs) are in part comparable to EXs. The recognition is in fact still performed by a computer, but instead of an expert system we rely on 'neural-networks' (cf. Parisi 1989; Cammarata 1990; De Guio 1992).

4. Gambling on the Table: the Risk Factor

There is an important issue to be considered in our object oriented' strategy: the risk-factor involved in gambling on the '*tabula praesentiae*'. The risk component is normally very high in every sub-domain of pattern recognition so far prospected, whether human or automatic. However, there is an enormous potential in incorporating this additional contextual information. Also, our 'object-oriented' approach does not prevent us from using the same (or a different) sampling design as our 'object-disoriented' colleague: we can use both and thus we are simply adding further sampling strata.

5. Operands, Operators, Operations

Some of the objects we have isolated can already contain valuable information. They are, however, basically still at the stage of 'operands' – in other words further 'operations' are required on them before their 'transform' alias can provide the way to our specific goals. For example we may explicitly address two major targets:

1) site morphological setting (statics);

2) site morphogenetic path (dynamics).

Following this problem orientation, we should now isolate a number of relevant object-operators. Two categories may be distinguished:

a) 'filtering' operators;

b) 'topo-logical' operators.

A variety of operators can be attributed to the first taxon, the main goal of which is basically noise-reduction for enhancing compositional or spatial properties of objects. Optical filters are the major type of filtering operators, currently applied to surface archaeology, but any kind of mathematical-statistical, multivariate, simulative and even expert operators which helps to individuate objects is useful.

The second set of operators can be instrumentally referred to as 'topo-logical', in the sense that they perform topological (spatial) as well as 'logical' relational operations between objects and components of objects. For the sake of clarity we may isolate four major subtypes of topo-logical operators: Physical, Set-theory, Logical and Spatial.

The physical operator is the most basic one, putting two or more objects in a physical contact: the coring process, and stratigraphic window inspection, for instance, both reveal a physical set of relations between objects.

Set-theory operators refer to relational properties between objects in terms of both spatial extent and components. We shall ascribe another set of operators to the proper 'logical' rank, referring to any possible 'logical' connection that may be found between objects in order to extract higher order inferences. The most obvious operators of this kind are the classic Harris stratigraphic relations (e.g. superimposition, correlation with spatial discontinuity, etc: we can further extend the coverage to non-Harris relational operators such as: contains/is contained; emanates/is emanated, 'in range', etc: De Guio 1991, 1992). A more generic 'corresponds to' logical operator can be used to relate two objects connected by a specific and recognisable transformational path. By exploiting physical, set theory and logical operators we may connect, in a chain of operations, a relevant number of objects.

The spatial operators are the constituents of the 'spatial analysis' toolkit which can be used for finding spatial objects (heuristics) and for tracing relevant spatial relations between objects and components. The subject, here, is enormous, with at least three successive generations of spatial analysis in archaeology since the seventies. The brilliant synthesis by Blankholm (1991) has put some order into the subject by examining and testing a critical subset of widely used techniques which are commonly recognised as key-references for the development of intrasite (but also intersite) spatial analysis, from 'k-means Analysis', to 'Unconstrained Clustering', to Carr's 'Coefficient of Polythetic Association', and his own 'Presab'.

We have recently (De Guio & Secco 1988) proposed a new method called 'Percolation', forming a substantial revision of a set of methods originally proposed by Tremolliers (1979) operating in the numerical taxonomy and pattern recognition domains. It has been purposely designed to cope with 'landscape of power' analysis and simulation, and has only recently been applied to the surface archaeology density domain, with interesting results and performances (e.g. size-effect compensation).

We are now coping with a huge number of operators which could be applied when approaching our objectives. What is urgently required is an optimising strategy for critical cognitive economy, tracing a 'minimum path' to our explanatory targets. In this case a critical path may reasonably be traced in the relational network among four key objects (fig. 4): remote-sensing objects (RSs), soil objects (SLs), core objects (CRs) and stratigraphic window objects (SWs). The scope is then to trace the minimum number of relations relevant to our target of reconstruction in the normally huge four-dimensional relational matrix. In fact a reasonable and workable relational subset is usually enough for our explanatory goals.

The starting point in this game is the identification of a number of RSs as legitimate SLs, which is often the case especially when the platform is not that remote (e.g. with ultra-light airplanes). The next critical step is the SLs<->CRs relation. A key concept is provided by the notion of 'Homomorphism' (Balista *et al.* 1988: 328), which is just a special case in the surface/subsurface relation, or , in more precise terms, between the Ploughzone (PZ) and its 'Root' (the underlying achaeostratigraphic unit or ASU) just below the plough level (cf. De Guio 1988a,b). In order to classify our SL we are therefore provided with a first rough dichotomy (homomorphism/non-homomorphism), dependent on PZ/Root relationships: we recognise as homomorphic the special case in which only one parent ASU originates a single soil object. Homomorphism can be the result of two possible processes:

a) continuous 'emergence' in the landscape of a whole ASU or a part of it ('primary homomorphism');

b) agrarian levelling (massive *décapages* or minor levelling and the like) with or without subsequent ploughing ('secondary homomorphism').

A special case (which we might call 'bi-morphism') is where two contiguous homomorphic islands are separated by a more or less narrow band (another composite SL), which, following compositional analysis, is found to be produced by the two parent ASUs. These ASUs, as sampled by cores, must therefore maintain an original depositional relation preserved *in situ* (covers/is covered and the like) underneath the band. Even when passing from a homomorphic island to a non-homomorphic patch, relevant stratigraphic relations are traceable between contiguous ASUs.

'Distant comparisons' are also analytically operable, for instance between SL and SW objects, even without an intermediate chaining (SL->CR) relational operation. In any case broken window objects (BWs) can sometimes offer precious 'connectivity-tools' to weave the web of relevant relations between separate objects.

As well as islands of Homomorphism and critical neighbouring transitional belts, there are various operations (set theory, spatial analysis, multivariate analysis, expert and neural filters, etc) which may be carried out even on noisy non-homomorphic SL objects, that are due to locally sensitive mixing between two or more parent ASUs.

What is really important is the general mental attitude *vis-à-vis* surfacies: it must be understood that the blurring processes are never completely devastating and that they normally leave residual discriminatory information. Normally a limited subset of the whole four-dimensional relational matrix is enough to trace back site-structure and morphogenesis at an acceptable resolution (see below). The basic four token game (RS, SL, CR, SW: cf. fig. 5) can be substantially upgraded with the addition of other objects (and operations on them), depending on the local universe, constraints and resource budget.

What has possibly been overlooked before now is the enormous potential impact of a critical mass of

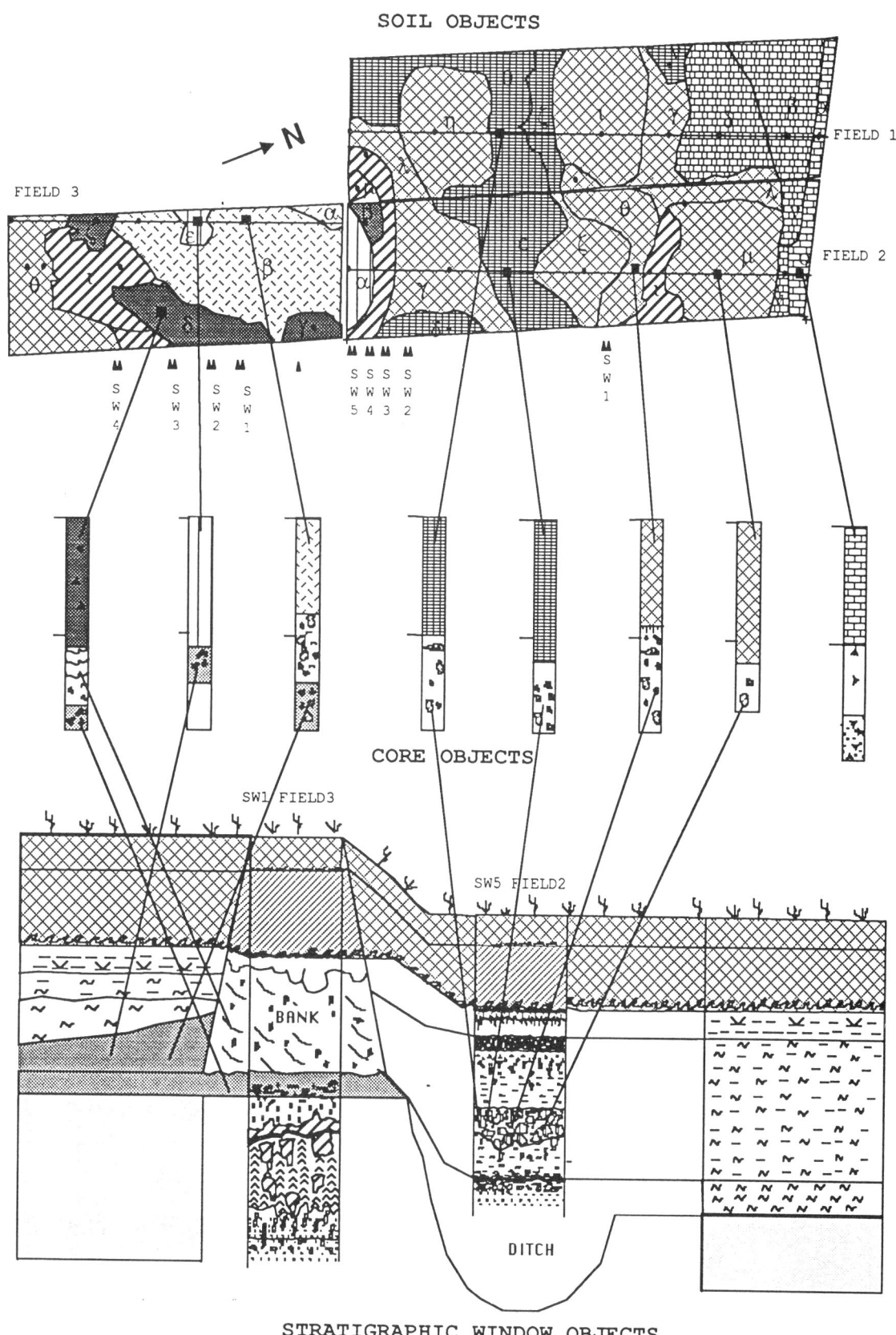

Fig. 5. The Canova case-study: a 'relational model' among 'Soil Objects', 'Core Objects' and 'Stratigraphic Window Objects'.

different operators acting on an equally critical range of objects within a self-consistent and minimum path strategy: the departure from *terra incognita* was a first move towards a promised land which we have just begun to sense 'remotely'.

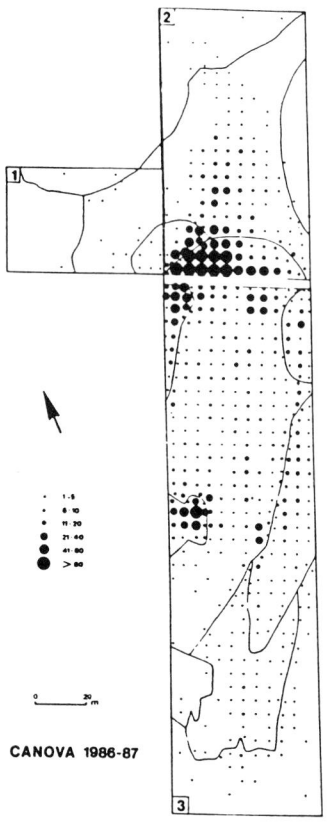

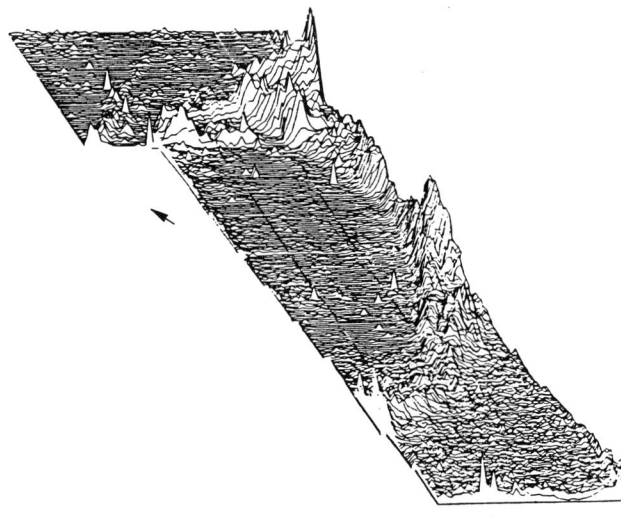

Fig. 6. The Canova case-study.
Above: 'Density Objects' as seen from a simple two-dimensional density plot (number of potsherds in the 5×5m collection units). Below: 'Prospection Objects'; three-dimensional representation of electrical resistivity survey on fields 1 (part), 2 (part) and 3 by C. Howard Davis and P. Howard (cf. Balista et al. 1988).

6. CASE STUDIES

The 'relational model' described above was designed as a minimum effort strategy to infer key statics and dynamics properties related to site-structure and site-formation processes, and has been progressively refined in the course of the project.

Its core was already present in the first, pilot, Canova case study in 1986 (Balista *et al.* 1986, 1988b, 1990; fig. 5), while its present configuration has been tested on the more complex site of Fabbrica dei Soci since 1990 (De Guio, Whitehouse & Wilkins 1989, 1990, 1992; Balista & De Guio 1990–91) and is a substantial upgrade, having now reached the stage of a distinct research domain within the AMPBV, which is called, provokingly, the 'Harris Project' (see below).

At Canova, a small Bronze Age banked settlement, the key operation has been the critical interfacing, in real time in the field, of three kinds of objects: SLs, CRs, SWs. Other objects were isolated and filtered, before, during and after the field campaign: their interfacing between each other and with the previous set has been a largely an *a posteriori* operation. The additional objects were:

– remote sensing objects (RS),
– prospection objects (PRs) (by electrical resistivity, effected by Phil Howard and Chris Howard Davis: a number of anomalies are clearly visible in the dot-density and three-dimensional graphs: fig. 6);
– density objects (DNs): clearly detectable by both direct inspection of simple graphs (fig. 6) and formal spatial analysis, such as our 'Percolation Model' (fig. 7);
– morpho-objects (MRs): there is a clear interference between agrarian morphologies (the multi-convex 'baulature') and the residual, instrumentally detectable, anthropogenic bank;
– expert objects (EXs): a number of 'expert objects', in both the morphocultural and eco-cultural domains, have been identified on the basis of 'previous knowledge' – e.g. the settlement itself with its infrastructure (bank and the ditch), a near-site manured zone, an intrasite secondary household refuse area, a palaeo-meander and various articulations ('point bars' close to the settlement), etc.

The n × n dimensional matrix (n being the number of objects examined) revealed a large number of inter-object relations, especially of the more simple 'corresponds to' type: particularly relevant are those among RSs, MRs, SLs and PRs, which have been related to the local stratigraphy by coring (fig. 8). It has thus been relatively easy to reconstruct the static and morpho-dynamic aspects of the local sequence.

In the case of Fabbrica dei Soci (Villabartolomea-VR) the situation was much more complex: we have

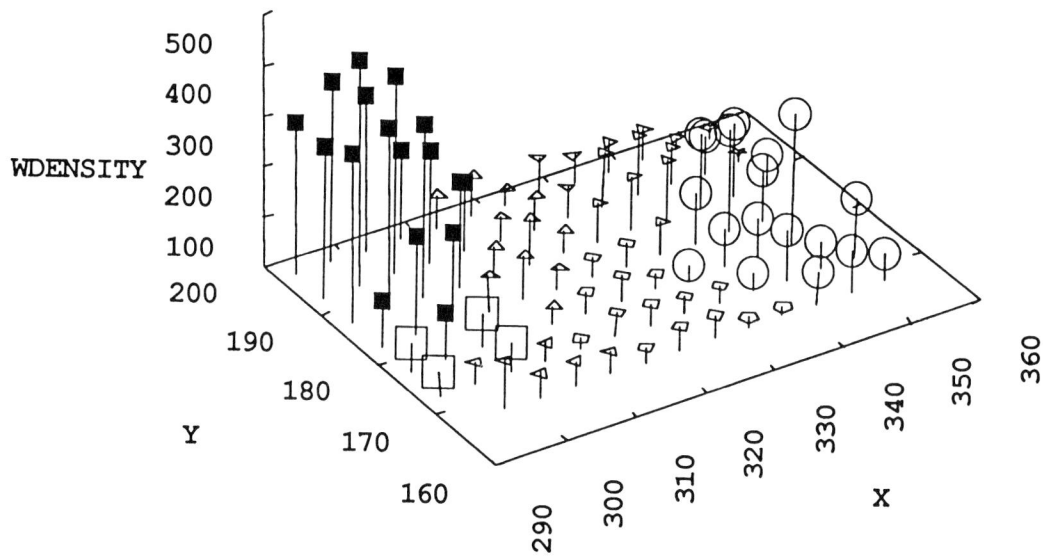

Fig. 7. The Canova case-study: 'Density Objects' highlighted by 'Percolation' (detail of the northern part of field 3: three-dimensional representation of 10 'objects', using a 'weighted density' function: De Guio & Secco 1988).

done an enormous amount of work there, from stratigraphy (no less than 500m of SWs opened), to remote sensing, prospections, phosphate analysis, artefactual and ecofactual sampling, high to medium intensity field surveys, etc. Fabbrica dei Soci (F.S.) has certainly represented a turning point in our expectations about surface archaeology, causing various traumas and failures in our critical path to surface 'complexity', and is still an open challenge to our capacity to manage it. This in fact been a story of hard 'impacts'.

The first, both complex and dramatic, has been the impact with the issue of agrarian impact, which has particularly affected the archaeological record over the last 20 years: its short term projection is very alarming (fig. 9).

The second, and possibly more relevant, impact along our F.S. track has been with what we might simply call 'complexity' (covering all the 'loci' from surface to subsurface and from intrasite to intersite, and all the morphogenetic processes involved). The archaeological complexity of F.S. still defies full understanding. It is amusing to recall here that our first approach to F.S. followed an 'easy' interpretation of the face value RS evidence, a well established *lectio facilior* in the Italian literature following which the site was assumed to be a self-evident and classic instance of a 'terramara' type settlement (cf. Bernabò Brea *et al.* 1987). According to this interpretation an artificial canal was thought to be derived from the nearby Tartaro river, to enter within the bank, to leave from its south-eastern side and finally flow back into the Tartaro.

This reconstruction has subsequently been definitively disproved by our field campaigns, especially by the raw evidence of our many 'Stratigraphic Windows'.

The whole surfacies now appears to be a very complicated palimpsest on which a variety of actors (human, biogenetic, physiogenetic and mechanical) have written and performed their intricate and puzzling scripts.

With a deliberate oversimplification we may select some key steps of this critical trajectory in terms of our so called 'Harris project'. This is a growing sub-domain of research, the target being to implement a working theoretical and methodological package aimed at disentangling the surface palimpsest, and specifically at managing the RSs->SLs->CRs->SWs optimal path discussed above.

The 'Harris' label (Harris 1989) is a deliberately provocative reference, which conceals a substantial post-Harris body of archaeostratigraphic theory. Our main goal is to fill the gap of what we have specifically addressed as the 'Harris matrix impasse', the delay caused by this mainstream-mechanical procedure, generally accepted by the establishment as a theory-proof apparatus for dismantling stratigraphic complexity (cf. our criticism in De Guio 1988a,b, 1991b, 1992; De Guio, Whitehouse & Wilkins 1990, 1992).

Theory apart, the practical 'Harris operation' starts from the compilation of a 'disordered' squared and symmetrical input matrix, with casual entry order for all the SLs considered. By applying specific relational operators to a limited subset of SL pairs we aim to produce a transformed, 'ordered' matrix (similar to a classical matrix seriation), in the stratigraphic sequence of the parent ASUs ('doubles').

Our example is deliberately limited to a small subset of the relevant objects (and relational operators), only five major SLs (fig. 9): they illustrate some critical

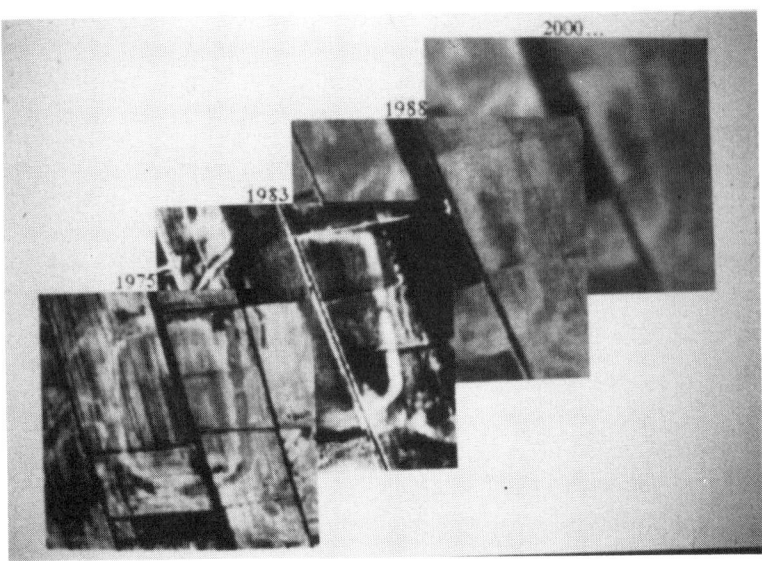

Fig.8. The Fabbrica dei Soci case-study: agrarian impact trough time (the last 2000... 'time-slide' represents an evocative short-term projection derived from the 1988 picture by an image-processing addition of 'gaussian noise': cf. Balista & De Guio 1990-91).

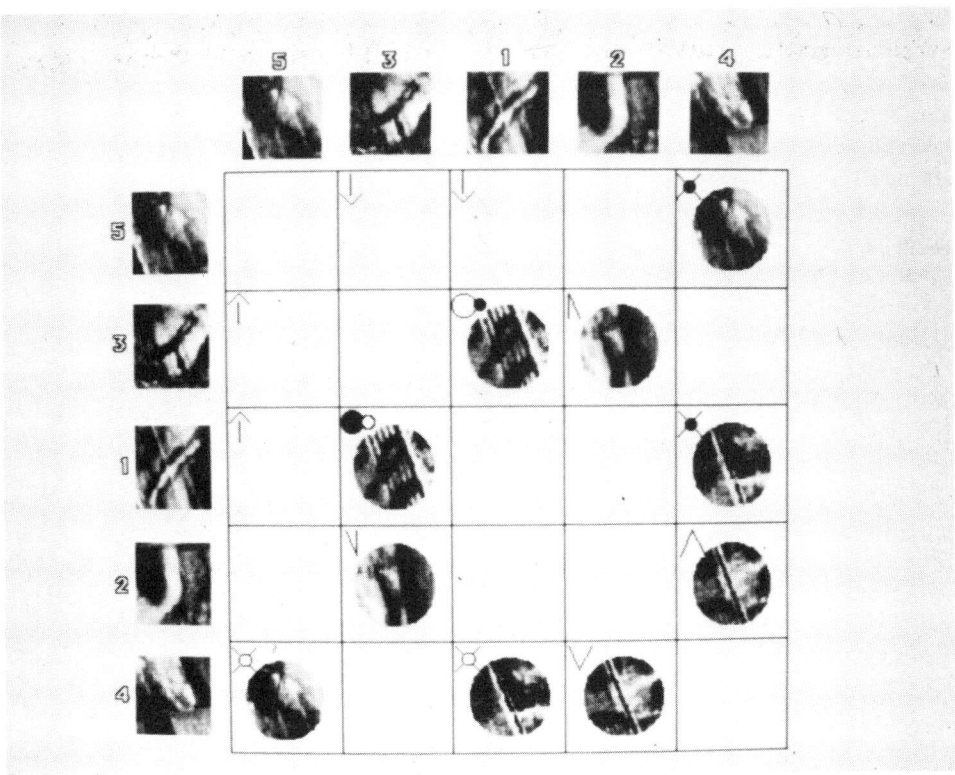

Fig. 9. The Fabbrica dei Soci case-study: aerial photograph (1983) of the site with 5 test 'Soil Objects' highlighted (equalised representative squared sections) and 'kinematic graph' (right) of the time-sequence (De Guio 1992).

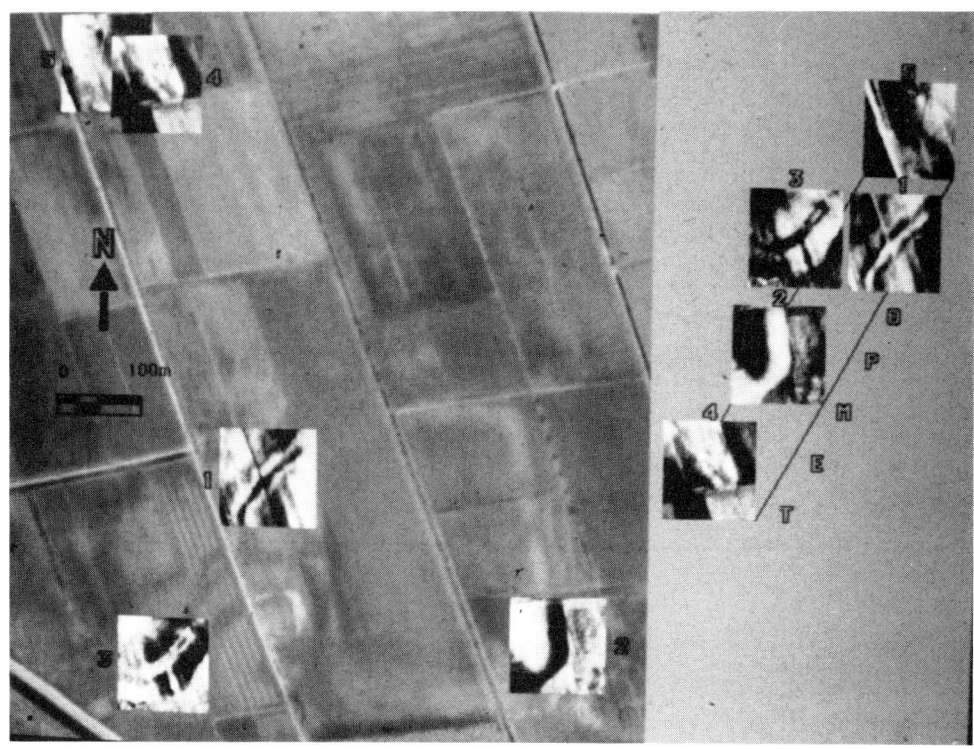

Fig. 10. The Fabbrica dei Soci case-study: the 'Harris project' ordered matrix (squares: representative samples of 'Soil Objects'; circles: representative samples of intersections between 'Soil Objects'; symbols near the circles: representing different Harris and non-Harris archaeo-stratigraphic relations: De Guio 1992).

sequential paths in the 'site formation processes', which disprove the previous simple explanation involved in the classic terramara interpretation.

SL 1 => ('corresponds to') a crevasse channel, that is its subsurface homomorphic counterpart or 'double' is an extinct crevasse channel);
SL 2=> the bank of the Bronze Age settlement;
SL 3=> a 'paleodosso' (an extinct river course) with an E-W direction;
SL 4 => a paleodosso with an NW-SE direction;
SL 5=> a fill of a Roman centuriation drainage channel.

The final sequence, whose restitution is based on teleobservation-eidomatics as well as expert previous knowledge and hard 'stratigraphic' evidence (CRs, BWs, SWs), is here visualised by the ordered, symmetrical matrix (fig. 10): here all the SLs, with their squared icons (referring to a representative segment), are compared and the physical or spatial/logical relations ascertained are expressed by a diagnostic symbol and a circular icon (referring to a representative segment of the spatial intersection, wherever existent, among SLs). The order from left to right and from top to bottom is referred to the seriation of the 'life cycle' of SLs 'doubles' (and specifically to their 'birth' stage).

The whole cartoon story can be simply read and is projected in the 'kinematic graph' on the right: the NW-SE 'paleodosso' (SL 4=>new branch of the palaeo-Adige river) in its senile-extinction phase, is covered by the bank of a settlement (SL 2), onto which another 'paleodosso' (SL 3, a probable Roman course of the Tartaro river) abuts, from which, in turn, a crevasse channel (SL 1) 'emanates', cutting the previous NW-SE 'paleodosso'. A Roman centuriation (SL 5: this is just an instance of a well known pattern: see Tozzi & Harari 1990), which 'cuts' the NW-SE 'paleodosso', is *a priori* conditioned ('logical implication') by both the E-W 'paleodosso' and its 'crevasse channel' (SL 3 and 1).

This easy 'Harris' operation is enormously complicated if we want to consider further SLs and even more so if we want to play our inter-object relational game, by comparing, for instance, SLs to MRs, PRs, DNs and EXs, not to mention the proper 'statigraphic' objects, that is CRs and SWs! Both Expert systems and 'neural networks' can be of some help but the prohibitive number of cross-references can dreadfully affect the neurons of the operators.

Once again an intelligent and minimum effort strategy is required: this is another critical path, which we have just begun to foresee in the misty, lost lands of our Po Plain.

Acknowledgements

The present paper is a selective review of a subject treated fully in De Guio, forthcoming. I am very grateful to Dr. Ruth Whitehouse, Dr. John Wilkins (co-directors of the AMPBV field survey project) and Dr. Mark Pearce for their invaluable suggestions and for their hard work in polishing my English; and also to Dr. Anna Malgarise for her long-term input to the theory, method and survival of the project.

Bibliography

Back, P. & Chen, K. 1991. 'La criticità autorganizzata', *Le Scienze*, 271, 22–30.

Baker, K.G. 1988. 'Towards an archaeological methodology for expert systems', in Ruggles, C. & Rahtz, S. (eds.), *Computer and Quantitative Methods in Archaeology 1987*, BAR International Series, Oxford, 393, 229–236.

Balista, C. & De Guio, A. (eds.) 1990–91. 'Il sito di Fabbrica dei Soci (Villabartolomea–VR): oltre la superficie...', *Padusa*, XXVI–XXVII, 9–85.

Balista, C., Blake, H., De Guio, A., Howard Davis, C., Howard, P., Whitehouse, R. & Wilkins, J. 1986. 'Progetto Alto Polesine. Marzo-Aprile 1986. Relazione preliminare', *Quaderni di Archeologia del Veneto*, II, 21–25.

Balista, C., De Guio, A., Ferri, R., Edwards, M., Herring, E., Howard Davis, C., Howard, P., Peretto, R., Vanzetti, A., Whitehouse, R. & Wilkins, J. 1988. 'Progetto Alto-Medio Polesine: secondo rapporto', *Quaderni di Archeologia del Veneto*, IV, 313–340.

Balista, C., De Guio, A., Ferri, R., Edwards, M., Herring, E., Howard Davis, C., Howard, P., Peretto, R., Vanzetti, A., Whitehouse, R. & Wilkins, J. 1990. 'Alto-Medio Polesine Project: second report', *Accordia Research Papers*, 1, 153–187.

Balista, C., De Guio, A., Ferri, R., Edwards, M., Herring, E., Howard Davis, C., Howard, P., Peretto, R., Vanzetti, A., Whitehouse, R. & Wilkins, J. 1991. 'Alto-Medio Polesine- Basso Veronese Project: third report', *Accordia Research Papers*, 2, 129–178.

Barker, G. & Lloyd, J. (eds.) 1991. *Roman Landscapes. Archaeological Survey in the Mediterranean Region*, London.

Bernabò Brea, M., Cardarelli, A. & Cremaschi, M. 1987. 'Le terramare dell'area centropadana. Problemi culturali e paleoambientali', in AA.VV., *Preistoria e protostoria del bacino del basso Po*, Ferrara, 145–192.

Bintliff, J. (ed.) 1988. *Extracting Meaning from the Past*, Oxford.

Blankhom, H.P. 1991. *Intrasite Spatial Analysis in Theory and Practice*, Aarhus.

Cammarata, S. 1990. *"Reti Neuronali". Un'introduzione all'altra Intelligenza Artificiale*, Milano.

Casati, G. (ed.) 1991. *Il caos. Le leggi del disordine*, Milano.

De Guio, A. 1985a. 'Archaeological applications of survival analysis', in Voorips, A. & Loving, S.H. (eds.), *To Pattern the Past*, P.A.C.T., 11, Strasbourg, 361–381.

De Guio, A. 1985b. 'Archeologia di superficie ed archeologia superficiale', *Quaderni di Archeologia del Veneto*, I, 176–184.

De Guio, A. 1988a. 'Archeologia stratigrafica come topica del corrente dibattito teorico-metodologico e tecnologico in archeologia: una proposta aperta alla "intelligenza artificiale" (I.A.)... e naturale', *Archeologia Stratigrafica dell'Italia Settentrionale*, I, 219–226.

De Guio, A. 1988b. 'Unità archeostratigrafiche come unità operazionali: verso le archeologie possibili degli anni '90', *Archeologia Stratigrafica dell'Italia Settentrionale*, I, 9–22.

De Guio, A. 1991a. 'Alla ricerca del potere: alcune prospettive italiane', in Herring, E., Whitehouse, R. & Wilkins, J. (eds.), *Papers of the Fourth Conference of Italian Archaeology*, 1, The Archaeology of Power, 1, London, 153–192.

De Guio, A. 1991b. 'Calcolatori ed archeologia: un progetto per gli anni '90', *Archeologia e Calcolatori*, 25–78.

De Guio, A. 1992. '"Archeologia della complessità" e calcolatori: un percorso di sopravvivenza fra teorie del caos, "attrattori strani", frattali e...frattaglie del postmoderno', in Bernardi, M. (ed.), *Archeologia del paesaggio*, Firenze, 305–389.

De Guio A., in press. 'Surface and subsurface: deep ploughing into complexity', in Hensel, W., Tabaczynski, S. & Urbanczyk, P. (eds.), *Theory and Practice of Archaeological Research*, II.

De Guio, A. & Secco, G. 1988. 'Archaeological applications of the "Percolation Method" for data analysis and pattern recognition', in Rahtz, S.P.Q. (ed.), *Computer and Quantitative Methods in Archaeology*, BAR International Series, Oxford, 446 (i), 63–93.

De Guio, A., Whitehouse, R. & Wilkins, J. (eds.) 1989. 'Progetto Alto-Medio Polesine – Basso Veronese: terzo rapporto', *Quaderni di Archeologia del Veneto*, V, 1989, 181–216.

De Guio, A., Whitehouse, R. & Wilkins, J. (eds.) 1990. 'Progetto Alto-Medio Polesine – Basso Veronese: quarto rapporto', *Quaderni di Archeologia del Veneto*, VI, 217–238.

De Guio, A., Whitehouse, R. & Wilkins, J. (eds.) 1992. 'Progetto Alto-Medio Polesine – Basso Veronese: quinto rapporto', *Quaderni di Archeologia del Veneto*, VIII, 173–190.

Doran, J. 1982. 'A computational model of sociocultural systems and their dynamics', in Renfrew, C., Rowlands, M.J. & Segraves, M.J. (eds.), *Theory and Explanation in Archaeology*, New York, 375–388.

Doran, J. 1986. 'A contrac-structure model of sociocultural change', *Computer Applications in Archaeology*, 171–178.

Flannery, K. 1967. 'Culture history vs. culture process', *Scientific American*, 217, 119–122.

Gleick, J. 1988. *Chaos: Making a New Science*, New York.

Harris, E.C. 1989. *Principles of Archaeological Stratigraphy*, London.

Hugget, J. 1985. 'Expert systems in archaeology', in Cooper, M.A. & Richards, J.D. (eds.), *Current Issues in Archaeologiacal Computing*, BAR International Series, Oxford, 271, 123–142.

Kauffman, S.A. 1991. 'Anticaos ed evoluzione biologica', *Le Scienze*, 228, 82–91.

Knapp, A.B. (ed.) 1992. *Archaeology, Annales and Ethnohistory*, Cambridge.

Malgarise, A. 1989–90. *Progetto Alto-Medio Polesine – Basso Veronese: un esempio di ricerca archeologica di superficie*, (unpublished dissertation: Università di Padova-Dipartimento di Scienze dell'Antichità).

Nikolis, G. & Prigogine, I. 1991. *La complessità. Esplorazioni nei nuovi campi della scienza*, Torino.

Parisi, D. 1989. *Intervista sulle reti neurali, cervello e macchine intelligenti*, Bologna.

Renfrew, C. & Bahn, P. 1991. *Archaeology. Theories, Methods, and Practice*, London.

Schofield, A.J. (ed.) 1991. *Interpreting Artefact Scatters. Contribution to Ploughzone Archaeology*, Oxford.

Schuster, H.G. 1989. *Deterministic Chaos. An Introduction*, Kiel.

Shutt, A. 1988. 'Expert systems, explanations, arguments and archaeology', in Rahtz, S.P.Q. (ed.), *Computer and Quantitative Methods in Archaeology 1988*, BAR International Series, Oxford, 446 (ii), 353–367.

Smith, T.R. 1987. *Mycenaean Trade and Interaction in the West Central Mediterranean 1600–100 B.C.*, BAR International Series, Oxford, 371.

Stein, J.K. 1986. 'Coring archaeological sites', *American Antiquity*, 51, 3, 505–527.

Tozzi, P. & Harari, H. 1990. *Tempi di un territorio. Atlante aerofotografico delle Valli Grandi Veronesi*, Parma.

Tremolliers, R. 1979. 'The Percolation Method for an efficient grouping of data', *Pattern Recognition*, 11, 225–269.

Trigger, B.G. 1989. *A History of Archaeological Thought*, Cambridge.

Wallerstein, I. 1974. *The Modern World-System*, New York.

Willey, G.R. (ed.) 1956. *Prehistoric Settlement Patterns in the New World*, (Viking Fund Publications in Anthropology no. 23), New York.

3

All or Nothing at all?
Criteria for the Analysis of Pottery from Surface Survey

ALISON MACDONALD

(Institute of Archaeology, University of Oxford)

Summary: *Investigation of ancient landscapes by surface survey is now a widely practised archaeological technique. Data collected by systematic field walking provide valuable information on poorly documented aspects of the ancient world, and in some cases determine a notable reassessment of the nature of rural life. While such new perspectives derive largely from the analysis of surface pottery, interpretations are rarely based on all pottery evidence available on sites. To gain a more complete understanding of the area under investigation, all types of pottery should be studied, not just the more closely dateable finewares. Details of all pottery collected on survey may be recorded using a computer database, which allows a large body of information to be effectively organised and manipulated. This paper reviews the different methodologies for the treatment of pottery and argues for a more rigorous theoretical and methodological approach to surface survey pottery analysis.*

This paper will examine the value of pottery from surface surveys in the identification, and more critically, the dating of sites and settlement patterns through time. Fine wares usually provide the date ranges for sites, even though they often comprise only a small proportion of the total surface collection. However, the bulk of most site assemblages is made up of coarse wares and although they are less easily dated, their potential for dating is significant. In this paper the limitations of surveys where fine wares alone have been used for dating will be outlined. Other research, where the importance of coarse wares has been recognised, will then be described. As a case study the procedure currently employed to examine Roman pottery from the Tuscania Project will be presented. This is an example of a recent survey where *all* pottery is being analysed in detail.

Surface survey depends fundamentally on pottery for various aspects of the interpretation of settled landscapes in antiquity. With tile, pottery is often the principal means of recognising ploughed out sites; occasionally pottery alone may identify a site. Together with other factors (such as extent of scatter) pottery may be used as an indicator of site status: those sites with a range of fine wares are often classed as wealthier than sites with none or very few. More importantly, however, fine pottery usually offers the best means of dating occupation and activity at a site. Other material such as coins, mosaics, sculptural fragments, and in particular fairly closely dated construction methods like *opus reticulatum* may be useful, but frequently the only dating tool available is pottery. This is largely a consequence of the more intensive nature of modern survey, which has been notably successful in discovering smaller, poorer sites (Cherry 1983: 375–416).

Maps of settlement patterns created by survey in the central Mediterranean region are almost always maps of the distribution of structural remains in the countryside, together with fine wares: Black Glaze for the Late Republic, Italian Terra Sigillata for late first century BC and first century AD, and African Red Slip ware subsequently. A fair degree of precision is possible as our knowledge of fine wares has improved over recent years. For example, survey of the Cosa area claims to date pre and post second century BC Black Glaze forms (Attolini *et al.* 1982: 365–385), with important implications for our understanding of the Gracchan period. Italian Terra Sigillata can be dated as close as twenty to thirty years (Ettlinger *et al.* 1990); dates for African Red Slip are generally broader (Hayes 1972, 1980).

Increasingly amphora evidence is being used for dating, for instance at Cosa (Attolini *et al.* 1991: 142–152) and in North Campania (Arthur 1991), although date ranges are usually wider than for fine wares. A preliminary study of the distribution of amphora sherds from surface survey around Cosa and the Albegna Valley, has allowed maps of Greco-Italic, Dressel 1 and Dressel 2/4 amphorae findspots to be made (Attolini *et al.* 1991: 148–150). At Cosa, for example, Dressel 1 sherds provide a broad chronological guide for sites occupied during the first century BC, and it has been suggested that this evidence dates the beginning of the villa system in the area to the period from the late second century to mid first century BC (Attolini *et al.* 1991: 148–149).

Fine wares often make up only a small percentage of the surface collection, and in some cases site dating is based on the presence of only one or two sherds. For instance, in the recently published survey of northern Keos in the Cycladic Islands (Cherry *et al.* 1991), some sites were dated by less than three fine ware sherds. Dating which depends on such a small number of sherds provides a poor basis for generating broad historical and archaeological interpretations, as the authors of the Keos report fully recognize (Cherry *et al.* 1991: 329), and in this rare example of a survey project published in detail, problems confronting survey pottery analysts are addressed: for example, graphs help to show how biases in frequency of pottery deposition may be counteracted (*ibid.*: 330–332).

A further complication is that uneven access to fine wares may have occurred through time. Assumptions are often made that the supply of fine pottery was constant, and that every site had equal access to the supply. However the volume of supply may have fluctuated significantly from period to period, as Fentress and Perkins (1989: 205–214) suggest in their quantitative analysis of African Red Slip. Other influential factors in the variations of access to pottery may include site function, status and economy. A method has been devised to allow for the supply variant by Millett (1991: 18–26) in his analysis of the pottery from the Ager Tarraconensis. Pottery is divided into broad chronological groups, and the amounts in each range are expressed as densities per hectare. The quantity ranges of pottery per hectare are arranged into quartiles and octiles (using the median value) so that the same part of two different distributions can be compared without concern for absolute values. Sites are represented by abnormal densities above background scatter: the top eighth of the values. Thus major divisions from the norm will be identifiable irrespective of absolute quantity of pottery found. As Black Glaze pottery was made in more places than Italian Terra Sigillata, it was more accessible, and this may explain why it has been found in greater quantities on surveys. The different quantities of pottery may not, therefore, relate to changing levels of population in the area. Scaling the results, as Millett describes, may permit more realistic assessments of population figures.

There are limitations to this approach, however, because the calculations only take into account part of the pottery assemblage. It seems to ignore the possibility of exploiting a further and readily available source: the coarse wares which make up the bulk of survey finds. In addition, the assumption of a 'steady state' rural population over long periods of time is questionable.

The value of coarse wares for dating certain phases of urban sites was realised many years ago. Commenting on the Wheelers' publication of excavations at the Romano-British town of Verulamium (Wheeler & Wheeler 1936), Frere suggests that the report:"...relies for its dating too greatly upon Samian and coins, too little on coarse pottery. Experience shows that, particularly in and after the second half of the second century, only a thorough study of the coarse pottery can give sufficiently accurate dates" (1981: 383). An important element of Frere's excavations at Verulamium between 1955 and 1961 was the identification of a large, well-dated sequence of coarse pottery (Frere 1972). As residuality of Samian at Verulamium gradually increases after the early second century AD, its reliability as a tool for dating decreases. From the late second century AD accurate dating becomes more dependent on information from coarse wares. Using this source of evidence, Frere suggested that some of the large houses, which Wheeler assigned to the late Antonine period, were probably built in the first half of the third century (1983: 14). This interpretation has obvious implications for the nature of Verulamium in the third century as a city in ruins or a place of considerable activity.

An awareness of the importance of coarse wares has been slow to reach rural studies, principally because lack of previous study allowed little to be done. Over the last years, however, more stratified deposits have become available in or near survey areas. Distinctive coarse wares, identified and dated from excavated deposits, may have parallels in surface pottery assemblages from the surrounding region. Thus evidence from excavation may assist in the dating of survey material, providing more accurate information on which to base the date range of sites.

An example of the use of coarse wares as tools for dating surface sites is the Biferno Valley in Samnium. Here Roberts, working from excavated data from Matrice and San Giacomo, has managed to group clibani (dome-shaped cooking vessels) into broad chronological groups (Cubberley, Lloyd & Roberts 1988: 98–119). Clibani from the Late Republic and Early Empire tend to be large, with diameters ranging from 24–50 cm, and with a pronounced rounded dome. Later forms tend to be considerably smaller, with flatter domes, and possibly smaller flanges. In addition, it was noted that clibani sometimes display crimped or 'pie-crust' decoration on, and above the flange, (this feature is also apparent on clibani flanges from the Tuscania survey). Although at present decoration does not seem to provide an accurate guide for dating, further research may allow certain features to be linked with a particular time period. Roberts' re-examination of survey finds using clibani and other dateable coarse wares, has revealed a more vigorous picture of rural settlement in the upper Biferno Valley under the early Empire than the fine ware evidence alone had suggested (Roberts pers. comm.). This would seem to support the view that, at least in some areas of the Roman world, access to Italian Terra Sigillata was restricted by comparison with the local Black Glaze of earlier times.

Information from excavation has also contributed to the dating of survey material on a recent project around the Hellenistic and Roman city of Balboura in Turkey. Here a number of distinctive coarse ware sherds were retrieved, characterised by thin vertical lines of burnishing, thought to have been made by the action of rubbing a small piece of stick down the vessel wall (Catling & Roberts 1991: 19). The date of these 'stick burnished' vessels was initially thought to be Late Roman. Recently, however, excavations at Xanthos (about fifty miles south of Balboura) have produced complete vessels in a very similar fabric and with similar burnishing (Catling, pers. comm.). They came from a sealed deposit of thirteenth century date. This indicates that the vessels were present in the Byzantine period, and calls for a reassessment of the survey site dating. As yet, it is unclear whether these vessels were only produced in Byzantine times, or whether production began at an earlier date.

For the Tuscania survey, excavations at Cosa provide local examples of fairly well dated coarse wares (Dyson 1976), while major publications, such as Ostia (1968, 1970, 1973, 1977) and Luni (1973, 1977), are useful for more common forms. At present I have found dated parallels for over fifty percent of coarse ware forms found on the survey, confirming the dates of some sites and providing new information for a number of others. In some cases these coarse wares fill in 'gaps' in date ranges; for example, sherds from coarse ware forms of Early Imperial date may suggest continuity of occupation on sites where sherds of Republican Black Glaze and Mid to Late Imperial African Red Slip were present, but Early Imperial Italian Terra Sigillata sherds were lacking. Republican and Late Imperial coarse wares have also been identified on a number of sites when no fine wares of these periods were present.

A different technique employed to assist the dating of coarse wares is to find parallels in fine ware forms. In his study of the coarse wares from Cosa, Dyson cites an example in the earliest deposit of a wide bowl (in coarse ware fabric) with a distinctive offset rim, which relates to a similar Black Glaze form. The date range of the Black Glaze vessel is early to mid Republic: a similar date range may be applicable to the coarse ware version (Dyson 1976: 32, CF66, fig. 5; Taylor 1957: 154-155). In a later deposit, he notes a deep wide-mouthed vessel with a heavy rolled rim which seems to reflect an African Red Slip form dated to the late Roman period (Dyson 1976: 162-163, FC6, fig. 64; Hayes Form 99). Likewise, imitations of African Red Slip wares in local clays have been noted in Northern Campania (Arthur 1991: 91). Examples include versions of Hayes Forms 8 and 23 (Arthur 1991: 122, Site S37) from the second century AD, and Hayes Forms 61A and 91 (ibid. 121, Site S24bis) from the fourth or fifth centuries AD (or possibly later).

Another approach, which I am using at Tuscania, is to focus on sherds from large, single period sites, as defined by fine wares and other evidence, in order to identify their typical coarse wares. Work of this kind, on the pottery from the Albegna Valley survey, is already providing important results (Cambi & Fentress 1989: 74-86). Here sherds from a distinctive type of jug, with globular body and strap handle, usually in a well-levigated buff fabric, were found on a number of sites along with sherds of late African Red Slip forms and clibani dating to the fifth and sixth centuries. On ten sites sherds from strap handle jugs were found when other dateable material was lacking, thus providing a fresh source of evidence for activity in Late Antiquity. These sites, it has been suggested, represent necropoleis for the inhabitants of nearby villas (Cambi & Fentress 1989: 80). At Tuscania, sherds from similar strap handled jugs have been found on a number of sites with associated African Red Slip, but also in isolation, again indicating otherwise unrecognisable activity in Late Antiquity.

Work of this kind is critical for recognising activity after the main fine wares cease arriving. In many parts of Italy, for example, there was a huge reduction of African Red Slip imports in the fifth century. But does this absence of fine ware evidence reflect a declining population and desertion of the countryside? The Cosa and Tuscania examples already suggest that it does not, and for the future, a better understanding of late sequences, obtainable from excavations such as that at Mola di Monte Gelato (Potter & King 1988: 253-311; Marazzi, Potter & King 1989: 38-40) and on the Rieti Project, will provide the opportunity to achieve more balanced perspectives.

As an example of current procedure for handling survey pottery, where entire assemblages of fine wares, amphorae and coarse wares have been recorded, the method used to examine the Roman material from the Tuscania Survey will be outlined. This project, directed by G. Barker, T. Rasmussen and A. Grant, is a modern, carefully conducted survey which took place around the town of Tuscania (Barker 1988: 772-785; Barker & Rasmussen 1988: 25-42; Rasmussen 1991: 106-114). The land under investigation covered the area within a 10km radius of the town. The sampling strategy involved the walking of 1km wide cardinal transects that stretched north, south, east and west from Tuscania. This was complemented by coverage of a random sample of 1 km squares in the survey zone and a number of judgement squares (to yield information about particular areas). Teams of four to six people, walking 5–10 m apart, surveyed accessible land in the sample area, and recorded the location and nature of finds, together with various other factors. All 'off-site' archaeological artifacts were collected, including a sample of the different tile fabrics. When a site was located, a gridding system was adopted, the size of grid depending on the area to be covered. A total pick up of pottery took place on all sites, apart from the largest, where a representative sample was collected.

A recording system devised for excavated material (Kenrick, unpub.) was adapted for the survey pottery. The framework of the system is the 'form' (shape and style) and 'fabric' series. All distinct variants of 'feature' sherds (rims, bases and handles) were numbered and placed together to establish the form series. Every sherd examined corresponds to one of the sherds in the form series. In the case of unique pieces, the sherd was numbered and added to the system. In the same way, the fabric of every sherd matches, in broad terms, a fabric series type. If a distinct fabric was identified, it joined the fabric series. By entering records onto a computer database, manipulation of the information can be achieved quickly, and more accurately than by manual sorting. The database can be formatted into a number of reports showing different selections of information. Although a considerable sample is dealt with, it is a simple process to search the data and find information on, for example, site, date, continuity of occupation, density and range of pottery. From initial analysis of the Tuscania material, it is apparent that different patterns emerge if the whole assemblage is examined, rather than finewares alone.

Manipulation of the data is still in process, but it is likely that systematic treatment of pottery will produce a more reliable framework for dating. Moreover, full presentation of evidence will provide a better basis for future scholars to re-calculate findings, in the light of new discoveries. A major limiting factor of survey reports so far published is that the ceramic data are not presented in detail. While historical texts are widely available in the original language and in translation, the source material of survey has tended to be only partially revealed. It is therefore virtually impossible to assess the validity of the interpretations, or attempt to draw different conclusions to those of the writer. Lack of primary evidence also means that accurate regional parallels cannot be made. As more survey work is reported, this criticism is becoming recurrent and should be taken very seriously indeed (Catling 1984: 98–103; Peia 1993: 183–185; Alcock 1993: 109–112). To maximise the usefulness of pottery analysis, future studies must develop a more vigorous theoretical and methodological approach, and ensure that data are presented in full.

Bibliography

Alcock, S. 1993. 'Review: G. Barker and J. Lloyd, (eds.) Roman Landscapes: Archaeological Survey in the Mediterranean Region', *Journal of Field Archaeology* 20, 109–112.

Arthur, P. 1991. *Romans in Northern Campania.* (British School at Rome Archaeological Monographs 1), London.

Attolini, I. *et al.* 1982. 'Ricognizione archeologica nell'ager Cosanus e nella valle dell'Albegna.Rapporto preliminare 1981', *Archeologia Medievale* 9, 365–385.

Attolini, I. *et al.* 1991. 'Political geography and productive geography between the valleys of the Albegna and Fiora in northern Etruria', in Barker & Lloyd (eds.), 142–152.

Barker, G. 1988. 'Archaeology and the Etruscan countryside', *Antiquity* 62, 772–785.

Barker, G. & Lloyd, J. (eds.) 1991. *Roman Landscapes. Archaeological Survey in the Mediterranean Region.* (British School at Rome Archaeological Monograph 2), London.

Barker, G. & Rasmussen, T. 1988. 'The archaeology of an Etruscan polis: the preliminary report on the Tuscania Survey', *Papers of the British School at Rome* 56, 25–42.

Cambi, F. & Fentress, E. 1989. 'Villas to castles: first millennium AD demography in the Albegna Valley', in K. Randsborg (ed.) *The Birth of Europe: Archaeology and Social Development in the First Millennium AD*, Analecta Romana Instituto Danici, Rome.

Catling, P. & Roberts, P. 1991. 'Balboura survey pottery study', *Anatolian Studies* XLI, 19.

Catling, R. 1984. 'Review: C. Renfrew & M. Wagstaff (eds.) An Island Polity. The Archaeology of Exploitation in Melos', *The Classical Review* 34, 98–103.

Cherry, J.F. 1983. 'Frogs round the pond: perspectives on current archaeological survey projects in the Mediterranean region', in Keller and Rupp (eds.), *Archaeological Survey in the Mediterranean Region*, BAR 155, Oxford, 375–416.

Cherry, J.F., Davis, J.L. & Mantzourini, E. 1991. *Landscape Archaeology, as Long-Term History. Northern Keos in the Cycladic Islands from Earliest Settlement until Modern Times.* (Monumenta Archaeologica 16), Los Angeles.

Coccia, S. & Mattingly, D. (eds.) 1992. 'Settlement history, environment and human exploitation of an intermontane basin in the central Apennines: the Rieti Survey, 1988–1991, part I'. *Papers of the British School at Rome,* 60, 213–289.

Cubberley, A.L., Lloyd, J.A. & Roberts, P. 1988. 'Testa and clibani: the baking covers of classical Italy', *Papers of the British School at Rome* 56, 98–119.

Dyson, S.L. 1976. *Cosa: The Utilitarian Pottery* (Monographs of the American Academy in Rome, 33), Rome.

Ettlinger, E. *et al.* 1990. *Conspectus Formarum Terrae Sigillatae Italico Modo Confectae*, Bonn.

Fentress, E. & Perkins, P. 1989. 'Counting African Red Slip Ware', *L'Africa Romana 5. Atti del V Convegno di Studio*, (Sassari 1987), 205–214.

Frere, S.S. 1972. *Verulamium Excavations Volume I* (Reports of the Research Committee of the Society of Antiquaries of London 28), Oxford.

Frere, S.S. 1981. 'Verulamium in the third century', in A. King & M. Henig, *The Roman West in the Third Century. Contributions from Archaeology and History*, BAR International Series 109 (ii), Oxford, 383–392.

Frere, S.S. 1983. *Verulamium Excavations Volume II* (Reports of the Research Committee of the Society of Antiquaries of London 41), London.

Hayes, J. W. 1972. *Late Roman Pottery*, London.

Hayes, J. W. 1980. *A Supplement to Late Roman Pottery*, London.

Kenrick, P.M. (unpub.). *The Cataloguing of Roman Pottery. A Manual Recommended for Use in Essex.*

Luni I 1973. *Scavi di Luni I. Relazione preliminare della campagna di scavo 1970–1971.* 3 vols., Rome.

Luni II 1977. *Scavi di Luni II. Relazione delle campagne di scavo. 1972-1974*, 2 vols., Rome.
Ostia I 1968. *Studi Miscellanei*, 13.
Ostia II 1970. *Studi Miscellanei*, 16.
Ostia III 1973. *Studi Miscellanei*, 21.
Ostia IV 1977. *Studi Miscellanei*, 23.
Millett, M. 1991. 'Pottery: population or supply patterns? The Ager Tarraconensis approach', in Barker & Lloyd (eds.), 18-26.
Marazzi, F., Potter, T.W. & King, A. 1989. 'Mola di Monte Gelato (Mazzano Romano -VT): notizie preliminari sulle campagne di scavo 1986-1988 e considerazioni sulle origini dell'incastellamento in Etruria Meridionale alla luce di nuovi dati archeologici', *Archeologia Medievale* 16, 103-119.
Peia, J.T. 1993. 'Review: P. Arthur, Romans in Northern Campania', *American Journal of Archaeology* 97, 1 183-185.
Potter, T.W. & King, A.C. 1988. 'Scavi a Mola di Monte Gelato presso Mazzano Romano, Etruria meridionale. Primo rapporto preliminare', *Archeologia Medievale* 15, 253-331.
Rasmussen, T. 1991. 'Tuscania and its territory', in Barker & Lloyd (eds.), 106-114.
Wheeler, R.E.M. & Wheeler, T.V. 1936. *Verulamium, A Belgic and Two Roman Cities*, (Reports of the Research Committee of the Society of Antiquaries of London 11), Oxford.

4

Survey Methodology and the Site: A Roman Villa from the Rieti Survey

D. J. MATTINGLY AND S. COCCIA

(with contributions by Paul Beavitt, Amanda Claridge, Hugh Elton, Ian George, and Paul Roberts)

Summary: *The Rieti Project (1988–1992) located c. 80 sites of Roman date in the hinterland of* Reate *(modern Rieti), including 2 large settlements (*vici*) and at least 6–7 sites that seemed to merit identification as luxurious villas, these being defined partly in terms of size, partly in terms of the presence of mosaic tesserae and/or marble fragments. Whilst survey cannot hope to emulate the degree of detail that an excavation can provide, what sort of a story can be put together on the basis of survey data alone? What are the limits to the knowledge that survey can provide about complex sites? These questions prompted the examination of one of the Rieti villas, site 1 at Ponte Capo d'Aqua, in great detail and using an array of techniques. This paper shows how sherding, gridded collection, plotting of surface distributions and soil marks, resistivity survey and coring were utilized to build a detailed picture of the chronology, architectural pretension and morphology of the site. The large quantity of marble, painted plaster fragments and mosaic tesserae recovered in gridding the site allow considerable insights into the decorative schemes used in the villa. We also consider what might and what might not be added by excavation at the site.*

INTRODUCTION

The Rieti Project has involved the intensive field survey of a sample of the different landscapes (plain, hills, mountains) that characterize the Sabina reatina in central Italy (Fig. 1). Three seasons of survey 1988–1990 and a study season in 1991 have been followed up by excavation at two sites in 1992 (Coccia & Mattingly 1992a/b; 1993; Barker & Mattingly 1989). Excavation was always seen as an essential complement to our survey methods and it must be made explicit at the outset that the argument of this paper is not a misguided attempt to claim some sort of primacy for survey methodology over excavation. Our purpose is to consider the extent to which survey may be used to build up a dossier of information on specific sites and thereby reduce the necessity to resort to excavation. The efficacy of these sorts of approaches is reasonably well-established in Italian archaeology, perhaps most dramatically by the recently published survey of the Etruscan town of La Doganella in the Albegna valley (Perkins & Walker 1990). We also believe that high quality survey data have a major role to play in the formulation of effective excavation strategies, particularly in research projects. At the very least they will give the excavated material a broader context and will focus the research design around key questions to which survey alone cannot provide the answer.

The existence of a Roman villa at Ponte Capo d'Aqua (site 1) was known to local archaeologists before the start of our survey (de Rossi 1973), but it is now clearer that, from a regional perspective, it was an exceptionally large and luxurious villa.

ARCHAEOLOGICAL EVIDENCE

Initial survey in 1988 quickly established that site 1 was large and complex. Part of the site lies beneath a vineyard of fairly recent creation, the rest below a patchwork of fields – some in regular cultivation, others normally fallow. Work was carried out over several seasons, involving:

1) the systematic walking of all fields under plough with collection of artefacts in relation to transects at 10m intervals;

2) more intensive collection and recording of all surface debris and artefacts within the rows of the vineyard (Figs. 3, 5, 6, 7, 8);

3) a separate gridded sherding exercise around the cistern at the E end of the site (Fig. 4);

4) resistivity survey of the entire area around the vineyard (Fig. 2);

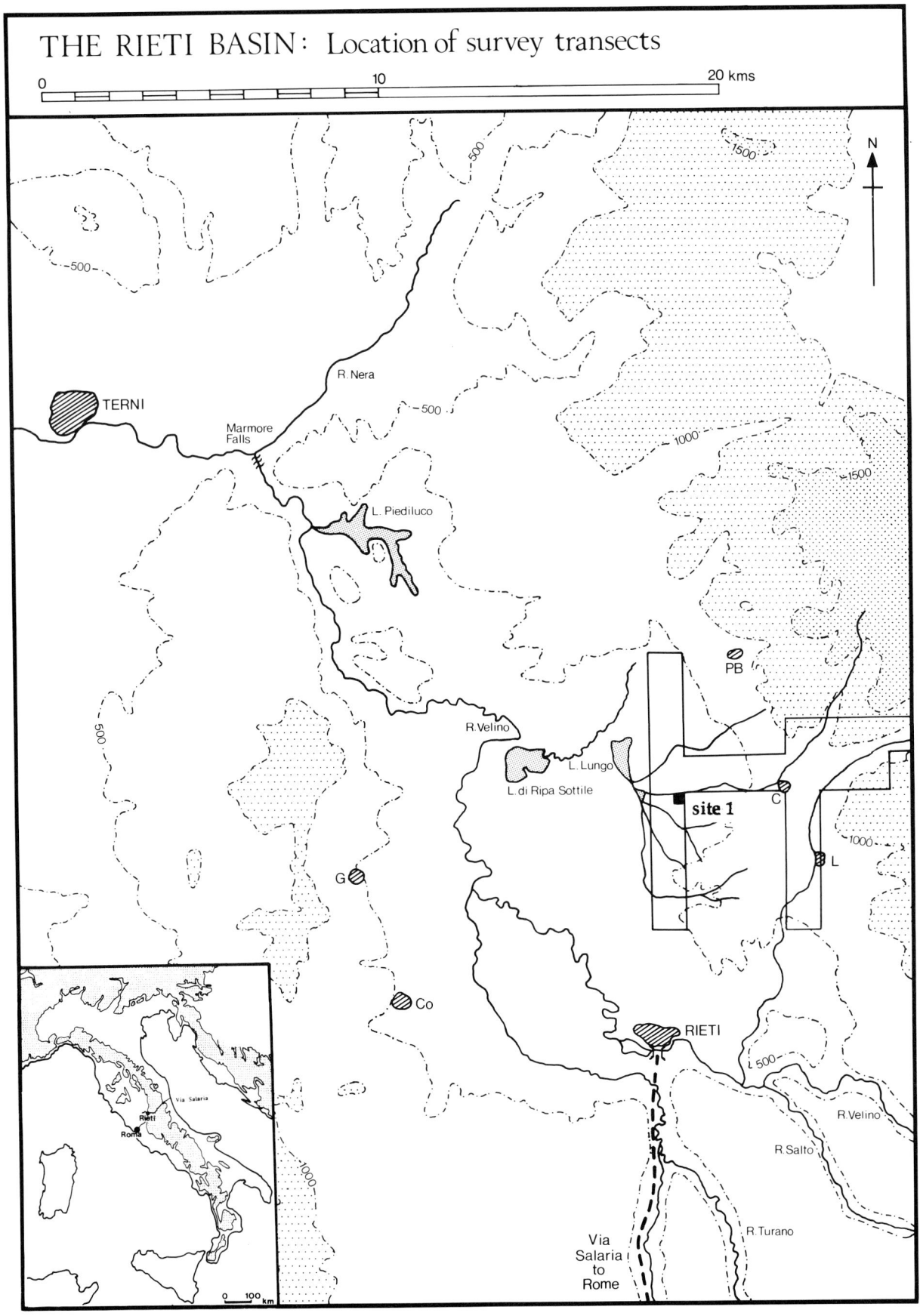

Fig. 1. The Rieti survey transect within the Rieti basin showing the location of the site 1 villa.

5) survey at 1: 200m of all physical traces of structures in relation to the topography of the site (this included many debris concentrations observed in the ploughsoil) (Fig. 3);

6) several grab samples of diagnostic pottery found during repeat visits to the site;

7) discussions with local farmers who had knowledge of the site.

The only architectural feature visible at the surface is a cistern, whose intact vault lies close to modern ground level. It is possible for a small person to descend through the original 0.75 m square access hole in the centre of the vault into the substantially infilled interior. The internal dimensions of the cistern are c. 3.5m (north-south) by 3.75m (east-west). Over and around the cistern a substantial cairn has been built up as a result of modern stone dumping.

Resistivity Survey (with IG, PB)

Resistivity survey was not practicable within the vine rows, but was carried out over an extensive area around the vineyard (Fig. 2). Along the southern edge of the vineyard, the adjacent resistivity grids contain a number of high resistance features (A, B) which must be building remains, running for a length of at least 40m. A number of linear features run up to them from the south, and the clearest of these may be the remains of an enclosure wall (C, D, E), contemporary with the villa and surviving for a distance of 40m north to south, then turning at a corner and running east for a further 80m before its trace becomes indistinct. Local farmers have independently confirmed the existence of this wall, noted by them in ploughing. Within this main outer wall there are several other high resistance anomalies, including two curving features of uncertain interpretation (F and G).

Two linear features were detected running away from the west side of the extant cistern (H, J) and one of these lines (H) probably represents a water channel draining from an overflow pipe (visible in the top of the west wall of the interior of the cistern). Local farmers report some sort of slab-lined channel running between the cistern and the vineyard and yellow tile and quite large pieces of mortar were observed in the ploughsoil in line with this feature. Additionally, both sherding and the resistivity plots suggest the possible presence of other buildings (M and N) in this area.

Resistivity results from the extreme western part of the site do not appear to reveal archaeological features, possibly due to the change in geology suggested by the existence of a spring and the change in slope. The soils in this area contain a significantly higher gravel component than those to the east.

Surface Observation (with IG, PB)

Various debris scatters and soil colour changes were observed in the ploughed areas to the east of the vineyard between 1988-1992. The long strip to the south of both this area and the vineyard was ploughed for the first time in many years in 1992, revealing further detail (Fig. 3). Most of the concentrations of surface debris are likely to represent plough damage to buildings below. Some of the surface concentrations comprised plentiful mortar, tile and building rubble (A, I), while other definite features contained abundant tile, but less mortar and large fragments (B, G, H, K, L, M) perhaps reflecting prolonged plough damage to the underlying structures. Slighter concentrations of tile (D, E) or pottery (C) pose interpretational problems, though the resistivity results and observation in other seasons suggest that they may also lie over structures.

The most suggestive minor scatters are those around the cistern. At B there was a concentration of pebbles, mortar, building stone, tile and pieces of dolium. To the north of the cistern (C,D,E) substantial amounts of pottery, tile, marble and mortar were observed, while to the west the plough soil was much darker, containing large amounts of tile, marble and mortar (A). In 1990 we recorded the amount and weight of pot and tile on the surface within 5m grid squares laid out over this end of the site. The results reveal a series of major concentrations and support the likelihood that there were structures to the north, west and southwest of the cistern (Fig. 4).

In 1992 a series of distinct grey clay linear features (J) was noted close to the spring at the west end of the site. The associated tile and pottery was somewhat abraded (with the spectacular exception of an intact late antique lamp). Augering along the line of these features failed to locate subsurface clay and hit gravel at a very shallow depth, indicating that these shallow features (water channels associated with the spring?) have been completely destroyed by ploughing.

To the south of the vineyard, a major rubble and mortar concentration (I) confirms the interpretation of the resistivity data. Within the vineyard rows, similar concentrations of building stone and mortar were plotted, tracing a major building extending northwards from this point. On the south side of the main concentration (I), a weaker 'shadow' of rubble and mortar was noted, petering out abruptly towards the west, beyond which point the dense debris continued as a narrow line. This sudden change corresponds with the point at which the putative enclosure wall joined the main villa (C on Fig. 2); this was evidently not at the corner of the villa itself. There was no trace in the ploughed area of the north-south enclosure wall itself. The southern edge of the main villa building appears to extend c. 7 m into the field beyond the posts marking the ends of the vine rows.

Resistivity Anomaly Figure 2	Surface Debris Figure 3	Interpretation
A, B	I	S edge of main villa building
C, D, E	change in width of J	Enclosure wall running up to S edge of villa
F, G	no surface trace	Possibly drains from the bath in S part of villa?
H		Thin trace of water pipe from cistern
J	B	Probable building (or broad wall?)
K	C,D,E,F	Possible building on N side of cistern
L	A	Probable building to W of cistern
M	G, H?	Possible structure (less clear from surface traces, than on resistivity)
N	L, M	Probable building (may connect with traces in extreme E part of vineyard)
high resistance area at W end of site	J	Clay filled shallow channels on gravel bed (that gives high resistance)

Table 1. Comparison between resistivity anomalies (letters in first column and on Fig. 2) and surface debris concentrations (letters in second column and on Fig. 3)

THE VINEYARD

Material was collected from the first 33 ploughed strips between north-south rows of vines, these being on average c. 75 m long by 2–2.5m wide with each row divided for collection purposes into three 25m sections numbered A, B, C (with A the most northerly – see Fig. 3, for numbering and layout). All marble and tesserae noted on the surface were collected in 1988 and 1989, plus all pottery in 1988 and significant diagnostics in 1989. The quantity of tile was such that, after counting and weighing a sample number of rows in 1988, we simply counted fragments on the ground and derived an estimated weight by extrapolation from a control sample, subsequently only collecting profile or near complete tiles. The quantities of material from an area of c. 0.75 ha (only 0.62 ha if the space taken up by the vines themselves is excluded) are striking: to give simply the 1988 figures, over 2,000 pottery sherds (weight, c. 13 kg), 10,000 tile fragments (with an estimated weight of 612kg), over 700 marble fragments (weighing 50 kg).

These figures are aggregates of the material collected across the entire vineyard. The peak densities were considerably higher and appear to indicate the position and something of the main building plan. There was far less material from rows 1–15 than from rows 16–33 and beyond row 33 the density rapidly reached negligible levels. It is possible that some archaeology had been lost from rows 1–15, since local informants reported that a natural 'hillock' was smoothed at the time the vines were dug in. This may coincide with a rather sterile area centred on rows 5C–10C and 11B-15B. On the other hand the absence of any trace of wall foundations in this area might indicate that it was originally open (perhaps a courtyard?). The overall distribution of building debris (Figs. 3 and 5) is suggestive of an L-shaped or U-shaped main building around some such open space.

Material	number	weight (kg)	per ha no (wt)	per 0.01ha no (wt)
Tile	10,187	612.34	16430 (988)	164 (9.88)
Pottery	2045	12.95	3298 (21)	33 (0.21)
Marble	730	50.1	1177 (81)	12 (0.81)
Tesserae	964	4.42	1555 (7.13)	16 (0.071)

Table 2. Counts and weights of material collected from the vineyard (0.62ha) in 1988 and extrapolated densities (counts and weights) for areas of 1 ha and 0.01ha.

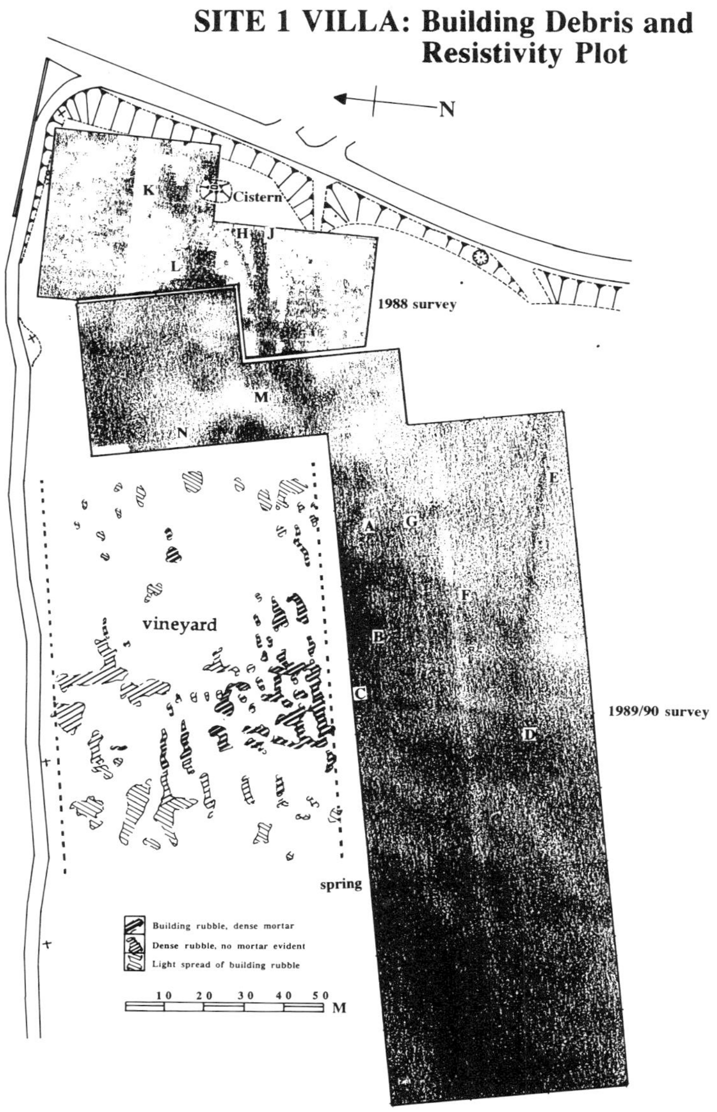

Fig. 3. Surface debris and ploughsoil concentrations at site 1. Note the numbering scheme for the vineyard rows (1–33) and their divisions into sectors A, B and C.

Fig. 2. Resistivity survey at site 1 (NB within the vineyard area building rubble and debris has been plotted for comparison).

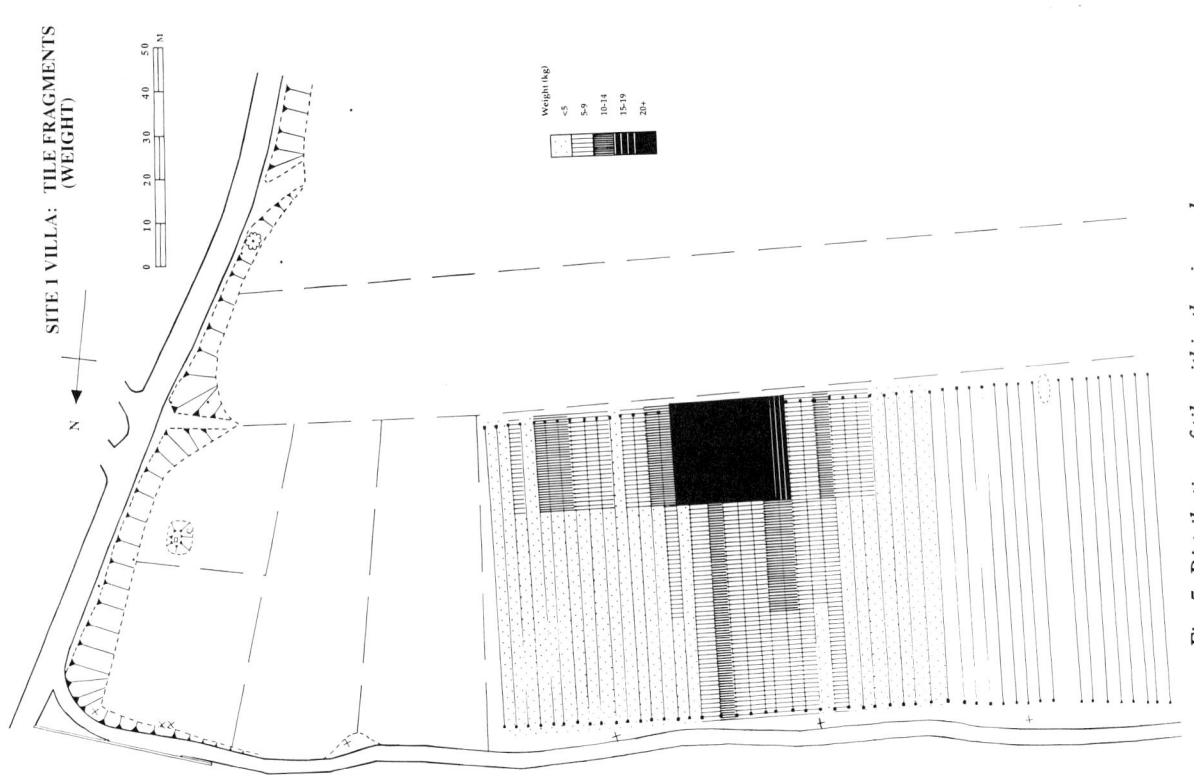

Fig. 5. Distribution of tile within the vineyard area (in kg – based on extrapolated weights from tile counts).

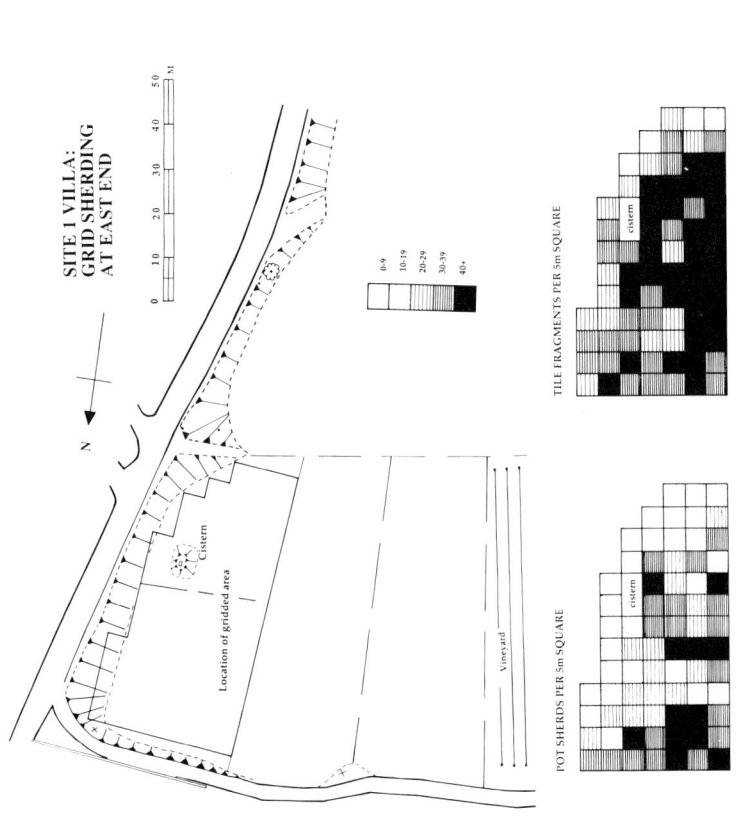

Fig. 4. Gridded sherding plots for the eastern end of site 1. The squares are 5 × 5 m. The high density of material may be compared with similar plots from a less imposing Roman farm (site 97), see Coccia & Mattingly 1993: fig. 15.

Pottery (with PR)

Several thousand sherds of pottery have been collected from this site over the years of study. The folowing list contains the main diagnostics recorded (noting number of sherds and references to the standard typological series: Bailey 1980; *Conspectus* 1990; Hayes 1972; Morel 1981) for the principal phases of occupation. In almost every period represented, this has been the most productive site from the entire survey zone. The Archaic/pre-Roman and Republican occupation (represented by impasto sherds, a calcite tempered ware and black gloss wares) is by the standards of the survey very strongly attested. The major concentration of early imperial wares is quite striking, but the mid- and later imperial presence is also well represented. A small group of probable late antique coarseware sherds and an intact lamp demonstrate that activity at the site continued to at least the late 5th century and likely into the 6th or later.

Archaic and Pre-Roman: Impasto 42 sherds; Calcite Tempered Ware 8 sherds.
Roman Republican: Black Gloss 15 (incl. Morel 2780, 2538).
Early Imperial: Italian Terra Sigillata 94 (incl. *Conspectus* 3 (×4), 13, 18/20 (×3), 19/21 (×6), 36, 37); Late Italian Terra Sigillata 4; Thin Walled Ware 3; Pompeian Red Ware 2.
Early Mid-Imperial: African Red Slip A Fabric 52 (incl. Hayes 6A (×2), 6B (×2), 8A, 9A (×2), 14); African Red Slip Cookwares 13 (incl. 23A (×2), 23B (×4), 196 (×2))
Mid-Imperial: African Red Slip Ware C Fabric 28 (incl. Hayes 45A, 50A (x3), 53B)
Late Imperial: African Red Slip Ware D Fabric 25 (incl. 58A, 91A (×4), 91B, 61B, 67); African Red Slip Lamps 2
Late Antique: Bailey type U Lamp (5thC +)
There were also numerous amphora fragments: diagnostics comprised Italian amphorae 37 (incl. Dressel 2/4 (×6), Dressel 1 (×3), Dressel 7/11 (×3)); African amphorae 21 (incl. Spatheion (×2)).

Tile and Brick (with HE)

Tile and brick fragments in the vineyard rows were counted and notional weights generated, based on an 'average' weight for a single fragment of 0.06kg. The resulting distribution plot fits well with other evidence suggesting the presence of a large tile-roofed building (Fig. 5), with a massive concentration in the area between rows 15 and 29 and a secondary concentration in rows 2C–7C that could relate to a separate building. As well as the usual *tegulae* and *imbrices*, the site yielded some unusual pieces, including three examples of red-painted tiles (21C × 2, 20C). Three column tiles were recovered from 22A, 23A, 24A and an *opus spicatum* brick from 9C. Some bath-house brick and tile was also noted, including two fragments of flue tiles (from 18A, 32A). Fragments of *opus signinum* flooring further suggested that there was a bath in this south facing wing.

Wall Plaster

All the fragments of painted wall-plaster came from the area of densest material in the vineyard (rows 23–28). Most plaster fragments were very small and fragile with no surviving pigment, but colour could be made out on 20 of them (one fragment had traces of two colours): red 8, pink 4, purple 4, yellow 1, black 2, powder blue 2. Although this is a meagre collection, the distribution coincides entirely with the zone of the vineyard below which lie mosaics and marble.

Mosaic Tesserae

Mosaic tesserae were most concentrated in rows 18C–28C, with a secondary concentration in 22B-26B (Fig. 6). Analysis of the different types and sizes of tesserae present reveals several distinct spatial groupings, suggesting that more than a single floor was involved (Appendix 1). For instance, it is noticeable that there is a higher concentration of coloured tesserae in the 22B-26B zone than in other sectors.

Type	Colour	Description	Av. dimensions (cm)	Area of face	Av. wt (g)
A	White	V. large rectangles/cubes	4×4×4.6	>15 cm²	177
B	White	Large thin rectangles	1.7×1.5×3.3	>2 cm²	20
C	White	Med. large thin rectangles	1.3×1.1×3	>1.4cm²	10–12
D	White	Medium rectangles	0.9×0.9×2	>0.5cm²	4–5
E	White	Large 'cubic'	1.5×1.5×1.6	>1.5cm²	9–10
F	White	Small rectangles	0.75×0.6×0.9	>0.25cm²	1–2
G	White	Small 'cubic'	0.5×0.5×0.5	<0.25cm²	0.5
H	Black	Large 'cubic'	1.5×1.4×1	>2cm²	6
I	Black	Medium'cubic'	1×1×0.8	>1cm²	2
J	Black	Small 'cubic'	0.5×0.5×0.5	<0.25cm²	0.5
K	Coloured	Small 'cubic' glass	0.4×0.5×0.8	<0.25cm²	0.5

Table 3: The types of mosaic tesserae (with average dimensions and weights) recovered from surface collection in the vineyard at site 1.

Non-white tesserae are underrepresented in the sample; possibly because they were more difficult to spot when dirty. Nonetheless the differing distributions of the various types would seem to reflect their use in combinations in a number of mosaics buried below the vineyard.

Type A tesserae were of unusually large size and were presumably used for some form of border decoration. The main concentration seems to lie in the 22B-26B and 23A-29A area. By contrast the type B large tesserae were more widely spread and seemed to have a second distinct concentration in the 18B-19B and 17C-20C area. Likewise, type C tesserae had only a moderate concentration in the 22B-27B/23C-25C sector, but a massive occurrence in 17C-20C. Type D also shows similarities to this pattern, with once again the highest values recorded for 18C-20C. However the smallest tesserae (types E, F, G, and the black and coloured tesserae) were overwhelmingly concentrated in the 23B-25B and 23C-28C.

On this evidence, it is plausible to infer the existence of a reasonably crude tesselated pavement below 18C-20C and a finer quality and more colourful mosaic or mosaics below rows 23B-26B/24C-27C. Local information has confirmed that a coloured mosaic (white, red, blue, yellow) was observed at a depth of *c.* 1.5m beneath row 26 during the machine trenching for installing the vines.

Marble (with AC)

The vast majority of the marble fragments collected came from the vineyard area. However, over 20 pieces (probably strays) were collected from the area to the east of the vines. The quantity of marble recovered through intensive sherding of the vineyard in 1988-1989, over 1100 fragments weighing >86kg, is interesting for a number of reasons (Fig. 7). The number and weight of fragments recovered in the 1989 was far less than in 1988 and continued observation (though not repeated collections) in subsequent years has suggested that the volume of material presented at the surface has fallen further. This would seem to indicate that the current ploughing between the vines is not reaching down to the Roman floor levels and the remarkable quantities and fresh state of much of the material recovered in 1988-89 was due to its recent disturbance by the cutting of the vine trenches. This is impressive testimony to the scale of destruction caused by the trenching operations.

Since the modern vine trenches cut randomly into well-preserved Roman levels, our surface sample should provide a useful indication of the range and scale of use of marble in the villa. The range of marbles represented is a broad cross-section of the major types of white and coloured marbles such as might be expected in a first or second century AD context (The 1988 material was fully analysed by AC and the 1989 finds were identified by DJM using a range of type samples provided by AC. The percentages of the various types of marble recovered were essentially very similar for the two seasons, sugesting that the conflated totals are broadly representative of the material from the site, Fig. 8). Overall, white and grey marbles made up over 25% of the total number of fragments, but nearly 50% of the total weight recorded. Of the coloured marbles the most significant in descending order were Giallo Antico, Africano, Portasanta, Pavonazzetto, Cipollino, with far smaller quantities of Breccias, Green Porphry, Red Porphyry, Rosso Antico. The most prominent white/grey marbles were Luna (including a significant presence of Bardiglio) and the granular 'Scritto' (from Cap de Garde, Algeria), with smaller quantities of Dokimeion, Skyrian (but very little Prokonessian) and a good deal of unassignable material, including some low grade marble and finer quality limestones (Dodge & Ward-Perkins 1992: 152-159 for a catalogue of marble types).

The disparity between the number of fragments of Cipollino (16% of the total) and its weight (only 7% of the total weight) is to be expected given the propensity for veneers of Cipollino to break into rather small pieces. Relatively few shapes were identifiable among these fragments. The other really striking disparity is between the number and weight of white/grey marbles as a percentage of the whole (26% and 48%). This is partly due to the fact that the majority of the bulkier mouldings

	1988 No.	1989 No.	Total No.	1988 Wt	1989 Wt	Total Wt
White/Grey	193	108	**301**	26023	15545	**41568**
Giallo Ant.	139	71	**210**	6701	5810	**12511**
Africano	89	62	**151**	5345	4372	**9717**
Portasanta	70	39	**109**	4345	2620	**6965**
Cipollino	117	67	**184**	3163	3012	**6175**
Pavonazzetto	83	70	**153**	2557	3533	**6090**
Other Cols.	39	17	**56**	1949	1208	**3157**
	730	434	**1164**	50083	36100	**86183**

Table 4: Number of fragments and weight (in g) of marble of different types found in 1988-1989.

Fig. 7. Distribution of marble fragments within the vineyard area by number.

Fig. 6. Distribution of mosaic tesserae within the vineyard area. Compare Appendix 1 for detail of distribution by type.

and thicker veneers or slabs were of white rather than coloured marbles. Although some white marbles were used in the *opus sectile* floor, those selected were primarily those with attractive coloured veining (Skyrian, Dokimeion, Cap de Garde).

The majority of the fragments came from thin, flat slabs of various shapes, probably deriving from one or more *opus sectile* pavements. The thickness of this material varied greatly, with a range from *c.* 0.4–2.3 cm and most fragments in the range 0.6–1.2 cm. The most common shapes were: strips (examples of *c.* 2.6, 3, 3.5, 4 or 4.5 cm wide, longest recorded was 9.5 cm+); rectangles (or possibly squares in some cases, based on a side length of c.7, 8 or 8.5 cm. The longest lengths recorded for rectangles were 10.5+×7cm and 10.5+×8+cm); large triangles – both acute and obtuse isosceles – (9.5×12×12 cm, 13+×10+×? cm, 13+×13+×? cm); points (acute angled triangles – probably from the large triangles); small obtuse angled isosceles triangles (typical examples are 6×4.5×4.5 and 7.5×5×5). Only a single piece with a sawn curved surface was found, that a very small fragment of Giallo Antico. Given the relatively large sample collected, it thus seems unlikely that the floor made use of circular modules.

Although hardly comprehensive, some idea of the appearance of the simple geometric floor (or floors) can be derived from all this. The marble was distributed quite densely between rows 17 and 33, with a progressive and marked fall off between sectors C and B and between B and A of most rows. The material reached exceptional densities between rows 21 and 27, with rows 25–27 marking the absolute peak levels. Although all the shaped pieces could conceivably belong to a single floor, the breadth of the distribution (*c.* 30×30m) and some differences in the distribution by type favours the possibility that more than a single floor lies buried here.

The fact that some of the rooms below the main concentration may have belonged to a small bath suite supports this notion.

Synthesis

Site 1 was a luxurious Roman villa, with the main group of buildings concentrated in an east-west strip (*c.* 170 × 60 m) and at least in part enclosed by a perimeter wall. The minimum area of the structures of the villa within this wall cover *c.* 1.62 ha and the site clearly extended further (especially to the east below the modern road). The villa would appear to have consisted of a number of distinct buildings, the most impressive of which was the main residential building. To the east of this was a number of smaller structures with tile roofs, clustered around a cistern. Some of these may have been farmyard buildings of the *pars rustica* of the estate. As well as the water-source that supplied the cistern at the east end of the site, the villa probably also made use of the still-extant spring just beyond the westernmost building.

Occupation of the site began in the pre-Roman period, perhaps no earlier than the fourth or fifth century BC. The main phase of villa building seems to have begun in the second half of the first century BC – early first century AD, with occupation of the site continuously down to late Imperial times and activity at the site even attested into the late antique phase.

The main residential block and some other walls made use of large ashlar footings supporting upper walls of coursed mortared blockwork. Roofs were tiled with *tegulae* and *imbreces,* typical of the region. Some bathhouse brick and tile elements were also utilized, indicating the presence of bath facilities in the southern-facing wing. The smallish quantity of such bath material suggests that this was a bath in a villa, rather than promoting an

Marble	Strip	Rectangle	L. Triangle	Point	S. Triangle	Moulding	Curved
Giallo	*	*	*	*		*	*
Africano	*	*	*	*	*		
Portasanta		*	*	*	*	*	
Pavonazzetto	*		*	*	*	*	
Cipollino	*	*					
Green Porphyry	*?	*					
Red Porphyry	*						
Rosso Antico	*					*	
Iasos Red (?)						*	
Skyros (?)	*	*					
Dokimian	*						
Luna			*			*	
'Scritto'			*				
Grey/white			*	*		*	

Table 5: Shapes and mouldings in the different types of marble.

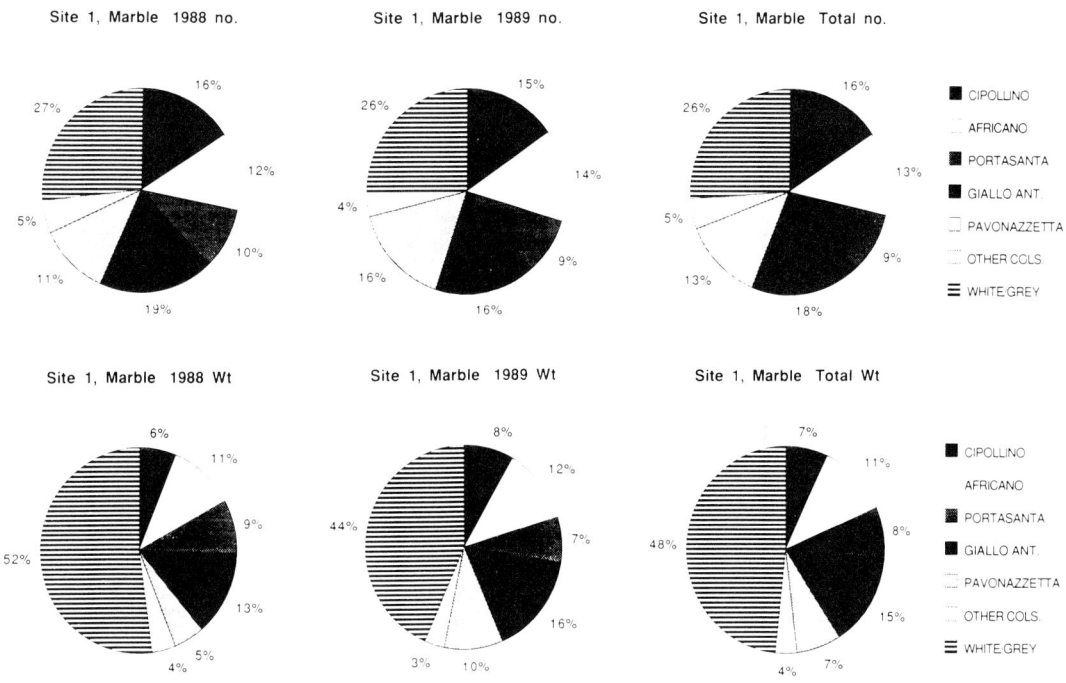

Fig. 8. Pie-charts illustrating the percentages by marble type of the fragments and weight of marble collected in 1988 and 1989 and for the two years combined.

alternative possibility, that this was a large specialized bath building. This main building was lavishly furnished with mosaics and marble floor and wall cladding. The *opus sectile* floors utilized primarily Giallo Antico, Africano, Portasanta, Cipollino and Pavonazzeto and a mixture of white marbles in the design modules (based on rectangles, squares and triangles). White and grey marbles were also used extensively as larger slabs (paving or cladding) and as mouldings. Some of the rooms had painted plaster on the walls. The plan of the main building was probably either L-shaped or possibly U-shaped around a central court.

The wealth of the site places it among a very small group of extraordinary villas in the Rieti basin, of which the Grotte di S. Nicola is the best known. These are the prime candidates for the estates of the leading Reatan families, who by the mid-first century BC had gained entrance to the Senate at Rome. M. Terentius Varro and Q. Assius are the best known figures from the first century BC. Quintus Assius (Axius) features in several of Varro's extended humorous conversations between Roman aristocrats comparing notes on correct farming practices (e.g. *rerum rustic.* 3.2.1–3.17.10), as does another Reatan, Fircellius Pavo (Di Flavio 1983; Pietrangeli 1976; Riposati 1976). T. Flavius Vespasianus capped their achievements by elevation to the imperial throne in the first century AD.

Much scholarly interest has focussed on the location and appointments of the two Reatan villas of Assius in the second half of the first century BC. One of these villas was situated *ad angulum Velini*, the other *in Rosea* (Colarieti-Tosti 1904; Menotti 1987; Spadoni Cerroni 1978; cf. other Sabine villas, di Manzano & Leggio 1980; Reggiani 1985). In comparing the Villa Publica on the Campus Martius to these villas of Assius near Reate, Varro commented on the richness of one of them: "Do you see anywhere here citrus wood or gold, or vermilion or azure, or any coloured or mosaic work? At your place everything is just the opposite" (Varro 3.2.4). The contrast is then drawn between the two villas of Assius: "Why you don't think that that place of yours on the bend of the Velinus, which never a painter or a fresco maker has seen, is less a villa than the one *in Rosea* which is adorned with all the art of the stucco worker and of which you and your ass are joint owners" (3.2.9). The villa by the bend of the Velinus is commonly identified with the Grotte di S. Nicola (though possibly mistakenly, since the extant structure is far grander than Varro's description would seem to allow). A case has been made on topographical grounds for identifying the second villa with site 1 (by Menotti 1989: 57–58), since the area described as the *Rosea* by the ancient sources was evidently the improved pasture land of the basin floor below *c.* 380 m elevation (Leggio 1989: 59–63) and site 1 lies on the upper margin of this zone. Although we do not ourselves propose to identify the villa with the name of Assius, we believe that the villa was constructed by one of the region's leading families (of Senatorial or

Equestrian status) in the first century BC. The villa may subsequently have passed into new hands as different families came to the fore in the first century AD. Certainly, the villa was still being embellished during the first and early second centuries AD. Site 1 is one of only a handful of sites in the Rieti region with clearcut evidence for continuing occupation down to late antiquity.

THE FUTURE: EXCAVATION OR WHAT?

So what exactly could excavation at this site add to the picture derived from survey? A clearer plan of the main building would obviously be an advance in knowledge, though the modern vineyard is an obstacle to achieving this A trench over the richest part of the villa would undoubtedly confirm that these were grandiose rooms with mosiacs, marble floors and painted walls. But the surface evidence suggests that these features have been severely damaged by the vine trenching, so we might uncover only a larger sample of broken fragments. Moreover, the area available for excavation within the vine rows or to the south in the open field is quite restricted. If, as seems almost certain, the southern wing of the villa contains a bath suite, that would no doubt provide some interesting structural detail, but the overall elaboration of its layout in such a confined area would be very problematic. Some small test trenches to check the alignment and dimensions of the structure might be equally revealing. The putative enclosure wall and the two faint curving features on the resistivity plot could also be checked (our best guess is that the latter are drains from the bath).

There is a faint possibility that the site might produce a spectacular find such as a piece of sculpture or a useful inscription. In real life such finds are extremely rare on villas and rural sites; the best site 1 can offer to date is a plain travertine table. Dragged up from close to row 26C, it comprises three sections, a plain rectangular top (2.06×0.65×0.16 m) and a pair of rectangular legs (0.88×0.30×0.27 and 0.88×0.32×0.32). It evidently stood against a wall, since one side of the legs was left rough, the other three being smoothed. The total weight of table and legs was $c.$ 0.9 tonnes. Local farmers have reported seeing lead pipes from the site, but this cannot be corroborated and it remains uncertain whether these would have carried stamped inscriptions (as did examples from a few other villas in the region, Spadoni Ceroni 1978). The main cemetery for the site appears to have lain across the modern road (tile graves reported), and is now for the most part under housing.

Survey has yielded an abundance of pottery from the various phases of the site's long life and it is by no means certain that excavation would substantially change our view of the overall chronology of the site. It would be helpful to be able to pinpoint with precision the points to excavate for the earliest and/or the latest phases of occupation. However, given the variables affecting pottery deposition, our best guesses from our survey data are not guaranteed to be sufficiently precise for a smallish excavation to hit the target. Pottery from stratified contexts would be valuable for advancing our knowledge of the local coarsewares, but well-swept villa floors are certainly not the places to choose to look for such assemblages. An attractive possibility is the cistern, open from the top, full of rubble and perhaps also rubbish. But again caution might be the best policy. When was this feature infilled? And for how long has the top of the vault and the access point remained exposed? The only safe conclusion is that the infilling could have been any time from the Roman period to the present.

The ancillary structures of the villa that cluster around the cistern are of immense interest, though there will almost certainly be plough damage to the later phases of occupation. The morphology of lesser rural buildings in Italy is still very imprecisely known and we might well gain considerable insights into the economic activities of the villa (some of the structures are certainly associated with dolia fragments – were these a few or from a large number of vessels?). Excavation of the suspected working area of the villa could also involve intensive palaeobotanical and faunal sampling. The detailed palaeoeconomic information that can be derived from systematic sampling and flotation of archaeological deposits simply cannot be recovered reliably by survey (and only in a limited way by minor intrusive procedures such as augering). Phosphate analysis and magnetic susceptibility testing could also be carried out on interior and exterior ground surfaces to build a clearer picture of the pattern of use by humans and animals.

The other advantage of working on this sector of the site is that it would be possible to excavate reasonably large areas at a time. Although at present we have no plans to dig any part of the site 1 villa, the excavation of such ancillary buildings on Roman villas is one of the prime desiderata of rural archaeology in Italy (Carandini 1985; Rossiter 1978).

Our site may never be as famous or as well-defined structurally as the scores of excavated villas across the length and breadth of Italy. But it may now enjoy the status of being one of the better-known unexcavated villas! The scale and luxury of the structure, its topographic position and the longevity of its dominance in this particular landscape are all significant gains in our knowledge of the villas of the Sabina reatina.

ACKNOWLEDGEMENTS

We are grateful to Tersilio Leggio for first drawing our attention to the existence of the site and for his continuing and generous encouragement of our work. The project was carried out under the aegis of the British School at Rome, with the permission and support of the Soprintendenza del Lazio. Sponsors of the fieldwork included the British Academy, the British School at Rome, the Universities of Leicester and Michigan, the Craven Committee, Oxford. This paper is dedicated to all those who worked on the investigation of site 1, notably Nick Whitehead, Bridget Brehm, Hugh Coddington, and Hugh Elton who supervised the vineyard sherding in 1988–1989; Peter Bellamy who was responsible for the 1:200m survey on which our plans are based, Tina Sudell and Eve Pugh who carried out the bulk of the resistivity survey with Ian George in 1988 and 1989. Finally much is owed to the people of the Rieti region, notably to the Comune di Cantalice, who have facilitated our work in innumerable ways.

Bibliography

Bailey, D. M. 1980. *A Catalogue of the Lamps in the British Museum, 2, Roman Lamps made in Italy*, London.

Barker, G. & Mattingly, D.J. 1989. 'The countryside of Roman Sabina: some current archaeological approaches', *Il Territorio* 5.1–2, 33–47.

Carandini, A. 1985. *Settefinestre, una villa schiavistica nell'Etruria romana*, Modena.

Coccia, S. & Mattingly D.J. (with P.Beavitt, H. Elton, P. Foss, I. George, C.O. Hunt, H. Patterson, P. Roberts) 1992a. 'The Rieti Survey 1988–1991', in N. Christie (ed.), *Leicester in Sabina. Field Surveys and Excavations in Central Italy, 1988–1991*. School of Archaeological Studies, University of Leicester, 5–23.

Coccia, S. & Mattingly, D.J. 1992b. 'La Rieti Survey 1988–1990', in E. Herring, R. Whitehouse & J. Wilkins (eds), *New Developments in Italian Archaeology. Papers of the Fourth Conference of Italian Archaeology, volume 2*, London, 113–120.

Coccia, S. & Mattingly, D.J. (with P. Beavitt, H. Elton, P. Foss, I. George, C.O. Hunt, T. Leggio, H. Patterson, P. Roberts) 1993. 'Settlement history, environment and human exploitation of an intermontane basin in the central Apennines: the Rieti Survey 1988–1991, Part I', *Papers of the British School at Rome*, 60, 213–289.

Colarieti-Tosti, G. 1904. *La villa d'Assio nella campagna Rosea*, Rieti.

Conspectus 1990 = Ettlinger, E. 1990. *Conspectus Formarum Terrae Sigillatae Italico Modo Factae*, Bonn.

De Rossi, E. 1973. 'Notiziario archeologico', *Rieti* 2, I-II.

Di Flavio, V. 1983. 'L'agro reatina in epoca romana', in R. Lefèvre (ed.), *Il Lazio nell'Antichità* (=*Lunario Romano* 12), 117–128.

Di Manzano, P. & Leggio, L. 1980. *Ville romane in opera poligonale nei dintorni di Cures Sabini*. Fara Sabina.

Dodge, H. & Ward-Perkins, B. (eds.) 1992. *Marble in Antiquity. Collected Papers of J.B. Ward-Perkins*, (British School at Rome Archaeological Monograph 6), London.

Hayes, J.W. 1972. *Late Roman Pottery*, London.

Leggio, T. 1989. 'Nota topografica sulla conca Reatina: la Rosea nelle fonti scritte medievali. Contributo alla sua delimitazione spaziale', in Menotti 1989, 59–63.

Menotti, E. 1987. 'La villa d'Assio e le ville rustiche romane', *Il Territorio*, 3.2, 31–59.

Menotti, E. 1989. 'La piana Reatina: la così detta villa d'Assio alle Grotte di San Nicola, un esempio di uso del territorio in età romana', *Il Territorio*, 5.1–2, 49–63.

Morel, J.-P. 1981. *Ceramique campaniennes les formes*, Rome.

Perkins, P. & Walker, L. 1990. 'Survey of an Etruscan city at Doganella in the Albegna valley', *Papers of the British School at Rome*, 58, 1–150.

Pietrangeli, C. 1976. 'La Sabina nell'antichità', in *Rieti e il suo territorio*, Milan, 9–164.

Reggiani, A.M. 1985. 'La villa rustica nell'agro sabino', in *Misurare la terra. Città, agricoltura, commercio: materiali da Roma e dal suburbio*, Modena, 61–65.

Riposati, B. 1976. 'Varrone e la sua terra sabina', in *Rieti e il suo territorio*, 213–236.

Rossiter, J.J. 1978. *Roman Farm Buildings in Italy*, BAR S 52, Oxford.

Spadoni Cerroni, M.C. 1978. 'La villa di Quinto Assio nel reatino', *Annali della facolta di lettere a filosofia Università degli studi di Perugia*, 16, ns 2, 169–74.

Appendix 1:

Finds of the different types of mosaic tesserae from the Site 1 vineyard.
Listings are by row (1–33) and sector (A, B or C), cf. Figs 3 and 6.

TYPE A

Row	A	B	C	Total
17				
18				
19		1		1
20			1	1
21		1		1
22		2		2
23		1	2	3
24		3	3	6
25		4	2	6
26		1	5	6
27	2		6	8
28		2	1	3
29	1		2	3
30				
31				
32			2	2
Total	3	15	24	42

TYPE B

Row	A	B	C	Total
17		1	2	3
18	2	6	7	15
19		11	1	12
20		1	4	5
21		3	3	6
22	3	5	2	10
23			5	5
24		8	3	11
25		5	5	10
26		6		6
27		1	3	4
28	1	1	1	3
29	1		2	3
30		1	3	4
31		1	7	8
32	1		1	2
Total	8	50	49	107

TYPE C

Row	A	B	C	Total
15			1	1
16				
17		2	12	14
18	4		15	19
19	2		17	19
20	2		14	16
21	3			3
22		2		2
23	1	4	8	13
24		9	7	16
25		5	5	10
26	1	3	1	5
27		6	1	7
28		1	2	3
29		1	2	3
30	1		1	2
31				
32				
Total	14	34	85	133

TYPE D

Row	A	B	C	Total
16		1		1
17			1	1
18			20	20
19			51	51
20	1		84	85
21		15	5	20
22		11	7	18
23	2	2	15	19
24	2	10	12	24
25		10	15	25
26	2	3	25	30
27		4	11	15
28	1	4	5	10
29			9	9
30		1	10	11
31			2	2
32			3	3
Total	8	61	275	344

TYPE E

Row	A	B	C	Total
5		1		1
13			3	3
14			1	1
15			3	3
16			1	1
17				
18				
19			4	4
20				
21			1	1
22	1	1	1	3
23		2	5	7
24		11	8	19
25		1	8	9
26		2	12	14
27	1	1	5	7
28	3	1	8	12
29				
30	1	1	2	4
31			2	2
32			4	4
Total	6	21	68	95

TYPE F

Row	A	B	C	Total
17			1	1
18				
19			4	4
20				
21		7	20	27
22		9	4	13
23	1	23	36	60
24	3	19	40	62
25		8	30	38
26		5	22	27
27	1	2	10	13
28	1	1	8	10
29	1		4	5
30			4	4
31			6	6
32			4	4
Total	7	74	193	274

TYPE G

Row	A	B	C	Total
21			9	9
22				
23		2	2	4
24		9	14	23
25		3	2	5
26	1		5	6
27		8	2	10
28			1	1
29		1	1	2
30		1		1
31			1	1
32	1			1
Total	2	24	37	63

TYPES H,I,J (BLACK)

Row	A	B	C	Total
21			4	4
22				
23		5	2	7
24		4	3	7
25		3	11	14
26		2	4	5
27		2	1	3
28				
29				
30				
31		1		1
32				
Total		16	25	41

COLOURED GLASS

Row	A	B	C	Total
4A			1	1
18	1			1
19				
20				
21	2		2	4
22		4	1	5
23	2	3	2	7
24		2	2	4
25		3	3	6
26		1	2	3
27		2		2
28		1	2	3
29		1		1
30		1		1
31			1	1
32		1		1
Total	5	19	16	40

5

Attività del Centro di Documentazione della Regione Lazio

Luigi Ramelli di Celle

(Centro Regionale per la Documentazione dei Beni Culturali e Ambientali del Lazio, Roma)

Sommario: *Un contributo sulle attività e metodologie in campo archeologico del Centro per la Documentazione dei Beni Culturali ed Ambientali del Lazio. Il CRD è una struttura regionale a carattere interdisciplinare di recente istituzione (1981), che si occupa di catalogazione dei Beni Culturali del territorio del Lazio in collaborazione con Soprintendenze, Università e altri istituti di ricerca ed ha avviato ed in parte condotto a termine numerosi progetti di ricognizione archeologica, di censimento e di studio di siti e di reperti.*

Istituto nel 1981, il Centro Regionale per la Documentazione dei Beni Culturali ed Ambientali (CRD) è stato riordinato con legge regionale 26.7.1991 n.31. Tale legge non costituisce solo una specie di testo unico riassuntivo della legislazione precedente: infatti essa affida al CRD nuovi compiti ed eleva il numero degli uffici per adeguare la struttura alle accresciute esigenze operative.

1. Documentazione in beni ambientali e cartografia storica;

2. Documentazione in materia archeologica, storico-artistica ed architettonica;

3. Documentazione in materia demo-etno-antropologica;

4. Documentazione in materia delle scienze della terra;

5. Informazione;

6. Amministrazione e contabilità;

7. Servizi tecnici.

Le competenze del CRD sono quindi piuttosto ampie e non limitte alla sfera di operatività del Ministero per i Beni Culturali e Ambientali.

Nell'adempimento della propria attività istituzionale, particolare importanza assumono i rapporti di collaborazione tra il CRD ed Enti Locali, Università, Istituti di cultura, enti pubblici e privati. A questo proposito debbono esssere ricordati quelli con il Ministero BB.CC. menzionato, con il quale è stata stipulata una apposita convenzione; in effetti, con le Soprintendenze, l'Istituto Centrale per il Catalogo e la Documentazione, l'Istituto Centrale per il Restauro sono in atto scambi ed iniziative concordate.

Il CRD cura principalmente il censimento e la catalogazione dei beni culturali ed ambientali, la realizzazione di ricerche, l'acquisizione, la elaborazione, la produzione e la pubblicazione di nuovo materiale documentario, nonchè la realizzazione di strumenti conoscitivi, informativi, didattici. Rientra in questo ambito anche la consistente attività di ideazione, realizzazione e sperimentazione di nuovi strumenti metodologici nei settori di competenza.

Particolare rilevanza possiede, nell'ambito della attività complessiva svolta dal CRD, l'impegno nel settore dell'archeologia. Le ricerche in corso comprendono indagini territoriali, volte sia alla verifica dell'esistente che alla prospezione sistematica, con relativa catalogazione di siti e materiali; documentazione e studio di collezioni archeologiche; allestimenti museali; rilevo e fotogrammetria finalizzati allo studio di monumenti; censimento di documenti filmografici e fotografici di interesse archeologico; ricerche bibliografiche, archivistiche ed inventariali.

Mentre in una prima fase, il censimento dei beni archeologici ha interessato solo tre aree campione, successivamente si è estesso a tutto il territorio laziale, con particolare attenzione a zone poco indagate finora o soggette a rischi di degrado ambientale o ad interventi distruttivi. A tale proposito attraverso la compilazione di apposite schede denominate 'conservative' – elaborate e sperimentale in collaborazione con l'Istituto Centrale per il Restauro – si è provveduto alla verifica dello stato di conservazione di reperti e monumenti.

Il CRD persegue l'obiettivo di riunire in una unica

banca dati territoriale tutte le informazioni raccolte, in modo da permetterne un'agevole fruizione.

Tra le ricerche definite o in corso di svolgimento si segnalano:

1. Indagini territoriali, in collaborazione con le Soprintendenze competenti, nel comune di Fara Sabina, nell'Agro Capenate, in alcuni comuni delle province di Latina e Frosinone, nel territorio costiero di Roma, nelle aree dell'Etruria meridionale interessate dai possedimenti del monastero di S. Paolo fino al 1300. I risultati di alcune di queste indagini sono oggetto di specifici contributi in questa sede (cfr. Arnoldus-Huyzendveld *et al.*; Belardelli; Turchetti & Bartolini; De Maria *et al.*);

2. Studio, catalogazione e documentazione di collezioni archeologiche pubbliche e private, ad esempio l'industria litica proveniente dalla Grotta del Fossellone (S.Felice Circeo – Latina); i materiali protostorici dei siti costieri del territorio di Civitavecchia; la collezione Oddone di Capena; i reperti del Museo Archeologico de Frosinone etc.;

3. Rilievo e fotogrammetria finalizzati alla documentazione e allo studio di monumenti archeologici, ad esempio i cosidetti Magazzini Traianei di Ostia Antica, l'Arco di Costantino a Roma etc.;

4. Ricerche inventariali su materiali laziali conservati nei musei, in particolare nel Museo Nazionale Romano;

5. Ricerca interdisciplinare finalizzata alla raccolta di dati riguardanti le collezioni di reperti archeologici e di opere d'arte del Lazio trasferite e conservate in altra sede.

Il CRD ha aderito inoltre, per aspetti sia organizzativi che scientifici, alla Campagna Europea per l'età del Bronzo (1994–1997), promossa dal Consiglio d'Europa, e al XIII Congresso dell'Unione Internazionale delle Scienze Preistoriche e Protostoriche (Forlì 1996).

Tra le pubblicazioni di interesse archeologico realizzate o promosse dal Centro si segnalano: la riedizione della *Forma Urbis Romae*, della *Storia degli Scavi di Roma* di Rodolfo Lanciani; il monumentale *Lexicon Topographicum Urbis Romae*; i volumi *La necropoli laziale di Osteria dell'Osa*; *Immagini fotografiche del Lazio nel fondo Thomas Ashby*; *La cartografia dei beni storici, archeologici e paesistici nelle grandi aree urbane. Dal cenismento alla tutela*; *Antichità tardoromane e medievale nel territorio di Bracciano*.

Si segnalano inoltre, in corso di stampa, un repertorio dei siti dell'età del Bronzo e della prima età del Ferro, relativo alle due province laziali di Rieti e di Latina, e le seguenti quattro monografie a carattere interdisciplinare relative ad altrettanti comuni del Lazio, che contengono i risultati derivanti dalla ricerca sul campo svolta negli ultimi anni: *Rocca Priora. Ricerca interdisciplinare sui beni culturali e ambientali*; *Capena e il suo territorio*; *Filacciano e il suo territorio*; *Monterotondo e il suo territorio*.

Altri studi collegati alle ricerche svolte sono stati resi noti attraverso la pubblicazione in atti di convegni, cataloghi di mostre e riviste specializzate.

6

Preliminary Results of the Malafede Survey, 1990–1992

A. ARNOLDUS-HUYZENDVELD, P. GIOIA, M. MINEO, P. PASCUCCI

(DIGITER Geoinformatica S.r.l., Roma; Sovrintendenza Comunale alle Antichità e Belle Arti, Roma; Soprintendenza Speciale al Museo Preistorico 'L. Pigorini'; Centro Regionale per la Documentazione BB.CC.AA., Regione Lazio)

Summary: *The systematic survey of Rome's coastal zone, begun in 1988, has identified many new sites of all periods, ranging from the Palaeolithic to the Roman period. The project has sought to define a methodology of recording the archaeological data to provide more accurate analyses of territorial change. The survey zone, the Valle di Malafede, set on the immediate fringes of the city of Rome, has in fact suffered badly through urban expansion and the application here of a rigorous methodology has been of immense value. Factors considered comprise: 1. quantity and type of finds; 2. surface of each site; 3. climatic and environmental conditions; 4. morphological and pedological conditions affecting finds survival. The paper summarises the changing methods of the Malafede survey and highlights the importance of excavation data to supplement the surface evidence.*

In 1988, promoted by the Sovrintendenza Comunale alle Antichità e Belle Arti of Rome and the Soprintendenza Archeologica di Ostia, a project of systematic survey was initiated in the coastal area of Rome (fig.1), designed in particular to identifiy and study the pre-protohistorical archaeological evidence for the zone (cf. Arnoldus-Huyzendveld, Gioia & Pascucci 1992; Anselmi *et al.* 1990; Arnoldus Huyzendveld, Crovato & Zarlenga 1991; Bedello 1994; Bedello, Gioia & Pascucci 1993).

The interdisciplinary project involves members of various organizations and institutions, who have co-operated in the study of the various aspects concerning the knowledge and conservation of the region; moreover a group of about twenty-five graduates and students of the University 'La Sapienza' of Rome have actively participated.

The methodology, initially defined on a theoretical base and then verified through fieldwork, underwent partial modifications resulting from both the practical situations encountered, as well as from experience through working with the databases created. Accordingly therefore three different sheets have been constructed for data collecting, replacing the previously-used recording sheet: a visit sheet, a survey unit (SU)/site sheet, and a trench sheet.

The visit sheet (fig.2a) records specific data collected during a single SU survey (e.g. meteorological conditions, visibility, surface conditions, archaeological finds). The SU/Site sheet (fig.2b) includes data which do not vary in time (topographical and geological data) and summarises also information collected during each single survey. The trench sheet includes the stratigraphical data related to each trench. The excavation of trenches and the registration of the data on a separate sheet were necessary to register as thoroughly as possible areas of imminent urbanisation, which would be impossible to explore in the future. In each SU, three to four trenches were excavated, reaching a maximum depth of 2 meters. In this way, a sampling of the subsoil was added to the surface investigation (the trench data are currently under study).

During the survey, which was carried out in groups of, on average, eight people walking at a distance of two meters apart, all the visible pre-protohistoric material was collected, whereas Roman artefacts were suitably sampled. Therefore, only the pre-protohistoric finds, i.e. the total number of which is known for each survey unit, will be considered here.

One of the specific purposes of the project is to reconcile research and conservation demands in the Rome suburbs. Therefore, activities were concentrated in the Malafede area, on account of the landscape transformations related to the urban expansion now underway (fig.3). Starting from autumn 1990, four survey campaigns were carried out covering *c.* 150 hectares in total. The survey has already added much new data to the knowledge of the area, important enough to justify government protection (cf. Bedello, Gioia & Pascucci, 1993).

Morphologically, the area consists of a slightly undulating plain at about 50–60 m above sea level, dissected by some minor tributaries of the Tiber river. From the geological viewpoint this is an Early Upper Quaternary coastal terrace, with fluvial, lagoonal and aeolean deposits. The soils encountered on the terrace's surface are predominantly of the composite type: sandy topsoil with fine-grained subsoil (Albic Luvisols; FAO/UNESCO 1988). The existing soil map of the coastal area of Rome, originally 1:50.000 in scale, has permitted the compilation of a map with distinct probability degrees of encountering pre- protohistoric artefacts; Malafede was evaluated as an area with a high probability (Arnoldus-Huyzendveld, Gioia & Pascucci 1992: fig.7).

Results are presented here of a first phase of data processing, aimed at a more refined interpretation of the artefact distribution. The processed data refer to the first three survey campaigns, carried out from autumn 1990 to summer 1992; another campaign took place from September 1992 to January 1993. Consequently, the sixty eight Survey Units here considered represent only a part of the actually surveyed area. They cover a total extension of 450.000 sq.m on the sheets 30N and

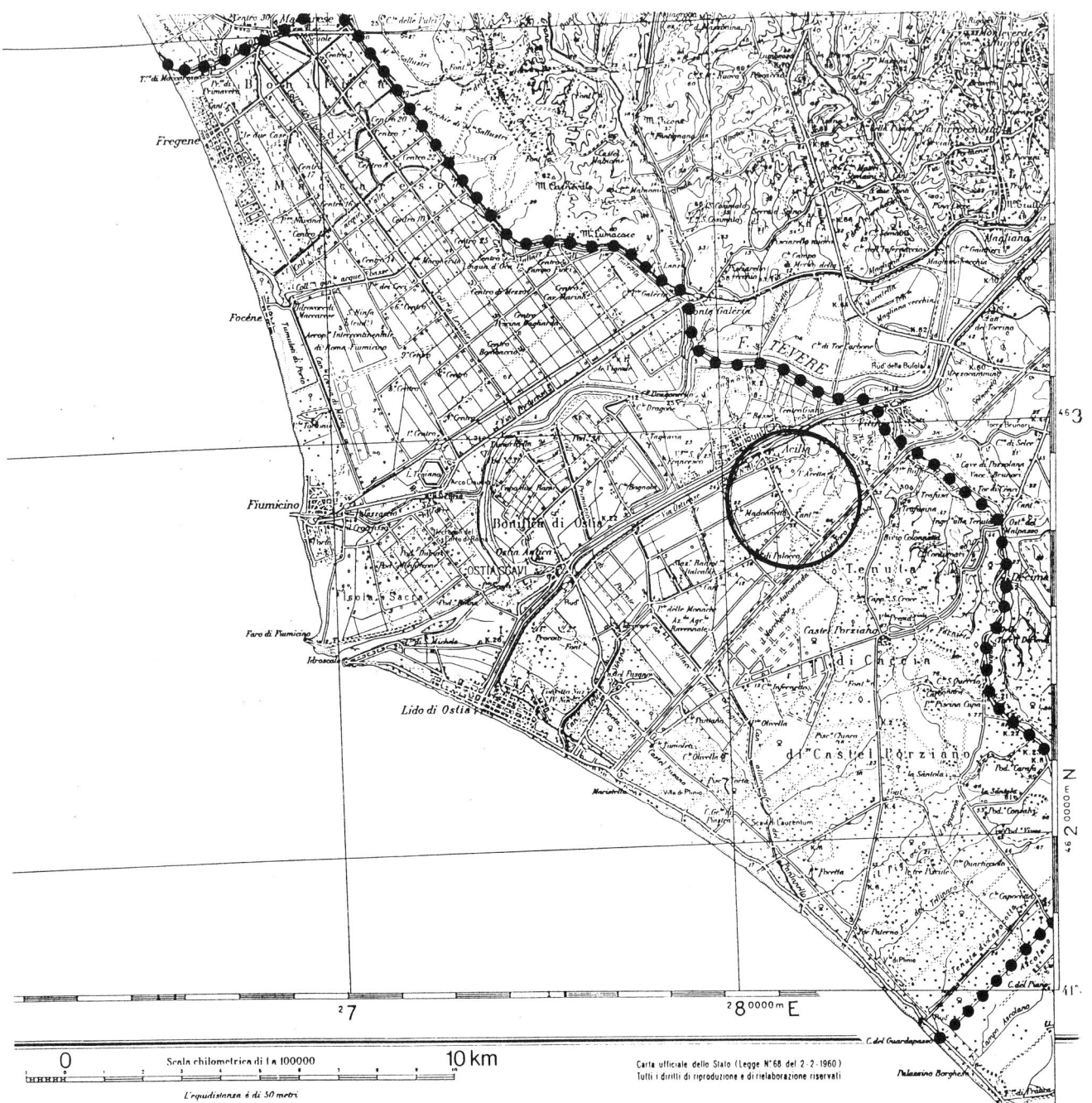

Fig. 1. Map of the coastal area of Rome showing the limits of the Soprintendenza Archeologica di Ostia.

a

b

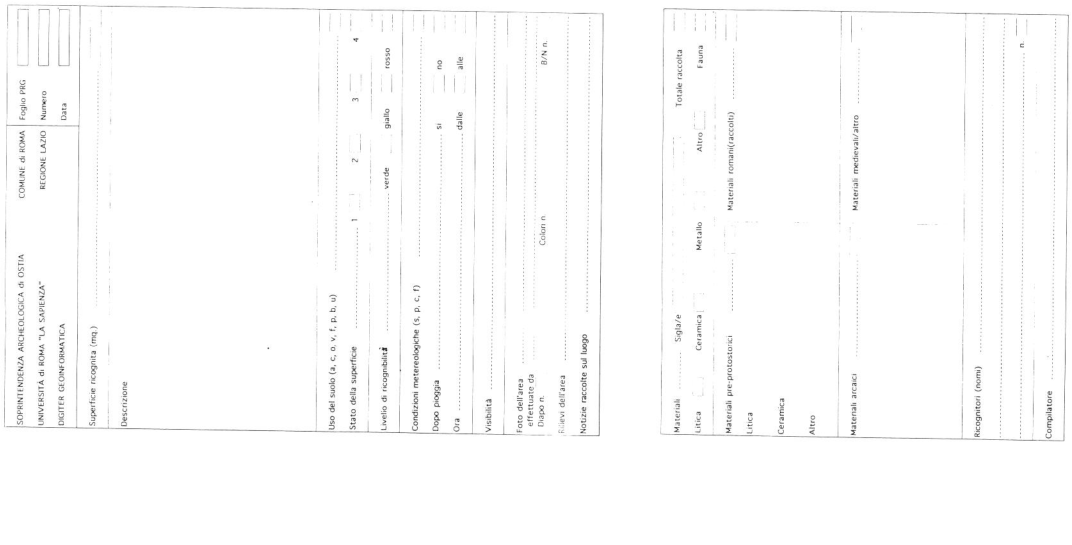

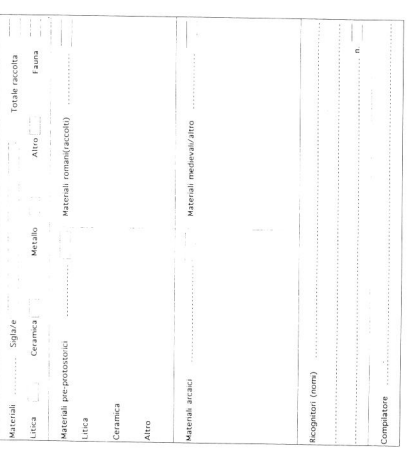

Fig. 2. The visit (a) and the SU/Site (b) recording sheets currently in use.

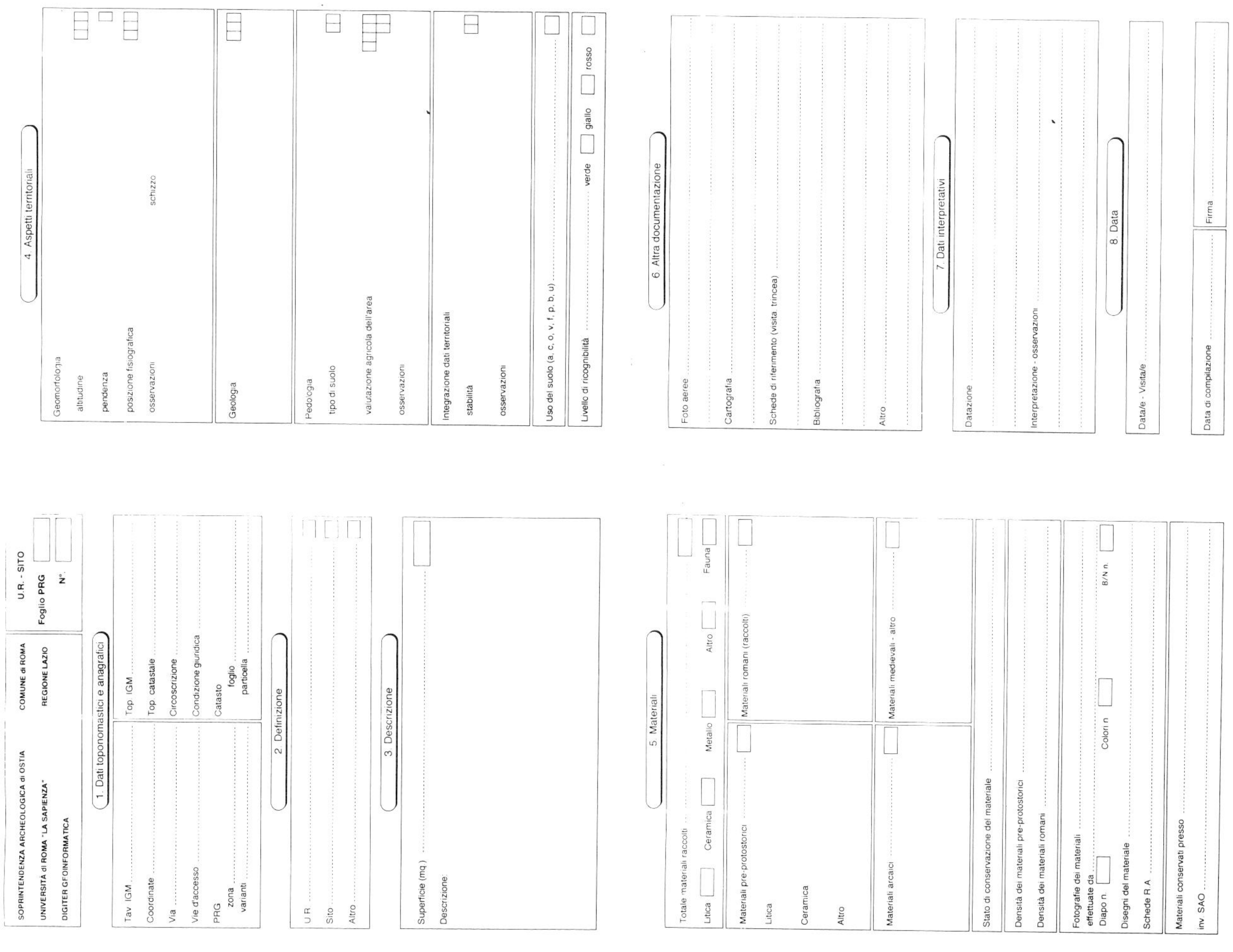

31N of the Rome town development plan, scale 10.000 (Arnoldus-Huyzendveld, Gioia & Pascucci 1992: fig.8). Their average size is about 6500 sq.m, slightly more than half a hectare. The survey units have been laid out in reference to fixed landmarks, trying to approach the selected standard size of 100 × 50 m (fig.3). Overall, 128 field visits were made, which means that every SU was visited on average about twice. A total of 11.500 items was collected, which comprised 8.500 lithic artefacts and 3.000 pottery fragments; their dating ranges from the Middle Palaeolithic to the Iron Age.

The main purpose of this paper is to compare various parameters in order to highlight significant connections and recurrencies, and to confirm quantitatively the observations made – multiple component analysis of the data is in progress at this moment. The parameters were selected from the sheet entries considered most significant: physiographic and soil data, land use, state of the surface and meteorological conditions during the survey, number of pre-protohistoric finds and their density.

1. Physiographic, geological and soil data.

The SU considered turned out to be situated mainly at the edges (56%) and on the summits (26%) of the slightly undulating plateaux (codes Oh1 and Oh2), and to a lesser extent (9%) on the hill slopes (code Cs2) (fig. 4a). Moreover, the dominant soil (72%) was shown to be of composite type, with a sandy topsoil (Albic Luvisol), whereas the remaining surface consists of clayey soils with vertic characteristics (fig.4b).

From these landscape data, a stability parameter was inferred, considered indicative of the survival strength of the surface. In this sense, stable areas are old surfaces on which erosion and accumulation processes were almost lacking, whereas unstable areas are those that have been subject to natural destructive processes. In the former, in contrast to the latter, it may be presumed that the find density approaches more the original value, whenever other variables (e.g. soil acidity) do not interfere with the destruction of the remains. The stability index thus represents a parameter, independent from

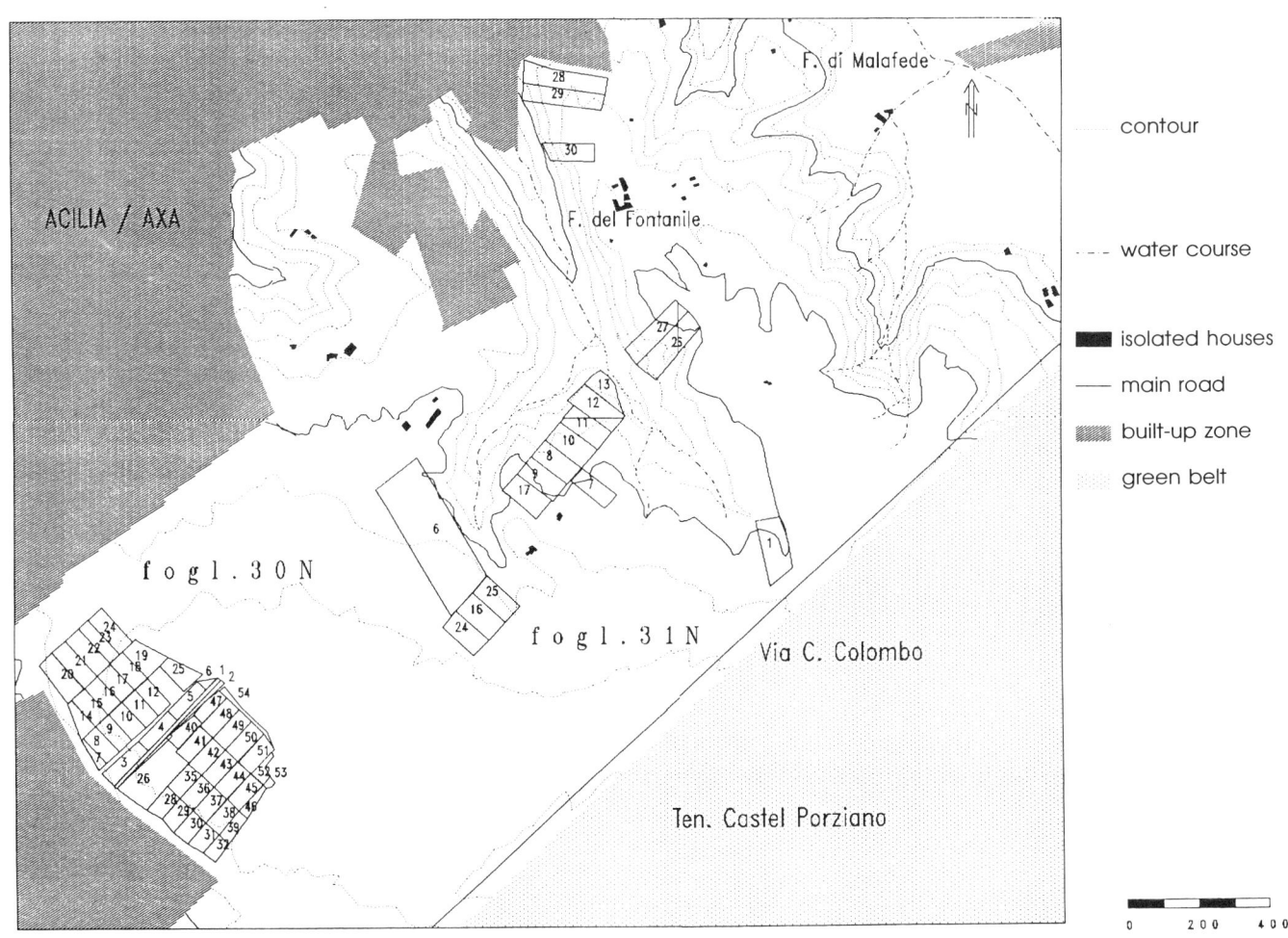

Fig. 3. Map of the Malafede district between the urban area of Acilia/AXA and the Castelporziano estate, illustrating the survey untis.

archaeological data, to evaluate artefact density and spatial distribution. The area surveyed has mainly been classified as stable: to 23% of the surface the highest stability index (1p) was assigned, to 57% a slightly minor stability index (1v) (fig.4c).

2. Land-use, state of the surface, level of survey potential

Overall, the area is characterised by a good level of survey potential, as it has been used lately as cropland (90%). Though a small portion of the area (10%) was recently raised with filling ground, it was surveyed anyway since the origin of the material was known.

The urgency to operate at Malafede required optimisation of the time and energy employed, in order to obtain maximum field visibility. Therefore, visits were concentrated in the ploughing season; moreover, in some cases it was possible to request ploughing in order to improve the visibility level. Thus a high degree of visibility was reached for most of the surface (63.5%); in the other cases, the visibility level was generally lowered through the presence of weeds or the initial crop growth (fig.4d).

3. Density of the prehistoric finds per survey unit

This value ranges from a minimum of zero to a maximum of 0,203 items/sq.m, with an average of 0,024. Six density classes have currently been applied to regroup the various SUs:

1 = 0–0,0049
2 = 0,005–0,0249
3 = 0,025–0,0499
4 = 0,05–0,0749
5 = 0,075–0,0999
6 = >0,1

The lowest density classes apply to most of the surveyed area (35% for class 1, 43% for class 2); the highest classes (5 e 6) occupy respectively 2% and 5% of the surface. One should bear in mind that the higher density values may be influenced by the application of a squared or positioned collection technique that were applied in the case of particular high concentrations of archaeological finds.

The find density has been first correlated with the geomorphological and soil variables, which are independent from the survey conditions, and secondly

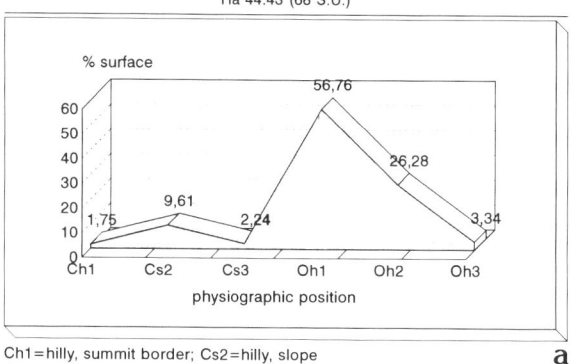

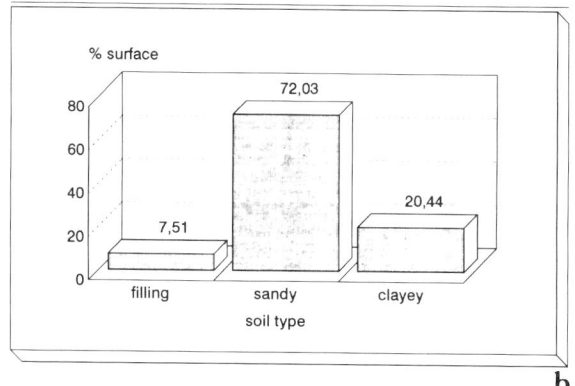

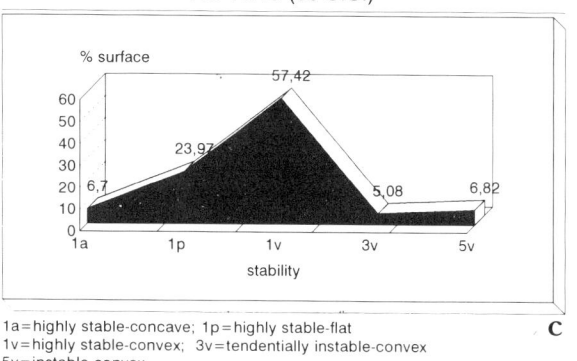

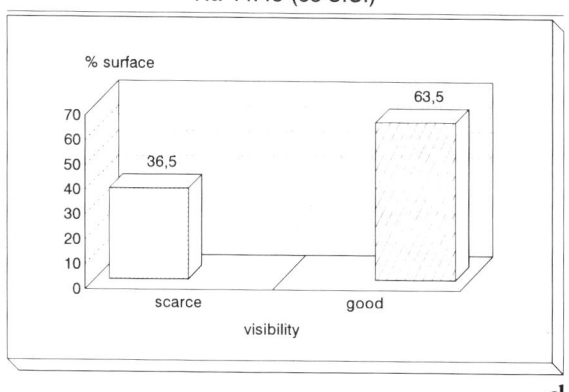

Fig. 4. Extension and morphological/soil data (a: physiographic position, b: soil type, c: stability index); extension and visibility level (d).

with the variables related to the modes and times of the survey, elements dependent mainly on the surveyer's choices. On the basis of the relationships between the parameters mentioned above, the following remarks are possible.

INCIDENCE OF THE LANDSCAPE VARIABLES

(i) Relationship between physiographic and soil data, stability index and artefact density

For each survey unit, the artefact density was compared with the minimum and maximum slope values, physiographic position, soil type and stability index, parameters not completely independent from each other.

a) *Minimum slope value and artefact density*: the lower slope value increases proportionally with the density classes (fig.5a). The correlation with the upper slope value is not significant.

b) *Physiographic position and find density*: the highest density classes (5 and 6) are found at the summit edges of the landscape (code Oh1) and on the upper parts of the hill slopes (code Cs2 e Cs3). Major find concentrations do not occur on the landscape summits (code Oh2, Oh3) (fig.5b).

c) *Soil type and artefact density*: this is essentially a comparison between the density on sandy and clayey soils. The minor concentrations are mainly related to the sandy soils (fig.5c).

d) *Landscape stability index and artefact density*: the highest concentrations are encountered in landscape positions considered to be less stable (code 3v and 5v) (fig.5d).

These results seem to emphasise that major artefact concentrations are related constantly to the following set of variables: the preferential position on the slope or the summit edge; the frequent association with higher minimum slope values; and the connection with the clays, often exposed along the slopes below the sands. This set of variables represents landscape conditions defined as unstable, i.e. those positions within the landscape where a dominance of erosive processes over

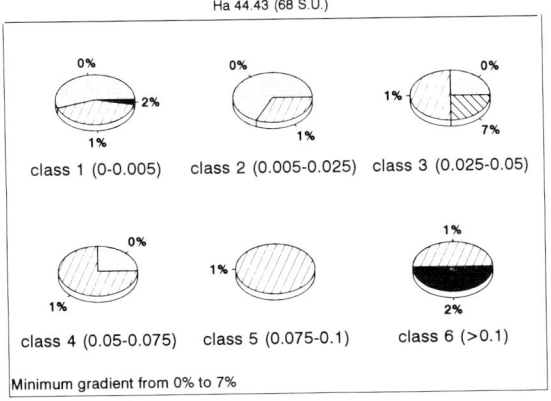

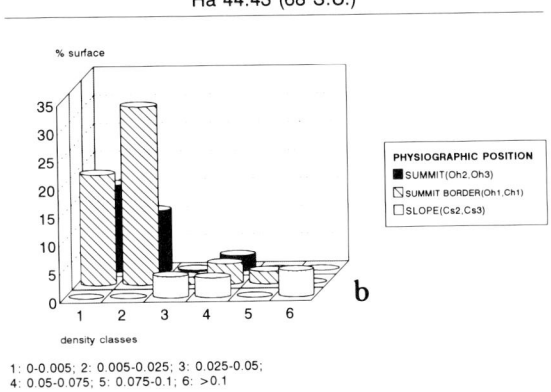

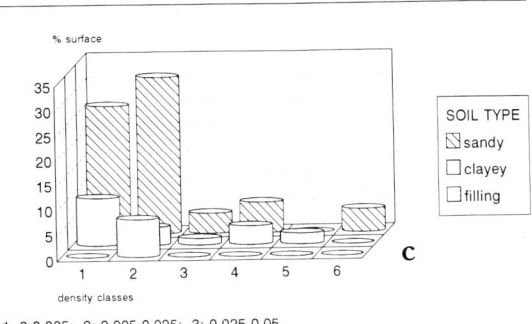

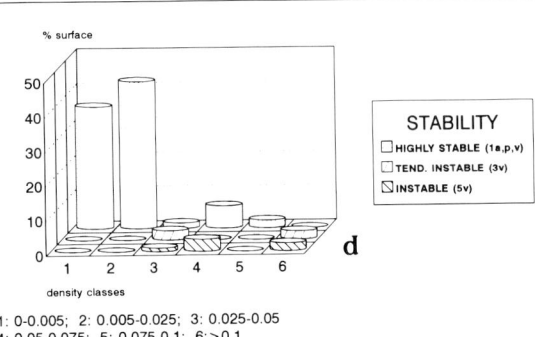

Fig. 5. Find density classes and morphological/soil data (a: lower slope value, b: physiographic position, c: soil type, d: stability index).

time may be presumed. This observation implies an early buried position of the finds, in the case of Malafede probably below a younger aeolian cover of the old coastal terrace. Such a cover was actually identified through sedimentological analysis (Anselmi *et al.*, 1990). Therefore it is particularly important to support the survey with subsoil data, collected through the excavation of trenches, in order to verify the presence, in stable positions, of possible concentrations of buried finds.

INCIDENCE OF THE SURVEY CONDITIONS

(i) Relationship between meteorological data and find density

We noted the relationship, although not very close, between the SU with major find concentrations and the meteorological conditions of covered or slightly clouded sky. This tendency can be connected to a higher visibility level in these conditions than with sunshine, the latter creating shadows and rendering the surface less readable. Our data fully confirm the known assumption that visibility improves after the rain. The graph in fig. 6, concerning SU 29 of sheet 30N, relates the number of finds collected during the various visits and the rain frequency. The contrast between the two situations can be clearly observed.

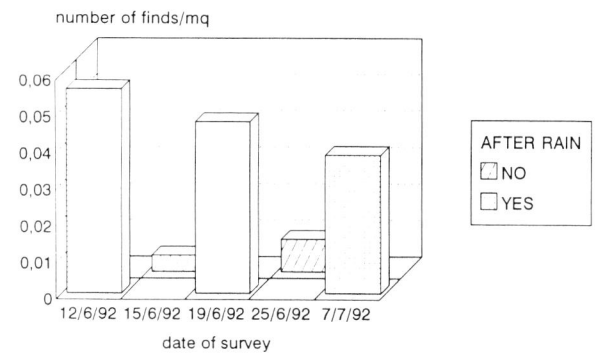

Fig. 6. Sheet 30N, Survey Unit 29: find density classes and rain frequency.

(ii) Relationship between level of survey potential and find density

The comparison between the find densities in the ploughed areas with a good visibility level, and those in the areas with a lower visibility level due to vegetation, shows that the find density in the former cases is on average higher (fig.7a). Thus it may be presumed that the spatial distribution in the well visible areas represents the best approximation to the number of preserved remains. Fig.7b shows the data concerning the SU of sheet 30N, situated in an area with uniform landscape characteristics: about half of this area was untilled during the survey, while the other part was ploughed. Although the two parts were about equal in size, the number of remains turned out to be definitely lower in the less visible areas.

DISCUSSION

This paper has offered a first description and interpretation of the collected data. A definition of the settlement models developed over thousands of years in this region is still out of reach. Our approach requires a constant trial based upon the matching of acquired data and actual problems put forward from time to time by the complex suburban reality of Rome. It is intended not only as a research tool, but also as a mean for correct land management planning, so that one may still catch the transition between the ancient world and the modern town.

Past populations made choices dictated by living conditions and social organization, in relation to the resources and the characteristics of the former environment. What the present landscape may tell about the past depends on a remarkable number of variables and their correlation.

A first series of variables are those that have allowed the conservation of the remains, or their partial or total destruction: for example, active erosion may destroy the traces of an archaeological deposit, but also partially expose buried layers; or else, the sedimentation of soil material over ancient remains may both favour a better conservation and hamper the discovery, except in case of earth moving. These variables are essentially linked to the intensity of natural transformation processes in time (erosion, accumulation, soil formation) and to environmental conditions (climate), but also partially to the numerous acts of transformation due to human activity. The latter have been particularly strong and destructive in the recent past and are still in progress. However, this complex of factors, determining sometimes drastic modifications, is beyond the researcher's control.

In contrast, another series of variables can be controlled by the researcher, and, according to our experience, they may strongly affect the results. Above all, they concern the research methodology. Homogeneous working procedures among various groups of operators can be obtained by strictly applied and constantly verified methods, with a data collection scheme which, even though simple to use, allows a complete and accurate registration. However, choosing the best terrain visibility conditions, whenever possible

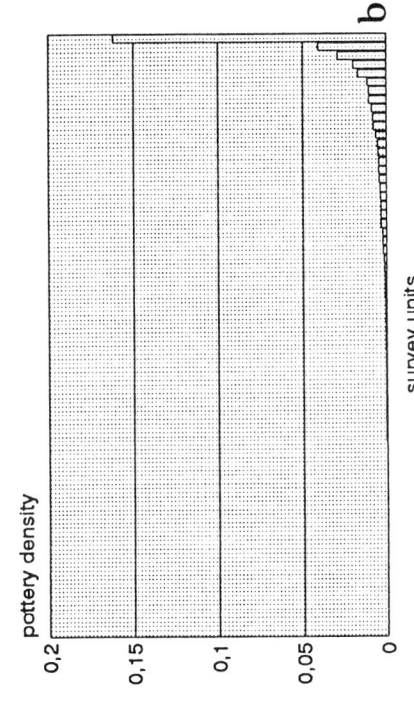

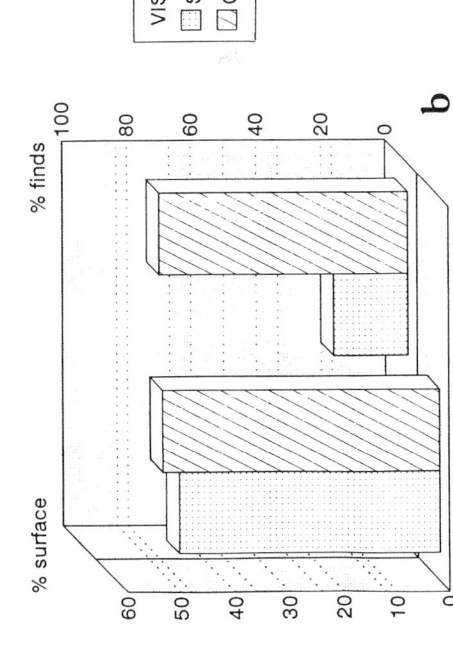

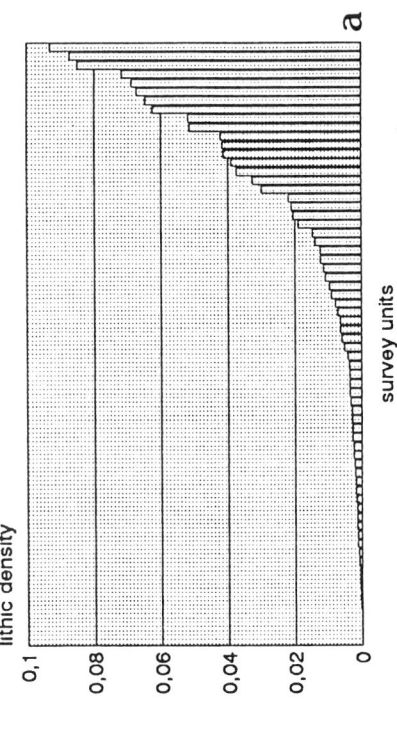

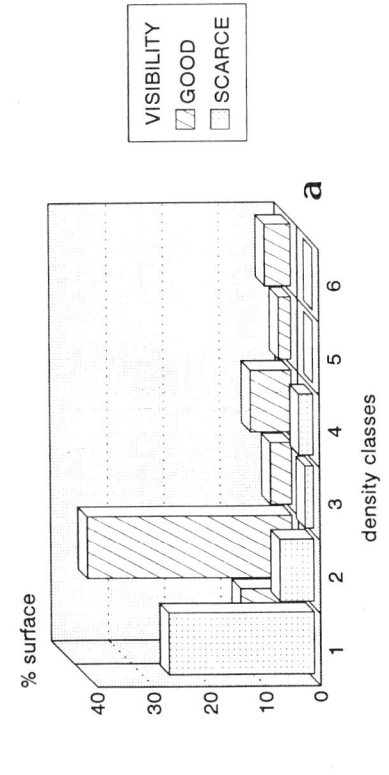

Fig. 7. (a) Find density classes and visibility level in the whole area here considered; (b) visibility level and extension, visibility level and finds in the survey units of sheet 30N.

Fig. 8. Density of (a) the lithic industry and (b) the pre-protohistoric pottery in the various survey units.

and particularly in cropland, seems to be a determining factor. Taking into account the impact of ground visibility is highly important in order to avoid that the layout of complex settlement patterns may somehow reflect the distribution of ploughed fields and/or fields surveyed after rain.

A clear distinction should be constantly made between three levels: the reality of the past, what of it is preserved, and what of it is encountered during the survey. Integration of archaeological and landscape data is therefore considered fundamental for the formulation of hypotheses on the relationship between the third level, the one actually within our reach, and the other two.

The survey project of the coastal area of Rome can be considered a 'non-site survey' (Dancey 1981; Dunnel & Dancey 1983); the primary aim is not to identify and catalogue 'sites', but to register the traces of human activity in relation to the environmental conditions. Within this context, a few small-sized areas have been identified, characterised by highly concentrated and typologically homogeneous records. In those areas registered as 'sites', a more detailed collection was carried out, including denser grid systems and sometimes also the location of the single items. Further research and excavations are planned in these areas.

The relationship between the actual settlement or intense activity areas defined as 'sites' and the remaining part of the region can be grasped also through a simple analysis of the different find densities in the various survey units. The two graphs in fig.8 highlight the different densities of lithic industry and pottery. The lithic industry, more abundant on the whole than the pre-protohistoric pottery, is distributed over all the SU and present in most density classes. This is obviously related to the long timespan of the Palaeolithic, testified in this area from the Mousterian onwards, but also to the widespread occupation pattern of the territory typical of hunter-gatherer societies.

In contrast, sherd finds are completely lacking or have low densities in the majority of SU; instead, they are highly concentrated in one area in particular. This can be connected to the different occupational patterns developed in ages following the Palaeolithic, implying a careful selection of steady settlement sites with concentrations in restricted areas. The Malafede district, only now being systematically surveyed, so far has not yet yielded traces of pre-protohistorical sites, though sites dating from the Neolithic to the Iron Age and important archaeological areas, like Ficana and Castel di Decima, are known in the neighborhood (Bietti Sestieri (ed.) 1984; Bedini *et al.*, 1976; Ficana 1981; Fischer Hansen 1990; Territorio di Roma 1986).

Typological study of the various classes of finds is in progress and might provide, together with the results of the planned excavations, more detailed information about each chronological phase, upon which further data processing will be based.

Acknowledgements

In addition to the authors, the project leaders comprise Dr Margherita Bedello (Soprintendenza Archeologica di Ostia), Drs Margherita Mussi and Daniela Zampetti (both Dipartimento di Scienze delle Antichità dell'Università di Roma 'La Sapienza'), and Dr Francesco Zarlenga (ENEA). The following graduates and students participated in the project from the outset: Drs B. Badei, S. Biondi, A. Curci, I. Fiore, S. Fogagnolo, B. Pino Uria, G. Recchia, E. Remotti, P. Toniutti, plus D. Albertini, I. Baroni, P. Boccuccia, E. Bonafede, R. Ciocchetti, C. Corsello, R. Piatti, E. Santucci; recent participants are G. Bertolani, S. Falzone, S. Marroni and L. Di Filippo. We would like to thank Dr G. Pisani Sartorio who is responsible for the Ufficio Monumenti Antichi e Scavi del Comune di Roma and Dr A. Zevi Gallina, Soprintendente Archeologo di Ostia, who have made this project possible; and moreover Dr L. Ramelli di Celle, responsible for the Centro di Documentazione BB.CC.AA. della Regione Lazio and Dr M. A. Fugazzola, Soprintendente al Museo Preistorico Etnografico 'L. Pigorini', who allowed the partecipation of two of the authors to the project. We also wish to thank Prof. G. Franciosa for his assistance in the graph composition and Dr E. J. Shepherd for editing the English text. Finally, special thanks are due to Dr M. Bedello for her continuous support and essential contributions.

Bibliography

Anselmi, B., Arnoldus-Huyzendveld, A., Catalano, C., Milli, S. & Zarlenga, F. 1990. *Analisi paleoambientale dei depositi (duna rossa) contenenti industria musteriana e affioranti nell'area di Castel Porziano – Pomezia (Roma)*, (ENEA/RT/AMB/90/39), Roma.

Arnoldus-Huyzendveld, A., Crovato, C. & Zarlenga, F. 1992. *Analisi paleoambientale dei depositi "intrawürmiani" e olocenici della Piana di Maccacese*, (Roma, ENEA/RT/AMB/91/26), Roma.

Arnoldus-Huyzendveld, A., Gioia, P. & Pascucci, P. 1992. 'Systematic survey project in the Roman coastal area', in Herring, E., Whitehouse, R. & Wilkins, J. (eds.), *Papers of the IV Conference of Italian Archaeology, New Developments in Italian Archaeology, Part 1*, London, 91–109.

Bedello, M. 1994. 'Un progetto di ricognizione territoriale nella Soprintendenza Archeologica di Ostia', in *La cartografia dei beni storici, archeologici, paesistici nelle grandi aree urbane – Dal censimento alla tutela* (Roma 26–28/4/1990), Roma, 49–55.

Bedello, M., Gioia, P. & Pascucci, P. 1993. 'Ricognizioni di superficie nel territorio costiero di Roma: prospettive di ricerca e di tutela', *Archeologia Laziale* XI, 131–141.

Bedini, A., Cordano, F., Guaitoli, M. & Zevi, F. 1976. 'Castel di Decima', in *Civiltà del Lazio Primitivo*, (Catalogo della Mostra), Roma, 252–290.

Bietti Sestieri, A.M. (ed.) 1984. *Preistoria e protostoria del territorio di Roma*, Roma.

Dancey, W. 1981. *Archaeological Field Methods: An Introduction*, Minneapolis.

Dunnell. R.C. & Dancey, W. 1983. 'The Siteless Survey: a Regional Scale Data Collection Strategy', *Advances in Archaeological Method and Theory* 6, 267–287.

F.A.O.- UNESCO 1988. *Soil Map of the World*, Revised Legend, Roma.

Ficana 1981. *Ficana. Una pietra miliare sulla strada per Roma*, (Catalogo della Mostra), Roma.

Fisher Hansen, T. 1990. *Scavi di Ficana, I. Topografia generale*, Roma.

Territorio di Roma 1986. AA.VV., 'Preistoria e protostoria nel territorio di Roma. Modelli di insediamento e vie di comunicazione', in *Il Tevere e le altre vie d'acqua del Lazio antico, Archeologia Laziale* VII, 2, 30–70.

7

Ricognizioni nelle Valli del Tevere e del Farfa: Indagini sulle Evidenze Pre-Protostoriche e Arcaiche

CLARISSA BELARDELLI
(Centro Regionale di Documentazione BB.CC.AA del Lazio)

Summary: *The territory of the Tiber and Farfa Valleys, in the Comune of Fara in Sabina (Rieti), has been the focus of systematic archaeological survey aimed at identifying pre-protohistoric and archaic sites around the ancient town of* Cures Sabini. *The survey project started in 1989 with the collaboration of the Soprintendenza Archeologica per il Lazio, is still in progress. This paper considers only the archaic period sites together with the bronze material from Piano San Giovanni, which probably derives from an Iron Age burial.*

A partire dal 1989*, entro i limiti comunali di Fara in Sabina (Rieti) veniva avviato dagli archeologi pre-protostorici del Centro Regionale di Documentazione BBCCAA del Lazio, ufficio 2, operanti nell'area 8 = media valle del Tevere e Sabina tiberina, un progetto di prospezione e ricognizione di superficie mirato al riscontro delle evidenze preistoriche, protostoriche e arcaiche già note e ad un nuovo esame del territorio con un analogo taglio cronologico (CRD 1992: 3).

La scelta di procedere ad un'indagine di settore, finalizzata alla comprensione dei modelli di occupazione del territorio nella pre-protostoria e in età arcaica, risultava particolarmente sollecitata dall'esistenza, nel territorio di Fara, dell'antico centro di *Cures Sabini*, abitato a partire dagli inizi dell'età del ferro e divenuto poi una tra le le più importanti città del comprensorio sabino tiberino (Muzzioli 1980; Guidi & Reggiani 1981: 75–82; Alvino & Guidi 1985: 77–92; Guidi 1988: 41–50; Guidi *et al.*, in stampa). La ricerca è venuta ad integrarsi utilmente con quelle portate avanti dalla Soprintendenza Archeologica per il Lazio, nella comune prospettiva di riuscire a definire e a studiare il territorio controllato da *Cures* agli inizi della sua storia (Reggiani Massarini 1992: 133); e dalla British School at Rome, che pure ha effettuato ed effettua nel comprensorio di Farfa ricerche ugualmente mirate, ma ad evidenziare presenze archeologiche tardo-antiche e altomedievali, o a ricostruire la fisionomia del paesaggio nell'antichità (Moreland 1986: 333–343; Christie 1992).

Ad una fase preliminare della ricerca, durante la quale sono stati censiti, schedati e riportati su base cartografica (IGM 1: 25.000 e aerofotogrammetrico 1: 5.000) i siti e le evidenze noti (AA.VV. 1988: 508–11), è seguita la definizione degli obbiettivi della ricerca:

– ricontrollo sistematico di quanto già conosciuto nel territorio in ambito pre-protostorico e arcaico;

– esplorazione del territorio immediatamente prossimo a *Cures Sabini*;

– esplorazione dei principali rilievi collinari;

– prospezione di alcune aree montuose di particolare conformazione (es. la dorsale di Fara);

– esplorazione dei terrazzi fluviali.

Essendo questo un progetto di ricerca mirata, non è stata effettuata una ricognizione a tappeto di tutto il territorio comunale, ma solo di alcune aree individuate in fase preliminare e ritenute più idonee all'esplorazione, sia da un punto di vista morfologico che strategico-insediamentale sulla base di comparazioni con modelli metodologici analoghi. Nell'ambito delle aree prescelte, la ricognizione è stata invece effettuata a tappeto e a

---

* Il censimento bibliografico fu avviato nel 1985 dagli archeologi dell'area 8 (QuadAEI 16: 508–11). Alle ricognizioni hanno preso parte, insieme a chi scrive, Maria Paola Moscetta (1989–90), Marco Bettelli (1989–90) e Massimo Briazzani (1991–92). La base cartografica del territorio comunale di Fara in Sabina, ottenuta dall'assemblaggio di varie tavolette IGM1:25000, è stata gentilmente fornita dall'Ufficio 1 del Centro Regionale di Documentazione BB.CC.AA del Lazio.

'maglie strette', con la registrazione puntuale di tutti i dati osservabili e dei punti di raccolta dei materiali archeologici, convenzionalmente definiti 'siti' (AA.VV. 1984; AA.VV.1986: 30–70).

La rilevanza numerica di nuovi punti di raccolta individuati nel territorio e la varietà degli ambiti cronologici in essi rappresentati ha consigliato di limitare in questa sede l'illustrazione dei soli siti dell'età del ferro e arcaici.

Colli Bernabei (Fig.1, 1).

IGM F 144 IV SE MONTOPOLI DI SABINA
Aerofotogrammetrico 1: 5000, Comune di Fara in Sabina, F5.
Ricognizioni: C. Belardelli, M. Bettelli, 6.11.1989.

Il sito è localizzabile sul lato destro di via di Colli Bernabei procedendo dalla strada che da Passo Corese porta a Talocci, sulle pendici del colle coltivato ad alberi da frutta o incolto fra ville di recente costruzione. Il materiale ceramico affiorava in superficie in seguito ad una parziale fresatura del terreno sotto gli alberi; una seconda concentrazione di frammenti era nell'orto di un'abitazione, ca. m.50 più avanti. Le raccolte consistono in frammenti di forma non ricostruibile, in impasto rossiccio grezzo, talvolta tornito, cui si aggiungono tegole e coppi, riferibili ad insediamento arcaico. Verso la fine della stessa via è un altro sito, a suo tempo individuato da M. P. Muzzioli (1980: 79, n.10).

Puzzaroli (Fig.1, 2)

IGM F 144 IV SE MONTOPOLI DI SABINA
Aerofotogrammetrico 1: 5000, Comune di Fara in Sabina, F5.
Ricognizioni: C. Belardelli, M. Briazzani, 7.2.1992 e 22.2.1992.

La località Puzzaroli era stata già segnalata da Muzzioli (1980: 78) relativamente ad una grande villa romana troncata in due dalla strada moderna. Il nuovo sito si riferisce alla sommità di una collina in prossimità di Corese Terra, delimitata a Est da un forte dislivello a strapiombo verso il Fosso di Corese. Il terreno è ad olivi ed alberi da frutta e reca traccia di arature non frequenti.

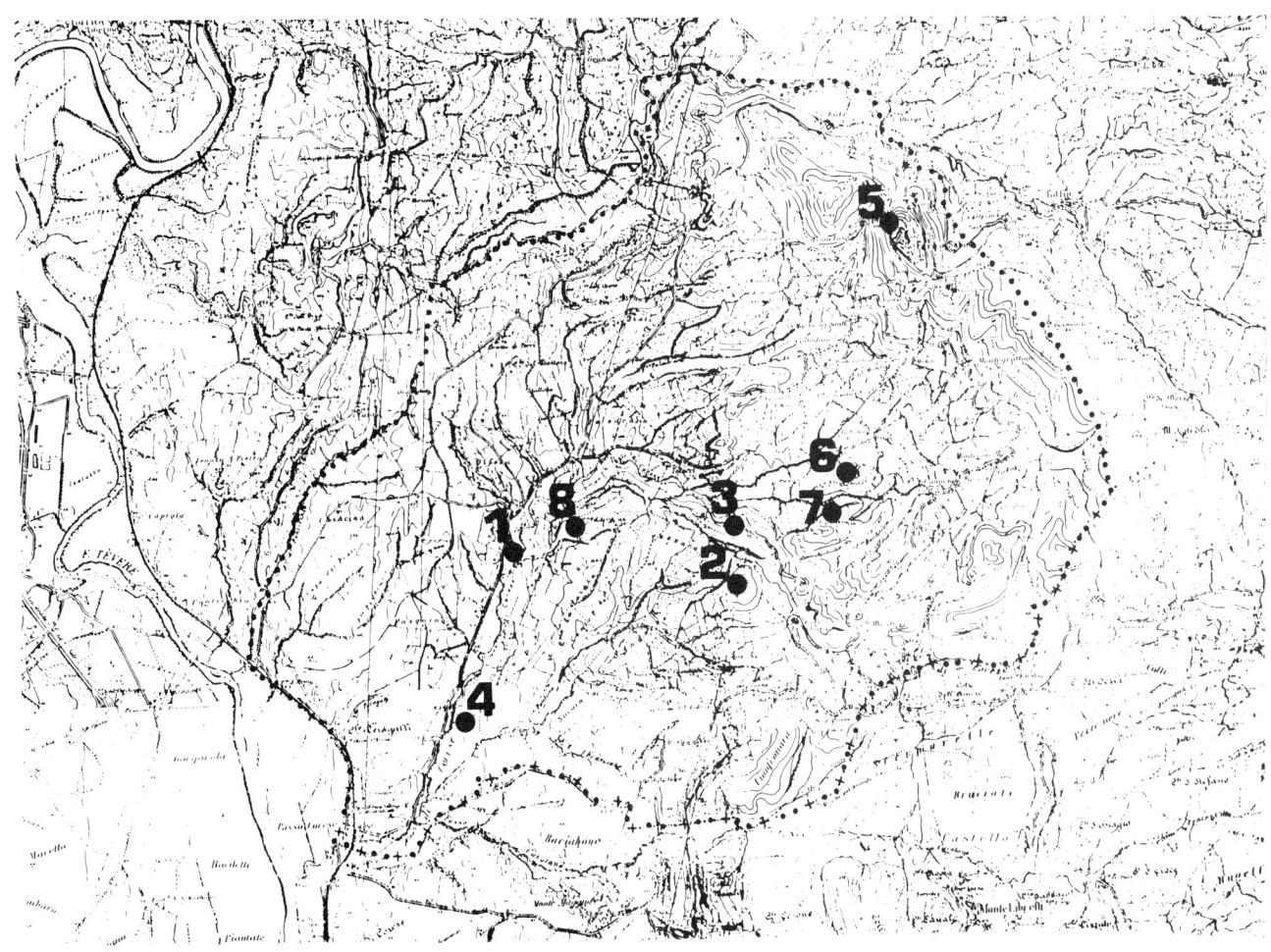

Fig. 1. Valli del Tevere e del Farfa: l'area oggetto di indagine. 1 – Colli Bernabei; 2 – Puzzaroli; 3 – Piano San Giovanni; 4 – Fosso di Corese/La Parata; 5 – Fara in Sabina; 6 – Colle Romito; 7 – Colle Peschiera/Le Cerquicarde; 8 – Cures Sabini.

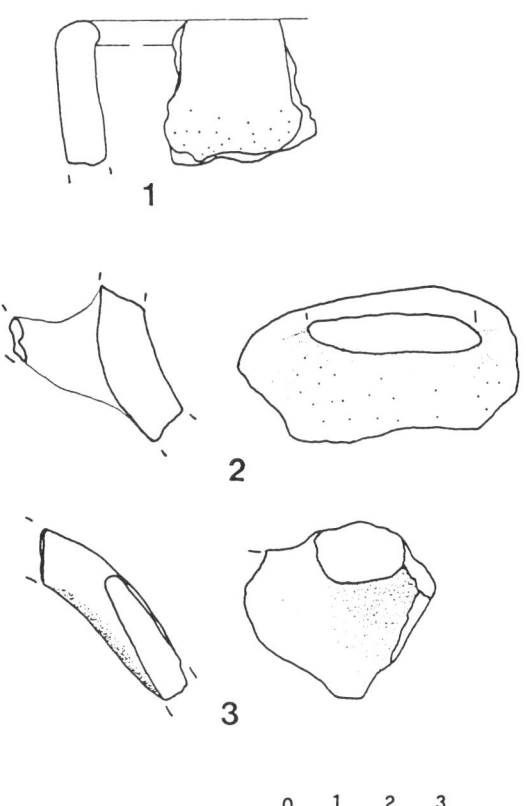

Fig. 2. Puzzaroli; frammenti di impasto.

In passato, T. Leggio e G. Filippi rinvennero nella stessa località, ma ad una certa profondità rispetto al piano di campagna, degli oggetti di bronzo (Guidi 1980), verosimilmente relativi ad un contesto funerario dell'età del ferro, fase II B laziale (DdA 1982: 79-96). Si tratta di: una piccola fibula ad arco a sezione quadrangolare rivestito di vaghi d'ambra (due conservati) e staffa simmetrica (Fig.4, 1a-1b); una spirale fermatrecce di filo di bronzo (Fig.4, 2); un frammento di verga di bronzo con decorazione incisa a puntini, forse parte di arco di fibula (Fig.4, 3); e due anelli da sospensione, in un caso con decorazione incisa a zig-zag, a sezione a losanga (Fig.4, 4-5). Il contesto appare cronologicamente omogeneo e trova confronti con corredi analoghi da Osteria dell'Osa, Tivoli e Valvisciolo, nonché da altri complessi laziali della fase II B (DdA 1982: 84, 95, tav. 10 n.16, 18, 20). Sempre in occasione delle medesime esplorazioni, Leggio individuò, di fronte al punto di rinvenimento degli oggetti di bronzo, tracce di probabili strutture abitative arcaiche; Filippi ricorda di aver raccolto nei pressi di un casale moderno pochi frammenti di impasto forse della media età del bronzo (informazioni da T.Leggio e G.Filippi). Poco più avanti, in prossimità del campo sportivo, è stata raccolta dell'industria litica (ricognizioni C. Belardelli, M. P. Moscetta, 1989-90).

Il materiale ceramico, in frammenti di piccole e medie dimensioni, era sparso su tutta l'area e sulla sommità del rilievo, dove affiorava anche materiale litico. Fra le forme riconoscibili se ne individuano alcune, chiuse, di medie dimensioni, e altre aperte, ansate, in impasto non lisciato in superficie e non tornito (Fig.2, 1-3).

PIANO S. GIOVANNI (Fig.1, 3)
IGM F 144 IV SE MONTOPOLI SABINA
Aerofotogrammetrico 1: 5000, Comune di Fara in Sabina, F5.
Ricognizioni: C. Belardelli, M. P. Moscetta, 10.11.1989 e 16.11.1989; C. Belardelli, M. Bettelli, 13.11.1989; C. Belardelli, 20.10.1990.

Il sito si identifica in una vasta piana di fondovalle fra i fossi di Corese e Peracalli, alla base delle alture di Colle Peschiera/Le Cerquicarde e Colle Romito (cfr. più avanti). Il terreno è raramente coltivato, più spesso lasciato a pascolo. Lungo la via di Piano S.Giovanni, oltre il campo sportivo e dopo una serie di casali, sono state effettuate le raccolte di materiale quantitativamente più significative (Fig.3, 1-8): si tratta di frammenti ceramici in impasto talvolta tornito, riferibili a fornelli, boccali, olle.

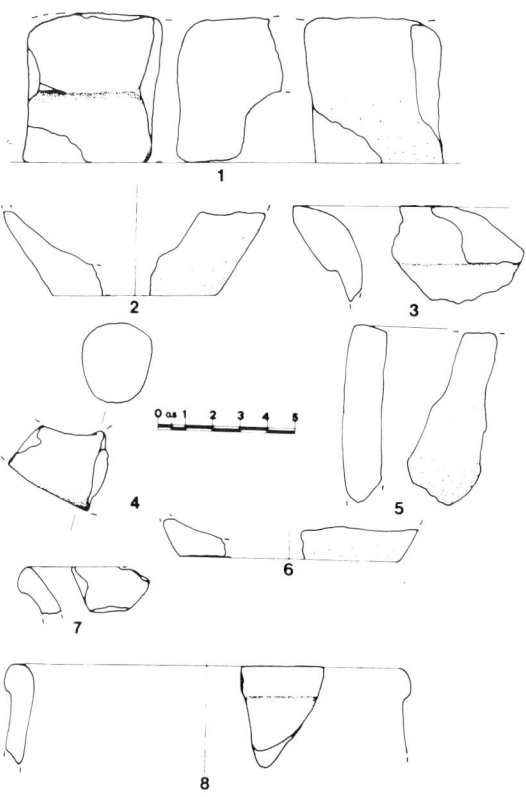

Fig. 3. Piano San Giovanni: materiali di impasto.

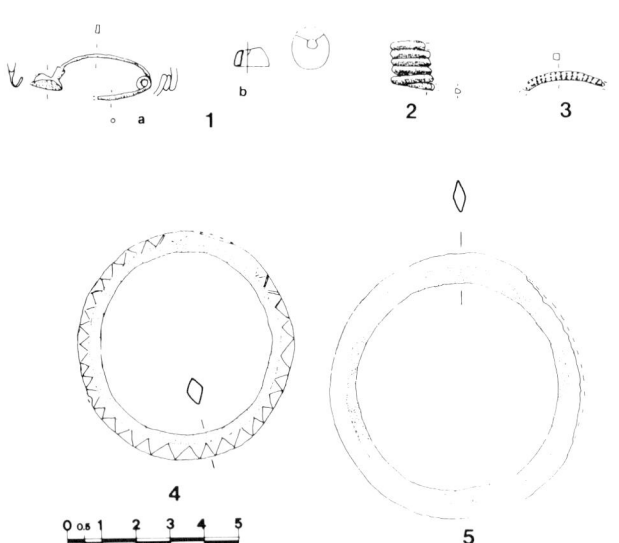

Fig. 4. Piano San Giovanni: oggetti in bronzo e ambra.

Fosso di Corese/La Parata (Fig.1, 4)
IGM F 144 III NE –PASSO CORESE
Aerofotogrammetrico 1: 5000, Comune di Fara in Sabina, F4.
Ricognizioni: C. Belardelli, M. Briazzani, 10.4.1991 e 10.11.1991.

La zona, molto ampia, in cui è localizzato il sito, è grosso modo compresa fra i fossi di Corese e Parata; il terreno è coltivato a seminativo. In corrispondenza di un grande viale di cipressi che conduce ad una villa, è stata osservata una concentrazione di materiale ceramico misto a frammenti di tegole. Le forme vascolari riconoscibili sono in impasto, analoghe a quelle di Piano S.Giovanni (Fig.5A, 1–4): vasellame comune da cucina e oggetti di uso quotidiano (Fig.5A, 3: fusaiola). Poco più avanti, su un terrazzo del Fosso di Corese, è stata raccolta dell'industria litica (ricognizioni C. Belardelli, M. P. Moscetta, 1989–90).

Fara in Sabina (sporadico) (Fig.1, 5)
IGM F 144 ISO – FARA IN SABINA
Aerofotogrammetrico 1: 5000, Comune di Fara in Sabina, F3.
Ricognizioni: C. Belardelli, M. Bettelli, 23.3.1990.

L'altura su cui sorge Fara in Sabina è una delle più importanti della zona; essa sale gradualmente da Farfa ai Quattro Venti, per poi proseguire, alquanto più ripida, fino al centro abitato. La raccolta, relativa a pochi frammenti ceramici, è stata effettuata lungo la strada antica e subito a ridosso delle prime abitazioni, fra la vegetazione spontanea a cespugli che ricopre le pendici del monte. Sul rilievo di Monte S.Martino, che fronteggia quello di Fara, era già stato identificato un sito dell'età del bronzo finale (Angle, Gianni & Guidi 1982; Filippi & Leggio 1982; Filippi 1985; Moreland 1986; Filippi & Pacciarelli 1991: 40–42), oggetto di una nuova esplorazione (ricognizioni 1989–90, C. Belardelli, M. Bettelli, M. P. Moscetta).

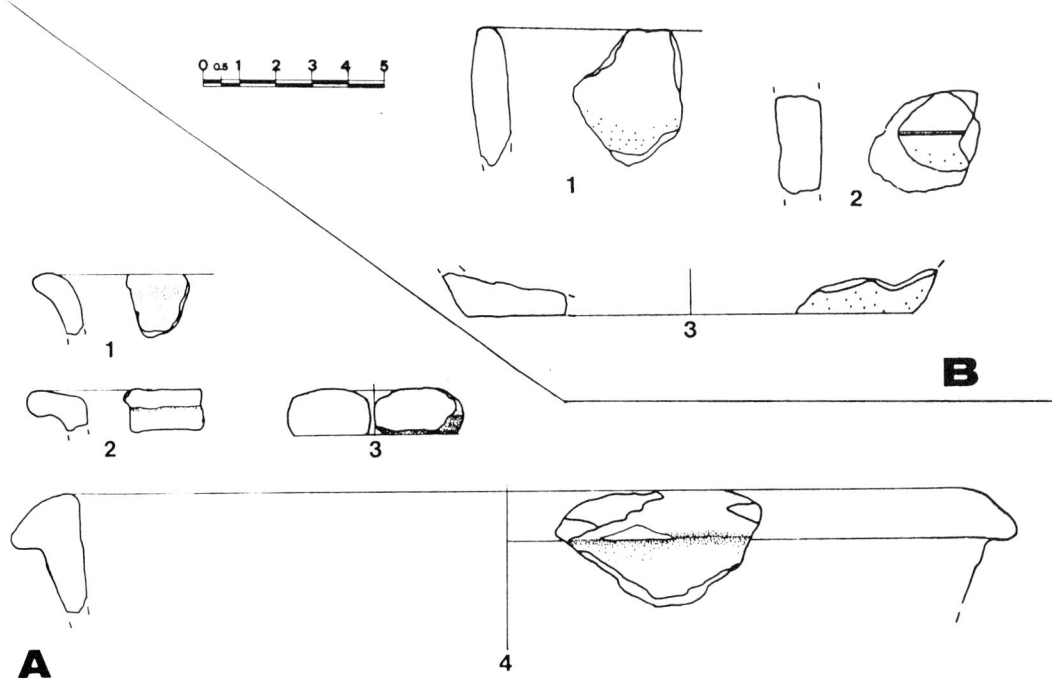

Fig. 5A. Fosso di Corese/La Parata: frammenti di impasto.
Fig. 5B. Colle Peschiera/Le Cerquicarde: frammenti di impasto.

Colle Romito (sporadico) (Fig. 1, 6)
IGM F 144 I SO – FARA IN SABINA
Aerofotogrammetrico 1: 5000, Comune di Fara in Sabina, F5-6.
Ricognizioni: C. Belardelli, M. Bettelli, 12.4.1990; C. Belardelli, 11.10.1990.

La collina, in fondo alla via di Piano S. Giovanni, è accanto ad un altro modesto rilievo. Fra le piante di olivi, il terreno è coltivato a cereali o lasciato a riposo. Lungo le pendici nord della collina e sulla sommità, in corrispondenza di un'area adibita a pascolo, sono stati raccolti alcuni frammenti in impasto.

Colle Peschiera/Le Cerquicarde (Fig.1, 7).
IGM F 144 I SO – FARA IN SABINA
Aerofotogrammetrico 1: 5000, Comune di Fara in Sabina, F5-6.
Ricognizioni: C. Belardelli, M. Bettelli, 12.4.1990; C. Belardelli, 11.10.1990.

La collina è stata recentemente rimboschita con giovani olmi ed il terreno intorno agli alberi viene coltivato regolarmente. Fra le zone fresate, subito a ridosso della strada che prosegue poi per Banditella da dove provengono materiali della media età del bronzo (Filippi 1985: 62-3), sono stati rinvenuti numerosi frammenti ceramici in impasto arcaico (fondi e orli di contenitori di medie dimensioni: Fig.5B, 1-3).

Il proseguimento delle ricerche in collaborazione con quanti operano sul territorio, la verifica sistematica di quanto già osservato e la diffusione dei risultati per un continuo aggiornamento, necessario anche per le modifiche repentine che talvolta si riscontrano (disboscamenti, urbanizzazione ecc.), sarà impegno per il futuro.

Ringraziamenti

Ringrazio Alessandro Guidi, già funzionario archeologo della Soprintendenza Archeologica per il Lazio, per avermi permesso di documentare e studiare i materiali in bronzo da Piano S. Giovanni e per aver seguito il lavoro; Tersilio Leggio, ispettore onorario della S.A.L., per le numerose notizie sulle sue ricerche in zona; Giorgio Filippi, direttore del museo territoriale di Forum Novum, per avermi fornito ulteriori dettagli in merito; e il prof. Renato Peroni per i suoi consigli. I disegni sono stati eseguiti da chi scrive.

Bibliografia

AA.VV. 1984. *Preistoria e Protostoria nel territorio di Roma.* Roma.

AA.VV. 1986. 'Preistoria e Protostoria nel territorio di Roma. Modelli di insediamento e vie di comunicazione', in *Il Tevere e le altre vie d'acqua del Lazio antico,* (QuadAEI 12), 30-70.

AA.VV.1988. 'Attività di censimento e catalogazione del settore archeologico della Regione Lazio', *QuadAEI* 16, 503-11.

Alvino, G. & Guidi, A. 1985. 'Cures Sabini'. *QuadAEI* 11, 77-92.

Angle, M., Gianni, A. & Guidi, A. 1982. 'Gli insediamenti montani di sommità nell'Italia centrale: il caso dei Monti Lucretili', *Dialoghi d'Archeologia*, 2, 80-91.

Christie, N. (a cura di) 1992. *Leicester in Sabina. Field Surveys and Excavations in Central Italy, 1988-1991*, University of Leicester, 1992.

CRD 1992. *Ufficio 2 - Documentazione in materia archeologica, architettonica e storico-artistica. L'attività di catalogazione 1985-1992*, Roma.

DdA 1982. *La formazione della città nel Lazio = Dialoghi d'Archeologia*, 1-2.

Filippi, G. & Leggio, T. 1982. *Nuove conoscenze sulle origini della città sabina di Cures* (Conferenza presso la Pontificia Accademia Romana di Archeologia).

Filippi, G. 1985. *Dialoghi d'Archeologia*, s.3, 2, 57-64.

Filippi, G. & Pacciarelli, M. 1991. 'Materiali protostorici dalla Sabina tiberina. L'età del bronzo e la prima età del ferro tra il Farfa e il Nera', *Quaderni del Museo Civico Archeologico di Magliano Sabina*, 1.

Guidi, A. 1980. 'Provincia di Rieti, Fara in Sabina: loc.Piano di S. Giovanni, Molino di Linguessa, Fosso di Banditella. Provincia di Roma, Montelibretti: loc.Capocotta', *RSP*, XXXV, 1-2, 389.

Guidi, A. 1988. 'Cures Sabini', *Quaderni della Soprintendenza Archeologica per il Lazio*, 1, 41-50.

Guidi, A. & Reggiani, A.M. 1981. 'Cures', *QuadAEI* 15, 75-82.

Guidi, A. et al., in stampa. 'Cures Sabini: lo scavo, le strutture, la cultura materiale, le attività economiche', in *Identità e civiltà dei Sabini*, (XVIII Convegno di Studi Etrusco-Italici, Rieti-Magliano Sabina, 30 Maggio-3 Giugno, 1993).

Moreland, J. 1986. 'Ricognizione nei dintorni di Farfa, 1985. Resoconto preliminare', *Archeologia Medievale*, 13, 333-43.

Muzzioli, M.P. 1980. *Cures Sabini*. Firenze.

Reggiani Massarini, A.M. 1992. In Reggiani Massarini, A.M. & Spadoni Cerroni, M.C. 1992. *Reate*. Pisa.

8

Ricognizioni Archeologiche nell'Ager Caeretanus: 1990–1992

FLAVIO ENEI

Sommario: *Si presentano i risultati delle ultime campagne di ricognizione (1990-1992) condotte nella fascia costiera dell'antico ager Caeretanus. Il progetto di ricerca, presentato nel 1990 a Londra, è finalizzato allo studio dei paesaggi antichi dell'immediato hinterland di Caere, una tra le più importanti città dell'Etruria meridionale costiera e del Mediterraneo in epoca etrusca. Si sta indagando di circa 400 kmq, subito circostante il centro urbano, comprendente realtà naturali molto diverse: dalla pianura litoranea, ai rilievi dei monti Ceriti, alle profonde valli fluviali. Emerge un quadro del popolamento, dalla preistoria al medioevo, in cui si delineano elementi di continuità e/o cambiamento nella gestione delle risorse naturali da parte delle comunità umane.*

INTRODUZIONE

Si presentano i risultati delle ricerche di superficie condotte nelle campagne dell'antica *Caere*, tra il 1990 e il 1992, nell'ambito del progetto *ager Caeretanus* (Enei 1992). La ricerca, destinata alla ricostruzione dei paesaggi antichi, riguarda l'immediato *hinterland* del centro urbano, esteso per un raggio di 15 km, tra il mare Tirreno e i Monti Ceriti, comprendente località distanti al massimo 4 ore di cammino dall'abitato. La città antica, oggetto d'indagine da parte del Centro di Studio per l'Archeologia Etrusco Italica del CNR, si trova quasi nel centro dell'area prescelta come campione: uno spazio geografico di circa 400 kmq, convenzionalmente diviso in 4 settori, coincidenti con le tavolette IGM di Cerveteri (149 IV NE), Castel Giuliano (143 III SE), Santa Severa (143 III SO), Stazione di Furbara (149 IV NO) (Fig. 1).

Nell'area prescelta sussistono realtà naturali molto diverse: dai Monti Ceriti, ai pianori tufacei, alle profonde valli fluviali, ai rilievi collinari calcarei, fino ai tratti di pianura litoranea. Varie morfologie, stratificazioni geologiche, processi pedogenetici e coperture vegetali interagiscono con i diversi assetti dell'idrografia disegnando un paesaggio complesso, articolato in numerose distinte unità topografico-ambientali la cui analisi costituisce il principale obiettivo della ricerca. Tra il 1985 e il 1989 è stato indagato sistematicamente il settore SE del campione, coincidente con la tavoletta IGM di Cerveteri, comprendente, in epoca storica, gli immediati dintorni sud-orientali della città antica e parte dell'*ager Alsietinus*, il territorio della colonia romana di *Alsium*, dedotta nel 247 a.C. nelle terre confiscate ai Ceriti. Il rinvenimento di oltre 900 siti d'interesse archeologico ha consentito la costruzione di una dettagliata cartografia di fase, estesa dalla preistoria al tardo medioevo, presentata in occasione della IV Conferenza di Archeologia Italiana (Enei 1992).

LE NUOVE ACQUISIZIONI

Le ultime ricerche, condotte tra il 1990 e il 1992, sono state indirizzate alla schedatura dei numerosi dati storico-archeologici noti in tutto il vasto territorio oggetto d'indagine, recuperati principalmente attraverso la lettura della notevole e dispersa bibliografia riguardante l'*ager Caeretanus*, e la ricognizione negli archivi della Soprintendenza Archeologica per l'Etruria Meridionale e del Gruppo Archeologico Romano.

L'attività sul campo, oltre che al ricontrollo dei siti noti e/o visibili in foto aerea, è stata invece finalizzata all'esplorazione di due specifiche aree campione prescelte per lo studio del paesaggio litoraneo antico, nel tratto di pianura alluvionale estesa tra *Alsium* e *Pyrgi*. Le ricerche hanno consentito l'allestimento di una carta archeologica preliminare dell'*hinterland* cerite comprendente 1374 segnalazioni di rinvenimenti, per la maggior parte di epoca etrusca e romana.

E' stato possibile definire delle prime carte di fase generali, con valore di appunti di lavoro, relative all'età del Bronzo, alla prima età del Ferro, all'epoca etrusca

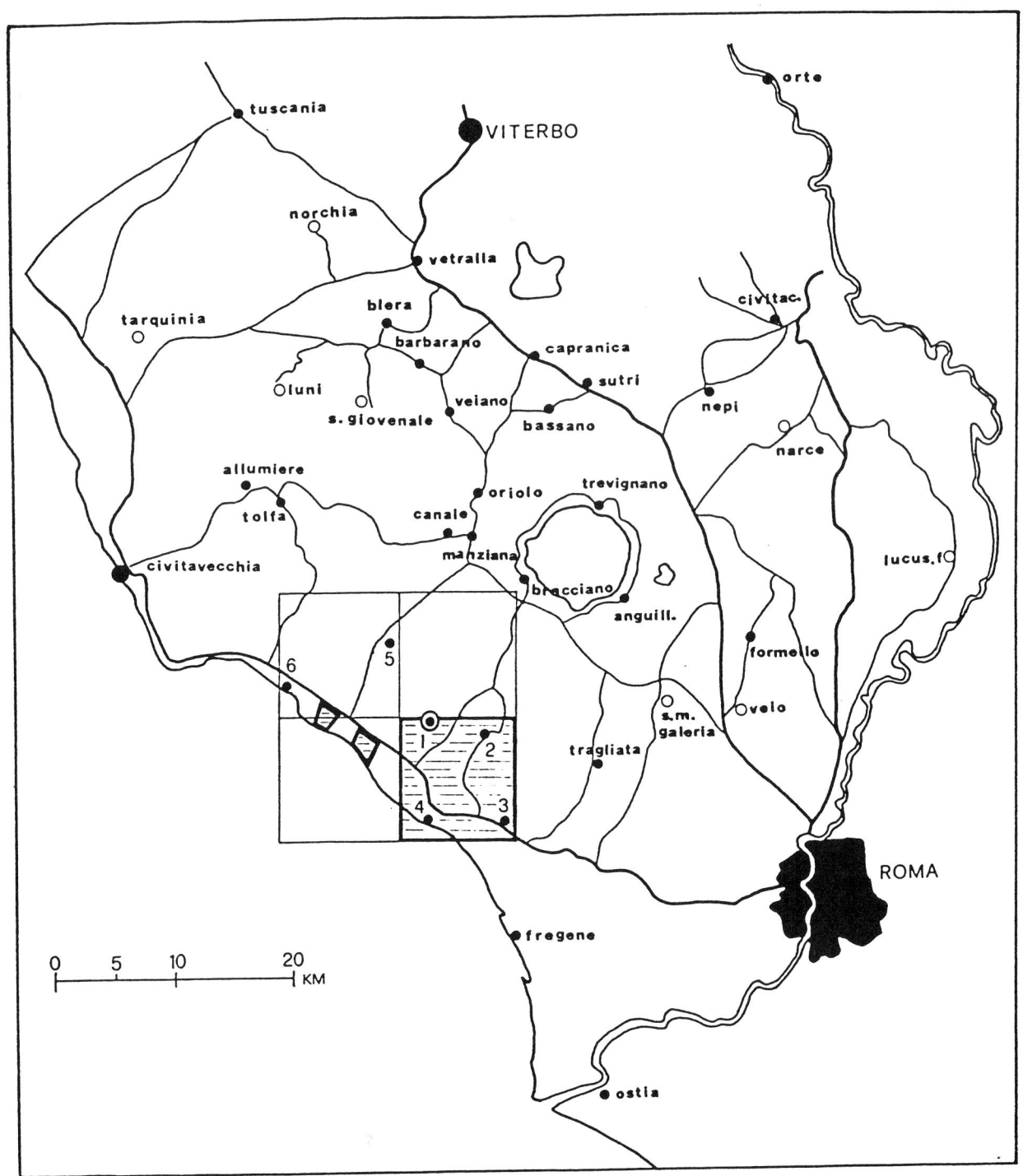

Fig. 1. Estensione dell'area interessata dal progetto di ricerca; il limite in neretto perimetra il settore e le aree campione indagate. I numeri corrispondono agli abitati di: Cerveteri (1), Ceri (2), Palidoro (3), Palo-Ladispoli (4), Sasso (5), Santa Severa (6).

arcaica, all'epoca romana primo-imperiale, al medioevo (XI-XII secolo).

Età del Bronzo (Fig. 2)

Le tracce di insediamenti inquadrabili nell'età del Bronzo, quasi tutti tra il Bronzo medio e il Bronzo finale, confermano quanto già osservato in molteplici zone dell'Etruria meridionale.

Le principali valli fluviali costituiscono importanti assi viari lungo i quali si distribuiscono piccoli siti abitati rinvenuti con una densità maggiore in prossimità dei punti di confluenza ricchi di acque sorgive. La frequentazione risulta più intensa intorno a specifiche compagini naturali formate da una valle fluviale sufficientemente ampia comprendente un punto di confluenza variamente articolato attorno ad una formazione tufacea, isolata per almeno tre lati, alla base della quale sussistono di solito una o più sorgenti perenni.

Tali habitat, spesso caratterizzati da suoli alluvionali facilmente lavorabili e in antico certamente ricchi di flora e fauna, sembrano costituire il paesaggio preferito dalle comunità agricolo-pastorali dell'età del Bronzo, in particolare per quanto riguarda il Bronzo recente e finale. Il polo urbano di *Caere* viene a svilupparsi nell'età del Ferro in coincidenza con una di queste tipiche compagini naturali, quella che tra tutte rivela comunque maggiori potenzialità in termini di spazi disponibili, ricchezza idrica, fertilità del terreno. Le caratteristiche degli elementi geo-morfologici, pedologici e idrografici, nonchè il numero delle sorgenti e la posizione geografica del pianoro occupato dall'abitato, indicano chiaramente le ragioni della scelta del sito e del suo successivo sviluppo e prevalenza rispetto alle comunità limitrofe.

Le ricognizioni stanno quindi documentando i presupposti preistorici del *populus* cerite, per la prima volta anche in zone strettamente collegate alla sede dell'insediamento etrusco-romano. Frammenti ceramici rinvenuti in località Sant'Angelo, Valle della Mola, Banditaccia – Manganello, fosso del Marmo, databili a partire dal Bronzo medio, sembrano assimilare la genesi di *Caere* a quella di molti altri importanti centri antichi dell'Italia tirrenica, in particolare quelli del *Latium Vetus*, Roma compresa (AA.VV 1980; Torelli 1984; Moscati 1985). Nel settore SE del campione, indagato a tappeto, la fase recente e finale dell'età del Bronzo registra un popolamento esteso a realtà ambientali molto diverse, e soltanto nel caso del piccolo pianoro delle Fornaci di Ceri può essere dimostrata l'occupazione di un rilievo naturalmente fortificato. Si riscontrano le soluzioni inquadrate nelle categorie I, 2 e II, 3 della tipologia proposta dalla Galassi (1986): insediamenti siti nell'interno delle valli, nelle fasce di terreno comprese tra i corsi d'acqua e i costoni rocciosi, in alcuni casi anche su piccoli terrazzi posti lungo le pendici presso la base dei pianori, secondo una logica molto simile a quella riscontrata nell'entroterra e nell'alta valle del Mignone (Pacciarelli 1982; Di Nocera & Enei 1990). Le testimonianze funerarie, finora ben attestate soltanto nella zona montana dell'acrocoro tolfetano-cerite e ristrette nella fascia costiera all'unica sepoltura protovillanoviana presente nella necropoli del Sorbo (Pohl 1972), vengono ampliate da due nuovi ritrovamenti. In località Porrazzeta (Croce Bianca), in seguito ad un profondo scasso agricolo sono emerse alcune grandi scaglie di calcare bianco associate a frammenti di olla biconica decorata e scodelle a pareti rientranti. In località Quarto del Cecio, si segnala il rinvenimento di due o tre sepolture ad incinerazione con olle biconiche, fibule, scodelle, contenute entro pozzetti e custodie circolari in tufo rosso.

I dati archeologici non consentono di stabilire gerarchie negli insediamenti ma permettono di valutare le scelte topografiche ed ambientali che nella parte esplorata sistematicamente dell'*ager Caeretanus* sembrano rivelarsi strettamente legate alla viabilità e alle esigenze di pacifici sistemi di vita rurale.

Allo stato attuale delle conoscenze, non sembrano emergere particolari necessità di ordine strategico-difensivo: nel settore SE del campione, all'unico esempio certo di abitato di sommità presso Le Fornaci di Ceri (considerando le rocche di Ceri e Castel Campanile potrebbero essere in totale tre) corrispondono comunque almeno 24 siti con materiali del Bronzo recente e/o finale situati in posizioni aperte o vallive. La documentazione raccolta sul campo sembra suggerire una presenza capillare di piccole comunità o singoli gruppi familiari distanti tra loro non più di 3 km, in alcune zone anche poche centinaia di metri.

Età del Ferro (Fig. 3)

Le ricognizioni condotte dai ricercatori del CNR nell'area urbana antica indicano già nella prima età del Ferro l'esistenza di numerosi nuclei di abitazioni, distribuiti sul pianoro, specie in prossimità dei margini NE e SO della vasta formazione tufacea. Ai diversi agglomerati di probabili capanne sembrano corrispondere altrettanti sepolcreti, posti nella fascia immediatamente suburbana: dal Sorbo, a Cava della Pozzolana al Laghetto, alla Via degli Inferi (Di Gennaro 1986; Cristofani 1986; Cristofani *et al.* 1986).

Nel settore SE del campione, il solo indagato a tappeto, i dati relativi a questa fase indicano una contrazione nel popolamento, avvertibile in particolare nelle aree periferiche, lontane dalla nascente città. Si rivelano deserte ad esempio le valli dei fossi Tavolato e Castellaccio, zone che fino alle soglie del primo millennio a.C. apparivano tra le più frequentate: il dato si allinea a quanto già osservato in altri settori del territorio, specie nell'entroterra, nel distretto tolfetano, nelle valli del Mignone e nell'area compresa tra *Caere* e il Tevere (Zifferero 1985; Delpino 1987). Negli immediati dintorni di *Caere* sono invece presenti almeno nove siti con materiali attribuibili all'età del Ferro. Si tratta di quattro necropoli (Casale San Paolo, Polledrara, M. Abbadoncino, M. Tosto) e sei probabili insediamenti (Tumulo Torlonia, f. della Maddalena, M. Abbadone, f. Sanguinara, M. Cucco, M. Vittoria, M. Tosto), alcuni con precedenti nell'età del Bronzo, distanti non più di 5 km dal pianoro dei Vignali.

Le necropoli sono disposte in posizione elevata, sui rilievi tufacei e calcarei, probabilmente non molto lontane dai rispettivi abitati; nei casi di Monte Tosto, Casale San Paolo e Monte Abbadoncino si rivelano sepolcreti consistenti, di certo superiori alle 30 unità.

La presenza di un polo urbano in via di definitiva

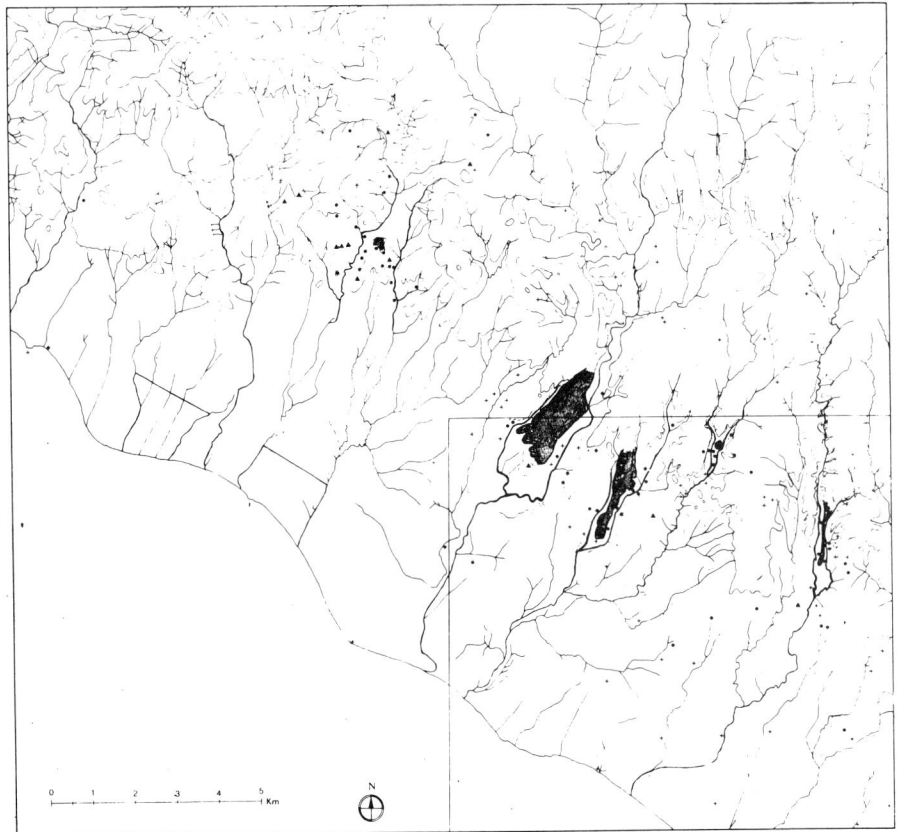

Fig. 2. Distribuzione dei siti dell'età del Bronzo (seconda metà del II millennio a.C.) : insediamenti (cerchi neri), sepolture 'protovillanoviane' (triangoli neri), presenze sporadiche (croci). In evidenza le formazioni tufacee dominanti i punti di confluenza.

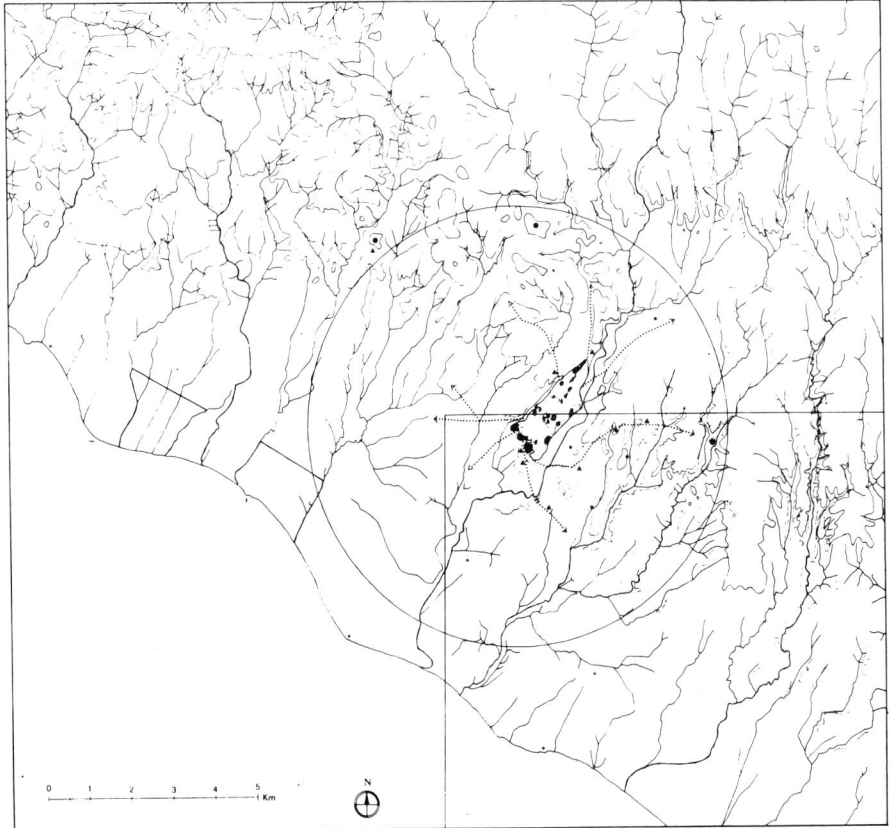

Fig. 3. Distribuzione dei siti dell'età del Ferro: ipotesi di viabilità nell'immediato hinterland cerite (5 km di raggio), insediamenti (cerchi neri), sepolcreti (triangoli neri), zone con probabili tracce di frequentazione (croci).

costituzione e la distribuzione dei ritrovamenti consentono di cogliere, anche se per un raggio molto limitato, l'esistenza di alcuni percorsi che, partendo da *Caere*, intersecano l'antichissima viabilità naturale, costituita dai fossi principali. Tali percorsi, disposti secondo uno schema stellare, forse anch'esso parzialmente originatosi nelle fasi precedenti, prefigurano gran parte delle linee generali della viabilità etrusca di epoca arcaica.

Le tracce documentate testimoniano che nell'età del Ferro soltanto le valli fluviali, i coni lavici di Monte Tosto e Monte Vittoria e alcuni pianori tufacei prossimi a *Caere* continuano ad essere abitati. Appare invece attenuata la frequentazione nelle zone periferiche dell'entroterra e forse lungo la costa, anche se in quest'ultimo caso lasciano molti dubbi varie segnalazioni relative al rinvenimento occasionale di materiali villanoviani nelle località Vaccina, Monteroni, Palo-San Nicola. Qualora tali segnalazioni ricevessero conferma, risulterebbero già esistenti nella prima età del Ferro i nuclei sepolcrali di Vaccina e Monteroni e forse anche l'approdo di *Alsium*, siti finora documentati a partire dal VII secolo a.C; apparirebbero quindi già definiti numerosi elementi del paesaggio etrusco.

Per lo studio di questa fase di formazione della città di *Caere* e del suo primitivo territorio è interessante sottolineare come almeno quattro dei sei abitati villanoviani riconosciuti nell'immediato *hinterland* cerite (Ceri, Monte Cucco, Monte Vittoria, Monte Tosto) siano localizzati su posizioni di altura, naturalmente fortificate, lungo altrettante probabili direttrici viarie (Fig. 4). Gli abitati vengono a trovarsi, a distanze tra loro quasi regolari, in coincidenza con i limiti teorici dello 'spazio economico basilare' della *Caere* villanovana. Tale spazio, riconosciuto come il minimo necessario per la sopravvivenza di una comunità agricola sedentaria, sufficientemente numerosa e con incipienti fenomeni di articolazione in classi, come fu senz'altro la *Caere* del IX-VIII secolo, viene indicato nel territorio compreso in un raggio di circa 5 km intorno il centro abitato principale (Vita Finzi & Higgs 1968).

I quattro siti di altura villanoviani potrebbero quindi rivestire precise funzioni strategiche, caratterizzandosi come potenziali *oppida* posti a controllo del 'cuore' dell'originario territorio ceretano che consisterebbe quindi in circa 80 kmq di terra in gran parte coltivabile, ricca principalmente di pascoli acqua e legname, estesa tra i boschi dei Monti Ceriti e il mare Tirreno con i suoi punti di approdo (Renfrew 1986; Di Gennaro 1986).

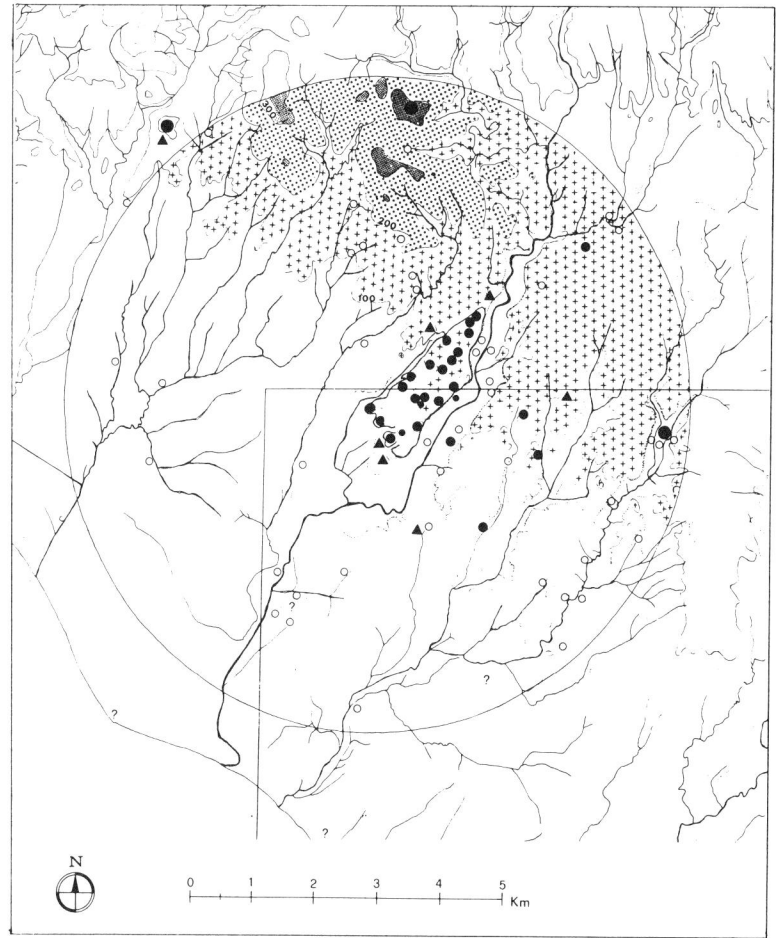

Fig. 4. Distribuzione dei siti dell'età del Ferro nell'immediato hinterland cerite (5 km dal pianoro di Caere): insediamenti (cerchi neri), sepolcreti (triangoli neri), sorgenti (cerchi bianchi), in evidenza le diverse altimetrie (m 100-300 s. l. m).

L'EPOCA ETRUSCA (Fig. 5)

In coincidenza con la fioritura della città di *Caere*, nel corso del VII, ma soprattutto nel VI secolo a.C., si registra un innegabile incremento demografico, probabilmente da collegare anche a forme di colonizzazione sistematica del territorio, aventi come risultato paesaggi molto simili a quelli indagati nel veientano (Potter 1985; Zifferero 1985). La ricognizione ha rilevato le tracce di almeno 203 insediamenti rurali, distribuiti nelle situazioni ambientali più diverse, dai rilievi tufacei a quelli collinari, dalle valli fluviali alla pianura costiera. Alcune concentrazioni particolari si notano sui terreni profondi, molto fertili e ben drenati, anche con ingenti opere di canalizzazione sotterranea, in località Migliorie di Zambra, Migliorie di San Paolo, Piano Sanguinara, Quartaccio, San Martino, Quarto del Cecio, Tenuta di Montetosto al Mare, Macchia Tonda-Poligono di Furbara.

In queste località, che si rivelano veri e propri distretti produttivi, gli insediamenti sono posti a breve distanza l'uno dall'altro (150–300 m), lasciando presumere, in alcuni casi, l'esistenza di divisioni agrarie regolari, composte da appezzamenti di limitata estensione, forse dell'ordine di 10–20 iugeri. Una particolare densità emerge nella zona collinare del Quartaccio, e soprattutto nella pianura litoranea presso la Tenuta di Montetosto al Mare e Macchia Tonda, dove la sostanziale contemporaneità degli insediamenti, molti vissuti tra la metà del VI e i primi decenni del V secolo a.C., lascia ipotizzare un vero e proprio fenomeno di colonizzazione agraria con distribuzione delle terre mediante una probabile forma di *limitatio* (Figg. 6, 7). I dati raccolti nel settore SE dell'*hinterland* cerite e nelle due aree campione esplorate nella pianura costiera tra *Caere* e *Pyrgi* rivelano comunque l'esistenza di un paesaggio litoraneo molto frammentato in cui realtà fortemente antropizzate coesistono con zone ancora selvagge. In epoca arcaica sembra verificarsi il primo tentativo di colonizzazione di alcuni settori della costa, senz'altro accompagnato da ingenti opere di bonifica per la messa a coltura di terreni idrologicamente instabili per vocazione naturale. Il fenomeno, verosimilmente scaturito in seguito ad importanti eventi di ordine politico-sociale verificatisi in seno alla comunità cerite, sembra determinare la nascita di numerose piccole proprietà distribuite nell'ambito di una parcellizzazione regolare dei terreni.

La spinta della 'bonifica' arcaica subisce un forte rallentamento nel corso del V e IV secolo a.C. E' probabile che siano venute meno le condizioni economiche, politiche e sociali che l'avevano determinata; ma se è lecito supporre che il tentativo di colonizzazione si arresti per motivi umani si deve comunque non sottovalutare l'influenza che la natura dei luoghi, rivelatasi forse troppo difficile, può aver esercitato sulle scelte e sull'esito complessivo dell'operazione.

Una realtà leggermente diversa si avverte nelle aree con substrato tufaceo, caratterizzate dalla presenza di pianori e castelline isolate dall'erosione fluviale. In queste zone si registra una diminuzione del numero degli insediamenti che soprattutto nella parte orientale del settore SE, lascia presupporre l'esistenza di un paesaggio ancora scarsamente antropizzato, con poche aree coltivate, dominate dalle estensioni boschive.

Un habitat ancora diverso, forse comprendente zone acquitrinose, è quello che con ogni probabilità qualificava il tratto di pianura costiera, esteso tra Palidoro e il fosso Cupino. Su questi terreni di formazione alluvionale olocenica è stata rilevato con certezza un solo insediamento, distante poco meno di 1 km dal mare, presso l'attuale corso del fosso Mentuccia; non si deve comunque sottovalutare la presenza di uno spesso strato di *alluvium* molto recente esteso su gran parte della zona.

Di grande interesse anche i nuovi dati relativi all'entroterra boschivo dei Monti Ceriti: questa particolare realtà ambientale, rimasta incontaminata dagli interventi moderni, rivela numerosi insediamenti, forse anche di sommità, dislocati lungo le principali vie per l'entroterra, in direzione delle valli del Lenta e del Mignone, dei Monti della Tolfa e del Lago Sabatino (Fig. 8).

All'indagine di superficie gli insediamenti etrusco arcaici si rivelano con l'affioramento di materiali ceramici ed edilizi sparsi su aree ampie in media 600 mq, variabili tra i 100 e i 6000 mq di superficie; su un campione di 97 siti rilevabili soltanto 6 superano i 1000 mq e 29 risultano compresi tra i 400 e i 900 mq. I dati raccolti sul terreno permettono di ricostruire alcune caratteristiche strutturali di queste costruzioni arcaiche. Nella maggior parte dei casi sembra si tratti di piccoli edifici, a pianta quadrata o rettangolare, di 20–50 mq^2, con pareti costruite in argilla mista a scaglie di tufo e/o calcare, alcuni forse con fondazioni in opera quadrata, tetti coperti con tegole e coppi. E' probabile che le ridotte dimensioni dell'edificio in muratura siano dovute alla presenza di altre strutture in legno, non rilevabili con la ricognizione di superficie. Questo tipo di edificio dal punto di vista volumetrico non molto dissimile dagli odierni 'casaletti', contiene dolii, fornelli, pesi da telaio, macinelli, associati sempre a ceramiche d'impasto rosso-bruno e bucchero, tra le quali spiccano rispettivamente bacini a vasca profonda, olle globulari ansate, *oinochoai*, calici, *kyathoi*, *kantharoi*. E' comunemente attestata la presenza di anfore di produzione etrusca mentre risultano molto più rare le fenicio-puniche, le samie e le corinzie. In alcuni casi si segnalano sporadici frammenti di ceramica attica a figure nere e/o rosse.

Soltanto tre insediamenti rinvenuti in località Monte Abbadoncino (Enei 1993), Boietto e Ponte del Lupo si rivelano con aree superiori ai 2000 mq (rispettivamente 2000, 6000, 8000 mq). Questi siti, in due casi (Boietto e Ponte del Lupo) frequentati tra il VI e il III secolo a.C., oltre al normale *instrumentum* domestico-agricolo, restituiscono frammenti di decorazioni architettoniche di I° (Ponte del Lupo) e II° fase (Monte Abbadoncino), oltre a ceramica attica a figure nere e rosse. Si tratta probabilmente di un genere d'insediamento rurale diverso, marcato da una maggiore estensione, articolato in più edifici e caratterizzato da un'architettura più vicina a quella urbana. Un gruppo particolare è rappresentato dai siti marittimi, probabili punti di approdo minori, certamente molto diffusi e attivi nello sfruttamento delle risorse dell'ambiente marino e litoraneo. Le ricognizioni hanno rilevato la presenza di insediamenti situati quasi sulla battigia, in località Macchia Tonda, San Nicola (*Alsium*?) e lungo il tratto di costa compreso tra Palo e Ladispoli. In quest'ultimo caso l'erosione marina ha esposto le tracce di numerose strutture lignee, canali di drenaggio (?), e quattro piccoli forni circolari, distribuiti lungo la riva per un tratto di circa 70 metri.

Sfuggono ancora ad una precisa definizione i tre centri di *Alsium*, Ceri e Castel Campanile. Il primo, di cui viene ricordata la fondazione pelasgica (Briquel 1984), è certamente esistito in epoca etrusca ed è localizzabile nella zona Palo-San Nicola. Viceversa, la presenza di abitati etruschi sulle rocche di Ceri e Castel Campanile, seppure logicamente ipotizzabile, non è stata mai confermata da sicuri ritrovamenti archeologici.

Per quanto riguarda Ceri, tracce di un insediamento etrusco, cronologicamente parallelo alla necropoli delle Fornaci, sono state individuate soltanto a 200 m a sud della rocca, nell'area pianeggiante compresa tra il fosso Sanguinara e un suo affluente. Una situazione analoga riguarda Castel Campanile, dove in realtà le uniche presenze arcaiche sono reperibili sul colle di Monte Bozzetta, situato a circa 250 m a sud del castello, in prossimità della confluenza tra i fossi Tavolato e Castellaccio. Il problema relativo all'esistenza di questi due siti fortificati in epoca etrusca va certamente approfondito con ricerche molto accurate, essendo di fondamentale importanza per la comprensione del territorio e la conseguente ricostruzione storica. La rocca di Ceri potrebbe anche essere stata soltanto la sede di un luogo di culto simile a quello rinvenuto nei pressi del fosso Sanguinara, su un alto colle isolato, all'altezza del Procoio di Ceri. In quel caso gli scavi rivelarono la presenza di un pozzo, presso il quale dovevano sorgere un'ara e un piccolo edificio, decorato con terrecotte architettoniche tardo-arcaiche, comprendenti lastre figurate (Ricci Portoghesi 1966; Nardi 1972). In epoca tardo etrusca sembrerebbero essere databili alcuni tratti delle murature in opera quadrata pertinenti al *castrum* medievale di Castel Dannato, posto a controllo di una delle più importanti antiche vie di accesso alla città di *Caere*. L'insediamento medievale potrebbe effettivamente essere sorto sui resti di una fortificazione etrusca avente analoghe funzioni strategiche.

L'analisi preliminare dei sepolcreti etruschi rilevati

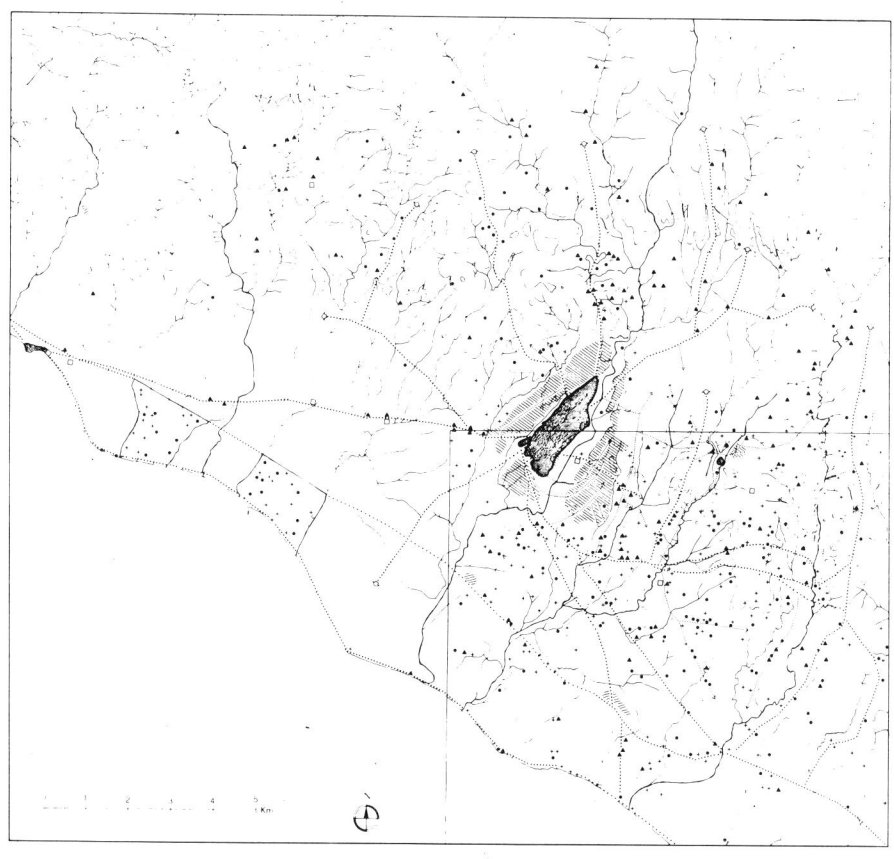

Fig. 5. Fase etrusca (VI secolo a.C.): Caere, Pyrgi, Ceri (aree puntinate), ipotesi di viabilità, piccoli siti rurali (cerchi neri), necropoli rurali (triangoli neri), presenze sporadiche (croci), necropoli estese (aree tratteggiate), luoghi di culto (quadrati bianchi).

nell'area esplorata permette di definire tre diverse categorie, distinguibili soprattutto in base all'estensione, alla consistenza numerica delle sepolture e alla disposizione topografica:

1) *Necropoli 'urbane'*: si tratta dei vasti nuclei cimiteriali situati a ridosso dell'area urbana di *Caere* e a questa direttamente riferibili. Vere e proprie città dei morti, risultano fornite di una propria viabilità interna, in alcuni tratti organizzata regolarmente; occupano centinaia di ettari in località Banditaccia, Cava della Pozzolana, Migliorie di Zambra, Prato Cavalieri (Sorbo), Polledrara (Monte Abatone), Macchia della Signora.

2) *Necropoli 'rurali'*: sono le necropoli relative agli insediamenti rurali sparsi nel territorio; risultano costituite da un numero limitato di tombe, spesso inferiore alle 10 unità, distribuite in aree non molto vaste, poco distanti dai rispettivi abitati. L'architettura delle tombe risulta assimilabile ai tipi tardo-orientalizzanti ed arcaici comunemente diffusi nell'area cerite: dalle camere con soffitto displuviato, columen centrale, letti laterali e banchina di fondo, fino alle soluzioni più articolate, a due camere in asse con celle nel dromos. Sono comunque attestati anche tipi semplicissimi di grotticelle, fosse, piccoli tumuli con camere semicostruite.

3) *Necropoli 'rurali estese e monumentali'*: in questa categoria sono inseribili le necropoli di Vaccina, Monteroni, delle Fornaci e di Pian Sultano, estese per alcuni ettari e comprendenti un elevato numero di tombe, anche entro tumuli monumentali. La presenza di questi nuclei cimiteriali sembra indicare l'esistenza di siti abitati collocabili in una posizione intermedia tra il centro urbano (*Caere*) e i piccoli insediamenti rurali sparsi nella campagna. I primi due sepolcreti (Vaccina e Monteroni), ricavati nei rilievi calcarei dominanti la pianura litoranea, potrebbero essere riferiti ad abitati costieri, forse coincidenti con punti di approdo posti alle foci dei fossi Vaccina e Cupino; *Alsium* nel caso dei Monteroni.

La necropoli localizzata sulla ristretta lingua tufacea delle Fornaci e nelle aree adiacenti, comprendente la Tomba delle Statue (Colonna & Hase 1986), può essere, invece, attribuita ad un centro avente come probabile fulcro la rocca di Ceri. Pian Sultano sembrerebbe invece essere in relazione ad un insediamento su terrazze localizzato nelle immediate vicinanze.

Dall'esame della distribuzione delle necropoli nel territorio si evince una scelta doppiamente funzionale, orientata a disporre i sepolcreti in zone dove l'affioramento della roccia facilita lo scavo o la costruzione di ambienti ipogei e nello stesso tempo pone forti limiti alle possibilità di sfruttamento agricolo del terreno. I dati indicano inoltre l'esistenza di un legame molto stretto tra sepolcreti e viabilità, verificabile per le necropoli maggiori così come per i piccoli nuclei cimiteriali riferibili al singolo insediamento rustico.

La disposizione degli abitati, la morfologia del territorio e la logica supposta continuità dei percorsi tra l'epoca etrusca e quella romana, consentono, insieme alle varie tracce ancora visibili, di ricostruire molti tratti della viabilità di epoca etrusca. Emergono chiaramente alcuni itinerari principali, assi portanti di uno schema 'stellare' a cui si lega una trama complessa e capillare di strade secondarie. Nel tratto compreso tra Palidoro e *Pyrgi* non può essere considerata casuale la concentrazione di insediamenti e necropoli lungo il tracciato che in epoca romana diventerà la via Aurelia. L'origine etrusca di tale percorso, proposta per il tratto Roma-Statua (Castagnoli 1968), va probabilmente estesa anche al restante tragitto, forse fino a Vulci e all'*ager Cosanus* (Celuzza & Regoli 1982). E' evidente, infatti, che la fascia costiera dell'Etruria meridionale, senza soluzione di continuità con quella del *Latium Vetus*, abbia costituito da sempre un'unica via naturale di collegamento 'veloce', sede di un asse stradale in qualche modo già codificatosi in epoca arcaica, al di là delle antiche divisioni politico-amministrative. Del resto su questa 'via litoranea' si affacciano fin dall'età del Ferro i maggiori centri della costa tirrenica con i relativi punti di approdo, e convergono numerosi percorsi provenienti dall'interno, attraverso le valli fluviali, compresi quelli di transumanza.

Un secondo tracciato è costituito dalla strada per Roma, anch'esso ricalcato dalla *Caere-Ad Turres*, documentata per l'epoca romana. Il percorso più breve e meno accidentato è indubbiamente quello che uscito dalla città antica, attraversata la valle della Mola, sale sulle Migliorie di San Paolo per proseguire in località Piano Sanguinara e Quartaccio fino a Statua dove confluisce nella via Aurelia. In epoca arcaica questo percorso attraversava alcune tra le aree più fertili e popolate del territorio cerite.

Un terzo tracciato, in gran parte già intuito dal Colonna (1981), sembrerebbe unire *Caere* al porto di *Alsium*, incrociando la via che diventerà l'Aurelia presso la necropoli dei Monteroni.

Il quarto è certamente la via *Caere-Pyrgi*, anch'esso con continuità in epoca romana (Giuliani & Quilici 1964; Colonna 1968); è probabile che la strada uscisse dal versante occidentale della città, forse transitando sul ponte scoperto di recente sugli argini del fosso Manganello (Cristofani *et al.* 1988). Nel settore NE del campione, ancora non esplorato sistematicamente, almeno altri tre importanti assi stradali di dirigono verso l'entroterra lasciando la città in corrispondenza della Via degli Inferi (Enei 1986), di Porta Coperta, e della porta in località Sant'Antonio (Nardi 1988).

Alla viabilità principale fanno capo numerose strade secondarie che costituiscono una complessa rete di

Fig. 6. Area campione n. 1 (loc. Tenuta di Montetosto al Mare): distribuzione dei piccoli siti rurali arcaici (quadrati neri) e delle presenze sporadiche (asterischi), zone con cattive condizioni di visibilità del terreno (aree tratteggiate).

Fig. 7. Area campione n. 2 (loc. Macchia Tonda): distribuzione dei siti rurali arcaici (quadrati neri), presenze sporadiche (asterischi), zone con cattive condizioni di visibilità del terreno (aree tratteggiate).

percorsi, solo parzialmente ricostruibile, sulla quale gravitano i singoli insediamenti rurali con le relative necropoli. A questa viabilità locale sembrano da riferire quasi tutte le numerose tagliate che pongono in comunicazione valli fluviali e pianori tufacei; questi tratti di strada, sfruttando depressioni naturali, localmente dette 'calatore', oppure scavati completamente nel tufo, collegano i percorsi di fondovalle di origine preistorica con quelli di crinale. Si tratta nella maggioranza dei casi di strade concepite per brevi distanze, non tutte carrabili, larghe in media 1,50-2 metri, alle quali non sembra possibile attribuire funzioni di collegamento con centri di primaria importanza. Al di là della sua probabile funzione sacra, l'immagine della strada etrusca a lunga percorrenza ci viene offerta dalla via *Caere-Pyrgi*, un asse in terra battuta, rivelatosi largo oltre 10 metri, carrabile in entrambi i sensi, fornito di crepidini laterali e sistema di drenaggio per le acque piovane (Colonna 1968). Un impianto analogo è probabilmente da ipotizzare per molti degli altri assi principali che attraversano il territorio oggetto d'indagine.

Una viabilità particolare è costituita dalle numerose strade a carattere sepolcrale che servono le vaste necropoli 'urbane' dalla Banditaccia a Monte Abatone. Queste vie, rivelate in molti casi con estrema precisione dalle ricerche geofisiche e aerofotografiche degli anni Cinquanta (Lerici 1957), mettono in comunicazione la città con i suoi principali sepolcreti, formando all'interno di essi un'articolata rete stradale a circuito chiuso.

I dati raccolti sul terreno sembrano documentare una forte contrazione dell'insediamento rurale nel corso del V e IV secolo a.C. Il vistoso calo del numero delle presenze, tuttavia, potrebbe derivare dalle indubbie difficoltà incontrate nell'identificazione e datazione dei materiali, in particolare dell'impasto e del materiale edilizio, attribuiti forse in maniera eccessiva alla fase precedente. I principali fossili guida per la cronologia dei siti sono stati la ceramica attica ed etrusca a figure rosse, alcune forme in bucchero, e in impasto chiaro-sabbioso, il tardo impasto grezzo con *internal slip* e la ceramica depurata dipinta tipo Casale Pian Roseto, il materiale architettonico di II° fase e alcune forme molto antiche a vernice nera.

In definitiva, l'impressione è che il calo delle presenze sia di proporzioni più limitate e che in realtà sussista gran parte del paesaggio di epoca arcaica con la complessa rete di strade, insediamenti e necropoli che lo caratterizza. Una rarefazione degli insediamenti si avverte tuttavia anche nell'entroterra cerite (Zifferero 1985) e seppure in maniera leggera anche nel vicino *ager Veientanus* dove scompaiono 10 siti (Potter 1985).

Nel IV secolo l'*ager* è ancora interamente *Caeretanus*, controllato dall'oligarchia gentilizia che amministra lo stato cerite, un'aristocrazia con ogni probabilità in larga parte terriera, proprietaria di grandi complessi sepolcrali nella necropoli della Banditaccia e di Greppe Sant'Angelo (Cristofani 1965; Proietti 1982 e 1983).

La produttività e la ricchezza del territorio in epoca tardo-etrusca è indirettamente testimoniata anche dai risultati degli scavi del santuario di *Pyrgi*: l'emporio, presso il quale dovevano verosimilmente confluire anche i prodotti dell'*ager*, risulta in piena attività, tanto da essere considerato dai siracurani degno di saccheggio nel 384 a.C. (Cristofani *et al.* 1988).

LA ROMANIZZAZIONE

Importanti cambiamenti di ordine politico, istituzionale e amministrativo, con ripercussioni certe nell'assetto del territorio, sembra si verifichino soltanto a partire dal primo trentennio del III secolo a.C. Le fonti, in particolare alcuni passi di Velleio, Diodoro, Strabone e Cassio Dione, illustrano le vicende che portano di fatto nel 273 a.C., alla fine dell'autonomia di *Caere*, divenuta prefettura, e alla confisca di metà del territorio trasformato in *ager publicus populi romani* (Sordi 1960; Humbert 1972; Cristofani *et al.* 1986). Estremamente difficile è identificare con certezza le aree confiscate ai Ceriti, ma la successiva colonizzazione lascia presumere che tra queste vi fosse larga parte del territorio costiero. Le colonie di *Castrum Novum* (264 a.C.?), *Pyrgi* (III sec. a.C.), *Alsium* (247 a.C.) e *Fregenae* (245 a.C.), si rivelano presidi romani posti a controllo e difesa del litorale tirrenico e degli interessi commerciali su questo gravitanti. Non a caso molti degli insediamenti militari vengono collocati in prossimità degli scali portuali, direttamente legati al percorso di epoca arcaica che in breve tempo, probabilmente a partire dal 241 a.C., diventerà la via Aurelia (Coarelli 1988). Uno di questi presidi è *Alsium*, colonia di diritto romano del 247 a.C., dedotta poco prima di *Fregenae*, in concomitanza con la prima guerra punica, presso uno degli antichi porti ceriti (Salmon 1969; Harris 1971; Humbert 1978). Si tratta di un fondamentale caposaldo topografico, situato lungo la costa, certamente all'interno del settore SE del campione. La posizione della colonia viene indicata nel luogo del castello di Palo (De Rossi *et al.* 1968), ma le nuove scoperte e una rivisitazione dei dati disponibili fanno in realtà oscillare la sua localizzazione in un ampio tratto di costa compreso tra la foce del fosso Cupino (San Nicola) e quella del fosso Sanguinara presso Ladispoli.

Nel territorio campione, dal 247 a.C. sussistono quindi tre diverse entità politiche ed amministrative, una prefettura (*Caere*) e due colonie (*Pyrgi, Alsium*), diret-

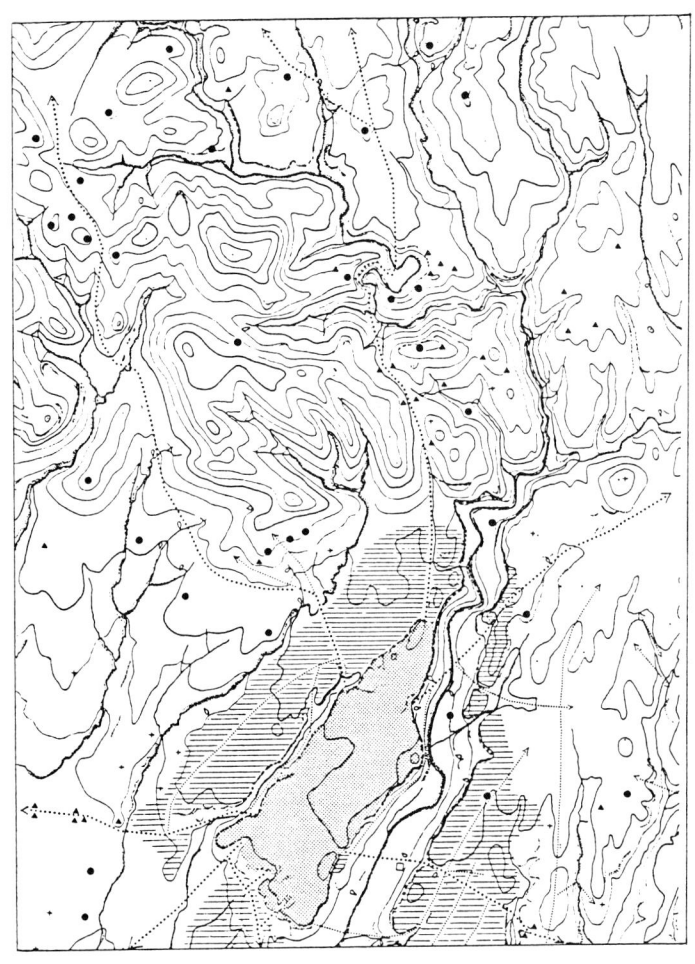

Fig. 8. Presenze etrusche di epoca arcaica sui Monti Ceriti: Caere (area puntinata), viabilità principale, necropoli 'urbane' (aree a tratteggio), insediamenti rustici (cerchi neri), necropoli e tombe isolate (triangoli neri), luogo di culto (quadrato bianco), presenze sporadiche (croci).

tamente confinanti. Molto difficile è rintracciare il confine tra i territori, due estesi lungo la costa, uno nell'entroterra; in via del tutto ipotetica nel caso di *Caere* ed *Alsium* potrebbe proporsi il corso del fosso Sanguinara o semplicemente la via Aurelia, qualora l'*ager Alsietinus* si limitasse a comprendere solo una ristretta fascia costiera. In questo caso una funzione di piccolo santuario di confine potrebbe aver avuto il luogo di culto ellenistico segnalato presso la foce del fosso Sanguinara nell'attuale città di Ladispoli (Colonna 1973; Nardi 1981).

Nel complesso la romanizzazione di *Caere* pare non implichi cambiamenti traumatici nel popolamento; la colonizzazione della costa, condotta in relazione al controllo dei porti e della viabilità litoranea, almeno nei casi di *Alsium* e *Pyrgi* sembra non sia seguita da distribuzioni di terre e quindi da ingenti iniziative di centuriazione. Sopravvive certamente gran parte del tessuto stradale etrusco, codificato in modo definitivo come nel caso della via Aurelia, adattato alle nuove diverse esigenze dell'insediamento rurale e marittimo nel caso delle numerose strade vicinali di collegamento locale. Anche la ricerca di superficie condotta nelle aree rimaste con ogni probabilità di pertinenza prettamente cerite, nell'ambito dell'istituita prefettura, indica una sostanziale continuità nell'occupazione del territorio, in particolare nelle zone più fertili, intensamente sfruttate fin dall'epoca etrusca (Migliorie di San Paolo, Piano Sanguinara, Quartaccio, San Martino).

Nel corso del III secolo a.C., rispetto alla fase tardo etrusca si percepisce comunque un incremento degli insediamenti rurali che altera in maniera profonda l'assetto di alcune aree destinando ad attività produttive spazi che fino a quel momento risultavano incolti o adibiti a differenti funzioni. L'occupazione di terre nuove è avvertibile nella fascia costiera situata subito a sud-est di *Alsium*, tra il mare e la via Aurelia. Forse in seguito alla deduzione della colonia inizia ad essere sfruttata anche l'estensione di terre alluvionali, a tratti acquitrinose, che in epoca giulio-claudia nei dintorni di *Fregenae* appariva a Silio Italico come uno *squalens campus* (Sil. It. 8, 475). Allo stato attuale delle conoscenze non si riscontrano comunque tracce certe di centuriazione.

Tra il III e il II secolo a.C. l'espansione degli insediamenti rurali non risparmia i terreni un tempo destinati a sepolcreto: sui rilievi di Vaccina, Monteroni e Monte Abatone si impiantano fattorie, al centro di un paesaggio in cui dovevano emergere in maniera ancora evidente i grandi tumuli orientalizzanti.

Le fonti antiche, i rinvenimenti effettuati nel santuario di *Pyrgi* e nell'area urbana di *Caere*, forniscono alcune indicazioni precise sull'uso del territorio in questa fase medio-repubblicana. Un passo di Licofrone descrive *Agylla* come una città ricca di greggi (Licofr. Alex. V, 1238) mentre la lista liviana degli aiuti inviati dalle città etrusche a Roma nel 205 a.C. ricorda, nel caso di *Caere*, la fornitura di *frumentum* e di altre vettovaglie (Liv.

XXVIII, 45). I resti lignei e vegetali, databili nella prima metà del III secolo a.C., rinvenuti nei pozzi del santuario di *Pyrgi*, indiziano un paesaggio vegetale ancora dominato da folti boschi in cui prevale il querceto misto (querce caducifoglie, carpini, olmi, pioppi, salici, ornielli) con abeti bianchi sottoquota. Si avverte tuttavia il diffondersi di una vegetazione tendente al *climax* mediterraneo delle querce sempreverdi associate a vite, olivo e lillastro (Coccolini & Follieri 1980). I materiali osteologici recuperati invece nell'area urbana testimoniano, sempre nella prima metà del III secolo a.C., la presenza di numerosi capi di bestiame ovino, bovino e suino (Enei 1987). I *torcularia* avvenuto nel corso delle ricognizioni, lasciano immaginare l'esistenza di un paesaggio estremamente diversificato comprendente grandi foreste ma anche vaste aree antropizzate, con piccoli insediamenti rustici circondati da estensioni seminate a frumento, interrotte da vigneti-oliveti e da ampie zone a pascolo.

I pochi siti medio-repubblicani, senza continuità di vita, si rivelano con affioramenti di materiali sparsi in aree variabili tra i 100 e i 600 mq come indicano in particolare i ritrovamenti avvenuti nei pressi del Centro Capanna a nord di Palidoro, a Furbara, Macchia Tonda e in altre ex proprietà dell'Ospedale del Santo Spirito. Permangono i piccoli edifici rurali documentati anche in epoca etrusca, costruiti con materiali e tecniche identiche a quelle arcaiche, contenenti doli e macinelli. Tra le ceramiche appare molto diffusa la vernice nera con piatti e coppe di varie forme, numericamente seguiti da *kylikes*, brocche, lucerne, piattelli su piede e *stamnoi*, di produzione locale, romana e forse in alcuni casi campana.

Numerose le ceramiche comuni tra le quali si distinguono olle e *pocula* con orlo a mandorla leggermente igrossato, alcuni bacini in impasto chiaro-sabbioso, tegami di varie fogge e tra le anfore le forme greco-italiche più antiche, assimilabili ai tipi Will A/C (Will 1982).

I materiali di superficie documentano soltanto l'esistenza di piccoli insediamenti rurali, ma già nel II secolo a.C. è certa la presenza di una grande villa, forse marittima, proprietà di M. Emilio Porcina, un facoltoso esponente dell'aristocrazia senatoria romana. Valerio Massimo ricorda la condanna di Porcina nel 125 a.C. proprio a causa della sua villa situata *in alsiensi agro* (Val. Max. 8, 1 *damn.* 7): il complesso, costruito nelle terre della colonia, viene reputato troppo alto e Porcina, su accusa di L. Cassio, fu costretto a pagare una forte ammenda.

Proprietà senatorie comprendenti grandi ville, sono quindi attestate nell'*ager Alsietinus* poco più di cento anni dopo la deduzione della colonia, come sembra indicare indirettamente anche la probabile epigrafe funeraria di un illustre membro della *gens Herennia* (*M. Herennius Rufus*) forse proveniente dal monumento funerario sito presso una grande villa marittima alla foce del fosso Sanguinara in Ladispoli, in tal caso attribuibuile in epoca tardo-repubblicana a tale famiglia (Shatzman 1975; *CIL* XI, 3717).

Ormai, nella seconda metà del I secolo a.C., molti personaggi, anche di primo piano, possiedono ville negli agri di *Alsium* e di *Pyrgi* divenuti amene località marittime a breve distanza dal centro del potere; per *Alsium* ne fornisce un elenco Cicerone ricordando i possessi di Pompeo, Cesare, Murena, Sallustio, Dida e Silio (Cic. *Pro Mil.* 20, 54; *Ep.* IX 6, 1,2; *Ep.* XIII 50, 3-5). Alcune di queste ville potrebbero essere riconosciute sotto le fasi imperiali dei grandi complessi di San Nicola, Palo e Ladispoli. Negli immediati dintorni di Pyrgi è probabile che fossero invece situati alcuni dei possedimenti dei Domizi Enobarbi (Suet. *Ner.* 5)

Tra la fine del I secolo a.C. e il II secolo d.C. il popolamento del territorio raggiunge i limiti massimi, rimasti insuperati per oltre 1800 anni, fino alla riforma agraria post-bellica che a partire dagli anni Cinquanta ha determinato la rinascita delle campagne (Fig. 9). I dati relativi all'entroterra cerite, nel distretto tolfetano, confermano l'apice della frequentazione nel I secolo d.C. in epoca giulio-claudia, così come nell'*ager Veientanus*, dove si registrano anche 2-3 insediamenti per chilometro quadrato (Gazzetti 1985; Potter 1985). Anche nel corso dell'epoca imperiale lo sviluppo delle campagne ceriti rivela forti analogie con quelle veienti: forse perchè in larga parte simili dal punto di vista naturale e con identici presupposti etruschi alle spalle, specie in relazione al regime della proprietà a al sistema di produzione, molto vicine a Roma, conoscono entrambe un lungo momento di espansione e un lento progressivo declino. Nella prima età imperiale il grande sviluppo produttivo dell'*ager Caeretanus* è verosimile che si rifletta in modo diretto nell'area urbana del *municipium* dove, forse anche con il contributo di personaggi locali di primo piano, vengono costruiti edifici pubblici monumentali tra i quali un teatro provvisto di ricca decorazione scultorea (*CIL* XI, 3620, 3621; Fuchs 1989), un *Templum Divorum* (*CIL* XI, 3614), un acquedotto (*CIL* XI, 3594). All'epoca di Traiano è certa la presenza di una sala per le adunanze degli Augustali, una curia, una *Basilica Sulpiciana* con annessi portici, un tempio di Marte (*CIL* XI, 3614).

Nell'hinterland cerite risultano complessivamente attivi almeno 331 insediamenti in gran parte ville rurali o *maritimae* dalle quali si distinguono in modo evidente alcune realtà più complesse, quasi urbane, sviluppatesi a partire dal II secolo a.C., attorno alle colonie di *Alsium* e *Pyrgi*, alle *Aquae Caeretanae* e alla *mansio* di *Ad Turres* (Cosentino 1989; Enei 1991).

Nell'ambito del settore NO del campione riveste grande importanza il luogo della *Aquae Caeretanae*, da sempre localizzato nei pressi del villaggio del Sasso e recentemente individuato con precisione in località Pian Della Carlotta, in seguito agli scavi della Soprintendenza

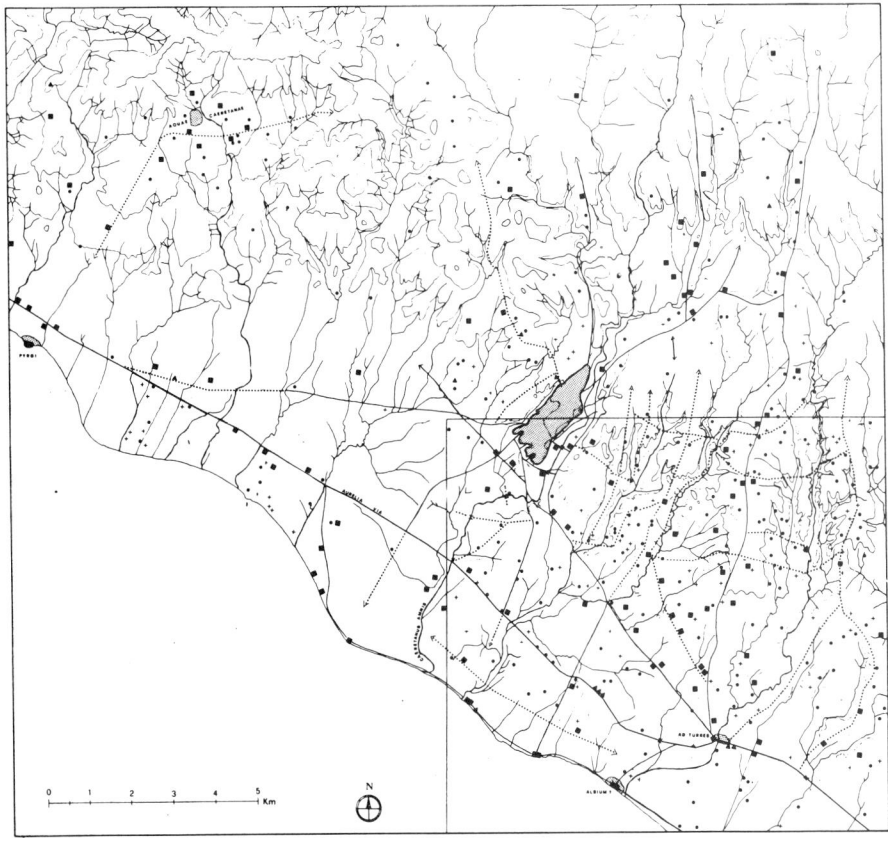

Fig. 9. *Fase romana primo-imperiale (fine I sec. a.C.-I sec. d.C.): Caere e centri urbani (aree puntinate), viabilità basolata (linee continue), ipotesi di viabilità in terra battuta (linee puntinate), ville di cat. A-B (quadrati neri), insediamenti rustici di cat. C (cerchi neri), tombe e mausolei (triangoli neri), presenze sporadiche (croci).*

Archeologica per l'Etruria Meridionale (Cosentino 1990).

La fortuita scoperta di due iscrizioni dedicate al *fons* della *Aquae*, una in particolare a Giove associato al culto del *fons*, presso i resti di un notevole impianto termale vissuto tra il I e almeno il III secolo d.C., ha fornito dati per la localizzazione dell'importante località terapeutica, ricordata da Strabone come più popolosa della stessa *Caere* e da Celio Aureliano come sede di alcune tra le più calde acque d'Italia (Strabo V, 2, 3; Cael. Aur. *Chron.* II, 1, 48). L'analisi preliminare dei dati bibliografici e di archivio, pertinenti ai dintorni del sito identificato con le *Aquae Caeretanae*, lascia intuire l'esistenza di un complesso sistema di ville e di impianti termali, sviluppatosi a partire dall'epoca medio repubblicana, attorno a diverse sorgenti, alcune calde e/o fortemente minerali, fino a costituire un fitto tessuto abitativo. E' probabile che la terma individuata dagli scavi, in qualche modo connessa con il culto di Giove associato a quello di una sorgente, sia da considerarsi soltanto uno dei molteplici complessi costituenti le *Aquae*, articolate in realtà, in diversi *fontes* localizzati senz'altro anche nei vicini Bagni di Costantino e presso altri resti di terme sparsi nell'area circostante. In uno di questi siti va probabilmente cercato il *fons Herculis* ricordato da Livio in occasione di prodigi avvenuti poco prima dell'inizio della seconda guerra punica (Liv. XXII, 1, 10).

Tra il I e il II secolo d.C. le terre ceriti, alsietine e pyrgensi sono divise tra numerosissime ville e insediamenti rustici, grandi e piccole fattorie, quasi tutte sorte, su precedenti etruschi, tra il III e il II secolo a.C., servite da una capillare rete di strade in terra battuta. Almeno 24 siti risultano comunque certamente frequentati per quasi un millennio, dall'epoca etrusca arcaica a quella romana imperiale come documentato anche nell'*ager Veientanus* (Potter 1980; 1985). Si registrano in media 2 insediamenti per chilometro quadrato, con punte massime di 4-5 siti nelle aree più fertili e meglio collegate. La media è comunque con ogni probabilità più alta considerando le scarsissime condizioni di visibilità del suolo, presenti in ampi settori della fascia costiera e sui monti.

L'esame dell'evidenza archeologica permette di individuare l'esistenza di tre principali categorie di insediamenti, per convenzione dette A, B, C, parzialmente confrontabili con quelle proposte per l'*ager Veientanus* e per il *Cosanus* (Enei 1992; Potter 1985; Celuzza & Regoli 1982). Si distinguono grandi complessi propriamente definibili *villae* (cat. A, B) e piccoli insediamenti rustici (cat. C), forse meglio definibili *tuguria*, mantenendo in sostanza la distinzione tra 'villas and farms' operata dal Perkins nel veientano (Kahane *et al.* 1968).

In epoca giulio-claudia, in quasi tutti i siti del territorio, anche nei più piccoli attribuibili alla categoria C, è documentata la presenza della sigillata italica, spesso accompagnata da frammenti di tardo-italica e sud-gallica e dalle anfore tipo Dressel 1 e 2/4.

Dalla fine del I secolo d.C. hanno forte diffusione i prodotti provinciali, anch'essi distribuiti in maniera capillare, come ad esempio le sigillate, le anfore e le ceramiche da cucina africane, le anfore vinarie galliche e le spagnole da olio e *garum*. Nei dintorni di *Alsium* e *Ad Turres* sono presenti tra gli altri, diversi prodotti delle officine laterizie Rutiliane, di *L. Rufus*, di *Q. Paconius (?) Lucrus*. Non è da escludere la possibilità che alcune di queste *figlinae* possano trovarsi all'interno del settore SE del campione: nella prima epoca imperiale vi risultano attivi diversi impianti per la produzione di tegole, coppi, mattoni e ceramica comune. Numerose cisterne in opera cementizia vengono costruite in posizione elevata, verosimilmente all'interno delle maggiori proprietà fondiarie. I resti conservati documentano edifici rettangolari con contrafforti esterni, a pianta semplice o divisa in navate rivestite in *opus signinum*, coperti con volte a botte sulle quali poggiano terrazze pavimentate in *opus spicatum*. Il deposito idrico del Quartaccio (settore SE), il più grande finora conosciuto nel campione, è diviso da 15 pilastri in due navate parallele con volte a botte e fornito di nove pozzetti di areazione. Misura 50 × 8,7 m, se riempito per soli 50 cm può contenere oltre 200 mc d'acqua. La costruzione di questi enormi serbatoi, quasi sicuramente gestiti dalle ville di categoria A e B, illustra forse meglio di ogni altra cosa l'intensità dello sfruttamento delle campagne ceriti, alsietine e pyrgensi.

Estremamente diversificate sono le attività che gravitano sulle ville e sugli insediamenti rustici del territorio, dall'allevamento del bestiame, soprattutto ovino e bovino, a quello ittico praticato soprattutto lungo la costa pyrgense, alla produzione di laterizi, tegole e ceramiche, all'estrazione di materiali da costruzione. Le fonti a disposizione documentano la preponderanza delle attività agricole con una massiccia sicura presenza della viticoltura e della cerealicoltura. Cento anfore a iugero produceva il fondo relativo alla villa di Columella, certamente situata *in (agro) ceretano* (Col. *R.r.* III 9,6); forse lo stesso vino *caeretanus* che in epoca flavio-traianea *Nepos*, l'amico di Marziale, riservava agli amici più intimi (Mart. *Ep.* XIII, 124). E' molto probabile che i numerosi dolii e i *torcularia* rinvenuti siano da collegare a questa diffusa viticoltura che ancora oggi caratterizza larga parte del territorio. Un frammento di dolio con il numero d'ordine LXVIII indica forse la consistenza minima del *doliarium* della villa dell'Osteriaccia (cat. A), sita lungo la via Aurelia, presso il fosso della Mentuccia, 1 km a sud-est di *Ad Turres*.

Accanto alla viticoltura appare molto diffusa anche la coltivazione dei cereali. Il *frumentum*, presente con ogni probabilità già in epoca arcaica e ricordato dalle fonti in epoca repubblicana, risulta prodotto in modo massiccio anche in seguito, come documentano i numerosi frammenti di macine rinvenuti nei siti di epoca imperiale.

Allo stato attuale della ricerca è ancora difficile azzardare ipotesi sulla distribuzione topografica e sullo sviluppo delle diverse colture. Nonostante l'intenso sfruttamento è molto probabile che vaste estensioni di terreno siano rimaste sempre incolte, allo stato naturale, soprattutto le zone con terreni poco profondi e roccia affiorante, come per esempio le aree montane e i margini delle ampie formazioni tufacee. A questo proposito è utile ricordare che la proprietà di Columella comprendeva *prata et pascua et silvas* (*R.r.* III, 33) e che all'epoca di Virgilio sussisteva un *ingens et gelidum lucus prope caeritis amnem* (Verg. *Aen.* VIII, 597). Nell'area indagata a tappeto (settore SE) la distribuzione degli insediamenti e dei connessi fenomeni di 'non site', lascia intuire l'esistenza di ampie zone incolte, pascoli ed estensioni boschive, soprattutto nelle località di Pian Cerese, Bosco e Valle del Ferraccio, Pianaccio, Tenuta di Castel Campanile. Altre zone non coltivate a causa della natura acquitrinosa, erano certamente situate lungo la costa, tra Palidoro e Ladispoli, un ambiente litoraneo che Silio Italico definisce *correptus stagnis* (V, 17).

Nell'*ager Caeretanus*, in particolare nei primi tre secoli dell'impero, emerge in maniera molto chiara l'esistenza di un tessuto economico-produttivo organicamente collegato e interdipendente, imperniato, come nel resto d'Etruria, sullo sfruttamento della manodopera servile, distribuita in grandi ville e insediamenti rustici. Nel controllo del sistema, in origine prerogativa dell'aristocrazia senatoria, subentrano, tra il I ed il II secolo d.C., i liberti arricchiti e il demanio imperiale. Quest'ultimo in epoca antonina e severiana comprende il gigantesco complesso della *villa alsiensis*, forse ormai un'unica cosa con *Alsium*, definito da Frontone *maritumus et voluptarius locus* (Fronto p. 223 Naber), amministrato da un *procurator* di nomina imperiale (*CIL* XI, 3720).

Il rapporto ville – insediamenti rustici lascia comunque presumere anche l'esistenza di piccole entità fondiarie verosimilmente amministrate da liberi coloni. Nel I-II secolo d.C. intorno ad ogni villa (cat. A, B), gravitano in media due insediamenti rurali (cat. C) ma in alcune località il rapporto diventa di 1:4, 1:5. La presenza del colonato nell'*ager Caeretanus* è indirettamente ricordata dai consigli di Columella a proposito della conduzione delle ville (*R.r.* I 7, 2-5) e da un epigramma di Marziale che, debitamente considerato, fornisce notizie interessanti forse proprio riguardanti il settore SE del territorio campione (*Ep.* VI, 73). L'epigramma è chiaramente destinato alla base di una statua lignea di Priapo, posta a protezione di un fondo di 14 iugeri compreso nelle vaste proprietà di un certo Hilarus, definito *caeretani cultor ditissimus agri*. La statua parlando di se dice: '*non rudis indocta fecit me falce colonus*'. E' quindi verosimile che i possedimenti di Hilaro, estesi su *laeta colles*, siano stati coltivati da coloni.

Tali possedimenti potrebbero essere localizzati, in via del tutto ipotetica, nella zona di Valcanneto (Pineto di Statua), circa un miglio a nord di *Ad Turres*, lungo un diverticolo Aurelia-Clodia. Può non essere, infatti, una semplice coincidenza il ritrovamento avvenuto in questa località dell'epigrafe *CIL* XI, 3701, databile nel I-II secolo d.C., relativa ad un *Hilarus* liberto di *C. Licinius*. Nei dintorni di Valcanneto, inoltre, zona collinare molto fertile, sono documentate due delle più estese e sontuose ville del settore SE.

I dati delle ricognizioni consentono di proporre un interessante confronto numerico tra le ville e gli insediamenti rustici, seguendone lo sviluppo nel periodo compreso tra il I e il VI secolo d.C. Nel corso del II secolo d.C. si avverte un leggero decremento dei 132 insediamenti rurali (cat. C), decremento che si presenta ormai come un crollo alla fine del III secolo d.C. Le 54 ville (cat. A, B), rimaste tutte in funzione nel corso del III secolo, iniziano ad essere abbandonate soltanto a partire dal IV secolo, in maniera costante e progressiva fino ad arrivare al VI secolo d.C., quando soltanto 14 di esse risultano ancora in qualche modo frequentate.

Anche nel territorio cerite si registra, quindi, durante l'epoca imperiale, il noto, progressivo, spopolamento delle campagne che nell'area indagata si avvia, in maniera quasi impercettibile, nel II secolo d.C. con l'abbandono di alcuni siti rurali, posti in zone periferiche e in alcuni settori della pianura litoranea. Quest'ultima, con l'eccezione delle grandi ville marittime, sembrerebbe completamente spopolata alla fine del IV secolo d.C.

Nel complesso, comunque, il sistema della villa sopravvive a lungo, seppure in una lenta agonia, paragonabile a quella riscontrata nelle vicine campagne veienti (Potter 1985). Evidente è invece la differenza con settori più settentrionali della costa tirrenica, come ad esempio il volterrano e il cosano dove la disgregazione e la morte del paesaggio rurale legato alle ville appare molto più veloce; già in epoca flavia si avvertono i primi segni di crisi. In epoca antonina, mentre nella Valle d'Oro scompaiono i 2/3 delle ville, gli agri di Cerveteri, *Alsium* e *Pyrgi* sono ancora in pieno sviluppo. Nel VI secolo d.C. l'*ager Cosanus* è ormai maremma deserta; nella parte esplorata della diocesi di *Caere* sono ancora frequentate almeno 14 ville (Celuzza & Regoli 1982; Attolini *et al.* 1982).

In epoca tardo-antica il popolamento del territorio sussiste lungo le vie principali concentrandosi nelle ville più grandi, molte delle quali saranno frequentate fino al VI secolo d.C. Nel V secolo d.C. risultano ancora in funzione molte *villae maritimae* e la *villa alsiensis* come documentano i ritrovamenti di Palo, San Nicola, *Pyrgi* (Nardi 1981; Caruso 1990) e il noto passo di Rutilio Namaziano relativo all'anno 417 (Rut. Nam. I, 223-226). Sopravvive certamente tutta la viabilità principale e il centro di *Ad Turres*, mentre tendono a scomparire le strade secondarie e vicinali in conseguenza del progressivo abbandono delle campagne; è verosimile che ingenti estensioni di terreno coltivato siano state in breve rioccupate dalla vegetazione spontanea o destinate al pascolo. Alla fine del IV secolo sono ormai scomparsi tutti i piccoli insediamenti rurali situati nella pianura costiera a sud-est di *Pyrgi* e di *Alsium*. Inizia con ogni probabilità la formazione di vaste zone acquitrinose tra le quali quella di Palidoro, bonificate soltanto nei primi decenni di questo secolo. Attorno al 400 d.C., nel settore SE, appaiono quasi deserti i pianori di Pian Cerese, Porrazzeta, Quarto di Montelungo e ampie zone collinari in località Boietto, Tenuta di Castel Campanile, Migliorie di San Paolo, Quartaccio.

Nonostante lo spopolamento, nell'anno 499 la città di *Caere* è amministrata da un vescovo della chiesa di Roma di nome Adeodato (Tomassetti 1913) e nelle ville ancora presenti nella diocesi continuano ad arrivare dall'Africa anfore e sigillata.

Seppure esposti alle operazioni militari connesse con le guerre greco-gotiche (Procopio *Bell. Goth.* III, 22), è probabile che punti di approdo sopravvivano ancora lungo la costa, forse in relazione con il grande complesso alsietino, con *Pyrgi* e con alcune altre ville marittime.

Le forme Hayes 99 n. 18, Hayes 104 A e 105 in sigillata africana D e le anfore tipo Keay XXXV B, XXXVI B, LVII, LXII A, sono gli ultimi prodotti africani che raggiungono la diocesi di *Caere*, tra la metà del V e gli ultimi decenni del VI secolo d.C.

Il medioevo (sec. xi–xii)

Nell'alto medioevo, scomparso il paesaggio delle ville e l'organizzazione agraria classica, il territorio appare deserto, ad eccezione di alcune sporadiche frequentazioni nel luogo di *Ad Turres* e in due ville romane. Rimane da approfondire la possibilità che l'antico sito di *Pyrgi* sia stato trasformato in una *domusculta*; sporadici indizi lasciano comunque presumere una possibile continuità di vita nell'area in seguito occupata dal castello di Santa Severa.

Frammenti di boccali in *Forum Ware* e di olle acquarie decorate a fasce di linee solcate, rinvenuti sulle pendici delle rocche di Castel Campanile e Ceri, rialzano la cronologia di fondazione di questi villaggi, finora documentati a partire dall'XI e XII secolo (Tomassetti 1913; Conti 1980). Gli scavi di recupero eseguiti dalla soprintendenza nel sito di *Ad Turres*, lungo la via Aurelia hanno invece portato all'individuazione di un probabile borgo rurale, attivo a partire dall'XI secolo, sviluppatosi sui resti dell'antica *mansio* (Cosentino 1990). Di grande interesse la presenza di questo insediamento di pianura medievale, formatosi direttamente sulle struttura romane prima della costruzione del *Castrum Statua*.

Nel settore SE del campione, nell'anno Mille sono ormai certamente una realtà tre insediamenti fortificati: Ceri (*Caere Nova* ?), Castel Campanile (*Fundus Campaninus*) e Cerveteri (*Caere Vetus* ?); i primi due di nuova fondazione, il terzo logica continuità del precedente centro urbano. E' probabile che in questa fase, nel resto del territorio campione, siano già presenti anche gli abitati di Castel Dannato, *Luternum*, Castel Giuliano, Monte Santo, Monte Sassone e Carcari.

I villaggi, arroccati su ristretti pianori tufacei dai fianchi scoscesi, dominano la viabilità e i punti di confluenza delle valli fluviali. Nel caso di Cerveteri, spopolatasi l'area urbana di epoca classica occupante l'intero pianoro dei Vignali, l'insediamento si restringe sulla probabile acropoli della città antica, un'appendice naturalmente fortificata da cui è possibile controllare la pianura costiera. Il Castello di *Caere*, feudo d'importante rilevanza strategica e ancora sede di diocesi, viene donato alla Chiesa nell'817 dall'imperatore del Sacro Romano Impero Lodovico I (Tomassetti 1913). Forse dall' 847 è documentato il luogo di culto *sub ripa* dedicato a San Michele Arcangelo, individuabile in località Sant'Angelo, subito sotto il costone sud-orientale della città antica. Nell'anno 999 il *castrum*, dopo essere stato occupato da Benedetto, un esponente della nobile famiglia romana dei Crescenzi, viene riconquistato dopo un violento assedio presenziato dall'imperatore Ottone III, dal Papa Gregorio V e dall'abate del Monastero di Farfa (Tomassetti 1913). Per Ceri e Castel Campanile non esistono invece notizie anteriori all'XI secolo.

Il paesaggio feudale del *Patrimonium Sancti Petri* sopravvive quasi immobile attraverso complesse vicende e passaggi di proprietà fino in epoca moderna. Nel settore SE, nel medioevo, Cerveteri, Ceri e Castel Campanile insieme al sito di Sant'Angelo scoperto a nord di Palidoro, e al villaggio di pescatori sviluppatosi attorno il *Castrum Pali*, rimangono gli unici poli abitati dell'area in esame. Nell'XI-XII secolo, circa 2 km a sud-est di Cerveteri, lungo la strada per Statua (antica *Caere-Ad Turres*), viene costruita una chiesa, forse dedicata a San Paolo o pertinente alle proprietà di detto monastero, sui ruderi di una grande villa romana. Il lato nord del Casale dei Guitti, in località Migliorie di San Paolo, si appoggia infatti su una struttura a tre absidi, alta circa 3 m: all'abside centrale maggiore fanno riscontro due laterali minori con finestrelle a feritoia strombate verso l'esterno, rispettivamente con ghiera in laterizi (lato est) e a piccoli conci di tufo (lato ovest). La struttura è costruita in blocchi di tufo squadrati, messi in opera senza regolarità, di testa e di taglio, con malta bianca, ricca di sabbia, con stilatura centrale.

Ringraziamenti

La carta archeologica del settore SE (Cerveteri) e i risultati dell'indagine sono in corso di pubblicazione nella serie della *Forma Italiae, Carta Archeologica d'Italia*, curata dalla Sezione di Topografia Antica del Dipartimento di Scienze dell'Antichità dell'Università di Roma. Si ringrazia la famiglia Fusaro per aver gentilmente messo a disposizione la Borsa di Studio intitolata a Daniela Fusaro consentendo l'ulteriore sviluppo della ricerca. Si ringraziano per la disponibilità e i numerosi consigli i professori Andrea Carandini e Paolo Sommella, preziosi punti di riferimento scientifico. Fondamentali per il riconoscimento dei materiali sono state le consulenze dei dottori: A. M. Conti, C. Persiani per i materiali preistorici; A. Naso, A. Zifferero per l'architettura funeraria cerite e i materiali di epoca etrusca; L. Caretta, A. Ciotola, S. Fontana, G. Gazzetti, M. Incitti, E.A. Stanco e la Prof. M. Steinby per i vetri, le ceramiche, i prodotti laterizi bollati di epoca romana; la Prof. G. Maetzke per i materiali medievali; il sig. A. Cavicchi per i reperti numismatici. Il lavoro sul campo è stato possibile grazie all'aiuto di F. Cauli, M. Cipriani, U. Fusco, A. Marziali, R. Paolelli, S. Principe, M. Romiti. Un grazie particolare va a Claudio Taddeo e a Laura Palma, inseparabili compagni di ricognizione. La ricerca è dedicata a Ludovico Magrini, vulcanico maestro di vita.

Bibliografia

AA.VV. 1980. *La formazione della città nel Lazio, Dialoghi d'Archeologia*, n.s. II, 2.

AA.VV. 1990. *Caere e il suo territorio. Da Agylla a Centumcellae*, (A. Maffei, F. Nastasi a cura di), Roma.

Attolini, I. Cambi, F., Celuzza, M., Fentress, E., Pasquinucci, M. & Regoli, E. 1982. 'Ricognizione archeologica nell'ager Cosanus e nella valle dell'Albegna. Rapporto preliminare 1981', *Archeologia Medievale*, IX, 365–86.

Briquel, D. 1984. *Les Pélasges en Italie*, Roma.

Caruso, I. 1990. 'La romanizzazione dell'Etruria', in AA.VV., *Caere e il suo territorio. Da Agylla a Centumcellae*, Roma, 305–309.

Castagnoli, F. 1968. in De Rossi et al., 'La via Aurelia da Roma a Civitavecchia', *Quaderni Topografia Antiqua*, IV, 6.

Celuzza, M. & Regoli, E. 1982. 'La Valle d'Oro nel territorio di Cosa', *Dialoghi d'Archeologia*, I n.s., 31–62.

Coarelli, F. 1988. 'Colonizzazione romana e viabilità', *Dialoghi d'Archelogia*, 35–48.

Coccolini, G. & Follieri, M. 1980. 'I legni dei pozzi del tempio A nel santuario etrusco di Pyrgi', *Studi Etruschi*, XLVIII, 277–91.

Colonna, G. 1968. 'La via Caere-Pyrgi', *Quaderni Topografia Antiqua*, IV, 75–87.

Colonna, G. 1973. 'Scavi e scoperte', *Studi Etruschi*, XLI, 541.

Colonna, G. 1981. in AA.VV. *Die Gottin von Pyrgi, Archäologishe Linguistische und Religionsgeschichtliche Aspekte*, (Akten des Kolloquiums, Tübingen, 1979), Firenze, 19.

Colonna, G. & Hase, F. 1986. 'Alle origini della statuaria etrusca: la Tomba delle Statue presso Ceri', *Studi Etruschi*, LII, 13–59.

Conti, S. 1980. *Le sedi umane abbandonate nel patrimonio di San Pietro*, Firenze.

Cosentino, R. & Sabbatini Tumulesi, P. 1989. 'L'edificio termale delle Aquae Caeretanae', *Miscellanea Ceretana*, CNR, 95–112.

Cosentino, R. 1990. in *Caere e il suo territorio. Da Agylla a Centumcellae*, Roma, 297–304.

Cristofani, M. 1965. *La Tomba delle Iscrizioni a Cerveteri*, Firenze.

Cristofani, M. 1986. 'Nuovi dati per la storia urbana di Caere', *BA*, 1–24.

Cristofani, M., Nardi, G. & Moscati, P. 1986. 'Ricerche nell'area urbana di Caere', *Archeologia nella Tuscia II*, Roma, 15–58.

Cristofani, M., Nardi, G. & Rizzo, M. 1988. *Caere 1. Il parco archeologico*, CNR, Roma.

Delpino, F. 1987. in M. Cristofani (a cura di), *Etruria e Lazio arcaico*, CNR, Roma, 23.

De Rossi, G., Di Domenico, P. & Quilici, L. 1968. 'La via Aurelia da Roma a Civitavecchia', *Quaderni Topografia Antiqua*, IV, 13–73.

Di Gennaro, F. 1986. *Forme di insediamento tra Tevere e Fiora, dal bronzo finale al principio dell'età del ferro*, Firenze.

Di Nocera, G. & Enei, F. 1990. 'Nuovi siti dell'età del bronzo nell'alta valle del Mignone', in Gazzetti, Zifferero (a cura di), 'Progetto Monti della Tolfa-Valli del Mignone, secondo rapporto di attività (1985–1989)', *Archeologia Medievale*, XVII, 440–442.

Enei, F. 1986. 'Alcune osservazioni sulla topografia cerite: la Via degli Inferi', *Ricognizioni Archeologiche*, 2, Roma, 25–29.

Enei, F. 1987. 'Cerveteri, recupero nell'area della città antica', *Ricognizioni Archeologiche*, 3, Roma.

Enei, F. 1991. 'Ad Turres sull'antica via Aurelia: osservazioni e ritrovamenti', *Studi Romani*, 1–2, 95–108.

Enei, F. 1992. 'Ricognizioni archeologiche nell'ager Caeretanus: rapporto preliminare', *Papers of the Fourth Conference of Italian Archaeology*, Part 3, London, 71–90.

Enei, F. c.s. 'Cerveteri: l'abitato etrusco di Monte Abbadoncino', *Studi Etruschi*, LVIII.

Fuchs, M., Liverani, P. & Santoro, P. 1989. *Caere 2. Il teatro e il ciclo statuario giulio-claudio*, CNR.

Galassi, R. 1986. 'Problemi di tipologia degli insediamenti dell'età del bronzo nell'Etruria meridionale', *Quaderni di Protostoria* 1, Perugia, 151–192.

Gazzetti, G. 1985. in Coccia *et al.*, 'Il progetto Monti della Tolfa-Valli del Mignone: una ricerca topografica nel Lazio settentrionale', *Archeologia Medievale*, XII, 517–34.

Giuliani, C. & Quilici, L. 1964. 'La via Caere-Pyrgi', *Quaderni Topografia Antiqua* I, 5–15.

Kahane, A., Threipland, L.M. & Ward-Perkins, J. 1968. 'The ager Veientanus, north and east of Rome', *Papers of the British School at Rome*, 36, 1–218.

Harris, W. 1971. *Rome in Etruria and Umbria*, Oxford.

Humbert, M. 1972. 'L'incorporation de Caere dans la civitas romana', *Mélanges de l'École Français de Rome, Antiquité*, LXXXIV, 231–268.

Humbert, M. 1978. *Municipium et civitas sine suffragio*, Roma.

Lerici, C. 1957. 'Campagna di prospezioni archeologiche nella necropoli di Monte Abatone', Milano, 3–31

Moscati, P. 1985. 'Studi su Falerii Veteres, l'abitato', *RAL* VIII, XL, 1–2, 71.

Brunetti Nardi, G. 1972. *Repertorio degli scavi e delle scoperte archeologiche nell'Etruria meridionale (1966–1970)*, Roma.

Brunetti Nardi, G. 1981. *Repertorio degli scavi e delle scoperte archeologiche nell'Etruria meridionale (1971–1975)*, Roma.

Nardi, G. 1988. 'I caratteri naturali e la viabilità antica', in *Caere 1, il parco archeologico* (M. Cristofani, G. Nardi, M.A. Rizzo), CNR, 11–27.

Pacciarelli, M. 1982. 'Economia e organizzazione del territorio in Etruria meridionale nell'età del bronzo media e recente', *Dialoghi d'Archeologia*, I n.s., 69–79.

Pohl, I. 1972. *The Iron Age Necropolis of Sorbo at Cerveteri*, (Acta Ist. Rom. Regni Sueciae XXXII).

Potter, T.W. 1980. in AA.VV., *Roman Villas in Italy, Excavation and Research*, Occasional Paper, British Museum, London.

Potter, T.W. 1985. *Storia del paesaggio dell'Etruria meridionale*, Roma.

Proietti, G. 1982. 'Osservazioni preliminari su un monumento sepolcrale in località Sant'Angelo di Cerveteri', *Archeologia della Tuscia* I, Roma, 104–108.

Proietti, G. 1983. 'L'ipogeo monumentale dei Tamsnie', *SE*, LI, 557–571.

Renfrew, C. 1986. 'Interazione fra comunità paritarie e formazione dello stato', *Dialoghi d'Archeologia*, n.s.1,1, 9–26.

Ricci Portoghesi, L. 1966. 'Una nuova lastra dipinta cerite', *Archeologia Classica*, XVIII, 16–22.

Salmon, E. 1969. *Roman Colonization under the Republic*, London.

Shatzman, I. 1975. *Senatorial Wealth and Roman Politics*, Bruxelles.

Sordi, M. 1960. *I rapporti romano ceriti e l'origine della civitas sine suffragio*, Roma.

Tomassetti, G. 1913. *La campagna romana, antica, medioevale e moderna*, vol. III, Roma.

Torelli, M. 1984. 'Veio: la città, l'arx e il culto di Giunone Regina', *Miscellanea Arch. T. Dohrn dicata*, Roma, 117–123.

Vita Finzi, C. & Higgs, E. 1970. 'Prehistoric economy in the Mount Carmel area in Palestine: site catchment analysis', *Proceedings of the Prehistoric Society*, XVI, 1–73.

Zifferero, A. 1985. 'Il periodo etrusco', in Coccia *et al.*, 'Il progetto Monti della Tolfa-Valli del Mignone: una ricerca topografica nel Lazio settentrionale', *Archeologia Medievale*, XII, 517–34.

Will, E. 1982. 'Greco-italic amphoras', *Esperia*, 51:3, 338–356.

PART 2

Religion and Ritual

9

From Secret Society to State Religion: Ritual and Social Organisation in Prehistoric and Protohistoric Italy

RUTH D. WHITEHOUSE

(Institute of Archaeology, University College London)

Summary: *Recent works on religion and ritual in prehistory have mostly been cast in structuralist and post-structuralist moulds. These offer important insights, but tend to neglect the connections between religion and society. The present paper returns to earlier functionalist models to explore these links in the prehistoric Italian context. The paper presents an overview of the development of religious ritual in later prehistoric Italy, starting with small-scale secret cults in the Neolithic, based on a series of 'underground' sites, including caves, rock-shelters, rock-cut tombs and hypogea. These continue into the Copper and Bronze Ages, but these later periods also witness the emergence of more public ritual monuments situated in the open, including megalithic tombs, menhirs and statue-menhirs and statue-stelae. In the Iron Age we find sanctuaries in the open, in the first place away from settlements, subsequently developing, in the context of the Etruscan civilisation, into true temples, found in both urban and rural situations, and presumably run by a specialist priesthood.*

The discussion associates this evolutionary sequence with the development of society. The secret cult of the Neolithic was appropriate for a small-scale non-hierarchical society, but as elites began to emerge in the Copper and Bronze Ages, there was a need for a more visible symbol system and we find the first ritual monuments in the open. The later sanctuaries of the Iron Age were associated with developed chiefdoms or emerging states, precursors of the full city-states which supported the temples and priesthoods known from the 6th century BC.

Recent works on religion and ritual in prehistory have mostly been cast in structuralist and post-structuralist moulds (e.g. papers in Garwood *et al.* 1991). These offer important insights, but tend to favour particularist interpretations rather than generalising ones; they also tend to neglect the connections between religion and society. My own book, on the cult of Neolithic and Copper Age Italy (Whitehouse 1992), while not ignoring social context, is also geared to the specific culture. However, it is indubitably the case that there is a close connection between the level of complexity of social organisation and the form of religion found in any community. We can see this clearly if we look at the extreme cases: no-one would expect to find shamans in an urban civilisation, nor a specialist priesthood in a hunter-gatherer band. The present paper attempts to explore the links between religion and society in prehistoric Italy. In doing this, I return to the ideas of early pioneers, who interpreted religion in functionalist terms, such as Durkheim (e.g. 1912), or more recent work in a similar vein, like that of Douglas (1966; 1970; 1975), or even early Sahlins (1968). This is likely to be regarded by some as a retrograde move, but I believe that these ideas can still provide helpful insights. In particular, they have a role to play in the study of social evolution in any area. Although much time and effort has been devoted in recent years to the study of the evolution of society in prehistoric Italy, to my knowledge few attempts have been made to integrate religion into our understanding of this evolution. Religion is considered quite often, it is true, in studies of Etruscan civilisation, but for prehistory few studies have looked at the social function of ritual (the work of Alessandro Guidi providing an honourable exception here (Guidi 1980; 1990; in press)). This paper is offered as a contribution to this area of study.

I make no attempt here to document the evidence for the reconstruction of social organisation in prehistoric and protohistoric Italy. Useful discussions for various periods, with bibliographies, can be found in Barfield 1986; Barker 1981: Chapter 11; Cazzella 1984; chapters by Cardarelli, Guidi and Pellegrini in Guido & Piperno 1992; Peroni 1989; Spivey & Stoddart: Chapter 8; Whitehouse 1984. For the purposes of this paper, I am taking as my base a generalised social evolutionary framework which I believe would be widely accepted by many scholars. Starting from a segmentary tribal organisation in the Neolithic, we find evidence for the emergence of some degree of ranking, and possibly also some degree of centralisation of settlement patterns, in the Copper Age and Early Bronze Age; later in the Bronze Age there are significant divergences between regions, with the processes of increasing social differentiation and increasing hierarchy of settlement organisation developing further in some areas, but not in others. Then, in the Early Iron Age we find a further development, restricted initially to west central Italy, with the emergence first of developed chiefdoms and subsequently of true urban states in Etruria and Lazio. This outline account provides the framework into which I shall attempt to fit the reconstruction of religious ritual.

I begin my study with the early farming societies of the Neolithic, since the evidence available on the religion of the earlier hunting and gathering societies of the Palaeolithic and Mesolithic is still too scarce to construct a coherent picture of even the most hypothetical type. I have argued elsewhere (Whitehouse 1984; 1992: Chapter 8) that the societies of peninsular Italy throughout the major part of the Neolithic period were small-scale and non-hierarchical in structure, i.e. they were of the type generally, if misleadingly, labelled 'egalitarian', where the main social divisions would have been based on age and gender. Although there is here and there some evidence suggesting co-operative constructive activities and some pointing to settlement nucleation, most noticeably in the *villaggi trincerati* of the Tavoliere (Brown 1991), we lack indicators of either hierarchical settlement organisation or marked differences in status between individuals. In other words, we are dealing with a segmentary tribal society.

What is the archaeological evidence for ritual and religion in peninsular Italy and Sicily during this period? There is in fact – and this may surprise some people – a wealth of data, considerable in quantity and varied in type. This material is presented in some detail in *Underground Religion* (Whitehouse 1992) and I shall provide only an outline here. The evidence for ritual comes predominantly from sites which I have described as 'underground': natural caves, crevices and rockshelters and, to a lesser extent, also artificial rock-cut structures; these latter become more common at the tail end of the Neolithic and in the Copper Age. These sites were used for a variety of cult purposes: many were used for burial and there is evidence for other types of cult too. In my book I describe a 'hunting cult', for which there is evidence in the form both of cave paintings and of apparently ritual deposition of bones of wild animals. There are also indications of what I have called a cult of 'abnormal water': the clearest evidence is of ritual attention being paid to stalactites and stalagmites (solid water), but there are also cases of cult sites associated with steam, with bubbling water and with pools of still water.

My interpretation of these data, presented in full in *Underground Religion*, and in summary form in a number of articles published over the last few years (Whitehouse 1990; 1991a; 1991b; 1991c; 1992), is multi-layered and involves approaches of different sorts. For the purposes of the present discussion, I shall emphasise a few basic points, related to social organisation.

a) We are clearly dealing here not with public rituals, but with small-scale, secretive rites (the underground cult sites, particularly the caves, are often hidden, difficult of access and cramped and uncomfortable internally). I have suggested that the rites that best fit this description are rites of passage, both life crisis rites (including burial rites, which are of course prime examples of this type of rite) and initiation rites into a religious sect or society.

b) There is an emphasis on secrecy in the cult activities, which I have interpreted on analogy with anthropologically documented societies where power is based on restricted access to secret religious knowledge.

c) Both the ritual emphasis on hunting in general (hunting is documented ethnographically as almost invariably a male activity) and the specific iconography of the Grotta di Porto Badisco paintings (where archers are shown as explicitly male) suggest that the cult was restricted to males. This suggests a primary social division of society along gender lines.

d) If the interpretation in terms of initiation rites into a secret religious society is accepted, anthropological analogy would suggest a graded series of initiations. From this we may deduce that there was another axis of division, based on age. Skeates (1991) has argued specifically in the case of sites in Abruzzo that there was an emphasis on age differentiation in burials.

e) Overall I argue that the cult provided a means of social control, in the first place control of men over women and secondly of older men over younger ones.

All this, if accepted, fits quite well with what we would expect religion to be like in segmentary tribal societies. Firstly, at the organisational level, we would expect religion to be 'embedded' in society; it would not be separated or institutionalised; religious leadership would tend to coincide with leadership of other kinds, such as lineage headship, or other status roles. A cult that placed emphasis on power relations based on gender and age would fit with a society with no instituted hierarchy.

In the next phase, the Copper Age and the earlier part of the Bronze Age, the archaeological record provides some evidence of changes in social organisation. Most noticeable is the evidence for increasing social differentiation: burials with rich grave goods increasingly distinct from those with poorer or no grave goods (see, for example, Barker 1981: 186–8). There are some indications too of incipient development of hierarchical settlement organisation: it has been suggested, for instance, that the settlement of Toppo Daguzzo in northern Basilicata might have served as a central place for its area (Cipolloni Sampò 1986). I should add, however, that these movements in the direction of greater social complexity were quite modest, especially by comparison with developments in some other parts of the Mediterranean – parts of the Aegean, for instance, or southeast Spain.

The evidence for ritual and religion at this time shows much continuity from earlier periods, but there are some new developments also. Caves, rock-shelters and crevices continue to be used for cult purposes, especially, though not exclusively, for burial. Indeed there seems to be more emphasis on burial in general, and the majority of all known sites of this period are funerary sites. The majority of the burial sites are still of 'underground' type, with natural caves and crevices preferred in some areas, e.g. Tuscany, artificial rock-cut tombs in others, such as Campania and Apulia. However, a new feature is the appearance also of some above-ground, highly visible monuments: megalithic tombs and simple menhirs in Apulia and statue-menhirs and statue-stelae in other areas, especially the Lunigiana (see, for example, Ambrosi 1972; 1988; Anati 1981; Whitehouse 1981).

Both the general continuity in cult practice and the new features that do occur seem to fit quite well with the other evidence for social organisation. The relatively modest scale of change indicated means that in general traditional religious practices and beliefs would have continued to serve their communities quite adequately. The new monuments are to a considerable extent still connected with funerary rituals. The megalithic tombs are, of course, directly funerary monuments and they were used, like most, though not all, contemporary tombs of other types, for collective burial. The statue-menhirs, statue-stelae and the undecorated menhirs are often also interpreted as connected with funerary ritual, although only in a few cases, such as at Aosta, are they directly associated with tombs (Mezzena 1985). Many authorities associate the statue-menhirs and statue-stelae with a cult of the ancestors, perhaps practised in association with funerary ritual (e.g. Peroni 1989). These monuments contrast with the cult sites of traditional type above all in their prominent visibility and this can be explained by the nature of the social changes that did occur. Clearly there was now a need for some more public ritual than before; religious leaders could no longer work only through secret rituals, the restriction of access to religious knowledge and the manipulation of arcane symbols. For some communities at least and some religious leaders it became appropriate to have public ritual displays. The flavour of these rituals may have been as community-oriented and collectivist in ideology as anything that happened earlier, but the public aspect of the rituals represents a real change. As I see it, in both the earlier and the later societies ritual leadership would have entailed real power, but now the power was making itself publicly manifest – 'coming out' as it were, not of the closet, but of the cave. This seems to me to fit well with a society that was increasingy differentiated and hierarchical in organisation. There is, however, no reason to believe that power was exercised on any level larger than the local community.

Apart from these modest developments, religion in the Bronze Age seems marked mainly by continuity with earlier periods, including use of caves and crevices in most areas. The next identifiable major stage in social evolution occurs in the later Bronze Age and earlier Iron Age, when both the socio-economic processes described previously – increasing differentiation of social statuses and increasing hierarchy of settlement organisation – developed much further and culminated in the emergence of early urban states, at least in Etruria and Lazio. The developments are best documented in west central Italy and indeed seem to have occurred earliest here. In terms of social hierarchy, still modest differentiation in grave goods characterises the record up to the second half of the 8th century BC; from this time on, and especially in the 7th century BC, we find some extremely rich burials; among the most famous examples are the Tomb of the Warrior at Tarquinia and the Regolini-Galassi Tomb at Cerveteri. This is clearly a different order of differentiation from that found earlier and suggests that we are now at the level of developed chiefdoms (see, for example, the recent discussion in Spivey & Stoddart 1990: Chapter VIII). By the 6th century the burial record would suggest the emergence of a society differentiated into true classes, normally associated with urban states. Over the same general period we find evidence also in the settlements for what has been described as a 'politicised landscape' or a 'landscape of power'. For instance, to take a single study by way of example, Guidi's rank-size analysis of settlements in the area supports the idea of a considerable degree of hierarchical organisation of settlements (described as 'protourban') in the 9th and 8th centuries BC and the emergence of a truly urban organisation, with the rank-size graphs conforming to the log normal distribution, emerging in the 7th century BC (Guidi 1985). To a lesser extent these same developments can be documented in many other parts of peninsular Italy, although only in Etruria and Lazio does it seem to have led to the early development of fully fledged states.

What can we say about religious sites during this phase of intensive social development? Cave sites continue to be used for cult purposes, especially in the earlier part of the period. But we find also a significant new development: the appearance of open-air sanctuaries. These date to the phase of 'protourban' development or complex chiefdoms. Both the chronology and typology of the cult sites of central Italy have been studied by Guidi (1980; 1990). He documents a three-phase development. In the Middle Bronze Age (c.1700–1300 BC) the vast majority of cult sites are in caves (both *grotte-santuario* and funerary caves), although there are also two cult sites he describes as being in the open (Guidi 1990: 409); however, even these sites – l'Eremita di Montecassino and Grotta delle Marmitte – have features indicating a characteristic 'underground' orientation. In the succeeding Late Bronze Age (c.1300–900 BC) the situation changes notably: on the Tyrrhenian side of the Apennines, the use of caves for funerary and other cult uses virtually disappears and, at the same time, we find the appearance of votive offerings, including food, especially cereals, in pits and ditches within settlement sites and, towards the end of the period, the earliest dated separate open-air cult site, associated with the Laghetto del Monsignore spring, near Campoverde, attributed to the 10th century BC (Guidi 1980: 149). Both these features of cult practice, i.e. the deposition of food remains within settlements and deposition of other materials, especially pottery, at the sites of natural springs, continued into the following period. Meanwhile, during the Late Bronze Age, according to Guidi, cult sites on the Adriatic side of central Italy continue to be predominantly caves and this in fact would seem to be the general pattern throughout the peninsula: the areas of Etruria and Lazio stand out as exceptional in this respect, as in other aspects of social evolution. For the succeeding Early Iron Age (900–700 BC) the evidence is poor, although there is enough to suggest that another significant development has occurred, with cult areas now within the settlements; certainly it is clear that in the area of *Latium vetus* some cult sites took the form of huts within settlements, e.g. at Satricum and Ardea. Guidi hypothesises that these are ancestral to the true sanctuaries of the 7th century BC and to the temples of the full city-states from the 6th century BC. Although the data have not been collected systematically for other parts of the peninsula, the development documented by Guidi for west central Italy can probably be seen elsewhere, but with a noticeable time-lag. In other words, there seems to have been a general move away from cult sites in caves to those in the open, but away from settlements. The later stage, involving the emergence of 'civic' cult sites – true sanctuaries – within settlements may also occur in some areas, although in many cases it does not antedate Romanisation.

I am interested here in the stage which saw the abandonment of the 'underground' cave sites and the establishment of cult sites in the open, a movement which seems to coincide with the phase of 'protourban' development or complex chiefdoms. A possible parallel is provided by the 'peak sanctuaries' of Bronze Age Crete, interpreted by Cherry (1986). The peak sanctuaries are ritual areas on or near mountain or hilltops, rarely with built structures, but yielding evidence of presumptively sacrificial fires and large numbers of votive objects. They were mostly established in MM I, were used throughout the MM period, but rarely survive into the LM period; in other words they belong with the early palace period of Minoan civilisation, but do not survive into the neopalatial phase of the mature civilisation. As Cherry says (1986: 32), 'There is thus a chronological correspondence between the emergence of state-like polities in Crete and the appearance of a new type of cult site throughout the island'. Cherry points to a close connection between the peak sanctuaries and the newly emerged palaces and interprets this as 'a deliberate attempt by the political and economic special interest groups in Minoan polities to consolidate their power by the communal performance of ritual activities revolving around unverifiable sacred propositions'. The same could be true of Etruria and Lazio, although we have too little evidence to pursue this idea much at this stage; it could, however, provide a useful framework for future research. At this stage, religious leadership may still have coincided with political leadership; what is probably new is the indication that power was being exercised beyond the bounds of the individual community, perhaps throughout the territory of each emerging city-state (or 'Early State Module' (Renfrew 1975)).

Finally, with the establishment of urban states on a firm basis, we find clear sanctuaries within cities, well established as monumental structures – easily recognisable as temples of classical type – by the 6th century BC. By this stage there is little doubt that we have a state religion: institutionalised, run by a specialist priesthood and geared to state aims and projects.

I do not propose to discuss either the evidence for, or the interpretation of, this form of religion, which is both familiar and the subject of a substantial literature.

Discussion

I have outlined an extremely brief history of ritual and religion in prehistoric and protohistoric Italy and have shown, I hope, how in the gradual evolution of society from small-scale tribal societies to fully fledged urban states, each stage has its appropriate form and organisation of religion. What I have not touched on so far is any discussion of the nature of the relationship, or the issue of which came first, the social or the religious organisation. The nature of the relationship is relatively easy to deal with. As I have already indicated in the foregoing discussion, I believe that the connection is that of *power*. Control of religious knowledge and ritual practices provides a source of social power in many societies, especially small-scale societies which lack institutionalised power structures of other kinds (economic, military or political). This is the source of power labelled 'ideological' by Mann (1986: 22–4), who describes how religious leaders can excercise power through a threefold mechanism. Firstly, 'power can be wielded by those who monopolize a claim to meaning', since the organisation of knowledge and meaning is essential to social life (Mann 1986: 22). Secondly, religious leaders may be the guardians of norms, shared understandings of appropriate moral behaviour, which are necessary for sustained social cooperation. Thirdly, they control ritual practices, which as Bloch has argued, serve to distance the exercise of power from the possibility of rational challenge (Bloch 1974). This is not the place to pursue this discussion further; for the purposes of this paper it is sufficient to show that if religion is closely associated with the exercise of power, it must clearly be considered in any discussion of social organisation or social evolution.

The other point – the question of whether society or religion was primary – is a classic example of the chicken or egg question and it may seem foolhardy to even try to say anything about it, but it would be cowardly to finish without even mentioning the subject. It is a question that Durkheim and many of the early anthropologists of the functionalist school would have had no difficulty in answering, firmly on the side of society. 'God is another name for society' said Durkheim; people made gods in their own image and set them apart, so that there would be something outside to make them behave in the way that was right for society. The assumption was clearly that society was primary, religion and indeed the entire world of ideas and symbols, secondary. These days, with the perspectives of structuralism and post-structuralism at our disposal, it certainly does not seem so simple. Structuralism would tend to assign primacy to the conceptual world, while post-structuralism challenges the very idea of society, at least as something consisting of fixed structures and roles and separate from the world of ideas. Rather, it is always in the process of being created, negotiated and renegotiated by the individuals and groups who constitute it, while the world of symbols and ideas provides the chief means by which it is so re-created and renegotiated. My own view is that the two are intimately interlinked, that it would be foolish to assign primacy to one or the other, to assume that change in one always precedes change in the other. I would think that change could emanate from either sphere, as indeed from others not considered here, such as economy or technology. It is the task of the archaeologist to attempt to interpret the specific archaeological record in this respect, as in others. Not that I am attempting to do this in the present paper. My aim here is altogether more modest: it is merely to put religion into the frame of discussion of prehistoric social evolution in Italy, where it has rarely figured in the past.

Bibliography

Ambrosi, A. 1972. *Corpus delle statue-stele lunigianesi*, (Collana Storica della Liguria Orientale, 6), Bordighera.
Ambrosi, A. 1988. *Statue-stele lunigianesi*, Genova.
Anati, E. 1981. *Le statue-stele della Lunigiana*, Milan.
Barfield, L. 1986. 'Chalcolithic burial in Northern Italy. Problems of social interpretation', *Dialoghi di Archeologia*, n.s. 4.2, 241–248.
Barker, G. 1981. *Landscape and Society. Prehistoric Central Italy*, London & New York.
Bloch, M. 1974. 'Symbols, song, dance and features of articulation or Is religion an extreme form of traditional authoriy?', *European Journal of Sociology*, 15, 55–81.
Brown, K. 1991. 'A passion for excavation. Labour requirements and possible functions for the ditches of the 'villaggi trincerati' of the Tavoliere, Apulia', *Accordia Research Papers*, 2, 7–30.
Cardarelli, A. 1992. 'Le età dei metalli nell'Italia settentrionale', in Guidi & Piperno, (eds.), 366–419.
Cazzella, A. 1984. 'Età del Bronzo: forme incipienti di stratificazione sociale nel II millennio a.C.', in AA.VV., *Palentologia. Metodi e strumenti per l'analisi delle società preistoriche*, Rome, 275–97.
Cherry, J.F. 1986. 'Polities and palaces: some problems in Minoan state formation', in Renfrew, C. & Cherry, J.F. (eds.), *Peer Polity Interaction and Socio-political Change*, Cambridge, 19–45.
Cipolloni Sampò, M. 1986. 'Dinamiche di sviluppo culturale e analisi archeologica: problemi interpretativi nello scavo di un sito', *Dialoghi di Archeologia*, 2, 225–235.
Douglas, M. 1966. *Purity and Danger*, London.
Douglas, M. 1970. *Natural Symbols*, London.
Douglas, M. 1975. 'Self-evidence', in Douglas, M. (ed.), *Implicit Meanings*, London, 276–318.
Durkheim, E. 1912. *Les formes élémentaires de la vie religieuse*, Paris. (English edition, *The Elementary Forms of the Religious Life*, London, 1915).
Garwood, P., Jennings, D., Skeates, R. & Toms, J. (eds.) 1991. *Sacred and Profane*, (Oxford University Committee for Archaeology Monograph No. 32), Oxford.
Guidi, A. 1980. 'Luoghi di culto dell'età del bronzo finale e della prima età del ferro nel Lazio meridionale', *Archeologia Laziale*, 3, 148–155.
Guidi, A. 1985. 'An application of the rank size rule to protohistoric settlements in the middle Tyrrhenian area', in Malone, C. & Stoddart, S. (eds.), *Papers in Italian Archaeology IV. Part iii. Patterns in Protohistory*. British Archaeological Reports International Series 245, Oxford, 217–42.
Guidi, A. 1990. 'Alcune osservazioni sulla problematica delle offerte nella protostoria dell'Italia centrale', *Scienze dell'Antichità*, 3–4, 403–414.
Guidi, A. 1992. 'Le età dei metalli nell'Italia centrale e in Sardegna', in Guidi & Piperno (eds.), 420–70.
Guidi, A. in press. 'Recenti ritrovamenti in grotta nel Lazio: un riesame critico del problema dell'utilizzazione delle cavità naturali', *Rassegna di Archeologia*, 10.
Guidi, A. & Piperno, M. (eds) 1992. *Italia preistorica*, Rome and Bari.
Mann, M. 1986. *The Sources of Social Power. Volume 1. A History of Power from the Beginning to AD 1760*, Cambridge.
Mezzena, A. 1985. 'La valle d'Aosta nella preistoria e protostoria', in *Archeologia in Valle d'Aosta*, Aosta (5th edition), 15–60.
Pellegrini, E. 1992. 'Le età dei metalli nell'Italia meridionale e in Sicilia', in Guidi & Piperno (eds.), 471–516.
Peroni, R. 1989. *Protostoria dell'Italia continentale. La penisola italiana nelle età del Bronzo e del Ferro*, Rome.

Renfrew, C. 1975. 'Trade as action at a distance', in Sabloff, J.A. & Lamberg-Karlovsky, C.C. (eds.), *Ancient Civilisation and Trade*, Albuquerque, 3–59.

Sahlins, M. 1968. *Tribesmen*, New Jersey.

Skeates, R. 1991. 'Caves, cult and children in Neolithic Abruzzo, Central Italy', in Garwood, P., Jennings, D., Skeates, R. & Toms, J. (eds.), 122–140.

Spivey, N. & Stoddart, S. 1990. *Etruscan Italy. An Archaeological History*, London.

Whitehouse, R.D. 1972. 'The rock-cut tombs of the Central Mediterranean', *Antiquity*, 46, 275–281.

Whitehouse, R.D. 1981. 'Megaliths of the central Mediterranean', in Evans, J.D., Cunliffe, B. & Renfrew, C. (eds.), *Antiquity and Man. Essays in Honour of Glyn Daniel*, London, 106–127.

Whitehouse, R.D. 1984. 'Social organisation in the Neolithic of southeast Italy', in Waldren, W.H., Chapman, R., Lewthwaite, J. & Kennard, R-C. (eds.), *Early Settlement in the Western Mediterranean Islands and their Peripheral Areas*, British Archaeological Reports, International Series, 229, Oxford, 1109–1133.

Whitehouse, R.D. 1990. 'Caves and cult in Neolithic Southern Italy', *Accordia Research Papers*, 1, 19–37.

Whitehouse, R.D. 1991a. 'The social function of religious ritual: the case of Neolithic southern Italy', *Origini*, 14 (1988–1989), 387–398.

Whitehouse, R.D. 1991b. 'Cult and culture in Neolithic Southern Italy', *Journal of Mediterranean Studies*, 1.2, 242–251.

Whitehouse, R.D. 1991c. 'Ritual knowledge, secrecy and power in a small-scale society', in Herring, E., Whitehouse, R., & Wilkins, J. (eds), *Papers of the Fourth Conference of Italian Archaeology, 1. The Archaeology of Power*, 1, London, 195–206.

Whitehouse, R.D. 1992. *Underground Religion. Cult and Culture in Prehistoric Italy*, London.

10

Analisi delle Strutture Tombali in Etruria nel Bronzo Finale

LAURA DOMANICO

(Istituto di Archeologia, Università degli Studi di Milano)

Sommario: *Nello studio vengono analizzati gli aspetti tecnici e costruttivi delle strutture tombali dell'età del Bronzo Finale presenti in Etruria. Dopo aver distinto tra necropoli vere e proprie, tombe isolate, rinvenimenti sporadici in area di necropoli più tarde e materiali del Bronzo Finale in tombe più tarde, vengono identificate 15 zone territoriali, alcune delle quali caratterizzate da un'alta concentrazione di ritrovamenti (Media valle del Fiora, Zona di Tolfa-Allumiere, Zona del Sasso di Furbara). Le caratteristiche costruttive osservate sono state suddivise in elementi strutturali, elementi aggiuntivi ed elementi esterni, raggruppati a loro volta in base alle loro diverse associazioni ed organizzate in tabelle riassuntive. L'analisi ha indicato l'esistenza di un'alta variabilità di tipi soprattutto nelle zone di Tolfa-Allumiere e del Sasso di Furbara, e l'esistenza di alcune strutture a carattere eccezionale, probabili indizi di una volontà di differenziazione sociale.*

Da alcuni anni lo studio delle necropoli e dei rituali funerari diffusi nella penisola italiana durante l'epoca pre-protostorica è tornato ad essere al centro degli interessi degli studiosi, soprattutto per le potenziali possibilità di ricostruzione del contesto sociale e del mondo ideologico delle antiche comunità. Le difficoltà interpretative che derivano da questo tipo di approccio, hanno stimolato un intenso dibattito che ha implicato una più attenta ed approfondita definizione delle premesse teoriche e metodologiche che devono essere alla base di un simile tentativo di ricostruzione (Gnoli & Vernant 1982; *Prospettive* 1987; Cazzella 1989). Ciò ha portato ad una diversa lettura di quegli aspetti tradizionalmente posti al centro dello studio delle necropoli, come ad esempio l'analisi dei corredi tombali e delle associazioni degli oggetti, non più affrontata unicamente da un punto di vista strettamente cronotipologico.

Va osservato tuttavia che spesso altri elementi ugualmente importanti, dall'analisi dei resti ossei all'osservazione della distribuzione spaziale delle tombe o dell'organizzazione delle necropoli sul territorio, vengono trascurati o non rappresentano l'aspetto prevalente negli interessi degli studiosi. Tra questi, anche l'analisi puntuale delle strutture tombali, le cui caratteristiche, se menzionate, restano quasi sempre marginali senza cioé divenire parte integrante dello studio delle necropoli antiche.

Ne deriva quindi che il nuovo approccio metodologico, se ha portato indubbiamente ad una maggiore consapevolezza nello studio delle manifestazioni funerarie, non ha ancora prodotto delle vaste sintesi in cui sia presa in considerazione la molteplicità degli aspetti che coinvolge il rituale di deposizione scelto da una comunità antica.

Questa carenza è particolarmente presente per le necropoli del Bronzo Finale dell'Etruria, pure assai note ed ampiamente studiate sotto altri punti di vista. Probabilmente lo stato frammentario ed incompleto di buona parte dei dati, frutto spesso di ritrovamenti occasionali pubblicati anche molti decenni fa, non ha finora incoraggiato un'analisi di questo tipo. Alcuni anni fa avevamo sottolineato come lo studio delle caratteristiche strutturali dei modelli abitativi diffusi in Etruria meridionale tra il Bronzo Finale e la prima età del Ferro potesse offrire interessanti spunti di riflessione per la comprensione dei fenomeni culturali di questo periodo (Negroni Catacchio & Domanico 1989). I risultati allora ottenuti, incoraggiano l'applicazione di un metodo di analisi simile anche per le strutture tombali.

In questo studio l'attenzione verrà quindi concentrata sugli aspetti tecnici che caratterizzano le strutture tombali del Bronzo Finale in Etruria, proponendone una preliminare sistemazione che possa costituire il punto di partenza per una più approfondita sintesi generale.

Va premesso che la natura dei rinvenimenti non è ovunque omogenea. Su un totale di 48 siti individuati (fig.1), 22 sono infatti necropoli vere e proprie, spesso costituite da non più di 4 o 5 tombe, 18 siti hanno restituito solo tombe isolate, mentre in 5 casi sono attestati ritrovamenti sporadici in aree di necropoli più tarde e in 3 casi materiali del Bronzo Finale sono stati trovati tra il corredo di tombe di epoca successiva (Appendice 1. I criteri di questa divisione sono stati già chiariti in Domanico & Miari 1991).

Il totale dei dati permette di osservare alcuni raggruppamenti che determinano altrettante zone territoriali, con particolare densità nel medio corso del Fiora e nelle zone di Tolfa-Allumiere e del Sasso di Furbara (Appendice 2). Tuttavia, l'esiguità delle presenze funerarie nel resto dell'Etruria potrebbe essere piuttosto collegata alla mancanza di ricerche sistematiche.

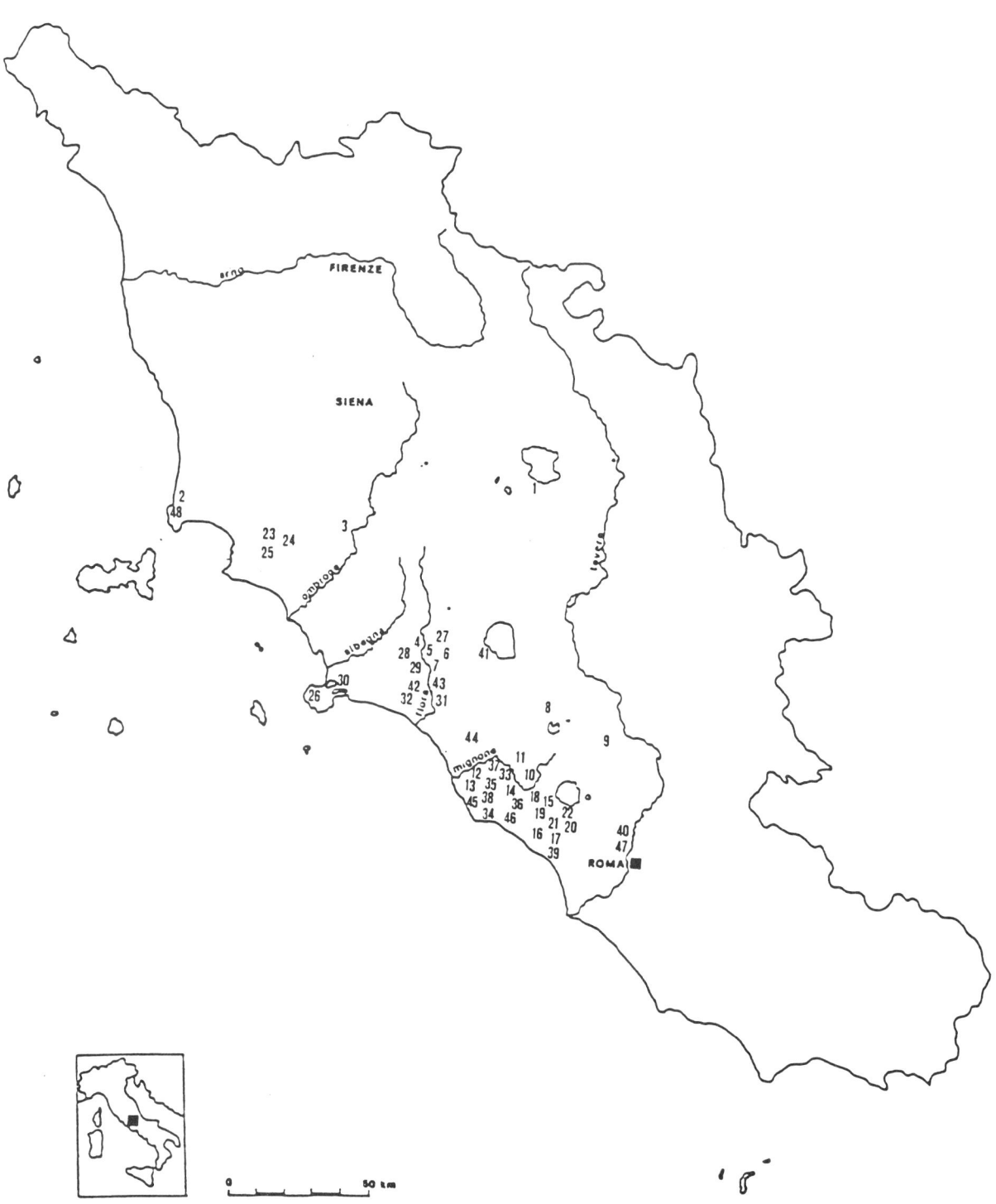

Fig. 1. Carta di distribuzione dei siti funerari del Bronzo Finale.

Assai raramente questi siti sono stati indagati in modo sistematico e per la maggior parte sono frutto di ritrovamenti casuali o di raccolte di superficie di materiali ormai distrutti dall'aratro. Il primo problema è quindi quello di rendere il più possibile omogenei i dati, ma soprattutto di affrontare un primo tentativo di sistemazione terminologica, in un ambito in cui la descrizione delle caratteristiche tecniche delle tombe può essere soggetta a facili equivoci. Non è sempre facile infatti, comprendere il significato, soprattutto dalle vecchie pubblicazioni, di termini come cista, cassetta, cassettone e cogliere la differenza tra questi e ad esempio il rivestimento del pozzetto, strutturalmente diverso. Ancora di recente tuttavia sono stati individuati, tra le forme costruttive tipiche delle tombe del Bronzo Finale, il 'pozzetto' e la 'buca', senza chiarirne il significato e l'eventuale differenza (Peroni 1989: 262).

Dall'analisi delle strutture tombali finora rinvenute, sono state individuate e distinte tre diverse 'modalità costruttive':

1. Pozzetto scavato nella terra
2. Pozzetto scavato nella roccia
3. Deposizione in anfratto naturale

La distinzione tra i tipi 1 e 2 è sembrata opportuna in seguito all'osservazione che alcuni elementi, come ad esempio la cassetta litica e il rivestimento, non appaiono mai nei pozzetti scavati nella roccia. Al contrario è forse interessante notare che la custodia litica, come anche la copertura con lastre, appaiono indistintamente in entrambi i tipi. Accanto a questi è stato aggiunto un quarto tipo costituito dal tumulo, riscontrato finora solo per le tombe di Crostoletto di Lamone e di Campaccio, la cui eccezionalità sembrava giustificarne una trattazione a parte.

Il pozzetto può presentare diversi aspetti costruttivi, riassunti nella Tabella riportata alla fig.4. Questi appaiono più o meno articolati in varianti che tuttavia nel loro insieme possono essere concettualmente raggruppate in *elementi strutturali*, che riguardano direttamente le caratteristiche del pozzetto, *elementi aggiuntivi* ed *elementi esterni* e comprendono ciascuno:

1. Elementi strutturali: copertura, rivestimento, base
2. Elementi aggiuntivi: custodia, cassetta
3. Elementi esterni: tumulo, segnacolo

Il pozzetto nel Bronzo Finale è prevalentemente del tipo semplice; due casi di pozzetto doppio – per es. la T.10 di Puntone al Norcino e la tomba del BF trovata nella necropoli del Sorbo di Cerveteri, delle quali si dirà più avanti – sembrano confermare una regola che vedrà poi numerose eccezioni a partire dalla prima età del Ferro (a questo proposito v. Cardosa in questi atti). I diversi elementi individuati si combinano tra di loro in modo molto vario, dando luogo ad alcuni raggruppamenti che possono essere così esemplificati (fig.5):

1. Pozzetto nella Terra
1a Semplice
1a1 urna deposta direttamente nella terra
1a2 copertura lastre litiche
1a3 pietre alla base
1a4 copertura lastre litiche – pietre alla base
1a5 rivestimento
1a5.a rivestimento lastre litiche – lastra alla base
1a5.b rivestimento lastre litiche – copertura lastre o pietre
1a5.c rivestimento lastre litiche – copertura lastre o pietre – lastre o pietre alla base
1a5.d rivestimento pietre – copertura lastra litica – lastra alla base – segnacolo
1a6 custodia
1a6.a custodia – anello di pietre alla base
1a6.b custodia – segnacolo
1a7 calotta litica
1a8 cassetta litica
1a8.a cassetta litica – segnacolo

1b Doppio
1b1 rivestimento a doppia fila concentrica di lastre litiche e pietre – copertura litica – cassetta – segnacolo

2. Pozzetto nella roccia
2a Semplice
2a1 copertura lastre litiche
2a2 custodia
2a2.a custodia – copertura lastre litiche
2a2.b custodia – segnacolo

2b Doppio
2b1 copertura pietre

3. Anfratto naturale

4. Tumulo
4a Semplice di pietre
4a1 pozzetto nella terra con rivestimento lastre litiche
4a2 pozzetto nella terra con cassetta (?)

4b Semplice di terra
4b1 pozzetto nella terra con rivestimento pietre – copertura lastre litiche – pietre alla base

4c Complesso di pietre
4c1 corridoio dolmenico

Tra i 40 siti nei quali si è riscontrata la presenza di necropoli o di tombe isolate (Appendice 1), in dieci casi non è stata trovata alcuna notizia che rendesse possibile la ricostruzione delle caratteristiche strutturali (figg. 4, 5).

Tra i siti rimanenti sembra che il pozzetto scavato semplicemente nella terra sia il più diffuso, tuttavia assai raramente l'urna appare deposta direttamente al suo interno, senza altri elementi strutturali (tipo 1a1). Più spesso le pareti appaiono rivestite con pietre o con lastre litiche (tipi 1a5.a/d), caratteristica diffusa soprattutto nella zona del Sasso di Furbara e in particolare nella necropoli di Puntone al Norcino, dove è attestato un gran numero di varianti (Brusadin 1964; 1989).

Se nella maggior parte dei casi il rivestimento appare alquanto sommario (Gangalante, con una lastra e un blocco informe di tufo; Cavallini del Bufalo (Poggiani 1988), con tre lastre infisse obliquamente nel terreno; Puntone al Norcino, T.6 con lastre rinforzate da pietre e T.7 con robuste pietre di forma rettangolare irregolare), a volte le lastre litiche sono così accuratamente accostate le une alle altre da dare l'impressione della volontà di costruire una struttura in realtà molto più complessa. Sembra questo il caso di una tomba rinvenuta nel 1881 dal Klitsche de la Grange a Poggio la Pozza, con otto lastre di calcare di rivestimento, due orizzontali di copertura e il fondo quasi lastricato con ciottoli. La struttura era lunga 70 cm e alta 30 cm e conservava intatte due urne cinerarie deposte orizzontalmente (Toti 1959).

Le pietre compaiono, sebbene molto raramente,

Fig. 2. Presenza e distribuzione delle tombe con custodia litica.

anche nelle coperture (fig.4), ma solo nella tomba 163 della necropoli del Sorbo hanno una funzione strutturale evidente (Vighi 1955). Nella maggior parte dei casi la copertura è costituita invece da una o più lastre litiche. Nelle necropoli della zona del Sasso di Furbara assai spesso questa sembra assumere una funzione più che altro simbolica, con una lastrina di piccole dimensioni posta in corrispondenza dell'urna cineraria sottostante (Brusadin 1964). Analogo valore simbolico è stato notato anche nella T.1, Trincea F di Poggio la Pozza, la quale però appare molto più complessa poiché al di sopra della lastrina vi erano alcuni frammenti ceramici di grosse dimensioni, anch'essi con probabile funzione di copertura (Peroni 1960). La struttura, con cassetta litica e segnacolo esterno, esemplifica un tipo a parte, attestato finora unicamente in questa necropoli (tipo 1a8.a).

Lastre litiche e pietre sono infine utilizzate anche alle basi, ma solo in una tomba di Grotte Barche, purtroppo depredata dai clandestini, queste ultime si disponevano ad anello alla base della custodia (tipo 1a6.a).

Il tipo più diffuso tra i siti considerati è senz'altro quello con custodia litica (fig.3), deposta in pozzetti

Fig. 3. Presenza e distribuzione delle tombe con cassetta litica.

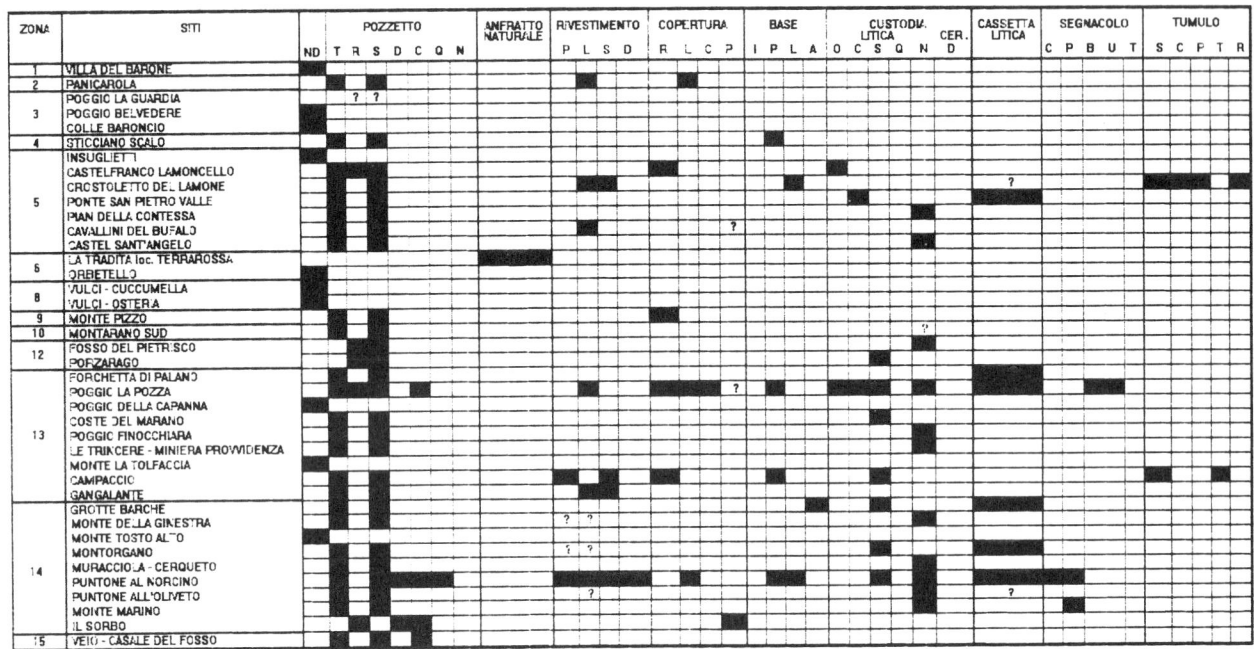

Fig. 4. Tabella dei singoli elementi attestati nelle strutture funerarie del Bronzo Finale in Etruria.

Legenda dei simboli: **Pozzetto**. *T: Terra; R: Roccia; S: Semplice; D: Doppio; C: Circolare; Q: Quadrangolare; N: Nicchia.*
Rivestimento. *P: Pietre; L: Lastre litiche; S: Semplice; D: Doppio.* **Copertura**. *R: Più lastre litiche; L: Lastra litica;
C: Calotta litica; P: Pietre.* **Base**. *I: Incavo nella roccia; P: Pietre; L: Lastra litica; A: Anello di pietre.* **Custodia litica**. *O: Ovale;
C: Cilindrica; S: Sferica; Q: Quadrangolare; N: Non determinabile; Cer.D: Dolio.* **Segnacolo**. *C: Circolo di pietre; P: Cippo;
B: Blocchi di pietre; U: Cumulo di pietre; T: Ciottoli.* **Tumulo**. *S: Semplice; C: Complesso; P: Pietre; T: Terra; R: Corridoio.*

scavati sia nella terra (tipi 1a6.a/b), che nella roccia (tipi 2a2.a/b) e presente anche nel caso della tomba di Campaccio, con tumulo di terra (tipo 4b1) (Toti 1959). In alcune tombe di Poggio la Pozza essa è anche associata ad una copertura costituita da grandi lastre di roccia trachitica (Bastianelli 1942; Toti 1959). La custodia, che assume forme e dimensioni differenti (fig.4), presenta a volte, soprattutto nelle tombe del Sasso, un incavo interno per ospitare l'urna oppure, nel caso della T.4 di Puntone al Norcino, una sorta di risega ricavata per appoggiare i vasetti del corredo (Brusadin 1964). Isolato anche il caso di una tomba trovata nel 1884 a Poggio la Pozza (Klitsche 1884) (tipo 1a7), dove una calotta litica copriva l'ossario formato da due ciotole poste l'una sull'altra.

La cassetta litica è stata invece riscontrata soltanto in otto siti (Fig.2B) e, come si è detto, non è mai presente nei pozzetti scavati nella roccia. Essa compare quasi sempre da sola, senza altri elementi strutturali (tipo 1a8), tranne nel caso della T.1, Trincea F di Poggio la Pozza, con un segnacolo costituito da un cumulo di pietre trachitiche (Peroni 1960) e nel caso di Crostoletto di Lamone, dove alcune cassette vuote sono state trovate tra le pietre del Tumulo VII (Negroni *et alii* 1979).

Tralasciando per il momento l'analisi puntuale dei tipi più diffusi ai quali si è finora accennato, vale forse la pena soffermarsi su alcuni casi particolari e per ora unici. Mi riferisco alla Tomba 10 di Puntone al Norcino (tipo 1b1), alla tomba isolata con deposizione in anfratto naturale della Tradita, loc. Terrarossa sul Monte Argentario (tipo 3), alle tombe ad incinerazione di Crostoletto di Lamone (tipi 4a1, 4a2, 4c1) e alla tomba di Campaccio (tipo 4b1) (fig.4).

Nel primo caso si tratta dell'unico esempio finora noto nella zona in esame durante il Bronzo Finale di pozzetto doppio scavato nella terra, con l'urna cineraria protetta da una cassetta di lastre litiche posta nella cavità più profonda, di forma quadrangolare. Il pozzetto superiore, circolare, aveva le pareti rivestite con una doppia fila di lastre disposte in modo concentrico, sostenute e rinforzate con alcuni ciottoli incastrati negli spazi vuoti. Una grande lastra copriva infine la struttura, segnalata all'esterno da un piccolo cippo eretto (Brusadin 1964).

Una struttura altrettanto complessa è quella della tomba isolata di Campaccio, trovata nel 1878 nella zona di Tolfa-Allumiere, in cui erano associate insieme le caratteristiche delle pietre di rivestimento e alla base, della custodia litica di forma regolare sferica e delle lastre di copertura. La tomba era segnalata all'esterno da un tumulo di terra, chiaramente visibile in un disegno particolareggiato dello stesso Klitsche de la Grange, che scopì la tomba, recentemente ripubblicato dal Toti (Toti *et alii* 1987, fig.102). Certamente il tumulo di terra doveva

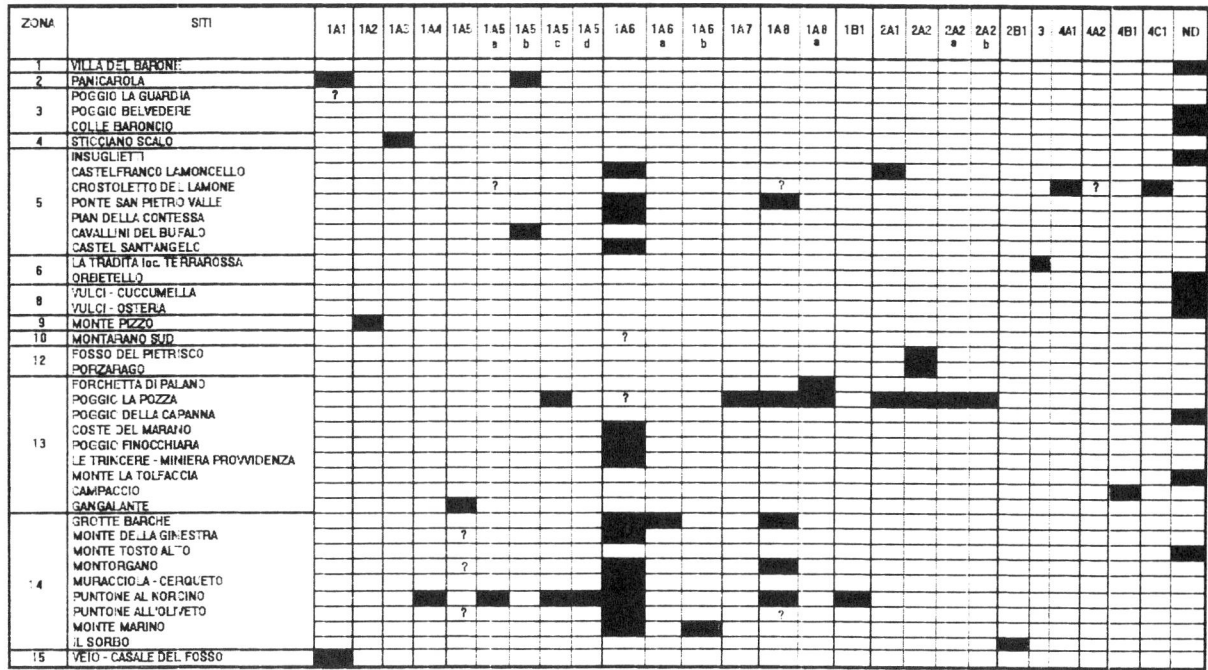

Fig. 5. Tabella dei raggruppamenti di elementi attestati nelle strutture funerarie del Bronzo Finale in Etruria.

essere in realtà più diffuso di quanto sembra, forse caratteristico proprio della zona di Tolfa-Allumiere e la sua rarità potrebbe essere piuttosto una conseguenza dell'uso attuale dei terreni. Tuttavia l'isolamento della tomba potrebbe indurre a riflettere su un fenomeno forse non casuale di volontà di differenziazione (Domanico & Miari 1991). Analogo problema riguarda anche i segnacoli, rinvenuti non numerosi e finora solo nelle zone di Tolfa-Allumiere e del Sasso di Furbara. Si tratta infatti spesso di tracce alquanto labili, come nel caso dei piccoli cumuli di pietre posti sulle tombe 1 e 2 della Trincea F e sulla T.4, Trincea D di Poggio la Pozza (Peroni 1960), o dei cippi di una tomba di Monte Marino e della già citata T.10 di Puntone al Norcino (Brusadin 1964 e 1989). In quest'ultima necropoli è stato notato anche un circolo di pietre visibile in superficie in corrispondenza del perimetro del pozzetto della Tomba 1.

I tumuli di pietre di Crostoletto di Lamone costituiscono invece un caso a parte che andrebbe diversamente approfondito. Non è possibile riprendere in questa sede la complessa problematica cronologica ed interpretativa relativa a questo sito, già d'altra parte ampiamente affrontata (Rittatore 1967 e 1972; Poggiani & Figura 1979). Ciò che interessa invece qui sottolineare è che le forme tipiche e diffuse del pozzetto, con rivestimento di lastre litiche o con cassetta compaiono in questo sito entro grandi strutture a carattere megalitico, nel caso del Tum.1 anche con un corridoio dolmenico a grandi lastre di travertino (Rittatore 1967, fig.5). Tracce di sepolture ad inumazione e alcuni frammenti attribuibili al Bronzo Medio e Recente indiziano l'antichità dei tumuli, riutilizzati poi per le incinerazioni del Bronzo Finale.

La presenza nell'area di grandi muraglioni a secco e di lenti di carbone e di concotto sottolinea infine l'eccezionalità del complesso, giustificandone la continuità d'uso (Rittatore 1967: 293).

Per quanto riguarda infine la tomba isolata rinvenuta sulle pendici orientali del Monte Argentario, in località La Tradita, si tratta della deposizione di un'urna cineraria biconica, coperta da una ciotola capovolta, in un piccolo anfratto naturale di roccia, quasi un pozzetto profondo circa 40 centimetri. L'analisi dei resti ossei combusti ha indicato che si trattava di un individuo di sesso femminile di 12–14 anni (Graziani & Rittatore 1961). Il caso resta finora unico, anche se si potrebbe osservare che sembra trattarsi quasi della ricerca di una tipologia già nota e diffusa altrove in questo periodo, cioè la deposizione in pozzetto scavato nella roccia, senza in questo caso procedere con un'azione costruttiva.

Come già dichiarato nell'introduzione a questo lavoro, lo scopo principale dell'analisi fin qui condotta vuole essere innanzitutto quello di attirare l'attenzione sulle caratteristiche strutturali delle tombe del Bronzo Finale dell'Etruria, ponendo l'accento sul modo assai vario in cui si combinano tra di loro i diversi elementi individuati. Questo aspetto in particolare permette di avanzare alcune considerazioni di carattere generale, che più che conclusioni, vorrebbero proporsi come indizi per orientare le future ricerche in questo territorio.

Innanzi tutto appare chiaro dall'osservazione delle Tabelle riportate alle figg. 4 e 5 che il tipo più diffuso e potremmo dire caratteristico di questo periodo, è la deposizione in custodia litica entro un pozzetto scavato nella terra o nella roccia. Tuttavia sarebbe riduttivo concludere che la custodia e la cassetta rappresentano gli elementi tipici delle strutture tombali del Bronzo Finale in Etruria.

Ciò che interessa è al contrario analizzare la frequenza con cui compaiono le varianti. Spesso alcune tombe rappresentano dei tipi a sé stanti, tale è l'originalità dell'associazione degli elementi (tipi 1a4; 1a5.d; 1a6.a/b; 1a7; 1b1; 2b1; 3; 4b1). Ciò potrebbe confermare l'ipotesi, già avanzata da R. Peroni, di una chiara volontà di differenziazione, forse sociale, tra gli individui (Peroni 1989: 262). In alcune zone, come ad esempio quelle di Tolfa-Allumiere e del Sasso di Furbara, questa varietà assume proporzioni interessanti non solo sul territorio in generale, ma anche all'interno di singole necropoli, come ad esempio nei casi di Poggio la Pozza e di Puntone al Norcino (fig.5). Certamente si tratta di necropoli almeno parzialmente indagate e che hanno restituito un numero elevato di deposizioni (più di 40 nel primo caso e almeno 12 nel secondo), mentre per altre zone mancano ricerche sistematiche e i dati, come già sottolineato, sono alquanto eterogenei. Tuttavia il confronto ad esempio con la zona del Medio corso del Fiora, da tempo attentamente studiata (*Sorgenti della Nova* 1981), potrebbe forse confermare questa impressione. Le necropoli sembrano infatti qui finora costituite prevalentemente da un numero ridotto di tombe (sei a Castelfranco Lamoncello; otto a Ponte San Pietro Valle). In esse, escludendo il caso eccezionale di Crostoletto di Lamone di cui si è detto, si ripete un modello strutturale abbastanza semplice, costituito prevalentemente da tombe con custodia litica. Se si aggiunge a questo la relativa povertà dei corredi, nei quali i vasi accessori e gli oggetti di ornamento, quando sono presenti, non sono mai più di uno per tomba, appare ancora più evidente la differenza con le due zone menzionate, dove al contrario una delle caratteristiche è appunto l'abbondanza e la varietà dei corredi. Inoltre sembrano esistere solo in queste zone altri aspetti peculiari, come ad esempio la lastrina di copertura ridotta a dimensioni simboliche (Poggio la Pozza, Puntone al Norcino), forse la presenza di segnacoli e la custodia litica con la calotta superiore di dimensioni maggiori.

Per un'analisi approfondita dei fenomeni funerari diventa infine quanto mai attuale la necessità, già in altre occasioni sottolineata (Domanico & Miari 1991), di individuare una più precisa suddivisione in fasi cronologiche all'interno del Bronzo Finale dell'Etruria, per evitare il rischio di porre a confronto situazioni in realtà lontane tra loro nel tempo e soprattutto per individuare l'eventuale esistenza di un'evoluzione nelle scelte costruttive e nei rituali di deposizione. Osservazioni di questo tipo proposte per il medio corso del Fiora, sembrano infatti suggerire, limitatamente a questa zona, una probabile anteriorità dell'uso della cassetta litica rispetto al pozzetto con custodia di tufo (*Sorgenti della Nova* 1981).

APPENDICE 1*

Elenco dei siti funerari del Bronzo Finale in Etruria

Necropoli
1. Panicarola (Castiglione del Lago, PG)
2. Villa del Barone (Piombino, LI)
3. Sticciano Scalo (Roccastrada, GR)
4. Insuglietti (Pitigliano, GR)
5. Castelfranco Lamoncello (Ischia di Castro, VT)
6. Crostoletto di Lamone (Ischia di Castro, VT)
7. Ponte San Pietro Valle (Ischia di Castro, VT)
8. Monte Pizzo (VT)
9. Montarano Sud (Civita Castellana, VT)
10. Fosso del Pietrisco (S. Giovenale, Blera, VT)
11. Porzarago (S. Giovenale, Blera, VT)
12. Forchetta di Palano (Allumiere, Roma)
13. Poggio la Pozza (Allumiere, Roma)
14. Poggio della Capanna (Tolfa, Roma)
15. Grotte Barche (Cerveteri, Roma)
16. Monte della Ginestra (Cerveteri, Roma)
17. Monte Tosto Alto (Cerveteri, Roma)
18. Montorgano (Cerveteri, Roma)

---

* Mentre questo articolo era ancora in stampa è stato pubblicato un altro mio lavoro sullo stesso argomento negli *Atti del II Incontro di Studi Preistoria e Protostoria in Etruria*, Farnese, 21/23 maggio 1993, Milano 1995, pp. 127–145, nel quale l'analisi delle strutture tombali del Bronzo Finale in Etruria viene affrontata in modo più approfondito sopratutto per quanto riguarda l'organizzazione tipologica dei dati. Nell'intervallo di tempo trascorso dalla *Fifth Conference of Italian Archaeology* tenuta ad Oxford nel 1992 sono inoltre apparsi nuovi elementi e scoperte o pubblicate altre necropoli, come ad esempio quella del Bagnatorio (Manciano, GR) nella valle del Fiora. Alcuni ripensamenti mi hanno infine indotto ad effettuare alcune modifiche, pur senza contraddire l'impostazione di fondo propria anche di questo lavoro. Per una migliore integrazione dei dati qui presentati si rimanda dunque all'articolo citato.

La bibliografia relativa alle necropoli del Bronzo Finale dell'Etruria è alquanto vasta e non può essere qui interamente riassunta. Vengono quindi citate le pubblicazioni principali rimandando a ciascuna di esse per eventuali riferimenti più dettagliati. Per le rassegne generali, nelle quali peraltro raramente vengono descritte le strutture tombali, v. Fugazzola Delpino-Delpino 1979; *Sorgenti della Nova* 1981; di Gennaro 1986; *Catalogo Manciano* 1988. Per Panicarola: Feruglio 1968 e 1969. Per i siti della Toscana marittima: Falchi 1891; Maetzke 1951; Galiberti 1970; Bergonzi & Cateni 1979. Per Orbetello: Ciampoltrini 1993. Per la tomba dell'Argentario: Graziani & Rittatore 1961. Per la valle del fiume Fiora: Rittatore 1972; Raddatz 1975; Rittatore, Falchetti & Negroni 1977; Negroni *et alii* 1979; *Sorgenti della Nova* 1981; Negroni 1985. Per Poggio Sopra Selciatello: Negroni 1987. Per Monte Pizzo: Scriattoli 1920. Per Montarano Sud: Pasqui-Bernabei 1894. Per San Giovenale: Berggren 1972; Gierow 1972. Per la zona di Tolfa-Allumiere: Toti 1959; Peroni 1960. Per la zona del Sasso di Furbara: Brusadin 1964 e 1989. Per Vulci: Fabbricotti 1972. Per Veio: Colini 1919; Vianello Cordova 1967.

19. Muracciola – Cerqueto (Cerveteri, Roma)
20. Puntone al Norcino (Cerveteri, Roma)
21. Puntone all'Oliveto (Cerveteri, Roma)
22. Monte Marino (Bracciano, Roma)

Tombe isolate
23. Vetulonia – Poggio La Guardia (Castiglione della Pescaia, GR)
24. Vetulonia – Poggio Belvedere (Castiglione della Pescaia, GR)
25. Vetulonia – Colle Baroncio (?) (Castiglione della Pescaia, GR)
26. La Tradita, loc. Terrarossa (Monte Argentario, GR)
27. Pian della Contessa (Pitigliano, GR)
28. Cavallini del Bufalo (Manciano, GR)
29. Castel Sant'Angelo (Manciano, GR)
30. Orbetello (GR)
31. Vulci – Cuccumella (Canino, VT)
32. Vulci – Osteria (Montalto di Castro, VT)
33. Coste del Marano (Tolfa, Roma)
34. Poggio Finocchiara (Tolfa, Roma)
35. Le Trincere, Miniera Provvidenza (Allumiere, Roma)
36. Monte la Tolfaccia (Fontanaccia, Allumiere, Roma)
37. Campaccio (Allumiere, Roma)
38. Gangalante (Allumiere, Roma)
39. Il Sorbo, Fondo Chiani (Cerveteri, Roma)
40. Veio – Casale del Fosso (Roma)

Rinvenimenti sporadici in area di necropoli più tarde
41. Monte Bisenzio (Capodimonte, VT)
42. Vulci – Poggio Maremma (Montalto di Castro, VT)
43. Vulci – Ponte Rotto (Montalto di Castro, VT)
44. Poggio Sopra Selciatello (Tarquinia, Roma)
45. Poggio Ombricolo (Allumiere, Roma)

Materiali del Bronzo Finale in tombe più tarde
46. Bandita Grande (Allumiere, Roma)
47. Veio – Quattro Fontanili (Isola Farnese, Roma)
48. Populonia (Piombino, LI)

APPENDICE 2

Zone territoriali

1. Zona di Populonia
2. Zona del Lago Trasimeno
3. Zona di Vetulonia
4. Zona di Sticciano
5. Zona del media valle del Fiora
6. Zona dell' Argentario
7. Zona del Lago di Bolsena
8. Zona di Vulci
9. Zona di Viterbo
10. Zona di Civita Castellana
11. Zona di Tarquinia
12. Zona di San Giovenale
13. Zona di Tolfa-Allumiere
14. Zona del Sasso di Furbara e di Cerveteri
15. Zona di Veio

Bibliografia

Bastianelli, S. 1942. 'Il territorio tolfetano nell'antichità', *Studi Etruschi,* XVI, 229–245.
Bergonzi, G. & Cateni, G. 1979. 'L'età del Bronzo Finale nella Toscana marittima', *Atti XXI Riunione Scientifica dell'Istituto Italiano di Preistoria e Protostoria, Il Bronzo Finale in Italia*, Firenze, 247–264.
Berggren, E. K. 1972. 'The Necropolis of Porzarago, Grotte Tufarine and Monte Vangone', in *San Giovenale, Acta Inst. Rom. Regni Sueciae I*, XXVI, fasc.5, Stockholm, 20–21.
Brusadin Laplace, D. 1964. 'Le necropoli protostoriche del Sasso di Furbara', in *Bullettino di Paletnologia Italiana* XV, 143–186.
Brusadin Laplace, D. 1989. 'Le necropoli protostoriche del Sasso di Furbara. II. Montorgano ed altri sepolcreti protovillanoviani', *Origini,* XIII, 1984–1987, Roma, 341–408.
Catalogo Manciano 1988. Museo di Preistoria e Protostoria della Valle del fiume Fiora, (a cura di N. Negroni Catacchio), Manciano.
Cazzella, A. 1989. *Manuale di Archeologia: Le società della preistoria,* Bari.
Ciampoltrini, G. 1993. 'Un insediamento del Bronzo Finale alla Puntata di Fonteblanda (Orbetello)', *Preistoria e Protostoria in Etruria, Atti del I Incontro di Studi,* (Saturnia- Farnese, maggio 1991), Milano, 387–389.
Colini, G. A. 1919. 'Veio. Scavi nell'area della città e delle necropoli', *Notizie degli Scavi di Antichità*, 3–12.
Di Gennaro, F. 1986. *Forme di insediamento tra Tevere e Fiora dal Bronzo Finale al principio dell'età del Ferro,* Firenze.
Domanico, L. & Miari, M. 1991. 'La distribuzione dei siti di necropoli in Etruria meridionale nel Bronzo Finale. Documentazione ed elaborazione dei dati', in Herring, E., Whitehouse, R. & Wilkins, J. (eds.), *Papers of the Fourth Conference of Italian Archaeology, The Archaeology of Power I,* London, 61–82.
Fabbricotti, E. 1972. 'Veio (Isola Farnese). Continuazione degli scavi nella necropoli villanoviana in località Quattro Fontanili. Quattordicesima campagna di scavo', *Notizie degli Scavi di Antichità,* XXVI, 342–353.
Falchi, I. 1891. *Vetulonia e la sua necropoli antichissima,* Roma.
Feruglio, A. E. 1968. 'Territorio della Soprintendenza alle Antichità dell'Umbria. Panicarola', *Studi Etruschi,* XXXVI, 161–162.
Feruglio, A.E. 1969. 'Panicarola (Castiglione del Lago)', *Studi Etruschi,* XXXVII, 281.
Fugazzola Delpino, M. A. & Delpino, F. 1979. 'Il Bronzo Finale nel Lazio settentrionale', *Atti XXI Riunone Scientifica dell'Istituto Italiano di Preistoria e Protostoria: Il Bronzo Finale in Italia,* Firenze, 275–316.
Galiberti, P. 1970. *La preistoria del promontorio di Piombino,* Associazione Archeologica Piombinese, Piombino.
Gierow, P. G. 1972. 'San Giovenale. The Tombs of Fosso del Pietrisco and Valle Vesca', *Acta Inst. Rom. Regni Sueciae* 4, XXVI, Stokholm, I, 8.
Gnoli, G. & Vernant, J-P. (a cura di) 1982. *La mort, les morts dans les sociétes anciennes,* Cambridge.
Graziani, E. & Rittatore Vonwiller, F. 1961. 'Tomba ad incinerazione protovillanoviana dell'Argentario', *Studi Etruschi,* XXIX, 293–295.
Klitsche de la Grange, A. 1884. 'Allumiere', *Notizie degli Scavi di Antichità,* 101–102.
Maetzke, G. 1951. 'Una necropoli ad incinerazione presso Sticciano Scalo (Grosseto)', *Rivista di Scienze Preistoriche,* VI, Not., 96.
Negroni Catacchio, N. 1985. 'Nuovi dati sulla preistoria e protostoria della valle del fiume Fiora', *Studi di Paletnologia in onore di S.M. Puglisi,* Roma, 833–850.
Negroni Catacchio, N. 1987. 'La fase di transizione bronzo-ferro in Etruria alla luce degli scavi di Tarquinia', in *Tarquinia: Ricerche Scavi e Prospettive* (a cura di M. Bonghi Jovino & C. Chiaramonte Treré), Milano, 219–232.
Negroni Catacchio, N., Ucelli Gnesutta, P., Poggiani Keller, P. & Figura, P. 1979. 'I centri protourbani del Bronzo Finale nella valle del fiume Fiora', *Atti XXI Riunione Scientifica dell'Istituto Italiano di Preistoria e Protostoria,* Firenze, 321–381.
Negroni Catacchio, N. & Domanico, L. 1989. 'I modelli abitativi

dell'Etruria preistorica', *Atti del Simposio Internazionale. I modelli insediativi dell'età del Bronzo*, (Cavriana, ottobre 1986), Annali Benacensi IX, 1988, 515-585.

Pasqui, A. & Bernabei, F. 1894. 'Degli scavi di antichità nel territorio falisco', *Monumenti Antichi Lincei,* IV, 5-588.

Peroni, R. 1960. 'Allumiere. Scavo di tombe in località "La Pozza"', *Notizie degli Scavi di Antichità,* XVI, 341-362.

Poggiani Keller, R. 1988. 'Una tomba del Bronzo Finale da Cavallini del Bufalo (Manciano-GR)', in *Catalogo Manciano*, 195-196.

Prospettive 1987. *Prospettive storico-antropologiche in archeologia preistorica*, (a cura di Bergonzi, G., Bietti Sestieri, A.M. & Cazzella, A.), Roma.

Raddatz, K. 1975. *Bisenzio I. Beobachtugen auf einem eisenzeitlich-frühetruskichen Siedlungskomplex, in Hamburgen Beiträge zur Archäologie* V.

Rittatore Vonwiller, F. 1967. 'Necropoli di età eneolitica e protovillanoviana della vallata del Fiora', *Studi Etruschi,* XXXV, 285-294.

Rittatore Vonwiller, F. 1972. 'Crostoletto di Lamone ed il megalitismo italiano', *Atti XIV Riunione Scientifica dell'Istituto Italiano di Preistoria e Protostoria*, Firenze, 27-34.

Rittatore Vonwiller, F., Falchetti, F. & Negroni Catacchio, N. 1977. 'Preistoria e protostoria della valle del fiume Fiora', *Atti X Convegno di Studi Etruschi*, Firenze, 99-195.

Scriattoli, 1920. *Viterbo e i suoi monumenti*, Viterbo.

Sorgenti della Nova 1981. *Sorgenti della Nova. Una comunità protostorica e il suo territorio nell'Etruria meridionale*, (a cura di N. Negroni Catacchio), CNR, Roma.

Toti, O. 1959. *I Monti Ceriti nell'età del Ferro*, Civitavecchia.

Toti, O., Caloi, L., Palombo, M.R., Maffei, A. & Conti, M. 1987, *La "Civiltà Protovillanoviana" dei Monti della Tolfa*, Civitavecchia.

Vianello Cordova, A. P. 1967. 'Una tomba protovillanoviana a Veio', *Studi Etruschi,* XXXV, 295-306.

Vighi, R. 1955. 'Caere II. Il sepolcreto arcaico del Sorbo', *Monumenti Antichi Lincei,* XLII, 24-199.

11

Analisi delle Strutture Tombali in Etruria nell'Età del Ferro: Le Tombe ad Incinerazione

Massimo Cardosa
(Centro Studi Preistoria e Archeologia – Milano)

Sommario: *Si delinea in questa sede una tipologia delle tombe ad incinerazione attestate in Etruria durante il periodo villanoviano, con particolare attenzione al centro di Veio, la cui articolazione cronologica interna a questa fase culturale è meglio conosciuta e studiata. Si cerca quindi di leggerne le caratteristiche sia in chiave cronologica che geografica, individuando delle linee evolutive costanti che legano senza soluzione di continuità il Bronzo Finale all'epoca storica.*

Un'analisi approfondita di questo particolare aspetto della cultura villanoviana trova, purtroppo, notevoli ostacoli in una serie di fattori negativi; oltre alla completa mancanza di un'edizione moderna, di numerosi importanti complessi dell'età del Ferro (come le necropoli di Vetulonia, Chiusi e Populonia), è infatti da lamentare, prima di tutto, la sommarietà con cui viene spesso descritta la struttura tombale, e, in secondo luogo, l'eccezionalità di pubblicazioni che coniughino la completezza dei dati di scavo con l'attendibilità delle seriazioni cronologiche, unico fattore che può permettere il superamento di una semplice analisi tipologica generica. L'eccezione, da questo punto di vista, è costituita da Veio, dove per la necropoli di Quattro Fontanili abbiamo la descrizione completa e precisa delle strutture e più studi sulla suddivisione in fasi cronologiche dei corredi. In questa sede, a causa della vastità della materia, ci si limiterà a proporre una classificazione degli elementi che costituiscono la struttura tombale, e a delineare un catalogo delle tombe ad incinerazione note in Etruria databili all'età del Ferro. In alcuni casi, per completezza di analisi tipologica, il limite cronologico inferiore della ricerca è stato superato, includendo tombe che, pur essendo databili tra la fine dell'VIII e l'inizio del VII sec. a.C., s'inquadrano perfettamente, concludendole, nelle linee evolutive di cui sono oggetto le strutture in esame durante l'età villanoviana.

Caratteri tipologici

Anche per le tombe dell'età del Ferro si è adottata l'impostazione analitica utilizzata per le sepolture del Bronzo Finale (vedi la relazione di Domanico in questi atti). Nel caso in esame (fig. 2), dal punto di vista degli elementi strutturali, il pozzetto può essere distinto in semplice (S) o doppio (D), circolare (C) o quadrangolare (Q); nel caso in cui sia stato scavato nella terra o in una roccia poco consistente le pareti possono essere rivestite da un paramento di ciottoli o scaglie di pietra (P) o da lastre infisse (L). La base può avere un incasso di profondità variabile per alloggiare il cinerario (I), oppure può esservi posta una pietra di piatto (L). La copertura, se esistente e conservata, consiste in una semplice lastra di pietra (L), talvolta rozzamente arrotondata, o da un blocco lavorato a calotta (C), in certi casi crestato; eccezionalmente è stata riscontrata la presenza di motivi decorativi incisi (per esempio tomba 2 a Puntone al Norcino: Brusadin Laplace 1964: fig. 6a).

Elementi aggiuntivi possono essere considerati la realizzazione nella parete del pozzetto (di quello superiore se doppio) di una nicchia per ospitare il corredo (N), e la presenza occasionale a protezione del cinerario di un dolio (D) o di una custodia di tufo, solitamente cilindrica (C), in pochi casi quadrangolare (Q), ovoidale (O), o sferoidale (S). All'esterno può essere presente un segnacolo, consistente in una lastra di pietra infissa (L), un grosso ciottolo (T), o un cippo lavorato (P).

Ciascuno di questi elementi caratteristici si combina con gli altri in un numero di associazioni potenzialmente vastissimo, con conseguente difficoltà nel delineare una tipologia senza cadere in una eccessiva parcellizzazione dei dati. In questo studio ci si limiterà alla segnalazione della presenza dei singoli elementi nei diversi siti funerari, alla distribuzione e all'esame sommario delle associazioni più significative di alcuni di questi, rimandando una trattazione più completa ad altra sede.

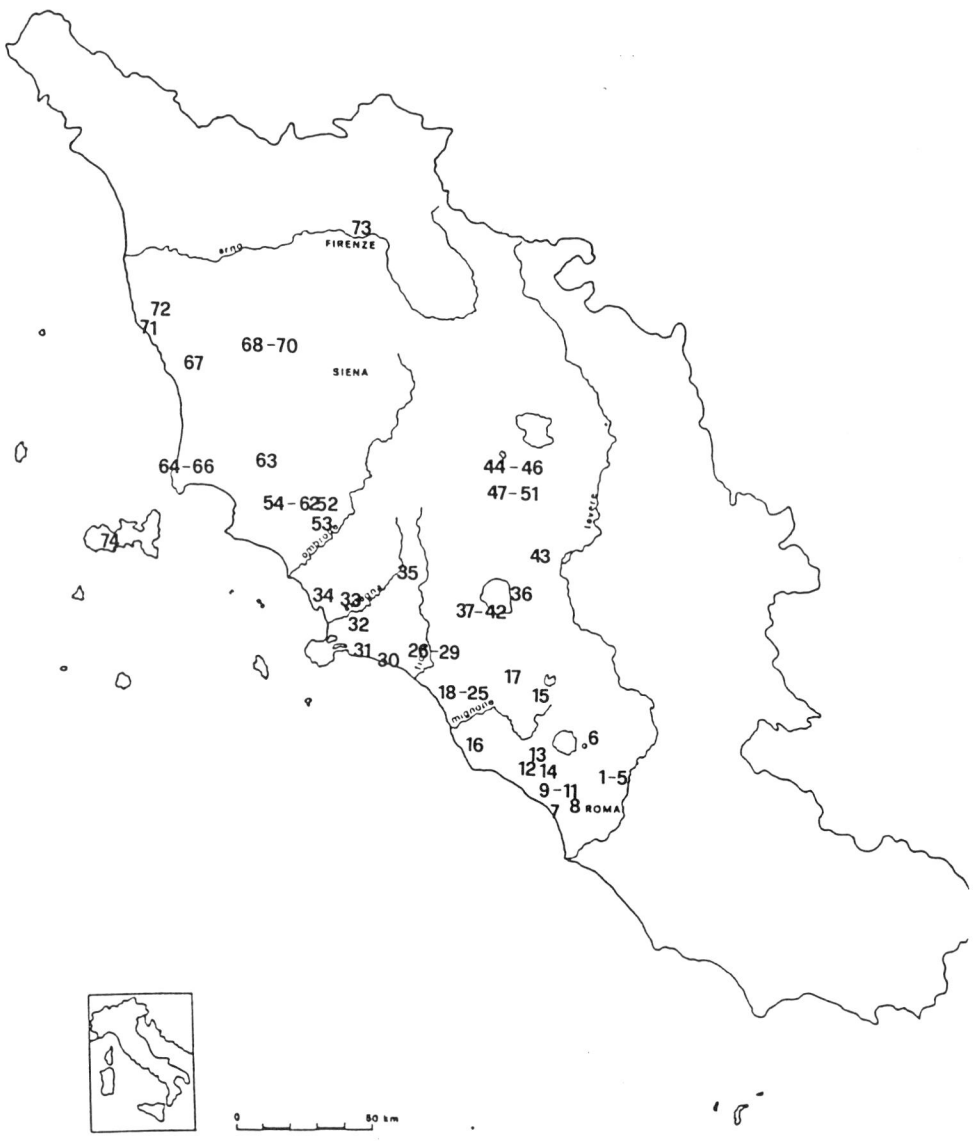

Fig. 1. Siti con tombe ad incinerazione.

Elenco delle necropoli ad incinerazione dell'età del Ferro in Etruria

1) *Veio – Quattro Fontanili*
Necropoli costituita da 651 tombe ad incinerazione ed inumazione databili alla prima e alla seconda età del Ferro (da Veio IB a Veio IIC – per i particolari v. *infra*).
Bibl. Toms 1986

2) *Veio – Valle La Fata*
Necropoli costituita da 4 tombe ad inumazione e 33 ad incinerazione databili alla prima e alla seconda fase iniziale dell'età del Ferro (da Veio IA a Veio IIA). 23 sono a pozzetto semplice (15 con custodia di tufo), 8 con pozzetto rivestito da scaglie di tufo (5 con custodia).
Bibl. Bartoloni Delpino 1979

3) *Veio – Casale del Fosso*
Necropoli costituita quasi esclusivamente da tombe ad inumazione, datata a partire da Veio IIB, all'interno della quale sono presenti due pozzetti semplici (t. 931 e 1094 -Veio IIA-) e quattro pozzi con custodia di tufo (t. 958, 969, 968 – Veio IB-IIA -, 1093 – Veio IB), oltre a pochi pozzetti e fosse con dolio (Veio IIB).
Bibl. Vianello Cordova 1967, p. 297

4) *Veio – Grotta Gramiccia*
Necropoli villanoviana costituita da nuclei sepolcrali distinti.
Bibl. Perkins 1961, p. 90

5) *Veio – Vaccareccia*
Necropoli villanoviana.
Bibl. Perkins 1961, p. 90

6) *Monte S. Angelo*
Piccolo nucleo sepolcrale che ha restituito 7 tombe ad incinerazione intatte e la traccia di numerosi pozzetti.
Bibl. Cozza Pasqui 1894, col. 70–87; di Gennaro 1986, p. 142

7) *Monteroni*
Notizia di materiali provenienti da contesti funerari della prima età del Ferro, raccolti nei pressi di Ladispoli, nella zona dei Monteroni.
Bibl. di Gennaro 1986, p. 140

8) *Palidoro (?)*
Probabile sepoltura sconvolta della prima età del Ferro.
Bibl. Peroni 1965; di Gennaro 1986, p.140

9) *Cerveteri – Cava della Pozzolana*
Necropoli villanoviana.
Bibl. di Genaro 1986, p. 137–138

10) *Cerveteri – Il Sorbo*
Necropoli costituita da 450 tombe, di cui 231 ad incinerazione e 219 ad inumazione, databili a tutto l'arco dell'età del Ferro. 123 sono a pozzetto semplice, di cui 22 con custodia, 35 con pietra di base per l'ossuario e 1 con incasso sul fondo; 106 sono a pozzetto doppio, di cui 1 con custodia e 43 con pietra di base.
Bibl. Vighi 1955; Pohl 1972

11) *Cerveteri – Monte Abbadoncino*
Sepolcreto villanoviano.
Bibl. di Gennaro 1986, p. 137–138

12) *Montetosto Alto*
Necropoli della prima età del Ferro sconvolta dai lavori agricoli, forse originariamente costituita da circa un centinaio di tombe.
Bibl. di Gennaro 1986, p. 139

13) *Puntone all'Oliveto*
Necropoli ad incinerazione sconvolta dai lavori agricoli, datata al Bronzo Finale e alla prima età del Ferro.
Bibl. Brusadin Laplace 1964, p. 175–178; di Gennaro 1986, p.91 e 139

14) *Puntone al Norcino*
Nell'ambito della necropoli del Bronzo Finale, alcune sepolture sono ancora databili alla prima età del Ferro (tombe 2, 3, 15).
Bibl. Brusadin Laplace 1964; di Gennaro 1986, p. 90 e 139

15) *Chiusa Cima*
Necropoli costituita da 32 pozzetti di incinerati 'senza custodia' e due fosse di inumati.
Bibl. Colonna 1967, p. 4 e tav. I

16) *La Mattonara*
Piccolo nucleo sepolcrale costituito da 4 tombe a pozzetto, violato in antico, di cui almeno una con dolio, coperte probabilmente da un tumulo di terra e databili alla seconda età del Ferro. Nell'area circostante sono state individuate tracce di altri pozzetti quasi completamente cancellati dall'erosione naturale.
Bibl. Barbaranelli 1956, p. 472–475; Guidi 1980, p.36

17) *Poggio Montano*
Necropoli costituita da 59 tombe di varia tipologia (a pozzetto, a fossa, a grotticella con corridoio e a camera) databile a partire dalla seconda età del Ferro. 9 sono le tombe ad incinerazione.
Bibl. Colini Rossi Danielli 1914; Colonna 1967, p.3–4; Cristofani Martelli 1971; Emiliozzi 1974, p. 29 -38; Guidi 1980, p. 35–36

18) *Tarquinia – Monterozzi (Poggio delle Arcatelle)*
Principale delle necropoli di Tarquinia, il cui nucleo centrale è costituito da tombe ad incinerazione. Circa 300 le sepolture individuate.
Bibl. Hencken 1968, p. 19–23

19) *Tarquinia – Poggio di Selciatello*
Nucleo sepolcrale costituito da 78 tombe, tutte ad incinerazione, 25 delle quali con custodia di tufo (1 rettangolare).
Bibl. Hencken 1968, p. 24

20) *Tarquinia – Poggio di Selciatello di Sopra*
Necropoli costituita da 204 tombe di cui una sola ad inumazione. 183 sono le tombe in pozzetto doppio, 19 quelle con custodia di tufo, 2 con dolio.
Bibl. Hencken 1968, p. 24

21) *Tarquinia – Poggio dell'Impiccato*
Necropoli costituita da 110 tombe. 28 in custodia di tufo, 3 in dolio.
Bibl. Hencken 1968, p. 24–25

22) *Tarquinia – Poggio Gallinaro*
Piccolo nucleo di tombe, delle quali alcune ad incinerazione.
Bibl. Hencken 1968, p. 25

23) *Tarquinia – Quarto degli Archi*
Tomba a pozzetto.
Bibl. Hencken 1968, p. 285

24) *Tarquinia – Le Rose*
Nucleo sepolcrale costituito da 69 tombe, 6 ad inumazione, 63 ad incinerazione. Di queste 15 con custodia di tufo.
Bibl. Moretti 1959; Hencken 1968, p. 424

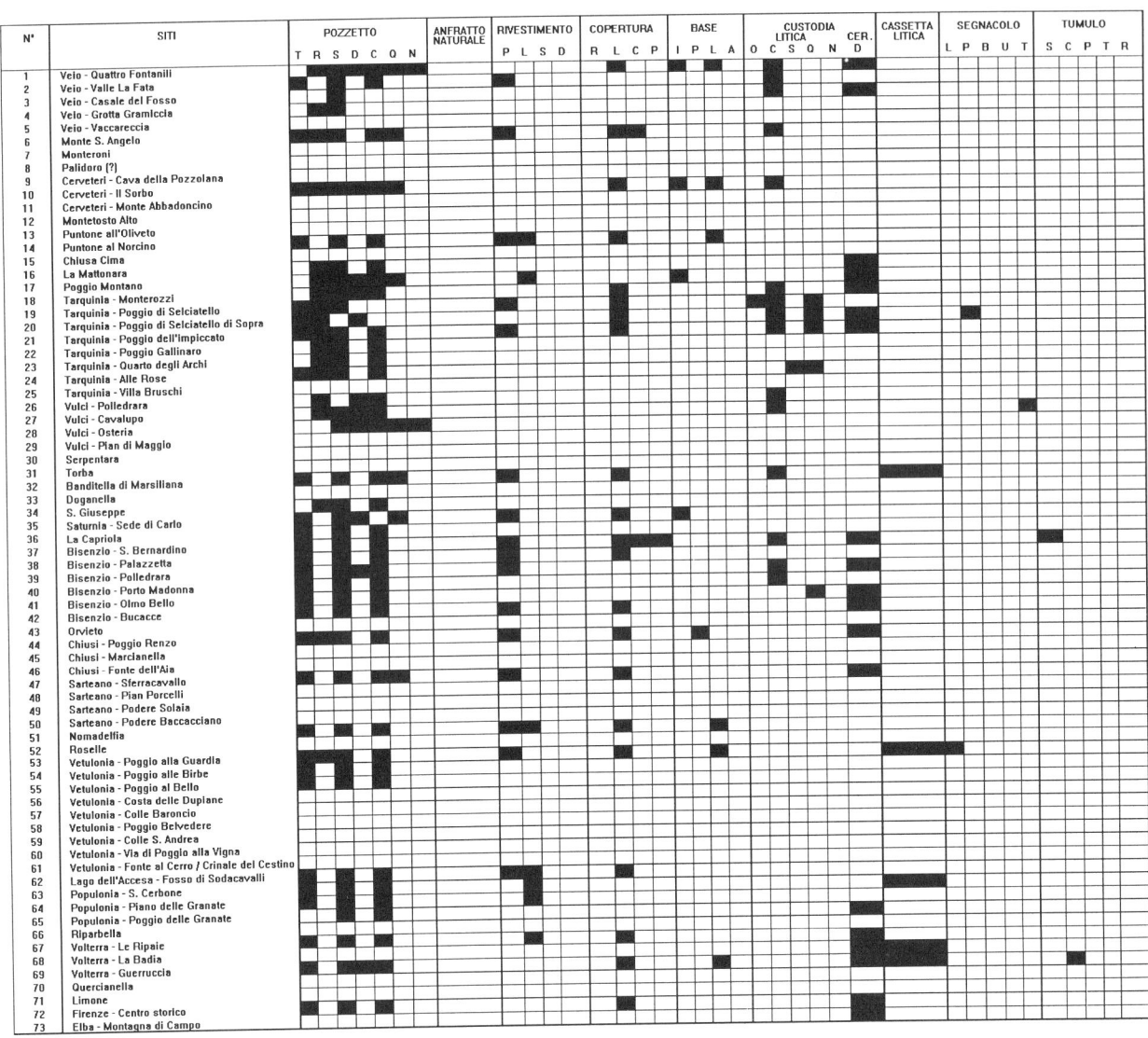

Fig. 2. Elementi caratterizzanti delle strutture tombali attestati nei diversi siti.

25) *Tarquinia – Villa Bruschi*
Recuperate due urne cinerarie sporadiche.
Bibl. Moretti 1959

26) *Vulci – Polledrara (Sopra Castellina, Sopra Longarina, Tomba del Trono)*
Necropoli scvata tumultuosamente soprattutto nel secolo scorso. Si ha notizia di 30 o 40 tombe a pozzetto, forse qualcuna con custodia di tufo.
Bibl. Helbig 1883, p. 168–170; Gsell 1891 p. 249, n. 2.

27) *Vulci – Cavalupo (Mandrione del Cavalupo e Ponte Rotto)*
Settore settentrionale della necropoli orientale di Vulci, costituita da numerosi nuclei sepolcrali, per lo più esplorati disordinatamente o vittime di scavi clandestini. Tre di essi sono stati esplorati dallo Gsell: il primo era costituito da due gruppi di tombe, uno, indicato da un rozzo segnacolo, di 6 tombe a pozzetto semplice, l'altro di tre tombe in custodia di tufo e 1 a pozzetto doppio. Il secondo nucleo era invece costituito da tre gruppi di tombe a pozzetto semplice comprendenti, rispettivamente, 3, 6 e 7 sepolture; quest'ultimo gruppo era fornito di un segnacolo di forma cubica. Nel terzo furono identificate 17 tombe a pozzetto doppio e 1 in custodia di tufo. In epoca più recente da ricordare il recupero della tomba dei bronzetti sardi, in custodia di tufo.
Bibl. Gsell 1891, p. 219–231; Colonna 1977, p. 194 n. 15; Falconi Amorelli 1966

28) *Vulci – Osteria (La Cantina, Marrucatello, Doganella, Poggio Mengarelli e Casal di Lanza)*
Necropoli settentrionale della città di Vulci, sede di numerosi nuclei sepolcrali di età villanoviana, per lo più oggetto di scavi inediti o interventi di recupero della Soprintendenza Archeologica dell'Etruria Meridionale. Questi ultimi hanno portato all'identificazione di almeno

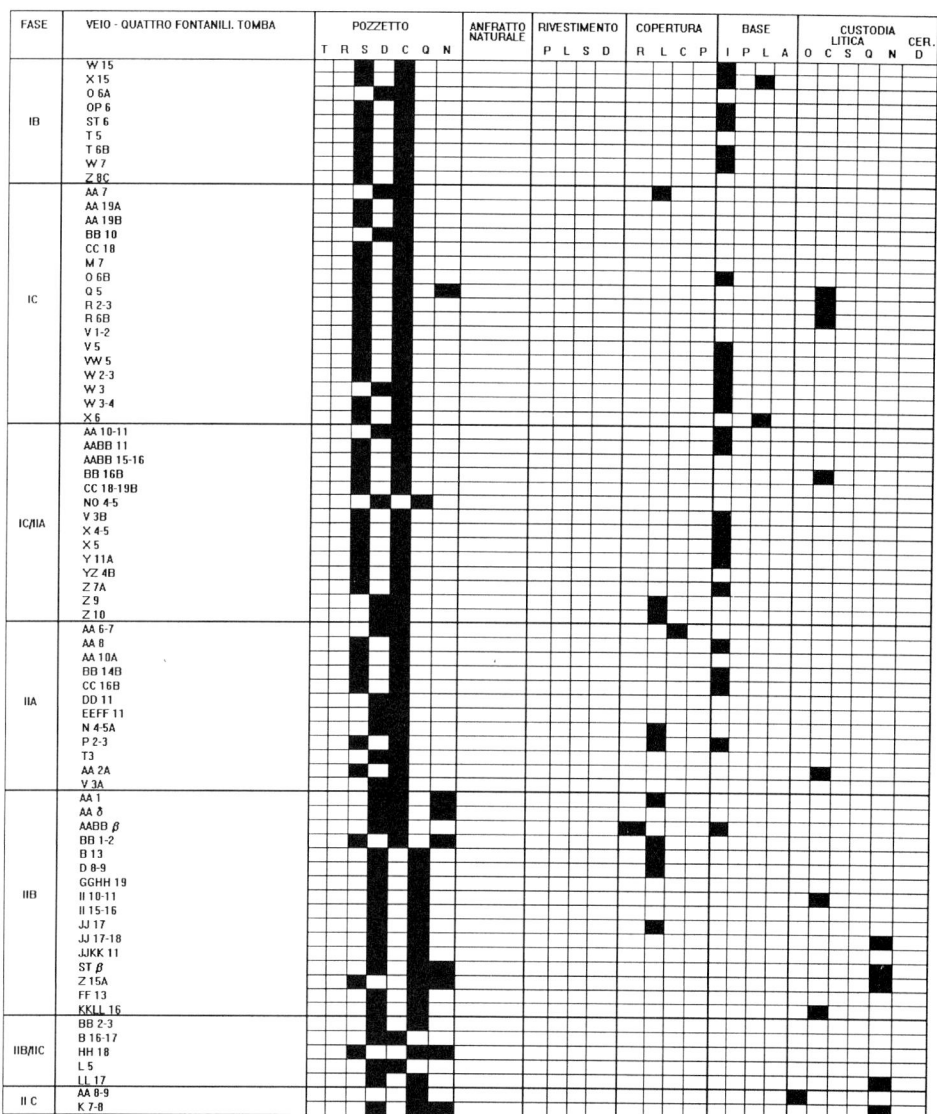

Fig. 3. Elementi caratterizzanti delle tombe ad incinerazione databili con precisione nella necropoli di Veio – Quattro Fontanili.

98 tombe villanoviane, di cui 10 a inumazione, 79 a pozzetto (32 databili alla prima età del Ferro, 25 alla seconda), 2 a pozzetto quadrato, 6 a fossa con incinerazione.
Bibl. Ricciardi 1989

29) *Vulci – Pian di Maggio*
Segnalata la presenza di tombe a pozzetto.
Bibl. Massabò 1979, p. 144

30) *Serpentara*
Resti di una necropoli dell'età del Ferro profondamente sconvolta dalle arature individuata durante la ricognizione della Valle dell'Albegna. In particolare è stata segnalata la presenza di una grossa lastra di scisto, alcune fibule e vari frammenti ceramici d'impasto villanoviani, fra cui urne con resti di ceneri. A questa stessa area probabilmente sono da riportare le notizie riguardanti una necropoli ad incinerazione che sarebbe stata individuata in passato "presso il Chiarone".
Bibl. Santangelo 1954, p. 28 e 53; Cardosa c.s.

31) *Torba*
E' segnalato il rinvenimento casuale di alcuni ossuari fittili con materiale vario "di corredo protoetrusco". Allo stesso complesso è probabilmente da riportare una tomba della seconda fase iniziale dell'età del Ferro citata da M. Cristofani.
Bibl. *SE* XXVII 1960, p. 439; Cristofani 1977, p. 240; Celuzza Regoli 1982, p. 34

32) *Marsiliana – Banditella*
Nella vasta necropoli di epoca orientalizzante pertinente all'abitato etrusco di Marsiliana, sono presenti alcune tombe ad incinerazione che sembrano poter essere datate ancora alla tarda età del Ferro. In particolare sono da ricordare la tomba XXXIII, con urna in custodia di

tufo, la XXXVI, l'unica con urna biconica anzichè ovoide, e corredo comprendente due rasoi, la LXXXIX, con ossuario biconico bronzeo e ancora un rasoio lunato tipo 'Marsiliana d'Albegna' che trova confronti nella fase II B di Tarquinia, da datarsi quindi alla seconda metà dell'VIII sec. a.C.
Bibl. Minto 1921; Cristofani 1977 p. 240-243; Peroni Bianco 1979, p.152; Cristofani & Michelucci 1981, p. 97-98

33) *Doganella*
In un campo arato individuati i probabili resti di una tomba ad incinerazione della quale è stato possibile recuperare solo una ciotola monoansata databile alla tarda età del Ferro.
Bibl. Michelucci 1982, p. 381

34) *S. Giuseppe*
Durante i lavori di bonifica dalla piana di Talamone, nel 1915-1916, sono andati distrutti i resti di almeno 3 sepolture ad incinerazione, costituite da altrettante urne biconiche (di cui almeno una decorata) con ciotola-coperchio, collocate in pozzetti scavati nella roccia. Alcuni sopralluoghi in epoca recente hanno dato esito negativo.
Bibl. Galli 1927, p. 8-9; Cristofani 1977, p. 249; Attolini *et alii* 1983, p. 441

35) *Saturnia – Sede di Carlo*
Nella necropoli pertinente all'insediamento etrusco di Saturnia, sono presenti alcune tombe ad incinerazione che hanno restituito ossuari biconici con coperchio a calotta convessa sormontata da un'espansione globulare collocabili cronologicamente tra la fine dell'VIII sec. e l'inizio del VII.
Bibl. Minto 1925, col. 629-633; Donati 1982

36) *La Capriola*
Necropoli costituita da 28 tombe. alcune delle quali ad incinerazione, databili alla seconda età del Ferro.
Bibl. Bloch 1963, p. 404-411; Colonna 1967, p. 5-6

37) *Bisenzio – S. Bernardino*
Necropoli posta all'interno di un ripiano rettangolare esteso per 150 mq, ricavato artificialmente scavando il terreno vergine per circa 80 cm, e costituita da 90 tombe, 39 ad inumazione, 51 ad incinerazione. Di queste 22 sono a pozzetto semplice (in 14 casi rivestito), 27 in custodia di tufo (in 5 casi con pozzetto rivestito), 2 a dolio; rinvenuti anche due rozzi segnacoli di pietra e una stele a forma di capanna. Individuata, infine, una grande fossa piena di ceneri, interpretata come fossa comune, e un'area circolare rialzata delimitata da una fila di grosse pietre dove probabilmente avveniva la cremazione dei corpi prima della sepoltura.
Bibl. Pasqui 1886, p. 177-205

38) *Bisenzio – Palazzetta*
Nucleo sepolcrale di epoca tardo-villanoviana, costituito da circa 30 tombe ad inumazione distribuite su tre livelli. In corrrispondenza di quello inferiore erano presenti anche 10 tombe di incinerati con urna in pozzetto rivestito da un paramento di piccole scaglie di pietra e chiuso da un 'coperchio' di tufo o nenfro.
Bibl. Pasqui 1986, p. 143-152

39) *Bisenzio – Polledrara*
Necropoli costituita da 34 tombe, 6 ad inumazione, 28 ad incinerazione. Di queste 2 sono in pozzetto semplice, 15 in pozzetto rivestito con un paramento di scaglie di pietra, 9 con custodia di tufo, 2 in dolio.
Bibl.Pasqui 1886, p. 177-205

40) *Bisenzio – Porto Madonna*
Necropoli ad incinerazione costituita da almeno 13 tombe a pozzetto con urna e corredo collocati entro custodia di tufo.
Bibl. Milani 1894, p. 123-141

41) *Bisenzio – Olmo Bello*
Nucleo sepolcrale che ha restituito 9 tombe a inumazione e 4 ad incinerazione, di cui 1 in pozzetto semplice, 1 in custodia di tufo e 2 in dolio.
Bibl. Paribeni 1928, p. 434-437

42) *Bisenzio – Bucacce*
Nucleo sepolcrale costituito da 10 tombe, tre ad incinerazione in pozzetto, di cui una a dolio, 6 ad inumazione.
Bibl. Galli 1912

43) *Orvieto*
Al Museo Archeologico di Firenze e al Museo Faina di Orvieto sono presenti alcuni ossuari biconici di sicura provenienza orvietana, indici dell'esistenza nei pressi della città, di tombe ad incinerazione. Notizie del rinvenimento nel XVI sec. di "un gruppo di vasi con resti di ossa e oggetti di Ferro e di rame" sono state interpretate come indici dell'esistenza di "tombe villanoviane in grotta".
Bibl. di Gennaro 1990, p. 32 con bibliografia precedente

44) *Chiusi – Poggio Renzo*
Si tratta della principale e più antica necropoli dell'età del Ferro di Chiusi, composta da tombe a pozzetto e a dolio.
Bibl. Bertrand 1874; Bianchi Bandinelli 1925, col. 440-442

45) *Chiusi – Marcianella*
Segnalata la presenza di tombe a pozzetto e a dolio.
Bibl. Bianchi Bandinelli 1925, col. 440-441

46) *Chiusi – Fonte dell'Aia*
Segnalata la presenza di tombe a pozzetto e a dolio.
Bibl. Bianchi Bandinelli 1925, col. 440

47) *Sarteano – Sferracavallo*
Necropoli ad incinerazione costituita da oltre 200 pozzetti, la maggioranza "di tipo villanoviano", una dozzina a ziro.
Bibl. Bianchi Bandinelli 1925, col 383–388; 440 e 442

48) *Sarteano – Pian Porcelli (o Piamporcelli)*
Tombe a pozzetto villanoviane e a ziro.
Bibl. Bianchi Bandinelli 1927, p. 7

49) *Sarteano – Podere Solaia / Albinaia*
Necropoli 'villanoviana' di tombe a pozzetto e a dolio.
Bibl. Bianchi Bandinelli 1927, p. 5–6

51) *Sarteano – Podere Baccacciano*
Tombe a pozzetto di tipo villanoviano.
Bibl. Bianchi Bandinelli 1927, p. 7

52) *Nomadelfia*
Piccola necropoli ad incinerazione databile alla prima età del Ferro profondamente danneggiata dai lavori agricoli.
Bibl. Laviosa 1969, p. 607–609; Bergonzi 1973, p. 5–13

53) *Roselle*
Al Museo Archeologico di Grosseto è conservata un'urna cineraria con indicazione di provenienza "Roselle" senza più precise indicazioni. Segnalata la presenza di tombe a pozzetto sul versante orientale del colle dove sorge la città.
Bibl. *L'età del Ferro nell'Etruria Marittima*, p. 37–38; Mazzolai 1977, p. 43 e fig. 8

54) *Vetulonia – Poggio alla Guardia*
E' la più estesa delle necropoli villanoviane di Vetulonia, costituita esclusivamente da tombe a pozzetto. Sono segnalate almeno 1000 sepolture databili alla prima e alla seconda età del Ferro. Ad una fase tarda di quest'ultima sono databili i cosiddetti 'ripostigli stranieri', tombe ad incinerazione senza cinerario, e i 'circoli interrotti', circoli di pietre infisse che circondano gruppi di tombe ad incinerazione.
Bibl. Falchi 1891, p. 31–56; Levi 1931, p. 22

55) *Vetulonia – Poggio alle Birbe*
Nucleo sepolcrale costituito da 34 tombe, 3 ad inumazione, 31 ad incinerazione in pozzetto.
Bibl. Falchi 1891, p. 56–59

56) *Vetulonia – Poggio al Bello*
Necropoli di tombe a pozzetto contigua a quella di Poggio alla Guardia.
Bibl. Levi 1931, p. 24

57) *Vetulonia – Costa delle Dupiane*
Necropoli che ha restituito anche un nucleo di tombe ad incinerazione in cattivo stato di conservazione. Riconosciute almeno 16 tombe (scavi Falchi).
Bibl. Falchi 1891, p. 59–63

58) *Vetulonia – Colle Baroncio*
Necropoli contigua alla precedente, costituita da 700 tombe a pozzetto e a fossa.
Bibl. Falchi 1891, p. 63–67

59) *Vetulonia – Poggio Belvedere*
Necropoli costituita da 93 tombe a pozzetto molto rovinati.
Bibl. Levi 1931, p. 25

60) *Vetulonia – Colle S. Andrea*
Gruppo di pozzetti rinvenuti vuoti, probabilmente resti di tombe.
Bibl. Levi 1931, p. 34

61) *Vetulonia – Via di Poggio alla Vigna / Strada del Casino*
Tombe a pozzetto isolate.
Bibl. Levi 1931, p. 35

62) *Vetulonia – Crinale del Cestino / Fonte al Cerro*
Notizie del rinvenimento di urne cinerarie villanoviane.
Bibl. Levi 1931, p.35–36

63) *Lago dell'Accesa – Fosso di Sodacavalli*
Nucleo sepolcrale del quale fanno parte 14 tombe a pozzetto.
Bibl. Levi 1933

64) *Populonia – San Cerbone*
Nella principale necropoli dell'abitato di Populonia, un gruppo di tombe è attribuibile già all'età del Ferro. Fra queste 11 sono ad incinerazione, 5 a pozzetto semplice, senza rivestimento nè lastra di copertura, 2 a pozzetto con massicciata di sassi sul fondo, e 4 in cassetta litica.
Bibl. Minto 1922, p. 16–21

65) *Populonia – Piano delle Granate*
Gruppo di tombe villanoviane ad inumazione ed incinerazione, piuttosto sconvolte a causa degli agenti naturali. Sono riconoscibili almeno 3 pozzetti semplici e 2 rivestiti.
Bibl. Minto 1922, p. 60–69

66) *Populonia – Poggio delle Granate*
Gruppo di tombe ad incinerazione distrutto dall'azione dell'erosione naturale.
Bibl. Minto 1922, p. 70–71

67) *Riparbella*
Sono segnalati materiali della prima età del Ferro provenienti da contesti funerari.
Bibl. Delpino 1981, p. 269

68) *Volterra – Le Ripaie*
Necropoli della prima età del Ferro costituita da almeno 22 tombe ad incinerazione, di cui almeno 11 in pozzetto semplice, alcuni in pozzetto rivestito con segnacolo di copertura, e 3 a dolio.
Bibl. Cateni 1981

69) *Volterra – La Badia*
Tomba a cassetta di grandi lastre ben squadrate con sepoltura in dolio.
Bibl. Ghirardini 1898, col. 101-112

70) *Volterra – Guerruccia*
Necropoli ad inumazione ed incinerazione posta sul margine delle balze di S. Giusto, databile a partire dalla prima età del Ferro fino al VII sec. a.C. Scavi della fine del secolo scorso hanno portato all'identificazione di 5 tombe a dolio, 2 a pozzetto quadrato con rivestimento di lastre (1 con dolio), 1 a pozzetto semplice, 2 a pozzetto doppio (con dolio).
Bibl. Ghirardini 1898, col. 117-204

71) *Quercianella*
Dalla località 'Cimitero', nei pressi di Quercianella, provengono alcuni cinerari databili alla prima età del Ferro, rinvenuti "circondati da pietre", forse indice dell'esistenza di pozzetti rivestiti.
Bibl. Mantovani 1884; Delpino 1981, p. 268

72) *Limone*
Da questa località sono noti materiali di corredi funerari smembrati di una fase avanzata della prima età del Ferro.
Bibl. Delpino 1981, p. 268

73) *Firenze – Centro*
E' indice dell'esistenza nel centro di Firenze di una necropoli villanoviana il rinvenimento di 6 sepolture ad incinerazione, di cui 4 a dolio e una in pozzetto semplice.
Bibl. Milani 1896

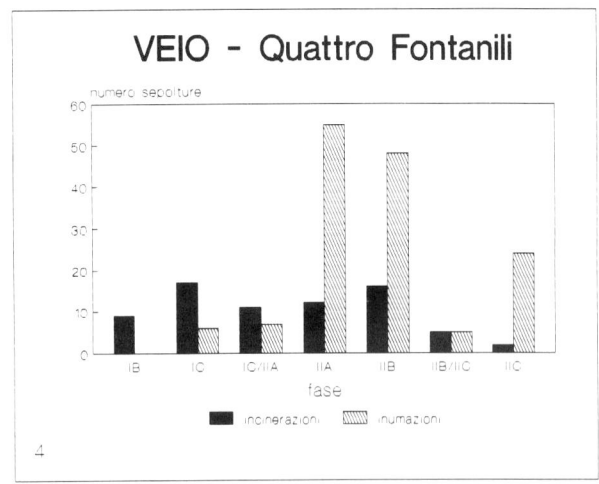

Fig. 4. Presenza di incinerazione e inumazione nella necropoli di Veio – Quattro Fontanili.

74) *Elba – Montagna di Campo (?)*
Rinvenimento di dubbia interpretazione, da alcuni inteso come ripostiglio, da altri come tomba a dolio. La tipologia degli oggetti che lo compongono, attribuibili alla prima età del Ferro, farebbero però pensare alla seconda soluzione.
Bibl. Delpino 1981, p. 272

LE TRASFORMAZIONI NEL TEMPO.
VEIO – QUATTRO FONTANILI

Veio – Quattro Fontanili è l'unico sito che, al momento, per le ragioni già anticipate, permette osservazioni di carattere cronologico a proposito dell'evoluzione delle strutture tombali. La necropoli, utilizzata per tutta l'età del Ferro, conta 169 tombe ad incinerazione su 651 complessive; di queste, 72 sono inquadrabili cronologicamente con precisione (fig. 3). Si può osservare come l'incinerazione sia esclusiva solo fino alla fase IB, nella IC compare l'inumazione in circa 1/4 dei casi (6

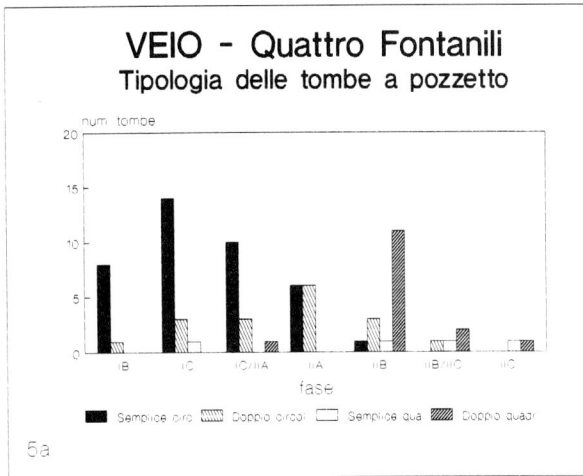
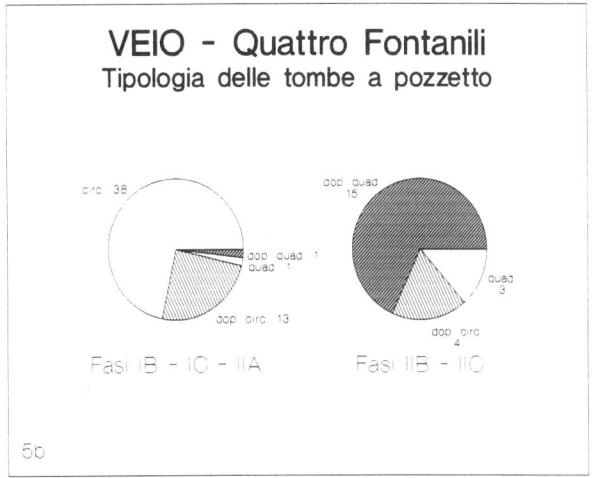

Fig. 5a e 5b. Suddivisione delle tombe a pozzetto per fasi e per forma.

su 23), in IIA e IIB il rapporto si capovolge (rispettivamente solo 12 incinerazioni su 67 sepolture e 16 su 64) e in IIC l'incinerazione è limitata a casi isolati (fig. 4) (vedi Bartoloni 1984).

Per quanto riguarda la tipologia delle strutture, osservazioni interessanti sono possibili considerando la forma del pozzetto (fig. 5). Fino alla fase IIA compresa, è da rilevare una sostanziale omogeneità di situazione, con la netta prevalenza del pozzetto circolare semplice, e la crescente attestazione del pozzetto circolare doppio (ma cfr. Toms 1986: 44, 47). Con la fase IIB si assiste invece ad una profonda trasformazione: il pozzetto circolare semplice scompare, la maggioranza delle tombe ad incinerazione è a pozzetto doppio quadrangolare, con spesso una nicchia per il corredo e/o un dolio a protezione del cinerario; a sottolineare l'appartenenza di questo elemento ad una fase tarda dell'evoluzione della tomba ad incinerazione, basti ricordare che la tomba a dolio (o 'a ziro' secondo la vecchia terminologia) è quella caratteristica di Chiusi arcaica, uno dei rari siti in cui l'incinerazione rimane pressochè esclusiva anche nelle fasi successive all'età del Ferro. La presenza di una custodia di tufo, invece, attestata in tutte le fasi, sembra non avere alcuna valenza cronologica.

LE TRASFORMAZIONI NELLO SPAZIO. CONSIDERAZIONI SULLA DISTRIBUZIONE DI ALCUNI CARATTERI TIPOLOGICI

Una caratteristica interessante della necropoli Di Quattro Fontanili è la diffusione dei pozzetti con incasso sul fondo (circa 1/3 dei casi, 59 su 169). Questo tipo di tomba (fig. 2) è diffuso nelle necropoli falische di Falerii e Narce (l'Agro Falisco per le sue peculiarità è stato escluso da questa indagine), ed è attestato nell'Etruria propria, per quanto è noto, solo nella necropoli del Sorbo di Cerveteri

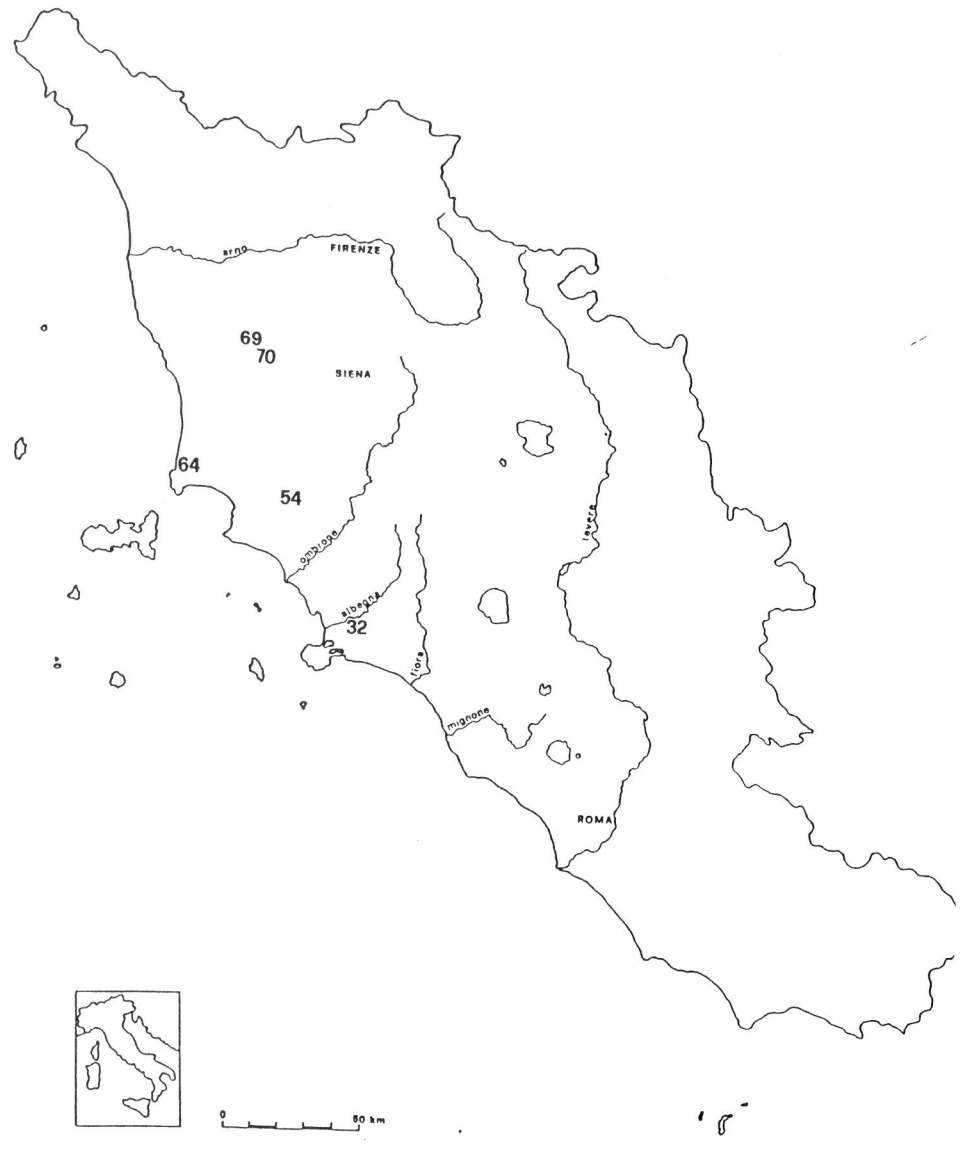

Fig. 6. Distribuzione delle cassette e dei rivestimenti di lastre litiche.

(1 esempio isolato) e in quella tarda di Saturnia – Sede di Carlo. Tale elemento tipologico potrebbe essere quindi da considerare caratteristico dell'area tiberino-falisca; non deve stupire la sua presenza in un centro apparentemente molto lontano come Saturnia, in una zona, quella dell'entroterra vulcente, i cui contatti culturali con l'area tiberino-falisca in età arcaica sono già stati infatti sottolineati in diversi aspetti della cultura materiale (Colonna 1973: 64).

Rimanendo a considerazioni generali, l'elemento che più si presta ad essere discusso è la distribuzione dei pozzetti con rivestimento di lastre litiche e delle cassette (fig. 6), tipologie attestate ampiamente anche nell'Etruria padana. Questi tipi sembrano essere caratteristici dell'Etruria settentrionale con l'unica eccezione del sito di Puntone al Norcino (no.14), nella zona del Sasso, dove però (caso eccezionale) si hanno poche tombe della prima età del Ferro iniziale, all'interno di complessi protovillanoviani. Tenendo conto di ciò e del fatto che, invece, nel Bronzo Finale il tipo è diffuso in tutta l'Etruria, si può forse parlare di una 'regionalizzazione', durante l'età del Ferro, di una tipologia in precedenza ad ampia diffusione, spiegabile con il carattere conservatore di quest'area periferica, noto anche per quanto riguarda i materiali dei corredi: si pensi che a Volterra si trovano ancora cinerari biconici di tipo villanoviano associati a materiali di piena epoca orientalizzante (Fiumi 1961). La distribuzione territoriale della custodia di tufo sembrerebbe, invece, essere legata semplicemente alla disponibilità della materia prima.

Bibliografia

A.A.V.V. 1983 = Attolini *et alii*. 'Ricognizione archeologica dell'Ager Cosanus e della valle dell'Albegna. Rapporto preliminare 1982/83', *Archeologia Medievale*, IX, 439-465.

Barbaranelli, F. 1956. 'Villaggi villanoviani dell'Etruria meridionale marittima', *BPI*, X, 455-489.

Bartoloni, G. 1984. 'Riti funerari dell'aristocrazia in Etruria e nel Lazio, l'esempio di Veio', *Opus* III, 1.

Bartoloni, G. & Delpino, F. 1979. *Introduzione allo studio delle necropoli arcaiche di Veio. Il sepolcreto di Valle la Fata*, (Monumenti Antichi, serie monografica, 1), Roma.

Bergonzi, G. 1973. 'Ricerche protostoriche nei dintorni di Roselle', *Studi Etruschi*, XLI, 3-25.

Bertrand, A. 1874. 'Sepoltures a incineration de Poggio Renzo, près Chiusi', *Revue Archeologique*, 27, 208-222.

Bianchi Bandinelli, R. 1925. 'Clusium. Ricerche archeologiche e topografiche su Chiusi e il suo territorio in età etrusca', *Monumenti Antichi dei Lincei*, XXX, col 210 ss.

Bianchi Bandinelli, R. 1927. *Edizione della carta archeologica d'Italia al 100.000. Foglio 129 (Santa Fiora)*, Firenze.

Bloch, R. 1963. 'Gli scavi della scuola francese a Bolsena', *Studi Etruschi*, XXXI, 399-124.

Brusadin Laplace, D. 1964. 'Le necropoli protostoriche del Sasso di Fubara', *BPI*, XV, 143-186.

Cardosa, M. c.s. 'La valle dell'Albegna nelle ultime fasi della protostoria', in A. Carandini E. Fentress & M.G. Celuzza (a cura di), *Paesaggi dell'Etruria tra l'Albegna e il Fiora dalla Preistoria al Medio Evo. I. La topografia*.

Cateni, G. 1981. 'La necropoli villanoviana delle Ripaie a Volterra', *Atti del XII Convegno di Studi Etruschi e Italici. L'Etruria Mineraria*, Roma, 193-198.

Celuzza, M.G. & Regoli, E. 1982. 'La valle d'Oro nel territorio di Cosa', *Dialoghi di Archeologia*, 31-62.

Colini, G.A. & Rossi Danielli, L. 1914. 'Vetralla – Necropoli di Poggio Montano', *Notizie degli Scavi di Antichità*, 297-362.

Colonna, G. 1967. 'L'Etruria meridionale interna dal villanoviano alle tombe rupestri', *Studi Etruschi*, XXXV, 3-30.

Colonna, G. 1977. 'La presenza di Vulci nelle valli del Fiora e dell'Albegna prima del IV sec.a.C.', *Atti Grosseto*, 189-213.

Cozza, A. & Pasqui, A. 1894. 'Il Monte S. Angelo e la sua necropoli', *Monumenti Antichi dei Lincei*, IV, col. 33-94.

Cristofani Martelli, M. 1971. 'La tomba XXX di Poggio Montano (Vetralla)', *Nuove letture di monumenti etruschi*, Catalogo della mostra, Firenze, 17-23.

Cristofani, M. 1977. 'Problemi poleografici dell'Agro Cosano e Caletrano in età arcaica', *Atti Grosseto*, 235-257.

Cristofani, M. & Michelucci, M. 1981. 'La valle dell'Albegna', in M. Cristofani (a cura di), *Gli Etruschi in Maremma*, Milano, 97-113.

Delpino, F. 1977. 'La prima età del ferro a Bisenzio. Aspetti della cultura villanoviana nell'Etruria meridionale interna', *Memorie dei Lincei*, s. VIII, fasc. 6, 1977, 453-493.

Delpino, F. 1981. 'Aspetti e problemi della prima età del ferro nell'Etruria settentrionale marittima', *Atti del XII Convegno di Studi Etruschi e Italici. L'Etruria Mineraria*, 223-264.

di Gennaro, F. 1986. *Forme di insediamento tra Tevere e Fiora dal Bronzo Finale al principio dell'età del Ferro*, Firenze.

di Gennaro, F. 1990. 'L'età del bronzo e la prima età del ferro a Orvieto. I materiali della Cannicella', in F. Roncalli (a cura di), *Gens antiquissima Italiae. Antichità dell'Umbria in Vaticano*, Perugia.

Donati, L. 1982. 'Un nuovo tipo di coperchio antropoide da Saturnia', *Studi in onore di G. Maetzke*, II, 273-279.

Emiliozzi, A. 1974. *La Collezione Rossi Danielli nel Museo Civico di Viterbo*, Roma.

Falchi, I. 1891. *Vetulonia e la sua necropoli antichissima*, Firenze.

Falconi Amorelli, M.T. 1966. 'Tomba villanoviana con bronzetto nuragico', *Archeologia Classica*, XVIII, 1-15.

Fiumi, E. 1961. 'La facies arcaica del territorio volterrano', *Studi Etruschi*, XXIX, 253 ss.

Galli, E. 1912. 'Il sepolcreto visentino delle Bucacce', *Monumenti Antichi dei Lincei*, XXI, col. 409-498.

Galli, E. 1927. 'Antiche vestigia nel dominio cosano dei Domizi Ahenobarbi', *Historia* I, 3-57.

Ghirardini, G. 1898. 'La necropoli primitiva di Volterra', *Monumenti Antichi dei Lincei*, VIII, col. 101-216.

Gsell, S. 1891. *Fouilles dans la necropole de Vulci*, Paris.

Guidi, A. 1980. *Studi sulla decorazione metopale nella ceramica villanoviana*, Firenze.

Helbig, W. 1883. 'Scavi di Vulci', *Bullettino Inst*, 161-170.

Hencken, H. 1968. *Tarquinia, Villanovans and Early Etruscans*, Cambridge.

Laviosa, C. 1969. 'Relazione preliminare della settima e della ottava campagna di scavi. Necropoli di Nomadelfia', *Studi Etruschi*, XXXVII, 607-609.

Levi, D. 1931. 'Carta archeologica di Vetulonia', *Studi Etruschi*, V, 13-40.

Mantovani, P. 1884. 'Oggetti del periodo archeologico di villanova trovati a Quercianella presso Livorno', *BPI*, X, 83-95.

Massabò, B. 1979. 'Vulci e il suo territorio in età etrusca e romana', *L'Universo*, LIX, 137-184; 369-400; 489-512.

Mazzolai, A. 1977. *Grosseto. Il Museo Archeologico della Maremma*, Grosseto.

Michelucci, M. 1982. 'Caletra, Kalousion, Heba: indagini sugli insediamenti etruschi nella bassa valle dell'Albegna', *Studi in onore di G. Maetzke*, 377-392.

Milani, L.A. 1894. 'Capodimonte – Nuovi scavi nella necropoli visentina nel comune di Capodimonte sul Lago di Bolsena', *Notizie degli Scavi di Antichità*, 123-141.

Milani, L.A. 1896. 'Reliquie di Firenze antica. I. Le tombe italiche', *Monumenti Antichi dei Lincei*, VI, 7-16.

Minto, A. 1921. *Marsiliana d'Albegna*, Firenze.

Minto, A. 1922. *Populonia. La necropoli arcaica*, Firenze.

Minto, A. 1925. 'Saturnia etrusca e romana', *Monumenti Antichi dei Lincei*, XXX, col. 586-702.

Moretti, M. 1959. 'Tarquinia – La necropoli villanoviana "alle Rose"', *Notizie degli Scavi di Antichità*, 112-139

Paribeni, R. 1928. 'Capodimonte – Ritrovamento di tombe arcaiche', *Notizie degli Scavi di Antichità*, 434-467.

Pasqui, A. 1886. 'Bisenzio. Scoperte della necropoli bisentina', *Notizie degli Scavi di Antichità*, 143-151; 177-205; 290-314.

Peroni, R. 1965. 'Significato degli scavi nel deposito a ceramiche di Palidoro', *Quartenaria*, VII, 309-311.

Peroni Bianco, V. 1979. *I rasoi dell'Italia Continentale, Prähistorische Bronzefunde, VIII Bd 2*, München.

Pohl, I. 1972. 'The Iron Age Necropolis of Sorbo at Cerveteri', *Acta Inst. Rom. R. Sueciae*, XXXII, Roma.

Ricciardi, L. 1989. 'La necropoli settentrionale di Vulci', *BdA*, 58, 27-52.

Santangelo, M. 1954. *L'Antiquarium di Orbetello*, Roma.

Toms, J. 1986. 'The relative chronology of the Villanovan cemetery of Quattro Fontanili at Veii', *AION Arch. Studi Antichi*, VIII, 41-97.

Vianello Cordova, A.P. 1967. 'Una tomba protovillanoviana a Veio', *Studi Etruschi*, XXXV, 295-306.

Vighi, R. 1955. 'Il sepolcreto arcaico del Sorbo', *Monumenti Antichi dei Lincei*, XLII, col. 1-76

Ward-Perkins, J.B. 1961. 'Veii – The historical topography of the ancient city', *Papers of the British School at Rome*, 29, 1-123.

12

Ricerca e Tesaurizzazione delle Offerte negli Edifici Cultuali della Sardegna Nuragica. Nota Preliminare

MARIA AUSILIA FADDA

(Soprintendenza Archeologica per le Provincie di Sassari e Nuoro)

Sommario: *Recenti campagne di scavo condotte nel territorio della provincia di Nuoro (nei Comuni di Orani, Villagrande Strisaili e Fonni) hanno portato alla luce quattro insediamenti di epoca nuragica che conservano fra le strutture di uso abitativo edifici di uso cultuale del tipo a pozzo e a megaron. L'elemento nuovo della ricerca è dato dalla scoperta di alcuni edifici adiacenti ai templi che al loro interno contenevano grandi accumuli di oggetti in bronzo, che ripropongono, per la loro tipologia, stretti contatti con le populazioni Protovillanoviane e Villanoviane della Costa Tirrenica e con il mondo Egeo orientale. Vi sono stati scoperti anche abbondanti materiali fittili e derrate alimentari contenute all'interno di silos e grandi contenitori. Gli scavi hanno inoltre documentato edifici cultuali di tipologia nuova, che un alcuni casi fondono elementi architettonici dei templi a pozzo con quelli a megaron, finora meno conosciuti in tutta la Sardegna.*

INTRODUZIONE

I numerosi luoghi di culto del periodo nuragico hanno sempre destato grande interesse fra gli studiosi. A partire dal 1865, anno della scoperta fortuita dei bronzi votivi nel santuario di Abini (Teti), Spano (1863), Pais (1884), Taramelli (1931), Lilliu (1955–57), hanno dato importanti elementi per la definizione, tipologia e l'inquadramento cronologico dell'architettura religiosa e per la ricostruzione dei riti purificatori ed ordalici. Recentemente, F. Lo Schiavo (1989–90) in uno studio sulle offerte nei templi della Sardegna Nuragica, alla luce dei nuovi dati acquisiti negli ultimi anni, proponeva una distinzione fra i templi riservati a piccole comunità ed i santuari, con architetture diverse da quelle di uso civile, intorno ai quali gravitano diverse comunità. Recenti censimenti nel territorio Nuorese, dell'Ogliastra e della Barbagia, ed una sostenuta opera di tutela volta a frenare il saccheggio dei monumenti hanno portato alla scoperta di diversi luoghi di culto, alcuni dei quali vengono illustrati in questa sede. Nelle schede dei siti di Nurdole (Orani), S'Arcu 'e Is Forros e sa Carceredda (Villagrande Strisaili) viene privilegiata la descrizione dell'architettura poichè per la loro complessità si discostano dalle tipologie più diffuse nella Sardegna. Ampio spazio viene dedicato alla descrizione del deposito archeologico dei vari monumenti in attesa di poter produrre un completo catalogo dei materiali dopo il completamento degli scavi in corso.

ORANI (NUORO) – TEMPIO DI NURDOLE

Cinque campagne di scavo hanno portato alla luce il tempio nuragico di Nurdole posto in cima ad un colle in agro di Orani (Fadda 1986, 1991). Il monumento sebbene sia stato ampiamente descritto in altre sedi necessita di una sintetica descrizione data la complessità dell'architettura e l'eccezionale quantità di materiali in esso rinvenuti.

Su un insediamento di Cultura Monte Claro che si colloca nell'ambito dell'eneolitico Medio della Sardegna, venne edificato, nel bronzo medio, un nuraghe di tipo complesso con una torre centrale e quattro torri ad addizione concentrica intorno al quale gravitano diverse capanne del villaggio (fig. 1.1). Una sorgente che sgorgava nel cortile del nuraghe, nella prima fase edilizia, veniva usata per il normale approvvigionamento dell'abitato. Nella seconda fase edilizia, da collocarsi nel bronzo recente, il nuraghe subì profonde trasformazioni architettoniche e l'acqua della sorgente venne incanalata in una fonte sacra costruita con blocchi di trachite, che veniva trasportata da lontano, perfettamente lavorata (Fadda 1992, 1993).

La fonte, analogamente ad altre di tipo isodomo presenta una copertura ad elementi architravati degradanti inseriti nello spessore murario degli otto filari di conci di trachite che delimitano le pareti laterali della fonte. Dalla fonte provengono diversi spilloni di bronzo infilati fra tre conci della muratura e olle ovoidi a colletto cilindrico con grandi anse a gomito rovesciato, decorate con fili di tacche e punti impressi, che costituiscono le forme tipiche del bronzo recente e finale sardo. Davanti alla fonte un basamento circolare, composto da vari elementi con incastri perfetti in trachite sosteneva una canaletta composta da vari elementi ad incastro che sviluppava una lunghezza di m 5,50 attraverso due ambienti di forma irregolare e conduceva l'acqua della fonte ad una grande piscina posta in un livello più basso di forma rettangolare (6,50 x 7,40 m) realizzata con conci di trachite e tufo ben lavorati e messi in opera con la tecnica dell'incastro alternato ottenuto con i conci a T e a coda (Fadda, Tuveri & Murru 1992).

Nonostante il precedente intervento degli scavatori clandestini che avevano infierito sopratutto sull'architettura, dopo la rimozione dei crolli, intorno alla vasca e nel cortile del nuraghe sono stati rinvenuti numerosissimi basamenti per le offerte in pietra, integre e frammentarie di cui molte conservano i piedi di figurine bronzee fissate con il piombo. Dell'area della vasca proviene un enorme quantità di oggetti votivi in bronzo tra cui spade votive, punte e puntali di lancia, pugnali a lingua da presa e con impugnatura massiccia, stocchi, stiletti e faretre votive. Fra gli oggetti di ornamento di elencano, fibule ad arco ribassato e a sanguisuga, una fibula cipriota (Lo Schiavo 1992) una ad arco serpeggiante, braccialetti, anelli, bottoni riproducenti nuraghi complessi, dischi in lamina bronzea con decorazioni geometriche, pendagli a pendolo, colossali vaghi di ambra circolari e oblunghi con scanalature parallele, di tipo Allumiere, seguono ancora amuleti egittizzanti in pasta silicea, uno scarabeo con castone in argento ed elementi di collana in faiance. Vi erano inoltre navicelle con protome cervina, numerose lamine di calderoni, attacchi a tripla spirale e frammenti di tripode di tipo cipriota. I bronzi figurati rappresentano numerosi guerrieri, offerenti, vasi miniaturistici, fiasche, tori, arieti, volpi, maiali ed un leoncino che trova strettissime analogie con i quattro leoni, di cui uno retrospiciente, applicati lungo il bordo di una phiale mesomphalica in lamina bronzea rinvenuta nella tomba del guerriero della necropoli di Cavalupo in Vulci (Ferragutti 1937). Alcuni offerenti rappresentati in una nudità rituale rimandano a contatti con il mondo orientale. I contatti commerciali con il mondo mediterraneo sono attestati dalla presenza di uno skiphos corinzio e da due brocche in lamina bronzea, delle quali una con orlo trilobato e una con orlo a fungo. Di una terza brocca con protome bovina sul ventre, abbiamo notizie indirette dal mercato clandestino. In prossimità della vasca sono stati esplorati alcuni ambienti che venivano usati come magazzini che contenevano derrate alimentari e materiale bronzeo frammentario, forse destinato alla riutilizzazione. I pithoi di grandi dimensioni erano decorati da motivi svariati a pintadera, da cordoni plastici ornati con tacche oblique o a pizzicato, o da larghe linee verticali e orizzontali impresse con le dita. I numerosi contenitori poggiavano su piani isolati da consistenti strati di argilla sui quali vi erano le impronte e i frammenti di corteccia di sughero usato ugualmente come materiale isolante. All'interno dei pithoi vi erano ancora abbondanti resti di grano, orzo e in piccole quantità fave e veccia. Altri ambienti usati come granai e dei vani privi di accesso usati come silos vennero costruiti nello spazio compreso tra il nuraghe e l'antemurale che conserva sul lato S-E un colossale ingresso architravato incassato tra le rocce affioranti. Anche una torre del lato Sud del nuraghe raggiungibile dal cortile attraverso una scala di 22 gradini, non aveva alcun accesso e veniva utilizzato come depositi di vasi particolarmente curati nell'esecuzione, fra cui un coperchio con presa zoomorfa, una fiasca del pellegrino con decorazioni geometriche, olle con falsi beccucci, ciotole carenate. Con il materiale ceramico erano associati diversi pugnali, una piccola ascia piatta, punte e pugnali di lancia e bronzi figurati.

Su tutti i lati del nuraghe sono affiorati numerosi conci di trachite decorati nella faccia a vista da motivi geometrici a losanga, zig zag, cruciformi a tridente, a greca, e con i motivi raggera delle pintadere fittili usate per decorare pani rituali. I conci appartenevano al coronamento della muraglia esterna del nuraghe (fig.1), e sono da attribuire alla stessa fase edilizia della grande vasca e della fonte sacra nel bronzo recente e finale. Nel lato N-E alcuni ambienti addossati al muro esterno del nuraghe hanno restituito enormi quantità di ossa di animali combuste sopratutto di suini, caprini, ovini, e roditori. E' possibile che in questi ambienti venissero offerti alla divinità anche animali e consumati durante riti propiziatori. All'esterno dell'antemurale nel versante S-E fra numerose rocce affioranti separate da profonde fessure naturali erano presenti a partire dagli strati più profondi materiali fittili dell'eneolitico evoluto, del bronzo antico e sopratutto del bronzo finale e prima età del ferro. Il repertorio dei materiali bronzei è sempre uguale e abbondantissimo e calcolabile in diverse migliaia tra il materiale integro e frammentario. Ancora diverse migliaia tra il materiale integro e frammentario. Ancora dall'area esterna provengono diversi grani di pasta vitrea ad occhi, una testina di kuros ionica e una statuina di Demetra (Madau 1991). Nonostante all'esterno dell'antemurale i materiali siano stati sconvolti dagli scavi clandestini attestano una continuità dell'uso dell'area almeno fino al V-IV sec. a. C.

VILLAGRANDE (NUORO) – TEMPIO A "MEGARON" DI S'ARCU È IS FORROS"

A seguito di un danneggiamento effettuato da ignoti scavatori clandestini, sono stati effettuati dalla Soprintendenza Archeologica per le province di Sassari e Nuoro, 3 interventi di scavo in località S'Arcu 'e Is Forros" in agro di Villagrande (Fadda 1985, 1989).

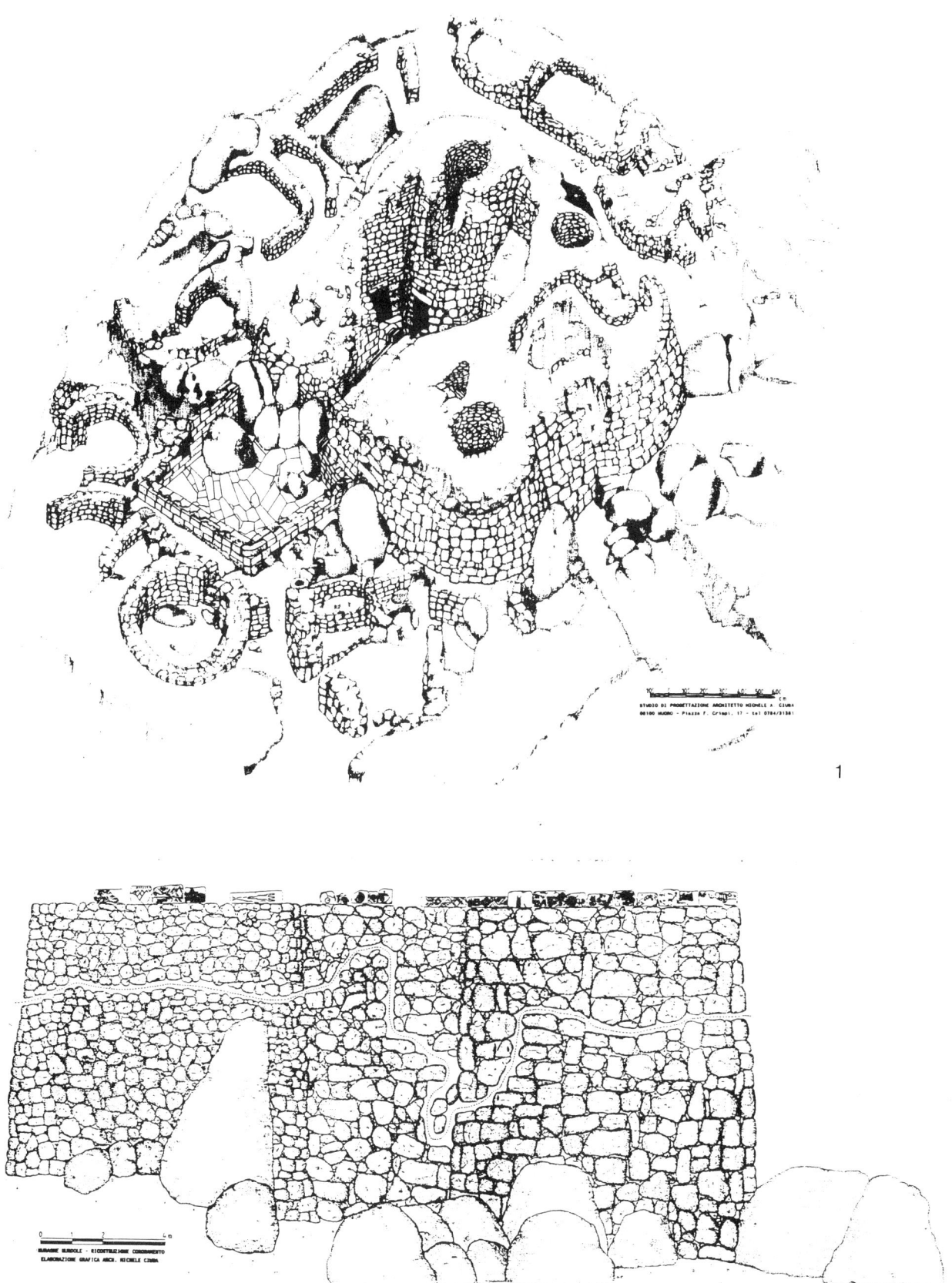

Fig. 1. Orani: 1.1. Veduta assonometrica del tempio nauragico di Nurdole. 1.2. Ipotesi di ricostruzione del paramento del lato S-E del nuraghe di Nurdole con una proposta di posizionamento dei blocchi decorati nei punti di rinvenimento.

L'insediamento preistorico è posto in una collina in prossimità del passo Correboi sotto la cima Allue in Fogu a quota 1300 m. s.l.m. La collina è circondata dai fiumi Bacu Alleri a Ovest e Iscra Abbatrula a Est, affluenti del Flumendosa. Si tratta di un imponente insediamento di età nuragica costituito da un nuraghe complesso a pianta tribolata costruito con pietre di medie dimensioni, appena sbozzate e disposte a filari irregolari.

Con esposizione ad Oriente disposte a mezza costa, affiorano le strutture di numerose capanne che degradano verso il fiume. Nella parte più alta della collina sono state portate in luce le strutture di un tempio a megaron costruite con poderosi muri di pietre appena sbozzate di granito degradato e di scisto, di dimensioni diverse, disposte a filari. Il tempio a pianta rettangolare, sviluppa una lunghezza esterna complessiva di m. 17 con larghezza non uniforme, che va da un minimo di m. 5,50 nella parte posteriore, a un massimo di m. 6,50, a causa della vistosa irregolarità dei muri perimetrale che hanno spessori diversi, con una misura minima di m. 1,10 fino ad un massimo di m. 1,50 (Fig. 2). Il tempio ha una planimetria complessa con una facciata che attualmente presenta un paramentro ad andamento rettilineo che conserva sette filari costruiti con blocchi poligonali di media grandezza, che mostrano una maggiore accuratezza nell'esecuzione in corrispondenza degli stipiti dell'ingresso. Un corridoio a pianta trapezoidale (lungh. m 2,10 × largh. m 1, m 1,50) strombato verso l'interno immette nel primo vano A di forma rettangolare (lungh. m 3,10 × largh. m 3,60). All'interno del vano A nell'angolo del muro sul lato sinistro a quota m 2,55 è stata rinvenuta un'olletta di forma aperta che aveva in fondo concavo inserito al di sotto del livello di un consistente battuto pavimentale di argilla che, a tratti, presentava delle lenti carboniose. Dalla stessa area di scavo provengono un frammento di spada votivo e una parte di brocca askoide con decorazioni geometriche tra il collo e il corpo.

Dal primo ambiente, attraverso un corridoio rettangolare (lungh. m 1,10 × largh. m 1,07) si accede al vano B (lungh. m 3,70 largh. m 1,80 m 1,65) anch'esso di pianta rettangolare irregolare, ma di dimensioni più piccole rispetto agli altri tre ambienti del tempio. All'interno del vano B sono stati raccolti pochi frammenti ceramici di piccole dimensioni e con impasti molto degradati. Nel corridoio (lungh. m 1,20 × 1,40) che conduceva al vano C, affiora un altro frammento di spada votiva e numerosi frustoli bronzei informi. Il corridoio del vano C conserva ancora l'ingresso architravato con soprastante finestrello di scarico a luce trapezoidale. I muri perimetrali che aggettano vistosamente, delimitano un vano a pianta rettangolare (lungh. m 2,30-2,50, largh. m 3,50) e all'interno di esso nella terza sconvolta dai clandestini, sono state raccolte numerose lastre di scisto e altre pietre piatte che sicuramente appartenevano alla copertura del tempio.

All'interno del vano C sono state rinvenute numerose lastre di calcaree arenaceo fossilifero, alcune di esse sono semplicemente sagomate e lisciate ai bordi, altre presentano dei regolari fori circolari. Fra le lastre giaceva un grosso concio in calcaree fossilifero de tipo a T che presenta nella faccia piana a vista una grossa bozza mammelliforme. Sempre dal vano C provengono vari conci in arenaria di forma rettangolare a base piana, nei quali sono stati praticati numerosi fori, talvolta disposti a file regolari o senza un ordine preciso; alcuni di essi conservano ancora residui di piccole colate di piombo che originariamente fissavano nei fori i bronzi votivi. Sempre nel vano C è stato rinvenuto un bacile calcare, spezzato, di forma quadrata, con una piccola conca circolare al centro e le superfici ben curate. Dal vano C provengono numerosi frammenti ceramici riferibili soprattutto a vasi a corpo globulare e a piccole tazze carenate e, sempre nel crollo, affiorano resti di lamine bronzee, piccoli frammenti di spilloni, resti di canali di adduzione risparmiati nei bronzi figurati ed usati come verghe di fissaggio nelle apposite basi presenti nei luoghi di culto.

Attraverso un corridoio a pianta quadrata (lungh. m 1,10 largh m 1,10) con i muri che aggettano formando un ingresso a ogiva s raggiunge il quarto vano D di forma rettangolare irregolare (lungh. m 2,60-2 largh. m 3,40).

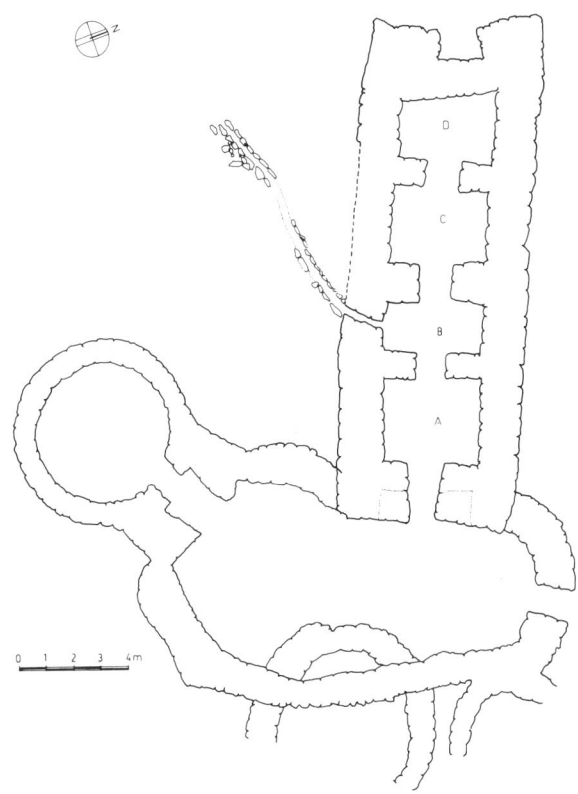

Fig. 2. Villagrande Strisaili, plainmetria generale del tempio a megaron di S'Arcu 'e Is Forros con la capanna el il recinto che delimitano l'area culturale.

Nel muro di fondo si apre una piccola nicchia sopraelevata di forma trapezoidale irregolare che risulta in asse a tutti i corridoi dei quattro vani. All'interno del vano D giaceva una enorme lastra in granito assottigliata all'estremità; fra i materiali ceramici sono presenti frammenti di tegami, ollette con basso collo cilindrico distinto, tazze di diverse dimensioni con carene molto accentuate e collo concavo estroflesso, ciotoline con prese forate, ecc. Nell'aria esterna sul lato destro della facciata poggiava un concio parallelepipedo (lungh. cm. 57, largh. cm. 24, alt. cm. 20) con sei grossi fori nella parte superiore e in uno di essi è ancora infissa la base di una spada votiva.

L'esplorazione nella parte anteriore del monumento ha evidenziato due distinte fasi edilizie che indicano una planimetria originaria, con due muri laterali prolungati oltre la linea d'ingresso (in antis), che successivamente sono stati riempiti con un muro, formando una facciata ad andamento rettilineo.

Nell'aria circostante il monumento si raccolgono numerosi segni di un'attività fusoria legata all'esistenza del tempio, infatti dal vicino nuraghe e dalle capanne provengono numerosi frammenti di lingotto di tipo egeo e di panelle, tre asce a margini rialzati, una fibula a sanguisuga, frammenti di bronzi figurati, un bronzetto di tipo orientalizzante che rappresenta un leone accosciato, numerosissimi frammenti di piombo e scorie di ferro che erano contenute all'interno di un bacile in lamina bronzea, con varie toppe di restauro (¢ di bocca cm. 40), e un coperchio circolare in piombo con due fori passanti (¢ cm. 47) che pesava kg. 11,700 e frammenti di tripode di tipo cipriota (Fadda 1985).

Nella seconda campagna di scavo effettuata nei mesi di ottobre e novembre 1990 è stata esplorata la parte posteriore del tempio sui lati N/O – N/E che risultava ancora coperta da un ammasso di crolli e di materiali di risulta provenienti dallo scavo clandestino che era stato effettuato solo all'interno dei quattro ambienti del tempio e nell'area antistante. Sul lato N/O dell'edificio a causa di una forte pendenza del terreno, che aveva formato un accumulo di terra di riporto, è stato esplorato il deposito archeologico che non aveva subìto manomissioni.

Lo scavo ha evidenziato chiaramente la planimetria del monumento con il prolungamento dei muri laterali dando luogo ad un edificio doppiamente in antis. Le appendici murarie della parte posteriore in antis si innestano al muro di fondo in modo molto irregolare, con una tessitura muraria diversa da quella dei muri perimetrali e con uno spessore maggiore che si accentua nella parte finale. Il prolungamento in antis nel lato dell'ingresso mostra invece maggiore regolarità nella composizione dei filari che non presentano discontinuità rispetto al lungo muro perimetrale. Fra il pietrame dei crolli si evidenziano numerose pietre piatte di piccolo spessore e diverse lastre che sembrano appartenere alla muratura degli ultimi ambienti del tempio, dove la muratura risulta molto più aggettante rispetto ai vani anteriori A,B,C. Lo scavo ha evidenziato uno zoccolo di rincalzo posto alla base della muratura del monumento e si sviluppa per tutta la lunghezza dei muri laterali. Lo zoccolo di contenimento, costruito con grossi blocchi appena sbozzati posti a coltello, oltre a garantire maggiore stabilità alla muratura poteva essere utilizzato come una sorta di panchina o come piano di appoggio. Nella trincea della parte posteriore sono stati individuati diversi strati di terra molto scura, misti a pietrame di tipo diverso, ciottoli fluviali di varia forma, usati probabilmente come pestelli o coti. Alcuni frammenti di calcare arenaceo che presenta su un lato dei fori di forma diversa, sono da riferire a basamenti per le offerte rinvenuti in grande abbondanza anche all'interno del tempio. La presenza di diversi frammenti di spada votiva e frammenti di piombo sono da mettere in relazione con la presenza delle basi stesse.

Dalla stessa trincea di scavo proviene la parte sommitale di un modellino di nuraghe in calcare arenaceo (alt. cm. 18,20 ¢ cm. 15 cad.) con sette fori ellittici disposti a cercio ed uno a centro. Il modellino che trova stretti confronti con altri modellini rinvenuti in Sardegna, sorreggeva in origine sette oggetti votivi fissati alla sommità con piccole colate di piombo.

La presenza delle basi e del modellino rinvenute nell'aria esterna dimostra le offerte del tempio venivano sistemate anche lungo le parti in antis. Il deposito archeologico conteneva sopratutto negli strati più profondi una rilevante quantità di frammenti ceramici riferibili al bronzo medio recente. Alla base dei muri esterni del tempio è presente, in modo uniforme, un consistente strato carbonioso, dovuto probabilmente all'incendio di strutture lignee che completavano l'aggetto della copertura fatta con lastre di pietra che poggiava sopra travi lignee. Non si esclude inoltre che l'incendio sia stata la causa delle successive modifiche apportate alla muratura delle parti in antis. Nella stessa campagna di scavo è stata completata l'esplorazione dell'ultimo vano D del tempio che, seppure stravolto dai clandestini, conservava parte del lastricato originario. Nel vano C lo scavo ha evidenziato uno strato culturale ricco di frammenti ceramici e due olle, una delle quali integra. I due contenitori risultavano incassati in due angoli della cella e sistemati al di sotto del piano di un battuto pavimentale che si conserva solo a tratti. I tre contenitori rinvenuti: uno all'interno del vano A nella prima campagna di scavo e nel vano C nell'ultima campagna di scavo, sono delle olle ovoidi di forma aperta con orli arrotondati, e fondo indistinto o piatto a margini arrotondati. Le anse delle olle sono del tipo a nastro piatto disposte a ponte nel punto di maggiore espansione della parete e del tipo a gomito rovesciato molto allargato all'imposta, a sezione concavo convessa. La disposizione dei contenitori incassati negli angoli degli ambienti del tempio può far supporre che venissero utilizzati per contenere dell'acqua che veniva usata nei riti purificatori. L'ipotesi viene rafforzata anche dalla presenza di bacili frammentari in arenaria e da un canale che si apre dal vano B. Le olle rinvenute all'interno del monumento rientrano in una tipologia di materiali nuragici molto diffusa in tutta la Sardegna e s'inquadrano nella fase recente e finale dell'età del bronzo (XII – IX sec. a. C.).

La terza campagna di scavo ha portato alla luce nella parte anteriore del tempio un grande recinto ellittico che parte dai lati del vestibolo. I muri che delimitano il recinto presentano alla base una panchina simile a quella rinvenuta sui lati esterni del monumento ed ugualmente utilizzata come piano d'appoggio per le offerte.

All'area ellittica si accede attraverso un ingresso, sul lato sinistro che conserva una singolare soglia composta da due blocchi di calcare arenaceo che su due piccole fossette conservano dei vasetti in lamina bronzea fissati col piombo e due fori rettangolari che in origine forse sostenevano i pali lignei dell'ingresso. I muri del recinto si sovrappongono, nel punto in asse all'ingresso, ad una capanna preesistente che ha restituito materiale del bronzo medio. Sul lato sinistro del recinto si apre un ambiente composto da un vestibolo rettangolare che conduce ad un vano circolare usato probabilmente come magazzino del tempio.

Tutta l'area esplorata dell'ultima campagna di scavo presentava tratti di battuto pavimentale mista a terra carboniosa, concentrata davanti all'ingresso del tempio che ha restituito numerosi frammenti di spade votive, pugnaletti, un pendaglio ad ascia, spilloni e diversi frammenti ceramici di ciotole carenate ornate da applicazioni plastiche, ciotole, olle a colletto che si collocano nell'età del bronzo recente e finale. Numerose basi per offerte, integre e frammentarie indicano che tutta l'area del recinto era destinata alla raccolta degli ex voto. Lo scavo del tempio a megaron ha riproposto sistemi di offerta, a tipologie di materiali identici a quelli documentati nei templi a pozzo più diffusi in tutta la Sardegna.

Recenti scavi condotti nei tempietti a megaron del villaggio nuragico di Serra Orrios (Dorgali) hanno restituito materiali che confermano i dati rinvenuti a Villagrande Strisaili e consentono infine di affermare che i templi a megaron, attribuiti da molti archeologi a contatti dei nuragici con Cartaginesi risultano invece contemporanei ai templi a pozzo del bronzo recente finale.

Villagrande Strisaili (Nuoro)
Il tempio nuragico di "Sa Carcaredda"

Nel 1991–92 è stato esplorato un tempio nuragico in località Sa Carcaredda in agro di Villagrande Strisaili dopo un danneggiamento della muratura affiorante. Il monumento (fig. 4.1) si compone di un vestibolo di forma trapezoidale irregolare, strombato all'esterno, che conserva alla base dei due lati due panchine in pietra, sul lato sinistro costituito da un unico masso rettangolare, e da due blocchi rettangolari sul lato destro. Il vestibolo è delimitato da un grosso muro a secco costruito in blocchi poligonali disposti a filari irregolari. Dal vestibolo, attraverso un ingresso con muri leggermente aggettanti, si passa a un ambiente di forma rettangolare, che presenta nei lati lunghi una linea che segna un distacco nella tessitura muraria. La linea è data dall'aggiunta di una parte del muro costruito in una diversa fase edilizia. In origine quindi il monumento si componeva di un vestibolo rettangolare, che conserva otto filari, e conduceva ad un ambiente circolare, costruito, anch'esso con blocchi di granito locale non lavorati, disposti a filari irregolari. I due ambienti sono pavimentati con lastrine di granito ben lavorate con incastri regolari. La parte antistante il vestibolo ha restituito un tesoretto di monete di epoca imperiale del III-IV sec. d. C. misti a frammenti di spade votive e pugnaletti, anelli in bronzo, graffe in piombo di epoca nuragica. La presenza del tesoretto potrebbe essere riferito ad un riutilizzo del tempietto in epoca romana o più probabilmente all'uso dell'edificio, ormai abbandonato, come nascondiglio del tesoretto. Questa seconda ipotesi può essere sostenuta dalla totale mancanza di materiale ceramico del basso impero in tutta l'area del monumento ove invece abbonda il materiale nuragico sopratutto frammenti di ciotole carenate, ollette di forma aperta e scarsi frammenti di tegami. Ancora dall'area antistante in uno strato non omogeneo provengono 50 vaghi di ambra di forma cilindrica decorata da solcature parallele di tipo Allumiere, grani discoidali piatti, grani a sezione ellittica, grani a sezione biconica, un grano di forma triangolare, misti a grani circolari di cristallo di rocca, e pasta vitrea associati ad una grandissima quantità di vaghi circolari schiacciati, in bronzo. Fra questi materiali giaceva un pendaglio in pasta silicea di divinità femminile egittizante che trova confronti con un pendaglio della necropoli di quattro fontanili (AA.VV. 1967) e con alcuni pendagli provenienti dalla tomba di Boccoris. Dal vano circolare provengono diversi blocchi in calcare arenaceo lavorati su tutti i lati con la faccia a vista decorata da profonde incisioni in rilievo a denti di lupo, che ricordano i conci provenienti da altri santuari della Sardegna. I blocchi si congiungono tra loro con larghe grappe in piombo, colate negli appositi incastri scavati sui lati nella parte superiore. I blocchi uniti, sono la rappresentazione di un mezzo nuraghe quadrilobato che in origine era collocato nell'ambiente circolare. Un muretto di piccoli mattoni (alti cm. 41) di calcare di cui si conservano quattro filari, rivestiti da uno strato di argilla, probabilmente sosteneva i blocchi decorati che all'interno delimitano un focolare, attestato da uno strato di terra nera carboniosa (spess. cm. 15).

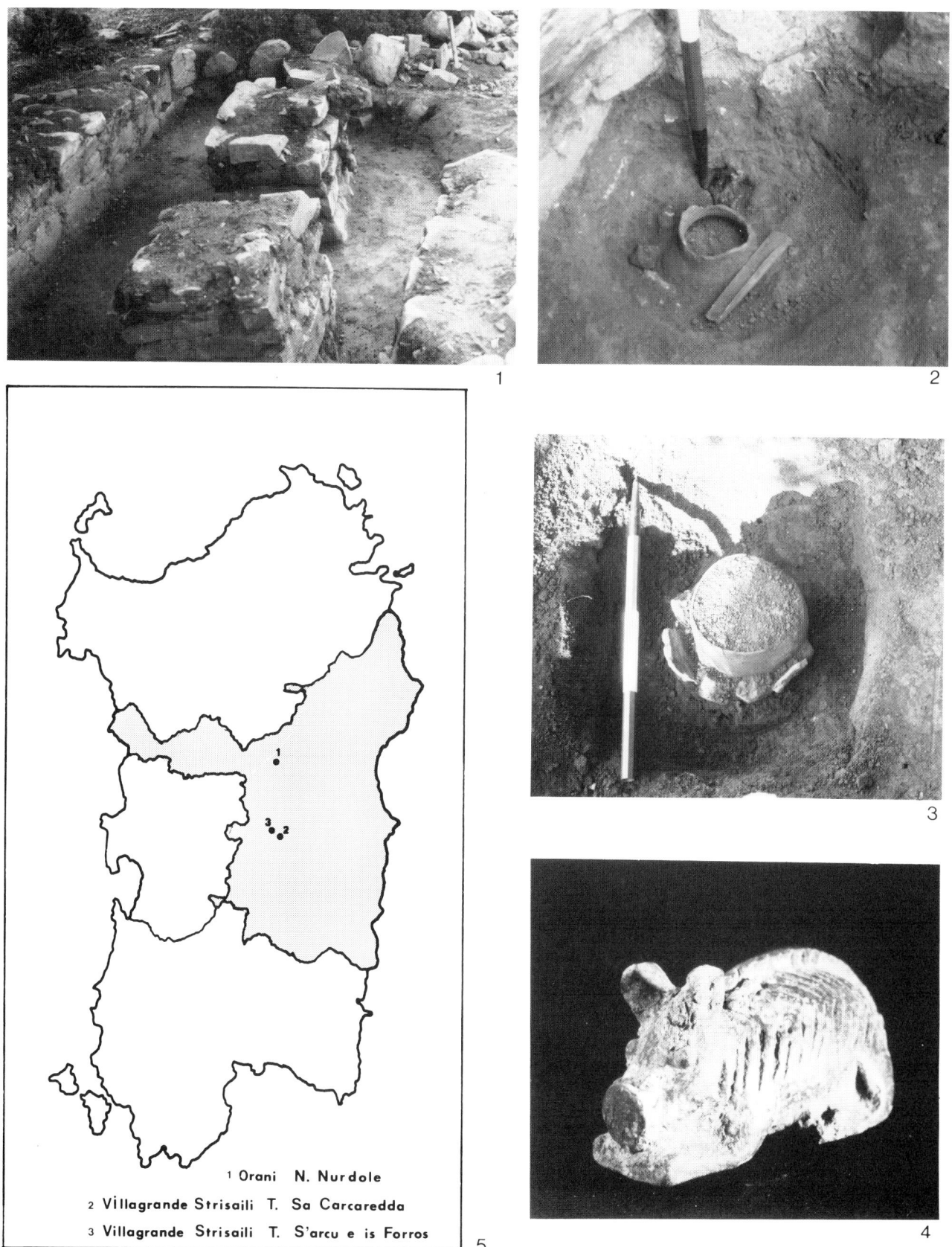

Fig. 3. Villagrande Strisaili. 3.1 Vano usato come deposito con pilastri. 3.2 Olla con ascia a margini rialzati rinvenuti nel deposito. 3.3 Olla rincalzata da lingotti e panelle rinvenute nel deposito. 3.4 Maiale miniaturistico in bronzo. 3.5 Carta della Sardegna con i luoghi di culto esplorati in Barbagia e Ogliastra.

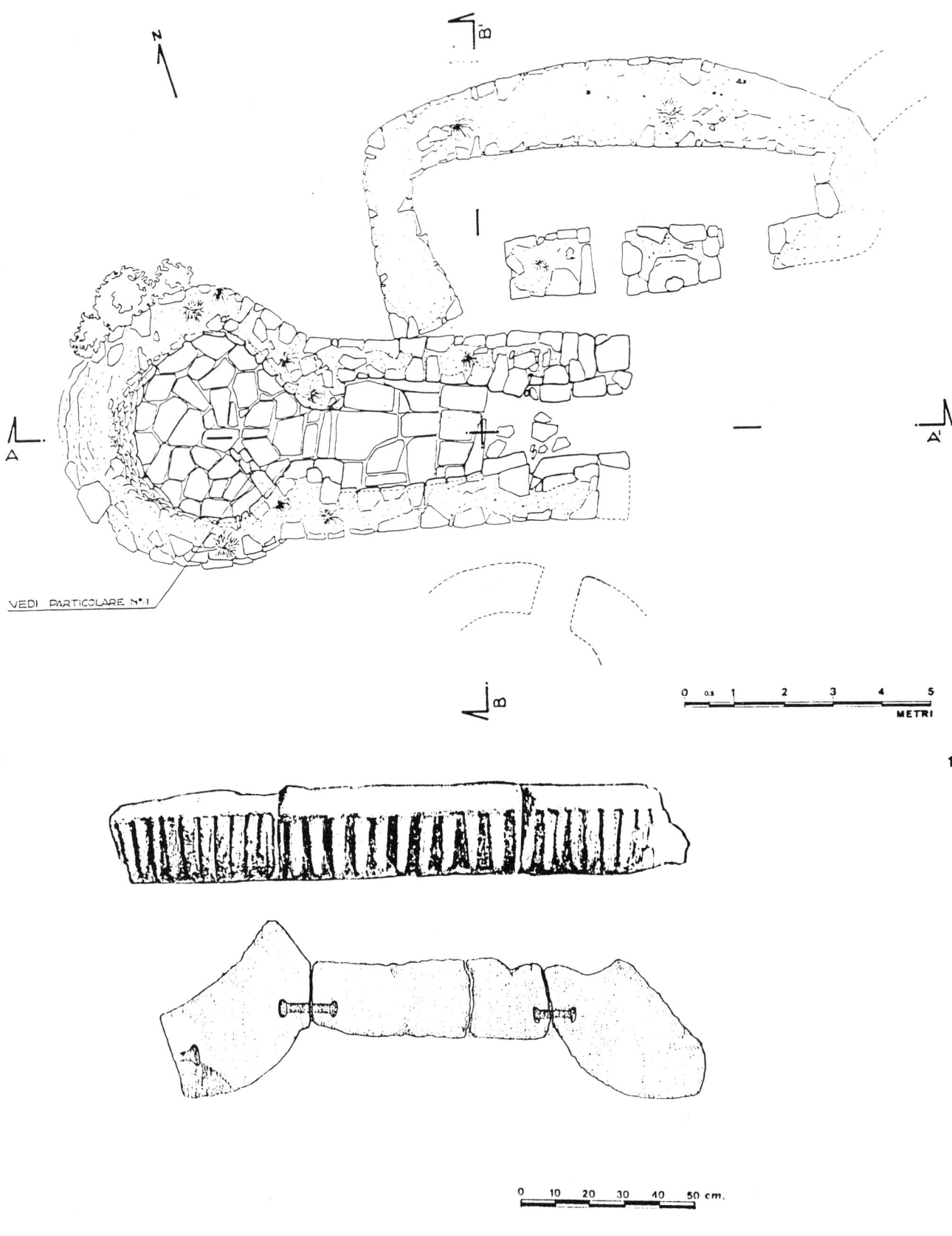

Fig. 4. Villagrande Strisaili. 4.1 Planimetria del tempio di Sa Carcaredda con vano rettangolare usato come deposito delle offerte. 4.2 Ricomposizione dei blocchi decorati che delimitavano il focolare all'interno del vano circolare del tempio.

Si raccolgono pochi frammenti ceramici, due anse di ollette, frammenti di parete, un frammento di lucerna a cucchiaio. La base del vano circolare è pavimentato con lastre di granito di forme diverse con connessure regolari. La muratura interna si compone di tre filari di base di blocchi di granito, più regolari rispetto agli altri filari superiori, formati da lastrine, e blocchi più piccoli disposti in modo irregolare.

Dai crolli provengono numerosissime lastre piatte di dimensioni diverse che appartenevano alla copertura originaria, fatta appunto di lastre che aggettavano. Sul lato sinistro del vano circolare, in corrispondenza del muretto di piccole pietre in calcare sopra lo strato carbonioso, che poggia sul lastricato, è leggibile un consistente strato di argilla di colore bruno, con uno spessore medio di 7 cm. Nella restante parte del vano, l'argilla si conserva a lenti e in modo non uniforme. Una grande lastra, posta a coltello, incastrata nell'ingresso che conduce al vano circolare, chiudeva l'accesso al vano circolare. Dal focolare provengono pochi frammenti ceramici, un elemento circolare in lamina bronzea vuoto all'interno con quattro fori passanti, che faceva parte dei finimenti di un cavallo, un pugnaletto a base triangolare con due chiodi di fissaggio, un anello a fascia decorata da linee verticali, uno spillone, ed altri frustuli di bronzo.

Lo scavo, ha portato alla luce, sul lato destro dell'edificio cultuale, un ambiente di forma rettangolare (lungh. m. 8 largh. m. 1,20) irregolare con gli angoli arrotondati, costruito con blocchi di granito locale non lavorati, disposti a filari irregolari. Il vano rettangolare si addossa al muro del tempietto in corrispondenza dell'innesto leggibile nel tratto di muro che delimita il vestibolo con le panchine laterali. All'interno del vano rettangolare si conservano due tratti di mura (lungh. m. 1,90 e m. 1,70) per un'altezza di m. 0,95, che fungevano da pilastri che anticamente reggevano una copertura aggettante ottenuta con lastre piatte. I pilastri, conservano cinque filari ottenuti da lunghi blocchi disposti in modo traversale rispetto alla faccia a vista del lato lungo.

L'edificio rettangolare per le caratteristiche della muratura è da attribuire alla prima fase edilizia del monumento cioè alla fase che ha preceduto la giunta della prima parte del vestibolo. Gli strati individuati all'interno dell'ambiente rettangolare presentano inoltre la stessa successione e la stessa quota degli strati del tempio circolare. Il vano rettangolare, conserva un deposito archeologico di 50 cm, composto da uno strato argilloso con pietre di crollo e ricco di materiali ceramici e bronzei e uno strato carbonioso, posto sotto uno strato di lenti di argilla non uniforme, che conteneva diverse olle e materiali bronzei prevalentemente di uso cultuale. Il primo strato ha restituito in corrispondenza dell'ingresso sul lato destro, sei elementi di collana in ambra di diverse forme e dimensioni e n° 120 elementi di collana in bronzo e altri elementi in pasta vitrea e cristallo di rocca. I numerosi vaghi, probabilmente appartenevano ad un unica collana a più fili che alternava ambra, bronzo e pasta vitrea. Dagli angoli sul lato destro del vano ripostiglio provengono un olla (fig. 3.3) di forma aperta con anse a nastro piatto a ponte, interrata per 15 cm. rispetto al piano contenente lenti di argilla. L'olla era rincalzata sul fondo da 5 frammenti di lingotto di tipo egeo e da 10 panelle per un totale di kg. 10. Dall'angolo opposto proviene un'altra olla a colletto, con anse a gomito rovesciato, interrata per cm. 20 rispetto allo stesso strato di argilla. Anche questa olla era rincalzata da 10 frammenti di lingotto di tipo egeo e da 10 panelle per un totale di 10 kg., ed inoltre, in corrispondenza del collo, poggiava un'ascia a margini rialzati lunga cm. 22, che può trovare una collocazione nelle fasi del bronzo medio recente (fig. 3.2).

E' importante sottolineare che per la prima volta i lingotti di tipo egeo vengano trovati associati a vasi di tipologia molto diffusa e con oggetti d'uso in bronzo con certa collocazione cronologica. La presenza di questi materiali contenuti all'interno di un magazzino di un luogo di culto offre ulteriori elementi cronologici per stabilire il periodo del primo impianto dell'intero edificio.

Adiacente al pilastro sul lato destro, è affiorata una ciotola carenata di forma aperta e diverse olle frammentarie. Dal lato sinistro del vano ripostiglio provengono diversi bottoni in bronzo, del tipo a calotta emisferica, a forma di nuraghe e a forma conica sormontata da una protome bovina. Dallo stesso lato provengono degli stiletti votivi ad elsa gammata, un elemento in bronzo a forma di ruota a raggi con una lavorazione a trecciolina, una figurina (Fig. 5.2) di donna ammantata che regge una ciotola decorata a raggera, diversi grummi di piombo che inglobano i piedi di figurine bronzee spezzate, un pendaglio. Dalla zona centrale dal lato sinistro sempre all'interno del vano ripostiglio proviene una olla con tre anse e due prese diametralmente opposte, che conteneva all'interno sei panelle, una fibula a sanguinga, un'ascia con appendici laterali, una doppia ascia a taglio ortogonale, un puntale di lancia, due frammenti di scalpello, un bracciale a verga a sezione circolare e appendici decorate a lobi, due anelli, un dente, un frammento di collo di vaso in lamina bronzea. Lungo la parete del lato lungo è affiorata una olletta di forma aperta con fondo ad anello con due anse a maniglia e due prese a lingua bifora, che trova confronti con quelli provenienti da S'Urbale (Teti) e del nuraghe La Speranza di Alghero databili al bronzo recente e finale.

Una terza campagna di scavo è stata volta all'esplorazione dell'area circostante per delimitare il muro esterno del tempio. Tutta l'area esterna era occupata da una grande abbondanza di lastre piatte disposte senza alcun ordine sopratutto in prossimità dei muri. Sotto lo strato di lastre c'era uno strato di terra sabbiosa di colore chiaro,

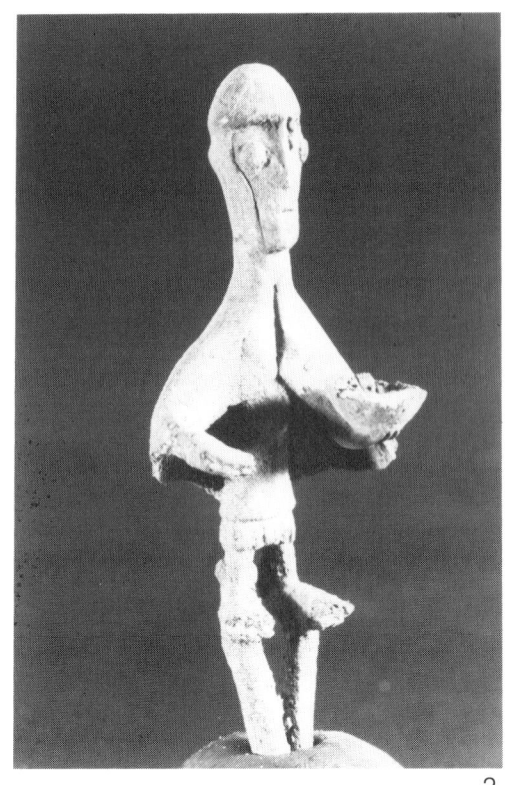
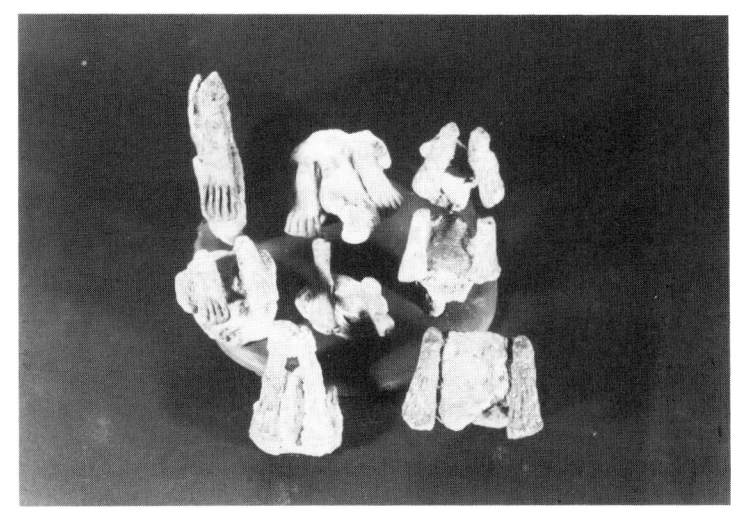

Fig. 5. Villagrande Strisaili, tempio di Sa Carcaredda. 5.1 Stiletti votivi in bronzo. 5.2 Figurina femminile di offerente. 5.3 Arciere orante con copricapo sormontato da lughe corna. 5.4 Gruppo di piedi di statuine con piombo di fissaggio.

compatta e durissima con qualche lente di carbone e ricchissima di materiali bronzei e ceramici, un secondo strato di terra chiara durissima ricca di materiali.

Lo scavo dell'area esterna a partire dal lato sinistro del vestibolo ha portato alla luce una porzione di muro che unisce parte del lato sinistro del vano circolare e si addossa, formando una porzione di cerchio, al muro di una capanna circolare posta sempre sul lato sinistro del vestibolo e con l'ingresso sullo stesso lato. L'area compresa tra il lato esterno del tempio e delimitata dal piccolo tratto di muro veniva sicuramente usato come luogo per la deposizione delle offerte o come secondo magazzino. Queste due ipotesi vengono indicate dalla presenza di diversi basamenti in pietra che conservano ancora l'impiombatura nei fori e da una straordinaria abbondanza di materiale bronzeo prevalentemente di uso cultuale.

L'uso cultuale è riscontrabile anche nell'accurata esecuzione di alcuni manufatti fittili che non trovano riscontro nei contenitori di uso quotidiano presenti negli abitati. Provengono dall'area destinata alla deposizione delle offerte una ciotola emisferica con orlo ondulato e fori passanti, e una olla decorata sul ventre da una spada sormontata da uno scudo, resi plasticamente.

Fra i materiali bronzei vi erano numerosi pugnali di diverse misure, a base semplice, spade votive, di cui alcune riutilizzate come pugnali, spilloni di diverse dimensioni, talvolta infilate in vaghi di collana in bronzo, punte e puntali di lancia, stocchi. Fra gli oggetti di ornamento vi erano numerosissimi anelli a fascetta piatta e a sezione circolare, con decorazioni geometriche e inornati, bracciali a fascetta aperta, bottoni a calotta emisferica con barretta interna sormontati da un pendice cilindrica, conica e zoomorfa. Seguono diversi pugnaletti ad elsa gammata singoli o in un caso con pugnale e spillone contenuti in un unica faretra. Tutti gli stiletti hanno due occhielli di sospensione per essere usati come pendagli, ma, residui di piombo fissati in corrispondenza dell'occhiello di uno di essi dimostra che venivano fissati anche nei basamenti con la punta rivolta in alto. Come basi per le offerte venivano utilizzati alcuni modellini frammentari di nuraghe realizzati in calcare arenaceo.

Ancora fra i pendagli sono presenti delle piccole sfere piene con anello e una sorta di grappolo d'uva con tre appendici nella parte superiore e anello di sospensione. Sono inoltre da interpretare come elementi ornamentali alcuni frammenti di disco in lamina bronzea con foro centrale, decorati da punti disposti nella circonferenza a raggi. Fra i materiali bronzei sono stati rinvenute due figurine con la base ed i piedi inglobati nel piombo. Si tratta di un orante con una coroncina sulla testa, sulla corta tunica porta una bandoliera e una stola. La seconda figurina rappresenta un'arciere con copricapo sormontato da lunghe corna con una daga sulle spalle (fig. 5.3). Dallo stesso ambiente provengono un porcellino (fig. 3.4) e decine di piedi inglobati parzialmente nel piombo, alcune mani di offerenti, uno scudo con umbone, una penna direzionale. Alcuni piedi, e lo scudo si riferiscono a bronzi figurati di grandi dimensioni che sono stati portati via dopo l'abbandono del monumento oppure sono stati saccheggiati durante una incursione nemica.

Dai dati disponibili sembra essere più probabile la seconda ipotesi perchè il deposito posto sul lato destro del tempio conteneva una grande quantità di lingotti, panelle, bronzi d'uso ed altri ex voto sopradescritti, integri e nascosti sotto il battuto pavimentale. Sembra quindi improbabile che gli abituali frequentatori del tempio abbiano potuto dimenticare un deposito così ricco prima di abbandonare il luogo di culto.

Discussione

La descrizione, seppure in modo sommario, dal deposito votivo di Sa Carcaredda conferma ancora una volta la grande disponibilità di materiali in bronzo nei monumenti cultuali delle zone interne della Sardegna, ove mancano i punti estrattivi che possano giustificare un'attività fusoria così intensa. Nel territorio circostante infatti sono presenti punti di estrazione di piombo e ferro peraltro di scarso rilievo. Il problema diventa più complesso se si considera l'enorme quantità di bronzi provenienti sopratutto dal territorio nuorese ove non solo mancano le testimonianze di luoghi di estrazione ma mancano tuttora chiari segni di attività fusoria.

Tale assenza di elementi che attestino un'autonomia nell' approvigionamento e nella lavorazione dei bronzi della Sardegna si complica se si considera la scarsa trasformazione del territorio che consentirebbe, una più facile individuazione delle cave e sopratutto la difficoltà di collegamenti determinata dall'aspra geomorfologia prevalentemente montana.

Tutte queste considerazioni rafforzano maggiormente l'ipotesi dell'esistenza di una forte presenza con valenza politico-religiosa capace di garantire la fornitura della materia prima dalle lontane miniere della Sardegna o a gestire scambi con i più importanti luoghi di produzione del mondo Egeo e sopratutto Cipriota.

I luoghi di culto sopradescritti risultano tutti integrati in insediamenti abitativi, che raggruppano costruzioni di carattere esclusivamente domestico ed altre strettamente legate ai templi. Queste ultime che non presentano necessariamente differenze nell'architettura venivano utilizzate per la raccolta di derrate alimentari, bronzi votivi e d'uso, manufatti ceramici ed oggetti ornamentali di varie materie e di diverse provenienze. All'interno dei depositi, sono stati ritrovati considerevoli quantità di panelle, lingotti di tipo egeo e bronzi d'uso che non sono strettamente pertinenti alle offerte votive e risultano sempre assenti fra i materiali degli altri luoghi di culto della Sardegna.

Questo aspetto nuovo nei metodi di tesaurizzazione delle aree di culto è forse da attribuire ad una gestione delle ricchezze da parte di personaggi che controllano anche il potere economico. Il tempio quindi diventa, come avveniva nel mondo Egeo Orientale, un punto di riferimento per la vita religiosa economica e politica.

Bibliografia

AA.VV. 1967. 'Veio. Continuazione degli scavi nella necropoli Villanoviana in località "Quattro Fontanili", *Notizie degli Scavi di Antichità*, serie 8, Vol. 21, fasc. 1–12.

Fadda, M.A. 1985. 'Il Tempio a megaron di S'Arcu 'e Is Forros', *N.B.A.S.*, 278–81.

Fadda, M.A. 1986. 'Il complesso nuragico di Nurdole (Orani – Nuoro)', *Bollettino Archeologico Sardo* 3, 308–314.

Fadda, M.A. 1989. 'Villagrande Strisaili (Nuoro) Megaron Temple at S'Arcu 'e is Forros', *Early Society in Cyprus*, Edinburgh.

Fadda, M.A. 1991. 'Un tempio nuragico in Barbagia punto di incontro di grandi civiltà', *Rivista di Studi Fenici* XIX, 1, 107–119.

Fadda, M.A. 1991. 'Nurdole. Il Nuraghe Santuario', *Bollettino di Archeologia del Min. dei Beni Cult. Amb.* 1/2 gennaio aprile 26 a.

Fadda, M.A. 1993. 'L'arte decorativa nell'architettura templare del periodo nuragico', *Rivista di Scienze Preistoriche. Atti. L'arte in Italia dal Paleolitico all'Età del Bronzo*, Firenze.

Fadda, M.A., Tuveri, C. & Murru, G. 1992. 'Le tecniche edilizie del periodo nuragico nell'architettura delle acque presenti nel territorio della Barbagia', in *Sardinia in the Mediterranean: A Footprint in the Sea*, 250–261.

Ferragutti, U. 1937. 'I bronzi di Vulci', *Studi Etruschi* 11, 107–55.

Lilliu, G. 1955–57 'Nuovi templi a pozzo della Sardegna Nuragica', *Studi Sardi*, 45–63.

Lo Schiavo, F. 1989–90. 'Per uno studio sulle offerte nei Santuari della Sardegna Nuragica', *Scienze dell'Antichità-Storia-Archeologia-Antropologia* 3–4., 535–549.

Lo Schiavo, F. 1992. 'Un'altra fibula "Cipriota" della Sardegna', in *Sardinia in the Mediterranean: A Footprint in the Sea*, 298–303.

Madau, M. 1991. 'Importazioni dal Nuorese e centralità delle aree interne. Nota preliminare', *Rivista di Studi Fenici* XIX, 1, 121–131.

Pais, E. 1884. 'Il ripostiglio di bronzi di Abini presso Teti', *Bollettino Archeologico Sardo*, ns, 66–181.

Spano, G. 1865. *Memoria sopra alcuni idoletti di bronzo trovati nel villaggio di Teti e scoperte archeologiche fattesi nell'isola in tutta l'area*, Cagliari.

Taramelli, A. 1931. 'Esplorazione del Santuario Nuragico di Abini', *Notizie degli Scavi di Antichità*, 45–63.

Vaghetti, L. & Lo Schiavo, F. 1989. 'Late Bronze Age long distance trade in the Mediterranean: the role of the Cypriots', *Early Society in Cyprus*.

13

Evidence of Households or of Ritual Meals?
Early Latin Cult Practices: A Comparison of the Finds at Lavinium, Campoverde and Borgo Le Ferriere (*Satricum*)

Marianne Maaskant-Kleibrink
(Department of Archaeology, University of Groningen)

Summary: *Excavations over the last fifteen years by Groningen University at Borgo Le Ferriere (*Satricum*), 60km south of Rome, have revealed several successive settlement phases. During all phases of construction (from 9th to 5th century BC) the site showed a division between the central sacred area and the surrounding zones: a space for the goddess and a space for the living, and a space for the dead too. In this paper an attempt is made to differentiate between these spatial types and their respective 'households' by relating the pottery to different 'meals' within each area. This paper further scrutinises the question of early Latin cult practices and compares* Satricum *with other Latial sites.*

Introduction

The topographical development of the site at Borgo Le Ferriere *(Satricum)*, 60 km south of Rome, recalls those at Piazza d'Armi at Veii, Colle della Noce at Ardea, the Palatine and the Forum Romanum. These ancient sites all contained central sacred spaces surrounded first by hut pits and later by monumental buildings. Since this type of lay-out seems to represent an essential characteristic of early Latin settlement, it may be valuable to examine closely the relations between the sacred centres and their surroundings. The above mentioned sites were excavated – fully or in part – during the late 19th or early 20th century; most of these remain only partially published. Of the sites which have been recently re-investigated, *Satricum* is one of the more thoroughly researched. The excavations (carried out by the Dutch Institute in Rome (NIR) and Groningen University on the 4 ha wide plateau of the 35m high hilltop at Borgo Le Ferriere near the river Astura over the past 15 years), have revealed five successive phases ranging from the 9th century BC to 490–80 BC (Maaskant-Kleibrink 1987; 1992a,b). For all phases the sacred centre with its three successive temples and its successive votive deposits has been distinguished from the surrounding dwellings, first hutpits and subsequently smaller *oikoi* and large courtyard houses. While the interpretation of the centre as a sacred zone is unquestionable (e.g. Graillot 1896; Mengarelli 1896; de Waele 1981; Colonna 1984; CatsSatricum 1982, 1985a,b); the identification of features around the temples as profane is unsatisfactory because many elements one would expect to be present in a hut settlement or an urban area are missing – the most obvious ones being solid walls for the huts and storage areas and infrastructural objects during the Archaic period (Maaskant-Kleibrink 1984; 1985; 1987; 1991; 1992a,b).

This paper offers a re-interpretation of the remains around the religious centre at Le Ferriere as associated with cult-practices of transhumance groups. Firstly a more general survey of the archaeology of early Latin cults is required. Fortunately, recent interest in the contents of the Latin votive deposits has brought forward much interesting new data (Anathema 1990), although until now no single early votive deposit has been satisfactorily published. By studying the various assemblages of votive gifts an insight is gained into the various different cult practices in Latium.

The archaeology of early Latin cults

Early protohistoric Latin society practised veneration in sacred areas in the open, a comparatively clear element being the donation of gifts. When and how these rituals started, and whether the development of early cult activities and their spatial arrangements must be considered to have been an entirely indigenous process in which sacred spaces were moved away from the sacred caves and burials into the settlement-centre, or whether the introduction of central cult-spaces in Latium was an abrupt borrowing of foreign religious practices, is still intensively debated together with the earliest possible dates for the Latin and Roman cults (Lowe 1978; Guidi 1980; Blagg 1985; Guidi 1990). Foreign influences in early Iron Age cult practices at sacred spaces are unlikely though, because of the continuity of a ritual veneration of water which is special to Italic and Latin religion and traceable by its use of miniature vessels already in the Bronze Age. The dedication of miniature vessels was practised early in Etruria – there are a number of caves in which a few Bronze Age miniature vessels were dedicated (Negroni Catacchio 1990: 588) – but this cult-practice seems not to have been very common: against the 29 Iron Age deposits from Latium, deposits with miniatures are until now few in Etruria (two deposits with miniatures pots date from the post-Archaic period: viz. the one near the necropolis at Vetulonia, where 2m below the grass 6 vessels were found, each filled with miniature pots, and the deposit at Pozzarello: Bonghi Jovino 1978). In South Italy cave-cults which made use of miniature pots were much more important, this is clear from the miniature vessels found at Pertosa (Salerno: Patroni 1899; Carucci 1907) and the Latronico Cave near Lagonegro at the upper Sinni valley (Rellini 1916: 461). In these caves miniature pots were piled up near the entrances or deposited along internal water channels. As the dates and continuity of these deposits have not been intensively studied; it is still unknown whether there are connections between late Bronze or Iron Age deposits.

Miniature vessels which, together with miniature weapons, represent the ritual behaviour of the early Latin population were found in Latial burials from the 10th and 9th centuries BC. The miniatures found in these graves are made of impasto ware. They are carefully manufactured and not mini-miniatures as the ones found in votive deposits and some of the types must have been used exclusively in tombs: e.g. the 'little boat' or lamp and the 'small table' or dish on three legs (e.g. CLP). Other shapes, such as the dish, 'focacce', the *askos*, the carinated cup and the collared amphora are also found (although until now sporadically) in the earliest votive deposits (CLP; Guidi 1980). Whether it is possible to divide the tomb-miniatures by their types into a group of impasto objects which imitate grave-furniture, and a set of vessels which copy more widely used domestic pots is a matter of further research.

The study of Latin votive deposits has concentrated for the most part on the earliest objects present. Opinions differ widely on this point because of the difficulty of dating the mini-miniature vessels, which often represent the bulk of the votive gifts (see Guidi 1980; 1990): Müller-Karpe dated the miniatures by comparing their types to full-sized vessels known from his periods I, II, etc.; Lowe did this only for some deposits, and for others extracted their dates solely from the full-sized objects, especially imported vessels. Sensibly Guidi has distinguished between the types of the miniatures and the type of their clay: early types of miniature vessels can only be called old-fashioned if they are made of a more recent ware or fabric (Guido 1990).

Apart from these different attitudes to the miniature vessels, students of Latial votive deposits also attribute different meanings to imported objects, especially in connection with the influences of foreign cult practices on the origin of the cults in Latium. The appearance of Greek objects in the last decades of the 8th century BC often is seen as proof of an origin in that period under foreign guidance. The theory of borrowing would fit the general assumptions that other developments in the societies of the late 8th and 7th centuries BC, e.g. the exchange of prestigious gifts among the elite and the ceremonial banquet with the drinking of wine, were introduced to Latin society from elsewhere. After the pioneering article on the influences of Orientalizing luxury (Formazione 1980), Rathje became one of the main advocates of Near Eastern influences (1984; 1988), pointing to the contents of elite tombs from the late 8th and the 7th century, which comprise evidence of burial in precious garments as well as objects belonging to elite courts, such as sceptres, thrones, carts, and horses, as well as precious furniture and valuable metal bowls. A general change in eating and drinking habits was also noted by Rathje during the same period: artefacts in use with banquets, or 'syndeipnoi', were Phoenician wine amphorae, vessels for mixing and drinking, vessels for cooking, fire-dogs, spits, plates and dishes. A special debris pit found at Ficana, near a building which was interpreted as a dwelling of the local elite, brought forth objects of sundeipnon sets and Rathje claims a similar set of banqueting vessels for the Archaic house found by Boni in the Forum Romanum (1988: 84). These banquet services often are made of a special ware, the impasto rosso (red slip ware), and consist of special types of vessels: holmoi, chalices, stemmed bowls, and dishes; the shapes probably were inspired by imported vessels from the Near East. Rathje and Ridgway stated that dishes of this type are known from the western Phoenician colonies and were found at Pithekoussai. It is noteworthy that none of these special objects until now have been found in association with the Latial cults: only later, in the second half of the 7th century, drinking sets, such as bucchero jugs, chalices, kantharoi, and cups make their appearance. The kind of status objects known from the elite tombs of the 8th and 7th centuries BC are largely absent from the cults as are the dishes, stemmed cups, or other artefacts of dinner services published by Rathje. In other words, the best recognizable elements from the symbolic/ritualistic behaviour in the tombs and daily life are not easily comparable with such behaviour in the contemporary cults. The 'foreign' dedications which are frequent in the votive deposits and which consequently must be considered to have been meaningful in the cults are small objects: perfume bottles such as aryballoi, alabastra, personal jewellery such as beads, bracelets etc., and thus objects which relate to personal care and attire.

This may also be concluded, among other things, from the recent excavations of the three deposits found at Lavinium, which provide a number of important facts about the objects present in the Latial cult-deposits and the symbolic uses to which they may have been put (Castagnoli 1975; CatEnea 1981; Fenelli 1984; 1990a,b; Fenelli & Guaitoli 1990).

LAVINIUM

Deposit IA The earliest intra muros deposit contained objects dating from the IVB period. It was found near the remains of huts and Archaic walls and it was part of a fill. It is a secondary deposit which contained material that had accumulated elsewhere. The somewhat poorly preserved remains consist for the larger part of miniature vessels (fig.1), mostly hand-made, two-handled impasto jars (circa 1527 complete vessels and fragments of 30,000). These miniatures are accompanied by fragments of full sized pots, among which are full-sized impasto jars of the same plump shape as the miniature ones, as well as fragments of bucchero vessels of open shapes and Italo-Geometric stamnoid vessels and a number of alabastra and kylikes (Fenelli 1990b).

Deposit IB A second, mid-Republican, deposit, found in the immediate vicinity of the older deposit, also contained impasto miniature jars, which, in the development of their types, demonstrate a gradual loss of the plump shape of jar (fig. 1). This later deposit was found in a ditch, but whether it was part of a secondary deposit or whether it is evidence of an original accumulation of gifts is unclear. Also, it is uncertain whether these two deposits were buried in a sacred or profane area. The latter seems to be implied by Fenelli;

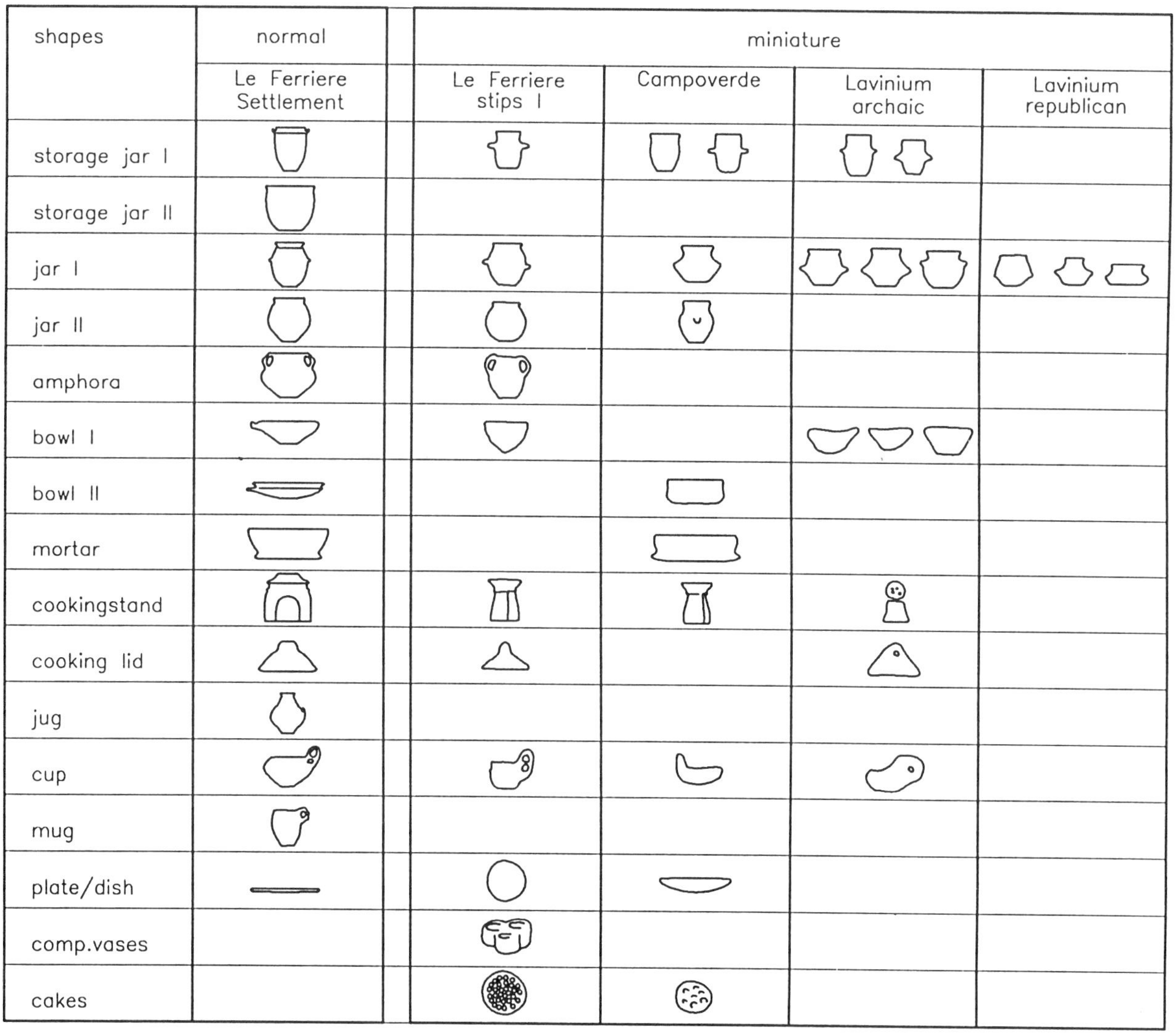

shapes	normal	miniature			
	Le Ferriere Settlement	Le Ferriere stips I	Campoverde	Lavinium archaic	Lavinium republican
storage jar I	⌴	⌴	⌴ ⌴	⌴ ⌴	
storage jar II	⌴				
jar I	⌴	⌴	⌴	⌴ ⌴ ⌴	⌴ ⌴ ⌴
jar II	⌴	⌴	⌴		
amphora	⌴	⌴			
bowl I	⌴	⌴		⌴ ⌴ ⌴	
bowl II	⌴		⌴		
mortar	⌴		⌴		
cookingstand	⌴	⌴	⌴	⌴	
cooking lid	⌴	⌴		⌴	
jug	⌴				
cup	⌴	⌴	⌴	⌴	
mug	⌴				
plate/dish	—	⌴	⌴		
comp.vases		⌴			
cakes		⌴	⌴		

Fig. 1. Borgo Le Ferriere-Satricum. Comparison of normal and miniature pot types; the miniature pots from Campoverde and Lavinium have been added.

however, that would make this deposit an exception to all other deposits in Latium as these always are buried in sacred precincts (Fenelli 1990b).

Fenelli stressed that hardly any 'female' shapes, such as lekythoi or aryballoi (often used by males too, however), were present in these deposits which were dominated by globular jars, but in which other miniatures shapes of well known impasto types of domestic vessels were present: e.g. dolium, fornello, lid-bowl. A well was found to exist near the spot where these deposits were found. If the content of the jars was the reason for the dedication rather than the vessel itself, then it must have consisted of a liquid; no grain or other material was present in the fills.

Deposit II The now famous Archaic deposit in the *extra muros* 'Minerva' sanctuary at Lavinium did contain 'female' votive gifts: a few fibulae, bullae, hair rings, silver rings, aryballoi and alabastra. This secondary deposit was dumped in a large area of 10 × 7m, and it was filled in layers: layers F and G date from the 7th and 6th centuries BC while layer E dates from the 6th century. A wall resting on a layer of stone chips and roof tiles separates these from the 4th and 3rd century specimens. In the pit there were many fragments of life-sized terracotta swaddled babies, and thymiateria. Most of the more outspoken gifts belong to the 4th and 3rd centuries. The different character of this deposit is related to rituals for young adults, for instance the preparation for marriage (Torelli 1984; Fenelli 1990).

Deposit III This deposit from Lavinium in fact comprises an area with objects which had accumulated near the altars at Lavinium (Castagnoli 1975). The area contained different objects again: from the Archaic period full sized imported Laconian and Attic kylikes, Etruscan bucchero kantharoi, chalices, and the valuable bronze statuettes are noteworthy: from the debris of the building near the altars many types of domestic pots such as dishes, bowls, and jars were found.

Thus Lavinium has rendered the remains of three markedly different votive deposits containing objects which show three markedly different kinds of gifts to the gods, each kind with a special symbolic value. Specific explanations may be devised for these specific types of offerings:

Deposit III The finds from the Archaic debris near the XIII-altars at Lavinium contained the debris of primary depositing, the objects being the remains of ritual acts carried out near the altars. Most votive gifts are full sized and extracted from daily circulation; they are gifts in the 'raw' (cf. Snodgrass 1990). The kylikes and mixing bowls are in all likelihood connected with sacrifices to the gods, sacrifices which ended in ceremonial eating and drinking in the building connected with the altars and build behind them. Near the altars a different type of dedication appears, a type which may be described as 'devotional'. All human figurines – either representing the dedicant in a devotional attitude or the deities – are in my opinion direct symbols of devotion: if the figurine represents the dedicant, then it expresses the direct devotion of this individual; if the figurine represents the deity, then it also expresses the devoted attention of the dedicant towards the god. Thus the offerings found near the altars at Lavinium are comparable to the ones Van Straten (1981: 81) has listed in his first category of votive gifts, which consists of participants and concomitants: "God, Man, Prayer and Sacrifice."

Deposit I The *intra muros* impasto-pots deposit clearly was a secondary deposit of a domestic character. This characteristic was ritually re-emphasized by the near-by depositing of, again, the same type of miniature vessels in a later period. The deposit presumably was connected with a spring (deity?). The category of gifts is clearly symbolic (by making the objects smaller than in daily life they are converted into symbols, the vessels are, however, not mini-miniatures as in other Latin votive-deposits). These miniature pots are connected with "Forces of domestic life", notably natural soil and water. This type of cult is probably Italic and connected with Lavinium itself since it lacks precise parallels elsewhere.

Deposit II The 'Minerva' deposit was also a secondary deposit of votive gifts, mostly of a 'female' character but in any case with objects referring to all kinds of ritual gifts of body-attire: fibulae, hair and body ornaments, perfume-flasks, etc. This category of gifts is always in the 'raw', i.e. the objects are taken unchanged directly out of the daily circulation: the objects were symbolic for the transition from one period to another in a person's life (compare also the cult for Fortuna at Praeneste: Champeaux 1982). In Lavinium the life-size terracotta statues of the dedicants hold many special objects, such as small chests, pomegranates, balls etc., objects which evidently were dedicated (but not found because they were of perishable materials) to a deity to mark these transitions. Most objects (those perishable as well as those re-found) in this deposit can be headed together under Van Straten's second category of cult practices: those connected with "initiation, 'course of life', illness etc." (1981: 81). The many bucchero drinking cups and jars belong to the same category as those found within the zone of the altars; they indicate that libation and drinking also took place in this sanctuary.

The differences in the early cult practices at Lavinium make it possible to scrutinise a number of traits present in other early Latial cults. Quite a number of the Latial votive areas contained miniature vessels, all in combinations similar to those found at Lavinium: jars, (lid) bowls, mugs, cups, cooking stands, votive dishes. These miniature types clearly imitate pots used in the Latin households, except perhaps for the special votive dish called 'focaccia' and the composite vases. The miniature dolium/jar and bowl are the most frequent dedications; it may be presumed – in view of the finds at Lavinium, Campoverde, and Satricum where the miniature dolii and jars were quite numerous – that the dolium and/or jar contained a food-offering, closed perhaps by a lid-bowl. It must be noted that these domestic sets of pots are not only present in miniature shapes: in full size they were also dedicated in contemporary sanctuaries. Later, during the 6th century BC, the symbolic use of miniatures vessels in some cases was replaced by the use of normal sized jars and bowls. This is evident from domestic deposits which contain only full-sized vessels. Many of the deposits with early miniature vessels in domestic shapes were found in connection with water, from natural as well as artificial sources; in later times these water-cults were respected, judging by the special protective platforms which were built over or quite near them.

Most objects from the well known deposit at the Laghetto del Monsignore (Crescenzi 1978) were retrieved from a small lake (depth 1.40/1.50m, diam. circa 5/7m) near a spring; but on its shore other assemblages of votive objects, amongst which the now lost sherds of 6th century Attic vases, seem to have been recovered. The fields around formerly were strewn with fragments of impasto pots and miniature vessels: no doubt these objects were dispersed from the nearby spring and lake by ploughing. The Campoverde deposit was not a closed deposit of objects which had accumulated elsewhere (contra Lowe 1978). It may have been an open deposit: either dedicants offered their gifts immediately in the waters of the spring of buried them in small pits around it. Dress-pins, fibulae, or other gifts of a personal nature were also present as were a few devotional dedications of figurines of sheet bronze. A deposit which resembles that at Campoverde more than the others was also associated with water: the mouth of the river Garigliano (Giglioli 1911; Mingazzini 1938; Guidi 1980). The original layout of this open-air sanctuary at Minturno, however, remains as unclear as that at Campoverde.

From this survey it is evident that cult practices which included – or consisted entirely of – the dedication of miniature vessels is fairly typical for Latium. The larger deposits of early miniature jars are often found near water; in later periods such miniatures were also dedicated in cults not connected with water. Although the lack of publication precludes any conclusive statements, it seems safe to say that in early deposits such personal objects as fibulae, pins, beads, hair-rings and small perfume pots are rarely found in combination with early miniature pots. The deposits which do contain such personal ornaments demonstrate an early interest in cults connected to the "course of life/rites de passage" type of veneration, which perhaps came into full swing only under foreign influences. The sheet bronzes are, however, often found in combination with the miniatures and seem in all periods to represent the connection to the family of the indigenous dedicants.

THE EARLY CULT AT LE FERRIERE-*SATRICUM*

The spatial organisation on the hilltop at Le Ferriere during the first period shows small hutpits and cooking pits grouped around a natural depression which presumably was filled with water. Grave pits were dug at the foot of the same hill. The oldest vessels from the hutpits and the grave pits must be dated in the IIB period of Latial culture, now generally dated 830–760 BC. However, we would do well to remember that the Groningen calibrated C14 dates for the carbon from the lowest levels in the debris-pits give earlier dates: they range from 1050 to 800 BC (Maaskant-Kleibrink 1987: Olde Dubbelink & Van der Plicht 1990).

From the arrangements of simple pits at Le Ferriere we learn that the early Latin occupants did not put much energy or skill in the construction of their dwellings, graves or sacred spaces. In all cases their activities were restricted to the digging and dressing-up of small pits in the loamy soil. Whatever kind of roofing or wall construction was used, it will not have amounted to much as firm post-holes or wall trenches for this period are totally absent. The earliest pits were arranged in a semi-circle around an open-air centre, which from the start seems to have functioned as a public, sacred space (fig.2). This space must have consisted of a natural depression – another pit, but larger and filled with water. Perhaps comparable is an opening in the natural rock, venerated in an early period, at the centre of the Civita plateau at Tarquinia: Bonghi Jovino 1990: 679ff.) The central cleft in the natural hill at Le Ferriere presumably was filled with the water of a small springlet. It left a layer of find-grained grey loam on the bottom of the depression. At some point in the 8th or 7th century BC (the clearances of the 19th century prevent any close precision) in this central area a round pond of diameter 12m was dug (cf. Piazza d'Armi at Veii: Stefani 1922; 1944–45). In and around the natural depression at *Satricum*, assemblages of votive gifts must have been deposited at least from the 10th and early 9th centuries onwards. This early origin of the cult may be substantiated as follows.

In the archaeological literature the oldest deposits (usually labelled No.I) found beneath the Archaic temple at Borgo Le Ferriere have usually been interpreted as a closed secondary deposit, with a closing date of c.530 and with the oldest gifts dating from 725 BC (e.g. CatsSatricum 1982; 1985a; 1985b; CatGrandRoma 1990: Guidi 1980; 1990). This deposit, the richest ever found in Latium, is thought to have contained gifts which

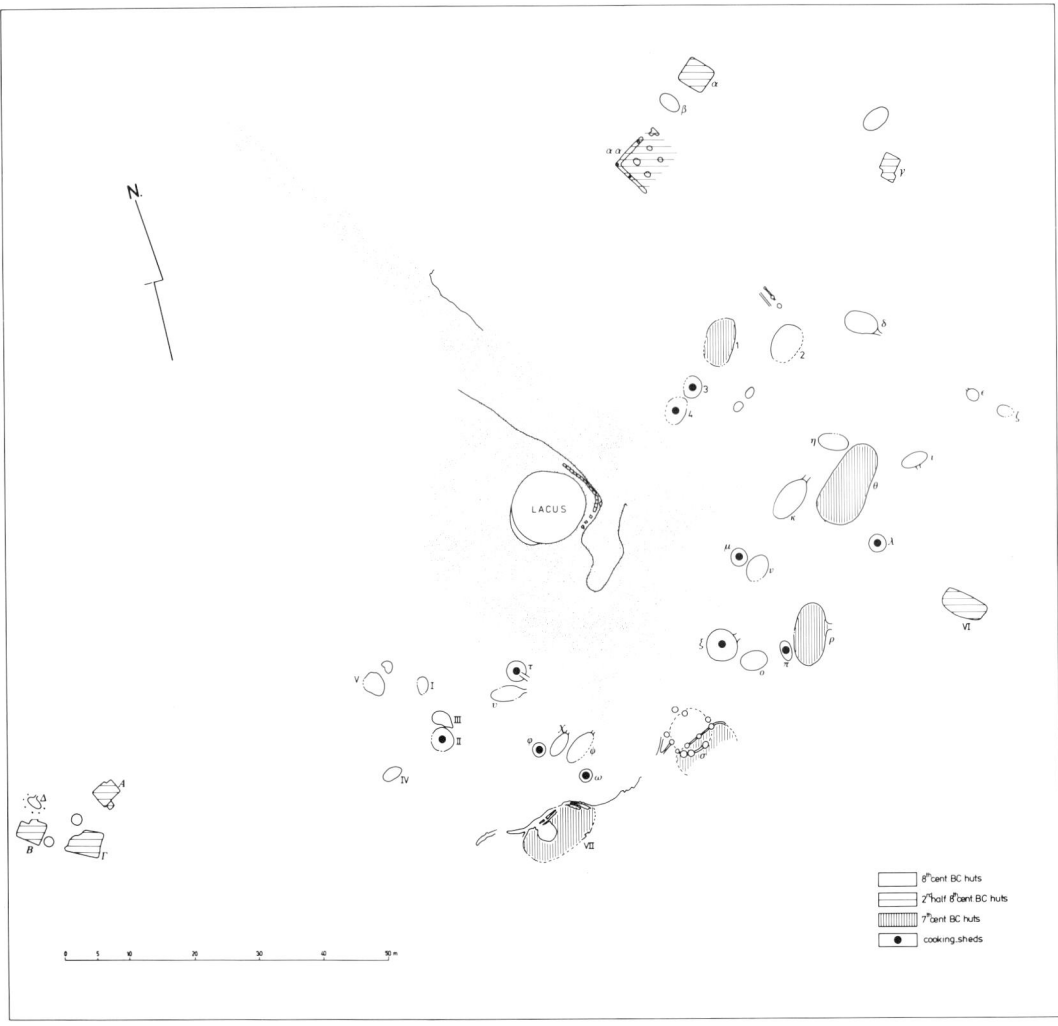

Fig. 2. Borgo Le Ferriere-Satricum. Plan of the earliest hutpits gathered around the lacus.

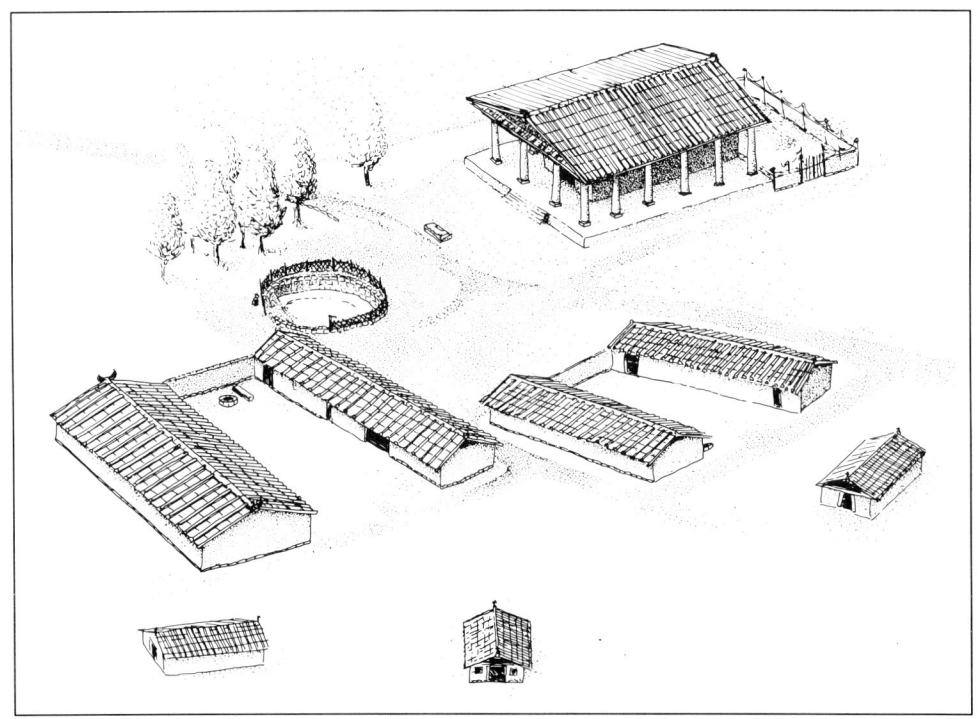

Fig. 3. Borgo Le Ferriere-Satricum. Reconstruction of the 'sacred zone' in the 6th century BC.

had accumulated elsewhere in the sanctuary and to have been deposited in a pit in the centre underneath temple I. There are a number of reasons to consider this deposit as consisting of primary votive assemblages and not as a secondary dump and to date its initiation much earlier, during the 10th or 9th century BC:

1. The first reason for a different interpretation comes from the small pits separately filled with gifts recently found below the temples. These pits indicate that around the centre dedicants had been digging small pits, bordering them with stones. In these pits they deposited small durable gifts as well as gifts of meat. The pits date from all the Latial periods except period I (from late 9th-7th century BC). The find contexts of these pits indicate that they must not be considered to be complete but 'topped off' by later activities (CatsSatricum 1985a: 138ff.; 1985b: 37ff.).

2. The second reason for a different reconstruction of the oldest votive practices is the evidence from the 19th century excavation journal, written up by the administrator of the Villa Giulia Museum, Finelli. His entries demonstrate that gifts came to light at numerous places beneath and around the central temples (see Della Seta 1918: 279–292; CLP, 108, pls. 87–88; CatGrandeRoma: 234–240; Maaskant-Kleibrink 1992a: 54 note 11; 1992b).

3. A third reason is the date and character of the gifts. The small votive vessels date from the 10th, 9th, and 8th centuries BC (fig.1). This early date rests on four arguments:

(a) The 9th century date of comparable miniature dishes and 'focacce' found as votive gifts in a number of early tombs in Osteria dell'Osa dedicated at special occasions (Bietti Sestieri interprets tomb 126 at Osa as the tomb of a priest: Bietti-Sestieri 1990).

(b) At Campoverde, a few kilometres from Borgo Le Ferriere, a votive deposit containing 10th and 9th century miniature vessels together with full-sized gifts was found (Crescenzi 1978: 51ff. CLP: 347). Of those available for study, the majority consists of the same miniature plain dolia, jars and bowls, which were also found among the oldest votives at Borgo Le Ferriere. In other words, similar gift-donation was practised as early as the 9th (or even earlier) and 8th centuries at the nearby small lake of the Laghetto del Monsignore. Consequently, there is no reason to date the start of gift giving at Borgo Le Ferriere later than that at Campoverde.

(c) From Borgo Le Ferriere itself there is corroborating evidence for such an early date of miniature pottery. In the hutpits a number of miniature vessels were found among sherds of full-sized pottery. All hutpits at Borgo Le Ferriere are closed finds: it is not possible that the miniatures were introduced later into these contexts. The miniatures which were found in the pits and thus date from periods II and III are: 14 miniatures of large storage jars (with knobs or plain); 9 miniatures of dishes or bowls; 5 miniatures cups (Maaskant-Kleibrink 1987; 1992a). Such miniatures vessels have been found in domestic contexts in other excavations as well: Ficana (CatFicana 1980: 57); Acquarossa, 5 jars, 1 bowl (Lundgren & Wendt 1986: 124); S. Giovenale 1 jar, 3 bowls (S. Giovenal III, 3: 89); Luni sul Mignone 2 miniature vases, 1 cup. In the latter case, Puglisi supposes that the small vessels were put to use in a domestic context (1959: 56–58). In view of the constant appearance in domestic contexts of the miniature vessels and the fact they are of the same make and types as the votive miniatures it may be suggested that miniature vessels were also sacred in the domestic sphere.

(d) Recent reanalysis of the miniature vessels found in the earliest votive deposits (I) at Satricum made clear that among the miniatures there are vessels which imitate 9th century reticulated jars, while other specimens imitate an early type of collared jar as well as a biconical pot. Moreover, among the sherds, were four specimens decorated with impressed 'Apennine' decoration. These recent re-analyses of the contents (1993) confirm the above arguments: the first votive assemblages on the hill-plateau of *Satricum* can be firmly dated to the 10th and 9th centuries and perhaps even earlier.

4. The fourth reason is the phenomenon of cult continuity: the character of the later votive deposits (No. II and in part No. III). They are open deposits consisting of assemblages of gifts bordered by stones and fragments of roof tiles (Maaskant-Kleibrink 1992a,b; Bouma 1995).

The veneration of sacred space in the centre of the hutpits initially was carried out through simple means. We may judge this from the many mini-miniature vessels recovered: the Villa Giulia Museum conserves *c.* 1800 specimens excavated below and around the central temples. The 19th century excavation journal of the 19th century Villa Giulia excavators makes it clear that these miniatures, together with other gifts, were in part found in separate areas around the natural central depression. Closer study of these miniatures shows that they are of the same types as the full-sized pots found in the hutpits (see below). This similarity is so close that it suggests a special meaning.

The domestic aspect of the early cult at Le Ferriere was later on supplemented with other aspects. From *c.* 700 BC onwards dedications of fibulae of normal and of miniature size, and gifts of beads, bracelets and scarabs as well as small perfume pots, indicate that the cult directed itself to the "'rites of passage' and/or 'course of life'" type of cult. Dedications of a devotional character, such as small bronzes and sheet bronzes, indicate that a divine presence was felt.

The cult-space and/or type of dwelling for the divine presence (at *Satricum* and elsewhere) already has been intensively debated (see Guidi 1980). Livy mentions the *fanum* as the oldest form of cult-place. It was interpreted as a place of worship in the open. Servius, citing Varro, says that the oldest type of temple had a convex roof (*ad Aen* I, 505). Boni and Müller-Karpe both reconstructed the original Vesta temple on the Forum Romanum as a hut. Gierow and Andrèn interpreted the miniature model of a dwelling, found in a votive context at Satricum, as the earliest sacred hut; Andrèn connected the same miniature with Villanovan huts by means of an intermediate sacred shape: the one known from the Tarquinian Selciatello cippus. However, Colonna (1980: 115) views the *Satricum* model as a miniature of a normal dwelling; Quilici interpreted it as a miniature hut-dwelling with a special function and saw the model as an evolved type, dating from the full 7th century BC. Staccioli (1990) interprets all miniature models as temples; he concludes that the miniatures have an opening of exaggerated width, to allow the sight of a small statue of a deity. Guidi and Simon associated the *Satricum* models with the oval hutpit found below the central temples on the plateau of Le Ferriere (Guidi 1980, 1990; Simon 1990).

EVIDENCE OF HOUSEHOLDS OR OF RITUAL MEALS?

As noted, the 9th and 8th century BC hutpits arranged in a semi-circle around the sacred centre are for the most part of an extremely simple nature. From these pits have come a great many closed assemblages of pottery fragments, charcoal, and bones (all pits were sealed by the same late-7th century destruction layer). Although the assemblages each belong to a different feature, clearly separated in time and in space, they are essentially – and surprisingly – similar. The features are large and oval, or smaller and roundish; they were never bordered by solid posts. The small holes found around the pits in a number of cases indicate that the features must have been covered with thin thatched straw roofs. The fills of the larger features all contained at least two horizontally separated areas mixed with charcoal ('hearths') around which the spread of fragments of cooking jars, bowls, cooking stands and animal bones was at its thickest (e.g. Maaskant-Kleibrink 1978; 1992a). As mentioned above, the top part of all the pits was filled with 7th century debris from the levelling layer below the Archaic buildings. In addition, finds from the oval hutpit NIR I found below the temple were likewise similar to the others (cf. CatsSat 1982: 35ff.; 1985b: 124ff.), making an identification of this hut as a different kind of dwelling from the other ones unlikely. The theory of Staccioli (1990) also militates against such an identification: an open view of a cult statue would mean an empty hut, not one used for cooking and eating, activities which are clearly indicated by the domestic finds in this hutpit. But if we do consider it to be of a special nature and of influence on the design of early sacred architecture then we must consider all the hutpits nearby also as special. The following observations offer support for this hypothesis.

The hutpits and their evidence

The evidence from the assemblages of pottery fragments, bones and ashes from the hutpits render eating and drinking archaeologically the most visible activities. This high visibility must not be considered as random but as testimony of the meaningfulness of eating and drinking in early settlement: they must be considered to be a reflection of very important socialisation processes. These pits contain rather uncomplicated and multifunctional, traditional vessels. These belong technologically to a single ware-group, hand-made of impasto, unpurified clay, on which only occasional traces of burnishing were left. The colours are usually blackish or brownish. The pots in the earliest period do not have profiled feet or stand rings, the rims of the vessels are mostly in curving (not fit for pouring) or upright and, if decorated at all, a plastic cord-band or a row of geometric incised motifs, for instance triangle, occur. To this waregroup belong storage jars, smaller jars, bowls, mugs, and cooking stands, a set of vessels which may be called the standard set of the early Iron Age (fig.1).

In the hutpits the multifunctional bowl is the shape that was most in use and the multifunctional dolii or larger jars were the second most frequent type of vessel. Only a few more sophisticated vessel shapes have been found, namely a number of cups, a few amphorae, and jugs. Such shapes may confidently be identified as used for ceremonial drinking. Only a single fragment from a Cycladic cup was found to be present in the hutpits; all other early hut-fills with these potsherds were not mixed with imported vessels: consequently, the hutpit-assemblages indicate an absolutely indigenous and pre-'international' Latial phase.

Because charcoal and bones were present among the pottery fragments in the hutpits, it is clear that these pits represent the debris of time sharing and food sharing activities of groups of people. But are we to presume that these pits contain the debris of households active all year round? This hardly seems the case: as mentioned before, the wall and roof structures must have been very flimsy indeed and the only activity that may be postulated from the remaining sherds is that of cooking and eating. Storage vessels and the remains of weaving activities are practically absent, which makes it unlikely that people dwelled here all year round. Presumably, therefore, the pits indicate the presence of visiting groups. If so, we must try to determine whether cooking was done only seasonally and/or during religious festivals. Only a small portion of the bones found in the pits are of sheep and/or goats, animals which are representative of the expected semi-nomadic pastoral/farming society in these regions. The presence of a relatively large proportion of cattle and pig bones is surprising: where pigs are present one expects a village-like infrastructure with pens, or one expects them to have roamed unpenned under the eye of a swineherd (Barker 1985: 33): a proper 9th/8th-century BC village was not found on the temples' plateau, and free roaming is unlikely because of the waterlogged area around it, which is also not compatible with cattle. Consequently, pigs and cattle may very well have been part of ritual meals. The quantity of animal bones in the pits (although in a very bad condition) indicate a rich consumption of meat, especially cattle and pig, which is certainly higher than may be expected for normal households. Meat consumption in this type of society is considered to be the consumption of surplus whereas the vegetarian diet is thought to have been the normal type of diet (Barker 1985). The special character of the consumption of cattle, sheep (goat) and pig at *Satricum* could be attested for the 5th and 4th century BC. The votive offerings (assemblages) of Votive Deposit II each contained either skull bones or leg bones from a cow, a sheep and a pig. This evidence indicates that a suovetaurilia was eaten during each religious meal, after which the skulls and/or a leg of the animals was dedicated to the goddess in a bowl or a cooking jar (Bouma 1995). Unfortunately, our excavations could not determine the presence of flora and other foodstuffs: despite sieving, carbonized seeds or other such remains have hardly come to light: these may have been absent or have been consumed by unfavourable soil conditions. Alternatively, they may have been absent from Latial hut-contents, because in these places only prepared foodstuffs may have been used.

To summarise, the semi-circle of flimsily-built huts around an open and early sacred centre (going back at least to the 10th–9th centuries BC), the traditional character of their fills, and the fact that the assemblages of pots are reflected in the miniature assemblages used in the early Latin domestic cults, draw us towards the conclusion that these hutpits are evidence of visiting groups cooking ritual meals while offering symbolic meals in mini-miniature vessels to the deity at the sacred centre. In my opinion the archaeological evidence points to sacred centres of transhumance families, during winter living at e.g. Campoverde and *Satricum*, and burying their dead and holding festivals. In view of the later developments at Le Ferriere, when, during the 6th century, we find large courtyard buildings with banqueting rooms flanking the central temples, and considering votive pit II (a 12 × 50m large area mainly filled with jars and bowls), a similar ritual function for the central features from the earliest period onwards is very likely. In the Greek sanctuaries several 'festival meadows' outside the temenoi and flanked by several stoai have been identified (Kuhn 1985: 254f; Sinn 1988: 149ff). Other – though later – evidence for the construction of special huts for the consuming of ritual meals is known from Samos, together with simple sets of pots, specially made in the sanctuary and used for the meals and afterwards deposited in the sacred area: the Samian pots date from the late 7th and full 6th century BC (Kron 1988: 135ff). The architecture at *Satricum* is different but the function of the structures around the temples may have been similar.

A NON-POSITIVIST CONCLUSION

The main question dealt with in this paper was whether we could designate the area around the sacred centre as a profane zone or whether the hutpits and buildings were actually functioning as part of the sacred area. Such a question has its own special difficulties, especially when the student of early Latin culture is dealing not only with material evidence stemming from badly published 19th and early 20th century excavations, but also with material which in antiquity itself may already have been put to secondary use, as is frequently the case with, for example, votive and debris deposits. The archaeologist in this case is interpreting phenomena which by actions of earlier people have at least been altered twice. In post-processual archaeology patterns of artefacts have been likened to texts: both are patterns of meaningful symbols which are removed from the original actors and which are open to re-interpretation. If we want to read sacred or profane meanings into the described patterns of artefacts we face the difficulty that now that it has been recognized that all material culture is imbued with symbolic meaning of one kind or another, we cannot easily distinguish materially between the sacred and the domestic. Human action recreates social structures by drawing upon existing symbols and conceptual schemata (Giddens 1987). Especially when we are dealing with an early period we must realize that the creation of ritual arises from the same material conditions as everyday life. For instance in the case of meals, how are we to distinguish between those of families or other groups and those intended for or shared with gods? Both will leave patterns of artefacts but to distinguish daily meals from ritual ones we must known the cultural dinner practices (Goody 1982). Barrett (1991) recently suggested that ritual may be regarded as a form of discourse characterised as 'textual' to distinguish it from the discourse of everyday 'talk'. Recognition of ritual traditions, then, may be rooted in the identification of 'textual' factors which will indicate the non-profane practices, necessarily reproduced over extensive tracts of time. Such elements are certainly present in the 'formulaic' sets of artifacts, full-sized and miniature, in the features of the plateau at Borgo Le Ferriere. Our difficulty is that notions such as profane or sacred may not be correct and that we must be satisfied – at least for early periods – with the description of these 'formulae' of artifacts.

ACKNOWLEDGEMENTS

For various helpful comments I am indebted to E. J. A. Borchert (for discussion of the miniature pots), R. A. Olde Dubbelink (hut contents), for the drawings to H. J. Waterbolk, and for corrections of the English text to Christina Williamson and Dr. Neil Christie.

Bibliography

Anathema 1990. Atti del Convegno Internazionale *Anathema*, Scienze dell'Antichità 3–4 (1989–1990) Università degli Studi di Roma 'La Sapienza'.

Antonielli, U. 1927. 'Tivoli, fossa votiva di età romana, repubblicana e con materiali arcaici, scoperta in contrada 'Acquoria', *Notizie degli Scavi di Antichità*, 215–256.

Barker, G. 1985. *Prehistoric Farming in Europe*, Cambridge

Barrett, J. 1991. 'Towards an Archaeology of Ritual', in *Sacred and Profane, Proccedings of a Conference on Archaeology, Ritual and Religion*, Oxford, 1ff.

Bartoloni, G. 1990. 'I depositi votivi di Roma arcaica', in *Anathema*, 747ff.

Bietti Sestieri, A.M., de Santis A. & La Regina, A. 1990. 'Elementi di tipo cultuale e doni personali nella necropoli laziale di Osteria dell'Osa', in *Anathema*, 65–88.

Blagg, T.F.C. 1985. 'Cult practice and its social context in the religious sanctuaries of Latium and South Etruria', *Papers in Italian Archaeology IV, The Cambridge Conference*, BAR International Series, Oxford, 35ff.

Bonghi Jovino, M. 1976. *Depositi votivi d'Etruria*, Milan.

Bonghi Jovino, M. 1990. 'Aggiornamenti sull'area sacra di Tarquinia e nuove considerazioni sulla tromba-litua', in *Anathema*, 679–695.

Boni, G. 1900. in *Notizie degli Scavi di Antichità*, 191ff.

Bouma, J.W. 1995. *Religio votiva, Archaeology and Early Republican Votive Religion in Latium – The Votive Deposit South-west of the Temples on the Acropolis of 'Satricum' Borgo Le Ferriere*, Groningen.

Carucci, P. 1907. *La grotta preistorica di Pertosa*, Napoli.

Castagnoli, F. 1975. *Lavinium II, Le tredici are*, Rome.

CatEnea 1981. Exhibition Catalogue: *Enea del Lazio, archeologia e mito*, Rome.

CatFicana 1989. Exhibition Catalogue: *Ficana, una pietra miliare sulla strada per Roma*, Rome.

CatRomaSott 1985. Exhibition Catalogue: *Roma sotterranea*, Rome.

CatGrandeRoma 1990. Exhibition Catalogue: *La grande Roma dei Tarquinii*, Rome.

CatSatricum 1982. Exhibition Catalogue (Latina): *Satricum, una città Latina*, Florence.

CatSatricum 1985a. Exhibition Catalogue (Leiden, Nijmegen): *Nieuw Licht op een oude stad, Italiaanse en Nederlandse opgravingen in Satricum*, The Hague.

CatSatricum 1985b. Exhibition Catalogue (Albano) *Area Sacra di Satricum, tra scavo e restituzione*, Rome.

Champeaux, J. 1982. *Le Culte de la Fortune I*, Rome.

CLP 1976. Exhibition Catalogue: *Civiltà del Lazio Primitivo*, Rome.

Colini, A. 1927. 'Le recenti scoperte sul Campidoglio', *Capitolium* 3, 383–388.

Colonna, G. 1981. 'Tarquinio prisco e il tempio di Giove Capitolino', *Parpas*, 43–44.

Colonna, G. 1984. 'I templi del Lazio fino al V secolo compreso', *Archeologia Laziale* 6, 396–411.

Colonna, G. 1985. 'Satricum, appunti sulla storia degli scavi, la storia della città e il soggetto degli altorilievi mitologici del tempio', in *Atti Latina*, 12–23.

Crescenzi, G. 1978. 'Campoverde', *Archeologia Laziale* 1, 51ff.

Della Seta, A. 1918. *Museo della Villa Giulia*, Rome.

De Rossi, M.S. 1878. 'Intorno ad un copioso deposito di stoviglie ed altri oggetti arcaici rinvenuto nel Viminale', *Bullettino communale* 3, 64–92.

De Waele, J.A. 1981. 'I templi della Mater Matuta a Satricum', *MededRom* 43, 7–68.

Fenelli, M. 1984. 'Lavinium', *Archeologia Laziale* 6, 325–344.

Fenelli, M. 1990a. 'Lavinio' in *BTCGI* V.

Fenelli, M. 1990b. 'Culti a Lavinium: le evidenze archeologiche', in *Anathema*, 487–506.

Fenelli, M. & Guaitoli, M. 1990. 'Nuovi dati degli scavi di Lavinium', *Archeologia Laziale* 10, 195–201.

Formazione 1980. *La Formazione delle città nel Lazio = Dialoghi di Archeologia* 1–2.

Giddens, A. 1980. *Social Theory and Modern Sociology*, Cambridge.

Giglioli, G.Q. 1974. 'Note archeologiche sul Latium Novum: Umbrosae regnae Maricaei', *Ausonia* 6, 38, 60–71.

Giuliani, C.F. 1966. *Tibur, Forma Italiae*, Rome.

Goody, J. 1982. *Cooking, Cuisine and Class. A Study in Comparative Sociology*, Cambridge.

Graillot, H. 1896. 'Le temple de Conca', *Mélanges de l'Ecole Française de Rome, Antiquité* 16, 131–164.

Gjerstad, E. 1960. *Early Rome* 3, Lund.

Guidi, A. 1980. 'Luoghi di culto dell'età del bronzo finale e della prima età del ferro nel Lazio meridionale', *Archeologia Laziale* 3, 148ff.

Guidi, A. 1990. 'Alcune osservazioni sulla problematica delle offerte nella protostoria dell'Italia centrale', in *Anathema*, 403ff.

Kron, U. 1988. 'Kultmahle im Heraion von Samos archaischer Zeit', in *Early Greek Cult Practices*, eds. R. Hägg, N. Marinatos & G. Nordquist, Stockholm.

Kuhn, G. 1985. 'Untersuchungen zur Funktion der Säulenhalle in archaischer und klassischer Zeit', *JdI* 100, 254f.

Lowe, C. 1978. *The Historical Significance of Early Latin Votive Deposits (up to 4th century BC)* BAR International Series 41, Oxford.

Lundgren, M.B. & Wendt, L. 1982. 'Acquarossa zone A', *Acta Romana* 4, 38, 3, Stockholm.

Maaskant-Kleibrink, M. 1984. 'L'urbanistica: il caso di Satricum', *Archeologia Laziale* 6, 351–357.

Maaskant-Kleibrink, M. & Olde Dubbelink, R. 1985. 'Stepping over or overstepping thresholds: on the identification of hutfloors, cooking areas and rubbish pits at the Site of Satricum', *Papers in Italian Archaeology IV: The Cambridge Conference iii*, BAR International Series 245, Oxford, 203ff.

Maaskant-Kleibrink, M. 1987. *Settlement Excavations at Borgo Le Ferriere <Satricum>, vol. I*, Groningen.

Maaskant-Kleibrink, M. 1991. 'Early Latin Settlement-plans at Borgo Le Ferriere (*Satricum*), Reading Mengarelli's Maps', *BABesch* 66, 51–114.

Maaskant-Kleibrink, M. 1992a. 'Gli scavi pi recenti svolti a Borgo Le Ferriere (<*Satricum*>)', *QuadAEI* 20, 53–64.

Maaskant-Kleibrink, M. 1992b. *Settlement Excavations at Borgo Le Ferriere <Satricum> Vol. II*, Groningen.

Mengarelli, R. 1898. 'Conca: Nuove scoperte nella tenuta di Conca nel territorio dell'antica città di *Satricum*', *Notizie degli Scavi di Antichità*, 167–171.

Mengarelli, R. 1903. 'Gli scavi di *Satricum* (Ferriere di Conca)', in *Atti del Congresso Internazionale di Scienze Storiche* vol. V, sezione IV, Roma, 267–272.

Mengarelli, R. 1905. in : G. Pinza, 'Monumenti primitivi di Roma e del Lazio antico', *Monumenti Antichi* 15, 476–487.

Mengarelli, R. & Paribeni, R. 1908. 'Scavi sulle terrazze sostenute da mura poligonali presso l'abbazia di Valvisciolo', *Notizie degli Scavi di Antichità*, 241–260.

Murray-Threipland, L. 1969. 'Veii. A deposit of votive pottery', *Papers of the British School at Rome*, 37, 1–14.

Negroni Catacchio, N., Domanico, L. & Miari, M. 1990. 'Offerte votive in grotta e in abitato nelle valle del Fiora e dell'Albegna nel corso dell'età del Bronzo: indizi e proposte interpretative', in *Anathema*, 579–598.

Olde Dubbelink, R.A. & van der Plicht, J. 1990. 'Le capanne II e VI a Borgo Le Ferriere <*Satricum*> e le datazioni al radiocarbonio', *QUADaei* 19, 234–236.

Patroni, G. 1899. 'Caverna naturale con avanzi preistorici in provincia di Salerno', *Monumenti Antichi* 9, 545–616.

Puglisi, S.M. 1959. *La civiltà apenninica*, Florence.

Quilici, L. 1979. *Roma primitiva e le origine della civiltà laziale*, Rome.

Rathje, A. 1984. *I Keimelia orientali, Aspetti delle aristocrazie fra VIII e VII a.C.*, Rome.

Rathje, A. 1988. 'Manners and customs in Central Italy in the Orientalizing Period: influence from the Near East', *Acta Hyperborea*, Copenhagen, 81ff.

Rellini, U. 1916. 'La caverna di Latronico e il culto delle acqua salutari nell'età del Bronzo', *Monumenti Antichi*, 24.

Simon, E. 1990. *Die Götter der Römer*, Munich.

Sinn, U. 1988. 'Der Kult der Aphaia auf Aegina', in *Early Greek Cult Practices*, eds. R. Hägg, No. Marinatos, & G. Nordquist, Stockholm.

Snodgrass, A.M. 1990. 'The economics of dedication at Greek Sanctuaries', in *Anathemai*, 288–300.

Stefani, E. 1922, 'Veio: Esplorazione dentro l'area dell'antica città', *Notizie degli Scavi di Antichità,* 19, 383ff.

Stefani, E. 1944–45. 'Scavi archeologici a Veio in Contrada Piazza d'Armi', *Monumenti Antichi*, 40: 182ff.

Torelli, M. 1984. *Lavinio e Roma; i riti iniziatrici e matrimonia tra archeologia e storia*, Rome.

Van Straten, F.T. 1981. *Gifts for the Gods, Faith, Hope and Worship*, Leiden.

14

Emblems of Identity
An Examination of the Use of Matt-Painted Pottery in the Native Tombs of the Salento Peninsula in the 5th and 4th Centuries BC

EDWARD HERRING

(Accordia Research Centre, University of London)

Summary: *By the end of the 6th century BC new pottery types, such as Greek-type glazed wares and local wheel-made banded wares, had superseded traditional matt-painted pottery in the domestic contexts of native sites in the Salento peninsula. These new wares reflect increasing contact between the natives and their Greek neighbours. This sequence is one witnessed all over Southern Italy in this period and is often taken as an indication of the assimilation of Greek culture by the native population. However, in the Salento area the introduction of these new wares did not signal the end of the matt-painted tradition: during the 5th and most of the 4th century, the natives here continued to use matt-painted pottery in their tombs. Indeed, almost every native tomb contained at least one matt-painted pot, normally a trozzella, as well as other grave goods of Greek type and actual Greek imports. It seems that this link with the past became an obligatory part of native funerary ritual. This paper examines this highly specific usage within the framework of 'emblemic style' as developed by Wiessner and suggests that these highly distinctive vessels were used as symbols of native identity.*

INTRODUCTION

The aim of this paper is to examine a fairly well-documented phenomenon in the archaeological record for Southern Italy according to a specific theoretical approach. The phenomenon in question involves the highly specific use of an otherwise obsolete pottery style in the tombs of the non-Greek population of the Salento peninsula. This form of theoretical interpretation, I believe, makes it possible to cast new light upon wider aspects of the non-Greek or native society of the area.

BACKGROUND

The Salentine peninsula features a number of important native sites which were flourishing during the 5th and 4th centuries BC. Many of these native sites seem to have been developing an urban form in this period; these sites include Muro Leccese, Oria, Rocavecchia, Rudiae, Ugento and Vaste (fig.1). The exact point which the native sites had reached in this process of urbanisation is a contentious issue which lies beyond the scope of this paper (Whitehouse & Wilkins 1989; Herring 1991a, 1991b). However, one can, I feel, fairly state that native society was growing in complexity during this time period. The same area contained the major Greek city of Taras and its surrounding territory or *chora* at the head of the Gulf of Taranto.

In the Salento peninsula, and in Southern Italy in general, the population can be divided into two broad groups, the Greeks and the non-Greek or native. Obviously there were many smaller political and cultural entities subsumed within these broad categories, and one should not underestimate the likely degree of mixing of the two populations through inter-marriage. From the end of the 8th century BC onwards with the foundation of the Greek colony of Taranto, the native population of the Salento area came into increasing contact with Greek culture. The nature of these relations is a complex problem: clearly there were all manner of if not friendly, then at least not openly hostile social relations, which can be attested in the archaeological record by the sheer volume of Greek artefacts found in native contexts, especially tombs. On the other hand, the ancient sources detail periods of violent conflict between the Greeks and their neighbours: for example, a number of authors tell how raids by the Lucanians and the Messapians (usually interpreted as coming from the Salento peninsula) forced Taranto to appeal for help from her mother-city, Sparta, in *c*. 343 BC (e.g. Diodorus Siculus 16.62.4 and Strabo 6.3.3–4 – only Strabo mentions the Messapians in this context). Herodotus (7.170) refers to an earlier Tarentine defeat at the hands of the Messapian Iapygians[1]; this same defeat is referred to by Aristotle (Politics, 1303^{a3}) in the context of his discussion of the creation of the Tarentine democracy, though Aristotle speaks simply of the Iapygians. Similarly, Diodorus Siculus (11.52) names only the Iapygians, although his is a fuller account than both Herodotus' and Aristotle's. From Diodorus Siculus (together with corroborative evidence from the Aristotle passage) a date of *c.* 473 BC can be ascribed to this event.

Contact between the Greeks and natives intensified over time and was most strong in areas where the two populations interacted most. This culture contact had profound consequences in the native communities, with native society undergoing considerable social and cultural transformations. Much of this change has been interpreted as a process of cultural assimilation; however, the phenomenon discussed in this paper I interpret as a sign of resistance to such assimilation.

THE CERAMIC PHENOMENON

The type of pottery under discussion is commonly referred to as geometric or matt-painted pottery. This pottery type now has a long tradition of scholarship stretching from the seminal work of Mayer (1914) up to Yntema's recent comprehensive treatment (1985. Cf. also Small 1971; De Juliis 1977). Yntema's general survey of these wares is, in my view, the fullest currently available and in this paper, I shall be following his typology and terminology[2]. Although his survey focusses more on the earlier phases of the matt-painted tradition than on the late surviving remnants, which are the topic of this paper, it does devote more attention to the Salentine wares than any other regional style.

Like much of Southern Italy, the Salento area had its own regional style of matt-painted geometric pottery from the late 9th century BC. This style, dubbed Salento Geometric by Yntema, developed from more general South Italian ancestors; Yntema's South Italian Early Geometric and South Italian Early Geometric.

This type of pottery was manufactured using slow wheel technology. Pots of this class have light surfaces and are decorated with geometric motifs executed in matt brown and red paint. This pottery type was considered suitable for use in both domestic and funerary contexts.

During the 6th century BC the native communities began to import Greek pottery in increasing quantity.

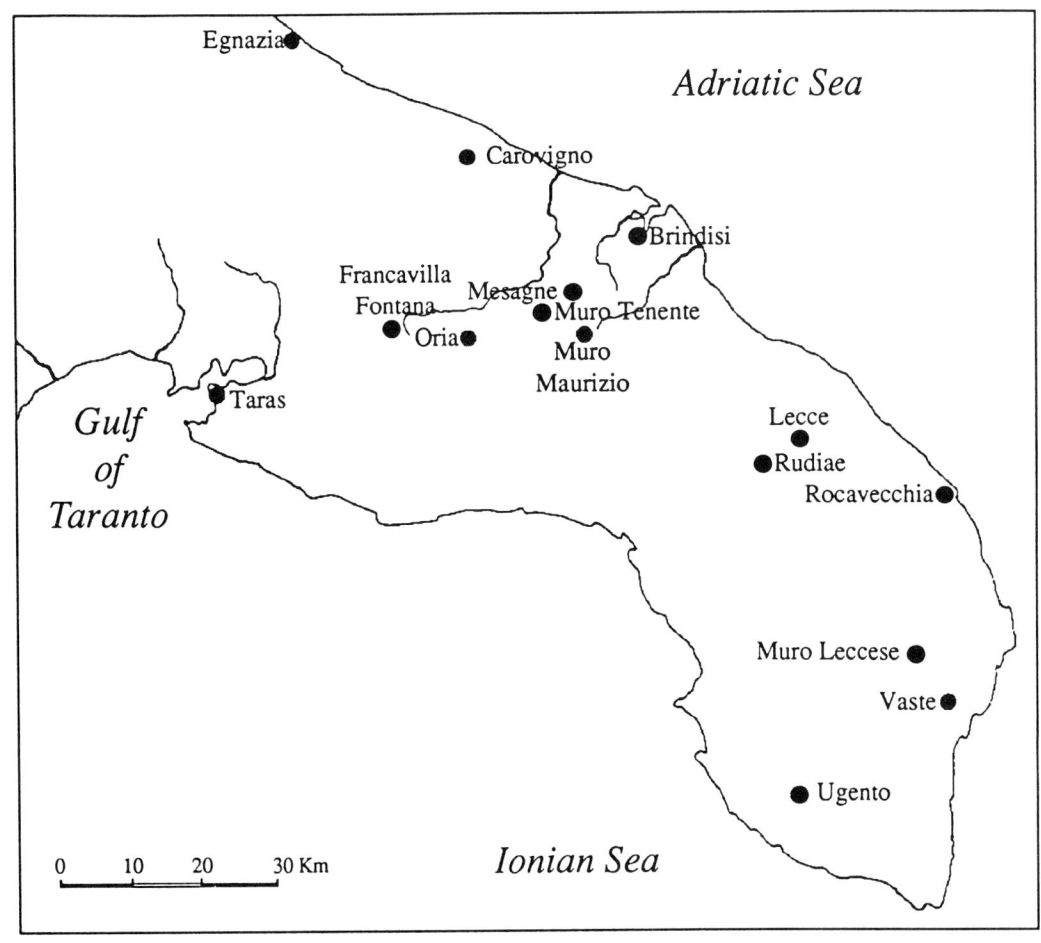

Fig. 1. Map showing sites mentioned in the text.

These imports included figured, glazed and banded wares. Moreover, during the course of the 6th century BC native potters began to produce new types of ware which were heavily derivative of Greek models. This type of pottery had a range of new vase forms and was decorated with bands and vegetal patterns. It was produced on a fast wheel which was a technological innovation learnt from the Greeks. This local wheel-made painted pottery is tremendously common in native domestic contexts and also occurs in tombs. This new pottery type quickly usurped the domestic rôle of the traditional matt-painted wares.

The phenomenon was repeated over most of Southern Italy. A broad pattern of the decline and ultimate demise of the matt-painted tradition can be observed in many areas. In general, the matt-painted wares were progressively reduced to a largely funerary function, and then following a period in which the stylistic coherence of the regional styles broke down, they more or less die out. In two areas of Southern Italy, however, matt-painted pottery managed to survive, albeit in a restricted context. These are North Apulia and the Salento peninsula (De Juliis 1977; Yntema 1985).

In the Salento peninsula, wheel-made painted pottery had completely taken over the domestic rôle once held by the matt-painted wares by the end of the 6th century BC. The matt-painted tradition survived, but in a highly restricted and specialised form. Yntema (1985: 455–461, updating his 1974 article) divides the peninsula into two halves for the purpose of his detailed study of these late wares. The first is the Oria-Mesagne area, which is close to the *chora* of Taranto, while the second is the coastal strip of the modern province of Brindisi and the province of Lecce, which may be assumed to have had less direct contacts with the Tarentines.

The Oria-Mesagne area contains such sites as Francavilla Fontana, Mesagne, Muro Maurizio, Muro Tenente and Oria. Each of these sites is likely to have been an important native settlement in the period but we still lack detailed knowledge of them. The Brindisi and Lecce zone is equally underexplored archaeologically but it is clear that Brindisi, Carovigno, Egnazia, Lecce, Muro Leccese, Rudiae, Ugento and Vaste were among the important centres.

In the first of these two areas (Oria-Messagne) only one traditional vase form survived: the trozzella. These late examples were produced solely for funerary purposes and as such they are unlikely to have been made in large numbers. Trozzelle with traditional decoration were still in production in the late 6th and early 5th centuries BC; however, at the same time, trozzelle with figurative motifs were also being made. Later, during the course of the 5th century, a series of fairly uniform trozzelle were made. These late productions were not uninfluenced by the introduction of newer wares: they were made on the fast wheel, the painting was monochromatic and had a semi-lustrous quality. On the other hand, the form itself was traditional as was the type of decoration (i.e. the motifs). Typically, the decoration consists of chains of cross-hatched lozenges arranged in a horizontal zone on the neck and upper body of the vessel. In the early part of the 4th century BC vegetal patterns began to be introduced as handle ornaments. Yntema referred to this group of trozzelle as the Early Oria Group (1974: 42–46) (fig.2). This type of trozzella was made through most of the 5th and into the 4th century BC. Later on in the 4th century trozzelle bearing some patterns on the vessel body derived from Gnathian, and perhaps also Apulian Red-Figure pottery, came into production. Such vessels are referred to as the Floral Oria Group (Yntema 1974: 46–48) and the Carovigno Group (1974: 74–80). This latter group spread beyond the Oria-Mesagne area to other parts of Brindisi province. Production of trozzelle in the Oria-Mesagne area seems to have gone into decline in the late 4th century, although other types of trozzella with less traditional patterning may well have survived into the 3rd century BC, at least in the Brindisino. This survival of the trozzella in the Oria-Mesagne area throughout the 5th and much of the 4th century BC is interesting in its own right but it is the pattern of use which is most striking. At least one trozzella is to be found in almost every native adult grave despite the fact that the remaining gravegoods are either Greek or of Greek type. It was only when this cultural practice declined in the late 4th century BC that trozzella production also tailed off.

In the coastal part of Brindisi and the province of Lecce, more traditional elements survived, although the pattern of use is very similar. In the Brindisino zone bichrome matt-painted, slow wheel manufactured trozzelle were still being produced until the late 5th century BC. Yntema (1974: 48–51) referred to these as the Geometric Zigzag Group. Wheel-thrown trozzelle with some vegetal motifs appear from the later 5th century BC. These have been termed the Floral Zigzag Group (Yntema 1974: 51–52). For much of the 4th century BC this area used similar trozzelle to the Oria-Mesagne territory.

In Lecce province, the trozzella was not the only surviving traditional form. A conical-necked olla with fungus handles and a narrow conical-necked jug were still being manufactured for much of the 4th century BC. Information for the 5th century is scant in this area, but it seems that bichromatic matt-painted trozzelle remained in production; some of these appear also to have been made using traditional technology. This poorly-represented period saw the floruit of Yntema's Middle and Late Southern Geometric (1974: 32–37) (fig.3). By the 4th century BC traditional manufacturing techniques had been replaced with fast wheel technology. Furthermore, over time bichromatic painting was

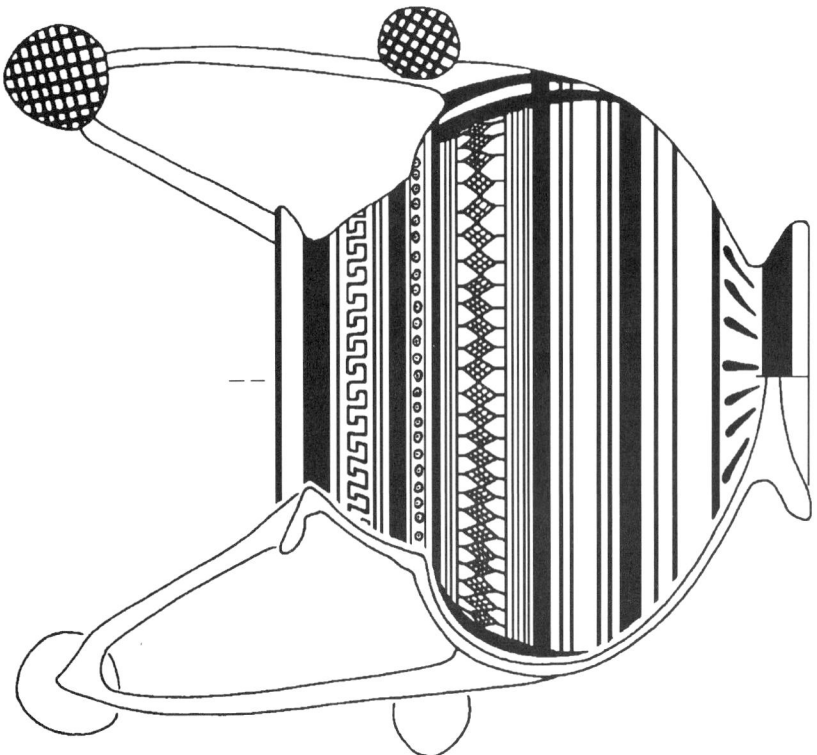

Fig. 3. Trozzella from Rudiae. Max height 227 mm. Date c. 475–425 BC. (After Yntema 1985: fig. 319).

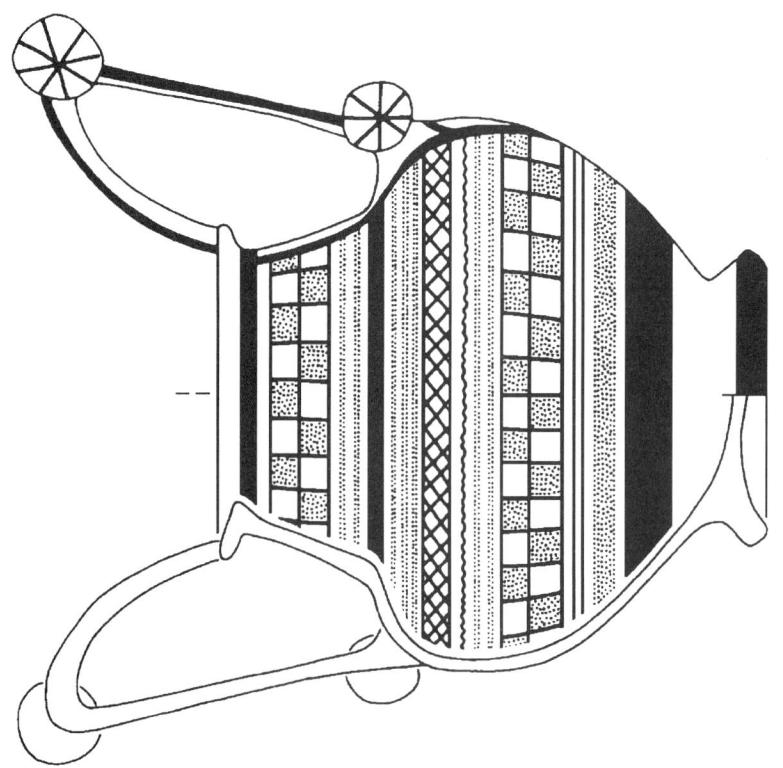

Fig. 2. Trozzella of the Early Oria Group from Mesagne. Max height 248mm. Date c. 475–425 BC. (After Yntema 1985: fig. 317).

replaced by the use of a monochrome semi-lustrous black paint. The decoration too moved away from traditional geometric motifs and towards vegetal patterns which echo those seen on the newer wheel-made painted wares. These processes took time and to some extent they can be mapped through vessels from the key site of Rudiae. Early on in the 4th century BC one finds wheel-thrown trozzelle with bichromatic, matt-painted, vegetal motifs (Early Floral Group of Rudiae. Yntema 1974: 55–58).

In time this group was superseded by one showing monochromatic, semi-lustrous painting, This group is called the Transitional Floral Group of Rudiae (Yntema 1974: 58–64). During the closing period of the 4th century BC and into the early 3rd century, a final coherent group of trozzelle with vegetal motifs was produced: the Late Floral Group of Rudiae (Yntema 1974: 64–71). By this final stage, the conical-necked olla with fungus handles and a narrow conical-necked jug had already ceased production.

Throughout the 5th and 4th centuries BC the same pattern of use as seen in the Oria-Mesagne area can be observed. By the start of the 3rd century BC, however, the trozzella had ceased to be a standard part of native tomb furniture. Once again, the pottery style died with the burial practice it accompanied.

The theoretical framework

I will now analyse this pattern of usage from one theoretical perspective, namely Polly Wiessner's theory of style. Wiessner (1983) developed her approach in a study of stylistic variation in Kalahari San projectile points. Her work belongs to a now rich body of anthropological/archaeological theory which sees stylistic variability as a means of communication. The development of various, divergent strands of this productive line of research may be traced in the work of Wobst (1977), Plog (1980), Sackett (1977; 1982) and Franklin (1989), as well as many others. The fertility of research into the rôle of stylistic variability in material culture may be attested by the recent spate of books on this topic (e.g. Hodder 1989; Conkey & Hastorf 1990 – the latter including useful revisions by Sackett and Wiessner).

Wiessner sees style as a non-verbal form of communication. The way that communication occurs and how specific the information communicated is, depends upon the degree of specificity of the social referent of the symbol. According to Wiessner, all styles have social referents. Some can be highly specific; for example, a school tie, in normal circumstances, strongly suggests that wearer is either a current or former pupil of a particular school. Others can have much vaguer associations: an ordinary tie, like the school tie, normally reveals the sex (as male) of the wearer, but beyond that one can say little with confidence. The wearer might be going to work, out for an evening, to a formal event, etc., but on the other hand, the person might simply like the particular image which wearing a tie forms part of. Thus, for Wiessner, style can be either assertive or emblemic depending on the degree of specificity. So, in assertive style a sign or symbol does not have a single or specific social referent; in emblemic style it does. Both types of style can convey information in an active way but examples of assertive style are likely to carry vaguer messages because the associations for the receiver are less specific. On the other hand, an artefact with a specific social referent will communicate information in an active and effective way to a receiver belonging to the same social group.

Taking the example of the late matt-painted pottery from the Salento area, one may ask two questions to help decide whether this is a case of assertive or emblemic style. These questions are:

1. How specific is the referent?
2. Is the communication conveyed in an active and effective way?

The first of these questions is, I feel, relatively easy to answer. Firstly, these vessels are highly distinctive. They are completely dissimilar to Greek and Greek type pottery, which was the most common type of pottery found in native tombs, and, although one must admit that they bear a somewhat closer resemblance to local Wheel-Made Painted vessels, their form and decorative syntax sets them apart from the rest of the ceramic assemblage found in such contexts. Secondly, they occur in only one type of context (i.e. native tombs). This context must have been highly charged with ritual symbolism, and these vessels are extremely likely to have had an important symbolic meaning. Thirdly, they are associated with a specific group (i.e. the native population). If one adds to this the fact that they had links with that group's past, this only strengthens the case. All of this suggests that this is a case of style having a distinct social referent.

For archaeologists the second question is always a difficult type to address. However, because one is dealing with funerary material it is easier to argue for an active and effective rôle in communication. This is simply because their deposition was deliberate. Indeed, it seems very clear that they were manufactured solely for this specific context. Simply by their physical appearance these vessels would have stood apart from the rest of the pottery placed in native tombs. The very fact that they were exclusively involved in funerary ritual would, together with their associations with the past, have given their symbolism a potency and, therefore, effectiveness as a means of communication.

I believe that one can view this specific usage of these vessels as an example of Wiessner's emblemic style. It would have communicated a specific message to a specific group. This message was, in my view, one of group identity. Funerary ritual is highly suited to the expression of group identity. By placing objects symbolic of group identity in a tomb, the participants in the funerary rites more than simply affirmed the deceased's status as a member of the group, they also reinforced their own sense of belonging. While one cannot assess in what terms these groups defined themselves, one can say that the symbolism used is entirely native. Moreover, the symbolism seems, in this context, to contrast with the Greek and Greek type pottery which forms the rest of the ceramic assemblage.

If then one accepts this view one might wish to ask the question 'Did matt-painted pottery always perform this function when used in tombs?' The answer, I feel, is negative. In the 5th and 4th centuries BC the social referent would have been much more specific than in earlier periods. After all, in earlier periods matt-painted pots were used in everyday life, and existed in a number of forms. Their use in funerary ritual is still likely to have communicated information to members of the social group but the associations would have been more vague. Indeed, the need to express native cultural identity may have been less keenly felt. In the earlier period, the use of matt-painted pottery in funerary ritual is perhaps better seen as an example of assertive style[3].

Another issue one may wish to address, if my basic argument is accepted, is if these vessels were a self-conscious expression of ethnic identity why did they cease to be used? I can suggest two answers. One simply ties in with theory of emblemic style; the other is more concerned with the historical context.

My first, and perhaps less satisfactory, answer would run that by the late 4th century BC these vessels had ceased to be an effective means of communicating ethnic identity. This can be explained by what gave potency to their use as an indicator of identity. I would argue that it was their very archaism that gave them potency and that they may have been seen as a link with the ancestral past. Eventually, however, as memory of their former use diminished so their efficacy as an ethnic indicator may have declined. One can perhaps help underpin this argument by considering these vessels from the point of view of their production. These late vessels are likely always to have been a rather occasional production; such marginal output is perhaps particularly vulnerable to falling out of production. Thus two factors may have worked in tandem to bring about the decline and ultimate demise of the cultural practice of placing at least one trozzella in every native adult tomb.

My second answer refers back to ancient history. In the later 4th century BC a number of native groups suffered under the military successes of various Tarentine champions. In the second half of the century the Tarentines called in a succession of foreign leaders to wage campaigns against Lucanians and Messapians, and later they used the same tactic against the Romans, who became an increasingly important force in the area in the early 3rd century BC. Strabo (6.3.4) lists the following champions: King Archidamus III of Sparta (killed in battle in c. 338 BC), Alexander I of Molossia (who enjoyed considerable success, having been called in in c. 333 BC, before being killed at Pandosia in c. 330), Cleonymus of Sparta (who, Diodorus Siculus (20.104.2) records, enjoyed the support of the Messapians), Agathocles of Syracuse (who campaigned around the turn of the century), and finally Pyrrhus of Epirus (called upon in c. 281 BC and, initially at least, successful against the Romans). Conflict seems to have been a feature of the period and the battle-lines were drawn (and re-drawn over time) not always on the simple basis of Greek versus native, but frequently on the basis of a Greek-native alliance against other native groups.

Against a debilitating backdrop of ongoing conflict which included a number of demoralising military defeats for the native population, the assertiveness of native cultural identity may also have declined; thus, explaining the decline of the cultural practice of putting a trozzella, as a symbol of identity, in every adult native grave. Such an interpretation would not be out of tune with the widely-held view that in the later 4th and early 3rd centuries BC a power vacuum developed in Southern Italy as both the Greek cities and the native tribes were seriously weakened by prolonged, and often inconclusive, warfare. It is often maintained that this power vacuum allowed Rome to become increasingly influential in Southern Italy from the 3rd century BC onwards.

THE WIDER IMPLICATIONS OF THIS VIEW OF NATIVE IDENTITY

If one accepts that throughout the 5th and 4th centuries BC the native population of the Salento area was making conscious expression of their cultural independence, then this sheds new light on native society of the period. Much is made in the archaeological literature of the extent of assimilation of elements of Greek culture by the native population. The process is one of integration leading to what has been described as a cultural *koiné*[4]. One hardly needs to comment on the applicability of the analogy between independent native Southern Italy and the conquered parts of the Near East where *koiné* Greek was spoken. Instead one should be looking for ways to interpret a more complex process of socio-cultural change, which includes elements of assimilation alongside counter-currents of assertive native independence[5].

Clearly, the native population of the Salento area did assimilate many aspects of Greek culture in the 5th and 4th centuries BC. However, native society remained, as the ancient sources tell us, fiercely independent and,

I suspect, highly dynamic (cf. Herring 1991a and 1991b). This dynamism can be witnessed in the moves towards urbanism and in the experimentation with writing[6]. Both of these developments may have been, indeed probably were, inspired by Greek models but, in my view, they were not taken on out of desire to be like the Greeks. Indeed, urbanisation and the building of city walls can be viewed as an attempt to resist assimilation and to defend native independence by military force if necessary. While the use of writing as an attempt to record native language can perhaps also be viewed as one to express ethnic identity. I would contend, therefore, that it was in this context of a vigorously independent native society that the matt-painted vessels were used in the tombs of the Salento area as emblems of identity.

Acknowledgement

I wish to thank Dr. Ruth Whitehouse for her helpful comments on an earlier version of this paper.

Notes

1. The use of the term Iapygians by ancient authorities is particularly problematic. In some instances it seems to be a generic name used of various south Italian tribes – as with the Herodotus passage and likewise, more clearly, in Polybius (3.88) who states that Iapygia is occupied by Messapians, Peucetians and Daunians. In other sources the name seems to refer to a specific group: for example, Pausanias (10.13.10) describes a Tarentine dedication at Delphi in honour of a victory over the Peucetians and their ally, the Iapygian king Opis. It has been suggested that the Iapygians were common ancestors to the three native tribes mentioned by Polybius. This type of usage has gone into the archaeological literature in the naming of geometric matt-pained pottery styles. Thus, traditionally, the earliest south Italian matt-painted styles were called Iapygian, while later regionalised styles were termed Messapian, Peucetian, Daunian, etc. (see note 2). Whatever the exact status of the name Iapygian, Herodotus clearly refers to those from Messapia. I therefore take this passage to refer to relations between the Tarentines and their native neighbours from the Salento area. This view is strengthened if one accepts Strabo's (6.3.6) suggestion that the Iapygian town of Hyria referred to by Herodotus can be equated with Uria, itself to be equated with modern Oria. Certainly, Oria was an important native site in this period.
2. Yntema in fact proposes a radical re-labelling of the various regional styles. Rather than using the tradional labels which are ultimately derived from tribal names given in the ancient sources, he uses geographical names based upon the distribution patterns of the various styles. Thus he refers to Salento Geometric not Messapian Geometric. This new terminology thus avoids implying links between the ceramic assemblages and any of the groups mentioned in the historical record. Moreover, the traditional terminology has not been applied consistently in all cases: for example, the term Peucetian has been applied to two groups identified by Yntema (Bradano Geometric and Bari Geometric), while some material belonging to Yntema's Bradano class has also been dubbed 'Oinotrian' (cf. Yntema 1985: 20).
3. Alternatively, the use of matt-painted pottery in funerary ritual in earlier periods may equally be an example of emblemic style, but we do not know what the specific social referent was. This would imply that the social referent and the message being conveyed changed over time. This is not incompatible with Wiessner's theory as she points out that this happens frequently. In her 1990 article she cites the example of blue jeans which started out as working men's clothes, but became a symbol of youth culture and revolution in the 1960s and by the 1980s had become part of designer fashion.
4. One does not need great insight to be able to assess the starting point of scholars who refer to a common culture developing between the Greeks and the natives by using a Greek term – clearly they feel the common culture was Greek culture.
5. The two are not mutially exclusive: one can find plentiful examples in anthropological contexts of the adoption or assimilation of those elements of a foreign culture which seem useful to, or compatible with, the 'indigenous' culture, while at the same time there can be firm evidence not only of political independence but also of wholesale rejection of other aspects of the same foreign culture. Nassanay (1989) quotes just such a situation in the case of interactions between Narragansett Native Indians and English settlers in 17th century New England.
6. The moves towards urbanisation (or at least some centralisation in the settlement pattern) are reasonably well attested in the Salento Peninsula in the 5th and 4th centuries BC (D'Andria 1989: 66–67). In terms of native writing, there is now a sizable number of inscriptions from Southeast Italy, which are grouped together by philologists into a language termed 'Messapic'. Written in a Greek script, they tend to be short and of dedicatory content (Parlangeli 1978). The majority sem to date from the 4th century BC.

Bibliography

Conkey, M. & Hastorf, C. (eds.) 1990. *The Uses of Style in Archaeology*, Cambridge.
D'Andria, F. 1989. 'Il Salento e le sue radici indigene: le origini Messapiche', in *Salento Porta d'Italia, Atti del Convegno Internazionale* (Lecce, 1986), Galatina, 63–69.
De Juliis, E.M. 1977. *La ceramica geometrica della Daunia*, Florence.
Franklin, N. 1989. 'Research with style: a case study of Australian rock art', in Shennan (ed.), 278–290.
Herring, E. 1990–91. *Cultural and social explanations for change and development in matt-painted pottery of southeast Italy from the 11th to the 4th centuries BC*, unpublished University of London Ph.D. thesis.
Herring, E. 1991a. 'Power relations in Iron Age southeast Italy', in Herring, E., Whitehouse, R. & Wilkins, J. (eds.), *Papers of the Fourth Conference of Italian Archaeology 2. The Archaeology of Power. Part 2*, London, 117–133.
Herring, E. 1991b. 'Socio-political change in the south Italian Iron Age and Classical periods: an application of the peer polity interaction model', *Accordia Research Papers*, 2, 31–54.
Hodder, I. (ed.) 1989. *The Meanings of Things. Material Culture and Symbolic Expression*, London.
Mayer, M. 1914. *Apulien vor- und während Hellenisierung mit besonderer Berücksichtigung der Keramik*, Berlin & Leipzig.
Nassanay, M. 1989. 'An epistemological enquiry into some archaeological and historical interpretations of 17th century Native American-European relations', in Shennan (ed.), 76–93.
Parlangeli, O. 1978. 'Il Messapico', in Prosdocimi, A. (ed.), *Lingue e dialetti dell'Italia antica*, Rome, 917–947.
Plog, S. 1980. *Stylistic Variation in Prehistoric Ceramics*, Cambridge.
Sackett, J.R. 1977. 'The meaning of style in archaeology', *American Antiquity*, 42, 369–380.
Sackett, J.R. 1982. 'Approaches to style in lithic archaeology', *Journal of Anthropological Archaeology*, 1, 59–112.
Sackett, J.R. 1990. 'Style and ethnicity in archaeology: the case for isochrestism', in Conkey & Hastorf (eds.), 32–43.
Shennan, S.J. (ed.) 1989. *Archaeological Approaches to Cultural Identity*, London.
Small, A.M. 1971. *Apulian Wares and Greek Influences*, unpublished University of Oxford D.Phil. thesis.
Whitehouse, R. & Wilkins, J. 1985. 'Magna Graecia before the Greeks:

towards a reconciliation of the evidence', in Malone, C. & Stoddart, S. (eds.), *Papers in Italian Archaeology IV. Part iii, Patterns in Protohistory*, BAR International Series 245, Oxford, 89–109.

Whitehouse, R. & Wilkins, J. 1989. 'Greeks and natives in Southeast Italy: approaches to the archaeological evidence', in Champion, T.C. (ed.), *Centre and Periphery. Comparative Studies in Archaeology*, London, 102–127.

Wiessner, P. 1983. 'Style and social information in Kalahari San projectile points', *American Antiquity*, 49: 2, 253–276.

Wiessner, P. 1989. 'Style and changing relations between the individual and society', in Hodder (ed.), 56–63.

Wiessner, P. 1990. 'Is there a unity to style?', in Conkey & Hastorf (eds.), 105–112.

Wobst, H.M. 1977. 'Stylistic behavior and information exchange', in Cleland, C. (ed.), *For the Director: Research Essays in Honor of James B. Griffin*, Museum of Anthropology Anthropological Paper 61, Ann Arbor, 317–342.

Yntema, D.G. 1974. 'Messapian painted pottery. Analysis and previsory classification', *Bulletin Antieke Beschaving*, 49, 3–84.

Yntema, D.G. 1985. *The Matt-painted Pottery of Southern Italy. A General Survey of the Matt-painted Pottery Styles of Southern Italy during the Final Bronze Age and Early Iron Age*, Utrecht.

15

Il Santuario di Diana a Nemi (RM): Nuove Ricerche

GIUSEPPINA GHINI

(Soprintendenza Archeologica per il Lazio)

Sommario: *Sulla riva settentrionale del lago di Nemi sorgono i resti monumentali di uno dei più importanti santuari dell'antichità, dedicato a Diana e ad altre divinità del Pantheon latino e orientale. I resti visibili, consistenti in un ampio recinto in opera incerta, un edificio ritenuto il Tempio e altre strutture in opera reticolata, sono databili al II sec. a.C., con restauri in età adrianea. Dal complesso provengono statue, iscrizioni e reperti esposti in vari musei italiani ed esteri. Nel 1989 la Soprintendenza Archeologica per il Lazio ha ripreso l'attività di scavo e ripulitura, in collaborazione con il Gruppo Archeologico Latino, in un'area finora inesplorata del complesso sacrale, riportando in luce i resti di un portico monumentale con colonne in opera incerta e mista rivestite con stucco rosso e trabeazione dorica in peperino. Un secondo saggio lungo il lato occidentale del cosidetto Tempio di Diana, ne ha evidenziato il podio in blocchi di peperino e l'elevato in conglomerato cementizio rivestito inferiormente in opera quadrata, superiormente in opera reticolata.*

INTRODUZIONE

"*Nemus locus haud longe ab Aricia, in quo lacus est, qui speculum Dianae dicitur*": così Servio (*Aen.*,VII,515) descrive il bosco sacro a Diana, situato poche decine di chilometri a sud-est di Roma, sulla riva settentrionale del lago di Nemi (fig.1). Qui, in un paesaggio estremamente suggestivo, miracolosamente preservatosi da un'incalzante espansione edilizia, sono ancora visibili i resti del complesso sacro, dedicato a Diana, che vi era adorata nel suo triplice aspetto di dea della caccia (Artemis-Diana), protettrice delle nascite (Lucina), dea della notte e della luna (Hecate e Selene) (Hyg. *Fab*.261; *Mit.Vat. I,112; II,25; Prop.* 32; Serv. *Aen*.2,116; Stat., *silv.* 3,1,55; Verg., *Aen*.,7,274). Il culto della dea, che risale per lo meno all'età arcaica, come prova l'elenco delle città latine facenti parte della lega che aveva la sua sede proprio nel Santuario e che ci é riportato da Catone nelle Origines, (fr.58) fu senz'altro preceduto da un culto "silvestre" risalente ad età protostorica, se ad esso si vuole attribuire un probabile ripostiglio di asce della media età del bronzo (XV sec.a.C.) conservate al British Museum (Giardino 1985) e il materiale in impasto, in bucchero e un centinaio di vasetti miniaturistici dell'età del ferro, rinvenuti nei pressi dell'area sacra e attribuiti dal Gierow nel suo studio sui Colli Albani ad un deposito votivo (1964: 363–364).

IL SANTUARIO DI DIANA A NEMI IN ETÀ ARCAICA

Anche il Tempio di Diana sull'Aventino a Roma, fondato secondo la tradizione da Servio Tullio (Liv. I,45; Dion. Hal., IV,26), era sede della lega latina, ma a quale dei due luoghi di culto vada attribuita la priorità di una funzione politica, oltre che religiosa, panlatina è tuttora materia di dibattito; sono a favore dell'anteriorità del Santuario di Diana Nemorense Merlin (1906: 106), Wissowa (1912: 247–252), Gordon (1934: 2), Alföldi (1961: 21–39), che, insieme a Grant (1971: 161), abbassa la fondazione del Tempio aventinese posteriormente alla battaglia del Lago Regillo, Schilling (1960), Ogilvie (1965: 181–184), Bayet (1957: 39–40), Dumezil (1977: 355–359); a favore dell'anteriorità del Tempio di Diana sull'Aventino Altheim (1930: 134 ss.), Momigliano (1962), Pena (1973). Pairault (1969) e Coarelli (1987: 165–185), pur ritenendo antichissimo il culto di Diana aricina, attribuiscono la priorità di centro della lega latina al Santuario aventinese, abbassando agli ultimi anni del VI sec.a.C., dopo la battaglia di Aricia del 504 a.C. e riducendola quindi a pochi anni(l'elenco riportato da Catone (*orig*., fr.58) in cui è citata *Pometia*, che venne occupata dai Volsci nel 495 a.C., deve essere anteriore a questa data) la funzione politica del Santuario nemorense.

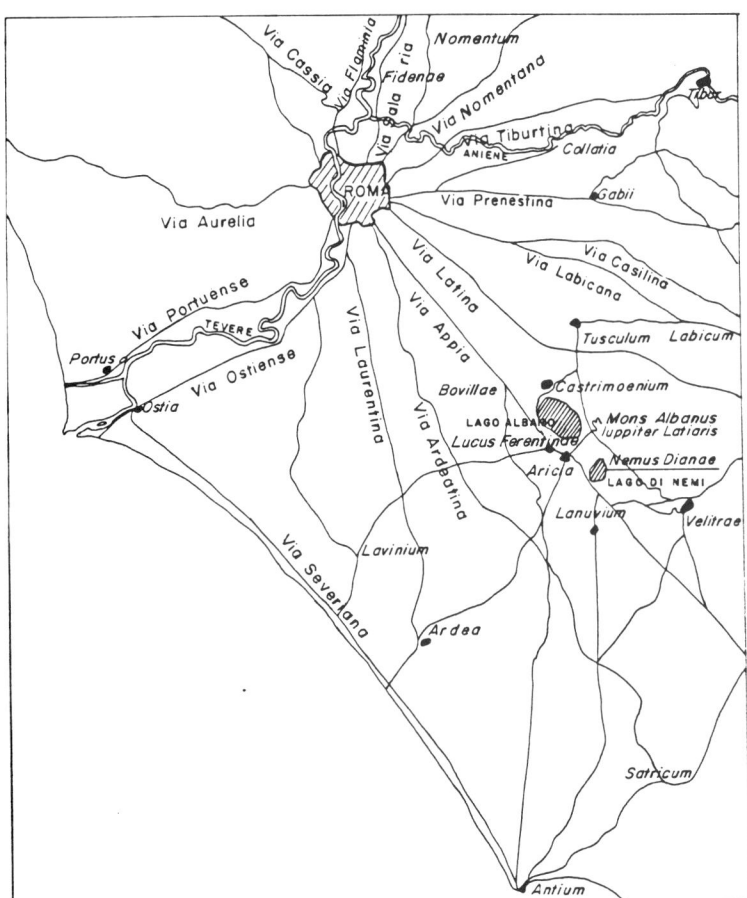

Fig. 1. Viabilità antica e principali siti archeologici nei Colli Albani.

Pur esulando dagli intenti di questo intervento affrontare e tantomeno risolvere il problema, vorrei appena porre l'accento su alcuni elementi della complessa questione.

La Diana nemorense (o aricina), nasce come divinità locale, italica, legata alla natura, alla luce notturna (Pairault 1969: 435; Dumezil 1977: 355–359), alla fertilità femminile (Morpurgo 1903: 346–351; Wissowa 1912; Gordon 1934: 8–9). Successivamente a questa originaria natura si sovrappone quella feroce dell'Artemis Taurica, importata secondo le fonti antiche (Hyg. *Fab*.261; Acr. *ad Hor*., C,1,7,10; Mit.Vat. II,202; Serv., *Aen*.2,116 ss.) tramite Oreste, che, fuggito in Tauride dopo il matricidio e ritrovata la sorella Ifigenia, divenuta sacerdotessa di Artemis, sarebbe fuggito con lei verso l'Italia, dopo aver ucciso il re del luogo Toante e rapito il simulacro della dea, che imponeva nel suo rituale sacrifici di schiavi stranieri. Portata sulle rive del lago nemorense, la dea avrebbe avuto come sacerdote uno schiavo fuggitivo, il *Rex Nemorensis*, che succedeva al predecessore dopo averlo ucciso in duello (Strab. *Geogr*.,V,12; Paus., *Descr*., II, 27,4), per morire poi nello stesso modo.

Probo, nel suo commento all'Eneide (Verg.*ecl*., proem.) riferisce che Oreste durante la sua fuga si fermò a Siracusa, fondando un Artemision e si purificò a Reggio. Questa notizia è stata interpretata da alcuni autori moderni (Ampolo 1970: 200–210; Bayet 1920: 128 ss.; Pairault 1969: 448) come un'introduzione del culto attraverso i rapporti commerciali che città quali Cuma avevano con i Focei. Vicino questo centro campano, a Capua, esisteva un importante tempio dedicato a Diana Tifatina (De Franciscis 1956) e nel 504 a.C. si svolse la battaglia di Aricia, tra latini e cumani da una parte e romani ed etruschi dall'altra, che può considerarsi senz'altro un'occasione di contatto e di scambio culturale (Coarelli 1987: 167). Pertanto l'Artemis Taurica giunge ad Aricia-Lago di Nemi verso la fine del VI sec.a.C. grazie alla Magna Grecia e in particolare a Siracusa, Regium, Capua, Cuma (tutte città, ad eccezione dell'ultima, dove pure è attestato il culto di Diana; cfr. RE). Anche la Diana Aventinese è importata: proviene da Marsiglia, tramite i Focei, che, esuli dalla loro patria nella Ionia, avevano portato con sé, qui come in altri insediamenti da loro fondati lungo le coste del Mediterraneo occidentale, il simulacro dell'Artemis Efesia (Saguntum, Hemeroskopeion, Rodhe, ecc.) (fig.2).

Da Marsiglia l'Artemis sarebbe poi giunta a Roma, in età arcaica e precisamente verso la metà del VI sec.a.C., o direttamente con i Focei (Pugliese Carratelli 1968) o per il tramite etrusco (Altheim 1950: 65 ss.), e in particolare attraverso *l'Artemidos limen*, in Corsica o l'isola di Giannutri, antica *Artemisia*, poi *Dianium*, che rientrava nell'orbita politica di Vulci (Colonna 1962). Secondo la testimonianza di Strabone (*Geogr*. IV,1,4–5) l'Artemis di Marsiglia (e quindi di Efeso) e quella dell'Aventino sono la stessa cosa: si tratta di xoana e forse lo stesso tipo iconografico si può ipotizzare anche per il simulacro dell'Artemis Taurica, rapito da Oreste e *"absconditum fasce lignorum"* (Serv., *Aen.* II,116), espressione che farebbe appunto pensare ad una statua lignea.

Probabilmente già in età arcaica Diana Nemorense assume un aspetto tricorpore e come tale viene rappresentata su una moneta di P. Accoleius Lariscolus del 43 a.C. (Alföldi 1960), in cui Riis (1966) ha voluto vedere la trasposizione numismatica della statua di culto arcaica, a cui ha riferito una testa arcaica in bronzo, ora conservata a Copenhagen, mentre già Paribeni (1960) vi aveva identificato una testina marmorea arcaicizzante del I sec.a.C., rinvenuta nel 1924 nell'area del teatro. La Diana Aventinese, a sua volta, in un periodo che Ampolo (1970) ritiene non precedente al IV secolo, subisce una trasformazione e assume, insieme all'Artemis Efesia e a quella marsigliese, il caratteristico aspetto polimaste.

Altro elemento che ricorre in tre dei quattro santuari è la presenza degli schiavi: ad Aricia-Nemi come sacerdote di Diana (*Rex Nemorensis*), sull'Aventino e ad Efeso come luogo di *asylia* (Ampolo 1970: 209; Van Berchem 1960) e di manomissione degli schiavi in occasione delle Idi di Agosto dedicate alla dea. La fondazione di entrambi i luoghi di culto è attribuita dalle

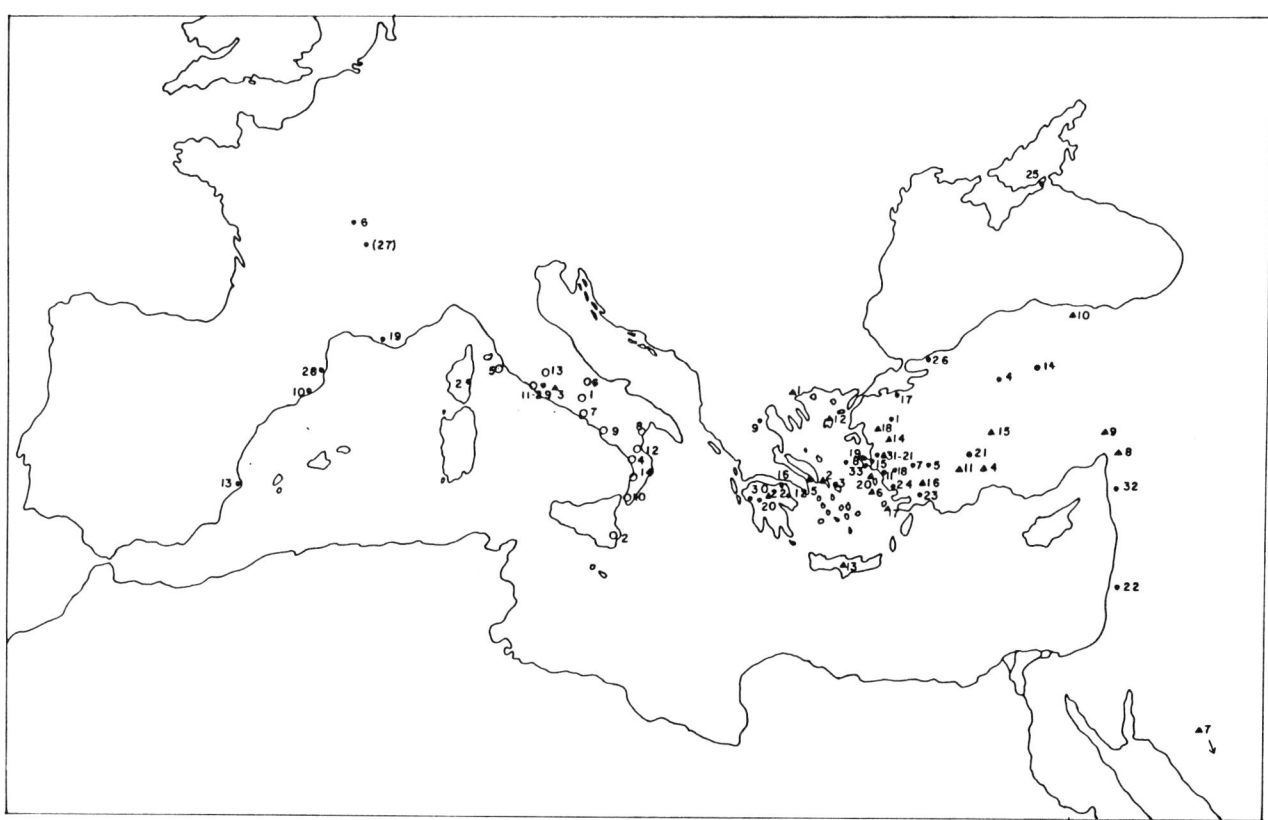

Fig. 2. Il culto di Artemis – Diana nel bacino del Mediterraneo: cartina di distribuzione.

Culto di Artemis-Diana in Italia ○
1. Capua
2. Syracusa
3. Aricia
4. Consentia
5. Dianum (Giannutri)
6. Larinum
7. Neapolis
8. Metapontum
9. Paestum
10. Reghion
11. Roma
12. Thurioi
13. Tibur
14. Hipponion-Vibo Valentia

Artemis Efesina ●
1. Akrasos
2. Aleria
3. Andros
4. Ancyra
5. Aphrodisias
6. Augustodunum
7. Bargasa
8. Chios
9. Dion
10. Emporion
11. Ephesos
12. Epidauros
13. Hemeroskopeion (Dianum)
14. Kidramos
15. Keazomenai
16. Korinthos
17. Kyzikos
18. Larisa (Ephesos)
19. Massalia
20. Megalopolis
21. Mossyna
22. Neapolis Samariae
23. Panamara
24. Panormos Mys
25. Pantikapaion
26. Prusa
27. Rodano
28. Rodhe
29. Roma
30. Skillus
31. Smirne
32. Siria
33. Teos

Artemis Tauropolos ◆
1. Amphipolis
2. Andros
3. Aricia
4. Hadrianopolis
5. Halai Araphenides
6. Ikaria (Samo)
7. Ikaria (golfo persico)
8. Hieropolis-Kastabala
9. Comana (Cappadocia)
10. Comana (Pontica)
11. Laodicea
12. Lemnos
13. Lyktos
14. Magnesia sul Sipylos
15. Metropolis
16. Mylasa
17. Patmos
18. Pergamo
19. Focea
20. Samos
21. Smirne
22. Sparta

fonti a figure di rilievo del mondo politico contemporaneo, sulla cui natura storica o leggenderia si è molto discusso: Manio Egerio di Ariccia (Fest., 128 L) o Egerio Bebio (o Levio), dittatore di Tuscolo (Cato, *orig.*, fr.58), per il Santuario Nemorense, Servio Tullio (Dion. Hal. X,32; Liv. III, 31; Fest. 467 L) per quello Aventinese. Entrambi i luoghi sacri sono anche sede politica di un culto federale latino, così come l'Artemision di Efeso, che avrebbe ispirato nella pianta il Tempio dell'Aventino, era sede della lega ionica (Liv. I,45).

Resta da definire il rapporto esistente tra la lega latina facente capo al Santuario nemorense e il *Lucus Ferentinae* (quindi un altro bosco sacro), luogo di riunione dei popoli latini, recentemente individuato pochi chilometri a nord-ovest del lago nemorense, sotto Castel Savelli (Ampolo 1981; Colonna 1985). Vicino a Nemi esisteva un altro tempio latino anfizionico, contrapposto ad uno romano, a sua volta situato vicino a quello di Diana Aventinese: si tratta del Tempio di Iuppiter Latiaris sul *Mons Albanus*, attuale Monte Cavo, che sembrerebbe fare da contraltare a quello di Giove Ottimo Massimo sul Campidoglio (Galosi 1979; Finocchi 1980).

Anche per questi due templi non si è potuta stabilire la priorità dell'uno sull'altro, poiché gli scavi condotti prima da Giovannoni (1912) e negli anni '20 da Lugli (1930) sul Monte Cavo non hanno riportato alla luce alcuna struttura sicuramente attribuibile all'edificio sacro, se si escludono dei blocchi squadrati di tufo non *in situ*.

I pareri degli studiosi sono discordanti, propendendo alcuni (De Sanctis 1907: 378 ss.; Brelich 1954: 33; Colonna 1974: 296) per la priorità del Santuario laziale, altri (Altheim 1951: 151 ss.) per quella del tempio romano. Si ricorderà solo che il Bayet (1957: 40) ritiene che l'appellativo di Ottimo sia stato dato proprio per sottolineare la superiorità di questa divinità, e indirettamente del potere che essa rappresentava, quello della Roma dei Tarquini, su quella latina.

Anche il Tempio di Iuppiter Latiaris era sede dei popoli latini, ma la lista che ci fornisce Plinio (*Nat.Hist.* III,5,68-70) non contiene gli stessi nomi di quella catoniana per il Santuario nemorense, quasi che, come ha ipotizzato Pairault (1969: 440) quest'ultima riflettesse una religione e un diritto più evoluti, mentre la prima fosse una federazione religiosa basata sulla legge del sangue fra tribù o gruppi dello stesso ceppo.

Sapere quando il Santuario di Iuppiter Latiaris, nato probabilmente come santuario d'altura e rimasto a lungo un recinto sacro con un'ara più che un vero e proprio tempio, abbia assunto il ruolo di sede anfizionica della lega latina, sarebbe determinante per comprendere quando questo avvenne anche per quello nemorense.

Ad ogni modo la lista catoniana delle città latine facenti capo al Santuario nemorense, come si è detto, cita *Pometia*, distrutta come è noto nel 495 a.C. e quindi deve essere precedente a questo evento. E' ormai considerata inaccettabile la datazione troppo bassa (IV sec.a.C) proposta dal Piganiol (1967: 177); infatti Catone riferisce che Egerio Levio (o Bebio) *"dedicavit lucum"*, ossia dedicò a Diana uno spiazzo sacro all'interno del bosco aricino: non fa menzione di alcun tempio che invece nel IV sec.a.C. è storicamente accertato. Gordon (1934: 1) propone la data della seconda metà del VI sec.a.C:, Coarelli (1987: 166) scende fino agli inizi del V. In questo periodo, e probabilmente per tutto il V sec.a.C., il culto si svolge nel bosco, intorno a un'ara.

Accettando una datazione 'alta' del Santuario nemorense, sembra più realistico ipotizzare una precedenza di questo rispetto a quello aventinese, per una serie di considerazioni: difficilmente Roma, in un periodo di predominio politico come quello compreso tra la seconda metà del VI sec. (dopo il regno di Servio Tullio) e l'inizio del V avrebbe permesso il costituirsi di un santuario federale latino politicamente avverso o potenzialmente pericoloso. Significativo in tal senso il silenzio che gli storici antichi, a cominciare da Tito Livio, hanno fatto calare su questo luogo di culto, mentre invece parlano di quello di Iuppiter Latiaris, che, persa la funzione federale, mantenne tuttavia quella di meta dei trionfi minori (*feriae latinae*) (Cic., *Pro Mil.* XXXI). Trasportata a Roma la sede della lega, il Santuario di Diana Nemorense continua a vivere, ma privato della sua valenza politica, divenuta ormai prerogativa di quello aventinese.

La fonte riportata da Servio nel commento all'Eneide (*Aen.* II,116; VI,136) e da Igino (*Fab.*,261) secondo cui il corpo di Oreste, morto a Nemi, sarebbe stato trasportato a Roma, nel Foro, davanti al Tempio di Saturno, quindi in un luogo significativo per la storia della città (in prossimità del *Lapis Niger* e del *Mundus* che poi verrà indicato come *Umbilicus Urbis*), potrebbe forse adombrare questo trasferimento della funzione politica e l'antichità dell'evento, quando nel Foro c'era ancora un'area riservata alle sepolture (Pairault 1969: 446). Della fase arcaica non si sono finora rinvenute tracce, ad eccezione dell'antefissa di Diana come Potnia Theron (Poulsen 1941: 8-9), che tuttavia recentemente Blagg (1983: 30-31) ha ritenuto opera arcaicizzante della fine del II-I sec.a.C., di una testa arcaica in bronzo (Riis 1966), e di un rilievo con l'uccisione di Egisto, proveniente da Vallericcia (Riis 1966: 71-72; Hafner 1967; Pairault 1969: 450-452). Tali reperti sono attualmente presso la Ny Carlsberg Glyptotek di Copenaghen.

Il Santuario di Diana a Nemi
nell'età repubblicana

Nel IV sec. a.C. quello di Diana è un tempio di tipo etrusco-italico, prostilo, tetrastilo, con timpano aperto, secondo la rappresentazione dei modellini fittili rinvenuti nel secolo scorso ed esposti al Museo di Villa Giulia (Von Rohden 1886; Rizzo 1910; Della Seta 1918: 229;

Andren 1940: 382-384, n.413-415, tav.117; Staccioli 1968: 41,31) e in quello di Nottingham, recentemente oggetto di studio da parte del Blagg (1983: 43-45) e di successiva revisione di Melis e Serra Ridgway (1987). Il significato politico del Santuario è ormai del tutto scomparso; Diana assume o ri-assume la sua caratteristica di dea protettrice delle nascite e guaritrice, che sembra essere ormai la sua prerogativa principale, come provano i numerosi ex-voto con anatomici e bimbi in fasce rinvenuti nelle fosse votive antistanti il Tempio durante gli scavi condotti da Lord Savile nel 1885 e ora conservati nel Castello di Nottingham (Blagg 1983: 46 ss.).

E' probabilmente in questo periodo che si conclude l'"ellenizzazione" della dea, ormai completamente assimilata alla Artemis Taurica, dea crudele che esigeva sacrifici umani di stranieri. Il mito si arricchisce di altre figure, quali Ippolito, il figlio di Teseo, morto e poi resuscitato da Asclepio come Virbio, la cui presenza è senz'altro successiva alla versione originale del mito e non precedente al V sec.a.C. e alle tragedie euripidee (Ifigenia in Aulide, Ifigenia in Tauride, Fedra). In memoria sua e della sua morte, causata dai suoi cavalli imbizzarriti (Ov., *fast.* III, 262-272; Verg., *Aen.* VII, 761-782; Paus., *Descr.* II,27,4) all'interno dell'area sacra era interdetto l'ingresso a questi animali.

Sul mito della Diana Nemorense e sul complesso rituale ad esso collegato è stato scritto molto da vari studiosi non sempre concordi; si cita solo, tra i più noti, James Frazer, autore di quel testo fondamentale per la storia delle religioni, nonostante sia passato più di un secolo dalla I edizione, che è *"Il ramo d'oro"* (1973), il cui titolo, riferito al vischio, richiama proprio quello che era il simbolo del potere del *Rex Nemorensis*.

Tra la fine del II e l'inizio del I sec.a.C. il Santuario subisce una completa trasformazione e una monumentalizzazione, analoga a quella dei vicini santuari di Praeneste, Tibur, Lanuvium, Gabii, e a quelli più lontani ma sempre di area centro-italica di Fregellae, Terracina, Pietrabbondante, Sulmona (La Regina 1966; Franchi dell'Orto & La Regina 1978: 449-461; Delbruck 1979; Coarelli 1987).

Questa fase è specchio di una mutata condizione economica e dell'ascesa sociale di una classe borghese arricchitasi prevalentemente con i commerci, che desidera "nobilitarsi" con atteggiamenti di evergetismo, contribuendo a proprie spese alle costruzioni o alle ricostruzioni di luoghi di culto (si ricordi che alcuni di questi ricchi commercianti menzionati per la loro attività edilizia a Praeneste e Pietrabbondante compaiono tra quelli attivi a Delo) (Coarelli 1976, 1981; Bodei Giglioni 1978, 1990).

I resti attualmente visibili appartengono a questa fase, in cui il Santuario è costituito da un recinto rettangolare di m. 200 × 175, delimitato da sostruzioni in opera incerta, triangolari nella terrazza inferiore, semicircolari in quella mediana, con colonnato dorico interno e Tempio situato, secondo una ricostruzione del Rosa (1856) accettata anche dal Coarelli, sulla terrazza superiore (fig.3-4).

Si è già detto che all'interno del Santuario erano venerate anche altre divinità e semidivinità, come Egeria, Virbio-Ippolito, a cui si aggiunsero dei orientali, come Iside, Bubastide, Arpocrate, ai quali erano dedicati sacelli o edicole (*CIL* XIV, 2215; Morpurgo 1903: 324). La statua di culto di Diana era costituita da un acrolito, conservato a Copenaghen, per il quale Moltensen (1986) ha proposto la stessa officina urbana che realizzò quello del Tempio B di Largo Argentina a Roma. Nella terrazza si trovavano anche altri edifici: bagni per abluzioni dei pellegrini, con funzione purificatoria e forse anche idroterapica, ambienti per i sacerdoti e probabilmente per i fedeli (fig.3,F), scavati nei secoli XVII e XIX e attualmente interrati, ad eccezione di un edificio in opera reticolata, identificato, con non totale soddisfazione, con il Tempio di Diana (fig.3,K).

Nel corso del I sec.a.C. viene chiuso il lato di fondo del colonnato dorico, realizzando così cinque celle donarie (fig.3,a-f), all'interno delle quali gli scavi condotti nel 1885 da Lord Savile Lumley riportarono alla luce statue ed erme, attualmente conservate parte a Nottingham (Blagg 1983; Devoti 1987), parte a Copenhagen (Poulsen 1941); vicino al Santuario, con una leggera deviazione verso nord, viene costruito il teatro, dove probabilmente si svolgeva la successione rituale del sacerdote di Diana, ormai trasformata in spettacolo (Morpurgo 1931).

Le strutture dell'età imperiale

L'attività medica del Santuario determinó evidentemente cospicue entrate economiche, se è vero quanto riferisce Appiano (*b.civ.*, V,24,97) che Augusto chiese finanziamenti a santuari e templi, tra cui quello di Giove Capitolino e quello di Diana Nemorense.

In età giulio-claudia si realizza una sesta cella (fig.3,g), che viene abbellita con statue della famiglia imperiale (Poulsen 1941). Adriano compie infine consistenti restauri, testimoniati sia da un'iscrizione (*CIL* XIV, 2216) sia dalle indagini condotte dalla Soprintendenza Archeologica per il Lazio nel 1989-90 (Ghini 1993).

Scavi al Santuario vennero condotti per volontà dei proprietari, prima i Frangipane, poi i Colonna, infine gli Orsini, fin dai secoli XVI e XVII (*CIL* XIV, 2213; Graevius 1732-37: 752-757); i ritrovamenti più consistenti furono quelli fatti dal Cardinal Despuig e confluiti parte a Palma de Maiorca (Bover Y Rosello 1845), parte alla Ny Carlsberg Glyptotek (tra questi il rilievo arcaico con l'uccisione di Egisto e la testa bronzea arcaica di Diana) (Poulsen 1941; Riis 1966); quelli che effettuò nel 1885 Lord Savile Lumley, ambasciatore a Roma, che, secondo la normativa allora vigente, portò parte del materiale a Nottingham, dove è tuttora esposto nel

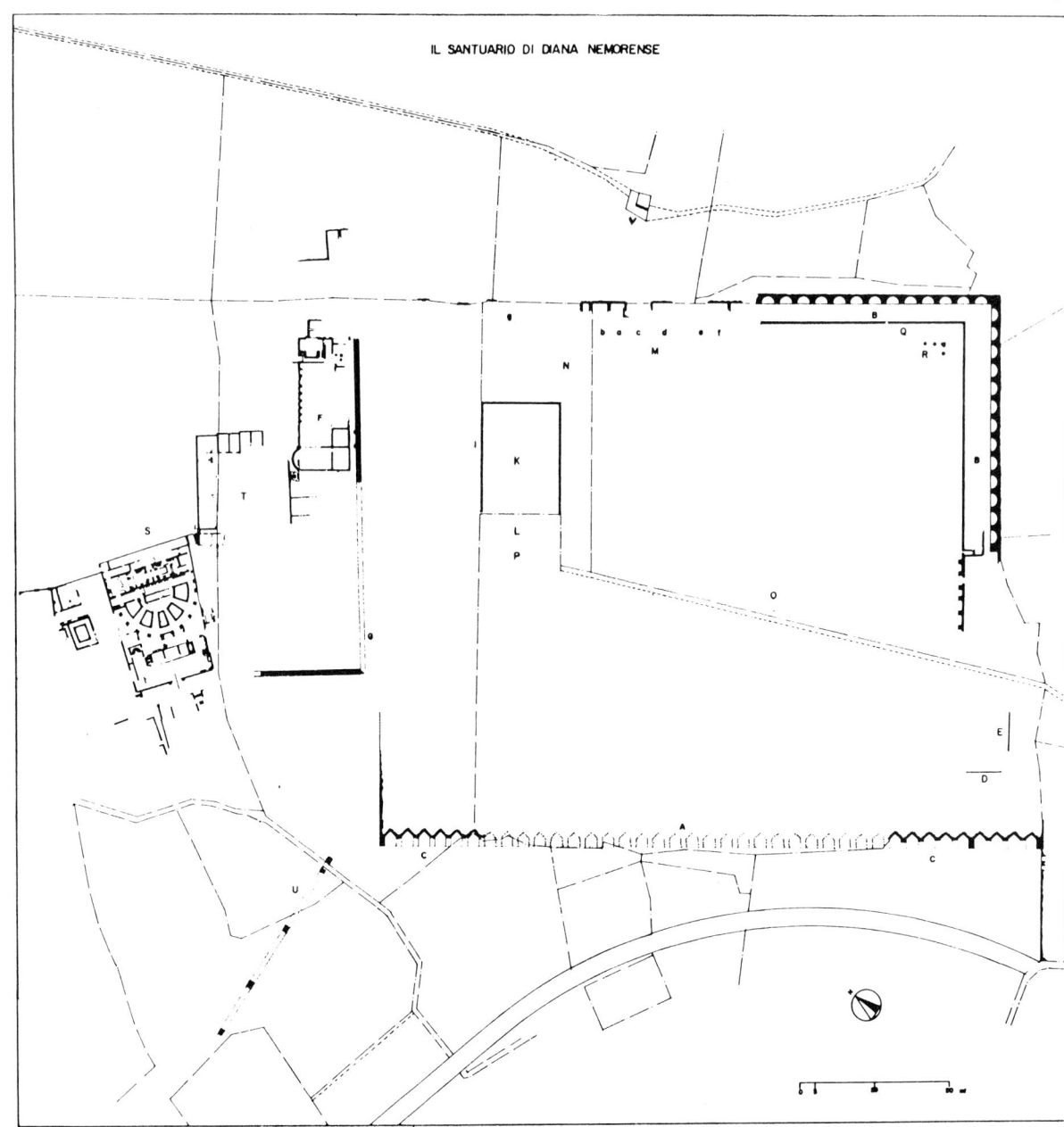

A   Muro di terrazzamento
BB Terrazzamento a nicchie semicircolari
CC Terrazzamento inferiore a nicchie triangolari
D   Prima trincea di Lord Savile
E   Seconda trincea di Lord Savile
F   Abitazioni dei sacerdoti
G   Strada basolata porticata
I   Recinzione medievale con cappella (sic)
K   Podio del supposto Tempio
L   Trincea di Lord Savile antistante l'entrata al Tempio
M   Stanze lungo il lato nord-orientale del recinto:
    a: stanza con il mosaico con il nome di M. Servilius Quartus, dove si rinvenne la statua di Fundilia Rufa
    b: bottega di scultore
    c: stanza con terrecotte architettoniche
    d: stanza con fregio in terracotta
    e: stanza con iscrizioni
    f: stanza con copertura a volta
    g: stanza absidata nella quale si rinvenne la statua di Tiberio
N   Struttura circolare identificata con un altare
O   Colonnato
P   Edificio in opera quadrata
Q   Recinto interno in opera incerta
R   Colonnato in opera incerta e mista
S   Teatro
T   Ambienti con vasche
U   via Virbia
V   Muro in conglomerato cementizio

Fig. 3. Il Santuario di Diana Nemorense, pianta (da Ghini 1993: 279).

Fig. 4. Il recinto a nicchioni semicircolari (B).

Fig. 5. Il colonnato R.

Museo della città (Blagg 1983), parte lo lasciò al principe Orsini, che successivamente lo vendette alla Ny Carlsberg Glyptotek. Solo il materiale rinvenuto alcuni anni dopo da Luigi Boccanera (Borsari 1887: 23-25, 120-121, 195-198; 1888: 193-194, 392-393; Lanciani 1889: 20-22) rimase al Museo Nazionale Romano e a quello di Villa Giulia (Della Seta 1918: 229 ss.); altri reperti finirono a Boston, nel Museum of Fine Arts (Robinson 1889).

Le indagini della Soprintendenza Archeologica per il Lazio, per motivi logistici e finanziari, sono state limitate all'angolo nord-est del complesso e hanno riportato in luce un secondo recinto (fig.3,Q) interno a quello dei nicchioni,(fig.3,B) da cui dista m. 6,30 (= 21 piedi), realizzato anch'esso in opera incerta di basalto e peperino, conservato per una lunghezza di m. 63 sul lato nord-est e di m. 20 su quello sud-est e un'altezza massima di m. 3,80 dalla quota antica. Nel muro si aprono ingressi ad arco formato da cunei di peperino alti m. 3 (=10 piedi), larghi m. 1,20 (=4 piedi), posti a intervalli regolari di m. 8,10 (=27 piedi), alcuni dei quali successivamente tamponati con opera reticolata poco accurata. Ne sono stati rinvenuti due sul lato sud-orientale, sei su quello di fondo, che sul lato posteriore presenta contrafforti in blocchetti di peperino posti alla distanza di m. 16,20 (=54 piedi), ossia ogni due aperture, e su quello anteriore reca tracce di uno spesso rivestimento in cocciopesto con funzione impermeabilizzante.

Parallelamente al muro Q e distante da questo m. 5,80 (=19 piedi) è venuto alla luce un portico (fig.3,R; fig.5) con colonne in opera incerta e mista di reticolato e laterizio rivestite di stucco rosso, del diametro di m. 1,10, conservate per un'altezza massima di m. 2,50, in corrispondenza della colonna angolare cuoriforme. Questa, come pure quella in opera incerta del lato sud-orientale, è attribuibile alla fase repubblicana del complesso, mentre quelle in opera mista del lato nord-orientale appartengono alla ristrutturazione adrianea. All'interno della muratura di queste ultime si sono rinvenuti due bolli laterizi, uno delle officine domizie di Lucanus e Tullius (*CIL* XV, 994), l'altro di quelle urbane di Papirius (*CIL* XV, 1356), databili fra l'età domizianea e gli inizi del II sec.d.C. L'intonaco che riveste le colonne è decorato a baccellature nella parte inferiore, mentre probabilmente superiormente doveva essere liscio o scanalato. Del colonnato si è riportata alla luce la trabeazione in peperino di tipo dorico a metope lisce alternate a triglifi con capitello a echino schiacciato; era costituita da quattro elementi: due pertinenti all'epistilio, uno alla cornice, l'ultimo alla gronda, con canaletta e fori con gocciolatoi per lo scolo dell'acqua.

L'altezza totale del colonnato era di circa 9 metri (=30 piedi), essendo la trabeazione alta m. 1,80 (=6 piedi) e le colonne all'incirca 7 metri (23 piedi); i nicchioni pertanto erano nascosti e la loro funzione non era scenografica ma puramente sostruttiva, il che spiega la loro posizione limitata ai lati dove maggiore era la spinta del terreno (fig.6). La trabeazione sosteneva un tetto di tegole e coppi, del quale si è rinvenuto il crollo tra il colonnato R e il muro Q.

Il rinvenimento di numerosi bolli ha confermato la datazione del tetto, e quindi del colonnato, all'età adrianea, confermando così un'iscrizione rinvenuta nel secolo scorso che cita appunto restauri voluti dall'imperatore Adriano (*CIL* XIV, 2216). Tra le officine attestate si ricordano le Caninianae (*CIL* XV, 134),le Sulpicianae (*CIL* XV, 595a), le Macedoniae (*CIL* XV, 287), quelle imperiali di Tetellus Donatus (*CIL* XV, 713); mentre la minor quantità di bolli delle officine imperiali di Lucio Vero (*CIL* XV, 737) e delle Oceanae Maiores di Marco Aurelio (*CIL* XV, 367) testimonierebbe interventi parziali di ripristino.

L'analisi stratigrafica ha rilevato che, ad una prima fase di abbandono, avvenuta probabilmente con il diffondersi del Cristianesimo, sono succedute fasi di crollo distinte ma abbastanza ravvicinate, o forse addirittura repentine, a causa della caduta dal monte soprastante di enormi massi di pietra. Lo strato contenente il crollo delle colonne e della trabeazione, in base al materiale ceramico rinvenuto, è databile tra la fine del XII e gli inizi del XIII secolo.

Ritrovamenti dalle celle donarie

Sospeso lo scavo per motivi finanziari, l'attività della Soprintendenza è proseguita in collaborazione con il Gruppo Archeologico Romano e Latino con la ripulitura delle celle donarie scavate nel secolo scorso da Lord Savile Lumley. Tra la terra di scarico lasciata nelle celle D ed E si sono rinvenuti frammenti di intonaco bianco e rosso e di lastre e antefisse dello stesso tipo di quelle rinvenute dal Savile.

I frammenti sono attribuibili alle lastre con motivo floreale che si diparte da un calice e a quelle con Diana alata con polos e corta tunica che tiene tra le mani elementi vegetali, secondo uno schema derivato dalla *Potnia Theron*, che si concluderà con il motivo detto 'della donna-fiore', in cui la figura femminile ha aspetto umano solo nella metà superiore, mentre quella inferiore è trasformata in un tralcio vegetale. Lastre con tale motivo decorativo sono diffuse nel periodo a cavallo tra il II e il I sec.a.C. (Campanelli, c.s.). I frammenti di lastre rinvenuti sembrano attribuibili al tipo A distinto dal Blagg (1983: 26,33-34, fig.5, N 741 A, N 741 B), che ha studiato gli esemplari conservati a Nottingham (fig.7).

Si sono inoltre rinvenuti due frammenti di fregio traforato, che sembrano attribuibili alla fase medio-repubblicana del santuario (probabimente quella con il Tempio di tipo etrusco-italico) e la parte inferiore di un'antefissa triangolare con busto di Diana (Blagg 1983: 27,33, pl.IV). La datazione proposta dal Blagg per le

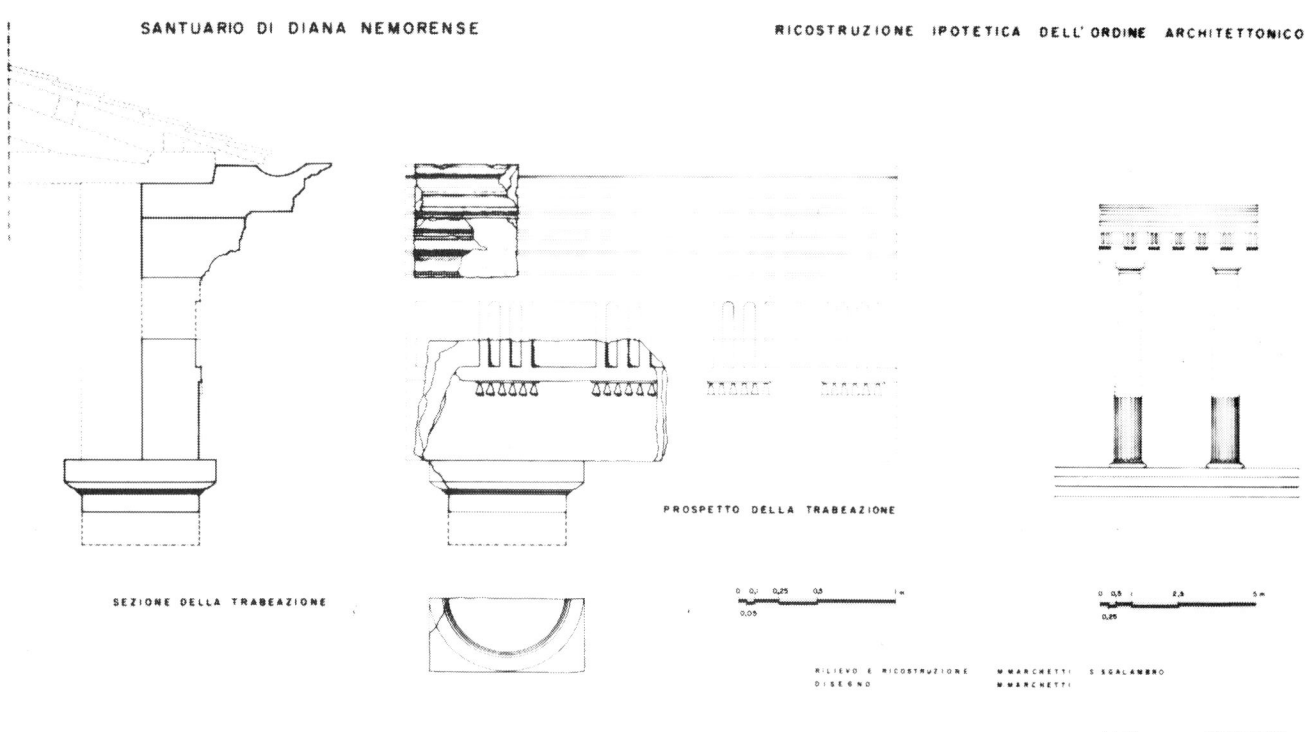

Fig. 6. Ricostruzione ipotetica del colonnato R e della trabeazione architettonica (da Ghini 1993: 283, fig.7).

Fig. 7. Celle E-F: lastra fittile con Diana alata (da Ghini 1993: 285, fig.11).

lastre è compresa fra la seconda metà del II sec.a.C. e gli inizi del I d.C., per le antefisse tra la fine del II e il I sec.a.C. (1983: 28, 33-35; cfr. Pensabene & Sanzi di Mino 1983: 114-117). Entrambe appartengono alla decorazione tardo-repubblicana del portico, consistente in lastre a motivi vegetali con o senza Diana, coronata da antefisse triangolari con la dea, probabilmente alternate ad altre a palmetta, pure attestate negli scavi del Savile (Blagg 1983: 31,33, fig.3, N 764, N 770), ma non rinvenute nel corso dei lavori.

Il rinvenimento di un votivo miniaturistico arcaico, simile a quelli citati dal Gierow, probabilmente proveniente dal terreno soprastante, potrebbe testimoniare l'esistenza di un luogo di culto arcaico, situato sulla terrazza superiore.

Discussione

Un secondo sondaggio è stato condotto lungo il lato occidentale dell'edificio identificato, non del tutto soddisfacentemente, con il Tempio di Diana. L'esatto rilevamento eseguito dai disegnatori della Soprintendenza ha mostrato che la pianta dell'edificio è molto meno allungata di quanto non appaia nel disegno redatto in occasione degli scavi di Lord Savile (Rossbach 1890: 152; Wallis 1891): m. 28.80 (= 96 piedi) × 35 (quelli conservati), anzichè 15,90 × 30. Si è riportato in luce il podio in peperino, già rinvenuto negli scavi del Savile e successivamente rinterrato, con modanatura inferiore a *cyma reversa* e rivestimenti in opera quadrata a diatoni e ortostati, secondo uno schema decorativo ellenistico elaborato in ambiente latino e campano, e diffuso in Italia centrale tra la seconda metà del II sec.a.C. e gli inizi del I, come, per citare solo alcuni esempi, il Tempio di Portuno a Roma, quello di Rieti, forse della Magna Mater (Reggiani 1987: 370-371, figg.7-8), il tempio B di Pietrabbondante, datato tra la fine del II e gli inizi del I sec.a.C. (Franchi dell'Orto & La Regina 1978: 453-461), il contemporaneo santuario sannitico di S.Giovanni in Galdo (ibid. 1978: 500-504), quello di Vastogirardi, posto dal Morel (1984: 38) tra il 125 e il 100 a.C. e attribuito ipoteticamente da La Regina anch'esso a Diana. Al di sopra del podio si conserva per un'altezza considerevole la cortina regolare in opera reticolata di peperino (fig.8). Le colonne erano costituite da rocchi di peperino scanalati alti cm.90 rivestiti in stucco bianco e i capitelli erano di ordine corinzio, come dimostra uno pertinente ad un'anta rinvenuto nel corso degli scavi.

La limitatezza delle indagini condotte non ha permesso di chiarire i problemi relativi sia all'attribuzione del tempio, sia alla pianta, che secondo la testimonianza di Vitruvio (*de arch.* IV.8-4) avrebbe dovuto avere cella trasversale, il che sembra essere in contraddizione con la pianta elaborata dal Wallis in occasione degli scavi del secolo scorso, in cui sono indicati tre muri che sembrano dividere in tre parti la cella; tuttavia, come è già stato notato (Blagg 1983: 19) si tratta di muri di fondazione, la cui presenza non è determinante per la ricostruzione dell'elevato e del resto anche per le misure la pianta non si è rilevata attendibile.

Fig. 8. Il cosidetto Tempio di Diana nel 1924 nell'area del teatro.

Resta comunque valida l'ipotesi del Rosa (1856) che il Tempio di Diana si trovi sulla terrazza soprastante, dove effettivamente, sotto una casetta diruta, si conserva un nucleo cementizio. L'edificio in questione potrebbe essere uno dei tanti tempietti dedicati alle varie divinità adorate nel Santuario.

La ricognizione effettuata nelle immediate vicinanze ha permesso di recuperare materiale ceramico della tarda età repubblicana e della prima età imperiale: ceramica a vernice nera, terra sigillata italica, ceramica di uso comune e alcuni frammenti di statuine fittili votive simili a quelle rinvenute dal Savile nella stipe antistante il tempio.

Il materiale finora rinvenuto, sia nello scavo sia nella raccolta di superficie, non sembra superare i primi due secoli dell'età imperiale, anche se sappiamo dalle fonti che il Santuario dovette essere frequentato perlomeno fino al IV (Rossbach 1890: 186). Poi l'oblio dovette avvolgere il sito, fin quando, in età medievale, sul luogo venne edificata la chiesa di S. Nicola e, sull'altura soprastante, il romitorio di S.Michele, con un'analogia che non appare casuale con il Tempio di Diana Tifatina a Capua, su cui sorgerà la chiesa di S.Angelo in Formis (De Franciscis 1956), con quello di Vastogirardi, su cui fu edificata la chiesa di S.Angelo Indiano (Morel 1984: 41) e con il Santuario di Diana a Chianciano, su cui si impianta la chiesa di S.Michele (Paolucci 1988: 57, n.64, n.65).

La limitatezza delle indagini, condotte nei secoli in maniera parziale e discontinua e ora appena riprese, non permette finora di esprimere ipotesi esaustive sulla reale topografia del luogo sacro e su molti problemi, tuttora insoluti, riguardo il culto e la datazione del complesso. Ulteriori indagini effettuate dalla Soprintendenza nel 1993 hanno riportato in luce un secondo colonnato, in peperino, di minori dimensioni, posto tra il muro Q e il recinto a nicchioni BB. Se ne dà notizia in G. Ghini, *I luoghi del mito della Diana Nemorense*, ed. Centro Bibliotecario dei Castelli Romani, Genzano 1994.

Bibliografia

Alföldi, A. 1960. 'Diana Nemorensis, *American Journal of Archaeology*, 64, 137–144.

Alföldi, A. 1961. 'Il santuario federale di Diana sull'Aventino e il tempio di Cerere', *Studi e Materiali di Storia delle Religioni*, 32, 21–39.

Altheim, F. 1930. *Griechische Götter im alten Rom*, Giessen.

Altheim, F. 1950. *Der Ursprung der Etrusker*, Baden-Baden.

Altheim, F. 1951. *Römische Religiongeschichte*, I, Baden-Baden.

Ampolo, C. 1970. 'L'Artemide di Marsiglia e la Diana dell'Aventino', *La Parola del Passato*, XXV, 200–210.

Ampolo, C. 1981. 'Ricerche sulla lega latina, I', *La Parola del Passato*, XXXVI, 219–233.

Andrén, A. 1940. *Architectural Terracottas from Etrusco-Italic Temples*, Lund-Leipzig.

Bayet, J. 1957. *Histoire politique et psychologique de la religion romaine*, Paris.

Blagg, T.F.C. et al. 1983. *Mysteries of Diana, the antiquities from Nemi in Nottingham Museum*, Nottingham.

Bodei Giglioni, G. 1978. 'Pecunia fanatica', in *Studi su Praeneste*, Perugia, 3–46.

Bodei Giglioni, G. 1990. 'Lavori pubblici ed evergetismo privato', in *Civiltà dei Romani. La città, il territorio, l'impero*, Milano, 99–110.

Borsari, L. 1887, 1888. *Notizie degli Scavi di Antichità*.

Bover Y Rosello, J.M. 1845. *Noticia historico-artistica de los Museos del Eminentissimo Señor Cardenal Despuig exsistentes en Mallorca*, Palma de Maiorca.

Brelich, A. 1954. *Introduzione allo studio dei calendari festivi*, I, Roma.

Campanelli, A. c.s. 'Le terrecotte architettoniche della Civitella di Chieti', in *Atti del convegno Cicli figurativi fittili di età repubblicana, Ostraka*, 1993.

Coarelli, F. 1976. 'Architettura e arti figurative in Roma', in *Hellenismus in Mittelitalien*, Gottingen, 21–37.

Coarelli, F. 1983. 'I santuari del Lazio e della Campania tra i Gracchi e le guerre civili', in *Les "bourgeoisies" municipales italiennes aux II et I siècle av.J.C.*, Paris-Naples, 217–240.

Coarelli, F. 1987. *I Santuari del Lazio in età repubblicana*, Roma.

Colonna, G. 1962. 'Sull'origine del culto di Diana Aventinensis', *La Parola del Passato*, XVII, 57–60.

Colonna, G. 1974. 'Preistoria e Protostoria del Lazio', in *Popoli e civiltà dell'Italia antica*, II, Roma, 275–317.

Colonna, G. 1985. 'Il Lucus Ferentinae ritrovato?', *Quaderni del Centro di studio per l'archeologia etrusco-italica*, 11, VII,1, 40–43.

De Franciscis, A. 1956. *Templum Dianae Tifatinae*, Caserta.

Della Seta, A. 1918. *Museo di Villa Giulia*, Roma.

Delbrück, R. (ed.) 1979. *Hellenistische Bauten in Latium*, Perugia.

De Sanctis, G. 1907. *Storia dei Romani*, I, Torino.

Devoti, L. 1987. *Speculum Dianae*, Frascati.

Dumézil, G. (ed.) 1977. *La religione romana arcaica*, Milano.

Finocchi, P. 1980. 'Il "Templum" di Iuppiter Latiaris sul Mons Albanus', *Quaderni del Centro di studio per l'archeologia etrusco-italica*, III, 156–158.

Franchi dell'Orto, L. & La Regina, A. 1978. *Culture adriatiche antiche d'Abruzzo e di Molise*, Roma.

Frazer, J.G. 1973. *Il ramo d'oro*, Torino.

Galosi, M.A. 1979. 'Mons Albanus – Un complesso sacrale', *Quaderni del Centro di studio per l'archeologia etrusco-italica*, II, 63–66.

Ghini, G. 1993. 'La ripresa delle indagini al Santuario di Diana a Nemi', *Quaderni del Centro di studio per l'archeologia etrusco-italica*, 21, XI, 277–289.

Giardino, C. 1985. 'Il ripostiglio di Nemi', *Documenta Albana*, 7, 7–16.

Gierow, P.G. 1964. *The Iron Age Culture of Latium, II,1, The Alban Hills*, Lund.

Giovannoni, G. 1912. 'Esplorazione dell'area del Tempio di Giove Laziale', *Notizie degli Scavi di Antichità*, 382–384.

Gordon, A.E. 1934. *The Cults of Aricia*, Berkeley.

Graevius, J.C. 1732-37. *Thesaurus Antiquitatum Romanarum*, Venezia.

Grant, M. 1971. *Roman Myths*, London.

Hafner, G. 1967. 'Das Relief vom Nemisee in Kopenhagen', *Jahrbuch des Deutschen Archäologischen Instituts* 82, 246–274.

Lanciani, R. 1889. *Notizie degli Scavi di Antichità*.

La Regina, A. 1966. 'Sulmona', *Quaderni dell'Istituto di Topografia Antica dell'Università di Roma*, 2, 107 ss.

Lugli, G. 1930. 'Saggi di scavo per la ricerca di Giove sulla vetta di Monte Cave, *Bollettino d'Arte*, IX, 162–168.

Melis, F. & Serra Ridgway, F. 1987. '"Mysteries of Diana". Sulla nuova esposizione dei materiali nemorensi nel Castle Museum of Nottingham', *Quaderni del Centro di studio per l'archeologia etrusco-italica*, 14, VIII, 218–226.

Merlin, A. 1906. 'L'Aventin dans l'Antiquite', *Bibliothèque des Écoles Françaises d'Athènes et de Rome*, 97.

Moltensen, M. 1986. 'To akroliton i Ny Carlsberg Glyptotek', *Musem Tusculanum*, 56, 289–309.

Momigliano, A. 1962. 'Sul dies natalis del santuario federale di Diana sull'Aventino', *Rendiconti dell'Accademia Nazionale dei Lincei*, s.VIII, XVII, 387–392.

Momigliano, A. 1966. *Terzo contributo alla storia degli studi classici e del mondo antico*, II, Roma, 545–598.

Morel, J.P. 1966. 'Les Phoceens en occident: certitudes et hypothèses', *La Parola del Passato*, XXI, 378–420.

Morel, J.P. 1984. 'Gli scavi del santuario di Vastogirardi', in *Sannio. Pentri e Frentani dal VI al I sec.a.C.*, (Atti del Convegno Novembre 1980), Matrice, 35–41.

Morpurgo, L. 1903. 'Nemus Aricinum', *Monumenti Antichi Lincei*, XIII, 297–368.

Morpurgo, L. 1931. 'Teatro ed altri edifici romani in contrada La Valle', *Notizie degli Scavi di Antichità*, n.s.VII, 237–305.

Ogilvie, R.M. 1964. *A Commentary on Livy Books 1–5*, Oxford.

Pairault, F-H. 1969. 'Diana Nemorensis. Déiesse latine, déiesse hellenisme', *Mélanges d'Archéologie et d'Histoire*, 425–471.

Paribeni, E. 1961. 'Note on Diana Nemorensis (AJA 1960: 137–144)', *American Journal of Archaeology*, 55–56.

Pauly-Wissowa. *Realencyclopaedie der Classichen Altertumswissenschaft.*

Peña, M.J. 1973. 'Artemis-Diana y algunas cuestiones en relación con su iconografía y su culto en Occidente', *Ampurias*, 35, 109–134.

Pensabene, P. & Sanzi di Mino, M.R. 1983. *Museo Nazionale Romano, Le terrecotte III*,1, Roma.

Piganiol, A. 1967. *Le conquiste dei Romani*, Roma.

Poulsen, F. 1941. 'Nemi Studies', *Acta Archeologica*, XII.

Pugliese Carratelli, G. 1968. 'Lazio, Roma e Magna Grecia prima del secolo quarto a.C.', *La Parola del Passato*, XXIII, 321–347.

Reggiani, A.M. 1987. 'Reate: avvio di un'indagine topografica', *Quaderni del Centro di studio per l'archeologia etrusco-italica*, VIII, 365–372.

Riis, P.J. 1966. 'The cult image of Diana Nemorensis', *Acta Archeologica*, XXXVII, 68–75.

Rizzo, G.E.. 1910. 'Di un tempietto fittile di Nemi e di altri monumenti inediti relativi al tempio italico-etrusco', *Bullettino della Commissione Archeologica Comunale di Roma*, XXXVII, 281–321.

Robinson, E. 1889. *Description of twenty-three objects found on the site of the Artemisium of Nemi "Nemus Dianae", during the excavations of Sig.Luigi Boccanera, in the Spring of 1887 and now in the Museum of Fine Arts in Boston*, Boston.

Rosa, P. 1856. 'Relazione dei ruderi esistenti in prossimità del lago di Nemi', *Annali dell'Instituto di Corrispondenza Archeologica*, 5–8.

Rossbach, O. 1890. 'Das Dianaheiligtum in Nemi', in *Verhandlungen der vierzigsten Versammlung Deutscher Philologen und Schulmanner in Görlitz 1889*, Leipzig.

Schilling, R. 1960. 'Une victime des vicissitudes politiques, la Diane latine', in *Hommages à J.Bayet*, (Coll. Latomus, 45), Bruxelles, 650–657.

Simon, E. 1984. 'Diana', in *LIMC*, II, 792–849.

Staccioli, R.A. 1968. *Modelli di edifici etrusco-italici, modelli votivi*, Firenze.

Van Berchem, D. 1960. 'Trois cas d'asylie archaique', *Museum Helveticum*, XVII, 21–33.

Von Rohden, H. 1886. 'Terrecotte di Nemi', *Mitteilungen des Deutschen Archäologischen Instituts-Römische Abteilung* I, 175–176.

Wallis, G.H. 1891. *Catalogue of Classical Antiquities from the Temple of Diana, Nemi, Italy*, Nottingham.

Wissowa, G. 1912. *Religion und Kultus der Römer*, Munchen.

16

I Luoghi della Penitenza: Strategie di Insediamento dei Complessi Mendicanti Femminili

Monica G. Sorti

Sommario: *Nell'ambito degli studi riguardanti gli insediamenti degli ordini mendicanti, esistono a tutt'oggi numerose lacune per quanto riguarda la comprensione e la definizione tipologica e funzionale degli insediamenti femminili. Il presente lavoro, ancora in fase preliminare, cerca di definire, nel quadro più generale di un sistema monastico-territoriale, le espressioni concrete di un* modus vivendi *penitenziale al femminile. Con questa chiave di lettura si procede alla verifica di queste esperienze; dall'eremo ai reclusori urbani agli insediamenti degli ordini mendicanti veri e propri, con il loro conseguente impatto nella realtà urbana del XIII secolo e successivi sviluppi (XIV-XVI sec.). A fronte di una cospicua mole di lavori di ricerca e di catalogazione degli insediamenti maschili, catalogati e analizzati nelle loro linee di condotta insediamentali, quelli femminili contano su una ben più ridotta attenzione degli studiosi, almeno per quanto riguarda il passato, e su una ancora più grave carenza di fonti attendibili cui poter attingere nel lavoro di ricerca. La mia ricerca, concentrandosi soprattutto sia nell'area che ho definito come 'Provincia Romana del Nord', compresa grosso modo tra il litorale tirrenico e il corso del Tevere, con la via Romea come asse centrale e comprendente le tre custodie francescane di Roma, Viterbo e Orvieto, sia nell'area Sabina, presenta un primo stralcio di schedatura dei diversi siti, differenziati per ordini e per epoca di insediamento e di eventuale soppressione.*

Questa ricerca rappresenta il tentativo di approfondimento di un tema – gli insediamenti degli ordini mendicanti – che ha già avuto una solida impostazione sia nelle sue linee generali storico-religiose che in quelle più specificamente storico-architettoniche; tuttavia questo tema presenta ancora oggi una attenzione ridotta se non inesistente riguardo alcuni aspetti particolari, quali, per esempio, la comprensione e la definizione tipologica e funzionale degli insediamenti femminili.

Le considerazioni che seguono hanno quindi lo scopo di puntualizzare alcuni aspetti storici di insieme della questione e vorrebbero essere il punto di partenza di un successivo approfondimento nel tentativo di ricostruire in termini attendibili un panorama che sia storicamente valido.

Senza fare una approfondita analisi degli studi che hanno avuto come centro di interesse la complessa realtà degli Ordini Mendicanti, voglio qui ricordare una data ed un testo che hanno rappresentato uno spartiacque nella considerazione del problema: la data è il 1968 e il testo è *L'apostolat mendiant et fait urbaine dans la France medievale. L'implantation geographique des Ordres Mendiant. Programme questionnaire pour une enquete,* l'autore è Jacques Le Goff (1968).

Anche se l'impostazione che Le Goff ha dato al tema in questione ha poi portato ad una serie di prese di posizioni critiche nella successiva storia degli studi (è stata soprattutto messa in dubbio la capacità reale di considerare gli insediamenti degli ordini mendicanti come parametri di definizione a livello matematico/statistico della realtà urbana della Francia medievale) ha avuto comunque il grandissimo merito di stimolare tutta una serie di ricerche successive, non solo francesi, che, in maniera più o meno specifica, hanno condotto ad una riconsiderazione di tutto il fenomeno.

Dallo sviluppo di questi studi è lentamente emersa l'importanza e la specificità dell'area 'femminile' che, lungi dall'essere un'appendice passiva nel panorama generale della realtà mendicante – e non solo mendicante – ne rappresenta un aspetto altrettanto fecondo del fenomeno maschile; essa è anzi parsa talmente carica di forme e di significati propri da porre in dubbio l'adattabilità di certe costanti proprie della realtà maschile, che sembrano aver acquistato ormai un carattere quasi definitivo.

Mi riferisco in particolare agli studi che in questi ultimi anni hanno messo in evidenza le linee principali di maturazione e assestamento di quella che è stata definita la 'rivoluzione mendicante': dai primitivi romitori e dagli insediamenti rurali, presenti soprattutto in area umbro-marchigiana ove la relativa viabilità, data l'economia di tipo agricolo-pastorale, è tracciata prevalentemente dai tratturi (Pellegrini 1979), al loro lento e progressivo affacciarsi sulla scena urbana con una manovra di avvicinamento che procede da un iniziale insediamento suburbano alla realizzazione della sede definitiva nel centro cittadino o nelle zone di immediata espansione (Bonelli 1982).

E' un meccanismo che, a parte qualche eccezione, si verifica con ampia generalità particolarmente nell'ordine francescano: di conseguenza anche la figura sociale del frate si modifica profondamente, dalla primitiva condizione di pellegrino itinerante e senza fissa dimora, fino a diventare una figura perfettamente integrata nel nuovo schema sociale della città.

Infatti lo sviluppo e il sempre maggior consenso che caratterizzarono gli ordini mendicanti e li resero protagonisti non solo a livello sociale ma anche nel campo edilizio e urbanistico, procede di pari passo con l'allargarsi del consenso popolare al fenomeno della predicazione, consenso che diventa causa-effetto della realizzazione di spazi sempre più grandi, adatti a contenere un pubblico in continuo aumento.

Ma la predicazione e quindi la necessità di ampi spazi contenitore non sono sicuramente stati ugualmente presenti negli ordini femminili, per i quali i 'grandi spazi' permessi e ricercati dalle monache stesse furono semmai quelli, altrettanto vasti ma ben definiti nel loro microcosmo edilizio, del ritiro spirituale e del raccoglimento interiore vissuti nell'esperienza comunitaria del convento di clausura.

In quale maniera dobbiamo quindi considerare i loro insediamenti, rispetto alla linea di sviluppo cui ho prima accennato? E' indubbio che stiamo parlando di una realtà che, pur provenendo da un medesimo *background* culturale e pur essendo frutto di uguali avvenimenti politici e sociali, rivendica a sè una diversità di soluzioni che già ora sono state parzialmente messe in evidenza dalla storiografia contemporanea. I tratti di questa specificità, infatti, sono stati oggetto di recenti convegni dedicati alla indagine del mondo religioso medievale femminile e soprattutto di quello francescano (vedi in particolare: Movimento religioso 1980; Rusconi 1984).

Il contesto da indagare è comunque molto complesso e difficile da decodificare soprattutto a causa del basso numero di fonti cui poter fare riferimento: è difficile avere elenchi attendibili sugli insediamenti femminili nel periodo in esame (tipo quello di Paolino da Venezia del 1300 per quanto riguarda i Frati Minori) e bisogna fare riferimento a fonti indirette quali la corrispondenza tra i vari monasteri o notizie di monasteri desunte da documenti tra i più disparati: per esempio si sa per certo che a Milano, nel 1034 – siamo ovviamente in un contesto culturale e temporale fuori del tema in esame – c'erano, all'interno della città, sette conventi femminili perchè citati nel testamento del vescovo Ariberto d'Intimiano (Pasztor 1986).

La stessa difficoltà si ha poi nel valutare l'attendibilità delle fonti a disposizione. Infatti la Pasztor (1986) afferma che *"gli studi sui singoli monasteri risentono ancora di una tradizione di storiografia ecclesiastica superata da tempo, che cerca di ricondurli – come si faceva una volta con le diocesi, che risultarono, quasi tutte, fondate dagli Apostoli – ad origini le più antiche possibili"*. Si tratta, dunque, di addentrarsi in un campo di ricerche dove quasi tutto è ancora da dire, o quanto meno, da approfondire: *"dalle visioni alla mistica vera e propria, alla santità, ai miracoli, all'immaginario"*, per dirla sempre con la Pasztor (1984).

Ritornando alla domanda che mi ero posta poco fa su quali potessero essere i possibili punti di contatto fra questa realtà femminile e il resto del movimento francescano e religioso in generale, quale cioè fosse la spinta unificante alla base di questa cultura, non si potrebbe tentare alcuna risposta senza inserire il nostro quesito in una prospettiva più ampia, che tenga conto di quelle che sono le *"forze profonde della storia (...) che si lasciano cogliere nei tempi lunghi"* (Le Goff 1980).

Chateaubriand, la cui prefazione degli *Studi storici*, secondo Le Goff, *"è un vero e proprio manifesto della nuova storia"*, affermava già a suo tempo che *"adesso la storia è un'enciclopedia; tutto vi rientra dall'astronomia fino alla chimica, dall'arte del finanziere a quella del fabbricante, dalla conoscenza del pittore, dello scultore, dell'architetto sino a quella dell'economista, dallo studio del diritto ecclesiastico, civile e penale sino a quello delle leggi politiche"*.

Siamo ai prodromi di quella che sarà poi la teorizzazione della 'nouvelle histoire' e della necessità di fare riferimento non più ad una storia evenemenziale bensì ad una storia costruita su un continuo dialogo multidisciplinare dove i tempi sono quelli del lungo periodo o meglio, per dirla con Vidal, del tempo *'mediamente lungo'*. Ciò che quindi può funzionare da griglia unificante della storia, come dice Le Goff (1980) riferendosi al metodo storiografico di Braudel, è la precisa individuazione di quelle *"forze particolari, ma contrassegnate da una certa permanenza: forze impersonali e collettive"* che agiscono in un determinato periodo storico.

Tra queste forze, nel periodo compreso tra XI e XV secolo di cui qui ci occupiamo, va sicuramente considerata come preminente la tradizione penitenziale. Questo fenomeno inizia infatti con il secolo XI quasi come risposta alla 'crisi della parola' in cui si dibattono soprattutto la chiesa e la cultura dotta (Magli 1977). Sin da allora la predicazione penitenziale si sviluppa come una modalità di conoscenza e di esperienza religiosa del tutto originale e alternativa rispetto alle speculazioni della teologia 'alta' della chiesa. In questo senso proprio la predicazione si pone come unico veicolo della cultura penitenziale, in contrasto con la codificazione scritta.

E' proprio questo il filo sottile, il 'rumore di fondo' dell'Occidente dall'XI al XV secolo, un modus vivendi culturale, che ha profonde radici psicologiche e religiose, ma che si rivela anche e soprattutto, come una visione totale del proprio modo di essere, e che si estrinseca 'culturalmente' in complesse e articolate istituzioni storiche e sociali.

La cultura penitenziale, scelta come chiave di comprensione e come ipotesi interpretativa di questo complesso periodo porta con sè, come suo immediato strumento, la 'povertà'. Così si esprime la Magli (1977): *"fin dai primi tentativi di predicazione penitenziale la povertà appare come l'aspirazione costante degli uomini della penitenza, ideale e simbolo di quel 'ritorno' a un cristianesimo primitivo che era la loro forza a la loro motivazione essenziale (...) Ci vengono incontro, circondati da un alone mitico, le figure suggestive del mendicante, del pellegrino e dell'eremita che, come categorie di 'diversi', incutono timore, perchè il timore si accompagna sempre al 'diverso', all'estraneo, all'altro (...) da essi proviene una forza, sono in qualche modo rappresentanti della 'potenza', e in quanto tali, potenti essi stessi".*

Ed è in questo contesto sociale e culturale che, nel passaggio tra XI e XII secolo, si assiste alla nascita di quel fenomeno tutto particolare che è l'eremitismo urbano, un modus vivendi 'privilegiato' delle donne. Proprio la città, dunque, fa da catalizzatore e da agente di trasformazione delle esperienze eremitico-penitenziali, consentendo la ricerca dei 'deserta' all'interno del tumultuoso mondo comunale.

Anna Benvenuti Papi (1984), in un suo studio sulla santità femminile, mette bene in evidenza come il fatto che il numero delle figure di sante non appartenenti all'area mendicante sia elevato soprattutto al nord dove è ancora forte la presenza signorile, mentre le altre sembrano prevalere soprattutto nell'Italia centrale: *"pochi casi nell'Italia nord-occidentale, poco più nel Veneto e nel Friuli, il fenomeno comincia a divenire degno di rilievo in Emilia Romagna, è notevolissimo in Toscana e in Umbria, diminuisce nell'area del Lazio, si fa sporadico nelle Marche, in Abruzzo e in Sicilia".*

Ciò evidenzia il rapporto sempre più stretto che sembra legare le figure di queste penitenti con le esigenze della nascente realtà cittadina, figure che sembrano assumere, talvolta, il significato quasi di mito di fondazione, o meglio sarebbe dire di ri-fondazione, come nel caso di Verdiana da Castelfiorentino, *"dove la comunità, che ha funzioni di 'sustentator' della donna, vede nella sua immolazione rituale un canale diretto di comunicazione col cielo. Questo mutuo scambio diviene al contempo strumento di legittimazione che la collettività cerca anche in ambiti sacrali mentre tenta di affrancarsi dalle dipendenze feudali che, nel caso di Castelfiorentino, erano legate alla sede episcopale fiorentina (...) Anche la successiva translatio simbolica in uno dei luoghi più cari alla tradizione fiorentina devota, la loggia del mercato di Orsanmichele, su un pilastro della quale l'effigie della santa non richiamava più la soggezione del castello vasldelsano al vescovo ma al comune di Firenze, è un simbolo chiaro di questa volontà di affrancamento"* (Benvenuti Papi 1979).

La scelta dell'eremitismo urbano (non necessariamente di carattere individuale: esistono infatti esempi di convivenza di due o più donne nel medesimo eremo) rende la città stessa il luogo privilegiato dell'esperienza religiosa. Il fatto stesso, poi, che la maggior parte dei cosiddetti 'reclusori' siano localizzati quasi esclusivamente in corrispondenza di punti di passaggio come *"ponti, zona delle mura non lontane dalle porte"*, oltre a rispondere alla necessità pratica di favorire le elemosine forse, a mio avviso, corrisponde anche ad un necessario e mutuo rapporto di legittimazione tra queste donne e la città, rapporto nel quale il romitorio stesso, posto su un limite topografico e sociale, assolve simbolicamente la funzione sacrificale legata ad un rito di passaggio.

Mi sto soffermando in maniera particolare su questo genere di 'applicazioni concrete' di un modo nuovo di accondiscendere ad un rinato spirito religioso, perchè le ritengo esperienze che in qualche modo fanno da prologo e da accompagnamento iniziale di quelle che saranno poi le strutture degli insediamenti mendicanti femminili veri e propri, cioè di quell'insieme di luoghi che sceglieranno o saranno cooptati sotto l'egida protettrice dei nuovi ordini: francescani, domenicani, agostiniani.

Sulle modalità di sviluppo degli insediamenti mendicanti maschili, si è scritto e teorizzato molto. Per i francescani il primo elenco che riassume le notizie sul numero dei loro insediamenti è quello di Paolino da Venezia, elaborato nel 1300, e come dice Pellegrini (1979), *"per un approccio globale al fenomeno della presenza francescana nell'Italia del secolo XIII nulla forse è tanto persuasivo quanto l'altissimo numero degli insediamenti".*

L'Ordine dei Frati Minori, o Francescani, era diviso in Provincie, le Provincie in custodie e le custodie nelle circoscrizioni dei singoli conventi, che risultano però non facilmente tracciabili. Una cosa da mettere in evidenza è la non corrispondenza tra le suddivisioni territoriali dei Francescani con le ripartizioni politiche ed ecclesiastiche.

Un esempio: per quanto riguarda la Tuscia *"la situazione (...) dimostra che l'organizzazione territoriale francescana risponde essenzialmente ad esigenze organizzative specifiche della struttura interna dell'ordine e del suo apostolato, adattando le une e le altre alla situazione ambientale esterna, ma senza lasciarsi, se non secondariamente, condizionare dalle strutture organizzative del territorio (ecclesiastiche o laiche esse siano)"* (Pellegrini 1979). Ecco quindi spiegati facilmente i confini geografici delle Provincie Francescane che diventano un modo semplice e concreto di organizzare funzionalmente un territorio.

Nell'area centro settentrionale, per esempio, lo spartiacque appenninico è il confine tra la *Provincia Bononiae* e la *Provincia Tusciae*, così come la Valle del Tevere diviene il confine naturale tra la *Provincia Tusciae* e quelle di S. Francisci e tra la medesima e la *Provincia Romana*. Lo stesso dicasi per il confine tra la Provincia della *Marca Anconetana* e la Provincia di S. Francesco rappresentato sempre dallo spartiacque dell'Appennino umbro-marchigiano o quello marchigiano-abruzzese che segna il confine tra la *Marca Anconetana* e la *Provincia Pennensis*.

La concretezza nel risolvere problemi di organizzazione del territorio è evidente anche nel fatto che le stesse suddivisioni tengono conto anche delle aree linguistiche, favorendo il raggruppamento in custodie e provincie che abbiano un medesimo substrato culturale-linguistico: ne è un esempio *"l'Alto Adige con i tre insediamenti di Bolzano, Villach e Brixen, dipendente dalla Provincia di Austria, (e quello della) Penisola Istriana (...) organizzate in una custodia, appartenente alla Provincia Sclavoniae, comprendente da nord a sud, gli insediamenti di Trieste, Muggia, Capodistria, Pirano, Parenzo, Pola e Valle"* (Pellegrini 1979).

Un altro esempio significativo è la mancanza di insediamenti a Sovana quando, in genere, i Francescani 'occupano' per così dire, tutte le sedi episcopali. Il fatto che Sovana ne sia tagliata fuori è sinonimo di un interesse per i centri che dimostrino di avere, per così dire, una dichiarata 'potenzialità espansiva'. Per Sovana, invece, *"Lo spopolamento del territorio dovuto all'impaludamento e alla malaria, e il conseguente decadimento degli agglomerati, ivi compresa la sede episcopale, è ormai fenomeno già evidente e in stadio avanzato nel secolo XIII, tant'è che il territorio pievano della sede episcopale annovera nelle* rationes decimarum *una sola chiesa solvente oltre la Cattedrale; passeranno ancora quattro secoli, prima che la sede episcopale venga trasferita alla vicina Pitigliano, ma la sorte di Sovana è ormai definitivamente segnata"* (Pellegrini 1979).

Del resto ci sono tutta una serie di contributi che hanno messo in evidenza la maniera 'programmatica' degli ordini mendicanti nel proporsi all'interno della dinamica del nuovo mondo comunale. Così scrive Guidoni (1989): *"ancor più che delle cattedrali - che interessano comunque soltanto un numero limitato di centri abitati - delle strutture comunali - che si sviluppano soltanto in ben determinate aree europee - le chiese e i conventi mendicanti coprono a tappeto quasi ogni regione, dalle città maggiori fino ai più piccoli paesi"*. E, come dice sempre Guidoni, questo inserimento sebbene i diversi ordini siano in concorrenza tra loro, non è mai il frutto di un agire 'spontaneo' e soprattutto 'isolato', ma concepito, in un certo senso, *"di comune accordo, almeno per quanto si riferisce alla collocazione nella città e alla spartizione delle risorse urbane; (...) è interesse del Comune (e anche del vescovo) evitare squilibri che potrebbero risolversi nella formazione di un nuovo polo monumentale contrapposto a quello vescovile e a quello comunale. Il bilanciamento tra le sedi degli ordini, invece, garantisce il mantenimento dei vecchi equilibri e delle vecchie localizzazioni contribuendo a consolidare la forma urbana piuttosto che a indirizzarla verso esiti nuovi"* (fig. 1).

Questo per quanto riguarda, dunque, i conventi maschili; per quelli femminili le modalità di insediamento sembrano ammantarsi soprattutto di valenze simboliche.

Con lo sviluppo del nuovo modello urbano, infatti, il topos alto-medievale del 'deserto-città', percorso da sentieri, disseminato di eremi, popolato da viandanti, devoti e residenti di ogni tipo, si è modificato profondamente ribaltandosi nei suoi termini: la città stessa,

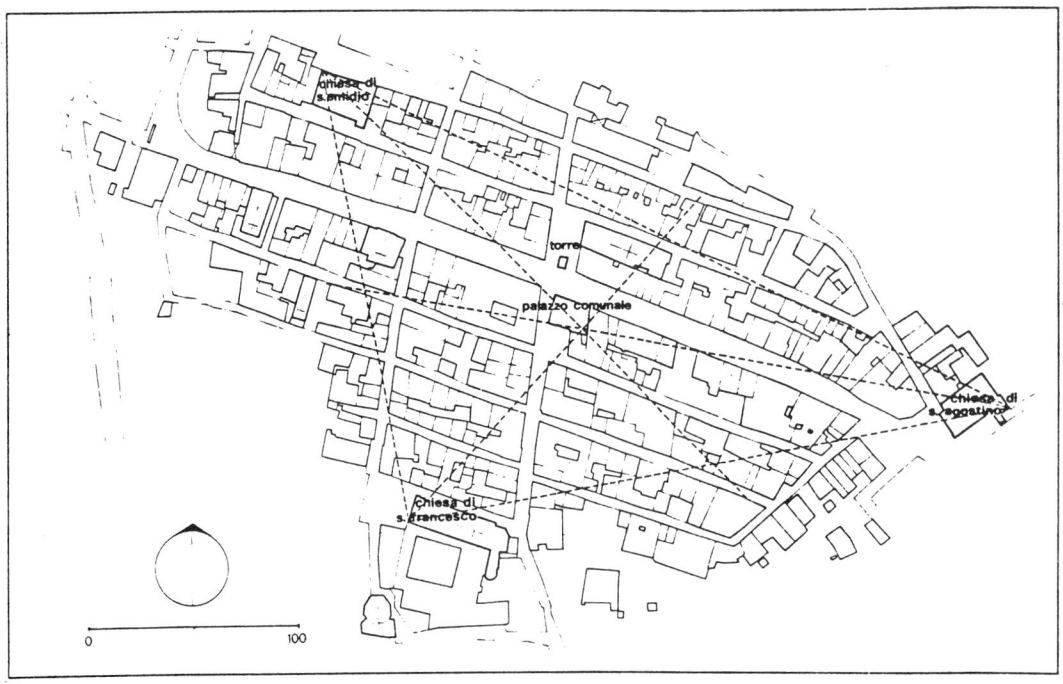

Fig. 1. Planimetria di Amatrice (Rieti) con la disposizione triangolare delle chiese degli ordini mendicanti (da Guidoni).

con i suoi eremi che attirano devoti e benefattori, la città con la sua crescente funzione di scambio e di passaggio diventa simile al deserto medievale, diventa 'città-deserto'.

E' il mondo urbano, soprattutto nell'Italia peninsulare, che si sostituisce nell'immaginario collettivo, diventando luogo di prove e di avventure, *"l'antico dualismo dell'Occidente medievale cultura-natura (che) si esprime di preferenza mediante la contrapposizione fra ciò che è costruito, coltivato e abitato (città, castello, villaggio ad un tempo) e ciò che è propriamente selvaggio (mare, foresta, equivalenti occidentali del deserto orientale), fra l'universo degli uomini che vivono in comunità e l'universo della solitudine"* (Le Goff 1984), si arricchisce di un nuovo termine creando spazi di 'frontiera' anche al suo interno: i reclusori urbani, spesso soltanto piccole celle con una tavola di legno per letto e, in seguito, soprattutto i conventi di clausura, sono vere e proprie fratture, e con Eliade (1973), potremmo definirle *"rivelazione di una realtà assoluta, in opposizione alla non realtà dell'immensa distesa che le circonda; (...) nulla può avere inizio, nulla può realizzarsi senza la premessa di un orientamento, ed ogni orientamento implica l'acquisizione di un punto fisso"*.

E quanto abbiano significato come 'centri' di riferimento questi soggetti privilegiati di comunione col sacro, lo si legge soprattutto nel valore sociale che assume la loro entrata nel reclusorio: qui, infatti, anche i 'frutti' di ogni scelta eremitica personali non sono più individuali, in quanto tutta l'intera collettività ne è beneficiata.

E' infatti la città che accompagna, in corteo funebre, la 'sua' reclusa per partecipare alla sua morte simbolica: si coglie la presenza di un atto di espiazione rituale volto al recupero di una purezza che sarà cristallizzata dalla 'liminalità' dell'accesso alla cella. L'isolamento monastico, da quel momento in poi, preserverà questa purezza da ogni contaminazione mondana: ed è appunto questa particolare condizione che fa della reclusa, *"vittima volontaria della morte rituale, una mediatrice per eccellenza tra il mondo dei vivi, al quale non appartiene più, e quello superiore, al quale ha accesso in virtù della sua funzione sacrificale"* (Benvenuti Papi 1979).

Anche la processione, insieme al culto dei santi, delle reliquie, delle ostensioni, è un fenomeno collegato al motivo del pellegrinaggio che è uno degli aspetti privilegiati del mondo penitenziale. *"Tutti si muovono, partono, camminano, si fanno nomadi, è un continuo viaggio verso la Gerusalemme celeste (dove) la vita terrena è come passaggio (...) e nel pellegrinaggio – come nella processione – è presente un significato ulteriore, il raggiungimento di uno spazio sacro"* (Magli 1977). Ed è lentamente, in questa realtà polimorfa e perennemente in movimento, che affiora l'esperienza religiosa mendicante; Pellegrini ha messo in evidenza come, nel francescanesimo delle origini, non esistesse nessuna sede privilegiata ma prevalessero luoghi privi di connotazioni particolari, come ricoveri, ospizi, funzionali soltanto ad una soluzione provvisoria, di fortuna.

Nell'area femminile tutto questo sembra non avvenire e i luoghi dell'origine danno l'idea di avere, fin dalla nascita, un loro carattere ben preciso. Come il reclusorio della cellana è uno spazio 'saturo' di sacralità, così il convento femminile, con il suo 'limen' più netto, invalicabile rispetto al recinto del convento maschile, riempie i suoi confini di una comunicazione più profonda con l'aldilà e chiude-apre nel tessuto urbano i suoi canali di rapporto con il sacro.

Per il movimento francescano al 'femminile' non è la piazza o la chiesa, spazio transitorio, sostituibile, il luogo dell'esperienza religiosa, bensì la fissità del chiostro. Ad una intercambiabilità degli spazi del sacro nell'esperienza mendicante maschile, soprattutto francescana, fa riscontro, nel movimento delle damianite-clarisse, per esempio, una fissità di riferimento radicata profondamente nel suo asse cielo-terra.

E non può essere un caso che, almeno inizialmente, il movimento che si coagula intorno alla figura di Chiara, le *Pauperes Dominae* di San Damiano, viene definito proprio dal luogo dove vivono la loro esperienza religiosa.

E' chiaro che questa originaria dicotomia di comportamento nel movimento francescano tra esperienza maschile e femminile è frutto non tanto di una diversa aspirazione, almeno non in termini così coscienti, quanto di oggettive situazioni socioculturali. Ma qualsiasi sia stato il fattore scatenante alla base di tutto ciò, è indubbio che questo ha portato al concretizzarsi di soluzioni differenti.

Nel cammino del sacro percorso dalla religiosità femminile dal XII al XVII secolo, infatti, si può individuare una strada che, seguendo modalità a volte molto articolate e complesse, è comunque tendente ad un progressivo 'abbandono' da parte dello spazio sacro femminile del suo rapporto con la città.

Nei reclusori urbani del basso medioevo, come abbiamo visto, la cella è spesso posta su un luogo di transito e assomma in sé *"la sacralità del ponte (che) 'sottomette' e 'domina' la parte della via spesso più pericolosa per il viaggiatore; (e così come) la sacralità del ponte è secondaria in paragone a quella del fiume e (...) sia nata quasi come un riflesso o piuttosto un antidoto della prima"* (Dinzelbacher 1990), così lo spazio abitato dalla reclusa diviene sacro in virtù della giovane realtà comunale che chiede protezione e 'antidoti' contro i demoni del 'nuovo mondo'. E' quindi uno spazio che pur nel sigillo che si è autoimposto è profondamente dialogante con la circostante realtà urbana.

Man mano che si approfondisce l'esperienza dei nuovi ordini il convento femminile sembra invece subire un fenomeno di 'implosione' e quindi di progressivo distacco dalla città. Mentre i conventi mendicanti maschili si aggrappano al tessuto urbano spinti come

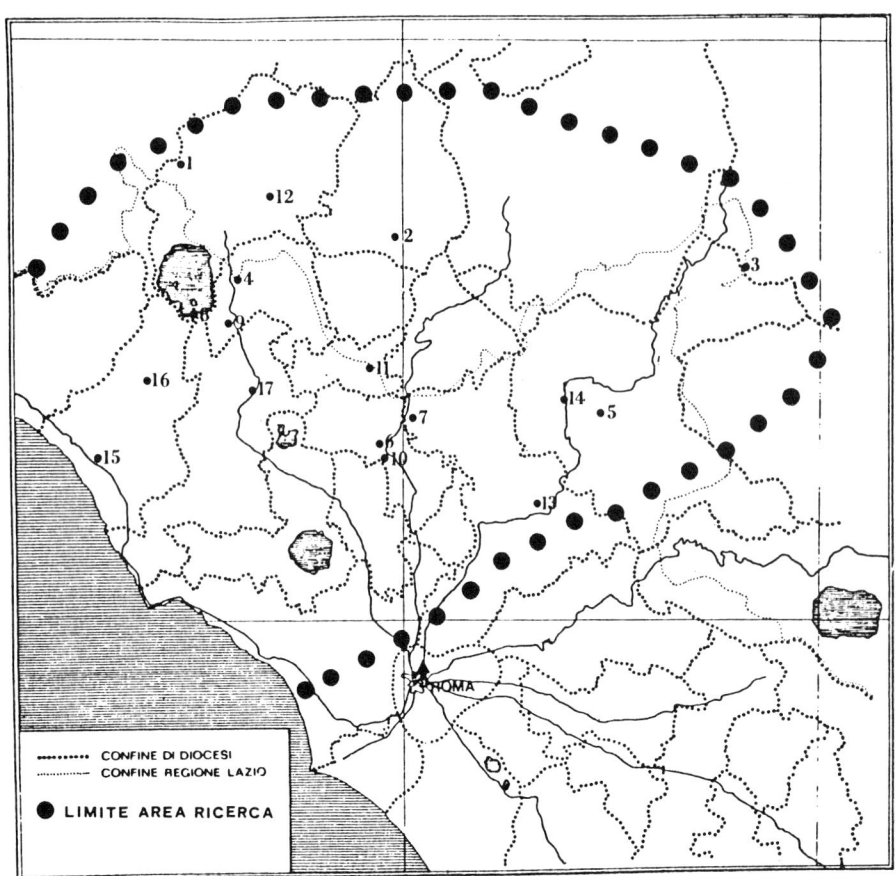

Fig. 2. Delimitazione dell'area oggetto di studio. I numeri individuano le località contenenti insediamenti femminili nei secoli XIII-XVI.

sono da una necessità di *"spazializzazione della parola sacra"* (Bologna 1990), il convento femminile, dopo una prima incerta fase pretridentina in cui si assiste ad un allentamento della clausura stessa, muove lentamente verso *"...la pace silenziosa nella caverna dell'interiorità (in latebris heremi)* (che) *rappresenta per suprema metafora il trasferimento della fatica contemplativa dall'esercizio del gesto, socializzabile ed 'urbano', dentro la caverna che è nel corpo"* (Bologna 1990). Ad un'esplosione della comunicazione, degli spazi, della luce, del tempo propria degli ordini maschili, il mondo femminile oppone il non tempo dell'interiorità: *"il tempio-monastero-luogo dell'interiorità si delinea come una regione immaginale, un utopistico spazio terrestre-celeste che coincide con l'anima, con quel non-luogo riconosciuto e perimetrato mediante elementi minimi, per tratti spesso eterogenei e incommensurabili, negli interstizi del corpo 'pensato dal di dentro'"* (Bologna 1990).

Questo chiudersi al mondo porta anche a rielaborare spazialmente alcuni elementi architettonici che caratterizzano gli edifici destinati ad un'utenza femminile: penso al muro divisorio che viene eretto per dividere talvolta le chiese femminili e che Grassi (1964) afferma essere, almeno con tale funzione, come una proposta originale del periodo cinquecentesco.

Infatti accanto alla programmatica semplicità degli edifici chiesastici propria degli ordini mendicanti, corrisponde soprattutto, come abbiamo visto, questa necessità di isolamento (a partire da quelle cistercensi):

"le religiose dovevano essere completamente isolate da tutto, anche dai confessori e dai preti che celebrano gli uffici. Il coro, direttamente comunicante con il chiostro, era chiuso in ogni sua parte, e separato dall'altare da una grata. I Sacramenti venivano somministrati attraverso un'apertura praticata nella grata stessa" (Grassi 1964).

Dopo il Concilio di Trento il convento femminile è ormai diventato un *hortus conclusus*, come sottolinea Zarri (1990), che ha dedicato un suo studio (uno dei pochi) alle modalità di inserimento degli insediamenti femminili mendicanti considerando come terreno di verifica tutta una città, in questo caso Bologna, e spaziando in un contesto temporale che lambisce il periodo storico che ci riguarda, essendo centrato soprattutto sul '500 e sul '600.

Nondimeno ripercorre in maniera suggestiva tutte le varie fasi di 'appropriazione' della città individuando tre fasi di insediamento: la prima tutta protesa a conquistarsi un posto immediatamente a ridosso delle mura, una zona non troppo popolata e soprattutto a costi ridottissimi ma che riveste anche una forte carica simbolica: *"la cura scenografica con cui vengono edificate le facciate dei piccoli oratori testimonia la rispondenza della localizzazione ad un proposito preciso, che assume l'inequivocabile valore simbolico di coronare la città affidandola alla protezione della Vergine"* (Zarri 1990); la seconda e la terza fase segnano invece un graduale allontanamento dei conventi di clausura, soprattutto dopo il Concilio di

N°	LOCALITA'	XIII	XIV	XV	XVI
1	Acquapendente		▲		
2	Acquasparta			▲	
3	Amatrice			○	○○
4	Bagnoregio	○			
5	Cittaducale		●	○	
6	Civita Castellana	▲			▲
7	Magliano Sabina	▲			
8	Marta			○	
9	Montefiascone			○▲	
10	Nepi				○
11	Orte		○		
12	Orvieto	▲ ●●		▲	▲
13	Poggio Nativo		○		
14	Rieti	▲	○	○○	○▲▲
15	Tarquinia			○	
16	Tuscania	▲			
17	Viterbo	▲	○	○▲	○

Fig. 3. Elenco dei centri con insediamenti femminili – sec. XIII–XVI.

○ BENEDETTINE*   ■ DOMENICANE**   ▲ FRANCESCANE   ● AGOSTINIAE

* Sono stati riportati, pur non rientrando nel tema in esame degli Ordini Mendicanti, anche gli insediamenti femminili benedittini solo per avere un quadro il più ampio possibile, di un sistema monastico territoriale.
** Gli insediamenti domenicani non sono riportati in questa tabella perche l'elenco dei loro insediamenti è ancora in fase di definizione.

Trento, dalla zona delle mura, dove *"cominciano a fervere attività artigianali e costituirsi stabilimenti manifatturieri. I bastioni che sovrastano le mura monastiche costituiscono, inoltre, ineliminabili prospetti dentro il recinto conventuale, rendendo la zona urbana fino allora privilegiata per gli insediamenti femminili inadatta alla clausura (...) Il centro cittadino è invece privilegiato dalle comunità di nuova istituzione che si costituiscono tra il XV e il XVI secolo, che avevano acquistato poche case nell'intento di espandersi successivamente (...)"*.

Questo il fenomeno che cercherò di verificare con l'area subito a nord di Roma compresa tra la fascia litorale tirrenica e la Sabina con la via Romea come asse centrale (fig. 2). Sono messe a confronto, relativamente allo stesso periodo, gli insediamenti degli ordini mendicanti femminili clarisse, domenicane, agostiniane, con quelli delle benedettine (fig. 3). Ciascuno degli insediamenti conventuali sarà corredato di una scheda indicante la cronologia e la storia, l'indicazione delle fonti archivistiche cui fare riferimento, l'eventuale rilievo se l'edificio è esistente (fig. 4). Uno studio del genere è stato approntato da Carbonara (1984), solo per quanto riguarda la Sabina, e comunque unicamente per gli insediamenti maschili. Tutto ciò nel tentativo di composizione di un sistema monastico territoriale che permetta la comprensione del valore della loro collocazione nel territorio.

Dai primi dati che ho potuto elaborare appare evidente una concomitanza di situazioni tra la realtà bolognese e l'area che ho preso in esame: per Bologna (Zarri 1973) si ha una soglia massima di nuove fondazioni tra la fine del Duecento e l'inizio del Trecento mentre si assiste ad un minimo nel periodo compreso tra l'inizio del '300 e la metà del '400, momento dopo il quale si assiste ad un nuovo incremento sia delle nuove fondazioni che ad un infoltimento demografico di quelle già esistenti (fig. 5).

Analogamente, per l'area che intendo analizzare, il grafico (fig. 6) mostra un andamento della curva che sembra confermare sostanzialmente – e soprattutto nell'ambito delle fondazioni femminili mendicanti piuttosto che benedettine – la situazione osservata a Bologna. L'andamento di tali grafici può essere spiegato da accadimenti di ordine generale, come la terribile epidemia di peste che flagellò l'Europa nel corso del XIV secolo, quanto da fattori locali che se per Bologna erano legati alle soppressioni dei conventi femminili (almeno sei) volute dal Cardinal legato Bertrando del Poggetto (Zarri 1973), per Rieti, prendendo uno dei centri principali dell'area interessata dal mio studio, possono avere un contorno meno chiaro: fatto certo è che così come nei testamenti del '300 si parla sempre più di monasteri e sempre meno di incarcerate – (nel corso del XIV secolo) *"...è possibile che le celle fossero ancora abitate e che la città di Rieti fosse un favo di reclusi, come la campagna attorno a Gualdo Tadino era stato un favo di eremiti negli ultimi anni del tredicesimo secolo, ma questa non è*

N° LOCALITA' 12	pagine scheda: ■ □ □	SCHEDA N° 2 6

DENOMINAZIONE

attuale: ORVIETO

precedente:

INTITOLAZIONE: S.Lorenzo in vineis/inter vineas

REGOLA/ORDINE: Clarisse

UBICAZIONE ATTUALE: /

FONDAZIONE: 1225 ca. Certamente esistente nel 1228.

DOCUMENTO PIU' ANTICO:

   Padre Casimiro da Roma: *fuori della Città di Orvieto, fu già un monastero di Clarisse, detto di S.Lorenzo in vineis, et inter vineas, edificato nel pontificato di Gregorio IX colle limosine delle monache e di altre persone pie. L'anno 1232, il di' 1 di ottobre, il vescovo Ranieri lo esentò "ab omne iure episcopali", riserbando solamente a sé ed ai suoi successori una libbra di cera, che ogni anno avrebbono dovuto presentare le dette monache nella vigilia dell'Assunzione di Maria Santissima. Nell'anno 1404, essendo esposto a molti pericoli, massimamente per cagione delle guerre civili, Monsignor F.Mattia degli Avveduti, frate minore e vescovo di Orvieto, sua patria, ritirò tutte le monache di detto monastero entro la città: Le quali, poi, nell'anno 1436, furono introdotte e unite al monastero di S.Lodovico.*

PASSAGGIO AD ALTRE OSSERVANZE:

SOPPRESSIONE: 1404

consultare: MF iv, 175
          AFH v, 445-6
          AM ii, 351,709-10
          MF iv, 174-8

Fig. 4. Esempio della scheda usata dall'autore.

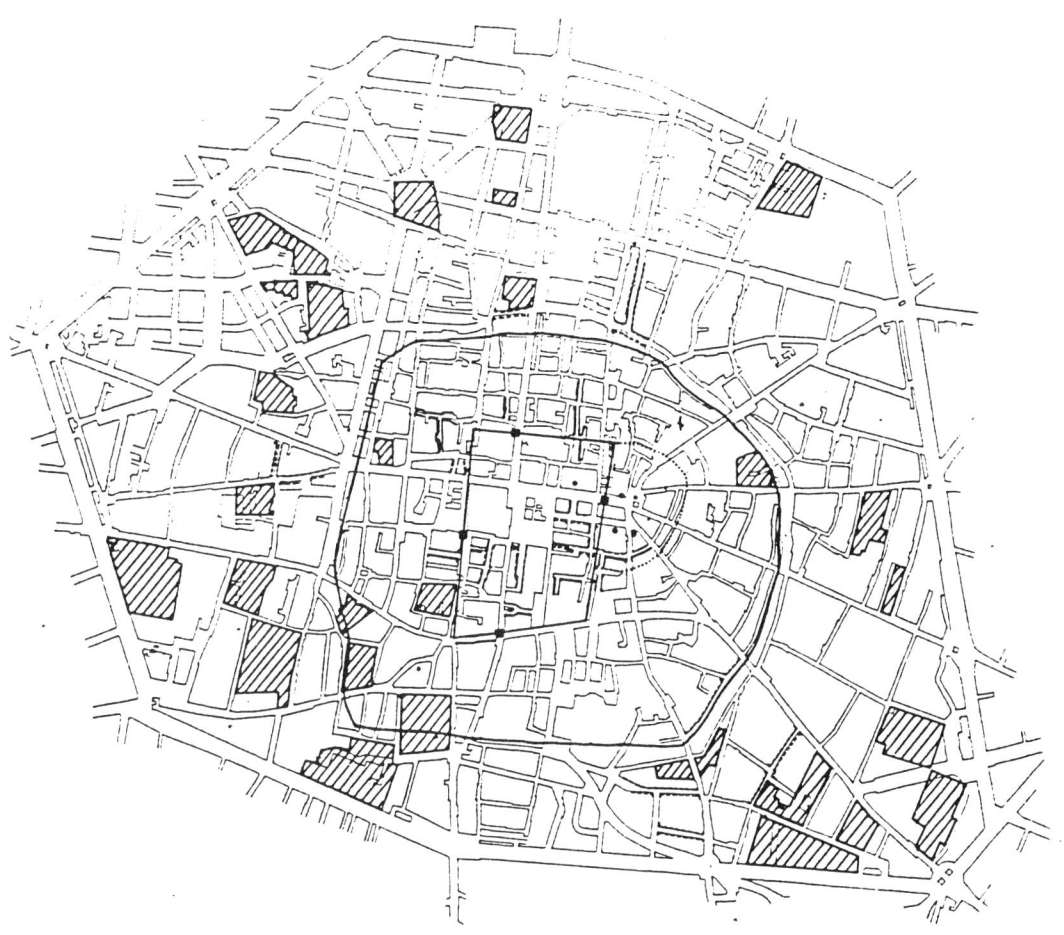

Fig. 5. Aree di insediamento dei monasteri a Bologna alla fine del secolo XVIII (da Zarri).

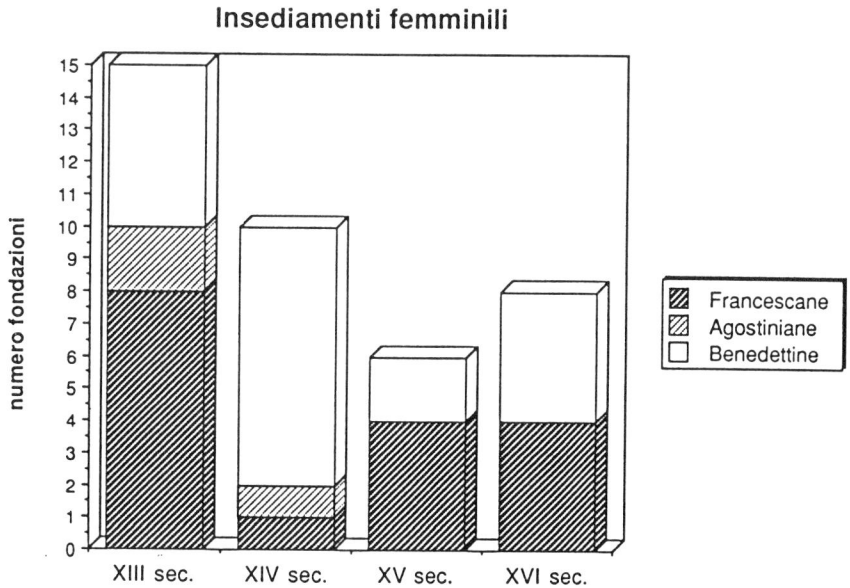

Fig. 6. Il graffico delinea l'andamento delle nuove fondazioni dei conventi femminili (escludendo quelli domenicani, ancora in fase di definizione) situati nell'area in esame.

l'impressione per chi legge i testamenti" (Brentano 1984) – così tra '300 e '400 ad aumentare è soprattutto la popolazione dei conventi benedettini a scapito delle nuove fondazioni mendicanti che riprenderanno, invece, nel corso del XVI secolo.

In sintesi si può quindi riassumere che per quanto riguarda una strategia di insediamento dei complessi mendicanti femminili in particolare, e dei monasteri femminili in generale, rispetto a quelli maschili (soprattutto in ambito mendicante) i dati distintivi sono:
– strutturarsi dello spazio sacro femminile come 'spazio del silenzio' rispetto alla necessità del movimento mendicante maschile di identificarsi sempre più con gli 'spazi della parola';
– spazio fisso femminile imperniato su una 'verticale' cielo-terra al contrario dello spazio transitorio maschile (soprattutto nelle fondazioni delle origini);
– lento ma continuo processo di allontanamento dal mondo (implosione) delle strutture femminili, soprattutto con l'irrigidimento della clausura successivo al Concilio di Trento contrapposto in ambito maschile al massimo dialogo con la realtà urbana fino ad un' ideale (ma non troppo) spartizione della città tra i maggiori ordini.

Nel corso del XVII secolo questo processo sembra ormai ben delineato e direi, praticamente concluso, tanto che così si può riassumere con queste brevi note: *"...separate dalla città e ridotte al silenzio con l'imposizione della clausura, le monache non hanno perduto un ruolo specifico nella gestione del sacro e nella promozione della religione cittadina. Cessa la funzione carismatica delle singole persone e non emergono figure dotate di eccezionali doni mistici o profetici, ma i chiostri si trasformano gradualmente in giardini recintati che si propongono alla città come immagini dell'Eden..."* (Zarri 1990).

Bibliografia

Benvenuti Papi, A. 1979. 'Velut in sepulchro: cellane e recluse', in S. Boesch & L. Sebastiani (a cura di), *Culto dei santi, istituzioni e classi sociali*, 367–455.

Benvenuti Papi, A. 1984. 'Una terra di sante e di città. Suggestioni agiografiche in Italia', in R. Rusconi (a cura di), *Il movimento religioso femminile in Umbria nei secoli XIII-XIV*, Città di Castello, 183–202.

Bologna, C. 1990. 'L'invenzione dell'interiorità (spazio della parola, spazio del silenzio: monachesimo, cavalleria, poesia cortese', in S. Boesch Gajano & L. Scaraffia (a cura di), *Luoghi sacri e spazi della santità*, Torino, 243–266.

Bonelli, R. 1982. 'Introduzione', in *Francesco d'Assisi. Chiese e conventi*, Milano, 7–12.

Brentano, R. 1984. 'Il movimento religioso femminile a Rieti nei secoli XIII-XIV', in R. Rusconi (a cura di), *Il movimento religioso femminile in Umbria nei secoli XIII-XIV*, Città di Castello, 67–83.

Carbonara, G. 1984. 'Gli insediamenti degli Ordini Mendicanti in Sabina', in *Lo spazio dell'umiltà*, (Atti del Convegno di Studi sull'Edilizia dell'Ordine dei Minori, Fara Sabina 3–6 Novembre 1982), Roma, 123–224.

Dinzelbacher, P. 1990. 'Il ponte come luogo sacro nella realtà e nell'immaginario', in S. Boesch Gajano & L. Scaraffia (a cura di), *Luoghi sacri e spazi della santità*, Torino, 51–60.

Eliade, M. 1973. *Il sacro e il profano*, Torino.

Grassi, L. 1964. 'Iconologia delle chiese monastiche femminili dall'alto medioevo ai secoli XVI-XVII', in *Arte Lombarda*, IX, vol.I, 131–150.

Guidoni, E. 1989. 'Gli Ordini Mendicanti nella città', in E. Guidoni (a cura di), *Storia dell'urbanistica: il Duecento*, 306–319.

Le Goff, J. 1968. 'Apostolat mendiants et fait urbaine dans la France medievale. L'implantation geographique des Ordres Mendiants. Programme. Questionnaire pour une enquete', *Annales E.S.C.*, 23, 924–958.

Le Goff, J. 1980. *La nuova storia*, Milano.

Le Goff, J. 1984. *Il meraviglioso e il quotidiano nell'Occidente medievale*, Bari.

Magli, I. 1977. *Gli uomini della penitenza*, Milano.

Movimento religioso 1980. *Movimento religioso femminile e francescanesimo nel secolo XIII*, (Atti del VII Convegno Internazionale di Studi, Assisi 11–13 Ottobre 1979, Società Internazionale di Studi Francescani), Assisi 1980.

Pasztor, E. 1984. 'I Papi del Duecento e Trecento di fronte alla vita religiosa femminile', in R. Rusconi (a cura di), *Il movimento religioso femminile in Umbria nei secoli XIII-XIV*, Città di Castello, 29–65.

Pasztor, E. 1986. 'Il monachesimo femminile', in *Dall'eremo al cenobio*, Milano, 155–180.

Pellegrini, L. 1979. *Gli insediamenti francescani nella evoluzione storica degli agglomerati umani e delle circoscrizioni territoriali dell'Italia del sec. XIII*, estratto vol.30, Italia sacra, Roma.

Rusconi, R. (a cura di) 1984. *Il movimento religioso femminile in Umbria nei secoli XIII-XIV*, (Atti del Convegno Internazionale di Studio, Città di Castello 27–29 Ottobre 1982), Città di Castello 1984.

Zarri, G. 1973. 'I monasteri femminili a Bologna tra il XIII e il XVII secolo', *Atti e Memorie della Deputazione di Storia Patria per le Province di Romagna*, XXIV, 133–224.

Zarri, G. 1990. 'Recinti sacri. Sito e forma dei monasteri femminili a Bologna tra '500 e '600', in S. Boesch Gajano & L. Scaraffia (a cura di), *Luoghi sacri e spazi della santità*, Torino, 381–396.

PART 3

Settlement and Economy

17

Economie di Allevamento in Italia Centrale dalla Media Età del Bronzo alla Fine dell'Età del Ferro

JACOPO DE GROSSI MAZZORIN
(Soprintendenza Archeologica di Roma)

Sommario: *Nel presente lavoro sono esposti i risultati delle ricerche zooarcheologiche condotte in Italia centrale negli ultimi anni, sottolineando in particolare le strategie economiche dei diversi insediamenti, in modo da proporre modelli di allevamento e caccia per le diverse aree geografiche e per le diverse fasi cronologiche. L'allevamento ha via via acquisito tecniche più specializzate che hanno prodotto un miglioramento nelle dimensioni delle diverse specie di animali domestici. Si è inoltre evidenziato come l'attività venatoria sia stata relegata, col passare del tempo, tra le attività di secondaria importanza, e come e quando nuove specie animali siano state introdotte nella regione considerata.*

Lo scopo di questa ricerca è quello di proporre modelli di allevamento attraverso lo studio del materiale zooarcheologico proveniente da diversi insediamenti della media e tarda età del Bronzo e dell'età del Ferro dell'Italia centrale, e di valutare se vi siano differenze tra le diverse aree esaminate (fig.1).

Numerose sono state le difficoltà incontrate nel corso di questa ricerca, soprattutto nel tentativo di confrontare i dati quantitativi di un sito con un altro. Poichè il numero minimo d'individui (NMI) non sempre era disponibile per tutti i campioni (alcuni pubblicano solo il numero di frammenti, altri solo percentuali) nel presente lavoro si è preferito fare riferimento solo al numero di frammenti, anche se questo porta a soprastimare alcuni animali a scapito di altri. Per questi ed altri problemi che sarebbe lungo elencare in questa sede si deve considerare questa ricerca il punto di partenza, piuttosto che un arrivo, teso alla comprensione della struttura socio-economica e delle attività di sussistenza ad essa riferibili, che andrà di volta in volta verificato con l'apporto di nuovi dati provenienti dagli scavi degli insediamenti delle comunità oggetto di questa ricerca.

I RESTI FAUNISTICI DEGLI INSEDIAMENTI DEL VERSANTE TIRRENICO

Per quanto riguarda i siti dell'età del Bronzo in Etruria e Lazio, gli animali domestici costituiscono la maggior parte dei campioni di fauna analizzati, sia come numero di frammenti che come numero minimo di individui; si notano tuttavia delle differenze a seconda del sito nei rapporti percentuali tra le tre principali categorie di animali domestici (fig.2,A).

A Luni sul Mignone (Gejvall 1967: 263-276) sono i bovini che predominano in tutti i periodi di occupazione con percentuali che oltrepassano il 40% circa dei resti. Il maiale si mantiene intorno al 20-25%: di conseguenza, potrebbe trattarsi di un insediamento fondamentalmente dedito all'agricoltura, soprattutto nel Bronzo medio, quando bovini e suini insieme costituiscono oltre il 75% degli animali domestici. L'attività pastorale sembra al contrario aumentare nel corso delle fasi abitative: i resti di ovicaprini passano dal 27% circa del Bronzo medio al 36% del Bronzo finale. Uno sviluppo analogo si registra anche nel campione faunistico di Pitigliano (De Grossi Mazzorin 1985a: 77-92). A M. Rovello (Caloi & Palombo 1986: 88-103) ugualmente si nota un aumento dell'attività pastorale nel Bronzo finale, anche se questa ha un peso considerevole già dalla fase recente (oltre il 30% di ovicaprini). In tutti e tre questi abitati si nota inoltre una progressiva diminuzione dell'allevamento suino.

A questo raggruppamento si contrappongono gli abitati di Narce (Barker 1976: 295-307) e San Giovenale (Sorrentino 1981a; 1981b) dove, al contrario, è attestata una economia caratterizzata dalla predominanza di pecore e capre. I nuovi dati di Castiglione e Ficana ben si inseriscono nelle medie delle rispettive fasi; a Castiglione nel Bronzo medio, prevalgono i bovini mentre nel Bronzo finale a Ficana si ha una netta prevalenza degli ovicaprini.

In generale si può concludere che nel corso della media e tarda età del Bronzo i bovini, tranne l'eccezione

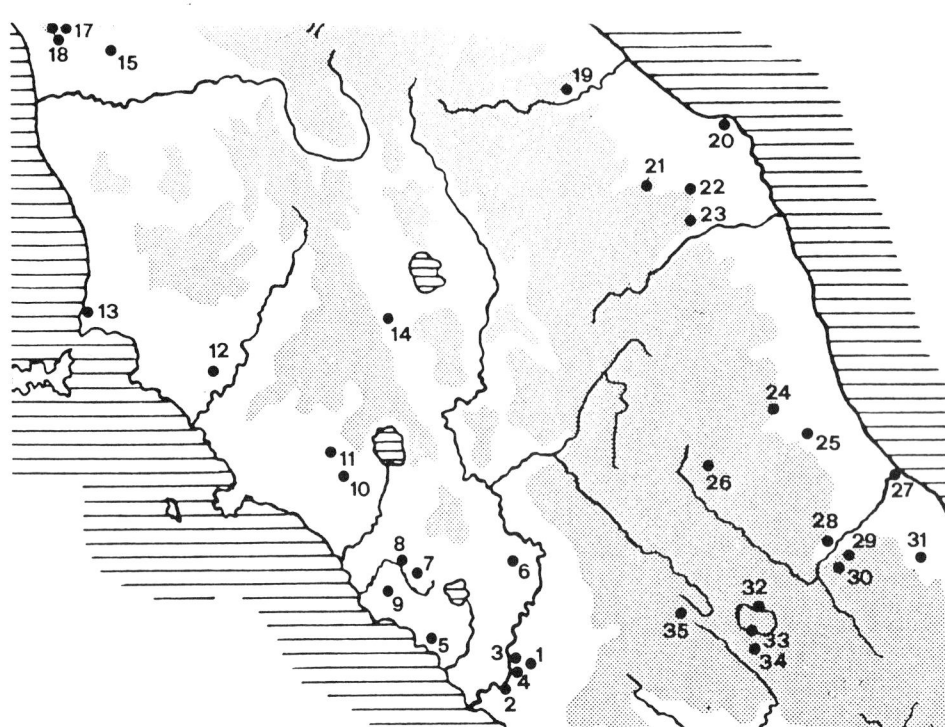

Elenco degli insediamenti di cui si sono confrontate le faune
1) Castiglione (Bronzo medio) De Grossi Mazzorin in studio
2) Ficana zona 2 (Bronzo finale) De Grossi Mazzorin in studio
   Ficana zona 3b-c (VIII-VI a.C.) De Grossi Mazzorin 1989
   Ficana zona 5a (VII a.C.) De Grossi Mazzorin 1989
3) Fidene A (VIII-VII a.C.) De Grossi Mazzorin 1989; Bietti Sestieri et al. 1990
   Fidene U.P.F. VIII a.C. De Grossi Mazzorin 1989
4) Roma - Palatino (VIII-VII a.C.) De Grossi Mazzorin 1989
5) Cerveteri (VI-V a.C.) Clark 1989
6) Narce (Bronzo recente, finale e VIII-VI a.C.) Barker 1976
7) S. Giovenale (Bronzo recente e finale, VIII-VI a.C.) Sorrentino 1981a; 1981b
8) Luni sul Mignone (Bronzo medio, recente e finale) Gejvall 1967; Lepiksaar 1975
9) M. Rovello (Bronzo recente e finale) Caloi, Palombo 1986
10) Sorgenti della Nova (Bronzo finale) Caloi, Palombo 1981
11) Pitigliano (Bronzo medio, recente e finale) De Grossi Mazzorin 1985
12) Roselle (VI a.C.) Corridi 1989
13) Populonia (III a.C.) De Grossi Mazzorin 1985
14) Grotta dell'Orso (Bronzo medio, recente e finale) Cremonesi 1968
15) M. Catino (V a.C.) Ciampoltrini et al. 1991
16) Riparo dell'Ambra (Bronzo medio, recente e finale) Bigini 1986
17) Riparo del Lauro (Bronzo medio) Bigini 1987
18) Riparo La Roberta (Bronzo medio, recente e finale) Bigini 1985
19) Grotta del Grano (Bronzo medio e recente) Ceccanti, Cocchi 1980-81
20) Colle dei Cappuccini (Bronzo finale - I età del Ferro) Wilkens 1990
21) M. S. Croce (Bronzo medio) Wilkens 1991-92
22) S. Paolina di Filottrano (Bronzo medio, recente e finale) Wilkens 1988
23) Moie di Pollenza (I età del Ferro) Wilkens 1988
24) Grotta S. Angelo (Bronzo medio) Wilkens 1991-92
25) Coccioli (Bronzo medio) Agostini et al. 1991-92
26) Grotta a Male (Bronzo medio, recente e finale) Pannuti 1969
27) Colle del Telegrafo (Bronzo finale - I età del Ferro) Di Fraia
28) Torre dei Passeri (Bronzo medio) Di Fraia
29) Grotta dei Piccioni (Bronzo medio, recente e finale) Cremonesi 1976
30) Madonna degli Angeli (Bronzo finale) Di Fraia
31) Fonte Tasca (Bronzo medio, recente e finale) Di Fraia
32) Celano (Bronzo medio e finale) Agostini et al. 1991-92; De Grossi Mazzorin 1991; 1991-92.
33) Trasacco (Bronzo medio) Wilkens 1991
34) Collelongo del Fucino (Bronzo medio, recente e finale) Wilkens 1991
35) Grotta B. Cenci (Bronzo medio) Agostini et al. 1991

Fig. 1. Distribuzione ed elenco degli insediamenti in esame.

di M. Rovello, sembrano diminuire col trascorrere delle diverse fasi cronologiche, mentre si ha un incremento degli ovicaprini e l'allevamento suino, mantenendosi su percentuali intorno al 20% per ogni fase abitativa non svolge ancora un ruolo di primaria importanza. Unica eccezione è il campione di Sorgenti della Nova (Caloi & Palombo 1981: 269-277): la fauna, proveniente essenzialmente da grotte artificiali scavate sul fianco della collina, è caratterizzata soprattutto da resti di maiale (oltre il 75%). Le ossa appartenevano in gran parte ad animali giovanissimi e a feti, ma purtroppo non è stato pubblicato da quali contesti dell'area scavata i singoli frammenti sono stati recuperati, anche se gli autori affermano che gran parte dei materiali proveniva dalla grotta n.10, interpretata dalla Negroni Catacchio (1981: 199-256) come area adibita alla funzione di 'cucina'. Altri resti furono inoltre recuperati nelle grotte n. 11, 13 usate come abitazioni, dalla grotta 12, un 'ambiente di servizio', dalla capanna 2 e infine dalla grotta n. 7 a cui è stata attribuita una funzione cultuale. Pertanto non si può escludere che le particolari funzioni di questi contesti abbiano influito sulla percentuale dei resti animali in modo da renderli non proprio corrispondenti all'economia dell'abitato.

Nei periodi successivi (fig.2,B), dalla I età del Ferro fino al V secolo a.C., l'allevamento bovino si mantiene costante e, tranne qualche eccezione, con percentuali attorno al 25-30%.

Gli ovicaprini, con percentuali più basse rispetto ai periodi precedenti, si mantengono sul 35% ca. A differenza dell'età del Bronzo, durante la I età del Ferro e ancor più nei periodi successivi, si ha un forte incremento dell'allevamento suino. Le mutate condizioni demografiche fanno sì che la carne di maiale divenga un'importante componente della dieta alimentare. A tale proposito è da notare che a Populonia (De Grossi Mazzorin 1985b: 131-171), in una fase urbana più avanzata, i suini costituiscono il 42% del campione (una percentuale impensabile per i periodi precedenti) e tale valore è molto vicino a quello riscontrabile negli scavi di città romane dove gran parte dei resti ossei animali appartengono a maiali.

I RESTI FAUNISTICI DEGLI INSEDIAMENTI DEL VERSANTE ADRIATICO

L'analisi degli insediamenti del versante adriatico ha comportato maggiori difficoltà per l'esiguo numero di siti di cui è stata studiata la fauna, soprattutto per quanto riguarda l'età del Ferro (fig.2,C). Inoltre è stato possibile utilizzare solo parzialmente i dati di alcuni abitati, come S. Paolina di Filottrano (Wilkens 1988a: 345-361), Collelongo (Wilkens 1991: 147-153) e Fonte Tasca (Di Fraia), in quanto essi non sono attribuibili a un preciso momento ma solo genericamente alla media e tarda età del Bronzo.

Come per i coevi insediamenti dell'Etruria e del Lazio le ossa degli animali domestici costituiscono la maggior parte di tutti i campioni di fauna esaminati, con proporzioni, tra le tre principali categorie, che variano sensibilmente a seconda dell'area e del periodo considerato.

Nell'area marchigiana si mantengono con valori percentuali più o meno costanti dall'età del Bronzo sino alla prima età del Ferro. Nell'abitato della media età del Bronzo di M. S. Croce (Wilkens 1991-92: 463-469) abbiamo circa il 22% di bovini, il 42% ca. di caprovini e il 37% ca. di suini. Nel Bronzo finale, a Colle dei Cappuccini (Wilkens 1990: 327-364), e nella I età del Ferro, sempre a Colle dei Cappuccini e a Moie di Pollenza (Wilkens 1988b: 137-144) si ha un leggero incremento, rispetto al Bronzo medio, dei bovini in concomitanza di un calo dei suini, e in almeno tre siti su quattro una riduzione delle attività pastorali. A S. Paolina le cui faune sono riferibili al Bronzo medio e tardo si ha un quadro molto simile a quello appena accennato.

In Abruzzo, invece, le percentuali delle tre categorie principali di animali domestici variano sensibilmente da sito a sito, specie per quanto riguarda il Bronzo medio. Per questo periodo abbiamo le faune di Coccioli, Celano (Agostini *et al.* 1991-92: 419-426), e Torre dei Passeri (Di Fraia) nonchè quelle riferibili alla fase media e recente di Trasacco (Wilkens 1991-92: 463-469), tutte con proporzioni percentuali molto diverse: a Celano e Torre dei Passeri prevalgono i bovini, a Trasacco e Coccioli i caprovini, i suini sono pochi in tutti e quattro i siti. Tale differenza nel modello di allevamento potrebbe essere ricercata nella posizione geografica dei diversi insediamenti che li porta ad assumere valenze economiche diversificate.

I due siti del Bronzo finale, Celano (De Grossi Mazzorin 1991: 165-173) e Madonna degli Angeli (Di Fraia), hanno invece un'economia di allevamento simile con una predominanza delle pecore e delle capre sui bovini e suini. Alle Paludi di Celano i bovini venivano allevati soprattutto per le pratiche agricole; dai dati sulla mortalità risulta che gli animali venivano macellati prevalentemente in età avanzata, quando ormai erano stati sfruttati per il lavoro nei campi. La curva di mortalità degli ovicaprini tracciata in base alla metodologia di Payne (1973: 281-303), lascia ipotizzare che gli scopi della pastorizia erano soprattutto la produzione di carne e di lana (fig.3). Infatti risulta che solo una parte del gregge (il 50% ca.) era macellata entro i primi tre anni, cioè quando la maggior quantità di carne viene resa con i più bassi costi di produzione, mentre circa il 13%, oltrepassava il quarto anno di vita, così da mantenere anche una certa produzione di lana. Allo stesso tempo la bassa mortalità infantile denota una scarsa attenzione per la produzione di latte; molti agnelli nel gregge, infatti, ne danneggiano la produzione sottraendo il latte alle madri.

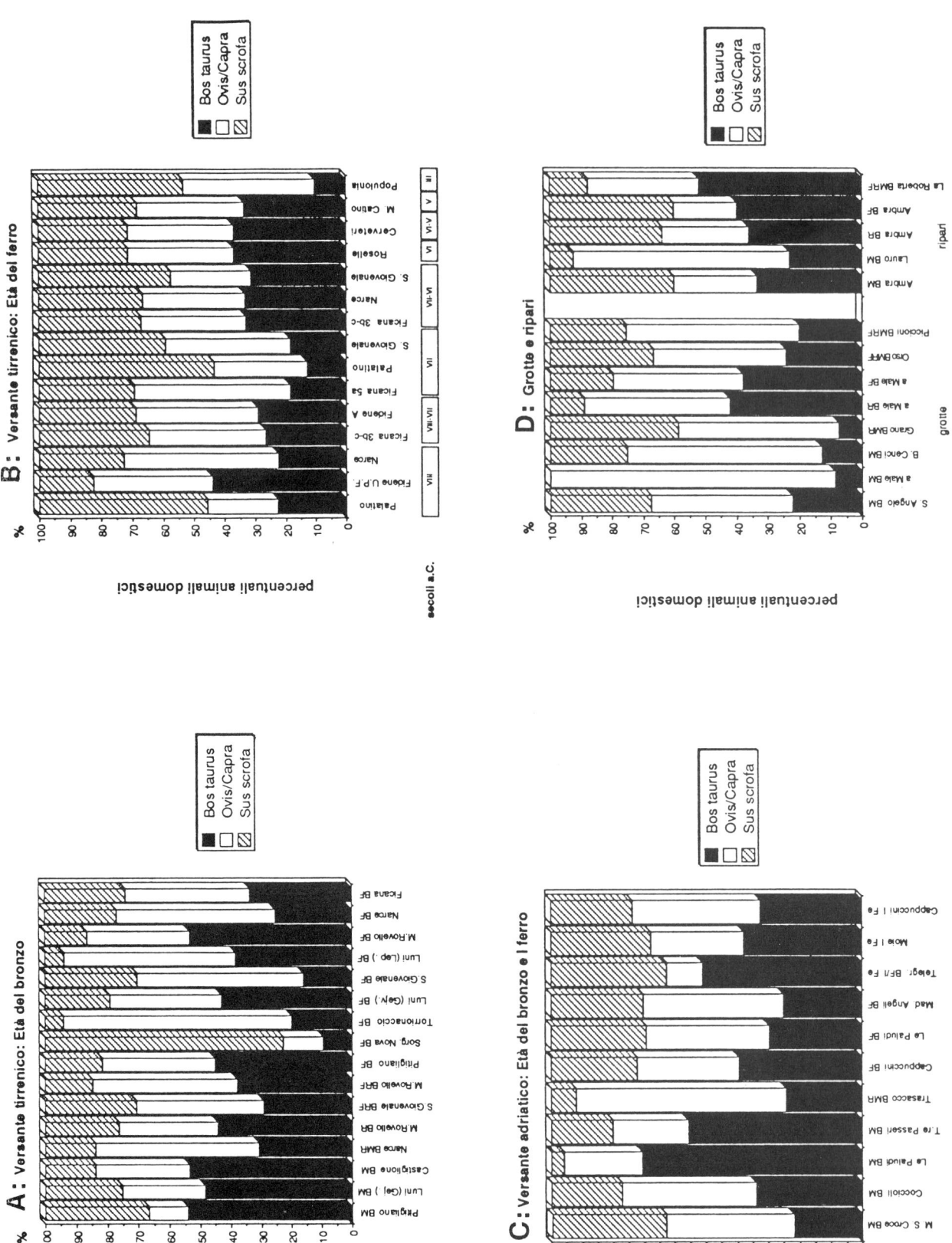

Fig. 2. Percentuali delle tre principali categorie di animali domestici in base al numero di frammenti.

Per quanto riguarda la I età del Ferro l'unico insediamento dell'Abruzzo di cui siano state studiate le faune, pur se frammiste a quelle del Bronzo finale, è Colle del Telegrafo (Di Fraia), dove si ha una forte prevalenza di bovini e suini sui caprovini.

I RESTI FAUNISTICI DI GROTTE E RIPARI

Un altro tipo di campione è costituito dai resti faunistici provenienti da scavi condotti in grotte o ripari. Spesso in diverse analisi paleoeconomiche si sono confrontati i dati zooarcheologici provenienti da scavi di questo genere e quelli di insediamenti all'aperto senza tener conto del tipo di contesto cui essi si riferiscono. E' ovvio che questi dati, vista la natura diversa dei giacimenti, devono essere analizzati separatamente. Le grotte erano infatti frequentate sporadicamente o stagionalmente da pastori, oppure spesso erano luoghi di culto se non addirittura luoghi funerari. La natura di questi luoghi pertanto influiva sulla tafonomia del campione.

Nel grafico della fig.2,D sono riportati i valori percentuali delle tre principali specie domestiche rappresentate nei campioni di resti ossei animali provenienti da diverse grotte o ripari. Nelle prime si può notare che per tutte le fasi della media e tarda età del Bronzo gli animali più rappresentati sono i caprovini con percentuali che oltrepassano il 40%. I valori sono soprattutto alti nella media età del Bronzo (oltre il 57%), specie a Grotta a Male (Pannuti 1969: 147-248) dove in questo periodo costituiscono la quasi totalità dei resti di animali domestici. Si vede inoltre che la percentuale degli ovicaprini tende a diminuire con le fasi più recenti. Anche i dati delle grotte dell'Orso (Cremonesi 1968: 247-331) e dei Piccioni (Cremonesi 1976), che non sono attribuibili come gli altri campioni a una fase cronologica precisa ma solo genericamente alla media e tarda età del Bronzo, mostrano una prevalenza di ovicaprini. I bovini hanno valori percentuali molto bassi, non oltrepassano mai il 20-25%, tranne che nella fasi recente e finale dell'età del Bronzo a Grotta a Male dove costituiscono il 40% circa degli animali domestici. Anche i suini si mantengono su percentuali abbastanza basse in confronto a quelle dei caprovini; nel Bronzo medio di Grotta a Male sono addirittura assenti, e solo nella Grotta del Grano (Ceccanti & Cocchi 1980-81: 121-172) sono abbastanza numerosi (il 40% ca.). La Grotta a Male di Assergi (AQ) è chiaramente, specie nella media età del Bronzo, un luogo di frequentazione stagionale, legato soprattutto alla transumanza verso i pascoli estivi. Anche la Grotta B. Cenci presso Cappadocia (Agostini *et al.* 1991: 66-70), nel Bronzo medio, sembra essere una cavità utilizzata prevalentemente da pastori, infatti i caprovini costituiscono il 62% degli animali domestici. Inoltre, dai dati sulla mortalità, risulta un'attenta strategia di allevamento che raramente si riscontra negli insediamenti coevi. Troviamo infatti che solo una parte del

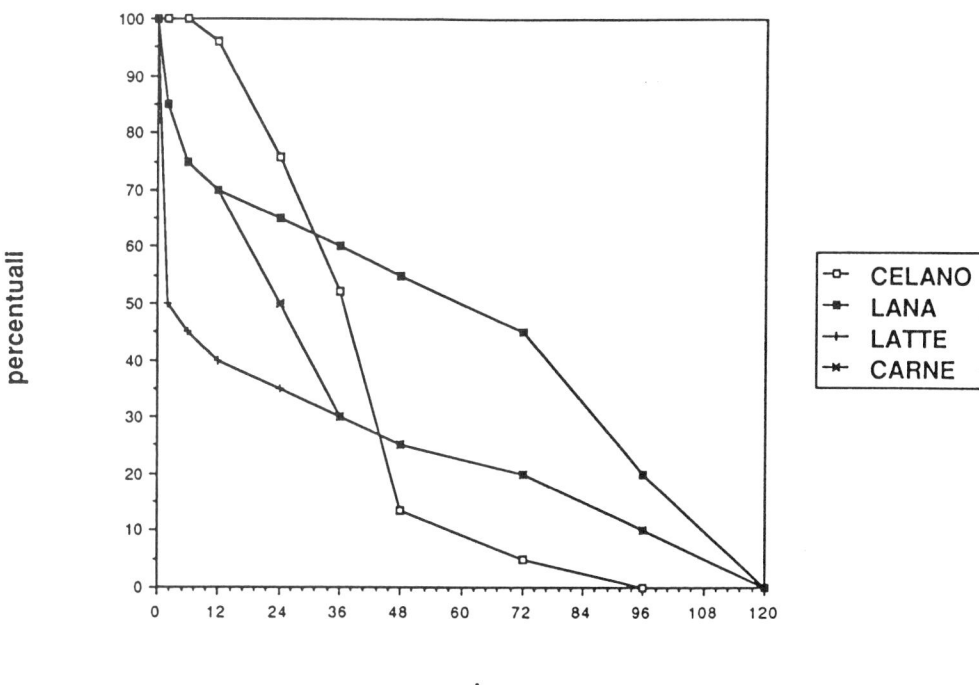

Fig. 3. Celano 'Le Paludi': modello di allevamento degli ovicaprini. Percentuali di sopravvivenza.

gregge (il 40% circa) era macellata entro i primi tre anni per la produzione di carne mentre circa il 35% oltrepassava il quarto anno di vita per mantenere quella della lana, inoltre la discreta mortalità infantile (il 25%) denota una certa attenzione anche per i prodotti caseari (come già detto troppi agnelli nel gregge danneggiano la produzione sottraendo il latte alle madri).

Per concludere, dal quadro sopraesposto, si evince come i campioni di resti faunistici provenienti da cavità naturali diano un'immagine deformata dell'economia di allevamento, in quanto fortemente influenzati dall'uso che i pastori facevano delle stesse.

La situazione appare invece più complessa nel caso dei ripari sotto roccia. Nel grafico della fig.2,D sono

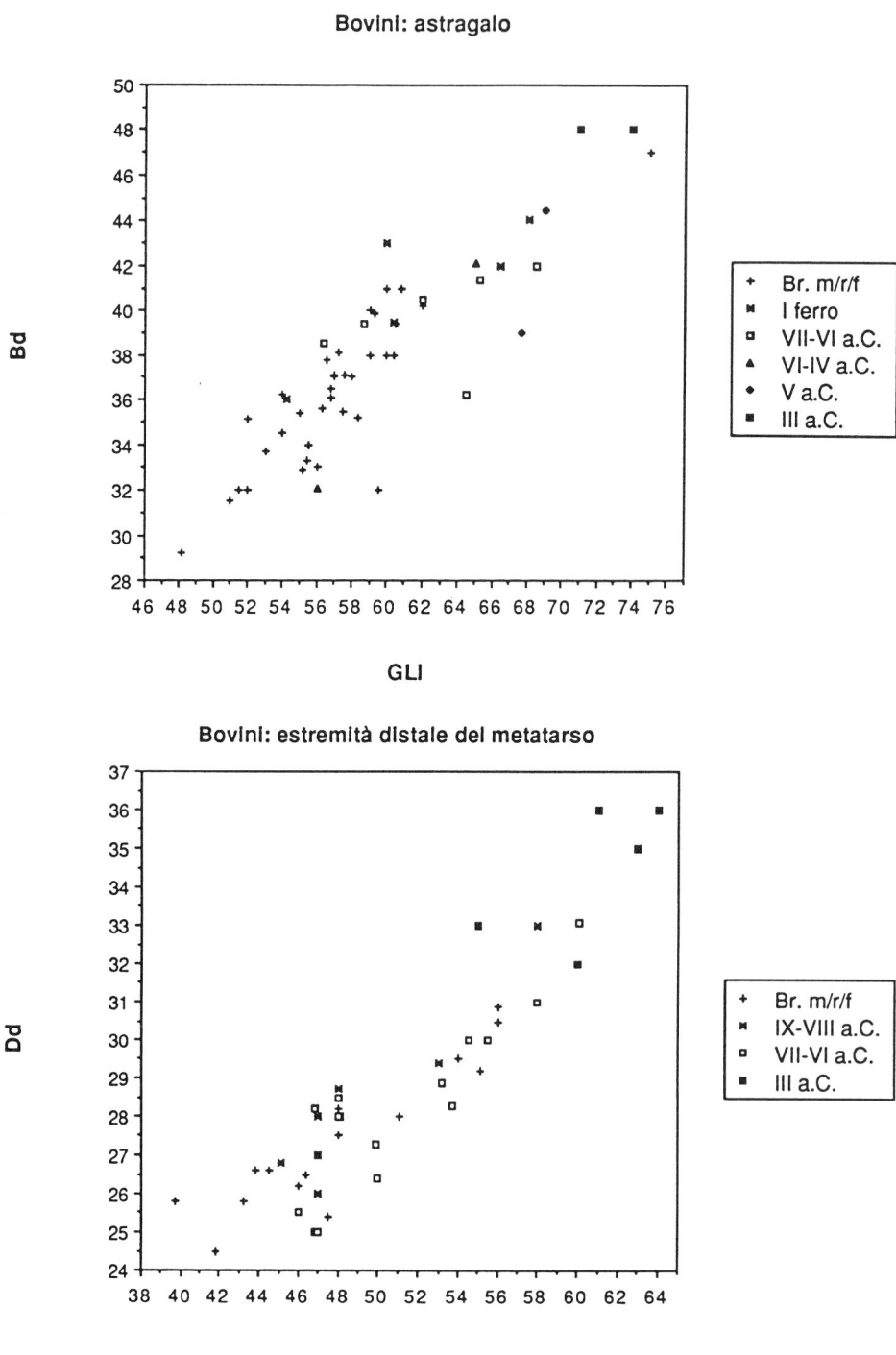

Fig. 4. Variazioni dimensionali dell'astragalo e del metatarso dei bovini in alcuni complessi dell'Italia centrale.

riportati i valori percentuali dei ripari del Lauro di Candalla (Bigini 1987), La Roberta (Bigini 1985) e dell'Ambra (Bigini 1986), tutti e tre situati sulle pendici del M. Penna nei pressi di Camaiore (LU).

Al riparo del Lauro, i cui dati faunistici si riferiscono alla fase iniziale del Bronzo medio, si ha una forte prevalenza di pecore e capre (il 70% ca.), mentre i suini sono scarsi (solo l'8%). Al Riparo dell'Ambra, nelle tre fasi del Bronzo medio, recente e finale, prevalgono invece bovini e suini. Questo riparo, posto sulla via che conduce ai pascoli del M. Matanna sembra aver costituito un luogo ideale per soste, forse stagionali, più o meno lunghe ricollegabili alla pratica della transumanza. Bisogna tuttavia sottolineare la natura esigua dei campioni, solo 26 frammenti determinati al Lauro e 46 per le tre fasi precedentemente menzionate del Riparo dell'Ambra, che rendono questi valori percentualmente poco attendibili.

Al Riparo la Roberta invece il campione è un po' più consistente (173 frammenti determinati) ma purtroppo i dati sono riferibili genericamente solo alla media e tarda età del Bronzo; anche qui, come al Lauro, i maiali sono scarsamente documentati (12%), ma in questo caso i bovini predominano sugli ovicaprini (52% contro il 36%).

La natura di questi tre campioni pertanto non ci permette di trarre conclusioni che siano di carattere generale.

L'EVOLUZIONE DELLE FAUNE DOMESTICHE

Durante l'età del Bronzo e parte dell'età del Ferro si assiste in Europa centrale a un forte calo dimensionale dei bovini (Bökönyi 1974) che poi ricominceranno ad aumentare di statura solo in seguito alla conquista romana. Anche in Italia settentrionale si assiste a un fenomeno analogo, infatti Riedel (1986) ha evidenziato, in base all'altezza al garrese dei bovini, che per tutta l'età del Bronzo questi animali diminuiscono da forme medie a forme molto piccole; l'uomo era più interessato ad una gran quantità di individui che ad animali con un importante forza di lavoro. Nell'età del Ferro e nei successivi periodi storici invece comincia uno sviluppo positivo che porta in età classica alla forza di lavoro e ad altre qualità.

Dalle altezze al garrese dei bovini dell'Italia centrale sembrerebbe che la statura di questi animali si sia mantenuta più o meno costante fino al periodo Arcaico (circa 112 cm) per crescere considerevolmente solo nel IV-III sec. a.C. (125 cm.) Purtroppo il numero dei reperti di cui è stato possibile stimare l'altezza al garrese è abbastanza esiguo: 11 per l'età del Bronzo, 6 per la I età del Ferro e solo 3 per i secoli dal VI al III a.C. Per verificare l'ipotesi sopra esposta su un campione statistico più attendibile, si sono elaborati due grafici (fig.4) che mostrano il campo di variabilità delle dimensioni degli astragali e dei metatarsi dei bovini provenienti da diversi insediamenti dei periodi in questione. Si può notare che in questi due casi i valori osteometrici dei resti della I età del Ferro si interpongono tra quelli dell'età del Bronzo e quelli dei periodi successivi come Montecatino (Ciampoltrini et al. 1991) e Populonia; sembrerebbe, cioè, che il processo di miglioramento della razza sia già in atto nella prima età del Ferro ma che questo fenomeno aumenti considerevolmente, come già osservato con le altezze al garrese, nei secoli successivi, dal V al III sec. a.C (fig.5).

Una situazione analoga si ha per i caprovini con altezze al garrese che si mantengono intorno ai 60 cm. fino al periodo arcaico; solo nel III sec, a Populonia, troviamo animali di statura considerevole (65 cm. di media). Anche in questo caso le misure di alcune ossa ci sono di aiuto per comprendere l'evoluzione di questi animali. Si ha un iniziale aumento delle dimensioni nella prima età del Ferro, ma il fenomeno diviene più consistente nei secoli successivi al periodo arcaico.

CONSIDERAZIONI SULLE ATTIVITÀ DI CACCIA E PESCA

Le specie selvatiche sono in genere poco rappresentate nei differenti campioni di resti osteologici, specie nell'età del Ferro. L'attività venatoria della media e tarda età del Bronzo sembra essere legata per lo più a necessità e condizioni locali (De Grossi Mazzorin & Di Gennaro 1992: 463-464); quasi inesistente a Luni sul Mignone e Narce, è maggiormente praticata a Pitigliano (con delle percentuali tra il 40 e il 20% a seconda delle diverse fasi abitative), M. Rovello, San Giovenale e Sorgenti della Nova in Etruria, e ad Ancona, Grotta a Male e Celano 'Le Paludi' sul versante adriatico. In tutti gli insediamenti, nei quali si può seguire il divenire di questa attività in senso diacronico, si assiste a una sua graduale diminuzione col procedere delle varie fasi abitative; come a Riparo dell'Ambra, Colle dei Cappuccini, Gr. a Male e Celano 'Paludi', M. Rovello e soprattutto a Pitigliano dove si passa dal 41% di fauna selvatica nel Bronzo medio al 18% nel Bronzo finale.

La caccia era volta soprattutto ai grossi mammiferi quali il cervo, il cinghiale e il capriolo, ma mentre in Etruria gli altri animali erano scarsamente cacciati, in Abruzzo era abbastanza praticata anche la caccia all'orso, alla volpe e al tasso, probabilmente cacciati sia per la carne che per la pelliccia.

Con l'età del Ferro comincia a praticarsi la caccia alla lepre e agli uccelli; probabilmente questo genere di caccia poteva essere effettuata da chiunque mentre la caccia al cervo e al cinghiale era divenuta una pratica dei ceti sociali più abbienti, data la quantità di tempo libero e la cooperazione di uomini necessari per un battuta di caccia (De Grossi Mazzorin 1989: 127-128).

A differenza della caccia è invece molto difficile

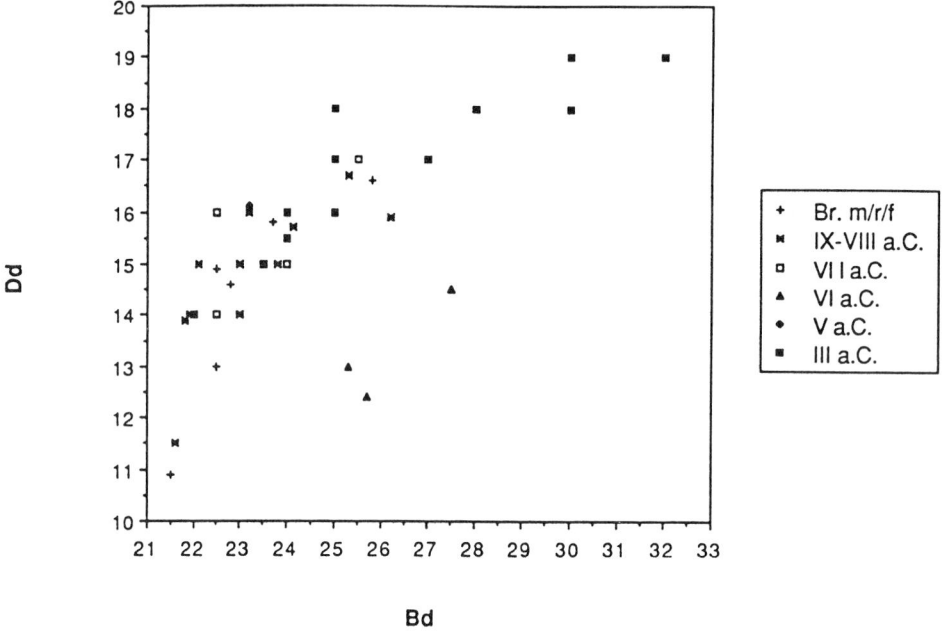

Fig. 5. Variazioni dimensionali del metacarpo degli ovicaprini in alcuni complessi dell'Italia centrale.

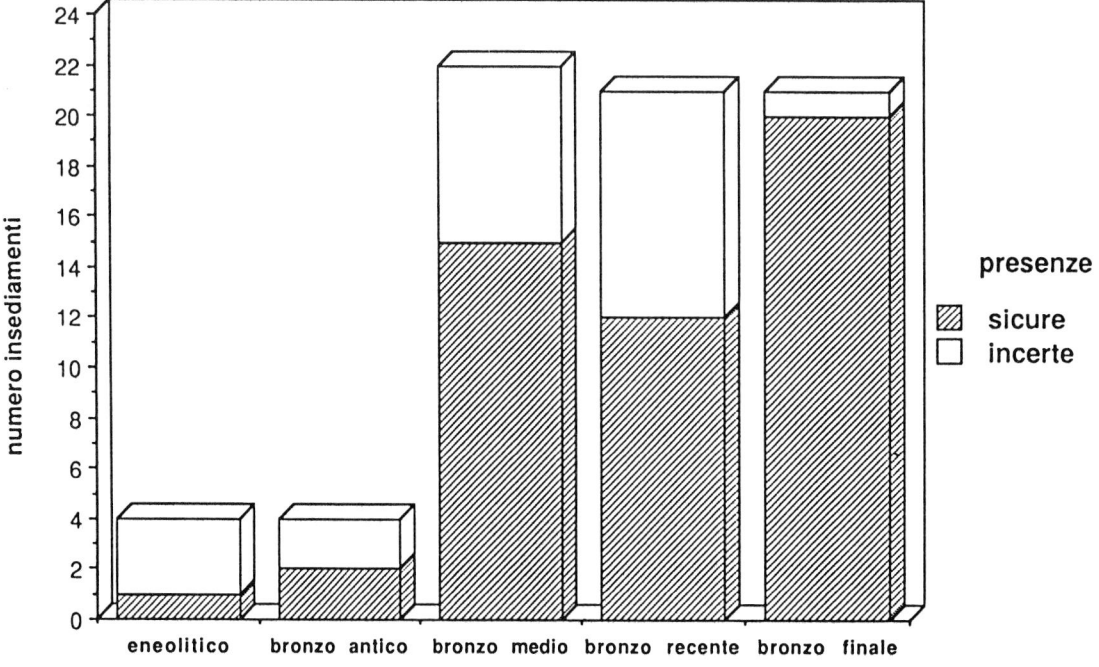

Fig. 6. Presenze del cavallo domestico negli insediamenti preistorici.

valutare l'importanza della pesca, poichè, anche se i resti di pesce si conservano benissimo, sono molto più difficili da reperire sullo scavo in quanto necessitano di operazioni di flottazione e lavaggio del terreno e di molta attenzione nel vaglio dei materiali. Poche sono, infatti, sinora le evidenze archeologiche, dirette o indirette, di attività di pesca documentate negli scavi. A Ficana zona 2, in livelli databili al Bronzo finale, si sono rinvenute 8 placche dermiche di storione, mentre in un'altra area dello stesso abitato sono stati recuperati un peso da lenza e due ami. Inoltre alcune lische di barbo e di cefalo sono state rinvenute nelle tombe della I età del Ferro a Roma nel sepolcreto del Foro (Gjerstadt 1956), mentre altri resti di pesce provengono dall'abitato di VIII-VII sec. a.C. di Cures (Ruffo 1987) e a Cerveteri (Clark 1989) e Populonia rispettivamente in contesti del VI sec. a.C. e del III sec. a.C.

L'INTRODUZIONE DI ALCUNI ANIMALI DOMESTICI NELL'ETÀ DEL BRONZO E DEL FERRO

Il recente ritrovamento di alcune ossa di cavallo nel villaggio 'campaniforme' di Querciola (Corridi & Sarti 1989-90) ha confermato la presenza del cavallo domestico in Italia sin dall'eneolitico. A parte vecchie segnalazioni – come ad esempio lo scheletro rinvenuto nella necropoli di Remedello (Colini 1898-1902) – poche erano sinora le segnalazioni di questo animale in contesti dell'Eneolitico e dell'antica età del Bronzo in Italia settentrionale: oltre ad alcuni denti rinvenuti al Segrino (Fedele 1984: 178-179), in un contesto databile all'Eneolitico-Bronzo antico, vi sono i resti del Bronzo antico di Sonnenburg e quelli forse dello stesso periodo di Barche di Solferino (Riedel 1986: 31-34). In Italia centrale oltre alla segnalazione sempre di Colini (1898-1902) nella necropoli di Cantalupo, vi sono i resti equini di Conelle d'Arcevia e Berbentina di Sassoferrato sulla cui datazione però sono stati espressi forti dubbi: Azzaroli (1979: 234) infatti sostiene che l'aspetto poco fossilizzato del dente equino di Conelle lascia intuire una intrusione recente, mentre dei denti di Berbentina, al contrario alquanto fossilizzati, asserisce che dovevano provenire da un qualche rimaneggiamento dello scavo perchè non vi erano fino ad allora segnalazioni così antiche in Italia. Tali argomentazioni sono state considerate come una posizione preconcetta da Peroni, che ha invece rimarcato come i resti di Conelle di Arcevia e Berbentina di Sassoferrato stiano a indicare *"...una presenza generalizzata, anche se forse poco consistente, del cavallo domestico in Italia durante l'Eneolitico e il Bronzo antico..."* (Peroni 1989: 128-129).

Se le recenti segnalazioni hanno definitivamente dissipato ogni dubbio sulla presenza del cavallo domestico in Italia sin dall'Eneolitico, rimane aperto il problema su quando l'allevamento equino sia divenuto effettivo patrimonio culturale delle comunità italiche.

La documentazione di resti di cavallo domestico nel Bronzo antico, come si è visto è scarsa e bisogna arrivare al Bronzo medio perchè vi sia una presenza diffusa del cavallo. A parte i vecchi rinvenimenti di ossa equine negli insediamenti terramaricoli, che purtroppo necessitano di conferma con nuovi dati di scavo più precisi, le numerose segnalazioni in questi abitati, come Montale, Castione dei Marchesi, Gorzano ecc., di montanti di morso in corno di cervo, indirettamente lasciano ipotizzare la presenza del cavallo già dal Bronzo medio. Inoltre è sempre in questo periodo che si ha la comparsa delle spade lunghe da fendente, la cui adozione è giustificabile dall'uso concomitante del cavallo (D'Ercole 1986: 324).

Nella fig.6 sono illustrati i siti dell'Eneolitico e dell'età del Bronzo di cui sono state studiate recentemente le faune e che hanno restituito resti di cavallo; si può quindi osservare come il numero di presenze aumenti in modo consistente nella media età del Bronzo e come questo si mantenga costante nelle successive fasi recenti e finale. Abbiamo infatti 15 segnalazioni sicure e 7 probabili per la media età del Bronzo, 12 sicure e 9 probabili per la recente e 20 sicure e 1 probabile per il Bronzo finale. La presenza per quegli insediamenti in cui i resti faunistici non sono attribuibili con certezza a una singola fase ma a un periodo più generico è stata considerata probabile per le fasi più antiche e sicura per quella più recente.

Dal numero crescente di segnalazioni di questi ultimi anni sembra che l'allevamento equino fosse alquanto diffuso sin dalla prima fase della media età del Bronzo, come testimoniano i resti degli insediamenti di Poviglio (Riedel 1989), di Tabina di Magreta (De Grossi Mazzorin 1988), delle Paludi di Celano (De Grossi Mazzorin 1991-92), di S. Mauro e Tufariello di Buccino (Barker 1973; 1975). Meno chiara è la loro posizione negli strati di Luni sul Mignone (VT): i reperti editi provenivano dalla trincea I, detta 'Tre Erici', e da alcune trincee nelle fondazioni delle tre case appartenenti all'abitato appenninico. Questi sono stati attribuiti ai periodi Luni Appenninico I + II e II senza specificarne i settori e i livelli di provenienza e sarebbe, quindi, interessante riesaminare questi materiali sulla base di dati di scavo precisi: non è escluso che i resti di cavallo in oggetto possano, anche in questo caso, riferirsi alla fase del Bronzo medio iniziale (facies di Grotta Nuova). Infine, pur se rinvenuti in un contesto subacqueo e quindi non del tutto sicuro per la loro giacitura, vi sono i resti equini associati a materiali del Bronzo antico e medio iniziale dei complessi sommersi di Vicarello e Vigna di Valle nel Lago di Bracciano (Fugazzola Delpino 1982) che avvalorano ulteriormente questa ipotesi.

E' stato ipotizzato che l'importazione si svolse attraverso i valichi del Brennero o di Dobbiaco e per la valle dell'Adige, fino al suo sbocco nella pianura Padana e la distribuzione dei siti sembra confermare questa supposizione.

I cavalli dell'età del Bronzo erano mediamente alti al garrese circa 123 cm. mentre nell'età del Ferro abbiamo un incremento dell'altezza al garrese con un valore medio di circa 135 cm. Le ossa rinvenute appartengono solitamente ad animali adulti, e si presentano poco frammentate e per lo più integre, ciò si spiega col fatto che i cavalli non erano consumati ma usati soprattutto come cavalcature o animali da tiro.

Altri due animali domestici introdotti in Italia nel periodo esaminato nel presente lavoro sono il gatto e il pollo. Per quanto riguarda il gatto, non è ancora chiaro come e quando questo animale raggiunga la penisola italiana; sue buone raffigurazioni sono già presenti in diverse pitture parietali delle tombe etrusche di Tarquinia, mentre la sua presenza è segnalata tra le faune di alcuni scavi dell' VIII e VII sec. a.C. Le ricerche condotte in questi ultimi anni dalla Soprintendenza Archeologica di Roma nell'area insediativa dell'antica Fidene hanno portato all'identificazione di una struttura abitativa della prima età del Ferro, databile nel complesso a un momento iniziale della III fase laziale, da collocare immediatamente prima o alla metà dell'VIII sec. a.C. (Bietti Sestieri *et al*. 1990). Di questa struttura, in eccezionale stato di conservazione, sono stati rimessi in luce lo strato di crollo delle pareti e la maggior parte degli elementi esterni. Tale crollo è stato determinato da un incendio di grande intensità che ha causato la quasi totale caduta delle pareti verso l'interno sigillando un momento di vita e uso della struttura. Nell'angolo sud-est, all'interno dello strato di crollo, sono stati ritrovati i resti calcinati dello scheletro di un gatto domestico, evidentemente rimasto intrappolato all'interno.

Altre segnalazioni di felini domestici si hanno in contesti probabilmente un po' più recenti a Cures (Ruffo 1988), e Ficana dove tra i materiali provenienti dalla zona 5A, in particolare dall'area del 'portico', se ne è rinvenuto un radio intero.

Molto probabilmente l'introduzione in queste regioni segue alla colonizzazione greca del sud-Italia; il gatto era senza alcun dubbio un animale di compagnia e forse, inizialmente, un lusso riservato alle classi aristocratiche.

Infine, anche per quanto riguarda il gallo domestico si ignora quando esso sia stato introdotto in Italia. La più antica attestazione di questo animale è segnalata in una tomba a incinerazione della prima età del Ferro laziale proveniente da M. Cucco presso Castel Gandolfo (Bartoloni *et al.* 1987: 229). E' comunque durante il periodo etrusco che si ha la più ampia diffusione di questo animale. Buone raffigurazioni di galli si trovano inoltre nelle tombe dipinte di Tarquinia, come ad esempio nella tomba del Triclinio o del Gallo (V sec. a.C.). Frammenti di ossa semicombuste provengono dalla tomba 47 c.d. 'del guerriero' della necropoli dell'Osteria a Vulci, databile all'ultimo quarto del VI sec. a.C., mentre frammenti di gusci di uova sono stati rinvenuti poggiati su un braciere della tomba 3 Maroi nella necropoli della Banditaccia a Cerveteri, databile alla seconda metà del VI sec. a.C. Altri resti ossei di gallo sono stati rinvenuti a Pyrgi sul fondo del pozzo situato nell'area sacra C, nell'insediamento agricolo di 'Le Pozze' a Blera (Ricciardi *et al.* 1987: 86), anche qui in un pozzo databile dal materiale ceramico associato tra la metà del IV e gli inizi del III sec. a.C. e infine a Populonia sempre nel III sec. a.C.

Bibliografia

Agostini, S., Coubray, S., De Grossi Mazzorin, J., d'Ercole, V. & Remotti, E. 1991. 'Cappadocia (L'Aquila). Località Oveto. Indagini preliminari nella Grotta B. Cenci', *Bollettino d'Archeologia*, 8, 61-71.

Agostini, S., De Grossi Mazzorin, J. & d'Ercole, V. 1991-92. 'Economia e Territorio in Abruzzo durante la media età del Bronzo', *Rassegna d'Archeologia*, 10, 419-426.

Azzaroli, A. 1979. 'Su alcuni resti di cavalli protostorici dell'Italia centrale', *Studi Etruschi*, 47, 231-236.

Barker, G. 1973. 'Faunal remains from the deposit at S. Mauro', in R.R. Holloway *et al.*, *Buccino. The Eneolithic Necropolis of S. Antonio and other Prehistoric Discoveries made in 1968 and 1969 by Brown University*, Roma, 115-116.

Barker, G. 1975. 'Stock economy', in R.R. Holloway, 'Buccino. The early bronze age village of Tufariello', *Journal of Field Archaeology*, 2, 59-71.

Barker, G. 1976. 'Animal husbandry at Narce', in T.W. Potter, *A Faliscan Town in South Etruria*, London, 295-307.

Bartoloni, G., Buranelli, F., D'Atri, V. & De Santis, A. 1987. *Le urne a capanna rinvenute in Italia*, Roma.

Bietti Sestieri, A.M., De Grossi Mazzorin, J. & De Santis, A., 1990. Fidene – la struttura dell'età del Ferro', *Quaderni di Archeologia Etrusco-Italica*, 19, 115-120.

Bigini, I. 1985. 'Resti faunistici', in D. Cocchi Genick, 'L'insediamento dell'età del Bronzo di Candalla', *Rassegna d'Archeologia*, 4, 105-148.

Bigini, I. 1986. 'La fauna', in D. Cocchi Genick, *Il riparo dell'Ambra. Una successione stratigrafica dal Neolitico tardo al Bronzo finale*, Viareggio, 203-205.

Bigini, I. 1987. 'La fauna', in D. Cocchi Genick, *Il riparo del Lauro di Candalla nel quadro del Bronzo medio iniziale dell'Italia centro-occidentale*, Viareggio, 189-190.

Bökönyi, S. 1974. *History of Domestic Mammals in Central and Eastern Europe*, Budapest, 1-597.

Caloi, L. & Palombo, M.R. 1981. 'Analisi dei resti ossei', in *Sorgenti della Nova. Una comunità protostorica e il suo territorio nell'Etruria meridionale*, Roma, 269-277.

Caloi, L. & Palombo M.R. 1986. 'La fauna dell'insediamento di Monte Rovello (fine del XII-IX secolo a.C.) e sue implicazioni paleoeconomiche', in 'La civiltà "Protovillanoviana" dei Monti della Tolfa', *Allumiere*, 88-103.

Ceccanti, M. & Cocchi, D. 1980-81. 'La Grotta del Grano presso Fossombrone (Pesaro)', *Rassegna d'Archeologia*, 2, 121-172.

Ciampoltrini, G., Rendini, P. & Wilkens, B. 1991. 'L'alimentazione nell'abitato etrusco di Montecatino in Val Freddana (Lucca)', *Studi Etruschi*, LVI, 271-284.

Clark, G. 1989. 'A group of animal bones from Cerveteri', *Studi Etruschi*, LV, 253-269.

Colini, A.M. 1898-1902. 'Il sepolcreto di Remedello Sotto nel Bresciano e il periodo eneolitico in Italia', *Bullettino di Paletnologia Italiana*, 24-28.

Corridi, C. 1989. 'Analisi preliminare dei reperti faunistici rinvenuti in due scavi archeologici in Roselle', *Studi Etruschi*, LV, 227-233.

Corridi, C. & Sarti, L. 1989-90. 'Sulla presenza di Equus nell'Eneolitico italiano: i ritrovamenti nel villaggio "campaniforme" di Querciola (Firenze)', *Rivista di Scienze Preistoriche*, 42, (1-2), 339-348.

Cremonesi, G. 1968. 'La Grotta dell'Orso di Sarteano. I livelli dell'età dei metalli', *Origini*, 2, 247-331.

Cremonesi, G. 1976. *La Grotta dei Piccioni di Bolognano nel quadro delle culture dal neolitico all'età del Bronzo in Abruzzo*, Pisa.

De Grossi Mazzorin, J. 1985a. 'I resti faunistici dell'insediamento protostorico di Pitigliano – Mulino Rossi (GR)', in Aranguren B.M., Pellegrini E., Perazzi P., *L'insediamento protostorico di Pitigliano. Campagne di scavo 1982-83*, Pitigliano, 77-92.

De Grossi Mazzorin, J. 1985b. 'Reperti faunistici dall'Acropoli di Populonia: testimonianze di allevamento e caccia nel III secolo a.C.', *Rassegna d'Archeologia*, 5, 131-171.

De Grossi Mazzorin, J. 1988. 'Tabina di Magreta: la terramara e i resti di età etrusca (campagne di scavo 1985-1986). Nota preliminare sulla fauna dell'insediamento della media età del Bronzo', in *Modena dalle origini all'anno mille. Studi di Archeologia e Storia*, vol. 1, Modena, 225-229.

De Grossi Mazzorin, J. 1989. 'Testimonianze di allevamento e caccia nel Lazio antico tra l'VIII e il VII secolo a.C.', *Dialoghi d'Archeologia*, 7, 125-142.

De Grossi Mazzorin, J. 1991. 'I resti faunistici dell'insediamento dell'Età del Bronzo finale delle Paludi di Celano. Campagne di scavo 1986-89', in *Il Fucino e le aree limitrofe nell'antichità*, Roma, 165-173.

De Grossi Mazzorin, J. 1991-1992. 'Il cavallo domestico e l'inizio della sua diffusione nell'Italia peninsulare', in Atti del Congresso "L'età del Bronzo in Italia nei secoli dal XVI al XIV a.C.", *Rassegna d'Archeologia*, 10, 760-761.

De Grossi Mazzorin, J. & Di Gennaro F. 1992. 'L'habitat et l'occupation du sol à l'age du Bronze en Étrurie méridionale', in *L'habitat et l'occupation du sol à l'age du Bronze en Europe*, (Documents Préhistoriques, 4), Paris, 459-465.

D'Ercole, V. 1986. 'Prima campagna di scavo alle "Paludi di Celano"', *Quaderni di Protostoria*, 1, Perugia, 317-343.

Di Fraia, T. *Nuovi contributi alla conoscenza dell'età del Bronzo nell'Italia centro-adriatica*, (Università degli Studi di Pisa, Facoltà di Lettere e Filosofia. Dottorato di ricerca in Archeologia).

Fedele, F. 1984. 'Note sulla fauna e sui manufatti ossei del Segrino (Canzo)', *Quaderni Erbesi*, 7, 177-180.

Fugazzola Delpino, M.A. 1982. 'Rapporto preliminare sulle ricerche condotte dalla Soprintendenza Archeologica dell'Etruria meridionale nei bacini lacustri dell'apparato vulcanico Sabatino', *Bollettino d'Arte*, suppl. 4, 123-149.

Gejvall, N.G. 1967. 'Esame preliminare del materiale osseo reperito negli scavi effettuati a Luni (Provincia di Viterbo, Comune di Blera) a cura dell'Istituto Svedese di Studi Classici in Roma', in *Luni sul Mignone e problemi della preistoria in Italia*, A.I.R.S.S., 4°, XXV, 263-276.

Gjerstadt, E. 1956. *Early Rome. The Tombs*, Lund.

Lepiksaar, J. 1975. 'Animal remains, in Luni sul Mignone', in *The Zone of the Large Iron Age Building*, A.I.R.S.S., 4°, XXVII, II, 2, 77-86.

Negroni Catacchio, N. 1981. 'L'abitato di Sorgenti della Nova nell'ambito dell'età del Bronzo finale', in *Sorgenti della Nova. Una comunità protostorica e il suo territorio nell'Etruria meridionale*, Roma, 199-256.

Pannuti, S. 1969. 'Gli scavi di Grotta a Male presso l'Aquila', *Bullettino di Paletnologia Italiana*, n.s. XX, vol. 78, 147-248.

Payne, S. 1973. 'Kill-off patterns in sheep and goats: the mandibles from Asvan Kale', *Anatolian Studies*, 23, 281-303.

Peroni, R. 1989. *Protostoria dell'Italia Continentale. La Penisola Italiana nell'età del Bronzo e del Ferro*, Roma.

Ricciardi, L., Costantini, L., Giorgi, J.A. & Scali, S. 1987. 'Blera', in *L'alimentazione nel mondo antico. Gli Etruschi*, Roma, 83-87.

Riedel, A. 1986. 'Archäozoologische Untersuchungen im Raum zwischen Adriaküste und Alpenhauptkamm', *Padusa*, XXII, 1-220.

Riedel, A. 1989. 'L'economia animale', in M. Bernabò Brea & M. Cremaschi (a cura di), *La Terramara di Poviglio. Le campagne di scavo 1985-1989*, Coopsette, 37-38.

Ruffo, M. 1987. 'Sintesi dei dati faunistici', in A. Guidi *et al.*, 'Cures', *Quaderni di Archeologia Etrusco-Italica*, 14, 321-332.

Ruffo, M. 1988. 'Cures: produzione, alimentazione e limiti territoriali, in A. Guidi *et al.*, 'Cures Sabini: risultati della sesta campagna di scavo', *Quaderni di Archeologia Etrusco-Italica*, 15, 319-333.

Sorrentino, C. 1981a. 'La Fauna', in *San Giovenale. Excavations in Area B, 1957-1960*, A.I.R.S.S., 4°, XXVI:II,2, 58-64.

Sorrentino, C. 1981b. 'La Fauna', in *San Giovenale. The Semi-Subterranean Building in Area B, 1957-1960*, A.I.R.S.S., 4°, XXVI:II,4, 85-89.

Wilkens, B. 1988a. 'S. Paolina di Filottrano (Marche): i resti faunistici', *Atti Società Toscana Scienze Naturali*, 95, 345-361.

Wilkens, B. 1988b. 'La fauna di Moie di Pollenza', *Le Marche. Archeologia, Storia, Territorio*, 1, 137-144.

Wilkens, B. 1990. 'La fauna del Villaggio del Colle dei Cappuccini (Ancona)', *Rassegna d'Archeologia*, 9, 327-364.

Wilkens, B. 1991. 'Resti faunistici ed economia preistorica nel bacino del Fucino', in *Il Fucino e le aree limitrofe nell'antichità*, Roma, 147-153.

Wilkens, B. 1991-1992. 'I resti faunistici di alcuni insediamenti dell'età del Bronzo nell'Italia centro-meridionale', *Rassegna d'Archeologia*, 10, 463-469.

18

Attività Agricole delle Comunità Nuragiche del Centro Sardegna: Alcune Annotazioni riguardo ai Dati Archeologici e agli Aspetti Socio-Economici

M. ASOLE, A. FOSCHI NIEDDU, F. NIEDDU

(Nuoro, Sardegna)

Sommario: Da parte degli autori è stata notata una continuità negli sviluppi economico-politici della Sardegna preistorica, che sembra dovuta ad uno stretto rapporto delle comunità stanziate nell'isola con le risorse e le caratteristiche del territorio e a processi di adattamento alle scoperte tecnologiche. Nei siti scavati e pubblicati è attestata quasi sempre l'agricoltura integrata dall'allevamento del bestiame. Come per altre schiatte italiche preromane si è riscontrata nei protosardi un'economia tendente all'autosufficienza con marcate resistenze a quella di scambio propria delle civiltà urbane e in particolare di Cartagine e Roma.

1. La realtà attuale del Centro Sardegna, corrispondente prevalentemente alla provincia di Nuoro e in parte a quelle di Sassari e Oristano, è ricca di indicazioni sul sostrato mediterraneo agro-pastorale precedente i disordinati aspetti di massificazione, urbanizzazione e industrializzazione tipici dell'Italia moderna, come da più parti è stato notato (Pais 1909; Le Lannoux 1941; Cherchi Paba 1974).

Nelle zone collinari e montuose del Marghine e delle Barbagie, dove la memoria di una vita rurale, dai tratti sorprendentemente arcaici nella tecnologia e nei criteri di distribuzione dei prodotti, ma ricca di valori culturali a cui taluni ritornano con nostalgia è assai recente, i sardi vedono la culla dei loro avi, indomiti e dai severi costumi. Per inciso, è probabile che i tentativi di raccordare l'antica solidarietà e i forti legami familiari alle moderne attività reddittizie e competitive abbiano esiti di conflittualità sociale e talvolta di violenza.

Gli scriventi presentano concordemente le seguenti considerazioni: ogni epoca ha avuto i suoi momenti di luce e di ombre anche se gli individui e i gruppi hanno reagito e reagiscono corrispondentemente al loro carattere e alla loro cultura (intesa come conoscenze, tradizioni, norme, tendenza all'isolamento o proiezione verso l'esterno, modo di pensare e linguaggio). Gli oggetti sia prodotti che importati nell'isola costituiscono dei residui, ancorchè interessanti e suggestivi, di aspetti culturali la cui ricostruzione – con le inevitabili lacune – è l'obiettivo della ricerca archeologica; nel passato remoto non si può cercare quello che non si riesce a trovare oggi e comunque è inutile indulgere a meri compiacimenti estetici o morali evitando ogni raffronto con i fenomeni della civiltà contemporanea, più complessi e inquietanti.

La raccolta delle testimonianze dirette riguardanti le attività agricole ha avuto scarsi risultati, in quanto per i circa dieci siti che hanno restituito semi carbonizzati gli studiosi parlano genericamente di grano, orzo, fava (già presenti negli insediamenti prenuragici); ancora più rare risultano le analisi e le elaborazioni sulle percentuali relative ai reperti faunistici (Lo Schiavo 1981; Fonzo 1987). In questa sede pertanto, come si è proceduto per i relativamente più lineari contesti sardi prenuragici (Foschi Nieddu 1993a), si danno indicazioni iniziali tratte da riflessioni e considerazioni sull'intero spettro delle espressioni culturali note come civiltà nuragica, che si irradiano dal Bronzo antico all'età del Ferro con scarse difformità apparenti in tutta la Sardegna.

2. Dagli elementi materiali e dagli studi editi finora sembra di poter osservare che le culture dell'età del Rame e del momento di passaggio all'età del Bronzo di Abealzu-Filigosa, Monte Claro, Campaniforme e Bonnannaro A, tramite un fenomeno di integrazione di cui è ovviamente arduo ricostruire i meccanismi, si risolvono nel crogiolo della civiltà nuragica protosarda, le cui manifestazioni saranno fra le più considerevoli dei popoli italici. La decisa tendenza verso modelli culturali analoghi riscontrabile dal sud al nord dell'isola è molto probabilmente in relazione a processi iniziali di sfruttamento locale delle risorse minerarie con le relative esigenze di organizzazione socio-economica per il procacciamento, la produzione e la distribuzione dei metalli e per la difesa da eventuali predatori.

Non si hanno prove certe, ma sembra lecito presumere che le comunità stanziate nelle valli e sugli altopiani della Sardegna, dopo aver importato oggetti in rame fabbricati da artigiani in possesso delle tecniche di martellatura e di fusione, riconosciutane l'utilità, abbiano acquisito i modi di sfruttare le miniere di piombo, zinco, rame, ferro, manganese, antimonio, queste ultime uniche in Italia con quella di Rosia presso Siena (Rollandi 1981; Lilliu 1986a). Gli equilibri delle società isolane, messi in crisi una prima volta nell'eneolitico da potenti gruppi tecnologicamente avanzati quasi sicuramente iberici, si ricompongono.

Anche se non sono da escludere apporti esterni via mare, le popolazioni indigene erano infatti riuscite ad esprimere culture notevolmente ricche e dinamiche che alle attività economiche basilari di agricoltura, pastorizia, caccia, pesca e raccolta avevano integrato il commercio dell'ossidiana del monte Arci (rinvenuta in villaggi e grotte della Corsica, dell'Italia settentrionale e della Francia meridionale) e probabilmente quello del sale, del legname e della selce; innegabili ed interessanti sono i confronti con le attività delle comunità che abitavano le isole Cicladi prima dell'occupazione cretese (Renfrew & Wagstaff 1982).

L'ampio e felice territorio dell'isola, ben protetto dalle coste alte o sabbiose con pochi approdi e dal clima mite, lodato dalle genti greche, costituiva evidentemente un potente deterrente alla stanzialità delle popolazioni preistoriche, le cui ceramiche e oggetti d'uso mostrano elementi di notevole originalità e solo tracce sporadiche di influssi di culture coeve extra-insulari.

La lavorazione in loco di strumenti in metallo determinò fin dalle prime fasi dell'età del Bronzo, verosimilmente, anche la crescita della produzione agricola e lo sviluppo dell'allevamento del bestiame, per la possibilità di dissodare terreni duri e di disboscare con migliori risultati.

Superata pertanto la fase dei contrasti sociali per il possesso dei terreni e delle risorse minerarie con la vittoria di una *leadership* guerriera, come sembra evincersi dalle deposizioni di facies Bonnannaro A2 della Tomba dei Guerrieri di Decimoputzu (Ugas 1990), la Sardegna viene capillarmente occupata da villaggi di capanne quasi senza eccezione circolari e dai primi nuraghi, la cui struttura megalitica si conserva ancora oggi in numerosi siti (Usai 1987). I protosardi ebbero inizialmente un'economia di allevamento e agricoltura che mirava all'autosufficienza; nelle capanne e nelle torri del Bronzo medio sono stati rinvenuti fittili, oggetti in ceramica e in pietra e rari strumenti in metallo (lesine, sgorbie) mentre mancano in genere prodotti di importazione (Ferrarese Ceruti 1981; Trump 1990). In questo periodo non necessariamente i capi e i guerrieri avevano rango diverso, poiché la società non era in grado di assumersi il peso di una casta avulsa dai normali lavori agro-pastorali e il compito della guerra a scopo di offesa e di difesa era dato occasionalmente agli uomini adulti.

All'età del Bronzo medio di tradizione Bonnannaro si riferisce (Foschi Nieddu 1995) la prima capanna delle riunioni nuragica finora rinvenuta, pertinente a un piccolo villaggio sito in regione Dore, agro di Orani (Nuoro); la presenza di un altarino o piedistallo a base circolare costituito da otto conci perfettamente sagomati e di tre vaschette 'liturgiche' indica nella direzione di implicazioni magico-religiose nel campo della organizzazione socio-economica o della politica, termine che riporta però ad epoche successive.

In comunità che lottavano per la sopravvivenza, per le quali l'interesse della collettività era senza dubbio superiore a quello dell'individuo (Polanyi 1968: 9–10), la cui coesione sociale è testimoniata dagli imponenti sepolcri collettivi con spazi per rituali e cerimonie, i sacrifici dei vecchi segnalati dalle fonti classiche potrebbero essere legati alla insostenibilità del loro mantenimento, soprattutto se malati o in tempi di carestia. E' però noto che i gruppi umani hanno schemi di parentela, credenze e tabù complicati che non aiutano l'utilizzazione razionale delle risorse umane e di quelle economiche più consona all'interesse comune, con conseguenti atteggiamenti contraddittori e paradossali.

Per necessità imposte dalle circostanze o per il volere di potenti oligarchie, dai dati emerge che a partire dal Bronzo recente o fase III nuragica (Lilliu 1982) le torri megalitiche raggiungono espressioni di monumentalità che le avvicinano, seppure con sviluppi paralleli (Contu 1980: 34–35), alle roccaforti achee di Tirinto, Argo e Micene.

Nei centri nuragici a partire da questa epoca si rinvengono molti strumenti in metallo: falci, asce, scuri, maleppeggi e oggetti quali ziri, macine e bacili per la panificazione (Lilliu 1955: 148 sgg; Fadda 1990: 106), che erano utilizzati in attività agricole fortemente connesse all'allevamento, a cui riportano i recinti che si trovano nei pressi delle dimore umane. Non sappiamo se e come i terreni fossero divisi, in particolare nelle zone di pianura a vocazione agricola dove il 'latifondo' poteva essere redditizio.

Le prime forme di monetazione accertate in Sardegna, i lingotti, forse nati come mezzi di pagamento e successivamente usati anche come riserve di metallo da fondere, hanno sagome estremamente riconoscibili quali pelli, macine, panelle (Lilliu 1987: 23; Ugas & L. Usai 1987).

I problemi di convivenza, preminenza e coesione all'interno delle comunità via via sempre più grandi e articolate (cfr. Nadel 1965) non dovettero essere risolti solo con la minaccia delle armi o direttamente con il loro uso: il nuraghe polilobato ciclopico, eretto con il quotidiano sforzo di moltitudini sicuramente prive di salario e della possibilità di abbandonare il lavoro, costituiva alla fine il simbolo e il segno del prestigio e della forza dell'intera tribù e ne venivano fatti modellini in pietra o in bronzo da esporre al centro delle capanne delle riunioni, come è stato documentato nell'Algherese (Moravetti 1980); le tombe sono quasi sempre monumentali e collettive, per cui re e membri di rango meno elevato, donne e bambini di diversa condizione sociale venivano in morte considerati ugualmente degni di memoria e di pianto e sepolti a poche centinaia di metri dal villaggio (cfr. Lilliu 1987).

Dai noti riferimenti alle abitudini dei Lestrigoni del Libro X dell'Odissea; che si attribuiscono ai protosardi, è molto probabile l'esistenza di monarchi temuti, di cospicue mandrie e greggi, di commerci agevolati da strade oltre che dal mare e dai fiumi. Contrariamente a quanto si verificò negli imperi orientali, le società nuragiche non attuarono sul territorio una differenziazione fra insediamenti volti alla produzione e centri prevalentemente di consumo, come si opererà nei castelli feudali del medioevo più di mille anni dopo.

A seguito dei commerci d'oltremare sulle vie dello stagno e dell'ambra (cfr. Lo Schiavo & Ridgway 1987) si diffuse un'economia a base sempre agro-pastorale ma che può definirsi monetaria, con maggiori possibilità da parte dei principi e dei mercanti di accumulo di beni. Poichè sembra difficile ipotizzare in comunità antiche fenomeni di speculazione economica (cfr. Mauss 1925; Barker 1986), si pensa ad accumuli per i tempi difficili in caso di carestie, epidemie, assedi o per una difesa migliore da parte di predatori.

3. Nell'età del Ferro è facilmente riscontrabile nelle comunità isolane una marcata gerarchia sociale: nei bronzetti sono raffigurati capi tribù, sacerdoti e sacerdotesse, guerrieri, atleti, pastori, contadini, donne di alto lignaggio e popolane (Lilliu 1966, 1981 e 1986b), mentre da particolari strumenti di lavoro è lecito ipotizzare l'esistenza di numerosi artigiani quali fabbri, cuoiai, armaioli e altri (Taramelli 1922). E' indicativo che i singoli individui oranti o offerenti siano rappresentati in effigie nei loro ruoli sociali e non per se stessi, devoti a divinità sconosciute protettrici di tutta la schiatta.

La civiltà nuragica resta in fondo estranea ai nuovi modelli culturali imposti dai colonizzatori fenicio-punici, improntati ad un'economia di scambio sostenuta da esigenze di consumo di gruppi 'elitari' e che presuppone dinamismo socio-economico, urbanizzazione e burocrazia. Le si addicono i misteri dei primordi mitologici della storia, le ideologie eroiche del patriottismo e del valore in guerra.

Eppure la precarietà dell'esistenza di questi antichi uomini, deducibile dell'alta mortalità per le fatiche, le malattie, gli scontri armati, è inversamente proporzionale all'impronta che hanno lasciato sia nelle opere in pietra, sia nell'immaginario collettivo che è parte inscindibile dell'odierna identità isolana.

Bibliografia

Barker, G. 1986. 'Una indagine sulla sussistenza e sull'economia delle società preistoriche', *Dialoghi di Archeologia*, terza serie, 4, n. 1, 51–60.

Cherchi Paba, F. 1974. *Evoluzione storica dell'attività industriale agricola caccia e pesca in Sardegna*, Vicenza.

Contu, E. 1980. 'La Sardegna preistorica e protostorica. Aspetti e problemi', in *Atti della XXII Riunione Scientifica dell'Istituto Italiano di Preistoria e Protostoria*.

Fadda, M.A. 1990. 'Il villaggio', in AA.VV., *La civiltà nuragica*, Milano.

Ferrarese Ceruti, M.L. 1981. 'La cultura di Bonnanaro', in AA.VV., *Ichnussa*, Milano.

Fonzo, O. 1987. 'Reperti faunistici in Marmilla e Campidano nell'età del bronzo e nella prima età del ferro', in *Atti del Convegno di Studi di Selargius: Un millennio di relazioni fra la Sardegna e i paesi del Mediterraneo. La Sardegna nel Mediterraneo fra il secondo e il primo millennio a.C.*, Cagliari.

Foschi Nieddu, A. 1993a. 'Considerazioni sulle attività agricole delle società prenuragiche', *Quaderni Bolotanesi*, XIX .

Foschi Nieddu, A. 1995. 'Primi risultati dello scavo nel villaggio nuragico di Dore (Orani, Nuoro)', *Bollettino di Archeologia del Ministero per i Beni Culturali e Ambientali*, 13-14-15, 1992, 163–166.

Le Lannoux, M. 1979 (ed. orig. 1941). *Pastori e contadini di Sardegna*, Cagliari.

Lilliu, G. 1955. 'Il nuraghe di Barumini e la stratigrafia nuragica', *Studi Sardi*, XII-XIII, vol. 1.

Lilliu, G. 1966. *Sculture della Sardegna nuragica*, Verona.

Lilliu, G. 1981. 'Bronzetti e statuaria nella civiltà nuragica', in AA.VV., *Ichnussa*, Milano.

Lilliu, G. 1982. *La civiltà nuragica*, Firenze.

Lo Schiavo, F. 1981. 'Economia e società nell'età dei nuraghi', in AA.VV., *Ichnussa*, Milano.

Lo Schiavo, F. & Ridgway, D. 1987. 'La Sardegna e il Mediterraneo occidentale allo scorcio del II millennio', in *Atti del Convegno di Studi di Selargius: Un millennio di relazioni fra la Sardegna e i paesi del Mediterraneo. La Sardegna nel Mediterraneo fra il secondo e il primo millennio a.C.*, Cagliari.

Mauss, M. 1954 (ed. orig. 1925). *The Gift. Forms and Functions of Exchange in Archaic Society*, London.

Moravetti, A. 1980. 'Nuovi modellini di torri nuragiche', *Bollettino Archeologico*, VI serie, XLV, n. 7.

Nadel, S. F. 1977 (ed. orig. 1965). *Lineamenti di antropologia sociale*, Bari.

Pais, E. 1909. *Sulla civiltà dei nuraghi e sullo sviluppo sociologico della Sardegna*, Roma.

Polanyi, K. 1980 (ed. orig. 1968). *Economie primitive, arcaiche e moderne. Ricerca storica e antropologia economica*, Torino.

Renfrew, C. & Wagstaff, M. 1982. *An Island Policy. The Archaeology of Exploitation in Melos*, Cambridge.

Rollandi, M. S. 1981. *Miniere e minatori in Sardegna: Dalla crisi del primo dopoguerra alla nascita di Carbonia*, Cagliari.

Taramelli, A. 1922. 'Ozieri. Ripostiglio di armi e strumenti in bronzo di età nuragica rinvenuto in regione Chilivani', *Notizie degli Scavi di Antichità*.

Trump, D. 1990. *Nuraghe Noeddos and the Bonu Ighinu Valley. Excavation and Survey in Sardinia*, Oxbow Archaeological Monographs 3, Oxford.

Ugas, G. 1990. *La Tomba dei Guerrieri di Decimoputzu*, Cagliari.

Ugas, G. & Usai, L. 1987. 'Nuovi scavi nel santuario nuragico di S. Anastasia di Sardara', in *Atti del Convegno di Studi di Selargius: Un millennio di relazioni fra la Sardegna e i paesi del Mediterraneo. La Sardegna nel Mediterraneo fra il secondo e il primo millennio a.C.*, Cagliari.

Usai, A. 1987. 'Tomba megalitica in località Mitzà e Fidi. Donori (Cagliari)', *Quaderni della Soprintendenza Archeologica per le Province di Cagliari e Oristano*, 4, vol. 1.

19

The Economy of an Early Latin Settlement, Borgo Le Ferriere-*Satricum*, 800–200 BC

J.W. Bouma, P.A.J. Attema, A.J. Beijer, A.J. Nijboer, R.A. Olde Dubbelink
(University of Groningen)

Summary: *The paper aims at a reconstruction of the economy of the protohistorical site known as* Satricum *situated in South Lazio at present-day Borgo Le Ferriere c. 60 km SE of Rome. Data relating to landscape potential, agriculture and production of goods, are used to comment on the means of subsistence of the community living at* Satricum. *To this end palaeobotanical and archaeozoological remains as well as ceramics are discussed. Furthermore a comparison of the pottery of the settlement, the necropolis and the votive deposits is undertaken to examine socio-economic changes during the period. The religious activity which characterised life at the site from the early beginning to the very end of occupation of the site, constituted a major component in its economy, if not the pivot, as appears from the votive deposits around the sanctuary of Mater Matuta. The contents of the subsequent deposits are here used as a reflection of the position of Satricum in the network of international, supra-regional and regional contacts.*

Introduction

This paper offers a review of aspects of the environment and material culture of the Latin site of *Satricum* with the aim of shedding light on the economic system of its community. To this end aspects of subsistence, industry, technology and contacts with other cultures will be examined. In the context of Latial archaeology, Borgo Le Ferriere – from now on referred by the supposedly ancient name *Satricum* –, offers good opportunities for such a study, having been subjected to detailed settlement excavations since 1977 (Maaskant-Kleibrink 1987; 1992), expanding greatly on evidence revealed here at the turn of the century.

As regards the nature of subsistence economy the evidence is still largely circumstantial, being mainly dependent on the evaluation of the landscape potential as obtained by regional archaeological and soil surveys, on research into the changing levels of technology over time, on the functional analysis of the pottery and on the information provided by the sacred areas. As yet sealed stratified deposits for the Archaic period are lacking, whereas on the whole bones are overrepresented with regard to seed remains.

Problematic is the question whether local resources were exploited for the on-site manufacture of building materials, ceramics and other artifacts, or whether raw materials had to be imported. The evidence for the production of pottery and iron artifacts at *Satricum* is for instance undisputable, whereas in the case of the use of pigments on the antefixes, the option for import of pigments remains open (cf. Nijboer, this volume). It is proposed that ceramic production developed from household production into more organised forms of manufacture. At the same time it is realized that such developments took place in other fields as well, as for instance in the field of planning, as evidenced by the 7th century BC levelling activities at the site which paved the way for the monumental lay-out that characterized the 6th century BC appearance of the acropolis (Maaskant-Kleibrink 1991).

Finally a study of imported artifacts in the votive-deposits and tombs excavated in and outside the settlement is used to discuss developments and fluctuations in trade contacts. Some general conjectures only can be made on the trading of, for instance, raw materials, needed for the artisans working at *Satricum*, or the foodstuffs and liquids that were used in the banquetting ritual, or the imported goods that are found in the cultplace and the tombs.

As this paper will show, through all periods much economic activity was focused on the sacred places: their deposits show that the sanctuaries, especially that on the acropolis, played a major role within the framework of international, interregional and regional contacts and local economic activities.

SETTLEMENT AND REGION

Satricum is situated at modern Borgo Le Ferriere, c. 60 km SE of Rome. In geological terms the area around the site belongs to the outer border of the tuff hills that cover the larger part of the Campagna Romana and the NW part of the Pontine Region. At the end of the 7th century BC, all along the contact area between this volcanic area and the coastal sediments, vast urban spaces developed at various sites: from NW to SE, sites as Castel di Decima, *Lavinium*, *Ardea* and *Satricum* occupied comparable environmental and geomorphological positions. A second row of sites of which *Satricum* formed part, was NE-SW oriented. Together with a large Archaic site surveyed north of Cisterna and one on the slopes of the Monti Lepini, still further inland at Caracupa/Valvisciolo, *Satricum* formed with the coastal settlement of *Antium* part of the easternmost settlements within the 6th century BC settlement pattern of *Latium Vetus* (fig.1).

Surveys by the University of Groningen and the University of Amsterdam have revealed that the environment of the Pontine plain, though put to marginal exploitation, was not favoured for the founding and subsequent development of urban sites during the 7th and 6th centuries. Findspots of this period are relatively few and limited in extension, suggestive of marginal subsistence activities only (Attema 1991; Attema 1993; Voorrips *et al.* 1991).

All sites represented in fig.1 have common spatial and material characteristics that convey a high degree of cultural unity. This unity was especially apparent during the Orientalizing and Archaic period (7th and 6th centuries BC). The elaborate lay-out and architecture known at some of the sites in combination with the possibly contemporary field drainage systems in the

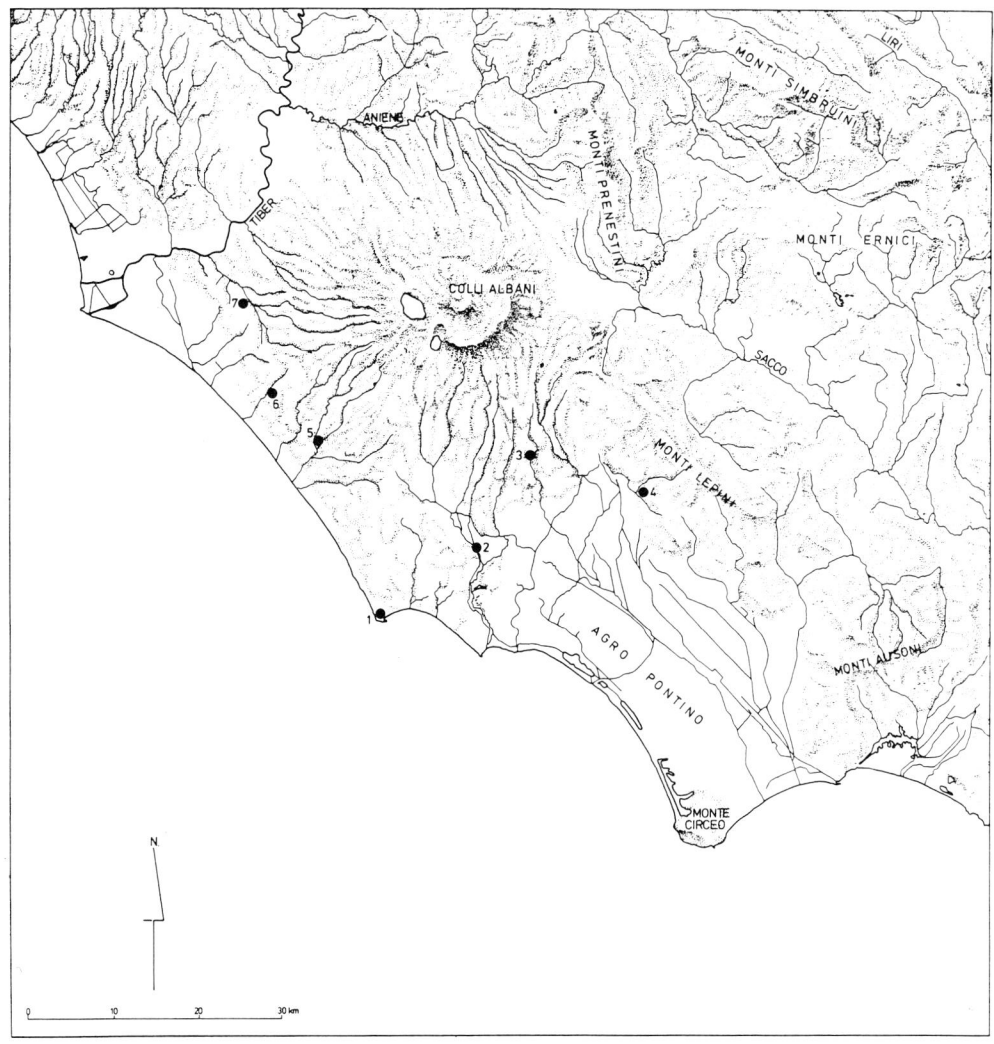

Fig. 1. Topographical map of south Lazio with protohistorical sites mentioned in the text (antique names in italics):

1 = *Antium*   2 = *Satricum*   3 = Cisterna
4 = Caracupa/Valvisciolo   5 = *Ardea*   6 = *Lavinium*   7 = Castel di Decima

volcanic area, presuppose a relatively high level of organisation, as do the earthworks and other forms of defence. Also, imported objects among the gravegoods and the votive gifts meanwhile point to widespread contacts of Latin society. At sites as *Satricum* and *Ardea*, and notably *Lavinium*, much time and energy was invested in the local cultus. The sacred areas here gained at least regional fame and remained in use well into the Republican period. As with many other sites in the Latial region, the settlement at *Satricum* had its roots in the early Iron Age (9th century BC) and came to full development in the Orientalizing and Archaic period (7/6th century BC), reaching its maximum expansion and occupying three plateaus amounting to a site-territory of ca. 58 ha. During the Republican period the site functioned mainly as a cultplace during which the temple and other sanctuaries remained frequented (5th to 3rd c. BC). Inhabitation of the site seems to remain restricted then to the western periphery (Attema *et al.* 1992), but during this latter period the site seems to suffer from its peripheral position with regard to Rome.

The natural environment

Satricum is situated on a number of tuff hills in the lower stream basin of the river Astura, a perennial river connecting the site with the sea. The easternmost plateau of the site borders on the river. The geomorphological characteristics of this landscape made settlement very attractive, as was already realized in the earlier Iron Age. The landscape furnishes well-confined elevated plateaus formed by watercourses that have deeply incised in the tuff bedrock. If complemented by artificial works of defence, as was common practice in the late Iron Age and Archaic period, the tuff hills that controlled the larger waterways, constituted militarily and economically strategic sites. In this respect *Satricum* may have been prominent since the Astura is the most substantial river south of the Tiber and forms the connection, if not economic life-line, between the Colli Albani and the Tyrrhenian coast.

However, conditions for a thriving mixed farming economy were less favourable. The agricultural potential of the clayey soils that result from the rapidly weathered tuff parent material of the hills is naturally very restricted. An evaluation of the volcanic landscape by means of a historical and cartographical survey of landuse showed that before recent land improvement schemes, only a very small portion was used for the cultivation of crops, the larger part being left to the shepherd. As regards cereal cultivation, the yields were notably low, chiefly due to bad drainage of the volcanic terrains due to the variable permeability of the underlying tuff. Waterlogging not only occurred in the valleys, but also on the plateaux creating local marshes (Attema 1993).

It has been argued that cereal cultivation played a fundamental role in the subsistence economy of Archaic society, but also that the production can hardly have gone out above the subsistence level, implying that no surplus production of grain was produced (Ampolo 1980). The main reason for such a supposition are the wet conditions that prevail in the area, which allow only the cultivation of inferior, low-yield cereal species. The network of underground field drainage channels recorded between Velletri and *Satricum* is proof of the wish to improve the conditions for agriculture, possibly from Archaic times onwards, in order to increase land productivity. Dating of the system is, however, not yet secure (Quilici-Gigli 1983).

Being situated in the transition zone between the eolian coastal sediments and the volcanic layers from the Colli Albani, at *Satricum* a good variety of soils was available: to the southwest of the site soils were formed in sandy deposits covering the tuff sediments, as were those on the acropolis hill itself; the valley of the Astura to the east (known as the *conca* of Le Ferriere) on the other hand, was most probably nothing less than a marsh. The *conca* is characterized by not well-developed fluvisols, and the first C14 dates indicate that since medieval times locally more than 1m. alluvial sediment was deposited in the conca due to colluviation of the surrounding hills (fig.2). Interestingly, the large landowners of the 18th and 19th century AD, thought it more profitable to leave large tracts of the hilly countryside to extensive grazing. This may reflect the exploitation patterns to which the landscape around *Satricum* was subjected during the later Republic and the Imperial period, when the region was likewise given over to the large extensively exploited farm estates, the so-called *latifundia*. It is therefore justifiable to conclude that this part of the Archaic landscape cannot have been the *granaio* which Rome sought to colonize (cf. Dion. Hal. V,26,3; Livy II.9.6, II.34.3); rather, it constituted an at places waterlogged and locally marshy environment that was not especially suited for the cultivation of cereals or other crops.

Nonetheless the evidence allows us to postulate a gradual shift in emphasis in the subsistence economy from pastoralism to farming practices (see for *Latium*: Bietti-Sestieri 1979 and Ampolo 1980; for the Tolfa Allumiere area: Östenberg 1967). The increase in pottery meant for storage found in the Archaic settlements, and more in general, the increasing complex structure of Archaic society, testifies to such a change. If the noted field drainage systems are to be dated to Archaic times, this would furnish another convincing argument for such a change. It must be concluded, however, that the natural environment did not greatly favour such a shift, which presupposes a continued strong dependence on either domestic stock-raising, transhumance or both, whereby the ecological variation, that is the marshy landscape, within the catchment of the site will have guaranteed

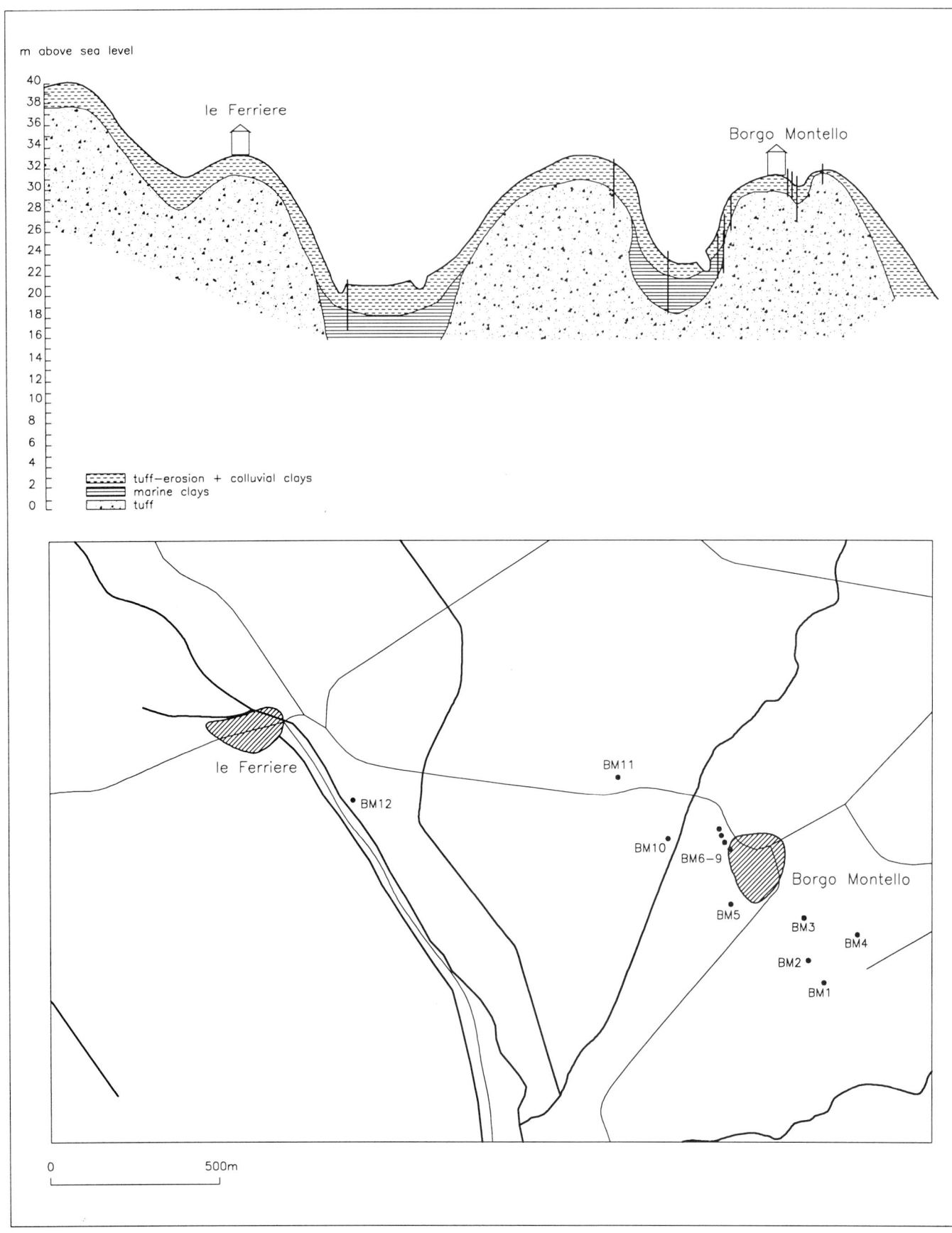

Fig. 2. Topographical map of the surroundings of Le Ferriere (Satricum) with locations of hand-augerings and reconstructed geological profile between Le Ferriere and Borgo Montello (the conca). Drawing after B. Haagsma.

extra food sources in the form of fish, fowl and other wildlife. Up till now surveys have only yielded a very limited number of rural sites dating to the Archaic period, which, though prematurely so, might point to a nucleated settlement pattern having developed at the end of the Latial Iron Age. The settlement and exploitation pattern in the region points to the development of a market system only well after the installment of new Roman colonies at *Cora*, *Norba* and *Setia* in the course of the 4th century BC. Of these colonies, *Cora* and *Setia* gradually grew out to the local centres of a villa-system. From then on landuse, as can be deduced from the settlement pattern, indicates the production of a larger variety of products, including wine and olives on a substantial scale (Attema 1993). The regional trend indicates that during the post-Archaic period (5/4th century BC), subsistence farming was still standard in Latial society (Attema & Bouma, 1995).

THE EVIDENCE FOR DIET

(i) The archaeozoological remains

In general the archaeozoological evidence in the settlement of *Satricum* is abundant, but the conservation of its remains rather poor. This may account for the fact that except for the bone remains of a fox in a hutpit and the remains of a duck and a turtle in one of the votive deposits (*deposit II*) chicken, waterbirds, fishes and small wild animals are absent, in spite of the fact that on ecological grounds it can be assumed that these were part of the diet at *Satricum*. Of the larger animals remains of cattle, caprine, pigs and antlers of roe deer have been found. Well stratified evidence comes from closed features as the cooking and rubbish pits of the 8th and 7th century BC. The 7th and 6th century archaeozoological material is on the other hand rather fragmentary as it relates to destruction layers, themselves partially disturbed by later activities. For the period after 500 BC we have evidence from a large votive deposit on the acropolis hill (*deposit II*), containing many animal offerings.

From the 8th century huts and cooking places clear evidence exists that both cattle (*bos taurus*), caprine (*ovis/capra*) and pigs (*sus domesticus*) were slaughtered and consumed. Of the bones the larger part belongs to cattle and caprine, cattle prevailing over pig. Remains of piglets and calfs show that young animals were also eaten. Some bones showed traces of gnawing. In the lower hearth of a hut (GRII) only pig and piglet bones were found, whereas the upper hearth revealed a great many bones of cattle and deer antlers (*cervus elaphus*).

Determined samples from the 7th century BC are smaller than those from the 8th century, but show a similar diversity: again cattle, caprine and pigs as well as antler of roe deer occur. Remarkable are the great fragments of cattle skulls in one of the features (hut GRV). The destruction layer of a large wooden building dating to this period yielded a great many bones among which cattle, caprine and a small dog. This period also shows a slight prevalence of cattle over other species.

Stratified bone fragments from the Archaic period are, like the pottery fragments from this period, few in number, due to the poor state of conservation of the strata of the Archaic houses, which lie directly under the surface of the acropolis, and which have been disturbed by recent ploughing. The few fragments which were excavated are from cattle and caprine.

Archaeozoological data for the post-Archaic and Republican period (5th to 3rd century BC) are restricted to a votive context. In *deposit II* caprine dominates, whereas cattle again prevails over pig. The same kind of animals (rams, cows and pigs or boars), but this time made of clay, has been recovered from a later Hellenistic deposit on the hill (*deposit III*, 4th/2nd century BC). They were found together with statuettes of cocks, pigeons (or young geese), horses and dogs (Della Seta 1918: 297; Moretti 1962: 252–255; Satricum 1982; Satricum 1985). Perhaps some of the animals raised at *Satricum* in the 5th/4th century were sold to pilgrims who visited the sacred areas, but in the course of the 4th century, this practice may have been replaced by the less expensive and more durable terracotta animal offerings (Thomasson 1961: 137).

In sum, cattle, sheep and goat formed a stable factor in the subsistence economy of the settlement, with a strong prevalence of cattle over pig, contrasting with data for Rome (Ampolo 1980: 35). A straightforward explanation is doubtless the different context of the finds. Cattle, sheep and goat meet the multiple needs of meat and milk, and will therefore have been valued highly in daily life. The spinning and weaving tools found in both the settlement and the votive deposits, indicate that sheep were also held for their wool, whereas oxen may have been used for plowing; pigs may well have been considered a luxury; the antlers of roe deer point to hunting, though the antler may also have been gathered to serve as tools.

(ii) The palaeobotanical remains

Specimens of seeds are few at *Satricum*. The earliest sample derives from a large late 8th century cup containing wheat grains of *triticum durum* (bread wheat), possibly *hordeum* (barley) and a horse bean (*vicia faba*) (cf. Hellstrom *et al.* 1975 on Luni sul Mignone). A 7th century sample yielded wheat as well. Of the samples that were taken from the hearths and fills of the huts and rubbish pits just one yielded data. The sample comes from a 6th century shallow rubbish pit that belonged to a courtyard house; the pit was found directly beneath the rooftiles of house A (Maaskant 1987: 52). The sample yielded many seeds including bitter vetch, sorrel, dandelion, butter-cups, a number of wild grasses and horse beans.

These remains give only slight and very general indications for the vegetarian part of the diet through the presence of cereals and beans. Though in general it is accepted that at the turn of the 8th century BC viticulture and olives were introduced in Latium under Greek influence, neither *Satricum* nor other sites have provided palaeobotanical proof. *Vitis* and *olea* are found in the Monticchio pollendiagram from the 5th c. BC onwards (ca. 20 km distance from Satricum) (Haagsma 1993). The pottery assemblages, however, indicate that wine consumption had become *usance* in the 7th century BC at the site.

LOCAL AND NON-LOCAL RESOURCES

While Nijboer (this volume) provides a discussion of the evidence for the production of pottery and iron artifacts at *Satricum*, here it is valuable to note other aspects of the site, namely the tuffs for the foundation of the 6th century buildings, the pigments for the decoration of the temple terracottas, and the copper alloys for the casting of *fibulae*. These combined, show that manufacture at *Satricum* had a partial dependency on imported raw materials, mainly metals like copper and lead. Pigments and iron bloom might have been imported, though local resources could have been exploited as well. This dependency on imported metals in the 7th and 6th centuries BC suggests an interregional trade with Etruria. These contacts are further highlighted through discussion of the contents of the votive deposits at *Satricum* (see below).

(i) Building materials

Most materials like loams for the plastering of walls and tuffs for the foundations are of local origin. Thin-sections of daub belonging to wattle and daub constructions and of samples from the gleyic luvisols covering the acropolis, show similarities in mineral composition, grain size and shape. Both the daub and the clay samples contained about 40% quartz, 1 to 2% volcanic rockfragments, some augites, biotites and plagioclases, indicating that the sandy clays of the acropolis were not processed before being used for the plastering of the huts and houses of the 7th and 6th century BC. Building foundations on the acropolis from the 6th c. BC were made from local tuffs, being either the yellowish lithoid tuff or a whitish tuff. Deposits of each occur in and around the site.

(ii) Pigments

The pigments used on the antefixes of the temple built around 500 BC were studied by microscopy and microprobe analysis. These terracottas were locally made, since wasters of white firing tiles with decoration were excavated in a kiln south of the temple (Nijboer, this volume). The pigments encountered on the samples were black, white and red, while the brown and violet on the antefixes were achieved by using alternating layers red and black. The black is most probably a manganese black which has the advantage that red and black colours can be obtained in one oxidising firing-cycle (Schweitzer & Rinuy 1982). Wasters show how the pigments were applied before firing, the temperature in the kiln being sufficient to obtain the black colour. Microchemical tests for lead and calcite in the white pigment were negative, showing it to have been a white earth; tests on the red pigment showed no lead or sulfide, but the microprobe analysis did reveal iron in varying quantities, indicating that the red pigment was a red ochre containing ironoxides. The analysis of the pigments used at *Satricum* implies the exploitation of current pigments available in several regions in Italy including Latium, but whether these were imported or local remains unclear.

(iii) Copper and lead

Copper and lead were definite imports, since no local resources are known. The nearest deposits of lead are in Etruria (Zifferero 1991: 212). Lead was used at the site in the 6th c. BC for the fastening of architectural terracottas, of which some still retain traces of plumbing. The evidence for the processing of copper alloys at *Satricum* is circumstantial, though the production of iron and copper-alloy artifacts, at one site, appears to be customary in this period (Klein 1972; Ostenberg 1983). Now that the on-site processing of iron is established (Nijboer, this volume), traces of manufacture of copper-alloy artifacts can be expected. There is indirect evidence for the casting of Cu-alloy *fibulae*, since several of the *fibulae* types represented in the oldest votive deposit (*deposit I*) are identical and cast from the same mould. Another indication of casting are droplets of Cu-alloy, which are occasionally found on the site. The difference between these droplets and the smallest *aes rude* is disputable, due to the fact that *aes rude* are created by fragmenting a Cu-alloy cake of the crudest form of casting, at a high temperature, by a blow with a hammer resulting in similar waste as compared to that of casting. The enormous amount of *aes rude* found at *Satricum* outside the *deposit* may indicate a workshop area as well (Haeberlin 1910: 3). Since some of these *aes rude* have a high iron content, they are probably the product of smelting of chalcopyrites, the nearest deposits of which occur in Etruria (Zifferero 1991: 212–13). The provenance of the metals processed at the site can, however, only be established by a research project using lead isotope analysis as has been done for the copper ore deposits of the eastern Mediterranean area (Gale & Stos-Gale 1986).

Economic aspects of the Iron Age and Archaic pottery

As well as providing dating evidence, the typological analysis of the *Satricum* pottery allows for a functional and economic interpretation. The pottery from the settlement features (in assemblages found in pits and layers) will be related to the finds from the contemporary necropolis situated to the northwest and the oldest cultplace (*deposit I*) in the centre of the settlement. The relationship between the people who visited the cultplace, those who lived on the hill and those who were buried in the NW-necropolis is clear from the distribution of identical pottery types in the three contexts (Beijer 1991a; 1991b).

The pottery can be divided into three main wares: *impasto* ware, depurated ware and *bucchero* ware. A classification of the pottery has been undertaken in which the pottery has been divided into classes based on morphological characteristics. In this classification, the functional meaning is implicit, although the real function as it was conceived by the potter or the user, is not known to us (Formazione 1980; Dizionari 1980; Rice 1987: 211–212). The classes are grouped in larger general functional categories as storing and processing or preparing (also labelled as 'kitchen ware') and transfer or serving and consuming ('table ware') (Rice 1987). A finer type division within each class is based on minor morphological, decorative and technological attributes (Beijer, in prep.).

(i) Variability in the wares

The three main wares impasto, depurated and *bucchero* are present in all three contexts, but in very different quantities (fig.3). Fragments of depurated clay and *bucchero*, so important for the chronology of the features, have a very low frequency in the habitation context (respectively 3,2% and 3,1%), whereas the *impasto* ware covers 93,7% of the pottery. Even considering chronological differences the non *impasto* fragments remain exceptional finds in the habitation. A different situation is offered by the tombs and the cultplace, where vases of depurated clay and *bucchero* form respectively 39,5% and 67,8% of the pottery (necropolis: 24,6% depurated, 14,9% *bucchero* and 60,5% *impasto*; votive deposit: respectively 33,9%, 33,9% and 32,1%).

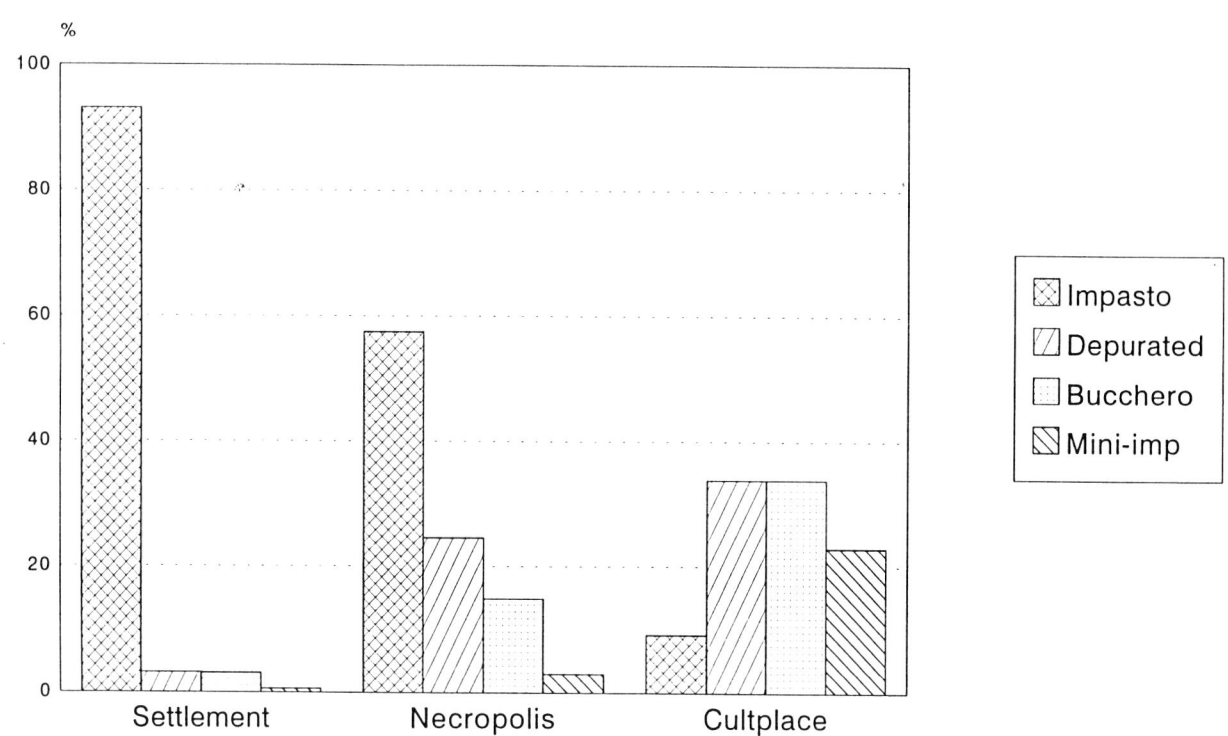

Fig. 3. Pottery wares, Satricum: quantities of impasto, depurated and bucchero pottery types.

The frequency differences in the wares have to be considered in relation to the various vessel types and thus to their function in relation to their specific context. Although both depurated and *bucchero* wares are generally considered luxury goods (in respect to *impasto* vases), they do not necessarily mean simply an economic progress in the community. The mainly Greek-inspired vase types of depurated clay are bowls, cups, jugs and plates. In Etruscan *bucchero* we find bowls, cups, jugs and amphoras. These are prevalent in the tombs and among the full-sized pottery in the oldest votive deposit. This frequency must have its explanation in their specific ritual or symbolic use in those contexts. A special group is formed by the *aryballoi* and *alabastra* (perfume containers) of depurated clay and *bucchero*, found mainly in the votive deposit (Beijer 1995).

The *impasto* ware found in the tombs consists exclusively of vessels belonging to the category of serving and consuming (fig.4). In the votive deposit the situation is different: the *impasto* can be divided into miniature pottery (22,9% of the total amount of pottery) and full-sized vessels (9,3%). The miniature pottery consists of various classes and categories, that are largely similar also in the relative frequency of the classes to those from the settlement. The *impasto* full-sized vessels are mainly amphoras, jugs and *kantharoi* (for pouring and drinking liquids, category serving/consuming). While the category storing/processing is absent in the tombs, a few small storing/cooking jars are present among the *impasto* vases in the votive deposit. Among the miniature pottery they are very well represented.

(ii) Variability in categories and classes

It is clear that the users of the vessels at *Satricum* choose different classes of pots for each occasion. In the tombs sets of fine serving and consuming vases accompanied the dead. These emphasize the importance and meaning of the use of this particular pottery in the funerary rituals. Moreover, the quality and quantity of this set of vessels play an important role in the way the community considered the former social position of the deceased: an image of the social *persona* (cf. Bietti Sestieri *et al.* 1989–90; Bietti Sestieri 1986; 1988–89; 1992; Ricerca 1979: 100–101 on Osteria dell'Osa). The relation between the pottery assemblages in the settlement and in the

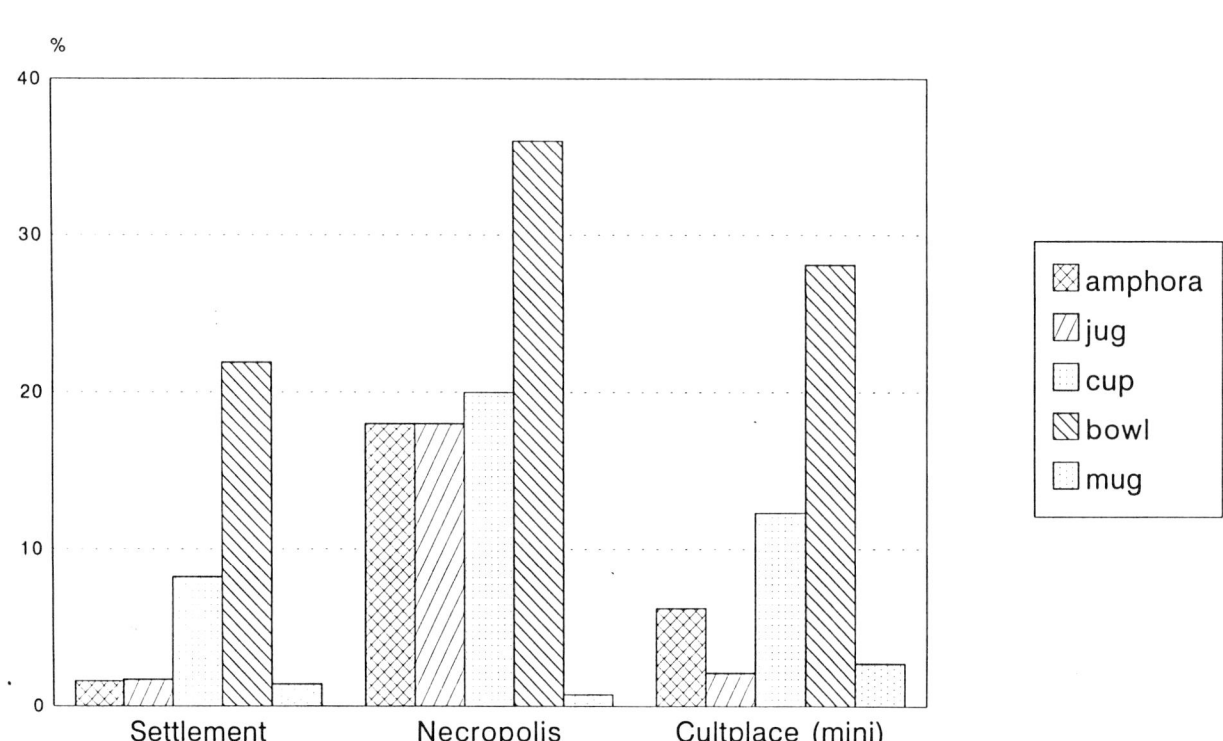

Fig. 4. Pottery shapes, Satricum*: chart comparing the frequency of the shapes of fine pottery from tombs with the same shapes from settlement features and with the miniature ones of the votive deposit.*

tombs is unclear, because there is a low frequency of pottery types in common (the fine pouring and drinking vases) (fig.4). Were the pots made exclusively for funeral purposes or were they first used in daily life and did most of the fine pottery finally end up in a tomb?

The interpretation of a specific meaning of the votive pottery can be based on its function in the cult as a container of gifts: symbolic small gifts (representing products that refer to the daily diet) in the miniature pottery, that in itself symbolises the daily pottery of the 8th and 7th centuries, liquids and perfumes in the other wares. The large quantity of *bucchero* and etrusco-corinthian drinking vessels of the late 7th and 6th century BC in the cult context stands in particular contrast with the finds from the settlement (tombs are not known from this period), where utilitarian pottery of *impasto* continues to dominate in the households.

Comparing the various assemblages of the settlement features, the frequency of the two main functional categories, storing/preparing and serving/consuming, vary considerably between the features. However, a tendency towards more serving/consuming vessels in the 7th century can be observed (fig.5). A similar tendency can be noted in the tombs of the same period, where the quantity and variety of drinking vessels increase considerably compared with the tombs of the earlier period. This might be due to an important variation in the food and drink supply and consumption, perhaps related to the introduction of ceremonial or aristocratic banquets. It must be noted that after this short period of variability the principal kind of pottery in the 6th century BC belongs again to the storing and processing category. Regarding the large storage jars only a few have been found in 8th and 7th century features, but a slight increase in the course of the Archaic period can be noted. This return to a predominance of traditional household vessels in the settlement of the 6th century probably continues in the post-Archaic and Republican period, when the jar is prevalent in the context of *deposit II*. The preference of jars (in miniature in the oldest *deposit* and of full-size in *deposit II*) in the same cultplace over a period of many centuries indicates clearly a continuous cult-practice linked with this vessel class.

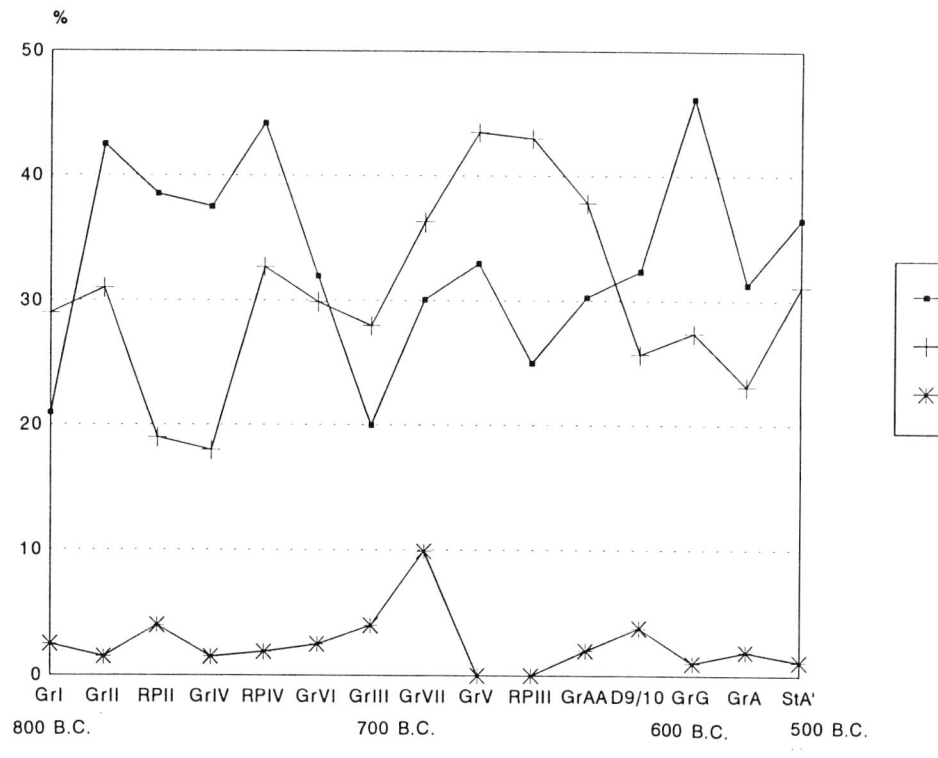

Fig. 5. Pottery categories, Satricum.

(iii) Variability in types

Among the *impasto* pottery a large variability in types could be observed. This is in strong contrast with the depurated and *bucchero* wares, which contain standardised types due to a different pottery production system. Some type varieties in the *impasto* ware have chronological implications, because their type-attributes are due to technological innovations and/or to morphological changes due to the import of new and foreign vessels. This import of vessels can be dated at the end of the 8th century, during the course of the 7th and the entire 6th century BC (Beijer 1991a). Earlier in the 8th century the many type varieties, which were based on minor morphological differences, are not due to chronological but to technomic differences. The large type variability observed in the classes might be caused by the pottery production system of the 8th century, when probably most of the handmade *impasto* pottery was produced within each single family. There is little overlap in types found in the features of this phase, except for lidbowls and incurved bowls, two traditional and simple Iron age shapes. From the late 8th century the type variety is no longer restricted to single features in the settlement: evidently a more organised pottery production system is at work. Technological innovations (use of wheel, slip, and purer clays), the copying of foreign types and, even in the *impasto* pottery repertoire, more standardised pots, confirm the idea of a more specialised production in organised workshops in the 7th and 6th centuries BC (Beijer 1991a).

The copying of foreign – Phoenician and Greek – types has also a functional implication. If we presume a close link between vessel type and content (=function/use), the increase of serving/consuming pottery: cups, jugs and plates, and the many type varieties in these classes in both settlement and tombs, imply a change to a more differentiated consumption pattern due to the introduction of a new diet, new foods and drinks (e.g. olives, wine?) from these countries. This differentiation is related to the social changes, that took place in the late 8th and 7th centuries BC (Beijer 1992). This implies also a change in the food production and food exchange.

ECONOMIC ASPECTS OF POST-ARCHAIC POTTERY

The evidence for local ceramic production in the successive post-Archaic and Republican period (5th to 3rd centuries BC) comes mainly from the cultplaces (*deposit II* and *deposit III*). The recent identification of a nucleus of workshops and kilns in the former Archaic settlement-area supports the idea of local production in this period (Attema *et al.* 1992). The local terracotta production comprised the processing of pottery, anatomical votives and small terracotta statuettes. In terms of the production of pottery, *impasto*, black-glazed and probably depurated wares can be assumed. The *impasto* pottery was found in great numbers in *deposit II*, the graves of the 5th-4th centuries BC, and to a lesser degree in *deposit III*, mainly comprising cooking-pots and bowls. Confirmation of local production in the early Republican period of at least part of this *impasto* ware, may be deduced from the scarcity of close parallels from the surrounding sites. Local production of part of the black-glazed pottery is proved by the presence of forms that do not occur in Campania, a different clay and a poorer quality of the glaze.

One of the most frequent types of *ex votos* in mid- and late Republican times (4th-2nd centuries BC) are the small terracottas statuettes of seated and standing females. For at least a part of these a local provenance is assumed (*Satricum* 1982: 108,118; *Satricum* 1985, nr.279).

Most of the votives produced in *Satricum* were intended for the local market. But some may have been sold also to other sanctuaries, or brought there by dedicants who had bought them in *Satricum* (e.g. *Satricum* 1985: nr. 303; Attema *et al.* 1992, fig.3, n.45). From this it is clear that in the post-Archaic and Republican period the cultplaces played an important role in the economic system of the site.

THE CULT PLACES

The rise, period of prosperity, and decay of the cultplaces of *Satricum* is strongly interrelated with the economic system of the site and its territory and a direct reflection of it. In the Archaic settlement-area at least three cultplaces are known (on the acropolis, in the S. Lucia and in the Macchia Bottacci – Maaskant-Kleibrink 1987; 1992; Attema *et al.* 1992: 79); in the territory two are present: one at Campoverde (BTCGI: 336–337) and one near the confluence of the Astura and the Fosso Pane e Vino (Tomassetti 1910: 388; Lugli 1936: 909).

The most famous cultplace within the territory is the sanctuary of Mater Matuta on the acropolis. Her cult is attested from the late 8th until the 3rd-2nd centuries by three successive votive deposits located underneath and in the direct vicinity of the later temple (in this paper referred to as *deposit I* (end 8th-*c*.540) *deposit II* (end 6th-3rd BC) and *deposit III* (4th-2nd BC)). This is the only cultplace where during a period of more than six centuries the cult can be traced without interruption. The contents of all three deposits on the acropolis reflect the importance of the site from an early period as a centre of local and wider economic activity. This picture is confirmed by the other cultplaces.

(i) Traces of contact

Whereas contacts on a regional and interregional level can be found during almost all periods of cult, those on an international scale are found especially in the earliest period. Thanks to the favourable location of the site, *Satricum* from early on played an important role in trade between Central Italy and the Eastern Mediterranean. The role of the site in this process is reflected in the number of imports which among others have been found in the oldest deposit of the sanctuary of Mater Matuta. The imports are of the highest quality and compared with other Latial cultplaces among the most abundant. The deposit yielded imports from Egypt, Rhodes, the Phoenician-Cypriot area, but mainly from Greece: proto-Corinthian and Corinthian pottery, and artifacts in faience, amber, bone, ivory and bronze. While the international component is predominant to c. 650 BC, after this date this contact gradually diminishes in favour of interregional import, marked by contacts with regions as Campania and the Sabine and Falisco-Capenan territory. The Etruria links are reflected in the great number of Etrusco-Corinthian and *bucchero* wares: *deposit I* contained more Etrusco-Corinthian vases than any other complex in all of Central-Italy. The strong relation with Etruria in the 7th and 6th centuries BC is also evident from the fact that *confronti* for specific artifacts from *deposit I* are known from Etruria only (*e.g.* Satricum 1985: nr.135,180; Bonacasa 1957: nr.2).

The high economic standard of the site in the late 7th and 6th centuries BC is further reflected in the presence in the oldest deposit of a considerable number of iron and bronze artifacts as well as gold, silver and gilted silver – in this period objects in gold and silver are nearly absent in sanctuaries elsewhere in Latium. Likewise objects in faience, amber and ivory are scarce in contemporaneous votive contexts in Latium (exceptions are S. Ombono in Rome, S. Cecilia, Anagni, Lavinium, Gabii, Antemnae Aquino (contrada Mèfete), and Campoverde).

In considering the relative frequency in each context, it can be noted that the number of imported pottery types in the earliest cultplaces, especially in the one on the acropolis, exceeds the number of imports in the necropolis. This leads to the conclusion that the international and interregional contacts mainly focused on the religious aspect of society and that this element of the economy must have had a very close relation with the cultplaces of the site.

From the mid-6th century BC onwards a clear shift in the contacts and relations can be observed. From this time *Satricum* and its direct surroundings almost totally lack imports from the Greek world. The rare instances include some black- and red-figured fragments from the acropolis (Della Seta 1918: 293; Stibbe 1978: 57; Satricum 1982: 108); fragments of some Attic *kylikes* from one of the earliest strata in *deposit II* and some black-glazed imports in the graves of the south-west necropolis (*Satricum* 1983: 29–30; Stibbe 1983a: 50; Stibbe 1985: fig.17; Knoop 1986: 42; Gnade 1992). In this lack of Greek imports, *Satricum* differs from other contemporaneous Latial sanctuaries as *Lavinium* and Rome (Stibbe 1981: 308 and n. 38). This international decline need not, however, be a direct indicator for a decrease in the economy: the economic situation in the second half of the 6th century and the start of the 5th still favoured the erection of two monumental temples of a Greek-inspired type on the acropolis.

It is only shortly after the beginning of the 5th century BC that the situation changes. Then the only traces of international and interregional contacts occur in the south-west necropolis, where the graves have yielded some imports from France, Etruria and South Italy (Satricum 1983: 29–30; Satricum 1985: 141; Gnade 1992). This reduction in the scale of trade goes hand in hand with the abandonment of the acropolis as a place for settlement and with spatial changes in the settlement-pattern as a whole (cf. Attema *et al.* 1992). Notable is the fact that the late Archaic sanctuary after it had fallen into ruins, was not rebuilt. In other Latial sites as *Lavinium* and *Ardea* a rebuilding or restoration of sanctuaries in the 5th century BC is not uncommon. A final indication of a changed economic situation in the late Archaic and Republican period may be the fact that in *deposit II* and *deposit III* precious metals are much reduced in number (Della Seta 1918: 295–296; Bouma, in prep.).

In the Republican period few clear settlement traces are known in the former Archaic urban area; the only traces known thus far were found near what may be interpreted as a production centre of terracotta material (Attema *et al.* 1992). Accordingly both the local production of pottery and votive offerings and the raising of cattle may be supposed to have been mainly intended for the immediate market and strongly related with the religious activities in the area. As it seems in this period, the economy of the site was mainly based on the demands set by the various cultplaces and by their pilgrims. Compared with the Iron Age and Archaic period the role of the sacred places in the economic system of the post-Archaic and Republican period seems even more dominant: judging from the available archaeological data the main justification for the existence of the site in this period seems the presence of cultplaces only. If so, the economic system during this Republican period therefore may well be characterized as a temple-economy proper.

Only as late as *c.* 400 BC can a more regular form of contact be traced again, with the import of black-glazed pottery and the so-called Tanagra-Myrina statuettes (Satricum 1985: nos.264, 278 and 284). For part of the black-glazed pottery a possible import from Etruria is suggested (Satricum 1982: 126), although a Campanian provenance cannot be excluded. As for the terracotta statuettes, for some a close relation with Sicily is supposed (Satricum 1985: no.282). Contacts with regions as

Umbria is reflected in a bronze Mars-statuette (Bonacasa 1957:no.22, fig.25); other contacts with Campania are given by the presence of a limited number of coins in the deposits: in *deposit II* two silver coins from Naples and two Roman-Campanian coins were found. The latter also occurred in *deposit III* (Barnabei 1896: 100). These coins are well-known in other Latial votive contexts (e.g. *Norba*, *Cora* and *Lanuvium*) where they occur in much greater quantitites.

When in the late Republican and early Imperial period in sites as Terracina, *Lanuvium*, *Praeneste* and *Nemi* sanctuaries were built on a scale which in splendour rivalled or even surpassed their predecessors, the religious activities at *Satricum*, and with them the existence of the site, already had come to an end to await the arrival of the first Roman *villae*.

CONCLUSIONS

This paper has examined various aspects of the economy of the Latin site of *Satricum*. The sections on natural environment and resources have shown that during all periods the subsistence in terms of landscape potential was limited. The agriculture around *Satricum* was mainly determined by domestic stock-raising since the soils around the settlement are not especially suitable for the cultivation of cereals and other crops. However, the presence of nearby marshes must have accounted for additional means like fuel, fish, fowl and other wildlife. Large quantities of cattle, caprine and pig bones survived, while the palaeobotanical remains, though meagre, do show a mixture of seeds like *triticum durum* (bread wheat), *vicia faba* (horse bean) and possibly *hordeum* (barley). Additional local resources were exploited, notably clays and tuffs and some metals, though copper and lead were imported as raw materials.

The limitations of the landscape potential in all periods reinforce the conclusion that the sanctuaries which characterised life at the site, constituted the major component of the economy of the settlement. This focal role in the late Iron Age and Archaic period of the sanctuaries is evident from the fact that most of the international imports are found in the sanctuaries. Also a comparison of the pottery in settlement, tombs and cultplace on the hill shows a predominance in this period in the sanctuary of depurated and *bucchero* ware, which are generally considered luxury goods in comparison with *impasto* pottery. However, in the tombs *impasto* prevails (approx. 60%) while in the settlement depurated and *bucchero* ware is almost absent.

The international and interregional contacts gradually disappear in the second half of the 6th and at the beginning of the 5th century BC respectively and subsequently the economy assumes a predominantly local aspect. The period sees the decay of the Archaic site, followed by severe turbulences for approximately 150 years in which the Pontine region became the stage of constant battles between Romans, Latins and Volsci. After the decline of the Archaic site, the cultplaces alone persist and even more than before the religious places become the focal point of – now local – economic activities. Though historiography recalls the Volsci in the Pontine region as exporting cereals as early as 508 and 491 it can hardly be imagined from our data that agriculture could produce a surplus and that cereals formed any medium of exchange. As concerns the role of *Satricum* in the process of international contacts in early Republican times, it seems unlikely that the economic system of the 5th-4th century BC based on stock-raising and terracotta production, can have provided any surplus to allow commerce and trade on a large international scale.

The revival of the interregional contacts from *c*. 400 onwards is explicable by in the fact that the combats in the region had by then ceased and Roman control extended over most of the Pontine region. But though *Satricum*, as many other sites in the 5th and 4th century BC, had become a Latin colony, this was shortlived. This and the fact that, according to the ancient sources, throughout the 4th century the site lay in the battle-ground between Volsci, Latins and Romans, certainly did not favour strong activities in the field of rebuilding or refounding of cultplaces as noticed elsewhere.

Nonetheless, the marginal economic position of the site was enhanced after the construction of the Via Appia in 312 BC. With this road many of the previously important sites in the coastal plain of Latium were ignored and gradually became isolated. The case of *Satricum* shows that except on a favourable location, natural resources and the presence of one of the most renowned cultplaces of ancient Latium, the economy of a site and its territory is dependent on and determined by the infrastructure of the region and by the role of the site and its territory in the political framework.

ACKNOWLEDGEMENTS

Our thanks go to Prof. A. Clason, Prof. H. van Zeist and Dr W. Prummel, Drs M. Vink and Drs T. Blokland for the analysis of the archaeozoological samples, and to Prof. W. van Zeist (Biological Archaeological Institute, Groningen) for the study of the seed remains.

Bibliography

Ampolo, C. 1980. 'Le condizioni materiali della produzione. Agricoltura e paesaggio agrario', *Formazione*, 15–46.

Attema, P.A.J., Bouma, J.W., Nijboer, A.J. & Olde Dubbelink, R.A. 1992. 'Il sito di Borgo Le Ferriere nei secoli V e IV A.C.', *Archeologia Laziale* XI, 75–86.

Attema, P.A.J. 1990. 'Tracce, siti ed insediamenti protostorici nel paesaggio pontino-lepino', *Archeologia Laziale* X, 238–240.

Attema, P.A.J. 1991. '"Quae arx in Pomptino esset", the emergence of the fortified settlement in the Pontine Lepine Landscape', *Papers* of the Fourth Conference of Italian Archaeology I, the Archaeology of Power, Part 1 (eds. E. Herring, R. Whitehouse & J. Wilkins), London, 83-92.

Attema, P.A.J. 1993. An Archaeological Survey in the Pontine Region: A Contribution to the Early Settlement History of Latium Vetus (900- 100 BC), Groningen 1993.

Attema, P.A.J. 1994. 'Roman colonisation of the Pontine region. Aspects of the rural landscape from the 6th to the 11th cent. BC', in Structures rurales et Sociétés Antiques, (Actes du Colloque de Corfou, 14-16 mai 1992), 273-282.

Attema, P.A.J. & Bouma, J.W. 1995. 'The Cultplaces of the Pontine region in the context of a changing human environment (900- 100 BC, South Lazio)', The Landscape of the Goddess, Caeculus II, Papers on Mediterranean Archaeology, Archaeological Centre, Groningen University.

Barnabei, F. 1896. 'Conca. Nuove scoperte nell'area dell'antico tempio presso Le Ferriere', Notizie degli Scavi di Antichità, 99-102.

Beijer, A.J. 1991a. 'Un centro di produzione di vasi d'impasto a Borgo Le Ferriere ("Satricum") nel periodo dell'orientalizzante', Mededelingen van het Nederlands Instituut te Rome, Antiquity 50, 63-86.

Beijer, A.J. 1991b. 'Impasto pottery and social status in Latium Vetus in the Orientalising period (725-575 BC): an example from Borgo Le Ferriere ("Satricum")', Papers of the Fourth Conference of Italian Archaeology, The Archaeology of Power, Part 2, (eds. E. Herring, R. Whitehouse & J. Wilkins), London, 21-39.

Beijer, A.J. 1992. 'Pottery and change in Latium in the Iron Age', Images of Ancient Latin Culture, Caeculus I, Papers on Mediterranean Archaeology, Archaeological Centre, Groningen Univ, 103-115.

Beijer, A.J. 1995. 'Greek and local pottery in Ancient Latium. The question of Greek influence in Latium in the Iron Age', Caeculus II, Papers on Mediterranean Archaeology, Archaeological Centre, Groningen Univ, in press.

Beijer, A.J. in preparation. Iron Age pottery from Ancient Latium. Analysis of the impasto ware from Borgo Le Ferriere (Dissertation).

Bietti Sestieri, A.M. 1979. 'La fase più antica della cultura laziale', Atti della XXI Riunione Scientifica dell'Istituto Italiano di Preistoria e Protostoria, Firenze, 399-413.

Bietti Sestieri, A.M. 1986. 'I dati archeologici di fronte alla teoria', Dialoghi di Archeologia, 249-263.

Bietti Sestieri, A.M. 1988-89. 'Esempi di lettura di materiali da contesti funerari', Origini, Preistoria e Protostoria delle Civiltà antiche XIV, 421-445.

Bietti Sestieri, A.M. (ed.) 1992. La Necropoli di Osteria dell'Osa, Roma.

Bietti Sestieri, A.M., De Santis, A. & La Regina, A. 1989-90. 'Elementi di tipo cultuale e doni personali nella necropoli laziale di Osteria dell'Osa', Atti del Convegno Internazionale Anathema: Regime delle offerte e vita dei santuari nel Mediterraneo antico, giugno 1989, Scienze dell'Antichità, Storia, Archeologia, Antropologia 3-4, 65-88.

Bonacasa, N. 1957. 'Bronzetti da Satricum', Studi Etruschi 25, 549- 565.

Bouma, J.W. in preparation. Religio Votiva: Archaeology and Early Republican Votive Religion in Latium. The Votive Deposit south-west of the Temple on the Acropolis at <Satricum> Borgo Le Ferriere (Dissertation).

BTCGI, Bibliografia Topografica della Colonizzazione Greca in Italia e nelle Isole Tirreniche (diretta di G.Nenci e G.Vallet).

CLP 1976. Civiltà del Lazio Primitivo, Exhibition Catalogue, Roma.

Crescenzi, L. 1978. 'Campoverde', Archeologia Laziale I, 51-55.

Della Seta, A. 1918. Museo Nazionale della Villa Giulia, Roma.

Dizionari 1980. Dizionari terminologici 1, Materiali dell'età del Bronzo e della prima età del Ferro, Roma.

Formazione 1980. La formazione della città nel Lazio, (=Dialoghi di Archeologia, nuova serie, 2).

Gale, N.H. & Stos-Gale, Z.A. 1986. 'Anatolian and Cycladic Metal Sources', PACT 15, 13-30.

Gnade, M. 1992. The Southwest Necropolis of Satricum. (Scrinium IV; Satricum II), Amsterdam.

Haagsma, B.J. 1993. Een pollenanalytisch onderzoek te Monticchio (Lazio, Italie), (internal report Mediterrane Archeologie), Rijksuniversiteit Groningen. (Also as an appendix in Attema 1993).

Haeberlin, J.E.J. 1910. Aes Grave, Frankfurt a.M.

Hellstrom et al. 1975. The Zone of the Large Iron Age Building, Luni Sul Mignone vol.II, fasc.2, Stockholm.

Kamermans, H. 1980. Verslag Fysisch Geografisch Onderzoek omgeving Le Ferriere, (internal report).

Klein, J. 1972. 'A Greek metalworking quarter, eighth century excavations on Ischia', Expedition 14.2, 34-39.

Knoop, R.R. 1986. 'Satricum a metà strada', in P. Chiarucci, Il Lazio antico dalla protostoria all'età medio repubblicana, Roma, 57-74.

Lugli, G. 1936. 'Satrico', Enciclopedia Italiana xxx, 908-909.

Maaskant-Kleibrink, M. 1987. Settlement Excavations at Borgo Le Ferriere <Satricum>, Vol. I, Groningen.

Maaskant-Kleibrink, M. 1991. 'Early Latin Settlement plans at Borgo Le Ferriere <Satricum>. Reading Mengarelli's maps', BABesch 66, 51-114.

Maaskant-Kleibrink, M. 1992. Settlement Excavations at Borgo Le Ferriere <Satricum>, Vol. II, Groningen.

Moretti, M. 1962. Il Museo Nazionale di Villa Giulia, Roma.

Östenberg, E. 1967. Luni sul Mignone e problemi della preistoria d'Italia, Lund.

Östenberg, C.E. 1983. 'Acquarossa, periodi Preistorici e Protostorici', Notizie degli Scavi di Antichità, 37, 79-97.

Quilici, L. & Quilici Gigli, S. 1984. 'Longula e Polusca', Archeologia Laziale VI, 107-132.

Quilici-Gigli, S. 1983. 'Sistemi di cunicoli nel territorio tra Velletri e Cisterna', Archeologia Laziale V, 112-123.

Rice, P.M. 1987. Pottery Analysis, A Sourcebook, Chicago/London.

Ricerca 1979. Ricerca su una comunità del Lazio protostorico. Il sepolcreto dell'Osteria dell'Osa sulla via Prenestina, Exhibition Catalogue, Roma.

Satricum 1982. Satricum, una città latina, Exhibition Catalogue, Firenze.

Satricum 1983. Satricum. Un progetto di valorizzazione per la cultura e il territorio di Latina. (Atti del convegno 'Satricum: una città latina', Latina.

Satricum 1985. Nieuw Licht op een oude stad: Italiaanse en Nederlands opgravingen in Satricum, Exhibition Catalogue, Leiden-Rome.

Schweitzer, F. & Rinuy, A. 1982. 'Manganese black as an Etruscan pigment', Studies in Conservation 27, 118-123.

Stibbe, C.M. 1978. 'Satricum', Archeologia Laziale I, 56-59.

Stibbe, C.M. 1981. 'Nuovi e vecchi dati su Satricum', Archeologia Laziale IV, 305-309.

Stibbe, C.M. 1983. 'I Volsci nell'agro Pontino ed a Satricum', Satricum, 24-32.

Stibbe, C.M. 1983a. 'La quinta campagna di scavo dell'Istituto Olandese di Roma a Satricum', Archeologia Laziale V, 48-53.

Stibbe, C.M. 1985. Satricum en de Volsken. Satricana vol.2.

Thomasson, B.M. 1961. 'Deposito votivo dell'antica città di Lavinio (Pratica di Mare)', Opuscula Romana III, 123-138.

Tomassetti, G. 1910-1926. La Campagna Romana. Antica, medioevale e moderna. II. Via Appia, Ardeatina ad Aurelia, Roma.

Tylecote, R.F. 1980. 'Furnaces, crucibles and slags', in Wertime & Muhly (eds.), The Coming of the Age of Iron, New Haven, 183-228.

Voorrips, A., Loving, S.H. & Kamermans, H. 1991. The Agro Pontino Survey Project, (Studies in Prae- en Protohistorie 6), Amsterdam.

Zevi, F. et al. 1975. 'Castel di Decima (Roma). La necropoli arcaica', Notizie degli Scavi di Antichità, 29, 298.

Zifferero, A. 1991. 'Miniere e metallurgia estrattiva in Etruria Meridionale: per una lettura critica di alcuni dati archeologici e minerari', Studi Etruschi, 57, 201-241.

Zitzmann, A. 1977-78. The Iron Ore Deposits of Europe and Adjacent Areas, Vol. I & II, Bundesanstalt für Geowissenschaften und Rohstoffe, Hanover.

20

Storia di un Tratturo

Prof. Emanuela Fabbricotti
(Dipartimento di Archeologia, Università di Chieti)

Sommario: *L'allevamento degli ovini che è stato la fonte economica predominante nell'Abruzzo e nel Molise fino a pochi decenni fa, è stato reso possibile dalla practica della transumanza dall'Appennino al Tavoliere delle Puglie in autunno e viceversa in estate. Questa si svolgeva sul tratturo e l'antichità dei tratturi è documentata in epoca anteriore alla conquista romana, sia dalla coincidenza che essi ebbero poi con le viae publicae romane, sia dalla frequenza di rinvenimenti di bronzetti rappresentati Eracle in atteggiamenti diversi, sia dalla presenza di santuari o di necropoli nelle vicinanze, quindi anche di insediamenti stabili, in genere piccoli, situati spesso all'incrocio di alcuni suoi bracci.*

Da anni, stiamo cercando di evidenziare il percorso delle antiche vie armentizie, cioè i tratturi, tratturelli ed i bracci minori. La ricerca si svolge sia in gruppo, sia con l'assegnazione di singole tesi su piccole parti del territorio abruzzese da scandagliare a fondo e da ricercare, ovviamente, sul terreno e in biblioteca, dove rare sono le notizie dei ritrovamenti del passato.

Questo studio ha ovviamente un fine scientifico, ma anche uno un pò meno scientifico, cioè quello di indurre la regione Abruzzo a prevedere e creare itinerari turistico-culturali a beneficio delle zone pedemontane più neglette perché economicamente meno valide di quelle di alta montagna e del mare. L'obiettivo è quello di costruire un futuro culturalmente positivo basato su un passato storico.

Quasi tutti i tratturi sono indicati nella carta della reintegra di Foggia del 1959, ma a noi interessano forse di più quelli dimenticati e quindi più difficili da individuare, quelli cioè che forse non sono entrati nell'ottica dei tratturi aragonesi.

Non sempre il tracciato è a fondo valle, spesso è misto. Se da una parte si disegna una carta dei tratturi di una certa zona e da un'altra quella archeologica, si vedrà che spesso esse si sovrappongono e che quindi il filo conduttore della geografia storica e archeologica d'Abruzzo è il tratturo. Ovviamente ci sono diversità cronologiche tra i vari rinvenimenti, forse per la preferenza di alcuni siti e l'abbandono di altri in un'epoca determinata, ma il periodo d'uso dei tratturi è molto lungo e la scelta o l'abbandono di alcune località può essere dovuto a ragioni varie, da quelle climatiche a quelle politiche, quindi è bene non tenerne conto, e considerare la via armentizia nel suo complesso. Infatti la vita dei tratturi inizia probabilmente dal momento cosiddetto appenninico dell'età del Bronzo, attraverso l'età del Ferro e quella storica (italica e romana in cui sono testimoniate regole precise ed anche soprusi) e poi avanti nel tempo, arrivando in molti casi fino a poco oltre la II Guerra Mondiale. E, considerando la cronologia dei vari rinvenimenti archeologici, abbiamo visto che ai periodi di maggiore instabilità politica corrisponda il maggior uso dei tratturi, specie minori, visto che i maggiori (L'Aquila-Foggia, Pescasseroli-Candela, Castel di Sangro-Lucera, Ateleta-Biferno) non conoscono, si può dire, momenti di utilizzazione, se non rari. I più piccoli vengono usati in momenti particolari e non continuativamente e quindi possono essere studiati meglio (come ad es. quello che scende dal Passo di Coccia sul versante orientale della Maiella) ed alcuni vengono poi trasformati in strade vere e proprie, specie in età romana (ad es. *Peltuinum* e, forse, Torricella Peligna). La transumanza aveva bisogno non solo di zone di pascolo, ma anche di zone di sosta provviste di acqua (spesso trasformate in aree cultuali) e di zone di rifugio in caso di pericolo. E non è raro il caso in cui si trovino insieme queste tre entità: tratturo, santuario e roccaforte (ad es. Sepino, *Iuvanum*).

E' ovvio che tutti i santuari sono situati lungo i tratturi e che non tutte le roccaforti siano luoghi di riparo per greggi e pastori. Ma nel primo caso, quello dei santuari, l'incidenza è grande. Sono infatti situati in zone poco accessibili, non altrimenti comprensibili: solo in Abruzzo posso citare quelli di *Iuvanum*, Atessa-Passo Porcari, Sulmona, Fontecchio, Navelli, Pescosansonesco, Vacri ed altri; molti caddero in disuso dopo la guerra sociale, perché soppressi per le loro ideologie politiche o perché i tratturi più accidentati, divenuti gli altri più sicuri per la *lex agraria* già dal II sec. a.C., furono in parte abbandonati a beneficio di quelli meno disagevoli. I santuari erano centri di potere nei quali, oltre le pratiche cultuali, veniva amministrata la giustizia, il controllo commerciale e la dogana. Servivano quindi non solo ai pastori, ma anche alla popolazione che viveva in campagna, erano sedi di mercato e di particolari attività legate alla pastorizia, come l'industria casearia e la vendita, lavorazione e tintura della lana. Fu infatti proprio la transumanza a ritardare la concentrazione di tipo urbano, mentre in età romana, alcuni divennero sedi di *municipia* come *Iuvanum* e l'attività giuridica, economica e politico-amministrativa fu sotto stretta sorveglianza del potere centrale (Roma prima e poi i monasteri in età medievale).

Molti sono i tratturi da esaminare in questo senso. Vorrei in questa sede segnalarne uno dei vari minori che si incontrano a Penne, in zona ex vestina, poi città romana tra le più fedeli a Roma.

Le località toccate dal braccio che segue il Vomano prima e poi il Piomba sono:

1. Montorio al Vomano, antica *Beregra* (rinvenimenti di bronzi, resti di edifici e di un ponte romano, probabilmente avanzi di un tempio ad Ercole: Cerulli Irelli 1971).

2. Basciano (notevole necropoli dell'età del Ferro in località La Brecciola; insediamento romano, probabile *vicus* del I sec. a.C.-II sec. d.C. in località S. Rustico con edificio templare medio-repubblicano e stipe votiva di I sec. a.C.; gruppo di iscrizioni romane (*CIL* IX, 5047, 5050, 5051) e di particolare interesse una tomba di VII sec. a.C. a S.Giovanni al Mavone con carro, fibule, borchie ed un interessantissimo pendaglio di tipo illirico che si trova anche nel Piceno (studiato dalla dott.ssa G.Martella): *Not.Sc.* 1896: 515–519; 1902: 261 ss.; AA.VV. 1986: 217; Cerulli Irelli 1971: 31, n. 13; Messineo & Pellegrino 1984).

3. Penna S.Andrea (necropoli con tre stele con iscrizioni in dialetto sabellico e pendagli punici figurati in pasta vitrea; probabile santuario italico; insediamenti rustici

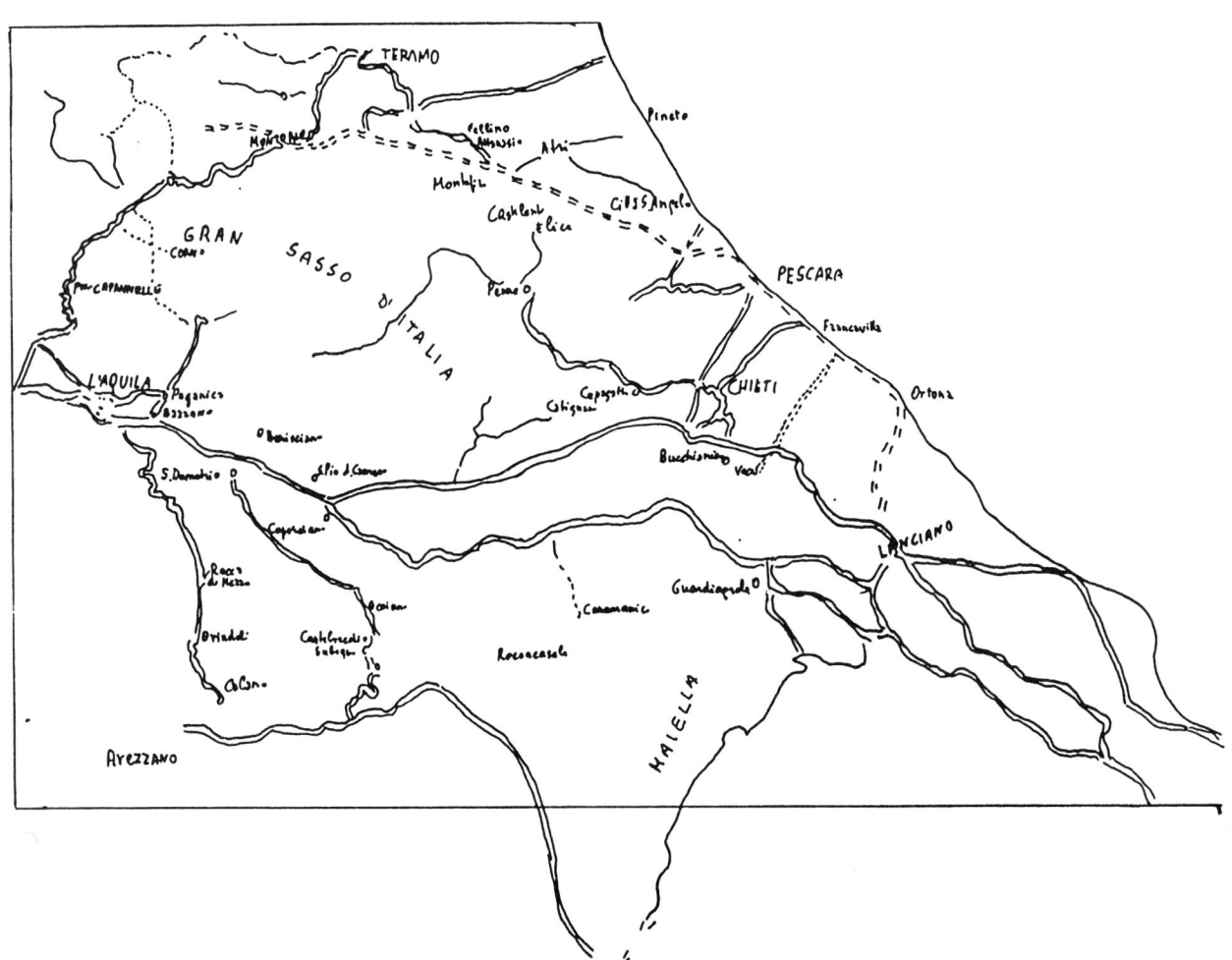

ed iscrizioni romane: AA.VV. 1978, 347–348; AA.VV. 1986: 125ss., 217).

4. Cermignano (tempio in località Monte Giove, edifici con mosaici ed iscrizioni romane: *Not.Sc.* 1888: 291; AA.VV. 1986: 217).

5. Cellino Attanasio (insediamento protostorico; tombe del Bronzo finale; insediamento e necropoli arcaici, di età romana e alto medievale; *vicus* e necropoli romana: *Not. Sc.* 1877: 15; 1895: 413–415; Cerulli Irelli 1971: 39, n. 12; AA.VV. 1986: 217 ss).

6. Castilenti (cippo miliario di Valentiniano I, 367–375 d.C., riferentesi alla strada romana che da Atri portava a Penne, citata anche nella *Tabula Peutingeriana*; tempio di S.Giorgio con ricca decorazione fittile: Lupinetti, 1962; *Not.Sc.* 1902: 260; Forni 1963; Cerulli Irelli 1971: 40, nn.4–6; AA.VV. 1978: 517 s.; La Regina 1968: 369 e 415 s.; Iaculli 1975: 253 ss.; 1981; 1983).

7. Città Sant'Angelo (necropoli romana; villa rustica tardo-imperiale in località Fagnani; forno ceramico; ripostiglio di monete romane repubblicane. *Not.Sc.* 1931: 615–637. Notizie concesse dal locale Archeoclub).

E potrei continuare ancora con le altre località sullo stesso tratturo, che hanno restituito materiale archeologico, cioè Pescara-Colle del Telegrafo, Francavilla, Tollo, Ortona, Crecchio.

Questo è solo un breve esempio della storia di uno dei tratturi minori che stiamo ricostruendo, anche se alle volte, con difficoltà. Alcuni furono abbandonati del tutto, altri potenziati come vie armentizie o trasformati in strade. Abbiamo l'esempio di Penne e di Lanciano che sono divenute prima *vici* e poi città romane di una certa importanza (*Pinna* e *Anxanum*) proprio perché strategicamente situate all'incrocio di vari tratturi e quindi economicamente valide per Roma, nel momento in cui, dopo le guerre sannitiche, vi era la necessità di creare nuovi centri amministrativi e allo stesso tempo centri di potere e di controllo all'interno di un territorio ostile attraverso il quale passavano non solo greggi e pastori, ma oggetti di mercato, influenze, propaganda ed idee.

Bibliografia
AA.VV. 1978. *Culture Adriatiche antiche di Abruzzo e Molise*, Roma.
AA.VV. 1986. *La valle del medio e basso Vomano*, Roma.
Cerulli Irelli, G. 1971. *Teramo, Carta archeologica d'Italia*, Firenze.
Forni, D. 1963. 'Sul miliario di Castilenti e la strada romana tra Hadria e Pinna', *Abruzzo,* I, 47 ss.
Iaculli, G. 1975. 'Terrecotte architettoniche da Colle S. Giorgio', *Archeologia Classica*, XXVII, 253 ss.
Iaculli, G. 1981. 'Ancora su Colle S. Giorgio', *Quaderni Istituto Chieti,* 2, 55 ss.
Iaculli, G. 1983. 'Architettura templare preromana', in *Storia come presenza*, Ancona, 19 ss.
La Regina, A. 1968. 'Note sugli insediamenti vestini', *Memorie Lincei.*
Lupinetti, D. 1962. *Il cippo romano di Castilenti*, L'Aquila.
Messineo, G. & Pellegrino, A. 1984. 'Ellenismo in Abruzzo: la stipe di Basciano', in *Studi in onore di Achille Adriani III*, Roma, 695 ss.

21

Evoluzione dell'Insediamento e dell'Economia nella Sabina in Età Romana

GIOVANNA ALVINO, TERSILIO LEGGIO
(Soprintendenza Archeologica per il Lazio; Museo di Farfa)

Sommario: *In questa breve nota vengono delineati i principali mutamenti del paesaggio avvenuti dopo la romanizzazione in una parte della Sabina e del territorio abitato dagli Aequiculi, attraverso l'analisi delle strutture economiche, delle forme insediative e degli interventi strutturali ed infrastrutturali che hanno assunto caratterizzazioni fortemente diversificate a seconda del mutamento delle condizioni ambientali, particolarmente rapido tra le varie aree. Da questa analisi emerge come in epoca romana siano stati differenti sia l'uso del suolo, sia la trama insediativa nella valle del Tevere, nella conca reatina, nelle valli del Velino, del Turano e del Salto. Anche la fine del mondo antico appare assumere connotazioni diverse tra le varie zone, con il precoce abbandono delle aree marginali e la maggior resistenza delle strutture economiche della valle del Tevere e della conca reatina.*

I moderni confini amministrativi non rispecchiano, se non marginalmente, le suddivisioni antiche e ciò è tanto più vero per la Sabina che è oggi inglobata da tre regioni: il Lazio, l'Umbria e l'Abruzzo. Obiettivo di questa nota sarà quello di delineare l'evoluzione dell'economia e dell'insediamento in età romana nella Sabina compresa nell'attuale provincia di Rieti e nel Cicolano, un'area che era in antico culturalmente differenziata dalla Sabina, essendo abitata dagli Equi, ma ad essa contigua e fortemente connessa, tanto da diventarne, almeno dall'alto medioevo parte integrante, pur conservando forti diversità culturali, sociali ed economiche.

DIFFERENZIAZIONI AMBIENTALI

All'interno di quest'area possono essere individuate un certo numero di sottozone nelle quali il paesaggio assume caratteristiche molto diversificate, condizionando in modo determinante l'articolazione e la tipologia delle forme insediative e delle strutture economiche. Ad una prima fascia collinare, normalmente definita Sabina tiberina, delimitata dal Tevere e dalla catena dei monti Sabini, segue, risalendo verso oriente, un paesaggio che diviene man a mano più aspro e montuoso, mentre il clima tende ad una maggior rigidità. La catena appenninica è intercalata poi dalle vallate del Velino, del Salto e del Turano, mentre, a quote diverse, si aprono alcuni bacini intermontani, il più ampio ed importante dei quali, quello reatino, era, in antico, ricoperto per la gran parte da un vasto lago, il così detto *lacus Velinus*, la cui estensione tendeva a variare fortemente in parallelo con i mutamenti climatici.

LA ROMANIZZAZIONE

Nel 290 a.C. il console Manio Curio Dentato, con una rapidissima campagna militare, conquistò in modo definitivo l'intera Sabina che, dalla valle del Tevere si estendeva verso l'interno, giungendo a comprendere l'attuale territorio di Norcia e parte dell'odierno Aquilano, l'alta valle dell'Aterno in particolare. Una regione che si era poco a volta differenziata tanto da un punto di vista politico-istituzionale, quanto da un punto di vista economico-sociale.

La conquista ebbe una vasta eco, perché in un sol colpo venne praticamente raddoppiata l'area controllata dallo stato romano. La romanizzazione della Sabina ne mutò ovviamente ed a fondo le strutture economiche e le forme insediative. Alcuni dei centri sabini, come *Cures, Reate* e *Trebula Mutuesca*, mantennero, pur nella mutata situazione, la loro funzione, restando i principali poli di gravitazione del territorio.

I vinti sabini ebbero anch'essi un ruolo in questa profonda riorganizzazione insieme ai cittadini romani, ai quali furono assegnate terre viritanamente o cedute attraverso l'alienazione di *ager quaestorius* nelle zone conquistate, senza quindi la deduzione di colonie, anche se l'inserimento dell'intera Sabina nel nuovo assetto politico-istituzionale fu contrassegnato da forti contrasti tra le diverse classi sociali romane. Nelle aree nelle quali invece i mutamenti furono più consistenti o la maglia del popolamento era più rada, furono creati centri nuovi, come *Forum Novum*, l'odierno Vescovio, lungo la valle dell'Aia e non lontano dal Tevere. Nella vallata del Salto, la regione degli Equi, appartenente oggi alla provincia di Rieti, ma in antico, fino a tutta l'età romana, sostanzialmente separata e differenziata dalla Sabina vera e propria, sopravvisse più marcatamente la struttura paganico-vicana.

La bonifica della piana reatina

Il definitivo inserimento della Sabina nel mondo romano innescò rapidi mutamenti del paesaggio, che ebbero un riflesso particolarmente rilevante nella conca reatina, prevalentemente occupata da un grande lago e da vaste aree paludose che condizionavano profondamente le strutture economiche del bacino, impedendo un deciso prevalere delle colture agrarie sull'allevamento, in grado di coesistere maggiormente con le acque e le paludi.

La palude ha costituito da sempre uno degli elementi caratterizzanti del paesaggio dell'Italia antica e medievale. Una presenza costante legata da un rapporto complesso con l'attività umana, cancellata soltanto dalle bonifiche integrali moderne e contemporanee (Traina 1988). Se la palude è stata di norma nel passato una componente marginale del paesaggio italiano, ben più più complesso è il caso di Rieti e della sua conca, dove il rapporto tra città ed acque è stato fortemente e costantemente condizionante per lo sviluppo economico dell'intera area.

La prevalenza dei fattori ambientali fu rotta nel III secolo a.C., secondo una tradizione ben consolidata, dallo stesso Curio Dentato che operò la bonifica della piana reatina per mezzo dello scavo di un canale alle Marmore. Una bonifica certamente non integrale, ma che dovette comunque prosciugare una parte notevole dell'area paludosa e ridurre fortemente la superficie dell'originario *lacus Velinus*, frammentato in specchi d'acqua minori e con le parcelle disposte a raggiera intorno ai laghi superstiti, dando vita ad uno dei maggiori e precoci mutamenti del «paesaggio italico» operato dai romani (Traina 1990: 30–40).

Se l'apertura della cava curiana fu senza molti dubbi l'intervento più macroscopico e spettacolare, basti ricordare la creazione della grandiosa scenografia della cascata delle Marmore, altre opere di bonifica minori dovettero assicurare il drenaggio delle acque sorgive e meteoriche (Leggio & Serva 1991). Un fitto reticolo di canali di scolo, individuabile in parte della conca reatina per mezzo delle foto aree e costituito probabilmente dalle *strigae* e dalle *scamnae* delle suddivisioni territoriali d'età romana, contribuì notevolmente, con ragionevole certezza, al completamento della bonifica della piana (Chouquer 1990).

E' probabile però che gli interventi per il controllo ed il rapido deflusso delle acque non si siano limitati soltanto a questi due aspetti. L'esperienza medievale dimostra che il semplice scavo alle Marmore, pur restando la chiave di volta della bonifica, non era di certo in grado di risolverne compiutamente tutti i problemi, che non erano ovviamente connessi soltanto con fattori antropici, come eventuali diboscamenti lungo le vallate del Velino, del Salto e del Turano, diboscamenti che, se effettuati massicciamente, come avvenne nel medioevo, potevano causare un rapido e violento afflusso delle acque nella conca reatina con conseguenti disastrose esondazioni ed un apporto detritico tale da essere in grado di colmare

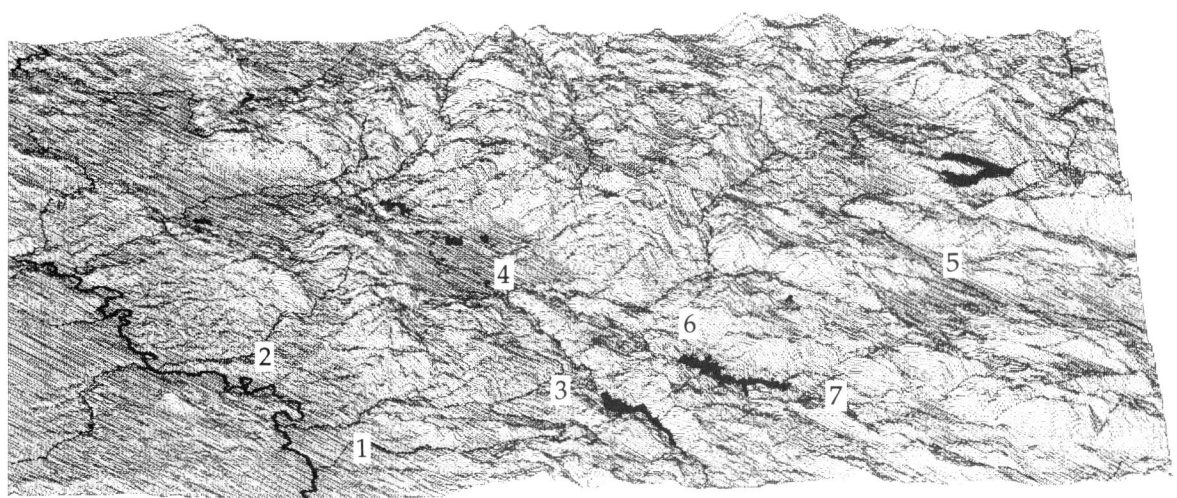

1. Cures Sabini *2. Forum Novum* *3. Trebula Mutuesca* *4. Reate* *5. Amiternum* *6. Cliternia* *7. Nersae*

Fig. 1. *Veduta tridimensionale della Sabina (Elaborazione Enea-Disp, G. Ursino).*

rapidamente i canali di bonifica, ma anche intimamente correlati alle fluttuazioni climatiche di breve e di lungo periodo, di rilevanza nel concorrere a modellare il paesaggio, in particolare in presenza di un importante reticolo idrografico (Veggiani 1990), mentre più controversa appare la valutazione della profondità del loro contributo nei mutamenti dell'agricoltura avvenuti nel lungo periodo (Grigg 1985: 97–108).

I dati ricavati dalle recenti indagini archeologiche di superficie compiute nella conca reatina dall'università di Leicester hanno ampiamente dimostrato e confermato la verosimiglianza di questa ricostruzione, pur sempre ampiamente provvisoria, evidenziando una fitta presenza di insediamenti romani, ville rustiche e fattorie dipendenti, in molti casi risalenti al periodo tardorepubblicano con una continuità di insediamento fino al V-VI secolo (Barker & Mattingly 1989; Coccia & Mattingly 1992), a quote molto basse, in quella zona che è stata recentemente identificata come la ben nota *Rosea*, ricordata dalle fonti classiche (Leggio 1989a).

Indubbiamente, oltre all'intervento umano, le oscillazioni stagionali ed i cicli di lungo periodo di maggior o minor piovosità potevano modificare sensibilmente i rapporti tra le superfici dei laghi, delle paludi e delle terre. La complessità di queste variabili e la difficoltà di ricavare dati oggettivamente affidabili non consente di scendere, in questa fase dell'indagine, in dettagli maggiori.

Le ville rustiche

La grande innovazione nel paesaggio agrario della Sabina tiberina, a partire dal II secolo a.C., fu l'abbandono degli antichi nuclei abitati e la costruzione di imponenti ville rustiche a conduzione schiavistica, che ne mutarono la fisionomia territoriale, anche se continuarono ad esistere, sparse per la campagna, le modeste abitazioni contadine, che potevano in taluni casi addensarsi in nuovi villaggi, sorti gradualmente lungo gli assi viari costruiti o ristrutturati all'indomani della conquista romana. Con la crisi della piccola proprietà contadina l'economia della Sabina dovette progressivamente mutare e concentrarsi su colture intensive che comportarono profonde trasformazioni del paesaggio agrario. L'economia delle ville rustiche in Sabina, si fondò su due basi ben definite: la conduzione schiavistica e la produzione di derrate alimentari destinate al grande mercato (Reggiani 1985; Migliario 1988: 16–22; Leggio 1992: 32–50).

Nella Sabina reatina, un processo simile, senza assumere però le stesse dimensioni dell'area tiberina, si sviluppò probabilmente dal I secolo a.C. nella piana intorno alla città, dove le fonti varroniane ricordano le due ville rustiche del senatore Assio. La prima, quella sita in *angulum Velini*, non aveva mai visto l'opera di un pittore o di un decoratore, mentre la seconda, che era collocata in *Rosea*, era invece adorna di eleganti decorazioni a stucco (Pietrangeli 1976: 35–41; Menotti 1989; Reggiani Massarini 1992: 155–156).

Lungo la valle del Velino, a ridosso della Salaria, sorsero alcune *villae rusticae* di grande imponenza e con grandi scenografie dominate dalle acque nella *pars urbana*, tra le quali le così dette ville di Vespasiano e Tito, il cui sistema economico si basò sia sulla

Fig. 2. Montopoli di Sabina, I Casoni, villa rustica.

coltivazione della fertile piana alluvionale del Velino, sia sulla utilizzazione delle retrostanti aree in quota dei monti Reatini come pascipascoli. In queste aree più interne fu probabilmente minore l'apporto della manodopera servile, mentre più importante fu il contributo della manodopera salariata stagionale. Non a caso un avo di Vespasiano era stato un reclutatore dei salariati che, ogni anno, dall'Umbria scendevano in Sabina per compiervi i lavori agricoli stagionali (Suet. *Vesp.* I, 7).

Le produzioni

L'economia agraria della Sabina tiberina si concentrò su colture specializzate come la vite e l'olivo, delle quali si hanno attestazioni precise fino a tarda epoca imperiale. L'olivicoltura in Sabina acquistò notevole importanza a partire dal I secolo d.C., come attesta Columella. Un grande estimatore dell'olio sabino fu nel II secolo d.C. Galeno, che lo considerava il migliore degli oli allora conosciuti, consigliandolo come base essenziale di molti preparati farmaceutici. Una fama che si mantenne a lungo inalterata.

Anche la viticoltura era abbastanza estesa. Le qualità coltivate erano la *visulla*, un vitigno bianco che allignava bene nelle zone temperate, e la *vinaciola*, ricordata da Plinio il Vecchio come un vitigno caratteristico della sola Sabina. Non ci sono note le caratteristiche dei vini prodotti da queste due qualità di uve, se non indirettamente. A partire dal III secolo d.C., però, dovette iniziare una trasformazione nei gusti del vino a Roma con l'affermarsi sul mercato di vini più leggeri, come i sabini, rispetto a quelli più liquorosi, tanto che, agli inizi del IV secolo d.C., il vino sabino fu calmierato al prezzo massimo nell'editto dioclezianeo. Il vino sabino rimase ancora sul mercato romano fino ai primi decenni del VI secolo d.C., come attesta Cassiodoro che nelle sue lettere lo ricordava ancora.

Un tipico prodotto, in particolare delle aree in quota, fu la così detta «erba sabina» usata sia come medicamento, sia da bruciare sul fuoco per profumare gli ambienti. Per le numerose qualità che possedeva era consigliata tra le erbe di base che un *pater familias* doveva tenere in casa. Altri prodotti caratteristici della Sabina furono i fichi, le pesche della varietà *supernatia*, le ghiande, le mele, oltre ai cereali. Per quanto riguarda l'allevamento, a parte quello degli gli animali domestici necessari alla vita stessa delle ville e delle fattorie dipendenti, fu ampiamente diffuso nella Sabina tiberina quello dei volatili. Un reddito molto elevato si ricavava soprattutto dall'allevamento dei tordi e numerosi erano i rivenditori romani che prendevano in affitto uccelliere in Sabina, per rivenderli nelle stagioni non di passo, al lievitare dei prezzi. Altrettanto importante per le *villae rusticae* più vicine al Tevere doveva essere la produzione dell'*opus doliare*, che, oltre all'autoconsumo ed al commercio locale, poteva essere agevolmente collocato sul grande mercato romano, grazie ai ridotti costi del trasporto via acqua (Leggio 1992: 41–51). Agli inizi del VI secolo è attestata la presenza di peschiere, costruite sbarrando il corso del Tevere, fortemente contraste da Teodorico perché ne impedivano la navigazione (Leggio 1989b: 172). La complessità delle opere, che dovevano fornire una quantità considerevole di pescato, fa ritenere che le peschiere, tra l'altro presenti in numerosi altri grandi fiumi italiani, potessero essere create soltanto nella zona settentrionale della Sabina tiberina, grazie alla minor portata del fiume ed alla minor larghezza dell'alveo.

Un quadro che però mostrava grandi variegature man mano che il paesaggio si modificava risalendo dal Tevere verso i monti Sabini o verso la valle del Turano, con la rarefazione delle ville e delle fattorie (Staffa 1984; Alvino 1993b), il probabile aumento delle dimensioni delle proprietà e dell'incolto e l'incremento delle aree destinate a colture estensive ed a pascipascolo. Dissimili erano infatti le strutture economiche nella Sabina interna. Le differenti caratteristiche climatiche, geomorfologiche e pedologiche hanno condotto alla formazione di un diverso modello di sviluppo economico che vedeva nell'allevamento una delle basi di maggior rilevanza (Pasquinucci 1979; 1990), secondo quanto tramandato da Varrone, che aveva egli stesso importanti interessi nella pastorizia transumante, con le greggi che scendevano fino nei pascoli invernali non soltanto in Puglia, ma anche nel Lazio meridionale, come attestato dalla diffusione di maschere rettangolari di produzione locale lungo gli itinerari di transumanza (Reggiani 1988: 27–28; Alvino 1995), ripresi poi nel medioevo, dopo la crisi tardoantica (Barker & Grant 1991: 40–41).

Oltre all'allevamento delle greggi ovine, un ruolo rilevante veniva svolto dall'allevamento di cavalli, di asini e di muli, che richiedeva un basso impiego di manodopera, servile o salariata, e di risorse. La razza degli asini reatini era una delle più famose in tutta l'area italica, tanto che, a quanto rammentava lo stesso erudito reatino, Rieti ne costituiva il mercato principale, come l'Arcadia lo era in Grecia. Particolarmente apprezzate erano anche le piccole lumache bianche di Rieti, le uniche ricordate dalle fonti come produzione italica, che contendevano il mercato a quelle africane di media dimensione ed a quelle provenienti dall'Illiria, le più grandi. Un ruolo non secondario, anche se quasi esclusivamente a livello locale, doveva poi avere la pesca nei laghi e nei corsi d'acqua, attestata dai numerosi pesi da rete rinvenuti durante le indagini archeologiche di superficie.

La fertilità della piana reatina, favorita dal persistere di condizioni microambientali umide e dallo sfruttamento delle aree limose prosciugate, particolarmente fertili, era così accentuata che una pertica piantata nel terreno il giorno successivo veniva ricoperta dall'erba

Fig. 3. Poggio S. Lorenzo, sostruzioni di villa rustica riutilizzate.

cresciutavi attorno. Conseguente la produzione di canne, mentre la viticoltura era praticata seguendo alcuni accorgimenti precipui, come il sollevare da terra i rami fruttiferi per mezzo di forcelle di legno, in modo da impedire l'azione nefasta dell'umidità (Pietrangeli 1976: 35–41; Menotti 1989; Spadoni Cerroni 1992: 47–55). Il vino prodotto nell'*ager Reatinus*, oltre all'autoconsumo, dovette alimentare esclusivamente il mercato locale, una produzione dunque di qualità non eccellente, dato che le fonti non ricordano vitigni caratteristici dell'area (Tchernia 1986).

Le zone più montuose dell'Appennino, poi, erano caratterizzate dallo sfruttamento come pascolo delle aree in quota e dalla conseguente espansione dell'allevamento transumante, mentre nelle conche intermontane si svilupparono forme di sfruttamento del suolo da parte di piccoli e medi proprietari sia attraverso una gestione diretta dei fondi, sia attraverso forme di mezzadria e di colonìa. Nell'area sabina oggi inclusa nell'Abruzzo, la zona di Amiterno presentava una economia abbastanza eterogenea, influenzata dalla posizione del municipio sabino, un importante punto di incontro di numerose direttrici viarie. Attestate sia attività artigianali, come le arti della falegnameria o della lana, sia attività connesse con l'allevamento, sia intense attività nel campo ortofrutticolo – cipolle, navoni – mentre destinata soltanto al mercato locale, come nel caso del Reatino, sembra essere la produzione del vino, pur essendo attestato un vitigno tipico per l'Amiternino, la *pumula* (Segenni 1985: 75–96; Buonocore 1986).

Il Cicolano

Risalendo la valle del Salto, sempre più profondi si fanno i legami con le aree più interne dell'Appennino. Lo stesso toponimo 'Cicolano' ricorda lo stanziamento nell'area degli *Aequiculi*. Qui le tappe della romanizzazione hanno seguito ritmi diversi, anche se non dissimili, rispetto alla Sabina. In quest'area, inoltre, la più difficile situazione ambientale ha profondamente condizionato le forme dell'insediamento, rarefacendone la trama e riducendone la consistenza.

Le indagini archeologiche di superficie condotte su alcuni altipiani intermontani della catena del Velino, Rascino, Aquilente, Campolasca, hanno mostrato una occupazione ed uno sfruttamento delle aree in quota concentrato tra la fine della repubblica ed i primi secoli dell'impero, con un rapido abbandono degli insediamenti da parte degli agricoltori residenti, dei pastori stanziali e di quelli transumanti, ad indicare una rapida crisi dello sfruttamento delle aree marginali appenniniche (Barker & Grant 1991), estesa, a quanto sembra, lungo la dorsale fino almeno all'area emiliana (Bollini 1971).

Il baricentro territoriale dell'alta valle del Salto in età romana fu il centro abitato di *Nersae*, che sorgeva non lontano da Pescorocchiano, nucleo di gravitazione della nebulosa di piccoli villaggi che costituivano la *Res publica Aequiculanorum*, mentre nella media valle del Salto sorgeva l'altro piccolo municipio della zona, *Cliternia* (Pietrangeli 1976: 75–86; Staffa 1984; Perotti 1989; Alvino 1993a).

Le strutture economiche del Cicolano dovettero essere fortemente influenzate da quelle dei municipi vicini di Carsioli e di Alba Fucens, situati lungo la via Valeria. In particolare Alba dovette fungere da centro di approvvigionamento di tegole e di mattoni prodotti in zona e di ridistribuzione del sale importato (Buonocore 1986), di estrema importanza nelle economie basate sulla pastorizia.

Peraltro un forte ostacolo allo sviluppo di forme di coltivazioni intensive dovette essere costituito dal forte contrasto del paesaggio che mutava con grande rapidità, passando dagli sterili terreni rocciosi difficilmente lavorabili degli angusti fondovalle (*duris Aequicula glaebis*, Verg. *Aen.* 7, 747; *rastrisque domant Aequicula rura*, Sil. It. 8,369), al fitto mantello vegetazionale che copriva buona parte della regione, ambiente ideale per la caccia (*multo venatu nemorum*, Verg. *Aen.* 7, 746–747). Un altro apporto non secondario all'economia della zona dovette essere dato dalla raccolta della *consiligo*, una pianta diffusa anche nella Marsica, scoperta in età pliniana e considerata estremamente efficace contro le malattie polmonari degli animali (Plin. *Nat.Hist.* 25, 86).

Le fonti epigrafiche ed i vari frammenti appartenenti a monumenti funerari o ad altri edifici pubblici e privati, riutilizzati ampiamente in pievi, chiese e cappelle del Cicolano, attestano, almeno tra la tarda repubblica ed i primi secoli dell'impero, una consistente occupazione ed una forte utilizzazione del suolo, centuriato ed assegnato, sia da un punto di vista agricolo, sia da un punto di vista dell'allevamento ovino, transumante verticalmente od orizzontalmente, che consentì l'affermazione sociale di alcune famiglie della zona, giunte fino al rango senatorio (Torelli 1982: 170, 192).

Le vie di comunicazione: le vie d'acqua

E' senza dubbio superfluo enfatizzare più di tanto l'importanza rivestita nell'antichità dal trasporto via acqua delle merci e delle derrate alimentari. Nella Sabina la più rilevante via d'acqua è stata senza molti dubbi il Tevere. Ovviamente l'attività principale concerneva il tratto del fiume che da Roma scendeva verso il mare, anche se, nel tratto a monte, si svolgeva un rilevante movimento di uomini e di merci. Non sono molti i porti sicuramente attestati lungo il Tevere in Sabina, il più noto è quello di *Cures Sabini*, ricordato in un frammento di epigrafe e sicuramente attivo a cavaliere tra III e IV secolo d.C.

L'importanza del Tevere come principale via commerciale che collegava la Sabina a Roma non scemò del tutto neppure con la grave crisi demografica e la profonda depressione economica che colpirono progressivamente l'impero romano a partire dal III secolo d.C., infatti un intenso traffico di battelli di varia dimensione che ne scendevano il corso è ricordato ancora tra V e VI secolo (Leggio 1989b: 172). Per quanto riguarda la Sabina interna, è il Velino, in collegamento con il sistema lacuale nato dalla bonifica curiana, l'unica via d'acqua che potrebbe aver avuto un ruolo non marginale, anche se soltanto a livello locale, considerato il punto di rottura alla cascata delle Marmore.

Le vie di terra

La via più importante che attraversava la Sabina era la Salaria, che, come induce a supporre il nome e come conferma Festo, era il tracciato lungo il quale, a partire già dall'VIII-VII secolo a.C., i Sabini importavano il sale dalle saline poste sulla sponda destra del Tevere, alla confluenza nel Tirreno. Dopo aver seguito per un certo tratto la valle del Tevere, la Salaria, il cui tracciato fu completamente ristrutturato dopo la romanizzazione con tempi e modi non completamente chiariti, se ne distaccava dopo il XVIII miglio, per dirigersi verso l'interno, mentre un diverticolo, ben evidenziato dalla *tabula peutingeriana*, procedeva verso nord, in parallelo al Tevere. Tra le principali opere d'arte da ricordare in questo tratto il ponte del Diavolo ed il ponte Sambuco. Giunta a Rieti, il principale nodo stradale dell'intera Sabina, dal quale si irradiava un fascio di importanti vie che si diramavano lungo le valli del Turano (Staffa 1983), del Salto e la conca reatina in direzione di Spoleto e Terni (Reggiani Massarini 1992: 141–148), la Salaria si dirigeva verso l'Adriatico risalendo la valle del Velino.

Dalle *Aquae Cutiliae*, dopo sei miglia si giungeva ad Antrodoco, importante nodo viario posto a 64 miglia da Roma, dove dal tracciato principale si staccava un diverticolo che conduceva a Pitino ed Amiterno, nell'alta valle dell'Aterno, mentre la Salaria proseguiva lungo l'alta valle del Velino, caratterizzata da alti picchi e anguste gole scavate nel calcare dall'erosione del fiume, costituendo la struttura portante dei collegamenti tra le aree appenniniche e transappenniniche e la conca di Rieti, prima di immettersi nella valle del Tronto, fatto questo che costrinse i romani a compiere grandi tagliate ed imponenti opere sostruttive (Pietrangeli 1976: 43–56; Radke 1981: 325–343; Wiseman 1987: 138–144; Coarelli 1988: 41; Alvino & Leggio 1994).

Epilogo

Per la Sabina tiberina, se le fonti scritte mostrano per la I metà del VI secolo un tessuto economico e sociale non ancora lacerato in profondità, ma sostenuto dalle richieste di derrate alimentari che dovevano provenire dal mercato romano, è dalla II metà del secolo che sembra determinarsi una frattura consistente, provocata non tanto dalle guerre gotiche, dato che la Sabina ne fu praticamente immune, o dalle ricorrenti epidemie, ma dallo stanziamento longobardo, che venne a sovrapporsi, aggravandole, alla crisi demografica ed alla depressione economica già presenti. Gli accadimenti del VI secolo dunque decretarono la fine del mondo antico e del suo sistema politico, economico e sociale nella Sabina tiberina.

Nel Reatino, invece, la sopravvivenza della curia fin sulla metà del VI secolo, attesta il perdurare di forme istituzionali locali legate ai *possessores* tardoantichi fin allo stanziamento longobardo e quindi una utilizzazione del suolo e forme di economia ancora in atto, anche se sfuggono molti dettagli, con Rieti che divenne sede di un importante gastaldato del ducato di Spoleto, a confine con il ducato bizantino di Roma.

Non si conoscono invece le tappe della crisi dei piccoli municipi interni, sorretti da una economia fragile, soggetta quindi, più rapidamente delle altre aree, alla depressione economica ed alla caduta demografica tardoimperiale. Peraltro il semplice fatto che nessuno di questi divenne sede di diocesi, dà conto delle ridotte

Fig. 4. Torricella, via Salaria, ponte Sambuco.

dimensioni degli insediamenti, anche se non possono essere sottovalutate le possibili resistenze alla penetrazione del cristianesimo in aree interne che potevano presentare forti difficoltà ad accettare una trasformazione non soltanto religiosa, ma anche sociale e culturale così profonda (Leggio 1989b: 170-176).

Bibliografia

Alvino, G. 1993a. 'Indagini sul sito di Nersae', *Archeologia Laziale*, XI, 225-233.
Alvino, G. 1993b. 'La valle del Turano in età romana. Evidenze archeologiche e prospettive di ricerca', *Il Territorio*, 9, 109-120.
Alvino, G. 1995. 'Santuari, culti e paesaggio in un'area italica: il Cicolano', *Archeologia Laziale*, XII, 2, 475-483.
Alvino, G. & Leggio, T. 1994. 'La Sabina e la Salaria', in *I sistemi vari del Lazio antico – La Salaria*, Atti del Convegno, Magliano Sabino c.s.
Barker, G. & Mattingly, D. 1989. 'The countryside of Roman Sabina', *Il Territorio*, 5, 33-44.
Barker, G. & Grant, A. (eds.) 1991. 'Ancient and modern pastoralism in central Italy: an interdisciplinary study in the Cicolano mountains', *Papers of the British School at Rome*, 59, 15-88.
Bollini, M. 1971. 'Semirutarum urbium cadavera', *Rivista Storica dell'Antichità*, 1, 163-176.
Buonocore, M. 1986. 'Insediamenti e forme economiche nell'Abruzzo romano dei due primi secoli dell'impero', *Studi Classici e Orientali*, 36, 279-292.
Chouqueur, G. 1990. 'Morphologie agraire antique du territoire de Reate', in Consiglio, R., *Rieti. Evoluzione di una struttura urbana*, Napoli, 40-56.
Coarelli, F. 1988. 'Colonizzazione romana e viabilità', *Dialoghi di Archeologia*, s. 3, 6, 35-48.
Coccia, S. & Mattingly, D. (eds.) 1992. 'Settlement history, environment and human exploitation of an intermontane basin in the central Appennines: the Rieti survey, 1988-1991, part 1', *Papers of the British School at Rome*, 60, 213-289.
Grigg D. 1985. *La dinamica del mutamento in agricoltura*, Bologna.
Leggio, T. 1989a. 'Nota topografica sulla conca reatina: la Rosea nelle fonti scritte medievali. Contributo alla sua delimitazione spaziale', *Il Territorio*, 5, 59-63.
Leggio, T. 1989b. 'Forme di insediamento in Sabina e nel Reatino nel medioevo', *Bullettino dell'Istituto Storico Italiano per il Medio Evo e Archivio Muratoriano*, 95, 165-201.
Leggio, T. & Serva, L. 1991. 'La bonifica della piana reatina dall'età romana al medioevo. Influenze sui mutamenti del paesaggio', *Sicurezza e Protezione*, 25/26, 61-70.
Leggio, T. 1992. *Da Cures Sabini all'abbazia di Farfa*, Passo Corese.
Menotti, E.M. 1989. 'La piana reatina: la così detta villa d'Assio alle Grotte di S. Nicola, un esempio di uso del suolo in età romana', *Il Territorio*, 5, 49-58.
Migliario, E. 1988. *Strutture della proprietà agraria in Sabina dall'età imperiale all'alto Medioevo*, Firenze.
Pasquinucci, M. 1979. 'La transumanza nell'Italia romana', in E. Gabba & M. Pasquinucci, *Strutture agrarie e allevamento transumante nell'Italia romana*, Pisa, 79-182.
Pasquinucci, M. 1990. 'Aspetti dell'allevamento transumante nell'Italia centro-meridionale fra l'età arcaica e il medioevo. Il caso della Sabina', *Rivista di Studi Liguri*, 56, 165-177.
Perotti, M.F. 1989. 'Per la storia degli Aequiculi in età romana', *Il Territorio*, 5, 15-31.
Pietrangeli, C. 1976. 'La Sabina nell'antichità', in Aa.Vv., *Rieti e il suo territorio*, Milano, 11-105.
Radke, G. 1981. *Viae publicae romanae*, Bologna.
Reggiani, A.M. 1985. 'La villa rustica nell'agro sabino', in *Misurare la terra: centuriazione e coloni nel mondo romano. Città, agricoltura, commercio: materiali da Roma e dal suburbio*, Modena, 61-65.
Reggiani Massarini, A.M. 1988. *Santuario degli Equicoli a Corvaro, oggetti votivi del Museo Nazionale Romano*, Roma.
Reggiani Massarini, A.M. 1992. 'Territorio e città', in Spadoni Cerroni, M.C. & Reggiani Massarini, A.M., *Reate*, Pisa, 125-193.
Segenni, S. 1985. *Amiternum e il suo territorio in età romana*, Pisa.
Spadoni Cerroni, M.C. 1992. 'Rieti in età romana', in Spadoni Cerroni, M.C. & Reggiani Massarini, A.M., *Reate*, Pisa.
Staffa, A.R. 1983. 'La viabilità romana della valle del Turano', *Xenia*, 6, 37-44.
Staffa, A.R. 1984. 'L'assetto territoriale della Valle del Turano nell'alto medioevo', *Archeologia Classica*, 36, 231-265.
Staffa, A.R. 1987. 'L'assetto territoriale della Valle del Salto fra la tarda antichità e il medioevo', *Xenia*, 13, 45-84.
Tchernia, A. 1986. *Le vin de l'Italie romaine. Essai d'histoire économique d'après les amphores*, Rome.
Torelli, M. 1982. 'Ascesa al Senato e rapporti con i territori d'origine. Italia: regio IV (Samnium)', in *Epigrafia e ordine senatorio*, II, Roma, 165-199.
Traina, G. 1988. *Paludi e bonifiche nel mondo antico*, Roma.
Traina, G. 1990. *Ambiente e paesaggi di Roma antica*, Roma.
Veggiani, A. 1990. 'Fluttuazioni climatiche e trasformazioni ambientali nel territorio imolese dall'alto medioevo all'età moderna', in *Imola nel medioevo*, I, Imola, 41-102.
Wiseman, T.P. 1987. *Roman Studies: Literary and Historical*, Liverpool.

22

Paesaggio Agrario e Produzioni Artigianali nell'Etruria Settentrionale Costiera (Ager Pisanus e Volaterranus)

MARINELLA PASQUINUCCI, SIMONETTA MENCHELLI
(Dipartimento di Scienze Storiche del Mondo Antico, Università di Pisa)

Sommario: *Ricerche condotte nella Toscana nord-occidentale permettono di delineare la storia del territorio pisano e delle aree adiacenti, quella del relativo popolamento e delle attività economiche in un arco cronologico compreso fra la preistoria ed il medioevo. Il territorio esaminato si articola in una fascia costiera e nel retroterra, esteso a Nord e a Sud del fiume Arno. Nel territorio, agli insediamenti preromani si sovrappone, alla fine del I sec. a.C., la centuriazione, connessa con la colonia* Opsequens Iulia Pisana *e accompagnata da una radicale riorganizzazione dell'insediamento rurale e delle attività produttive. In età tardorepubblicana ed imperiale le fonti letterarie documentano attività cantieristiche, commercio del legname, lo sfruttamento delle cave di pietra del Monte Pisano. In questo contributo si esamina in modo particolare lo sviluppo dell'economia dell'*ager Pisanus *e* Volaterranus.

INSEDIAMENTO E PAESAGGIO (M.P.)

Presentiamo una breve sintesi di ricerche topografico-archeologiche effettuate in alcune aree dell'Etruria settentrionale costiera, comprese fra la Bassa Versilia (Pietrasanta), il Monte Pisano, il fiume Era e la Bassa Val di Cecina, grosso modo corrispondente, nell'assetto municipale, all'*ager Pisanus* (confine settentrionale l'antico corso del Versilia; confine meridionale il fiume Fine; orientale il fiume Era?) e a parte del *Volaterranus* occidentale (Bassa Val di Cecina) (Fig.1). Il nostro lavoro si articola in indagini di superficie (con copertura totale, da estendere all'intero territorio sopra citato e monitoraggio delle aree non arate), saggi di scavo, recupero di dati di archivio, studio della toponomastica. L'arco cronologico si estende dalla più antica frequentazione (paleolitico inferiore nel territorio livornese, paleolitico medio nel basso Valdarno) a tutto il Medioevo.

Ricerche interdisciplinari hanno permesso di delineare l'evoluzione geomorfologica, cospicua nella fascia costiera da Luni a Livorno, e in particolare le oscillazioni della linea di riva, databili, in epoca storica, in base alla distribuzione degli insediamenti antichi e post-antichi (Mazzanti & Pasquinucci 1983; Mazzanti *et alii* 1990) (Fig.2). Fra questi, costituiscono un sistema di porti e di approdi, attivi, con aspetti di continuità e di discontinuità, dall'età arcaica al tardo-antico e in alcuni casi oltre, i seguenti siti ubicati a Nord del promontorio livornese e lungo la linea di riva di (almeno) V-I sec. a.C.:

- Foce del Versilia, presso l'odierna Pietrasanta (area Pisanica: età arcaica, Bonamici 1990: 158 ss.; età romana, Menchelli 1990: 412 ss.) (Fig. 1, P).

- San Rocchino (VIII-III sec. a.C., Maggiani 1990: 69 ss.; età romana, Cristofani 1975: 191; età tardo-romana e alto-medievale, Ciampoltrini, Notini & Rendini 1991: 712 ss.) (Fig. 1, SR).

- Isola di Migliarino, alla foce del Serchio (dal VII sec. a.C. al V-VI sec. d.C., Vecchiano 1988: 79 ss.) (Fig.1, CM).

- San Piero a Grado (dal VII sec. a.C. al II sec. d.C., Coltano 1986: 181 ss.) (Fig. 1, SP).

- *Portus Pisanus* (utilizzato almeno dall'età tardo-repubblicana e sino al tardo-antico, esplicitamente menzionato nell'*Itinerarium maritimum*, databile agli inizi del III secolo: Pasquinucci & Mazzanti 1987; Pasquinucci & Rossetti 1988) (Fig. 1, PP).

A Sud di Livorno la fascia costiera è caratterizzata, in epoca storica, da stabilità nella porzione rocciosa, e da modeste oscillazioni della linea di riva a Sud di Castiglioncello; sono intuibili o documentati scali alla foce delle vallette del promontorio livornese, e porti a Castiglioncello e a Vada, loc. Pontile (*Vada Volaterrana*): Cherubini 1987; Del Rio 1987; Cherubini, Del Rio & Mazzanti 1987 (Fig. 1). Per quanto riguarda il complesso problema della idrografia, sono da segnalare modifiche, anche moderne, del corso dell'Arno e soprattutto del

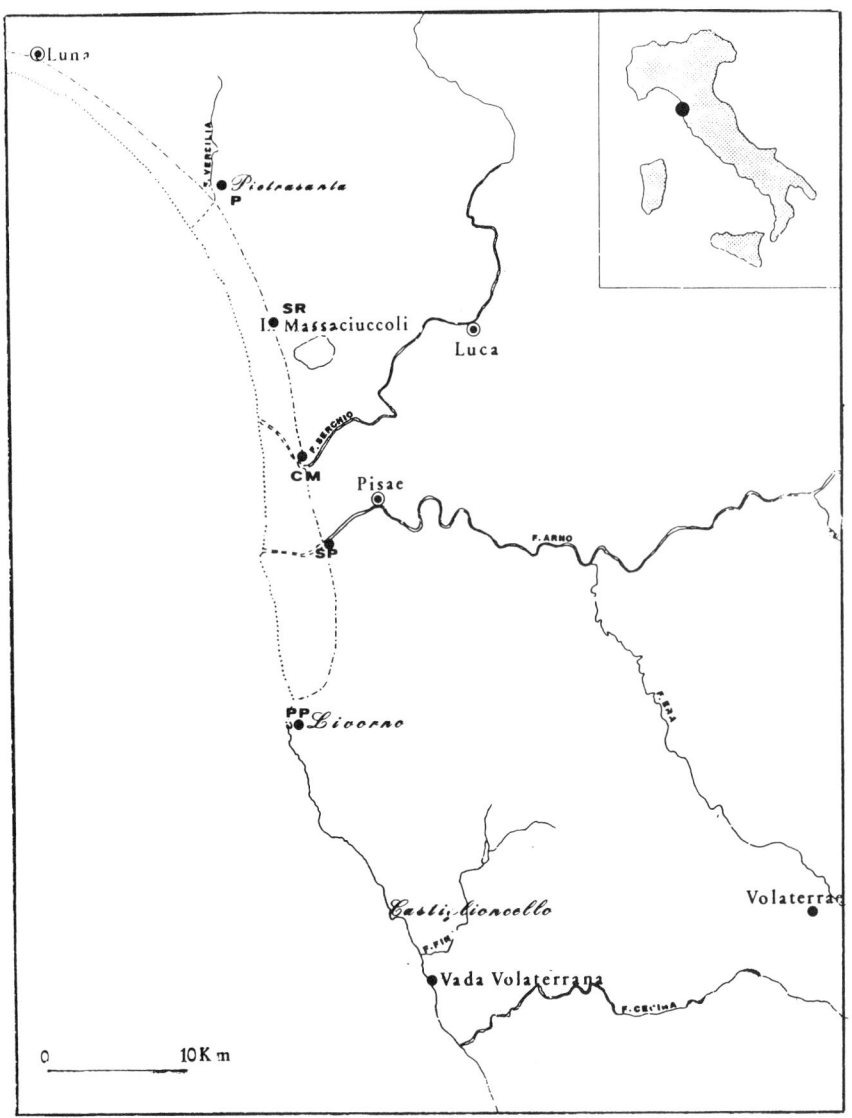

Fig. 1. Il territorio in esame con i principali porti/approdi:
P = Pisanica
SR = San Rocchino
CM = Isola de Migliarino (Cava Mori)
Pisae
SP = San Piero a Grado
PP = Portus Pisanus
Vada Volaterrana
------------ Linea di riva del I–II sec. a.C.

Serchio-*Auser-Auserculus*, secondo le fonti antiche e indagini aerofotografiche confluente nell'Arno a Pisa e attualmente, nel suo corso inferiore, con andamento Est-Ovest e foce a Nord-Ovest di Pisa: Federici & Mazzanti 1989 (fig. 1).

Le ricognizioni hanno permesso di individuare tracce della frequentazione preistorica, di presenze protostoriche e del successivo popolamento etrusco, l'organizzazione del territorio conseguente alla deduzione della *Colonia Opsequens Iulia Pisana* effettuata negli ultimi decenni del I sec. a.C., a quanto pare ad opera di Ottaviano, e aspetti del tessuto insediativo di età medievale (Pasquinucci & Storti 1989; Pasquinucci 1992). I siti di età ellenistica, distribuiti sia nelle aree di pianura che in quelle collinari, costiere ed interne (fig. 3), hanno restituito, accanto a vasellame di produzione locale, materiali importati da aree italiche ed extra-italiche: anfore greco-italiche di produzione campano-laziale; "petites estampilles" dal territorio rurale a Nord di Pisa; piattello "Genucilia" e anfore puniche dalle aree costiere a Sud della città; ceramica iberica ("sombreros de copa") dal retroterra di *Vada Volaterrana* (Coltano 1986; Cherubini 1987; Vaggioli 1990: 144 ss.). Questi ritrovamenti sono un indice della vitalità degli insediamenti al momento identificati, nella cui economia doveva avere un ruolo importante la produzione di vino, attestata da manifatture locali di anfore greco-italiche, individuate su base minero-petrografica (argille della piana terminale dell'Arno: Vecchiano 1988: 130 ss.; D'Ambrosio, Mannoni & Sfrecola 1989).

Il vasellame di manifattura locale, le cui fornaci cominciano ad essere individuate (fig. 4), e la cui produzione accertata su base minero-petrografica e chimica (Coltano 1986; Vecchiano 1988; Pasquinucci & Storti 1989; Von Schnurbein 1982), consiste in ceramica a scisti microclastici, "grigia" e a vernice nera. Presumibilmente, oltre che in ambito "pisano", tali ceramiche erano commercializzate lungo le coste alto-tirreniche e liguri (Milanese & Mannoni 1986: 117 ss., con riferimento al vasellame a scisti microclastici). La deduzione della colonia di veterani sopra citata comportò un riassetto urbano (le cui caratteristiche ed entità sono in parte documentate da recenti scavi in corso di studio), e un cospicuo intervento territoriale, con l'impianto di una *limitatio* estesa nella bassa Versilia e dalle rive meridionali (antiche) del lago di Massaciuccoli a Coltano e almeno al fiume Era (fig. 3). Il modulo risulta di 20 *actus* (710 m circa), l'orientamento NE-SW, con declinazione leggermente diversificata nei vari settori (ad esempio nel territorio a Nord di Pisa (Vecchiano) di 29° 25' dal Nord; nell'area di Cascina 28° 33'; a Coltano 31° 25'), non apprezzabile nella fig. 3 in conseguenza della scala (Fraccaro 1939; Ciampoltrini 1981; Menchelli 1984 e 1990; Pasquinucci 1986; Vaggioli 1990; Mazzanti 1994).

Nelle aree al momento indagate il popolamento

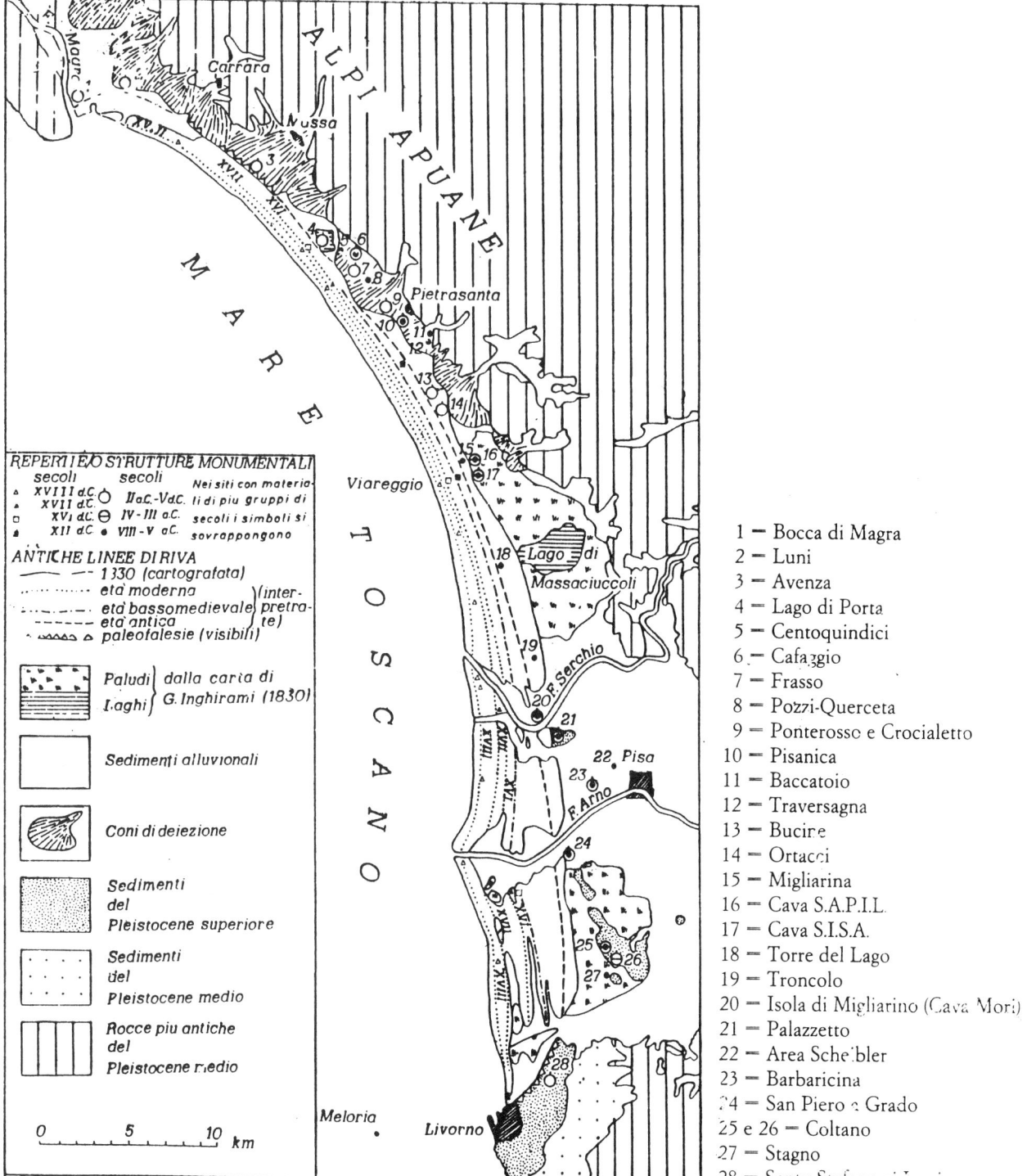

Fig. 2. *Lineamenti geo-morfologici del territorio lunense-pisano (da Mazzanti et alii 1990).*

rurale, sia nel territorio centuriato sia nelle zone collinari apparentemente esterne alla *limitatio*, gravitanti sulla grande viabilità e sulle vie d'acqua, appare capillare e consiste in unità insediative (*villae*) di una certa dignità architettonica (strutture in pietra, mattone crudo o semicotto intonacato, pavimentazione in parte litoide, colonne in laterizio, copertura con *tegulae* e *imbrices*, finestre a vetri). Tali edifici, dei quali spesso sono state identificate le relative necropoli, sono contestuali alla deduzione della colonia di veterani e in massima parte attivi sino al IV-V sec. d.C.. Essi documentano una capillare diffusione e razionalizzazione del popolamento rurale in tutte le aree di pianura e in quelle collinari meridionali sino ai fiumi Fine e Cecina. Tale popolamento in parte si sovrappose o si giustappose (senza soluzione di continuità?) ai siti di età ellenistica. Allo stato attuale delle conoscenze sembra fare eccezione l'area dei Monti dell'Oltre Serchio, caratterizzati da siti d'altura di IV-III sec. a.C. (fig. 3), rioccupati soltanto in età (alto)-medievale.

Nel paesaggio agrario dell'*ager Pisanus* un ruolo importante doveva ricoprire la coltivazione dei cereali: secondo Plinio (*Nat. Hist.* 18, 86–87), Pisa era nota per la produzione di una varietà di grano comune (*siligo*), un cereale d'inverno la cui farina permetteva di ottenere pane e *pistrinarumque opera* della più alta qualità. In particolare, la mescolanza della *siligo* campana con quella "pisana" garantiva i risultati più apprezzabili (*Nat. Hist.* 18, 86). Un altro cereale che Plinio ricorda prodotto nel territorio pisano è l'*alica*, coltivata in Italia in parecchie località, fra cui il territorio veronese e la Campania, dalla quale proveniva la più nota (18, 109). Plinio (*Nat. Hist.* 14, 39) menziona Pisa anche per la produzione di uva detta *Pariana* (forse dall'antroponimo *Parius/Parianus*: tale dato trova conferma archeologica nelle manifatture locali di anfore vinarie (cfr. oltre). Il territorio pisano doveva essere inoltre ricco di boschi che fornivano abbondante e pregiato legname, utilizzato in loco per la cantieristica navale, e a Roma per l'edilizia (Strabone 5, 2, 5).

Fabri navales e *fabri tignarii* sono attestati anche epigraficamente (CIL XI,1436), e la loro attività è documentata sino al tardo-antico (Claudio, *Bell. Gild.*, 483); Strabone dà rilievo anche all'attività di estrazione e lavorazione della pietra, con tutta probabilità proveniente dalle cave del Monte Pisano (Strabone 5, 2, 5 - su cui Pasquinucci 1988; Ciampoltrini 1991).

Economia e "Industria" (S.M.)

Per quanto riguarda la produzione di ceramiche, di anfore e di laterizi, sono già note manifatture di terra sigillata italica e tardo-italica in Pisa (fornace di *Ateius* e dei suoi lavoranti in area S. Zeno: Taponecco Marchini 1974; matrice per terra sigillata tardo-italica rinvenuta fuori contesto in Lungarno Pacinotti: Pucci 1975) e nel territorio (fig. 1, CM: Isola di Migliarino: Menchelli & Vaggioli 1987; Vecchiano 1988: 95 ss.). Ad esse si aggiunge un recente rinvenimento (estate 1991) nel suburbio settentrionale di Pisa romana, in prossimità dell'antico *Auser*. Sotto tombe alla capuccina di età imperiale avanzata è stato individuato uno scarico di terra sigillata italica e tardo-italica, con 1145 frammenti pari ad almeno 493 esemplari, molti dei quali con difetti di cottura. 9 esemplari sono bollati da *Cneus Ateius Arretinus*, 2 da *Cneus Ateius Mahes* e 36 da vasai tardo-italici; dallo scavo provengono inoltre alcuni nuclei di argilla vetrificata. Evidentemente nell'area erano ubicate una o più manifatture gestite da lavoranti di *Ateius* nel periodo grosso modo compreso, a giudicare dalla cronologia delle forme prodotte, fra l'estrema età augustea e il 40–50 d.C. Nella stessa area si impiantarono una o più manifatture tardo-italiche, la cui attività è testimoniata sino all'80–90 d.C. (Menchelli 1992). Questo rinvenimento costituisce un'ulteriore prova del legame, spaziale e temporale, fra le manifatture pisane di *Ateius* e la produzione tardo-italica, già evidenziato dalle strette analogie fra i corpi ceramici e dalle modalità tecniche di produzione (Menchelli & Vaggioli 1987; Vecchiano 1988, 95 ss.; Menchelli 1994).

Altre fornaci con prodotti bollati da *Cneus Ateius* e da *Lucius Rasinius Pisanus* sono state individuate nell'*ager Pisanus* meridionale e nel limitrofo *Volaterranus* costiero, fra Rosignano M.mo e Cecina, in particolare in prossimità del fiume Fine (Cherubini & Del Rio 1992; 1994; Del Rio *et alii* 1995) (Fig. 4). Il toponimo Rosignano documenta l'antica presenza dei *praedia* appartenenti ai *Rasinii*. Si sta dunque delineando un sistema di molteplici centri produttivi ubicati in Pisa e lungo la costa, gestiti prima da *Ateius* e dai suoi lavoranti e poi, in prosieguo di tempo, dai vasai tardo-italici. L'elemento costante è la vicinanza ai corsi d'acqua: come è noto l'acqua è indispensabile nel processo produttivo della ceramica; la prossimità di un fiume poteva inoltre garantire un veloce rifornimento delle altre materie prime (ad esempio il legname, tramite fluitazione), nonchè una rapida commercializzazione del vasellame prodotto. Studi recenti (Von Schnurbein 1982; Ettlinger 1983 e 1990; Moutinho De Alarcao 1975; Lavizzari Pedrazzini 1984; Pucci 1985; Guery 1987; Medri 1992) hanno rivelato sia la cospicua quantità, sia l'ampia area di commercializzazione della terra sigillata "pisana" (e in particolar modo di quella prodotta nelle botteghe di *Ateius*) lungo il *limes* germanico (ad Haltern, *Vindonissa*, *Novaesium*), nella Gallia meridionale, a *Conimbriga*, in *Britannia* e nella fascia costiera del Mediterraneo occidentale. Dall'età augustea ad almeno gli inizi del II sec. d.C. la produzione della terra sigillata rivestì dunque un ruolo importante nell'economia pisana, anche in connessione con le forniture all'esercito (Crawford 1981: 271 ss.; Pucci 1985: 370).

Produzioni locali di anfore databili dall'età tardo-

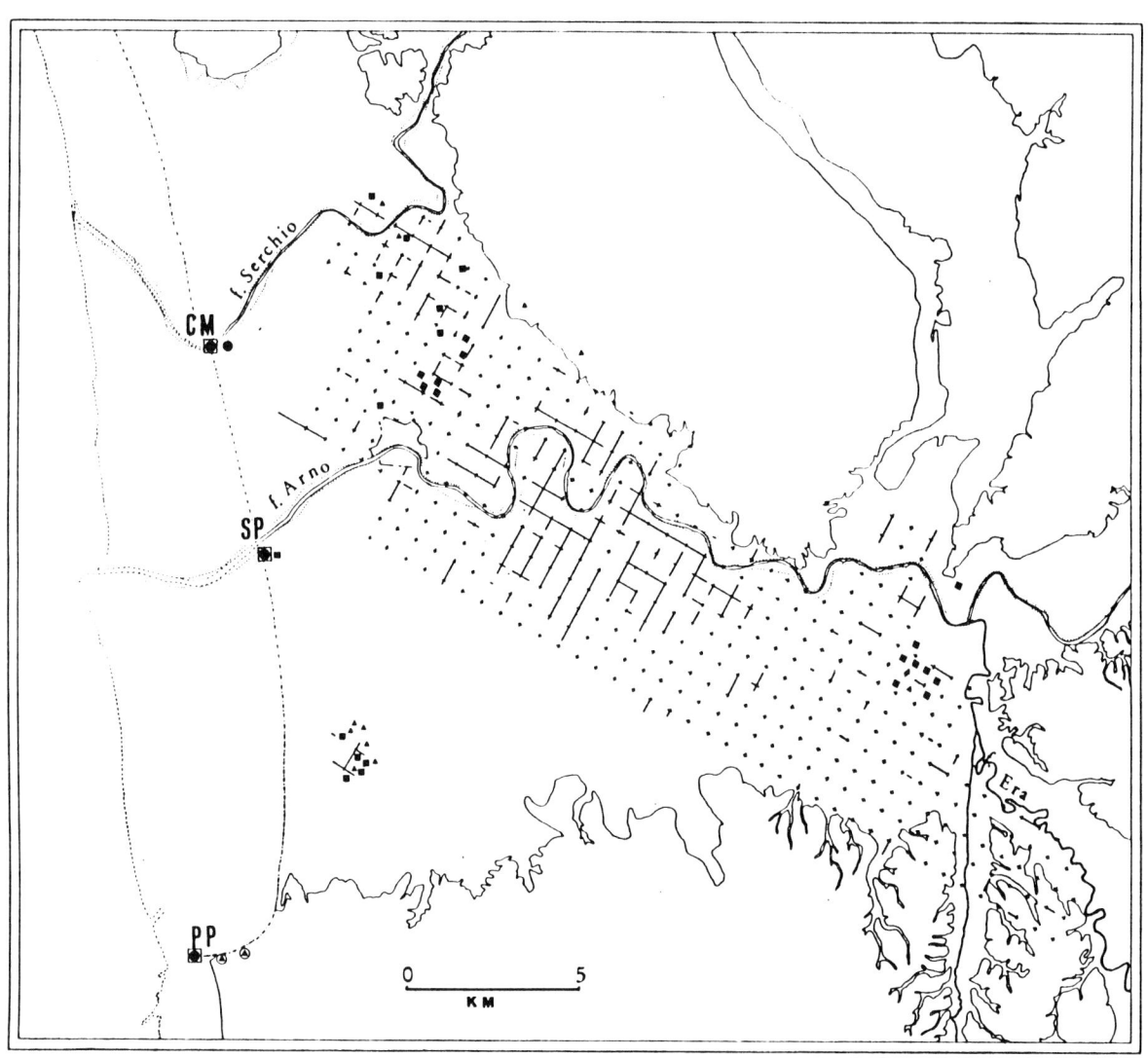

Fig. 3. La centuriazione dell'ager Pisanus.
▲ siti di età preromana   ■ fattorie di età romana   ⊙ fornaci

repubblicana al tardo-impero, già individuate su base minero-petrografica (Pasquinucci *et alii* 1989; D'Ambrosio, Mannoni & Sfrecola 1989), sono state confermate dal rinvenimento di fornaci in una decina di località dell'*ager Pisanus* centro meridionale e nel limitrofo *ager Volaterranus* costiero (fig. 4: loc. Campacci, loc. Vallimbuio: Dressel 2–4; fra Rosignano M.mo e Cecina: Dressel 1, Dressel 2–4, anfora cosiddetta di Forlimpopoli (Ostia IV, 440-441; Ostia I, 452/Ostia IV, 442: Menchelli 1990–1991; Esposito 1992; Cherubini & Del Rio 1994; Del Rio *et alii* 1995). Tali fornaci risultano distribuite, quasi esclusivamente, nella fascia costiera, o comunque in prossimità di corsi d'acqua e della grande viabilità, sia in connessione con *villae*, sia in aree apparentemente adibite alle sole attività artigianali (ad esempio loc. Vallimbuio, nell'immediato retroterra di *Portus Pisanus*; loc. Mazzanta, in destra del Cecina: scavi Soprintendenza Archeolgica della Toscana).

Ai contenitori vinari citati va aggiunta la produzione locale di anfore cosiddette "di Spello" (Ostia II, 521/ Ostia III, 369–370) e di Empoli (Ostia IV, 279), delle quali al momento non sono stati individuati scorti di fornace, ma le cui paste ceramiche presentano strette analogie con quelle di esemplari sicuramente "pisani" o "volterrani" (cfr. bibl. sopra citata).

La notazione pliniana (*Nat Hist.* 14, 39) relativa all'uva *Pariana* del territorio pisano trova riscontro archeologico nella manifattura di contenitori vinari, la cui commercializzazione è difficile da definire attraverso il materiale edito, in assenza di numerosi bolli e *tituli picti*, nonchè di sistematiche indagini archeometriche. Analisi chimiche effettuate su anfore Dressel 2–4 di località elvetiche, peraltro, hanno rivelato ad *Augusta Raurica* (Augst) e forse ad *Aventicum* (Avenches) esemplari prodotti in un'area compresa fra Rosignano M.mo e Cecina (Thierrin Michael 1992: 50 ss.).

La produzione e commercializzazione del vino del medio e basso Valdarno e dell'*ager Volaterranus* costiero,

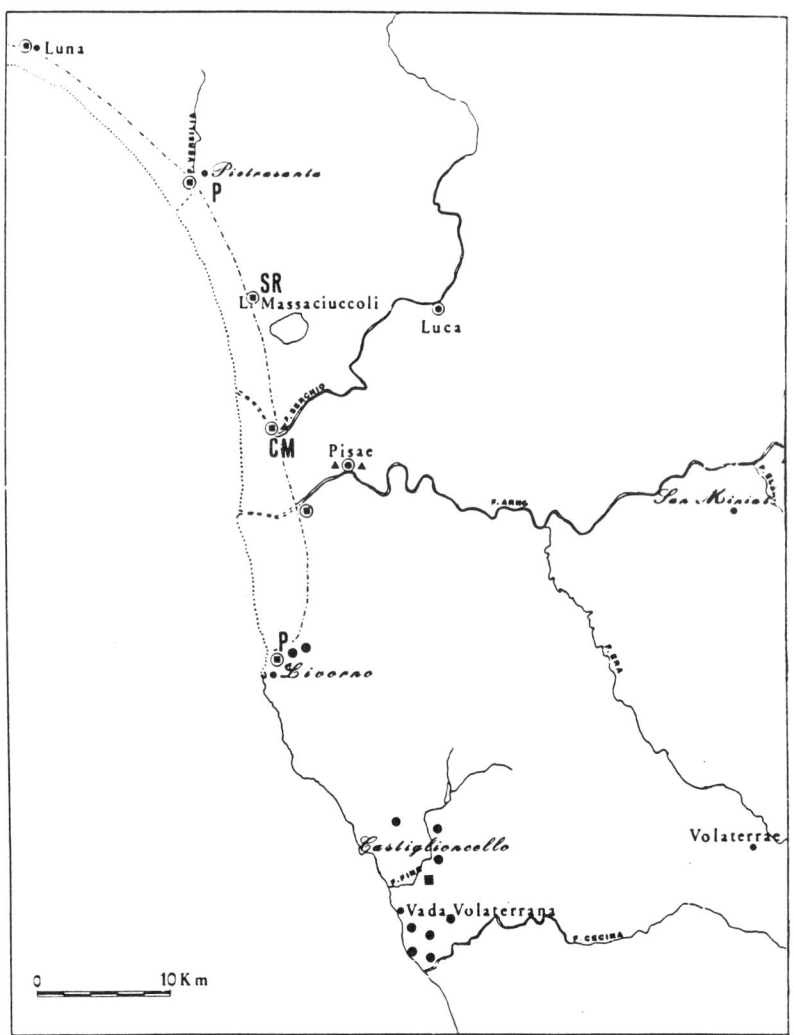

Fig. 4. Le fornaci dell'ager Pisanus e Volterranus

▲ fornaci di terra sigillata italica
■ fornaci di terra sigillata e altro
● fornaci di anfore

al momento appena intuibile per la tarda Repubblica e la prima età imperiale, è meglio definibile per la media e la tarda età imperiale. Le anfore cosiddette "di Spello", "di Forlimpopoli" e "di Empoli", oltre che, come è ovvio, nelle aree di produzione, risultano infatti diffuse anche a livello interregionale e interprovinciale. E' verosimile che parte di esse, e soprattutto di quelle rinvenute in ambito Mediterraneo occidentale, (arcipelago toscano, Corsica, Sardegna, Ostia, Roma, Ponza, Lipari, Ventimiglia, Francia, Spagna) provenisse dalle fornaci e dai porti della zona in esame (Menchelli 1990-1991).

Fornaci di laterizi, per certo largamente diffuse sul territorio, sono state individuate nell'*ager Pisanus* meridionale e nel *Volaterranus* costiero, in connessione con *villae* (fig. 4). In base alla documentazione epigrafica risulta sicuramente coinvolta nella manifattura di laterizi la famiglia senatoria dei *Venuleii Aproniani*, i cui prodotti non solo venivano utilizzati localmente (villa di Massaciuccoli; acquedotto di Pisa/Caldaccoli: Pasquinucci 1990), ma anche commercializzati, come dimostrano i rinvenimenti effettuati presso il porto di Populonia (Shepherd 1985: 183 ss.; Ciampoltrini & Andreotti 1990-1991 anche per le figline dei *Rasinii*).

La vitalità di Pisa e di gran parte degli insediamenti rurali nell'area in esame sino al tardo antico emerge da quanto detto e dalla documentazione relativa ad importazioni di vasellame e di anfore dall'intero bacino del Mediterraneo, in particolare dalla Penisola Iberica e dal Nord-Africa (Coltano 1986; Vecchiano 1988; San Giuliano 1990; Pasquinucci & Storti 1989; Del Rio *et alii* 1995). Nei porti/approdi dell'area in esame, come nell'intera Etruria settentrionale (Celuzza & Rendini 1991) continuarono ad arrivare, senza soluzione di continuità sino al V-VI secolo, prodotti veicolati dal commercio transmarino; questi venivano distribuiti nel retroterra, tramite la viabilità maggiore (che includeva una via in sinistra dell'Arno che ne seguiva il corso) e minore, o tramite vie d'acqua (fig. 5: Ceccarelli Lemut & Pasquinucci 1991).

Tutti gli insediamenti sorti in età tardo-repubblicana finora identificati, con l'eccezione dei siti rurali più interni, risultano ancora attivi in età tardo-antica, quali che fossero, in prospettiva diacronica, il regime di proprietà e i modi di conduzione. La produzione di vino

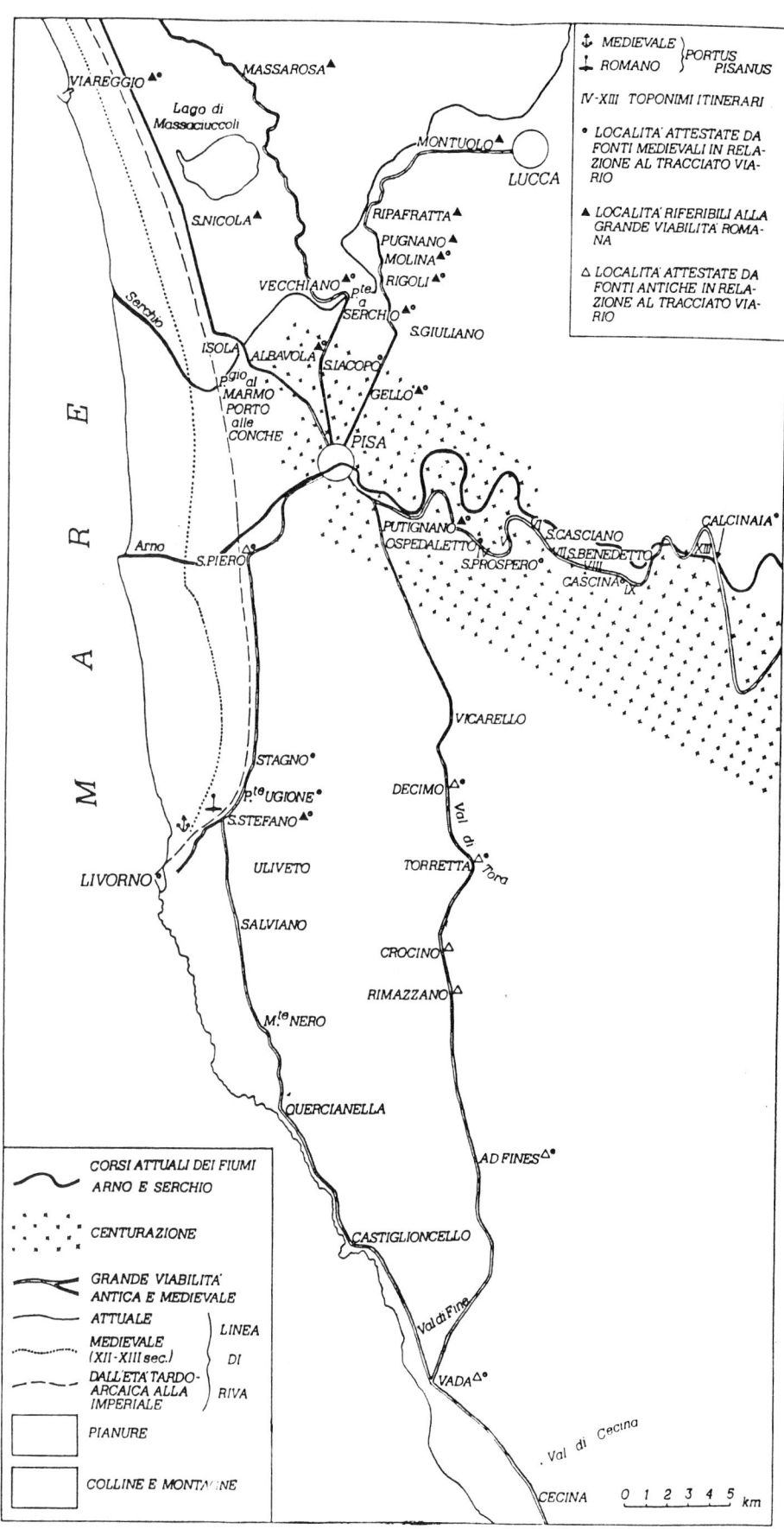

Fig. 5. La viabilità del territorio in esame (Da Ceccarelli Lemut-Pasquinucci 1991)

e di ceramiche fu anche in età medievale uno dei cardini dell'economia pisana, come attestano le fonti archeologiche ed archivistiche (Tongiorgi 1964; Andreolli 1981; Menchelli 1993).

Ringraziamenti

Alle ricerche sul terreno hanno partecipato: Donatella Alessi, Susanna Bianchini, Desirée Bonet, Patrizio Bonet, Massimo Brando, Linda Cherubini, Antonella Del Rio, Chiara Favilla, Claudia Guarguaglini, Beatrice Guiggi, Francesca Nalli, Sandra Pecori, Antonietta Pisano, Paolo Giovan Battista Sangriso, Paola Spinesi, Simonetta Storti, Maria Adelaide Vaggioli, Marina Vallebona. Figg. 1, 3, 4: disegni e lucidi di Desirée Bonet.

Bibliografia

Andreolli, B. 1981. 'I prodotti alimentari nei contratti agrari toscani dell'alto medioevo', *Archeologia Medievale* 8, 117 ss.

Bonamici, M. 1990. 'I monumenti funerari di marmo', in *Etruscorum ante quam Ligurum. La Versilia tra VII e III sec. a.C.*, a cura di E. Paribeni, Pontedera, 151 ss.

Ceccarelli Lemut, M.L. & Pasquinucci, M. 1991. 'Fonti antiche e medievali per la viabilità del territorio pisano', *Bollettino Storico Pisano*, 60, 111 ss.

Celuzza, M.G. & Rendini, P. 1991. *Relitti di storia*, Siena.

Cherubini, L. 1987. 'Vada e il territorio limitrofo in età preromana (III-I secolo a.C.)', in *Terme romane e vita quotidiana*, a cura di M. Pasquinucci, Modena, 116 ss.

Cherubini, L. & Del Rio, A. 1992. 'Appunti su fabbriche del territorio pisano e volterrano', in *Ateius e le sue fabbriche*, (Atti Convegno Pisa, dicembre 1992), in stampa.

Cherubini, L. & Del Rio, A. 1994. 'Produzioni ceramiche della bassa valle del Fine e del Cecina', in *Archeometria e ceramica romana*, (Atti Convegno Montelupo, aprile 1993), 217 ss.

Cherubini, L., Del Rio, A. & Mazzanti, R. 1987. 'Sviluppo e prosciugamento dei paduli della Provincia di Livorno', in *La gestione delle risorse idriche*, Roma, 149 ss.

Ciampoltrini, G. 1981. 'Note sulla colonizzazione augustea nell'Etruria settentrionale', *Stud. Class. Orient.*, 31, 41 ss.

Ciampoltrini, G. 1991. 'I porti dell'Etruria augustea', *Athenaeum*, 79, 256 ss.

Ciampoltrini, G. & Andreotti, A. 1990-1991. 'Figline pisane', *Opus*, 9-10, 161 ss.

Ciampoltrini, G., Notini, P. & Rendini, P. 1991. 'Materiali tardo-antichi ed alto-medievali dalla Valle del Serchio', *Archeologia Medievale*, 18, 699 ss.

Coltano 1986. *Terre e paduli. Reperti, documenti, immagini per la storia di Coltano*, Pontedera.

Crawford, M. 1981. 'Intervento', in *Società romana e produzione schiavistica*, a cura di A. Giardina & A. Schiavone, III, Bari, 271 ss.

Cristofani, M. 1975. 'Osservazioni preliminari sull'insediamento etrusco di Massarosa', in *Archaeologica. Scritti in onore di A. Neppi Modona*, Firenze, 183 ss.

D'Ambrosio, B., Mannoni, T. & Sfrecola, S. 1989. 'La provenienza delle anfore romane di alcuni contesti italiani: possibilità e limiti del metodo mineralogico', in *Amphores romaines et histoire économique*, Roma, 130 ss.

Del Rio, A. 1987. 'Vada e il territorio limitrofo in età romana (I sec. a.C. - VI sec. d.C.)', in *Terme romane e vita quotidiana*, a cura di M. Pasquinucci, Modena, 118 ss.

Del Rio, A., Mannoni, T., Menchelli, S. & Pasquinucci. M. 1995. 'Importations et productions locales de la haut Etrurie Tyrrhénienne, de la période de la romanisation jusqu'au VIᵉ siècle apr. J.-C. Un example d'étude archéométrique', *Revue d'Archéométrie*, in stampa.

Esposito, A.M. 1992. 'Presenze etrusche nel territorio livornese', *Atti del I Seminario Storia del Territorio Livornese*, Livorno, 23 ss.

Ettlinger, E. 1983. *Die Italische Sigillata von Novaesium*, Berlin.

Ettlinger, E. 1990. 'Die Klassische Zeit', in *Conspectus formarum terrae sigillatae italico modo confectae*, Bonn, 4 ss.

Federici, P.R. & Mazzanti, R. 1989. 'The Pisa Plain (Italy) and its hydrological hazards', *Suppl. Geogr. Fis. Dinam. Quat.*, 2, 41 ss.

Fraccaro, P. 1939. 'La centuriazione romana dell'agro pisano', *Studi Etruschi*, 13, 221 ss.

Guery, R. 1987. 'Les marques de potiers sur terra sigillata découvertes in Algérie II, Sigillée tardo-italique', *Antiquites Africaines*, 23, 149 ss.

Lavizzari Pedrazzini, M.P. 1984. 'Terra sigillata italica', in *Ricerche a Pompei. L'insula V della Regio VI dalle origini al 79 d.C.*, Roma, 214 ss.

Maggiani, A. 1990. 'San Rocchino (Massarosa)', in *Etruscorum ante quam Ligurum. La Versilia tra VII e III secolo a.C.*, a cura di E. Paribeni, Pontedera, 69 ss.

Mazzanti, R. et alii . 1990. 'La Pianura Versiliese nel contesto geomorfologico, in *Etruscorum ante quam Ligurum. La Versilia tra VII e III secolo a.C.*, 33. ss.

Mazzanti, R. & Pasquinucci, M. 1983. 'L'Evoluzione del litorale lunense-pisano fino alla metà del XIX secolo', *Boll. Soc. Geogr. Ital.*, 10-12, 605 ss.

Mazzanti, R. 1994 (a cura di). *La pianura di Pisa e i rilievi contermini. La natura e la storia*, Roma.

Medri, M. 1992. *Terra sigillata tardo-italica decorata*, Roma.

Menchelli, S. 1984. 'Contributo allo studio del territorio pisano: Coltano e l'area dell'ex Padule di Stagno', *Stud. Class. Orient.*, 34, 255 ss.

Menchelli, S. 1990. 'Materiali per la storia della Versilia in età romana', *Stud. Class. Orient.*, 40, 387 ss.

Menchelli, S. 1990-1991. 'Una fornace di anfore Dressel 2-4 nell'ager Pisanus ed alcune considerazioni sui contenitori vinari prodotti nell'Etruria settentrionale', *Opus*, 9-10, 169 ss.

Menchelli, S. 1992. 'Ateius e gli altri: produzioni ceramiche in Pisa e nell'ager Pisanus fra tarda Repubblica e primo impero', in *Ateius e le sue fabbriche*, (Atti Convegno Pisa, Dicembre 1992), in stampa.

Menchelli, S. 1993. 'Ceramica medievale priva di rivestimento', in *Piazza Dante: uno spaccato della storia pisana*, Pontedera, 473 ss.

Menchelli, S. 1994. 'Da Cn. Ateius ai vasai tardo-italici: alcune considerazioni sulla terra sigillata "pisana"', *Boll. Stor. Pisano*, 63, 1 ss.

Menchelli, S. & Vaggioli, M.A. 1987. 'Ricerche archeologico-topografiche nell'ager Pisanus settentrionale: il sito costiero di Isola di Migliarino', *Stud. Class. Orient.*, 37, 495 ss.

Milanese, M. & Mannoni, T. 1986. 'Etruschi a Genova e il commercio Mediterraneo', *Studi Etruschi*, 52, 127 ss.

Moutinho De Alarcao, A. 1975. 'Sigillées italiques', *Conimbriga* 14, 26 ss.

Pasquinucci, M. 1986. 'L'area di Cascina nell'antichità', in M. Pasquinucci, G. Garzella & M.L. Ceccarelli Lemut, *Cascina II, Dall'antichità al Medioevo*, Pisa, 13 ss.

Pasquinucci, M. 1988. 'Strabone e l'Italia centrale', in *Strabone e l'Italia antica*, a cura di G. Maddoli, Perugia, 47 ss.

Pasquinucci, M. 1990. 'L'acquedotto romano', in *San Giuliano Terme. La storia, il territorio*, Pisa, 165 ss.

Pasquinucci, M. 1992. 'Colonia Opsequens Iulia Pisana', in *Ateius e le sue fabbriche*, (Atti Convegno Pisa, dicembre 1992), in stampa.

Pasquinucci, M. *et alii* 1989. 'Ricerche archeologico-topografiche nella fascia costiera tirrenica (ager Pisanus e Volaterranus occidentale). Risultati preliminari', in *Amphores romaines et histoire économique*, Roma, 620 ss.

Pasquinucci, M. & Mazzanti, R. 1987. 'La costa tirrenica da Luni a Portus Cosanus, in *Déplacements des lignes de rivage en Méditerranée*, (Colloque Internationale C.N.R.S.), Paris, 95 ss.

Pasquinucci, M. & Rossetti, G. 1988. 'The Harbour Infrastructure at Pisa and Porto Pisano from Ancient Times until the Middle Ages', *Proceedings of the First International Symposium 'Cities on the Sea. Past and Present'*, Haifa, 137 ss.

Pasquinucci, M. & Storti, S. 1989. *Pisa antica: scavi nel giardino dell'Arcivescovado*, Pontedera.

Pucci, G. 1975. 'Una matrice per terra sigillata tardo-italica decorata da Pisa', *Ant. Pis.*, 2, 4, 1 ss.

Pucci, G. 1985. 'Terra sigillata italica', in *Atlante delle forme ceramiche II. Ceramica fine romana nel bacino Mediterraneo (tardo-ellenismo e primo impero)*, Suppl. E.A.A., Roma, 359 ss.

San Giuliano 1990. *San Giuliano Terme: La storia e il territorio*, vol. I, Pisa.

von Schnurbein, S. 1982. *Die unverzierte Terra Sigillata aus Haltern*, Munster Westfalen.

Shepherd, E.J. 1985. 'Testimonianze di commercio marittimo a Populonia in età romana', *Rassegna di Archeologia*, 5, 173 ss.

Taponecco Marchini, P. 1974. 'La fabbrica pisana di Ateio', *Ant. Pis.*, 2, 3 ss.

Thierrin Michael, G. 1992. *Römische Weinamphoren*, Freiburg.

Tongiorgi, L. 1964. *Pisa nella storia della ceramica*, Faenza 50, 3 ss.

Vaggioli, M.A. 1990. 'Il territorio di San Giuliano in età romana', in *San Giuliano Terme. La storia, il territorio*, Pisa, 125 ss.

Vecchiano 1988. *Il fiume, la campagna, il mare.* (Reperti, documenti, immagini per la storia di Vecchiano, coordinamento M. Pasquinucci), Pontedera.

23

Il Soratte ed il suo Territorio:
Un Esempio di Modellamento Territoriale Monastico

Stefania Fidanza

Sommario: *L'area in esame si trova a circa 40km da Roma, in quello che le fonti definiscono 'territorio collinense', delimitato dalla via Flaminia a sud/ovest e dal percorso del Tevere a nord, che segna anche il limite tra la 'Collina' e la 'Sabina'. Elemento caratterizzante del paesaggio è il monte Soratte, che rappresenta fin da secoli remoti un luogo di particolare interesse soprattutto dal punto di vista religioso ma non secondario neppure da quello produttivo. Un momento particolarmente significativo per l'assetto del territorio è la donazione del monastero di S. Silvestro sul Monte Soratte a Carlomanno di Francia, e la successiva fondazione di S. Andrea in Flumine, in quanto le due strutture, proprietarie di molta parte del territorio, diedero impulso alla fondazione di circa sette castelli. Di questi sono sopravvissuti solo Sant'Oreste e Ponzano. Il territorio degli altri, almeno quelli di totale proprietà monastica, venne poi ridistribuito alle 'terre' superstiti.*

L'area considerata in questa relazione si trova a circa 40 km a nord di Roma ed è caratterizzata dalla presenza di quattro elementi, tre geografici ed uno politico-amministrativo che ne hanno determinato l'assetto e lo sviluppo. I primi tre sono costituiti dal Monte Soratte (m.691 slm) che, essendo l'unico rilievo in una vasta pianura, ha da sempre rappresentato un punto di riferimento ed un luogo di culto per le popolazioni della Collina e della Sabina; il Fiume Tevere che separa e, contemporaneamente unisce questi due organismi territoriali e che venne usato come direttrice per i traffici commerciali verso Roma; la via Flaminia che rappresenta il mezzo e l'esito della conquista romana a partire dal III secolo a.C. e che continuò ad essere praticata anche nel Medio Evo. Il fattore politico-amministrativo è rappresentato dai monasteri di S.Silvestro sul Monte Soratte e di S.Andrea in Flumine che, a partire dal VI secolo videro aumentare, attraverso donazioni ed acquisti il loro potere sul territorio fino ad assumerne il diretto e totale controllo.

Scopo del presente contributo è quello di chiarire le modalità di questo possesso e di delineare le vie attraverso cui esso si esplicò considerando le fasi altomedioevali e propriamente medievale, caratterizzate dall'insediamento sparso, dall'incastellamento e poi dall'abbandono di buona parte delle fondazioni per arrivare all'assetto attuale che vede il territorio diviso tra due soli centri: S. Edisto (oggi S. Oreste) e Ponzano Romano.

Da qualche anno a questa parte, un vero e proprio fervore di studi si è rivolto a questa porzione dell'Agro Romano che fino a qualche tempo fa sembrava non riscuotere alcun interesse, di fatto, però, la bibliografia è ancora abbastanza povera e la parte più impegnativa del lavoro deve ancora essere fatta. La parte più interessante e meno esplorata è comunque quella delle fonti documentarie che possono essere suddivise in quattro grandi gruppi:

a) Fonti cronachistiche[1];

b) Documenti pubblici attestanti benefici pontifici ed imperiali e carte private quali atti di compravendita, di permuta, di enfiteusi stipulati tra privati o tra privati ed enti monastici[2];

c) Catasti abbaziali e dello Stato Pontificio[3];

d) Cause rotali o atti del Buon Governo relativi a diritti comunitari da esercitare sui territori appartenenti de iure ai monasteri di S. Andrea e S. Silvestro[4].

Per delineare quale fosse la situazione altomedioevale è indispensabile considerare il tipo di insediamento tardo romano che qui, come del resto ovunque, era caratterizzato dalla presenza di *fundus* e *villae* sia a carattere produttivo che residenziale. La ricognizione permette di individuare almeno una decina di ville dislocate lungo la fascia pedemontana e collegate con la viabilità di riferimento, data dal Tevere e dalla Flaminia, attraverso una fitta rete di percorsi in buona parte ancora utilizzati. Un esempio di come poteva essere organizzato un *fundus* di quest'epoca può forse essere individuato in una iscrizione funeraria di provenienza sconosciuta attualmente collocata sulla facciata di S. Maria Hospitalis[5]; in essa vengono nominate varie strutture costituenti il '*dotalicium*' del sepolcro: un roseto, una viniola col suo solario, una vigna e il terreno compreso tra la zona della piscina, i canali, i magazzini, gli edifici di abitazione, le cisterne, il canneto ed i relativi percorsi, un insieme quindi di strutture di produzione e di strutture residenziali.

La situazione dovette permanere così almeno fino alla seconda metà dell'VIII secolo, come testimonia l'elenco dei beni costituenti il Dotalicio di S. Andrea costituito tra il 747 ed il 750[6] e dovette subire un cambiamento radicale forse a partire dal IX secolo.

S. Silvestro, la cui fondazione viene posta dal *Chronicon* di Benedetto addirittura al IV secolo[7], avrebbe ricevuto in dono nel VI secolo, alcuni beni nell'ambito del territorio del Soratte da Galla, figlia del prefetto Simmaco[8], che avrebbe fondato anche un porto sul Tevere, un mulino ed alcune chiese tra cui una dedicata a S. Andrea. Da questa donazione di cui è ancora possibile riscontrare l'effettiva consistenza, in quanto la toponomastica si è ben conservata, emerge una attività del territorio prevalentemente agricola con colture incentrate sulla produzione cerealicola, come dimostrerebbe anche la fondazione di un mulino sul fosso della Calva, e probabilmente ancora esportata verso Roma come sembrerebbe indicare la fondazione del porto, e sulla coltivazione dell'olivo, come si evince dai 'Dialoghi' di Gregorio Magno[9] in cui ci sono precisi riferimenti alla raccolta delle olive.

Come ho già detto, la costituzione del Dotalicio di S.Andrea in Flumine fatta da Carlomanno di Francia tra il 746 ed il 750, anno in cui il nostro si trasferì a Cassino, conferma ancora per la metà dell'VIII secolo questa situazione. Il documento[10] elenca 5 *curtes cum colonis et colone* di cui fa parte, oltre alla *Curtis S. Heristi* da cui si originò S. Oreste, anche la *Curtis Priscani* dalla quale dipendevano tre *funda: Flabianello, Robelli* e *Corbiani* sulla quale era edificata la chiesa di S. Vittore (citata come monastero in una lettera di Paolo I)[11]. L'attestazione della dipendenza dalla *Curtis Priscani* di questi tre fondi è probabilmente la spia della pratica, abbastanza diffusa, della *commendatio* di proprietari in difficoltà a personaggi più potenti che potessero assicurare loro protezione. Viene citato poi un *casale*, anch'esso dotato di coloni e colone e ben 61 *funda*; di questi, 54 vengono donati *in integro* e per 6 di essi si parla di coloni e colone; 3 sono provvisti di una propria chiesa, in un caso si parla di due mulini e in un altro di *aliis vocabulis cum famulis, famule, casinis, casale*. Sempre nel *Chronicon* si parla di un *castrum* nominando i *fratres de castro Babiano* a cui Carlomanno si sarebbe rivolto per avere aiuto e consilio nella fondazione del monastero di S. Andrea[12], ma non sappiamo deve si trovasse e se, essendo Carlomanno un monaco e parlando la fonte di Fratres, fosse un insediamento monastico o laico.

Col X secolo la situazione sembra parzialmente cambiare: innanzitutto inizia l'espansione sulla riva Sabina del Tevere attraverso gli acquisti fatti dall'abbate Leone[13]. L'insediamento è ancora per *Funda et Massae* ma viene citato un *Castro de Summavilla*. Non sappiamo se in questo momento i monasteri avessero già iniziato ad accentrare l'abitato sparso che abbiamo visto dominare l'habitat nei secoli precedenti, ma un indizio in questo senso proviene dal privilegio di Leone VIII a favore di Ottone I nel 964: *montem Siraptim cum oppidis suis*[14].

Certamente non era ancora stato accentrato l'insediamento di Ponzano che dal Liber Floriger[15] risulta ancora nel 1028 abitato da coloni di Farfa che lo cederà a S. Andrea solo nel 1052 attraverso uno scambio di beni in Sabina con beni in Collina operato dall'abbate Stefano[16]. E' evidente, a questo proposito, la volontà dei monasteri di razionalizzare i loro possessi e di affermare con sempre maggiore forza la propria supremazia innanzitutto nelle loro immediate vicinanze.

Il documento che fotografa meglio la situazione nel basso medioevo, quando ormai il territorio si era già definito nella sua forma attuale, è il privilegio di Nicolò IV del 1290 circa. Esso ci informa dell'esistenza in vita di sei castelli nell'arco di pochi kilometri quadrati: Sant'Edisto, Versano, Ramiano, Poggio della Merla, Ponzano e Cusignano. Tutti questi, tranne Versano, sono posseduti integralmente dai monasteri che esercitano il mero e misto imperio su di essi. Non sappiamo quando si sia proceduto all'accentramento dell'insediamento, ma per la maggior parte di essi è possibile ricostruire il passaggio dal *Fundus* o dalla *Curtis* al *Castrum*.

SANT'EDISTO

Sant'Edisto nasce dall'omonima *curtis* localizzabile nei pressi dell'attuale cimitero di S. Oreste dove resta oggi solo una chiesa dedicata al santo, mentre fino a qualche anno fa erano ancora visibili i resti di imponenti strutture ora rase al suolo. E' interessante notare come la chiesa sia associata a livello popolare, con l'apparizione del martire durante l'invasione longobarda dalla quale avrebbe difeso gli abitanti del luogo. Probabilmente il passaggio dall'insediamento curtense sparso a quello accentrato, con il conseguente spostamento dalla fascia pedemontana sudorientale alla cresta rocciosa, dovette avvenire nel X secolo in seguito alle invasioni saracene (Benedetto chiama gli arabi '*agarenis*') che secondo il nostro cronista avrebbero messo a ferro e fuoco la regione e avrebbero danneggiato gravemente anche i monasteri[17]. E' anche interessante rilevare la presenza, in vicinanza della corte, della Pieve dei SS. Epimaco e Gordiano. Essa dovette nascere come chiesa fundanea della villa del Giardino ed essere elevata alla dignità plebana solo nell'VIII o IX secolo. Tale dignità, però, dovette essere persa ben presto, probabilmente in seguito alla fondazione delle chiese castrensi; infatti essa venne donata all'inizio dell'XI secolo al monastero di S. Agnese sulla Via Nomentana da papa Benedetto IX (1033–1048)[18]. Il ricordo di questa antica funzione si trova in un documento di visita del 1551 ed in un Protocollo notarile settecentesco[19] nei quali si afferma che essa è membro della chiesa vescovile di Civita Castellana, ma che il Vescovo non possiede alcun atto attestante ciò. Si fa presente che tutto il territorio è '*Nullius Diocesis*', cioè svincolato dall'autorità episcopale.

Ramiano

Ramiano nasce dal *fundus Damiano*, donato anch'esso da Carlomanno al monastero di S. Andrea in Flumine[20]. Questo territorio era già abitato in età falisca e romana[21], come testimoniano la necropoli delle Cimate e le strutture romane trovate nei pressi. La sua importanza è facilmente comprensibile analizzando la sua posizione geografica: si trova infatti su una collina prospiciente il Tevere, vicino al Porto di Pignatta, ed è collegato con la Via Flaminia attraverso la Via Ponzano.

La prima attestazione, peraltro indiretta, di un insediamento in questo luogo viene da un documento farfense del 1084[22] nel quale compare un *Rusticus de Ramiano* commerciante *de macinis* e di altri che frequentano il mercato di Caballaria in Sabina. L'atto lascia sostanzialmente aperta la questione sul tipo di insediamento, in quanto non vi è alcuna esplicita menzione di un *castrum*; è ipotizzabile perciò che i monasteri si fossero limitati a favorire un accentramento dell'abitato, più che un incastellamento vero e proprio, tenendo conto anche che nel X secolo era già stato fortificato il monastero di S. Andrea il quale si trova a poco più di un kilometro dal sito del castello.

Ponzano

Sostanzialmente analoga è la situazione di Ponzano che venne acquisito solo nel 1050[23]. Il Liber Floriger[24] riferisce i nomi dei coloni di Farfa che lo abitavano ed è probabile che essi passassero alle dipendenze di S. Andrea quando venne operato lo scambio. Per quanto riguarda il tipo di insediamento è da notare l'esistenza di una struttura detta

Legenda
■ *Abbey*
● *Castra*

'Castellazzo' (da *castellarium*, termine col quale si designa un centro fortificato abbandonato) di cui non è possibile identificare il tenimento, che si trova molto vicino a S. Angelo Vecchio, una delle chiese fondate da Galla[25]. Tale situazione potrebbe far pensare ad un primo accentramento dell'abitato su questo sito, peraltro mai indagato archeologicamente, che al momento dell'incastellamento vero e proprio del territorio sarebbe stato abbandonato per andare ad occupare la posizione attuale, molto più favorevole perchè domina il 'fiasco' del Tevere e perchè è frontale rispetto ai due insediamenti farfensi di Stimigliano e Forano.

Cusignano, Poggio della Merla

La mano ordinatrice dei monasteri è perfettamente visibile anche nei casi di Cusignano e Poggio della Merla, dislocati lungo la direttrice viaria della Via Piana già identificata dal Jones con l'antica Via Tiberina[26].

Il *Chronicon* di Benedetto dice che Galla, figlia del prefetto Simmaco, donò nel VI secolo *un agro cum monte de Campana* al monastero di S.Silvestro[27]. Un catasto del 1847 conserva ancora il toponimo *Monte de Campana o S. Silvestro* in una posizione compatibile con le indicazioni confinarie riportate dal cronista[28]. E' lecito perciò pensare che i monasteri ad un certo punto, non meglio precisabile, avessero favorito l'organizzazione dei coloni in due insediamenti abitati accentrati ma forse non ancora fortificati e che successivamente, seguendo un impulso generalizzato in tutto il territorio Collinense e Sabino avessero premuto verso l'attuazione di un modello castrense vero e proprio.

Versano

Un caso particolare, per ragioni legate più che alle modalità di insediamento agli aspetti della gestione della proprietà, è rappresentato da Versano, che nel 1208 risulta essere un *castrum* di proprietà di privati[29], Romano di Cinzio e suo fratello Enrico. Romano ricorda nel documento in questione di aver acquistato questo ed altri castelli da 5 personaggi di cui fa esplicito ricordo. Il fatto curioso è che il *Fundum Bersiano*, all'interno del quale il castello sorge, faceva parte di quei beni che costituivano il Dotalizio di S. Andrea e perciò, almeno in questo caso, i monasteri sembrerebbero qualificarsi essenzialmente come soggetti 'passivi' dell'incastellamento, come lascerebbe pensare anche tutta la documentazione anteriore al 1290: nel testamento di Onorio IV, per esempio, il castello viene nominato e si dice che appartiene per metà al papa e per il resto ad un tale Rainerio, ovvero a sua nuora.[30]

A Versano sono legati anche due altri centri che non trovano spazio nella documentazione: la *Rocca muntis Sirapti* che risulta solo dal documento del 1208 e Vallecomo, noto solo induttivamente come *castrum* da fonte catastale[31] e da documenti rotali[32].

Il primo si trova sull'estrema propaggine nord-occidentale del Soratte in evidente posizione strategica, potendo controllare il percorso della Flaminia e quello del Tevere. Di questo resta solo una torretta e qualche resto di altre strutture non meglio identificate. Il suo tenimento doveva essere localizzato, per quanto ci consta, sul versante sud/ovest del monte, dove resta ancora il toponimo 'Fossarocca'. Non è chiaro perchè i monasteri abbiano permesso che venisse edificato nelle immediate vicinanze di S. Silvestro un *castrum* svincolato dal loro potere a meno che non si ammetta che la sua fondazione sia avvenuta in un momento particolare, per esempio in concomitanza colle invasioni saracene, proprio ad opera di S. Silvestro che, successivamente, essendo venuto meno il pericolo, potrebbe averlo 'affittato' a *boni homines Romani*.

Situazione altrettanto complessa è quella di Vallecomo che in un catasto cinquecentesco[33] risulta di totale proprietà di S. Silvestro e S. Andrea in Flumine e dotato di un tenimento che, stando a documenti rotali[34] assommerebbe a 300 rubbia (circa 600 ettari). Spia dell'irregolarità della sua posizione è l'attribuzione del suo tenimento al solo castello di S. Edisto mentre, come vedremo, la prassi seguita per i tenimenti degli altri castelli abbandonati, fu quella di distribuire il territorio tra S. Edisto e Ponzano ed inoltre colpisce il fatto che esso venga reclamato come pertinenza della loro proprietà dai condomini di Versano. La questione può essere sciolta facendo riferimento al Privilegio di Nicolò IV già citato: in esso si dice che i monasteri possedevano solo *quadam partem* del *castrum Bersiani* con le sue pertinenze. E' probabile perciò, che Vallecomo fosse una pertinenza di Versano, la parte posseduta dai monasteri, appunto, che aveva essenzialmente funzioni di controllo della Via Flaminia, che in età medievale lo costeggiava e che, proprio in relazione a questo possesso, sia potuto entrare direttamente a far parte del tenimento di S. Edisto.

La Riorganizzazione Basso Medioevale

A questo punto è lecito chiedersi quando si sia passati dai sei castelli nominati nel Privilegio di Nicolò IV ai due che attualmente si dividono il territorio e perchè, contrariamente a quanto è avvenuto in Sabina, dove nonostante l'alto numero di fallimenti c'è comunque una forte densità di centri abitati, si sia proceduto ad una razionalizzazione così radicale del territorio. Premetto che la risposta a queste domande è tutt'altro che semplice soprattutto perchè nessuno di questi insediamenti è mai stato scavato e quindi non ci sono dati di riscontro obbiettivo.

Partiamo dal Privilegio di Nicolò IV che attesta nel 1290 tutti e sei i castelli e dice che tutti essi, tranne Versano, sono posseduti *pleno iure* dai monasteri di S. Andrea e S. Silvestro. Tutti questi compaiono in un documento coevo alla Bolla del Rettore del Patrimonio tassati per 26 denari *pro foco* ogni anno e pertanto è lecito presumere che a quest'epoca fossero ancora tutti abitati[35]. Le Chroniche Viterbesi, però, affermano che Ramiano fu distrutto nel 1228 insieme con Vignanello (un paese che si trova sui monti Cimini)[36] ma è probabile che continuasse ad essere abitato in quanto compare col solo S. Edisto in una relazione del Rettore del Patrimonio da cui consta che doveva pagare II fiorentini per la custodia delle strade insieme con S. Edisto che ne pagava VIII[37]. Nessun altro dei nostri castelli è ricordato ma questo non è una prova del loro abbandono. Lo spopolamento non dovette essere di molto posteriore però, considerando che solo quattro di essi, Cusignano, Versano, S. Edsito e Ponzano, compaiono nella Lista Base del sale e del focatico del Comune di Roma; di questi, Cusignano è compreso nella lista del 1416 tra le *Terrae Inhabitatae*, e Versano risulta tassato per cinque rubbia *pro foco* ma non paga mai, non sappiamo se ciò fu possibile perchè dotato di una qualche esenzione o perchè, come è più logico, era già stato abbandonato[38].

Se è fuori discussione che i monasteri abbiano agito nel senso dell'incastellamento, premendo affinchè si costituissero dei centri abitati che potessero procurare reddito e sui quali si potesse agire anche ai sensi di un miglioramento del paesaggio, come lascerebbe pensare la menzione di 'Novalia' ancora nel Privilegio del 1290, ci si chiede a partire da quali condizionamenti si sia agito in senso contrario approvando, se non promuovendo l'abbandono della maggior parte dei centri incastellati. Obbiettivamente la risposta non è semplice: se è infatti possibile invocare congiunture poco favorevoli al popolamento in questi secoli del basso medioevo, rimane inspiegabile perchè i monasteri non abbiano cercato di 'rimpiazzare' i vassalli, cosa avvenuta a partire dal XVI secolo con l'immigrazione di numerosi marchigiani ed emiliani, ed abbiano invece accettato che essi si trasferissero a S. Edisto e a Ponzano, come farebbe supporre la presenza in questi centri di *Homines* che erano proprietari di beni nei tenimenti delle *terrae* abbandonate.

L'ipotesi più plausibile è che si sia cercato di razionalizzare lo sfruttamento delle terre, che durante la vita dei castelli erano certamente adibite a colture varie, tali che potessero soddisfare le necessità degli abitanti, come vigneti, frutteti, arativi, pascolativi e, naturalmente, bosco. I documenti che possediamo per i secoli posteriori all'abbandono dei *castra* presentano innanzitutto la ridistribuzione delle terre dei tenimenti tra i *castra* superstiti accompagnata da una lunga litania di liti giudiziarie[39]. Il materiale più interessante è quello pertinente a Ramiano che era dotato di un tenimento di 325 rubbia (circa 650 ettari). Negli atti processuali che lo riguardano[40] si dice che era incolto da tempo e che l'assegnazione venne fatta secondo lo *Ius Coloniae Perpetuae*. Sembrebbe che la distruzione del 1228 ad opera dei viterbesi fosse stata radicale e comunque tale da provocare un abbandono irreversibile. Le terre assegnate vennero totalmente adibite alla produzione di cereali per i quali il monastero di S. Paolo prima, e quello delle Tre Fontane poi, ricevevano il quarto del prodotto. E' attestato anche un frutteto all'interno del tenimento ma, appartenendo ai Signori Caccia di S.Edisto, *boni Homines* molto vicini all'abbate, non fa testo[41].

Simile è la situazione di Poggio della Merla e di Cusignano; è probabile che il primo dei due ad essere abbandonato fosse Poggio della Merla, che dei due è anche quello conservato meglio. Dai documenti i loro territori risultano adibiti a colture cerealicole, a canapine che per Poggio della Merla è attestata ben 25 volte, e a bosco. L'importanza di quest'ultimo per l'economia locale ed abbaziale è attestata chiaramente da un inventario di beni dell'abbazia delle Tre Fontane redatto nel 1600 da Domenico Balada[42], nel quale si riferisce dell'uso di portare a Roma il legname sfruttando il Porto Vecchio pagando per ogni 40 passi di legname, un passo all'abbazia. Nello sfruttamento del bosco rientra anche la prassi della vendita del taglio, fatta dai monasteri o, più spesso, dalle comunità e la pratica delle 'Carbonarie' citate spesso nella documentazione.

L'attività impreditrice degli enti monastici, non direttamente individuabile nel caso di Versano, è comunque visibile nei casi di Vallecomo e della Rocca. Entrambi questi tenimenti entrarono a far parte del territorio di S. Edisto e vengono comunemente citati nella prassi riguardante i controlli esercitati dai 'guardiani delle biade': quindi anch'essi vennero adibiti a colture cerealicole, vista anche la distanza dal centro abitato, probabilmente quando tutta la fascia pedemontana venne ad essere occupata dagli oliveti, a cui corrisponde dentro il *castrum* la costituzione di quattro mulini da olio di proprietà o dei monasteri o di personaggi eminenti ad essi legati, e quindi il territorio destinato al pascolo ed ai cereali si trovò ridotto di molto.

Conclusioni

Riepilogando possiamo dire che il sistema di organizzazione del territorio è strettamente dipendente dalla volontà dei monasteri che lo possedevano per la maggior parte. Essa si esplicito dapprima nella razionalizzazione dei possedimenti attraverso acquisti o permute con Farfa e attraverso l'affitto di beni da monasteri romani sotto forma di atti enfiteutici. A questo 'compattamento' della proprietà seguì un iniziale accentramento degli abitati che divenne incastellamento vero e proprio a seguito di eventi traumatici, quali l'invasione saracena. Le mutate condizioni storiche, che portarono alla nascita dei comuni anche in quest'ambito, ridussero notevolmente gli ambiti di manovra economica e, associati a condizioni demografiche svantaggiose, indussero al ridimensionamento del numero dei centri abitati ed alla ridistribuzione delle terre tra gli insediamenti maggiori in modo da poter contare su una gestione dei suoli più produttiva e redditizia.

Note

1. Ci si riferisce in modo particolare al *Chronicon* di Benedetto monaco di S. Andrea del Soratte, edito dallo Zucchetti, Istituto Storico Italiano, *Fonti per la Storia d'Italia*, 55, Roma 1920; nello stesso volume è contenuto il *Libellus de Imperatoria Potestate in urbe Roma*, probabilmente dello stesso autore. Sono stati utilizzati anche *Il Chronicon Farfense di Gregorio di Catino* a cura di U. Balzani (*Fonti per la storia d'Italia*, 33) Roma, 1903; il *Liber Largitorius* edito dallo Zucchetti in due volumi (*Regesta Chartarum Italiae*, 9/1, 9/2) Roma, 1913 e 1932; il *Liber Floriger* a cura di M.T. Maggi Bei in Misc. della Società Romana di Storia Patria vol. XXVI, Roma, 1984; Il *Regestum Pharphensis* edito da I.Giorgi e U.Balzani in 5 vol. per la Biblioteca della Società Romana di Storia Patria, Roma, 1879-1914.
2. Il più importante di questi documenti è un privilegio di Nicolò IV, *Religiosam vitam eligentibus* pubblicato dal Galletti nel 1776 Appendice doc. LXXIV che sarà oggetto di un mio studio in fase di preparazione. Molti documenti privati sono contenuti in B.Trifone, 'Le carte del monastero di S. Paolo', *Archivio della Società Romana di Storia Patria*, 31, 1908, 267-313; 32, 1909, 29-106.
3. Si fa riferimento ai catasti abbaziali conservati nell'Archivio Segreto Vaticano nel fondo delle Tre Fontane con le segnature: A 17, A18, A 69, C 37, C.38, C.41.
4. I documenti rotali, che coprono un arco di tempo che va dall'inizio del 700 alla seconda metà dello stesso secolo, non sono stati finora analizzati ai fini di uno studio del nostro territorio. sono conservati nel fondo della Sacra Rota dell'Archivio Segreto Vaticano.
5. Il testo è edito in *CIL* XI che presenta anche una ricostruzione del monumento. LICTORIAE CHAERUSAE VIXIT ANNIS XV /MENSIBVS VII DIEBUS V FECER L.VETVRIVS PVDENS/VIR ET LARCIA AVCTA MATER HVIC MONIMENTO/CEDIT ROSARIVM CVM VINIOLA SOLO SVO FINE VINIAE/ET A REGIONE PISCINAE ET CANALIS VSQVE AD ARIAM/ET AREA CVM EDIFICIS ET HORREO ET CISTERNA E../SOLAR ET REGIONE EIVS VSQVE ADARVNDINETVM CVM ITIN/QVE SVNT DETERMINATA ET COLLIGE IVG.../
6. Benedetto, *Chronicon*, 75- 76.
7. Benedetto, *Chronicon*, 6.
8. Benedetto, *Chronicon*, 25-26.
9. Gregorio Magno, *Dialoghi*, in Migne, Patr. Lat. LXXVII. Parisii, 1849.
10. Benedetto, *Chronicon*, 75-76.
11. Salubri Providentia: Annales O.S.B. II,122; Jaffé 2349.
12. Benedetto, *Chronicon*, 75.
13. Benedetto, *Chronicon*, 167- 168.
14. *Privilegium Maius* di Leone VIII. ed. Watterich, I, 680.
15. *Liber Floriger*, 187 e 252.
16. *Liber Floriger*, 261, n.525; *Chronicon*, 167-168.
17. Benedetto, *Chronicon*, 167-168
18. Kehr, Gott. Nachr., 1900, p.140, n.2.
19. I documenti relativi a questa chiesa sono contenuti in un Cabreo del 1867 delle monache di S. Croce di S. Oreste alle pp.42 e 43; e nel Protocollo VII (anni 1769-1772) del notaio G.F. Clerici di S. Oreste alle pp.398-406; Notizie del ritrovamento della chiesa sono contenute in De Carolis, cit., pp.354-356
20. Benedetto, *Chronicon*, 75-76.
21. Cfr. Jones 1962-63; Ashby 1924.
22. *Regestum Pharphensis*, IV.
23. *Liber Floriger*, 261-262.
24. *Liber Floriger*, 187 e 252-253.
25. Benedetto, *Chronicon*, 25-26.
26. Jones 1962-63.
27. Benedetto, *Chronicon*, 25-26.
28. Archivio Segreto Vaticano (A.S.V.), fondo Tre Fontane A 69.
29. Archivio di Stato in Roma, Fondo dell'Ospedale di S. Spirito in Sassia cassetta n. 59. coll. B (1193-1300). Colgo l'occasione per ringraziare Jean Coste che non solo mi ha indicato questo documento ma mi ha anche sostenuto incoraggiato e corretto in questi anni e che immodestamente considero il mio maestro.
30. Registro di Onorio IV, ed. Prou doc.823, p. 578-582.
31. A.S.V. fondo Tre Fontane, C.37.
32. A.S.V. fondo della Sacra Romana Rota, Positiones nn.1005, 1006, 1007,2029,2030.
33. A.S.V. fondo Tre Fontane, C.37.
34. A.S.V. fondo della Sacra Romana Rota, Positiones nn. 1005,1006,1007,2029,2030.
35. Theiner, *Codex Diplomaticus Dominii Temporalis S. Sedis*, I, 1861, Roma. doc. CCCCLVII pp. 303-304.
36. Egidi, P. 1901. 'Le Chroniche di Viterbo scritte da frate Francesco D'Andrea', *ASRSP*, XXIV, 193-371.
37. *ASRSP*, XVIII, 1895, p. 467
38. J. Coste, 'Nota sulle liste del sale e focatico' in *Monti Lucretili. Un paese naturale del Lazio*, a cura di G. de Angelis e P. Lanzara, III ed. Roma, 1988, 409 ss.
39. I materiali sono conservati, oltre che negli archivi della Sacra Romana Rota, anche negli archivi dei due Comuni interessati. Per quanto concerne l'Archivio Storico di S. Oreste essi si trovano nelle buste 90, 91, 92, 94, 96, 98.
40. A.S.V. fondo Sacra Romana Rota 2292-2293; 974, 975, 976; 2211, 2212.
41. Carta della Tenuta di Ramiano, redatta il 10-10-1732 da A. Tomai, conservata nell'Archivio Storico di Ponzano.
42. A.S.V. fondo Tre Fontane, C.38.

Bibliografia

Ashby, T. 1924. 'La Via Tiberina e i territori di Capena e del Soratte nel periodo romano', *Memorie della Pontificia Accademia di Archeologia*, I, 129-179.

Carta Archeologica 1881-1897, 1972. G.F. Gamurrini, A. Cozza, A. Pasqui & R. Mengarelli, *Carta Archeologica d'Italia Materiali per L'Etruria e la Sabina*, Forma Italiae, s. II,1, Firenze, 1972.

Conti, S. 1980. *Le sedi umane abbandonate nel patrimonio di S.Pietro*, (Comitato dei Geografi Italiani, 5), Firenze.

De Caprio, S. 1979. 'Abbazia di S.Andrea in Flumine', in *Vita Italiana, Documenti e Informazioni*, 29, 11-18.

De Carolis, M. 1950. *Il Monte Soratte e i suoi santuari*, Roma.

Degli Effetti, A. 1675. *Memorie di S. Nonnoso, del Soratte e dei luoghi circonvicini e loro pertinenze*, Roma, Tinassi.

Galletti, P.L. 1776. *Del primicerio della Santa Sede Apostolica e gli altri uffiziali maggiori del Sacro Palazio Lateranense*, Roma.

Grisar, H. 1915. 'Il Soratte, note di storia, ecclesiastica e di archeologia', in *La Civiltà Cattolica*, III, Firenze, 583-596.

Jones, J.D.B. 1962-63. 'Capena and the ager Capenas', *Papers of the British School at Rome*, 30, 116-207; 31, 100-158.

Martinori, E. 1934. *Lazio turrito. Repertorio storico ed iconografico*, II, Roma.

Mastrocola, M. 1962. 'Il monachesimo nelle diocesi di Civita Castellana, Orte e Gallese fino al secolo XII', in *Miscellanea di Studi Viterbesi*, Viterbo, 352-368.

Potter, T.W. 1985. *Storia del paesaggio dell'Etruria Meridionale. Archeologia e trasformazioni del territorio*, Roma.

Ramieri, A. 1987. *Ponzano, la storia, i monumenti, il territorio. Comune di Ponzano*, Roma.

Savio, F. 1911. 'Notizie varie sui monasteri del Soratte', *Rivista Storica Benedettina*, VI, 169-174.

Tomassetti, G. 1913. *La Campagna romana, antica, medievale e moderna*, III, (rieditata nel 1979 a cura di L. Chiumenti e F. Bilancia).

PART 4

Settlement and Society

24

L'Abitato di Torre Mordillo nel Quadro dello Sviluppo dell'Insediamento Protostorico nell'Alto Ionio (Sibaritide)

Maria Letizia Arancio, Vittoria Buffa, Isabella Damiani,
Antonio Tagliacozzo, Flavia Trucco, Lucia Vagnetti

Sommario: L'abitato di Torre Mordillo è situato in Italia meridionale, sul versante ionico della Calabria settentrionale (Sibaritide). Il sito fu abitato per un lunghissimo arco di tempo, dagli inizi della media età del bronzo (XVII sec. a.C.) fino all'età ellenistica. Sono presenti inoltre sporadici indizi di una più antica frequentazione risalente al Neolitico. Il presente studio prende in considerazione le fasi abitative di età protostorica, con particolare riguardo all'età del bronzo finale. Ciò attraverso l'analisi di evidenze archeologiche frutto di ricerche condotte in tempi e con modalità diverse: da una parte gli scavi effettuati negli anni '60, finalizzati allo studio dell'insediamento di epoca storica, che hanno incontrato sporadicamente strati e strutture protostorici, dall'altra gli scavi 1987-90, questi finalizzati specificatamente all'indagine dell'abitato di età protostorica. Le evidenze archeologiche vengono distinte per specifici ambiti cronologici ed inquadrate nello sviluppo culturale del comprensorio della Sibaritide. Di particolare interesse risulta, tra l'altro, la presenza dell'elemento egeo ed il suo ruolo nei confronti dello sviluppo dell'assetto sociale ed economico delle comunità protostoriche della regione.

Lo studio del popolamento della Sibaritide tra media età del bronzo e prima età del ferro è stato affrontato in modo sistematico a partire dal 1979. In due dei siti maggiori sono state condotte campagne di scavo estensivo da parte di diverse equipe di ricerca: a Broglio di Trebisacce nella Sibaritide settentrionale, iniziati nel 1979 ed ancora in corso (Bergonzi *et al.* 1982a, b; Peroni 1984a, b; Peroni & Trucco 1994; Peroni & Vanzetti 1994), e a Torre Mordillo nella Sibaritide centrale dal 1987 al 1990 (scavi Museo L. Pigorini: Trucco 1987-88; 1989; Trucco *et al.* 1992; Arancio *et al.* 1994), scavi che hanno indagato su ampie superfici i depositi protostorici, ed i cui risultati sono almeno in parte editi od in corso di edizione. L'indagine stratigrafica in questi due siti è stata affiancata da ricognizioni di superficie, integrate dallo studio accurato della geografia della regione e dalla sistematica classificazione dei litotipi collegati agli insediamenti individuati (Peroni 1984b: 229-250; Peroni & Trucco 1994).

L'insieme di tali ricerche rende certamente questa parte della Calabria ionica un'area dalla documentazione privilegiata, che, benchè lungi dall'essere esaustiva, potrà presto permettere la ricostruzione di un quadro complesso ed articolato. Infatti, sono sino ad oggi ben 14 i siti noti databili alla media età del bronzo (Peroni & Trucco 1994: fig. 227), posti per lo più sulla prima fascia collinare, spesso su pianoro, generalmente al centro di un comprensorio, di limitata estensione, i cui confini sono segnati dalle fiumare.

Nella Sibaritide centro-settentrionale i siti sono relativamente fitti, posti a breve distanza l'uno dall'altro, mentre nella Sibaritide meridionale le presenze si diradano, rispecchiando forse, più che una lacuna nelle ricerche, una reale minor densità insediativa. Nelle fasi successive il quadro insediativo va progressivamente mutando, rispecchiando dinamiche socio-economiche complesse. Il numero complessivo degli insediamenti noti al momento della colonizzazione non è però di molto superiore a quello della fase iniziale del processo qui in studio: 18 sono infatti i siti attestati nella prima età del ferro (Peroni & Trucco 1994: fig. 235). Abbandono di numerose sedi e fondazione di nuovi abitati caratterizzano in particolare l'età del bronzo finale, sintomo della ricerca di nuovi equilibri economici e politici tra le comunità della Sibaritide. Solo i siti su pianoro con superficie superiore ai 10 ettari, occupati in una fase non avanzata della media età del bronzo, restituiscono testimonianze di continuità insediativa per tutto il periodo in esame. Da una articolazione territoriale fondamentalmente costituita da cellule monocentriche, si può cogliere il progressivo affermarsi della comunità territoriale policentrica; processo che, alle soglie della colonizzazione greca, sembra essersi pienamente realizzato solo nel caso di Torre Mordillo, sito per il quale è stato ipotizzato il ruolo di vero e proprio *central place* (Peroni 1989; Peroni 1994).

In questa sede abbiamo scelto di presentare alcuni dei risultati delle ricerche da noi condotte a Torre Mordillo, privilegiando la documentazione relativa alle fasi avanzate dell'insediamento indigeno, per le quali abbiamo potuto utilizzare anche i materiali degli scavi effettuati tra il 1963 ed 1967 dall'Università di Pennsylvania e dalla Soprintendenza Archeologica della Calabria. Questa missione, creata per la ricerca e l'indagine della colonia greca di *Thurii*, mise in luce sull'altura di Torre Mordillo un grande centro di età ellenistica (Colburn 1977). Nel corso di tali indagini fu raggiunta più volte la parte del deposito archeologico sottostante gli strati di età classica, rinvenendo e parzialmente scavando strati e strutture dell'abitato protostorico. Materiale di impasto in giacitura secondaria era, poi, presente pressochè in tutte le trincee aperte in più punti del pianoro.

Il nuovo ciclo di ricerche, per la prima volta finalizzato all'indagine dell'abitato di età protostorica, iniziato nel 1987, si è purtroppo interrotto nel 1991 per volontà dell'Istituto promotore della ricerca: per questo motivo i dati che presentiamo per ciò che riguarda l'indagine sul terreno di alcune strutture e complessi stratigrafici sono incompleti. Le campagne di scavo annuali sono state affiancate da indagini di superficie e dallo studio geopedologico dei suoli per una valutazione complessiva, anche attraverso carotaggi e prospezioni geomagnetiche, della presenza e del grado di integrità del deposito protostorico su tutta l'altura (studio prezioso effettuato da A. Arnoldus Huyzendveld).

L'insediamento protostorico occupava l'estremità di un'ampia struttura terrazzata di origine marina, prospiciente la piana di Sibari e posta al centro dell'arco di rilievi che le fanno corona, circa 1 km a valle della confluenza tra Esaro e Coscile, corso d'acqua, quest'ultimo, che costeggia la base del pianoro a settentrione. Il rilievo naturalmente munito, sulla cui sommità sorgeva l'abitato, è collocato in posizione favorevole per il controllo del territorio: con un dislivello di 70-80 m. rispetto alla piana, domina il territorio circostante sia verso l'interno che verso il mare, da cui dista oggi circa 19 km. Il pianoro sommitale, che ha attualmente una superficie di circa 14 ettari, è delimitato da bordi netti e fianchi ben acclivi, intatti lungo il margine settentrionale, ma fortemente alterati a sud dall'azione delle cave; i ripidi cigli perimetrali che garantivano la difendibilità dell'insediamento si interrompono solo a sud-ovest, dove il pianoro è collegato al terrazzo retrostante da una sorta di sella, che presenta oggi una pendenza più accentuata che in passato (fig. 1,a).

Sulla base della documentazione disponibile, è stata accertata l'esistenza sul pianoro di un ininterrotto ciclo insediativo che dall'orizzonte più antico del Bronzo medio (protoappenninico B, fase 1) giunge sino alla fine dell'VIII secolo.

Non sono però quelle dell'età del bronzo le testimonianze più antiche della presenza umana sull'altura. Un esiguo numero di frammenti (Arancio *et al.* 1994: fig.2,1-3), rinvenuti in giacitura secondaria, in strati databili a fasi diverse dell'età del bronzo, è da attribuire al Neolitico antico e medio. Lo scarsissimo numero di reperti identificati non consente di formulare per ora ipotesi sull'entità di un eventuale insediamento di questa età sul pianoro, ma la scoperta si inserisce in un quadro di conoscenze che privilegiano ancora, nella Calabria settentrionale, i giacimenti in grotta (Tinè 1987), come le Grotte di S. Angelo e Pavolella a Cassano allo Ionio (Carancini & Guerzoni 1987), poco a nord di Torre Mordillo, e la grotta della Madonna a Praia a Mare (Cardini 1970), sul versante tirrenico; l'unico insediamento all'aperto noto ed indagato nella Sibaritide è quello di Favella della Corte (scavi ancora in corso), posto nella piana alle spalle di Sibari. I nuovi dati di Torre Mordillo fanno dunque intravvedere l'esistenza, anche per questo periodo, di una occupazione differenziata del territorio.

Gli elementi che consentono di assegnare al Bronzo medio iniziale la nascita del ciclo insediativo provengono soprattutto da raccolte di superficie effettuate nell'area F (fig. 1,a). Le fasi avanzate del Bronzo medio, come pure quelle relative al Bronzo recente, oltre ad essere state indagate con lo scavo di due grandi trincee, aperte presso il margine sud-occidentale del pianoro in corrispondenza della sella (area AO), sono documentate anche tra il materiale raccolto al centro e all'estremità orientale del pianoro (area L). Pur nell'assenza di dati utilizzabili per una lettura della densità delle strutture abitative, è quindi possibile ipotizzare che l'insediamento interessasse l'intero pianoro già nel corso del Bronzo medio (Trucco *et al.* 1992).

Ad un momento piuttosto avanzato del Bronzo recente si datano i resti di un'imponente opera a carattere difensivo (Arancio *et al.* 1994: figs. 3-4), che fu costruita per proteggere il lato più vulnerabile dell'abitato. Una fortificazione ad aggere, di cui si conservano cospicue tracce, individuate sia attraverso lo scavo che i carotaggi per una lunghezza di 50 m, seguiva il margine del pianoro prima in corrispondenza della sella, proseguendo poi, almeno per un tratto, verso nord-ovest, là dove il pendio diviene più scosceso. Il profilo esterno della struttura si presenta fortemente alterato a causa delle trasformazioni subite dal ciglio del pianoro in questa zona. Il lato interno, non soggetto ad erosione e ricoperto da numerosi apporti di terreno depositatisi dopo la distruzione dell'aggere, è quello meglio conservato, ma lo scavo è stato interrotto prima di raggiungerne i livelli di base.

La costruzione dell'aggere, almeno per quanto riguarda la parte indagata, comportò lo spianamento dei livelli immediatamente sottostanti, attribuibili ad una fase antica del Bronzo recente (Damiani 1991: 27, fig.14c).

Gli strati che compongono l'aggere contengono

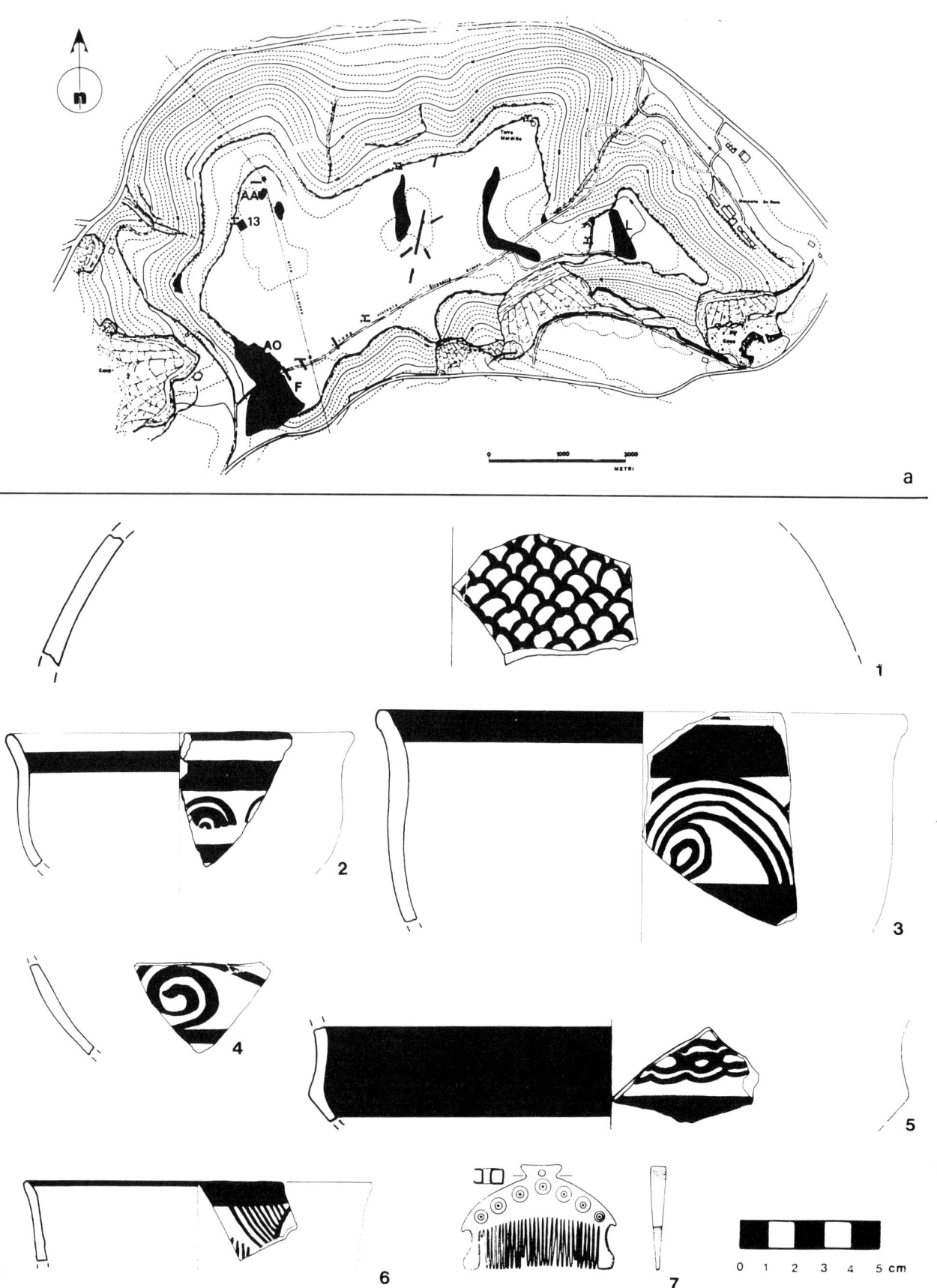

Fig. 1. a: Torre Mordillo: in nero le aree in cui è stato rinvenuto materiale protostorico in superficie o in scavo. (Rilievo V. Di Grazia). 1-6: Ceramiche di tipo egeo. 7. Pettine in avorio.

materiali attribuibili al Bronzo medio (sia di fase protoappenninica che appenninica) e in misura maggiore al Bronzo recente. La ceramica del Bronzo recente in particolare è documentata da un cospicuo numero di forme e dalle particolari classi di produzione, già note a Broglio di Trebisacce, vale a dire la ceramica grigia tornita acroma e dipinta e la ceramica italo-micenea.

A Torre Mordillo, come a Broglio, le ceramiche egee coprono un arco di tempo che si può prevalentemente fissare tra il XIV e il XII sec. a. C., corrispondente alle fasi ceramiche del Tardo Elladico IIIA-IIIC non finale. Qualche indizio, in corso di approfondimento, non fa escludere che a Torre Mordillo questo tipo di documentazione sia iniziato in epoca un po' più antica, anche se i pezzi significativi sono collocabili fra il pieno TE IIIA (fig. 1,1), il TE IIIA-B (fig. 1,2–3,6) e il IIIC (fig. 1,4–5). Per quanto riguarda Broglio, ad una limitata quantità di importazioni certe e probabili, fa riscontro un'abbondante produzione locale di ceramica dipinta di stile miceneo. Tale produzione, inizialmente sospettata in base ad osservazioni macroscopiche, sia qualitative, sia tipologiche e stilistiche, è stata confermata da analisi archeometriche di vario tipo (Jones et al. 1994). Un programma di analisi parzialmente simile, in corso di applicazione per Torre Mordillo, ha confermato l'abbondante presenza di materiali di tipo egeo prodotti nella regione.

I caratteri tipologici e stilistici della documentazione rinvenuta nei due siti si differenziano abbastanza nettamente. Ad una abbondanza di elementi decorativi derivanti dal repertorio cretese presenti a Broglio, fa riscontro una maggior varietà di ispirazione per i materiali da Torre Mordillo, che, pur nella limitata dimensione dei frammenti, hanno addentellati con la produzione della Grecia micenea, anche regionale, e solo in misura assai limitata con Creta. La manifattura della maggioranza dei reperti è da localizzare nella stessa Sibaritide, anche se è probabile che più di una bottega fosse attiva in questo settore produttivo (Vagnetti 1982a, b; 1984a, b; Vagnetti & Jones 1988; Jones & Vagnetti 1990; Vagnetti & Panichelli 1994).

Ad ispirazione tecnologica egea sono da riportare anche la ceramica grigia depurata e tornita, e i dolii cordonati, presenti in ambedue i siti. Dobbiamo constatare come a Torre Mordillo la ceramica grigia sia rappresentata da una quantità di frammenti, tipologicamente significativi, decisamente inferiore rispetto a Broglio, fatto questo che potrebbe essere spiegato con la localizzazione della trincea di scavo in una zona periferica dell'abitato. Anche la ceramica grigia dipinta, produzione limitata e quasi esclusiva della Sibaritide, è rappresentata a Torre Mordillo da scarsi frammenti.

La distruzione dell'aggere è da collocarsi tra il Bronzo recente ed il Bronzo finale antico: lo scarso materiale proveniente dagli strati di distruzione non ne consente una più precisa datazione. Questo evento segna, nelle nostre trincee di scavo, un cambiamento nella composizione degli strati archeologici, interpretabile come l'indizio di una sopravvenuta instabilità abitativa. Nel deposito formatosi sopra l'aggere, in un arco di tempo che comprende il Bronzo finale ed il principio dell'età del ferro, si alternano, infatti, a resti di abitazione strati costituitisi per il degrado di strutture abitative, caratterizzati da matrice argillosa e ceneri, contenenti frammenti vascolari e d'incannucciata; questi strati possono raggiungere spessori anche elevati, in una zona nei pressi della sella fino a 80 centimetri, ed hanno restituito una grande quantità di materiali riferibili al Bronzo finale, sia d'impasto che di argilla depurata. Oltre a questi, di particolare interesse è un pettine decorato a cerchielli concentrici (fig. 1,7), probabilmente realizzato con avorio di elefante (determinazione del prof. F. Poplin del Museo di Storia Naturale di Parigi). Il pettine appartiene ad una foggia presente nel ripostiglio di Frattesina, a Pianello di Genga e a Timmari e ha un confronto stringente a Cipro nella tomba 6 di Enkomi, le cui ultime deposizioni non dovrebbero essere più recenti del Tardo Cipriota III B1 che, in termini di cronologia assoluta, si pone alla transizione fra il XII e l'XI secolo a. C (Vagnetti 1986). Sempre da uno strato formatosi con il degrado di strutture abitative proviene un altro frammento di avorio, probabilmente di elefante, che può essere interpretato come elemento semilavorato o come scarto di lavorazione.

La scoperta più rilevante, all'interno della sequenza stratigrafica riferibile al Bronzo finale, è costituita dai resti di un'abitazione, purtroppo indagata per una superficie molto limitata, venuta in luce subito a monte dell'aggere e parzialmente incavata nel primo degli strati di abbandono costituitisi al di sopra di esso. Della struttura abitativa, distrutta da un incendio e ricoperta da un imponente crollo di pietre e concotto, è stata individuata e scavata solo una stretta porzione, comprendente un angolo e due lati, seguiti l'uno per 5, l'altro per 1 metro. Lo scavo ha messo in luce i resti delle pareti in argilla e in legno di quercia, in parte crollate all'interno dell'abitazione, in parte ancora infisse nel terreno, ed alcuni buchi di palo posti subito all'interno di queste (fig. 2,1).

I frammenti ceramici rinvenuti negli strati di distruzione e sul fondo dell'abitazione costituiscono un complesso databile al Bronzo finale non iniziale. Elemento caratteristico è il grande vaso con collo tronco-conico e spalla pronunciata in argilla depurata (fig. 2,8), decorato sul collo con un motivo a metope campite a graticcio, sulla spalla con triangoli inscritti e sulla parte interna dell'orlo con serie di tratti perpendicolari all'orlo; mentre il graticcio è uno dei motivi più caratteristici del proto-geometrico enotrio-iapigio, la versione in forma metopale non risultava attestata finora fra il materiale edito; quanto alla forma essa è nota in Puglia,

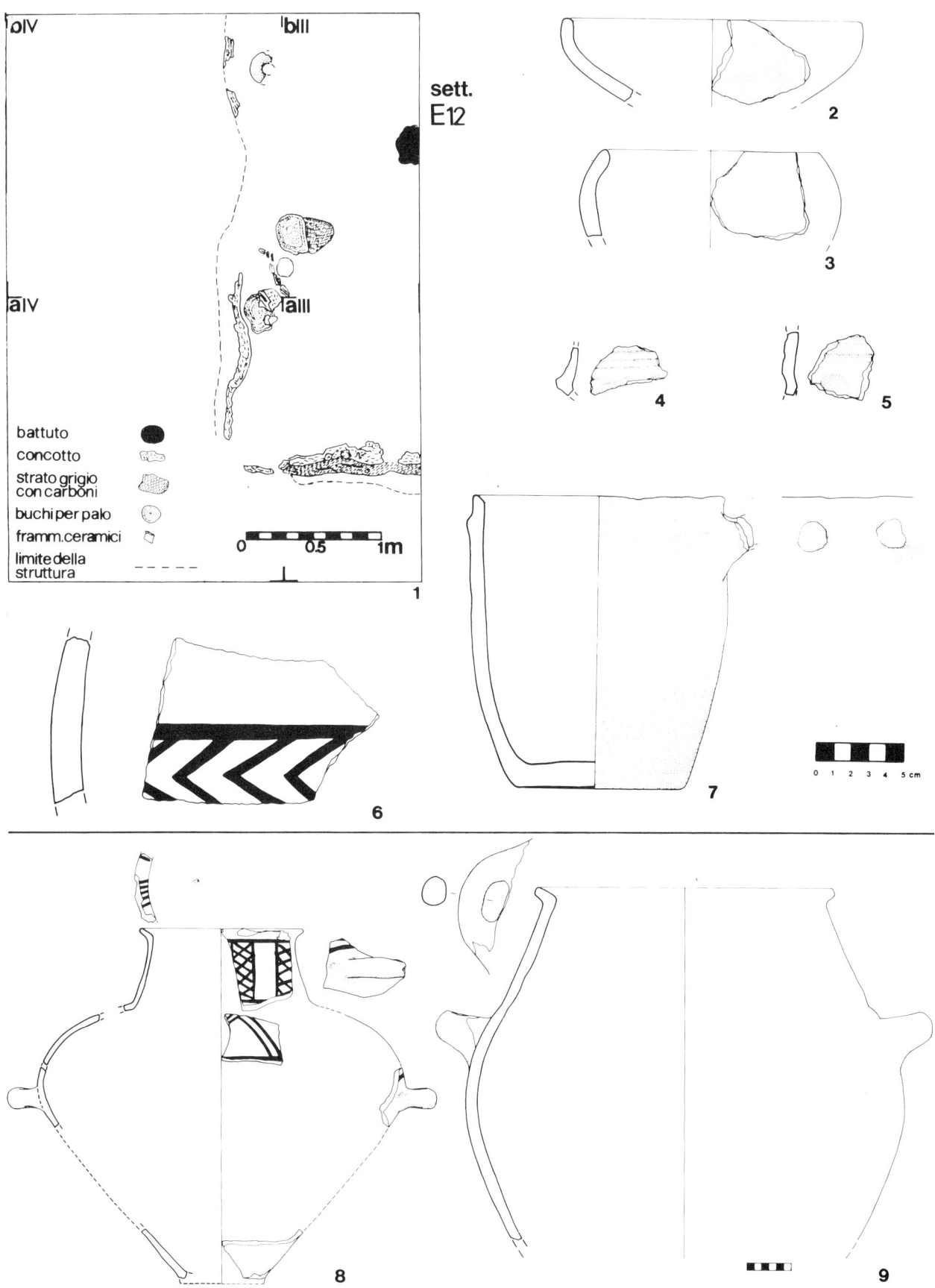

Fig. 2. *La casa del Bronzo finale (scavo 1990). 1. Planimetria. 2-9: Materiali rinvenuti all'interno.*

a S. Maria di Leuca (Orlando 1990: 14, fig. 35), a Torre Castelluccia (Biancofiore 1967: tav. XL,u) e nella Sibaritide, in genere, però, con spalla meno pronunciata (Buffa 1994: forma f14). Un frammento di grande dolio per derrate in argilla depurata reca una decorazione dipinta a spina di pesce giacente (fig. 2,6), motivo conosciuto nel protogeometrico enotrio-iapigio (Buffa 1994: motivo XI); la decorazione dipinta su dolii è elemento noto, anche se non molto frequente, a Broglio di Trebisacce (Bergonzi & Cardarelli 1982: 97, tav. 22,8) e in Puglia. Un altro grande contenitore è il vaso con collo troncoconico appena distinto, corpo ovoide e ansa a maniglia orizzontale, in impasto (fig. 2,9). Due elementi tipici di questo orizzonte sono il piccolo frammento in impasto decorato con una grossa cuppella e due solcature piuttosto larghe (fig. 2,5) e la ciotola (fig. 2,4), o più probabilmente la tazza, con carena accentuata, decorata con costolature oblique sormontate da solcature (Buffa 1994: forma 3). Sono state inoltre rinvenute due scodelle ad orlo rientrante (fig. 2,2-3) ed un'olletta cilindro-ovoide quasi interamente ricostruita (fig. 2,7).

Per quanto riguarda lo studio delle faune, vengono presentati in questa sede i risultati dell'analisi relativa ai resti rinvenuti nelle unità stratigrafiche databili al Bronzo finale in ambedue le trincee di scavo. Sono stati presi in considerazione oltre 5.000 resti ossei, di cui 1089, di almeno 183 individui, sono stati determinati a livello specifico (fig. 3a). Il campione è composto prevalentemente di mammiferi domestici (91,5%) con più rari mammiferi selvatici quali cervo, volpe e un grosso gatto selvatico, uccelli, due specie di tartarughe e rarissimi pesci. Sono inoltre presenti alcune conchiglie di molluschi marini, in prevalenza *Dentalium* (da utilizzare forse come elementi di collana) e di *Patella*, *Monodonta* e *Cerastoderma*. Tra gli uccelli, oltre al gufo reale, sono da segnalare la cicogna e l'oca lombardella; la loro presenza, assieme ai resti di testuggine d'acqua (*Emys orbicularis*), indica che alla base del pianoro dovevano estendersi zone acquitrinose ed umide. Analizzando complessivamente il rapporto tra i mammiferi (fig. 3b), si nota che le specie più comuni sono il maiale, gli ovicaprini ed il bue, segue quindi il cervo, raro cane e rarissimi cavallo, volpe e gatto selvatico, con lievissime variazioni a seconda del metodo di conteggio utilizzato (NR o NMI).

Il cavallo è presente con due individui adulti di piccole dimensioni; il cane con cinque individui di almeno due differenti razze. Il cervo è rappresentato prevalentemente da resti craniali e delle estremità degli arti di individui adulti, oltre che da frammenti di palco con tracce di lavorazione. L'allevamento era basato in maggioranza su bovini, ovicaprini e suini, con questi ultimi leggermente prevalenti. Per la differente mole erano, però, i buoi che fornivano la maggior quantità di carne. Evidenti tracce di macellazione sono rilevabili sulle ossa di queste specie, che erano uccise nel sito essendo presenti resti dell'intero scheletro. I buoi erano in maggioranza di piccole ed a volte piccolissime dimensioni; anche tra gli ovicaprini, tra i quali le pecore sono più numerose delle capre, prevalgono individui di taglia ridotta. I suini, rappresentati in maggioranza da maschi, sono invece di grosse dimensioni e non è esclusa la presenza di cinghiali o di incroci con essi.

Diversificata appare la modalità di sfruttamento riguardo l'età di macellazione (fig. 3c). I buoi erano uccisi in maggioranza in età adulta, dopo essere stati sfruttati anche come forza lavoro e per i prodotti caseari; rarissimi i vitelli, sono però ben rappresentati individui uccisi tra il secondo ed il quarto anno di età. Anche tra gli ovicaprini sono rare le uccisioni di capretti e agnelli, mentre oltre la metà dei resti apparteneva a giovani e giovani-adulti di meno di tre anni; molti erano tenuti in vita fino ad oltre i 6-8 anni per la lana ed il latte. Numerosi porcelli (15%) erano invece uccisi a meno di sei mesi e oltre il 60% dei maiali era ucciso sotto i tre anni, anche se non mancano prove di uccisioni di animali senili.

Complessivamente, nel Bronzo finale di Torre Mordillo, l'economia di allevamento risulta ben sviluppata e varia; l'alimentazione era basata su una forte incidenza di bovini-suini, integrata dai prodotti della pastorizia ovina e caprina, da rara cacciagione e da ancor più rari prodotti ittici.

Durante la campagna del 1966, nella trincea 13, aperta nella parte occidentale del pianoro presso il pilone Nord (fig. 1,a), lo scavo interessò, come si è già accennato, i livelli protostorici, mettendo in luce una complessa situazione stratigrafica (Colburn 1967: 37-38; 1974: 81-88; 1977: 451-454; 491-496; fig. 38-39). Al disotto di alcuni ambienti di età ellenistica, si rinvennero i resti di quelle che furono interpretate dall'autore dello scavo come due strutture abitative protostoriche sovrapposte, entrambe distrutte da un incendio. Occorre precisare, tuttavia, che non sembra possibile una puntuale ricostruzione della sequenza stratigrafica e, soprattutto, della dinamica di formazione degli strati: questo a causa del carattere tutt'altro che esaustivo delle pubblicazioni di scavo. Altro elemento di incertezza è costituito dalla presenza, nei depositi della Soprintendenza, di materiali databili dal Bronzo medio-recente (fig. 5,1) alla prima età del ferro, indicati come provenienti dai due complessi. Ciò rappresenta, evidentemente, un limite alla lettura che in questa sede si propone. L'abitazione più recente venne indagata solo in parte (m. 3 × 4 ca.) a causa della presenza delle soprastanti strutture di età ellenistica: non se ne conoscono pertanto nè l'estensione complessiva nè la pianta. Sulla base della documentazione edita, all'interno di uno degli ambienti ellenistici, ad una ventina di cm. sotto il pavimento, si rinvenne uno strato di bruciato contenente frammenti di incannuc-

	Settore E9 US 2		US 19		Settore D12 US 20		US22		Totale Bronzo finale			
	NR	NMI	NR	NMI	NR	NMI	NR	NMI	NR	%	NMI	%
Equus caballus	4	1			1	1			5	0,5	2	1,2
Bos taurus	182	21	8	2	74	14	12	4	276	27,6	41	24,3
Ovis vel *Capra*	155	22	16	4	81	16	33	6	285	28,5	48	28,4
Sus scrofa dom.	178	31	16	4	109	16	27	9	330	33,0	60	35,5
Canis familiaris	12	3	1	1	6	1			19	1,9	5	3,0
Mammiferi domestici	531	78	41	11	271	48	72	19	915	91,5	156	92,3
Cervus elaphus	38	4	3	2	28	4	12	1	81	8,1	11	6,5
Vulpes vulpes					2	1	1	1	3	0,3	2	1,2
Felis silvestris	1	1							1	0,1	1	0,6
Mammiferi selvatici	39	5	3	2	30	4	13	2	85	8,5	13	7,7
Totale mammiferi	570	83	44	13	301	52	85	21	1000		169	
Uccelli	2	2	1	1	2	2			5		5	
Tartaruga	67	5	1	1	14	1	1	1	83		8	
Pesci			1	1					1		1	
Totale complessivo	639	90	47	16	317	55	86	22	1089		183	
Molluschi marini	8	8					2	2	10		10	

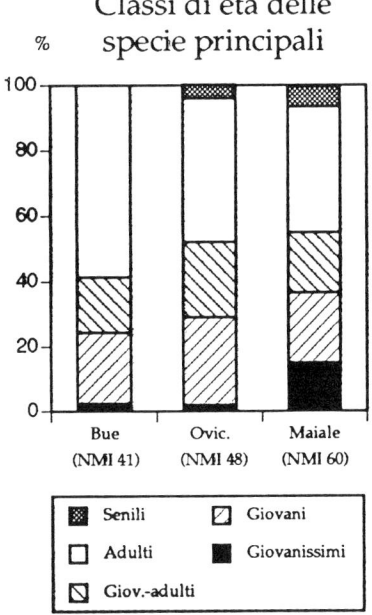

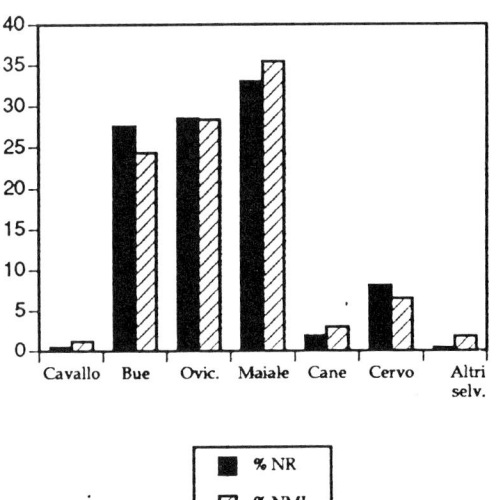

Fig. 3. Faune del Bronzo finale (scavi 1987–90).

ciata e carboni, relativo al crollo delle pareti e della copertura dell'abitazione a seguito di un violento incendio.

Questo strato, denominato 8, dello spessore di una trentina di cm., poggiava sul pavimento della struttura.

Qui, oltre ad un certo numero di recipienti di impasto integri o in frammenti e ad abbondanti resti di maiale, cervo e pecora, fu rinvenuta una piastra rettangolare di argilla cotta (m. 0,93 × 0,97, alt. m. 0,15), nella quale si riconobbe un 'focolare', su cui poggiavano alcuni vasi

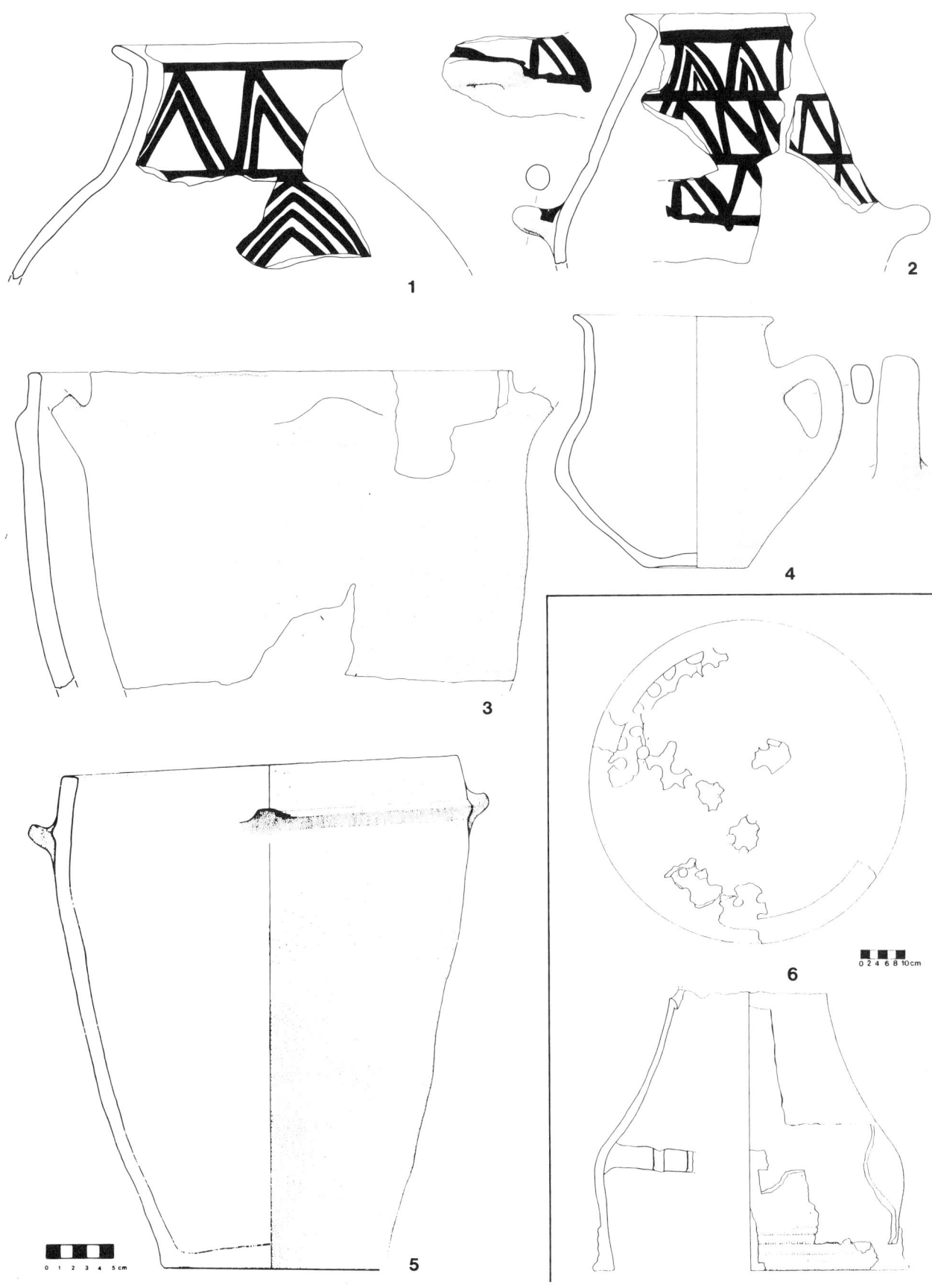

Fig. 4. Scavi 1966: trincea 13. 1-2: strato 9. 3-6: strato 8.

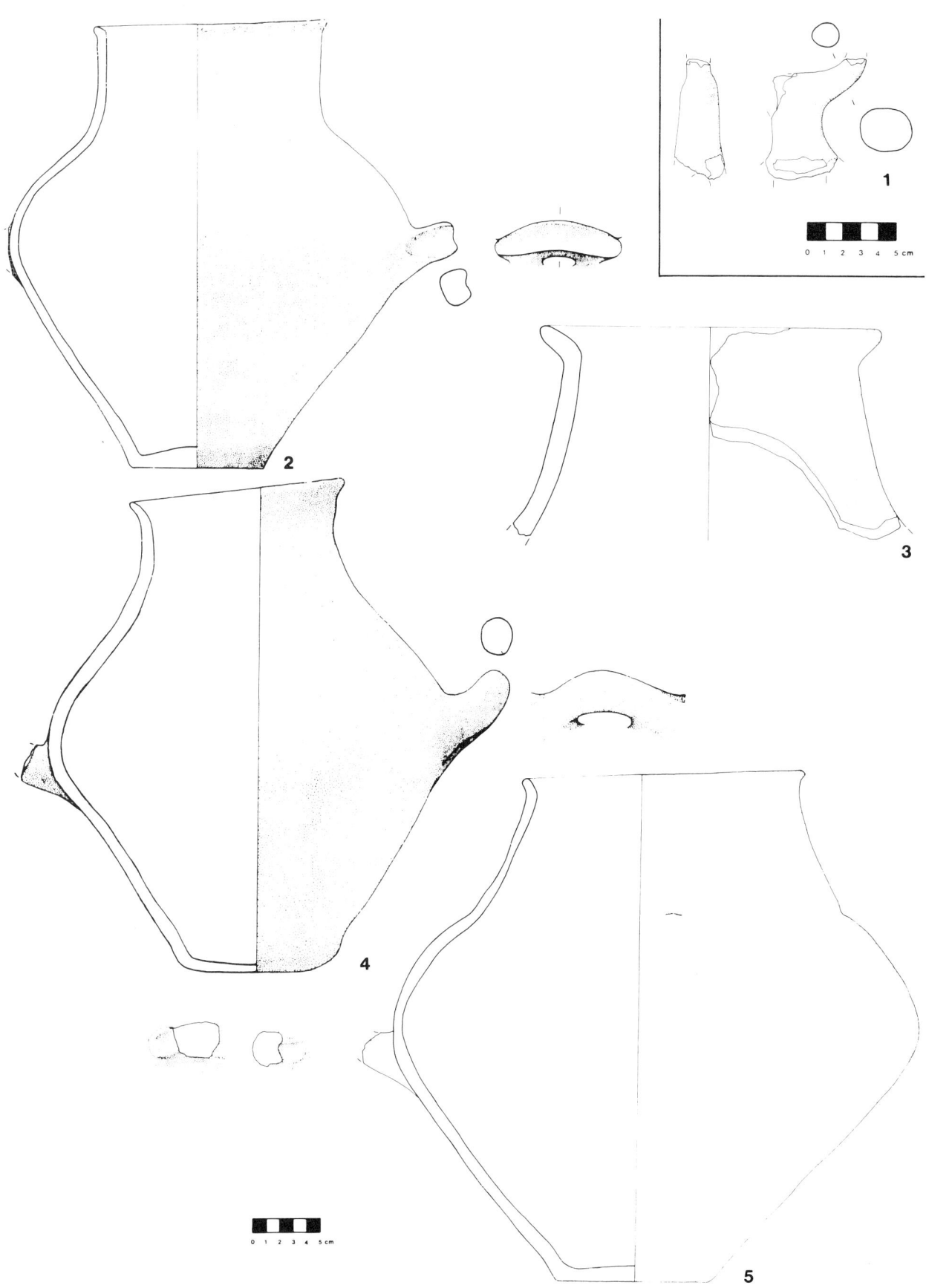

Fig. 5. Scavi 1966: trincea 13. Strato 8.

e un vero e proprio forno (fig. 4,6). La superficie di scavo venne quindi ampliata su una limitatissima area, dove si potè constatare la presenza del medesimo livello di bruciato, sovrapposto al pavimento dell'abitazione, sul quale si rinvennero numerosi altri recipienti, fra cui un grosso dolio in argilla depurata.

Non potendosi, per le ragioni sopra esposte, ampliare ulteriormente la superficie di scavo, vennero effettuati alcuni saggi in profondità, nel corso dei quali fu individuata la seconda struttura. Uno dei sondaggi venne eseguito nell'area occupata dal focolare, dopo averlo rimosso. Qui, ad una profondità di ca. 10–20 cm, fu messo in luce uno strato, denominato 9, contenente alcuni frammenti sia di impasto che di argilla depurata dipinta, attribuibili all'età del bronzo finale (fig. 4,1–2), in rapporto con l'abitazione più antica, indiziata dalla presenza di grossi frammenti di intonaco di capanna; le tracce di bruciato riscontrate dagli scavatori attesterebbero, anche in questo caso, una distruzione violenta per incendio. Un altro sondaggio, posto circa un metro a sud-ovest del precedente (Colburn 1967: 38; 1974: 86), permise di individuare un secondo focolare, forse pertinente alla struttura abitativa più antica.

I materiali provenienti dal sondaggio sotto il 'focolare', strato 9, sono, come già noto (Colburn 1977: fig. 73), databili all'età del Bronzo finale. Un vaso biconico in argilla depurata, dipinto con i motivi dei triangoli inscritti e dello zig-zag continuo su registri sovrapposti (fig. 4,2), tipici del 'protogeometrico enotrio-iapigio', ed un altro, decorato con un motivo simile (fig. n. 4,1), trovano confronti in esemplari dagli strati del Bronzo finale di Broglio di Trebisacce (Buffa 1994: motivo VI) e a Salapia (Alberti et al. 1981: 166, fig. 10,5). Allo stesso ambito cronologico appartengono vari frammenti di un vaso in impasto decorato a solcature e cuppelle (Colburn 1977: 491, fig. 73, P5).

Nella letteratura archeologica i materiali provenienti dallo strato 8 (Colburn 1977: figg. 77–78) sono stati considerati pertinenti alla prima età del ferro, anche se Bergonzi ed Cardarelli (1982: 107, 112: fig.17; 1984: 144–145, 148) avevano espresso dubbi sulla pertinenza di tutti i materiali ad un complesso unitario, soprattutto per la presenza di un dolio a fasce tricostolate tipico del Bronzo finale. Il ritrovamento dei materiali, il loro restauro (dal Laboratorio di Restauro dell'Ufficio Scavi di Sibari della Soprintendenza Archeologica della Calabria) e il conseguente riesame di tutto il contesto hanno consentito di precisarne meglio la cronologia.

Un nucleo consistente di reperti è databile al Bronzo finale. Il grande vaso biconico in impasto (fig. 5,5) ha numerosi confronti in Italia meridionale, per esempio a Torre Guaceto (Guerreschi 1966: 296, fig. 12,1), Scoglio del Tonno (Saeflund 1939: 464, fig. 6) e a Timmari, tomba 199 (Quagliati & Ridola 1906: 51, fig. 40). Gli altri due biconici (fig. 5,2,4) trovano confronti a Milazzo, tomba 91 della necropoli dell'Istmo (Bernabò Brea & Cavalier 1959: tav. XXXIV, 7) e a Lipari, fra i materiali dell'Ausonio II (Bernabò Brea & Cavalier 1980: tav. CCXXIII,5; CCXIX,10). Il grande dolio in argilla depurata con fascia tricostolata ed ansa verticale a costolature oblique appartiene ad un tipo ampiamente documentato nel corso dell'età del bronzo finale a Broglio, fase in cui è presente anche un tipo di tazza carenata (Buffa 1994: forma 13) a cui appartengono due degli esemplari di Torre Mordillo qui presentati (fig. 6,1,5). I due piccoli vasi cilindrici, muniti l'uno di cordone orizzontale con prese (fig. 6,10) e l'altro di quattro prese (fig. 6,8), trovano confronti fra i materiali dell'Ausonio II di Lipari (Bernabò Brea & Cavalier 1980: tav. CCXXXVII,7).

Un altro nucleo di materiali è rappresentativo della fase iniziale della prima età del ferro e più precisamente dell'orizzonte iniziale di tale fase, come indicano i confronti con materiali dalla necropoli di Torre Galli; si tratta del piccolo vaso (fig. 6,4) con collo distinto troncoconico e spalla rigonfia (Orsi 1926: tav. II, 25) e dell'orciolo (fig. 4,4) con ansa a bastoncello, vicino al tipo F21 di Kilian, con molti esemplari da tombe datate alla I fase (Kilian 1970: 310, beil. 7). La scodella ad orlo rientrante decorata con elementi angolari a rilievo sotto l'orlo (fig. 6,7) e la ciotola carenata con orlo indistinto, svasato (fig. 6,2) hanno invece confronti non proprio puntuali fra i materiali (non distinti per corredo) di Castiglione di Paludi, necropoli inquadrabile nella fase iniziale della prima età del ferro (Guzzo 1975: 145, fig. 76; 147, fig. 80,638).

A questa fase potrebbero essere attribuite anche la scodella ad orlo lievemente rientrante con ansa a maniglia orizzontale (fig. 6,9) ed il dolio tronco-conico in impasto (fig. 4,5), che rientrano agevolmente nelle tipologie elaborate per tali fogge della prima età del ferro. La tazza a corpo arrotondato con costolature oblique sul punto di massima espansione (fig. 6,6) non trova confronti puntuali fra i corredi ceramici nè della necropoli di Torre Mordillo, nè delle numerose necropoli, note nella Sibaritide e in genere in area enotria, datate alla fase avanzata della prima età del ferro, tanto da farla ritenere anch'essa databile alla fase iniziale.

Al di sopra della piastra rettangolare denominata 'focolare' era stato rinvenuta una 'graticola di terracotta' (Colburn 1977: 451): si tratta di un forno a campana (fig. 4,6), parzialmente ricostruito (lavoro di V. Pitrelli dell'Ufficio Scavi di Sibari), con base profilata e piastra fissa a circa un terzo dell'altezza, che non sembra trovare al momento confronti puntuali.

Lo strato 8, dunque, è costituito da almeno due complessi cronologicamente distinti, l'uno pertinente al Bronzo finale, l'altro alla fase iniziale della prima età del ferro, mentre sembrerebbero assenti elementi attribuibili alla fase recente.

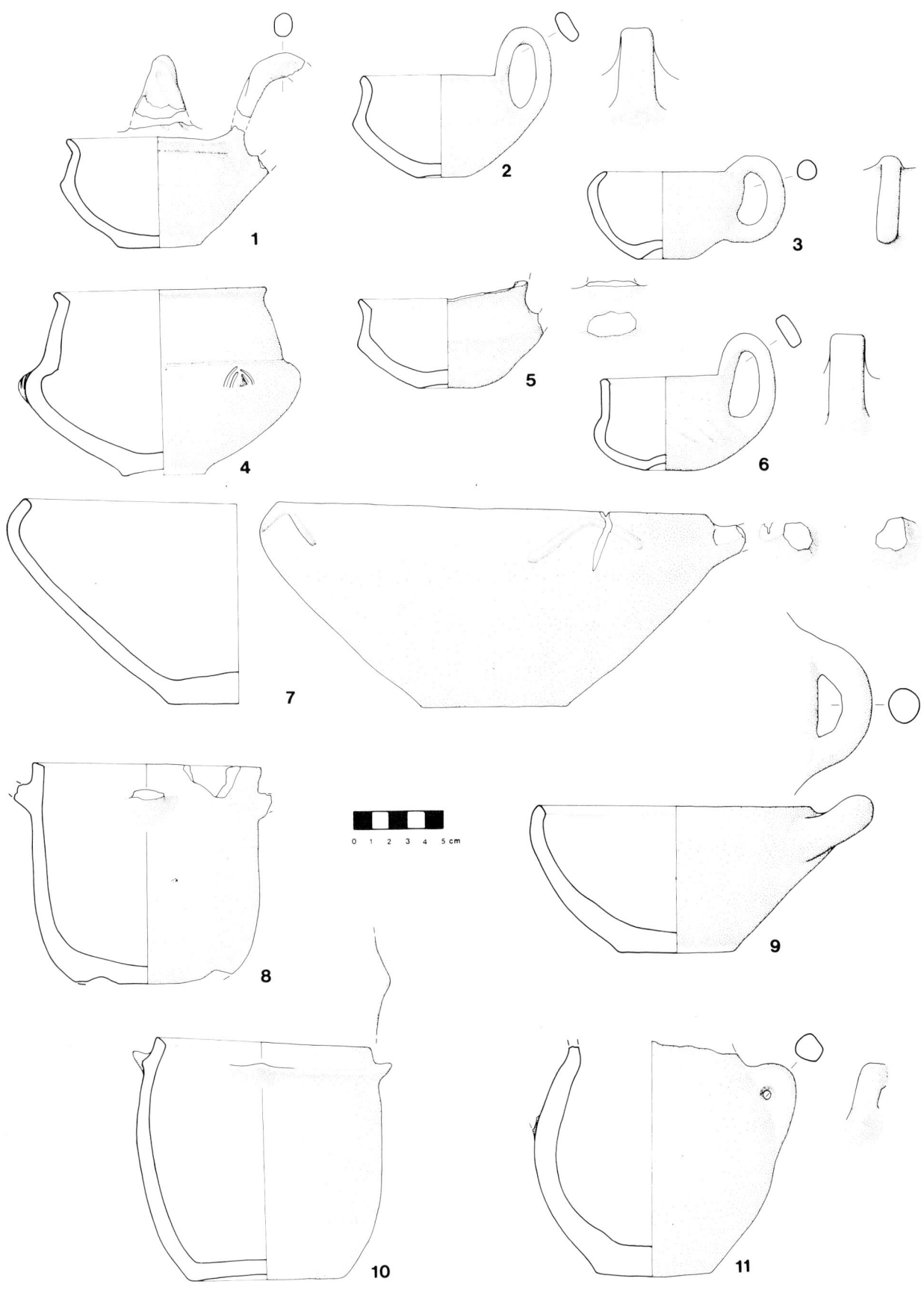

Fig. 6. Scavi 1966: trincea 13. Strato 8.

Lembi di strati riferibili alla prima età del ferro sono presenti anche nelle trincee scavate sulla sella, fortemente disturbati dagli interventi di età successiva (Arancio *et al.* 1994). Pur nell'assenza di strutture abitative riferibili a tale fase, la documentazione raccolta in questi livelli più superficiali testimonia il perdurare dell'insediamento per tutto il corso dell'VIII secolo a.C.

Ringraziamenti

Il progetto di ricerca a Torre Mordillo è stato voluto e reso possibile dal prof. F. Zevi, ai tempi Soprintendente al Museo L. Pigorini, e dalla dott.ssa E. Lattanzi, Soprintendente Archeologo della Calabria. Particolare gratitudine dobbiamo a Silvana Luppino, direttore dell'Ufficio Scavi di Sibari, per la pazienza e la disponibilità dimostrataci dall'inizio di tale ricerca. Desideriamo anche ringraziare, per l'appoggio ed i consigli datici nel corso della ricerca, Renato Peroni e Giovanni Scichilone, ed anche E. Pellegrini che ha partecipato alle prime tre campagne di scavo a Torre Mordillo. La documentazione grafica presentata in questa sede, oltre che agli autori, è dovuta a C. Damiani e a G. Mieli.

Bibliografia

Alberti, M.A, Bettini, A. & Lorenzi, I. 1981. 'Salapia (Foggia). Notizia preliminare sugli scavi nella città dauna di Salapia. Campagne 1978-1979', *Notizie degli Scavi di Antichità*: 159-182.

Arancio, M.L., Buffa, V., Damiani, I. & Trucco, F. 1994. 'Recenti indagini protostoriche nella Sibaritide. 2-Torre Mordillo', *Atti XXXII Convegno Studi Magna Grecia*, 145-162.

Bergonzi, G. & Cardarelli, A. 1982. 'Due produzioni dell'artigianato specializzato', in Bergonzi *et al.* 1982a, 94-118.

Bergonzi, G. & Cardarelli, A. 1984. 'Due produzioni dell'artigianato specializzato: ceramica grigia e dolii per derrate', in Peroni 1984a, 101-163.

Bergonzi G., Cardarelli A., Giardino C., Guzzo P. G., Peroni R. & Vagnetti L. 1982a. *Ricerche sulla protostoria della Sibaritide*, 1, Napoli.

Bergonzi G., Buffa V., Cardarelli A., Giardino C., Peroni R. & Vagnetti L. 1982b. *Ricerche sulla protostoria della Sibaritide*, 2, Napoli.

Bernabò Brea L. & Cavalier, M. 1959. *Mylai*, Catania.

Bernabò Brea L. & Cavalier, M. 1980. *Meligunìs Lipàra IV*, Palermo.

Biancofiore, F. 1967. *Civiltà micenea nell'Italia meridionale*, Roma.

Buffa, V. 1994. 'I materiali dell'età del bronzo finale e della prima età del ferro', in Peroni & Trucco (a cura di), 455-569.

Carancini, G.L. & Guerzoni, R.P. 1987. 'Gli scavi nella Grotta Pavolella presso Cassano allo Jonio (CS)', in *Il Neolitico in Italia, Atti XXVI Riunione Scientifica IIPP*, Firenze, 783-792.

Cardini, L. 1970. 'Praia a Mare. Relazione degli scavi 1957-1970 dell'Istituto Italiano di Paleontologia Umana', *Bullettino di Paletnologia Italiana*, 79, 31-59.

Colburn, O. C. 1967. 'A habitation area of Thurii', *Expedition. The Bulletin of the University Museum* 9, 3, 30-38.

Colburn, O.C. 1974. *The Quest for Thurii, 1963-1967*. (Dissertation in Classical Archaeology, Faculty of the Graduate School of Arts and Sciences of the University of Pennsylvania (1973), University Microfilms International, Ann Arbor).

Colburn, O.C. 1977. 'Torre del Mordillo (Cosenza). Scavi negli anni 1963, 1966 e 1967', *Notizie degli Scavi di Antichità*, 423-526.

Damiani, I. 1991. 'Aspetti ceramici dell'età del bronzo recente in Italia peninsulare e nelle isole Eolie: la facies subappenninica a trent'anni dalla sua definizione', *Dialoghi di Archeologia*, 5-33.

Damiani, I. 1992. 'Caratteri dell'insediamento nell'Italia sud-orientale', in *L'età del Bronzo in Italia nei secoli dal XVI al XIV a.C.*, (Atti del Congresso, Viareggio 1989), Firenze, 742-43.

Edwards, G. R. 1969. 'Torre Mordillo 1967', *Expedition* 11, 2, 30-35.

Guerreschi, G. 1966. 'I reperti del promontorio di Torre Guaceto (Brindisi)', *Memorie Museo Civico Storia Naturale Verona*, 15, 239-302.

Guzzo, P.G. 1975. 'Paludi (Cosenza): località Castiglione. Necropoli dell'età del ferro', *Klearchos* XVII, 97-177.

Jones, R.E., Lazzarini, L., Mariottini, M. & Orvini, E. 1994. 'Studio minero-petrografico e chimico di ceramiche protostoriche dal Broglio di Trebisacce (Sibari)', in Peroni & Trucco (a cura di), 413-453.

Jones, R.E. & Vagnetti, L. 1990. 'Traders and craftsmen in the Central Mediterranean: archaeological evidence and archaeometric research', in Gale, N.H. (ed.), *Bronze Age Trade in the Mediterranean*, (Conference in Oxford, 1989), Sima, XC, Jonsered, 127-147.

Kilian, K. 1970. *Früheisenzeitliche funde aus der Südostnecropole von Sala Consilina (provinz Salerno)*, Heidelberg.

Orlando, M.A. 1990. 'S. Maria di Leuca. Punta Meliso', in D'Andria, F. (a cura di), *Archeologia dei Messapi. Catalogo della Mostra*, Lecce, 5-16.

Orsi, P. 1926. 'Le necropoli preelleniche calabresi di Torre Galli e di Canale Janchina, Patariti', *Monumenti Antichi dei Lincei*, XXXI, 5-376.

Pasqui, A. 1888. 'Territorio di Sibari. Scavi nella necropoli di Torre Mordillo nel comune di Spezzano Albanese', *Notizie degli Scavi di Antichità*, 239-268; 462-480; 575-592; 648-671.

Peroni, R. (a cura di), 1984a. *Ricerche sulla protostoria della Sibaritide*, 3, Roma.

Peroni, R. (a cura di), 1984b. *Nuove ricerche sulla protostoria della Sibaritide*, Roma.

Peroni, R. 1987. 'La Protostoria', in S. Settis (a cura di), *Storia della Calabria antica*, Roma, 67-136.

Peroni, R. 1989. *Protostoria dell'Italia continentale. La penisola italiana nelle età del Bronzo e del Ferro*, Roma.

Peroni, R., 1994. 'La Sibaritide prima di Sibari', *Atti XXXII Convegno di Studi della Magna Grecia*, 1992, 103-135.

Peroni R. & Trucco F. (a cura di) 1994. *Enotri e Micenei nella Sibaritide*.

Peroni R. & Vanzetti, A. 1994. 'Recenti indagini nella Sibaritide. 1 - Broglio di Trebisacce', *Atti XXXII Convegno di Studi della Magna Grecia*, 1992, 137-145.

Quagliati, Q. & Ridola, D. 1906. 'Necropoli arcaica ad incinerazione presso Timmari nel Materano', *Monumenti Antichi dei Lincei* XVI, 5-166.

Säflund, G. 1939. 'Punta del Tonno. Eine griechische Siedlung bei Tarent', in *DRAGMA Martino P. Nilsson*, 458-490.

Tinè, S. 1962. 'Successione delle culture preistoriche in Calabria alla luce dei recenti scavi in provincia di Cosenza', *Klearchos*, 13-14, 38-48.

Tinè, S. 1964a. 'Il Neolitico in Calabria alla luce di recenti scavi', *Atti VIII-IX Riunione Scientifica IIPP*, 277-289.

Tinè, S. 1964b. 'La grotta di S. Angelo III a Cassano Jonio', *Atti e Memorie della Società della Magna Grecia*, n.s. V, 11-55.

Tinè, S. 1987. 'Il Neolitico', in S. Settis (a cura di), *Storia della Calabria antica*, Roma, 41-62.

Trucco, F. 1987-88. 'Torre Mordillo (Spezzano Albanese, Prov. di Cosenza)', *Notiziario, Rivista di Scienze Preistoriche*, XLI, 1-2, 421-422.

Trucco, F. 1989-90. 'Torre Mordillo (Spezzano Albanese, Prov. di Cosenza)', *Notiziario, Rivista di Scienze Preistoriche*, XLII, 1-2, 389.

Trucco, F., Pellegrini, E., Tagliacozzo, A., Arancio, M.L., Buffa, V., Damiani, I. & Vagnetti, L. 1992. 'La fase iniziale dell'abitato di Torre Mordillo (Spezzano Albanese, Cosenza): scavi 1987-89', in *L'età del Bronzo in Italia nei secoli dal XVI al XIV a. C.*, (Atti del Congresso, Viareggio 1989), Firenze, 752-753.

Vagnetti, L. 1982a. 'I frammenti micenei', in Bergonzi *et al.* 1982a, 119-128 e 159-160.

Vagnetti, L. 1982b. 'Ceramica micenea e ceramica dipinta dell'età del bronzo', Bergonzi *et al.* 1982b, 99-113.

Vagnetti, L. 1984a. 'Ceramiche d'importazione egea e ceramica dipinta dell'età del bronzo', in Peroni (a cura di), 1984a, 164–184.

Vagnetti, L. 1984b. 'Ceramica d'importazione egea e ceramica dipinta dell'età del bronzo', in Peroni (a cura di), 1984b, 169–196.

Vagnetti, L. & Jones, R.E. 1988. 'Towards the identification of local Mycenean pottery in Italy', in French, E.B. & Wardle, K.A. (eds.), *Problems in Greek Prehistory. Papers presented at the Centenary Conference of the British School of Archaeology at Athens* (Manchester, 1986), Bristol, 335–348.

Vagnetti, L. 1986. 'Cypriot elements beyond the Aegean in the Bronze Age', in *Cyprus between the Orient and the Occident* (Atti del Simposio), Nicosia, 210–214.

Vagnetti, L., Panichelli, S. 1994. 'Ceramica egea importata e di produzione locale', in Peroni & Trucco (a cura di), 373–413.

25

Siti Costieri dal Bronzo Medio al Bronzo Finale nella Calabria Centro-Orientale (Italia Meridionale)

DOMENICO A. MARINO & SILVIA FESTUCCIA
(Università di Roma 'La Sapienza')

Sommario: *Dai momenti iniziali dell'età del bronzo medio all'età del bronzo finale ed oltre la fascia costiera ionica della Calabria centrale, in particolare il tratto compreso tra Crotone (a Nord) e il capo di Le Castella (a Sud), viene occupata da numerosi siti su promontorio. Uno di questi siti è quello di Capo Piccolo che spicca nel panorama regionale per alcune sue caratteristiche. Questo sito, infatti, ha restituito alcune tra le più antiche testimonianze di contatti tra l'area egea e l'Italia peninsulare: si tratta di ceramiche datate al TM I A/TE I–II. Lo stesso sito ha restituito importanti materiali confrontabili con la* facies *siciliana di Rodí-Tindari e testimonianze della lavorazione locale di armi bronzee. Sempre dai momenti iniziali del bronzo medio è documentata la frequentazione di altri promontori (Capo Pellegrino, Capo Cimiti, Le Castella) che si prolunga fino a tutto il bronzo recente. E' ipotizzabile una significativa apertura nei confronti delle correnti di traffico tra oriente e occidente. Solo nel bronzo recente ha inizio l'occupazione del promontorio di Crotone che ha restituito anche significative testimonianze di frequentazione nel bronzo finale e poi, più intensamente, nella prima età del ferro.*

Dai momenti iniziali del bronzo medio fino al bronzo finale ed oltre, la fascia costiera ionica della Calabria centrale, in particolare il tratto compreso tra Crotone (a Nord) e il capo di Le Castella (a Sud), viene occupata da numerosi siti. La costa a Sud di Crotone, costituita da una piattaforma di arenarie pleistoceniche poggianti su argille plioceniche, mostra una articolata sequenza di promontori, dalle falesie rocciose e a picco sul mare, e di ampie spiagge.

Il tipo di insediamento preferito è quello posto su un promontorio naturalmente difeso e dominante su due baie o rade che permettano duplice possibilità di approdo e di riparo dai venti, similmente a quanto si verifica, a partire dall'età del bronzo, nell' area di Tropea, nella vicina Puglia e in altre aree (Bernabò Brea 1982: 15; Bianco 1992: 509; Laviosa 1982: 334–5; Pacciarelli 1989–90: 10; Radina 1992: 526). La durata di questi abitati è variabile, così come nel resto dell'Italia meridionale (Cazzella & Moscoloni 1989: 403), ma è spesso più lunga rispetto ai siti interni (con l'esclusione del sito di Corazzo: Geniola 1989–90: 389–90).

I DATI ARCHEOLOGICI (D.A.M.)

Il sito che ha restituito le testimonianze più cospicue per i momenti iniziali del bronzo medio è quello di Capo Piccolo, un promontorio (m.16 slm.- sup.ha.3) proteso nel golfo che va dal Capo Rizzuto a Le Castella (fig.1.6). Sul versante occidentale sfocia in mare il fiume Vorga che poteva offrire ottimo approdo. Nel 1977 uno sbancamento mise in luce, nella fascia sud-orientale, materiali archeologici in situ: numerosi vasi d'impasto vennero recuperati pressoché integri. Alcuni elementi (un vaso a fruttiera, un frammento di ansa ad 'orecchie equine' ed una grande tazza globulare con ansa a nastro verticale 'pizzuta', sopraelevata sull'orlo e impostata sul punto di massima espansione del vaso) riportano alla facies siciliana di Rodí-Tindari (Marino 1987: 26–36). Tra le altre forme d'impasto si distinguono diverse ciotole carenate. Una ciotola ha vasca profonda, fondo piatto ed orlo svasato con diametro leggermente superiore a quello della carena, dove conserva l'attacco di un'ansa a nastro verticale, probabilmente sopraelevata sull'orlo (fig.4.8). Il profilo ci rimanda a forme simili presenti a Monte Fellino (Albore Livadie 1985: 22–4, 27–8, tavv.1–2). Gli stessi confronti valgono anche per un framm. di ciotola con vasca profonda ed orlo svasato con diametro leggermente inferiore a quello della carena (fig.4.10). In più vi sono confronti con la fase antica di Mursia (Tozzi 1968: 343, fig.15.2) e Tindari (Cavalier 1970: fig.12). Un frammento di ciotola con fondo ombelicato (fig.4.9) ha ugualmente confronti con Tindari (Cavalier 1970: fig.12). Un'altra ciotola con vasca profonda, parete breve, orlo svasato con diametro

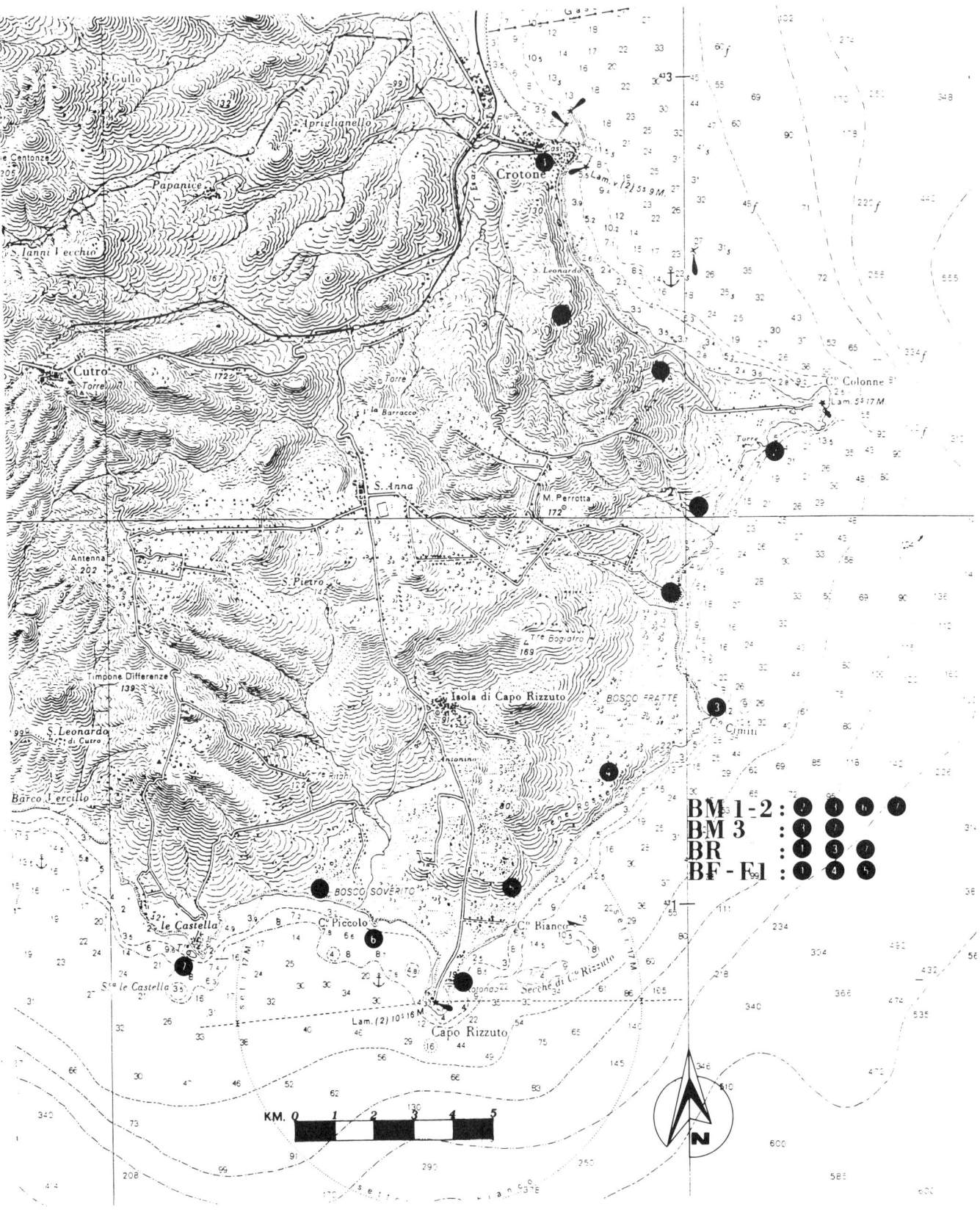

Fig. 1. Carta topografica con la distribuzione dei siti protostorici costieri (nn.1-6). Con il punto nero privo di numero sono indicati i siti di incerta attribuzione.

leggermente inferiore a quello della carena (fig.4.11) mostra confronti generici con Vivara-Punta d'Alaca (Damiani 1984: fig.5.4), più stringenti con Giovinazzo (Cataldo & Radina 1989-90: fig.4.1-2). Una ciotola con vasca profonda, parete rientrante, orlo svasato con diametro inferiore a quello della carena (fig.4:12) presenta confronti con Vivara-Punta di Mezzogiorno (Damiani 1984: fig.3.7). Può richiamare Coppa Nevigata (Cazzella & Moscoloni 1987: fig.71.8) una ciotola a vasca profonda e parete rientrante con diametro dell'orlo inferiore a quello della carena (fig.4.13). Un'ultima ciotola con vasca profonda a profilo convesso, parete rientrante, breve orlo svasato (fig.4.14) ha confronti con Broglio (Capoferri & Trucco 1992: 748-9, fig.14) e, più generici, con Vivara-Punta d'Alaca (Damiani 1984: fig.4.4).

Altre forme vascolari ben rappresentate sono le scodelle e gli scodelloni. Uno scodellone con orlo a tesa (fig.5.1) ha confronti con Broglio (Capoferri & Trucco 1992: 748-9, figg.12-13), con Grotta Cardini (Bernabò Brea 1989: 115, fig.101) e con Pignataro di Fuori (Tusa 1983: fig.65). Stessi confronti, ma anche con Torre Mordillo (Trucco 1992: 753), valgono per un'altro scodellone con orlo a tesa (fig.5.2). Una scodella con orlo a tesa (fig.5.3) ha confronti con Broglio (Capoferri & Trucco 1992: 748-9, figg.12-13) e con Grotta Cardini (Bernabò Brea 1989: 115; fig.101.g).

Tra i molti esemplari di vasi contenitori va ricordata l'olla con leggera carena sulla spalla ed orlo svasato (fig.5.4) che mostra un certo confronto con Mursia (Tozzi 1968: fig.19.13). Vi sono poi alcune anse a nastro verticale, a volte leggermente insellato (fig.6.3-4) e, in particolare, un'alta ansa a nastro verticale rastremata alla sommità (fig.5.5) che ha confronti con Santa Domenica di Ricadi (Pacci 1987: fig.1.3) e con Torre S.Irene (Pacciarelli & Varricchio 1992: 756-7, fig. A.3). L'unico frammento di sopraelevazione a nastro con margini rilevati e foro circolare (fig.6.2) richiama stretti confronti con la facies protoappenninica (Damiani 1984: fig.9; Peroni 1989b: 52). Questo tipo di ansa, con apici accentuati, è attestata nel territorio a Corazzo.

Altre forme vascolari documentate sono le teglie, a volte provviste di anse impostate sull'orlo (fig.5.6-7), e il coperchio - bollitoio per la lavorazione del latte, del tipo tronco-conico con fori fitti e sottili (fig.6.1).

Un frammento di ceramica figulina tornita presenta un motivo dipinto a spirale piuttosto irregolare. Potrebbe essere pertinente alla spalla di un vaso chiuso di medie dimensioni. I confronti riportano alla produzione cretese insulare o a produzioni 'minoicizzanti' del Peloponneso riferibili al TM I A o al TE I-II (Vagnetti 1987: 37-42, figg.6-7).

Altro importante elemento è dato dal frammento di valva di matrice litica (fig.6.5) che, secondo la ricostruzione grafica da noi proposta, veniva utilizzata per la fusione, non necessariamente contemporanea, del manico (fig.6.5c) e della lama (fig.6.5d) di un pugnale del tipo a manico fuso (Marino 1987: 28; Bianco & Marino 1992: 754). Su uno dei lati è presente una solcatura (fig.6.5a) che poteva consentire l'allineamento con un'altra valva.

Nel 1986 e nel 1988 sono stati condotti una serie di saggi. I saggi del 1986 nella fascia centrale hanno permesso di individuare livelli residui di una facies iniziale del bronzo medio con evidenti influssi proto-appenninici ed apporti delle contemporanee facies siciliane ed eoliane. Da sottolineare la significativa presenza di scorie metalliche. Tra le ceramiche d'impasto vi sono ciotole carenate di vario tipo tra le quali alcune provviste di anse a nastro con breve sopraelevazione asciforme impostate sull'orlo e sulla carena, anse a nastro verticale 'pizzute', vasi a fruttiera e sostegni a clessidra (Bianco 1992: 509-11, fig.1.3). E' rilevante un frammento di ceramica figulina tornita con due bande di colore bruno, collocabile, come il precedente, nel periodo iniziale dei contatti con il mondo egeo. In un saggio si mise in luce un lembo di una 'struttura' costituita da scaglie di arenaria e intonaco concotto e in un altro alcune scorie metalliche.

Dai saggi effettuati nel 1988, nella fascia meridionale, vengono numerosi vasi contenitori, quasi interamente ricomponibili (Bianco 1992: fig.1.1). Di particolare rilievo un focolare, posto entro una fossa tagliata nella roccia di base. Anche in questa campagna si rinvenne un frammento di ceramica figulina con tracce di una banda di colore bruno (Bianco & Marino 1992; Bianco 1992). Altri siti che hanno restituito materiali attribuibili ai momenti iniziali del bronzo medio sono, partendo da Nord, Capo Pellegrino, Capo Cimiti e Le Castella.

Il Capo Pellegrino è un promontorio (m.15 slm. - sup.ha.2) che protegge una piccola baia riparata dai venti, collocato nel g olfo delimitato a Sud da Capo Cimiti (fig.1.2). Sul versante orientale sono stati rinvenuti alcuni frammenti di ceramica d'impasto (segn. di L.Cantafora, che si ringr.). E' probabile che il sito protostorico sia stato distrutto dall'edificazione della torre medievale ivi esistente. Tra i pochi reperti spiccano un framm. di orlo a tesa (fig.2.7) e due frammenti di scodelle di forma tronco-conica, più o meno rigida, con orlo a tesa ben distinto dalla parete (fig.2.8-9). I confronti sono con Mursia (Tozzi 1968: 354, fig.20.11) ed anche con Grotta Cardini (Bernabò Brea 1989: 114, fig.100). Una ciotola poco carenata con orlo leggermente svasato, vasca profonda ed emisferica, diametro dell'orlo e della carena uguali (fig.2.10) mostra confronti con Capo Piccolo (Bianco & Marino 1992: 755, Fig.3), con la fase più antica di Mursia (Tozzi 1968: 339, fig.13.9) e con Vivara (Damiani 1984: fig.2.7).

Di notevole interesse un frammento di vaso a fruttiera (fig.2.13) che ha confronti con il vicino sito di Capo Piccolo e, sempre in Calabria, con l'area di Tropea (Pacciarelli & Varricchio 1992: 756-7, fig.A.1-2).

Alcuni frammenti di anse con sopraelevazione a nastro

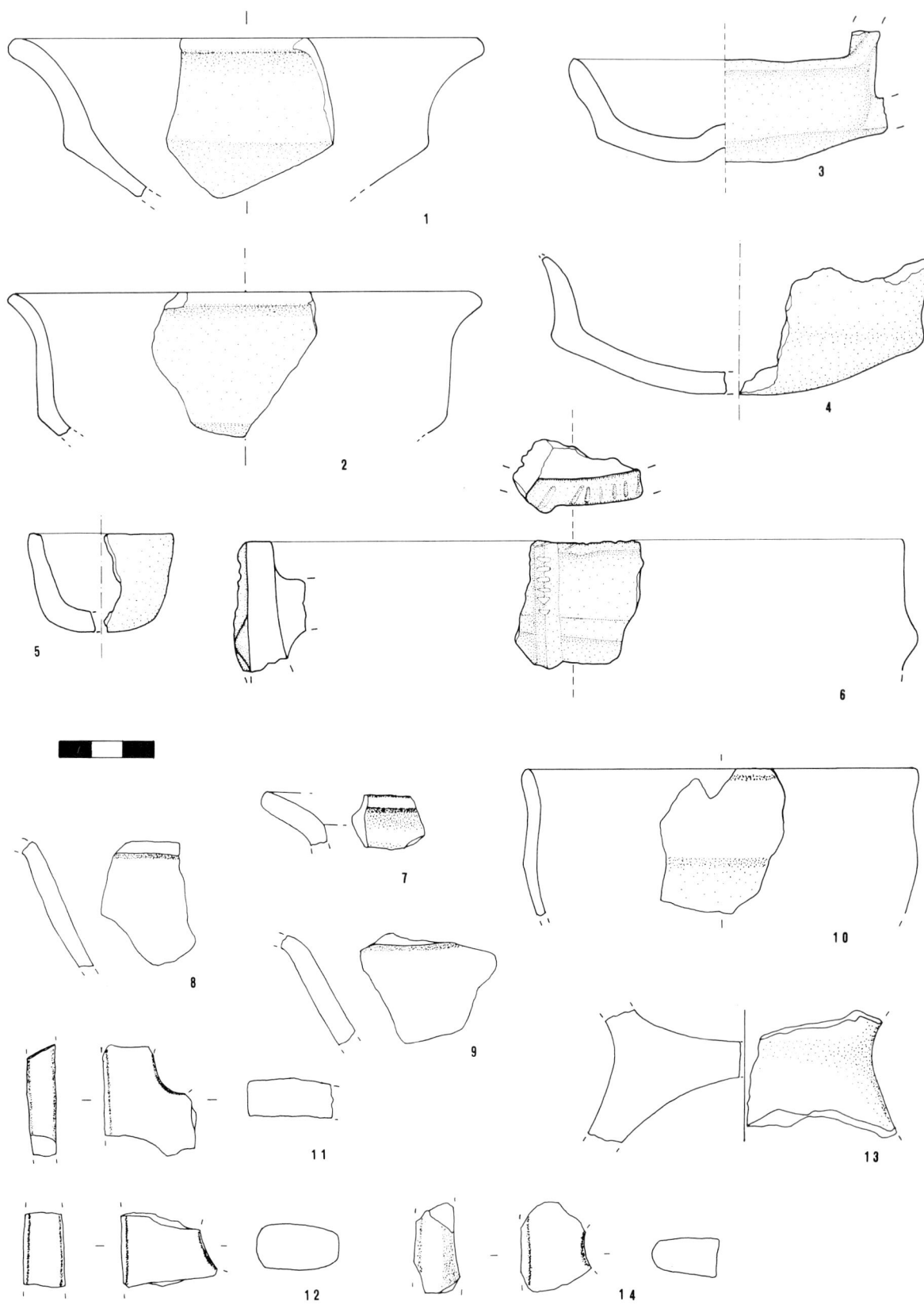

Fig. 2. Reperti del sito 1: Crotone (nn.1-6) e del sito 2: Capo Pellegrino (nn.7-14).

piatto con foro circolare (fig.2.11, 12–14) possono avere confronti con Grotta Cardini (Bernabò Brea 1989: fig.69) ed anche con Giovinazzo (Cataldo & Radina 1990: fig.6.8). E' comunque netta la pertinenza alla facies protoappenninica (Peroni 1989b: 50; Damiani 1992a: 80–88). Anse con sopraelevazioni ad ascia o a nastro piatto di notevole larghezza sono attestate nel vicino sito di Corazzo (Bianco 1992: 512). Ancora più a Sud, l'ampio promontorio del Capo Cimiti si protende nello Jonio con una serie di tre punte (fig.1.3). Sulla punta più settentrionale (m.12 slm. – sup.ha.3) un saggio stratigrafico, effettuato nel 1981 in un piccolo lembo libero dalle strutture di una splendida villa d'età imperiale, ha restituito ceramiche d'impasto con forme vascolari databili dagli inizi del bronzo medio fino al bronzo recente (Lattanzi 1981: 158–9; Marino 1990: 139–40).

Tra i reperti attribuibili a momenti iniziali del bronzo medio spiccano due frammenti di scodelloni con orlo a tesa (fig.3.1 -2) che hanno confronti con Grotta Cardini (Bernabò Brea 1989: 115, fig.100–1), Broglio (Capoferri & Trucco 1992: 749, fig.12) e Pignataro di Fuori (Bernabò Brea 1985: 55, fig.25). Nel territorio sono stretti i confronti con Capo Piccolo (fig.5.1) e Le Castella (fig.6.7). La forma è anche ben attestata a Corazzo (Scavi 1987 dell'Univ. di Bari).

Un'ansa a nastro verticale, 'pizzuta' e insellata (fig.3.3) mostra nettissimi confronti con Capo Piccolo (Scavi 1986=Bianco 1992: 511). Un'altra ansa a nastro con sopraelevazione ad ascia, impostata sul punto di massima espansione del vaso (fig.3.4), ha confronti con Torre Mordillo (Trucco 1992: 752-3, figg.1–2) e Broglio (Capoferri & Trucco 1992: 748-9, figg.10–11).

A momenti più avanzati del bronzo medio sono riferibili altri reperti quali alcuni frammenti di manici a nastro ad apici revoluti, con foro triangolare (fig.3.5-6). Tra i molti confronti possibili sono significativi quelli col vicino sito di Corazzo (Bianco 1992: 512) ed inoltre con Broglio (Capoferri & Trucco 1992: 748-9, fig.1), Torre Mordillo (Trucco 1992: 752 -3, fig.9,12), Grotta Cardini (Bernabò Brea 1989: fig.104–105).

L'ultima fase di vita, relativa al bronzo recente, è documentata nel sito di Capo Cimiti da alcuni tipici reperti quali un framm. di apofisi a corna di lumaca (fig.3.7) e un framm. di ansa con sopraelevazione a bastoncello con appendici a corna (fig.3.8) che trovano significativi confronti a Santa Domenica di Ricadi (Pacci 1987: fig.2.12) e con l'Ausonio I di Lipari (Bernabò Brea & Cavalier 1980: 574-5, tavv.201–202). Si tratta, comunque, di una forma piuttosto diffusa in ambito subappenninico (Peroni 1960: 80-4, Tav.IX; 1989b: fig.21; Broglio= AA.VV. 1982a: tav. 10.1; 1984b: tav.5.12, 11.5; Termitito= Bianco 1982: tav. XXVII.11; Coppa Nevigata= Puglisi 1982: 47-8, tav.VII.4; Cazzella & Moscoloni 1987: fig.80.4). La presenza di questo tipo a Capo Cimiti va vista anche in connessione con il tipo presente a Timpa dei Santi (Marino 1990).

Doppiato il Capo Rizzuto, spostandosi verso occidente, si incontra il promontorio di Le Castella. Sull'isolotto (m.9 slm. – sup.ha.1) (fig.1.7), collegato da un istmo al promontorio, un piccolo saggio stratigrafico, effettuato nel 1981, ha restituito una complessa documentazione delle varie fasi di occupazione del sito e del castello medievale ivi esistente (Lattanzi 1981: 139–40, 157-8 ; Marino 1990: 139).

A momenti iniziali del bronzo medio sono attribuibili un framm. di scodella con orlo a tesa (fig.6.6) con confronti simili a d un esemplare di Capo Piccolo (cfr. fig.5:2) ed un framm. di scodellone con orlo a tesa (fig.6.7) che ha i medesimi confronti di due esemplari presenti a Capo Cimiti (cfr. fig.3.1-2). Ad un momento più avanzato del bronzo medio va riferito un framm. di manico ad apici revoluti (fig.6.8), mentre il bronzo recente è documentato da un frammento di ciotola carenata ad orlo poco distinto, parete rettilinea pressochè verticale, carena bassa, forma complessiva larga e poco profonda, orlo con diametro superiore a quello della carena (fig.6.9), che trova significativi confronti a Broglio (AA.VV. 1982b: fig.10.1; 1984a: 34, tavv.15.19, 16.3; 1984b: 49, tav.3.10 ,13).

Solo nel bronzo recente ha inizio l'occupazione dell'ampio promontorio di Crotone (fig.1.1) che proseguirà anche nel bronzo finale e nella prima età del ferro. A Crotone, nel 1975, durante lavori edilizi nell'area delle ex Ferrovie Calabro-Lucane, venne recuperato (per merito di V.Fabiani) un gruppo di reperti, inquadrabile nell'età del bronzo recente (Marino 1990: 139–40).

Due frammenti di ciotole carenate con parete fortemente concava, orlo svasato, diametro massimo all'orlo e carena bassa (fig.2.1–2) hanno confronti con Broglio (AA.VV. 1984a: 36, 97, tav.1.3) ed anche con Serra Ajello (Luppino 1981: 76, tav.9.2). E' attestato anche il tipo della ciotola carenata con parete concava, non a gola, carena bassa, diametro all'orlo superiore a quello della carena, attacco di ansa a bastoncello verticale sopraelevata impostata sull'orlo, fondo ombelicato (fig.2.3) e quello della ciotola carenata con concavità della parete formante una gola, carena bassa, diametro dell'orlo superiore a quello della carena (fig.2.4) che trova confronti a Broglio (AA.VV. 1982b: 29–30, tav.8.1-2; 1984b: 51, tavv.8.6, 13.4).

Di un certo interesse è un vasetto miniaturistico tronco-conico, a fondo convesso (fig.2.5), forse connesso alla lavorazione del latte come, sicuramente, lo è il vaso con listello interno, orlo diritto, decorato con cordone verticale a tacche e cordone orizzontale liscio (fig.2.6) che mostra confronti con Broglio (AA.VV. 1984a: 45, 95, tav.5.4) e con l'area di Tropea (com.pers. di M.Pacciarelli).

Sempre a Crotone, nell'attuale area del quartiere S.Francesco, si ha notizia dello scavo, ai primi del '900, di una sepoltura probabilmente riferibile al bronzo

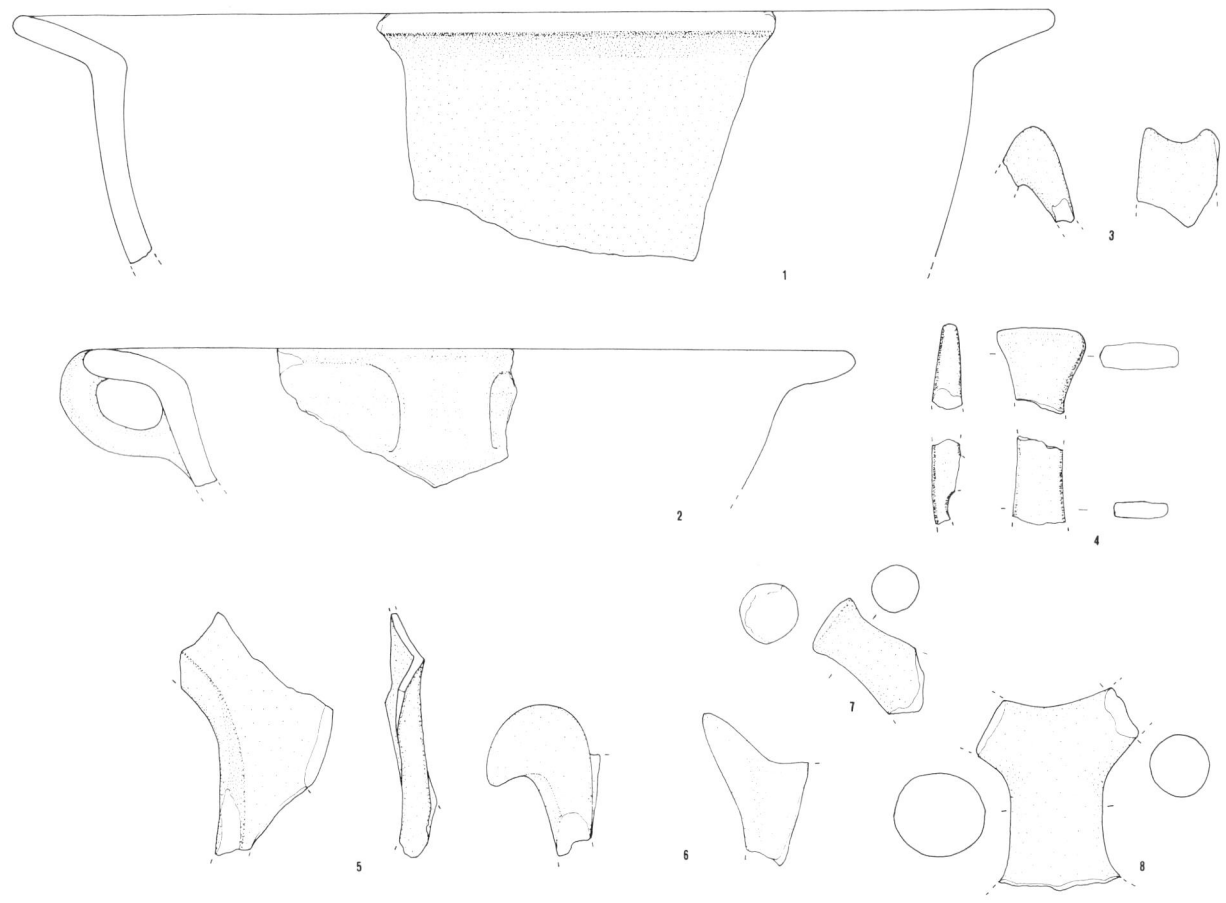

Fig. 3. Reperti del sito 3: Capo Cimiti (nn.1–8).

finale. E' N.Sculco (1905: 25-26) che ce ne dà notizia con le seguenti parole: "... scavarono il contenuto di una tomba a cremazione. L'urna grande di arte locale, di colore nero, conteneva con le ceneri, coperte da una pietra, una fibula ad arco semplice piatto e due punte di frecce in bronzo".

Per l'età del ferro le testimonianze sono numerose anche se legate più all'espansione edilizia della città che ad una ricerca programmata. I dati ci mostrano però, in vari punti dell'area urbana moderna, occupata anche dalla polis greca, la presenza di materiali indigeni. Gli elementi più interessanti sono quelli relativi ad un intervento d'urgenza effettuato nel 1984 nell'area di Vigna Nova, nei pressi di un importante santuario arcaico. Negli strati inferiori furono rinvenuti materiali d'impasto ed una fibula bronzea a spirali, purtroppo frammentaria (Borrello 1987). E' possibile si trattasse di una sepoltura sconvolta già in antico. Invece, nel 1991, sempre durante un intervento d'urgenza nell'area centrale di Crotone, è stato individuato un livello di frequentazione riferibile alla prima età del ferro.

Nel bronzo finale e nella prima età del ferro non sono noti altri siti su promontorio, ma risultano invece attivati due siti costieri (individuati dalla Missione Archeologica della University of Texas at Austin) collocati tra Capo Cimiti e Capo Rizzuto, dove la costa presenta il tipico aspetto a falesia. Il sito di Mendolicchio (fig.1.5) è posto in posizione arretrata, ma dominante (m.50 slm.) rispetto al promontorio di Capo Bianco (m.18 slm.). L'area dell'insediamento sembra svilupparsi su una superficie di poco superiore agli ha.2, ma l'area a disposizione, naturalmente delimitata, è superiore agli ha.20.

Tra i reperti più significativi va menzionata una scodella ad orlo rientrante (fig.4.5) che ha confronti con Broglio (AA.VV. 1982a: tav.29.3; 1982b: tav. 30.5). Di grande interesse sono un framm. di ceramica figulina rosata, tornita, con due fasce orizzontali di colore rosso-arancio (fig.4.6) ed un secondo framm. di ceramica figulina rosata, tornita, con due fasce curvilinee di colore rosso-arancio, ma con ingubbio giallo-biancastro (fig.4.7). I confronti con Broglio (AA.VV. 1982b: 136-7; 1984a: 217-9) se per il secondo frammento ci permettono di ipotizzare una datazione entro l'età del bronzo finale nell'ambito del proto-geometrico enotrio, per il primo frammento lo attribuiscono ad una categoria di lunga durata.

Più a Nord, il sito di Fossa dell'Acqua (fig.1.4) è collocato sempre in posizione arretrata, ma dominante (m.34 slm.) rispetto al promontorio di Punta Fratte (m.26 slm.). La superficie occupata dall'abitato non è superiore agli ha.4, ma l'area naturalmente delimitata a disposizione è anche in questo caso superiore agli ha.20.

Tra i materiali è di un certo interesse una scodella con breve orlo rientrante (fig.4.1) che mostra confronti, piuttosto generici, con Broglio (AA.VV. 1982b: tav.34.10) e, molto più netti, con Castiglione di Paludi (Guzzo 1975: 150, 165, 174, fig.59). Una ciotola carenata (fig.4.2) ha confronti con Broglio (AA.VV. 1982a: tav.29.2; 1984a: tav.49.26). Tra gli altri elementi vi sono una ronde lla fittile (fig.4.3) e un peso da telaio tronco-piramidale con svastica incisa su una faccia (fig.4.4) che trova confronti, anche se non stringenti, a Broglio (AA.VV. 1984a: 201, tav. 51.19).

Nella fascia costiera e sub-costiera sono presenti altri siti protostorici che, però, non hanno ancora restituito reperti diagnostici. Si tratta, partendo da Nord, dei siti di Vrica (m.160 slm.), Campione (m.149 slm.), Domine Maria (m.70 slm.), Marinella (m.5 slm.), Torre Tonda (m.19 slm.) e Bosco Soverito (m.15 slm.). Nel sito di Torre Tonda, sul Capo Rizzuto, ai materiali d'impasto sono associati frustuli di metallo e scorie di fusione. La presenza di questi siti mostra come la frequentazione protostorica della costa della Calabria centro-orientale fu intensa, così come le nostre ricerche stanno dimostrando anche per il territorio interno.

Sulla base degli elementi portati è possibile svolgere alcune considerazioni sui siti. Nella facies documentata a Capo Piccolo alcuni confronti con il sito di Monte Fellino (Albore Livadie 1985), riferibile alla facies di Palma Campania, e con la fase più antica di Mursia (Tozzi 1968; Damiani 1984: 24–5), lasciano intravedere connessioni, almeno a livello tipologico, con gli aspetti avanzati del bronzo antico. Ciò ci fa ipotizzare che l'attivazione del sito possa essere avvenuta in un momento decisamente iniziale del bronzo medio (cfr. Cazzella & Moscoloni 1992: 539–41). Ben attestate appaiono, comunque, la componente siciliana, strettamente connessa alla *facies* di Rodí-Tindari, la componente eoliana, nettamente influenzata dalla facies di Capo Graziano, e quella più continentale tipicamente protoappenninica (Cazzella & Moscoloni 1989: 404; Damiani 1992a: 81).

Nei siti di Capo Cimiti e Le Castella le affinità con la facies proto-appeninica dell'Italia meridionale appaiono piuttosto nette, ma non mancano evidenti nessi con le facies eoliane. Limitandosi all'esame della tipologia delle anse si può notare che a Capo Piccolo compaiono tipi attribuiti sia alla fase 1 che alla fase 2 del protoappenninico, mentre a Capo Pellegrino e Capo Cimiti il tipo documentato viene attribuito alla fase 1 (Damiani 1984; 1992a: 80–8; Peroni 1989b: 50–52).

Per i momenti più avanzati del bronzo medio che, attraverso i reperti, si possono cogliere nei siti di Capo Cimiti e, in misura più limitata, Le Castella, va rilevata l'assenza della tipica decorazione appenninica documentata, invece, nel sito interno di Corazzo (Bianco 1992: 512). Va qui ricordato che l'appenninico 'classico' di Corazzo (dove è prevalente la decorazione ad intaglio) costituisce l'attestazione più meridionale, lungo la costa ionica, di questa facies così come Santa Domenica di Ricadi lo è per la tirrenica (Peroni 1987: 81; 1989a: 144; 1989b: 363). A queste attestazioni va ora aggiunta quella relativa alla presenza di ceramica con decorazione appenninica (a punteggio) nel sito di Monte Tiriolo, collocato a controllo della via più breve tra lo Jonio e il Tirreno, la stretta di Catanzaro.

Nel bronzo recente i confronti operabili ci riportano tutti in ambito subappenninico anche se appare possibile rilevare, nel sito di Capo Cimiti, un certo legame con la facies liparese dell'Ausonio I, i cui nessi con i coevi aspetti dell'Italia continentale sono ben noti (Marino 1990 ivi bibl.).

Per il bronzo finale e la prima età del ferro i dati sono ancora molto limitati. Di notevole interesse appare la notizia della sepoltura a cremazione in ossuario scavata a Crotone ai primi del '900. Tale notizia ci riporta a problematiche meglio documentate nei siti di Tropea ed Amendolara (Peroni 1987: 98–108; 1989a: 170–2; 1989b: 290). Anche la presenza, nel sito di Mendolicchio, di rari frammenti di ceramica figulina dipinta attribuibili, almeno in parte, al proto-geometrico enotrio costituisce un elemento di novità e di discussione ancora troppo labilmente documentato.

La frequentazione nella prima età del ferro è attestata nei siti di Fossa dell'Acqua e di Crotone. Nel caso di Crotone la presenza indigena, anche dopo la fondazione della polis, deve avere avuto una consistenza maggiore di quanto lascino intravedere i dati archeologici. A riprova di questo va ricordato il rinvenimento, nel cosiddetto 'Edificio B' dell'Heraion di Capo Colonna, di un pendaglio in bronzo, decorato a cerchi concentrici, del tipo noto nelle tombe di Alianello (Lattanzi 1987: 652, tav.90.1).

Per quanto riguarda i contatti con l'area egea, il dato di Capo Piccolo, testimonianza di scambi a lunga distanza (Pacciarelli 1992: 270), che spicca nel panorama generale per la sua notevole antichità, appare isolato nel contesto territoriale. Nel caso degli altri siti, infatti, è solo ipotizzabile una apertura nei confronti delle correnti di traffico tra oriente e occidente che, però, non ha ancora trovato un chiaro riscontro archeologico. Certamente il consistente numero di siti costieri può essere riferito allo sviluppo di attività di scambio e delle connesse attività artigianali (Bernabò Brea 1982: 15; Cazzella 1991: 51).

Un altro elemento che potrebbe adombrare, per il sito di Capo Piccolo, un ruolo politico e/o economico

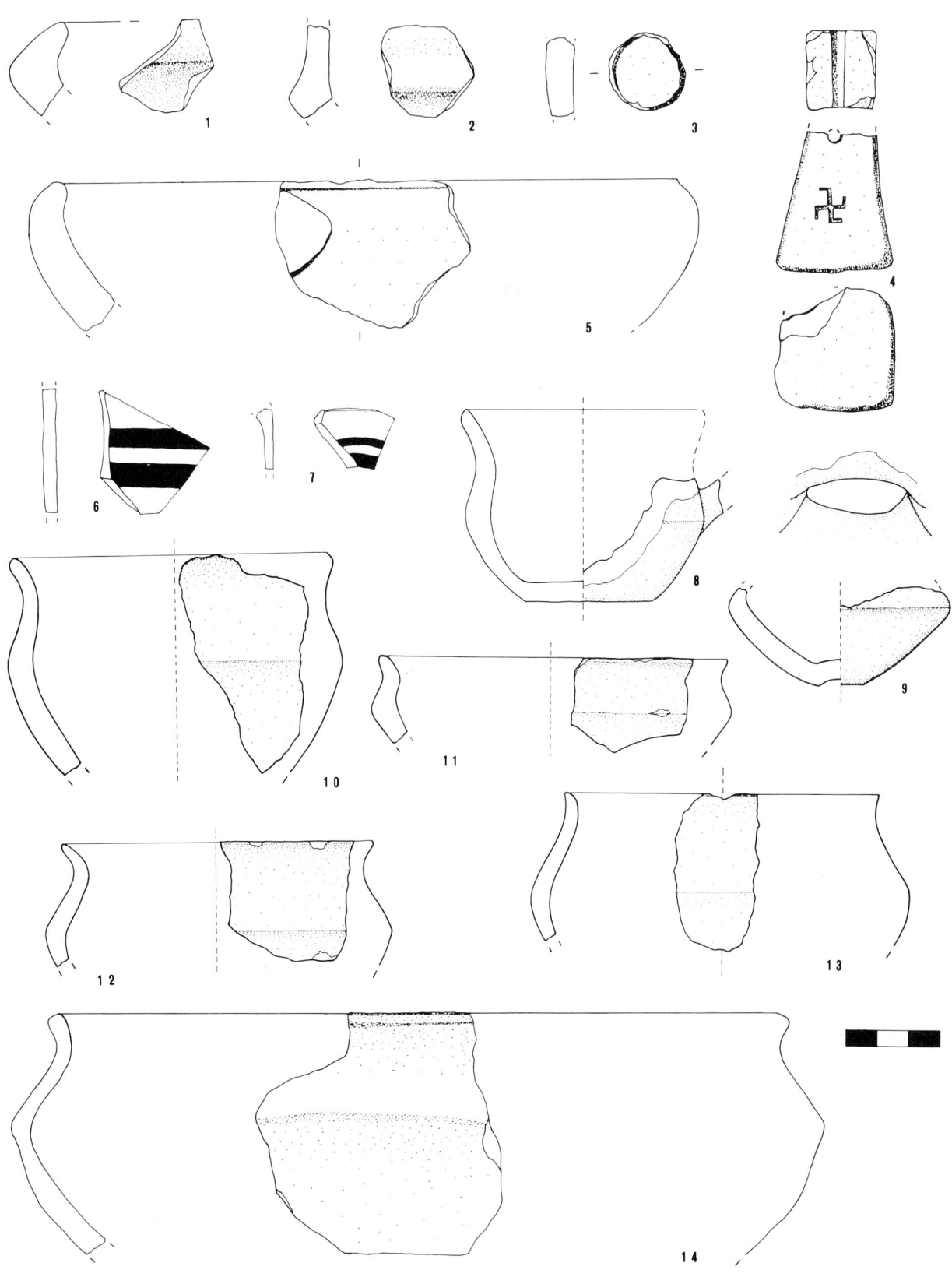

Fig. 4. Reperti del sito 4: Fossa dell'Acqua (nn.1-4), del sito 5: Mendolicchio (nn.5-7) e del sito 6: Capo Piccolo (nn.8-14).

differenziato (Cazzella & Moscoloni 1992: 541; Pacciarelli 1992: 270), è la documentazione, seppure in tracce, di una complessa attività metallurgica. La presenza della forma di fusione e di scorie metalliche, segnalate anche a Torre Tonda, ci pone infatti un rilevante quesito sulla provenienza del metallo. Nell'area in esame sono note presenze di oggetti metallici fin da una fase finale del bronzo antico: è il caso del ripostiglio di asce a margini rialzati ed alabarde del Lago Ampollino (Tiné 1962–63: 227–33), dove di recente abbiamo individuato resti di un insediamento (Marino 1990: 134) e labili tracce di attività fusoria, e del corredo di una sepoltura di Roccabernarda, costituito da due asce a margini rialzati (Lattanzi 1987), associate in origine ad un pugnale, andato disperso. Sempre nell'area rientra il rinvenimento a Strongoli di un'alabarda bronzea (Topa 1927).

Al bronzo finale e alla prima età del ferro si riferiscono, invece, un gran numero di cosiddetti ripostigli nell'area tra Cirò e Crotone. Notissimo è quello di Cirò-Sant'Elia composto da sei asce ad occhio allo stato di getto di fusione (Topa 1933). A questo se ne aggiungono ora altri con la medesima composizione o costituiti da oggetti finiti. Dall'area a Sud di Crotone proviene un gruppo di oggetti in frammenti e scorie di fusione, interpretabile, quindi, come un 'ripostiglio di fonditore'. In quest'ultimo ripostiglio si va delineando la possibile presenza di oggetti di tipologia cipriota.

Da tutti questi dati appare abbastanza chiaro che nella Calabria centro-orientale, tra bronzo antico e prima età del ferro, vi è una notevole presenza di oggetti in metallo, per lo più rinvenuti in 'ripostigli' (ma notevolissime sono le presenze nelle sepolture). Non può essere escluso che la materia prima venisse estratta in aree limitrofe, dove compaiono affioramenti di minerale di rame (l'area di Catanzaro, l'area tirrenica del Savuto, la Sibaritide meridionale), e non può essere del tutto esclusa la presenza di minerale in aree ancora più vicine, poco note dal punto di vista geologico, come la Sila.

Ritornando al sito di Capo Piccolo, risulta evidente che la presenza di attività metallurgica 'secondaria' (produzione di manufatti) deve necessariamente avere a monte un'attività estrattiva mineraria e un'attività metallurgica 'primaria' (produzione di metallo – sul tema dei ripostigli del processo metallurgico cfr. Pellegrini 1992: 486–7). In questo contesto si inserisce perfettamente l'individuazione nel sito di Praia Longa, posto pochi chilometri ad Ovest di Capo Piccolo, di lingotti metallici concrezionati alla scogliera sommersa e di una grande ancora in pietra di forma tronco-piramidale: si tratterebbe, quindi, di un relitto e del relativo carico (segn. di L.Cantafora). Uno dei lingotti, recuperato e ripulito dalle concrezioni, si è rivelato essere una panella di forma sub-rettangolare a sezione piano-convessa (lungh. cm.27,5; largh. cm. 17; spess. cm. 4,5; peso ca. kg.12).

Certamente è da chiedersi se per il sito di Capo Piccolo si possa supporre il superamento del semplice ruolo di mediazione tra i micenei e i gruppi interni (Cazzella & Moscoloni 1985: 543) o se questo ruolo vada, invece, letto in rapporto alle strette connessioni con la facies di Rodí-Tindari attestata, in Sicilia, anche in alcuni insediamenti dal carattere spiccatamente marittimo, posti a controllo di rotte costiere e in punti chiave per i collegamenti con la Calabria e le Eolie. La facies di R.-T. riceve forti apporti dalla facies eoliana di Capo Graziano, fortemente proiettata sul mare e legata al commercio marittimo (Bernabò Brea 1982: 29; 1992: 107–11). Non va dimenticato che è stata ipotizzata una partecipazione attiva delle comunità locali eoliane alle fasi iniziali delle navigazioni egee, limitatamente alle coste tirreniche dell'Italia centrale e meridionale. Data la vicinanza, non solo geografica, tra le facies di Capo Graziano e R.-T. è stato ipotizzato, inoltre, che anche quest'ultima abbia avuto parte nel sistema di contatti nelle acque del basso Tirreno (Bietti Sestieri 1980–81: 34–5). Queste considerazioni potrebbero essere estese anche all'area costiera della Calabria centrale ionica.

Potrebbe essere chiaramente riconosciuta a Capo Piccolo una funzione di scalo intermedio per navigazioni destinate a raggiungere gli arcipelaghi eoliani e flegrei (Vagnetti 1987: 41; 1989; Marazzi 1988: 12, carta 1; Bianco 1992: 511). D'altro canto non sembra errato supporre che i navigatori egei si inserissero ed integrassero in una complessa trama di contatti locali (Bietti Sestieri 1980–81: 32; 1982: 49–52; 1988: 39–49; Damiani 1984: 15). L'attestazione di attività metallurgica insieme alla presenza di ceramiche di produzione egea non può non ricordarci che il movimento dall'Egeo verso l'Italia è diretto all'acquisizione di materie prime tra cui, probabilmente, grande importanza dovevano avere i metalli (Bietti Sestieri 1980–81: 30; 1982: 41).

Discussione (S.F.)

Lo stato delle ricerche nell'area permette di svolgere alcune considerazioni relative all'organizzazione del territorio e al l'ampiezza degli insediamenti, anche se la valutazione di quest'ultima, in assenza di scavi estensivi, è basata essenzialmente sui l imiti orografici e, ove possibile, sulla dispersione dei materiali.

Nelle fasi iniziali del bronzo medio, documentate nei siti di Capo Pellegrino, Capo Cimiti, Capo Piccolo e Le Castella (fig. 1.2–3–6–7), l'insediamento non supera i limiti del promontorio che, nel caso di Capo Cimiti, sembrerebbe chiuso alla base da un fossato artificiale non attribuibile, però, ad una fase in particolare. Si tratterebbe, in questo caso, dell'unica struttura di tipo difensivo nota nell'area in esame, priva di strette analogie con i coevi insediamenti fortificati pugliesi. I siti, che occupano una superficie variabile da uno a tre ettari, sono posti, nell'ambito dei relativi golfi, alla distanza di 6–7 km. l'uno dall'altro. Tale distanza risulta inferiore a

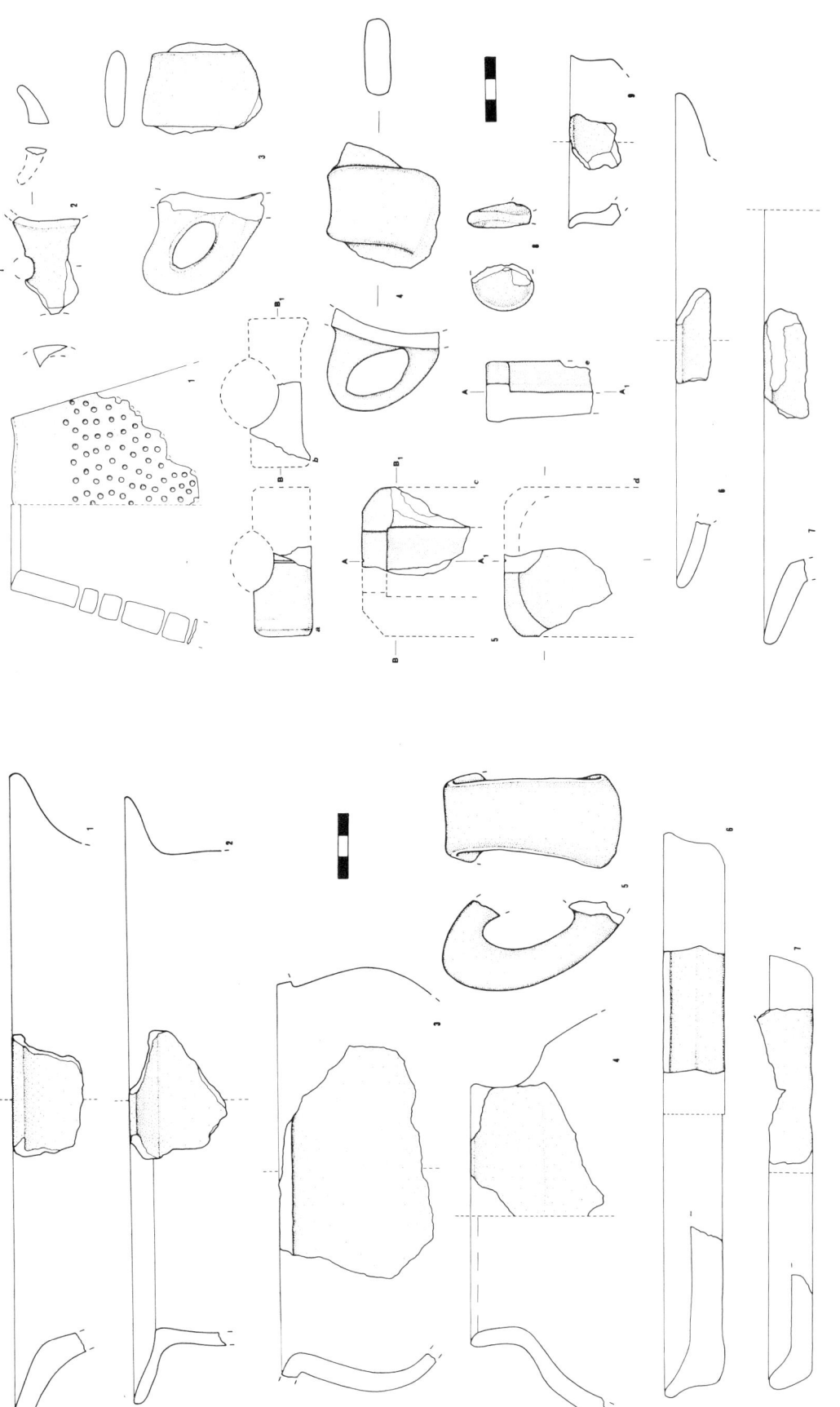

Fig. 6. Reperti del sito 6: Capo Piccolo (nn.1-5) e del sito 7: Le Castella (nn.6-9).

Fig. 5. Reperti del sito 6: Capo Piccolo (nn.1-7).

quella rilevata tra coppie di insediamenti costieri in Puglia, dove si aggira intorno a 10 km., mentre la superficie occupata appare simile (Cazzella 1991: 51-3). Vi è una certa densità di insediamento che richiama un'analoga situazione del promontorio del Poro o di Tropea dove l'ubicazione dei siti costieri appare relazionata al controllo di un punto di approdo (Pacciarelli 1989-90:10).

I dati riferibili ai momenti avanzati del bronzo medio evidenziano, accanto alla mancata attivazione di nuovi siti, un compl essivo diradarsi dell'occupazione della costa: mentre i siti collocati sui promontori intermedi (fig.1.2-6) non mostrano continuità di vita, perdurano i siti di Capo Cimiti e Le Castella (fig.1.3-7), posti alla reciproca distanza di 14 km., delimitanti rispettivamente a Sud e ad Ovest i golfi di pertinenza, in posizione di notevole controllo sul mare. La superficie occupata dagli abitati rimane invariata. Questa situazione rimanda all'area del promontorio del Poro dove, sulla costa, è solo il centro 'maggiore' di Tropea a perdurare dal la fase precedente. Analoga appare la situazione della Puglia ionica dove si assiste ad un apparente decremento numerico degli abitati (Pacciarelli 1989-90: 10-17; Pacciarelli & Varricchio 1992: 758-9; di Gennaro 1992: 203-4).

Nel bronzo recente si nota da un lato continuità di occupazione rispetto alla fase precedente e dall'altro l'attivazione del nuovo sito di Crotone, collocato su un promontorio delimitante a Nord il golfo di pertinenza. L'insediamento, posto alla distanza di 14 km. dal sito più prossimo, ha a disposizione un'area molto ampia, teoricamente superiore a i 10 ha., se consideriamo come limiti naturali il torrente Pignataro e le pendici della collina del Castello, ma molto più estesa, fino a 50 ha., se si prende in considerazione l'intero promontorio. L'ampiezza dell'area, unitamente alla possibilità di forte controllo sul territorio oltre che sugli approdi e sul mare, offerta a Crotone dalla presenza di un'acropoli (m.30 slm.) naturalmente connotata in senso difensivo, sembrano costituire un dato discriminante per le fasi successive. L'occupazione del promontorio di Crotone prosegue, infatti, anche nel bronzo finale e nella prima età del ferro, mentre gli altri siti del bronzo recente, che non posseggono le stesse caratteristiche di ampiezza e forte controllo territoriale, vengono definitivamente abbandonati. Il cambiamento a livello di scelte insediative è testimoniato, infine, dal nuovo impianto dei siti di Fossa dell'Acqua e Mendolicchio (fig.1.4-5) che sono collocati nella fascia sub-costiera, in aree naturalmente delimitate superiori ai 20 ha., in netta posizione di controllo sul territorio interno e sugli approdi sottostanti.

Le variazioni a livello insediativo osservate nell'area di Crotone, a partire dai momenti avanzati del bronzo medio, sembrano trovare riscontro con quanto avviene nell'area di Tropea, nella stessa fase, e in altre aree a partire dal bronzo tardo (Pacciarelli 1989-90: 10; Peroni & di Gennaro 1986).

I processi di differenziazione sociale in atto, col conseguente aumento della competizione tra le varie comunità, potrebbero offrire una spiegazione della generale tendenza, in una fase avanzata dell'età del bronzo, ad un più deciso controllo territoriale, comportante anche la scelta di siti su altura (Cazzella 1991: 56).

Bibliografia

AA.VV. 1982a. *Ricerche sulla Protostoria della Sibaritide*, 1, Napoli.
AA.VV. 1982b. *Ricerche sulla Protostoria della Sibaritide*, 2, Napoli.
AA.VV. 1984. *Ricerche sulla Protostoria della Sibaritide*, 3, Roma.
AA.VV. 1985. *Nuove ricerche sulla Protostoria della Sibaritide*. Roma.
Albore Livadie, C. 1985. 'Il complesso preistorico di Monte Fellino', *Atti del Circolo Culturale B.G.Duns Scoto di Roccarainola*, 10-11.
Bernabò Brea, L. 1982. 'Dall'Egeo al Tirreno all'alba dell'età micenea', *Atti del XXII Convegno di Studi sulla Magna Grecia*, Taranto.
Bernabò Brea, L. 1985. 'Gli Eoli e l'inizio dell'età del bronzo nelle isole Eolie e nell'Italia meridionale', *Annali dell'Istituto Orientale*, Napoli.
Bernabò Brea, L. 1989. *La grotta Cardini: giacimento del bronzo*, Roma.
Bernabò Brea, L. 1992. 'La Sicilia e le isole Eolie', *Rassegna di Archeologia*, 10.
Bernabò Brea, L. & Cavalier, M. 1980. *Meligunis Lipara IV*, Palermo.
Bianco, S. 1982. 'Termitito. Aspetti del contesto locale', *Magna Grecia e mondo miceneo. Nuovi documenti*, Taranto.
Bianco, S. 1992. 'Nuovi dati da Basilicata, Calabria e Puglia meridionale', *Rassegna di Archeologia*, 10.
Bianco, S. & Marino, D.A. 1992. 'L'insediamento di Capo Piccolo di Isola di Capo Rizzuto', *Rassegna di Archeologia*, 10.
Bietti Sestieri, A.M. 1980-81. 'La Sicilia e le isole Eolie e i loro rapporti con le regioni tirreniche dell'Italia continentale dal neolitico alla colonizzazione greca', *Kokalos*, 26-27.
Bietti Sestieri, A.M. 1982. 'Implicazioni del concetto di territorio in situazioni culturali complesse: le isole Eolie nell'età del bronzo', *Dialoghi di Archeologia*, 2.
Bietti Sestieri, A.M. 1988. 'The "Mycenaean connection" and its impact on the central Mediterranean societies', *Dialoghi di Archeologia*, 1.
Borrello, L. 1987. 'Comunicazione', in *Atti del Convegno Internazionale "Crotone tra IV e III sec. a.C."*, Napoli.
Capoferri, B. & Trucco, F. 1992. 'Broglio di Trebisacce', *Rassegna di Archeologia*, 10.
Cataldo, L. & Radina, F. 1990. 'L'insediamento protostorico di Giovinazzo', *Rivista di Scienze Preistoriche*, 42.
Cavalier, M. 1970. 'La stazione preistorica di Tindari', *Bullettino di Paletnologia Italiana*.
Cazzella, A. 1991. 'Insediamenti fortificati e controllo del territorio durante l'età del Bronzo nell'Italia sud-orientale', in E. Herring, R. Whitehouse & J. Wilkins (eds.), *Papers of the 4th Conference of Italian Archaeology*, 1, London.
Cazzella, A. et al. 1980. 'Vivara. Terza campagna di ricerche sull'isola', *Bullettino di Paletnologia Italiana*, 24.
Cazzella, A. & Moscoloni, M. 1985. 'Dislivelli culturali nel Mediterraneo centro-orientale fra terzo e secondo millennio a.C.', in *Studi di Paletnologia in onore di S.M. Puglisi*, Roma.
Cazzella, A. & Moscoloni, M. 1987. 'Età del bronzo. La ricerca archeologica', in *Coppa Nevigata e il suo territorio*, Roma.
Cazzella, A. & Moscoloni, M. 1989. 'La Civiltà Appenninica: prospettive di ricerca', *Origini*, 14.
Cazzella, A. & Moscoloni, M. 1992. 'La sequenza cronostratigrafica di Coppa Nevigata fra XVI e XIV sec.a.C.', *Rassegna di Archeologia*, 10.
Damiani, I. et al. 1984. 'Le facies archeologiche dell'isola di Vivara e alcuni problemi relativi al protoappenninico B', *Annali dell'Istituto Orientale*, Napoli.

Damiani, I. 1992a. 'Facies protoappenninica', *Rassegna di Archeologia*, 10.
Damiani, I. 1992b. 'Caratteri dell'insediamento nell'Italia sud-orientale', *Rassegna di Archeologia*, 10.
di Gennaro, F. 1992. 'Insediamento e territorio', *Rassegna di Archeologia*, 10.
Geniola, A. 1989-90. 'Isola di C.Rizzuto', *Rivista di Scienze Preistoriche*, 42.
Guzzo, P.G. 1975. 'Paludi: Loc. Castiglione. Necropoli dell'età del ferro', *Klearchos*, 65-68.
Lattanzi, E. 1981. 'Attività della Soprintendenza Archeologica della Calabria', *Klearchos*, 89-92.
Lattanzi, E. 1987. 'L'attività archeologica in Calabria', *Atti del XXVII Convegno di Studi sulla Magna Grecia*, Taranto.
Laviosa, C. 1982. 'La navigazione micenea, dal mito alle testimonianze archeologiche', *Atti del XXII Convegno di Studi sulla Magna Grecia*, Taranto.
Luppino, S. 1981. *Il versante nord-occidentale del fiume Savuto. Temesa e il suo territorio*, Perugia-Trevi.
Marazzi, M. 1988. 'La più antica marineria micenea in occidente', *Dialoghi di Archeologia*, 1.
Marino, D.A. 1987. 'Nota preliminare sul sito protostorico di Capo Piccolo presso Crotone', *Klearchos*, 113-116.
Marino, D.A. 1990. 'Considerazioni sul sito protostorico di Timpa dei Santi e il Bronzo recente nella Calabria centro-orientale', *Annali della Facoltà di Lettere dell'Università di Bari*, 33.
Marino, D.A. 1992. 'Il Neolitico nella Calabria centro-orientale. Ricerche 1974-1990', *Annali della Facoltà di Lettere dell'Università di Bari*, 35.
Pacci, M. 1987. 'Revisione e nuove proposte d'interpretazione per i materiali delle tombe di Santa Domenica di Ricadi', *Sicilia Archeologica*, 64.
Pacciarelli, M. 1989-90. 'Ricerche nel promontorio del Poro e considerazioni sugli insediamenti del primo ferro in Calabria meridionale', *Rivista Storica Calabrese*, n.s.X-XI, nn.1-4.
Pacciarelli, M. 1992. 'Considerazioni sulla struttura delle comunità del bronzo medio dell'Italia centromeridionale', *Rassegna di Archeologia*, 10.
Pacciarelli, M. & Varricchio, M.R. 1992. 'Il Promontorio di Tropea', *Rassegna di Archeologia*, 10.
Pellegrini, E. 1992. 'Le età dei metalli nell'Italia meridionale e in Sicilia', in Guidi, A. & Piperno, M. (eds), *Italia preistorica*, Bari.
Peroni, R. 1960. 'Per una definizione dell'aspetto culturale "subappenninico" come fase cronologica a sè stante', *Atti e Memorie dell'Accademia Nazionale dei Lincei*, Roma.
Peroni, R. 1987. *'La Protostoria'. Storia della Calabria Antica*, Roma-Reggio Calabria.
Peroni, R. 1989a. *'Enotri, Ausoni, Itali e altre popolazioni dell'estremo Sud d'Italia'. Italia omnium terrarum parens*, Roma.
Peroni, R. 1989b. *Protostoria dell'Italia continentale*, Roma.
Peroni, R. & di Gennaro, F. 1986. 'Aspetti regionali dello sviluppo dell'insediamento protostorico nell'Italia centro-meridionale alla luce dei dati archeologici ed ambientali', *Dialoghi di Archeologia*, 2.
Puglisi, S.M. 1982. *'Coppa Nevigata'. Magna Grecia e mondo miceneo. Nuovi documenti*, Taranto.
Radina, F. 1992. 'Contributo alla conoscenza dell'età del bronzo nell'area murgiana tra XVI e XIV sec.a.C.', *Rassegna di Archeologia*, 10.
Sculco, N. 1905. *Ricordi sugli avanzi di Crotone*, Crotone.
Tinè, S. 1962-63. 'Ripostiglio di armi da Cotronei', *Bullettino di Paletnologia Italiana*, 71-72.
Trucco, F. et al. 1992. 'La fase iniziale dell'abitato di Torre Mordillo: Scavi 1987-1989', *Rassegna di Archeologia*, 10.
Topa, D. 1927. *Le civiltà primitive della Brettia*, Palmi.
Topa, D. 1933. 'Scoperta di una sepoltura preistorica a Ciró', *Rivista di Antropologia*, 30.
Tozzi, C. 1968. 'Relazione preliminare sulla I e II campagna di scavi effettuati a Pantelleria', *Rivista di Scienze Preistoriche*.
Tusa, S. 1983. *La Sicilia nella preistoria*, Palermo.
Vagnetti, L. 1987. 'Frammento miceneo', *Klearchos*, 113-116.
Vagnetti, L. 1989. 'Ricerche recenti sulle relazioni fra l'Egeo e l'Occidente mediterraneo', *Seminari dell'Istituto per gli Studi Micenei ed Egeo-Anatolici - C.N.R.*, Roma.

26

Note sulla Società della Sardegna Nuragica e sulla Funzione dei Nuraghi

ALESSANDRO USAI

(Soprintendenza Archeologica per le Province di Cagliari e Oristano, Cagliari)

Sommario: *Il problema della comprensione della società nuragica e quello dell'interpretazione funzionale dei nuraghi sono strettamente connessi. Vengono discusse alcune teorie antitetiche sulla struttura sociale nuragica, specialmente per l'età del bronzo. Viene proposto un quadro diacronico articolato in stadi di sviluppo sociale, in analogia con quello elaborato per la protostoria della penisola italiana. In questo quadro viene esaminata la complessa funzionalità dei nuraghi, sia nella loro effettiva destinazione pratica (a fini di difesa, abitazione, immagazzinamento, quindi come deposito votivo o luogo di culto), sia nei significati simbolici considerati all'interno delle singole comunità e nel rapporto competitivo fra le diverse comunità protosarde.*

1. INTRODUZIONE

Il problema della comprensione della società nuragica e quello dell'interpretazione funzionale dei nuraghi sono strettamente connessi, al punto che molte ipotesi sul primo argomento sono fondate quasi esclusivamente su teorie relative al secondo. La questione della funzione dei nuraghi ha attirato l'attenzione degli studiosi dal sec. XVI fino ad oggi (Lilliu 1981); per lungo tempo, oltre a molte teorie fantasiose e stravaganti, le interpretazioni prevalenti hanno considerato i nuraghi come edifici sepolcrali o cultuali, e quest'ultima opinione è stata riproposta anche recentemente. Nell'ultimo secolo, ad opera del Taramelli e soprattutto del Lilliu (1962, 1963, 1988), si è imposta una teoria che, nell'ambito di una società prevalentemente pastorale e guerriera, interpreta i nuraghi come fortini e fortezze distribuiti strategicamente sul territorio, e insieme come abitazioni dei capi. Recentemente è stata osservata una frequente connessione dei nuraghi con pratiche di culto nell'età del ferro, nel quadro di importanti mutamenti di organizzazione socio-politica (Lilliu 1988: 433–434; Tronchetti 1988: 20; Ugas 1989–90).

Tuttavia non si può dire che il problema della funzione dei nuraghi sia stato fino ad oggi ben definito, anzi esso pare sfuggire ancora ad una penetrazione critica e metodologicamente corretta. Numerosi studiosi, sia sardi che stranieri, hanno trattato l'argomento anche recentemente, proponendo ipotesi ora sostanzialmente simili, ora completamente antitetiche (ultimamente Webster 1991).

Pertanto credo che sia necessario studiare la complessa funzionalità dei nuraghi nell'ambito di una corretta e penetrante analisi socio-economica del mondo protosardo durante le età del bronzo e del ferro. Per questo motivo mi accingo a trattare l'argomento con solo scopo di mediare fra le diverse posizioni e di fornire spunti di riflessione. Infatti ritengo che l'interpretazione funzionale dei nuraghi debba ancora progredire, considerando non solo l'effettiva destinazione ma in generale tutti i possibili ruoli svolti dal nuraghe nella società isolana.

2. I NURAGHI E LA SOCIETÀ NURAGICA

Lo studio della società protosarda e della funzione sociale dei nuraghi fu impostato da Lilliu negli anni '50 e '60 con la consueta estrema lucidità, segnando anche in questo campo una direzione di ricerca ancor oggi fondamentale. Egli considera la società nuragica dell'età del bronzo una società tribale patriarcale fondata prevalentemente sulla pastorizia, organizzata in piccoli cantoni territoriali con popolamento sparso, caratterizzata da una rigida gerarchia socio-politica e da un innato spirito guerriero. Egli vede nei nuraghi una funzione militare effettiva e permanente; in particolare, i nuraghi semplici sarebbero fortini con funzione di controllo territoriale diffuso e di intervento armato ausiliario, mentre i nuraghi complessi sarebbero vere e proprie fortezze destinate alla resistenza a oltranza contro gli invasori. Nei nuraghi complessi avrebbero inoltre sede e dimora i re-pastori, capi delle tribù cantonali e detentori di un potere assoluto monarchico-teocratico.

Accanto alle fortezze o reggie stanno i villaggi, abitati dalla plebe in stato semi-servile; un ceto distinto è composto dai sacerdoti, dai guerrieri e dai patriarchi di rango inferiore (capi-famiglia e capi-clan) che formano il consiglio degli anziani. Nell'età del ferro il Lilliu suppone un processo di riorganizzazione generale, che sul piano politico comporta il passaggio dal regime monarchico a quello aristocratico. È interessante l'ipotesi che i nuraghi fossero costruiti da schiavi, forse prigionieri di guerra (Lilliu 1962: 13-15; Lilliu 1963: 176-177, 244, 249-251, 307-310).

Molte obiezioni si possono muovere a questa ricostruzione, fondata su una concezione pastoralistica molto in voga alcuni decenni fa, su suggestioni delle civiltà egee e vicino-orientali, su reminiscenze omeriche, su analogie coi castelli medievali e infine sulla convinzione di una continuità morale e culturale dei Sardi attraverso i millenni. Tuttavia il quadro tracciato risulta nel complesso convincente e avvincente, ed entro le sue linee si sono mossi numerosi studiosi, soprattutto sardi (Contu 1974: 161-163; Contu 1981: 76-81; Santoni 1980).

In particolare Ugas, accentuando alcuni aspetti della teoria del Lilliu anche sulla base delle fonti mitografiche antiche, asserisce l'esistenza di una 'parentela strutturale socio-politica' tra la società protosarda del Bronzo Recente e quella micenea (Ugas 1987: 87). In sostanza egli attribuisce il fenomeno nuragico ad una struttura socio-economica protourbana molto più complessa della società tribale patriarcale definita dal Lilliu. In particolare egli sostiene l'analogia del monarca nuragico e del *wanax* miceneo, residenti rispettivamente nel nuraghe e nella cittadella fortificata; anzi ritiene che il nuraghe fosse, almeno nel Bronzo Medio e Recente, del tutto isolato dall'abitato, configurandosi come sede del potere monarchico separato dai ceti sociali intermedi e subordinati (sacerdoti, guerrieri, popolo) (Ugas 1992: 204-209).

Queste ultime ipotesi necessitano di approfondite verifiche con le ricerche future; per il momento, a parte la questione dell'abitabilità dei nuraghi, su cui tornerò in seguito, non è inutile ricordare che il palazzo miceneo presenta una complessità strutturale e funzionale inimmaginabile in un nuraghe, anche solo pensando alla macroscopica differenza di strutture, spazi utili, ornamenti, arredi e suppellettili; è evidente che tali differenze non possono non rispecchiare un corrispondente dislivello di complessità dei rapporti sociali, nei quali il palazzo e il nuraghe esplicano i propri rispettivi ruoli. Inoltre, è ben noto che l'insieme dei caratteri culturali, socio-politici ed economici che contraddistinguono il sistema palaziale miceneo (fra cui è importantissima la scrittura) non è diffuso in tutto il mondo miceneo, ma si sviluppa organicamente solo nei quattro centri palaziali finora noti (Micene, Tirinto, Pilo, Tebe), mentre il resto del continente greco e le isole egee dovevano avere un'organizzazione sostanzialmente meno complessa (Darcque 1989: 430-433). Pertanto se il modello palaziale non costituisce un paradigma valido per tutto il mondo miceneo, non è prudente assumerlo per la Sardegna nuragica, in mancanza di prove specifiche e sulla sola base di una struttura sociale definita 'piramidale'. È assai probabile che i contatti diretti con i navigatori micenei abbiano stimolato una vivace evoluzione della società nuragica; tuttavia ciò è troppo poco per confermare l'ipotesi di una complessiva analogia strutturale fra la società nuragica e quella micenea. Per esempio, in Sardegna non si conoscono sepolture definibili come regali, anche lontanamente confrontabili con quelle micenee; pertanto mi sembra necessario negare l'esistenza di regimi monarchici propriamente detti, mentre sarebbe certamente preferibile un modello più sfumato e adattabile come quello denominato *chiefdom* (Cazzella 1989: 239-241, 251-252).

Comunque è degno di attenzione il confronto formulato da Ugas fra l'edificio complesso *gamma* di Monte Zara (Monastir) e l'*anaktoron* di Pantalica, cioè una struttura certamente più funzionale del nuraghe allo scopo di abitazione di personaggi di rango sociale e politico eminente (Ugas 1992: 212).

In modo del tutto opposto, il Trump vede nell'età del bronzo sarda una società egualitaria composta da comunità cantonali suddivise in famiglie estese di 10-20 persone; secondo l'autore inglese ciascuna famiglia erige il proprio nuraghe monotorre in un rapporto dialettico di competizione e collaborazione con le altre famiglie della stessa comunità. Egli ritiene che i nuraghi semplici, come quelli a corridoio e con camera embrionale, siano costruzioni caratterizzate da complesse valenze funzionali in senso difensivo e soprattutto simbolico, significanti il possesso della terra e il prestigio della famiglia e dell'intera comunità. Egli accetta l'esistenza di una marcata differenziazione sociale e politica solo per l'età del ferro, in concomitanza con lo sviluppo dei nuraghi complessi, che considera fortezze destinate soprattutto ad assicurare il dominio dell'aristocrazia sul popolo (Trump 1990: 44-49).

Il ragionamento del Trump presenta alcuni punti deboli. Innanzitutto l'esistenza dei nuraghi complessi è attestata già dal Bronzo Medio avanzato, anzi in molti casi la costruzione dei bastioni turriti sembra essere stata programmata fin dall'erezione della torre centrale; pertanto la connessione delle strutture più complesse con una forma di potere politico autoritario e con una corrispondente articolazione sociale deve essere estesa almeno all'età del Bronzo Medio e Recente. Inoltre proprio i nuraghi più arcaici, con corridoi o camera embrionale, sono caratterizzati da dimensioni e da masse murarie così imponenti e da blocchi di pietra così enormi, nonchè da una collocazione strategica così evidente (Santoni 1980), che mi riesce molto difficile immaginarli costruiti spontaneamente da gruppi di famiglie come simboli di un possesso e di un prestigio familiare; mi sembra invece chiaro che anch'essi fossero opera dell'intera comunità distribuita in un territorio naturalmente delimitato, e che dell'intera comunità difendessero gli interessi.

Nelle due posizioni esposte esistono elementi comuni, soprattutto riguardo all'organizzazione cantonale e al popolamento sparso con comunità di tipo policentrico articolate su più insediamenti. Tuttavia il divario è notevole: esso riguarda specialmente la ricostruzione della società nuragica nell'età del bronzo, giacchè non vi è sostanziale divergenza su quella dell'età del ferro. Pertanto tenterò di mediare fra le due posizioni antitetiche esposte, l'assolutismo monarchico di stampo orientale e l'egualitarismo su base familiare.

3. STADI DI SVILUPPO DELLA SOCIETÀ PROTOSARDA

La ricostruzione degli schemi di organizzazione sociale e territoriale nella Sardegna protostorica si presenta ancora assai problematica sia per la carenza di dati utili, sia per l'insufficiente elaborazione concettuale, sia per l'obiettiva difficoltà di trasferire nell'ambito isolano i modelli teorici formulati per la penisola italiana, per l'Europa e per l'Egeo. Malgrado certe differenze appariscenti o almeno apparenti che sembrano distinguere l'isola dei nuraghi da gran parte del mondo contemporaneo, non posso evitare di prendere in considerazione la ricostruzione dello sviluppo socio-economico e politico elaborata da Peroni per la protostoria dell'Italia continentale (Peroni 1989, 1992); infatti, contro il parere dello stesso Peroni (1992: 264, 669-70) e in accordo con l'opinione di Guidi (1992: 448-458), ritengo che i rapporti culturali fra la penisola italiana e la Sardegna, ben documentati lungo tutta l'età del Bronzo, abbiano contribuito a creare ideologie, gusti formali, strutture socio-economiche e politiche in certa misura affini, pur in una sostanziale diversità di tradizioni culturali. Pertanto non mi propongo di estendere automaticamente questa ricostruzione alla Sardegna, ma di esaminarne le implicazioni e i possibili contributi alla spiegazione dei vari aspetti della civiltà nuragica.

La società della cultura di Bonnanaro del Bronzo Antico (Lilliu 1988: 276-316) sembra, almeno sulla base delle sepolture, molto legata alla tradizione eneolitica delle *facies* di Filigosa, Abealzu e Monte Claro; resta ancora da precisare l'effettiva natura di quell'associazione di manufatti e tipologie funerarie solitamente definita come 'cultura del vaso campaniforme', con cui Bonnanaro ha stretti rapporti (Lilliu 1988: 160-176). Persiste il costume della sepoltura in grotte naturali ed ipogei artificiali riutilizzati, per lo più senza corredi personali distinti e senza oggetti denotanti un particolare rango individuale o di gruppo; unica eccezione nota in questo senso è rappresentata dalle spade in bronzo della 'tomba dei guerrieri' di Decimoputzu, che sembrano connotare personaggi distinti dalle altre deposizioni (Ugas 1990: 129-135). Per il resto si ha un'impressione generale di indifferenziazione sociale, di fluidità territoriale e di scarso sviluppo delle attività artigianali specializzate: sono quasi sconosciuti gli abitati all'aperto, che erano ben noti nelle fasi precedenti; sono assenti i ripostigli di bronzi, così importanti nello stesso periodo nell'Italia continentale, anzi sono scarsissimi i reperti metallici in genere. Tutto ciò induce a considerare la società del Bronzo Antico in Sardegna come una società ancora di tipo eneolitico, fondata su gruppi di parentela con differenziazioni interne poco sensibili e forse non permanenti; per adoperare la terminologia del Peroni (1989: 200-201), si potrebbe definire come una *società di lignaggio* con incipienti differenziazioni interne tendenti alla formazione di un embrione di aristocrazia guerriera.

Da questo punto di partenza è molto difficile immaginare come abbia potuto svilupparsi il fenomeno nuragico fin dagli inizi del Bronzo Medio (Lilliu 1988: 317-354). A questo proposito poco importa la continuità dell'evoluzione ceramica; una netta frattura rispetto al periodo precedente è evidenziata dalla ricomparsa degli abitati all'aperto, dalla cessazione quasi totale dell'utilizzo delle grotte e delle tombe ipogeiche più antiche, dallo sviluppo generale e diffuso delle sepolture megalitiche monumentali sulla base dell'antica tradizione dolmenica, dalla comparsa dei primi nuraghi, per lo più del tipo a corridoio. Ciò sembrerebbe attestare una società improvvisamente più evoluta: le grandi sepolture collettive, con un numero di deposizioni molto più elevato che nelle fasi precedenti, indicano una maggiore consistenza demografica; l'imponenza dell'impegno profuso nella costruzione di nuraghi, tombe e villaggi testimonia una coesione ragguardevole dei gruppi parentelari componenti le varie comunità cantonali; la funzione strategica e non solo tattica dei nuraghi (a corridoio, monotorri e complessi) evidenzia un interesse per il controllo del territorio in funzione dell'intera comunità e non delle singole famiglie. Non sarà forse azzardato ipotizzare l'esistenza anche in Sardegna, come nell'Italia continentale durante lo stesso periodo, di comunità territoriali organizzate secondo il modello definito dal Peroni (1989: 201-203) come *società tribale*, caratterizzato dalla fusione dei vecchi lignaggi in gruppi di alcune centinaia di individui, dalla relativa dissoluzione dei precedenti rapporti di parentela, da un assetto sostanzialmente egualitario ma con una presenza sensibile del ceto dominante. Contrasta però con questo quadro la persistenza di un insediamento sparso assai frazionato, per cui gli abitati non sembrano avere la consistenza di quelli noti in Italia, almeno nella regione padana.

Ancora più problematico è ricostruire gli sviluppi successivi. Sulla base dei dati disponibili è assai arduo ipotizzare anche in Sardegna un'ulteriore evoluzione parallela a quella riconosciuta nell'Italia continentale, che secondo il Peroni (1989: 298-302) porta le comunità tribali a forme di maggiore articolazione e complessità socio-economica e politica definite come *comunità gentilizio-clientelari preurbane*. Gli esiti di tale processo sono visibili nella penisola italiana fin dal Bronzo Recente e Finale, nella regione padana solo con la prima età del ferro. In Sardegna una simile articolazione mi sembra chiaramente compiuta nel periodo geometrico e orientalizzante (Lilliu 1988: 417-433), quando la formazione di un'aristocrazia gentilizia è rivelata da svariati fenomeni, fra cui le sepolture individuali con corredi di pregio e le sculture monumentali di Monti Prama (Lilliu 1988: 431, 547-550; Tronchetti 1988: 73-76), l'altare con figura in rilievo di Cann'e Fadosu (Cabras) (Ugas 1980), e le figurine in bronzo rappresentanti guerrieri superumani con quattro occhi e quattro braccia. Nello stesso tempo il rapporto di dipendenza che secondo il Peroni lega i ceti inferiori della popolazione all'aristocrazia gentilizia e che egli riconosce nella qualifica di soldato e quindi nella presenza o rappresentazione generalizzata di armi, sarebbe testimoniato, in mancanza di un'adeguata documentazione funeraria, dall'abbondanza di spade, lance e pugnali nei ripostigli e come offerte votive nei santuari, e dalle numerosissime figurine di guerrieri in bronzo. Non è da credere che lo sviluppo in senso aristocratico riconoscibile in tutta l'Isola e testimoniato specialmente dall'eccezionale complesso di Monti Prama, sia dovuto soltanto agli stimoli provenienti dalle colonie fenicie e specialmente da Tharros nella piena età del ferro; anzi vi è motivo di ritenere che il processo di riorganizzazione sociale avesse potuto avviarsi in tutta la Sardegna già qualche secolo prima, in condizioni assai simili a quelle definite dal Peroni (1989: 210-215, 241-251) per l'Italia meridionale e per la fascia mediotirrenica. Mi riferisco specialmente agli stimoli esercitati nel corso del Bronzo Recente e Finale dai contatti coi traffici micenei e con la metallurgia specializzata cipriota; proprio la metallurgia, approfonditamente studiata dallo Lo Schiavo, offre significativi indizi di un ruolo importante svolto dal ceto dominante nello sviluppo delle attività di estrazione, fusione e circolazione del metallo, e più generalmente nello sviluppo economico complessivo della Sardegna nuragica (Lo Schiavo 1981, 1986; Ferrarese Ceruti, Lo Schiavo, Vagnetti 1987). Tuttavia, aspetti discordanti da quelli che caratterizzano l'Italia meridionale e mediotirrenica nel Bronzo Recente e Finale si osservano nella mancanza di una contrapposizione fra sepolture monumentali e sepolture comuni, nell'assenza di differenziazioni individuali all'interno delle offerte funebri collettive, e soprattutto nella struttura degli insediamenti. Questi sono generalmente articolati in un certo numero di agglomerati di capanne raccolti intorno a cortili (Lilliu 1988: 366), secondo uno schema che sembra funzionale alla persistenza di gruppi parentelari intermedi che avrebbero dovuto essere già scomparsi o fortemente indeboliti; infatti una simile articolazione planimetrica è documentata dagli abitati eoliani di Capo Graziano e del Milazzese nel Bronzo Antico e Medio, ma fin dalla stessa fase essa tende a scomparire in tutta l'Italia per lasciare il posto a schemi modulari con abitazioni singole giustapposte in modo più o meno ordinato (Peroni 1989: 179-181).

Malgrado la difficoltà di definire in positivo la società nuragica nel corso del suo sviluppo, mi sembra necessario supporre che essa fosse fin dal Bronzo Medio caratterizzata da forme di potere tribale, pertanto più complessa e articolata di quella egualitaria e su base familiare proposta dal Trump; per altro verso l'immagine dei re-pastori evocati da Lilliu sembra inadeguata, lasciando in ombra il ruolo svolto dal potere politico nell'organizzazione delle attività industriali e nello sviluppo economico generale dell'Isola; infine è evidente che la Sardegna nuragica non arrivò mai allo stadio di organizzazione protourbana e monarchica delle società micenee o egee in genere.

4. La funzione dei nuraghi

In questo quadro ancora incerto si inserisce il tema della funzione dei nuraghi. In effetti i nuraghi, sparsi a migliaia in tutta l'isola, spesso raggruppati o allineati a brevissima distanza gli uni dagli altri, impressionanti per la mole e le ardite soluzioni architettoniche, talvolta veramente giganteschi (Lilliu 1962), costituiscono un fenomeno di enormi proporzioni, che sfugge ad una spiegazione funzionale intesa in senso stretto. L'investimento di beni e forza-lavoro direttamente o indirettamente connesso all'edificazione non tanto dei singoli nuraghi semplici e complessi, quanto di veri e propri sistemi fortificati territoriali in continuo sviluppo, sembra assolutamente sproporzionato e comporta considerazioni d'ordine simbolico, come giustamente sottolinea il Trump.

È evidente la destinazione ultima in senso militare di molti nuraghi complessi, vere fortezze composte dalla torre centrale, dai bastioni turriti e dagli antemurali, e provviste di numerosi espedienti difensivi (feritoie, botole, piombatoi, ecc.); sembra pertanto giustificata un'interpretazione analoga, sebbene in tono ridotto, anche per i nuraghi semplici e per i nuraghi di tipo più arcaico. A questo riguardo non condivido l'opinione del Trump (1990: 47) sullo scarso valore difensivo dei nuraghi, opinione fondata sull'osservazione del fenomeno dei nuraghi abbandonati precocemente; infatti ciò si può facilmente spiegare ammettendo che la funzione strategica di un nuraghe potesse decadere in seguito a spostamenti di centri abitati o a mutamenti dei confini cantonali, ovvero a cambiamenti nelle strategie di sfruttamento delle risorse locali.

Sulla base di queste considerazioni non concordo

neanche con l'ipotesi formulata dal Santoni (1985: 184), secondo cui durante il Bronzo Recente e Finale il nuraghe perde il proprio ruolo di centro di riferimento degli abitati ed è sostituito in tale funzione dai luoghi di culto (pozzi sacri e templi a *megaron*). Per analoghe ragioni, in attesa dei necessari riscontri, non condivido l'ipotesi opposta di Ugas (1992: 204–209) sopra accennata, circa la separazione dell'abitato dal nuraghe durante il Bronzo Medio e Recente.

Infatti le recenti ricerche territoriali hanno dimostrato che vi è un'interdipendenza, pur senza perfetta coincidenza topografica, tra sistema difensivo e sistema insediativo, in quanto la distribuzione dei nuraghi segue criteri prevalentemente strategici, mentre quella degli abitati obbedisce a scelte essenzialmente economiche. Sulla base delle conoscenze acquisite, io credo che durante il Bronzo Recente e Finale lo sviluppo dell'economia primaria e delle attività indsutriali e di scambio abbia provocato non tanto il regresso funzionale del nuraghe, quanto l'esplosione del sistema insediativo, non più costretto entro la maglia difensiva impostata nel corso del Bronzo Medio.

Tuttavia, proprio la frequente separazione fra nuraghi e abitati fa sorgere dubbi circa la reale efficacia difensiva dei sistemi fortificati nuragici. Al riguardo è istruttivo notare come nella penisola italiana, a partire dal Bronzo Medio e sempre più nelle fasi successive, gli insediamenti si trovano normalmente su posizioni strategiche e spesso sono essi stessi fortificati (Peroni 1989: 140); invece in Sardegna gli abitati non sono frequentemente arroccati o cinti da mura e spesso sono del tutto indifesi, trovandosi ad una certa distanza dal nuraghe più vicino. Questo fatto, se da un lato consentiva una distribuzione del popolamento più funzionale alle necessità produttive, dall'altro esponeva tutto il sistema economico al pericolo della paralisi in caso di aggressione. La vecchia ipotesi del Lilliu (1963: 251), secondo cui in caso di attacco la popolazione e il bestiame potevano rifugiarsi nei nuraghi, è chiaramente insostenibile per mancanza di spazi utili: gli abitanti dovevano spostarsi in luoghi più sicuri fino al termine del pericolo, e ciò doveva provocare gravi squilibri nella vita della comunità. Pertanto mi sembra chiaro che la proliferazione dei sistemi fortificati nuragici non presupponeva uno stato di guerra permanente, e che la strategia difensiva doveva essere essenzialmente preventiva, fondandosi sul valore deterrente delle grandi fortezze e delle torri dislocate lungo i confini cantonali e lungo le vie di penetrazione, che costituivano segni ben visibili di una presenza vigile e costante a controllo del territorio. Questa deve essere almeno una delle funzioni anche dei tipi più arcaici di nuraghi, caratterizzati da corridoi e da camere embrionali, che sarebbero altrimenti enigmatici se considerati solo dal punto di vista dell'uso degli angusti spazi interni e dei terrazzi superiori (Lilliu 1988: 180–186; Trump 1990: 43–44; Santoni 1980).

Un utilizzo abitativo dei nuraghi è certo innegabile; le ceramiche e gli strumenti d'uso comune e i resti di pasto rinvenuti nei vari ambienti dimostrano che alcune persone vivevano o almeno svolgevano certe attività, preparavano e consumavano il cibo dentro i nuraghi. Per esempio il Trump (1990: 46) pensa che vi si svolgessero banchetti, tipica attività sociale connessa al prestigio della famiglia ospitante. Tuttavia ritengo che la destinazione abitativa fosse del tutto secondaria e dipendente da altre funzioni. Parlare di nuraghe come abitazione fortificata mi sembra assurdo sia per l'impegno costruttivo sproporzionato all'effettiva utilità domestica, sia per l'umidità e l'oscurità che rendono difficilmente abitabile una tale struttura.

A maggior ragione, l'interpretazione del nuraghe complesso come abitazione del capo o monarca mi sembra insostenibile, anche per l'assoluta mancanza di suppellettili o ornamenti distinti o di speciali simboli del potere, insomma di qualsiasi indizio che possa riferirsi ad un monarca assoluto, di cui mancano tracce anche in ambito funerario. A mio parere, quello della reggia nuragica è certamente un mito da sfatare.

Inoltre nella protostoria d'Italia e del Mediterraneo occidentale non esiste una differenziazione strutturale così esagerata ed una totale separazione fra le abitazioni comuni e quelle più importanti: queste ultime si trovano insieme alle prime e si distinguono solo per l'ampiezza relativamente maggiore e per la pianta più complessa (Peroni 1989: 227–232, 284–286). Lo stesso *anaktoron* di Pantalica (al quale può essere accostato l'edificio complesso *gamma* di Monte Zara presso Monastir) ha un costo di gran lunga inferiore ad un nuraghe complesso, ma la sua funzionalità abitativa è senz'altro molto superiore.

In effetti, l'uso della fortezza nuragica come abitazione del monarca presuppone un'appropriazione esagerata di beni e prestazioni forniti dalla comunità: appropriazione accettabile nel modello orientale di disponibilità assoluta dei mezzi di produzione, simile a quello supposto da Lilliu ed Ugas, ma inconciliabile col controllo indiretto dei mezzi di produzione e con l'impulso allo sviluppo delle attività industriali e di scambio, che secondo il Peroni (1989: 251–261) costituiscono la base della capacità d'intervento economico e politico dell'aristocrazia gentilizia.

Questo rapporto fra il nuraghe e l'autorità politica, ritenuto così diretto ed esclusivo, mi sembra più opportuno immaginarlo mediato attraverso ulteriori funzioni e significati simbolici, soprattutto ai fini della ricerca del consenso e della stabilizzazione del potere, che in un organismo sociale assimilabile al modello del *chiefdom* non è mai assolutamente saldo e sicuro. In altre parole, il nuraghe non può essere considerato solo come 'segno del potere', secondo la definizione coniata da Santoni (1980), ma come simbolo dei rapporti sociali complessi e instabili esistenti nella comunità nuragica, che legano l'aristocrazia dominante e il popolo. Infatti da un lato è evidente l'esercizio di un potere autoritario che impone prestazioni di lavoro e forniture di beni per la costruzione del nuraghe; anzi è assai probabile che la costruzione stessa dei nuraghi, come delle tombe, dei santuari e perfino dei villaggi, fosse anche uno strumento di controllo e dominio sociale esercitato dai ceti egemoni su comunità subordinate di tipo tribale o clientelare; ma ritengo che la giustificazione di tali sacrifici sociali fosse comunque un'utilità collettiva, in qualche modo sentita e accettata dalla comunità. La richiesta di forniture e prestazioni tanto onerose necessarie alla costruzione doveva certamente dare l'avvio ad un'organizzazione di produzione e scambio tale da consentire periodicamente il distacco di un gran numero di uomini dalle normali attività e porli a carico dell'intera comunità; è assai probabile che ciò si traducesse in un rafforzamento dei detentori del potere e in un aumento del consenso sociale, in virtù del beneficio comune derivante dalla garanzia di sicurezza o da altre funzioni svolte dal nuraghe nella vita comunitaria.

Per esempio, si potrebbe ipotizzare che il nuraghe avesse un ruolo anche nei processi di circolazione di beni appartenenti all'aristocrazia dominante o alla comunità, posti sotto il controllo del potere politico: si può pensare alla concentrazione e redistribuzione di beni il cui uso fosse regolato da norme, e pertanto accuratamente protetti. Espongo questa idea con la massima cautela, senza voler certo affermare che la destinazione originaria e prevalente dei nuraghi fosse quella di magazzini organizzati; ma non mi sembra assurdo pensare che gli edifici più imponenti della Sardegna nuragica, solo saltuariamente adoperati in funzione difensiva, fossero invece stabilmente impiegati per una destinazione civile essenziale in tutte le società protostoriche evolute, direttamente connessa con l'ordinaria gestione dei mezzi di produzione e coi rapporti economici e politici. Mi sembra chiaro che molti vani sia principali (camere) sia secondari (nicchie, garitte, cellette, diverticoli, pozzi, cisterne ecc.) potevano essere adoperati come depositi di beni di vario genere (alimentari, materie prime, armi, strumenti, oggetti di prestigio, altri manufatti, ecc.). Ad esempio, il vano *a* del Nuraghe Antigori (Ferrarese Ceruti 1981), contenente gran quantità di ceramica micenea, deve essere interpretato a mio avviso come un deposito di beni di prestigio esotici, piuttosto che come un sacello, per la mancanza di specifici reperti e di caratteri strutturali e funzionali indicanti lo svolgimento di attività rituali; analogamente, i non rari ripostigli con lingotti e panelle di rame grezzo o manufatti in bronzo possono costituire riserve metalliche tesaurizzate o da distribuire ai fonditori.

Questa destinazione, forse secondaria nell'età del bronzo ma sempre presente e via via più importante fino all'età del ferro, contribuì probabilmente alla trasformazione di numerosi nuraghi in depositi votivi e in veri e propri luoghi di culto nel periodo geometrico; d'altra parte questo fenomeno, che spesso si accompagna a parziali distruzioni e ristrutturazioni di nuraghi, va ben al di là di un semplice mutamento funzionale e si inquadra in un generale processo di riorganizzazione sociale, economica e politica della Sardegna nel corso dell'età del ferro (Lilliu 1988: 433–434). Esso segna una fase di grave instabilità, a cui l'*élite* dominante sarda reagì rafforzando il proprio potere con evidenti sviluppi in senso teocratico (Tronchetti 1988: 20). I recentissimi rinvenimenti nel nuraghe Nurdole di Orani (Fadda 1991) confermano l'importanza di tali mutamenti, sottolineata dall'impianto di strutture sacrali e votive e dall'accumulo di offerte e di derrate alimentari.

Tuttavia credo che la complessa funzionalità dei nuraghi oltrepassi il loro uso effettivo, sia militare che civile; anzi ritengo che il fenomeno dei nuraghi non riveli una logica puramente economica, e che al contrario, se considerato solo sotto questo aspetto, esso rappresenterebbe un enorme spreco di energie per un'utilità comunque inadeguata all'investimento.

Per comprendere appieno la funzione sociale del nuraghe è senza dubbio necessario approfondire l'indagine sui suoi significati simbolici, che per quanto adombrati nell'effettiva destinazione d'uso, devono essere studiati nel quadro ancora lacunoso dell'ideologia della civiltà protosarda.

Ho già accennato al nuraghe come simbolo dei rapporti sociali vigenti all'interno delle singole comunità tribali o clientelari; tale significato è evidente nei numerosi modelli di nuraghi a grande o piccola scala, in pietra e in bronzo, che nell'età del ferro vengono posti al centro delle grandi capanne per riunioni o adoperati come altari in edifici di culto o offerti come doni votivi (Moravetti 1980).

In relazione ai rapporti fra le varie comunità nuragiche, sono utili alcune considerazioni del Trump, elevate però dal livello familiare a quello comunitario, poiché è impossibile ridurre il ruolo dei nuraghi alla competizione e collaborazione fra singole famiglie. Per la sua grandiosa monumentalità il nuraghe si presta ancor meglio delle tombe megalitiche ad affermare la proprietà e il controllo del territorio e ad assumere un valore simbolico come manifestazione di potenza e superiorità nei confronti delle comunità nuragiche vicine e lontane. Certamente fra le varie comunità isolane si innescò una spirale di rivalità ed emulazione, ma anche di collaborazione reciproca, che doveva esprimersi anche nella moltiplicazione abnorme del numero dei nuraghi e nella costruzione di fortezze sempre più gigantesche, anche al di là della loro potenziale efficacia difensiva.

Questa ed altre possibili ragioni di ordine ideologico, accanto alle motivazioni difensive ed economiche, offrono valide prospettive alla ricerca sul fenomeno più imponente e complesso prodotto dalla civiltà della Sardegna antica.

Bibliografia

Cazzella, A. 1989. *Manuale di archeologia. Le società della preistoria*, Bari.

Contu, E. 1974. 'La Sardegna dell'età nuragica', in AA. VV., *Popoli e Civiltà dell'Italia Antica*, 3, Roma, 143-203.

Contu, E. 1981. 'L'architettura nuragica', in AA. VV., *Ichnussa. La Sardegna dalle origini all'età classica*, Milano, 3-175.

Darcque, P. 1989. 'L'histoire du monde mycenien', in Treuil, R., Darcque, P., Poursat, J.-C. & Touchais, G., *Les civilisations egeennes*, Paris, 424-457.

Fadda, M. A. 1991. 'Nurdole. Un tempio nuragico in Barbagia. Punto d'incontro nel Mediterraneo', *Rivista di Studi Fenici*, XIX, 1, 107-119.

Ferrarese Ceruti, M. L. 1981. 'Documenti micenei nella Sardegna meridionale', in AA. VV., *Ichnussa. La Sardegna dalle origini all'età classica*, Milano, 605-612.

Ferrarese Ceruti, M. L., Lo Schiavo, F. & Vagnetti, L. 1987. 'Minoici, Micenei e Ciprioti in Sardegna nella seconda metà del II millennio a. C.', in AA. VV., *Studies in Sardinian Archaeology III: Nuragic Sardinia and the Mycenaean world*, BAR International Series 387, 3-37.

Guidi, A. 1992. 'Le età dei metalli nell'Italia centrale e in Sardegna', in AA. VV., *Italia preistorica*, Bari, 420-470.

Lilliu, G. 1962. *I nuraghi, torri preistoriche della Sardegna*, Cagliari.

Lilliu, G. 1963. *La civiltà dei Sardi dal Neolitico all'età dei nuraghi*, Torino (I ed.).

Lilliu, G. 1981. 'La preistoria sarda e la civiltà nuragica nella storiografia moderna', in AA. VV., *Ichnussa. La Sardegna dalle origini all'età classica*, Milano, 487-523.

Lilliu, G. 1988. *La civiltà dei Sardi dal Paleolitico all'età dei nuraghi*, Torino (III ed.).

Lo Schiavo, F. 1981. 'Economia e società nell'età dei nuraghi', in AA. VV., *Ichnussa. La Sardegna dalle origini all'età classica*, Milano, 255-347.

Lo Schiavo, F. 1986. 'Sardinian metallurgy: the archaeological background', in AA. VV., *Studies in Sardinian Archaeology II: Sardinia in the Mediterranean*, Ann Arbor, 231-250.

Moravetti, A. 1980. 'Nuovi modellini di torri nuragiche', *Bollettino d'Arte*, LXV, s. VI, 7, 65-84.

Peroni, R. 1989. *Protostoria dell'Italia continentale*, (Popoli e Civiltà dell'Italia Antica, 9), Roma.

Peroni, R. 1992. 'Per un quadro culturale dell'Italia centrosettentrionale tra XVI e XIII sec. a. C.', in AA. VV., *La Sardegna nel Mediterraneo tra il Bronzo Medio e il Bronzo Recente (XVI-XIII sec. a. C.)*, Cagliari, 249-264; discussione, 667-671.

Santoni, V. 1980. 'Il segno del potere', in AA. VV., *Nur. La misteriosa civiltà dei Sardi*, Milano, 141-187.

Santoni, V. 1985. 'I templi di età nuragica', in AA. VV., *Sardegna preistorica*, Milano, 181-207.

Tronchetti, C. 1988. *I Sardi*, Milano.

Trump, D.H. 1990. *Nuraghe Noeddos and the Bonu Ighinu Valley. Excavation and survey in Sardinia*, Oxford.

Ugas, G. 1980. 'Altare modellato su castello nuragico di tipo trilobato con figura in rilievo dal Sinis di Cabras (Oristano)', *Archeologia Sarda*, 10, 7-32.

Ugas, G. 1987. 'Un nuovo contributo per lo studio della tholos in Sardegna. La fortezza di Su Mulinu – Villanovafranca', in AA. VV., *Studies in Sardinian Archaeology III: Nuragic Sardinia and the Mycenaean world*, BAR International Series 387, Oxford, 77-128.

Ugas, G. 1989-90. 'Il sacello del vano e nella fortezza nuragica di Su Mulinu – Villanovafranca (CA)', *Scienze dell'Antichità*, 3-4, 551-573.

Ugas, G. 1990. *La tomba dei guerrieri di Decimoputzu*, Cagliari.

Ugas, G. 1992. 'Note su alcuni contesti del Bronzo Medio e Recente della Sardegna meridionale. Il caso dell'insediamento di Monte Zara – Monastir', in AA.VV., *La Sardegna nel Mediterraneo tra il Bronzo Medio e il Bronzo Recente (XVI-XIII sec. a.C.)*, Cagliari, 201-227.

Webster, G.S. 1991. 'The functions and social significance of nuraghi: a provisional model', in AA. VV., *Arte militare e architettura nuragica. Nuragic architecture in its military, territorial and socio-economic context*, Acta Instituti Romani Regni Sueciae, XLVIII, Stockholm, 169-185.

27

Grave Dimensions as a Diagnostic Tool for Palaeodemography and Social Ranking The Example of Veio-Quattro Fontanili

WOLF-RÜDIGER TEEGEN

(Georg-August-Universität, Göttingen)

Summary: *Few early Iron Age tombs in Etruria have been anthropologically studied, and for these, the cemetery of Veio-Quattro Fontanili represents the only published material on a large scale. The material studied here consists mainly of human teeth: 109 individuals from 98 graves – dating back to the 8th century BC – were aged; only 23 could be sexed. This paper examines the distribution of the different age classes, the size and depth of graves and the variety of grave-goods. Analysis shows that the mortality rate of children under 10 years was 43% and for young individuals under 15 years 49%; very few children under 2 years were found. Tombs depths vary from between 0,2m to almost 3.0m, but amongst children the associated grave-goods indicate that graves at a depth of up to 0.9m can be considered 'poor' and those at more than 1.2m as 'rich'. Grave size may also be viewed as a likely indicator of status.*

INTRODUCTION

Only very few anthropological investigations have been carried out on early Iron Age tombs in Etruria. The cemetery of Veio-Quattro Fontanili, dating to the 9th/8th century BC, is the only cemetery for which osteological material has been published on a large scale. G. Alciati and P. Passarello studied the remains, mainly consisting of human teeth, of 112 individuals. Of these only 109 (from 91 graves) could be aged and only 23 could be sexed (see tab. 1 and fig. 1). There are two types of graves at Veio-Quattro Fontanili: 'pozzo' and 'fossa'. The former is circular and the latter rectangular, both cut into the tufa bedrock. Of 112 individuals studied 11 cremations were found in 5 pozzo tombs, 91 inhumations were found in 76 fossa tombs, and the remaining 10 indivdiduals come from 10 graves which are given incomplete labels in the publication of G. Alciati and P. Passarello, and are therefore unidentifiable.

Figure 2 show the mortality rate of the ontogenetic age classes (after Vallois 1960) for the 109 individuals from the Veio-Quattro Fontanili cemetery. The mortality rate of children under the age of 10 years is around 43%, and for the young individuals under the age of 15 years is around 49%. For all sub-adults the mortality rate is up to 55%. Figure 3 is a histogram of the age

Table 1. Veio-Quattro Fontanili (fossa-graves).
Anthropologically sexed and aged individuals (data after Alciati & Passarello 1963; Passarello 1965; 1967). For distribution maps and plots only the information in the normal typed columns was used (76 graves).

	n (ind.)	n (grave)	Sex n.d.	M	M arch.	F	F arch.
Inf. I	22	17	14	3	6	2	2
Inf. II.	15	12	10	0	2	3	3
Inf.	7	4	4	0	1	1	1
Juv.	6	6	3	2	2	1	1
Ad.	25	22	15	2	3	5	11
Mat.	16	15	7	2	1	6	7
n	91	76	53	9	15	14	25

M/F arch. = archaeologically sexed individuals. Bold = 91 individuals from 76 graves.

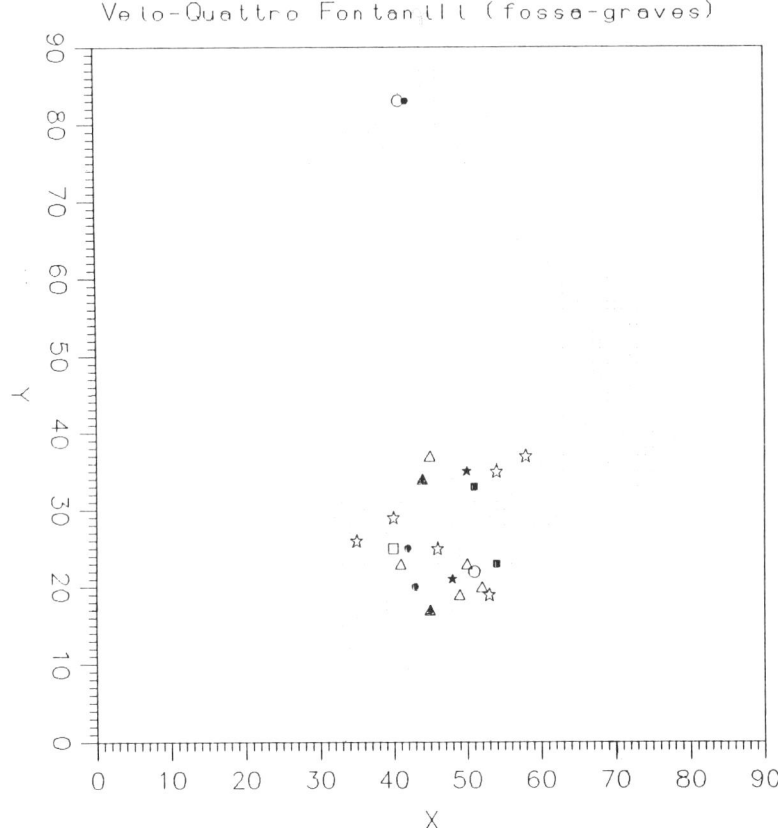

Fig. 1. Veio-Quattro Fontanili. Distribution of anthropological sexed and aged graves in the cemetery.
X-axis (0–90) = 225m,
Y-axis (0–90) = 225m (0/0 = SS-TT/44–45).
Bold signature = M,
light signature = F,
circle = inf.,
square = juv.,
triangle = ad.,
star = mat;
n=23
(data after Alciati & Passarello 1963; Passarello 1965; 1967).

classes for the 91 individuals buried in fossa-graves. The darker bars of figure 3 shows the 76 selected individuals from the original 91, of the 76 fossa-graves. Figure 4 shows the distribution of the 76 fossa-graves in the cemetery.

The age class of young infants under the age of 2 years is missing in many cemeteries of the early Italian Iron Age, like Veio- Quattro Fontanili. The latter has one exception, the grave II18-19 with an infant between the age of 1–2 years. The extremely high mortality rate among young people under the age of 20 can also be observed at the Forum necropolis in Rome. Here the mortality rate runs up to 56%. In a previous publication I have argued that perhaps only weaned infants were buried in the cemetery and the breast feaded babies mainly in the settlements (see Teegen [in press]). The inhumation graves from settlements of the Cultura laziale like Rome (Forum Romanum), Fidenae, Ficana, Ardea, Lavinium, Satricum contain not only newborns and infants but also older children. An analysis of mortality tables of cemeteries of the Cultura laziale also indicates missing sub-adults (see Teegen 1987).

The distribution of finds like greek import vessels or gold indicates that at Veio-Quattro Fontanili there are at least three different grave groups: the NE group, SE group and SW group. Concerning the few material that has been studied anthropologically, an age- and sex-classification of each group was not possible.

At first all graves with anthropologically aged (and sexed) individuals were analyzed. The correlation between grave-length and breadth (fig. 5) resp. depth (fig. 6) was plotted considering also the age of the buried individuals (inf., juv., ad., mat.). The dimension of a tomb directly indicates the age group of the burried individual: children or adults. Extraordinary large children's graves generally contain a large amount of grave-goods.

Figure 5 describes the age at death with the length and the breadth of the tomb. Two groups strike: children (infans I/II) and adults. Due to the length of the tomb, the graves of – anthropological determined – juvenile individuals are as well in the first group "child" as in the second one of the "adults". The grave goods often gave a good clues to decide whether the individual is considered as an "adult" ($\geq$15/17 years) or still as "children" (<15/17 years). The attribution to one or another group is justified. The critical value, separating children from adults, for Veio-Quattro Fontanili seems to be fixed at about 2m length of the tomb with a deviation of ± 10cm (at max. 20cm), about a breadth of a spade. Both groups can be rather certainly separated with the help of its length/breadth-index (see later).

The depth of children's graves gives first information about their social status (fig. 7). According to the children's grave goods a depth up to 90cm can be considered as "poor" (0 grave goods = average depth

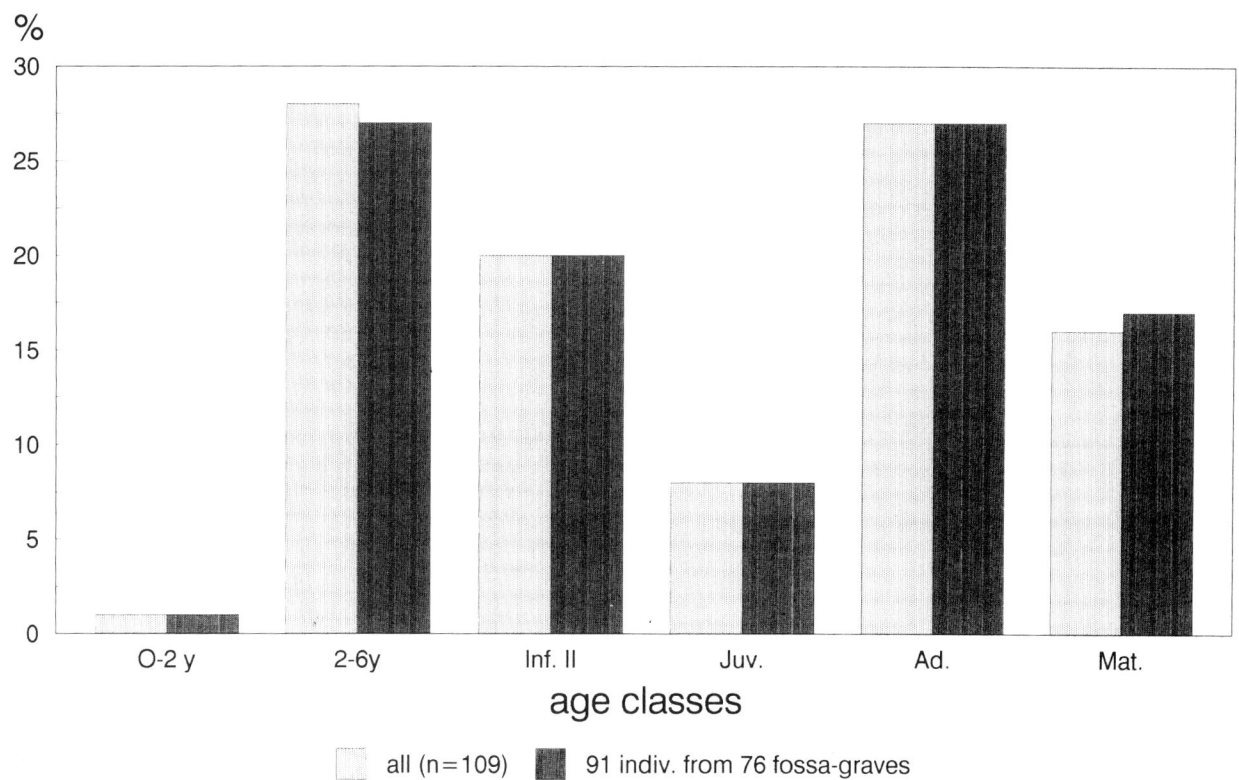

Fig. 2. Veio-Quattro Fontanili. Distribution of anthropological aged individuals on ontogenetic age classes in %. Light grid = all individuals (n=109), dark grid = 91 individuals from 76 fossa-graves (data after Alciati & Passarello 1963; Passarello 1965; 1967).

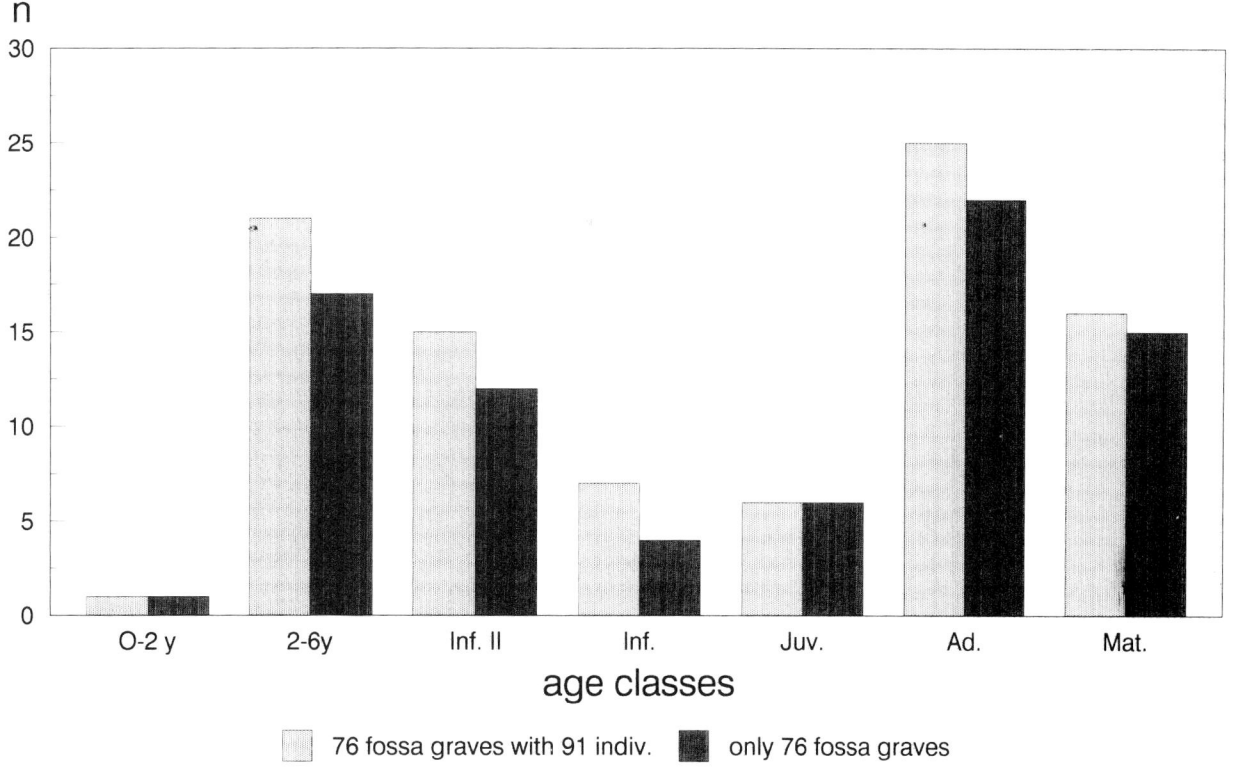

Fig. 3. Veio-Quattro Fontanili. Distribution of anthropological aged individuals on ontogenetic age classes. Light grid = 91 individuals from 76 fossa-graves, dark grid = only the major individuals from the same 76 fossa-graves (data after Alciati & Passarello 1963; Passarello 1965; 1967).

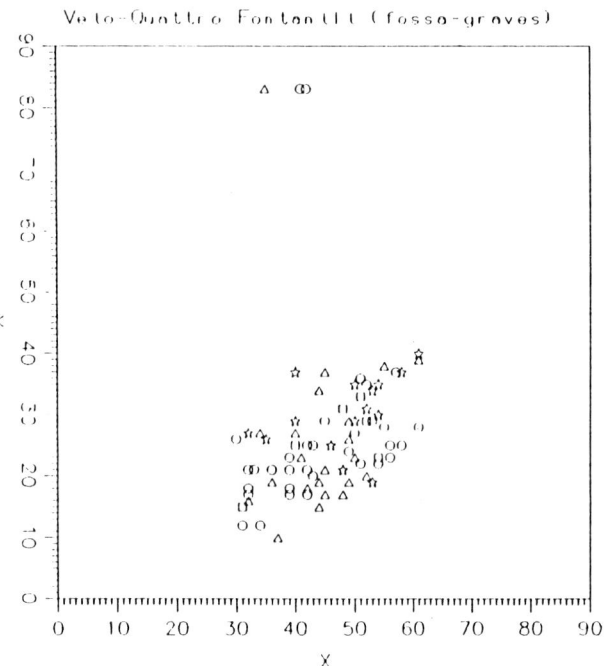

Fig. 4. Veio-Quattro Fontanili (fossa-graves). Distribution of anthropological aged graves on the cemetery (n=76). X-axis (0-90) = 225m, Y-axis (0-90) = 225m (0/0 = SS-TT/44-45). Circle = inf., square = juv., triangle = ad., star = mat (data after Alciati & Passarello 1963; Passarello 1965; 1967).

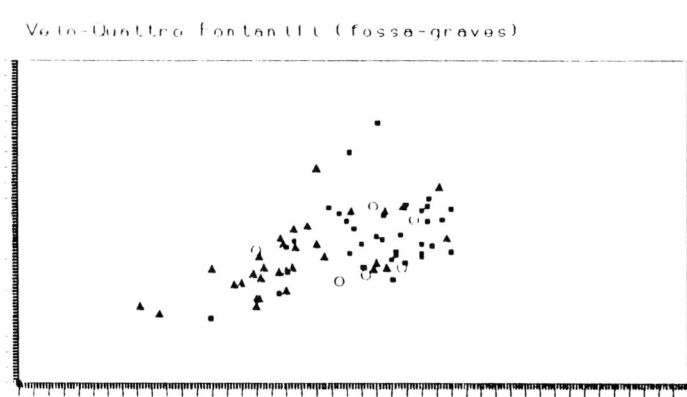

Fig. 5. Veio-Quattro Fontanili (fossa-graves). Correlation between grave length (L) and breadth (B) and age at death (n=76). Triangle = inf., circle = juv., square = ad./mat. X-axis = 0–450cm, Y-axis = 0–210cm.

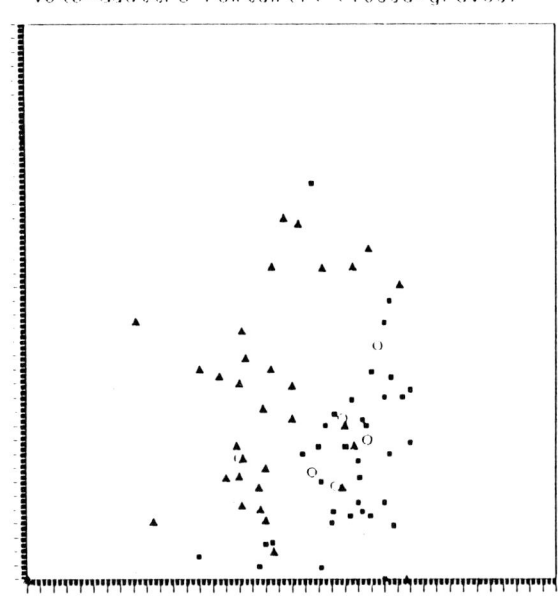

Fig. 6. Veio-Quattro Fontanili (fossa-graves). Correlation between grave length (L) and depth (D) and age at death. (n=76). Triangle = inf., circle = juv., square = ad./mat. X-axis = 0–400cm, Y-axis = 0–400cm.

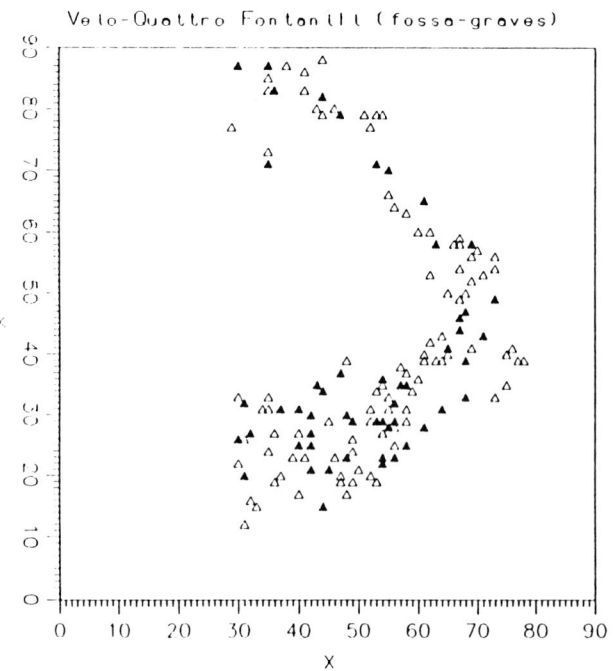

Fig. 7. Veio-Quattro Fontanili (fossa-graves). Distribution of archaeological sexed graves in the cemetery (minimum). Bold triangle = M (n=52), light triangle = F (n=94).

60cm; 1–9 grave goods: 92cm) and more than 120cm as "rich" (10–19 grave goods = average depth 143cm; >20 grave goods: 202cm; fig. 6). There is a great variety in the group of the adults. It is more difficult to explain their averages, although there is a slight trend: adult indivduals: 1–10 grave goods: average depth = 72cm; >10 grave goods: 103cm; mature individuals: 1–10 grave goods: average depth = 67cm; >10 grave goods: 83cm. The preserved tomb-depth varies between 20cm and almost 3m (see below). To explain this phenomena you have to consider the irregular erosion, caused by agricultural working of the terrain.

All fossa-graves (n=435) publicated in QF1–7 were recorded with a relational database. The following attributes were used: grave-number, grave status (0/1 [disturbed/destroyed]), grave dimensions (L, B, D in cm), coffin dimensions (L, B in cm), presence and no. of loculus, loculus dimensions (L, B, H in cm), chronology (after J. Toms 1986), archaeological determined sex (fibula serpeggiante, razor, arms = M; fuso, fusaiola, rocchetto = F), anthropological determined sex and age (after Alciati & Passarello 1963; Passarello 1965; 1967), grave goods (no.), ceramic vessels (no.), imported vessels (0/1), other painted vessels (0/1), other imported finds (0/1), bronze objects (no.), ferrous objects (no.), gold and silver objects (0/1). Every grave gets X/Y-coordinates (0/0 = SS-TT/44–45). Area and volume of the graves were calculated automatically using the grave dimensions (L, B, D).

The archaeological sexed graves (M/F; distribution: fig. 7) only represent a minimum because only a few sexing attributes were taken into consideration. Further studies on this subject are needed. It seems to be, that the males' graves are not so significant in their grave goods as the females' are. There are 52 graves with arms and/or fibula serpegiante which are classified as male. There are 94 graves that contain fuso and/or fusaiola and/or rocchetto; they were therefore classified as "female". At least two graves (HHII9, ZAA17–18) contain grave goods of both sexes. There is a slight sex difference in grave length. The grave length of the male are naturally longer. Females' graves have a greater amount of goods: M (arch. det.; n=52) average grave length = 241cm and average no. of grave goods = 10; F (arch. det.; n=94) average grave length = 239cm and average no. of grave goods = 15.

The distribution of the grave length indicates two significant maxima, separated by a minimum of 190–199cm graves (fig. 8). This reflects the distribution of childrens (inf. I-II) and adults (ad.-mat.). Probably behind there is a third covered peak representing the juvenils. Considering the range of the length of children's graves (inf. I: range 130–287cm, average 168cm [n=17]; inf. II: range 82–247cm, average 202cm [n=12]; inf.: range

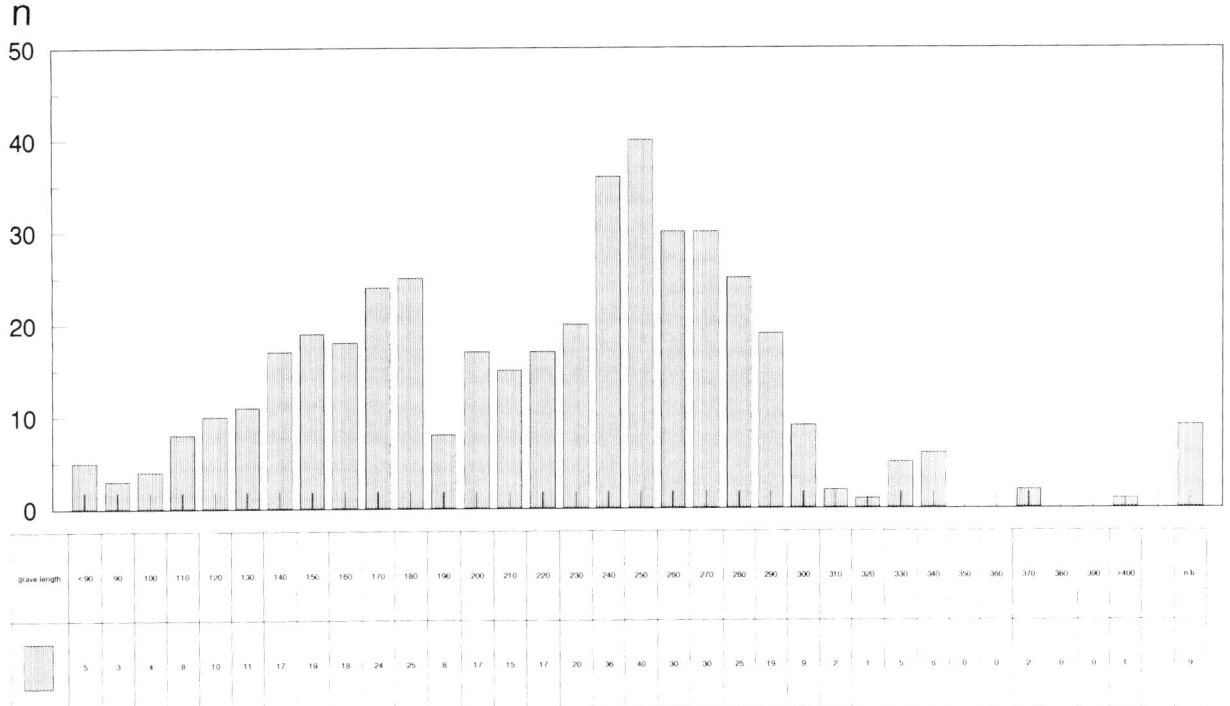

Fig. 8. Veio-Quattro Fontanili (fossa-graves). Distribution of grave length (n=435; not determined [n.b.] = 9).

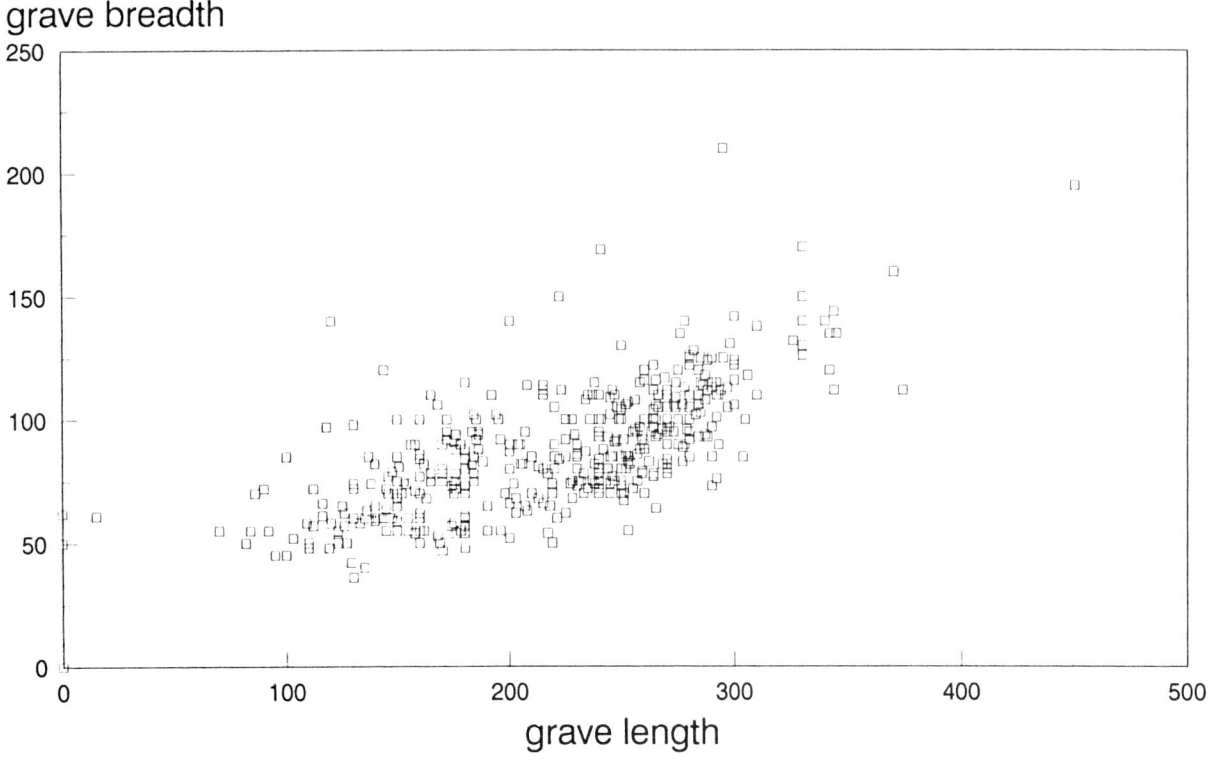

Fig. 9. Veio-Quattro Fontanili (fossa-graves). Correlation between grave length and breadth (n=435).

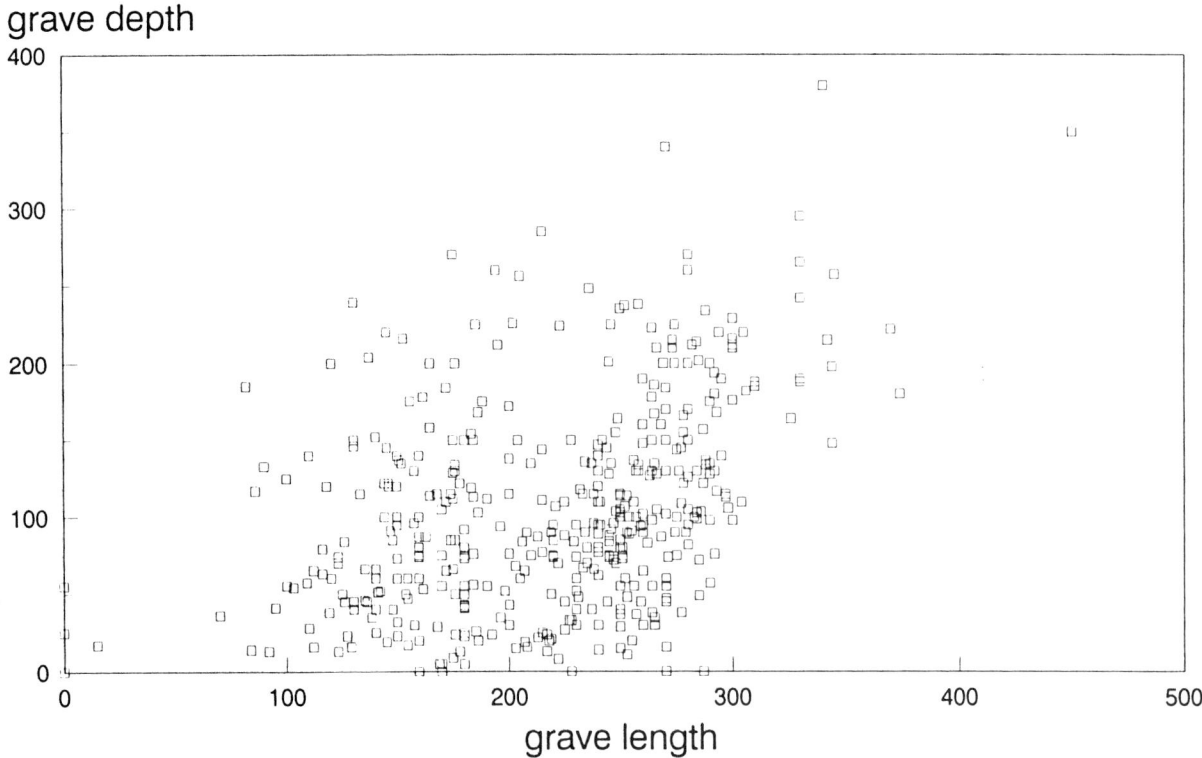

Fig. 10. Veio-Quattro Fontanili (fossa-graves). Correlation between grave length and depth (n=435).

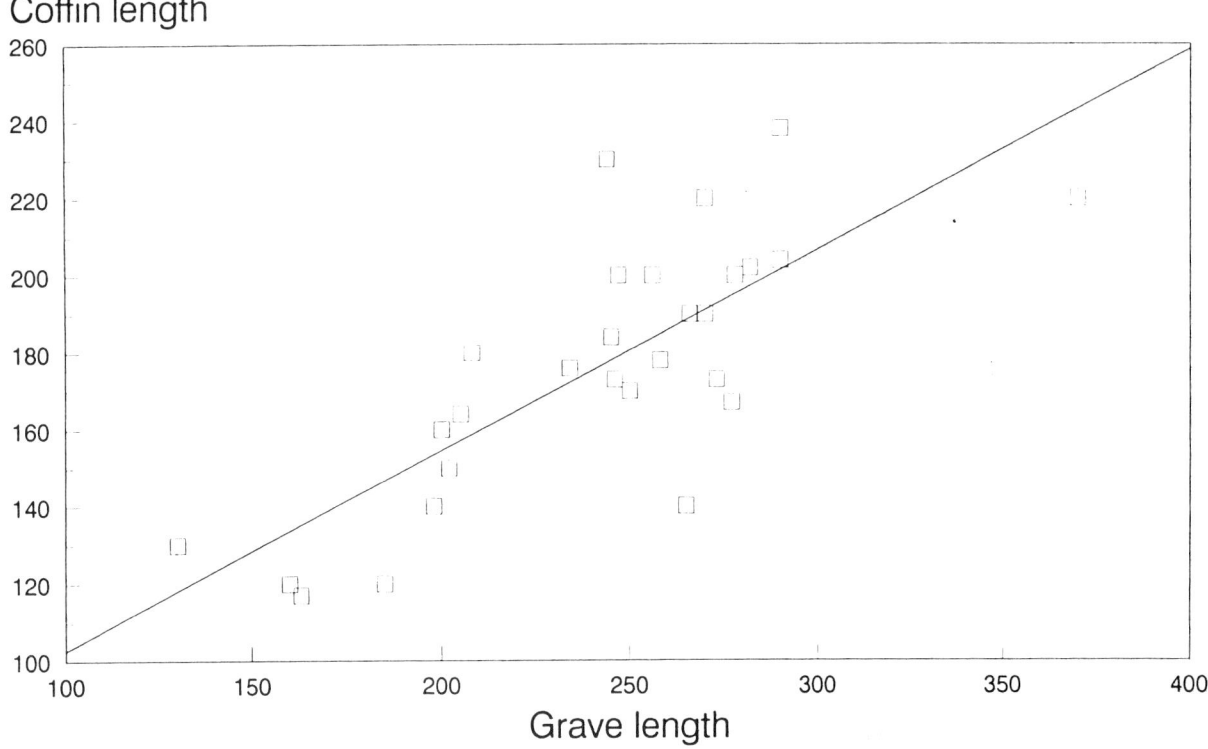

Fig. 11. Veio-Quattro Fontanili (fossa-graves). Correlation between grave length and coffin length (n=28). Regression: R^2 1:0.5968174, b 0.5207180, a 50.532306.

95–184cm, average 140cm [n=2]), graves of juvenils (range 160–257cm, average 228cm [n=6]) and graves of adults (ad.: range 129–290cm, average 244cm [n=21]; mat.: range 175–277cm, average 239cm [n=15]) support this hypothesis. It seems to be certain that the graves smaller than 200cm of length at Veio-Quattro Fontanili predominant contain children resp. sub-adults (37.8% [100% = 426]).

The large number of sub-adults (>50%), determined by anthropological analyses, cannot be only estimated by the grave length. It is more suitable to use the length/breadth-index (fig. 10). The plot indicates two clusters (centre 1 at ca. 160cm, centre 2 at ca. 280cm). It is possible to seperate the two clusters by a deduced line y=-x+300 (analysing 50 anthropological studied fossa-graves; fig. 5).

There is a correlation between grave and coffin length (R^2 1:0.5968174 b 0.5207180; a 50.532306); only 28 graves could be used (fig. 11). A correlation between body height and coffin length seems not to be possible.

To estimate the correlation between grave length and body height the recent values from the former GDR (Flügel *et al.* 1986) were taken into account. Fig. 12 shows the development of the body height from birth to adult, separated by sex (P5 to P95 and average). Considering the formula of Manouvrier the average body height of the Italian Iron Age (9.-6. cent. BC) is for man 164.98cm (n=131) and for females 155.52cm (n=40) (Teegen 1987, Tab. 3). Therefore the average body heigth of the middle-European man is 7cm (average body height 172cm), the female ca. 6cm taller (average body height 161cm) in comparison to the Italian Iron Age.

Social ranking

Number and quality of grave goods are an expression of social status. Figure 13 represents the number of grave goods, fig. 14 their distribution in the cemetery. The size of the grave (in m^3; fig. 15–16) is another important indicator for the social status. The correlation between grave dimensions (p.e. depth or size) and number of grave goods is already documented by the average values: 0 grave goods: average depth 76cm/average 1.3m^3; 1–9 grave goods 96cm/2.2m^3; 10–19 grave goods 133cm/3.4m^3; ≥20 grave goods 160cm/5.3m^3. The grave with the greatest amount of grave goods (Y alpha; n=101 with more than 1100 parts) is one of the three non-disturbed graves with a greater volume than 10 m^3. The two others contain 65 (FFGG7–8) resp. 34 (FF7–8) grave goods. Many other distribution maps were plotted but cannot be presented here.

LIVING POPULATION

According to the published data (n=109) the age distribution of the 'living' population was estimated by the formula of M. Gebühr (1976, 303 note 9); Sexratio: M=F. If a visitor could have seen the settlement that belongs to the cemetery, he would have met numerous infants, children and juvenils (at least 58%); 30% the adults from 20-40 years, 9% 40-55 years, and 1% 55-65 years.

The population size of the corresponding settlement is difficult to measure, because many of the tombs are destroyed. At least an amount of 651 graves was excavated (Toms 1986; 435 fossa-graves); totally more than 900 findspots are published in QF1-7 (Kampffmeyer & Teegen 1986).

The whole duration of the cemetery could be considered as 130 years (middle of the 9th cent. BC to the last quarter of the 8th cent. BC). There is a peak in the 8th cent. BC. A duration of 50 years would be underestimated. Concerning the minima/maxima values it is possible to evaluate the contemporary living

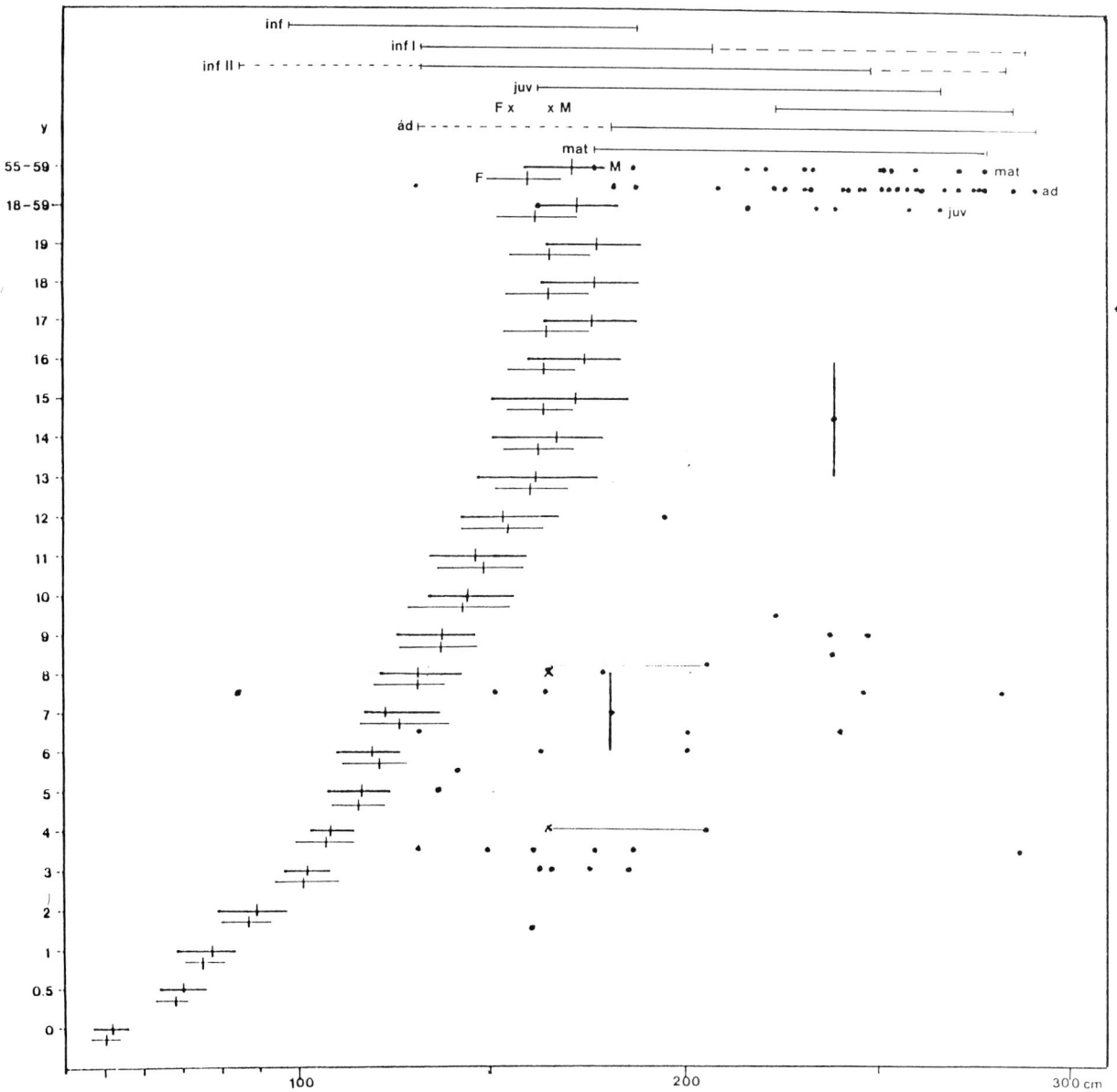

Fig. 12. Recent development of body height from birth to 59y in Middle Europe (GDR [data after Flügel et al. 1986]). Upper, bold lines = M, lighter lines = F. For 0-2y the range and the average is indicated, for 3-59y the P5/P95 and average. Points represents the individuals from Veio-Quattro Fontanili (fossa-graves; n=76) in their age classes (1-15 and in juv., ad., mat.). The upper lines indicate the total range in the single age classes (inf., inf. I, inf. II, juv., ad (20-25), ad., mat.).
xM = average body height of man in the Italian Iron Age (9th-6th cent. BC),
xF = average body height of female in the Italian Iron Age (9th-6th cent. BC).
X-axis = 40-310cm, Y-axis = age (in y).

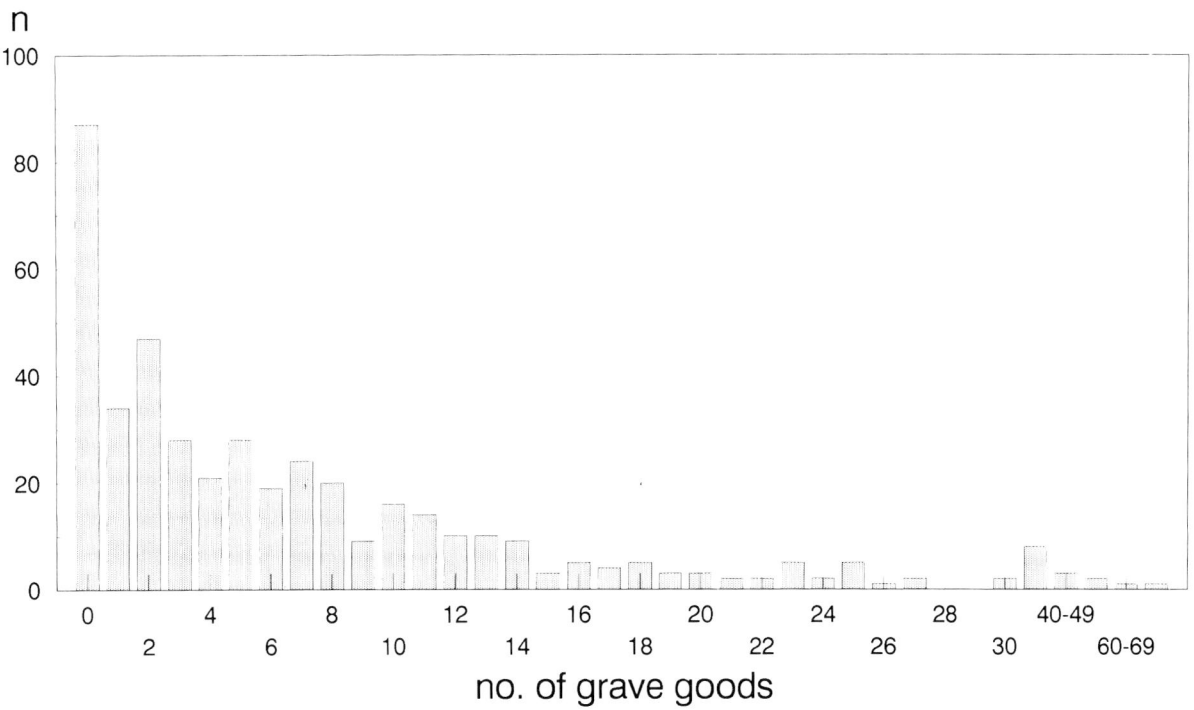

Fig. 13. Veio-Quattro Fontanili (fossa-graves). Distribution of the number of grave goods (0–101).

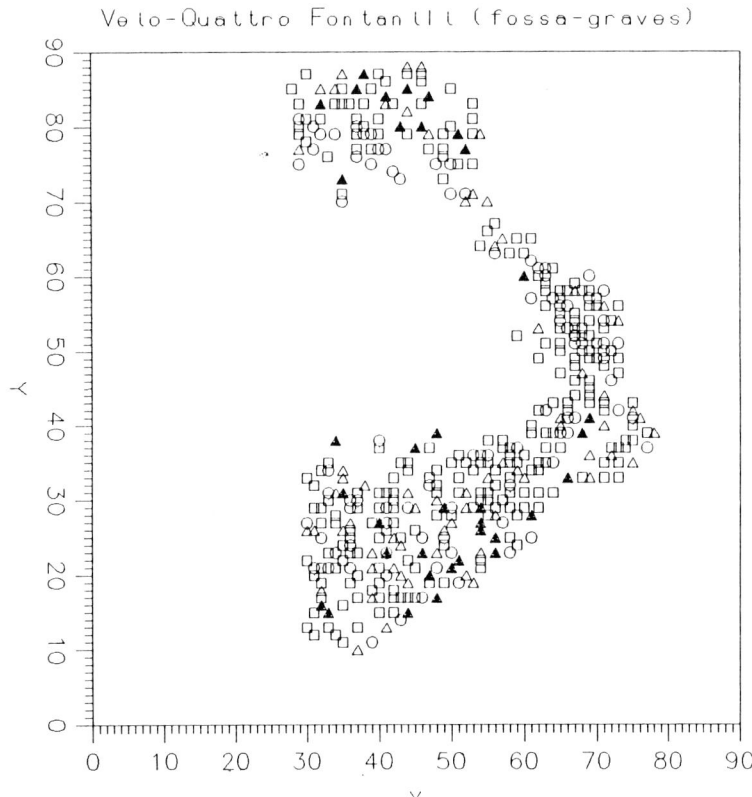

Fig. 14. Veio-Quattro Fontanili (fossa-graves). Distribution of graves with 0 (circle), 1–9 (square), 10–19 (triangle) and ≥20 (bold triangle) grave goods in the cemetery. X-axis (0–90) = 225m, Y-axis (0–90) = 225m (0/0 = SS-TT/44–45).

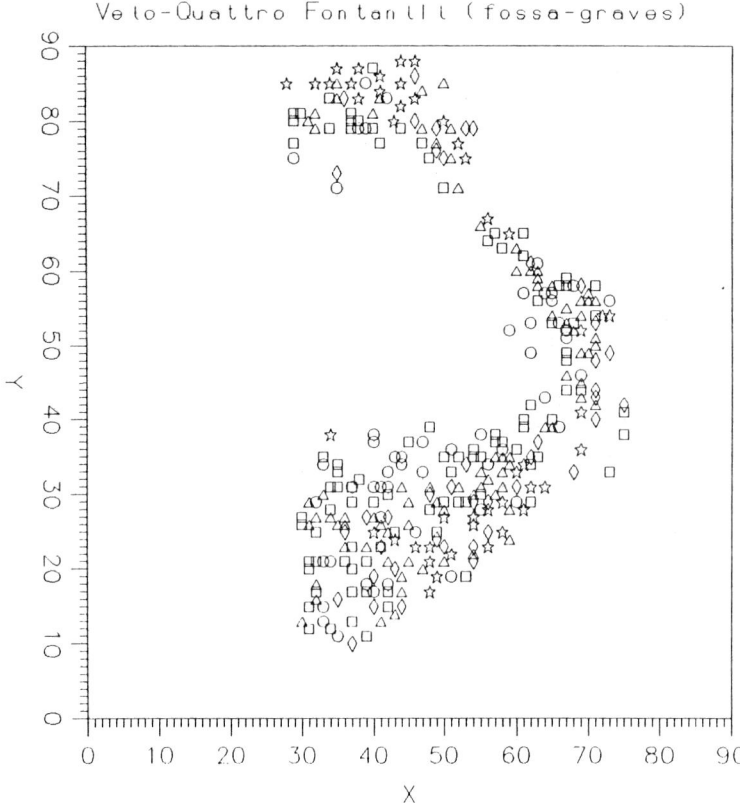

Fig. 15. Veio-Quattro Fontanili (fossa-graves). Distribution of graves with volumes of
<0.50 (circle),
0.5–1.5 (square),
1.5–3.0 (triangle),
3.0–4.5 (rhomb) and
>4.5 m^3 (star).
X-axis (0–90) = 225m,
Y-axis (0–90) = 225m (0/0 = SS-TT/44–45).

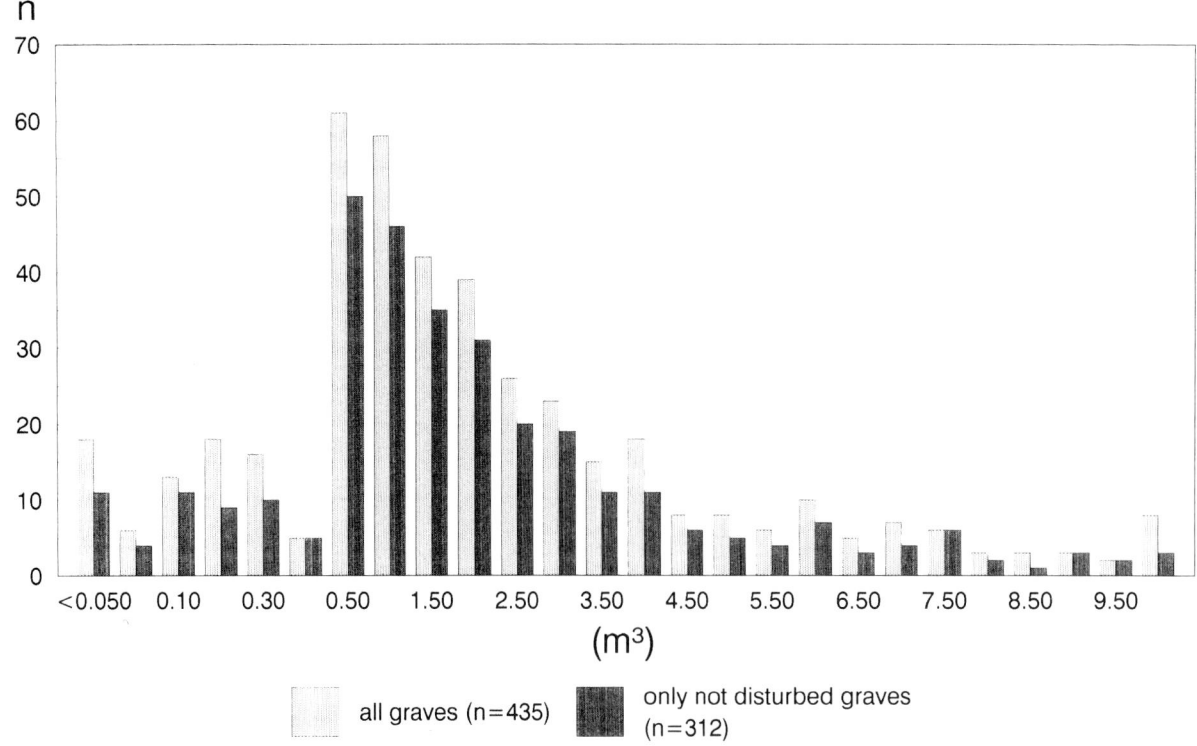

Fig. 16. Veio-Quattro Fontanili (fossa-graves). Distribution of grave size (in m^3).
Light grid = all graves (n=435), dark grid = only not disturbed graves (n=312). X-axis = <0.050 to > $10m^3$.

population by the following formula: B = n * e0/xa (n=number of graves, e0 = life expectency at birth, xa = duration; Drenhaus 1977). That means that for Veio-Quattro Fontanili the e0 = 22.2 years (Teegen 1987, 60; Tab. 13) and 651 graves: 111 (duration 130 years) to 289 (duration 50 years), average ca. 200 inhabitants; 900 graves: 153 (duration 130 years) to 399 (duration 50 years), average ca. 289 inhabitants. This leads to a settlement size of ca. 200–280 inhabitants (ca. 20–30 families with the same number of huts).

RESULTS

The analysis of the amount of grave goods, grave size and depth, correlates with age and sex. This gives interesting informations. It is remarkable that the amount of grave goods of the older adults (mat.) seems to be far beyond of the adults (ad.). A difference in the burial customs could be considered as a cause for the former described situation (older indiviuals are more "conservative", the younger ones are more "progressive"). Considering the single grave inventories it is necessary to go into detail.

It is difficult to decide, whether the validity of these results on a large scale, e.g. in Etruria or of their restricted significance to the local place, is typical for Veio-Quattro Fontanili. Additional anthropological examinations on large cemeteries of the early Iron Age are necessary. In case of the confirmation of these results, it will be possible to analyze roughly the social and demographical structures of a cemetery even when "tombaroli" looted the graves.

Note (June 1995)
For age estimation by grave length see now: Rösing, F.W. 1994. 'Die Menschen von Liebenau Paläodemographie und Grabsitte', *Das sächsische Gräberfeld bei Liebenau, Kreis Nienburg/Weser, Teil 5. Studien zur Sachsenforschung 5, 4* (Hannover 1994), 189–245.

Bibliography
Alciati, G. & Passarello, P. 1963. 'Relazione su alcuni reperti ossei umani della necropoli dei "Quattro Fontanili"', *Notizie degli Scavi di Antichità*, 273–279.
Drenhaus, U. 1977. 'Paläodemographie, ihre Aufgaben, Grundlagen und Methoden', *Zeitschrift für Bevölkerungswissenschaft* 3, 3–40.
Flügel, B., Greil, H. & Sommer, K. 1986. *Anthropologischer Atlas. Grundlagen und Daten*, Frankfurt.
Gebühr, M. 1976 'Das Gräberfeld Hamfelde, Kr. Hzgt. Lauenburg – Grösse und Altersaufbau der bestattenden Bevölkerung', *Die Heimat (Neumünster)*, 83, 296–303.
Kampffmeyer, U. & Teegen, W.-R. 1986. 'Untersuchungen zur rechnergestützten Klassifikation von Gefässformen am Beispiel der eisenzeitlichen Keramik des Gräberfeldes von Veio, Quattro Fontanili (Provinz Rom, Italien)', *Die Kunde NF* 37, 1–83.
Passarello, P. 1965. 'Relazione sui resti dentari di 35 individui della necropoli dei "Quattro Fontanili"', *Notizie degli Scavi di Antichità*, 232–236.
Passarello, P. 1967. 'Relazione sui resti dentari di una necropoli villanoviana in località "Quattro Fontanili"', *Notizie degli Scavi di Antichità*, 281–286.
Passarello, P. 1973. 'Aspetti paleodemografici sull'età del ferro in Italia. I villanoviani di Veio', *Rivista di Antropologia*, 48, 149–156.
QF1-7 AA.VV. 'Veio (Isola Farnese). - Scavi in una necropoli villanoviana in località "Quattro Fontanili"', *Notizie degli Scavi di Antichità*, 1963, 77–272; 1965, 49–231; 1967, 87–280; 1970, 178–329; 1972, 195–384; 1975, 63–184; 1976, 149–220.
Teegen, W.-R. 1987. 'Problemi della paleodemografia con particolare riferimento all'età del bronzo finale e dell'età del ferro in Italia e in Europa centrale', Unpublished Seminar paper, Università degli Studi di Roma "La Sapienza", Anno Accademico 1986/87 (Roma 1987) (138pp.).
Teegen, W.-R. in press. 'Mittelitalische Kindergräber des 9.-8. Jhs. v. Chr. und ihre Aussagemöglichkeiten. Demographie der Bronzezeit'.
Toms, J. 1986. 'The relative chronology of the Villanovan cemetery of Quattro Fontanili at Veii', *AION Arch. St. Ant.*, 8, 41–97.
Vallois, H. 1960. 'Vital statistics in prehistoric populations as determined from archaeological data', in R. F. Heizer & S. F. Cook (eds.), *Quantitative Methods in Archaeology*, Chicago, 186–222.

28

Human Skeletal Remains from the Pre-Colonial Greek Emporium of Pithekoussai on Ischia (NA): Culture Contact in Italy from the Early VIII to the II Century BC

MARSHALL JOSEPH BECKER
(West Chester University of Pennsylvania)

Summary: *By 775 BC Greek traders from Euboea had established a trading post on a promontory on the island of Ischia in the Bay of Naples, Italy. From this location, on the southern fringe of the Etruscan cultural sphere, these enterprising merchants brought spices, silks, as well as lesser goods from the Orient in exchange for metals and various other products of central Italy. Excavations at Pithekoussai have revealed more than 100 cremation burials among over 700 tombs. Problems with ground water and the intense heat generated by thermal springs have reduced the bones in most of the inhumations to powder, but had little effect on the teeth or the cremations. High temperature alteration of human remains through the cremation process allowed these bones to withstand these soil conditions, providing us with material by which age and gender can be evaluated. A double blind system of analysis demonstrated an extremely high reliability in the determination of gender where at least 100 grammes of bone could be recovered. These results both verify the accuracy of gender evaluation based on associated artifacts as well as providing gender evaluations for the majority of tombs, which have no associated offerings. Age and gender evaluations provide clear insights into mortuary patterning during this period. Studies of the skeletal biology of the residents of the Greek outpost of Pithekoussai reflect daily life and death as well as the social dynamics taking place between these Euboean settlers and their Native hosts as the settlement developed into a major Greek colony. Gender ratios provide information concerning patterns of intermarriage, as well as suggesting the presence of polygyny, slavery, and other cultural behaviours which are difficult to elicit from the archaeological record. Evidence for Canaanite mortuary rituals as recorded in the Bible is here presented for the first time, in addition to further examples of the Roman custom of burying an os resectum with the dead.*

INTRODUCTION

By the end of the first quarter of the VIII century BC, or decades before any Greek city states attempted to establish colonies in the area of western Italy, merchants from Euboea had established a trading post on an island now known as Ischia (fig.1) near the southern edge of the Etruscan realm. From this easily defended emporium in the Bay of Naples, with its excellent harbor systems for sailing vessels which had limited manoeuverability, these entrepreneurial Greeks gained access to the market for Etruscan metals and other resources from this rich market. In exchange they delivered ceramics and other luxury goods into the local exchange systems. The knowledge which these Greek traders gained about the lands situated between Ischia and their home cities facilitated the development of the first Greek colonies.

Ultimately, colonists from Euboea came to settle at the trading station of Pithekoussai, joined at some point in time by merchants from the Phoenician or Carthaginian realm. Cumae, a nearby and related Greek colony on the Italian peninsula, probably was occupied soon after, when the traders at their station on Pithekoussai felt militarily comfortable and could risk exposure to possible attack by the local peoples (Becker 1991). The skeletal remains of the inhabitants of Cumae would provide useful data for comparative studies. Buchner (1977) offers an important review of the archaeological information from Cumae, where the preservation of skeletal materials does not appear to have been a priority during that early period of excavation.

Local Oscan people also must have lived and married among these Euboeans and Phoenicians, creating a rich cultural cluster and an interesting subject for study. The impact of this emporium, and its subsequent colony, on the Iron Age people of this part of Italy was far more extensive than just the material results of trade. The biological impact must have been considerable, and it is this influence which we now hope to reveal.

Excavations at Pithekoussai began during the 19th century; more recently the cemetery area for these ancients was identified along the lower margins of the

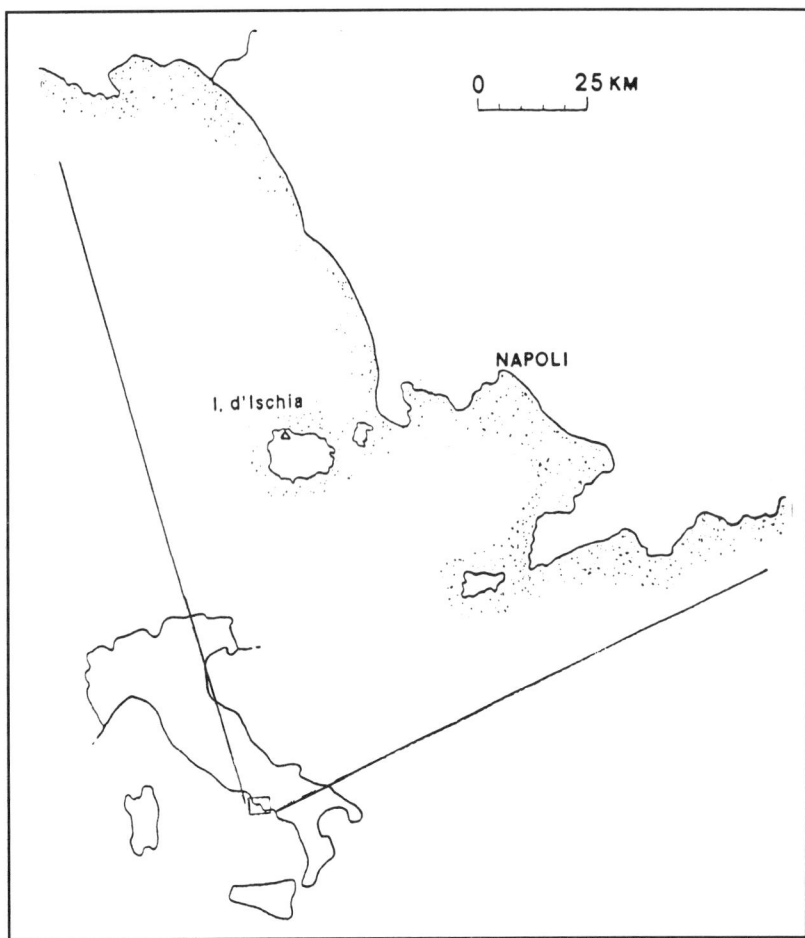

Fig. 1. Location map of Pithekoussai, Ischia.

hill on which the settlement was perched. A constant flow of detritus from the heavily occupied hilltop rapidly covered the graves of all periods, deeply burying them even before occupation of this settlement ended. Today, the most recent of these graves, dating to the Roman period, lie nearly four meters below the modern surface of the ground; the tombs of those first merchants and early colonists lie another four meters lower, or eight meters below the present surface of the ground. This limits access to these graves, with the fortunate effect of restricting casual treasure hunting and weekend looting.

These archaeological conditions protected these skeletal remains until the middle of the 20th century. Modern excavations at the site began in 1952 (Buchner & Ridgway 1993), but found that the preservation of the skeletal material was not particularly good. The excavators recovered all available skeletal material and stored these few remains with care. Initial identification of the gender of each individual in these tombs, as is often the case, has been made on the basis of associated artifacts, where such grave offerings are present. All of the fibulae found in these graves are of a local variety and usually are found as one or more pairs. One subset of these is identified as the dragon type, believed to be the only form associated with males. A bow type, as well as other forms, are believed to be associated only with women. For those graves lacking such diagnostic artifacts, as well as a means of verifying the initial gender assignments, skeletal analysis is critical. Also important in this research is the determation of the ages of these people at death. This information provides insights into the structure of this society as it progressed from a trading station to a colony.

To date all the known graves excavated from Pithekoussai appear to be those of common folk, or what Buchner describes as middle class Euboean colonists. The unusually deep overburden inhibits systematic and extensive testing of the cemetery, and the aristocratic graves such as those found at Velletri and Cumae remain undiscovered at Pithekoussai. Thus studies of social class variation, so important at other sites (d'Agostino 1969, 1977; Becker 1990, 1993) are not now a part of this program. However, the extensive data from this site offers outstanding comparative information for examining the bones of Greek colonists and others throughout this region.

Even more important to the understanding of the general history of this site (Buchner 1971) is the potential for skeletal research to decode information regarding the ethnic origins of these individuals. Although

Euboean colonists may be the primary inhabitants of these graves, we can have no doubt that many married Oscan women, both to consolidate trade relationships as well as to forge other alliances. Phoenicians also appear to have been resident at Pithekoussai (Moscati 1986, 1989), giving yet another dimension to this potentially rich study. Considerable archaeological evidence suggests that by 750 BC Phoenicians were being buried in this cemetery. Remains of Phoenicians may be identifiable using the information from previously studied colonial Carthaginian populations (cf. Becker 1985, in press), and study of the skeletal material has revealed traces of their customs.

Prior to 1992 only Munz (1970) had discussed this skeletal material, focusing on the dentition from the tombs excavated during the field seasons from 1952 to 1961. In addition to placing these remains in their archaeological context and describing the materials extremely well, this report notes the problems of bone preservation at this site. The determination of gender from the teeth, so successfully achieved at Osteria dell'Osa (Becker & Salvadei 1992), was not attempted.

This report summarizes data from the cremated human skeletal materials from Pithekoussai (Becker ms., c; Becker & Donadio 1992) as well as from 17 of the inhumations more recently studied. While cremations are most commonly found in the period from the second half of the VIII century to the early VI century BC (111 of the 591 tombs known from this period), several examples are known from later periods. In general, however, cremations appear most characteristic of adult burials of the early period of colonization, although some individuals as young as eight years of age now can be identified among these tombs. Table 1 lists data from 112 cremations where human bones have been recovered for study. Data also are provided from the teeth and few traces of bone from 17 of the 126 inhumations studied to date (Table 3). The inhumations will be the subject of a separate study.

Materials and Methods

The project described here continues the interest established by the excavators of Pithekoussai in using current scientific techniques to augment our ability to solve archaeological problems (cf. Deriu *et al.* 1986; Becker 1987; Becker & Salvadei 1992). The study of the skeletal materials was conducted at the Villa Arbusto in Lacco Ameno, Ischia, where they were stored. Available for study were 112 cremations recovered from that portion of the burial area including the earliest interments at Pithekoussai, dating primarily from the period from 750 to 675 BC. Also included are two later examples (Roman) of the cremations interred over the next 5 centuries. These data largely relate to those tombs included in the first comprehensive publication of the archaeological data (Buchner & Ridgway 1993). The analysis of a second set of cremations (number unknown), which appear to be those excavated more recently, relate to an area in which inhumations dominate (to appear in *Pithekoussai II*). Gender and age evaluations (Table 1) are followed by the weight of the bones *recovered* for analysis and by an estimate of the temperature of the pyre on which the recovered materials appear to have been burned. In most cremations the large pieces of bone which normally survive the burning process were crushed to fit them into small containers (Becker, ms., b). Those cremated individuals whose remains were placed in larger containers, such as an Attic krater or a Villanovan biconical urn, need not be subjected to a comminution process. The fire normally causes cracks and fissures to open in the bone. Comminution and/or the processes of soil compaction in a tomb may leave burned bones in an even more fragmentary state. Where joins were found between the bone fragments recovered from these tombs, they were glued using a water soluable polyvynal acetate solution. Other materials found with the human bone, including animal bone and ceramic fragments, were separated and where possible the categories were repackaged as separate units for future study.

Comparative skeletal data from the Greek homeland is being sought, but at present almost no skeletal remains from Euboea have been recovered and studied. The Early Helladic (3,000 BC) tombs from Manika in Chalkis (Euboea) have been excavated and published (Sampson 1985): these deep chamber tombs are from a period in time nearly as distant from the colonial period at Pithekoussai (2,200 years) as Pithekoussai is from modern times (2,800 years). Although the genetic distance may not be great, at Manika only 22 graves with some 40 people were excavated and preservation was poor. Even the stature of these ancient people from Manika was difficult to calculate (Fountoulakis 1985 focuses on dubious cut marks on the human bones, a recent vogue, but offers no data useful in making biological comparisons).

Goals

Three general goals sought by this research are:

1. Basic information of concern to the archaeologists, including age and gender of each individual, the possibility that multiple cremations or burials were placed in a single tomb (cf. Becker 1993), and other data useful in reconstructing culture and culture history;

2. Ethnic identification of individuals (Greek, Oscan, Phoenician), which may be revealed both by the skeletal material itself or by the ways in which these bones have been treated in their respective mortuary rituals;

3. Biological change over time, as a reflection of degree or rate of intermarriage as revealed by the odontometric data. As of this date the odontometric data from the inhumations of adults (N=9, see Table 3) includes insufficient numbers to permit valid statistical comparisons.

Discussion

A total of 112 cremations were sought for review during the 1991 study season, of which two (39 and 116) could not be located (see Table 1). In the 110 cremations evaluated, bones representing 112 separate individuals were identified, including three children. Gender evaluations based on skeletal evaluation were attempted for 95 individuals age 19 or older. At the end of this study an evaluation of gender based on archaeological evidence (fibula form, etc.) was provided by the excavators for those individuals which were accompanied by diagnostic grave goods (52 of 95, or 53%). Agreement was found in the majority of *all* cases, but eight of the nine cases in which there are differences in gender evaluations are those which are represented by minimal amounts of bone (e.g. only two grams for T. 149 and 50+ grams for T. 169). If cases in which under 100 grams of bone were available for evaluation are eliminated from the sample, then we have agreement between archaeological and biological evidence in 51 out of 52 cases (98%). In many instances an evaluation was attempted when less than 100 grams of bone was recovered, such as Tomb 179 where only fragments of a femur shaft were used to form the gender evaluation. Surprisingly, accuracy in providing gender data is quite good in these examples. However, the male in Tomb 167 was identified as a female based on the size of a radius head, a trait which was not confirmed as problematical until the end of this research. The male in Tomb 149 was incorrectly identified using only a piece of right maxilla. Age evaluations are, of course, believed to be more than 95% accurate within the range stated in the study (Becker in review). The skeletal evaluation made of the very fragmentary bones from cremation Tomb 223 indicates that they derive from a female of age 60 years (±10), and are not the bones of a child as suggested earlier (see Buchner & Boardman 1966:10).

Among the many questions posed by this study is one concerning possible status variables within the society as revealed by these graves. Although the excavators do not believe that high status graves are apparent, the vast differences in tomb offerings suggest that status differences are considerable. The individual in Tomb 159 was identified as male on the basis of long bone robusticity, but the grave goods indicate that this may be a female. Quite possibly this is an extremely robust female who was a well nourished member of a high status family (Becker 1988). Alternatively, this may be a case of confusion in gender by these Greeks, or even a case of a male playing a female role.

Two of the cremations studied (114 and 220) were found to include the remains of a second individual; thus a total of 112 people were evaluated. In Tomb 114 the bones of a young female were found with those of an old adult male, who was more completely represented. While the woman's remains may have been mixed accidentally, she may have been deliberately included with the male and possibly they were cremated together, as may be the case of some tombe principesce (d'Agostino 1969, 1977; Becker 1993). The single fragment of a bone representing the second woman with the female of Tomb 220 is probably an accidental inclusion, and should not considered a double burial.

A number of questions may be asked regarding differential survival of cremated remains. Quite possibly cremation pyres were of relatively standard size, which would result in smaller individuals (women) being cremated at higher temperatures since their body fluids would not be as highly retardant to the burning process. A pyre which fails to porcelainize the bone of a large male allows that poorly burned material to decay in the ground, resulting in a smaller amount of surviving bone. These factors may result in an apparently larger number of females being represented by surviving bone.

Conclusions

1. Gender evaluation, where possible, has not been made on the basis of cranial morphology, which has been the focus of many other studies. While cranila dimorphism provides useful indications of gender in northern European populations, Becker and Salvadei (1992) demonstrate that cranial morphology is a poor predictor of gender in central Italy. Therefore, emphasis was placed on the evaluation of the postcranial skeleton. This entire population appears relatively slender. Several specific features of the anatomy, such as the size of the radius head (see Tomb 167), are not considered to be reliable indicators of gender. Despite these difficulties, gender was evaluated (blind) accurately for nearly all (if not all) cremated individuals for whom 100 grams of bone or more were recovered, as confirmed by artifacts from those tombs where these items serve as an independent means of evaluating gender.

2. The ratio of adult males to females, approximately 40/60 as determined through the archaeological evidence (associated artifacts, where present), now has been independently confirmed through the skeletal analysis. This extremely interesting finding may be interpreted as reflecting an extremely high incidence of polygyny, or at least the presence of large numbers of female slaves (concubines?) in these households. This suggests that these colonists may have had a high rate

Table 1. Age & Gender Evaluations of the Cremations, plus weight of skeletal material recovered and temperature of cremation.

Tomb number	Age	Skeletal evaluation of gender	Archaeological evaluation of gender	Weight of Bone	Temperature of Pyre (estimated)
19	65	F	F	19	900
21	65	F	-	43	900
27	70	F??	-	1062	950+
39	The ossilegium in this Roman period glass urn, not found				
40	65	F?	-	1531	950
42	70	M???	M	834	950
61	55	F	F?	197	950
62	50	M???	M	716	950
86	70	M	M	1014	950
87	MA	F	-	187	950
91	55	M	-	1255	900±
93	10	-	-	854	900
94	70	M	-	1988	900
114	65	M	M	1263	875±
114	21	F	/	16	875±
115	OA	M???	F??	46	950
116	No evaluation	M [not located in 1991, 1992]			
117	45	F???	F?	365	950
118	70	F	-	201	925±
119	65	M	-	548	900+
120	65	F???	F	142	925
135	65	F?	-	53	925
136	50	F???	-	189	875
137	65	F?	-	340	875
138	65	F??	-	23	900
139	65	M???	-	167	825
140	8???	-	-	3	900
142	23	F	-	196	900
145	20	F?	F	131	925
146	60	F???	F?	40	875
147	A???	F???	-	26	925
148	A	F???	-	78	900
149	A??	F???	M	2	900
150	A	F??	-	173	925
152	A??	F	F	5	925
154	50	F?	-	1263	925
155	A	-	-	3	900
156	60	M	-	204	875+
157	65	F	F	233	875
158	60	F???	F	227	900
159	75	M	F	296	850±
160	60	F	F	295	875
161	50	M?	-	398	875
162	YA	M	-	341	925
163	MA	F??	-	134	900
164	MA	-	M/F	66	925
165	YA??	-	F	195	875+
168	14	-	M	289	925
170	MA	-	-	34	900+
172	60	-	M	166	875
173	MA	F	F	63	900
174	50	F	F	349	900+
175	60	F??	-	240	900
176	60	M???	-	317	900
177	A	M?	-	41	875
178	60	-	-	38	900
179	YA???	-	F	77	900

Tomb number	Age	Skeletal evaluation of gender	Archaeological evaluation of gender	Weight of Bone	Temperature of Pyre (estimated)
181	A	F???	F	55	900
182	MA	F???	F	49	950
183	70	M???	0	275	900+
184	70	-	0	238	950
185	A	-	unc.	9	950
186	A??	-	unc.	12	950
188	OA	–	F	13	825
189	A	F???	F	161	950
190	60	M	0	460	950
191	45	F???	F	873	950
192	65	F??? (intr.?)	M?	164	900
193	40	M???	0	179	875
194	MA	M???	-	185	950
195	50	F???	F	153	950
196	50	F??	F	627	925
197	70	M??	M???	534	950
198	45	F	F?	903	950
199	YA	F	F	228	925
200	A	F???	-	19	900
201	70	M???	M??	647	950
203	60	M	-	329	900±
204	MA	M?	-	91	900±
206	A	F???	M??	110	950
208A=209B	50	F?	F	870	900
209A=208B	65	M??	–	203	900
210	19	F???	F	97	900±
211	A	M???	-	44	900±
212	55	F??	M?	68	950
213	70	M	M	299	875±
215	MA	M?	M	157	900
216	60	?	M?	124	900+
218	50	F	F	141	900±
219	A	M???	-	183	900
220	A	F	F	285	900
220	A	F	/		
225	YA???	M???	M??	603	900
226	A	F???	F??	99	925
227	40	M?	M??	176	875
229	MA	F???	M???	144	900+
230	55	F	F	117	900+
232	A	F???	F	117	900
235	50	F???	M??	120	900+
236	A	F???	-	61	900+
238	A	F???	-	143	900
239	60	M???	M???	278	900
240	50	M???	-	101	900+
241	MA	M?	M	156	875
242	-	-	-	13	900
243	A	F	F	124	900+
N=112	112	M=36 (38%) F=58 (62%)	M=26 (41%) F=38 (59%)		

A = Adult   MA= Mature adult   YA= Young adult   OA= Old adult
M/F = Associated artifacts provide conflicting gender data.
/ = Second individual, not noted in excavation.
0 = No fibula found in grave.
Unc.= Noted by excavators as *incerto*.

of intermarriage with native (local) women, rather than bringing women from Euboea.

3. The very preliminary data from the study of the inhumations (see Table 3) shows the ratio of adult males (N=3) to females (N=6) as 33/67. This is not drastically distinct from the 40/60 ratio noted in 2, above. However, the eight *inhumed* children for whom we can evaluate gender show a male/female ratio of 63/37, suggesting the possibility that the skewed adult ratio may result from an extremely high male infant and child mortality rate.

4. Only three children below the age of 17 are noted in this sample of cremations (Tombs 93, 140, 168: ages 10, 8, and 14 respectively). Gender could not be determined for any of these cremated children. The low incidence of identifiable children among these graves suggests that many of the tombs from which no skeletal remains were recovered may have been those of children (individuals below the age of 17). The age of ritual passage into personhood (entitled to a burial in the cemetery; see Becker 1986a) in this population appears to have been less than eight, but cannot be made more specific from the data now at hand. Neonates, foetuses, and children under the age of one year (the largest number of deceased individuals expected in such populations) may have been buried in very simple fashions within the residential zone. One jar found beneath a floor in the settlement area, in which no trace of bone was detected, may well have been an *enchytrysmos*; several such containers were found in the necropolis and probably represent the burials of infants or young children (see Ridgway 1984: fig. 17; Buchner 1982: 277).

5. Excellent dental health (Table 2) appears to be the rule during all periods at Pithekoussai as reflected by the limited data from the cremations. When tabulated by general period we find that the cremated early colonial population appears to have had an extremely low rate of dental loss (approximately 8%) and that the later people had a similarly low rate. Note should be

Table 3. Summary of age and gender for each inhumation (cf. Becker & Donadio 1992).

Tomb	Gender	Age (in years)
4	M	5.8
22	F?	3.8
23	M?	3.5
29A	F	6.8
B	F	50
33	F?	45
48	F	25
49A	M???	65+
B	F???	45
53A	F??	45
B	F???	4
78	M???	10
389	M???	7
390	To Do	4
395	M??	A
	[M?	A] possible mix
458	F???	20
470	To Do	2
515	To Do	11
519	To Do	[5.5]
529	M	7.5

N=17	N=21	N=21 (9 adults
	M=8	and 12 children, ages 2–11)
	F=9	
	(4 not yet determined)	
Adults:	M=3 (33%)	
	F=6 (67%)	
Children:	M=5 (63%)	
	F=3 (37%)	

made that molars as well as anterior teeth are represented in the sample of tooth spaces represented among the cremated remains. However, note also should be made that in the case of cremations, alveolar survival itself may be a function of dental health. Individuals from whose jaws teeth have been lost become reduced in

Table 2. Dental attrition from the cremations only, not factored for age (Becker & Donadio 1992).

	No. of Individuals	No. of Tooth spaces	No. of Teeth lost	Loss Rate
End VI-Roman Period	9	136	14	10%*
VIII-VI Century	26	178	14	8%**

* Seven of the 14 teeth lost came from the person in Tomb 27. Removing this individual from the sample reduces the loss rate to about 6%.
** Four of the 14 teeth lost came from the person in Tomb 184, a person of 70 years of age. Removing this person from the sample reduces the loss rate to under 6%.

In both periods dental attrition rates are very low, suggesting dietary and cultural stability. These data should be compared carefully with the findings from the inhumations.

size and therefore more subject to destruction in the context of the cremation process.

6. Although the significance of the incidence of bifurcate roots on maxillary first premolars is not yet clear, note is made of this trait (e.g. Tomb 149) where the actual root is preserved or is suggested by the configuration of the tooth socket. Note should be made that the examination of the tooth socket of the person in Tomb 149 did not easily reveal the bifurcation. Thus many more examples may exist than are specified in the field record. Bifurcation of the root of maxillary first premolars is a trait commonly found in central Italy, particularly during the period from *ca.* 900–600 BC.

7. Disease among these people generally appears in the form of geriatric exostoses. The woman (?) in Tomb 175 has fused cervical vertebrae as well as numerous exostoses on the other surviving examples. The male (?) in Tomb 176 has similar exostoses, as do many other individuals in this sample. While some pitting was noted on the interiors of skull fragments, no inventory of these examples was made. No broken bones or malformations were noted among these sparce remains. The individual in Tomb 150 appears to have had an anaemic disorder, possibly malaria or thalassemia.

8. The cremated bones of the child in Tomb 93 (dated to the V Century BC) include an unburned terminal phalange of an adult which I believe to be an os *resectum*. These artifacts are described indirectly in ancient Roman texts and recently have been documented many times in the archaeological record (Bowmer & Molleson 1986; Becker 1988, ms., a). However, this example from Pithekoussai of an unburned terminal phalange with a child's burned bones, first thought to be an unburned *os resectum*, derives from an adult female. The context of this find, in a red figure Attic krater of the V century which had been placed in a cube of tufa (see Boardman 1980) appears to rule out the possibly that this may be a stray bone; furthermore, the absence of other examples or fragments of unburned bone from this burial context suggests that this phalange was deliberately placed in this krater. This suggests that an adult, probably the mother or a near female relative of the deceased child, had a terminal finger joint cut from a digit (possibly the third on the right hand) to be buried with the *ossilegium* of this child (cf. Becker 1986b). Such customs are known from various parts of the world and this may be the traditional Canaanite mortuary custom noted in the Old Testament, but previously unreported in the archaeological literature of either the Levant or from Italy. This practise appears to be similar to, but not necessarily related to, the custom of taking an *os resectum* so widely known at this time from sites throughout central Italy.

The bones of the female in Tomb 137 also have with them an *os resectum*. This terminal phalange, however, appears likely to have derived from her own hand.

9. The bones found in Tomb 114 suggest that two cremated individuals were placed in this single tomb, possibly having been burned on separate pyres rather than a single pyre. Although it is possible that the inclusion of the remains of two people in this context may not have been intentional, the presence of young females in inhumation tombs of old adult males certainly has been noted elsewhere in central Italy (Becker 1990). Joint interments have been confirmed but infrequently in cremation burials (Becker 1987, ms., a). However, the cremated remains of an older male together with a young female have been well documented from several tombe principesche of the Orientalizing period (Becker 1993). Burials of secondary individuals with old males may be a reflection of status in these communities (Becker 1990). The second adult female represented in Pithekoussai Tomb 220 is represented by a single bone fragment which probably is an accidental admixture.

10. Burned remains of mammals (generally sheep or goat) also are found among the cremated bones in several of the Pithekoussai burials (e.g. Tombs 94, 114, 167, 184, and possibly Tomb 200). While some of these animal bones may be accidental inclusions, most appear to be the remains of funerary meals or offerings.

ACKNOWLEDGEMENTS

Sincere thanks are due Dr G. Buchner for his kind invitation to study these human remains, and for his extensive aid in arranging for this aspect of the research to be completed. Thanks also are due the Soprintendenze Archeologica for Naples for permission to study these materials, and to Dott.sse Costanza Gialanella (Ispetrice per Pozzuoli e Ischia) for her co-operation in every aspect of this study. The comments of several colleagues at the Fifth Conference of Italian Archaeology (Oxford) are very much appreciated. Thanks also are due Professor Erminio Braidotti (West Chester University) for his aid with translations, to Dr. A.M.G. Rè, Sig. Ignazio Di Meglio and his family (Lacco Ameno), and all the other people on Ischia who assisted this project in so many ways. Special thanks are due Prof. Mennella, Sindaco of the Municipio di Lacco Ameno, for his kind permission to use the facilities at the Villa Arbusto to initiate this project (May-June 1991 and 1992), and to Alessia Donadio for her invaluable assistance in the field aspect of this project. Portions of this paper were presented in the symposiun *Social Dynamics of the Prehistoric Central Mediterranean* organized by Jon Morter for the 1992 meetings of the Society for American Archaeology. Partial funding for this project derived from small grant for travel and research from West Chester University of Pennsylvania. Any errors of interpretation or presentation are the responsibility of the author alone.

Bibliography

d'Agostino, B. 1969. 'Pontecagnano. Tombe orientalizzante in Contrada S. Antonio', *Notizie degli Scavi di Antichità*, 75–196.

d'Agostino, B. 1977. 'Tombe "principesche" dell'orientalizzante antico da Pontecagnano', *Monumenti Antichi* (Serie Miscellanea II, 1) 49, 1–74.

Bartoloni, G., Buranelli, F., D'Atri, V. & De Santis, A. 1987. *Le Urne a Capanna rinvenute in Italia*, Rome.

Becker, M.J. 1982. Anthropological Appendix (pp. 479–481) to 'Cremation among the Lucanians', by M. Gualtieri, *American Journal of Archaeology* 86, 475–479.

Becker, M.J. 1985. 'Metric and Non-metric data from a series of skulls from Mozia, Sicily and a related site', *Antropologia Contemporanea*, 8 (3), 211–228.

Becker, M.J. 1986a. 'Mandibular Symphysis (Medial Suture) closure in modern Homo sapiens: Preliminary evidence from archaeological populations', *American Journal of Physical Anthropology* 69, 499–501.

Becker, M.J. 1986b. 'An ethnographical and archaeological survey of unusual Mmortuary procedures as a reflection of cultural diversity: Some suggestions for the interpretation of the human skeletal deposits from excavations at Entella, Sicily, Italy', *La Parola del Pasato: Rivista di Studi Antichi*, 226: 31–56.

Becker, M.J. 1987. 'Analisi Antropologiche e Paleontologiche: Soprintendenza di Roma. Appendice I', in *Le Urne a Capanna Rinvenute in Italia*, G. Bartoloni, F. Buranelli, V. D'Atri & A. De Santis, Rome, 235–246.

Becker, M.J. 1988. 'The contents of funerary vessels as clues to mortuary customs: identifying the Os Exceptum', *Proceedings of the 3rd Symposium on Ancient Greek and Related Pottery* [Copenhagen, 1987], ed. J. Christiansen and T. Melander, Copenhagen, 25–32.

Becker, M.J. 1990. 'Etruscan social classes in the VI Century BC: evidence from recently excavated cremations and inhumations in the area of Tarquinia', *Die Welt der Etrusker* (International Colloquium, 1988), ed. H. Heres & M. Kunze, Berlin, 23–25.

Becker, M.J. 1991. 'European trade and colonization in the territory of the Lenape of Pennsylvania during the 17th century: An historical model for Greek colonization in Italy', Paper presented at the International Congress of Americanists, New Orleans.

Becker, M.J. 1993. 'Human Sacrifice ... the "Tombe Principesche", Numbers 926 and 928 at Pontecagnano (Salerno)', Italy, *Old World Archaeology Newsletter*, 16(2): 23–30.

Becker, M.J. in press. 'Human Skeletal Remains from the 1987 excavations in Marsala, Sicily', *Annali della Scuola Normale Superiore di Pisa*.

Becker, M.J. ms., a. 'The os resectum: A review of the literary and archaeological evidence', Manuscript on file, West Chester University of Pennsylvania.

Becker, M.J. ms., b. 'Tarquinia Tomb 6322: An example of a cremation showing extreme comminution', Manuscript in circulation.

Becker, M.J. ms., c. 'Cremated human remains from Pithekoussai, primarily from the period ca. 770–600 B.C.'.

Becker, M.J. & Donadio, A. 1992. 'A summary of the analysis of cremated human skeletal remains from the Greek colony of Pithekoussai at Lacco Ameno, Ischia, Italy', *Old World Archaeology Newsletter*, 16 (1), 15–23.

Becker, M.J. & Salvadei, L. 1992. 'Analysis of the human skeletal remains from the cemetery of Osteria dell'Osa', in *La Necropoli Laziale di Osteria dell'Osa*, ed. A.M. Bietti Sestieri, Rome, 53–191.

Boardman, J. 1980. *The Greeks Overseas: Their Early Colonies and Trade*, New York.

Bowmer, M. & Molleson, T. 1986. 'Appendix: Identification of human remains from the hut urns, in "Le urne a capanna: ancora sulle prime scoperte nei Colli Albani,"' by G. Bartoloni, in *Italian Iron Age Artefacts in the British Museum*, ed. J. Swaddling, London, 238–239.

Buchner, G. 1966. 'Pithekoussai: oldest Greek colony in the West', *Expedition* 8 (4), 4–12.

Buchner, G. 1971. 'Recent work at Pithekoussai (Ischia), 1965–71', *Archaeological Reports for 1970–71*, 63.

Buchner, G. 1975. 'Nuovi aspetti e problemi posti dagli scavi di Pithecusa con particolari considerazioni sulle oreficerie di stile orientalizzante antico', in *Contribution l'étude de la société et de la colonisation eubennes*, Naples, 61–71.

Buchner, G. 1977. 'Cuma nell'VIII Secolo a.C., Osservata dalla Prospettiva di Pithecusa', in the Proceedings of the International Congress *I Campi Flegrei nell'Archeologia e nella Storia* (Roma, 1976), Rome, 131–148.

Buchner, G. 1979. 'Early Orientalizing: Aspects of the Euboean connection', *Italy Before the Romans: The Iron Age, Orientalizing and Etruscan Periods*, ed. D. & F. Ridgway, London, 129–144.

Buchner, G. 1982. 'Articolazione sociale, differenze di rituale e composizione dei corredi nella necropoli di Pithecusa', in *La Mort, Les Mortes dans les Societes Anciennes*, ed. G. Gnoli & J.-P. Vernant, Cambridge, 275–287.

Buchner, G. & Boardman, J. 1966. 'Seals from Ischia and The Lyre-Player Group', *Jahrbuch des Deutsches Archäologischen Instituts* 81, 1–62.

Buchner, G. & Ridgway, D. 1993. *Pithekoussai I. La Necropoli: tombe 1–723, scavate dal 1952 al 1961*, (Monumenti Antichi, Serie Monografica), Roma.

Buchner, G. & Ridgway, D., ms., a. *Pithekoussai, Scavi della Soprintendenza alle Antichit di Napoli, II*, (Monumenti Antichi, Serie Monografica).

Deriu, A., Buchner, G. & D. Ridgway. 1986. 'Provenence and firing techniques of Geometric pottery from Pithekoussai: A Mosbauer investigation'. Annali: Istituto Universitario Orientali, Naples (AION), *Archaeologia e Storia Antica* VIII, 99–116.

Dunbabin, T.J. 1948. *The Western Greeks*, Oxford.

Fountoulakis, M. 1985. The skeletal remains from the Early Helladic Cemetery of Manika-Chalkis, Appendix in Sampson 1985.

Graham, A.J. 1964. *Colony and Mother City in Ancient Greece*, Manchester.

Moscati, S. 1986. *Italia punica* (with S.F. Bondi). Milan.

Moscati, S. 1989. 'Fenici e Cartaginesi in Italia', *Bollettino di Archeologia* I, 38–41.

Munz, F.R. 1970. 'Die Zahnfunde aus der griechischen Nekropole von Pithekoussai auf Ischia', *Archaeologischer Anzeiger* 85, 452–475.

Ridgway, D. 1984. *L'Alba della Magna Grecia*, Milano.

Ridgway, D. in press. 'The eighth century pottery at Pithekoussai: an interim report'. La ceramique grecque ou de tradition grecque au VIIIe siècle en Italie centrale e meridionale, Naples.

Sampson, A. 1985. *Manika: An Early Helladic Town in Chalkis*, Chalkis.

Stevenson, P.H. 1924. 'Age Order of Epiphyseal Union in Man', *American Journal of Physical Anthropology* 7, 53–93.

Ubelaker, D.H. 1989. *Human Skeletal Remains: Excavation, Analysis, Interpretation*, Washington.

29

Gentes Romane dei Monti della Tolfa

Enrico Benelli

Sommario: *Si esamina la documentazione epigrafica latina dei Monti della Tolfa, che consiste prevalentemente di bolli laterizi e di iscrizioni su grandi monumenti sepolcrali. Per molti bolli laterizi è possibile rintracciare la fornace in cui vennero prodotti. L'analisi delle testimonianze epigrafiche, combinate con i dati archeologici, permette di delineare la nascita di un ceto di grandi proprietari terrieri in età augustea.*

Il massiccio tolfetano si estende come una barriera che interrompe la pianura costiera medio-tirrenica; anche se la morfologia è generalmente dolce e le elevazioni sono sempre modeste, l'estensione del massiccio, che si sviluppa dalle alture dell'Etruria meridionale interna fino al mare, rende la frattura molto marcata.

La mancanza di altri complessi simili su un tratto di qualche centinaio di chilometri permette di dominare dalle cime più alte buona parte delle piane costiere con le loro città e i loro porti; tuttavia, il valore strategico del comprensorio è abbastanza modesto, dal momento che la morfologia offre numerose vie di penetrazione, tutte più o meno ugualmente agevoli, e non esiste nessuna posizione chiave in grado di impedirne l'attraversamento.

Sulle alture l'humus ha di solito pochi centimetri di spessore, e lascia scoperta in più punti la roccia sottostante, mentre nelle valli predomina un terreno argilloso incoerente, costantemente impregnato d'acqua e continuamente eroso e spostato dai torrenti. In conclusione, l'agricoltura si può praticare con qualche profitto quasi solo sulle modeste formazioni tabulari tufacee dell'area orientale e nelle piane della bassa valle del Mignone.

Le risorse minerarie, se si eccettua l'allume, la cui estrazione nell'antichità è ancora tutta da provare, sono piuttosto scarse, appena sufficienti a uno sfruttamento di carattere locale (Zifferero 1991). Prima della penetrazione romana i Monti della Tolfa probabilmente non erano altro che un diaframma facilmente attraversabile tra i territori costieri di Caere e Tarquinii. Con la fondazione di Forum Clodii e delle colonie marittime di Pyrgi e Castrum Novum il comprensorio tolfetano si trova ad essere circondato da piccoli centri indipendenti. La disposizione degli insediamenti viene a ricalcare così la realtà ambientale: una zona marginale e scarsamente produttiva circondata da territori molto più ricchi. Coerentemente con questa particolare situazione i Monti della Tolfa sono un grande vuoto per le fonti letterarie.

Tutto quello che si conosce si riduce a due toponimi. In primo luogo il fiume *Minio*, oggi Mignone, che è riportato in testi di carattere corografico quali Vibio Sequestre (I, 99) e Pomponio Mela (II, 72); nella tradizione manoscritta di quest'ultimo compare però un fiume *Anio*, la cui foce è posta fra Pyrgi e Castrum Novum. Anche accettando la verosimile correzione in *Minio*, proposta già dal Cluverius, la posizione geografica è comunque errata. Rutilio Namaziano (I, 279) ricorda come si dovesse passare al largo dalla foce del Mignone a causa di pericolosi banchi sabbiosi, dovuti certamente alle forti variazioni stagionali nella portata.

Nell'Eneide (X, 183), fra le zone da cui vennero alleati per i Troiani, si trovano gli *arva Minionis*. L'uso del termine è certamente poetico, ma potrebbe far pensare alla mancanza di un termine unitario per i Monti della Tolfa. Il *Minio* si ritrova infine naturalmente anche in Servio, in due passi distinti (*ad Aen*. X 183 e VIII 597); nel secondo il commentatore sostiene, certamente a torto, che *Minio* è un altro nome del *Caeritis amnis*, che invece doveva scorrere sotto il pianoro urbano di Caere.

Il secondo toponimo antico si trova nella *Tabula Peutingeriana* e nell'*Itinerarium Antonini*, che tramandano, con leggere varianti, un percorso che attraversa i Monti della Tolfa e che poteva servire da via alternativa a quella costiera, sul quale si trovava una stazione chiamata '*Aquae Apollinares*'. Il tracciato è ancora oggi ricostruibile in molti punti, e la stazione va certamente identificata con i resti di antiche terme venuti alla luce a più riprese presso gli attuali Bagni di Stigliano (v. Fontana 1990).

Secondo una recente ipotesi, un altro toponimo sarebbe rintracciabile sempre nella *tabula Peutingeriana*, in una didascalia 'volante' sul segmento che unisce *Aquae Apollinares* a Tarquinia. Questa indicherebbe una stazione da identificare con il santuario in loc. Grasceta dei Cavallari, con un piccolo tempio periptero (da ultimo Gazzetti 1985: interpretazione errata della planimetria). Se così fosse, si dovrebbe supporre che sui Monti della Tolfa si trovasse l'estrema propaggine di quel vasto diaframma boschivo chiamato *silva Cimina* (AA. VV. 1990: 101).

Per conoscere la storia del territorio bisogna allora rivolgersi ai dati dell'archeologia, e particolarmente a quelli che si vanno accumulando a partire da due decenni attraverso scavi sistematici e soprattutto ripetute campagne di ricognizione, i cui risultati sono stati presentati a più riprese (da ultimi cfr. i contributi di Gazzetti, Stanco, Incitti in AA.VV. 1990). In questa sede è importante riprendere in considerazione un aspetto della storia del popolamento che a nostro avviso non è stato ben sottolineato.

In età imperiale, la struttura dell'occupazione del territorio sembra profondamente diversa rispetto all'età repubblicana. Le carte di fase in questo sono ingannevoli, perché mostrano una continuità pressoché totale almeno fino al II secolo d.C. (AA. VV. 1990: 105-107). In realtà si può rilevare una marcata differenza gerarchica tra i siti, che in età repubblicana non esisteva, o almeno non doveva essere così vistosa. I due livelli degli insediamenti si possono distinguere agevolmente non tanto dalla quantità dei materiali rinvenuti, che può essere frutto di fattori casuali, quanto piuttosto dalla qualità, ossia in base alla presenza di determinate classi di materiali. La validità della distinzione è rafforzata dal fatto che i parametri o non compaiono del tutto o compaiono quasi tutti insieme. Il passaggio dalla struttura egualitaria del popolamento alla struttura gerarchizzata andrà collocato in un momento coincidente o non troppo lontano dall'età di Augusto.

Esistono alcuni indizi di una ristrutturazione diffusa nel primo impero. I paramenti murari degli edifici rustici sono sempre in opera reticolata, tranne due eccezioni che presentano opera mista, e uno solo in laterizi. Indubbiamente nella zona sono frequenti pietre da costruzione particolarmente adatte a questo tipo di paramento, ma non c'è ragione per supporre un notevole attardamento rispetto alle cronologie urbane. Infatti, come si vedrà meglio in seguito, in tutto il comprensorio erano attive numerose fornaci laterizie, che avrebbero potuto agevolmente fornire i mattoni per i paramenti in *opus testaceum:* la sua assenza può essere allora un indizio cronologico importante dell'abbandono delle fornaci e quindi del ristagno dell'edilizia. D'altra parte, negli stessi Monti della Tolfa l'acquedotto che alimentava il Porto di Traiano a Centumcellae è costruito in laterizio: i mattoni del paramento, a giudicare dai bolli, non sono prodotti sul posto, ma da una fornace pubblica del porto stesso (*CIL* XV, 6; Brunori 1990, da consultare con riserva).

Le decorazioni architettoniche fittili rinvenute in almeno cinque siti dell'area tolfetana sono tutte dei primi decenni dell'impero, e non è nota al momento alcuna decorazione architettonica, né fittile né lapidea, certamente posteriore, nonostante sia stato scavato più di un sito vissuto per tutto l'impero. Anzi, in questi casi tutti gli indizi hanno sempre datato la fase di costruzione in età augustea, spesso senza rilevare alcun intervento costruttivo posteriore (molti dati sono inediti: si veda comunque De Carolis 1974 per M. S. Angelo e AA. VV. 1990, passim).

Un ulteriore elemento da considerare è il gran numero di siti romani che non hanno restituito in superficie materiale databile. Quattro di questi, scelti in maniera assolutamente casuale, sono stati scavati: in tutti i casi la loro storia era analoga. Si trattava sempre di fattorie di età repubblicana abbandonate in momenti compresi fra l'età di Augusto e quella dei Flavi (per tre di questi v. AA. VV. 1990: 127-128 e 130-132; un quarto è ancora inedito). Il campione è molto ristretto ma non privo di valore.

Alla fine di questa disamina, lunga ma necessaria, si può asserire con un buon margine di certezza che in un periodo di durata imprecisabile, forse pochi decenni o forse un secolo, la struttura del popolamento di età repubblicana fu alterata sensibilmente. In questo contesto, che vede il passaggio da una struttura indifferenziata ad una gerarchizzata, un certo numero di edifici rustici fu profondamente ristrutturato, generando un momento di accelerazione dell'attività edilizia.

La premessa è importante dal momento che una fonte primaria per la conoscenza dell'onomastica degli abitanti della zona sono i bolli laterizi, che, grazie all'intensità delle ricerche di superficie, sono venuti in luce in numero ragguardevole, spesso in connessione con i resti delle fornaci.

In base a quanto si è visto e, in qualche caso, grazie ai materiali che accompagnano in superficie le fornaci, l'attività produttiva è da collocare entro il primo secolo dell'impero; un ulteriore dato a favore di questa cronologia si ricava anche dall'osservazione dei pochi bolli di provenienza esterna importati nel comprensorio tolfetano.

Il bollo *CIL* XV, 6, evidentemente relativo ad una manifattura pubblica, che si è già visto impiegato nell'acquedotto di Traiano, è attestato in più esemplari dall'edificio rustico in loc. Castellina del Quarto (Fig. 1, 1; Gasperini 1976: 35-37, nn. 6-9, con lettura errata), a breve distanza dall'acquedotto stesso: è possibile che

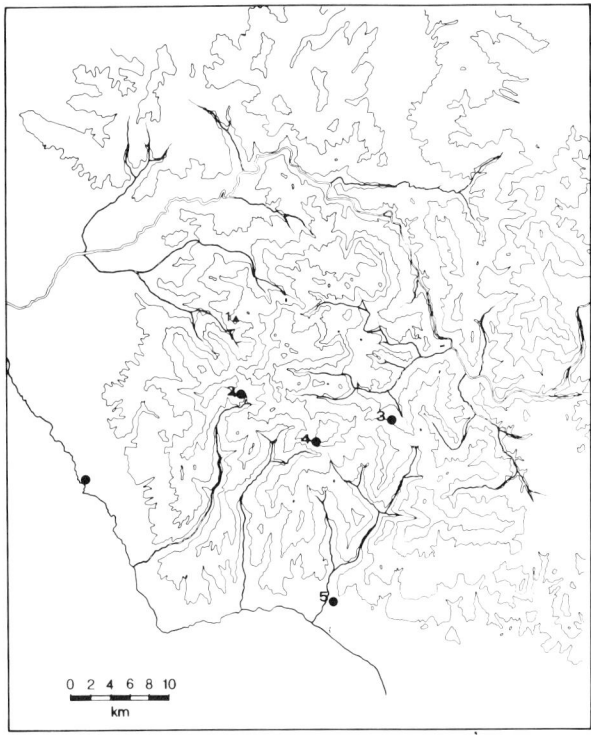

Fig. 1.

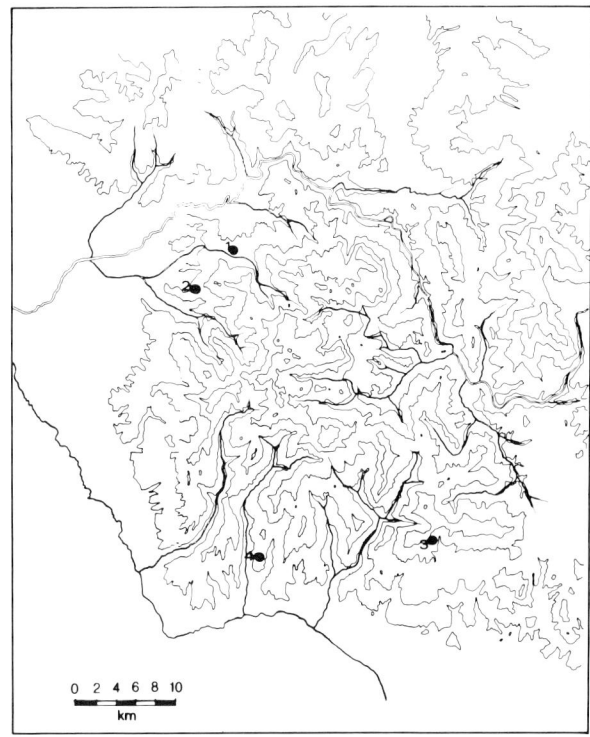

Fig. 2.

vi siano state ristrutturazioni proprio in concomitanza con l'edificazione di questo.

Forse provengono da Centumcellae anche le tegole con bollo *CIL* XV, 2168, piuttosto diffuse nell'area tolfetana (Fig. 1, 2: Brunori 1984: 29 fig. 11; 1, 3: Del Chiaro 1962: 53; 1, 4: due esemplari inediti dalla villa in loc. Fontanaccia; presenti sulla costa anche in loc. Poggio Smerdarolo: Fig. 1, 5; Vitali Rosati *et al.* 1992: 113). In base alla forma il bollo si puo' datare tra la fine del I e la prima metà del II secolo d.C.

Solo due sono le attestazioni di bolli urbani del pieno impero, di tipi noti anche a Centumcellae e in generale sulla costa tirrenica: un esemplare di *CIL* XV, 261 b (inedito al Museo di Allumiere, da M. Sassetto, Fig. 2, 2) e uno di *CIL* XV, 1051 (inedito al Museo di Tolfa, da M. S. Ansino, Fig. 2, 3); le località di provenienza sono entrambe nei pressi dell'area costiera.

Anche i bolli urbani più antichi si ritrovano nella medesima zona, direttamente legata ad un tratto di costa tirrenica che puo' considerarsi virtualmente un prolungamento dell'urbe. Nel borgo della Farnesiana si trovavano reimpiegati sul bordo di un pozzo moderno sei mattoni bipedali con un bollo di forma rettangolare (Fig. 2, 1; inediti; *CIL* XV, 970), purtroppo oggi scomparsi; è probabile che fossero stati raccolti in un insediamento nei pressi.

In loc. Prato Rotatore fu rinvenuto un bollo (Fig. 2, 4; inedito) che per i caratteri e la formula abbreviata va considerato piuttosto antico, probabilmente ancora del I secolo a.C. Un altro esemplare identico è noto a Roma (*CIL* XV, 1388). In questo caso però non si può dare per scontato che il centro di produzione sia Roma stessa, perché per i laterizi di quest'epoca è documentata piuttosto una vivace produzione da parte di grandi impianti rustici.

Nell'interno la situazione è molto diversa. I bolli urbani non vi penetrano; quelli centocellesi vi penetrano tardi, in un momento in cui evidentemente le fornaci locali dovevano essere già state abbandonate. Infatti i Monti della Tolfa sono piuttosto ricchi di argilla e, a giudicare dalle maglie larghe del popolamento, che diventano ancora più larghe nelle zone più elevate, dovevano essere provvisti di una sufficiente copertura boschiva che doveva rendere agevole e conveniente una produzione locale.

Dalla ricerca di superficie sono state individuate otto fornaci rustiche (Fig. 3), tre delle quali (f-h) non hanno restituito per ora alcun bollo: una di queste ultime (f) è stata scavata, e se ne è potuta datare l'attività al II e I secolo a.C. (Camilli 1992).

Per quanto riguarda le restanti cinque, si dà qui un quadro schematico dei dati, per la maggior parte editi.

1) Fornace in loc. M. Cerreto (Fig. 3, d; 4, d), indiziata da alcuni materiali di scarto rinvenuti in superficie insieme ad altri reperti che testimoniano l'esistenza di un cospicuo

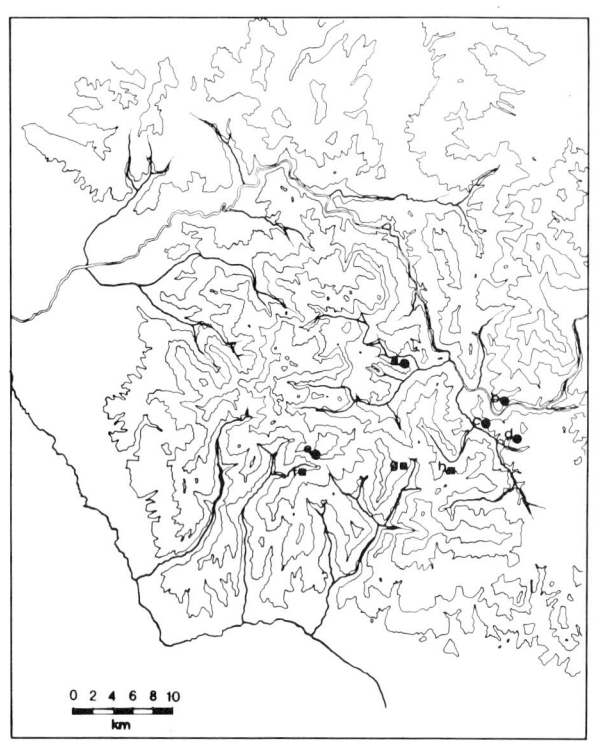

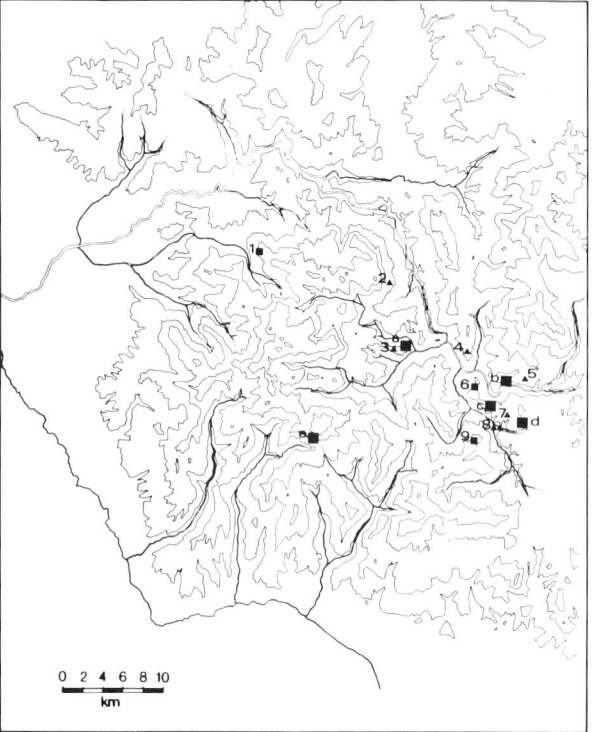

Fig. 3.

Fig. 4.

sito rustico di età repubblicana e imperiale. Il bollo è molto probabilmente *A. Tucci Cyri* (Gasperini 1961: 32, n. 4). Tegole recanti questo marchio sono state poi rinvenute a breve distanza, in loc. Colonnetta del Bagno (Fig. 4, 7; Gasperini 1961: 32-33), e negli scavi delle *Aquae Apollinares* (Fig. 4, 8; Gasperini 1976a: 28-29, n. 18). Altri esemplari hanno raggiunto località più lontane: Pignano (Fig. 4, 5; inedito al Museo di Tolfa) e Grottino del Marano (Fig. 4, 2; Gasperini 1976a: 28-29, n. 18).

2) Fornace in loc. Piana di Stigliano (Fig. 3, c; 4, c), indicata chiaramente da numerosi scarti rinvenuti in superficie nei pressi di un sito romano (prime notizie in Zifferero 1980: 87) insieme a quattro esemplari, inediti, del bollo *C. Calpetan(i)*. Altri esemplari provengono dai nuovi scavi delle *Aquae Apollinares* (Fig. 4, 8: "Il Messaggero" 18 maggio 1990: 37). Nella costruzione degli edifici termali furono impiegati quindi laterizi prodotti da due diverse fornaci.

3) Fornace in loc. La Conserva (Fig. 3, a; 4, a), anche questa ben visibile dai reperti di superficie, fra i quali numerosi mattoni refrattari e ingenti quantità di scarti (primi cenni in Naso 1980: 11 ss.). I materiali di superficie che accompagnano i resti della fornace sono in questo caso cronologicamente circoscritti fra la metà del I secolo a.C. e la metà del successivo. Il bollo, noto da cinque esemplari, è *M. Lolli/Felicis D(- - -) f(ecit)* (nuovo scioglimento rispetto alla prima edizione in Benelli & Naso 1986: 33, n. 1). Altri esemplari provengono da una piccola struttura produttiva poco distante (Fig. 4, 3; AA. VV. 1990: 130: sembra che qui si sia rinvenuto anche un esemplare recante il bollo *Lolli*, ma il dato è da verificare, e non è stato possibile ritrovare il pezzo).

4) Fornace in loc. Poggio Fortino (Fig. 3, b; 4, b), indiziata da resti di vasche e strutture scavate nel banco di tufo immediatamente a ridosso di cospicui banchi di buona argilla. La situazione del terreno non permette l'affioramento di molti reperti, ma è certa la presenza di un sito di età romana. Scavi clandestini sulla sommità hanno portato alla luce numerosi frammenti di ceramica di uso comune, alcuni dei quali chiaramente malcotti e non utilizzabili. È probabile che vi vada connesso il bollo *Bov(- - -)Ari(- - -)* (Gasperini 1961: 33-34, n. 7 = Del Chiaro 1962: 52), un altro esemplare del quale fu rinvenuto a breve distanza in loc. Poggio S. Pietro (Fig. 4, 4; Zifferero 1985: 24).

5) Fornace in loc. Fontanaccia (Fig. 3, e; 4, e), connessa con una villa di notevoli dimensioni (da ultimi Felici *et al.* 1993), da cui proviene un bollo inedito, troppo frammentario per essere utilizzato in questa sede.

A questo elenco vanno aggiunti tre bolli rinvenuti in un esemplare ciascuno, senza alcuna traccia dell'impianto che li possa aver prodotti.

1) Loc. Monte Seccareccio (Fig. 4, 6): bollo *A. Fur(i)* (Del Chiaro 1962: 52), probabilmente tardo-repubbli-

cano, rinvenuto negli scavi di un modesto impianto produttivo (cfr. AA. VV. 1990: 130-132).

2) Loc. Il Termine (Fig. 4, 9): bollo *L. Nivelli/L. Nivelli* (Benelli & Naso 1986: 34, n. 2), con una iterazione del medesimo testo su un solo punzone, sinora senza confronti. Proviene da una raccolta di superficie, accompagnato da materiale che indica l'esistenza di un cospicuo sito rustico vissuto almeno dal II sec. a.C. al tardo impero.

3) Loc. Monte S. Angelo (Fig. 4, 1): bollo *Meni*, speculare (errata la lettura in Gasperini 1976: 34-35, n. 5), rinvenuto in due esemplari nei saggi di scavo eseguiti in una grande villa rustica (v. anche AA.VV. 1990: 130).

Tutti i bolli qui elencati sono su tegole, anche se alcuni furono erroneamente pubblicati come su mattoni.

La relativa densità di piccoli impianti è dovuta forse all'abbondanza della materia prima e all'isolamento dell'area tolfetana dalle grandi correnti di commercio, ma è probabile che vi abbia giocato un ruolo importante anche l'intensità della ricerca di superficie.

Naturalmente non è possibile esaminare in questa sede tutti i tipi di rapporto tra fornaci e territorio che si sono riscontrati in varie parti d'Italia; va notato comunque che la situazione dei Monti della Tolfa si presenta sinora senza puntuali confronti. Infatti la maggior parte degli studi, che hanno raggiunto una concentrazione notevole soprattutto per l'area padana, si sono rivolti a impianti di maggiori proporzioni, con aree di diffusione di alcune decine di chilometri, mentre la presenza diffusa di piccole fornaci rustiche, rilevata in diverse zone, ma difficilmente connessa con una simile concetrazione di bolli, è rimasta spesso abbastanza al margine. Un rapido spoglio del volume XI del *CIL* conferma che situazioni analoghe, per quanto riguarda i bolli, si potrebbero trovare nei territori di Chiusi, Arezzo, Tifernum Tiberinum e di qualche altro centro. In questi casi però si tratta di realtà molto diverse, legate a territori ad alta produttività agricola, con una popolazione delle campagne probabilmente molto fitta.

Uno dei problemi principali il motivo che spinge, a un certo momento, a bollare la produzione. Infatti è difficile pensare a ragioni puramente commerciali, perché per quanto si possa rilevare un commercio di carattere locale, il raggio è piuttosto limitato, e non esce comunque mai dalla ristretta area tolfetana interna. Nel nostro caso si può escludere la possibilità che il bollo distinguesse le diverse partite cotte in una sola fornace: come si è visto la pluralità dei centri di produzione è certa a differenza di quanto ipotizzato per Roma (Steinby 1993). Quindi, anche se la causa della bollatura resta per ora aperta, nel bollo si identifica certamente qualcuno che ha a che vedere con la produzione stessa: sia che questa persona fosse il proprietario del fondo su cui avveniva la produzione, sia che fosse un suo dipendente, a qualunque titolo, resta certo che nei bolli leggiamo i nomi di persone presenti fisicamente o tramite loro proprietà nel territorio tolfetano.

Il problema se i proprietari del fondo, della fornace e delle cave di argilla si identificassero probabilmente in questo caso non si pone. Le fornaci che conosciamo nei Monti della Tolfa sorgono sempre presso banchi d'argilla, e, se si considera la scarsa commercializzazione sinora attestata delle tegole, è improbabile che i proprietari degli impianti fossero dei liberi imprenditori che lavoravano su terreno altrui. È molto più verosimile che la produzione laterizia fosse legata direttamente alla proprietà terriera.

In questo senso può essere interessante richiamare un passo dell'opera dei Saserna conservato da Varrone (r. r. I, 2, 22), che indica proprio come la produzione laterizia si potesse inserire nel più generale contesto produttivo di una *villa rustica*, quando vi fossero le materie prime disponibili e, aggiungiamo noi, se la produzione doveva superare le necessità dell'autoconsumo, adeguate possibilità di commercializzazione (Di Porto 1984: 3244-3247).

Le iscrizioni lapidarie sono molto meno abbondanti: infatti nella zona manca qualunque centro di addensamento della popolazione, e l'epigrafia risente molto di questa situazione. Anche il centro di Monterano, pure abbastanza consistente in età arcaica, in seguito è probabilmente del tutto trascurabile (Gasperini 1963). Le *Aquae Apollinares* (Fig. 5, 1), insieme stazione stradale, impianto termale e luogo di culto, sono su una strada troppo poco frequentata per essere un centro primario. Non è un caso però che proprio nei pressi delle *Aquae Apollinares* si trovi l'unica necropoli romana di tipo canonico, collocata lungo una strada basolata. Nessuna iscrizione sepolcrale vi è stata rinvenuta, mentre dagli scavi delle terme provengono due dediche (Gasperini 1976a). Oltre a queste esiste un'altra iscrizione votiva, a Diana (Vitali Rosati 1994). Alcuni chilometri a nord di Allumiere stessa fu rinvenuto un cippo probabilmente di confine, sul quale la formula onomastica è troppo abbreviata per giungere ad uno scioglimento univoco (*CIL* XI, 3571; Zifferero, c. s.).

Per il rapporto delle famiglie con il territorio sono invece molto più importanti le scarse iscrizioni funerarie. Le necropoli romane di norma sono formate da semplici tombe alla cappuccina intorno agli impianti rustici, prive di strutture monumentali e anche probabilmente di iscrizioni, se ci eccettuano due miseri frustuli di lettura molto incerta (Gasperini 1976: 53-54, n. 4; inedito dalla Fontanaccia, e *CIL* XI, 3552).

In più casi sono individuabili reimpieghi di tombe a camera etrusche: da un riutilizzo nella necropoli in loc. La Conserva (Fig. 5, 2) proviene il più antico testo latino del comprensorio, la cui datazione si può fissare al I secolo a.C. (Naso 1986).

Ma, a parte questo caso, il fenomeno più interessante

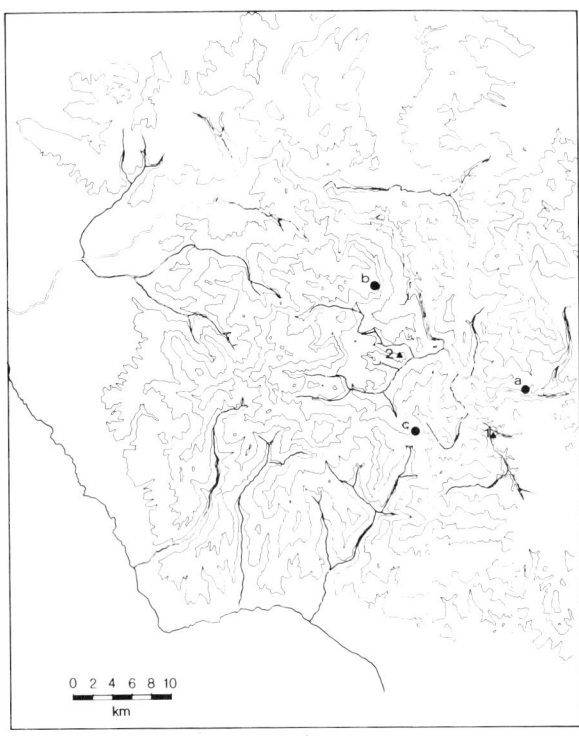

Fig. 5.

è rappresentato da alcuni monumenti funerari, regolarmente provvisti di iscrizioni, collocati in posizioni del tutto peculiari, su speroni rocciosi elevati, spesso lontano non solo dalla viabilità ma anche dagli stessi impianti rustici. L'unico chiaramente visibile, già segnalato in passato, si trova su una collina in posizione dominante la valle del Mignone di fronte a Monterano (Fig. 5, a). Si tratta di un monumento di forma circolare, con un tamburo in blocchi di tufo. Un blocco di marmo curvo, e quindi inserito in questo tamburo, recava l'iscrizione principale, a grandi caratteri, *C. Pescennius M. f. / Vol(tinia)* (Benelli 1990, purtroppo interpolato dalla redazione; Gasperini 1990: 157-158). Dal formulario, dalla grafia e dalla forma del monumento si ricava una datazione all'età augustea, piuttosto verso l'alto che verso il basso. Nei pressi fu rinvenuta un'ara funeraria (Gasperini 1961: 34-36, n. 8), chiaramente più tarda.

Un altro monumento analogo si doveva trovare a Monte Piantangeli, in una posizione del tutto analoga (Fig. 5, b). Di questo resta soltanto un blocco di marmo, con l'iscrizione dedicatoria sempre a grandi caratteri, *P. Plotius P. [f.] / Macer* (Gasperini 1976: 26, nota 8). La datazione non deve essere lontana dal precedente. Il blocco era reimpiegato in una chiesa medievale, ma non vi deve essere stato portato da lontano, dal momento che i paramenti sono realizzati con pietra cavata sul posto (in generale v. AA. VV. 1984), che è un ottimo materiale da costruzione. In effetti a breve distanza dalla chiesa scavi clandestini intercettarono una necropoli di tombe alla cappuccina, a quanto sembra di età romana (relazione inedita presso l'archivio del G.A.R., 1979).

Qualcosa di simile si trovava certamente anche presso Monte Castagno (Fig. 5, c). Anche in questo caso ritorna la costante della posizione isolata e dominante. Un'iscrizione monumentale fu rinvenuta tra i ruderi di un *castrum* medievale sulla sommità del monte (Gasperini 1990: 156-157), mentre in un punto imprecisato del medesimo fu rinvenuta una parte di un'altra iscrizione (*CIL* XI, 3544: il quarto miglio della strada ottocentesca da Tolfa a Cerveteri cade proprio ai piedi di Monte Castagno), che doveva occupare almeno tre blocchi differenti.

Venendo a concludere dopo questa rapida disamina dei documenti, i gentilizi presenti offrono considerazioni di grande interesse. Molti di questi sono troppo diffusi per poterne definire con certezza l'origine. Ma colpisce subito il fatto che la maggior parte sono di evidente derivazione non etrusca. Alcuni, come *Pescennius, Bovius/ Bovianius* e *M(a)enius* rimandano all'area campana o in generale appenninica centro-meridionale; un altro, *Nivellius,* è rarissimo; gli uomini hanno sempre *praenomen Lucius* (*CIL* VI, 22997 e 35920; XIV, 2992): non è impossibile che esistesse un legame di parentela fra i personaggi, che comunque restano nella totale oscurità. Tutti gli altri gentilizi sono in genere troppo diffusi per afferrarne l'origine; si può dire solo che non è etrusca.

Plotius è di larghissima diffusione, e non si può definire specifico di nessuna area dell'Italia peninsulare in particolare. In questo caso però, nella scarsissima documentazione epigrafica etrusca dei Monti della Tolfa compare un *plavte* dalla vicina necropoli di Pian della Conserva (Rix 1991, Cr 2.67), che potrebbe essere in qualche modo un antenato del nostro. In ogni caso il *cognomen Macer* non è attestato altrove con questo gentilizio.

Molto più interessante è *Calpetanus:* questo gentilizio è probabilmente etrusco, ed abbastanza raro per tentare delle connessioni. La famiglia, prima ignota, compare sulla scena politica in età augusteo-tiberiana, arrivando più tardi anche in Senato (Groag & Stein 1936: s.v.). I *Calpetani* romani, tutti con il medesimo *praenomen* che si trova nei bolli tolfetani, sono molto attivi, tramite loro liberti, nella produzione laterizia urbana, già dall'età giulio-claudia (Bloch 1947: 220). Fino ad ora l'origine della famiglia è rimasta molto incerta; così si pensò ad Histonium, in base a una modesta iscrizione funeraria, o più spesso a Volsinii a seguito del rinvenimento di una tegola bollata, peraltro frammentaria, e di un dolio, bollato questo da un *L. Calpetanus Rufus* (v. Syme 1959: 318). Ma il *praenomen* e la certa presenza della fornace, che non doveva essere trascurabile se rifornì anche le vicine *Aquae Apollinares,* sembrano dare maggiori probabilità ai Monti della Tolfa come luogo di origine della famiglia.

A parte quest'ultimo caso, si è visto come quasi tutti i gentilizi siano chiaramente di origine esterna. In questa sede naturalmente non si considera il fenomeno per cui, all'atto della romanizzazione del patrimonio gentilizio, si tendeva a 'normalizzare' in senso romano l'onomastica: fenomeno che indubbiamente esiste, ma che è certamente molto meno generale di quanto si possa pensare, e che soprattutto colpisce l'Etruria (e particolarmente l'Etruria meridionale) in maniera molto minore di altre zone d'Italia. Anche supponendo un margine di dubbio, il fatto che di tutto il patrimonio gentilizio tolfetano di età romana soltanto due nomi possano richiamarsi con un certo grado di probabilità ad elementi preesistenti è già di per sé significativo di apporti esterni non indifferenti.

C'è da chiedersi quando questi si siano verificati. In un primo momento verrebbe da pensare alla ripresa del popolamento nel III secolo a.C., o alla sua intensificazione nel II (AA. VV. 1990: 104-107). Ma è difficile che, anche con tutta la mobilità che poteva essere facilitata dalla cittadinanza *sine suffragio* di Caere, un'area marginale come quella tolfetana potesse attirare numerosi abitanti dall'esterno.

In realtà c'è un altro momento di rottura nella storia del popolamento, e cioè quel momento che prelude alla generale ristrutturazione del territorio. Si è visto che archeologicamente questa va collocata in età augustea. Allo stesso periodo rimandano i grandi sepolcri come quello di Pescennio, quello di Plozio e forse il terzo a Monte Castagno, la cui posizione ricorda molto da vicino il ruolo dei monumenti funerari come segno di confine di proprietà descritto nell'anonimo trattatello *de sepulchris* (Grom. vet. 271-272 L.). Quindi anche da qui viene il segno di un mutato rapporto con il territorio, che non è più quello delle piccole fattorie dell'età repubblicana, impianti sempre piuttosto modesti. La creazione di grandi proprietà in un'area marginale a bassa produttività è segno nient'altro che di un rilancio economico generale della produzione agricola, che ben si colloca in età augustea. Allo stesso tempo, la massiccia presenza di personaggi evidentemente provenienti dall'esterno, ed altrettanto evidentemente nel ruolo di grandi proprietari (bolli e monumenti funerari), coincide con quella tendenza generale sviluppatasi nell'ultimo secolo della repubblica alla rapida creazione di nuovi patrimoni fondiari distribuiti in zone diverse sulla penisola e al di fuori. Su un piano più generale, è interessante come l'età augustea, nel contesto del processo di decantazione delle aristocrazie municipali, riveli abbastanza costantemente un inserimento nelle comunità di elementi allotri, anche dove non vi siano tracce precise di assegnazioni coloniarie.

La tribù *Voltinia*, attestata nel territorio da due iscrizioni, merita qualche attenzione. Nell'antico territorio cerite questa tribù ricompare più volte, ma sempre con qualche incertezza. Secondo il Bormann (*CIL* XI, 531), alla *Voltinia* apparterrebbero gli abitanti di Castrum Novum. La base di questa affermazione però è debole, perché si limita ad un'iscrizione urbana di interpretazione incerta (cfr. *RE*, Sb. X, s.v. *Voltinia tribus*, 1116-1117).

Maggior margine di sicurezza ci potrebbe essere per Forum Clodii. In effetti anche in questo caso non mancano i dubbi, perché si conoscono una coppia di duoviri ascritti uno all'*Arnensis* e l'altro alla *Quirina*. Tuttavia va presa in considerazione seriamente la *Voltinia*, perché a questa tribù era ascritto un personaggio onorato a Forum Clodii nel 174 d.C., che doveva essere un discendente di un altro onorato sempre a Forum Clodii nel 18 d.C.: la continuità mostrerebbe che la famiglia aveva una solida pertinenza locale, mentre i duoviri potrebbero provenire da centri vicini, dove figurano appunto sia l'*Arnensis* che la *Quirina* (*RE*, Sb. X, s.v. *Voltinia tribus*, 1123).

Un caso dubbio potrebbe esserci anche a Caere (*CIL* XI, 3257 = 3615): secondo la migliore lettura tràdita vi sarebbe menzionata la *Voturia*, ma una recente fotografia permette di riconoscervi piuttosto la *Voltinia* (Liou 1969: tav. 10). Le iscrizioni sui cippetti funerari ceriti non sono da prendere in considerazione, poiché non di rado vi si abbreviano anche i cognomina, e quindi le abbreviazioni che sembrano tribù potrebbero essere ben altra cosa.

La certezza è ancora molto lontana, ma va considerata la possibilità che gli abitanti di tutto l'antico territorio cerite siano stati riuniti nella tribù *Voltinia*, come è avvenuto certamente in quello tarquiniese con la Stellatina e in quello vulcente con la Sabatina (Torelli 1984: 273; 1985. La proposta fu già avanzata in Pfiffig 1966: 38-41, che però si basava solo sulla supposta tribù *Voturia* di *CIL* XI 3257 = 3615).

L'ascrizione dei Ceriti alla *Voltinia* potrebbe aver avuto un valore strategico notevole nel quadro delle lotte politiche dei decenni successivi alla guerra sociale. Infatti, a parte Lucus Feroniae, che è molto probabilmente colonia triumvirale, in Italia sono ascritti alla tribù *Voltinia* solo i Sanniti Pentri, con l'esclusione della colonia di Aesernia.

I Sanniti sono costantemente un elemento di opposizione e di turbolenza; al contrario Caere ha già da secoli la cittadinanza romana, sia pure senza diritto di voto, e l'aristocrazia cerite è già certamente da tempo integrata a quella romana; Pyrgi, Castrum Novum, Alsium (e Fregenae) sono colonie romane; Forum Clodii è sede di prefettura: anche per la sua contiguità geografica è molto verosimile che l'antico agro cerite fosse ormai legato indissolubilmente a Roma a tutti gli effetti.

È evidente che, al momento di procedere a una votazione per tribù, i Pentri, per quanto fossero molte volte più numerosi dei Ceriti, erano fortemente ostacolati dalla distanza. In questo modo la classe dirigente romana poteva agevolmente neutralizzare ogni iniziativa pericolosa.

Bibliografia

AA.VV. 1984. *L'abbazia di Piantangeli*, Roma.
AA.VV. 1990. *Caere e il suo territorio. Da Agylla a Centumcellae*, Roma.
Benelli, E. 1990. 'Un mausoleo romano con iscrizione funeraria presso Monterano', in AAVV 1990, 133.
Benelli, E. & Naso, A. 1986. 'Nuovi bolli laterizi e doliari dei Monti della Tolfa', *Ricognizioni Archeologiche* 2, 33–38.
Bloch, H. 1947. *I bolli laterizi e la storia edilizia romana*, Roma.
Brunori, E. 1984. 'Ritrovato l'antico Castrum Ferrarie', *Notiziario del Museo Civico di Allumiere* 6, 13–42.
Brunori, E. 1990. 'L'acquedotto di Traiano', in AA.VV. 1990, 215–219.
Camilli, A. 1992. 'Nuove scoperte archeologiche nei Monti della Tolfa, I: La villa di Freddara', *Papers of the Fourth Conference of Italian Archaeology*, 4, London 99–103.
De Carolis, E. 1974. 'Gruppo di elementi decorativi in terracotta provenienti da Monte S. Angelo', *Notiziario del Museo Civico di Allumiere* 3, 35–39.
Del Chiaro, M.A. 1962. 'An Archaeological-topographical Study of the Tolfa-Allumiere District: Preliminary Report', *American Journal of Archaeology* 66, 49–55.
Di Porto, A. 1984. 'Impresa agricola ed attività collegate nell'economia della villa', *Sodalitas. Scritti in onore di A. Guarino*, Napoli, 7, 3235–3277.
Felici, F., Gazzetti, G. & Vitali Rosati, B. 1993. 'La villa della Fontanaccia: rapporto preliminare', *Archeologia, Uomo, Territorio* 12, 59–88.
Fontana, S. 1990. 'La viabilità di epoca romana nel territorio tolfetano', in AA.VV. 1990, 119–121.
Gasperini, L. 1961. 'Materiali epigrafici di età romana dal territorio di Canale Monterano', *Epigraphica* 23, 26–42.
Gasperini, L. 1963. 'Monterano. Un centro minore dell'Etruria meridionale', *Etudes Etrusco-italiques*, Louvain, 19–70.
Gasperini, L. 1976a. 'Materiali epigrafici del Museo Civico di Allumiere (Roma)', *Epigraphica* 38, 25–33.
Gasperini, L. 1976b. *Scoperte archeologiche a Stigliano* (cat. della mostra), Bracciano.
Gasperini, L. 1990. 'Etruria tributim discripta: supplementa nonnulla', *Quaderni Catanesi di Cultura Classica e Medievale*, 2, 149–173.
Gazzetti, G. 1985. 'Il santuario di Grasceta dei Cavallari sui Monti della Tolfa', *Santuari d'Etruria* (cat. della mostra), Milano, 155–156.
Groag, E. & Stein, A. 1936. *Prosopographia Imperii Romani saeculi I-II-III, editio altera, pars II*, Berolini-Lipsiae.
Liou, B. 1969. *Praetores Etruriae XV populorum*, Bruxelles.
Naso, A. 1980. *La necropoli etrusca di Pian della Conserva*, Roma.
Naso, A. 1986. 'Un'epigrafe funeraria latina dalla necropoli etrusca di Pian della Conserva (Tolfa)', *Epigraphica*, 48, 191–198.
Pfiffig, A. 1966. *Die Ausbreitung des römischen Städtewesen in Etrurien und die Frage der Unterwerfung der Etrusker*, Firenze.
Rix, H. 1991. *Etruskische Texte. Editio minor*, Tübingen.
Steinby, M. 1993. 'L'organizzazione produttiva dei Laterizi: un modello interpretativo per l'instrumentum in genere?', *The Inscribed Economy. Proceedings of a Conference, Rome 1992*, Ann Arbor, Mi., 139–143.
Syme, R. 1959. Recens. a A. Jagenteufel, Die Statthalter der römischen Provinz Dalmatien von Augustus bis Diocletian, Wien 1959, *Gnomon* 31, 510–518.
Torelli, M. 1984. *Storia degli Etruschi*, II ed., Roma-Bari.
Torelli, M. 1985. 'I duodecim populi Etruriae', *Annali della Fondazione per il Museo Claudio Faina* 2, 37–57 (= M. Torelli, *La società etrusca. L'età arcaica. L'età classica*, Roma 1987, 97–115).
Vitali Rosati, B., Rinaldoni, C. & Felici, F. 1992. 'Nuove scoperte archeologiche nei Monti della Tolfa, III: La villa di Poggio Smerdarolo – Piana di Rio Fiume', *Papers of the Fourth Conference of Italian Archaeology*, 4, London, 111–117.
Vitali Rosati, B. 1994. 'Iscrizione votiva dalla villa in località La Fontanaccia ad Allumiere (Roma)', *Archeologia, Uomo, Territorio* 13, 87–91.
Zifferero, A. 1980. *L'abitato etrusco di Piana di Stigliano*, Roma.
Zifferero, A. 1985. 'Nuove presenze etrusche e romane a Poggio S. Pietro (Tolfa): osservazioni preliminari', *Ricognizioni Archeologiche* 1, 21–31.
Zifferero, A. 1991. 'Miniere e metallurgia estrattiva in Etruria meridionale: per una lettura critica di alcuni dati archeologici e minerari', *Studi Etruschi*, 57, 201–241.
Zifferero, A. c.s. 'Ricerche archeologiche ad Allumiere nel XIX secolo: un documento inedito del card. T. Mertel', *Notiziario del Museo Civico di Allumiere*, 8, c.s.

30

La Villa Romana di Marina di S. Nicola a Ladispoli

IDA CARUSO

(Soprintendenza Archeologica dell'Etruria Meridionale)

Sommario: *La zona archeologica di Marina di S.Nicola, già nota nella cartografia del 1600 e negli studi topografici del 1800, è stata oggetto di scavi e ricerche sul terreno da parte della Soprintendenza Archeologica in questi ultimi anni. Pressanti progetti di edificazione hanno reso necessario l'avvio di una serie di campagne di scavo finalizzate alla delimitazione topografica della zona archeologica soprattutto mirata alla tutela della medesima. Il risultato di queste indagini è stato il seguente: la villa romana, articolata in vari settori e residenziali e commerciali, dimostra un periodo di frequentazione che va dalla fase originaria di costruzione intorno alla fine del I sec.a.C. sino a tarda età imperiale intorno al VI sec.d.C. Non si può ancora attribuire la villa ad un preciso proprietario, ma si può ipotizzare, in base all'estensione del complesso e alla raffinatezza di alcuni suoi particolari architettonici e decorativi, un personaggio di notevole rilievo. Per il momento solo le fonti antiche danno un nome all'illustre personaggio, mentre mancano i dati archeologici di conferma. Le future eventuali campagne di scavo dovranno chiarire alcuni punti oscuri dell'intero complesso archeologico che va, comunque, considerato uno dei più importanti della costa tirrenica compresa tra l'attuale Palidoro e il Fosso di Zambra.*

INTRODUZIONE

La zona archeologica di Marina di S.Nicola, distante da Roma circa 35 Km lungo la Via Aurelia, si affaccia sul litorale tirrenico tra il centro di Palo Laziale a Nord e la foce del fosso Cupino a Sud. Già nota e studiata dal Nibby, limitatamente ad uno dei settori del corpo principale, la zona era già riportata nella cartografia del 1600, in una pianta di Jacomo Oddi (1662) con l'attuale denominazione di S.Nicola. Solo qualche anno più tardi nelle tavole topografiche il sito non compare più con il nome moderno dell'odierna località balneare; compaiono, invece, sempre Palo-*Alsium*, Statua e, nell'area adiacente il Fosso Cupino, viene segnalata la presenza di un bacino lacustre. Di contro, nelle due carte rispettivamente di G.B. Cingolani (al foglio IV) e di G.F.Arneti (al foglio IV) nel 1692 e nel 1696 i resti archeologici emergenti sono menzionati come *Rudera portus Alsiensis* e *Vestigia Alsiensis portus*, mentre *Alsium* viene ubicata presso l'attuale Statua (fig.1).

Altre testimonianze preziose alla conoscenza della topografia della zona provengono dagli scrittori antichi (Cicerone, *Ad Fam.* 9,6,1; *Ad Att.* 13,50; *Pro Milone,* 20,54; Valerio Massimo, VIII,1,7) che tendono ad identificare l'imponente complesso residenziale costruito presso *Alsium* con la villa di Pompeo.

In realtà, le ricerche operate sul territorio, anche in tempi precedenti all'attività di scavo da parte della Soprintendenza Archeologica per l'Etruria Meridionale, non consentono di confermare l'ipotesi di un proprietario così illustre per il grandioso complesso, sebbene l'estensione delle presenze archelogiche e la raffinata qualità di alcuni ambienti portano automaticamente a riconoscere un importante personaggio nel padrone di casa.

Prima di poter affrontare una serie di indagini sistematiche sul terreno, le uniche notizie relative all'area risalivano a quelle raccolte dal De Rossi, per altro di contenuto più che esauriente: senza dubbio la zona archeologica aveva un'estensione notevole che lasciava ipotizzare non solo la struttura complessa di una grandiosa villa ma anche, in successione di tempo, la presenza di un piccolo, popoloso borgo così come riportato da Rutilio Namaziano (*De Reditu suo*, I,223).

Negli anni settanta la Soprintendenza ha effettuato numerosi interventi di scavo e restauro sull'intera area, portando alla luce numerosi muri che definiscono alcuni settori del grandioso complesso, mentre si operavano consolidamenti alle strutture del lungo criptoportico e dell'area prospiciente il lato mare.

GLI SCAVI 1986–1990 E
LE STRUTTURE DELLA VILLA ROMANA

Un'attività di ricerca più estesa è stata intrapresa negli

Fig. 1. Carta del 1696.

anni 1986-90. Pressanti progetti immobiliari su due zone del complesso, solo parzialmente esplorate, hanno reso necessarie una serie di campagne di scavo finalizzate soprattutto alla tutela di tutta l'area, già in parte compromessa dalla presenza di moderni villini residenziali.

La collaborazione scientifica da parte dell'Università di Strasburgo ha consentito di ottenere eccezionali risultati in tempi alquanto brevi. Il programma di scavo su alcuni settori dell'area archeologica mirava essenzialmente a comprendere l'estensione del complesso, l'articolazione architettonica del medesimo, le fasi cronologiche di ciascun 'quartiere'. Alla luce delle recenti indagini sugli insediamenti lungo la costa laziale (v. Sperlonga, Astura, Terracina, ecc.), nonchè sulla base degli studi relativi ai complessi residenziali, i rinvenimenti di Marina di S.Nicola possono essere interpretati non più isolatamente ma in diretta e reciproca connessione e vanno riferiti al tipo di villa c.d. costiera e marittima.

Forte risulta l'influenza dell'architettura ellenistica sull'intera struttura: abile è lo stratagemma di costruire terrazze artificiali quali *basis villae* con lunghi porticati atti a godere un ampio panorama sulla costa.

Resta ancora incerta l'esatta identificazione o, meglio, un'assegnazione tipologica per questo complesso monumentale di Marina di S.Nicola, in base alla sua struttura architettonica: secondo il Lafon essa appartiene al genere di ville costiere e non propriamente marittime, in quanto mancano strutture murarie sotto la superfice marina a pochi metri dalla linea di battigia pertinenti a vasche usate per la piscicoltura, caratteristica, invece, delle vere e proprie ville marittime.

In realtà, durante le indagini operate sul terreno interessato dalla presenza delle strutture murarie, è stato osservato che a pochi metri dalla linea di costa si intravvedono scarse tracce di probabili vasconi, per buona parte corrose dall'azione distruttiva del mare. Inoltre, va considerata la pianta della villa (fig.2), il cui nucleo principale va identificato nel c.d. settore A costituito dall'imponente *basis villae*, grandioso e massiccio sperone in cementizio caratterizzato da un criptoportico con finestre a 'gola di lupo' lungo circa m. 80, a cui si sovrappone un portico probabilmente

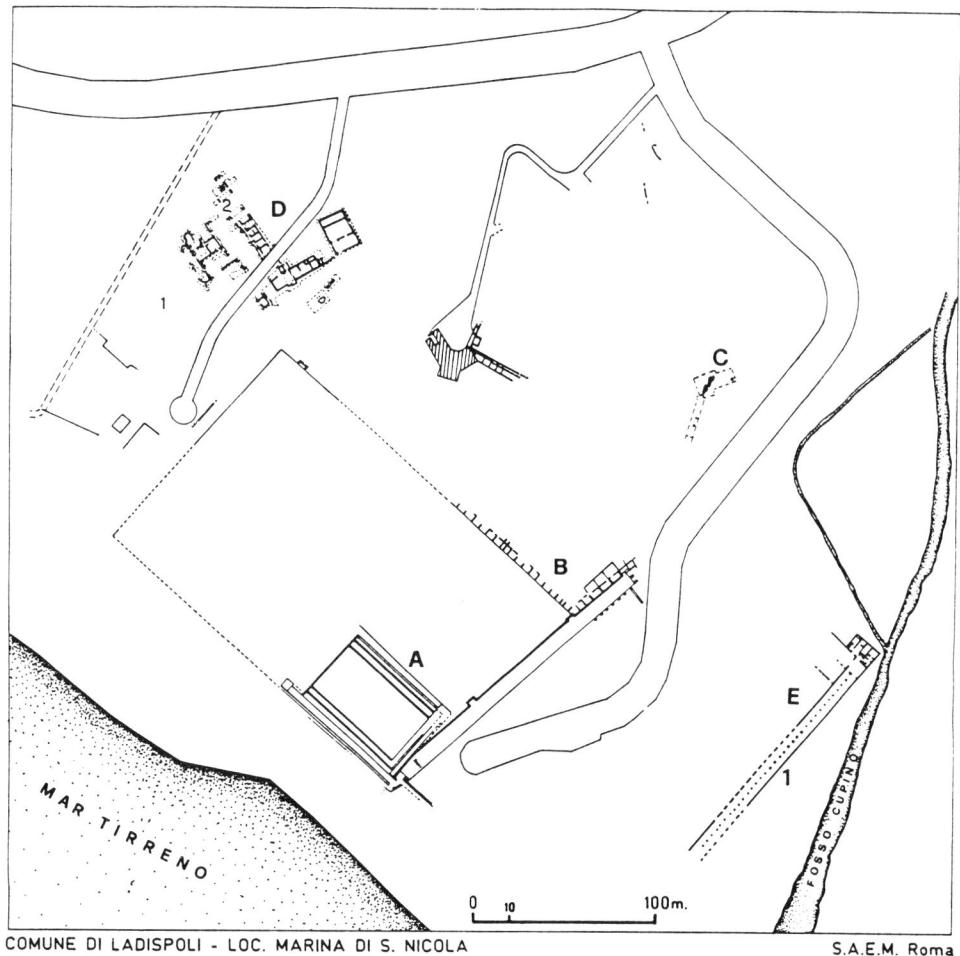

Fig. 2. Pianta della villa romana a Marina di S.Nicola

coperto, che si affacciava sul lato mare (fig.3). Questo settore, solo in parte esplorato, era inserito all'interno di un grande muro perimetrale realizzato in *opus reticulatum* e lungo, per ciascun lato, rispettivamente m. 200 e m. 13. Sul fronte interno di questo nucleo – settore C – si aprivano alcuni ambienti costituiti da due vani in successione, riferibili a probabili *tabernae*. L'area antistante tale settore, infatti, era costituita da un ampio piazzale usato per traffici commerciali nonchè da zona di ingresso all'intero complesso: prova ne é la massicciata di strada con direzione N-NO, probabile diverticolo della *via Aurelia* che consentiva l'accesso alla villa; va sottolineato che la struttura geomorfologica del piano di preparazione della strada, ovvero la massicciata, è costituita da un tipo di calcare che ricompare come lastricatura della piazza stessa.

Un secondo settore, nella zona Nord Ovest della villa, dimostra una funzione diversa dal nucleo principale: un'aula porticata affiancata da due ambienti rettangolari adibiti a magazzini si aggiungono ad una serie di vani intercomunicanti che costitiuscono un quartiere con una particolare pianta ad L. I muri perimetrali in *opus*

Fig. 3. Il criptoportico nel settore A della villa

reticulatum comproverebbero la coeva cronologia con l'intera struttura della villa – fine I sec.a.C. inizi I sec.d.C. – ma il riutilizzo di molti degli ambienti, alcuni addirittura risultano trasformati in vasche per l'acqua, una stratigrafia costituita da frammenti di ceramica romana imperiale, dimostrano che questo settore deve essere stato utilizzato in epoca successiva alla prima fase abitativa della villa. La cronologia muta ancora nella fascia più settentrionale del complesso, dove anche i muri perimetrali si ispessiscono, mostrando una tecnica costruttiva sciatta e di qualità mediocre: la presenza, inoltre, di materiale ceramico tardo imperiale avvalora l'ipotesi di una fase avanzata della villa adibita, forse, non più a residenza di lusso ma a zona di servizio.

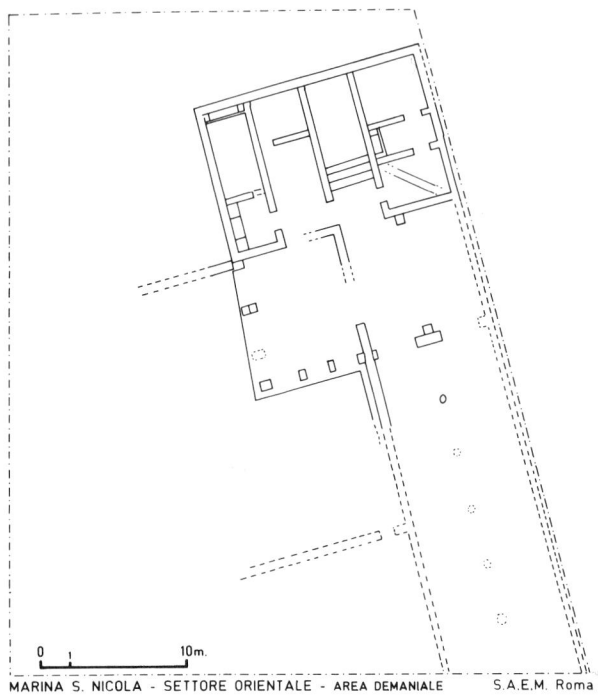

Fig. 4. Pianta delle strutture nel settore orientale

I risultati più sorprendenti dello scavo restano quelli del settore orientale (fig.4). Quivi, lungo l'asse del fosso Cupino erano stati effettuati alcuni sondaggi, in occasione di alcuni sbancamenti per la costruzione di un gruppo di villette: all'estremità del portico est una serie di ambienti messi in luce vanno identificati con una c.d. *diaeta*, mentre una scala ampia (fig.5) dimostra la presenza di due livelli di costruzione di questo settore della villa. Facile è il confronto, ipotizzato anche dal Lafon, con le ville coeve caratterizzate da una torre-belvedere, ove il proprietario usava accogliere i suoi ospiti, o ritirarsi in contemplazione del paesaggio antistante (Plinio il Giovane, *Epist*.II, 17,20–24). Ad un livello inferiore del portico erano, invece, un gruppo di piccoli ambienti adibiti al servizio della villa (cucina e *latrina*).

Particolarmente interessanti sono le pitture sulle pareti dei locali che si affacciano sul porticato e quelle ancora della c.d. *ambulatio sub divo*, quasi una sorta di cortile quadrangolare che rafforzavano il carattere residenziale del settore (fig. 6). Da un'analisi delle pitture parietali si può delimitare una cronologia di questo gruppo di ambienti intorno alla fine dell'età repubblicana – inizi età imperiale, mentre l'asimmetria della pianta rispetto a tutto il nucleo principale, poco ricalca gli impianti tardo ellenistici particolarmente rigorosi nelle partizioni planimetriche. Interessante e contrastante è invece l'uso del cortile-*viridarium* che fiancheggia il nucleo secondario della villa.

Discussione

Concludendo, anche se con opinioni incomplete ed ipotesi ancora aperte, la villa romana di S. Nicola mostra di aver avuto una vita particolarmente lunga: dal I sec.a.C al VI sec.d.C., con una progressiva costruzione di settori e, a volte un successivo e diverso riutilizzo dei medesimi; restano ancora aperti tanti quesiti, non da ultimo quello relativo al ricco o famoso proprietario. Sino ad oggi l'unica testimonianza di un'iscrizione è rappresentata da una *fistula aquaria* in piombo rinvenuta nel settore periferico nord-occidentale durante la campagna di scavo degli anni settanta. Il bollo presente recava l'iscrizione DEI SOL ELAG. da leggersi: *Dei Solis Magni Elagabali* che rimanderebbe ad una cronologia piuttosto certa e circoscrivibile intorno al 220 d.C.

Ciò tuttavia non consentirebbe comunque di attribuire la proprietà della villa all'imperatore Eliogabalo mentre è da considerarsi come elemento interessante ad una migliore datazione di questo settore già utilizzato in epoca successiva alla prima fase di costruzione. Più labili sembrano i riferimenti letterari a personaggi illustri, eventuali proprietari della fastosa residenza. Valerio Massimo (VIII,1) abbina la zona di *Alsium* alla presenza di M.Aemilius Porcina; Cicerone (Att. XIII,5; *Mil.* 20,54) rispettivamente a Murena Silius o a Pompeo; Plinio (*Epist.* VI,10,1) a Verginius Rufus; Frontino (*De Fer. Als.*) a Marco Aurelio. L'unica attribuzione ancora utilizzata per la villa resta quella a Pompeo che, per quanto ipotetica, risponde però ad una determinazione e circoscrizione cronologica valida che trova conferma nei ritrovamenti e nell'analisi delle tecniche murarie nonchè nello stile della pitture parietali del settore orientale.

Inoltre ritengo importante sottolineare, a diffferenza di quanto è stato di recente riferito, che non vada assolutamente esclusa l'ipotesi di una originaria fase costruttiva e di un primo sviluppo dei settori principali in epoca pompeiana: l'*opus reticulatum* dei muri perimetrali degli edifici principali è direttamente confrontabile con quello coevo e soprattutto con quello che caratterizza il teatro proprio di Pompeo.

Fig. 5. Settore orientale: la scala ampia

Fig. 6. Il cosidetto ambulatio sub divo.

Altro problema è quello di ordine topografico: la villa messa in luce va considerata esclusivamente una 'villa marittima', l'antica *colonia* di *Alsium* o una delle tante ville litoranee del territorio di *Alsium* che si affacciano sulla costa tirrenica tra l'attuale Torre di Palidoro e la villa di Fosso di Zambra? Se localizziamo *Alsium* nell'area moderna di Marina di S.Nicola cade l'identificazione della *colonia* romana con l'attuale Palo Laziale, teoria da sempre sostenuta da molti topografi. A sfavore di detta identificazione sta anche la mancanza di un porto che, comunque, allo stato attuale delle indagini non è stato ancora messo in luce. Se di ricovero di natanti si può parlare, va considerata la naturale insenatura creatasi alla foce del Fosso Cupino. Ma non vedrei in questa sorta di incavo sabbioso e costiero altro che un approdo di modeste dimensioni ed esclusicamente privato, senza il particolare rilievo che, invece, doveva avere un sito costiero come *Alsium*. In previsione di una futura campagna di scavo andrà analizzato proprio questo problema, orientando la ricerca sul settore nord occidentale, ancora parzialmente esplorato.

Va comunque rilevato, al di là delle singole e puntuali ricerche finalizzate ad una migliore conoscenza topografica del sito e ad una sua effettiva identificazione, il fattore architettonico della villa: la tutela del monumento, perché anche e soprattutto di tutela si deve parlare, non riveste solo le strutture emergenti ma il complesso residenziale in tutte le sue articolazioni. Gli spazi c.d. 'aperti' nel settore interno della zona settentrionale, là ove insiste la carreggiata di una strada di accesso dalla *via Aurelia* alla villa, non sono vuoti architettonici, bensì 'pause' tra i vari corpi di fabbrica, soluzioni architettoniche all'interno di un complesso residenziale che non va visto come affollamento di costruzioni a distinte funzioni ma come aree di respiro e di movimento e di valorizzazione del paesaggio circostante e della villa stessa.

Solo in questa ottica sarà possibile salvare un monumento ricreando quanto era nel progetto antico e non certo scontornando, dagli spazi occupati dalle costruzioni, le zone libere da corpi di fabbrica così come vorrebbe la mentalità di chi fa dell'edilizia moderna l'unico falso interesse nei confronti del paesaggio antico e moderno.

Bibliografia

Bastianelli, S. 1954. *Centumcellae-Castrum Novum*, Roma.
Del Bufalo, A. 1968. In *La Via Aurelia,* (Quaderni dell'Istituto di Topografia dell'Università di Roma), Roma, 45–57.
Frutaz, A.P. 1972. *Le carte del Lazio*, rist. Roma, tavv.76, 163, 181.
Huelsen, C. 1984. 'Alsium', *RE* I,2, coll.1639–1640.
Lafon, X. & Caruso, I. 1990. 'Marina di S. Nicola. Il complesso archeologico', *Bollettino d'Archeologia*, 4, 15–29.
Nenci, G., Vallet, G. 1984. *Bibliografia topografica della colonizzazione greca in Italia e nelle isole tirreniche*, III, Pisa-Roma, 185–188 (Alsio di D.Gallo).
Nibby, A. 1849. *Analisi storico-topografica-antiquaria della Carta dei contorni di Roma*, Roma, 527–29.
Proietti, G. 1980. 'La villa imperiale di Marina S. Nicola', *Archeologia Romana*, 2, 39–44.
Tocco, L. 1867. 'Alsium', *Bullettino Inst.*, 209–212.
Torelli, M. 1971. 'Contributo dell'archeologia alla storia sociale, I, L'Etruria e l'Apulia', *Dialoghi d'Archeologia*, IV-V, 431–442.
Torelli, M. 1980. *Etruria*, Bari.

31

La Villa Romana in Località Selvicciola (Ischia di Castro-VT.)

GIANFRANCO GAZZETTI
(Soprintendenza Archeologica per l'Etruria Meridionale)

Sommario: *Lo scavo sistematico dell'insediamento in località Selvicciola a Ischia di Castro (VT), iniziato nel 1982, è stato eseguito, sotto la direzione dello scrivente, Archeologo della Soprintendenza Archeologica per l'Etruria Meridionale, da volontari del Gruppo Archeologico Romano. Gli ambienti della villa romana, impostata su di un insediamento rustico tardo etrusco, si dispongono su tre livelli secondo uno schema planimetrico molto articolato in cui è stato possibile distinguere la pars rustica e la* pars dominica *relativamente alle diverse fasi cronologiche. Queste sono state così definite: fase mediorepubblicana (seconda metà del III secolo a.C.); tardorepubblicana (seconda metà del II secolo a.C.); augustea; medioimperiale (fine del II - prima metà del III secolo d.C.); seguono una fase di abbandono databile al V secolo d.C. ed una rioccupazione longobarda (secc. VII-VIII d.C.), sia relativa ad una modesta presenza abitativa impostata sui ruderi della villa romana, sia ad una vasta necropoli di oltre 200 sepolture intorno ad una chiesa.*

Lo scavo in località Selvicciola ha avuto inizio nel 1982, in seguito ad una segnalazione della Guardia di Finanza che aveva fermato il proprietario del lotto di terreno mentre con alcuni amici stava scavando clandestinamente una cisterna romana affiorante in parte sul terreno. Il primo intervento d'emergenza eseguito dalla Soprintendenza Archeologica per l'Etruria Meridionale nel maggio dello stesso anno, rivelò l'esistenza di un vasto complesso rurale romano e di una necropoli longobarda. Dall'agosto 1982 iniziò la campagna di scavo stratigrafico sistematica eseguita sotto la direzione di Funzionari della Soprintendenza Archeologica per l'Etruria Meridionale, da volontari del Gruppo Archeologico Romano e dei Gruppi Archeologici d'Italia. Tale campagna di scavo, tuttora in corso, ha dimostrato la validità della collaborazione tra Associazioni di volontariato ed Enti preposti anche nella ricerca scientifica, realizzando quel fondamentale rapporto tra interventi sul territorio e coinvolgimento di chi lo abita essenziale alla tutela dei beni culturali; le modalità con cui si è svolta questa attività di ricerca hanno infatti favorito e promosso interventi del Comune di Ischia di Castro e della Regione Lazio sia nel parziale finanziamento di alcune attività connesse allo scavo come i restauri delle murature e delle pavimentazioni venute alla luce, sia nell'organizzazione di mostre sulle attività di ricerca in corso nel territorio comunale e del locale Museo Civico dove, con una rotazione parziale dei materiali esposti, è possibile anno per anno presentare i materiali di maggiore interesse provenienti dallo scavo, rispondendo al dovere di divulgazione che dovrebbe sempre essere presente a tutti gli studiosi. Una prima scelta del materiale proveniente dallo scavo della Selvicciola fu presentato alla mostra di Orbetello sulla Romanizzazione del territorio di Vulci, organizzata dalla Regione Toscana nell'estate 1985, nel quadro delle manifestazioni relative al Progetto Etruschi; nel catalogo della mostra, unitamente ad una prima sintesi degli studi sul popolamento, trovò spazio anche un preliminare sulla campagna di scavo nell'area della villa (Toiati & Pontacolone 1985: 149–151). La necropoli longobarda fu invece presentata in via preliminare alla Quarta Conferenza sull'Archeologia Italiana svoltasi a Londra (Incitti 1990: 213–217). In questa sede si forniranno pertanto i risultati degli scavi della villa ormai in via di conclusione, suscettibili di ulteriori modifiche col prosieguo dell'attività di scavo e di documentazione dei materiali raccolti.

La villa, fortemente danneggiata da lavori agricoli con mezzi meccanici di notevole portata fin dagli anni '50, è disposta su tre livelli altimetrici cui si sono adattati gli ambienti secondo uno schema planimetrico articolato. La natura del terreno ha fortemente condizionato i sistemi e le tecniche costruttive: si tratta infatti di un banco di travertino che copre uno strato di tufiti giallastre; i due livelli più alti sono relativi al banco di travertino e quello più basso allo strato di tufiti. Questa

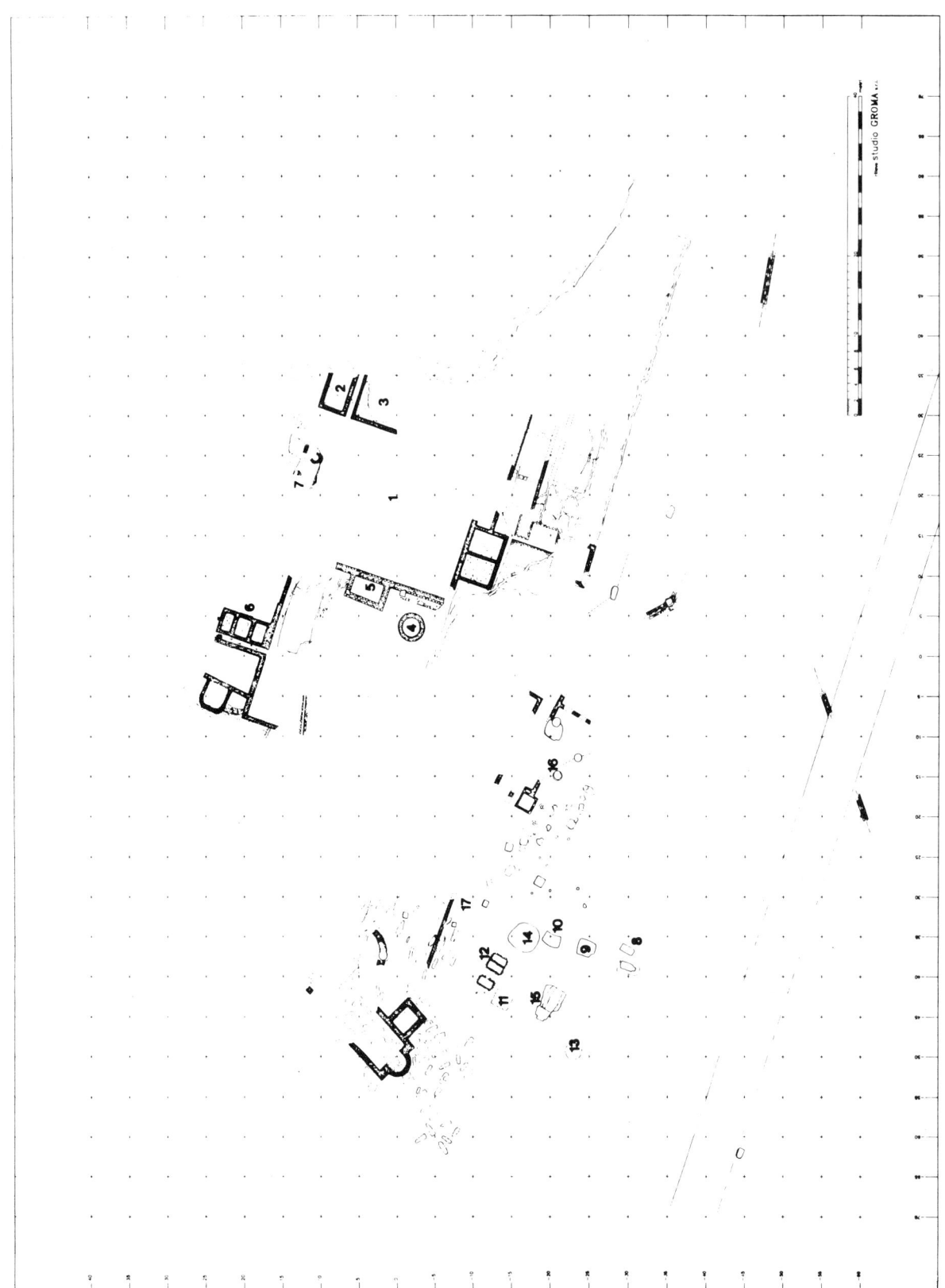

Fig. 1. Pianta della villa romana di Selvicciola (Ischia di Castro).

conformazione del terreno ha determinato la creazione di numerosi vani ipogei (soprattutto nel livello inferiore) e di livellamenti del piano di appoggio degli ambienti (soprattutto nei livelli superiori). Allo stato attuale dello scavo sembra emergere una tripartizione funzionale del grande complesso rurale; la parte residenziale si estende attorno ad un peristilio quadrangolare (Fig.1.1) e poggia sul livello superiore del banco di travertino, regolarizzato e 'foderato' con un muro a blocchetti parallelepipedi in pietra locale, sul lato sud est, in modo da costituire una sorta di *basis villae*. Parte degli ambienti situati sul lato orientale del peristilio (Fig.1.2,3) è franata nella sottostante forra costituita nei secoli dal torrente Strozzavolpe; il settore sud orientale di questa area della villa è ancora da indagare.

Sul secondo livello del banco travertinoso si dispongono attorno all'atrio con cisterna (Fig.1.4) e vasca – serbatoio (5) gli ambienti di lavorazione tra i quali il frantoio oleario (Fig.1.6) e il relativo *doliarium* (Fig.1.7). Sul livello di tufite sono stati individuati gli immondezzai purgatoria (Fig.1.8,9,10,11), la concimaia (Fig.1.12), depositi sia terragni (Fig.1.13,14,15) che in *dolia* (Fig.1.16) di cui al momento non si è potuta dare alcuna identificazione e l'aia (Fig.1.17), questa zona risulta di difficile lettura per il sovrapporsi di più interventi, dal primo impianto della villa in età medio repubblicana all'estendersi della grande necropoli longobarda dal VII secolo d.C. in poi. L'area coltivata relativa al podere della villa si estendeva con ogni probabilità su tutta la rimanente parte del pianoro a ovest e sud ovest dei resti individuati; la costruzione della strada interpoderale di bonifica ha tagliato tale pianoro come risulta evidente dal rilievo planimetrico del complesso.

Allo stato attuale delle ricerche sembrano delinearsi sei fasi di vita del complesso: un primo impianto di seconda metà III secolo a.C. sorto su una precedente fattoria etrusca di fine IV-inizi III secolo a.C.; un ampliamento del complesso trasformato in grande villa produttiva nella seconda metà del II secolo a.C.; un vasto intervento di ristrutturazione realizzato in età giulio claudia (probabilmente sotto Augusto); alcuni interventi di modeste dimensioni in età medio imperiale (fine II – inizi III secolo d.C.); e l'abbandono da collocarsi nell'ambito della seconda metà del V secolo d.C. L'intervento longobardo sembra aver riguardato anche una parziale riabitazione con strutture lignee della parte residenziale della villa, oltre alla costituzione dell'area sepolcrale e della relativa chiesa (VII-VIII secolo d.C.).

L'esistenza di numerosi vani ipogei e di ambienti ricavati almeno in parte dal banco di travertino ha consentito, in una situazione di notevole distruzione moderna del complesso, la sopravvivenza di lembi consistenti della stratigrafia che indagati per estensione in questi anni consentiranno un inquadramento sufficientemente attendibile del sito.

LE TRACCE DELL'INSEDIAMENTO TARDO ETRUSCO

Le uniche tracce riscontrate riferibili a fasi precedenti il primo impianto della villa sono quelle relative alla presenza di tre pozzi, un deposito scavato nel banco di tufite e un butto; i materiali raccolti all'interno dei pozzi sono relativi a riempimenti di seconda metà III secolo a.C. e comprendono frammenti di vasellame di fine IV e inizi III secolo a.C.

Negli strati di riempimento d'età repubblicana si rinvengono anche materiali protostorici e arcaici, purtroppo non riferibili allo stato attuale delle ricerche ad alcuna presenza sicuramente identificabile anche se dimostrano una continuità abitativa del sito tra le più ampie dell'area.

I tre pozzi cilindrici profondi in media dall'attuale piano di calpestio 6/7 metri, presentano pedarole di accesso e sembrano 'pescare' da una falda acquifera oggi situata ad un livello molto più basso. Il pozzo più settentrionale risultava coperto dal muro circolare di un edificio d'età longobarda, quello meridionale è stato tagliato e coperto dalla costruzione dell'attuale via di bonifica, mentre quello sud orientale era stato obliterato dai muri della *pars rustica* della villa di II secolo a.C.

LA FASE MEDIO-REPUBBLICANA SECONDA METÀ III SECOLO A.C.

Le tracce di tale fase sono desumibili, allo stato attuale delle ricerche, quasi esclusivamente dai materiali rinvenuti negli strati di riempimento dei pozzi e dei manufatti del periodo tardo etrusco. Non sembra tuttavia, ad una prima analisi delle seriazioni stratigrafiche, che l'estensione e il posizionamento della fattoria di quest'epoca varino rispetto alla fase precedente. Sono infatti con ogni probabilità da ascrivere a tale periodo tracce di alloggiamenti di *dolia effossa*, buchi di palo per strutture lignee, parte dei cunicoli di drenaggio scavati nel banco di tufiti giallastre. I materiali cronologicamente riferibili al III sec. a.C. rinvenuti in riempimenti in altre zone del complesso, realizzati durante l'ampliamento del secolo successivo non permettono di identificare strutture o aree di provenienza relative. Tra i reperti appartenenti a questa fase un'ansa di un *askos* in ceramica comune del Gruppo Rufvies con bollo in cartiglio rettangolare [ATRAN]E databile alla seconda metà del III secolo a.C.

LA FASE TARDO-REPUBBLICANA: SECONDA METÀ DEL II SECOLO A.C.

Nella seconda metà del II secolo a.C. si impianta la villa di ampie dimensioni. Il settore meridionale dell'area con banco di tufite è l'unico ad aver restituito tracce

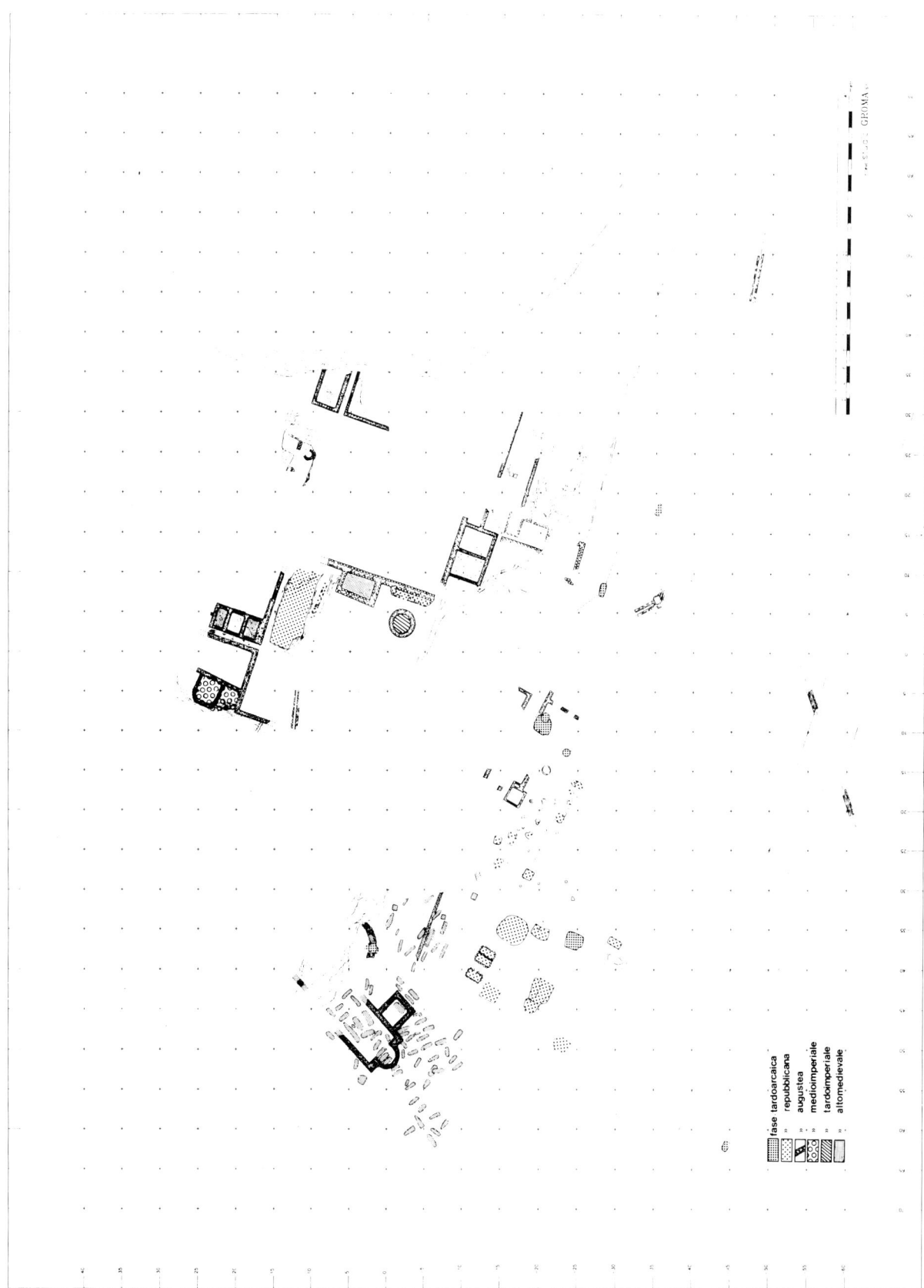

Fig. 2. *Selvicciola: le fasi principali dell'insediamento e l'estensione della necropoli longobarda.*

murarie e ambienti scavati relativi a questa fase. Si tratta di due serie di ambienti separati da un corridoio di cui al momento non è ancora possibile dare una precisa identificazione, di una vasca di raccolta del frantoio oleario, di dolii probabilmente ad esso relativi, di un dolio e di una vasca con pavimento in tessellato fittile e rivestimento in *signinum* e di un pozzo collegato ad una cisterna a cunicoli. Numerose tracce di buche di pali e di incassi quadrangolari, emerse dallo scavo e cronologicamente appartenenti alle fasi repubblicane, non sono state ancora analizzate compiutamente. Nell'area occidentale due vasche simili a quella sopra descritta con pavimento in tessellato fittile di forma rettangolare, disposte a livelli diversi e comunicanti tra loro, sono forse relative ad una concimaia; nella stessa zona sono stati rinvenuti tre *purgatoria* e tre depositi scavati nel terreno di incerta identificazione. In età augustea tutti questi ambienti sono stati coperti con una colmata di detriti e materiali ceramici di II-I secolo a.C. Tra i materiali relativi a questa fase rinvenuti nei riempimenti, numeroso vasellame fittile in ceramica a vernice nera di produzione vulcente, tuscano-tarquiniese e romana, lucerne a vernice nera del tipo sud-etrusco, un denario d'argento del 108 a.C. di L.Flaminio Cylo e alcuni assi in bronzo della serie sestantaria della prora. Materiali appartenenti a questa fase si trovano in tutti gli strati sottopavimentali del rifacimento augusteo in tutti i settori del complesso. Scarse tracce di muri in opera quadrata cimati e obliterati nella fase augustea si trovano nella zona dell'atrio e in quella dei bagni, ma non è al momento possibile stabilirne la relazione planimetrica.

Sembra comunque ormai certo che la villa abbia raggiunto in quest'epoca la massima espansione occupando tutte e tre le terrazze su cui si articola il complesso archeologico.

Nei riempimenti della fase augustea sono stati rinvenuti nel settore residenziale della villa due embrici con bolli in cartiglio rettangolare MINUCIUS.C.F, MINUCI e L.MINUC(I) che potrebbero essere relativi ai proprietari della villa. La *Gens Minucia*, di antica origine, presente in Senato già dal IV secolo a.C., è attestata in Italia centro meridionale; non si conoscono *Minucii* nell'Etruria Meridionale e in particolare nel Vulcente; non è certo infatti che alla *Gens* in questione vada collegato *L.Minicius Natalis* ufficiale di Traiano che dedica un altare ad Apollo a *Maternum* (sui Monti di Canino).

La fase augustea

La ristrutturazione di questo periodo riguarda la maggior parte degli ambienti della villa. Appartengono a questa fase l'atrio con la cisterna e la vasca serbatoio, gli ambienti del frantoio oleario e la parte residenziale attorno al peristilio. Per ampliare questo settore verso est viene riempita una piccola cava di materiale travertinoso, servita probabilmente per la costruzione della villa alla fine del II secolo a.C.

Tra gli ambienti della *pars dominica* sono riconoscibili l'ipocausto del *calidarium* con tracce della vasca e due ambienti contigui pavimentati in cocciopesto, forse la cucina nell'ambiente a sud est contiguo ai bagni, il *doliarium* a nord est e due ambienti non identificabili separati da un fognolo a est. Il frantoio oleario non ha mostrato traccia dell'ara, distrutta sicuramente durante gli scassi agricoli moderni (l'incasso in travertino degli *arbores* è stato rinvenuto insieme ad altri elementi decorativi nei mucchi di pietre creati dal proprietario dopo le arature) ma solo delle tre vasche relative alla fasi della lavorazione e disposte a livelli parzialmente differenti. L'ambiente del *torcular* era forse quello a oriente delle vasche. Sull'area produttiva della fase repubblicana si imposta la corte rustica con l'aia in ciotoli e frammenti fittili. A questa fase è attribuibile anche la costruzione dell'acquedotto di alimentazione della villa di cui sono stati scavati tre tratti in direzioni diverse; quello orientale si collegava al grande acquedotto che serviva l'area della centuriazione in cui era collocata la villa e che attraversava su arcata il torrente Strozzavolpe a oriente del complesso. L'acquedotto proveniva come quello di Vulci dai vicini Monti di Canino.

Per effettuare i rifacimenti degli ambienti è stata eseguita una colmata con materiali ceramici delle fasi precedenti della villa tra questi figurano frammenti di sigillata italica delle prime fasi di produzione (ultimo quarto del I secolo a.C.), questo dato unito a quello di altri reperti rinvenuti nei masselli pavimentali e nelle murature, datano tale fase alla prima età augustea.

Gli interventi di età medio imperiale

Scarsi elementi dimostrano l'esistenza di rifacimenti di alcuni ambienti e settori della villa tra la fine del II e la prima metà del III secolo d.C. Nella zona residenziale gli ambienti con pavimento in cocciopesto vengono parzialmente ristrutturati, nella fossa di fondazione del muro divisorio tra i due ambienti sono stati rinvenuti una firmalampen e una moneta di Filippo l'Arabo; viene rialzata la cisterna dell'atrio e nella zona del frantoio viene scavato e rivestito con muratura a blocchetti di travertino un deposito ipogeo di difficile identificazione. Anche le vasche del frantoio vengono parzialmente modificate soprattutto quella centrale che viene rialzata. Un muro di recinto della corte rustica viene costruito con andamento nord ovest sud est.

La fase di abbandono: V secolo d.C.

I materiali rinvenuti nelle occlusioni dei cunicoli di drenaggio e nel riempimento della cisterna datano con sufficiente attendibilità l'abbandono della villa. In particolare il riempimento della cisterna ha dato risultati di notevole interesse. Il mantenersi di un sedimento limoso ha consentito la conservazione di materiali deperibili come legni e vegetali e ha consentito di acquisire dati di estrema importanza sulla vita del complesso e sulle sue strutture. Lo strato di abbandono risultava coperto da un riempimento (probabilmente relativo alla fase longobarda) con i frammenti del *puteal* di travertino dell'atrio e di un trapezoforo a grifone in marmo lunense pertinente ad un tavolino sempre situato nell'atrio. Nello strato di abbandono oltre a numerosi resti lignei di un tavolato sono state rinvenute 11 brocche fittili in ceramica comune verniciata in rosso e cinque in rozza terracotta con decorazioni incise databili al V secolo d.C., due piatti d'imitazione della forma Hayes 61 in sigillata chiara africana D con decorazioni in rosso sul fondo interno, noti da rinvenimenti effettuati negli strati tardo antichi di Fiesole e da altre testimonianze dell'Etruria centrale e settentrionale, una coppa tipo Hayes 53b in sigillata africana C3 con decorazione a rilievo applicata sul fondo interno (figura di leonessa), una coppa tipo Lamboglia 35/Atlante LXVII/5 in sigillata africana C3, due piatti tipo Hayes 67 in sigillata africana D1 e uno tipo Hayes 61a in D1.

Una brocca conteneva capperi ancora conservati. Sono stati rinvenuti anche una brocca in bronzo e una pentola in bronzo ricolma di ceci. Tutti questi reperti unitamente ai rimanenti materiali dello strato portano a datare l'abbandono della villa tra il 400 e il 450 d.C.

I materiali vegetali sono attualmente in studio presso la Facoltà di Botanica dell'Università di Roma 'La Sapienza' mentre il materiale ligneo è conservato così come quello in bronzo presso i laboratori di restauro della Soprintendenza Archeologica per l'Etruria Meridionale di Civitavecchia e Viterbo. Parte del materiale fittile è esposta nel Museo Civico di Ischia di Castro così come il *puteal* in travertino ricomposto da più frammenti e il trapezoforo a grifone.

La fase longobarda: VII-VIII sec. d.C.

Tra la fine del VI e gli inizi del VII secolo d.C. sulle rovine della villa si imposta una presenza abitativa modesta testimoniata da fori di palo nei pavimenti in cocciopesto degli ambienti termali, da tracce di altri incassi nella zona del peristilio e dai riempimenti delle vasche del frantoio oleario e del serbatoio dell'atrio. In questi strati oltre a numeroso materiale di V secolo d.C., compaiono alcuni vasi in sigillata africana D2 che datano la costituzione dello strato e quindi l'impostazione della fase abitativa altomedievale nell'ambito del primo quarto del VII secolo d.C. Di particolare importanza a tale riguardo la presenza dei piatti tipo Hayes 104/Atlante XLIII/4 e tipo Hayes 103b in sigillata africana D2, del piatto fondo/teglia tipo Hayes 109 e dalla coppa tipo Hayes 80b/99/Atlante XLVIII/9 in sigillata africana D2. A questa fase è ascrivibile anche il primo impianto della vasta necropoli sviluppatasi fino al IX secolo e comprendente a tutt'oggi circa 200 sepolture a fossa.

La chiesa cimiteriale si è impostata verso la metà del VII secolo su parte dei nuclei più antichi del sepolcreto con tombe a fossa coperte da tegole disposte 'alla cappuccina' (Incitti 1990: 213–217).

La complessità dello scavo e la ricchezza di dati che ha fornito richiedono ancora un ulteriore approfondimento della documentazione in nostro possesso e l'ultimazione del catalogo dei materiali rinvenuti tuttora in avanzato stato di elaborazione. Il proseguimento dello scavo previsto per l'estate 93 potrà infine chiarire meglio alcuni particolari soprattutto in merito alla pianta della fase repubblicana e all'estensione della parte residenziale della villa sul lato orientale in età imperiale.

Ringraziamenti

I dati qui esposti sono tuttavia già sufficientemente indicativi e sono stati elaborati dall'equipe interdisciplinare che segue la documentazione dello scavo da me coordinata (Fanno parte di questo gruppo di lavoro: Mauro Incitti per le anfore e le ceramiche dipinte altomedievali, Giuseppina Ghini per la Ceramica a Pareti Sottili, Enrico Stanco per la Ceramica a Vernice Nera e le ceramiche dipinte d'età repubblicana, A.Camilli per i balsamari in ceramica e le ceramiche preromane, L.Caretta per i vetri, L.Pontacolone per la Sigillata Chiara Africana, oltre a L.Carta, T.Conti, D.De Giovanni, A.De Laurenzi, G.De Santis, M.De Simone, S.Fontana, A.Guarino, G.Innocenti, P.Rossi, P.Toiati, P.Turi, che hanno coordinato le aree di scavo e che aiutano chi scrive nel catalogo e nello studio delle ceramiche d'uso comune da mensa e da fuoco.

Bibliografia

Carandini, A., Tortorici, E. & Tortorella, S. 1989. 'Ceramica Africana. Terra Sigillata vasi', in *E.A.A, Atlante delle Forme ceramiche I*, Roma, 9–183.

Hayes, J.W. 1972. *Late Roman Pottery*, London.

Incitti, M. 1990. 'La necropoli longobarda della Selvicciola', *Papers of the Fourth Conference of Italian Archaeology, 4, New Developments*, 213–217.

Toiati, P. & Pontacolone, L. 1985. 'La Villa della Selvicciola', in *La Romanizzazione dell'Etruria. Il territorio di Vulci*, Firenze, 149–151.

32

The Evolution of Rural Settlement in *Regiones* V and VI: From the Roman to the Early Medieval Period

UMBERTO MOSCATELLI

(Istituto di Archeologia, Università di Macerata)

Summary: *The author examines the evolution of the rural settlement in some territories of the V and VI regiones. Here the available archaeological data are often inadequate, but we possess a satisfactory basic knowledge on the field of land property toponymy. Moreover, from research made on Roman centuriation we gain essential pieces of information for the study of rural settlement. As regards the Early Middle Ages, it is interesting that the* curtes *are located in those areas in which the percentage of place-names relating to names of Roman land owners is very high. Finally, the author briefly presents some data relative to the territory of* Urbs Salvia, *where detailed topographical investigations are underway.*

INTRODUCTION

It is very difficult to examine diachronically the changes in rural settlement within the *regiones* V and VI (at present, corresponding to the Marche region); this is due to a variety of problems which are usually connected with the conditions of local archaeological research. Our general archaeological knowledge is often inadequate, especially in the topographic field. Only a small part of the territory has been subjected to systematic research, while very large areas (mostly belonging to the main ancient towns) still remain unexplored. Indeed, on a regional scale, we still refer to the map formulated by Mercando, Brecciaroli and Paci in 1981. That map, as the authors themselves admit, was created by analysing data deposited intermittently in the Archaeological Soprintendenza archives over a period of more than one hundred years. Its relative unreliability has recently been highlighted by work by the author and others (e.g. Moscatelli 1988, 1990).

Even our knowledge of Roman villas is limited: since publication of the results of the excavation of a small group of settlements (Mercando 1979), research on rural settlement seems to have stopped. Some sites are now being subjected to investigation, but only a few preliminary data are yet available on them, but enough to indicate that these sites had been used from the end of the 1st century BC and the beginning of the 1st century AD to the 6th and in some cases perhpas even into the 7th century AD.

These gaps in our knowledge obviously have a negative effect on studies of the evolution of the rural settlement during the Early Middle Ages and the Middle Ages. Indeed, it could be argued that medieval archaeology is still very much underdeveloped in the Marche and that at present research remains at an archive level (cf. Cruciani Fabozzi 1991).

THE LAND PROPERTY TOPONYMY

Despite the many gaps, we possess a satisfactory basic knowledge on the field of toponymy. The map in Figure 1 is based on the assessment of the toponymic units present in the maps (scale 1:25000) of the Istituto Geografico Militare Italiano, with additional pieces of information taken from the medieval documents and, in particular, from the Codice Bavaro for the *VI regio* (Baldetti 1988), and from the Farfa documentation for the *Picenum*, corresponding to the lands subjected to the Longobard domination (*Chronicon Pharphense, Liber Largitorius, Regestus*; Ferranti 1985).

The main limitation of the map is in the lack of historical depth: it shows only the final result of the complex set of divisions and joinings of the land properties over time. Nonetheless, we are able to date the formation of many place-names relating to landowners to the period spanning from end of the Republic to the beginning of the 1st century AD. This coincides with a phase of strong municipalisation, during which many *viritanae adsignationes* and foundations of *coloniae*, such as Falerio, Urbs Salvia, Firmum, Ancona, Fanum, Pisaurum, were realised (Luni 1984; Moscatelli 1985; 1988b).

Looked at from a quantitative viewpoint, much can be discerned regarding toponymic units, which are especially concentrated in the *Picenum*. Within this area two sub-areas seem to be particularly rich in place-names relating to Roman landowners' names: namely the area surrounding *Camerinum-Attidium-Tuficum* (*regio VI*) and the area between the upper Tenna Valley and the town called S. Vittoria in Matenano (south-west of *Falerio, regio V*). The first appears to be strictly connected with a road which ran through Umbria, entering the modern Marche region through the Nera Valley, and went through *Camerinum* to reach the Esino Valley (Moscatelli 1994).

In the *ager Urbisalviensis* the situation is different: here, for a few kilometres around the ancient town, we lack information about this type of place-name. Even the Catasto Gregoriano and the (edited) documents belonging to the Cistercian Abbey of Chiaravalle di Fiastra (see below) fail to add any further data.

In terms of the relationship between the toponyms and the ground morphology, the highest number of place-names refers to the hilly areas with an altitude varying from 200 to 500 metres, which are the most suitable ones for growing grain, olives and fruit trees, as reflected in the ancient sources (Sirago 1982). In contrast, the percentage of place-names in the bottom of the valleys is very low (5%) and this is very likely due to the characteristics of the landscape during the Roman period. Recently, Coltorti has argued that, during Roman times and up to AD 1000 and beyond, there had been a rather stable 'a meandri' fluvial dynamic, characterised by the presence of sheets of water and a luxuriant vegetation along the river banks. Indeed, the archaeological surveys confirm the low number of land owner place-names in the bottom of the valleys. In these valleys the Roman roads systematically run very near to the northern side of the hills, and the rural settlements tend to be on the hillsides, not far from the plain (Mercando, Brecciaroli & Paci 1981).

Land divisions

From research on ancient centuriation we gain essential pieces of information for the study of rural settlements. The *Libri coloniarum* contain many details on the allotments made in *Umbria* and in *Picenum*, especially during the age of strong municipalisation (1st century BC – 1st century AD). In fact, the *Libri Coloniarum* contains explicit references to the cities of *Ancona, Asculum, Attidium, Auximum, Camerinum, Cingulum, Cupra, Fanum Fortunae, Falerio, Firmum, Matilica, Ostra, Pausulae, Pisarum, Potentia, Ricina, Sena, Septempeda, Tolentinum, Trea, Tuficum, Urbs Salvia*.

The study of Roman centuriation in the Marche region is negatively affected by an approach developed on the prejudice according to which the mostly hill-like morphology of the region caused the loss of the ancient

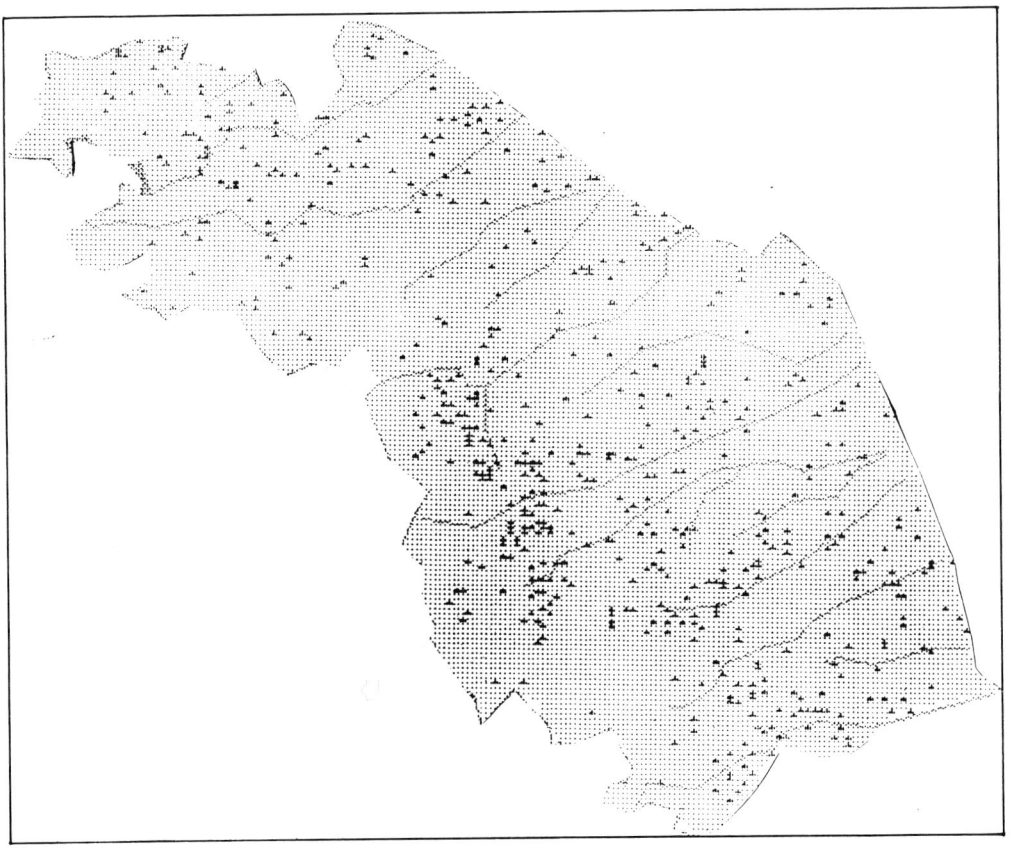

Fig. 1. Marche – distribution of place-names derived from Roman land owner names.

limites. This approach, improperly based on an old preliminary research made by Nereo Alfieri (Alfieri 1968), has now been carried on by Giovanna Bonora and Pier Luigi Dall'Aglio (Dall'Aglio 1987; Bonora 1987; Dall'Aglio & Bonora 1991). In their research they always make use of the 20 *actus* form; but this form, largely known and used in the Po Valley, often produces questionable results when used in the Marche region. In this kind of study, if we make use of the 15 or the 16 *actus* forms (or other forms that we will examine later), rather than the 20 *actus* one we can obtain very different results (Moscatelli 1993).

It is helpful to recall that the recourse to those forms is fully justified by the numerous references present in the *Corpus Agrimensorum: Lib.Col.*, I, 216, 16 Lach.; Boeth. *(Plerumque sunt agri quam multi adsignati, quorum mensura limitum licet diuersa sit, tamen distant a se alius ab alio in pedes C, in pedes CL, in pedes CCXL...); Lib. Col. I, 214, 3-9; 216, 11; 217, 14; 220, 13 – 221, 2; 221, 14 – 222, 10; 222, 14 – 223, 9; 228, 4-15; 240, 10-15; 243, 3-10.* Moreover, French scholars have detected in central southern Italy grids based on 15 and 16 *actus* (Chouquer, Levèque, Favory & Vallat 1987). While the authors do not always apply the method in a correct way (Moscatelli 1990b), nevertheless, they maintain the modular differentiation of the centurial grids as a guiding principle. Not only do they explicitly formulate the principle, but they also satisfactorily demonstrate its validity in some of the proposed reconstructions, many of which are based on the 15 or 16 *actus* forms.

Finally, the same conclusions can be reached by analysing the boundary stone of Amandola, coming from an almost-mountainous area, and well known in the international scientific literature (see Moscatelli 1991). If we connect the co-ordinates relative to the *kardines* (at least 11 intervals) with a 20 *actus* form, we find that the centurial grid is 8 kilometers long, a result which is totally incompatible with the morphology of the location. But if, however, we use a grid made with rectangular lots of 1020 × 1400 Roman feet (measures which, although unusual, are described in the *Libri Coloniarum* and have been used for the nearby *ager Adteiatis: Lib. Col. I, 240, 10-15* Lach) we can convincingly connect the information presented in the boundary stone with the many traces still visible on the ground.

Thus it is largely a question of method: without taking into due consideration the Gromatic information on the variety of forms of ancient centuriations we run the risk of creating a very poor and inaccurate framework – and this, of course, would negatively affect the quality of the historical reconstruction of rural settlement. In other words, it is not proper to apply the model used for the Po Valley in a completely different morphological context. In fact, if we use the modular differentiation which was part of the ancient surveyor's technical knowledge, we can recognise a larger number of centurial grids; moreover we can greatly improve the quality of the results in all the cases where the 20 *actus* form was not very effective. Hence, we can attain a better definition of the ways through which both the land control and the degree of land exploitation were realised. For example, the noted existence of the centurial grid in the uneven land between Amandola and Sarnano shows the intensive level of occupation in the countryside. We could suppose that the choice of that special *ager* had been conditioned by the presence of large land properties, widespread to such a degree that the amount of land available for division was very limited. But this is only a theoretical possibility. In fact, the available archaeological and epigraphical data recommend a different frame. In the areas under study, the density of archaeological sites is usually rather high, so that we can reasonably think that the land ownership had to be very divided, at least during the age of large allotments. According to our present knowledge, the distribution of sites within the centuriated areas seems to show that the internal divisions were thought to denote no more than two farms for each *centuria*. Such a ratio does not seem to change according to the form: this is what happens for the centuriations of *Cluana* and *Pausulae*, respectively based on the 15 and 20 *actus* forms (figs. 2 and 3).

For historical reasons, and according to the Roman land surveyors, we can date back those grids which have been identified to the period of the Triumvirate-Augustan Age. Choquer *et al.* (1987) have suggested their own dating criteria for south Italy based on forms, arguing that the 15 and 16 *actus* forms belong to the Augustan era (cf. Moscatelli 1990b). But these might not be fully valid criteria. Indeed, it is possible that the choice of forms was due to some needs singled out during the planning stage. It is difficult now to read and describe these needs in their totality, but we can at least reconstruct some of them: the size of the average share of land to be assigned; the land morphology; the width of the *ager* available for the division. Comparison between the actual land morphology and *Cluana* centurial axes shows many concomitances between the natural elements (hollows, ridges, ridge-lines, and so on) and the system of *kardines* and *decumani*. Also the disposition of the axes clearly shows the purpose of choosing the longitudinal axis of the valley and the Fosso Pontignano water-course as the guiding structures of the grid. Of course, we can not expect a perfect superimposition of the geometrical scheme on the natural reality. Therefore, the choice of the 15 *actus* form was very likely forced by a variety of factors. In the Amandola-Sarnano system, the uneven surface morphology surely played a fundamental role in the choice of a form which had the significant advantage of being based on a set of short measurements. They were the only possible measurements which could enable the surveyors to overcome the technical problems created by the presence of a various natural obstacles obstructing the view.

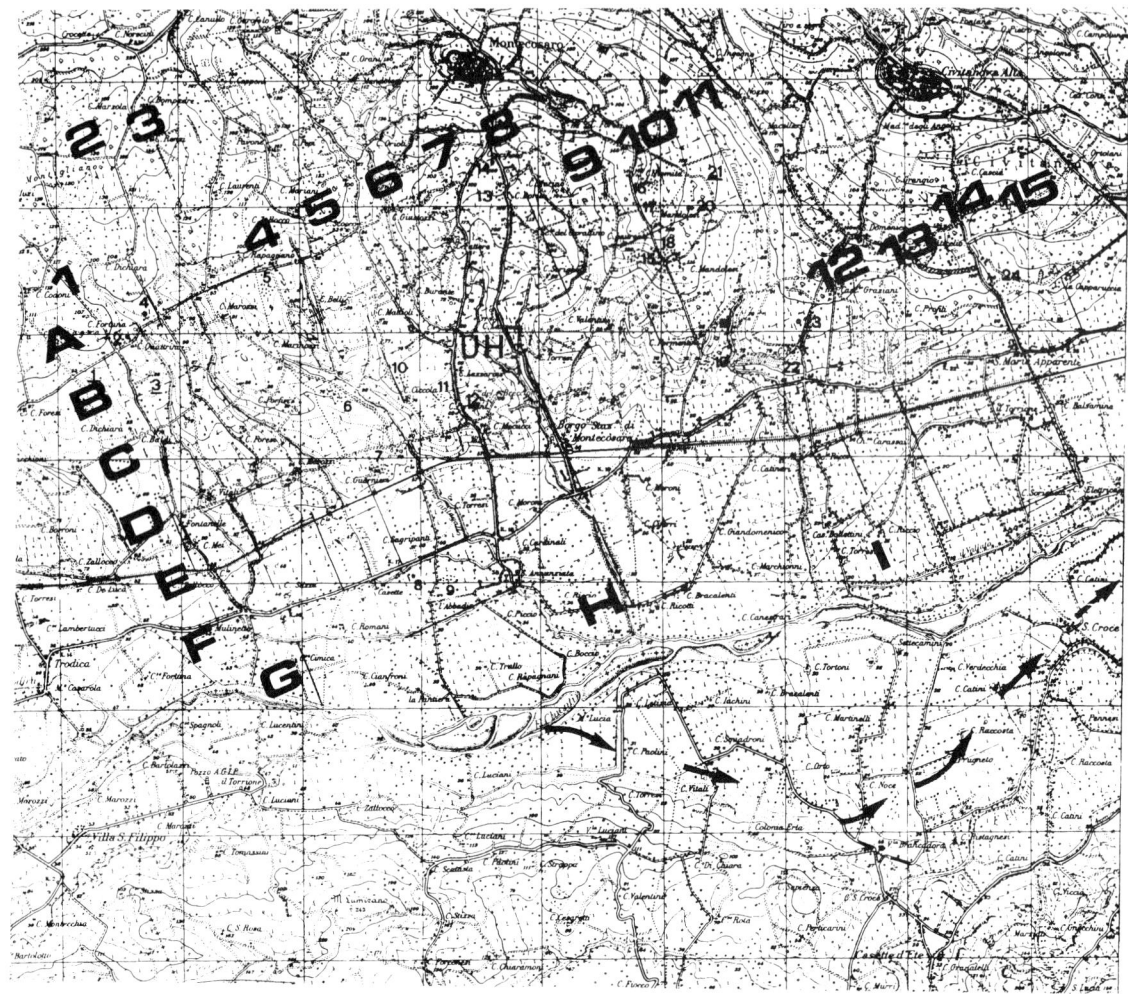

Fig. 2. Centuriation pattern in the territory of Cluana.

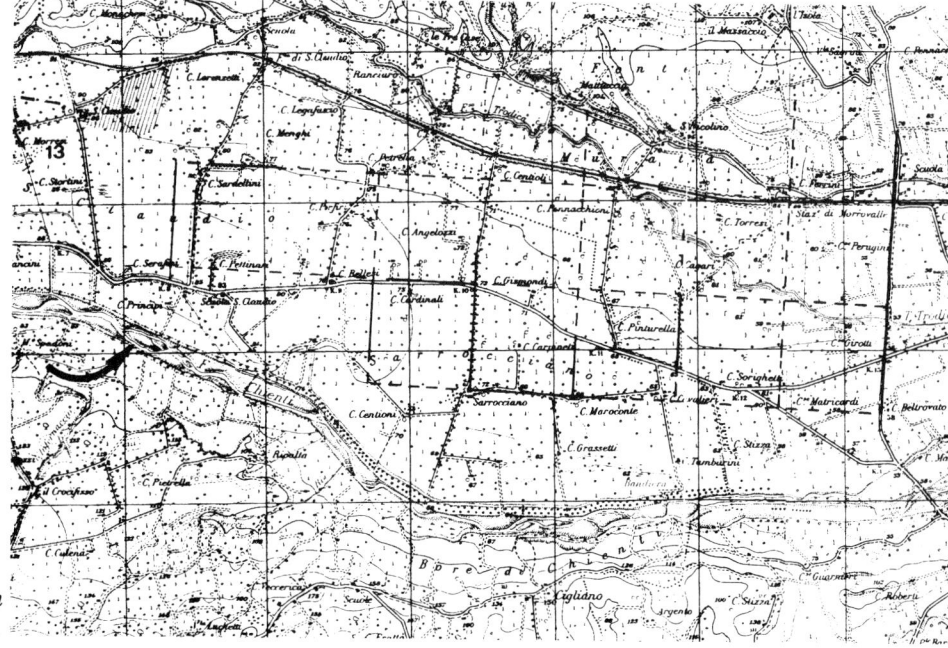

Fig. 3. Centuriation pattern in the territory of Pausulae.

The evolution of rural settlement in the Early Middle Ages: first approaches

In general, scholars maintain that, during the passage from the late Roman period to the Early Middle Ages, the Marche region went through a period of decay, during which many changes in the landscape took place. This happened particularly in those lands subjected to the Lombard domination, where the spread of woods, uncultivated areas and swamps was considerable. (Fumagalli 1992: 33, 76; Luzzato 1979: 26; Montanari 1981: 15; Sereni 1976: 69–72). And yet there are insufficient data to support these claims, particularly given the limited archaeological investigation of the land; scholars indeed have normally looked purely at events within the urban centres, which has had the consequence that only one aspect of the whole reality has been portrayed (Alfieri 1977; 1981). Indeed, the documentation is too poor to enable us to formulate any kind of thesis, especially since we lack any details about the dynamics of land property structures during the late Roman period.

Only from the middle of the 9th century AD can we claim a more reliable image, when we gain the invaluable evidence of the archives of the monastery of Farfa. These data describe an agrarian reality in which the woods, the uncultivated areas and the swamps do not seem to prevail over the cultivated fields. We find clear confirmation of this in the already mentioned studies on the Marchigian environment, thanks to which we can establish that many characteristics of the early medieval landscape already existed during Roman times. Of value in this respect is my research on the survival of place-names such as Salto/Salti, Gualdo, Spescia and Selva. The lemma *saltus* is present in both the cartographic documentation and the medieval documents describing differentiated morphological areas: the bottom of the valleys, areas close to the sea, hilly territories, interiors. Moreover, it is possible to find some cases of toponymic continuity. For example: close to Camerino (an area belonging to the Trevenano Court) are two place-names, Pian di Salto and Gualdo, which refer to the same place; while the area of *c.* 720 hectares between *Urbs Salvia* and *Falerio* features a concentration of place names such as Salti, Selva, Selva Grande and La Selva. This second example is of particular interest, since the place-names relating to Roman land owners virtually gird the whole area.

In brief, in accordance with recent scholarly thought (e.g. Verzar 1986: 683; Wickham 1983: 24; Migliario 1988: 57–58, 74–75), it seems reasonable to say that, although it is true that there was some extension to the woods and the uncultivated areas, this developed from an already existing basis.

Despite the poverty of the framework within which I operate, I think that it is possible to outline some working hypotheses. If, for example, we examine the map containing the positions of the *curtes* mentioned in the Farfa documents as existing before AD 1000 in the large territory between the Chienti Valley (in the north) and the Aso Valley (in the south), we observe that the *curtes* are located in those areas in which the percentage of Roman landowner place-names is very high. To take a few examples: in the territory of *Camerinum*, the data on the *curtis* of Trevenano are particularly interesting, with the *Largitorius* and *Regestus* indicating that the *curtis* occupied a large territory on both sides of the Chienti river, strongly characterised by the presence of place-names relating to landowners. Among the different districts present on this territory, we find the following *fundi: Trevenano, Fereliano, Galuniano, Bocariano, Borgiano, Manciano, Toreliano, Rosiano, Seneizano, Carpiniano, Vintiliano, Terrentiano, Verculiano, Salto*. Since the medieval documents show the boundaries of the above *fundi*, it is possible to go back to the original positions of most place-names, only a few of which still survive in the present cartography (fig. 4).

Similarly the *curtis in fundo Vestiliano*, a few kilometres

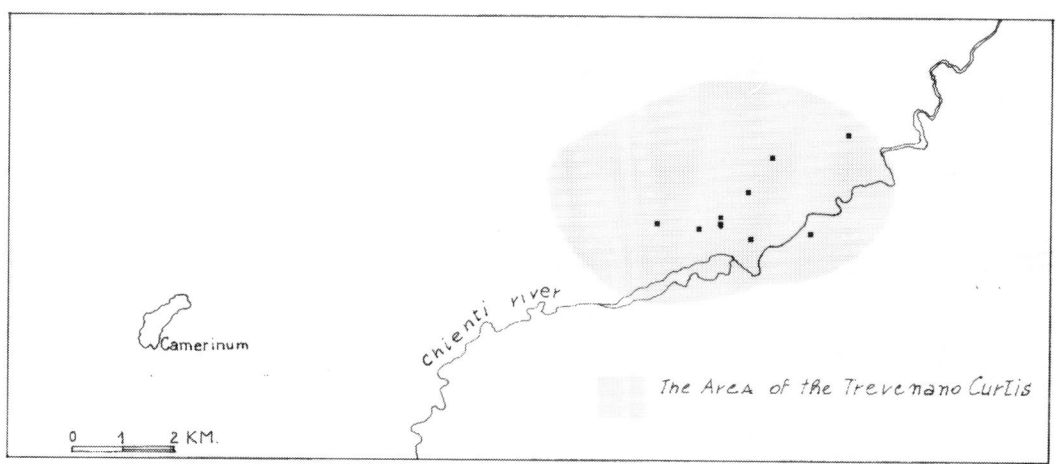

Fig. 4. Territory of the Trevenano curtis with land owner place-names marked.

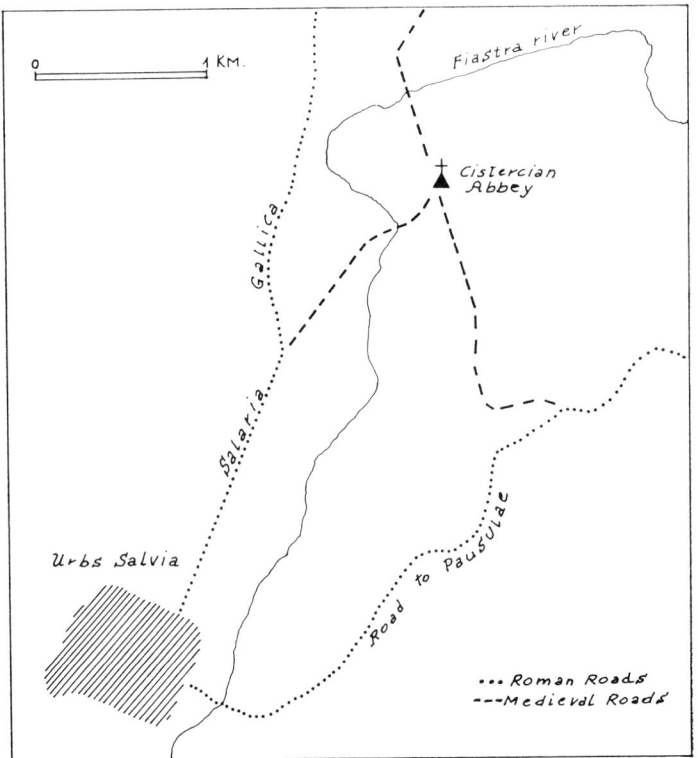

Fig. 5. Chiarvalle di Fiastra abbey: location and roads

south-west of *Trevenano*, seems to be somehow connected with an ex-Roman *fundus*. This *curtis* is first mentioned in a document dated from 833 (*Larg. I*, n.59).

In the *Urbs Salvia* (Urbisaglia) territory, the *curtis de Molliano*, mentioned several times in the *Liber Largitorius*, may be the closest to the Roman city in the 9th century AD. The *curtis* lay outside the *ager urbisalviensis* belt of land in which, as noted, there are no land-owner place-names.

Thus there seems to exist, at least on a geographical basis, a precise relationship between the rural organisation with a Longobard tradition and the Roman landed structure. Clearly we need to understand the historical meaning of such connections, through both topographical research and archaeological excavation. The rural settlements so far identified nearby the sites where the later *curtes* established themselves, are too little known; therefore, they cannot yet provide us with useful elements for detailed discussion.

If we look at the territories of *Urbs Salvia*, *Pausulae*, *Cluana* (two *municipia* along the Chienti Valley) and *Camerinum* from the perspective of settlement evolution, then we find far more data. In the specific case of *Urbs Salvia*, the town's territory clearly covered a very large area, containing the whole Fiastra Valley. It is reasonable to think that the *ager* extended inland and south-east for many kilometres, as far as the beginning of the Appennines, where its boundaries met those of *Camerinum* in the north and of *Falerio* in the south. As to the northern administrative boundaries of the colony, they went beyond the Chienti river, as it is proved by the still recognisable remains of the Roman centuriation on both banks of the river (Vettorazzi 1990).

The Roman roads running within the *ager Urbisalviensis* comprised one section of the *Salaria Gallica* (Alfieri, Gasperini & Paci 1985), and the roads connecting *Urbs Salvia* to *Tolentinum*, and *Pausulae* to *Falerio* (Moscatelli 1990). The rural settlement gravitates around the roads. Many sites have been identified within and around the centuriated area, and these suggest a rather capillary occupation of the *ager*. On the basis of the surface pottery, this occupation probably began at the end of the 1st century BC and lasted until the 4th-5th century AD. A good number of funerary monuments and villa sites exist. Particularly interesting is the case of a modern farm built on the walls of a Roman rural settlement, located along the *Salaria Gallica*. By examining the walls which have survived – a very good *opus latericium* – we can identify some rooms. The complex made use of a sizeable aqueduct situated in the south. The agrarian divisions were realized in the north-east sector of the territory, an area surrounded by the main roads. Studies on landscape changes following the realisation of agrarian allotments are underway.

During the Early Middle Ages, a few kilometres east of the Roman city and, therefore, distant from the ancient roads built on the valley bottom, the *curtis de Molliano* took shape. According to some scholars, this *curtis* had belonged to the Farfa monastery since the beginning of the 8th century AD (Pacini 1966). Certainly it is clear that the *fundus Molianus* played a very significant role and within this *fundus* lay the *fundus Pappianus*, mentioned in a document from July 948: *Domnus Hildebrandus abbas concessit cuidam Ramperto filio Alberici in .III. generationem res iuris huius monasterii, in fundo Moliano vocabulo Pappiano, terre et silve modia .CC. adunata* (*Lib. Larg.*, n. 235).

The *castrum Moliani* (present Mogliano) was built at the start of the 11th century. More than a century later (1142) the Cistercian Abbey of Chiaravalle di Fiastra was founded (fig.5) in the centuriated area, next to one of the main crossroads of the grid. This event modified the network of roads and added two new roads: one which ran west of the *Salaria Gallica*, the second one which connected the Abbey with the ancient road going to *Pausulae*. Only at this date can we see significant changes to the Roman system emerging.

Acknowledgement

I wish to thank Dr. Sergio Cicconi, who kindly translated this paper.

Bibliography

Alfieri, N. 1968. 'La centuriazione romana nelle basse valli del Potenza e del Chienti', *Studi Maceratesi*, 4, 215–225.

Alfieri, N. 1977. 'L'insediamento urbano sul litorale delle Marche durante l'antichità e il Medioevo', in *Themes de recherches sur le villes antiques d'Occident*, Paris, 87–96.

Alfieri, N. 1981. 'Le Marche e la fine del mondo antico', in *Istituzioni e società nell'alto Medioevo marchigiano, Atti del Convegno della Deputazione di Storia Patria per le Marche*, Roma, 9–34.

Alfieri, N., Gasperini, L. & Paci, G. 1985. 'Marci Octavii lapis Aesinensis', *Picus*, V, 7–50.

Baldetti, E. 1988. *Aspetti topografico-storici dei toponimi medievali nelle valli del Misa e del Cesano*, Bologna.

Bonora, G. 1987. 'Rapporti tra centuriazione e viabilità nella valle del Tenna', in *Le strade nelle Marche. Il problema nel tempo, Atti del Convegno della Deputazione di Storia Patria per le Marche*, 417–430.

Chouquer, G., Clavel Levèque, M., Favory, F. & Vallat, J.P. 1987. *Structures agraires en Italie centro-meridionale. Cadastres et paysages ruraux*, Roma.

Cruciani Fabozzi, G. 1991. 'Per una revisione dei lineamenti di studio e di tutela dei castelli medievali delle Marche', *Studi Maceratesi*, 24, 23–46.

Dall'Aglio, P. 1987. 'La viabilità romana nelle medie a alte valli del F. Cesano e del F. Misa, in *Le strade nelle Marche. Il problema nel tempo, Atti del Convegno della Deputazione di Storia Patria per le Marche*, Ancona, 325–348.

Dall'Aglio, P. & Bonora, G. 1991. 'La centuriazione', in *Archeologia delle valli marchigiane Misa, Nevola e Cesano*, Perugia, 28–34.

Ferranti, P. 1985. *Memorie storiche della città di Amandola*, Ripatransone.

Fumagalli, V. 1992. *L'uomo e l'ambiente nel Medioevo*, Bari.

Luni, M. 1984. 'Topografia storica di Pisaurum e del territorio', in *Pesaro nell'antichità. Storia e monumenti*, Venezia, 109–180.

Luzzatto, G. 1979. *Breve storia economica dell'Italia medievale*, Torino.

Mercando, L. 1979. 'Marche. Rinvenimenti di insediamenti rurali', *Notizie degli Scavi di Antichità*, 180–280.

Mercando, L., Brecciaroli, L. & Paci, G. 1981. 'Forme d'insediamento nel territorio marchigiano in età romana: ricerca preliminare', in *Società romana e produzione schiavistica*, I, Roma, 311–354.

Migliario, E. 1988. *Strutture della proprietà agraria in Sabina dall'età imperiale all'alto Medioevo*, Firenze.

Montanari, M. & Baruzzi, M. 1981. *Porci e porcari nel Medioevo*, Bologna.

Moscatelli, U. 1985. 'Municipi romani della V regio augustea: problemi storici ed urbanistici del Piceno centro-settentrionale (III-I sec. a.C.)', *Picus*, V, 51–97.

Moscatelli, U. 1988. *Trea*, Firenze.

Moscatelli, U. & Vettorazzi, L. 1988. 'Aspetti delle divisioni agrarie romane nelle Marche', in *Le Marche. Archeologia storia territorio*, 7–84.

Moscatelli, U. 1990a. 'Urbs Salvia: lettura preliminare di un territorio', *Studi Maceratesi*, XXIII, 79–86.

Moscatelli, U. 1990b. 'A proposito di alcune recenti ricerche in Italia centro-meridionale', *Annali della Facoltà di Lettere e Filosofia dell'Università di Macerata*, XXII-XXIII, 659–677.

Moscatelli, U. 1991. 'Resti di divisioni agrarie nel territorio tra Amandola e Sarnano in età romana', *Annali della Facoltà di Lettere e Filosofia dell'Università di Macerata*, XXIV, 529–550.

Moscatelli, U. 1993. '*Mensuram aacipere debebunt*. Sulla pratica agrimensoria romana in collina', *Ancient Society*, 24, 103–118.

Moscatelli, U. 1994. 'Approci complementari per lo studio della toponomastica prediale romane nelle Marche', in *Le Marche. Archeologia storia territorio*, 1991–93, 99–140.

Pacini, D. 1966. 'I Monaci di Farfa nelle valli picene del Chienti e del Potenza', *Studi Maceratesi*, 2, 129–174.

Sereni, E. 1976. *Storia del paesaggio agrario italiano*, Bari.

Sirago, V.A. 1982. 'I catilinari piceni', *Picus*, II, 69–85.

Verzar Bass, M. 1986. 'Le trasformazioni agrarie tra Adriatico nord-orientale e Norico', in *Società romana e impero tardoantico. III Gli insediamenti*, Bari, 647–685.

Vettorazzi, L. 1990. 'Ricerche topografiche nel territorio a nord di Urbs Salvia', in *Le Marche. Archeologia storia territorio*, 97–136.

Wickham, C. 1983. *L'Italia nel primo Medioevo*, Milano.

33

Late Antique Cavemen in Northern and Central Italy

NEIL CHRISTIE

(School of Archaeological Studies, University of Leicester)

Summary: *The usual image of the late antique-early medieval transition in Italy is one of dislocation of settlement, marked by a shrinkage or even an abandonment of the urban landscape, and by a collapse of the open farm system and a flight to the hills. The archaeology of this period is still only crudely understood, making it hard to refine this image of decay, which remains far too simplistic. Besides examining the fate of towns and the origin of hilltop villages, a potentially useful avenue of research may be to scrutinise the evidence for the reuse of caves as shelters and as permanent homes. This paper briefly discusses the limited data so far available for investigating these late antique cave dwellers.*

INTRODUCTION

The present disastrous conflicts in former Yugoslavia have provided some horrendously clear indicators of the effects of war on urban civilian and peasant populations: these include, amongst many others, the destruction of town structures, the displacement of populations, the advent of disease and polluted water supplies, and the enforced abandonment of large scale rural activities. Although the weapons of war, the level of conflict and the means of communications differ drastically from those of the ancient world, it can be argued nonetheless that it is possible to tie in the present martial events and effects into pre-modern and antique contexts. A key period for comparison is the break-up of Roman rule when, as well as external invaders, the Roman social fabric was collapsing, as marked by civil disorders, barbarisation of the army, highway robbery, land depopulation and general urban decay. In many regions of the old Empire the transition from Roman to Germanic rule was indeed very long drawn-out: there was nowhere (as often is presumed) a straightforward abandonment of villas, towns and material culture, but everywhere a piecemeal decay or transition in settlement systems, sometimes strongly contrasting with the classical Roman set-up but in other cases denoting merely a reduced continuity of life and style.

The problem has been that, archaeologically, these transitions have as yet been little examined systematically within the old Empire, with the result that broad statements like Roman 'collapse' or 'decline and fall' still hold sway and continue to suggest rapid overnight change. On paper at least, political changes may well have been sudden – as in the termination of official Roman control in Britain in 410 or in Italy in 476 – but these changes do not always register, even in contemporary documents. On a lower, human level, namely that of the peasant farmer or the town dweller, any transition may have been only barely perceptible: the failure to maintain a highway, a decline in foreign wines or a rise in their price, or the absence of a supply of coin. But it is impossible for us to visualise the impact of such changes on the immediate level: how widely was a decline, decay or transition recognised? Was it even viewed as a decline, or was it the case that each person adapted to modifying circumstances without recognising the much wider trends? When dealing in centuries or decades as is the wont of an historian or an archaeologist, broad changes may well be obvious, but yearly, let alone day-to-day changes which more closely affected past populations, are not easily perceived unless one thinks of a destruction of a site by fire or earthquake when a single moment in time can be touched. Modern populations, even in war-torn Bosnia, are served by modern news and communications networks which allow for the broader picture to be observed: each community can thus recognise the political machinations, the economic dealings and the manoeuvrings which are affecting the situation – but of course these instantaneous sources of information were lacking in antiquity and we cannot really be certain how well informed, if at all, a 5th century Italian peasant farmer was of contemporary politics and wars.

Only now are archaeological data becoming available for attempting to address some of these problems in the wider theme of transition from the Roman to the medieval world. Of high importance is urban archaeology and its realisation that the fragmentary and impoverished culture and structures of the early medieval centuries can indeed be recognised between the Roman quality layers and the late medieval and modern intrusions (Brogiolo 1984). Yet the very fragility of the data means that patterns remain uncertain and conclusions regarding settlement are still a long way off. The urban finds do however mean that slightly more can be said of events in the countryside, where over thirty years of field survey work in parts of central Italy have largely failed to provide a clear vision of the sequence of rural change in the period AD 500 – 1000 (cf. Potter 1979: 138–167). The material poverty identified through close scrutiny in the urban centres is even harder to identify in disturbed contexts in the ploughed countryside. This impoverishment has too frequently led both historians and archaeologists to claim massive depopulation of the land and even a complete cessation of lowland farming activity. The picture offered comprises a shelter of peasants in towns, or a flight to the heights of hills to eke out a prehistoric existence. Only with a fuller resumption of documentary sources and a tangible appearance of castles on hills from the 10th and 11th centuries does the picture once more gain a fairly clear definition.

The usual picture for the post-Roman centuries is too simplistic by far. Certainly it cannot be denied that in some areas rural depopulation was intense, brought about by exposure of a zone to consistent or aggravatingly intermittent insecurity; in other areas, however, villa excavations might suggest some level of habitation persisting well into the 9th century. For towns, meanwhile, excavations are now showing that there was life in them but that these centres were economically distraught and with many parts of their civic landscape ruinous or turned over to cultivation (cf. Brogiolo 1989; La Rocca 1986). And yet, often in stark contrast with this archaeological image, the few documentary sources available continue to speak of thriving political and religious affairs within the walls of towns and a continued ornamentation of churches, all suggesting that nothing much had really changed (cf. Balzaretti 1991). The documentary sources are of course restricted and restrictive: some speak of barren fields and barbarian hordes on the rampage, yet others list church income from estates and land transactions. No single image should be expected: different areas responded and were affected differently from others; abandonment in one area does not mean regional abandonment; likewise survival of one villa need not denote the general survival of open farming patterns. The argument is clear: we are still at far too early a stage to make any sort of conclusion; far more data need to be accumulated before anything solid can be said.

Insecurity ancient and modern:
a return to the caves

This paper seeks to add a few more scraps of information to the databank of post-Roman settlement by highlighting an often overlooked feature of the period, namely the reoccupation of cave sites. The evidence available for this is in many cases extremely slight, but sufficient to suggest that it was a fairly common phenomenon in the period of the break-up of Roman rule and beyond. Returning to the theme of modern warfare in former Yugoslavia, brief news coverage was given to the instance of the occupation of various caves in the hinterland of bombarded towns and villages by refugee families. A particular instance concerned the east Bosnian centre of Zepa, whose Muslim population of 6000 persons, swollen by the addition of over 20,000 refugees, lay under siege by the Serbs for fourteen months, before days of bombardment by tanks forced the vast majority of the inhabitants to flee in desperation into the mountains, leaving Zepa a ghost town. The families took with them what few personal belongings remained and hid out in caves and other shelters, gathering what few natural food resources existed in the vicinity. Only when Zepa was declared a UN-protected town did the "desperate Muslim civilians, hungry and clad in makeshift garments stitched together from US parachutes, emerge from caves and shelters in the east Bosnian mountains and begin to trickle back" (report by Ian Traynor, *The Guardian*, 12 May 1993. The very recent Serb capture of Zepa on 25 July, 1995, despite the nominal UN protection, prompted further recourse to caves as well as flight to Sarajevo: report by Emma Daly, *The Independent*, 26 July 1995).

In this and in most other cases, the cave-dwelling was a brief phase of panic activity, marking simply a retreat from exposed and undefended settlements and a temporary sheltering in an upland location. Subsequently most families withdrew to towns or camps offering some degree of protection, with these refugee town dwellers unused to the inconvenience of hunter-gathering and more than fearing their fate in the hills. But in some instances occupation seems to have continued as the residents held out for better days to come, with stability allowing for them to reoccupy their former homes.

In transferring this image of panic response to the setting of the late and post-Roman Italy, some modifications should be made. An important factor to bear in mind is that the inhabitants of 5th century Italy lacked the range of modern civilising conveniences such as canned food, electricity, heating, etc., and so a transfer of residence from house to cave or from riverside to hilltop will have been one of superable inconvenience and not a wholesale changeover in lifestyle. Obviously food pressures could have been intense, but most 5th century citizens would have been part-time farmers at least and in no way dependent on local supermarket times. The uprooting of residence will have been traumatic of course, but there may have been a comparably less intense desire on the part of these refugees to return to the towns once the level of insecurity diminished. Much of this is speculative, but should be considered when analysing the archaeologically-recognised decline of both town and country in late antique Italy. Nor can the picture be applied wholesale since responses will have differed from zone to zone depending on the level of insecurity felt, the strength of nearby towns and forts, the local topography, and, just as importantly, human resilience. Hence the recognition of cave reoccupation in 6th century Liguria does not require the contemporary reuse of caves in Tuscany.

As noted above, the evidence for cave reuse in Late Antiquity is scattered and not well documented. Only in Sicily and southern Italy, where extensive cave villages and towns ('insediamenti rupestri') exist and in some cases persist, has much academic research been focussed on early medieval and medieval cave dwelling, although here greatest emphasis is placed on art historical studies of church wall paintings. In southern Italy at least it is the case that fairly small scale initial settlement activity – perhaps going back to late Roman times or alternatively to the Byzantine-Longobard period – expanded through permanency to create large scale medieval and later village communities, as viable alternatives to open, above-ground settlements (similar, of course, to the well known Cappadocian sites in central Turkey) (The data for Puglia in particular are well summarised in Fonseca 1970; *La civiltà* 1975; De Vitis 1990. Extensive continuity in sites like Grottaglie, Mottola and Massafra in the province of Taranto has, however, removed most tangible traces of early activity).

Leaving aside the south Italian cave settlements, the following section instead briefly seeks to consider the data for cave usage in northern and central Italy where the level or frequency of subterranean activity was nowhere sufficient to create permanent cave communities. The causes for this disparity between north and south remain to be investigated. Here the aim is merely to offer a summary of the main archaeological evidence, with a view to highlighting the current inadequacies of research in this field.

LATE ANTIQUE CAVE DWELLERS IN ITALY

Although cave sites abound in the Alpine zones of Italy, recognition of post-prehistoric and pre-modern usage of such caves and shelters is extremely limited, and where recognised the attention given to the archaeological data is cursory at best. A few exceptions exist, however. For example, in Piedmont, prov. of Vercelli, the site of Monfenera offers three caves (Ciota Ciara, Belvedere and Ciutarun), each of which yielded finds spanning the late Roman to medieval periods (Fedele 1975). The strongest evidence came from the Belvedere cave with historic period finds commencing from the 3rd/4th century (and including a coin of mid-4th century date) and extending into the 6th or 7th century. Although a possible gap is claimed before resumption of settlement activity in the 10th-12th centuries, the break might be not be real and instead merely reflect the absence of any closely datable early medieval ceramic type. Alternatively, if there was a break, this would correspond reasonably to the hypothesis of relative stability in northern Italy during the period of later Longobard and early Carolingian rule. Nonetheless, the excavators claimed that Belvedere witnessed "una intensa occupazione altomedievale e medievale" (Fedele 1975: 278).

Fairly substantial data are available for the modern region of Liguria with late antique activity recognised at a series of well-excavated coastal and inland cave sites, such as Arene Candide, Le Manie and Pollera, with a particular concentration of activity in the Finalese zone in Western Liguria (Mannoni 1983: 263; Christie 1990: 256–257. Only in a few cases, however, has a full publication appeared and not always with full consideration of the historic period materials. Most of the relevant finds are displayed or stored at the Museo Civico d'Archeologia Ligure at Pegli-Genova). Best studied of the Ligurian sites is the Caverna delle Arene Candide, with occupation extending from the 4th millennium BC into the 1st millennium AD (fig.1). Over 0.5m of disturbed stratification existed for the Roman to post-Roman period, whose latest finds comprised sherds of pietra ollare and a glass stem beaker – again seen as sufficient to indicate that the "caverna ha continuato ad essere ancora intensamente frequentata fino agli inizi del medio evo" (Bernabò Brea 1946: 33–35, 253–255). Pietra ollare or soapstone appears a common find in late Roman and early medieval contexts in Liguria and its presence in these cave sites must signify that these settlements were not isolated but enjoyed contacts with the local urban markets (cf. Murialdo *et al*. 1986: 236–241); indeed, there is good evidence to show that the region remained fairly prosperous into the 7th century with urban sites like Finale and Albenga receiving various foreign imports (cf. Christie 1990). The Longobard take-over of Liguria from the mid-7th century may well have contributed to the decline in both trade and markets and perhaps consolidated this phase of cave settlement although, of course, frustratingly, dateable finds to verify such continuity are absent.

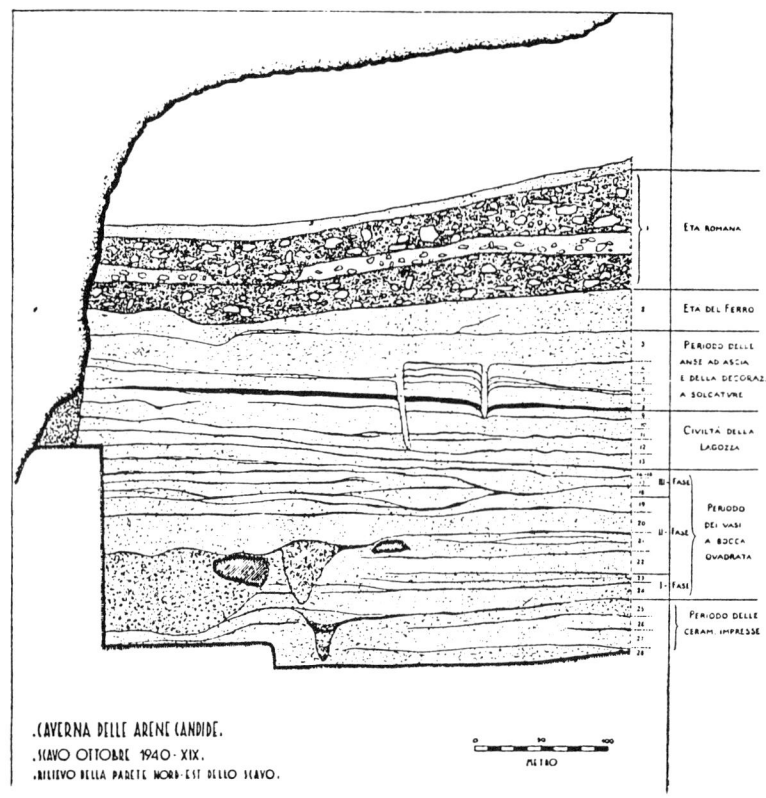

Fig. 1. Internal stratigraphy in part of the Caverna delle Arene Candide, revealing extensive 'Roman'-period site activity (Bernabó Brea 1946: fig. 4).

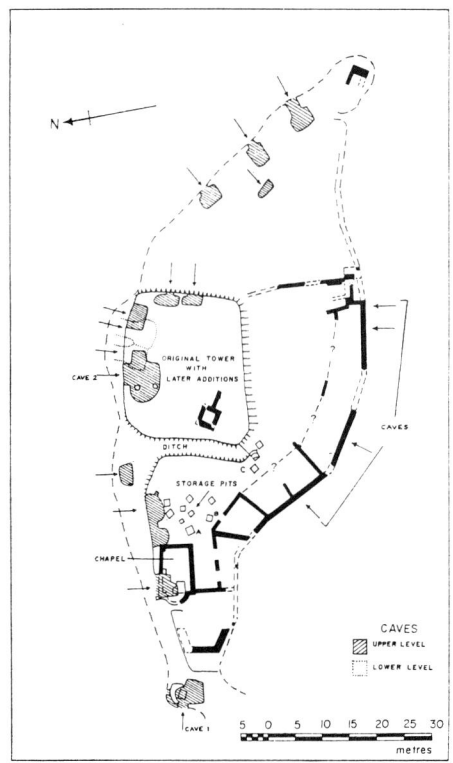

Fig. 2. Plan of Castel Porciano, showing the location of numerous rock-cut dwellings and stores (Mallett & Whitehouse 1967: fig. 5).

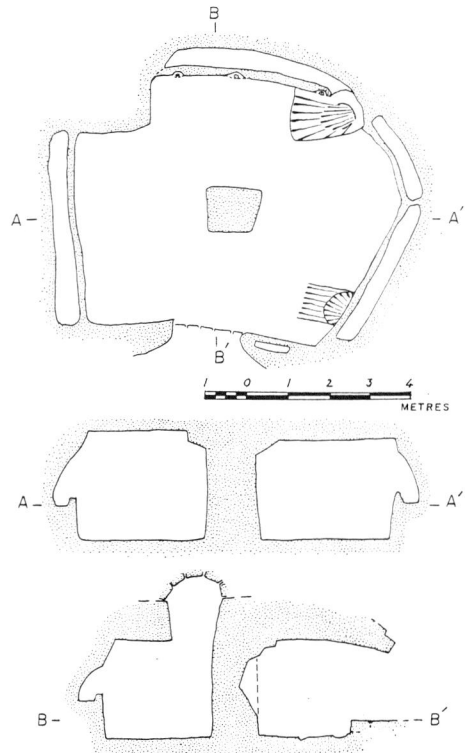

Fig. 3. Castel Porciano. Plan and cross-sections of cave no. 2 (Mallett & Whitehouse 1967: fig. 9).

Central Italy, and Northern Lazio and South Etruria in particular, features numerous instances of cave dwellings cut into the tufa of hills, promontories and spurs such as Castel Porciano (Mallett & Whitehouse 1967: 133–134), Salce (Andrews 1981: 318–319), Ponte Nepesino (Cameron *et al.* 1984: 72–73) and Belmonte (Stiesdal 1962). In most cases dating is difficult and the occupation of these subterranean spaces can generally only be broadly set to a pre-12th century period; problematic of course is the start date to many of these sites, although finds of *ceramica a vetrina pesante* ('Forum Ware') are sufficient in some cases to verify 10th or 11th century activity, while in other cases documentary sources push this date back still further (for example, Salce is first documented in 796) with the possibility also offered of origins, as yet archaeologically invisible, in the 6th-8th centuries (cf. Christie 1987: 458–463). Useful in this regard is the identification and partial excavation of a cave at Mola di Monte Gelato, whose period of occupancy can be set to the 9th-10th centuries AD on the basis of finds from an abandonment deposit – the use of this cave, and, probably, others in the vicinity, thus coincides with the fully examined 9th-11th century church complex (Potter, forthcoming).

Problematic in most cases is determining the function of these caves: do they denote the primary occupational points of the site or are they secondary storage areas used in conjunction with above-ground stone-built houses? In some cases habitational use seems clear, but in others changing functions from living to storage are apparent. In the case of Castel Porciano the tufa had been cut to provide rectangular rooms, some of which contained central columns, cupboard areas, and chimneys while others featured troughs and mangers (cf. Mallett & Whitehouse 1967: 133–134; Potter 1979: 158) (figs. 2 and 3). Potentially also the caves may have functioned both as storage points and as shelters, used in case of external threat.

Discussion

It could be argued that the reuse or reoccupation of caves in late antique and early medieval Italy relates to two diverse responses: firstly, a rural/civilian response, in which 'peasants' utilise such shelters as an immediate haven, avoiding insecurity, but with a progressive evolution of such sites from refuge to home. After all, caves were cheap to maintain (and, where the stone permitted, extendable), offered warm and relatively constant internal temperatures, and for the most part were suitably secluded (cf. Kempe 1988, passim). The second response could be deemed to be of military origin, whereby hilltops were chosen for their defensive capabilities and, where available, caves were adopted as an accepted mode of habitation. The tufaceous South Etrurian promontories of Ponte Nepesino and Castel Porciano could fit into this context, although the dispute here remains of whether these hilltop centres were indeed military in scope (Mallett & Whitehouse 1967; cf. Christie 1987: 458–463). In parts of southern Italy various towns, villages and monasteries feature a honeycomb network of cave dwellings – ostensibly civilian in content, although as ever, some military involvement in their foundation cannot easily be excluded. Potentially it could be argued that survival of such a site might signify a civilian origin, and that abandonment indicates a military one, where the loss of its former military significance negated its existence. The interpretative framework is perhaps flimsy, but should at least provide initial models for testing.

A further necessary comment is that caves need not denote second-class or isolated settlements: in the case of the Caverna delle Arene Candide in Liguria the finds of *pietra ollare* and also part of a stem goblet might well indicate that such sites remained involved in farming and market activity. Elsewhere non-urban settlement was presumably in timber huts perhaps on hills and these huts would require constant repair or rebuilding; in this respect caves had one solid advantage, namely that of permanency. For most of the period AD 500–1000 we know nothing of these timber built farms – hence the caves at least offer us some initial guide as to material culture/poverty for this dark epoch.

Overall it can be stated that late antique and medieval cave dwelling in northern and central Italy has been very much ignored, due to the potentially more interesting data to be derived from an in-depth study of the prehistoric phases. Even in southern Italy, recent studies have focussed too far on church structures and their wall paintings and far too little on their broader social contexts. Caves tend of course to be excavated by specialists in prehistory and 'recent' or historic phase material is accordingly sidelined in reports (cf. Branigan & Dearne 1992). In part this is due to the fragility of these upper, historic layers, disturbed through modern inspection or reuse, but should no longer be so in a time when more exacting excavation techniques are practised and all archaeological data are in theory retrieved and interpreted. Until this changes we will remain in the dark regarding the level of such historic reuse of caves – was it commonplace or atypical in the early medieval era in northern and central Italy? How far did this reuse signify temporary/seasonal/permanent occupation of the caves? Why do cave settlements evolve in southern Italy and not in the north? The basic temporal limits of such reuse likewise remain wholly vague as yet, and thus it is impossible to discern whether a shelter or fixed occupational status persisted only until the insecurity which may have instigated reuse lessened or whether occupation, once begun, continued even beyond this. The trouble is of course that our best answers to these questions lie in unexplored sites.

Acknowledgements

My thanks to Hugh Porter of the The Guardian and Tony Barber of The Independent newspapers for their kind assistance in hunting out references to the instance of cave occupation around Zepa in east Bosnia. I must also acknowledge the generous assistance of Dott.ssa Eugenia Isetti at the Museo Civico d'Archeologia Ligure, Pegli (Genova) in allowing me access to late antique finds from the Finalese cave sites. Finally, my thanks to Dr. Tim Potter of the Department of Prehistoric and Romano-British Antiquities at the British Museum for allowing me to read the final Monte Gelato report in advance of publication.

Bibliography

Andrews, D. 1981. 'The archaeology of the medieval castrum in Central Italy', in G. Barker & R. Hodges (eds.), *Archaeology and Italian Society: Papers in Italian Archaeology II*, British Archaeological Reports S-102, Oxford, 313–334.

Balzaretti, R. 1991. 'History, archaeology and early medieval urbanism: the north Italian debate', *Accordia Research Papers* 2, 87–104.

Bernabò Brea, L. 1946. *Gli scavi nella Caverna delle Arene Candide, I. Gli strati con ceramiche*, Bordighera.

Branigan, K. & Dearne, M. 1992. *Romano-British Cavemen. Cave use in Roman Britain*, (Oxbow Archaeological Monograph 19), Oxford.

Brogiolo, G.P. 1984. 'La città tra tarda antichità e medioevo', in *Archeologia in Lombardia*, Modena, 48–55.

Brogiolo, G.P. 1989. 'Brescia: transformations in a Lombard city', in K. Randsborg (ed.), *The Birth of Europe. Archaeology and Social Change in the First Millennium A.D.*, Rome, 156–165.

Cameron, F., Clark, G., Jackson, R., Johns, C., Philpot, S., Potter, T.W., Shepherd, J., Stone, M., & Whitehouse, D. 1984: 'Il castello di Ponte Nepesino e il confine settentrionale del Ducato di Roma', *Archeologia Medievale*, XI, 63–148.

Christie, N. 1987. 'Forum Ware, the Duchy of Rome, and Incastellamento: problems in interpretation', *Archeologia Medievale*, XIV, 451–466.

Christie, N. 1990. 'Byzantine Liguria: an imperial province against the Longobards, A.D. 568–643', *Papers of the British School at Rome*, 58, 229–271.

De Vitis, S. 1990. 'Il territorio ionico: insediamenti urbani e rurali in età altomedievale', *XXXVII Corso di Cultura sull'Arte Ravennate e Bizantina: L'Italia Meridionale fra Goti e Longobardi*, Ravenna, 169–183.

Fedele, F. 1975. 'Scoperte e ricerche di archeologia medievale sul Monfenera (Valsesia)', *Bollettino Storico-Bibliografico Subalpino*, LXXIII, 269–287.

Fonseca, C.D. 1970. *Civiltà rupestre di terra jonica*, Milan.

Kempe, D. 1988. *Living Underground. A History of Cave and Cliff Dwelling*, London.

La civiltà 1975. *La civiltà rupestre medievale nel Mezzogiorno d'Italia*, Genoa.

La Rocca, C. 1986. '"Dark Ages" a Verona. Edilizia privata, aree aperte e strutture pubbliche in una città dell'Italia settentrionale', *Archeologia Medievale*, XI, 31–78.

Mallett, D. & Whitehouse, D. 1967. 'Castel Porciano: an abandoned medieval village in the Roman Campagna', *Papers of the British School at Rome*, 35, 113–146.

Mannoni, T. 1983. 'Insediamenti poveri nella Liguria di età romana e bizantina', *Rivista di Studi Liguri*, XLIX, 254–264.

Murialdo, G., Fossati, A., Falcetti, C. & Bonora, E. 1986. 'La pietra ollare nel Finalese', *Atti della giornata di studio, "Archeologia in Liguria: la pietra ollare"* (*Rivista di Studi Liguri*, lii), 217–242.

Potter, T.W. 1979. *The Changing Landscape of South Etruria*, London.

Potter, T.W. (ed.), forthcoming. *The Mola di Monte Gelato*, London.

Stiesdal, H. 1962. 'Three deserted medieval villages in the Roman Campagna', *Analecta Romana Instituti Danici*, II, 63–100.

34

L'Abruzzo Tardoantico ed Altomedievale nelle Fonti Archeologiche: Urbanesimo, Popolamento Rurale, Economia e Cultura Materiale

Andrea R. Staffa

(Soprintendenza Archeologica dell'Abruzzo, Chieti)

Sommario: *Sulla base di numerosi nuovi scavi condotti fra 1988 e 1992, di ricognizioni sistematiche di vaste aree della regione, si propone uno studio sulle principali dinamiche di riassetto urbano e territoriale della regione Abruzzese fra la tarda antichità e l'epoca di riassetto connesso all'incastellamento ed allo sviluppo del Regno Normanno (secc. IV-XII). Si analizzano i fenomeni di trasformazione e persistenza dell'abitato in numerosi centri urbani, l'evoluzione dell'abitato rurale dalle ville antiche occupate sino al VI sec., all'insediamento dei Longobardi, ai villaggi a capanne tipici dell'età altomedievale, di cui si propongono vari esempi fatti oggetti di recenti indagini, delineando infine un panorama delle dinamiche che portano all'incastellamento, comunque non uniformemente diffuso.*

I. Nota introduttiva

Le ricerche archeologiche condotte in Abruzzo negli ultimi anni sono andate concentrandosi finalmente anche sulle problematiche dell'assetto dei centri urbani e del territorio come va progressivamente trasformandosi fra tarda antichità ed altomedioevo, sino alla definizione in età medievale più avanzata di un quadro urbanistico e rurale che resta sostanzialmente quasi immutato sino all'età contemporanea. Sono al proposito già disponibili i primi contributi analitici, dedicati ad un esame complessivo delle problematiche del popolamento e della cultura materiale (cfr. numerosi contributi di Staffa; Feller & Giuntella 1992). Ad essi si rinvia per eventuali approfondimenti sul panorama di dati che costituiscono la base della presente proposta di sintesi preliminare.

II. Urbanesimo in Abruzzo fra tarda antichità ed altomedioevo

II.1 La crisi tardoantica (sec.IV-VI)

Le città abruzzesi si conservavano ancora in età tardoantica per lo più nell'assetto che era andato definendosi fra I a.C. e I secolo d.C., periodo a cui erano seguiti l'inserimento di qualche edificio pubblico, opere di ampliamento ancora riferibili al II secolo, e qualche limitato intervento di riassetto e ristrutturazione già inquadrabile nel III. Con il IV secolo l'economia del latifondo, che va anche qui prevalendo, si accompagna alla progressiva decadenza e perdita di importanza dei centri urbani, che passa anche attraverso la creazione di mercati (*nundinae*) nell'ambito delle grandi proprietà, e la progressiva elusione del ruolo dominante del centro urbano nel territorio. Non è dunque casuale che molti municipi, come *Amiternum* (n.2), *Interamnia* (n.12), *Aveia* (n.9), e *Cluviae* (n.100), facessero ricorso alla protezione proprio dei grandi proprietari terrieri dell'aristocrazia senatoria, a cui si devono ormai quei pochi lavori di restauro che permettono ai centri monumentali di sopravvivere ancora per qualche tempo (Staffa 1992e: 790; Giardina 1986: 26-8).

Non possono inoltre dimenticarsi i gravissimi danni che erano stati provocati nell'intera regione da devastanti terremoti (quale ad es. quello del 346 d.C.), a cui può imputarsi, come hanno evidenziato chiaramente gli scavi, il crollo traumatico di gran parte degli edifici pubblici nell'area forense di *Alba Fucens* (n.1), lo sconvolgimento di tanti altri abitati sino a *Peltuinum* (Prata d'Ansidonia, n.4), *Histonium* (Vasto, n.19) e *Iuvanum* (n.20), e la conseguente crisi traumatica dell'assetto delle città come si erano sostanzialmente assestate nella prima età imperiale (Staffa 1992e: 790-5).

Nei centri urbani dell'interno gli interventi successivi alla prima metà del IV secolo sono molto limitati o del tutto inesistenti, a differenza degli abitati dell'area adriatica interessati da numerosi interventi di recupero successivi al sisma e da ultime consistenti opere di riassetto correlabili alle esigenze difensive bizantine all'epoca della Guerra Gotica (VI sec.) (Staffa 1992e: 819-20; I Bizantini in Abruzzo). Interventi sono attestati ad *Aternum* (n.16), con il recupero della fronte dell'abitato verso il fiume e probabilmente delle stesse strutture portuali (Staffa 1991a: 288-9), ad *Anxanum* (Lanciano, n.18) ove sembra plausibile l'impianto di strutture difensive nell'ambito dei settori del tessuto antico sino ad allora sopravvissuti (area del c.d. castello longobardo) (Staffa 1992d: 23-7), ad Ortona (n.17) ove le fonti documentarie testimoniano dell'esistenza di una cinta difensiva edificata *ex novo* o allora rinnovata (Staffa 1992e: 819-20).

II.2 Il tracollo dei centri urbani (secc. VI-VII)

I danni provocati in molti centri della regione dalle vicende della Guerra Gotico, carestie e pestilenze ad essa seguite, ed infine le devastazioni connesse all'invasione longobarda, ben evidenti ad esempio nel grande incendio di Pescara alla fine del VI secolo, dovettero tradursi in un rapido degrado del paesaggio urbano, connesso all'abbandono di vasti settori dell'abitato (Staffa 1991a: 214, 238, 289-91; 1992e; 1993a).

Fenomeni del genere sono attestati ad *Interamnia* (Teramo), nell'area fra Madonna delle Grazie e Largo Melatini e nella zona della primitiva cattedrale (S. Anna) e della Domus del Leone, ove deve rilevarsi l'inserimento di varie sepolture probabilmente databili fra VI e VII secolo fra i ruderi dell'abitato antico (Staffa 1990a: 19-26; 1992e: 829-31); a *Truentum*, ove su un piano di voluto obliteramento di parte dei resti vanno a collocarsi sepolture alla cappuccina databili al tardo VI-inizi VII secolo (Staffa 1992e: 815-816, 832); a Pinna, ove, oltre a due sepolture alla cappuccina collocate presso resti antichi a viale Ringa, sono state scavate due sepolture a cassone ricavate nel livellamento della sommità del colle del Duomo e databili fra VI e VII secolo; ad *Aternum* (Pescara) ove viene abbandonato l'intero settore di abitato antico distrutto dagli incendi alla fine del VI secolo nell'area di piazza Unione, mentre vengono ripristinate, già nel VII secolo, varie strutture lungo il fiume Pescara (Staffa 1991a: 292); a *Teate* (Chieti) ove nei pressi dell'anfiteatro ormai cadente per i danni del sisma è stata scavata una sepoltura forse riferibile al primo altomedioevo (studio di A. Campanelli); ad Ortona, ove la presenza di una necropoli del tardo VI-inizi VII secolo sulla passeggiata orientale a mare fa supporre che si fossero qui attivate, nonostante la presenza dei Bizantini, forme di progressivo degrado ed abbandono di consistenti settori dell'abitato antico (De Nino 1882; Staffa 1992e); ad *Anxanum* (Lanciano), ove negli ultimi livelli di vita di un complesso antico ancora occupato agli inizi del VII secolo e forse di pertinenza pubblica vanno a collocarsi due sepolture con elementi di corredo forse ascrivibili ad una presenza già longobarda (Staffa 1992d: 27; I Bizantini in Abruzzo).

Deve comunque in proposito notarsi che a Penne, Chieti, Lanciano, Teramo, le sepolture vanno a collocarsi nei pressi di settori d'abitato in cui non può dubitarsi della persistenza di forme di popolamento, in aree probabilmente pubbliche a Chieti e Penne, e forse private a Teramo ove le tombe vanno ad insediarsi fra i ruderi di alcune *domus*. Questo diffondersi delle sepolture all'interno delle città è almeno in parte indubbiamente correlabile a fenomeni di parziale disgregazione del tessuto civile ed amministrativo, ricandosene un'immagine particolarmente efficace e significativa dello stato di totale crisi e degrado del vivere civile in ambito urbano in quell'epoca.

II.3 L'inserimento degli episcopii e delle chiese

Considerato che tuttavia che in qualche caso, a Teramo e Penne, l'area in cui vanno a collocarsi le sepolture è quella in cui fonti documentarie e monumentali di più avanzato periodo altomedievale (secc. VIII-IX) testimoniano dell'esistenza delle loro cattedrali, potrebbe supporsi che almeno in questi due casi i fenomeni di crisi attivatisi nel tardo antico avessero trovato, già nel VII secolo, un qualche sia pur mediocre punto di equilibrio, non casualmente collegato all'insediarsi di strutture vescovili nell'ambito dell'abitato. Particolare importanza dovette essere rivestita proprio dal progressivo insediamento degli *episcopia*, che venivano a concretizzare nell'ambito del tessuto urbano ormai degradato nuovi punti di attrazione tali da innescare fenomeni di riassetto di particolare ampiezza (Staffa 1992e: 807-09).

Eloquente al proposito è l'esempio di *Hatria* (Atri), in cui la cattedrale, forse già insediatasi in età tardoantica, catalizza la progressiva trasformazione del quadro viario nelle sue adiacenze, attraendo i percorsi antichi a motivo anche dell'abbandono di vasti settori di abitato ad essa circostanti (Azzena 1987: 91-9; Pannuzi 1991; Staffa 1992e: 831-2). Fenomeni analoghi sembrano ipotizzabili anche a Chieti, ove la cattedrale di S. Giustino, collocata in ambito periferico rispetto al centro romano e comunque non menzionata prima del IX secolo, sembra attrarre uno dei due poli di concentrazione del popolamento altomedievale con l'abbandono di parte del tessuto antico intermedio; ad Ortona ove la sede originaria della chiesa locale, soggetta in età medievale ad una traslazione a S. Tommaso, doveva essere in qualche modo correlata all'assetto dell'ambito antico.

Numerose strutture analoghe di fondazione tardo-antica vengono tuttavia meno fra VI e VII secolo, a motivo della crisi profonda dei relativi abitati. Esempi in tal senso solo le sedi di *Aufinum* (Ofena), *Truentum* (Martinsicuro), e *Aveia* (Fossa), trasferita presso il vico antico di *Forcona* (Monachino 1968: 81-5; Staffa 1992e: 808). Un caso analogo è attestato a Sulmona ma il fenomeno si lega probabilmente alla preminenza assunta della vicina Valva per la presenza del gastaldo longobardo; più che un collasso dell'abitato sembrano infatti qui delineabili consistenti forme di continuità insediativa, testimoniate dalla parziale persistenza del tessuto regolare romano e dal recentissimo rinvenimento

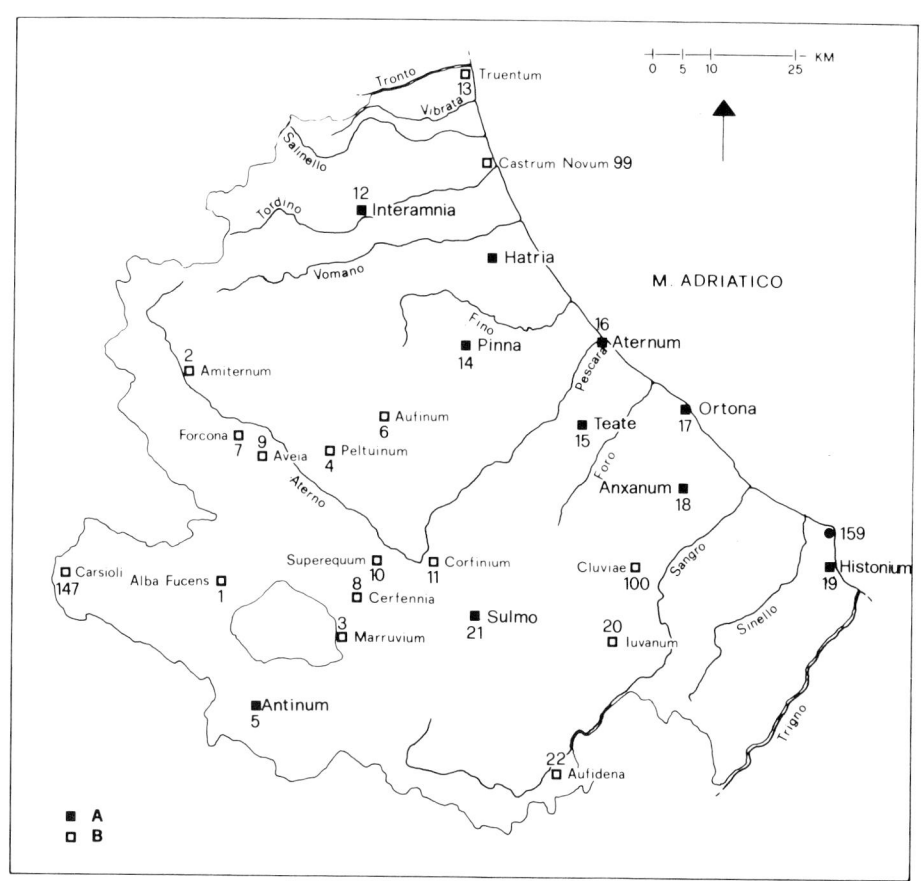

Fig. 1. I centri urbani abruzzesi fra tarda antichità ed altomedioevo (A: centri a continuità di vita fra altomedioevo e medioevo; B: centri sottoposti a fenomeni di destrutturazione ed abbandono).

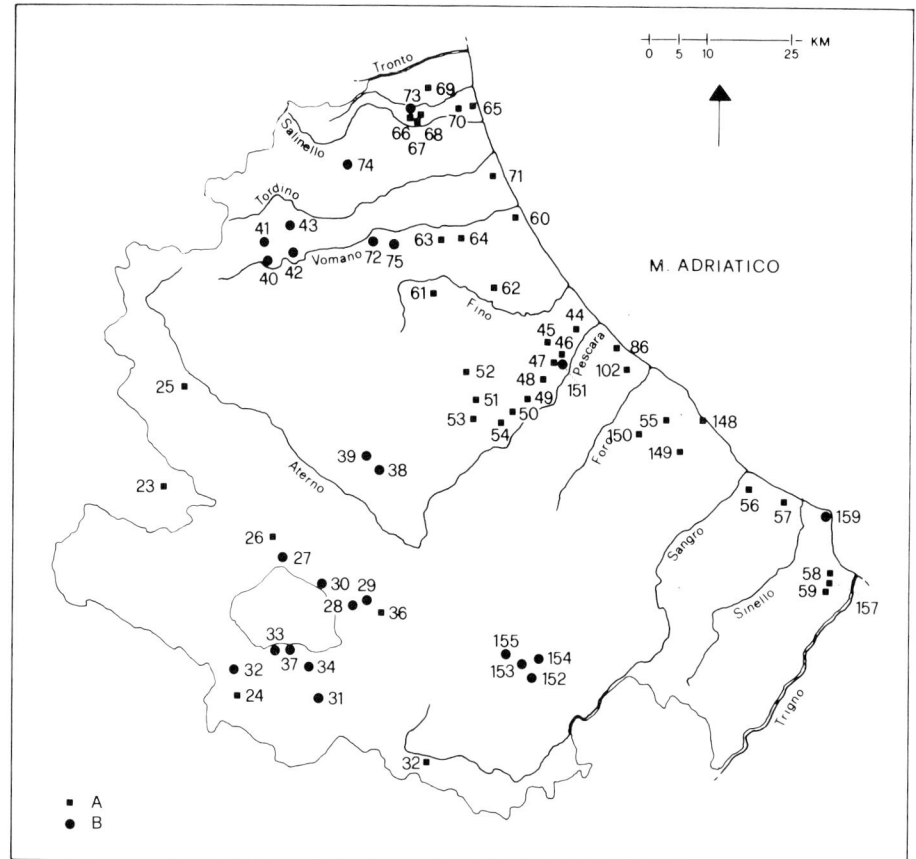

Fig. 2. Il territorio abruzzese nella tarda antichita con indicazione della ville (A) e degli abitati vicani (B) ancora occupati sinora noti.

di strutture religiose di probabile origine antica con fasi di VIII secolo (Feller & Giuntella 1992).

Da questi esempi appare in tutta evidenza la necessità di prestare particolare attenzione alla localizzazione non solo delle sedi vescovili, ma anche delle strutture pievane e monastiche di età altomedievale e medievale, per meglio focalizzare le tracce di quegli abitati antichi, che risultano sovente abbandonati o del tutto modificatisi nella più avanzata età medievale. Solo per proporre qualche esempio ricordiamo *Aternum* (Pescara), ove nell'area di ubicazione della chiesa di S. Salvatore, attestata dalle fonti solo in età altomedievale (secc.IX-XIII), sono stati rinvenuti resti di un pluteo tardoantico (Staffa 1991a: 300–01, 310); *Alba Fucens* ove, nell'ambito del tessuto antico poi quasi del tutto abbandonato sono localizzate tre chiese, l'una riferibile ai secoli VI-VIII nell'ambito dell'area forense, la seconda riferibile ai secoli X-XI nei pressi del lato orientale delle mura, ed infine S. Pietro sovrapposta ai resti di un precedente edificio templare antico (Mertens 1989: 390; Staffa 1992e: 828); *Amiternum* (L'Aquila), ove le fonti attestano la presenza di una cella farfense, e si è supposta la presenza dell'episcopio altomedievale nei pressi dell'Anfiteatro (Pani-Ermini 1980); *Antinum* (Civita d'Antino) con chiare tracce di abitato tardoantico ed altomedievale nei pressi della chiesa pievana di S. Stefano (Staffa 1992c: 139–40); e *Cerfernia* (Collarmele), ove la chiesa altomedievale di S. Felicita *in Cerfennia* conservava nel nome il ricordo dell'abitato antico (Reg. Farf.: Balzani V, doc.1280, p.274; Grossi 1989: 207, n.9).

II.4 Aspetti urbanistici delle città in età altomedievale

In sede di esame delle dinamiche attivatesi nei centri urbani abruzzesi nel primo altomedioevo vanno anzitutto evidenziati i limiti di un approccio al problema mediato solo dalle scarsissime fonti documentarie (cfr. Feller & Giuntella 1992), anche perchè un siffatto esame viene ad eludere quello che sembra un elemento centrale nella ricostruzione di un corretto quadro generale di riferimento, e cioè la forte differenziazione evidente fra aree interne e versante adriatico della regione. In quest'ultimo ambito sembra infatti notarsi un esito dei fenomeni di crisi attivatisi nel tardo antico che si traduce in una sostanziale continuità dei principali centri ivi esistenti nella loro dimensione urbana, anche aldilà degli articolati fenomeni di riassetto d'età altomedievale. Non mancano tuttavia anche qui casi di progressivo abbandono, tradottisi nell'età medievale più avanzata nel totale venir meno dell'abitato (*Truentum, Castrum Novum, Cluviae, Iuvanum*).

Al contrario nell'Abruzzo interno gli insediamenti sopravvissuti perdono quasi ovunque dimensioni ed assetto propriamente urbani, riproponendosi forme di popolamento sparso di ben più antica tradizione articolate per nuclei nell'ambito dell'antica estensione urbana. Eloquenti al proposito sono i casi di *Alba Fucens* divenuto il villaggio di Massa d'Albe, *Marruvium* divenuto S. Benedetto dei Marsi, *Corfinium* divenuta Pentima, *Superequum* divenuto Castelvecchio Subequo.

A tali fenomeni si collega la progressiva trasformazione dello stesso tessuto urbanistico delle città, come evidenziato da vari esempi per lo più relativi all'Abruzzo adriatico. A tal proposito si è già enfatizzata l'importanza assunta dal progressivo inserimento di strutture religiose, che venivano a costituire nuovi poli d'attrazione sovente del tutto estranei a quella che era stata la pianificazione degli spazi in età precedente, provocando modifiche profonde della viabilità ad essi connesse. Un esempio è *Truentum*, ove un tracciato altomedievale, diretto al superstite nucleo altomedievale (Case Feriozzi), oblitera il tessuto antico occupato sino al VI secolo stravolgendone l'orientamento. Dinamiche di trasformazione di più lungo momento sono attestate ad *Hatria* (Atri), ove sono stati ipotizzati fenomeni di progressivo consumo della pianificazione regolare antica forse già attivatisi in età tardoantica, con invasione dei tracciati viari probabilmente ad opera di strutture insediative povere, ed un quasi totale stravolgimento della rete viaria probabilmente correlato ad un collasso vero e proprio dell'abitato (Azzena 1987: 91–9; Gizzi & Pannuzi 1988; Pannuzi 1991: 589–91).

Forme di maggiore continuità sono attestate ad *Aternum*, ove si è direttamente constatata una consistente persistenza della viabilità antica, che va lentamente trasformandosi solo fra VIII e IX secolo a seguito dei crolli e dell'invasione dei tracciati di origine antica ad opera di case di legno e terra (Staffa 1991a: 298–9); e ad *Anxanum* ove deve notarsi la presenza di livelli dell'abitato altomedievale sull'intero colle di Lanciano Vecchia ove doveva essere localizzato il municipio, con persistenza degli orientamenti dell'abitato antico e forse di un asse viario principale non molto difforme da via dei Frentani (Staffa 1992d). E' significativo che questi ultimi due contesti rientrino in quell'area costiera che era rimasta più a lungo collegata all'impero bizantino. Analoghe forme di continuità insediativa sembrano collegarsi alla persistenza di un impianto regolare di probabile origine antica, attestato a Sulmona, e ad *Interamnia* nell'area adiacente gli edifici da spettacolo in cui doveva essersi concentrato il popolamento superstite.

Accanto a casi del genere sono tuttavia numerosi gli esempi di precoci forme di 'arroccamento' del popolamento all'interno dell'abitato antico: a *Peltuinum* si conservano consistenti tracce di abitato altomedievale presso il Teatro; ad *Interamnia* si è ricostruita l'esistenza di resti di fortificazione nell'area circostante il teatro ed il anfiteatro (Staffa 1992e); a Penne ore recentissimi scavi archeologici (1992–95) hanno rivelato la presenza di un abitato fortificato altomedievale intorno al Duomo sull'omonimo Colle; a *Teate*, ove l' abitato altomedievale appare ristretto a due nuclei distinti, l'uno nei contorni della città antica nell'area dell'Anfiteatro, e l'altro intorno alla sede vescovile di S. Giustino, facendosi inoltre nelle fonti distinzione fra una *Civitas Teatina Vetus*, abbandonata nel IX secolo probabilmente a seguito del saccheggio franco dell'801, ed una *Civitas Nova* che non pare tuttavia sovrapporsi esattamente all'area di S. Giustino (cfr. Falla-Castelfranchi 1991).

Dinamiche di riassetto sembrano attestate anche nelle aree interne, ove si traducono fra X e XII secolo nel definitivo venir meno delle forme di abitato ancora attestate all'interno dei centri d'età imperiale (Staffa 1992e: 833-4), nel accennato definitivo ritorno degli abitati a dimensioni di villaggio, con la concentrazione del popolamento su siti in qualche modo 'arroccati' ma ancora prossimi agli impianti antichi: per esempio, ad *Aveia* l'abitato medievale di Fossa si riduce alla fascia collinare sovrastante il piano dell'impianto regolare antico; a *Corfinium* il villaggio medievale segna il ritorno del popolamento al probabile sito del più antico abitato italico precedente la Guerra Sociale.

II.5 Aspetti economici

Nell'analizzare complessivamente su ambedue i versanti della regione gli articolati fenomeni attivatisi fra tardoantico ed altomedioevo nei centri urbani è sorta spontanea la domanda se, nella diversificazione delle dinamiche e nel differente esito dei processi di crisi sin qui evidenziati, non potessero ricercarsi motivazioni e logiche connesse non esclusivamente agli aspetti politici, storici ed istituzionali delle vicende che coinvolgono anche l'Abruzzo alla fine del Mondo Antico. Questi aspetti sono ovviamente prevalenti nelle fasi traumatiche succedutesi fra VI e VII secolo, ma appare evidente che nei successivi accadimenti del pieno altomedioevo sono anche altri i fattori che entrano in gioco nel determinare crisi o ripresa dell'abitato.

Per vari centri dell'interno determinante nei successivi sviluppi è il venir meno di quel ruolo dominante nel territorio la cui programmatica affermazione aveva rappresentato l'elemento più caratteristico dell'urbanesimo diffusosi dopo la Guerra Sociale, con il conseguente ritorno a più modeste dimensioni adatte all'economia di sussistenza consentita dalle risorse economiche disponibili, e il connesso sostanziale riproporsi di forme di abitato sparso di ben più antica tradizione. E' questo probabilmente il caso di centri quali *Alba Fucens*, *Amiternum*, *Aveia*, *Marruvium*, *Antinum*, *Superequum*, anche se ovviamente le varie situazioni presentano sfumature connesse allea peculiarità di ognuna.

Per altri centri dell'Abruzzo costiero, in antico vissuti su un fecondo ruolo di centri di scambio e mercato per un territorio in cui l'economia agricola rivestiva un ruolo preminente, qualche ripresa economica sembra attivarsi già nel IX secolo in connessione ad una rinnovata intensificazione delle forme di uso del territorio circostante, al progressivo sia pur ridotto potenziamento delle strutture del potere civile (es. Teramo, Penne, Chieti), ed al riallargarsi di forme di scambio in ambito locale.

Non è forse casuale che fra IX e X secolo le scarse fonti documentarie ed i dati archeologici di recente rinvenimento restituiscano memoria di un uso delle strutture portuali antiche, ad esempio *Truentum* e *Aternum*, uso che doveva essere finalizzato a forme di cabotaggio lungo la costa su rotte non sempre marginali. L'acclarata presenza in vari contesti abruzzesi del IX secolo di materiali quali la pietra ollare qui importata dal settentrione e confrontabile con analoghi reperti da centri portuali altomedievali dell'alto Adriatico è al proposito ben eloquente (Staffa 1991a: 354-9; 1991c). Diverse erano state le vicende di quei centri della costa che erano rimasti sotto il controllo bizantino sin nel VII secolo. Il venir meno dei contatti con l'impero d'oriente nel passaggio anche di queste aree al ducato longobardo di Benevento dovette probabilmente tradursi nella consistente riduzione delle funzioni dei centri portuali minori, e tuttavia sembra plausibile che il porto più importante, quello di Ortona, sia riuscito a conservarsi come approdo di rilevante importanza.

Per quanto riguarda quei centri dell'interno con una prevalente economia pastorale, devono invece rilevarsi forme di crisi lenta ma comunque irreversibile, ad esempio per *Peltuinum*, *Iuvanum* e forse *Cluviae*, a seguito del venir meno della grande transumanza in età tardoantica.

II.6 Le forme dell'abitato altomedievale

Numerosi scavi condotti di recente hanno evidenziato come l'uso di strutture in legno connesse a poveri focolari a terra vada riproponendosi nell'ambito dei centri antichi abruzzesi già nella tarda antichità, non diversamente da altri centri dell'Italia settentrionale, come evidenziatosi a *Truentum*, ad *Aternum*, e a *Iuvanum* (Staffa 1992e). Trattasi indubbiamente della ripresa di tecniche costruttive di ben più antica origine, conservatesi anche in età romana nelle campagne e con ogni plausibilità anche in aree periferiche e 'povere' degli stessi centri urbani antichi. Mentre i pochi centri del potere civile e religioso vanno probabilmente conservandosi almeno parzialmente in muratura, il paesaggio delle città sopravvissute va caratterizzandosi per la progressiva sempre più diffusa sostituzione a quanto restava del tessuto antico della dominante presenza di strutture in legno, capanne, case in terra. In particolare gli scavi condotti a Pescara hanno evidenziato il quasi totale assorbimento nel tessuto abitativo della nuova città altomedievale dei ruderi antichi, o parzialmente riutilizzati a fianco di strutture in legno, oppure del tutto crollati o demoliti perchè fatiscienti, ed il progressivo rialzamento dei livelli di vita con la formazione di strati di 'terre nere', dovute allo smaltimento e riuso nell'ambito dello stesso insediamento dei rifiuti prodotti (Staffa 1992a: 220, 225, 240-53, 296-7).

Vanno prevalendo in ambito urbano strutture realizzate in legno, argilla cruda, pietre senza leganti. Trattasi di semplici capanne rettangolari realizzate con strutture a telaio ligneo e farcitura interna di argilla o pietrame, talvolta poggiate su un cordolo di grandi pietre. Le strutture a telaio erano talvolta rinforzate da pali interni poggiati su appositi incassi di pietre a terramentre all'esterno dovevano essere rinforzate da tavolati lignei. Le capanne erano costituite da una struttura portante a pali, con copertura lignea probabilmente a travetti intrecciati, a sorreggere uno strato di graticcio ed argilla, o una copertura a piccoli assi lignei. I pavimenti sono in terra battuta, ghiaia o sabbia, talvolta con frammenti fittili e ciotolame inseriti. Ogni unità insediativa presenta per lo più un focolare, e il frequente rinvenimento, nei pressi di questo, di frammenti di un piccolo 'forno' testimonia come il pane venisse cotto direttamente sul piano di cottura a fianco delle braci. Per conservare gli alimenti erano scavate nei pavimenti delle fosse di dimensioni variabili (Staffa 1993c).

Un simile paesaggio urbano dovette conservarsi a lungo, cedendo il passo al progressivo ritorno a più consistenti strutture in muratura solo fra X e XII secolo. E' questa infatti l'epoca in cui una delle case altomedievali di Pescara, realizzata in terra con basamento di grandi pietre, viene demolita e sostituita da un edificio in muratura che ne riprende orientamenti ed ingombro; ad analoga cronologia possono inoltre riferirsi i più antichi contesti monumentali d'età medievale presenti nei centri storici della regione (Staffa 1991a: 226).

III. IL POPOLAMENTO RURALE FRA TARDA ANTICHITÀ ED ALTOMEDIOEVO

III.1 La crisi del quadro insediativo antico nelle campagne (sec.IV-VII) (Fig.2)

Fra la fine del IV ed il V secolo emergono indubbi segni di progressiva crisi del quadro insediativo tardoantico nelle campagne come si era assestato agli inizi della tarda antichità nel sistema dei grandi latifondi (Staffa 1992e: 795–801). Anche se le prime testimonianze di abbandono sembrano già riferibili all'avanzato IV secolo, complessivamente l'abitato rurale di origine antica imperniato sul sistema delle ville sembra conservarsi almeno sino alla seconda metà del V secolo (nel Fucino, nella Valle del Vomano, nelle Valli del Salinello e Vibrata, a Coppito: nn.36, 35, 24, 60, 61, 63, 64), se non anche sino al secolo successivo (per es. nella Val Pescara, a Coppito e Corvaro di Borgorose, nn. 25, 23). Alcuni complessi, particolarmente lungo la fascia costiera rimasta sotto il controllo bizantino, restano occupati addirittura sino agli inizi del VII secolo (locc. S. Maria delle Grazie-Villanesi e S. Cecilia di Francavilla, nn.86, 102; Murata Alta di S. Vito Chietino, n.148; Casino Vezzani-Vassarella di Crecchio, n.55; Moccoli di Torino di Sangro, n.56; Stefano in Rivo Maris di Casalbordino, n.57 (Staffa 1991a: 337, n.145; Tulipani 1991); Colle Pizzuto di Vasto, n.59), e forse oltre (loc. Guastameroli di Lanciano, Orni di Canosa Sannita, nn.149–150). Un'occupazione protratta sino ai secoli V-VI appare attestata anche per vari abitati vicani dell'interno (Fucino, nn.27, 33), e del versante costiero (locc. Castellana-Piano Leone-Masseria Simeone di Pianella, n.151; Telesio-Case Di Sante di Cellino Attanasio, n.63; Marrocchi-S. Giovanni di Campli; S. Rustico di Basciano, n.72) (Staffa 1992e: 796–7, 800–01).

III.2 Elementi di continuità e fenomeni di riassetto territoriale nelle campagne (secc. VII-XI) (Fig.3)

Determinante nella transizione delle campagne all'altomedioevo appare il perpetuarsi di una tradizione di abitato sparso paganico-vicano di ben più antica origine, che mosse indubbiamente da forme di popolamento che si erano conservate per tutta l'età imperiale. Ci sono esempi oggi di tanti vici antichi trapassati probabilmente senza soluzioni di continuità in successive forme d'abitato altomedievale, ed abbandonati solo nella piena età medievale (per es. *Vicus Supinum* (n.37), trapassato nell'abitato di Trasacco, probabilmente gli insediamenti antichi corrispondenti agli attuali abitati di Moscufo e Spoltore nella Val Pescara) (Staffa 1992e: 800–01, 834–41).

In qualche caso la continuità sembra porsi da un insediamento d'età tardoantica riconoscibile come *villa*, dovendosi supporre che vi fossero giustapposte povere forme di abitato vicano poi conservatesi *in situ* anche al venir meno dell'assetto organizzato dell'impianto. Qui la continuità insediativa può essersi collegata a una struttura domocoltile inserita nell'economia curtense, presso i resti del precedente complesso antico. Casi del genere sono gli abitati di *Apinianicum* di Pescina (n.28), Case Egler di Castilenti (n.62), l'abbazia di S. Clemente a Guardia Vomano (n.80), e vari siti della Val Pescara (vedi Staffa 1992e).

Non dovettero tuttavia mancare fenomeni di discontinuità insediativa, con il precoce spostamento (secc.VIII-IX) di nuclei di popolamento su siti d'altura, come ad esempio ipotizzabile per gli abitati in località Castellina di Navelli (n.116) (Mattiocco 1986: 92; Staffa 1992e: 835–6), Il Castello-Floriano di Campli (n.145), ed altri abitati della Val Vomano e zona di Atri. In alcuni casi le testimonianze archeologiche disponibili danno conto di una rioccupazione vera e propria di siti antichi in precedenza abbandonati, come nel caso della villa di S. Potito di Ovindoli (n.26) (Gabler & Redo 1989: 484), essendo plausibile che un forte impulso fosse derivato dal diffondersi delle strutture monastiche (secc.IX-X).

Che anche queste forme di riassetto andassero comunque correlandosi alla riproposizione di modelli insediativi di ben più antica origine è esemplificato da un esame dei villaggi a capanne di origine altomedievale in località Ventignano-Case Fiucci di Cepagatti (n.138) (Staffa 1989: 565–78), Coccetta di Villabadessa di

L'ABRUZZO TARDOANTICO ED ALTOMEDIEVALE NELLE FONTI ARCHEOLOGICHE 323

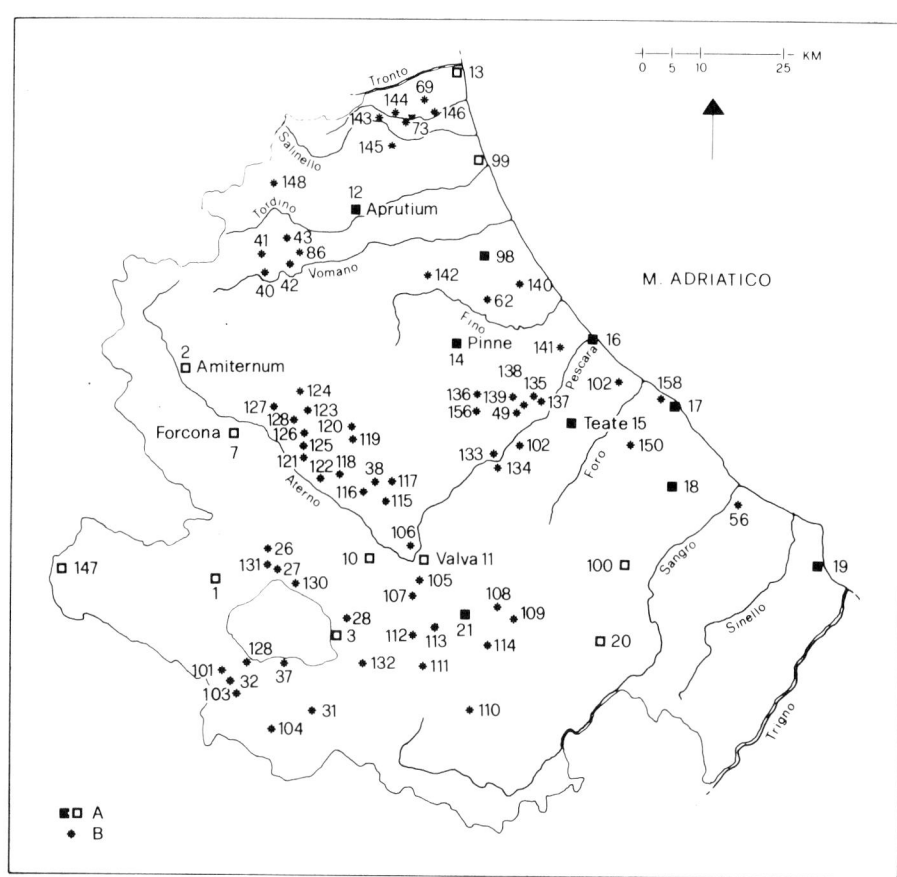

Fig. 3. L'Abruzzo nell'Altomedioevo con indicazione dei centri urbani (A) e degli abitati rurali (B) menzionati nel testo.

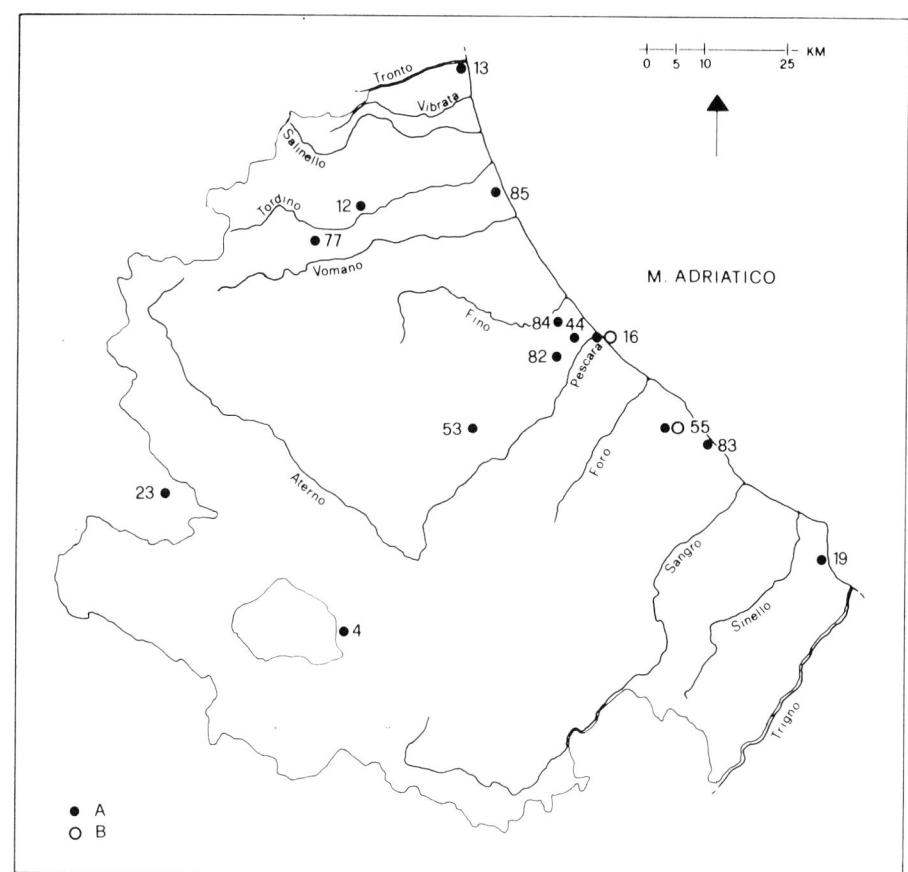

Fig. 4. Carta distributiva di rinvenimenti sinora noti di anfore di produzione africana (A) ed orientale (B) in Abruzzo.

Rosciano (n.139), Colle S. Giovanni d'Atri (n.140), Sperpara di Catignano (n.156), confrontabili per tipologie costruttive e strategie insediamentali con analoghe situazioni abitative di età ben precedente.

Questi esempi offrono un'eloquente conferma del lavoro dal Feller nell'esame del popolamento rurale altomedievale, sulla base della sola evidenza documentaria (in Feller & Giuntella 1992). Lo studioso, nel delineare i caratteri dell'azienda contadina del IX secolo, ricorda come nel paesaggio agrario dell'alta Valle del Pescara corte ed allodio vivessero in osmosi, realizzando un sistema che era stato ben compreso dai cronisti dell'XI secolo, da loro considerato quasi ideale, ed era sopravvissuto anche all'azione demolitrice della presenza monastica tendente a monopolizzare la forza lavoro dei contadini dipendenti assorbendone finanche la proprietà allodiale. Si sofferma inoltre sul fatto che il territorio da lui esaminato non risulta ancora polarizzato dalle corti o da altri centri di sfruttamento minori, ma resta diviso in unità topografiche del tutto autonome dalla struttura fondiaria, i c.d. casali delle fonti documentarie, riconoscibili come uno spazio comunemente percepito, anche se dai limiti incerti.

Considerato che numerosi di questi casali presentano una toponomastica prediale di presumibile origine antica, appare evidente come una loro persistenza nel IX secolo vada a collegarsi proprio all'evidenza del quadro archeologico sopra ricostruito nel disegnare diffuse forme di continuità di un assetto abitativo di sostanziale origine antica, non sembrando possibile riferire un quadro insediativo così fortemente radicato solo a dinamiche di ricolonizzazione agraria che potevano essersi avviate da non più di un secolo. Il quadro interpretativo risulta confermato dalla sopravvivenza di una toponomastica prediale ampiamente diffusa, almeno nell'Abruzzo adriatico. I primi studi sistematici dedicati a queste problematiche, condotti su ampi comprensori quali le Valli del Pescara (Staffa *et al.* 1991: 662–6) e del Vomano (Staffa 1985b: 50–1) ed i Monti della Laga (Staffa 1991b: 255–6), vanno evidenziando un quadro complessivo in cui alla persistenza dei toponimi corrisponde sovente la presenza di resti archeologici antichi, rendendosi talora possibile definire ambiti territoriali in qualche modo riconoscibili come i fundi antichi di loro pertinenza (Moscatelli 1992).

III.3 L'inserimento delle strutture religiose nel territorio

In considerazione dei fenomeni sin qui delineati appare evidente come un esame di quel tessuto di strutture religiose che costituivano in età altomedievale e medievale una vera e propria rete di punti di riferimento per il popolamento rurale, possa rappresentare un potente strumento per una ricostruzione sia delle principali forme di continuità insediativa, sia per una comprensione delle dinamiche di riassetto che vanno avviandosi con il VII-VIII secolo. Numerosissime sono le strutture pievane che vanno a collocarsi in ambiti abitati già in antico e comunque il quadro del popolamento sparso come appare ancora attestato da tante chiese rurali menzionate nelle *Rationes Decimarum* presenta ancora moltissimi punti di contatto con quello antico (Staffa 1992e).

Particolare importanza nel riassetto delle campagne fra IX e X secolo rivestono infine quei gruppi monastici che erano andati diffondendosi a seguito della presenza di proprietà delle grandi abbazie, quali Farfa, S. Vincenzo al Volturno, Montecassino, ed all'insediamento dell'importante centro locale di S. Clemente a Casauria, anche se in Abruzzo il ruolo da essi rivestito ha forse conseguenze di minor impatto sull'assetto fondiario delle campagne (cfr. Feller & Giuntella 1992). Da un esame generalizzato di queste situazioni è apparso inoltre plausibile che la attestata rioccupazione da parte di tali strutture monastiche di siti abitati già in antico altro non sia che l'adattamento di tali insediamenti ad un quadro insediativo d'età altomedievale, che proprio su quei siti si era in qualche modo conservato (Staffa 1992e: 843). Questa appare la situazione per l'insediamento casauriense di S. Clemente di Guardia Vomano-Notaresco, quello cassinese di S. Massimo di Torano Nuovo, e quello di incerta pertinenza di S. Maria di Mejulano presso Corropoli. Sono numerosi altri i casi in cui, pur in assenza di dati archeologici che permettano di meglio precisare le dinamiche del popolamento in loco fra VII e IX secolo, deve constatarsi su siti di insediamento monastico la preesistenza di resti di abitato antico (Staffa 1992c).

Il quadro ecclesiastico rurale così definito va conservandosi quasi cristallizzato sino al basso medioevo, pur in presenza di consistenti fenomeni di riassetto insediativo che vedono fra XI e XII secolo, particolarmente sul versante adriatico, lo svilupparsi dei nuovi centri incastellati su siti d'altura, e la conseguente nascita delle nuove chiese castrali.

La geografia del popolamento va così sempre più marcatamente divergendo da quella delle strutture religiose d'inquadramento, ma bisognerà attendere il Concilio di Trento e le visite pastorali ad esso immediatamente successive, per assistere al generalizzato affidamento formale della *cura animarum* alle summenzionate chiese castrali, con il progressivo e successivo venir meno di tante chiese pievane e curate ormai isolate nelle campagne circostanti e sui piani sottostanti i nuovi villaggi, a testimoniare un assetto insediativo definitivamente tramontato.

III.4 Aspetti organizzativi delle forme di abitato rurale altomedievale

Quali dovessero essere logiche insediative ed assetto strutturale del popolamento rurale in età altomedioevale può intuirsi sulla base dell'esame di qualche esempio, e tuttavia deve notarsi che trattasi sovente, particolarmente in presenza di forme di continuità insediativa da abitati d'origine precedente, di logiche connesse al preesistente quadro insediativo sparso d'età romana, logiche che sembrano perpetuarsi in qualche modo sino all'incastellamento (secc.XI-XII).

Diffuse, specie nell'Abruzzo adriatico, sono forme d'abitato su terrazzo fluviale che riprendono tipologie insediative di origine ben più antica. Sono attestati anche villaggi su dorsale collinare, sovente in continuità insediativa rispetto a forme d'abitato antiche, ed anche quelli abitati ubicati su siti d'altura e sovente sulle parti sommitali di articolati complessi collinari.

In qualche caso gli insediamenti d'età altomedievale vanno infine ad occupare una posizione collinare dominante i sottostanti pianori già abitati in antico. Scavi esaustivi di uno di questi villaggi, localizzato sul Colle S. Giovanni di Atri, restituiscono l'immagine di un abitato a case di terra collocate a fuso su due o tre file sulla cima del colle, con un terrapieno verso il lato meno difeso naturalmente (Staffa 1993c). Elementi difensivi quali un fossato e resti di muri sono presenti anche ad Astignano-Case Scipione di Pianella, Colle della Sala di Alanno, e Castellare S. Egidio Vecchio di S. Egidio alla Vibrata. Sulla montagna sembrano infatti perpetuarsi forme d'abitato di lungo momento, condizionate nel loro conservarsi sui medesimi orizzonti dalla forte influenza dell'habitat naturale, e soggette a forme di riassetto solo a partire dalla media età medievale, anche per il riattivarsi della grande transumanza appenninica.

III.5 Le forme dell'abitato rurale altomedievale

Nell'Abruzzo pre-protostorico ed italico gli abitati erano realizzati con strutture in legno e terra, capanne-case più o meno articolate, ma comunque riferibili a quelle tipologie costruttive che in più avanzata età romana Vitruvio venne a definire *opus craticium*, e che presentano amplissima diffusione in ambito mediterraneo e continentale.

Il recentissimo rinvenimento di resti di due strutture del genere riferibili alla tarda età repubblicana (II-inizi I sec.a.C.), a Penne con pavimentazione scutulata e muri in terra intonacata, e a Lanciano con basamento in grandi pietre destinato a supportare un alzato in terra cruda (Staffa 1992d: 11, 13), evidenzia chiaramente come queste forme costruttive di ben più antica origine fossero allora diffuse in Abruzzo addirittura all'interno dei centri urbani. Anche più ampia doveva essere la diffusione nelle campagne, come evidenziato dalla recentissima esplorazione di strutture con basamento in ciotoloni ed alzato in terra riferibili ad un abitato occupato dalla tarda Età del Ferro all'età repubblicana (secc.V-II a.C.) in località Piane di Valle S. Giovanni di Teramo (Staffa 1991b: 190), e dal rinvenimento di resti di un villaggi d'età romana con strutture in terra, pavimenti battuti e copertura in argilla spalmata su graticcio, in località Marrocchi-S.

Giovanni e Battaglia-Il Colle di Campli (Staffa 1993b), ed in località Castellana-Masseria Simeone di Pianella, quest'ultimo occupato sin nei secc. III-VI d.C.

In età altomedievale appare documentato un ricorso generalizzato anzitutto a strutture lignee, come dimostrato dal fatto che ancora nella prima metà dell'XI secolo l'importante complesso monastico di S. Salvatore a Majella (Serramonacesca, PE), risalente all'VIII secolo, fosse costituito da edificia lignea et vestusta e che, dovendosi procedere a vaste opere di ristrutturazione dell'abbazia di S. Clemente a Casauria nella seconda metà del XII, si facesse ricorso ancora a *strutture lignee* (Feller 1985: 148). Chiaramente il legno doveva anzi rappresentare un materale di un certo pregio, mentre per le abitazioni della gente comune specie in ambito rurale si faceva ricorso quasi solo all'uso della terra. Resti di unità insediative con strutture in terra e copertura e graticcio sono infatti presenti, solo per fare qualche esempio, sui siti dei villaggi altomedievali in località Astignano (Lesteniano) di Pianella, Cordano di Loreto Aprutino corrispondente alla *Curtis* casauriense *de Ocretano*, Ventignano-Case Fiucci di Cepagatti, Sterpara di Catignano, e soprattutto Colle S. Giovanni di Atri.

Le tecniche costruttive trovano confronti in numerosi altri esempi d'età altomedievale e medievale anche aldilfuori dell'Abruzzo, per esempio in Calabria, Lucania, Piemonte meridionale, Sardegna meridionale, e soprattutto nell'intera fascia adriatica fra Marche ed Abruzzo (cfr. Francovich *et al.* 1980).

Proprio il soffermarsi su tecnologie costruttive e schemi organizzativi ancora utilizzati sino a poco tempo, ma di cui va ormai perdendosi finanche il ricordo, può risultare di particolare interesse per una migliore comprensione delle forme dell'abitato rurale altomedievale come sopra delineate esclusivamente sulla base delle fonti archeologiche. I metodi adottati nella costruzione erano essenzialmente due, compattazione dell'argilla modellata in opera (pisé), o utilizzo di blocchi di terra precedentemente realizzati ed essiccati all'aria a realizzare muri spesssi da 60/80 cm sino ad un metro, quasi sempre privi di fondazioni (adobe) (Profico 1986). "Si preparava anzitutto il piano di posa della casa, scavando eventualmente sul lato a monte se il sito era in pendio": talvolta il terreno era preparato scavando all'interno del perimetro una fossa profonda da 50 cm ad 1 m, per rimettervi poi la stessa terra a strati di 30/40 cm, dopo averla mescolata con acqua e paglia di grano e avena, pestandola per compattarla (Gandolfo *et al.* 1986: 35). Nello stesso modo si lavorava la terra per tirar su le pareti, e "quando si arrivava ad avere la giusta consistenza con la zappa si staccavano delle zolle che venivano portate su una zona in piano e ammassate con le mani, cioè lavorate come la pasta".

Non appena l'impasto si era alquanto consolidato, si costruiva il muro perimetrale della struttura accumulando l'una su l'altra e lavorando tali zolle (tecnica

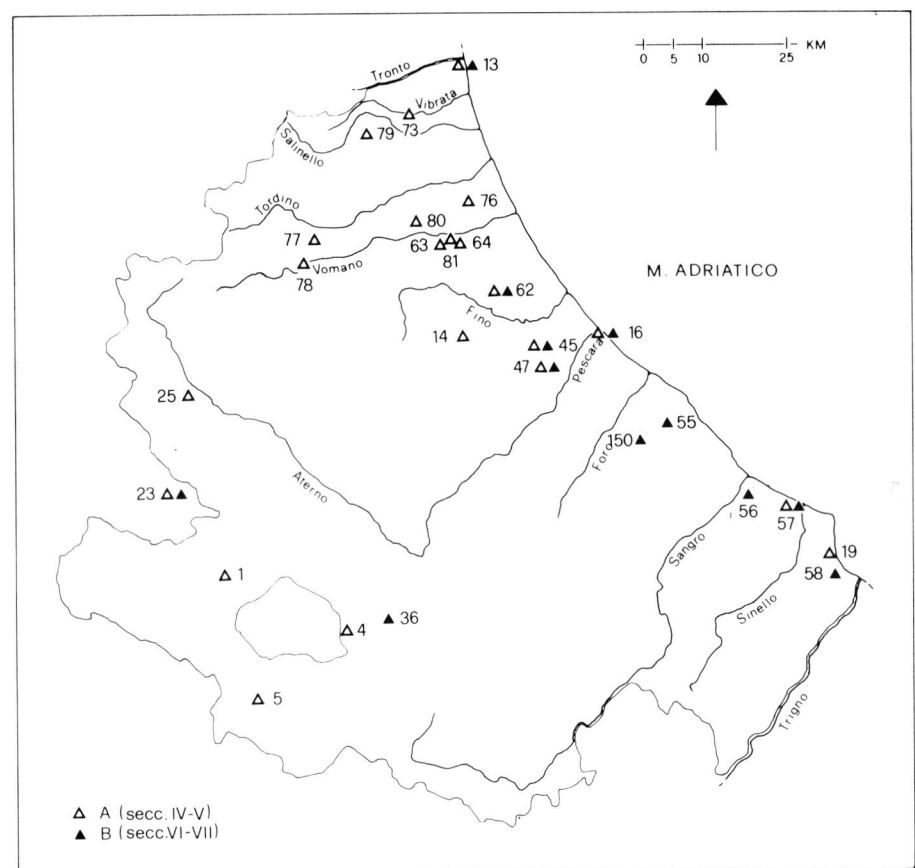

Fig. 5. Carta distributiva dei rinvenimenti sinora noti di sigillate africane (A: secc.IV-V; B: secc.VI-VII).

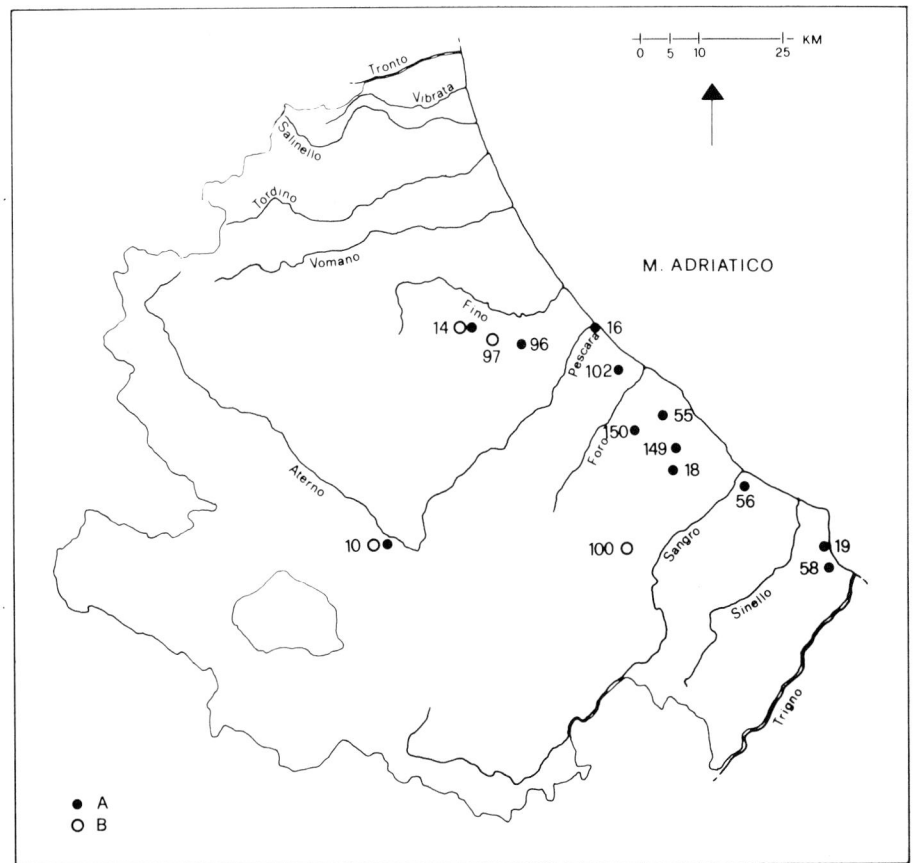

Fig. 6. Carta distributiva dei rinvenimenti sinora noti di ceramica dipinta a bande (secc.VI-VII) in Abruzzo (A: ceramica tipo Crecchio; B: imitazioni locali).

a pisé), "fino a che si formava *Lu bbanghe*, una parete alta circa 80 cm e larga 60/70 cm, che era il primo strato della costruzione", parete che poteva essere larga sino ad un metro ed alta 2; man mano che saliva i lavoranti vi salivano sopra standovi a cavalcioni mentre da sotto altri passavano loro l'impasto, questo sino ad giungere ad un'altezza di circa metri 2. Il tutto richiedeva non meno di due settimane e si attendevano poi una decina di giorni circa, che la struttura si fosse consolidata, per poi rifinirla e se del caso innalzarla ulteriormente sino al primo piano (Gandolfo *et al.* 1986: 35).

Una tecnica non dissimile si conservava sino a qualche tempo fa anche nel territorio a sud di Arezzo, compreso fra Val di Chiana e Cortonese, con realizzazione delle strutture in armature lignee (Francovich *et al.* 1980: 213). I solai di tradizione più antica poggiavano su grandi travi di sostegno ed erano in canne ed argilla, o realizzati con assicelle di legno. Assi di legno servivano altresi da architravi di porte e finestre, mentre i tetti, che potevano essere ad una, due o quattro falde, erano anch'essi sorretti da un struttura lignea su cui poggiavano assi di legno e poi i coppi. Le coperture, a due falde o a padiglione erano sorrette da una struttura di travi lignee con piano di posa per i coppi costituito più anticamente da canne ed argilla, e più di recente da mattoni (Profico 1986: 21–4. Per quanto riguarda l'ubicazione, vedi Gandolfo *et al.* 1986: 37).

Nel Teramano e nel Chietino il modello più diffuso era quello a schema rettangolare, ben raramente quadrato, con un unico piano e stalla direttamente collegata agli altri locali di abitazione (Spinozzi & Conti 1986: 16). Questo modello è costituito da tre elementi – cucina, camera e stalla – aventi dimensioni simili, allineati su un solo asse, orientato Est-Ovest, con prospetto principale esposto verso Sud. Ciascuno dei tre vani, che sono collegati fra loro, presenta un autonomo accesso dalla fronte della struttura, integrando così ai suoi spazi interni l'area collocata di fronte alla casa, l'aia (Profico 1986: 18–32). Uno schema rettangolare analogo appare attestato nella maggior parte delle unità insediative del villaggio altomedievale di Colle S.Giovanni d'Atri (secc.VIII-XI).

In Abruzzo le case in terra sembrano dunque localizzate sulla costa e nell' entroterra adriatico, mentre nelle aree montane dovevano al contrario essere utilizzate, oltre che dimore stagionali in legno ad uso di carbonai e pastori, strutture realizzate con muri in grandi pietre legati insieme da terra (Staffa 1991b: 216, 249). Questa tecnica appare già impiegata in antico, come appare evidente da resti di villaggio d'età romano-imperiale identificati in località Pie di Serra Secca di Rocca di Botte (AQ), e consistenti di semplici unità insediative quadrangolari (ringr. D.ssa C. Morelli).

Ne sono ulteriore esempio i resti esistenti presso i gli abitati in località Altavilla-Il Castello di Montorio (TE), Piano di Crognaleto, Piano Vomano-Colle del Vento di Crognaleto, Casagreca-Piano S. Maria di Cortino, abbandonati in età medievale (vedi Staffa 1991b: 210–1, 226–30, 238–9). Queste strutture medievali permettono di conferire la necessaria prospettiva temporale ai numerosissimi esempi di capanne in pietre a secco di epoca più recente schedate da Micati (1983, 1990) sulla Montagna Teramana, sul Gran Sasso, nell'Aquilano e sulla Majella.

III.6 Crisi dell'abitato sparso e sviluppo dei nuovi centri incastellati (secc.XI-XII)

Fra X e XII secolo il quadro territoriale sin qui esaminato va incontro a dinamiche di forte stravolgimento, con il progressivo abbandono dei fondovalle e la nascita di nuovi centri incastellati o meglio fortificati, talvolta con la rioccupazione di antichi siti italici, ma più sovente con lo sviluppo di abitati di nuova fondazione, anche se non mancano casi di incastellamento di abitati di ben più antica origine altomedievale.

Si conferma oggi anche sulla base di un esame ormai vasto di varie situazioni territoriali dell'Abruzzo costiero, che "l'incastellamento non sembra presentarsi come un momento di rottura così immediato e totale con le precedenti forme di occupazione del territorio, ma piuttosto una fase in cui confluiscono nuove fondazioni, centri d'altura già esistenti, strutture insediative collocate in contesti occupati in età romana". L'articolazione di tali processi appare evidente anche dalla complessità del quadro territoriale di riferimento in cui vanno ad operare, come ben delineatosi nelle varie situazioni esemplificate in questa sede. Questi fenomeni sono particolarmente diffusi nell'Abruzzo adriatico costiero e collinare a prevalente economia agricola, ove sembrano presentarsi con manifestazioni di rinnovamento del quadro insediativo rurale quasi totalizzanti.

Le fonti documentarie disponibili (vedi Clementi 1988; Feller 1985, 1989; Staffa 1985b, 1986, 1989, 1991b, 1992c; Vultaggio 1983) sono eloquenti al proposito e trovano preciso riferimento nei primi dati archeologici da alcuni di questi nuovi abitati d'altura quali Rosciano, Civitaquana nella Valle del Pescara, dati che confermano le fonti documentarie nel delineare lo sviluppo delle forme più diffuse di abitato incastellato nei secoli XI-XII (Staffa *et al.* 1991: 665). La situazione si presenta tuttavia fortemente differenziata, tanto che in alcune zone (ad es. Valva, forse parte della fascia pedemontana dei Monti della Laga) il sistema curtense sembra conservarsi sino agli inizi del XIII secolo (Feller 1989: 124; Wickham 1982: 59–71).

Nelle aree montane infine, come sembrerebbe suggerire l'esame sistematico della montagna teramana, sembra che "il passaggio a forme di abitato concentrato su siti alti" sia attestato "quasi solo ed esclusivamente nelle aree a prevalente economia agricola della fascia pedemontana…in precedenza interessate da articolate forme di abitato sparso collegabili prima al sistema antico delle ville e poi al sistema altomedievale delle *curtes*..., mancando quasi completameamente sulla montagna ove continuano a sopravvivere forme aperte di abitato sparso" (Staffa 1991b: 260).

Nelle aree montane della regione dunque queste forme di riassetto si manifestano in misura molto contenuta, conservandosi il popolamento su molti siti di tradizione antica sin nei secoli centrali del medioevo. La definitiva trasformazione del paesaggio in tante aree montane della regione si deve probabilmente alle conseguenze della crisi economica e demografia del XIV secolo, ed agli effetti devastanti dei due terremoti del 1349 e 1457.

IV. LA TRANSUMANZA

Per concludere è utile soffermarsi su un aspetto particolarmente importante dell'economia della regione in età medievale, quella grande transumanza che va riprendendo fra Abruzzo e Puglia all'epoca del Regno Normanno (sec.XII), dopo un una lunga interruzione in età altomedievale, e che ha rappresentato a lungo l'elemento più distintivo ed evidente dell'intera economia regionale (vedi AA.VV. 1984). Va ricordato che forme di transumanza a lungo raggio erano esistite già in età romana, probabilmente connesse nel periodo imperiale anche all'esistenza di una rete di fondi del *Fiscus* imperiale diffusi nell'intera area adriatica media e meridionale (Gabba & Pasquinucci 1979; Barker 1984). Se ne è sottolineato il venir meno nella tarda antichità, connesso alla sopravvivenza in età altomedievale di più ben contenute forme di spostamento stagionale degli armenti dal piano alla montagna. La grande transumanza presupponeva infatti l'esistenza di un forte potere statuale che, nel garantire l'incolumità e l'incontestato possesso del bestiame in un lungo arco spaziale, salvaguardasse nel contempo il forte investimento messo in opera dal proprietario. Non erano evidentemente queste le condizioni dell'età altomedievale, in cui i tracciati poi percorsi dalle greggi nella più avanzata età medievale ricadevano nel territorio di due ducati longobardi (Spoleto, Benevento), e nell'ambito dei domini bizantini in Italia e dovettero conservarsi solo casi di piccola transumanza legati all'esistenza di articolati domini monastici. La grande transumanza va dunque riprendendo solo in età normanna, ripercorrendo spesso tracciati viari di origine antica che erano rimasti in uso nell'intera età altomedievale (Staffa 1989: 562-5).

Recenti scavi condotti lungo il tracciato di uno dei tratturi più importanti, quello L'Aquila-Foggia presso i resti della città antica di *Peltuinum* (Prata d'Ansidonia) e, in località Villa Oliveti di Rosciano, hanno al proposito evidenziato l'esistenza dei resti della città antica e delle strutture di un complesso antico che occupano quasi interamente la fascia del tratturo, assestatosi pertanto in età di molto successiva all'abbandono e successivo crollo di quelle strutture.

Se in questi due casi appare accertato che il tracciato tratturale vada a riprendere antichi itinerari viari quali la *Claudia Nova*, ed il tracciato che dalla Forca di Penne discendeva la prima catena di colline a nord del Pescara, non è invece sempre detto che sia vero il contrario, cioè che i tratturi debbano per forza di cose, ed in assenza di testimonianze archeologiche, riprendere sempre percorsi antichi.

L'età normanna vede dunque non la ripresa di forme economiche che a scala più ridotta si erano conservate per l'intero periodo altomedievale, ma il loro rinnovato proiettarsi aldifuori dell'ambito regionale, nell'ambito di collegamenti che segnano una nuova stagione di di scambi economici e commerciali.

Bibliografia

AA.VV. 1984. *Giornate Internazionali di Studio sulla Transumanza*, L'Aquila-Sulmona, Campobasso, Foggia 1984, L'Aquila 1990.

AA.VV. 1986. *Le case di terra nel territorio abruzzese*, (Quaderni del Museo delle Genti d'Abruzzo), Pescara.

AA.VV. 1988a. *Il territorio del Parco Nazionale d'Abruzzo nell'Antichità*, Atti del I Convegno Nazionale d'Archeologia, Villetta Barrea 1987, Civitella Alfedena.

AA.VV. 1988b. *Homines de Carapellas, Storia e archeologia della Baronia di Carapelle*, L'Aquila.

Angeletti, G. 1990a. 'Lo scavo di S. Maria Aprutiensis,"Mondo Edile"', *Trimestrale della Cassa Edile della Provincia di Teramo*, n.9, Gennaio-Marzo 1990, 18-21.

Angeletti, G. 1990b. 'Ricerche archeologiche a S. Maria Aprutiensis', in AA.VV., *Ricerche archeologiche a S. Maria Aprutiensis. La Domus, la necropoli*, Teramo, 5-10.

Azzena, G. 1987. 'Atri', *Città antiche in Italia*, 1, Roma.

Baldacci, O. 1958. 'L'ambiente geografico della casa di terra', in Studi geografici in onore del Prof. Renato Biasutti, *Rivista Geografica Italiana*, LXV, Supplemento.

Balducci, A. 1926. *Regesto delle pergamene della curia arcivescovile di Chieti, I (1006-1400)*, Casalbordino.

Barbieri, G. & Gambi, L. 1970. *La casa rurale in Italia*, Firenze.

Barker, G. 1984. 'Possiamo riconoscere la transumanza nelle testimonianze archeologiche?', in AA.VV. 1984, 39-52.

Biasutti, R. 1952. *La casa rurale della Toscana*, Firenze.

Buonocore, M. 1983a. 'Regio IV - Sabina et Samnium, Teate Marrucinorum', *Supplementa Italica*, 2 (Nuova serie), Roma, 145 ss.

Buonocore, M. 1983b. 'Histonium', *Supplementa Italica*, 2 (N.S.), Roma, 97 ss.

Buonocore, M. 1986a. 'Insediamenti e forme economiche nell' Abruzzo romano dei primi due secoli dell'Impero', *Studi Classici e Orientali*, XXXVI, 279-292.

Buonocore, M. 1991. 'La vita cittadina dal sorgere dei municipia al tardo impero', in *Chieti e la sua provincia*, 187-196.

Calderoni, G. & Petrone, V. 1990. 'Datazioni radiometriche con il metodo del carbonio-14 di una necropoli medievale scoperta nel centro storico di Teramo', in AA.VV., *Ricerche archeologiche a S. Maria Aprutiensis. La domus, la necropoli*, Teramo, 11-12.

Campanelli, A. 1983. 'L'anfiteatro di Chieti: nuovi dati sull'urbanistica della città romana', *Quaderni dell'Istituto di Archeologia e Storia Antica dell'Università di Chieti*, 3, 163-170.

Cecchelli-Trinci, M. 1982. 'Il Paleocristiano in Abruzzo', *Atti del V Congresso Nazionale di Archeologia Cristiana*, 563-573.

Chiappa-Mauri, L. 1980. 'Dimore rurali nella bassa Lodigiana', *Archeologia Medievale*, VII, 95-125.

Chieti e la sua provincia = AA.VV., *Chieti e la sua provincia*, Chieti 1990.

Chronicon Casauriense = Chronicon Casauriense, sive Historia Monasterii Casauriensis...auctore Ioanne Berardi, in RR.II.SS., vol.II, t.II, Milano 1726, col.767 ss.

Chronicon Volturnense, a cura di V.Federici, Fonti per la Storia d'Italia, nn.33-34, Roma 1925-38.

Clementi, A. 1988. 'Gli ordini monastici nell'organizzazione del territorio abruzzese', in AA.VV., *Abruzzo dei castelli*, Brescia, 70-79.

Coletti, A., Giuntella, A.M., Saladino, L., Sereni, A., Somma, M.C. & Saladino, L. 1990. 'Corfinio (AQ). Campagne di scavo 1988-89', *Archeologia Medievale*, XVII, 483-514.

Colonna, G.1959. 'Un miliario poco noto della via Claudia Valeria', *Epigraphica*, XXI, fasc.1-4, 51-59.

Conta, G. 1982. *Asculum II, vol.I, Il territorio di Asculum in età romana*, Pisa.

Conti, A. 1984. *Le case di terra cruda nel territorio di Casalincontrada*, Chieti.

Coppa-Patrini, A. 1929. *Costruzioni edilizie in terra battuta*, (Annuario Scolastico del Liceo Ginnasio Plana di Alessandria, vol.34).

D.A.T. II = AA.VV., *La Valle del Medio e Basso Vomano*, (Documenti dell'Abruzzo Teramano), II, Roma 1986.

D.A.T. III = AA.VV., *La Valle dell'Alto Vomano e i Monti della Laga*, (Documenti dell'Abruzzo Teramano), III, Firenze 1991.

De Angelis D'Ossat, G. 1950. 'Cimiteri antichi della via Valeria e del bacino del fiume Aterno', *Rivista di Archeologia Cristiana*, 36, 5 ss.

D'Emilio, L. 1991. 'Il porto romano di Atri', in AA.VV., *Il porto di Atri: un invito alla ricerca archeologica*, Mosciano S.Angelo.

De Nino, A. 1882. 'Ortona a Mare', *Notizie degli Scavi di Antichità*, 419-420.

De Petra, G. & Calore, P. 1900-01. 'Intepromium et Ceii', *Atti della Regia Accademia di Napoli*, XXI, 155 ss.

De Pompeis, C. 1980. 'Coccetta di Villabadessa (Prov. di Pescara); indagini archeologiche di interesse postclassico, *Archeologia Medievale*, VII, 461-466.

Donati, A. 1974. 'I miliari delle Regioni IV e V dell'Italia', *Epigraphica*, 36, 152-222.

Fabbricotti, E. 1985. 'Iuvanum: scavi e ricerche 1980-93', *Papers in Italian Archaeology, IV, 4*, British Archaeological Reports, International Series, Oxford, 119-163.

Falla-Castelfranchi, M. 1991. 'L'età paleocristiana ed altomedievale: testimonianze archeologiche', in *Chieti e la sua provincia*, 199-221.

Faraglia, N. 1892. 'Saggio di Corografia Abruzzese medievale',*Archivio della Società Napoletana di Storia Patria*, 140 ss.

Feller, L. 1985. 'Casaux et *castra* dans les Abruzzes: San Salvatore a Maiella et San Clemente a Casauria (XIe-XIIIe siècle)',*Melanges de l'Ecole Française de Rome, Moyen Age-Temps Modernes*, 97, 144-182.

Feller, L. 1989. 'L'incastellamento inachevé des Abruzzes', *Archeologia Medievale*, XVI, 121-136.

Feller, L. & Giuntella, A.M. 1992 c.s. 'L'Abruzzo', in Atti del Convegno *'La storia dell'altomedioevo italiano (V-X secolo) alla luce dell'archeologia'*, (Siena, Dicembre 1992).

Floridi, V. 1976. 'La formazione della regione abruzzese e il suo assetto territoriale fra il tardo periodo imperiale ed il XIII secolo', Abruzzo, *Rivista dell'Istituto di Studi Abruzzesi*, XIV, n.2, 19-32.

Fonseca, C.D. 1984. 'Longobardia minore e Longobardi nell'Italia meridionale', in AA.VV., *Magistra Barbaritas*, Milano, 127-184.

Fraccaro, P. 1957. 'Iscrizioni della via Valeria', in *Opuscula, Scritti vari di P.Fraccaro raccolti per iniziativa dei discepoli in occasione del suo LXX genetliaco*, Pavia, 273-287.

Franchi d'Orto, L. & Staffa, A.R. 1991. 'L'insediamento italico di Colle del Vento', in *D.A.T. III*, 167-174.

Francovich, R., Gelichi, S. & Parenti, R. 1980. 'Aspetti e problemi di forme abitative minori attraverso la documentazione materiale nella Toscana medievale', *Archeologia Medievale*, VII, 173-246.

Gabba, E. 1985. 'La transumanza nell'Italia romana, evidenze e problemi', in AA.VV., *L'uomo di fronte al mondo animale nell'Alto Medioevo*, Atti della Settimana di Studi sull'Alto Medioevo, Spoleto, 373-389.

Gabba, E. 1988. 'La pastorizia nell'età tardo-imperiale', in AA.VV., *Pastoral Economies in Classical Antiquity*, Cambridge, 134-142.

Gabler, D. & Redo, F. 1988. 'Gli scavi a S.Potito di Ovindoli 1985-86. Seconda relazione preliminare', in *Specimina nova dissertationum, ex Instituto Historico Universitatis Quinque-ecclesiensis*, 69-94.

Gabler, D. & Redo, F. 1991. 'Gli scavi della villa romana di S. Potito di Ovindoli', in *Il Fucino nell'antichità*, Roma, 478-500.

Galie, V. 1984. *Castrum Truentum e Turris ad Truntum*, Macerata.

Gandolfi, A., Severini, A. & Gennaro, E. 1986. 'Viaggio nel vissuto della casa di terra: un percorso di memorie', in AA.VV., 33-38.

Genito, B. 1988. 'Lo scavo della necropoli di Vicenne. Materiali e problemi', *Conoscenze*, 4, 49-68.

Giammarco, E. 1984-86. 'Il dominio longobardo in Abruzzo', *Aprutium*, II-1984 (Gennaio-Aprile), 5-17; III-1985, 5-16; IV-1986, 5-13.

Giardina, A. 1986. 'Le due Italie nella forma tarda dell'Impero', in *Società Romana e Impero Tardoantico*, 1, 1-30.

Giardina, A. 1989. 'Uomini e spazi aperti', in AA.VV., *Storia di Roma, 4. Caratteri e morfologie*, Torino, 71-100.

Gizzi, E. 1986. 'Tombe altomedievali in agro di Notaresco', in AA.VV., *La Valle del Medio e Basso Vomano, Documenti dell'Abruzzo Teramano*, III, Roma, 260-272.

Gizzi, E. & Pannuzi, S. 1988. 'Atri, Centro Storico: riutilizzo medievale di un isolato romano', *Archeologia Medievale*, XV, 587-608.

Grossi, G. 1989. 'Topografia antica del territorio del Parco Nazionale d'Abruzzo (III sec.a.C.-VI sec.d.C.)', in AA.VV., 111-133.

Grossi, G. 1990. 'Topografia antica della Marsica (Aequi-Marsi e Volsci): quindici anni di ricerche, 1974-1989', in *Il Fucino nell'antichità*, 199-238.

I Bizantini in Abruzzo 1993 = AA.VV., *I Bizantini in Abruzzo*, Catalogo della Mostra, cura di A.R. Staffa & W. Pellegrini, Crecchio.

Il Fucino nell'antichità = Atti del Convegno *Il Fucino e le aree limitrofe nell'antichità*, (Avezzano 1989), Roma 1991.

Il Territorio e la sua storia = *Il Territorio e la sua storia. Un anno di ricerche archeologiche in Abruzzo*, Atti del Convegno, (Chieti, Dicembre 1991), in preparazione.

Lanzoni, F. 1927. *Le diocesi d'Italia dalle origini al principio del secolo VII*, Faenza.

La Regina. A. 1968. 'Ricerche sugli insediamenti Vestini', *Atti della Accademia Nazionale dei Lincei, Memorie*, ns.VIII, vol.XIII, 363-446.

La Torre, G.F. 1988. 'Il processo di urbanizzazione nel territorio vestino: il caso di Aveia', *Archeologia Classica*, XXXVII, 154-170.

Letta, C. 1988a. 'Oppida, vici, e pagi in area marsa. L'influenza dell'ambiente naturale sulla continuità delle forme d'insediamento', in AA.VV., *Geografia e storiografia del Mondo Classico*, a cura di M.Sordi, (Contributi dell'Istituto di Storia Antica dell'Università Cattolica del Sacro Cuore, XIV), 217-233.

Letta, C. 1988b. 'Confini vicani e confini municipali a sud del Fucino', in AA.VV., 203-207.

Lo Cascio, E. 1985-90. 'I greges oviarici dell'iscrizione di Sepino (CIL IX,2438) e la transumanza in età imperiale', in *Scritti offerti a Ettore Paratore ottuagenario*, (Abruzzo, XXIII-XXVIII), 557-569.

Mattiocco, E. 1981. *Centri fortificati preromani nella conca di Sulmona*, Chieti.

Mattiocco, E. 1985. 'La terra murata di Leporanica', *Bullettino della Deputazione Abruzzese di Storia Patria*, LXXV, 361-385.

Mattiocco, E. 1986. *Centri fortificati vestini*, Sulmona.

Mattiocco, E. 1989. 'Reinsediamenti medievali nell'ambito dei recinti fortificati preromani in Abruzzo', in AA.VV., *Mura poligonali, I Seminario Nazionale di Studi*, (Alatri, Ottobre 1988), Alatri, 71-81.

Mercano, L. 1970. 'Matelica (Macerata). Rinvenimenti di età gallica e medievale', *Notizie degli Scavi di Antichità*, XXIV.

Mertens, J. 1989. 'Recenti scavi ad Alba Fucens', in *Il Fucino nell'antichità*, 387-402.

Micati, E. 1983. *Le capanne a tholos della Majella*, Quaderni del Museo delle Genti d'Abruzzo di Pescara, 8-9, Pescara.

Micati, E. 1990. *La capanna abruzzese in pietra a secco, censimento, schedatura e studio*, Quaderni del Museo delle Genti d'Abruzzo di Pescara, 20, Pescara.

Monachino, V. 1968. 'La prima diffusione del Cristianesimo in Abruzzo', *Abruzzo*, VI, 1, 79-102.

Moretti, G. 1928. 'Torricella Peligna (Chieti). Elmo barbarico in rame dorato', *Notizie degli Scavi di Antichità*, 471–478.

Moscatelli, U. 1992, c.s. 'Evoluzione dell'insediamento rurale dell'età romana al medioevo nelle regiones augustee V e VI', *Fifth Conference of Italian Archaeology*, Oxford.

Ortolani, M. 1961. *La casa rurale negli Abruzzi*, Firenze.

Palagiano, C. 1976. 'Carta dei nomi territoriali dell'Abruzzo nell'alto medioevo', *Abruzzo*, XIV, n.2, 34–39.

Pani, G.G. 1986. *Incriptiones Christianae Italia, III, Regio IV*, Bari.

Pani-Ermini, L. 1971–72. 'Contributo alla storia delle diocesi di Amiterno, Forcona e Valva nell'alto medioevo', *Rendiconti della Pontificia Accademia di Archeologia*, XLIV, 257 ss.

Pani-Ermini, L. 1975. *Il santuario del martire Vittorino in Amiternum e la sua catacomba*, L'Aquila.

Pani-Ermini, L. 1976. Echi e tradizioni diverse nella scultura altomedievale in Abruzzo', *Abruzzo*, XIV, 1, 41–60.

Pani-Ermini, L. 1980. 'Possessi farfensi nel territorio di Amiterno. Note di archeologia altomedievale', *Archivio della Società Romana di Storia Patria*, 103, 41–52.

Pannuzi, S. 1991. 'Interventi di archeologia medievale ad Atri', *Archeologia Medievale*, XVIII, 547–586.

Paoletti, M. 1989. 'L'insediamento di Amplero e la Vallelonga', in *Il Fucino nell'antichità*, 299–321.

Paratore, E. 1976. 'La viabilità in Abruzzo nell'alto medioevo', *Abruzzo*, XIV, n.2, 42–47.

Pasquinucci, M. 1984. 'La transumanza ed il paesaggio', in AA.VV., 1984, 29–38.

Pellegrini, L. 1990. 'La città e il territorio nell'alto medioevo', in *Chieti e la sua Provincia*, 227–278.

Pinto, G. 1980. 'Le dimore mezzadrili nella Toscana medievale', *Archeologia Medievale*, VII, 153–171.

Profico, F. 1986. 'Caratteristiche tipologiche ed elementi costruttivi delle case di terra abruzzesi', in AA.VV. 1986, 18–32.

Quilici, L. 1966. 'Antino', *Quaderni dell'Istituto di Topografia Antica* (Università di Roma), 2, 35 ss.

Quilici, L. 1982. 'La rete stradale del ducato di Spoleto nell'alto medioevo', *Atti del IX Congresso Internazionale di Studi sull'Alto Medioevo*, Spoleto.

Rationes Decimarum = *Rationes Decimarum Italiae. Aprutium-Molisium, ledecime dei secoli XIII-XIV*.

R.F. = *Il Regesto Farfense di Gregorio da Catino*, a cura di U. Balzani, 5v., RR.II.SS, Roma 1879–1914.

Russi, A. 1971. *L'amministrazione del Samnium nel IV e V sec.d.C.*, (III Miscellanea Greca e Romana), Roma.

Santamaria-Scrinari, V. 1975. 'Note di archeologia paleocristiana abruzzese', *Atti del IX Congresso Internazionale di Archeologia Cristiana*, Roma, (Città del Vaticano 1978), II, 457 ss.

Santoponti-Emiliani, C. 1941. *Dimore primitive nelle Marche*, (Bollettino della Reale Società Geografica Italiana, s.VII, vol.VI).

Savini, F. 1898. *S. Maria Aprutiensis ovvero l'antica cattedrale di Teramo. Studio storico-artistico*, Roma.

Segenni, S. 1985. *Amiternum e il suo territorio in età romana*, Pisa.

Sgattoni, M. 1983. 'Le antichità cristiane e altomedievali nel Teramano. Proposte per una ricerca', in *Atti del VI Congresso Nazionale di Archeologia Cristiana*, (Pesaro-Ancona 1983), Firenze, 627–636.

Sommella, P. 1985. 'Centri storici ed archeologia urbana in Italia. Novità dall'area meso-adriatica', in AA.VV., *Arqueología de las ciudades modernas superpuestas a las antiguas*, Madrid, 359–392.

Sommella, P. 1988. *Italia antica. L'urbanistica romana*, Roma.

Sommella, P. & Tascio, M. 1989. 'Ricerche sull'urbanistica romana nell'area fucense: Marruvium', in *Il Fucino nell'antichità*, 456–477.

Spagnuolo, D. 1991. 'Altipiani maggiori d'Abruzzo', *Quaderni del Museo delle Genti d'Abruzzo di Pescara*, 21, Pescara.

Spinozzi, L. & Conti, G. 1986. 'La diffusione della casa di terra nel Teramano e nel Chietino', in AA.VV. 1986, 13–17.

Staffa, A.R. 1985b. 'Assetto territoriale fra la tarda antichità ed il medioevo', in *D.A.T., II*, 21–56.

Staffa, A.R. 1986. 'Ricognizioni nel territorio di Atri: problemi di una presenza volturnese', *Archeologia Medievale*, XIII, 437–460.

Staffa, A.R. 1987. 'L'assetto territoriale della Valle del Salto fra la tarda antichità ed il medioevo', *Xenia*, 13, 45–84.

Staffa, A.R. 1989a. 'Interventi della Soprintendenza archeologica dell'Abruzzo in contesti altomedievali della Valle del Pescara', *Archeologia Medievale*, XVI, 561–582.

Staffa, A.R. 1989b. 'Contributo alla ricostruzione dell'assetto antivo del territorio di Alba Fucens. Ricognizioni a Valle Solegara (1988)', in *Il Fucino nell'antichità*, 414–422.

Staffa, A.R. 1990a. 'Teramo: nuovi dati per la ricostruzione dell'assetto antico della città', *Xenia*, 19, 19–30.

Staffa, A.R. 1990b. 'Chieti, Palazzo De Majo. Scavo nei sotterranei', *Bollettino di Archeologia del Ministero per i Beni Culturali a Ambientali*, 1/2, 222–224.

Staffa, A.R. 1991a. 'Scavi nel Centro Storico di Pescara, 1: primi elementi per una ricostruzione dell'assetto antico ed altomedievale dell'abitato di Ostia Aterni-Aternum', *Archeologia Medievale*, XVII, 201–367.

Staffa, A.R. 1991b. 'Contributo per una ricostruzione del quadro insediativo dall'età romana al medioevo', in *D.A.T., III*, 189–267.

Staffa, A.R. 1991c, c.s. 'Contributo per un primo inquadramento delle produzioni ceramiche in Abruzzo fra tarda antichità e medioevo', *Atti del Convegno La Ceramica medievale nel Mediterraneo Occidentale* (Rabat, Novembre 1991).

Staffa, A.R. 1992a. 'Ceramica altomedievale a vetrina pesante e sparsa in Abruzzo', *Atti del Seminario su La ceramica invetriata tardo-antica ed alto-medievale*, (Siena-Pontignano, Feb. 1990), Firenze, 475–480.

Staffa, A.R. 1992b. 'L'Abruzzo dalla Romanizzazione alla fine dell'Alto Medioevo', in AA.VV., *L'Archeologia nel Museo delle Genti d'Abruzzo di Pescara*, Mosciano S.Angelo, 38–59.

Staffa, A.R. 1992c. 'La Valle Roveto dalla Tarda Età Imperiale al XII secolo', in AA.VV., *Antinum e la Valle Roveto nell'Antichità*, (Atti del Convegno, Civitad'Antinono 1990), Roma, 111–121.

Staffa, A.R. 1992d. *Lanciano fra preistoria ed altomedioevo*, Lanciano.

Staffa, A.R. 1992e. 'Abruzzo fra tarda antichità ed alto medioevo: le fonti archeologiche', *Archeologia Medievale*, XIX, 789–854.

Staffa, A.R. 1993a, c.s. 'L'Abruzzo fra tardoantico ed altomedioevo', *Keiron*, X.

Staffa, A.R. 1993b, c.s. 'Contributo per una ricostruzione del quadro insediativo dall'età romana al medioevo', in AA.VV., *Le valli del Salinello e della Vibrata, Documenti dell'Abruzzo Teramano, IV*.

Staffa, A.R. 1993c. 'Forme di abitato altomedievale in Abruzzo: un approcio etnoarcheologico, in *"L'edilizia residenziale tra V e VIII secolo"*, Atti del IV Seminario sull'Italia centrosettentrionale tra tarda antichità e alto medioevo, Montebarro 1993, Brescia 1994.

Staffa, A.R., Marrone, A., Petrone, D., Scorrano, S., Siena E, Troiano, D. & Verrocchio, V. 1991. 'Progetto Valle del Pescara. Secondo rapporto preliminare di attività', *Archeologia Medievale*, XVII, 643–666.

Staffa, A.R. & Moscetta, M.P. 1986. 'Contributo per una carta archeologica della Valle del Medio e Basso Vomano', in AA.VV., *La Valle del Medio e Basso Vomano, Documenti dell'Abruzzo Teramano, II*, Roma.

Tulipani, L. 1990. 'Il complesso cultuale di S. Stefano ad Rivum Maris', in *Chieti e la sua provincia*, 223–226.

Von Wonterhem, F. 1984. *Superaequum, Corfinium, Sulmo. Forma Italiae IV, 1*, Firenze.

Von Wonterghem, F. 1987. 'Scavi e ricerche di De Nino a Corfinium e Superequum', in AA.VV., *La figura e l'opera di A. De Nino*, (Atti del Convegno, Castelvecchio Subequo, 1987), 123–143.

Vultaggio, C. 1983. 'Vicende politiche e aspetti del quadro insediativo in età medievale', in *D.A.T., I*, 33–54.

Wickham, C. 1982. *Studi sulla società degli Appennini nell'Alto Medioevo*, (Quaderni del Centro Studi Sorelle Clarke), Bologna.

Wickham, C. 1985. *Il problema dell'incastellamento nell'Italia centrale. L'esempio di S. Vincenzo al Volturno*, Firenze.

35

Considerazioni intorno alle Valutazioni Demografiche di Paolo Diacono sul *Samnium*

Gianfranco De Benedittis

(Istituto Regionale per gli Studi Storici del Molise "V. Cuoco")

Sommario: *Con questa relazione si offre una discussione sulle fonti documentarie ed archeologiche per la* provincia Samnii *nei IV-VIII sec. d.C. In particolare si esaminano i risultati dello scavo della villa romana posta in località Casalpiano, in comune di Morrone (Campobasso), in una zona intermedia tra i due centri romani di Bovianum e Larinum. Lo scavo ha permesso di evidenziare una serie di fasi cronologiche che vanno dal III sec. a.C. fino al V sec. d.C.; ad essi ha fatto seguito una ulteriore fase collocabile tra il VI e l'VIII sec. documentata da un'ampia necropoli sovrappostasi alle rovine della villa stessa.*

Introduzione

Il notevole risveglio di attenzione degli studiosi sulla realtà storica del Sannio di questi ultimi decenni ha determinato un certo progresso delle nostre conoscenze su questa regione, grazie anche alla più intensa attività archeologica svolta ed ai relativi studi pubblicati (per es., Hodges & Mitchell 1985; Hodges, Barker & Wade 1982; Lloyd & Cann 1984; Hodges & Wickham 1981; Hodges & Patterson 1986; Hodges, Moreland & Patterson 1985; Hodges *et al.* 1988; Pantoni 1980).

Il recente rinvenimento della necropoli altomedievale di Vicenne presso Campochiaro (Ceglia 1988; Ceglia & Genito 1988; Genito 1988, 1991a, 1991b) si è posto al centro dell'attenzione degli studiosi determinando un nuovo rilancio degli studi sul passaggio dal tardo impero all'alto medioevo nel Sannio. Ricognizioni sui vecchi materiali (De Benedittis 1988b; De Tata 1988; De Benedittis 1991) hanno messo in evidenza tutta una serie di dati topografici rimasti in precedenza sostanzialmente inutilizzati; ad essi va aggiunta una serie di nuovi rinvenimenti archeologici che determinano la necessità di un loro riesame complessivo.

La quantità di nuovi documenti, grandi e piccoli, che si sono accumulati in questi ultimi anni, meritano un minimo di ripensamento onde dare nuovo slancio alla ricerca. La nostra relazione vuole perciò tentare non tanto di risolvere i problemi che ci sono, quanto di dare un minimo di ordine ai dati che conosciamo.

La *Provincia Samnii*

Il primo aspetto, preliminare a quanto si esaminerà in seguito, è il riesame dei confini di quello che si intende per *Samnium* nel periodo cronologico da noi considerato: IV-VI sec. d.C. Una recente nostra ricerca ci ha permesso di arrivare alla conclusione che nel periodo indicato la *provincia Samnii* abbia mantenuto come confini i fiumi *Aternus* a Nord e, all'incirca, il fiume *Fertor* a Sud, mentre, sul lato occidentale, almeno per questo periodo, non ne faccia parte *Beneventum*, città che dal VII sec. verrà a costituire, insieme al *Samnium*, una nuova entità territoriale, nota come ducato longobardo di Benevento. In questo periodo verrà esaltato il carattere sannita di Benevento alimentato forse dalle tendenze centrifughe del ducato longobardo che portarono a sottolineare l'antica identità etnica, pur non rispondendo ai reali limiti geografici della *Provincia Samnii* (De Benedittis 1988a).

Il riesame dei confini del *Samnium* tra IV e VI sec. d.C. ha permesso di ricollocare topograficamente alcuni eventi di questo periodo che spesso venivano erroneamente attribuiti a località poste in regioni limitrofe. Basti come esempio il caso di Felice IV, pontefice dal 527–530, che dalla pubblicistica locale veniva considerato, in quanto *natione Samnium*, erroneamente nativo di *Beneventum.*

In questo intervento vogliamo esaminare una frase di Paolo Diacono che, narrando gli avvenimenti del 667, descrive buona parte del *Samnium* come quasi del tutto deserto; il brano dello storico longobardo, riferendo l'assegnazione di terre al bulgaro Alkzeco, inviato al duca di Benevento Romualdo dal padre Grimoaldo, afferma testualmente di affidargli *"...spatiosa ad habitandum loca, quae usque ad illud tempus deserta erant..."*

tra cui *"Sepinum, Bovianum et Iserniam et alias cum suis territoriis civitates"* (*Hist. Lang.*, V,29).

Questa affermazione trova conferme anche in altre fonti relative a zone di pertinenza del *Samnium*; questo vale ad esempio per il territorio di *Aufidena* in cui ricade la chiesa di S. Maria *in duas basilicas*, posta presso il fiume Sangro; in un documento della fine del VII sec. viene detto che attorno alla chiesa *"...ab antiquo tempore nulla habitacio hominum fuisse memoratur sed tantum silva puplica ..."* (CV, I, 135, 11-13).

Lo stesso documento ci parla della chiesa di S. Maria *iuxta fluvium Trinium* (S. Maria in Canneto), che appare *"...incendio combusta et a cunctis habitatoribus derelicta..."* (CV, I,135,10-11). La cronaca di Farfa, per un periodo leggermente successivo, la fine del VII sec., quando viene fondato il monastero di S. Vincenzo al Volturno, oltre a ribadire che il viaggio dei tre nobili beneventani *"per Samnii provinciam habuit iter"*, ricorda che l'oratorio dedicato a S. Vincenzo Martire, era circondato da una *"densissima quoque ex utraque parte fluminis silva..."* ed aggiunge che *"nulla ibidem erat habitatio praeter ferarum ac latronum fortasse latibula"*. (CF, I,14).

Il concetto viene ripetuto a più riprese anche nelle cronache di S. Vincenzo:

– *"in Samnii partibus super ripam Vulturni fluminis ... situm est oratorium martyris Christi Vincentii nomine dedicatum; ex utraque vero parte fluminis silva densissima, que habitacionem tantum praestat ferarum latibulaque latronum"* (CV, I,111);
– *"ex utraque parte condensa silva ferarum habitacio et latronum latibula"* (CV, I,129);
– *"omnis hec regio vacabat habitatoribus rarusque viator aut agricola videbatur"* (CV, II,42);
– *"adhuc autem locus iste bestiis et avibus latibula prebens, hominibus omnino vacabat"* (CV, II,85).

Se però analizziamo le altre fonti relative a questo periodo, le conclusioni non sembrano, almeno in parte, collimare con quelle di Paolo Diacono, anzi, nonostante la violenza dei tempi, appaiono elementi che ci consentono di parlare di una certa vitalità.

La creazione della *Provincia Samnii* può oggi considerarsi cronologicamente collocata in concomitanza con il terremoto del 346 d.C. (Gaggiotti 1978; Buonocore 1992). La documentazione dell'impegno profuso da *Fabius Maximus* e dai *rectores* che a lui successero, pur se ci propone un territorio certamente non autosufficiente, mostra che gli edifici più significativi dei municipi romani ricadenti in questa zona sono urbanisticamente ancora ben strutturati; le iscrizioni del IV sec. d.C. ci propongono sostanzialmente efficienti edifici pubblici, terme, mura, teatri, anfiteatri ed ogni altro edificio che meglio possa rappresentare un centro urbano. L'ultimo elemento epigrafico che sia coerente con questa situazione ci viene da *Venafrum* (*CIL* X, 4859) da cui proviene un'iscrizione di età ostrogota che ci attesta il nome dell'ultimo dei *rectores provinciae Samnii* a noi noto: *Flavius Pius Marianus* (Gaggiotti 1978), ma mentre le attestazioni di questi funzionari appaiono molto diffuse nel IV sec. d.C., pochissime sono quelle per i secoli successivi.

STORIA ED ARCHEOLOGIA

Dal punto di vista ecclesiastico le notizie che abbiamo su questa zona per il V e VI sec., soprattutto per il periodo che è a cavallo tra i due secoli, ci permettono di sapere che erano vitali le diocesi di *Telesia* (465-487), di *Histonium* (492-496), di *Aufidena* (494-495), di *Venafrum* (496), di *Alifae* (499), forse di *Aesernia* (501-De Benedittis 1991b), di *Saepinum* (501), di *Bovianum* (501-502), di *Larinum* (493-501 e 556-561) e di *Ortona* (591-649).

Se ci volgiamo al territorio, la documentazione d'archivio non è moltissima, tuttavia è certamente d'aiuto. Una lettera risalente al 494-495 di papa Gelasio I al vescovo larinate Aprilis ricorda il fenomeno, diffuso soprattutto nell'Italia meridionale, della fuga degli schiavi che, ordinati sacerdoti, perdevano il loro stato servile, ma non ci aggiunge altro (Kehr 1962). Qualcosa in più ci dice una bolla databile tra il 556 ed il 561 di papa Pelagio I al vescovo di Larino (Gassò & Battle 1969). Il papa invia al vescovo di Larino Giovanni una lettera in cui si affronta il problema dell'ingerenza dei laici nell'amministrazione dei beni ecclesiastici; in essa si fa chiaro riferimento alle proprietà agricole *de monasteriis in Lucania et Samnio constitutis*; il vescovo Giovanni era invitato infatti a vigilare sul loro buon andamento produttivo. Al di là delle valenze teologiche e giuridiche, il documento sul piano puramente topografico ci attesta la presenza di aziende agricole rette da organizzazioni monastiche; dal documento è anche possibile ipotizzare la presenza di aziende agricole gestite da laici che hanno interesse ad ottenere vantaggi da quelle ecclesiastiche con soprusi.

I dati archeologici ci consentono di ipotizzare una certa vitalità nei centri abitati. Seppure documentata dal corredo di tombe, la presenza umana è attestata a *Saepinum*, a *Larinum* come nella stessa *Fagifulae*, municipio presso Montagano di cui sappiamo ancora poco (Samnium 1991: 259-260, 354-355).

La stessa situazione è attestata nel territorio da un congruo numero di ville attive anche in periodo tardo-antico; è questo forse il caso della villa romana di S. Maria in Canneto, di S. Fabiano (Di Niro 1982; 1984; 1991), dove è presente ceramica di V-VI sec. d.C., di S. Martino (Ceglia 1991), di Matrice – S. Maria della Strada (Lloyd & Cann 1984), ma anche dei resti di una villa presso Castropignano, non scavata, da cui provengono corredi tombali di VI e VII sec. d.C., a S. Giacomo degli Schiavoni (Roberts 1991; Ceglia 1985); un'altra è

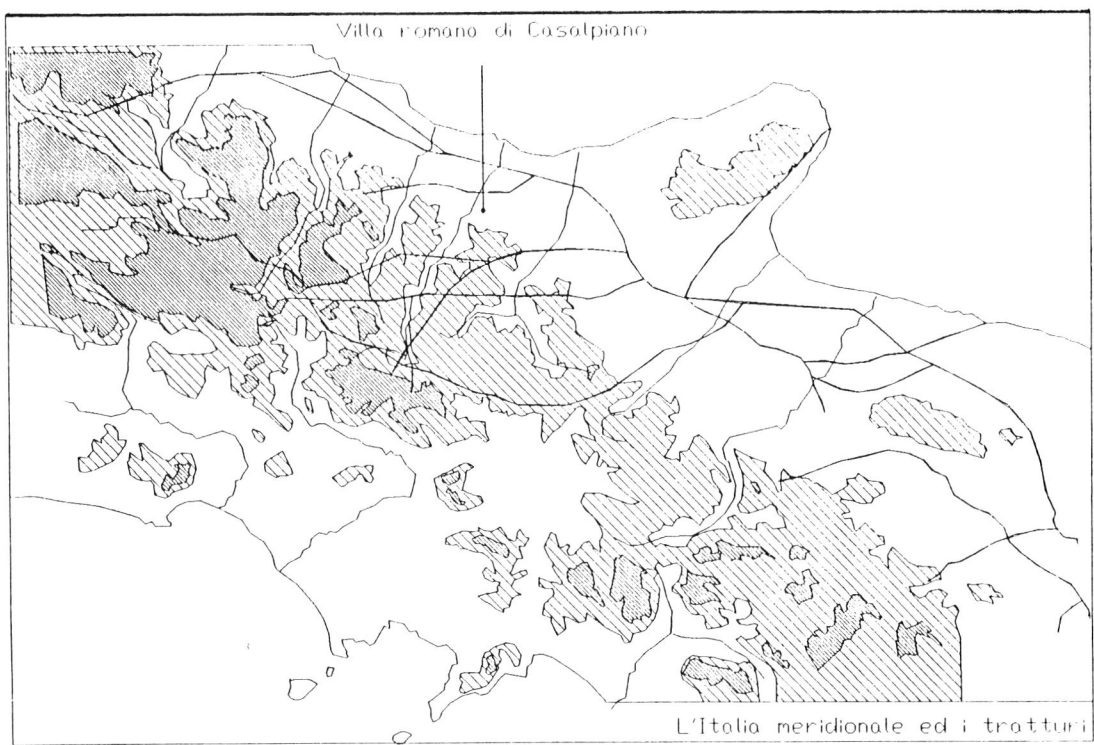

Fig. 1. Ubicazione della villa romana di Casalpiano.

presente in località S. Angelo, presso Civitacampomarano, villa questa, che dalla ceramica presente in superficie può considerarsi utilizzata anche nel V sec. d.C., fino alla costa dove da una tomba parzialmente manomessa da Termoli proviene una lucerna del tipo Dressel 31 (Di Niro 1991). I dati relativi al V-VI sec. d.C. appaiono tuttavia in tutti casi, se si esclude la villa di Matrice, ancora provvisori, i reperti archeologici ancora insufficienti per chiarire la situazione di questo periodo cronologico.

Casalpiano – scavi e risultati

Ad una migliore conoscenza di questa epoca può oggi forse contribuire un recente scavo effettuato in località Casalpiano, presso Morrone; esso ha di recente permesso il rinvenimento di parte di un'ampia villa romana da cui sono ricavabili non pochi dati utili al nostro discorso (De Benedittis 1991a; 1993).

La zona archeologica di Casalpiano (fig. 1) si colloca in un'ampia superficie pianeggiante di media collina posta ai margini del basso Molise attraversata dal corso del fiume Biferno. Il paesaggio è caratterizzato dal tratturo Celano – Foggia, importante strada in terra battuta che trova qui uno dei tratti meglio conservati. La presenza di una villa in questa zona era già indirettamente nota attraverso il rinvenimento di un'iscrizione romana che ricorda *Rectina, domina* romana resa famosa da una lettera di Plinio il giovane all'amico Tacito (*Epistulae*, VI,16) in cui lo scrittore latino ricorda gli ultimi attimi di vita dello zio durante l'eruzione del Vesuvio del 79 d.C.; l'iscrizione romana rinvenuta a Casalpiano era stata fatta a ricordo del ritorno di questa donna, scampata all'eruzione del Vesuvio; da ciò l'ara, quale ex voto, innalzata da un liberto per il ritorno della *domina* (Van Buren 1940).

La zona di Casalpiano propone dal punto di vista archeologico tre fasce d'interesse:

a) quella della villa romana (fig. 2);
b) quella della necropoli altomedioevale (fig. 3);
c) quella dell'insediamento benedettino (fig. 4).

Di queste le prime due rivestono particolare interesse per il Sannio in quanto, nonostante gli interventi fino ad ora effettuati in situazioni analoghe, poco si sapeva di queste strutture per il periodo repubblicano come non si avevano elementi per capire quale uso ci fosse del territorio sannita nel periodo che possiamo definire di passaggio tra il tardo impero e l'alto medioevo.

La stratigrafia, soprattutto nella zona interessata da ristrutturazioni successive, come nel caso della canonica o della stessa chiesa, si è presentata particolarmente articolata; meno complicata è apparsa all'esterno, dove tuttavia una relativamente recente arbitraria risistemazione della zona posta alle spalle della chiesa ha praticamente trinciato gli strati superiori, impedendo così la lettura delle fasi più recenti, almeno nella zona fino ad ora scavata; questo lavoro, effettuato mediante l'uso di macchinari pesanti, ha in qualche caso asportato anche grossi brandelli di muri antichi, che sono stati

Fig. 2. La villa romana di Casalpiano.

Fig. 3. La necropoli di VI-VII sec. di Casalpiano.

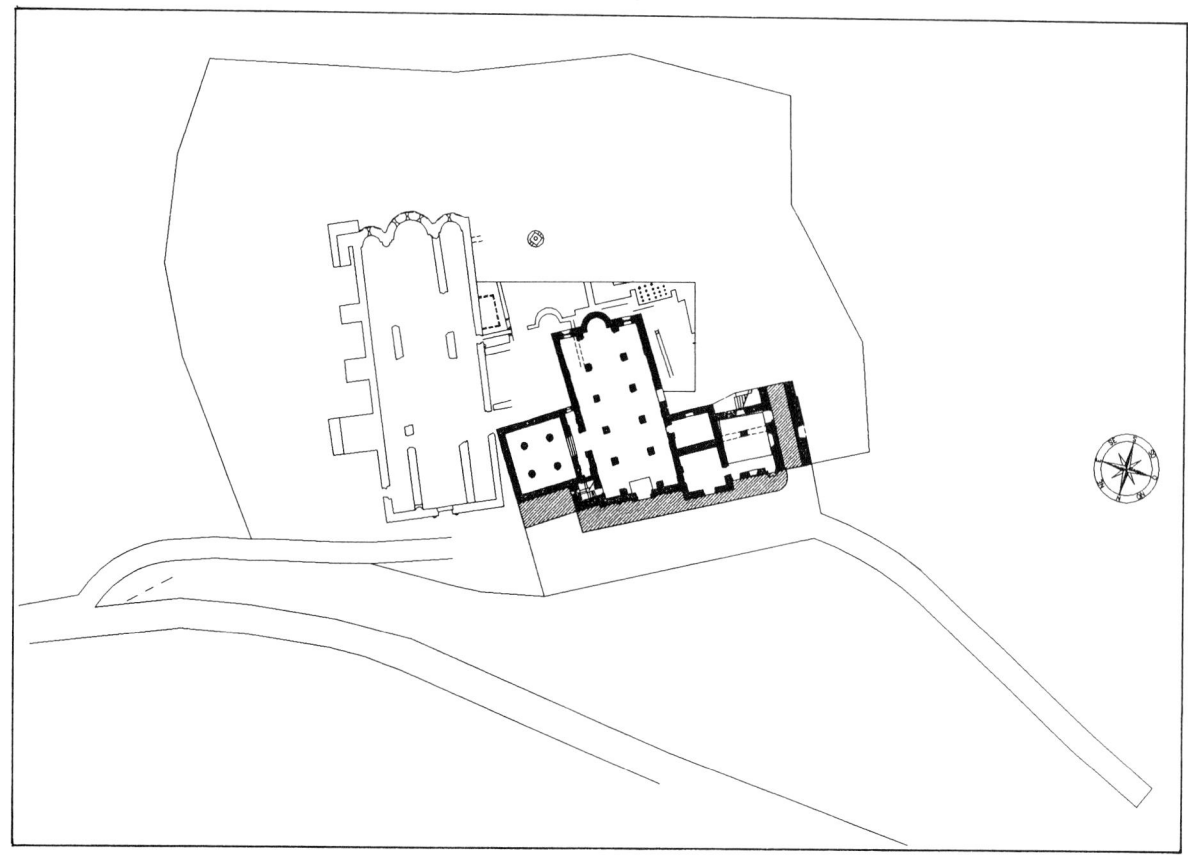

Fig. 4. Il complesso benedettino di Casalpiano.

poi riversati ai margini del terreno di pertinenza della badia. Ciò nonostante, la necropoli è rimasta sostanzialmente intatta ed i dati ricavati dallo scavo appaiono confortanti.

Il materiale archeologico rinvenuto sul lato dell'attuale ingresso della chiesa, frutto verosimilmente di un butto, ci rimanda cronologicamente al III-II sec. a.C. Se questi appaiono per ora come elementi atti a documentare solo una frequentazione della zona o tutto al più a permetterci di ipotizzare la presenza di una fattoria, vi sono motivi che ci consentono di parlare già di villa in epoca di poco posteriore: II-I sec. a.C. Sono stati rinvenuti infatti quattro pavimenti in cocciopisto, mentre vi sono elementi per pensare di trovarne almeno un altro. Uno di questi propone una massicciata di calcestruzzo composta di calce bianca, pozzolana, polvere e forse scaglie di marmo decorato da un ordito a reticolo di losanghe delimitato da semplice riquadratura lineare di piccole tessere nere.

Subito a lato del precedente è un pavimento in signino caratterizzato da piccole tessere bianche disposte ad intervalli regolari con al centro cerchi concentrici a tessere bianche ed azzurre fiancheggiati da riquadro campito con squame a tessere azzurre; un ordito a reticolo di losanghe s'interpone tra il riquadro centrale ed un meandro di svastiche e quadrati; al centro, sotto i cerchi corre l'iscrizione *C. Volusius Gallus fecit* (Terzani 1993); il gentilizio, forse di origine etrusca, è quasi del tutto assente nella *IV Regio* augustea. Di un secondo pavimento in signino restano pochi brandelli all'interno della chiesa sotto il livello pavimentale; esso è caratterizzato da grandi tessere irregolari di colore verde disposte verosimilmente secondo un reticolo di esagoni, forma questa riconoscibile almeno nella fascia più esterna; subito sotto l'altare vi sono resti di un altro pavimento in signino decorato da piccole tessere bianche disposte secondo un reticolo di piccoli rombi; a questi andranno aggiunti altri pavimenti che fino ad ora trovano documentazione in frammenti rinvenuti fuori contesto come le piccole mattonelle relative ad un pavimento in *opus spicatum*.

A Casalpiano è stato individuato con certezza il *calidarium*; gli elementi strutturali ad esso connessi fanno pensare anche a trasformazioni subite dalle stesse terme (un cunicolo tamponato in antico è ben visibile sulla parete laterale dell'ambiente che segue il *calidarium*). L'impianto di Casalpiano si presenta nella forma più elaborata in quanto qui sono stati rinvenuti i *tubuli* (Adam 1984: 294–295). Gli ambienti termali a Casalpiano presentano un orientamento leggermente diverso dagli altri più antichi; di dimensioni diverse, hanno anche pareti accostate fra di loro senza omogeneità alla forma generale della pianta della villa; ciò in quanto l'impianto termale dovette adattarsi alle strutture precedenti.

Se è ancora prematuro trarre conclusioni sulla pianta generale della villa, siamo nella condizione di ipotizzare una distribuzione degli ambienti su terrazze digradanti lungo il pendio; l'articolazione dei locali fino ad ora noti fanno proporre un *atrium* centrale; sul lato sud è stato invece rinvenuto un portico dei cui pilastri restano le basi quadrangolari. Alla villa dei pavimenti in signino, collocabile cronologicamente tra il II ed il I sec. a.C. si sovrappone dunque la costruzione di un impianto termale che ne modifica anche lo schema ampliandolo. Sono da attribuire a questa fase anche due tratti murari in opera reticolata, collocati uno a ridosso del *calidarium* ed uno nei pressi dell'attuale canonica.

La ceramica rinvenuta e gli elementi stratigrafici ci permettono di affermare che le strutture della villa mantengono le loro funzioni almeno fino al IV-V sec. d.C., quando tra le sue rovine troverà spazio una necropoli relativa ad un piccolo insediamento di cui si sono rinvenuti i resti di un focolare sotto i livelli pavimentali della chiesa di S. Maria. I dati fin qui raccolti su di essa non sono entusiasmanti essendo le tombe quasi sempre prive di corredo, tuttavia siamo ottimisti su quanto potrà ricavarsi dalle indagini successive.

Sono state scavate più di 50 tombe; la maggior parte è da attribuire ad una stessa fase cronologica, pur se qualche volta sono evidenti le sovrapposizioni o, in un caso, l'asportazione di parte delle strutture per la messa in opera di altri loculi. Le tombe sono del tipo a fossa con copertura a lastroni; un segnacolo in pietra senza decorazione sporge dal livello di calpestio per molte di esse; la fossa era raramente sistemata anche nella parte inferiore mediante lastroni; per lo più il defunto veniva adagiato su pavimentazioni antiche, ma comunque non vi era l'intento di sistemarne la base; le fosse non presentano sempre la stessa dimensione e vengono probabilmente adattate alla conformazione del defunto; le pareti vengono invece sistemate mediante lastre di pietra portate ad un livello omogeneo nella parte superiore dove veniva collocata la copertura a larghe lastre di pietra; la copertura come le pareti della fossa non sono a secco, ma vengono sigillate con un legante a base di arenaria di colore prevalentemente giallo. Il defunto presenta sempre lo stesso orientamento con il capo rivolto ad ovest e le braccia unite sull'addome; le tombe sono quasi sempre prive di corredo.

Per lo più le tombe sono di adulti di entrambi i sessi; in pochi casi sono di adolescenti, quattro sono di bambini piccoli; in qualche occasione lo stesso loculo viene riutilizzato per una seconda deposizione. Le tombe vengono collocate un po' dovunque secondo un preciso orientamento (est-ovest) a coprire almeno una metà della villa, in particolare quella dei mosaici.

I pochi oggetti rinvenuti nelle tombe rimandano tutti ad ambiente culturale latino. Tra i materiali di corredo sono da annoverare una brocchetta monoansata a bande rosse sottili, una fibbia ad occhielli di bronzo e una tremissis d'oro di Giustino II (565–578) (Terzani 1993); questi materiali consentono di collocare la necropoli in un contesto cronologico di VI sec. d.C. che non esclude proiezioni nel VII sec. d.C.

Se dunque da una parte abbiamo una completa distruzione della villa tra IV e V sec., non c'è dubbio che la zona sia stata ampiamente utilizzata tra V e VI sec. d.C.; se poi non è da escludere che sia stata utilizzata anche nel VII sec. d.C., non vi sono elementi per ora che ci consentano di parlare di fruizione della zona oltre questo lasso di tempo. La cronologia dei corredi della necropoli lascia ipotizzare che la zona non abbia subito drastiche trasformazioni durante il periodo della guerra greco-gotica. Una situazione analoga è ricavabile anche dal recente studio della villa di Avicenna, località posta presso Cagnano Varano, in agro sostanzialmente di *Teanum Apulum*, ancora *Samnium* dunque (D'Angela 1988).

Anche se lo scavo non può considerarsi ultimato, appare ipotizzabile che a determinare la crisi della villa, se si dà credito ai dati cronologici fino ad ora esposti, non sia stata solo la guerra greco-gotica; se poi si escludono cause specifiche a questo solo insediamento nella determinazione dei motivi della crisi, non possiamo che fare riferimento agli episodi connessi con Alarico ed in particolare al saccheggio con i suoi Visigoti di Roma (410) e dell'Italia meridionale. A seguito di questo episodio con decreto dell'amministrazione centrale datato 8 maggio 413 le province di Tuscia, Picenum, Samnium, Apulia, Calabria, Brutium e Lucania, a causa dei danni subiti, ebbero l'esonero dalle contribuzioni per cinque anni (*Cod.Theod.*, IX,30,1).

Che cosa succederà qui dopo il VII sec. d.C. non possiamo che ipotizzarlo; dobbiamo attendere l'anno mille per avere nuove notizie certe su Casalpiano. Nell'agosto del 1017 infatti il presbitero Pietro offre all'abate Atenolfo di Monte Cassino la sua parte della chiesa di S. Maria di Casalpiano; nell'ottobre dello stesso anno Martino, anch'egli monaco e presbitero, offre sempre all'abate Atenolfo la parte di sua pertinenza della chiesa di S. Maria di Casalpiano e la chiesa di S. Apollinare in Casalpiano (Bloch 1986: 276–277).

Il dato d'archivio ci consente di affermare che il toponimo Casalpiano è altomedioevale; inoltre lascia intravedere la presenza qui di uno di quei piccoli insediamenti denominati anche *fundi, vici, curtes*, o *loci*; i casali tuttavia, a differenza dei fundi e delle curtes, più che organismi patrimoniali, sembrano essere centri amministrativi minori; la probabile tradizione romana del toponimo indurrebbe a pensare ad una continuità dell'antico insediamento e che quindi il *casalis* non sia altro che la villa tardo-antica ribattezzata.

Certo le due chiese di S. Apollinare e S. Maria dovevano esistere già prima dell'anno 1000; probabilmente una delle due va riconosciuta nel rudere che fiancheggia l'attuale chiesa in stile romanico; va infine sottolineato che Casalpiano rappresenta un'ulteriore struttura benedettina sovrappostasi ad un'antica villa romana.

Discussione

Se si dà credito a quanto emerge dai dati archeologici sopra esposti se ne potrebbe concludere che la situazione della *provincia Samnii* era già prima del VI sec., e quindi anteriormente alla guerra greco-gotica, oppressa da una consistente crisi strutturale e demografica che investiva non solo le campagne, ma anche le città.

Certamente le vicende belliche connesse con il conflitto tra Goti e Bizantini non possono considerarsi estranee a questa regione (*Additamentum*, 105) dove la presenza dei Goti è ampiamente documentata (*Cassiodori, Variarum*, PL, Migne, 69,III,13; IV,10; V, 26; V, 27; XI,36), anche da reperti archeologici (Staffa & Pellegrini 1993: 15; Moretti 1918) ; al tracollo di questa realtà non certo florida non saranno estranei gli effetti dell'avanzata longobarda verso l'Italia meridionale e la spedizione condotta da Costante II; la frase di Paolo Diacono relativa alla completa desertificazione del Sannio nel 667 non può dunque che considerarsi la conseguenza di vicende accadute in tempi diversi alle quali non furono estranei fenomeni generali di lunga durata che hanno coinvolto il Sannio, ma anche tutta l'Italia meridionale; proprio per questo il giudizio espresso dal cronista longobardo sulle condizioni demografiche del Sannio può essere ridimensionato nella sua negatività se lo si confronta con la realtà dell'Italia meridionale, da cui quella del Sannio non appare affatto dissimile.

Se il giudizio di Paolo Diacono viene inquadrato in questo modo, non appaiono più contraddizioni i vari insediamenti rurali del Sannio ricordati dalla bolla di papa Pelagio I al vescovo di Larino della seconda metà del VI sec. d.C. o la fondazione verso la metà del VII sec. nei pressi del Biferno, del monastero di S. Maria in Castagnetum, da parte di Teoderada, madre del duca di Benevento Gisulfo, i cui resti oggi vengono riconosciuti dai più nei pressi della chiesa dell'Annunziata presso Casalciprano (CV, II, 14–18), o la documentazione di un'azienda agricola come quella di Camposinarcone, presso Campobasso, nel 774 (Chr. SS, 431) o il rinvenimento recente di un tesoretto di venti monete di denari franchi della fine dell'VIII sec. all'interno dell'anfiteatro di *Larinum*.

Bibliografia
Adam, J.P. 1989. *L'arte di costruire presso i Romani, materiali e tecniche*, Milano.
Additamentum = *Additamentum Marcellini Comitis, Monumenta Germaniae Historica*, XI, 2, 105.
Bloch, H. 1986. *Monte Cassino in the Middle Ages*, I-III, Roma.
Buonocore, M. 1992. 'Una nuova testimonianza del *rector Provinciae* Antonius Iustinianus e il *macellum* di Saepinum', *Athenaeum*, LXXX, 2, 484–486.
Cangemi, G. 1987. 'Osservazioni sulla rete viaria antica in Irpinia', AA.VV., *L'Irpinia nella società meridionale*, II, Avellino, 117–122.
Ceglia, V. & Genito, B. 1991. 'La necropoli altomedievale di Vicenne a Campochiaro', in *Samnium*, 329–334.
Ceglia, V. 1985. 'S. Giacomo degli Schiavoni: campagna di scavo 1984', *Conoscenze* 2, 135–137.

Ceglia, V. 1988. 'Lo scavo della necropoli di Vicenne", *Conoscenze* 4, 31-48.

Ceglia, V. 1991. 'La villa rustica di S. Martino in Pensilis: le anfore del rinvenimento del pozzo', in *Samnium*, 273-276.

CF = *Il Chronicon Farfense di Gregorio di Catino*, voll. I-II, Fonti per la Storia d'Italia, nr. 33-34, Roma 1903.

ChrSS = *Chronicon Beneventani Monasterii S. Sophiae*, in Ughelli F. & Coleti N., *Italia Sacra*, Venezia 1722 (rist. Forni Bologna 1974).

CIL = *Corpus Inscriptionum Latinarum*.

CV = *Chronicon Vulturnense del monaco Giovanni*, ed. V. Federici, FISI, 58,1, Roma, 1925.

D'Angela, C. (a cura di) 1988. *Gli scavi del 1953 nel Piano Carpino (Foggia): le terme e la necropoli altomedioevale della villa di Avicenna*, Taranto.

De Benedittis, G. 1988a. 'Considerazioni preliminari sul toponimo Sannio tra tardo impero e alto medioevo', *Conoscenze* 4, 23-29.

De Benedittis, G. 1988b. 'Di alcuni materiali altomedioevali provenienti dal Molise centrale ed il problema topografico della necropoli di Vicenne', *Conoscenze* 4, 103-108.

De Benedittis, G. 1991a. 'La necropoli di Casalpiano a Morrone del Sannio', in *Samnium*, 346.

De Benedittis, G. 1991b. 'Crisi e rinascita: il VII secolo d.C., Introduzione', in *Samnium*, 324-328.

De Benedittis, G. 1991c. 'Morrone del Sannio (Casalpiano)', in *Samnium*, 354.

De Benedittis, G. 1991d. 'Fagifulae', in *Samnium*, 259-260.

De Benedittis, G. 1993. 'La problematica storica', AA.VV., *S. Maria di Casalpiano, storia e restauro*, Pescara, 13-36.

De Tata, P. 1988. 'Sepolture altomedievali dall'anfiteatro di Larinum', *Conoscenze* 4, 94-103.

De Tata, P. 1991a. 'Larino (Anfiteatro)', in *Samnium*, 354-355.

De Tata, P. 1991b. 'Montagano (S. Maria a Faifoli)', in *Samnium*, 355.

Di Niro, A. 1982. *La villa romana di S. Fabiano e il sistema di produzione schiavistico*, Campobasso.

Di Niro, A. 1984. 'Roccavivara, villa rustica', *Conoscenze* 1, 213-215.

Di Niro, A. 1991. *Canneto, villa romana*, Termoli.

Gaggiotti, M. 1978. 'Le iscrizioni della basilica di Saepinum e i rectores della provincia del Samnium', *Athenaeum*, LVI, 1-2, 145-169.

Gassò, P.M. & Battle, C.M. 1969. *Pelagii I papae epistulae quae supersunt*, Abbatia Montisserati 1956 = *Patrologia Latina, Serie Latina, Supplementum*, vol. IV, Paris, col. 1310.

Genito, B. 1988. 'Materiali e problemi', *Conoscenze* 4, 49-67.

Genito, B. 1991a. 'Tombe con cavallo a Vicenne', in *Samnium*, 335-338.

Genito, B. 1991b. 'Campochiaro (Vicenne) T. 33, T. 25, T. 42, T. 46, T. 76', in *Samnium*, 347-354.

Hist. Lang. = *Historia Langobardorum*, Paolo Diacono, a cura di L. Capo, Vicenza, 1992.

Hodges, R., Barker, G. & Wade, K. 1980. 'Excavations at D85 (Santa Maria in Civita): an early medieval hilltop settlement in Molise', *Papers of the British School at Rome*, 48, 70-124.

Hodges, R. & Mitchell, J. 1985. *The Archaeology, Art and Territory of an Early Medieval Monastery*, British Archaeological Reports (Internat. Series 252), Oxford.

Hodges, R., Moreland, J. & Patterson, H. 1985. 'San Vincenzo al Volturno, the Kingdom of Benevento and the Carolingians', in C. Malone & S. Stoddart (eds.), *Papers in Italian Archaeology IV. Part III*, British Archaeological Reports (Iternational Series), Oxford.

Hodges, R. & Patterson, H. 1986. 'San Vincenzo al Volturno and the origins of the medieval pottery industry in Italy', in Francovich, R. & Mannoni T. (eds.), *La Ceramica Medievale nel Mediterraneo Occidentale*, Firenze, 13-27.

Hodges, R. & Wickham, C., 1981. 'Vetrana: un villaggio abbandonato altomedievale presso Guglionesi nella valle del Biferno (Molise)', *Archeologia Medievale*, VIII, 492-502.

Hodges, R. et al. 1984. 'Excavations at Vacchereccia (Rocchetta Nuova) - A late Roman and medieval Settlement in the Upper Volturno Valley', *Papers of the British School at Rome*, 52, 18-94.

Kehr, P.F. 1962. *Regesta Pontificum Romanorum, vol. IX, Samnium, Apulia, Lucania*, ed. W. Holzmann, Berlin.

La Regina, A. 1991. 'Sepino (Altilia)', in *Samnium*, 355.

Lloyd, J. & Cann, S. 1984. 'Late Roman and early medieval pottery from Molise', *Archeologia Medievale*, XI, 425-436.

Moretti, G. 1928. 'Torricella Peligna (Chieti): elmo barbarico in rame dorato', *Notizie degli Scavi di Antichità*, 471-478.

Pantoni, A. 1980. *Le chiese e gli edifici del monastero di San Vincenzo al Volturno*, Montecassino.

PL = *Patrologia Latina, Serie Latina*, ed. Migne.

Roberts, P. 1991. 'The late Roman pottery from S. Giacomo degli Schiavoni', in *Samnium*, 277-278.

Samnium 1991 = AA.VV., *Samnium, Archeologia del Molise*, Quasar, Roma.

Staffa, A.R. & Pellegrini, W. (a cura) 1993. *Dall'Egitto copto all'Abruzzo bizantino (sec. VI-VII)*, Crecchio.

Terzani, C. 1991. 'Tremissis d'oro', in *Samnium*, 354.

Terzani, C. 1993. 'Gli scavi archeologici', in *S. Maria in Casalpiano. Gli scavi archeologici e il restauro architettonico*, Pescara, 39-41.

Van Buren, A.W. 1940. 'Saggi di prosopografia', *Rendiconti dell'Accademia Pontificia di Archeologia*, XV, 73-86.

Vitolo, G. 1980. 'Vescovi e Diocesi', *Storia del Mezzogiorno* III, 75-91.

PART 5

New Research in South Etruria

36

Nuove Acquisizioni sulla Protostoria dell'Etruria Meridionale

Vincenzo d'Ercole & Flavia Trucco

con contributi di

Carlo Casi, Bianca Fossá, Gianfranco Mieli, Nuccia Negroni Catacchio, Maurizio Pellegrini & Rita Vargiu

Sommario: *Si presentano i risultati di tre interventi d'emergenza – differenti per problematica ed ambito cronologico – effettuati dalla Soprintendenza Archeologica dell'Etruria Meridionale in contesti protostorici. Con il primo è stata messa in luce a Prato di Frabolino, nella Selva del Lamone, una tomba a camera con dromos utilizzata nel corso dell'orizzonte iniziale della media età del Bronzo. Il secondo ha portato a riprendere gli scavi nella necropoli protovillanoviana di Poggio della Pozza e ha permesso di riaffrontare la problematica delle aree sepolcrali del Bronzo finale nella Tuscia, mentre l'ultimo intervento ha portato alla scoperta, nei pressi di Vulci, di un luogo di culto all'aperto villanoviano, con antecedenti nell'età del Bronzo, alla sorgente di Banditella.*

Si presentano in questa sede alcuni rinvenimenti effettuati dalla Soprintendenza Archeologica dell'Etruria Meridionale nel corso del 1992 in varie località del suo territorio. Pur trattandosi di scoperte fortuite, risultato di interventi d'emergenza in differenti contesti geografici e cronologici, esse ben si inseriscono in una serie di problematiche storico-archeologiche attualmente al centro del dibattito scientifico. Si tratta di rinvenimenti tutti collocabili tra il XVII e l'VIII secolo a.C., in quel periodo cioè che vede compiersi il processo della proto-urbanizzazione e della differenziazione sociale, che porterà l'Etruria dalle comunità di villaggio alle città di epoca storica.

Nello specifico, lo scavo di una tomba a camera con dromos presso Farnese (Viterbo) consente di affrontare, con dati di fatto obiettivi, la problematica dei rituali funerari della media età del bronzo e, attraverso di essi, dell'organizzazione sociale delle comunità relative, di cui molto si è sino ad oggi ipotizzato valendosi soprattutto dei dati, meglio noti, relativi all'Italia meridionale (Casi *et al.* 1995).

La ripresa delle ricerche nella necropoli di Poggio della Pozza presso Allumiere (Roma) permette invece di riesaminare la problematica della consistenza demografica delle comunità dell'età del Bronzo finale nell'Etruria meridionale (D'Ercole 1995).

Infine, il deposito votivo rinvenuto alla sorgente di Banditella presso Vulci apre un primo spiraglio sui luoghi di culto e sulla religiosità delle comunità protourbane e sui possibili antecedenti nel corso dell'età del Bronzo (D'Ercole & Trucco 1995).

Questa serie di 'fortunati' rinvenimenti testimonia come una consapevole attenzione alle incessanti trasformazioni a cui è da anni sottoposto il territorio possa fornire dati non irrilevanti per la comprensione della storia della regione. Infatti, ogni rinvenimento, per quanto casuale, se inserito in un critico contesto di lettura, può contribuire a colmare lacune e a dare maggior consistenza al quadro storico in esame.

Ciò non toglie che solo una ragionata programmazione della ricerca e conseguentemente della 'tutela', con adeguate e costanti risorse finanziarie ed umane, può permettere la lettura e l'interpretazione di dati archeologici che, in tempi ormai rapidissimi, i continui processi di trasformazione e degrado del territorio offrono e contemporaneamente cancellano per sempre. Non è poi un caso che gli interventi che si presentano in questa sede siano il risultato della collaborazione instauratasi nel corso del 1992 tra studiosi di enti diversi, i quali, ognuno per quanto di propria competenza, hanno permesso, con risorse certamente limitate, di acquisire elementi significativi per la comunità scientifica.

Prato di Frabolino (Farnese – Viterbo)

La prima segnalazione del rinvenimento di materiali preistorici nell'area denominata Prato di Frabolino (fig. 1,1), IGM F. 136 IV SE, risale al 1981 (Cf. Negroni Catacchio 1988: 72, tav.33,B. Inform. anche del Dr. Antonio Baragliu, Assessore alla Cultura del Comune di Farnese). Nell'occasione furono rinvenuti frammenti ceramici riferibili ad un abitato inquadrabile cronolo-

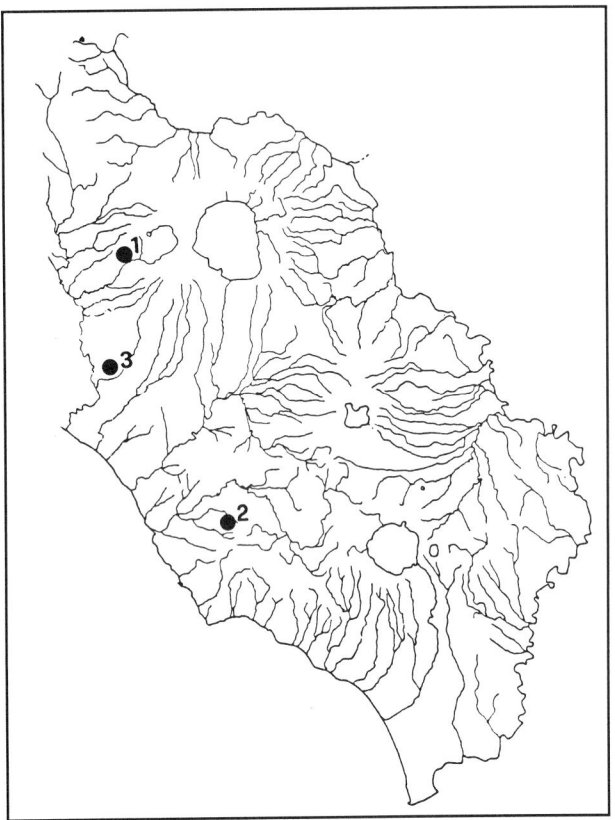

Fig. 1. 1: Prato di Frabolino. 2: Poggio della Pozza. 3: Banditella.

gicamente tra l'orizzonte evoluto del Bronzo antico ed il Bronzo medio iniziale.

Dal punto di vista geologico, l'abitato insiste sul bordo dell'ultima eruzione vulcanica, che ha originato uno degli ambienti naturali più impervi d'Etruria. La tomba è posizionata immediatamente al di fuori della colata lavica recente ed è scavata nel bancone tufaceo originatosi in seguito al vulcanismo volsiniese, caratterizzato da piroclastiti incoerenti, utilizzate anche successivamente, nel periodo etrusco, a fini sepolcrali. L'idrografia della zona è caratterizzata dal torrente Olpeta, che scorre circa 500 m a valle dell'abitato e che ha originato la profonda solcatura del plateau lavico, intervallata da terrazzi, che costeggia la Selva del Lamone sul versante meridionale.

La sepoltura risultava violata dai clandestini, che avevano asportato quasi integralmente il riempimento della camera sepolcrale, lasciando in posto solo alcuni lembi di terreno presso le pareti, senza invece intervenire sul dromos. La tomba è costituita da una camera approssimativamente quadrangolare (m. 2,16 × 2,32; fig. 2,1), attualmente conservata per un'altezza massima di circa 1 m, priva dell'originaria copertura che è stata asportata dai lavori agricoli. Ad essa si accedeva tramite un'apertura appositamente sagomata per alloggiare due lastre sovrapposte di chiusura; la camera era preceduta da un corridoio (m 3,6 × 1,3), scavato anch'esso nel tufo, il cui riempimento, rinvenuto intatto, era costituito da un ammasso di pietre laviche che, poste a puntello della porta della camera, andavano decrescendo allontanandosi da essa. Al di sotto di queste, sul pavimento del dromos, è stato asportato un sottile e compatto strato, contenente diversi frammenti ceramici, riferibili a più forme aperte non interamente ricostruibili, per lo più d'impasto ben depurato, con superfici accuratamente lucidate. Tra di essi sono riconoscibili una ciotola con carena a spigolo e parete concava fortemente inclinata all'esterno (fig. 2,8); una ciotola con orlo quasi a tesa distinto da spigolo interno fortemente ingrossato (fig. 2,7) ed un'ansa con soprelevazione ad ascia breve (fig. 2,6).

Nel corso dell'indagine stratigrafica sono stati rinvenuti resti scheletrici umani da cui sono stati identificati quattro individui, di cui tre di età adulta (due di sesso femminile e uno di sesso indeterminato) e uno di età infantile. I resti di due individui (individuo A e individuo B) sono stati ritrovati in posizione non fisiologica nello strato intatto, mentre i resti degli altri due (individui C e D) sono stati recuperati dallo strato di violazione recente.

L'individuo A, i cui resti erano deposti nei pressi dell'angolo est della camera, probabilmente di sesso femminile, risulta avere un'età alla morte compresa tra i 33-39 anni. L'analisi della ipoplasia dello smalto ha permesso di ipotizzare che l'individuo sia stato soggetto a fattori di stress durante i primi cinque anni di vita. In connessione con questa deposizione è stato rinvenuto un frammento di ciotola carenata con parete convessa rientrante e breve orlo a colletto, di forma complessiva schiacciata, che presenta sulla vasca, subito al di sotto della carena, tre fori, forse di riparazione, a sezione biconica, uno completo, due incompleti lungo l'attuale linea di frattura (fig. 2,3). E' questo l'unico elemento vascolare di corredo rinvenuto *in situ*: la ciotola, infatti, era posta a pochi centimetri dalla calotta cranica dell'individuo A.

L'individuo B, i cui resti sono stati raccolti nei pressi dell'angolo ovest della camera funeraria, risulta di sesso femminile e di età alla morte di 23-31 anni. Su quasi tutti i denti analizzati sono state rilevate linee di arresto nella deposizione dello smalto: l'individuo sembra essere stato soggetto a fattori di stress durante l'accrescimento con particolare gravità tra 1.5-3 anni e a circa 4 anni. Ad esso è da attribuire una collana, probabilmente in faïence azzurra, costituita da almeno 84 vaghi discoidali di differenti dimensioni, di forma sovente irregolare, con diametri compresi tra cm 0,2 e cm 0,5 e da un elemento distanziatore di forma irregolarmente rettangolare, con tre fori passanti posti a intervalli irregolari (determinazione ancora in corso a cura di Paola Santopadre dell'I.C.R.). Della medesima parure facevano parte anche tre fermatrecce, incompleti, a tre o quattro spirali ad estremità assottigliate in argento.

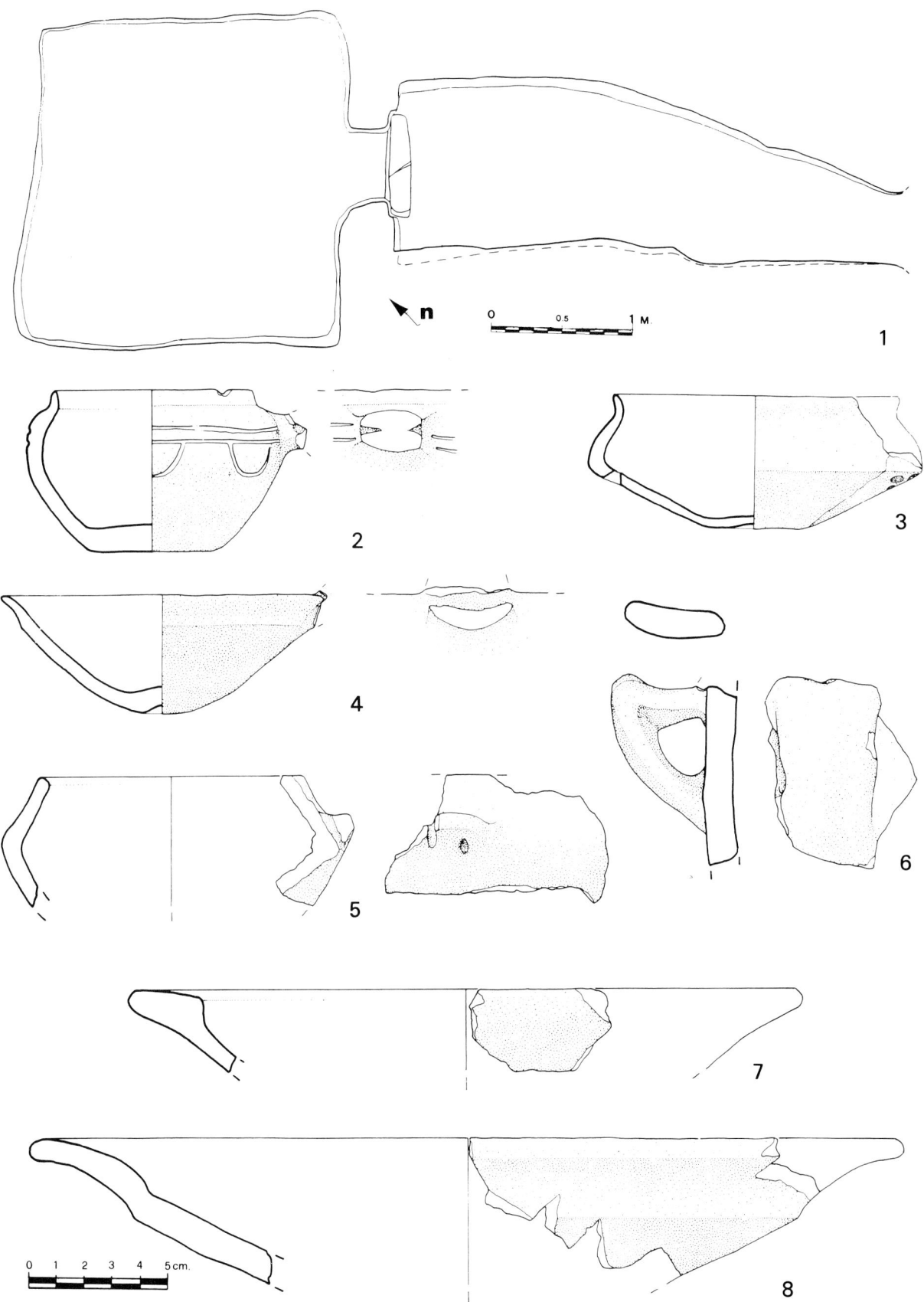

Fig. 2. Prato di Frabolino. 1: Pianta della tomba. 2-5: Corredo vascolare dalla camera. 6-8: Materiali del dromos.

Scarsi resti di un'ulteriore deposizione (individuo C) sono stati rinvenuti nello strato di violazione ed erano pertinenti ad un individuo di sesso non più determinabile, di età alla morte compresa tra i 25 e i 35 anni. Anche questo individuo sembra essere stato soggetto a fattori di stress tra i 2 e i 5 anni.

La presenza in questo stesso strato di un secondo molare deciduo destro del mascellare inferiore attesta la presenza di un altra inumazione: in questo caso si trattava di un bambino di età compresa tra i 6 e i 10 anni.

Lo scavo clandestino ha asportato dalla camera il resto dei corredi vascolari, di cui non è più possibile ricostruire con certezza la posizione. Verosimilmente dal centro della camera provengono una tazza con alta carena appena accennata, con attacco di ansa a nastro dall'orlo alla carena (fig. 2,4) ed una tazza globulare con colletto, decorata a festoni, con attacco di ansa a nastro, probabilmente formante anello, impostata sul punto di massima espansione. Ai lati dell'ansa é presente una decorazione a solcature, dal disegno relativamente irregolare: un motivo a 6 festoni, ben distanziati e disegnati da una sola solcatura, pendenti da due solcature parallele orizzontali (fig. 2,2). Un frammento di ciotola con carena arrotondata e parete fortemente rientrante, con presa trapezoidale a margini arrotondati e due fori verticali passanti (fig. 2,5), è stato recuperato nel corso dell'asportazione del terreno già manomesso dallo scavo clandestino, in prossimità dell'angolo est della camera.

I quattro vasi provenienti dalla camera hanno in comune diverse caratteristiche morfologiche: si tratta di 4 forme aperte, probabilmente tutte da leggere come tazze, di piccole dimensioni – se non delle vere e proprie miniaturizzazioni – le cui vasche hanno altezze comprese tra i 4,3 e i 5,6 cm. Presentano tutte l'impasto accuratamente depurato e le superfici lucidate.

I due frammenti provenienti dall'angolo est hanno in comune alcuni caratteri tipologici. La ciotola carenata con parete convessa rientrante e breve orlo a colletto rientra in una famiglia tipologica dall'ampia diffusione in area medio-tirrenica che, in particolare, caratterizza l'orizzonte iniziale della *facies* di Grotta Nuova. La ciotola ha un confronto puntuale con un frammento con vasca decorata da Luni, dallo strato 3 della trincea 11 (Fugazzola Delpino 1976: fig. 36,13).

Di più difficile inquadramento, invece, il frammento di ciotola carenata con parete fortemente rientrante, che non trova riscontri puntuali nel panorama vascolare dei complessi databili alla media età del bronzo, sia per l'assenza di un orlo distinto, sia per la forte rientranza della parete. Confronti generici possono essere istituiti con frammenti provenienti da Grotta dei Piccioni (Cremonesi 1976: fig. 63,5–6) e da Dicomano (Sarti 1980: fig. 17,2,9); più strette analogie si colgono con un frammento di ciotola, con decorazione incisa e a punteggio, dallo strato 6 del Riparo dell'Ambra (Cocchi Genick 1986: fig. 38,1).

Rientra in una famiglia tipologica sempre di ampia diffusione in area medio-tirrenica la tazza con alta carena appena accennata, presente ad esempio a Cetona (Calzoni 1962: tav. XVIII,b), Mezzano (Franco 1982: 64, tav. XVI, 11), Grotta dell'Orso (Cremonesi 1968: fig. 11,10; 14,12).

Del tutto originale, invece, la tazza globulare a colletto, forma per la quale non sono rintraciabili confronti tra il materiale edito da siti delle fasi iniziali dell'età del bronzo. Anche la decorazione si discosta alquanto dal canonico motivo a festoni, quale ci è noto in numerosi complessi di questa età dalla Liguria al Lazio (Bagnoli & Panicucci 1992), per il numero ridotto delle incisioni con cui esso è ottenuto. La distanza tra un festone e l'altro lo avvicina al vasetto da Felcetone (Rittatore Vonwiller 1951: 166, fig. 7), con il quale sembrerebbe esservi qualche analogia anche per la forma.

Pur con le incertezze, dovute alla scarsità di dati da contesti chiaramente stratificati, che ancora presenta l'articolazione in fasi del 'gruppo di Grotta Nuova', sembra possibile inquadrare i materiali della tomba di Prato di Frabolino nell'ambito dell'orizzonte più antico della media età del bronzo dell'area medio-tirrenica.

Più generiche indicazioni offre la parure ornamentale dell'individuo A. Infatti, le perle in faïence o in pasta vitrea sono attestate sia in Italia settentrionale che in Italia meridionale fin dal Bronzo antico (Mercurago, Bande di Cavriana, Lucone, Lavagnone 2, Caverna dell'Acqua di Finale Ligure), ma sono più ampiamente presenti nei contesti, soprattutto funerari, del Bronzo medio (Montale, Montata t. 16, Franzine t. 32, 247) (Bergonzi & Cardarelli 1992: 218). Recentemente Renato Peroni (1989: 167) e Andrea Cardarelli (1992: 393) hanno ripresentato l'ipotesi della produzione locale della faïence, in particolare per i bottoni di Mercurago, Montale, Quingento e Santa Rosa di Poviglio, la cui datazione ad una fase iniziale del Bronzo medio sembrerebbe ormai sicura. Alcune spirali d'argento sono state rinvenute in contesti funerari eneolitici, mentre per quanto attiene l'età del Bronzo medio rinvenimenti in argento sono assai più limitati: si conoscono infatti una perla da Castellaro Lagusello, una lamina da Isolone del Mincio ed uno spillone da S. Polo (Guidi 1992b: 449).

Più complesso si presenta, invece, il quadro restituito dai materiali ceramici provenienti dallo strato a contatto col pavimento del dromos. Si tratta di frammenti di non grandi dimensioni, appartenenti a forme vascolari per lo più aperte e di formato normale, probabilmente senza uno stretto rapporto con la dimensione funeraria. Il frammento di ciotola carenata con parete concava fortemente inclinata all'esterno trova confronto in Italia centrale con esemplari da complessi non stratificati come il deposito della grotta dell'Orso (Cremonesi 1968: fig. 10,16) e Colle Palumba nel territorio di Roma (Bietti

Sestieri *et al.* 1992: 441, fig. 2,2); il tipo ha qualche analogia con alcuni degli esemplari della forma 44 (gruppo C) di Coppa Nevigata (Cassano *et al.* 1987: fig. 74,12), che permetterebbero una sua datazione alla media età del Bronzo. Dubitativamente allo stesso periodo possono essere inquadrati i due frammenti di ciotola con orlo quasi a tesa (uno solo dei quali qui riprodotto: fig. 2,7). Per essi è possibile istituire confronti con esemplari dallo strato 4 del Riparo Grande di Camaiore (Cocchi Genick 1991: fig. 1,9), dallo strato 2, orizzonte superiore di S. Maria in Belverde (Cuda, Sarti 1992: 387, fig. 1,1), da Pian Sultano Crepaccio (di Gennaro 1992: 704, n. 4), da Tolfa, punto 2 (di Gennaro, Pacciarelli & De Grossi 1974: tav. II,1). In Italia meridionale la foggia è presente nella capanna 2 di Cavallino (Pancrazzi 1979: fig. 112,7-8) e con esemplari meno articolati anche a Muro Maurizio 2 (Cremonesi 1977: fig.3,1-6). La famiglia tipologica potrebbe avere rapporti con i cosiddetti scodelloni di Capo Graziano, anche se in essi è sempre presente una maggiore articolazione dell'orlo. La sua presenza in Italia centrale in contesti stratificati permettono di inquadrarla in un momento antico della media età del Bronzo, senza per altro escludere la possibilità di una evoluzione a partire da forme simili nella fase finale dell'antica età del Bronzo. Anche per le anse a gomito con sopraelevazione a breve ascia o ad ascia accennata si ripropone un discorso simile. Esse sono considerate un fossile guida della fase finale dell'antica età del Bronzo, ma la loro presenza in contesti con sicuri elementi della successiva media età del bronzo (Cocchi Genick 1987: 61), più che indicare una commistione di elementi potrebbe essere letta come una sopravvivenza, contemporanea all'allungamento della sopraelevazione.

Anche per il materiale rinvenuto nel dromos è quindi possibile avanzare, se pure con maggior cautela data la possibile non omogeneità del contesto, l'ipotesi dell'attribuzione all'orizzonte iniziale della media età del Bronzo.

Avendo, purtroppo, l'intervento clandestino interessato la quasi totalità del livello deposizionale della camera sepolcrale, ricostruire un quadro complessivo delle deposizioni risulta quanto mai arduo; come pure è difficile proporre una lettura verosimile dei fenomeni rituali che generalmente intervengono nella formazione di depositi all'interno di sepolture.

Come è possibile evincere dallo studio dei resti osteologici, la tomba venne destinata alla sepoltura di più individui, almeno quattro sulla base di quanto recuperato. E' ipotizzabile che i primi due individui ad essere stati seppelliti siano stati quelli identificati come A e B, successivamente spostati e rideposti nei pressi degli angoli est ed ovest della camera, per lasciare posto, al centro, per gli individui C e D, quelli cioè più disturbati e manomessi dall'intervento dei clandestini.

Sulla base di ciò si è portati a pensare che il dromos, lasciato agli inizi probabilmente vuoto e percorribile, sia stato riempito e sigillato con le pietre laviche, dopo la riapertura della camera funeraria in conseguenza del seppellimento degli individui C e D. A questa prima fase di utilizzo della tomba sarebbero quindi pertinenti i frammenti ceramici trovati sul pavimento del dromos.

Per quanto attiene i corredi non può non colpire la perfetta corrispondenza tra il numero dei vasi presenti nella tomba, quattro, ed il numero degli individui in essa sepolti. Solo in un caso, però, quello dell'individuo A, abbiamo l'associazione *in situ* della ciotola carenata con orlo a colletto con il relativo inumato. Il frammento di ciotola con presa forata, trovato durante lo scavo nella terra di riempimento e i due vasi, rinvenuti precedentemente all'intervento di scavo, potrebbero essere riferiti, indistintamente agli altri tre inumati.

In Italia meridionale durante il Bronzo medio sembra essere caratteristica la deposizione, per ogni individuo sepolto, di una tazza, che veniva collocata prevalentemente nei pressi del cranio (Cipolloni Sampó 1992: 283).

Gli oggetti di pregio, i grani di collana in faïence ed i fermatrecce in argento, sembrano appannaggio dell'individuo B, con l'eccezione di alcuni grani, rinvenuti nei pressi dell'angolo nord della camera, per i quali non si può stabilire con certezza se appartenessero sempre alla collana dell'individuo B o se invece facessero parte dell'eventuale parure ornamentale degli individui C o D.

Appare evidente come la camera sepolcrale, dalle dimensioni abbastanza ridotte di poco più di 4,5 mq, sia stata utilizzata fino alla pressoché completa saturazione dello spazio disponibile. Sulla base dei dati raccolti è presumibile che l'accesso alla tomba sia stato selezionato in base al sesso a favore delle donne e dei bambini. La composizione numerica ed antropologica del gruppo sepolto a Prato di Frabolino ricorda quella formata dai tre inumati del vicino tumulo IV di Crostoletto di Lamone, fra cui vi erano una donna, un bambino e nessun maschio antropologicamente accertato.

La presenza nei corredi di Prato di Frabolino di oggetti di pregio, come la faïence e l'argento, ben si inserisce in quel processo che vede, nella media età del bronzo soprattutto in Italia meridionale (Pacciarelli 1992: 274), la fine dell'accumulazione 'statica' dei beni di lusso nei ripostigli (caratteristici dell'eneolitico/bronzo antico) a favore di un lusso ostentato nell'abbigliamento e negli ornamenti (gioielli) particolarmente evidente negli individui di sesso femminile, così come l'emblema eroico del comando è attestato dalla presenza delle spade nelle coeve deposizioni maschili.

Poggio della Pozza (Allumiere – Roma)

Nel mese di agosto 1992 é stato effettuato un'intervento di recupero sul versante di Poggio della Pozza (fig. 1,2) cartograficamente denominato Quarto delle Bufale (Allumiere): lo scavo è stato condotto su di una lingua di terra posta a quota 375 m slm (IGM F 152 I SE; foglio 13, particella 131, del Catasto del comune di Allumiere).

La zona in cui è stato effettuato l'intervento è ben nota nella bibliografia archeologica: infatti, alla fine del secolo scorso Adolfo Klitsche de La Grange vi aveva scavato parecchie decine di tombe protovillanoviane (1881; 1884a; 1984b); altre tombe furono portate alla luce nella prima metà di questo secolo (Bastianelli 1939; idem 1942), mentre negli anni sessanta, Peroni, con due diverse campagne, scavava altre 20 sepolture (1960: 341–362). La zona oggetto di queste indagini è situata nella particella 135, in una fascia posta 100–200 m a valle dell'area oggi indagata.

Lo scavo ha interessato un'area di 30 mq, sondata per una profondità variabile tra i 15 e i 40 cm, in cui sono state identificate otto tombe.

La tomba 6 è stata rinvenuta intatta: il pozzetto foderato di pietre conteneva una brocca a corpo globulare, che fungeva da urna ed una ciotola carenata con ansa a nastro canaliculata, in funzione di coperchio (fig. 3). La brocca, dalla superficie fortemente abrasa, è decorata a solcature con motivi lineari ed angolari con cuppelle ai vertici. All'interno, oltre ai resti compiutamente cremati di un individuo adulto (20–40 anni) e di un infante (0–6 anni), era deposto un frammento di rotella in osso, decorata a cerchielli.

Fig. 3. Poggio della Pozza: tomba 6 (foto M. Pellegrini).

La tomba 8 (fig. 4), in cassetta litica, conteneva un'urna biconica, decorata a cordicella, solcature e cuppelle, coperta da una ciotola a vasca arrotondata, parete a gola rientrante e presa forata sulla carena. All'interno dell'urna, oltre a resti della cremazione di un individuo adulto, probabilmente di sesso maschile (25–45 anni), vi era una fibula in bronzo con arco a doppia piegatura decorato ad incisioni parallele.

La tomba 2 conteneva un vaso bivalve biconica d'impasto non decorato, rinvenuto in frammenti e non completamente ricostruibile, deposto nel terreno senza alcuna protezione litica.

Della tomba 5, in cassetta litica, rimanevano *in situ* solo alcuni frammenti di una scodella non decorata d'impasto e scarsi resti di ossa combuste (indeterminabili), mentre del corredo della tomba 3, anch'essa in struttura litica, sono stati recuperati alcuni frammenti di vaso biconico decorato con motivi angolari continui ed una banda orizzontale a solcature.

La tomba 1 consisteva in una custodia bivalve biconica di tufo, la cui parte inferiore era ancora *in situ*, con all'interno uno strato di terra di rogo; il coperchio era in frammenti a causa della manomissione subita dalla tomba.

Delle tombe 4 e 7 rimanevano sul terreno solo le lastre che costituivano la base della cassetta litica, in cui le ceneri potevano anche essere state deposte senza urna, come già attestato in questa necropoli.

Risulta evidente a questo punto delle ricerche come la necropoli protovillanoviana della Pozza, considerata già, con le sue circa 100 sepolture, come la più estesa dell'Etruria meridionale, sia numericamente molto più consistente.

Considerando, infatti, la densità delle tombe riscontrata nell'ultimo saggio di scavo effettuato (una tomba ogni 4 mq circa), è ipotizzabile che sulla lingua di terra posta tra q. 375 e q. 400, la cui superficie supera l'ettaro, vi fossero parecchie centinaia di deposizioni, in un tessuto discontinuo, costituito da più gruppi di tombe, sulla cui entità numerica non è per ora possibile pronunciarsi, separate da aree non utilizzate per il seppellimento, ma in alcuni casi interessate da strutture ad esso accessorie (aree per i roghi, acciottolati, ecc.). Sempre per ciò che riguarda Poggio della Pozza, le sepolture scavate nei vari periodi si collocano lungo il pendio sud-orientale della collina, su di una fascia che supera abbondantemente i 100 m in senso est-ovest, suggerendo una dislocazione a semicerchi concentrici – avente come fulcro la cima della collina – che utilizzava il pendio naturale, adattandolo artificialmente ove necessario. Infatti, pur nella limitatezza del campione noto, sembra di intravedere un'organizzazione spaziale su più file parallele, in cui le deposizioni si collocano a distanze costanti.

A questo quadro vanno aggiunte la tomba sul versante di Monte Rovello verso Valle del Campaccio, come pure quelle di Forchetta di Palano. E' ovvio ipotizzare che

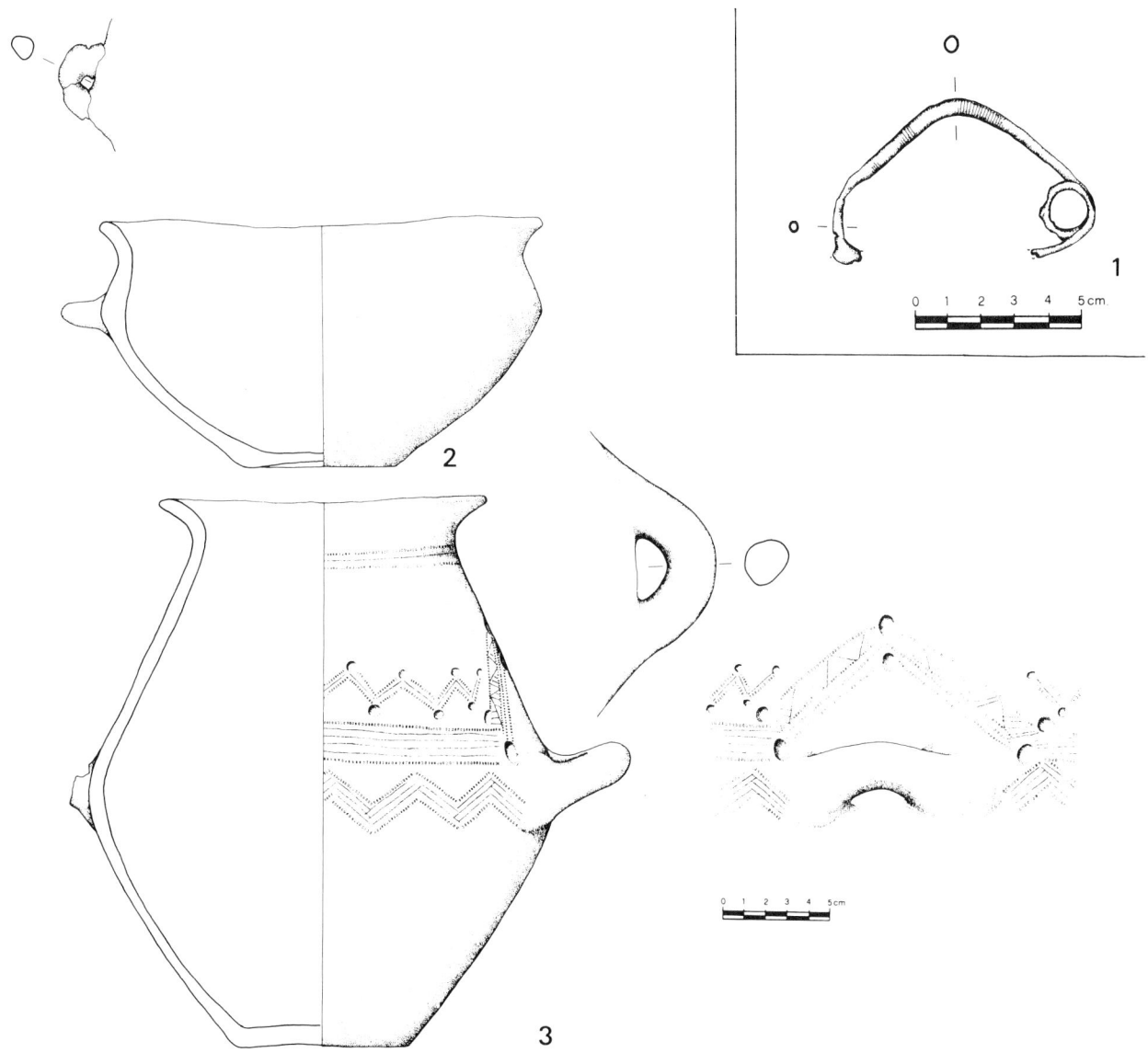

Fig. 4. Poggio della Pozza: tomba 8.

esse siano tutte riferibili all'abitato di Monte Rovello. Inoltre, la presenza di frammenti ceramici, probabilmente da situazione insediativa, sulla cima del vicino colle a quota 375, come pure sulla cima del Poggio della Pozza, lascierebbero presumere che tale insediamento comprendesse anche nuclei posti sulle due alture meridionali, mentre le aree sepolcrali dovevano occupare, in modo non omogeneo, gran parte delle pendici.

Resta aperto nella Tuscia, come per buona parte della penisola, il problema della dicotomia tra l'elevato livello demografico che è possibile desumere sulla base della documentazione relativa agli insediamenti (quantità e dimensioni) ed il limitato numero di sepolture note per l'età del Bronzo finale (Domanico & Miari 1992). Infatti, nelle 20 località sepolcrali conosciute, molte delle quali con una sola tomba, a fronte di circa un centinaio di abitati (di Gennaro 1990: fig. 5), si contano un totale di circa 150 tombe. Anche volendo ipotizzare una fortissima selezione nel seppellimento, appare evidente che si è di fronte ad una vera e propria lacuna delle fonti documentarie, anche se meno marcata che nelle precedenti fasi dell'età del Bronzo. D'altra parte risulta ormai evidente che per il seppellimento, già a partire dall'età del Bronzo recente, non vengono più utilizzate le cavità naturali (Guidi 1992a). Proprio l'assenza di scavi esaustivi nelle aree sepolcrali protostoriche d'Etruria ha portato a far considerare La Pozza come un'eccezione in un quadro generale costituito da necropoli apparentemente composte da 3–12 sepolture. In realtà, si potrebbe invece proporre quello della Pozza come vero e proprio modello: più nuclei di sepolture distribuite su ampie estensioni, localizzate per lo più sui pendii o comunque su morfologie scarsamente redditizie dal punto di vista economico.

Banditella (Canino – Viterbo)

Lo scavo di Banditella (fig. 1,3) ha interessato l'area di un'antica sorgente, con relativo piccolo stagno, frequentata dalla media età del bronzo fino ad epoca arcaica. Lo scavo scientifico ha potuto indagare una superficie limitata (poco più di 200 mq) su un'area archeologica presunta di almeno 1000/1500 mq, già compromessa dalle opere di adeguamento dell'acquedotto di Montalto di Castro (IGM F. 136 III SE).

In particolare, sul fondo del piccolo specchio d'acqua, in un livello di limi lacustri, spesso cm 10/15 e che poggia sulle ghiaie di base, sono stati messi in luce numerosi manufatti databili dal Bronzo medio al finale (XVII-XI sec. a.C.). La presenza di elementi diagnostici per ognuna delle fasi cronologiche note in Etruria testimonia una frequentazione ininterrotta del sito. Tra i reperti (fig. 5) rinvenuti si segnalano, infatti, anse a lobi con doppio foro verticale caratteristiche delle fasi non avanzate della media età del bronzo, anse a nastro a gomito, ceramiche decorate in stile appenninico, vasi a listello interno, anse a capocchia bilaterale caratteristiche dell'età del bronzo recente, ceramiche decorate in stile protovillanoviano, fornelli.

Tali materiali archeologici appaiono del tutto simili, sia dal punto di vista funzionale che per lo stato di frammentazione, a quelli che normalmente si rinvengono in un abitato; stessa indicazione fornisce la presenza di faune nelle consuete proporzioni (studio in corso da parte di Jacopo De Grossi Mazzorin). Fanno eccezione le numerose rotelle in osso (fig. 6,1–2) e i molti vaghi di collana in pasta vitrea (fig. 6, 8–10), rinvenuti sui bordi dello stagno, riferibili all'età del Bronzo finale, la cui concentrazione appare estranea ad un normale contesto abitativo.

Con l'età del Bronzo finale le modalità di utilizzo del sito sembrano cambiare. Può essere significativo notare che nel decimo secolo a.C. ha inizio l'occupazione stabile del pianoro della città di Vulci e cominciano le prime sepolture in quelle che diverranno le necropoli 'storiche vulcenti' (Pacciarelli 1991).

Nello stesso ambito cronologico si colloca la fine di tutti gli insediamenti dell'età del Bronzo noti nella zona, quali Pontecchio, Rogge di Canino, Poggio Olivastro, Poggio Martino, Castellina del Formiconcino (Casi & Mandolesi 1993) e forse Banditella stessa, nei cui dintorni

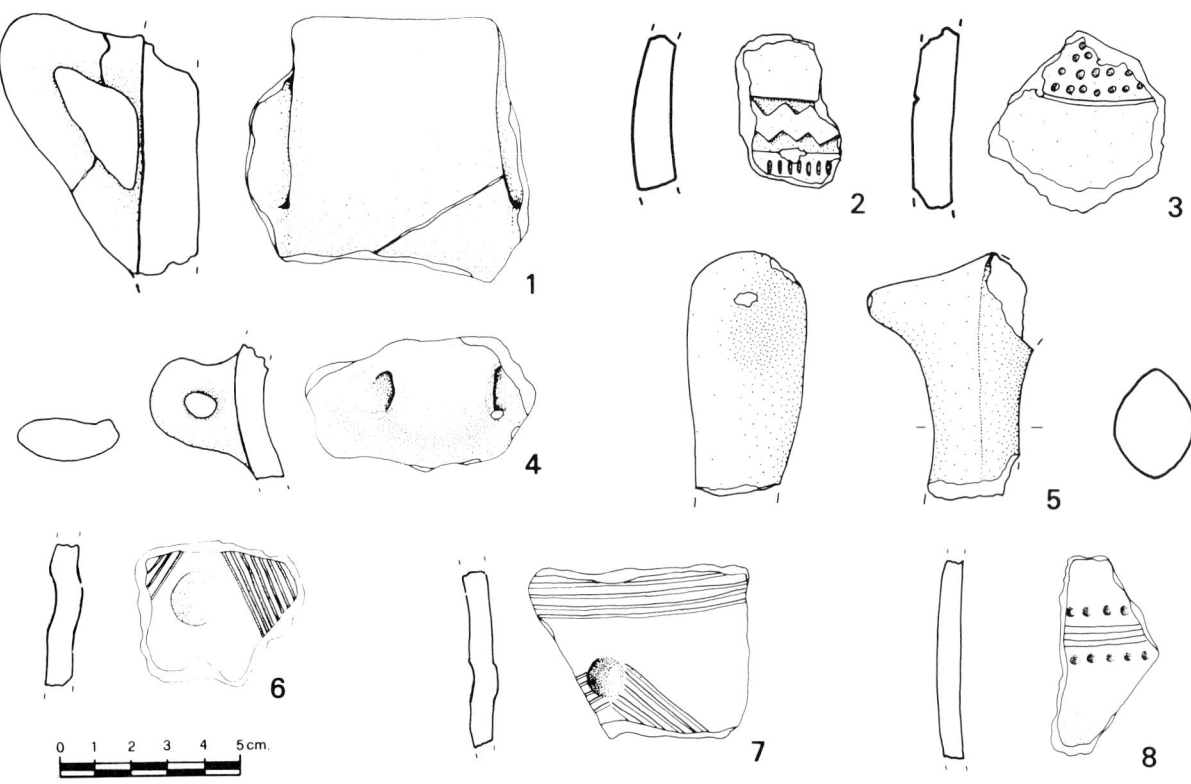

Fig. 5. Banditella: materiali dell'età del Bronzo.

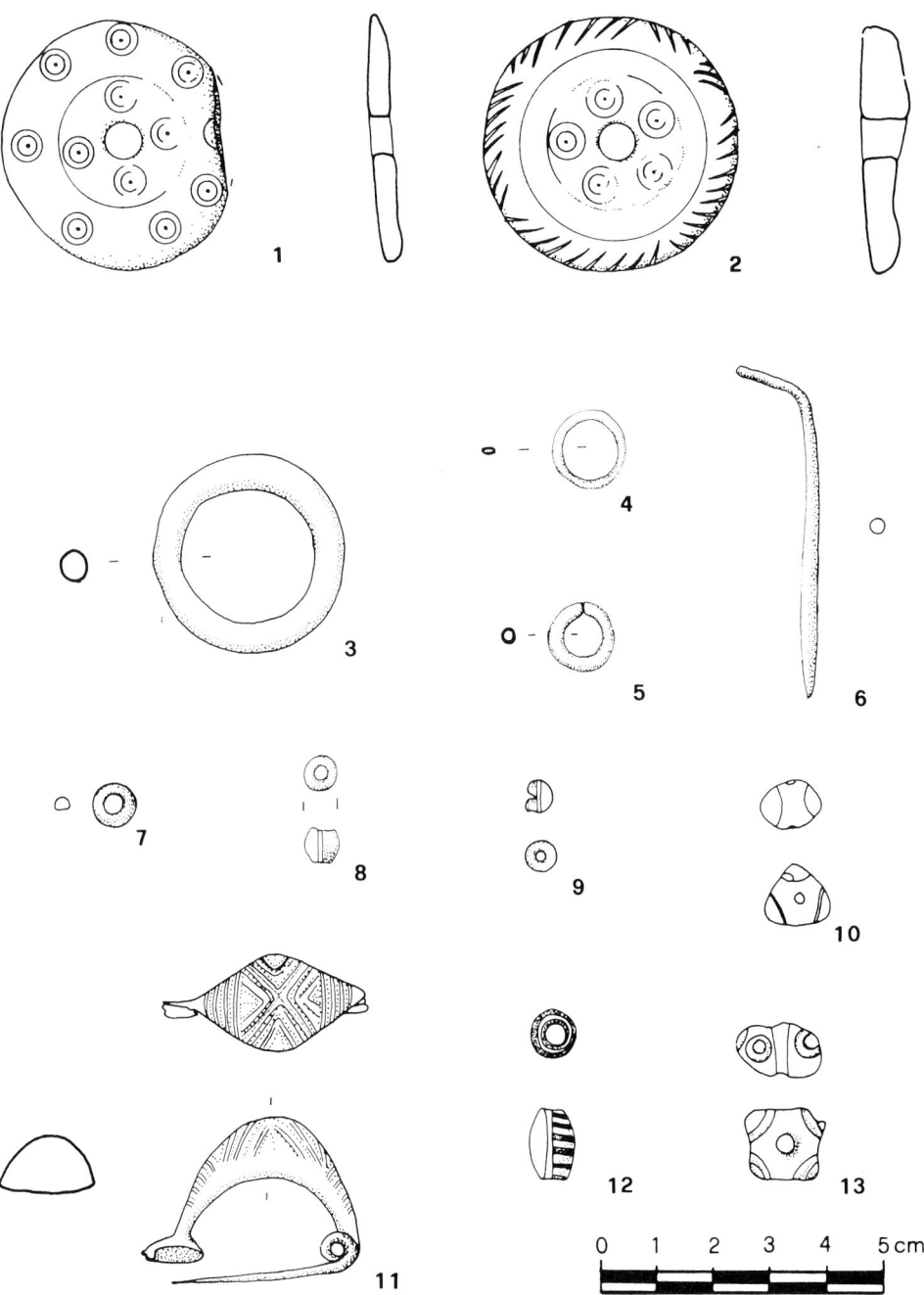

Fig. 6. Banditella: materiali dell'età del Bronzo finale e dell'età del Ferro (1-2: osso; 3-6,11: bronzo; 7-13: pasta vitrea).

sono stati raccolti, in superficie, reperti dell'età del Bronzo.

Il mutato assetto del territorio si riflette anche sulla sorgente di Banditella. Tra la fine dell'età del Bronzo e la prima età del Ferro un consistente apporto di lapilli e di pomici di origine vulcanica ricopre il piccolo specchio d'acqua intorbidendone il fondo. In età villanoviana, la sorgente viene 'bonificata' con un muro di grosse pietre a secco, ad andamento rettilineo, posto di fronte al punto da cui sgorgava l'acqua, creando così un artificiale specchio d'acqua quasi a forma di triangolo isoscele con la sorgente al vertice. Sulle due sponde laterali della sorgente, formate da sabbione, lo scorrere di piccoli rivoli d'acqua provenienti dalle sorgenti secondarie, creava sottili cascatelle con minuscole pozze, in cui veniva deposto il materiale archeologico appositamente selezionato ad uso votivo. Un settore di queste pozze è stato rinvenuto intatto ed ha restituito circa 150 vasi di impasto miniaturizzati, per lo più integri, alcuni dei quali a lamelle metalliche, oltre ad un vaso di bronzo, a vaghi di collana in pasta vitrea e in osso (fig. 6,12-13), ad anelli in bronzo e in argento (fig. 6,3-5), ad una fibula in bronzo a sanguisuga (fig. 6,11); in

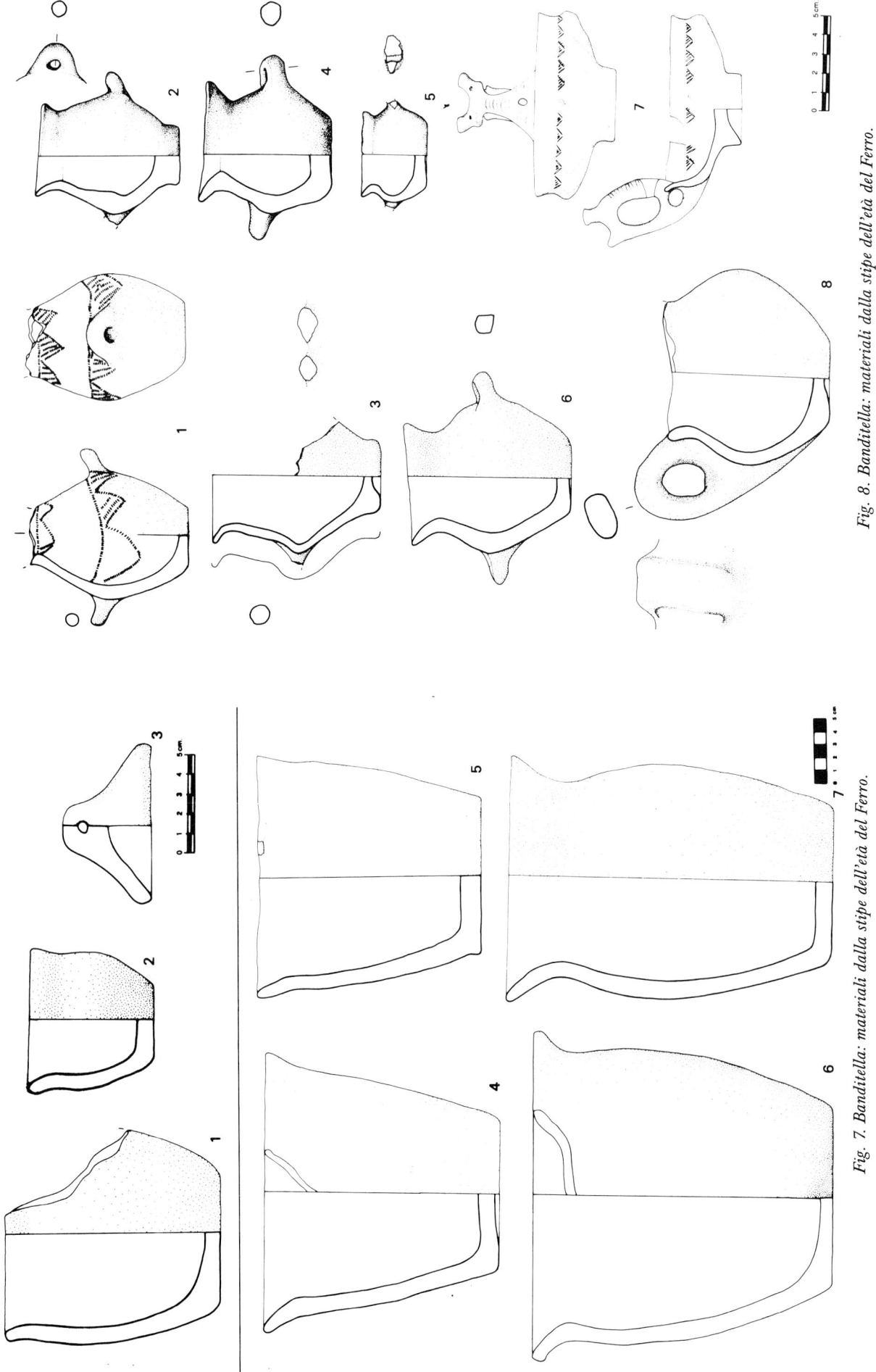

Fig. 8. Banditella: materiali dalla stipe dell'età del Ferro.

Fig. 7. Banditella: materiali dalla stipe dell'età del Ferro.

questo contesto avevano dimensioni normali solo due olle ovoidi ad orlo svasato (fig. 7,5) e tre tazze (fig. 8,7-8), due delle quali d'impasto nero decorato, di fattura particolarmente accurata. Del tutto assenti qui i resti osteologici ad eccezione di un frammento di calotta cranica, attribuibile ad un individuo adulto.

Abbondanti reperti, riferibili alle fasi villanoviana ed orientalizzante, sono stati rinvenuti nella terra di risulta proveniente dall'area del moderno manufatto in cemento (costruito per fungere da camera di manovra per l'acquedotto). Tra essi si segnalano una fibula ad arco serpeggiante in bronzo, alcuni vasi biconici, di cui uno con decorazione a lamelle metalliche applicate; numerosi dolii ed olle ovoidi e troncoconici con orlo svasato a grandezza naturale, di forma relativamente standardizzata; molto limitato – non superiore alla decina – il numero delle tazze; alcune centinaia i vasi miniaturizzati, per lo più biconici e olle, forme ambedue biansate (fig. 8,1-6); molto più rari gli esemplari miniaturizzati di tazze, fornelli, coperchi ed olle prive di anse (fig. 7,1-3).

Del tutto eccezionale poi la presenza di un bronzetto raffigurante un piccolo cavallo (fig. 9), realizzato a fusione piena (lunghezza cm 10, altezza cm 9). E' ancora da stabilire se il cavallino di bronzo sia un elemento isolato o piuttosto non faccia parte di un gruppo, composto forse da un altro bronzetto simile e da una figura umana maschile o femminile sul genere 'signore/a degli animali', ad esempio poggiante sulla cima di un coperchio di bronzo. Tale ipotesi potrebbe essere suffragata dalla disposizione delle zampe del cavallino, che sembrano essere fatte per poggiare su di un piano inclinato, data anche la maggior lunghezza di quelle posteriori e dalla presenza, al di sotto di esse, di tracce di perni.

Particolarmente accurata è la resa con graticcio della bardatura alla base del collo; sulle cosce è disegnato ad incisione un complesso motivo che potrebbe essere letto come resa della muscolatura o come elemento di protezione delle stesse. La resa geometrizzante degli occhi e della criniera, disegnati in modo più accurato sul lato destro, farebbe pensare ad una volontà di privilegiare questo punto di vista.

L'uso cultuale dell'area sembra perdurare sino alle soglie dell'età arcaica. I reperti più recenti sembrano, infatti, essere le ollette miniaturistiche tornite (fig. 8,5) ed un kyathos miniaturizzato di bucchero grigio. Verrebbe quasi spontaneo collegare la fine di questo luogo di culto extra-urbano con il sorgere dei grandi santuari urbani di età arcaica a Vulci, da cui Banditella dista circa 5 km in linea d'aria.

E' ipotizzabile che, durante l'età del Ferro, il culto, che aveva per oggetto la sorgente, consistesse soprattutto in libagioni e che gli offerenti, dopo averle effettuate, depositassero nelle acque un modellino simbolico da lasciare in offerta alla divinità.

Per quanto riguarda le fasi villanoviana ed orientalizzante non si conoscono finora, in Etruria, testimonianze del genere, al contrario di quanto accade nel mondo laziale con la stipe, in acqua, del laghetto del Monsignore presso Campoverde ad Aprilia (Crescenzi 1978) e forse dell'Acquoria a Tivoli (De Palma 1981).

Molte sono le similitudini fra i laghetti di Banditella e di Monsignore: una distanza simile (5-4 Km) con le relative città (Vulci-Satricum), una analoga durata nel tempo (dal Bronzo medio all'età arcaica), offerte differenziate tra l'età del Bronzo (frammenti di vasellame d'uso comune) e l'età del Ferro (vasellame miniaturizzato ed oggetti preziosi). La stipe di Banditella si può collegare alla cultura laziale per l'aspetto strutturale: presenza di un muro di delimitazione, documentato ad esempio a Tivoli, Roma e Satricum. Assai meno evidenti appaiono i legami con la cultura materiale: mancano ad esempio le focaccine fittili, le figurine metalliche ritagliate o la ceramica figulina.

Alcune analogie si trovano anche con il mondo atestino: numerosi stipi extraurbane legate all'acqua (Vicenza, Baratella, Cortellazzo, S. Pietro Montagnon) presentavano opere artificiali di terrazzamento o di arginatura (Fogolari & Prosdocimi 1987), in parecchie di esse (S. Pietro Montagnon, Baratella, Lagole, Caldevigo) erano deposti bronzetti di cavalli (De Min 1976), al punto di far ipotizzare un culto, con sacrificio rituale dei cavalli, in onore di Diomede, quale citato dalle fonti. Il santuario di S. Pietro di Montagnon presentava anche uno strato dell'età del Bronzo.

Ringraziamenti

Le istituzioni che hanno collaborato con la Soprintendenza Archeologica dell'Etruria Meridionale alle ricerche oggetto di questo contributo sono l'Istituto

Fig. 9. Banditella: bronzetto dalla stipe dell'età del Ferro (foto M. Pellegrini).

Centrale del Restauro, l'Istituto di Archeologia dell'Università di Milano, la Sezione di Antropologia del Dipartimento di Biologia Animale e dell'Uomo dell'Università 'La Sapienza', l'ENEA, il Comune ed il Museo Civico di Farnese, i Gruppi Archeologici d'Italia. Desideriamo ringraziare il Soprintendente Archeologo per l'Etruria Meridionale Giovanni Scichilone ed il funzionario di zona Gianfranco Gazzetti. Particolare gratitudine dobbiamo all'amico Francesco di Gennaro per i consigli generosamente datici in vari momenti di queste ricerche. I restauri sono stati curati da Bianca Fossà, Antonella Catalano e Grazia Cordelli. La documentazione grafica è opera di Simonetta Massimi (Ufficio tecnico Soprintendenza Archeologica Etruria Meridionale), Alessandra Stoppiello, Alessandro Mandolesi.

Bibliografia

Bagnoli, P.E. & Panicucci, N. 1992. 'L'insediamento del Paludetto di Coltano nell'ambito dell'Italia centrale', in *L'età del Bronzo*, 672–73.

Bastianelli, S. 1939. 'Allumiere – Rinvenimento di tombe arcaiche', *Notizie degli Scavi di Antichità*, 45–48.

Bastianelli, S. 1942. 'Il territorio tolfetano nell'antichità', *Studi Etruschi* XVI, 229–260.

Bergonzi, G. & Cardarelli, A. 1992. 'Status simbol e oggetti d'ornamento nella media età del Bronzo dell'Italia settentrionale: ambra, faïance, pasta vitrea, metalli preziosi', in *L'età del Bronzo*, 217–220.

Bietti Sestieri, A.M., Belardelli, C., Capoferri, B., Moscetta, M.P. & Saltini, A. C. 1992. 'La media età del Bronzo nel territorio di Roma', in *L'età del Bronzo*, 439–54.

Calzoni, U. 1962. 'Le stazioni preistoriche della montagna di Cetona', in *Belverde. II. La ceramica*, (Quaderni di Studi Etruschi, Ser. I, Quad. II).

Cardarelli, A. 1992. 'Le età dei metalli nell'Italia settentrionale', in Guidi S., Piperno M. (a cura di), *Italia Preistorica*, Bari, 366–419.

Casi, C. & Mandolesi A. 1993. 'Paesaggi d'Etruria tra Fiora e Albegna nel Bronzo finale', *Informazioni. Periodico del Centro di Catalogazione dei Beni Culturali – Viterbo*, n.s.- anno II, n. 8: 35–44.

Casi, C., D'Ercole, V. Negroni Catacchio, N. & Trucco, F. 1995. 'Prato di Fabulino (Farnese, VT) – Tomba a camera dell'età del Bronzo', *Atti del II Incontro di Studi sulla Preistoria e la Prtostoria d'Etruria*, 81–110.

Cassano, S. M., Cazzella, A., Manfredini, A. & Moscoloni, M. (a cura di), 1987. *Coppa Nevigata e il suo territorio. Testimonianze archeologiche dal VII al II millennio a. C.*, (mostra Manfredonia 1987).

Cifarelli, F. M. & di Gennaro F. 1993. 'I bacini della Paternale e della Vesca nella preistoria. Informazioni sullo sviluppo del territorio della Tuscia dallo studio dei valloni torrentizi', *Atti I Incontro di Studi sulla Preistoria e la Protostoria d'Etruria*, 223–233.

Cipolloni Sampò, M. 1992. 'Le sepolture collettive nel sud-est italiano', in *L'età del Bronzo*, 281–285.

Cocchi Genick, D. 1986. *Il Riparo dell'Ambra. Una successione stratigrafica dal Neolitico tardo al Bronzo finale*, Viareggio.

Cocchi Genick, D. 1987. *Il Riparo del Lauro di Candalla nel quadro del Bronzo medio iniziale dell'Italia centro occidentale*, Viareggio.

Cocchi Genick, D. 1991. 'La media età del bronzo al Riparo Grande (Camaiore, Lucca)', *Origini* XV, 283–300.

Cremonesi, G. 1968. 'La Grotta dell'Orso di Sarteano. I livelli dell'età dei metalli', *Origini* II, 247–331.

Cremonesi G. 1976. *La Grotta dei Piccioni di Bolognano nel quadro delle culture dal Neolitico all'età del Bronzo in Abruzzo*, Pisa.

Cremonesi, G. 1977. 'Materiali protoappenninici di Muro Maurizio (Mesagne)', *Ricerche e Studi* X, 23–46.

Crescenzi, L. 1978. 'Campoverde', *Archeologia Laziale* I, 51–55.

Cuda, M.T. & Sarti L. 1992. 'Nuove ricerche a Belverde di Cetona', in *L'età del Bronzo*, 384–392.

De Min, M. 1976. 'Stipe di S. Pietro Montagnon', *Padova Preromana*, Padova 197–218.

De Palma, G. 1981. 'Tivoli', in *Enea nel Lazio. Archeologia e mito*, Roma, 38–42.

d'Ercole, V. 1995. 'Ripresa dagli scavi nella necropoli protovillanoviana di Poggio della Pozza ad Allumiere (Roma), *Atti del III Incontro di Studi sulla Preistoria e la Protostoria d'Etruria*, 177–186.

d'Ercole, V. & Trucco, F. 1995. 'Canino (Viterbo). Località Banditella. Un luogo di culto all'aperto presso Vulci', *Bollettino di Archeologia*, 13–15, 77–85.

di Gennaro, F. 1990. 'Aspetti delle ricerche sull'assetto territoriale dell'area mediotirrenica in età protostorica', *Gedenkschrift für Jürgen Driehaus*, Mainz, 204–224.

di Gennaro, F. 1992a. 'Pian Sultano (Tolfa, RM)', in *L'età del Bronzo*, 704–705.

di Gennaro, F. 1992b. 'Gli insediamenti dell'età del bronzo del territorio di Barbarano', *Informazioni. Periodico del Centro di Catalogazione dei Beni Culturali – Viterbo*, n.s.- anno I, n. 7, 33–49.

di Gennaro, F., Pacciarelli, M. & De Grossi, J. 1974. 'Prima nota sul complesso preistorico di Tolfa', *Notiziario del Museo Civico di Allumiere* III, 13–24.

Domanico, L. & Miari, M. 1991. 'La distribuzione dei siti di necropoli in Etruria meridionale nel Bronzo finale: documentazione ed elaborazione dei dati', *Papers of the Fourth Conference of Italian Archaeology* 1, 61–82.

Fogolari, G. & Prosdocimi, A. 1987. *I Veneti antichi*, Padova.

Franco, C. 1982. *L'insediamento preistorico del Lago di Mezzano*, Roma.

Fugazzola Delpino, M. A. 1976. *Testimonianze di cultura appenninica nel Lazio*, Firenze.

Guidi, A. 1992a. 'Recenti ritrovamenti in grotta nel Lazio: un riesame critico del problema dell'utilizzazione delle cavità naturali', in *L'età del Bronzo*, 427–437.

Guidi, A. 1992b. 'Le età dei metalli nell'Italia centrale e in Sardegna', in Guidi S., Piperno, M. (a cura di), *Italia Preistorica*, Bari, 420–470.

Klitsche de La Grange, A. 1881. 'Allumiere', *Notizie degli Scavi di Antichità*, 88–89.

Klitsche de La Grange, A. 1884a. 'Tombe antichissime scoperte in contrada della Pozza', *Notizie degli Scavi di Antichità*, 101–103.

Klitsche de La Grange, A. 1884b. 'Rapporto sopra nuove scoperte di tombe antichissime in contrada della Pozza', *Notizie degli Scavi di Antichità*, 152–153.

L'età del Bronzo = *L'età del Bronzo in Italia nei secoli dal XVI al XIV a. C.* (Atti del Congresso, Viareggio 1989), Firenze.

Negroni Catacchio, N. (a cura di), 1988. *Museo di Preistoria e Protostoria della Valle del fiume Fiora*, Manciano.

Pacciarelli, M. 1991. 'Ricerche topografiche a Vulci: dati e problemi relativi all'origine delle città medio-tirreniche', *Studi Etruschi*, LVI, 11–48.

Pacciarelli, M. 1992. 'Considerazioni sulla struttura delle comunità del Bronzo medio dell'Italia centro-meridionale', in *L'età del Bronzo*, 265–280.

Pancrazzi, O. 1979. *Cavallino I*, Galatina.

Peroni, R. 1960. 'Allumiere. Scavo di tombe in località La Pozza', *Notizie degli Scavi di Antichità*, 341–362.

Peroni, R. 1989. 'Protostoria dell'Italia Continentale', *Biblioteca di Storia Patria*, 9, Roma.

Rittatore Vonwiller, F. 1951. 'Nuove scoperte dell'età del bronzo lungo la valle del fiume Fiora', *Rivista di Scienze Preistoriche*, VI, 3-4, 151–180.

Sarti, L. 1980. 'L'insediamento dell'età del Bronzo di Dicomano (Firenze)', *Rivista di Scienze Preistoriche*, XXXV, 1-2, 183–247.

37

The Role of Interregional Contact in the Development of Latial Society in the Early Iron Age

ANNA MARIA BIETTI SESTIERI

(Soprintendenza Archeologica di Roma)

Summary: *The cemetery of Osteria dell'Osa, near Rome, in the region of ancient Lazio, comprises 600 graves spanning the whole sequence of the local Iron Age (IX-VII century BC). One of the results of the study of this complex was a better understanding of the role and significance of interregional contact throughout this period. During the Latial period II (c. 900-770 BC), systematic relationships involved two areas of peninsular Italy: the southern Tyrrhenian regions (the so-called fossa-grave and southern Villanovan complexes of Campania and Calabria) and southern Etruria (the classic Villanovan complexes of Veii, Cerveteri, Tarquinia and Vulci). The evidence of the cemetery points to a systematic and uninterrupted connection with the southern Tyrrhenian area, apparently through the arrival of small groups of people of south-Italian origin and their systematic integration within the local community. The relationship with Etruria in the same period was less intense, and apparently based on economic exchange and exogamy. The systematic and rapid integration of groups and individuals of foreign origin probably depended on the kinship-based, 'egalitarian' structure of the community of Osteria dell'Osa, within which no permanent social division can be identified prior to Latial period III. The significance of this phenomenon, as well as its intensity, is clearly shown by the fact that 'foreigners' had access to high status and role positions in the community. In the subsequent phases (Latial periods III and IV, c. 770-580 BC) the main flow of interregional contact shifted from southern Italy to Etruria, in close coincidence with the emergence of complex socio-political structures and the beginning of urbanization in the Tyrrhenian regions.*

OSTERIA DELL'OSA:
SITE AND CEMETERY EVOLUTION

The study of the Iron Age cemetery of *Osteria dell'Osa* (*c*. 900–580 BC – according to the conventional archaeological chronology) was based on the integration of three main categories of information: gender and age determination, analysis of the relative spatial distribution of the graves, and formal (typological) and physico-chemical analyses of the artifacts (*Osteria dell'Osa* 1992; Bietti Sestieri 1992). The main effort aimed at exploiting the potential of the whole range of material culture represented in the cemetery as a source of information on the structure and organization of the corresponding community, as well as their evolution over time. By this approach, it has been possible to propose a relatively sound reconstruction of several important aspects of the community, especially as regards its earliest period of development (Latial period II, *c*. 900-770 BC; in the cemetery of Osteria dell'Osa, this has been further subdivided into phases IIA, *c*. 900-840 BC and IIB, *c*. 840-770 BC). A brief summary of these aspects is valuable for considering the specific evidence of interregional contact in a wider perspective.

The site of the cemetery lies 17,5 km east of Rome, on the later *via Praenestina*, in the Gabii-Castiglione district, which extends around and within the extinct volcanic crater of Castiglione. During the earliest phases of the local Iron Age, the district was occupied by several small settlement units (both villages and individual households) and by a number of cemeteries, two of which have been excavated: Osteria dell'Osa, on the outer western edge of the crater, and Castiglione, on the opposite inner side. The different communities which occupied the Castiglione district during these phases apparently belonged to a territorial and socio-political organization of tribal type.

The Latial period II cemetery

One of these communities – possibly the largest one – has been reconstructed by analysing the cemetery of Osteria dell'Osa, in which 450 graves – out of a total of 600 – can be dated to the Early Iron Age. Based on the

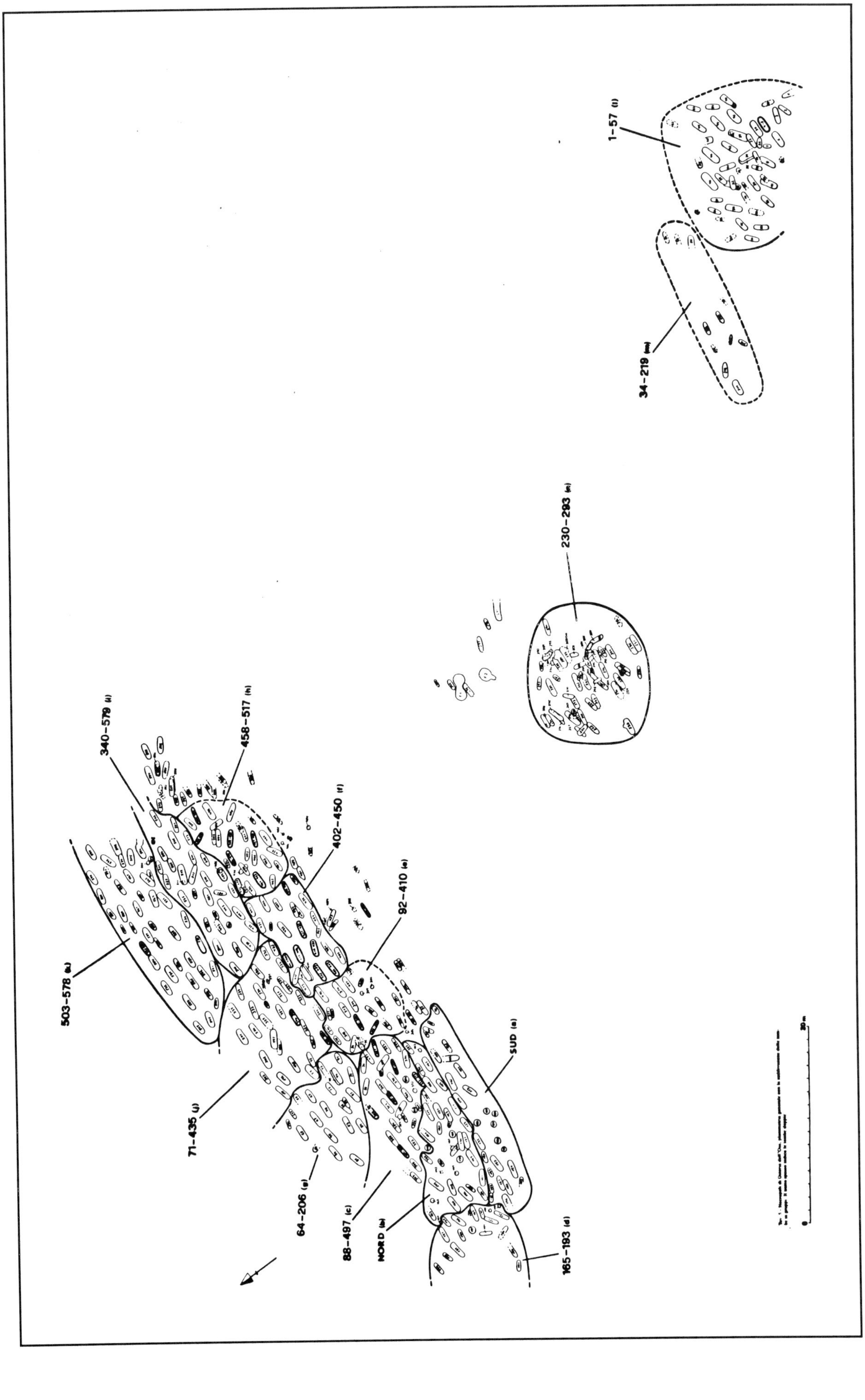

Fig. 1. Plan of the cemetery of Osteria dell'Osa, showing the division by grave-clusters during Latial periods II and III.

anthropological and demographic study of the cemetery, by M.J. Becker and L. Salvadei (1992), the average size of this community can be estimated to between one and three hundred people.

The burial ground in this period was organized by individual grave-groups, each comprising *c.* 30–50 graves, apparently the funerary equivalents of kinship groups (fig. 1; see *Osteria dell'Osa* 1992: pl. 5). These have been identified as extended families, that is, family groups comprising a nuclear family and the wives and children of the original pair's children; within the approximate time-span of two generations, the group would usually split into two or more similar units (Goody 1969; Keesing 1975: 35–38). The grave-groups develop over a mean archaeologically-defined time-span of a few decades. The single extended families identified in the cemetery probably belonged to at least two different lineages, apparently surviving throughout period II.

The following archaeological indicators point to an 'egalitarian' structuring of the community as well as to a relatively simple socio-political organization during this period:

- The grave-clusters (which correspond to the family groups of the community) are not spatially separate, except for a single group (1–57) dating from phase IIB; within each cluster, the individual graves are usually isolated, though relatively close to one another. This specific combination of internal and external spatial relationships of the single grave-groups is considered to indicate the solidarity of the community as well as the emphasis of the funerary ritual on the individual deceased rather than on the grave-groups as units.

- The artifacts which constitute the funerary outfits (handmade *impasto* pottery, bronze fibulae, amber, faïence and glass beads and pendants) point to a limited degree of technical and technological development in the local craftsmanship. Moreover, exotic prestige items are almost totally absent.

- The specific features of the funerary outfit of the individual graves show a close correspondence between gender, age-group and the distribution of horizontal roles.

- The most important indicators of status and of vertical social roles are connected with the age group of adult males.

This consistent combination of features characterizes the cemetery throughout Latial period II, although a few elements apparently indicating a slow process of social change can be identified towards the end of the period.

The most significant feature which appears in the cemetery, essentially during the first half of the 9th century BC, is the specialized ritual of cremation, which was exclusive to young adult and adult males, apparently the weapon-bearers of the community. The grave-goods, including the weapons, are all miniature, with the urn usually reproducing a hut. The most important vertical roles, which can be identified in a limited number of burials within this category, are those connected with cult (the grave-goods comprise a statuette in an offering attitude, as well as a knife, probably indicating a sacrificial function) and with war (a sword is included with three cremated adult men). These men can probably be identified respectively as the priest and the war chief of the community.

A few indicators of cult-related functions or roles are also found in female burials; the most important one is the knife, which is present in two graves only (153 and 433). Horizontal roles, which are more clearly identifiable in female burials, include spinning (a single spindle-whorl, usually found in the graves of adult, mature adult and old women) and weaving (several spindle-whorls and spools, mostly among the grave-goods of young and young adult women). A function of food redistribution, marked by a large vessel with a cup intentionally placed inside, probably corresponds to an important vertical role; this feature appears in a limited number of adults' to old adults' burials of both genders, which are usually characterized by a rich set of grave-goods.

The Latial period III cemetery

The most recent grave-group identified in the cemetery (graves 230–293), can be dated to Latial period III (*c.* 770–730/20 BC), with a few burials belonging to the subsequent Orientalizing period (Latial period IV, *c.* 730/20–580 BC). The evidence of this grave-group indicates a significant change in the basic structure of the community: the emergence of permanent social inequality, marked by the incipient formation of the *gens* system. The following archaeological indicators of this change, all marking significant differences from period II, appear in grave-group 230–293:

- The grave-cluster is spatially isolated in a wide open area (fig. 1), considerably distant from the two earliest cores of the cemetery.

- The graves concentrate in a limited area, with a pair of burials (a male inhumation, 262, and a female cremation, 259) in the centre, and are usually superimposed on one another, with later burials disturbing earlier ones.

- Traditional indicators of gender, such as fibula types used by women and men respectively, or spindle-whorls and spools, exclusive to female burials, are found in a few graves only, while the number and variety of vessels per grave is significantly reduced as compared with period II. In the earliest part of period III, even in burials which include important role-markers, the most common set of vessels consists of two cups of different size.

- Real, functional weapons appear for the first time in the cemetery in the graves of a few adult and mature adult men.

- Finally, a significant percentage of the burials (*c.* 15%) lack grave-goods.

This consistent set of features probably indicates the emergence of a funerary ideology which emphasizes group membership and descent rather than individual role and gender and age differences as in the previous period. Especially in the earliest part of period III, wealth is not included among the funerary indicators of this process of social division.

In its late phases, from the second half of the 8th to the beginning of the 6th century BC, the cemetery no longer corresponds to a natural community. The few burials (*c.* 70) of this period comprise an unusually high percentage of adult, mature and old adult individuals; the graves are loosely distributed over the whole cemetery, either isolated or in groups of no more than a few units.

The survey of the area showed that, around the mid-8th century BC, the sparse villages and individual households which characterized the Castiglione district in the Early Iron Age were undergoing a fast process of settlement nucleation on the site of the future city of Gabii. The specific characteristics of the burials dating from this period at Osteria dell'Osa possibly indicate that some members of the original residential community were still buried in the cemetery.

Interregional contacts in Latial period II

The evidence of interregional contact for the earliest phases of the cemetery (Latial period II) will be examined in the following section (the evidence for periods III and IV are analysed in detail by A. De Santis, this volume).

The archaeological aspect which appears at Osteria dell'Osa is identical to the one already known in ancient Lazio as seen mainly in Rome in the cemeteries of the Roman Forum and the Esquiline (Gjerstad 1956), and in the Alban Hills (Gierow 1964). A distinctive feature of the pottery of Latial period II (early Iron Age) is its close affinity to that of the contemporary complexes of the so-called fossa-grave culture of southern-Tyrrhenian Italy as exemplified by the long-known cemeteries of Cumae in Campania (Gabrici 1913) and Torre Galli in

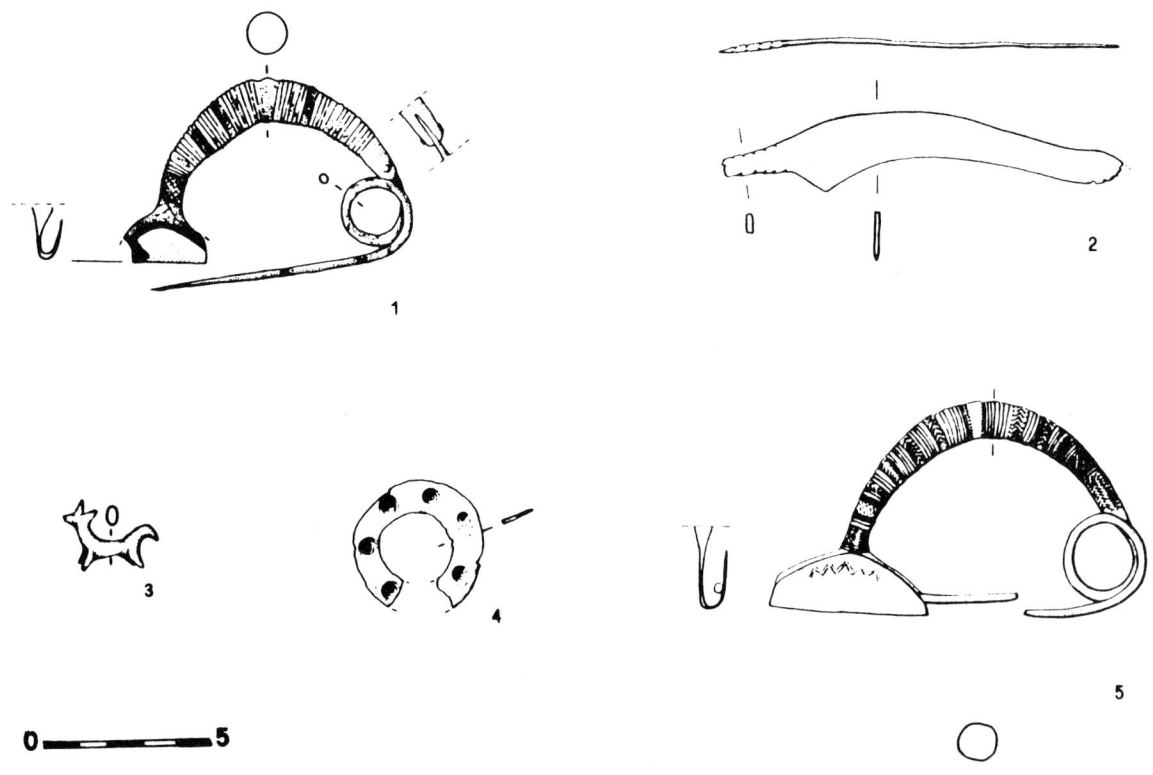

Fig. 2. Bronzes with parallels in the fossa-grave complexes of southern Italy. 1. Fibula with incised and plastic decoration. 2. Knife of Torre Galli type. 3. Animal-shaped pendant. 4. Sheet-bronze ring decorated with incised circlets. 5. Fibula of south-Italian type.

Calabria (Orsi 1926), which affects the near totality of the pottery shapes. Some good parallels for the Latial impasto pottery can be found also in the so-called southern Villanovan complexes, such as Pontecagnano and Sala Consilina; however, it is probably significant that these usually concern precisely those shapes which apparently are of local, south-Italian origin and are not represented in the Villanovan complexes of Etruria.

The overall similarity between the Latial and fossa-grave pottery was already acknowledged in the earliest studies on the Italian Iron Age. The evidence of Osteria dell'Osa, the first Latial cemetery in which the Early Iron Age is documented on a relatively wide basis, indicates that the connection also extends to several categories of bronze objects. The most important one is constituted by arch fibulae with short symmetrical foot, decorated with both incised and plastic patterns (fig. 2.1; see *Osteria dell'Osa* 1992: pl. 33), which are frequent among the grave-goods of the female burials of the cemetery. The decorative technique of this group of fibulae is quite similar to the one which was adopted for fibulae of similar shape in the fossa-grave cemeteries of Calabria and Campania, especially Torre Galli, S.Onofrio di Roccella Jonica and Cumae (e.g. Orsi 1926: figs. 25, 26, 42, 78, 135; Chiartano 1981: figs. 9, 19; Gabrici 1913: figs. 38, 43, pls. 20/2,3, 21/3).

The Latial and fossa-grave arch fibulae are similar both in general shape and decoration; as a whole, they differ significantly from the most common types of arch fibulae from the contemporary Villanovan cemeteries, in Etruria as well as in southern Italy, which are characterized by incised decorations and disc-foot. This consistently different distribution of arch fibula shapes and decorations apparently indicates that the circulation of formal models and technical know-how for the manufacture of these objects followed two fairly separate routes, one comprising the Latial and fossa-grave area, the other the Villanovan centres.

Apart from the arch fibulae with incised and plastic decoration, which are quite common among the grave-goods of female burials, and presumably of local manufacture, a few bronze objects probably imported from southern Italy also appear in the cemetery. These comprise the following categories:

- Razors with square or trapezoidal blade (fig. 3; see *Osteria dell'Osa* 1992: pl. 42, types 61b, 61c, 61e, 61f; these can be attributed to the types Sopra Selciatello, Torre Galli, Torre Mordillo and the razor with foliate blade and nervatures as defined by Bianco Peroni 1979).

- A knife from grave 433 (fig. 2.2; see *Osteria dell'Osa* 1992: pl. 41, type 58e, similar to the so-called Torre Galli type as defined by Bianco Peroni 1976).

- A small animal-shaped pendant from grave 163 (fig. 2.3; see *Osteria dell'Osa* 1992: pl. 45, type 88v and figs. 3a.42–43), with close parallels at Torre Galli and Cumae

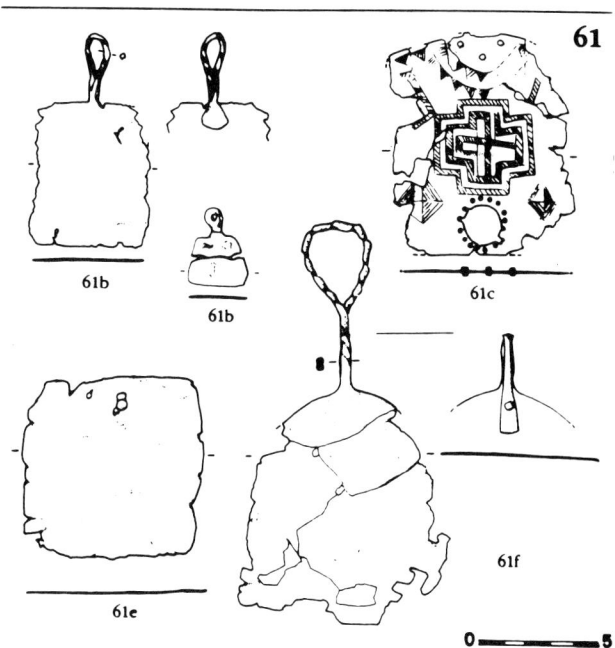

Fig. 3. Quadrangular razors with parallels in southern Italy.

(Orsi 1926: figs. 26, 58, tombs 45 and 118; Gabrici 1913: fig. 33a,b).

- A small spectacle pendant and a few spiral rings from graves 163, 475 and 499 (*Osteria dell'Osa* 1992: pls. 45, type 88z, and 40, type 45e; figs. 3a. 42–43, 218, 237), with several parallels in south-Italian cemeteries.

- Small sheet-bronze rings with a typical incised decoration of concentric circlets from graves 88, 160, 317 and 348 (fig. 2.4; see *Osteria dell'Osa* 1992: pl. 40, type 45d and figs. 3a.83, 56–57, 144, 103), with parallels in Lucania and Calabria.

- An arch fibula with incised and plastic decoration from grave 490 (fig. 2.5; see *Osteria dell'Osa* 1992: pl. 36, type 38e and fig. 3a.231), shows a decorative pattern quite close to those seen on fibulae from Cumae, and might therefore be an import from Campania.

Although the evidence of the bronzes of Osteria dell'Osa offers some important information on the links between ancient Lazio and southern Italy, its significance is ambiguous. Since metal objects are likely to circulate over long distances within interregional networks of exchange or actual trade, the appearance in a Latial context of bronzes of south-Italian type, or indeed imports from southern Italy, need not imply a direct contact between the regions involved.

It is worth mentioning that the chemical and metallographic analyses of some of the fibulae from the cemetery of Osteria dell'Osa did not show significant differences in both alloy composition and metallurgical technique between 'local' and 'imported' pieces (Guida & Marabelli 1992: 479–484)

From this point of view, pottery dating from Latial period II at the cemetery of Osteria dell'Osa certainly is more likely to provide significant information. In this period, the pottery manufacture of ancient Lazio, as well as of many other regions of peninsular Italy, was organized on a domestic basis. According to the categories proposed by Van der Leeuw (1976) and Peacock (1981), the pottery production as documented at Osteria dell'Osa should be classified either as household production or, more probably, as household industry. The vessels were hand-made, the firing technology did not yet include the use of permanent kilns, and the final products, though not lacking in aesthetic quality, were clearly meant for everyday use and were not circulated as exotic prestige items.

Thus a clearly identifiable formal relationship in the impasto pottery production of distant regions points to a systematic direct connection between the areas involved, and a close scrutiny of the vessels as well as of their contexts should provide important clues about the specific characteristics of these contacts.

The grave-goods of a limited number of burials of Osteria dell'Osa comprise some pottery types clearly differing from the bulk of the local pottery production. These types (represented by one or by no more than a few vessels) are marked by typological or stylistic features which are specifically south-Italian in character. The most common of these traits include a bulging neck (fig. 4.2, 3; see *Osteria dell'Osa* 1992: pl. 18, jug types 11i and 11j) and a plastic cordon or a slight fold separating the neck from the body (fig. 4.4; see *Osteria dell'Osa* 1992: pl. 18, jug type 11h). The few jugs with these features are easily distinguished from the most common local types (fig. 4.1), although the overall characteristics of the two groups of vessels are rather similar.

Another small group of vessels, in which each type is represented by no more than one or two pieces, is consistently different from the local pottery and is connected to south-Italian types by the whole set of formal features which characterizes each piece. The group comprises the following types and *unica*:

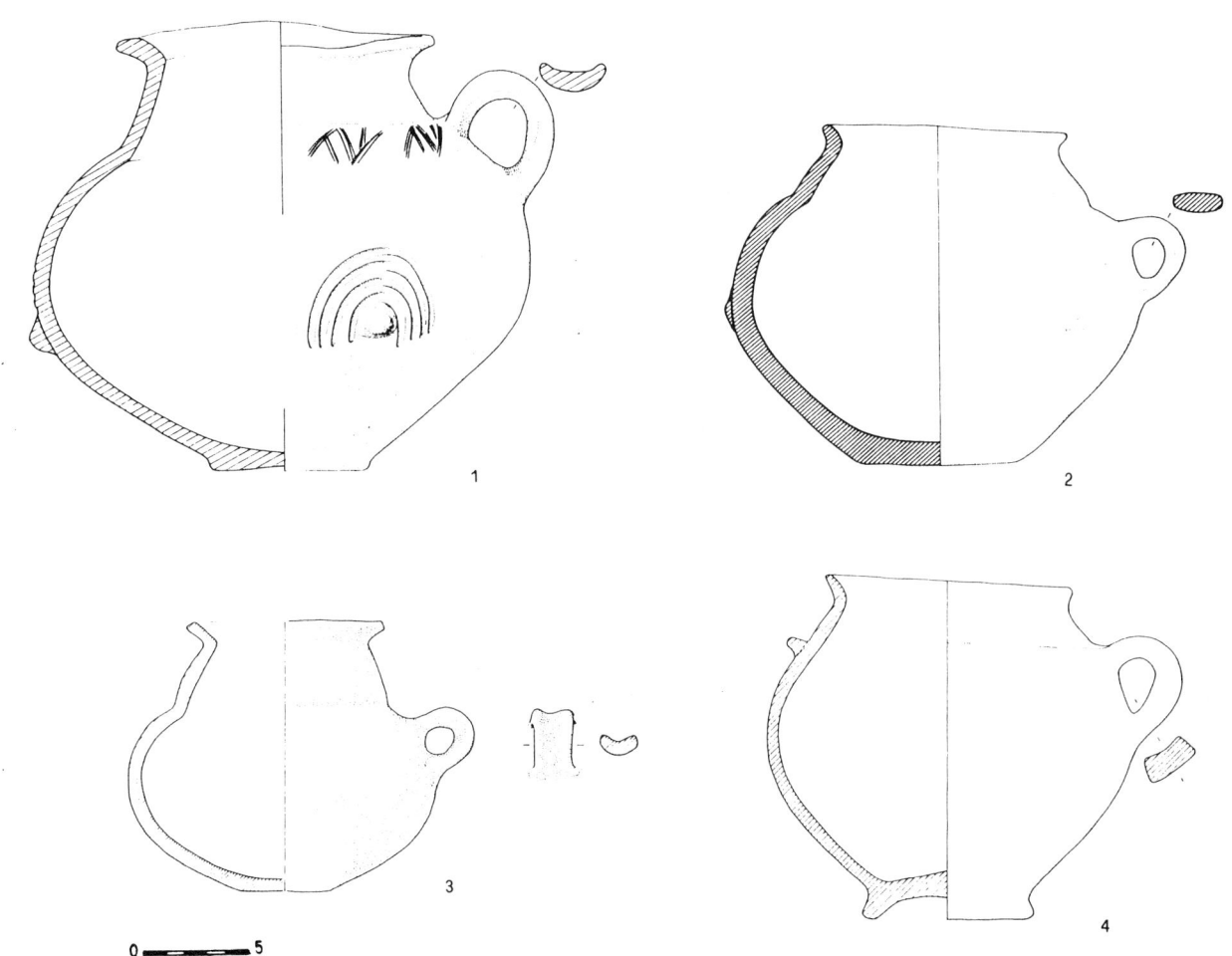

Fig. 4. Impasto jugs. 1. Jug of local type (11a). 2–4. Jugs showing typological features with south-Italian parallels.

- A cup with bulging neck, decorated with oblique parallel nervatures, from grave 371 (fig. 5.1; see *Osteria dell'Osa* 1992: pl. 23, type 21 *unicum* I and fig. 3a. 122/9), with some good parallels at Torre Galli (Orsi 1926: pls. II/1, III/17).

- A pair of two-necked biconical jugs from graves 84 and 122 (fig. 5.2; see *Osteria dell'Osa* 1992: pl. 19, type 12f and figs. 3a. 205/1, 34/3), similar to pieces from Pontecagnano and Sala Consilina (d'Agostino & Gastaldi 1988: pl. 9, type 5a; Kilian 1970: fig. 8.2, type F5c).

- A carinated cup with horned handle from grave 122 (fig. 5.3; see *Osteria dell'Osa* 1992: pl. 23, type 22 *unicum* I and fig. 3a. 34/1) comparable with cup types from the so-called Ausonian II aspect of Lipari (Bernabò Brea & Cavalier 1980: pls. 224/3; 236/1,2; 240/3; 241/3).

– A two-handled ovoid jar from grave 460 (fig. 5.4; see *Osteria dell'Osa* 1992: pl. 16, type 8 *unicum* II and fig. 3a. 243/2), with good parallels in the cemetery of Canale in Calabria (Orsi 1926: fig. 172, pl. X/20).

- A small jar with in-turned rim from grave 363 (fig. 5.5; see *Osteria dell'Osa* 1992: pl. 12, type 5 *unicum* I and fig. 3a. 121/2), identical to a type from Sala Consilina (Kilian 1970: fig. 9, type H3d; Ruby 1990: pl. 153, type H1212).

Neither these vessels nor the jugs characterized by single formal traits of south-Italian type are in any respect remarkable or exotic. All appear to be the product of the same 'domestic' technology which characterizes the Latial impasto pottery in this period.

Thin-section analyses, performed by N. Cuomo di Caprio (1992: nos. 12, 14, 15), did not show significant differences in clay composition between the vessels belonging to the most common local types and those with south-Italian features. However, the analyses also indicated some specific technical features of the vessels of south-Italian type, especially as regards surface treatment. The smooth, slightly polished surface of the local impasto pottery came from rubbing the finished vessel with a stick or small pebble; this treatment apparently was not used on the south-Italian type vessels, which usually have opaque and slightly coarse surfaces.

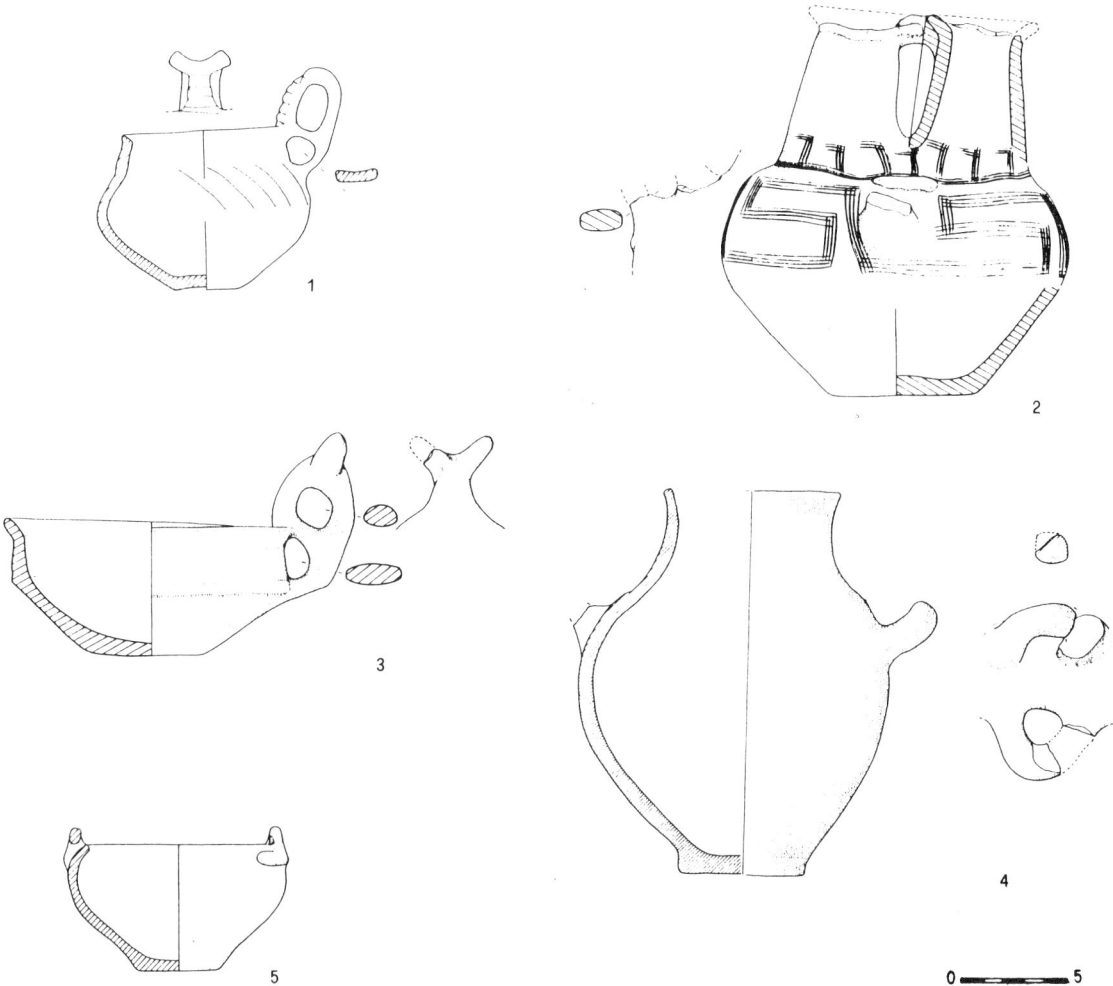

Fig. 5. Impasto vessels of south-Italian type. 1. Cup decorated with oblique parallel nervatures. 2. Two-necked jug. 3. Carinated cup with horned handle. 4. Ovoid jar. 5. Jar with in-turned rim.

The surface of a globular jug with bulging neck from grave 508 (fig. 4.2; see *Osteria dell'Osa* 1992: fig. 3a. 267/3) is coated with a thick, opaque slip of whitish clay, reminiscent of the colour of the so-called *ceramica a tenda* of Sala Consilina, whereas the carinated cup with horned handle from grave 122 (fig. 5.3) has a glossy reddish-brown slip.

Overall, the analyses of the vessels showing formal connections with the south-Italian pottery production seem to indicate that they were locally made in Lazio (i.e. they were not the object of long-distance trade), by potters who possessed formal and technical knowledge differing slightly from that of the local craftsmen.

A brief examination of the specific burial contexts which comprise these pieces provides some further important elements as to their significance. As already noted, the vessels appear in the cemetery in a rather limited quantity; moreover, they are often present in more than one piece per burial. The total amounts to seventeen vessels, distributed among eleven graves. Two vessels appear in six graves respectively, while in the remaining five graves there is only a single vessel.

The eleven burials, which date from the whole course of Latial period II, can be attributed to individuals of both sexes, with a wide range of age-classes. The elements relating to these pieces as well as to their context and relative chronology are summarised in the table 1.

The most important elements concerning the vessels with south Italian features can be summarised as follows:

1 – they appear in the cemetery in a rather limited number;

2 – they are probably locally made and do not differ significantly from the local impasto pottery as regards manufacture and general appearance;

3 – they are objects of everyday use, mostly showing traces of wear or of ancient breakage, as do many of the vessels of local type in the cemetery;

4 – they are often found in more than one piece in the same burial;

5 – they are included among the grave-goods of individuals of both genders and of all age-classes.

The hypothesis which seems best suited to this specific combination of features is that, throughout period II, individuals, or, more probably, small groups originating from southern Italy joined the community of Osteria dell'Osa, into which they were systematically integrated.

However, while the vessels which have been described can be considered as the most significant archaeological indicator of long distance intercommunal relationships, their number probably does not constitute a quantitatively accurate description of the phenomenon. For one thing, we cannot exclude that some of the 'foreigners' who merged with the community of Osteria dell'Osa were buried with a set of grave-goods entirely of local type. Moreover, in the perspective outlined above, the few imported bronzes of south-Italian type

Table 1

TOMB		TYPE	SEX/AGE*	GROUP	PHASE**
122	2	22 un I (cup) 12f (two-necked jug)	F1	North	IIA1
383	1	11h (jug)	F7	88–497	IIA
84	1	12f (two-necked jug)	F5	64–206	IIA1
435	1	11i (jug)	F3	71–435	IIA2
508	2	11i (jug) 11j (jug)	F7	340–579	IIB2
517	2	11i (jug) 11i varI (jug)	F7	458–517	IIB1
216	1	11i (jug)	F4	34–219	IIB2
371	2	11h (urn) 21 un I (cup)	M7	88–497	IIA1
363	2	11i (jug) 5 un I (jar)	M7	88–497	IIA1
440	1	11j (jug)	M4	340–579	IIB2
460	2	8 un II (two-handled jar) 11h (jug)	M5	458–517	IIA2

* F = female; M = male. Age classes: 1–2 infant-child, 0/11 years; 3 juvenile,11+/19+years; 4 young adult, 20/30 years; 5 adult, general, 20/40 years; 6 adult, 30+/40 years; 7 mature adult, 40+/60 years; 8 old adult, 60+ years.
**IIA: ca. 900–840 BC; IIB: ca. 840–770 BC.

identified in the cemetery can be best understood as being personal possessions of individuals of south-Italian provenance.

A similar hypothesis also applies to the inscription in Greek letters on the impasto vessel from grave 482, dating from phase IIB2, which might indicate contact with the regions of southern Italy in the pre-colonial period (Bietti Sestieri, De Santis & La Regina 1989–90).

As already noted, the evidence concerning this specific kind of contact is quite steady throughout period II; this probably implies the continuous and systematic character of the contact during the corresponding timespan.

The hypothesis which has been proposed can be further developed. The interregional connection between ancient Lazio and southern Italy, which quite probably went in both directions, might have been carried on by small groups of people, possibly whole families. This possibility is indicated by the presence of vessels of south Italian type among the grave-goods of a few extremely young individuals, such as the little girl buried in tomb 122. We can also try to identify some elements concerning the specific features of the integration of individuals or groups of foreign origin in the community of Osteria dell'Osa. Two aspects of the evidence seem particularly informative in this respect. First, there is no apparent spatial separation between the graves of 'foreigners' and those with grave-goods exclusively of local type. Since throughout period II the graves' spatial setting constitutes the main indicator of the structure of the corresponding community and of its division by individual kin-groups, the underlying implication is that the 'foreigners' were full-right members of both kin-groups and community at large.

The second important element is that, within the overall context of the cemetery, some of the foreigners' burials comprise the usual indicators of high status and role. Among these are tomb 371 (a mature adult male's cremation with miniature grave-goods; *Osteria dell'Osa* 1992: figs. 3a.122, 123), tomb 508 (a mature adult female's inhumation, with a rich set of grave-goods and occupying a central place in the burial ground of group 340–579; *Osteria dell'Osa* 1992: figs. 3a. 267, 268). The double burial 482 and 483 (old adult female's cremation and young adult male's inhumation respectively; *Osteria dell'Osa* 1992: figs. 3a.269, 270, 275, 276), whose grave-goods include the impasto vessel with inscription in Greek letters, belongs to the same group. Apparently, foreigners were wholly integrated in the local community and had access to the main status and role positions in the host group.

If this reconstruction is acceptable, then the pervasive similarity between the Early Iron Age pottery of Osteria dell'Osa (as well as of the rest of ancient Lazio) and that of the fossa-grave complexes of Camapnia and Calabria can be understood as the archaeologically perceptible outcome of the specific kind of relationship which has been described; moreover, it probably indicates the main direction of the contact.

The essential condition for the rather generalized acceptance of newcomers which can be identified from the archaeological record would be the open character of the host community. In a kinship-based society, such as the one of Early Iron Age Lazio, this condition could be achieved by means of a classificatory kinship system, in which *"the social similarity is embodied in a common kinship designation. Classificatory kinship has a logic of expandability: however remote genealogically, kinsmen need not be lost track of, nor in fact conceived remote in kinship class"* (Sahlins 1968: 11). In a system of this kind, the mechanisms of affiliation allow the enlargement of the local kin-groups, thus representing the means to form and maintain relationships.

Another important implication of the wide permeability to interregional contact as seen at Osteria dell'Osa is that, quite probably, the Latial Early Iron Age communities had an 'egalitarian' structure. In egalitarian communities, access to basic resources such as land is not controlled by a permanent elite (Fried 1967: 175–178). This is clearly an essential condition for foreigners to be systematically integrated in the local kin-groups.

OSTERIA DELL'OSA AND VILLANOVAN ETRURIA

The similarities between the pottery and bronze artifacts of Osteria dell'Osa and those of the Villanovan centres of Etruria are less numerous and, moreover, far less pervasive than those involving southern Italy. As regards pottery, a clear formal similarity links together a few types which are specific to the ritual of cremation in both regions between the end of the Late Bronze Age and the Early Iron Age: hut urns, conical lids, jars with in-turned rim, two-handled bowls, miniature bowls on a high stand, three-legged miniature tables (*Osteria dell'Osa* 1992: pls. 10, 11, 12, 24, 26, types 2a-f, 4a, 5a-d, 24a-b, 25a, 27a).

As far as the Villanovan, Early Iron Age complexes are concerned, it is well-known that the cemetery of Sorbo at Cerveteri shares several ritual and typological features in common with ancient Lazio (Pohl 1972), while a few elements of the same kind have been recently identified at Veii, Quattro Fontanili (Berardinetti Insam 1990). As regards the bronzes, arco serpeggiante fibulae with disc foot and lunate razors are quite similar in Villanovan Etruria and ancient Lazio; however, these objects are widely diffused in several Italian Early Iron Age complexes.

A more significant indication is provided by a small group of arch fibulae with disc-foot from Osteria dell'Osa (fig. 6.1; see *Osteria dell'Osa* 1992: pl. 36, types 38q, 38r, 38s) from a few female burials, which are very close to well-known Villanovan types as well as being consis-

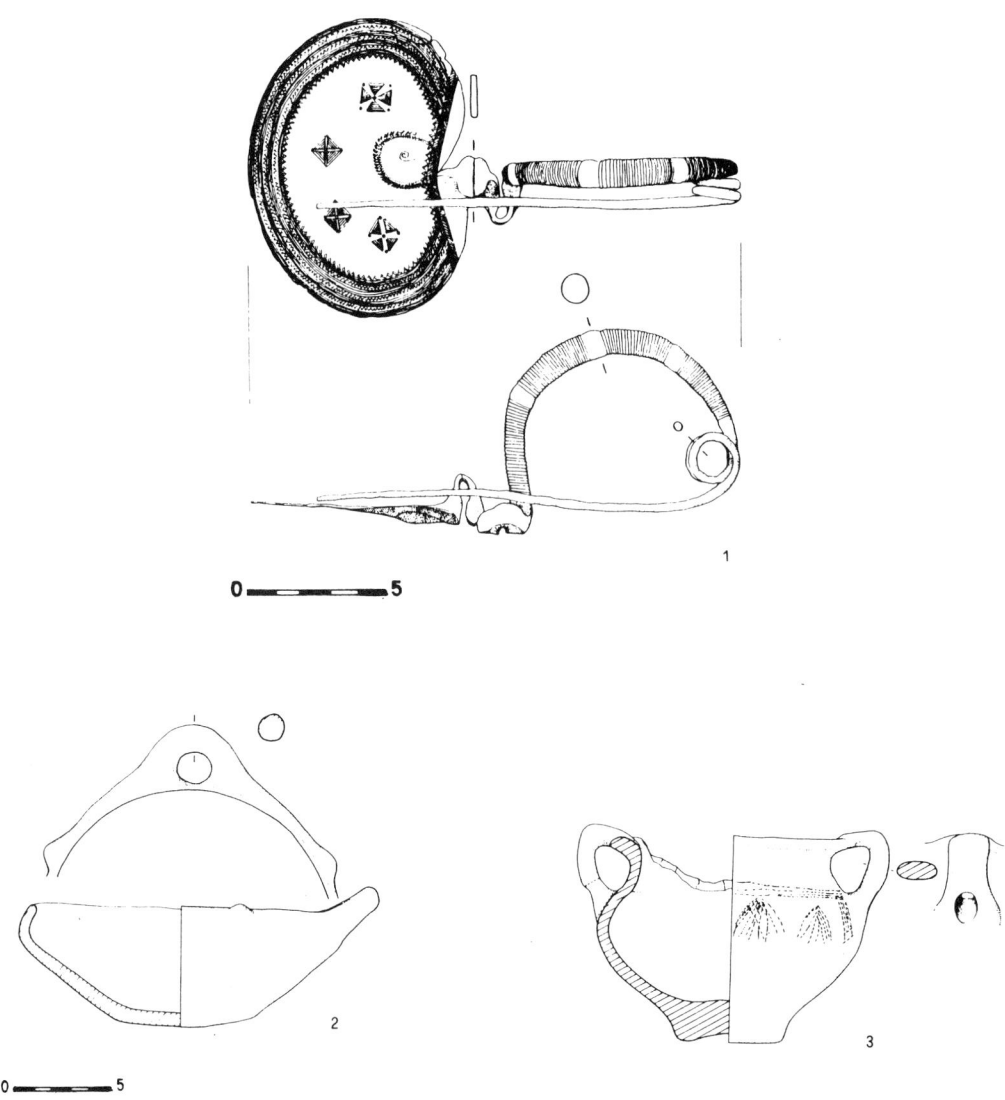

Fig. 6. Bronzes and pottery of Villanovan type. 1. Arch fibula with disc-foot. 2. Bowl. 3. Amphora.

tently different from the most common local types both in overall shape and in decoration. Quite probably, although, as already noted, no significant differences from the local types have been identified by the analyses, these fibulae are imports from the Villanovan area (cf. Tarquinia: Hencken 1968: figs. 32a, 51b-e, 43a, 55g-j; Pontecagnano: d'Agostino & Gastaldi 1988: pl. 19, types 32b13a2, 32b15a, 32b15b).

It is interesting to note that in two graves with Villanovan type fibulae (*Osteria dell'Osa* 1992: figs. 3a.45,46/7,15, 254/7,9, tombs 119 and 439) the grave-goods include a distaff (*Osteria dell'Osa* 1992: pl. 41, type 51a), also a Villanovan type, constituted by a wooden stick covered with small bronze rings (see for example Veii: *Quattro Fontanili* 1965: fig. 61e, tomb HH14).

Villanovan type vessels are only present in two female burials (91, a very young girl, and 198, a young adult: *Osteria dell'Osa* 1992: figs. 3a. 198/3, 316/1). These are a bowl with small projections on both sides of the handle (fig. 6/2; see *Osteria dell'Osa* 1992: pl. 25, type 26 *unicum* II), from grave 91, and a small amphora (fig. 6.3; see *Osteria dell'Osa* 1992: pl. 14, type 7 *unicum* I) from grave 198. For parallels in Villanovan complexes see for example Veii (*Quattro Fontanili* 1965: fig. 5, type 11; *Quattro Fontanili* 1986, fig. 15c, type X1, bowl) and Tarquinia (Hencken 1968: figs 62d, 95f, amphora). Thin-section analyses of these two vessels (Cuomo di Caprio 1992: nos. 11, 13) did not entirely rule out the possibility of a local manufacture. However, several features of the amphora from grave 198 indicate that it was probably an import from Villanovan Etruria: this vessel is not remarkable for its aesthetic quality, but is quite different from the local amphora types both in shape and decoration; some technical details, such as the light reddish colour of the impasto, which possibly implies firing in an updraft kiln, could indicate that it was not made locally. Moreover, it shows clear traces of wear, which are also present along the edge of an ancient breakage. This vessel was probably a personal possession, which had seen long use.

Grave 91 was not characterized by other unusual elements besides the bowl of Villanovan type, whereas grave 198 occupied a central place in its grave-group, along with a male burial (tomb 197: *Osteria dell'Osa* 1992: figs. 3a.336, 337) characterized by important indications of prestige and role. The funerary outfit of grave 198 comprised several personal ornaments, including an arch fibula with disc foot, possibly another import from Villanovan Etruria.

Overall, the evidence concerning objects of Villanovan type from the burials of Osteria dell'Osa is substantially different from the one concerning objects with south-Italian affinities. The differences can be briefly summarised as follows:

- Vessels of Villanovan type are far less numerous, as well as being more sharply separate from the local pottery shapes and types.

- The number of bronzes which can be identified as Villanovan and south Italian imports respectively is more or less equivalent. However, the former are almost exclusively objects used by women, such as the arch fibulae with disc foot and the distaffs, whereas the latter comprise objects used by men (essentially razors) as well as ornaments used by women.

- The two vessels of Villanovan type both come from female burials, while those vessels showing south-Italian features were found in the graves of individuals of both sexes and of all age-classes.

As was the case for the material of south-Italian type, these data indicate the possiblity that a few individuals coming from Villanovan Etruria also entered the community of Osteria dell'Osa. This seems quite likely as regards the woman buried in grave 198 and perhaps the little girl of tomb 91, and could also apply to some of the women who used fibulae or other bronzes of Villanovan type. As regards the latter group, one should also consider the possibility that these imported Villanovan bronzes were simply a category of exotic goods, more prestigious than their widely diffused local equivalents, rather than indicating the region of origin of the deceased.

However, the relationship with Villanovan Etruria as it appears from the archaeological evidence does not seem to be identical to that with southern Italy, the main difference being that the foreigners involved in the Villanovan connection were exclusively, or almost exclusively, women. This probably implies that the social mechanism for integration was marriage rather than the incorporation of whole families of outside origin in the local kin-groups.

The specific features of tomb 198, as well as some elements appearing in many of the graves furnished with bronzes of Villanovan type, indicate that for these women, too, access to high social status was possible.

Discussion

In general terms, the main features of the contacts with southern Italy and Etruria respectively which appear in the cemetery of Osteria dell'Osa also involve the rest of ancient Lazio. The similarity with the pottery of the fossa-grave groups is generalized in the region throughout Latial period II, and the hypothesis concerning an openness to foreign contact probably applies to all the local communities.

However, local differences can be identified. In the cemetery of the Roman Forum, near the temple of Antoninus and Faustina, vessels of Villanovan type appear in graves, B, male, and X, female, respectively (Gjerstad 1956: figs. 32/7, 14/2). In the Alban Hills complexes, vessels with specific features of south-Italian type apparently are less frequent than they are at Osteria dell'Osa, while Villanovan imports are rather numerous (impasto vessels: Gierow 1964: figs. 193/16; 202/36, 37; 205/6, 7, from Castel Gandolfo; fig. 233/2–4, unknown provenance. Bronzes: Gierow 1964: figs. 48/23; 209/23, *arco ingrossato* fibulae with disc-foot from Villa Cavalletti and Castel Gandolfo; Gierow 1966: 343, belt from Velletri). In the cemetery of Tivoli, the grave-goods of several graves, all dating from a late phase of Latial period II, include bronzes of Villanovan type (CLP, pls. 34/12a, 36A, 38B/10: *arco ingrossato* fibula with disc foot, tomb 45; belt, tomb 43; bronze-sheet vessel, tomb 24b).

It would appear that although all the communities of ancient Lazio were involved in interregional relationships, the specific features as well as the main direction of the contact should be examined within each individual context. The interregional connections of ancient Lazio may also have had some implications of economic nature: within the Latial communities, which possessed a relatively simple, 'egalitarian' structure and a political and territorial organization of tribal type, contacts such as the ones which have been described probably constituted the main vehicle of economic exchange. In a region almost totally lacking in mining resources, it seems rather likely that the acquisition of metal was linked to the systematic integration in the local communities of people from ore-rich areas, such as Etruria and, possibly, Calabria.

Overall, it can be argued that the evidence from Osteria dell'Osa provides an insight into an important mechanism of long-distance contacts, which can be seen as a vital structural component of the Italian Early Iron Age society.

Postscript: Latial period III contacts

Finally, while the subsequent development of the interregional relationships of ancient Lazio will be analyzed in the paper by A. De Santis (this volume), it is worth mentioning some of its most significant features.

The beginning of Latial period III, from about 770 BC, marked a substantial change in the direction as well as in the characteristics of the connection. The generalized similarity in pottery shapes between Lazio and the fossa-grave complexes of the southern Tyrrhenian regions did not continue; many Latial pottery shapes characteristic of period III have close parallels in Villanovan Etruria, especially in the cemetery of Quattro Fontanili at Veii. As far as bronzes are concerned, 8th century Latial metal production is almost indistinguishable from that of Etruria; once again, the closest parallels are with Veii. This change in the main flow of interregional contact, as it appears from the archaeological record, is quite striking, since it altered the long established tradition of systematic relationships between Lazio and southern Italy which, quite probably, depended on a strong cultural and ethnic affinity.

A possible explanation can be based on the overall consideration of the differences in political and economic complexity between the central and southern Tyrrhenian regions throughout the Iron age. The archaeological evidence indicates that the political and economic structure of the proto-urban Villanovan centres of Etruria was considerably more complex and organized than those of both ancient Lazio and the fossa-grave groups of Campania and Calabria. As already noted, during Latial period II the main flow of interregional communication of Lazio was addressed towards Campania and Calabria; apparently, the strongest interregional links of Lazio were those based on cultural and ethnic affinities with relatively distant areas. Economic factors probably played some role in this connection, whereas political ties were weak or non-existent.

The new ties between Lazio and adjacent Villanovan Etruria which appeared at the beginning of Latial period III, around 770 BC, seem to mark a shift towards political and economic factors as the main basis for interregional relationships. This possibly coincided with the growing role of Veii – the Villanovan centre more directly connected with Lazio and, mainly, with Rome – among the centres of Etruria. The relationship with Etruria was further enhanced with the start of the Greek colonization in Campania, around the mid-8th century BC. Ancient Lazio became the terrestrial route between the Greek colonies in southern Tyrrhenian Italy and the Villanovan centres of Etruria, in which the strategic location of Rome, on the best ford of the Tiber and within a distance of a few kilometres of Veii, played a central role.

Bibliography

Becker, M.J. & Salvadei, L. 1992. 'Analysis of the human skeletal remains from the cemetery of Osteria dell'Osa', in *Osteria dell'Osa*, 53–191.

Berardinetti-Insam, A. 1990. 'La fase iniziale della comunità villanoviana di Quattro Fontanili. Rapporti con le comunità limitrofe', *Dialoghi di Archeologia*, 1, 5–28.

Bernabò Brea, L. & Cavalier, M. 1980. *Meligunis Lipara IV*, Palermo.

Bianco Peroni, V. 1976. *I coltelli nell'Italia continentale*, (Prähistorische Bronzefunde VII/2), München.

Bianco Peroni, V. 1979. *I rasoi nell'Italia continentale*, (Prähistorische Bronzefunde VIII/2), München.

Bietti Sestieri, A.M. 1992. *The Iron Age Community of Osteria dell'Osa – A Study of Socio-Political Development in Central Tyrrhenian Italy*, Cambridge.

Bietti Sestieri, A.M., De Santis, A. & La Regina, A. 1989–90. 'Elementi di tipo cultuale e doni personali nella necropoli laziale di Osteria dell'Osa', in *Scienze dell'Antichità*, 3–4, 65–88

Chiartano, B. 1981. 'Roccella Jonica (Reggio Calabria). Necropoli preellenica in contrada S.Onofrio', *Notizie degli Scavi di Antichità*, 491–539.

CLP 1976. *Civiltà del Lazio primitivo*, Roma.

Cuomo di Caprio, N. 1992. 'Studio tecnologico e analisi di microscopia ottica di 63 campioni ceramici dalla necropoli di Osteria dell'Osa', in *Osteria dell'Osa*, 449–478.

d'Agostino, B. & Gastaldi, P. 1988. *Pontecagnano II. La necropoli del Picentino. 1. Le tombe della prima età del Ferro*, Napoli.

Fried, M. H. 1967. *The Evolution of Political Society. An Essay in Political Anthropology*, New York.

Gabrici, E. 1913. *Cuma dalle origini ai principii del sec. VI a.C.* (Monumenti Antichi dei Lincei, 22).

Gierow, P.G. 1964. *The Iron Age Culture of Latium II. The Alban Hills*, (Acta Instituti Romani Regni Sueciae 4°, XXIV, 2), Lund.

Gierow, P.G. 1966. *The Iron Age Culture of Latium. I. Classification and Analysis*, (Acta Instituti Romani Regni Sueciae 4°, XXIV, 1), Lund.

Gjerstad, E. 1956. *Early Rome II – The Tombs*, (Acta Instituti Romani Regni Sueciae 4°, XVII:2), Lund.

Goody, J. 1969. 'The fission of domestic groups among the Lodagaba', in J.Goody (ed.), *The Developmental Cycle in Domestic Groups*, Cambridge, 53–90.

Guida, G. & Marabelli, M. 1992. 'Studio metallografico di fibule degli scavi di Osteria dell'Osa', in *Osteria dell'Osa*, 479–484.

Hencken, H. 1968. *Tarquinia, Villanovans and Early Etruscans*, American School of Prehistoric Research – Peabody Museum, Harvard University, Bulletin n. 23, Vol. I-II.

Keesing, R.M. 1975. *Kin Groups and Social Structure*, New York.

Kilian, K. 1970. *Früheisenzeitliche Funde aus der Südostnekropole von Sala Consilina (Provinz Salerno)*, (Archäologische Forschungen in Lukanien III).

Orsi, P. 1926. *Le necropoli preelleniche calabresi di Torre Galli e di Canale, Ianchina, Patariti*, (Monumenti Antichi dei Lincei 31)

Osteria dell'Osa 1992. A.M. Bietti Sestieri (ed.), *La necropoli laziale di Osteria dell'Osa*, Roma.

Peacock, D.P.S. 1981. 'Archaeology, ethnology and ceramic production', in H. Howard & E.L. Morris (eds.), *Production and Distribution: A Ceramic Viewpoint*, BAR International Series 120, Oxford, 187–194.

Pohl, I. 1972. *The Iron Age Necropolis of Sorbo at Cerveteri*, (Acta Instituti Romani Regni Sueciae 4°, XXXII), Lund.

Quattro Fontanili 1965. AA.VV. 'Veio (Isola Farnese). Continuazione degli scavi nella necropoli villanoviana in località "Quattro Fontanili"', *Notizie degli Scavi di Antichità*, 49–236.

Quattro Fontanili 1986. J. Toms, 'The relative chronology of the Villanovan cemetery of Quattro Fontanili at Veii', *AION ArchStAnt*, 8, 41–97.

Ruby, P. 1990. *Le crepuscule des marges* (Thèse de Doctorat- Université Paris I – Pantheon-Sorbonne).

Sahlins, M.D. 1968. *Tribesmen*, New Jersey.

Van der Leeuw, S.E. 1976. *Studies in the Technology of Ancient Pottery*. (Ph.D. Dissertation, University of Amsterdam).

38

Contatti fra Etruria e Lazio Antico alla Fine dell'VIII sec. a.C.: La Tomba di Guerriero di Osteria dell'Osa

ANNA DE SANTIS

(Soprintendenza Archeologica di Roma)

Sommario: *Nel 1972, nei pressi della necropoli di Osteria dell'Osa, nella zona a sud-ovest della via Prenestina antica, venne recuperata una deposizione di guerriero (tomba 600 nella numerazione della necropoli), sconvolta dai lavori agricoli. La tomba, probabilmente isolata, presentava un ricco corredo di bronzi laminati costituito da un vaso di forma biconica, un elmo crestato, probabilmente due scudi da parata, quattro patere baccellate, una 'paletta', un 'carrello rituale', forse un pettorale quadrangolare; completavano il corredo una spada, due lance, un'ascia e due spiedi di ferro; unici elementi di corredo personale un bracciale e un anello digitale di bronzo. Per quanto riguarda il rituale della deposizione, la presenza nel corredo di più di uno scudo di bronzo, caratteristica in generale delle sepolture a inumazione, sembrerebbe contraddire l'uso dell'incinerazione, suggerita dal vaso biconico. I materiali permettono di datare il complesso nell'ultimo trentennio dell'VIII secolo a.C.*

Si tratta indubbiamente dei resti di un corredo del tutto eccezionale fra le tombe coeve della necropoli di Osteria dell'Osa e che trova piuttosto riscontro per il tipo di 'segni di prestigio' nelle tombe di guerriero più o meno contemporanee di ambiente laziale (tomba 21 di Castel di Decima, tomba 94 dell'Esquilino a Roma) ed etrusco (ad es. tombe Z15A di Quattro Fontanili, più antica, 871 e 1036 di Casale del Fosso a Veio, tomba del Guerriero a Tarquinia). Particolarmente stringenti appaiono i confronti soprattutto con le tombe veienti. Il carattere eccezionale e non locale di questo corredo pone il problema del significato di questa sepoltura nell'ambito della comunità di Osteria dell'Osa e quello più ampio dei contatti fra Lazio antico ed Etruria alla fine dell'VIII sec. a.C.

L'evidenza archeologica offerta dalla necropoli di Osteria dell'Osa durante il IX e il primo trentennio dell'VIII sec. a.C., fasi laziali IIA-IIB, documenta l'esistenza di un'ampia trama di rapporti e di scambi che coinvolge l'Italia centro-meridionale, in particolare tirrenica e soprattutto una notevole apertura delle comunità laziali alla circolazione di oggetti e persone di origine 'straniera' (cfr. Bietti Sestieri, in questi atti). Con l'inizio del III periodo laziale (770–730/720 a.C.), il quadro offerto dalla necropoli e dal resto del Lazio più in generale mostra alcune trasformazioni sostanziali nei modi tradizionali dei contatti e degli scambi quali si erano andati precisando e consolidando nel periodo precedente.

A partire da questo momento infatti i rapporti con l'Etruria acquistano un peso maggiore e i collegamenti più intensi e sistematici si spostano dall'Italia meridionale all'Etruria villanoviana. Le strette affinità nei tipi della ceramica e soprattutto in tutta la produzione metallica che si colgono specialmente tra Veio e i centri laziali sembrano indicare infatti una più ampia circolazione di persone tra le due regioni e soprattutto un intensificarsi dei legami economici.

Le trasformazioni che si colgono nelle produzioni artigianali nell'area centrale tirrenica riflettono un importante cambiamento che si verifica nei rapporti interregionali fra la fine del IX e l'inizio dell'VIII sec. a.C. In questo momento infatti, Cerveteri, il centro costiero villanoviano più vicino al Lazio, sembra perdere importanza rispetto agli altri centri, in particolare Tarquinia e Veio; nel Lazio questi nuovi equilibri determinano la rapida decadenza, per i collegamenti con l'Etruria, della via parallela alla costa che metteva direttamente in contatto i centri laziali con Cerveteri e il suo entroterra e l'intensificarsi al contrario dei rapporti con Veio. Questo spostamento dell'asse principale dei contatti con l'Etruria determina fra i centri laziali la crescita di importanza di Roma, direttamente collegata con Veio. Roma assume pertanto un ruolo fondamentale non solo come punto di passaggio obbligato per i collegamenti fra Lazio ed Etruria, ma anche come tramite dei collegamenti fra Etruria e Campania, che diventeranno particolarmente rilevanti a partire dalla metà dell'VIII secolo, con l'inizio della colonizzazione greca (Bietti Sestieri 1992a: 72ss, figg. 3.17a.b. Sul ruolo di Veio durante la prima età del ferro, cfr. Bartoloni 1986; Colonna 1986; Berardinetti Insam 1990; Bartoloni 1991).

L'inizio dello stanziamento euboico a Ischia verso il 770 ca. a.C. e del collegamento sistematico fra l'Etruria e il Lazio antico – e in particolare tra Veio e Roma, favorito dalla posizione geografica e dal Tevere, determinano l'intensificarsi degli scambi. Una conferma delle strette relazioni tra Roma e Veio e del loro diretto coinvolgimento con gli stanziamenti greci in Campania è data dalla presenza precoce nei due centri di ceramica greca importata e imitata (Bartoloni 1981; Colonna 1988: 298-300; da ultimo sul problema con ampia bibliografia, Bartoloni 1991: 43-44).

Fin dall'inizio del III periodo laziale le forme e i tipi della ceramica di impasto di Osteria dell'Osa, e in generale di tutti i centri del Lazio antico, mostrano affinità strettissime con il repertorio ceramico dei complessi villanoviani dell'Etruria, e in modo particolare di Veio (fasi IIA-IIB: Toms 1986). Queste affinità si estendono anche al repertorio metallico, come mostrano le fibule sia maschili che femminili, gli oggetti di ornamento, le armi (Bietti Sestieri 1992: 523-525).

Le relazioni dirette con l'Etruria appaiono ancora più significative nella seconda metà dell'VIII secolo, quando l'affermarsi e il consolidarsi nel Lazio di una classe aristocratica basata sulla strutturazione della società per gentes determina una specializzazione dei contatti interregionali attraverso lo stabilirsi di relazioni economiche e politiche sistematiche fra le elites dominanti delle due regioni (*Dialoghi di Archeologia* 1980). La necropoli di Osteria dell'Osa offre una conferma importante delle strette relazioni che coinvolgono in questo momento le classi dominanti del Lazio e dell'Etruria.

Al momento finale del III periodo appartiene infatti nella necropoli una isolata tomba di guerriero con un ricco corredo di armi e vasi di bronzo che non trovano confronti nel resto del sepolcreto, ma che al contrario presentano caratteristiche tipicamente villanoviane.

La tomba (600 nella numerazione della necropoli: cfr. De Santis in Bietti Sestieri 1992: 845-847, 875-877, tavv. 47-49), venne scoperta casualmente nell'autunno del 1972 in un terreno incolto nella zona a Sud-ovest della via Prenestina (fig.1, n.8) dove uno scasso agricolo, della profondità di ca 50 cm., aveva rimesso in luce un'area, approssimativamente quadrata di ca m. 1,50 di lato, interamente cosparsa di frammenti di metallo. Gli oggetti, tutti in cattivo stato di conservazione e molto lacunosi, fra i quali due patere baccellate ancora impilate l'una sull'altra, erano contenuti in una lente di terra nera, frammisti ad alcune lastrine di crosta di travertino e a piccole pietre.

Del corredo ceramico, probabilmente andato completamente distrutto con le arature, rimaneva solo un frammento di anforetta di impasto con anse crestate (parte della spalla e di un'ansa), attualmente non conservata, mentre non si rinvenne nessuna traccia della deposizione.

Gli oggetti recuperati furono consegnati prima al Gruppo Archeologico Romano e successivamente, nel 1974, al Museo Pigorini, dove sono tuttora conservati. Il complesso dei materiali, costituito da un'associazione di armi e recipienti di bronzo con caratteristiche tipicamente villanoviane, fece avanzare seri dubbi sulla sua effettiva provenienza dalla zona di Osteria dell'Osa. Subito dopo la consegna, venne pertanto effettuato un saggio di scavo nell'area indicata come quella del rinvenimento. In questa occasione si recuperarono altri minuti frammenti di lamina di bronzo con decorazione a sbalzo, del tutto analoghi a quelli trovati in precedenza. Inoltre i risultati di un'analisi comparata compiuta su campioni di terreno sul sito e di terra prelevata da alcuni oggetti del corredo hanno confermato definitivamente l'appartenenza di questa deposizione al complesso della necropoli.

In base alle osservazioni compiute sul terreno, la tomba era isolata e relativamente distante da altri piccoli gruppi di sepolture identificati sempre nella stessa area, fra la Prenestina antica e la nuova, databili da un momento avanzato del III periodo a tutto il IV (fig.1 nn.11-12). Sempre da questo settore proviene anche la deposizione in tronco d'albero scoperta nel 1889 riferibile alla fase IVA2, cioè agli anni centrali del VII secolo a.C., conservata nel Museo Nazionale di Villa Giulia (fig.1 n.7; per questa tomba, 601 nella numerazione della necropoli di Osteria dell'Osa, cfr. De Santis in Bietti Sestieri 1992: 851-853, figg. 3c.70-73). Questo gruppo di tombe non fa parte di un tessuto continuo ma è caratterizzato da una scarsa consistenza numerica e da una distribuzione spaziale rada. Le stesse caratteristiche contraddistinguono le tombe contemporanee nella necropoli. Le deposizioni delle fasi finali della necropoli, databili dalle ultime decadi dell'VIII secolo a tutto il VII (un totale di poco più di settanta tombe per un arco cronologico di circa 150 anni) sono distribuite infatti su tutta l'area del sepolcreto, isolate o in gruppi di poche unità. Un'altra importante caratteristica di queste tombe, e soprattutto di quelle del periodo orientalizzante, è l'anomala distribuzione per classi di età, con una netta prevalenza di individui adulti e anziani. Tutti questi elementi che caratterizzano le tombe delle fasi finali, e cioè numero limitato, distribuzione sparsa, rappresentazione anomala delle classi di età, sembrano indicare che la necropoli non corrisponde più in questo momento ad una comunità residenziale. L'inizio della fase avanzata del III periodo segna probabilmente il momento della concentrazione delle comunità presenti nel comprensorio sul sito di Gabii (fig.1 n.13). E' probabile che alcuni importanti membri della comunità originaria, che hanno ormai spostato la loro residenza a Gabii, come probabilmente è avvenuto per le altre comunità sparse

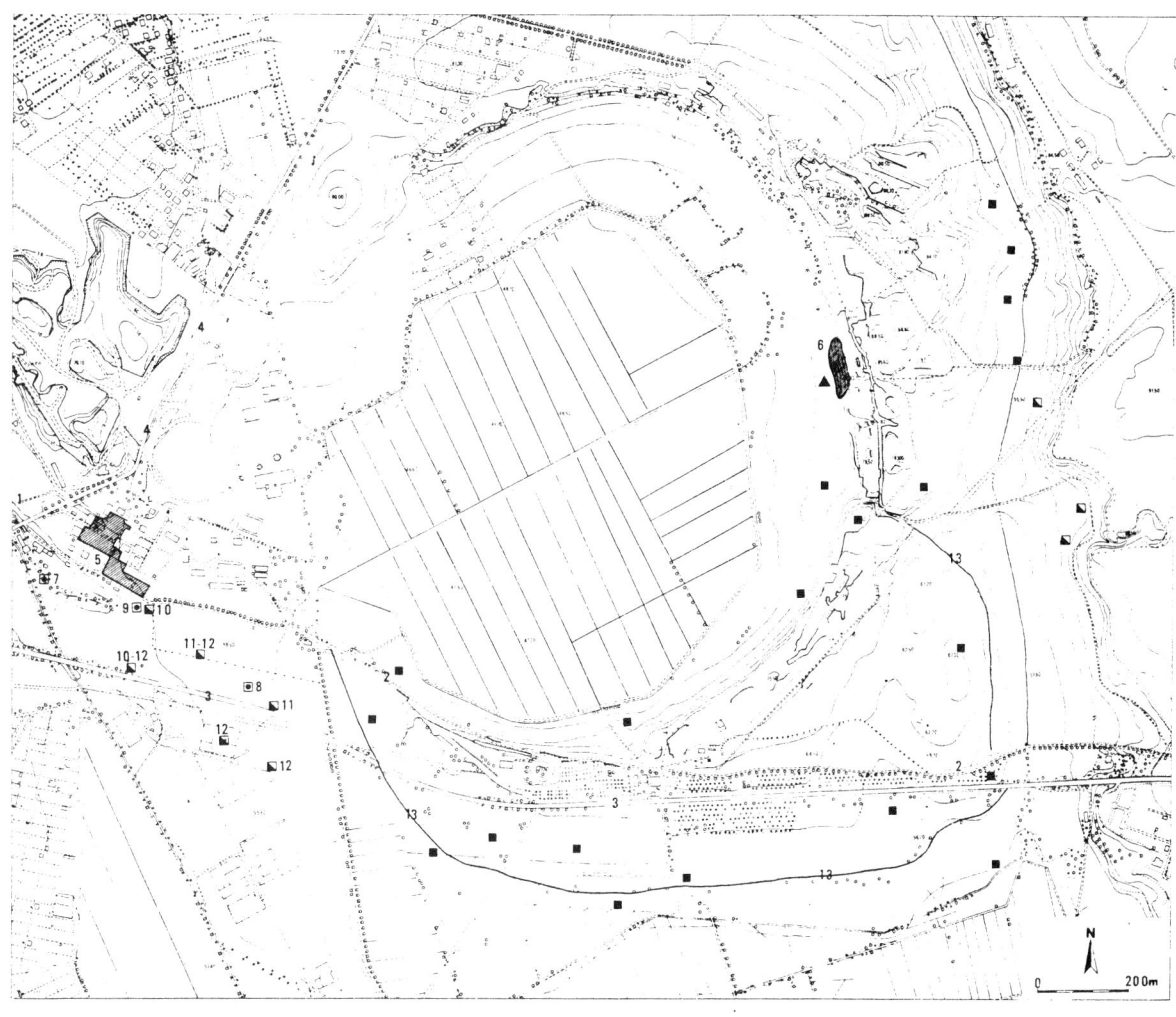

Fig. 1. Comprensorio Osteria dell'Osa-Gabii-Castiglione: 1: fosso dell'Osa, 2: via Prenestina antica, 3: via Prenestina nuova, 4: via di Poli, 5: necropoli diOsteria dell'Osa, 6: necropoli di Castiglione, 7: tomba del 1889 (601), 8: tomba del guerriero (600), 9: tomba a camera 602, tratteggio: le necropoli esplorate sistematicamente, quadrato campito a metà: tracce di necropoli dell'età del ferro, triangolo nero: abitato dell'età del bronzo, quadrato nero: tracce di abitati dell'età del ferro, 10: fase IIB, 11: III periodo; 12: Orientalizzante; 13: limite della città arcaica.

intorno al cratere di Castiglione (fig. 1 – i quadrati neri indicano le tracce di abitati della prima età del ferro), continuino ad usare la tradizionale area di necropoli. Una possibile lettura di questo fenomeno potrebbe essere che i membri della antica comunità residenziale rafforzino la propria posizione nel nuovo centro conservando un legame visibile con l'area di origine. Nello stesso tempo, la collocazione di queste sepolture in un'area relativamente distante dal nuovo insediamento (ca. km 2) costituiva probabilmente anche un mezzo per assicurare il controllo sul territorio.

Nel caso della tomba 600, il maggiore isolamento rispetto alle altre sepolture presenti nella stessa area non è probabilmente casuale ma costituisce un mezzo per sottolinearne ulteriormente la particolare importanza (cfr. la necropoli di Casale del Fosso a Veio, nella quale è stata osservata una disposizione a coppie di sepolture importanti distanziate negli ultimi decenni dell'VIII secolo, Buranelli 1981: 39).

La tomba di Osteria dell'Osa, sicuramente maschile e riferibile ad un guerriero, presenta infatti un corredo eccezionale anche se certamente incompleto e con i materiali in uno stato di conservazione tale da consentirne in genere una ricostruzione esclusivamente grafica.

Il defunto era stato sepolto con la sua armatura, completa di elmo crestato (fig.2.1), almeno due scudi (fig.3) e probabilmente un pettorale quadrangolare di bronzo (fig.2.24), spada di ferro, probabilmente lunga, con fodero di materiale deperibile e fascia trasversale di osso o avorio (fig.2.8), lancia (fig.2.9), giavellotto (fig.2.10) e ascia a cannone di ferro (fig.2.12) e con un ricco corredo di vasellame di bronzo, comprendente un vaso biconico (fig.4.2), quattro patere baccellate

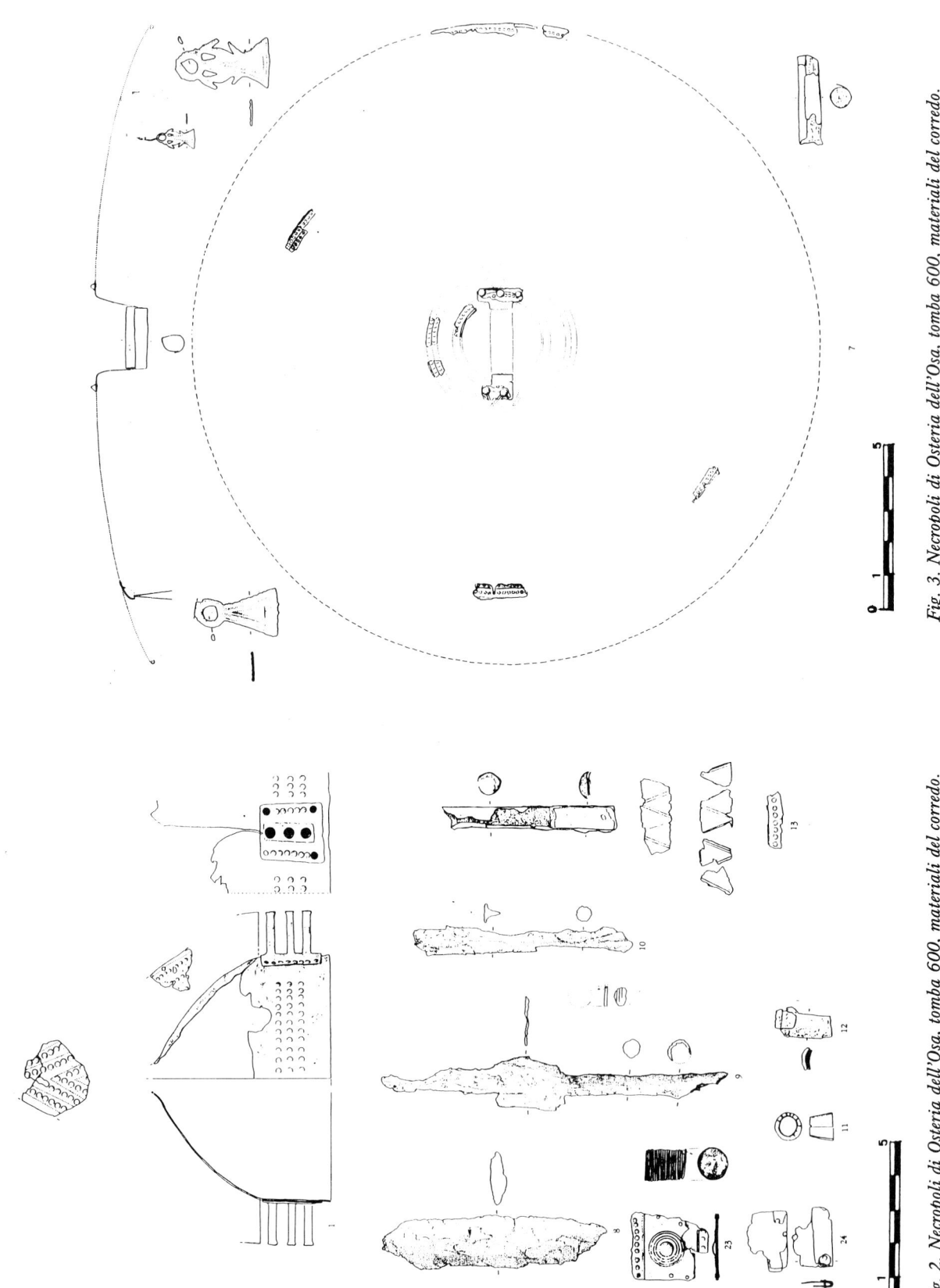

Fig. 3. *Necropoli di Osteria dell'Osa, tomba 600, materiali del corredo.*

Fig. 2. *Necropoli di Osteria dell'Osa, tomba 600, materiali del corredo.*

(fig.5.15-18), un bacile troncoconico con orlo perlato (fig.4.14), un altro recipiente con fondo ombelicato (fig.5.19), un coperchio con raffinata decorazione geometrica incisa a bulino (fig.4.20), un carrello-incensiere su quattro ruote (fig. 6), una paletta-flabello (fig.2.13) e due spiedi di ferro (fig.5.22). Gli unici oggetti di ornamento sono costituiti da un bracciale e da un anello digitale di bronzo; il corredo doveva comprendere anche altri oggetti di bronzo e ferro, dei quali restano alcuni frammenti, e altri vasi di bronzo, come mostrano i frammenti di lamina riferibili, rispettivamente, ad un bordo e ad un fondo (De Santis, in Bietti Sestieri 1992: tavv. 47 nn. 3-6, 49 nn. 25-27), e un'anforetta con anse crestate di impasto, perduta. Il complesso di questi materiali, databile verso la fine del terzo quarto dell'VIII sec. a.C., cioè alla fine della III fase laziale (Osteria dell'Osa fase IIIB: Bietti Sestieri 1992: 535-537), testimonia l'alto livello sociale del personaggio, che si distacca in modo significativo dallo standard delle tombe contemporanee della necropoli.

Appare interessante la presenza, segnalata al momento del rinvenimento, di lastrine di crosta di travertino insieme ai materiali. La crosta di travertino infatti costituisce uno degli elementi che nella necropoli di Osteria dell'Osa caratterizzano fin dalle fasi iniziali le sepolture dei membri più importanti della comunità e in particolare quelle degli uomini portatori di armi (Bietti Sestieri e De Santis, in Bietti Sestieri 1992: 491). Pietre di colore bianco, alle quali si attribuiva probabilmente un particolare valore rituale, compaiono anche in alcuni corredi maschili con armi di VIII secolo della necropoli veiente di *Quattro Fontanili* (LL12-13: frammenti di tufo bianco nel riempimento, *Quattro Fontanili* 1963: 241; Z1a: fossa con coperchio di tufo con pietra bianca al centro, *Quattro Fontanili* 1970: 283; AA1: un grande blocco di tufo chiaro nel riempimento, *Quattro Fontanili* 1970: 296) .

Una particolare attenzione meritano alcuni oggetti che permettono di definire meglio il carattere della deposizione: l'elmo, la paletta-flabello e il carrello-incensiere. Si tratta infatti di un insieme chiaramente definito con caratteristiche tipologiche completamente estranee al repertorio laziale e che riportano invariabilmente all'area villanoviana.

L'elmo (fig. 2,1) appartiene al tipo definito da Hencken 'with pointed cap' (Hencken 1971: 78ss., figg. 52-53, 55-67) e rientra nella variante II dei 'Kammhelme mit pickelhaubenartiger Kalotte' di von Hase, documentata nella versione in bronzo solo nell'VIII sec.a.C. (von Hase 1988: 196ss., nn. 5-11; figg.2,2; 4,1; 3,2; K55). Particolarmente vicini all'esemplare da Osteria dell'Osa sono gli elmi dalla tomba I della necropoli di Poggio Impiccato di Tarquinia, databile nella prima metà dell'VIII secolo (Hencken 1968: 115ss., fig. 105; Hencken 1971: 85ss, fig. 59; von Hase 1988: 196 n.5, figg.2,2; 4,1) e quello dalla tomba 1036 della necropoli di Casale del Fosso, databile al terzo venticinquennio dell'VIII sec. a.C. (Hencken 1971: 90, figg. 61-62; von Hase 1988: 196 n.6. Da ultimo su questa deposizione, una delle più notevoli fra le 'tombe di guerrieri' finora note in Italia, Colonna 1991: 63ss., fig. 16/16).

Ancora ad ambiente etrusco, e in particolar modo veiente, riportano sia il tipo di paletta-flabello che quello del carrello-incensiere. La paletta-flabello (fig.2.13) presenta infatti la forma trapezoidale che appare caratteristica di tutti i flabelli rinvenuti in Etruria meridionale in area veiente (Casale del Fosso tombe 871 e 1031: Müller-Karpe 1974, taff. 25,10 e 28,g; Monte Michele tomba 5: Boitani 1985: 554-555, tav.CI,a) e in area falisca (Narce tomba 63 e 19M: Pasqui 1902: 595; Hall Dohan 1942: 37, tav. XIX,11). Caratteristica di tutti gli esemplari laziali (Castel di Decima, tombe 15 e 50, Laurentina tombe 70, 93, 73, 74, 103, 121) è invece la versione a lamina circolare (Bedini 1990: 55-56 n. 20, 63 n. 27 con bibliografia). L'esemplare della tomba 600, ancora piuttosto stretto, appare confrontabile soprattutto con la 'paletta' dalla tomba Z15A della necropoli veiente di Quattro Fontanili (*Quattro Fontanili* 1965: 178, fig. 83t, databile alla fase IIB Toms), considerato l'esempio più antico di flabello (Bedini 1990: 56).

Anche il carrello-incensiere (fig.6.21) compare nella tomba di Osteria dell'Osa nella versione tipicamente etrusca su quattro ruote (Woytowitsch 1978: 54-66). Si tratta di un oggetto di particolare valore e prestigio presente esclusivamente nei corredi 'principeschi' di Palestrina, Veio, Cerveteri e Vetulonia (Pareti 1947: 290-291, n. 240; Woytowitsch 1978: 54-56, tavv. 21-22). L'origine della forma va probabilmente ricercata nei vassoi su ruote fenici, menzionati nei poemi omerici (Odissea, IV: 128). L'esemplare da Osteria dell'Osa appare particolarmente vicino, per le soluzioni tecniche, le dimensioni, gli elementi decorativi accessori (ocherelle e pendagli trapezoidali), soprattutto a quelli veienti, come i carrelli dalla tomba 871 di Casale del Fosso (Müller-Karpe 1974, tavv. 22-23) e quello da una tomba femminile sempre di Veio (Woytowitsch 1978, tav. 22/121; un altro esemplare è probabilmente presente, sempre a Veio, nella tomba 5 di Monte Michele, cfr. Boitani 1985: 547, tav. CI,b,c). L'elemento esterno che collega le ruote dell'esemplare di Osteria dell'Osa e che non compare nei carrelli menzionati, si ritrova invece su un carrello dal Circolo dei Lebeti di Vetulonia (Woytowitsch 1978, tav. 22/124a,b). Frammenti di un altro carrello probabilmente dello stesso tipo di quelli citati sono conservati nell'Ashmolean Museum di Oxford. La provenienza indicata per questo oggetto è la zona di Lezoux, Puy-de-Dome in Francia; si può pensare verosimilmente ad un'importazione dall'Etruria (Brown 1980: pl. VIb).

Nel Lazio, appare più diffuso invece un altro tipo di vassoio-incensiere, identico per forma generale, misure e funzione, ma che si differenzia per il sostegno a calotta

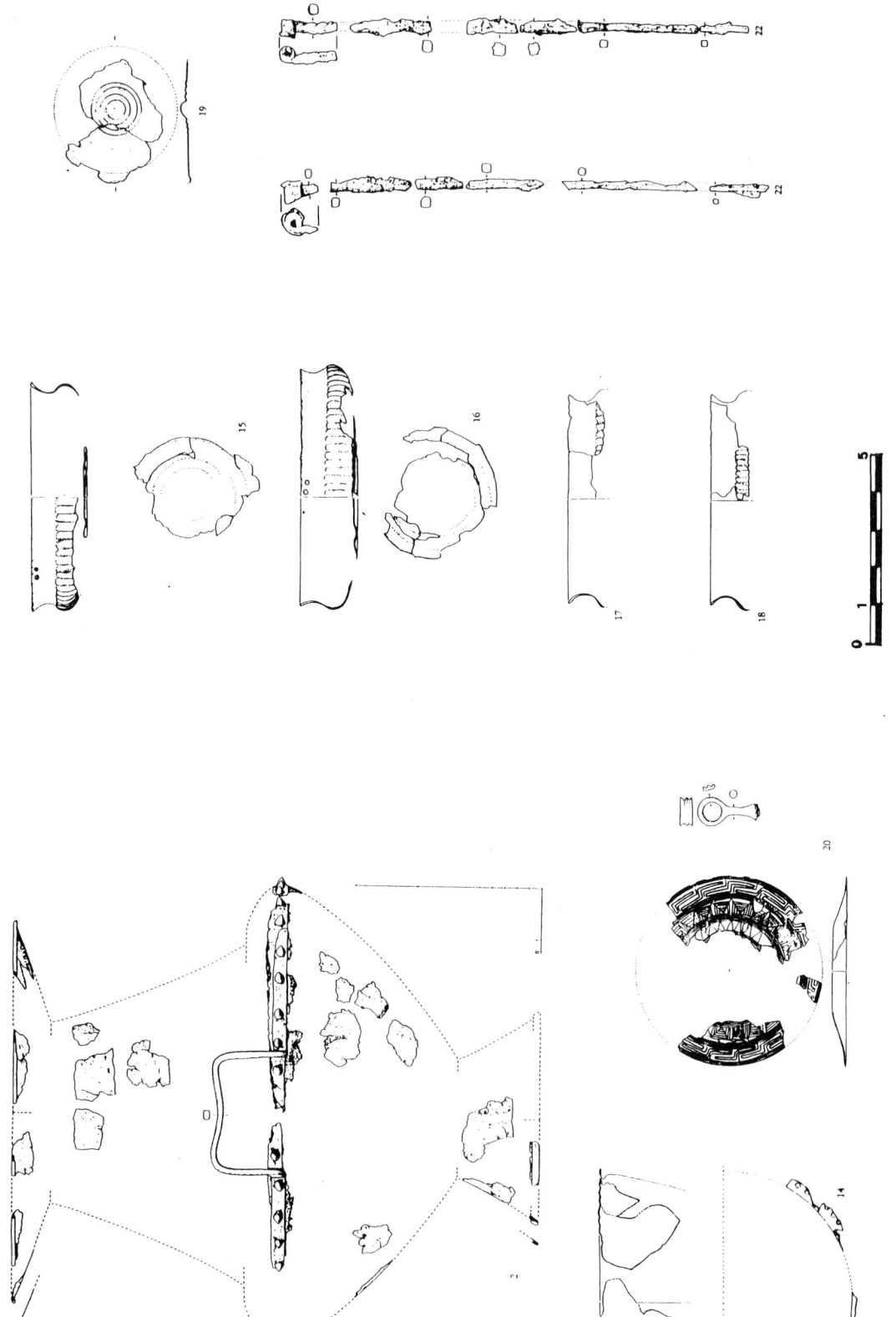

Fig. 5. Necropoli di Osteria dell'Osa, tomba 600, materiali del corredo.

Fig. 4. Necropoli di Osteria dell'Osa, tomba 600, materiali del corredo.

troncoconica e per la fattura a due lamine separate (tre esemplari identici dalla necropoli della Laurentina, tombe 70, 93 e 121 e forse un esemplare dalla tomba sotto il cosiddetto Heroon di Enea di Pratica di Mare: Bedini 1990: 57-58, n.22). Vassoi analoghi ai tipi laziali, ma di dimensioni minori e con redazioni anche in impasto, appaiono diffusi in area bolognese nel Villanoviano III (Tovoli 1989: 254-255, tav.115/72 in bronzo). Sia i flabelli che i carrelli-incensieri costituiscono oggetti di particolare distinzione, che caratterizzano i corredi 'principeschi' maschili e femminili dell'area tirrenica a partire dai decenni finali dell'VIII sec. a.C. Gli esemplari laziali sembrano comunque in generale più recenti e non comparire prima dell'inizio dell'Orientalizzante.

Anche l'ascia (fig.2.12) è un oggetto in genere poco diffuso nei corredi laziali al contrario di quelli etruschi.

Di particolare interesse sono il vaso biconico e gli scudi soprattutto per le implicazioni sul tipo di rituale utilizzato per la deposizione. Come tutti gli esemplari dello stesso genere, il vaso (fig.4.2) appare costituito da lamine separate, martellate a freddo, sovrapposte nei punti di giuntura e tenute insieme mediante borchie coniche. Sul punto di giuntura tra spalla e corpo e fissate con lo stesso sistema mediante borchie, sono applicate le anse, ottenute a fusione. L'esemplare della necropoli è estremamente frammentario e la ricostruzione della forma generale non è del tutto sicura. Anche la funzione del vaso non è precisabile, anche se non si può escludere una utilizzazione come cinerario.

Vasi di forma biconica di bronzo, con varianti nella forma generale e nella decorazione, utilizzati spesso come contenitori delle ceneri, compaiono nei corredi più ricchi di tutti i centri dell'Etruria meridionale e settentrionale a partire da un momento avanzato della seconda fase villanoviana (cfr. ad es. per Veio: *Quattro Fontanili* 1970: 300, n. 17; figg. 72-73, t.AA1; per Tarquinia: Hencken 1968, figg. 169a, 178a, 182, 352, Monterozzi, tt. 4, 9, del Guerriero, 12; per Vulci: Fugazzola Delpino 1984: 71s, n.7, necropoli dell'Osteria, loc. La Cantina, t. 23; Falconi Amorelli 1983: 159, n. 211, figg. 69-70, loc. La Cantina, scavi 1923; per Vetulonia: Falchi 1891, tavv. XIV/6, XV/21bis, 1° e 2° Circolo delle Pelliccie). Ossuari biconici di bronzo sono attestati anche in area bolognese in contesti databili tra l'ultimo quarto dell'VIII secolo e la prima metà del VII (Tovoli 1989: 250, tipo 60). La diffusione di questo tipo di vaso presuppone più centri di produzione (sul problema, Kilian 1977: 80-83; La Rocca 1978: 467, n.9, che ipotizza l'esistenza di un atelier a Vulci).

La forma appare invece abbastanza estranea al repertorio laziale e documentata solo sporadicamente come nella tomba 110 di Castel di Decima (*Dialoghi di Archeologia* 1980, tav. 15, tipo 29). Anche il bacile con orlo perlato con vasca rigidamente troncoconica (fig.4.14) appartiene al tipo di bacile di questa classe più diffuso in Etruria durante la fase avanzata del II periodo villanoviano (Albanese Procelli 1985: fig.10,1), mentre nel Lazio, lo stesso tipo appare documentato contemporaneamente nella versione tripode (la produzione laziale sembra distinguersi da quella etrusca per alcune caratteristiche della decorazione e della forma dell'orlo, Albanese Procelli 1985: 186).

Per quanto riguarda gli scudi (fig.3), il diametro ricavato dai frammenti di orlo conservati, abbondantemente superiore al metro, è probabilmente eccessivo per un unico esemplare; inoltre la presenza di due maniglie e di quindici pendagli fusi, di forma triangolare e a protomi di uccello stilizzate (Geiger 1994: 13-15. Abb.10,B, tipo 2), indica la presenza di almeno due esemplari. La maniglia più grande, costituita da un blocco cilindrico di piombo rivestito di lamina di bronzo, trova un confronto significativo in uno scudo deposto piegato nella tomba LL12-13 della necropoli veiente di Quattro Fontanili (fase IIC Toms; *Quattro Fontanili* 1963: 241-248, figg. 109-110). La decorazione sbalzata conservata sui frammenti di lamina dalla tomba 600, mostra file di nervature concentriche alternate a file di borchiette e, almeno in uno degli scudi, una fila di zig-zag a doppio e triplo tratto presso l'umbone che richiama la decorazione presente su un esemplare dalla tomba Castellani di Palestrina (Ström 1971: 23, cat. n. 12, fig. 9b, tipo AIV4; Geiger 1994: 65, cat.n.37, taf. 44-45, tipo 1d).

Nella seconda metà dell'VIII secolo la presenza di più di uno scudo è relativamente rara, e documentata esclusivamente in tombe a fossa. A Veio, due scudi compaiono in una tomba riferibile ad un guerriero, pubblicata da Garrucci (Ström 1971: 156). Il corredo di questa deposizione, andato completamente perduto, comprendeva, oltre ai due scudi, un elmo crestato simile a quello della tomba 871 della necropoli veiente di Casale del Fosso, databile alla fine del terzo quarto dell'VIII sec. a.C. (Müller-Karpe 1974, tav. 24/4), due spade di ferro con impugnatura di avorio e ambra, una punta di lancia di bronzo, alcune fibule di bronzo e i resti di un carro.

Nella tomba 21 della necropoli laziale di Castel di Decima, tre scudi erano deposti in modo da coprire interamente il cadavere (Bedini 1977: 287; Bartoloni, Cataldi Dini e Zevi 1982: 263). Lo stesso rituale compare, in epoca leggermente precedente, nella tomba 1036 di Casale del Fosso di Veio. In questo caso però sono stati utilizzati due scudi bilobati, secondo la ricostruzione della deposizione recentemente proposta da G. Colonna (Colonna 1991: figg.16-19).

Nel VII secolo la presenza di più di un esemplare sembra invece meno eccezionale: tre scudi sono stati rinvenuti in area di abitato a Verucchio (Gentili in Bermond Montanari 1987: 258ss, nn. 161-163), nella tomba 3 di Fabriano (Stary 1981: 259ss), nelle tombe Castellani di Palestrina e 70 della Laurentina, dove probabilmente erano appesi alle pareti (Canciani in *Civiltà del Lazio primitivo* 1976: 220ss nn.13-15; Bedini 1990: 52); due scudi sono documentati nel Lazio nelle tombe 93 e 121 della Laurentina, entrambe maschili (Bedini 1990: 54 e 61-64). Anche i supposti scudi fittili associati con il carro, generalmente in tombe maschili eminenti, sono documentati spesso in più di un esemplare (Colonna 1991: 81, nota 39; Bartolini & De Santis 1995).

Per quanto riguarda la tomba 600, proprio la presenza nel corredo di più di uno scudo di bronzo, caratteristica in generale delle sepolture a inumazione, sembrerebbe contraddire l'uso dell'incinerazione, suggerita invece dal vaso biconico di bronzo. A questo proposito va comunque notato che l'area di dispersione dei frammenti sul terreno era piuttosto ristretta per una tomba ad inumazione e che del resto più di uno scudo è documentato anche in associazione con tombe ad incinerazione (per es. a Veio nella tomba 5 principesca di Monte Michele, Boitani 1985 e nella tomba 93 della Laurentina, Bedini 1990: 53, entrambe con deposizione maschile).

L'eccezionalità di questo corredo appare evidente soprattutto se lo si confronta con le uniche due sepolture maschili con lancia e spada contemporanee della necropoli. Le due tombe, 239, leggermente più antica e 414 (De Santis in Bietti Sestieri 1992: 807, figg. 3b.3, 42 e 845, figg. 3c. 58-59), pur presentando infatti elementi di prestigio, come spada, lancia, dischi decorativi del balteo e, nel caso della seconda, anche uno spiedo, un coltello e una fibula a drago, non sono nemmeno lontanamente paragonabili al livello espresso dai materiali dalla tomba 600. Quest'ultima si inserisce infatti a pieno titolo fra le 'tombe di guerrieri' che compaiono più o meno contemporaneamente nella seconda metà dell'VIII sec. a.C. nel Lazio: a Roma la tomba 94 dell'Esquilino (Gjerstad 1956: 232-234, fig. 209), a Decima la tomba 21 (Bartoloni, Cataldi Dini & Zevi 1982: 263), nei pressi di Velletri in località Vallone di Lariano (Drago Troccoli 1989: 38-42) e in Etruria: a Veio nella necropoli di Quattro Fontanili le tombe Z15A e AA1, più antiche della tomba 600 (*Quattro Fontanili* 1965: 171ss.; 1970: 296ss.), e nella necropoli di Casale del Fosso le tombe 1036 e 871 (Müller-Karpe 1974; Buranelli 1981; Colonna 1991); a Tarquinia la tomba del Guerriero (Kilian 1977).

Queste deposizioni sono contraddistinte dai medesimi segni di status sociale: lance, spada, pettorale, scudo, ricco corredo di vasellame di bronzo e di ceramica e in molti casi un carro. Soprattutto appare costante l'associazione di pettorali quadrangolari e scudi rotondi (v.ad es. tombe del guerriero di Tarquinia, 21 di Decima, e probabilmente 94 dell'Esquilino e 600 di Osteria dell'Osa). Da questo costume militare, che potremmo definire 'normale', sembra divergere soltanto la tomba 1036 di Casale del Fosso, contraddistinta dall'associazione inconsueta di due dischi-corazza e due scudi bilobati. La presenza in questo corredo di oggetti che sottolineano la particolare dignità del personaggio, quali una mazza, uno scettro, tre lance, elmo, ascia, due spade, e soprattutto la combinazione mazza, scudo bilobato e disco-corazza, ha fatto ipotizzare un collegamento con il costume dei sacerdoti salii (Colonna 1991).

Le affinità che legano fra loro queste deposizioni di guerriero della seconda metà dell'VIII secolo sono strettissime, sia nella tipologia che nella quantità e qualità degli oggetti. Tuttavia in Etruria questo fenomeno, soprattutto in centri come Veio, si afferma in una dimensione quantitativamente molto più rilevante e le tombe di questo genere non presentano il carattere di eccezionalità delle analoghe sepolture del Lazio (Bartoloni 1987: 46-47).

La fisioniomia del tutto particolare e non locale della tomba 600 di Osteria dell'Osa pone infine il problema del significato di questa sepoltura nell'ambito della comunità alla fine dell'VIII sec. a.C. I confronti più stringenti per tutti gli oggetti più significativi del corredo sono, come si è visto, quelli istituibili con i materiali delle tombe di guerriero veienti contemporanee. E' pertanto possibile pensare che il guerriero della tomba 600 fosse un personaggio di alto rango, probabilmente un 'principe' originario dell'Etruria villanoviana, forse proveniente da Veio.

L'evidenza relativa alla tomba, che si inserisce nel contesto delle strette relazioni esistenti in questo momento tra le classi dominanti del Lazio e dell'Etruria, sembra indicare che il defunto, pur non appartenendo alla comunità laziale, sia vissuto al suo interno, completamente integrato nella società locale, conservando il rango elevato che ricopriva nella comunità di origine.

La tradizione letteraria relativa ai periodi successivi, Orientalizzante e arcaico, mostra chiaramente l'esistenza di una mobilità aristocratica, non solo dovuta a legami matrimoniali, ma anche allo spostamento di individui o gruppi verso le maggiori comunità dell'Etruria e del Lazio. Il conosciutissimo racconto del corinzio Demarato, profugo a Tarquinia, che si colloca negli anni centrali del VII secolo, sembra trovare in particolare una interessante conferma archeologica e epigrafica nel caso di *Rutile Hipucrates*, con prenome di origine latina e gentilizio di origine greca, sepolto in una tomba probabilmente monumentale dell'Orientalizzante medio di Tarquinia (Ampolo 1976-77: 333-345; Bartoloni 1987: 52-53). Sempre in questo contesto, si inserisce la tradizione relativa agli ultimi re di Roma, i Tarquinii, di origine etrusca. Alla fine del VII secolo a.C. a Veio è documentato un *tite latine*, sepolto con un ricco corredo nella tomba 17 della necropoli di Picazzano (Palm 1952: 56-57, tavv. IV-V n.8). Le evidenze, relative ai periodi Orientalizzante e arcaico, sembrano rappresentare in forme diverse, legate allo sviluppo di differenziazioni sociali permanenti, una diretta continuazione di una

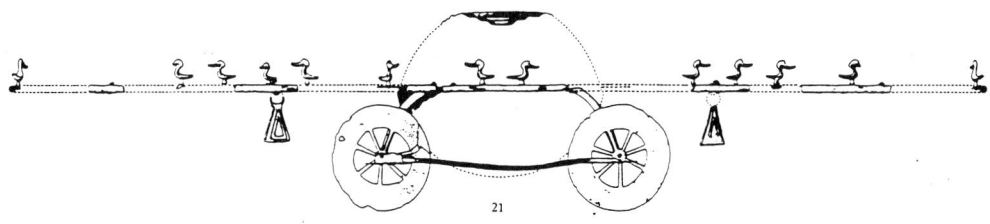

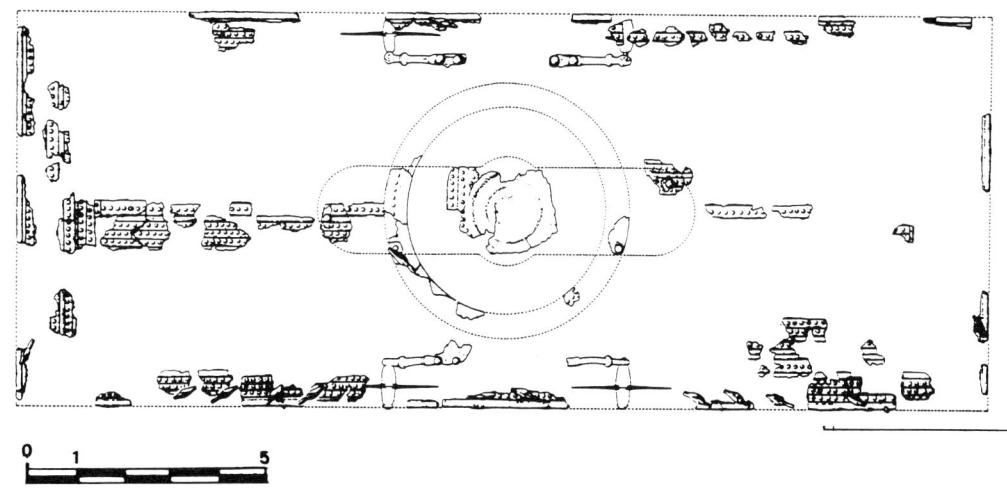

Fig. 6. Necropoli di Osteria dell'Osa, tomba 600, materiali del corredo.

prassi già lungamente stabilita durante l'età del ferro nelle stesse regioni.

E' interessante notare come questa apertura che coinvolge ai livelli più alti la società etrusca e latina in questi periodi non è un fenomeno isolato ma al contrario appare abbastanza diffuso a livello etnografico. A proposito di società basate essenzialmente su sistemi di parentele e lignaggi, è stato infatti osservato come spesso il governante che sta al di sopra della società venga concepito come estraneo ad essa; pertanto i capi e i re non appartengono al popolo che governano ma sono di provenienza straniera. Questo fenomeno è stato ampiamente analizzato da Sahlins nell'illustrare l'incontro fra il capitano Cook e gli abitanti delle isole Hawaii e le ragioni culturali che portarono alla sua identificazione con il dio-re Lono (cfr. Sahlins 1986: 65-91).

Nel caso della necropoli di Osteria dell'Osa, la tomba 600 documenta probabilmente la presenza a Gabii di un 'principe' etrusco, provvisto di tutte le insegne connesse con il suo ruolo e potere. Siamo di fronte ad un fenomeno che si collega direttamente, in un contesto sociale profondamente mutato, alla consuetudine dell'integrazione di persone o gruppi di provenienza esterna, con la possibilità per singoli individui di accedere a posizioni sociali elevate, che costituisce uno dei tratti essenziali della comunità di Osteria dell'Osa fin dal IX secolo a.C.

Ringraziamenti

Desidero ringraziare la dott.ssa Anna Maria Bietti Sestieri, la prof. ssa Gilda Bartoloni, e il dott. Alessandro Bedini per gli utili suggerimenti e scambi di idee. Le ricostruzioni grafiche del vaso biconico e del carrello-incensiere (Figg. 4.2 e 6) sono di Sergio Barberini, quella dello scudo (Fig. 3) di Adelheid Heil, i disegni del resto dei materiali sono di Monica Sorti.

APPENDICE

Elenco dei materiali della tomba 600 della necropoli di Osteria dell'Osa, conservati nel Museo Preistorico Etnografico L. Pigorini di Roma:

1 – elmo crestato di lamina. h 29,3+; h ric. 34ca; diam 22,7ca.

2 – vaso biconico formato da lamine separate. Ricostruzione ipotetica. h 42,9 ca; diam bocca 30,0; diam piede 16,8; diam max 36,2.

3 – bracciale di verga a sezione quadrangolare irregolare. diam 7,8 ca; h 0,4; spess 0,2.

4 – anello digitale (?) di lamina sottile a sezione triangolare. diam 2,1ca; h 0,25; spess 0,15.

5 – anello di verga spessa a sezione circolare con capi accostati. diam 3,0; 2,4.

6 – anello di verga spessa a sezione circolare. lungh cons 1,7; spess 0,5.

7 – frammenti probabilmente di due scudi circolari di lamina. Rimangono trentatrè frammenti dell'orlo: lungh totale 344,2; un frammento di lamina più sottile arrotolata con orlo di lamina ribattuto: lungh 5+; spess 0,4×0,2; tre frammenti di lamina con decorazione a sbalzo a file di borchiette alternate a nervature: 2,3×8,6; 1,9×6,71,9×7,4; due maniglie: a) lungh 10ca; diam 2,8-3,7; b) lungh 14+; diam 3,5-3,7; gli attacchi di una delle maniglie sullo scudo: 6,5+×7,5+; 5,5+×5+; una staffa per la sospensione sul retro dello scudo delle coppie di pendagli: h 4+; quindici pendagli fusi: quattro pendagli triangolari: h 5,5; largh 3,2-1,1; undici pendagli a protomi di uccelli (?) stilizzate, matrice a (cinque): h 6,0-6,4; largh 3ca; diam anello 2,0; matrice b (quattro): h 6,2ca; largh 3,2; diam anello 2,0; matrice c (due): h 6,2; largh 2,6ca; diam anello 2ca. fr, lac, ric.

8 – spada lunga con fodero in materiale deperibile (probabilmente cuoio) con fascia trasversale di avorio o osso. lungh 21+; largh 5,0.

9 – punta di lancia di ferro. lungh 32,3+; diam cannone 2,0-2,5; largh max lama 4,7.

9a – cilindretto di filo sottile a sezione piano-convessa avvolto a spirale fitta. lungh 3,2; diam 3,0.

10 – punta di giavellotto di ferro. lungh 20,5+; diam cannone 1,7-2,0; largh max lama 2,5.

10a – cilindretto di filo sottile a sezione triangolare avvolto a spirale fitta. h 0,7+; diam 2,2ca.

11 – oggetto troncopiramidale internamente cavo, ottenuto a fusione, superficie esterna con dodici leggere sfaccettature, all'interno resti di legno mineralizzato. h 2,2; diam 2,0-2,5.

12 – ascia a cannone di ferro; occhiello verticale poco aldisotto dell'orlo. lungh 5,3+; largh 2,7+.

13 – paletta-flabello di lamina trapezoidale con manico cilindrico applicato all'estremità minore. Decorazione a sbalzo. lungh totale ric 34,7ca; manico: lungh 16,1+; diam 2,2; largh base 2,6; largh max 12,3+.

14 – bacile di lamina sottile; ampio labbro a tesa orizzontale decorato con una fila di borchie a sbalzo. h 6,6+; diam bocca 22 ca.

15 – patera baccellata di lamina; baccellature fitte e sottili; fondo rientrante distinto da due scanalature circolari; presso l'orlo, due fori per la sospensione. h 4,7ca; diam bocca 18,8.

16 – patera baccellata di lamina; baccellature fitte e sottili; fondo rientrante distinto da una scanalatura circolare; presso l'orlo, due fori per la sospensione. h 4,8ca; diam bocca 19,4.

17–18 due patere baccellate di lamina; vasca con baccellature fitte e sottili. h 3,1+; diam 17ca. h 3,2+; diam bocca 17,3ca.

19 – frammento di lamina con decorazione a sbalzo: al centro una borchia circondata da nervature concentriche e da una larga scanalatura concentrica distanziata. Forse il fondo di un recipiente. 7+×10+. diam fondo 10,5 ca.

20 – coperchio troncoconico di lamina con presa verticale di verga terminante ad anello con tre costolature parallele. Decorazione incisa a bulino. Disco: h 1,1; diam 15,0; spess 0,1. presa: h 5,0; largh 0,6; diam anello 2,3.

21 – carrello-incensiere composto da un bacile emisferico inserito in un piano di lamina rettangolare sostenuto da quattro ruote. h totale: 20ca; h carrello: 12,8; piano: lungh 1,03; largh 40,0; bacile: h 9ca; diam esterno 25,9; diam interno 20,9; ruote: diam 10,7 ca.

22 – almeno due spiedi con testa a rotolo di ferro. lungh 40,6+; spess 0,8; lungh 39+; spess 0,9.

23 – oggetto formato da almeno due elementi quadrangolari separati, forse collegati con parti in materiale deperibile. Decorazione a sbalzo sulla lamina esterna. h 6,1+; largh 7,2+. h 2,5+; largh 3,6+.

24 – frammento di lamina con margine ripiegato, trattenuto da un ribattino e con resti di una lamina sovrapposta per restauro antico (forse resti di pettorale quadrangolare). h 3,3+; largh 5,5+.

25 – tre anellini di filo a sezione circolare con capi accostati. diam 1,0; 1,5; 1,5.

26 – frammento di lamina rettilinea con estremità ripiegata (frammento di bordo di recipiente?). 2,0×5,2.

 - frammento di lamina rettilinea con estremità ripiegata (frammento di piede di vaso?). 0,85×2,6.

 - fascetta di lamina piatta rettangolare piegata ad angolo al centro; ad una estremità, dalla parte interna, un frammento di lamina trattenuto da un ribattino. lungh 5,7; largh 0,8.

27 – sette frammenti di ferro e di bronzo con tracce di sostanza organica mineralizzata, non identificabili. lungh 3,5+; 1ca. 4,5+; 1,2ca; 5,3+; 1,2; 5,4+1,2ca; 6,1+; 1,8+.2,1×2.2,7×2,8.

Bibliografia

Albanese Procelli, M.R. 1985. 'Considerazioni sulla distribuzione dei bacili bronzei in area tirrenica e in Sicilia', in *Il commercio etrusco arcaico*. (Quad. AEI, 9), Roma, 179–206

Ampolo, C. 1976–1977. 'Demarato. Osservazioni sulla mobilità sociale arcaica', *Dialoghi di Archeologia* IX-X, 333–345

Bartoloni, G. 1981. 'Precisazioni sulla produzione di ceramica geometrica in Italia', *La Parola del Passato* 196-198, 90–101.

Bartoloni, G. 1984. 'Riti funerari dell'aristocrazia in Etruria e nel Lazio. L'esempio di Veio', *Opus*, 3, 13–29.

Bartoloni, G. 1986. 'I Latini e il Tevere', in *Il Tevere e le altre vie d'acqua del Lazio antico, (Archeologia Laziale* VII, 2), Roma, 98–110.

Bartoloni, G. 1987. 'Le comunità dell'Italia centrale tirrenica e la colonizzazione greca in Campania', in M. Cristofani (a cura di), *Etruria e Lazio arcaico*, (*Quaderni AEI* 15), Roma, 37–53.

Bartoloni, G. 1991. 'Veio e il Tevere. Considerazioni sul ruolo della comunità tiberina negli scambi tra Nord e Sud Italia durante la prima età del ferro', *Dialoghi di Archeologia*, 2, 35–48.

Bartoloni, G., Cataldi Dini, M. & Zevi, F. 1982. 'Aspetti della ideologia funeraria nella necropoli di Castel di Decima', in G. Gnoli & J.P.Vernant (a cura di), *La mort, les morts dans les societés anciennes*, Paris-Cambridge, 257–272.

Bartolni, G. & De Santis, A. 1995. 'La deposizione di scudi nelle tombe di VIII e VII secolo a.C. nell'Italia centrale tirrenica', in *Preistoria e Protostoria in Etruria. Atti del II Incontro di Studi*, (Firenze 1993), Milano, 277–287.

Bedini, A. 1977. 'L'ottavo secolo nel Lazio e l'inizio dell'orientalizzante antico alla luce di recenti scoperte nella necropoli di Castel di Decima', *La Parola del Passato*, 175, 274-309.

Bedini, A. 1990. 'Abitato protostorico in località Acqua Acetosa Laurentina', in M.R. Di Mino & M. Bertinetti (a cura di), *Archeologia a Roma. La materia e la tecnica nell'arte antica*, Roma, 48-64.

Berardinetti Insam, A. 1990. 'La fase iniziale della comunità villanoviana di Quattro Fontanili. Rapporti con le comunità limitrofe', *Dialoghi di Archeologia*, 1, 5-28.

Bermond Montanari, G. (a cura di) 1987. *La formazione della città in Emilia Romagna*, Bologna.

Bietti Sestieri, A.M. (a cura di) 1992. *La necropoli laziale di Osteria dell'Osa*, Roma.

Bietti Sestieri, A.M. 1992a. *The Iron Age Community of Osteria dell'Osa - A Study of Socio-political Development in Central Tyrrhenian Italy*, Cambridge.

Boitani, F. 1985. 'Veio: La tomba "principesca" della necropoli di Monte Michele', *Studi Etruschi*, 51, 534-556.

Brown, A. C. 1980. *Ancient Italy before the Romans*, Oxford.

Buranelli, F. 1981. 'Proposta di interpretazione dello sviluppo topografico della necropoli di Casale del Fosso a Veio', in *Necropoli e usi funerari dell'età del ferro* (a cura di R. Peroni), (Archeologia, Materiali, Problemi 5), Bari, 19-45.

Civiltà del Lazio Primitivo 1976, Roma.

Colonna, G. 1986. 'Il Tevere e gli Etruschi', in *Il Tevere e le altre vie d'acqua del Lazio antico* (*Archeologia Laziale* VII,2), Roma, 90-97.

Colonna, G. 1988. 'La produzione artigianale', in *Storia di Roma, I, Roma in Italia*, Torino, 291-316.

Colonna, G. 1991. 'Gli scudi bilobati dell'Italia centrale e l'ancile dei Salii', *Archeologia Classica* 43/1, 55-122.

Dialoghi di Archeologia 1980. C. Ampolo, G. Bartoloni, A. Bedini, G. Bergonzi, A.M. Bietti Sestieri, M. Cataldi Dini & F. Cordano, *La formazione della città nel Lazio*, (*Dialoghi di Archeologia* 1, 2).

Drago Troccoli, L. 1989. In AA.VV., *Il Museo Civico di Velletri*, 29-45, Roma.

Falchi, I. 1891. *Vetulonia e la sua necropoli antichissima*, Firenze.

Falconi Amorelli, M.T. 1983. 'Vulci. Scavi Bendinelli (1919-1923)', *Collana di studi sull'Italia antica*, 1, Roma-Cagli.

Fugazzola Delpino, M.A. 1984. *La cultura villanoviana. Guida ai materiali della prima età del Ferro nel Museo di Villa Giulia*, Roma.

Geiger, A. 1994. *Treibuerzierte Bronzerundschilde der Italianischen Eisenzeit aus Italien und Griechenland*, (*Prähistorische Bronzefunde III*, 1), Stuttgart.

Gjerstad, E. 1956. *Early Rome II. The Tombs*, (Acta Instituti Romani Regni Sueciae 4°, XVII:2), Lund.

Hall Dohan, E. 1942. *Italic Tomb-Groups in the University Museum*, Philadelphia.

von Hase, F. 1988. 'Früheisenzeitlichen Kammelhelme aus Italien', in *Antike Helme*, (*Römisch-Germanisches Zentralmuseum. Monographien, Band* 14), Mainz.

Hencken, H. 1968. *Tarquinia, Villanovans and Early Etruscans*, (American School of Prehistoric Research - Peabody Museum, Harvard University, Bulletin n.23), Harvard.

Hencken, H. 1971. *The Earliest European Helmets: Bronze Age and Early Iron Age*, Cambridge (Mass.).

Kilian, K. 1977. 'Das Kriegergrab von Tarquinia. Beigaben aus Metall und Holz', *Jahrbuch des Deutschen Archäologischen Instituts*, 92, 24-98.

La Rocca, E. 1978. 'Crateri in argilla figulina del geometrico recente a Vulci', *Mélanges d'Archéologie et d'Histoire de l'École Française de Rome*, 90, 465-514.

Müller-Karpe, H. 1974. 'Das Grab 871 von Veji', *Präistorische Bronzefunde* XX, 89-97

Palm, J. 1952. 'Vejian tomb groups in the Museo Preistorico, Rome', *Opuscula Archaeologica*, 7, 50-86

Pareti, L. 1947. *La tomba Regolini Galassi nel Museo Gregoriano Etrusco e la civiltà dell'Italia centrale nel VII sec. a.C.*, Città del Vaticano.

Pasqui, A. 1902. 'Mazzano Romano-Scavi del principe del Drago nel territorio di questo comune', *Notizie degli Scavi di Antichità*, 321-355; 593-627

Quattro Fontanili 1963. AA.VV., 'Veio (Isola Farnese). Scavi in una necropoli villanoviana in località "Quattro Fontanili"', *Notizie degli Scavi di Antichità*, 77-297.

Quattro Fontanili 1965. AA.VV., 'Veio (Isola Farnese). Continuazione degli scavi nella necropoli villanoviana in località "Quattro Fontanili"', *Notizie degli Scavi di Antichità*, 49-236

Quattro Fontanili 1970. AA.VV., 'Veio (Isola Farnese). Continuazione degli scavi nella necropoli villanoviana in località "Quattro Fontanili"', *Notizie degli Scavi di Antichità*, 178-329.

Sahlins, M. 1986. *Isole di storia: società e mito nei mari del Sud*, Torino.

Stary, P.F. 1981. *Zur eisenzeitlichen Bewaffnung und Kampfweise in Mittelitalien (ca. 9. bis 6. Jhr. v. Chr.)*, Mainz.

Ström, I. 1971. *Problems concerning the Origin and Early Development of the Etruscan Orientalizing Style*, (Odense Univerity Classical Studies. Vol. 2).

Toms, J. 1986. 'The relative chronology of the Villanovan Cemetery of Quattro Fontanili at Veii', *AION Arch.St.Ant*, 8, 41-97

Tovoli, S. 1989. *Il sepolcreto villanoviano Benacci Caprara di Bologna*, Bologna.

Woytowitsch, E. 1978. *Die Wagen der Bronze- und frühen Eisenzeit in Italien*, (*Prähistorische Bronze-funde* XVII/1), München.

39

Nuovi Elementi nello Studio del Ponte Romano sul Fosso dei Tre Ponti

VINCENZO ANTONELLI

(Soprintendenza Archeologica per l'Etruria Meridionale)

Sommario: *Il ponte romano posto sulla* Via Amerina *per l'attraversamento del Fosso dei Tre Ponti nei pressi dei* Falerii Novi *è stato oggetto di recenti lavori di restauro da parte della Soprintendenza Archeologica per l'Etruria Meridionale. I primi dati emersi da questi lavori hanno contribuito ad allargare le conoscenze sul monumento. Si sono potute confermare alcune ipotesi formulate da precedenti studiosi, M.W. Frederiksen e J.B. Ward Perkins, circa la presenza del nucleo interno in conglomerato o l'assenza di malte come leganti. Inoltre avendo avuto modo di esaminare la struttura nel suo interno, è stato possibile individuare un particolare e inedito tipo di foro per l'alloggiamento dei* ferrei forfices *per mezzo del quale era possibile procedere all'accostamento finale dei blocchi senza dover ricorrere all'impiego dei paletti sfilando la tenaglia ad accostamento avvenuto. Inoltre è stata individuata nei prospetti del ponte la presenza di un sottile stato di malta di calce che potrebbe essere stata impiegata per una intonacatura o scialbatura dei paramenti o per la stuccatura e stilatura dei giunti dei blocchi. Anche per quanto concerne l'aspetto architettonico del ponte sono emersi nuovi elementi conoscitivi: in seguito a saggi di scavo è stato individuato un allargamento in pianta della struttura del ponte in prossimità della testata Sud e l'esistenza nel prospetto SO di un contrafforte che si va ad aggiungere ai quattro già noti offrendo nuove interpretazioni compositive.*

Dopo la distruzione della falisca *Falerii* (241 a.C.) e in relazione alla fondazione ex novo della città di *Falerii Novi* i conquistatori Romani, anche utilizzando tracciati preesistenti, realizzarono un nuovo asse viario che, distaccandosi dalla Via Cassia al XXI miglio in corrispondenza della *mansio* di *Vacanas*, raggiungeva con un percorso di sole 56 miglia l'umbra *Ameria*, l'attuale Amelia. Questa strada, nota dal II – III sec. d.C. in poi come *Via Amerina* dal nome della città di *Ameria*, costituiva il collegamento più rapido con l'Umbria, si è stimato in soli due giorni il viaggio tra Roma e Amelia, attraversando il territorio Falisco secondo l'itinerario riportato nella *Tabula Peutingeriana* che indica le principali stazioni lungo il percorso quali: *Vacanas* (Valle di Baccano), *Nepe* (*Nepet* – Nepi), *Faleros* (*Falerii Novi* ora Santa Maria di Falleri), *Castello Amerino* (*Castellum Amerinum*, l'antico porto fluviale di Seripola nei pressi di Orte) e infine *Ameria*.

Nel tratto tra le città di *Nepet* e *Falerii Novi* la strada attraversava su ponti numerosi corsi d'acqua: il Fosso dell'Isola, il Fosso dei Tre Ponti, il Fosso Maggiore, il Rio Calello e il Rio Purgatorio. Tra queste opere d'ingegneria ormai dirute il ponte che scavalca, con orientamento Nord – Sud, il Fosso dei Tre Ponti nei comuni di Nepi e Castel Sant'Elia (prov. di Viterbo) è quello che è giunto fino a noi in migliori condizioni al punto che, apparentemente integro, è tutt'ora utilizzato da una strada comunale (fig. 1).

La Soprintendenza Archeologica per l'Etruria Meridionale (organo del Ministero per i Beni Culturali e Ambientali Italiano), che da più anni svolge un'opera di recupero generale della *Via Amerina* nel tratto tra Nepi e *Falerii Novi* anche con la collaborazione fattiva dei volontari del Gruppo Archeologico Romano (cfr. Caretta *et al.*, nei presenti atti), è intervenuta tra il dic. 1991 e il feb. 1992, per fronteggiare il pericolo di un imminente crollo di una porzione di questo ponte e attualmente sta procedendo ad un secondo lotto. L'intervento, eseguito dall'Impresa *Edil Concordia S.r.l.* di Nepi, è stato progettato e diretto dal sottoscritto con la collaborazione archeologica della dott.ssa M.A. De Lucia Brolli, dell'assistente L. Caretta e del geometra M. Novello, tutti della Soprintendenza. In occasione di tali lavori si è avuto modo di acquisire una prima serie di dati utili sia alla conoscenza del monumento stesso sia alla maggiore comprensione della tecnica esecutiva dell'*opus quadratum*.

Di questo monumento si hanno scarse notizie; Gazzola gli dedica poche righe confrontandolo con il Ponte del Diavolo a Manziana (Roma) del quale lo ritiene

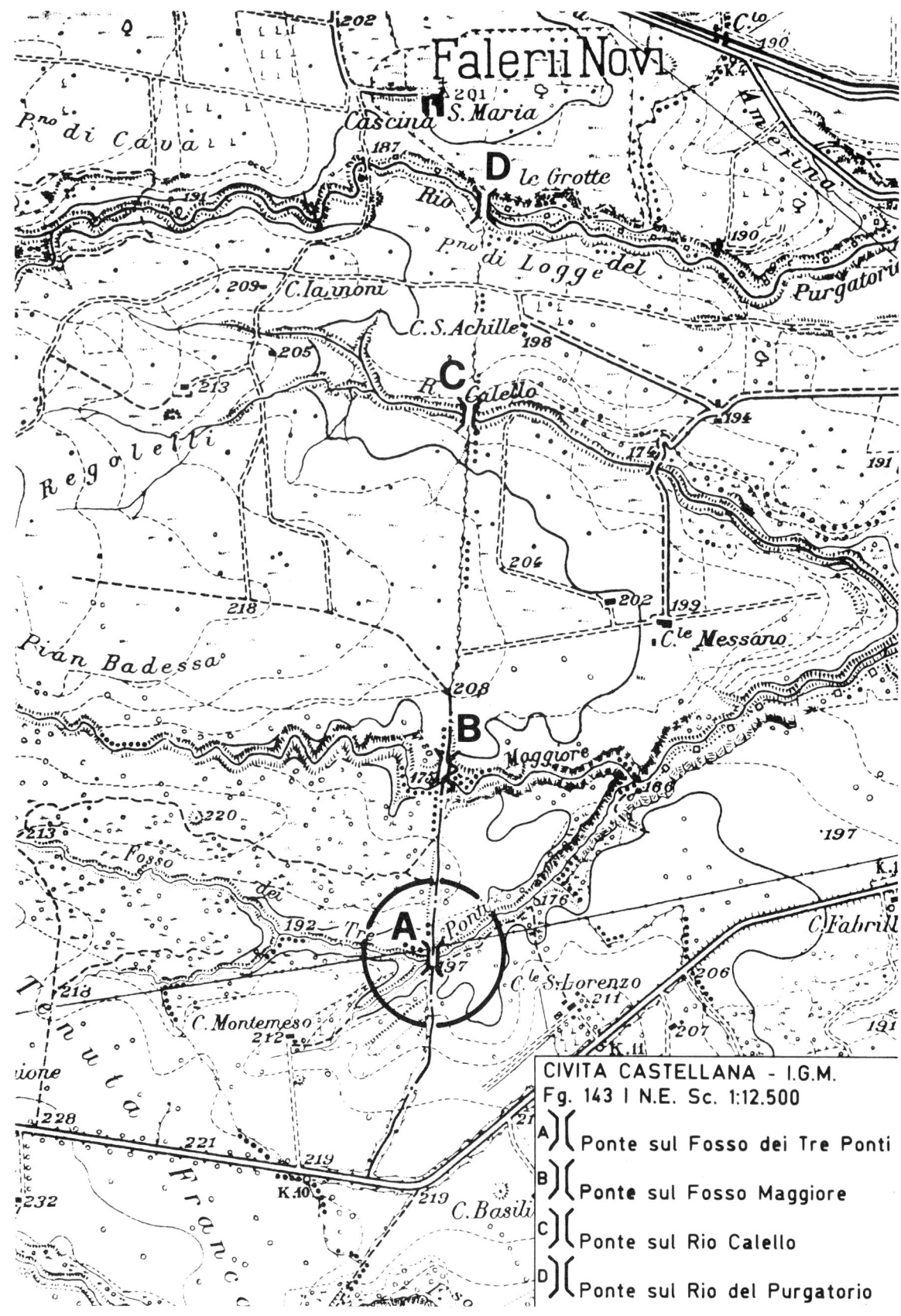

Fig. 1. Stralcio del Foglio I.G.M. 143 I NE.

"(...) coetaneo e parente (...)" senza peraltro avanzare ipotesi su una qualche datazione. Più estesa e accurata è la trattazione che ne fanno Frederiksen e Ward Perkins i quali mettono in relazione la sua costruzione con le opere di riassetto e di pavimentazione stradale compiute dai Romani sulla *Via Amerina* collocandolo nel terzo quarto del III sec. a.C.

Il ponte, dalle linee massicce ma assi semplici, ha una larghezza massima in sommità di m. 8,10 e uno sviluppo longitudinale di circa m. 45 e presenta un unico fornice a tutto sesto basato su una robusta zoccolatura ottenuta dall'aggetto delle assise di spiccato (fig. 2). (Nel presente testo, le quote e la numerazione dei ricorsi dei blocchi verranno riferite alla quota di m. 0,00 che verrà definita dal piano superiore della zoccolatura del fornice).

Il fornice, lungo circa m. 7,60 all'imposta, presenta una luce massima di circa m. 4,80 che si riduce a circa m. 4,20 in corrispondenza della zoccolatura; l'imposta dell'arco è a circa quota m. +4,85 e la quota dell'intradosso in chiave è circa m. +7,25 mentre attualmente la quota media della superficie dell'acqua del fosso in regime di magra è di circa m. −0,80; confrontando tale quota con le misurazioni e i rilievi pubblicati da Frederiksen e da Ward Perkins si può dedurre che il fosso dal 1957 a oggi ha subito un interro di circa m. 1,05.

I 17 conci dell'arco non presentano la più comune e più antica disposizione ad arco estradossato individuabile, tra i numerosissimi altri esempi, nelle porte urbiche della vicina *Falerii Novi*, ove con conci di uguale forma l'estradosso descrive un semicerchio concentrico all'intradosso. Nel ponte sulla *Via Amerina* presso Nepi i conci hanno una forma molto allungata e sono sagomati per permettere l'innesto con i blocchi dei filari orizzontali. Questa particolarità costruttiva trova numerosi confronti in realizzazioni del periodo augusteo dalle quali però se ne discosta per un disegno che, abbastanza incerto nella delineazione dei conci d'innesto con i filari orizzontali, non presenta la tipica simmetria bilaterale riscontrabile in altri archi, tra i quali il più antico esempio è costituito dal così detto Arco dei Pantani al Foro di Augusto come era stato opportunamente evidenziato da Frederiksen e da Ward Perkins. Al contrario la decisa impostazione compositiva dei sette conci in chiave tagliati superiormente secondo un unico piano orizzontale, riconduce il riferimento tipologico ad esempi tardo repubblicani quali il portico del *Forum Holitorium* a Roma e l'arco d'ingresso al *vomitorium* settentrionale dell'anfiteatro di Pompei, databile intorno all'anno 80 a.C.

La struttura dei paramenti murari è realizzata in *opus quadratum* di buona e accurata esecuzione in tufo litoide rosso giallastro dalla pasta compatta e con inserzioni carboniose. I blocchi presentano misure relativamente costanti con l'altezza di circa m. 0,60 e una larghezza media di m. 0,60 (sono presenti sporadicamente anche misure inferiori fino ad arrivare a m. 0,35 o superiori fino a m. 0,80) e una lunghezza oscillante tra i m. 1,00 e m. 2,25. I ricorsi dei blocchi hanno un andamento rettilineo e un'altezza costante di circa m. 0,60; in un solo caso, a circa m. 3,00 a destra dal contrafforte II SO, si riscontra una repentina variazione dell'altezza (circa m. 0,68) nelle assise VIII e IX con la presenza in quella VIII di un blocco sagomato per permettere di assorbire tale variazione. L'isodomia dei ricorsi dei blocchi è quindi generalmente rispettata e questi sono diligentemente disposti a filari alterni di testa e di taglio la qual cosa fa intuire a prima vista che lo spessore del paramento esterno sia 'a due teste' (fig.3).

Nel ponte presso Nepi la tessitura del paramento murario è analoga a quella delle mura urbane di *Falerii Novi*, realizzate dopo il 241 a.C., o a quella del muro di basamento del *Tabularium*, più tardo in quanto venne ricostruito ex novo nel 78 a.C., o ancora a quella delle superstiti murature (seconda fase) del vicinissimo ponte sul Fosso Maggiore, distante dal nostro monumento soli m. 500 circa in direzione Nord sulla *Via Amerina*. Un più appropriato parallelo può essere fatto con il così detto Ponte di Nona, al IX Miglio della Via Prenestina, databile al 100 a.C.; a questo, che presenta la zoccolatura nei fornici, si deve far riferimento anche per il tipo di trattamento superficiale dei blocchi, non presente nell'intradosso della volta, a leggero bugnato che tuttavia è riscontrabile pure nel ponte sul Fosso Maggiore. Un paramento assai simile a quello del ponte presso Nepi, per tessitura e bugnatura, è però riscontrabile anche nel muro di fondo del Foro di Augusto, più recente di circa un secolo rispetto al Ponte di Nona.

La composizione architettonica di ogni prospetto, ad un primo esame visivo, si mostra caratterizzata dalla presenza di due coppie di contrafforti che, secondo quanto suggerisce il Gazzola, servono ad aumentare lo spessore delle murature e a determinare l'effetto di grave solidità del monumento. Forse proprio la presenza di tali contrafforti può aver indotto il Gazzola a pensare a una somiglianza tra questo ponte e quello presso Manziana, fatto risalire al III sec. a.C., dal quale però, a un più approfondito esame, se ne discosta per una differente sintassi costruttiva e una diversa impostazione compositivo – architettonica.

Nel Ponte del Diavolo l'arco è estradossato, i ricorsi dei blocchi hanno un andamento leggermente sinuoso e presentano elementi lapidei di misure assai variabili e con altezze non costanti, quindi sono frequenti gli elementi sagomati per permettere l'inserzione del blocco contiguo di altezza differente. La disposizione di tutti i blocchi con il lato più lungo in prospetto può suggerire il fatto che il paramento ha il semplice spessore di una testa e che e privo di ammorsature con il nucleo interno; quindi, i contrafforti esterni, estesi su tutto lo sviluppo dei prospetti, assolvono l'importante ruolo d'irrigidimento della struttura e di contenimento dei paramenti.

Fig. 2. Nepi, Ponte sul Fosso dei Tre Ponti, prospetto Ovest; si notino: la cornice marcapiano superiore, la cornice d'imposta; la disposizione dei conci dell'arco; (da sinistra) il contrafforte II NO; la base del contrafforte I NO ora distrutto; il contrafforte I SO con due blocchi di sommità; il contrafforte II SO (V. Antonelli).

Fig. 3. Nepi, Ponte sul Fosso dei Tre Ponti, spalla Nord del fornice, paramento murario; si noti la disposizione a filari alterni di testa e di taglio dei blocchi, è visibile, soprattutto nelle assise inferiori, la presenza di malta di calce nelle connessure orizzontali e verticali (V. Antonelli).

Due contrafforti assai simili a quelli del ponte sul Fosso dei Tre Ponti sono riscontrabili nel ponte sul Fosso Maggiore, ma per quanto si può vedere della struttura, attualmente allo stato di rudere, non è possibile formulare un attendibile parallelo compositivo architettonico tra i due monumenti.

Contrariamente a quanto è riscontrabile nel ponte sul Fosso Maggiore o nelle mura urbane di *Falerii Novi*, nella maggior parte dei blocchi del ponte sul Fosso dei Tre Ponti sono presenti i tipici incavi utilizzati per l'alloggiamento dei *ferrei forfices*, strumenti a doppia tenaglia impiegati per il sollevamento e per la posa in opera degli elementi lapidei. Nei prospetti sono visibili in corrispondenza delle linee di posa orizzontali dei blocchi le tipiche fossette per l'inserimento delle barre impiegate per l'allineamento dei conci in facciata; invece non sembrano essere presenti sui piani orizzontali dei filari gli incassi in cui venivano inseriti i paletti per lo spostamento orizzontale e l'accostamento dei blocchi gli uni agli altri come pure non sono state individuate le sedi delle grappe di collegamento, mentre in alcuni casi sono visibili le linee di fede utilizzate per l'esatta posa in opera degli elementi lapidei.

In ogni prospetto del ponte sul Fosso dei Tre Ponti la coppia di contrafforti più esterna raggiunge la quota stradale mentre l'altra coppia, in corrispondenza delle spalle dell'arco, termina all'imposta dello stesso inglobando una massiccia cornice priva di modanature che, ottenuta dall'aggetto per circa m. 0,30 dei blocchi dell'assisa VIII, corre lungo i fianchi del ponte fino a raggiungere i contrafforti più esterni. Questo tipo di cornice, che sottolinea l'imposta dell'arco e rimanda ad altri esempi di ponti, quali il ponte di Nona e lo stesso Ponte del Diavolo a Manziana, era destinata a sostenere la centinatura lignea per la costruzione della volta in quanto non sono presenti i tipici fori per l'alloggiamento delle travi della centinatura.

Il ponte presenta un'altra cornice marcapiano che, in parte conservata, è ottenuta anch'essa dall'aggetto di un filare di blocchi, il XV. Contro questa cornice, che sottolinea e delimita lo sviluppo verticale dei prospetti in corrispondenza del piano stradale, si attestano i sette conci in chiave dell'arco (fig. 2).

Prima di passare alla descrizione delle novità emerse dall'intervento di consolidamento è opportuno fare alcune riflessioni sulla possibile datazione del ponte che viene collocato al terzo quarto del III sec. a.C. Le particolarità esecutive e compositive osservate, quali la tessitura del paramento, il tipo di bugnatura, il disegno e la composizione dei conci dell'arco rimandano a confronti con monumenti che trovano la loro collocazione cronologica più antica tra il periodo tardo repubblicano e il periodo augusteo con riproposizioni frequenti nel periodo imperiale. Quindi la datazione del ponte sul Fosso dei Tre Ponti potrebbe essere riferita al periodo tardo repubblicano; forse la sua costruzione, o il suo rifacimento ex novo al posto di una precedente struttura verosimilmente lignea, potrebbe essere messa in relazione all'elevazione a municipio romano di *Falerii Novi*, nel cui territorio ricadeva il ponte, evento che, collocabile al tempo delle guerre sociali, troviamo attestato epigraficamente dal 89 a.C. in poi.

L'intervento di restauro odierno può essere considerato il primo di particolare rilevanza che il monumento subisce forse dal tempo della costruzione in quanto il ponte, come già era stato notato dal Frederiksen e dal Ward Perkins, non mostra segni di rifacimenti o di ricostruzioni che invece sono visibili in altri ponti come in quello sul Fosso Maggiore.

Si può affermare a ragione che il primo risultato conseguito negli attuali lavori è stato quello di aver liberato il ponte dalla fitta e invasiva vegetazione che si era sviluppata sulla struttura stessa e nelle sue immediate vicinanze consentendo così la visione completa del monumento e creando le premesse per un accurato rilievo fotogrammetrico. Ci si riserva, a lavori ultimati, di pubblicare tale rilievo, in corso di esecuzione da parte dello *Studio Groma S.r.l.* di Roma.

Sul monumento, ricoperto di Edera, avevano trovato dimora alberi di Elce, di Quercia, di Cerro, di Sorbo e di Carpino mentre nell'intorno la vegetazione ad alto fusto era costituita anche da alberi di Ontano, di Corniolo, di Orniello e di Nocciolo Selvatico. Ora, dopo le operazioni di decespugliamento e di disboscamento, effettuate senza l'impiego di prodotti chimici, il monumento si mostra nella sua reale consistenza con evidenti gravi dissesti; risultano crollati e quindi perduti i contrafforti I SE del prospetto Est, a valle (fig.4), e II NO del prospetto Ovest, a monte (fig. 2). Nel studio del Frederiksen e del Ward Perkins viene segnalata la mancanza del solo contrafforte I SE, imputando il crollo alla probabile insufficiente ammorsatura con la struttura interna, mentre non si hanno notizie del I NO in quanto viene riferita l'impossibilità di esaminare il relativo prospetto a causa della vegetazione infestante. Nel corso dell'attuale intervento non sono state rinvenute tracce di recenti crolli, per questo si può pensare che il contrafforte I NO sia andato perduto già prima del suddetto studio.

Il Frederiksen e il Ward Perkins segnalano la presenza al di sopra del contrafforte I NE di un blocco isolato la cui collocazione sembra loro originale ma dallo scopo oscuro. Ora, l'esame ravvicinato del blocco, che presenta un'altezza di m. 0,68, conferma tale ipotesi e dalla ubicazione dei fori dei *ferrei forfices* si può stabilire che l'elemento lapideo, attualmente fratturato, aveva una lunghezza di circa m. 1,90 e una ammorsatura di circa m. 0,75 con la retrostante struttura; la parte inserita nella muratura si mostra sagomata per permettere l'inserzione del II concio NE dell'arco. Inoltre la presenza di differenti tipi di fori per l'alloggiamento dei *ferrei forfices*, del *Tipo A* a Nord e del *Tipo B* (fig.5) a Sud (tipi che

Fig. 4. Nepi, Ponte sul Fosso dei Tre Ponti, prospetto Est, particolare spalla Sud del fornice; sono visibili i blocchi basamentali del contrafforte I SE e, tra i ponteggi, il contrafforte II SE dopo lo smontaggio e la radice che lo attraversa (V. Antonelli).

descriveremo meglio in seguito) permette di dedurre che tale blocco, posto di testa, era il centrale dei tre che costituivano un ulteriore e ultimo filare di prolungamento del contrafforte al di sopra della cornice. L'esame del paramento murario al di sopra del contrafforte esclude la possibilità dell'esistenza di ulteriori assise. Rimane in ogni caso oscuro il suo ruolo; forse potrebbe trattarsi di una sorta di attico o di basamento per qualche elemento decorativo ora perduto. Nel contrafforte I SO si ripropone un'analoga situazione con la presenza di due blocchi al di sopra della cornice (fig.2).

Un'attenta analisi della tessitura muraria dei contrafforti induce a pensare che non esista un vero e proprio difetto costruttivo nella realizzazione delle ammorsature ma che all'origine del crollo vi siano state le radici della vegetazione infestante che, soprattutto nei contrafforti, si insinuano in profondità. In una situazione simile si trovano tuttora i contrafforti superstiti che per la loro costituzione e posizione nel contesto del manufatto risultano essere più esposti all'aggressione della vegetazione così come lo sono stati i parapetti ora completamente perduti.

L'intervento della Soprintendenza si è concentrato di conseguenza proprio su un contrafforte, il II di SE, che si mostrava in condizioni statiche estremamente critiche rispetto agli altri in quanto le radici degli Elci, cresciuti spontaneamente sul monumento, avevano completamente frantumato alcuni blocchi e lesionato quelli di ammorsatura creando una soluzione di continuità tra il contrafforte e la restante struttura (fig.4).

La struttura del contrafforte oggetto dei lavori di consolidamento era a tal punto dissestata dalle radici penetrate in profondità che l'unico tipo d'intervento possibile si è pensato essere quello dell'asportazione meccanica totale delle radici stesse e il successivo risarcimento della struttura lesionata. Sono stati tagliati quindi gli apparati arborei superiori, poi si è smontato il contrafforte blocco dopo blocco asportando via via le radici e i tronchi che erano cresciuti nella muratura e ricollocando poi nella posizione originaria i blocchi precedentemente smontati e opportunamente restaurati. Per circa 7 metri, dalla assisa IV alla XV alla sommità del ponte, il contrafforte era attraversato verticalmente da una radice con circonferenza massima pari a circa m. 0,94.

Il piano stradale del ponte attualmente è privo di basolato; questo è stato rinvenuto in ottimo stato di conservazione, sotto un interro mediamente di circa m. 0,35, a circa m. 21,00 dalla testata Sud del ponte. Qui, inserita in una tagliata di tufo ampia circa m. 11,50, la strada romana tra le crepidini in parte conservate ha una larghezza di circa m. 2,76 che rientra nella larghezza media della *Via Amerina* riscontrabile lungo il suo tracciato. Non è dato sapere con certezza l'ampiezza della carreggiata sul ponte ma si può ipotizzare che si estendesse priva di *crepidines* tra i due parapetti, in questo caso costituiti verosimilmente dallo spessore del paramento murario (circa m. 1,20) per una larghezza di circa m. 5,20, come è possibile rilevare in più punti. Anche nel Ponte del Diavolo presso Manziana non sono presenti i marciapiedi e il lastricato stradale è esteso tra un parapetto e l'altro per m. 5,50 circa, senza soluzione di continuità.

Prima di procedere alle fasi dello smontaggio del contrafforte II SE, in prossimità del contrafforte stesso, sono stati eseguiti alcuni saggi di scavo al di sotto del piano di calpestio del ponte al fine di individuare eventuali tracce del basolato stradale, di accertare la consistenza della struttura e la reale natura del nucleo interno che il Frederiksen e il Ward Perkins, non essendo allora visibile in alcun punto, avevano ipotizzato essere in muratura per analogia con gli altri ponti della *Via Amerina*.

Nell'area interessata dai saggi non sono emerse tracce di basolato *in situ* o di altra pavimentazione originaria, probabilmente asportata o distrutta in epoca passata, me è stato possibile accertare la stratigrafia che può essere così schematizzata dall'alto verso il basso: strato di calpestio attuale costituito da materiale inerte di color bianco – beige (testina di Narni); deposito alluvionale, grigio sabbioso; strato di notevole compattezza con la presenza di piccole scaglie di basalto pressate con terra marrone corrispondente al *rudus*; battuto di tufo e terra assimilabile allo *statumen*; conglomerato di *coementa* di tufo e malta grigiastra aderente ai paramenti esterni che ne costituiscono la cassaforma di contenimento. Risulta quindi evidente la mancanza degli strati superiori costituenti la tipica sezione stradale: il *summum dorsum* di *silex* e il *nucleus* di allettamento.

Il risultato dei saggi ha confermato l'ipotesi dell'esistenza di un nucleo interno costituito da conglomerato che rende la struttura del manufatto notevolmente robusta. Infatti, il ponte sul Fosso Maggiore in cui il nucleo interno appare costituito da terreno costipato ha subito devastanti crolli. Nel Ponte del Diavolo, il nucleo interno è costituito da terreno di riporto costipato e il paramento in *opus quadratum* è stato realizzato esclusivamente da blocchi posti nel senso della lunghezza, aventi lo spessore di circa m. 0,70 senza ammorsature con il nucleo interno, come si è potuto constatare nel corso degli interventi di consolidamento a suo tempo effettuati dal sottoscritto; i paramenti hanno subito una notevole rotazione verso l'esterno con la conseguente modifica dell'equilibrio statico; inoltre il piano stradale basolato risulta dissestato a causa dell'acqua meteorica che, infiltratasi al di sotto del lastricato, è penetrata nel nucleo di terra sottostante causando cedimenti del piano stradale e provocando poi il dilavamento e la perdita di gran parte del terriccio di riempimento attraverso le connessure dei blocchi, fenomeni di dissesto questi che non sono presenti nel ponte sul Fosso dei Tre Ponti.

Altri saggi di scavo in corrispondenza della testata Sud del ponte, a circa m. 14,60 dal contrafforte II SO, hanno portato ad accertare l'esistenza, in quel punto, di un cambiamento di direzione planimetrico di circa 45° verso Ovest della struttura, realizzato verosimilmente per ottenere una piazzola necessaria a permettere l'incrocio o la sosta dei carri prima d'impegnare la carreggiata del ponte. Inoltre si è constatato che qui l'opera muraria, in corrispondenza dell'assisa IX, poggia direttamente sul *solidum* costituito dal banco tufaceo che, in quel punto abbastanza superficiale, è stato scavato e livellato per creare la sede di allettamento dei blocchi, anche con l'ausilio di un calcestruzzo gettato a sacco in analogia a quanto è visibile delle opere fondali del ponte sul Fosso Maggiore.

Lungo lo stesso lato del ponte sono stati eseguiti dei saggi di scavo circa m. 5,00 a destra del contrafforte II SO che, non ancora ultimati, hanno portato all'individuazione delle assise basamentali di un ulteriore contrafforte, il III SO crollato in antico, del quale non si conosceva l'esistenza. Tracce della presenza di tale contrafforte potevano essere già lette nel paramento di prospetto il quale, in quel punto, presenta oltre a un irregolare trattamento superficiale e a mancanze di materiale, dovute al distacco traumatico del contrafforte dalla struttura, due blocchi nell'assise IX con i fori per l'alloggiamento dei *ferrei forfices* di *Tipo B* che, come vedremo in seguito, non vengono posti abitualmente sulla faccia visibile all'esterno.

Sempre con lo scopo di constatare lo stato delle fondazioni, è stato effettuato un altro saggio alla base della spalla Sud del ponte nel letto del fosso ma, dopo aver raggiunto in profondità la quota di circa m. -2,15, si sono incontrate difficoltà tecniche tali da non consentire di raggiungere il piano fondale; si è potuta esaminare però la zoccolatura che prosegue almeno per altri quattro ricorsi di blocchi con le stesse caratteristiche costruttive riscontrabili nella parte superiore del paramento murario fatta eccezione per l'assisa negativa IV in cui è prevalente la disposizione per testa dei blocchi.

Un ulteriore elemento di novità emerso nel recente intervento sul monumento è l'individuazione di un leggero strato di malta in alcune zone dei prospetti. Tale strato di malta di calce quasi allo stato puro, molto compatto e di sottile spessore, è stato individuato in corrispondenza di alcuni giunti dei blocchi e in parti ben protette dall'azione degli agenti atmosferici sul prospetto Est, tra il contrafforte II SE e il I SE ormai perduto, tra il I e il II NE e all'interno del fornice sulla parete della pila Nord in prossimità della spalla di NE (fig.3).

Il Frederiksen e il Ward Perkins, e conseguentemente il Gazzola, riferiscono che l'*opus quadratum* di questo ponte fu realizzato senza l'impiego di leganti di malta o di grappe. In effetti durante le operazioni di smontaggio del paramento murario non sono state individuate le sedi delle grappe né è emersa alcuna traccia di malte sulla superfici di contatto dei blocchi, quindi, almeno per quanto è stato possibile accertare, si può escludere l'impiego di queste come leganti o anche l'utilizzo del grassello di calce come mezzo per diminuire l'attrito e facilitare lo scivolamento dei blocchi nelle fasi di accostamento che, come vedremo in seguito, venne effettuato direttamente con gli stessi strumenti meccanici per il sollevamento.

Sono state eseguite fotomicrografie della sezione sottile di un campione di tale malta dalle quali è risultato che lo spessore sovrapposto alla massa lapidea tufacea, con ben visibili granuli di calcite e quarzosi, appare come un deposito a base di calce con componenti gessose con aderenza al substrato continua e diretta, cioè senza apparente interposizione di strati di sudicio e di depositi: ciò induce a pensare che questo strato non sia stato il frutto di un intervento successivo alla realizzazione del ponte ma sia stato posto in opera contemporaneamente all'esecuzione del paramento lapideo.

Si può avanzare l'ipotesi che la malta individuata, sulla quale appare chiarissimo l'intervento di uno strumento di ferro per lisciarne la superficie, possa essere stata impiegata, in sottilissimo strato quasi una scialbatura, come un leggero rivestimento con lo scopo di proteggere e garantire una maggiore conservazione della superficie lapidea o anche con l'intenzione di nobilitare un materiale altrimenti povero come è il tufo. Il tufo vulcanico è un materiale facilmente attaccabile dagli agenti atmosferici e ha una forte tendenza al decoesionamento superficiale, inoltre l'impiego d'intonaco sulle superfici di tufo esterne è una tecnica assai antica che trova attestazioni in Etruria con funzioni sia decorative sia protettive; si pensi ad alcune tombe rupestri della necropoli di Norchia dove si hanno testimonianze di un leggero strato d'intonaco di malta di calce con tracce di pigmenti a rivestimento della superficie tufacea.

Si potrebbe formulare anche l'ipotesi che tale malta sia stata impiegata semplicemente per stuccare e stilare i giunti dei blocchi con fini estetici e tecnici, quali potrebbero essere l'eliminazione delle infiltrazioni d'acqua o l'impedire lo sviluppo della vegetazione infestante nelle connessure degli elementi lapidei.

Altri nuovi elementi emersi nel corso di questo intervento riguardano alcuni particolari costruttivi del ponte e un inedito aspetto della tecnica esecutiva dell'*opus quadratum* per quanto concerne i metodi di accostamento orizzontale dei vari blocchi.

Come testimoniato dalla presenza dei tipici fori di alloggiamento sulla superficie a vista dei blocchi, anche per la costruzione di questo ponte sono stati impiegati i *ferrei forfices* per la presa dei blocchi di tufo durante le operazioni di sollevamento. Questi strumenti a forma di tenaglia, descritti già da Vitruvio e dei quali esistono versioni moderne impiegate ai giorni nostri in particolari lavori, erano realizzati in ferro, schematicamente costituiti da due coppie di leve di primo genere aventi il fulcro in comune costituito da un perno intorno al quale risultano girevoli; all'estremità della parte corta della tenaglia, detta ganascia, erano presenti delle sporgenze o dei ganci che venivano introdotti nei fori predisposti, prevalentemente nelle facce lunghe, a metà della lunghezza e a circa due terzi dell'altezza del blocco da sollevare. I bracci opposti alla ganascia, in corrispondenza del loro estremo superiore, erano attrezzati con anelli o corde per il collegamento con il gancio della macchina di sollevamento; quando questa entrava in funzione e quindi in tiro, il peso del blocco stesso stringeva le ganasce che serravano la pietra assicurando la presa.

Il Lugli evidenzia il limite di impiego dei *ferrei forfices* a presa laterale nell'accostare i blocchi l'uno con l'altro nel senso della loro lunghezza in quanto *"(...) bisognava prima togliere i forfices* (dal blocco) *e poi assestarlo al filo degli altri (...)"* limite questo superabile, sempre secondo il Lugli, o con i *forfices* a divaricamento applicati sulla faccia superiore del blocco, o con l'impiego della *olivella*, anch'essa applicabile sul piano superiore del blocco; in entrambi i casi era così possibile posizionare con il solo ausilio di macchine il blocco nella sua sede definitiva a contatto con l'elemento vicino, in caso contrario,

Fig. 5. Nepi, Ponte sul Fosso dei Tre Ponti, prospetto Est, particolare del blocco di sommità del contrafforte I NE; è visibile l'alloggiamento di Tipo B per i ferrei forfices (V. Antonelli).

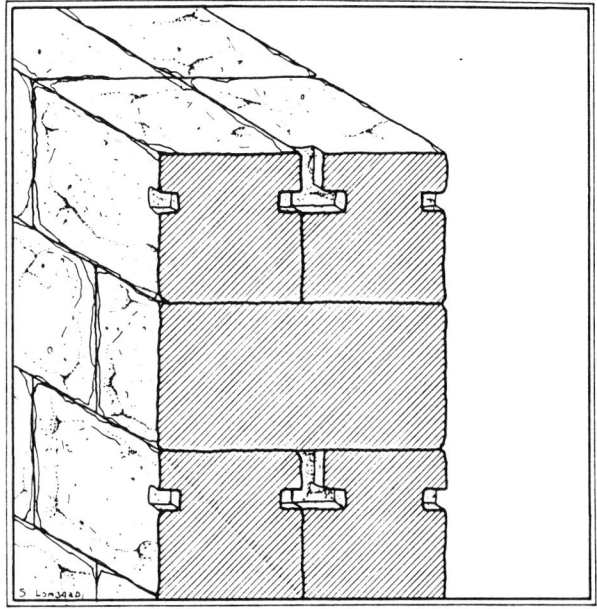

Fig. 6. Sezione schematica tipo di paramento in opus quadratum con in opera blocchi con fori di Tipo A e di Tipo B per l'alloggiamento dei ferrei forfices. Il blocco a sinistra presenta entrambi i fori di Tipo A, è un elemento del paramento esterno ed è stato posto in opera per primo; il blocco di destra presenta a sinistra il foro di Tipo B e a destra il foro di Tipo A, è un elemento interno ed è stato posto in opera per secondo (Ricostruzione grafica arch. Silvana Lombardi).

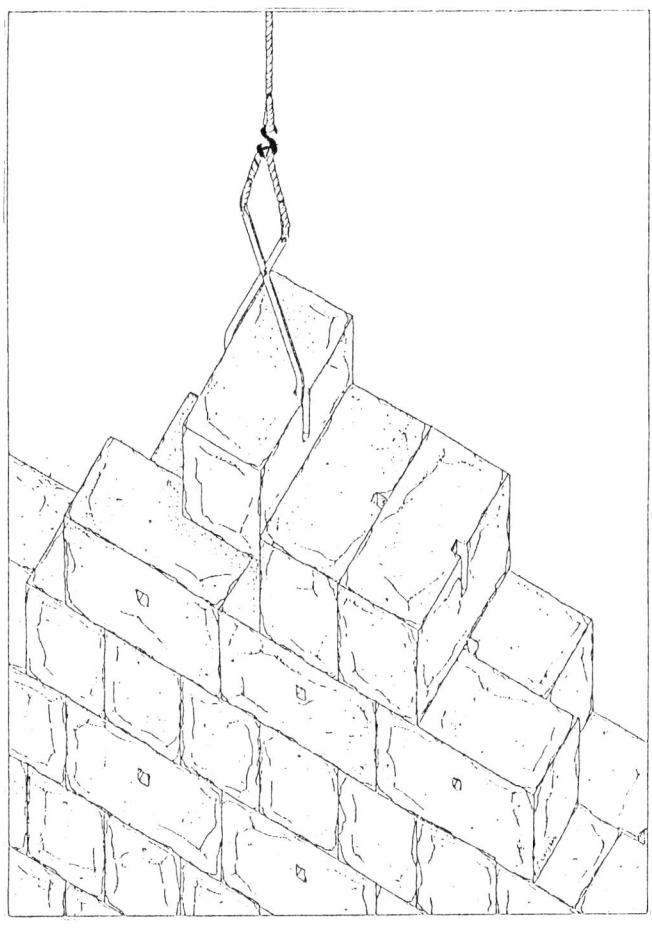

Fig. 7. Schema di assemblaggio dei blocchi dell'opus quadratum *con l'impiego dei* ferrei forfices *utilizzando fori di alloggiamento* Tipo B *(Ricostruzione grafica arch. Silvana Lombardi)*.

prosegue il Lugli, *"(...) la tenaglia del forcipe avrebbe disturbato l'accostamento (...)"* che si sarebbe dovuto poi effettuare con leve e paletti.

Questo inevitabile limite d'impiego dei *ferrei forfices*, ribadito recentemente anche da Adam, poteva al contrario essere agevolmente superato. Infatti nelle operazioni di smontaggio del contrafforte II SE del prospetto a valle del ponte e di parte dell'attiguo paramento murario, si è potuto determinare che i costruttori romani nella realizzazione dell'opera avevano adottato un espediente, fino ad ora inedito, con il quale risultava possibile l'impiego dei *ferrei forfices* a tenaglia anche nella fase di accostamento dei blocchi, senza ricorrere ad altri sussidi, con una conseguente notevole riduzione generale dei tempi costruttivi.

Nei ricorsi di taglio mentre i blocchi delle assise di prospetto mostrano in entrambe le facce i tipici alloggiamenti dei *ferrei forfices* a forma di fossetta quadrangolare di uguali dimensioni e fattura, che chiameremo *Tipo A*, nelle assise interne e nei ricorsi posti di testa i blocchi presentano su una faccia un foro di alloggiamento di fattura tradizionale, *Tipo A*, e su quella opposta un foro di forma inedita. Questo foro che distingueremo come *Tipo B* (fig.5) presenta una sezione verticale a 'L' di cui il braccio orizzontale è costituito dal classico foro di alloggiamento con una profondità di circa m. 0,18, cioè quasi il doppio rispetto a quella degli altri, il braccio verticale è costituito da un incasso che, largo circa m. 0,08 e profondo circa m. 0,09 con un'altezza di circa m. 0,29 (le presenti misure si riferiscono al foro *Tipo B* del blocco di sommità del contrafforte I NE), raggiunge la superficie superiore del blocco (fig.6). Dall'osservazione della posizione dei fori *Tipo B* nel contesto dell'intera struttura si è potuto dedurre che l'incasso verticale, una sorta di guida, permetteva di effettuare lo sfilamento della tenaglia di *ferrei forfices* con il blocco già collocato nella sua posizione finale (fig.7).

Le informazioni emerse dai lavori eseguiti e in corso di esecuzione sul ponte sul Fosso dei Tre Ponti non possono considerarsi conclusive ma costituiscono un primo piccolo passo verso una più approfondita conoscenza archeologica e architettonica del monumento. Non è possibile escludere infatti che nel corso della prosecuzione dei lavori possano emergere ulteriori dati tali da rimettere in discussione quanto conosciuto fino ad ora. Già l'individuazione del quinto contrafforte, il III di SO propone una nuova lettura compositiva del ponte infrangendo l'ormai codificata immagine simmetrica che avevamo di esso suggerita dalle due coppie di contrafforti. Gli scavi programmati potrebbero portare all'individuazione di altre simili strutture di rinforzo che potrebbero ricondurre l'insieme ad una composizione simmetrica. E ancora è da chiarire il significato dell'allargamento della struttura del ponte in corrispondenza della testata Sud. Infine un ulteriore e più approfondito studio della superficie dei paramenti murari, soprattutto nelle parti ancora interrate, potrebbe fornire una risposta definitiva all'affascinante ipotesi di una scialbatura o di una intonacatura dell'intera struttura.

Bibliografia

AA.VV. 1991. *Viae Publicae Romanae*, Roma.
Adam, J.P. 1990. *L'arte di costruire presso i Romani*, Milano.
Antonelli, V. 1987. 'Il ponte del Diavolo a Manziana', *Antiqua*, XII, n. 5-6, 69-76.
Blake, M. 1947. *Ancient Roman Construction in Italy from the Prehistoric Period to Augustus*, Washington.
De Lucia Brolli, M.A. 1987. 'La Via Amerina', *Antiqua*, XII, n. 5-6, 27-41.
De Lucia Brolli, M.A. 1991. *L'Agro Falisco*, Roma.
Frederiksen, M. & Ward Perkins, J.B. 1957. 'The ancient road systems of the Central and Northern Ager Faliscus', *Papers of the British School at Rome*, 25, 67-208.
Gazzetti, G. 1987. 'Le campagne sistematiche di scavo nella Valle di Baccano, *Antiqua*, XII, n. 5-6, 24-26.
Gazzola, P. 1963. *Ponti Romani*, vol.II, Firenze.
Lugli, G. 1957. *La tecnica edilizia romana, con particolare riguardo a Roma e Lazio*, Roma.
Ward Perkins, J.B. 1974. *Architettura romana*, Venezia.

40

Considerazioni sugli Insediamenti in Area Falisca: I Periodi Arcaico e Tardoantico

GABRIELE CIFANI, MASSIMILIANO MUNZI

Sommario: *Gli studi più recenti e nuove scoperte nell'area falisca inducono ad alcune riflessioni sul sistema insediativo di età arcaica e tardoantica. Per la fase arcaica si registra in particolare l'inserimento di Nepi nella dialettica insediativa tra i centri dell'area falisca, la presenza di una estesa necropoli in località Tenuta Franca cui possono essere riferiti più insediamenti rurali, la presenza accertata di un insediamento nel sito di Castel S. Elia. Per la fase tardo antica quattro temi sono messi in evidenza dalla ricerca: la sopravvivenza dello status urbano di* Falerii Novi *almeno fino al VI sec. d.C.; l'ininterrotta funzionalità del suburbio meridionale di* Falerii Novi *come area di sepoltura; la continuità d'uso della via Amerina dal periodo romano a quello bizantino-longobardo e medievale; la persistenza del popolamento rurale fino al V–VI sec. d.C., anche lungo la via Amerina.*

I processi insediativi nell'area falisca sono stati ampiamente indagati dalle ricerche della British School at Rome a partire dagli anni Cinquanta (Potter 1992), di cui un valido antecedente erano stati i lavori per la realizzazione della Carta Archeologica d'Italia tra il 1881 ed il 1887 (Gamurrini *et al.* 1972). Il quadro delineato è rimasto da allora per molti versi immutato, anche se, a partire dagli anni Settanta, sono state condotte diverse indagini sulla zona, in particolare dall'Istituto di Topografia antica dell'Università di Roma (Morselli 1980, Moscati 1990), cui più recentemente si sono aggiunti numerosi recuperi e studi sulla fase protostorica della regione (Di Gennaro 1988a). Notevole contributo alla storia della città di *Falerii Novi* è stato quindi apportato dalle ricerche di Di Stefano Manzella con la revisione sistematica del materiale epigrafico mentre una panoramica delle maggiori problematiche archeologiche della regione è stata offerta dai contributi al XV *Convegno di Studi Etrusco Italici* dedicato alla Civiltà dei Falisci nel 1987. Parallelamente allo svolgersi di questo vivace dibattito scientifico, diversi dati venivano raccolti dal G(ruppo) A(rcheologico) R(omano), che dalla prima metà degli anni Settanta, ha svolto un'azione di controllo e ricognizione del territorio, nonchè di valorizzazione di alcuni siti monumentali, quali la Via Amerina (Caretta *et al., infra*), segnalando tempestivamente i recuperi effettuati, in larga parte confluiti nei repertori delle scoperte nell'Etruria Meridionale (Brunetti Nardi 1980). Con questo contributo ci si propone, pertanto, di fornire nuovi dati per la discussione sugli insediamenti nell'Agro Falisco, in particolare nelle fasi arcaica e tardoantica.*

1. NEPI E GLI INSEDIAMENTI RURALI IN ETÀ ARCAICA (G.C.)

L'area falisca è nota nelle sue dinamiche insediative a partire dall'età del Bronzo con vari siti documentati, in modo ancora incompleto, da ricerche di superficie, soprattutto per le fasi più recenti. Narce rivela una frequentazione a partire dal Bronzo Medio e, trattandosi dell'unico insediamento indagato stratigraficamente, può indicare un più diffuso modello di sviluppo (Potter 1976; Petitti 1990). Di più antica tradizione sono gli insediamenti aperti o connessi a piccole alture difese, o

---

* Dedichiamo questo contributo alla memoria di Ludovico Magrini, fondatore dei Gruppi Archeologici d'Italia recentemente scomparso. I materiali dei siti di Tenuta Franca, Casale Messano, Pian Badessa, Tre Ponti, Monte La Macina, Grotta Arnaro, S. Marcello (F. IGMI 143 I NE; 143 I SE), sono stati raccolti da ricognizioni del GAR tra il 1984 ed il 1989. Hanno contribuito allo studio della ceramica M. Incitti e N. Marletta. Si ringrazia per gli utili consigli il prof. G. Colonna; ed inoltre A. Augenti, P. Carafa, L. Caretta, F. Di Gennaro, F. Marazzi, C. Morselli, A. Naso e N. Terrenato per aver discusso parte delle problematiche affrontate.

addirittura la frequentazione di grotte (Rellini 1920), che sembrano superare il tipo caratterizzato da unità orografiche a superficie difesa, consolidatosi nettamente nel Bronzo Finale sia con esempi di larga estensione, come quello del Vignale (circa 13 ettari) che con esempi più ridotti come l'insediamento di La Torre (Di Gennaro 1988a: 71-72).

Complessa la problematica relativa all'origine dei centri urbani, che sembra porsi in leggero ritardo rispetto a quelli dell'Etruria costiera (Peroni 1989: 439). E' stata infatti proposta per *Falerii Veteres* (da ora in poi *Falerii*) l'esistenza di un abitato protourbano solo dalla fine dell'VIII sec. a.C., con la ripresa e la successiva espansione, dopo un parentesi di apparente abbandono, dell' insediamento protovillanoviano del Vignale a tutto il pianoro dell'attuale Civita Castellana. La nascita di una compagine protourbana di circa 45 ettari inserisce il centro falisco tra i maggiori del periodo (Judson & Hemphill 1975; Moscati 1990). Diversamente, il processo per la formazione urbana di Narce è stato spiegato tramite il sinecismo, sia pure condizionato dall'ambiente fisico, dei villaggi di cinque colli (Monte li Santi, Calcata, Pizzo Piede, Narce e la collina della q. 210), tali da creare una compagine di 50 ettari (Colonna 1990a: 137-140).

Alla base di questi processi, riscontrabili nel resto dell'Etruria Meridionale, vengono posti una serie di cambiamenti nella gestione della terra a favore di gruppi aristocratici (Peroni 1989: 218 ss; inoltre Zifferero 1991: 109 con bibl.) gli stessi che, verosimilmente, in area falisca detengono il controllo dei traffici tra il territorio veiente ed i bacini dell'alto Fiora e dell'Albegna (Baglione 1986), nonché degli itinerari relativi all'allevamento transumante della limitrofa Sabina (Pasquinucci 1990: 167-8). Connesso a questi fenomeni è il popolamento rurale che si verifica dal VII sec. a.C. con l'irradiazione dai nuovi centri urbani individuabili nelle città di *Falerii*, Narce e negli insediamenti minori di Vignanello, Corchiano e Nepi (Potter 1985: 85-88).

Per quanto riguarda la zona di Nepi tra orientalizzante ed età arcaica tre aspetti in particolare sembrano emergere dalla raccolta di dati già editi e da nuovi recuperi effettuati negli ultimi anni:

1) l'inserimento completo di Nepi nella dialettica insediativa tra i centri dell'area falisca;

2) la presenza di una nuova necropoli, relativamente estesa, in località Tenuta Franca cui possono essere riferiti almeno quattro insediamenti rurali;

3) la presenza accertata di un insediamento nel sito di Castel S. Elia.

1.1. Nepi

Per il centro etrusco è stata individuata una frequentazione almeno dall'VIII sec. a.C. (Edwards, Malone & Stoddart *infra*). Del VII sec. a.C. sono le prime sepolture a fossa con loculo (Stefani 1910 e 1918) con caratteristiche comuni all'area falisca, di probabile origine veientana (Di Gennaro 1988b:114-115), e quella inedita, recuperata nel 1914 in località La Massa. Si tratta di una deposizione in tronco di quercia entro una piccola camera sepolcrale circolare databile, per il corredo, alla metà del VII sec. a.C. (Archivio Saem Villa Giulia). A questi rinvenimenti seguono altri gruppi di tombe negli immediati dintorni a partire dal VI sec. a. C. di tipologia analoga a quella falisca (Morselli 1980: 129 ss.; Rizzo 1985). Al carattere falisco della cultura materiale si contrappone la presenza di iscrizioni di lingua etrusca che caratterizzano nettamente il ruolo di Nepi come città di confine (Renzetti Marra 1974: 351). Ad essa possono correlarsi tra VII e VI sec. a. C. i numerosi insediamenti rurali documentati dalla British School at Rome (Potter 1985: 86-87; 1991, 175; 1992, fig.4) che mostrano un'occupazione analoga al resto del territorio.

1.2. Il sito della Tenuta Franca
(F. IGMI 143 I NE) (Fig. 1)

La località comprende un ampio pianoro di tufo delimitato a Nord dal Fosso dei Tre Ponti, a Sud dal Fosso dell'Isola, ad Est dalla tagliata di età romana della Via Amerina, a poca distanza dal sito protovillanoviano di La Torre, dove si installò in età medievale l'insediamento noto come *Insula Conversina*. Geologicamente il pianoro è composto da uno spesso strato di tufo rosso litoide che ricopre un deposito di sabbie ed argille plioceniche. Queste caratteristiche rendono possibile la presenza di sorgenti di cui almeno una individuabile al di sotto della quota 232. Il solo margine meridionale si presenta in pendenza e poco adatto ad un uso agricolo a causa anche dell'erosione del suolo, che ha favorito invece la realizzazione di vie di collegamento con il sottostante Fosso dell'Isola.

Presso il margine orientale della località è presente una tagliata ad andamento rettilineo lunga 65 m ca, di larghezza variabile dai 2 ai 3 m, con altezze delle pareti piuttosto bassa a Nord, fino a raggiungere i 3-4 m nell'estremità meridionale, dove è interrotta da una frana. Il suo orientamento Nord Ovest/Sud Est può riferirsi ad una viabilità verso settentrione, in età romana codificata dalla via Amerina, che lambisce la stessa tagliata, con un rampa tra il Fosso dell'Isola e la Tenuta Franca (Quilici 1989: 453). Una seconda breve via scavata nel tufo, larga 2 m e con un'altezza di 3 m con orientamento Nord Sud, è stata documentata a circa 1 Km ad Ovest della precedente, sopra la quota 182, per una lunghezza di 10 m. Un'altro percorso è individuabile al di sotto della quota 232, presso un facile guado del Fosso dell'Isola ed un'agevole risalita al pianoro della Tenuta dell'Isola, in direzione di Nepi.

Presso la quota 232 sono stati raccolti frammenti di ceramica di impasto di uso domestico e tegole, che

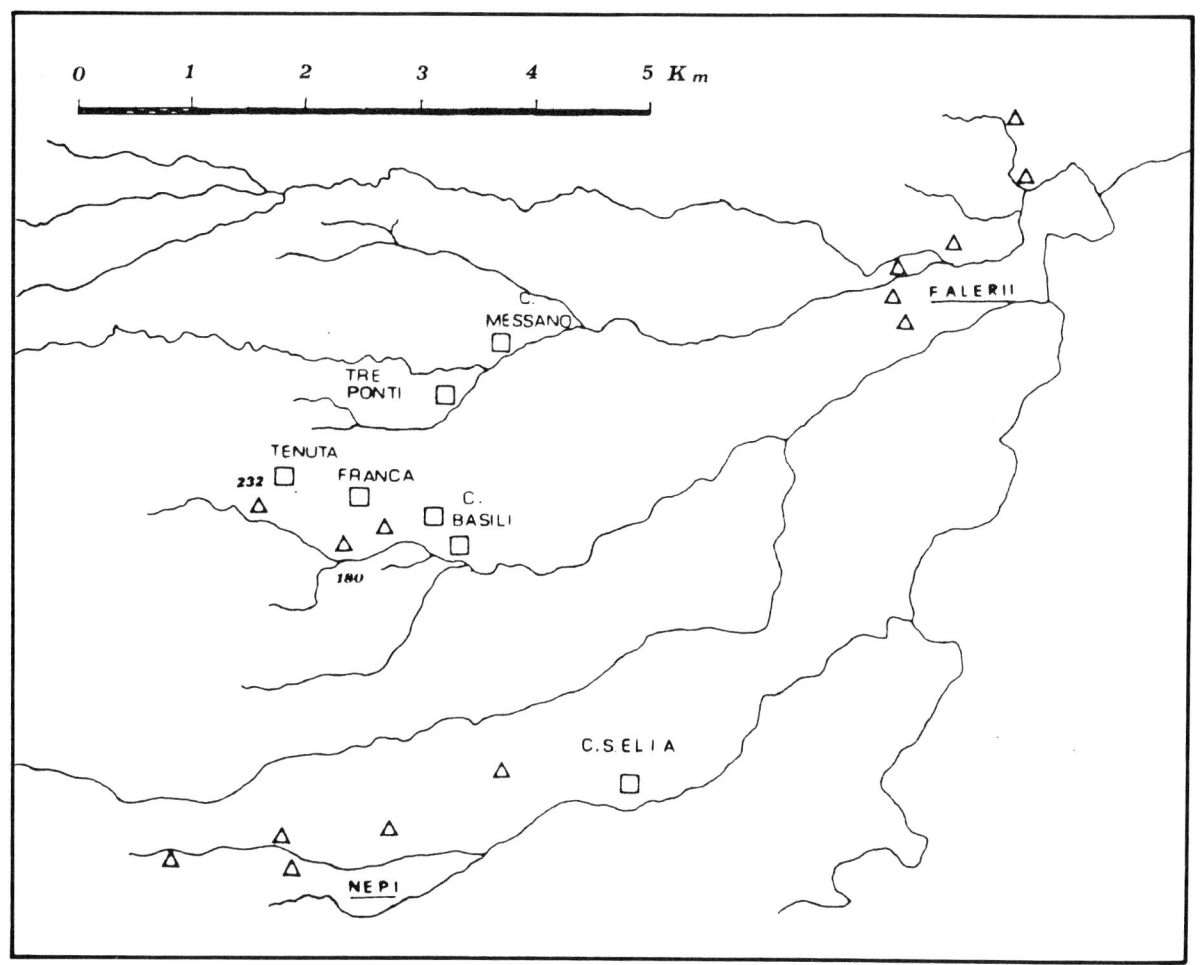

Fig. 1. Insediamento della Tenuta Franca e siti circostanti:

□ *Insediamento* △ *Necropoli*

coprono un periodo tra la fine del VII e tutto il VI sec. a. C., oltre a cospicui quantitativi ceramici relativi ad una fattoria di età romana. Altre aree di frammenti fittili di età arcaica, sono state individuate a circa 1 Km ad Est, presso la via Amerina e a Sud Est di Casale Basili; entrambe possono rientrare nello stesso comparto della Tenuta Franca, caratterizzato quindi da piccoli agglomerati rurali di tipo familiare, di cui il maggiore presso la quota 232.

Più distanti invece due nuove fattorie arcaiche individuate in località Tre Ponti e Casale Messano, che sembrano porsi a controllo di distinti pianori.

Un'estesa necropoli, presente sul margine meridionale del pianoro, era probabilmente utilizzata dai vari insediamenti, come sembrerebbe mostrare la disposizione in gruppi di tombe al suo interno, in prossimità delle vie prima descritte. La necropoli, per il numero di tombe documentate, inferiore, in ambito locale, solo a quelle urbane di *Falerii*. Si tratta, infatti, di circa 30 tombe a camera scavate nel tufo, con pianta quadrangolare, precedute da breve *dromos* e loculi alle pareti. La tipologia è quella tipica a partire dall'orientalizzante recente in area falisca (Colonna 1988: 523), cui non mancano influssi dell'architettura funeraria di *Caere*, come lunette intagliate sopra le entrate, gambe di *kline* sotto i loculi e, più raramente, letti di deposizione. Caratteristico è anche il precoce utilizzo di tegole per la chiusura dei loculi in età orientalizzante, il cui uso su larga scala, testimonierebbe la presenza di un'officina locale e di un'evoluzione della tecnica edilizia alla pari con i maggiori insediamenti del periodo. Particolare è il recupero di un frammento di tegola per la chiusura di un loculo, decorata con una pantera dipinta a tecnica *white-on-red*, di iconografia affine alla prima produzione etrusco-corinzia e databile tra il 630 ed il 600 a. C. (Cifani 1992).

Gli insediamenti della Tenuta Franca possono datarsi solo genericamente tra la fine del VII ed il VI sec. a.C., mentre la necropoli mostrerebbe una frequentazione più sicura già dall'ultimo quarto del VII sec. a. C. Alla fase tardo arcaica è ascrivibile un'iscrizione funeraria su tegola recuperata nel 1975 (Polidori 1977; Colonna 1993: 66–67). Pochi frammenti ceramici di età ellenistica rinvenuti all'interno di una tomba farebbero ipotizzare un parziale utilizzo ancora nel IV-III sec. a. C.

1.3 Castel S. Elia

Il nuovo rinvenimento avvenuto nel 1992, durante lavori edilizi nella zona Nord Est del pianoro del moderno abitato (quota 214) di resti di strutture in blocchi di tufo associate a frammenti di impasto (Archivio Saem Villa Giulia), permette di suffragare l'ipotesi di un insediamento arcaico sul sito di Castel S. Elia (Frederiksen & Ward Perkins 1957: 139). L' abitato medievale e moderno si estende, infatti, su di un pianoro prospiciente il Fosso del Ponte, all'incrocio di un'antica via di collegamento tra Nepi e *Falerii* ed una viabilità Nord/Sud. All'insediamento arcaico andrebbero riferite anche alcune sepolture, rinvenute nel 1879, databili al VI–V sec. a. C. (Fiorelli 1879: 262).

La formazione degli insediamenti satelliti a carattere rurale (Potter 1985: 87, fig.21; inoltre Rendeli 1991: 27–28) può ricondursi ad un aumento demografico, conseguenza di una crescita economica che investe tutta la valle tiberina nel VI sec. a.C dove si esercita il commercio dei metalli provenienti dalla Toscana, in concorrenza con i centri dell'Etruria costiera (Colonna 1973: 68–69; Cristofani 1988: 21). La loro presenza denota una sistematica occupazione delle aree coltivabili, in genere pianori di origine vulcanica adatti alle colture agricole ed all'allevamento stanziale, necessaria a soddisfare la domanda interna dei centri urbani. Questi siti rurali sono probabilmente da vedersi diffusi in modo capillare nell'ambito di una più complessa gerarchia insediativa.

Tali osservazioni, parziali e provvisorie per il tipo di dati utilizzati, potranno essere confermate attraverso l'analisi dei territori non ancora compresi nelle precedenti ricerche.

2. LA CITTÀ DI *FALERII* E L'AGRO FALISCO IN ETÀ TARDOANTICA (M.M.)

Con questo studio ci si propone di apportare un contributo alla discussione delle dinamiche insediative, che interssarono l'area falisca in età tardoantica. In particolare si tenterà di delineare l'asetto della città di *Falerii* (Di Stefano Manzella 1977) e di tracciare un quadro dell'insediamento rurale nell'agro falisco. Quattro aspetti emergono dalla raccolta di dati già editi, principalmente epigrafici e da nuove ricognizioni di superficie:

1. per quanto riguarda la città non sembra più sostenibile l'ipotesi che lo status urbano non si fosse mantenuto oltre il IV sec. d.C. e che la frequentazione fosse estremamente ridotta già intorno al 400 d.C. (Potter 1985: 155–157); al contrario viene restituita l'immagine di una città ancora sufficentemente strutturata almeno tra IV e VI sec. d.C. e abitata in modo sporadico forse fino all'VIII sec. d.C., quando con ogni probabilità anche l'episcopato si spostò a Civita Castellana; la popolazione urbana dovette ridursi costantemente e gradualmente nel corso dei secoli, forse concentrandosi nell'area intorno la chiesa di S. Maria di Falleri (Potter 1991: 179);

2. si individua una ininterrotta funzionalità del settore suburbano meridionale come area di sepoltura, nonostante uno spostamento topografico (dalla via Amerina alla via verso Sutri) e una variazione nel tipo dell'area cimiteriale (da necropoli rupestre a catacomba), avvenuti nel IV sec. d.C.;

3. si riscontra una sostanziale continuità d'uso della via Amerina dal periodo romano a quello bizantino-longobardo e medievale;

4. per quanto riguarda le campagne si individua una continuità insediativa fino al V-VI sec. d.C. lungo la viabilità principale, in questo caso l'Amerina.

2.1. La città

Documenti epigrafici e letterari ci informano su due elementi peculiari della vita pubblica ed amministrativa della città tardoantica: la presenza ideale dell'imperatore e quella reale del vescovo.

(i) Onori epigrafici all'imperatore

La serie documentaria epigrafica, aggiornata dal Di Stefano Manzella nel 1981, permette oggi di credere ad una maggiore vitalità del centro urbano almeno tra IV e V sec. d.C. La lacuna nella documentazione epigrafica, sottolineata in passato (Potter 1985: 157), va ridimensionata. Un'epigrafe (*CIL*, XI 3086), in base alla menzione di voti trentennali, può essere datata tra IV e V sec. d.C. (Di Stefano Manzella 1981: 117). La tavola marmorea doveva far parte di una complessa iscrizione onoraria, dedicata ad un imperatore tardoantico. Essa testimonia l'esistenza di una comunità urbana, ancora vitale e con possibilità economiche sufficienti alla realizzazione di monumenti onorari, verosimilmente posti in luoghi pubblici ancora sottoposti a manutenzione.

La documentazione epigrafica tardoantica comprende almeno altri quattro testi: due, databili al IV sec. d.C., sono stati rinvenuti nella catacomba dei SS. Gratiliano e Felicissima (vedi oltre); un altro, un tempo conservato a Civita Castellana e oggi non più rintracciabile, in base al formulario cristiano sembra posteriore alla metà del IV sec. d.C. (*CIL*, XI 7539; Fiocchi Nicolai 1988: 266); infine la base onoraria di *Lunius Bassus, praefectus Urb.* nel 359 d.C., testimone di possedimenti della famiglia senatoria degli *lunii Bassi* nei dintorni di Aquaviva (Di Stefano Manzella 1981: 136–137). Dalla serie documentaria falisca vanno invece espunte due iscrizioni non pertinenti: l'una (*CIL*, XI 7538) è stata rinvenuta in località Le Cese, nel territorio di *Horta*

(Fiocchi Nicolai 1988: 287); l'altra, conservata nel vescovado di Civita Castellana, è probabilmente di provenienza romana (Di Stefano Manzella 1981: 171–172 n. 65; Fiocchi Nicolai 1988: 265).

(ii) L'episcopato

La presenza di un vescovo a *Falerii* tra V e VI sec. d.C. sembra provare la persistenza almeno ideale del rango urbano del centro in quel periodo. Nel 499 d.C. la sede è ufficialmente aggregata a quella di Nepi, visto che un certo Felix, *episcopus nepesinus* tra 499 e 501 d.C., può qualificarsi nel 499 d.C. anche come *episcopus ecclesiae Faliscae et Nepesinae*. Va aggiunto che dal 465 al 502 d.C. anche la *mutatio* di *Aquaviva* sulla via Flaminia ha un suo vescovo; a questa diocesi evidentemente è assegnato almeno parte del settore orientale del territorio della colonia romana, negli anni in cui le sedi episcopali di *Falerii* e Nepi sono formalmente unite. Di conseguenza l'estinzione della diocesi di *Aquaviva* e la creazione di una diocesi indipendente di *Falerii* sono forse da vedere come avvenimenti tra loro strettamente connessi. E' perciò probabile che nel 595 d.C., quando *Falerii* ha, per la prima volta nella documentazione pervenutaci, un proprio titolare, la diocesi falisca sia estesa su tutto il territorio dell'antica colonia (sulle tre diocesi: Duchesne 1892: Raspi Serra 1974a: 56–57 e 1974b: 392; Fiocchi Nicolai 1988: 241, 263–264).

(iii) L'attività edilizia

Le indagini archeologiche nella città hanno spesso individuato strutture tardoantiche (ad esempio Pasqui 1903: 15). Anche i recenti lavori nell'*insula* a Est del monastero di S. Maria di Falleri hanno messo in luce strutture di tarda età imperiale, che invadono le sedi stradali (Potter 1991: 179 e 1992: 660). Il rinvenimento di maggior interesse fu tuttavia effettuato nel corso dei grandi sterri pontifici del secolo scorso. Già tra il 1821 e il 1823 fu scavato un edificio 'd'epoca tarda', probabilmente termale, non sappiamo se pubblico o privato, in un'area non precisabile all'interno del circuito murario urbano. Nella pavimentazione erano reimpiegate molte epigrafi, tra le quali una con dedica a Gallieno e Salonina (Di Stefano Manzella 1981: 110), che permette di datare l'edificio a dopo il 268 d.C. Oltre che come sintomo della decadenza della città, l'edificio e la sua decorazione di recupero potrebbero forse essere visti come l'indizio della sopravvivenza di una certa vitalità edilizia, coerente tuttavia con uno stato di assottigliate disponibilità economiche.

(iv) Le mura urbiche

Si può ragionevolmente presumere che il circuito murario della città, realizzato in occasione della creazione della nuova *Falerii* nella seconda metà del III sec. a.C. e ancor oggi in buono stato di conservazione, fosse quasi intatto in età tardoantica. *Falerii* poteva quindi fruire di un antico ma efficiente sistema di fortificazione, in un periodo in cui tutte le città importanti si trinceravano dietro nuove cinte murarie, giungendo ad identificarsi, agli occhi dei contemporanei, con le mura stesse (La Rocca 1992: 164; Wickham 1981: 80).

2.2. La basilica cimiteriale extraurbana, la catacomba e le antiche necropoli rupestri

A 500 m dalla Porta di Giove, sulla via verso Sutri, è situata una catacomba scavata nel banco tufaceo, contenente approssimativamente un migliaio di tombe. La paleografia di due iscrizioni, qui rinvenute, indica una datazione al IV secolo d.C. dell'intero complesso. Le gallerie della catacomba furono in parte tagliate per la costruzione di una chiesa absidata, incassata nel banco tufaceo. Si tratta molto verosimilmente della chiesa dei SS. Gratiliano e Felicissima, per la quale è altamente probabile una fase (quella costruttiva) tardoantica o altomedievale, anche in considerazione dei sarcofagi tufacei entro *formae* scavate nel banco, in passato rinvenuti a più riprese nell'area (Fiocchi Nicolai 1988: 266–283. Vedi anche Le Louet 1880; Duchesne 1892: 492; Gamurrini *et alii* 1972: 396; Frederiksen & Ward Perkins 1957: 162).

In pieno accordo con Fiocchi Nicolai ritengo che la catacomba e l'annessa basilica, di chiaro carattere cimiteriale, rappresentassero il cimitero ufficiale di *Falerii* dal IV sec. d.C. In diretto collegamento con la creazione di questa area sepolcrale cristiana va visto l'abbandono della necropoli rupestre lungo la Via Amerina, concentrata soprattutto nel tratto tra la città e il Fosso dei Tre Ponti. Non è un caso che questa area cimiteriale, utilizzata ininterrottamente dalla seconda metà del III sec. a.C., restituisca elementi di corredo non più tardi della seconda metà del III sec. d.C. (Munzi 1994: 56–57). D'altra parte non si può completamente escludere che la necropoli sia stata utilizzata saltuariamente anche in seguito, vista la presenza sporadica di materiale ceramico più tardo, che tuttavia è preferibilmente spiegabile in relazione alla continuata frequentazione della via (Caretta *et al., infra*).

2.3. La via Amerina

L'abbandono (o l'uso estremamente limitato) della necropoli rupestre ci riconduce al problema della funzionalità della via Amerina stessa in età medio e tardoimperiale. Un piccolo saggio di scavo, impiantato sulla sede stradale in località Cavo degli Zucchi, ha mostrato che la funzionalità e la manutenzione del lastricato stradale dovettero rimanere inalterate almeno fino al IV sec. d.C. (Munzi 1994). Questi dati, unitamente alla presenza lungo la via di siti rurali occupati in età tardoantica (vedi oltre) e alla notizia della 'riapertura' della via nel VI sec. d.C. da parte dall'esarca Romano

(Bullough 1966; Quilici 1983: 413; Potter & Whitehouse 1984: 65; Christie 1987: 456), contribuiscono ad indicare che l'Amerina rimase in funzione senza interruzioni nei periodi tardoimperiale e altomedievale. Il tracciato dell'Amerina ancora nel 700 d.C. ca., così come lo descrive l'Anonimo Ravennate (IV, 33), è rimasto pressochè immutato, nonostante l'inserimento in posizione errata di Gallese: *Perusia, Petona, Tuder, Ameria, Ortas, Faleris, Galenese, Nepe, Bacanis*. Come lascia intendere il toponimo *Faleris* (Di Stefano Manzella 1977: 161) la via continuava a toccare la città romana e non Civita Castellana (Potter & Whitehouse 1984: 65).

2.4. Gli insediamenti rurali (Fig. 2)

In area falisca si assiste ad un costante decremento numerico dei siti rurali tra il II e il V-VI sec. d.C. (Potter 1985: 153). Tuttavia il diradarsi degli insediamenti non pare aver comportato un cambiamento nella distribuzione spaziale dei siti, che continua ad interessare sia le zone interne che la fascia lungo la via Amerina (ma cfr. Cambi 1993: 237-238). All'ininterrotta funzionalità della strada corrisponde una presenza di siti nelle sue adiacenze almeno fino al V sec. d.C., in alcuni casi fino al VI sec. d.C.

Nuove ricognizioni hanno individuato, nel tratto tra *Falerii* e Nepi, cinque siti, sicuramente ancora frequentati in età tardoantica. Di ognuno di essi, oltre al rango (villa o fattoria) si ritiene opportuno segnalare la cronologia dell'ultima frequentazione, fornita dalla ceramica più tarda rinvenuta (sigillata africana D): ville a Pian Badessa (VI sec. d.C.) e a Monte la Macina (IV-V sec. d.C.); fattorie a Tenuta Franca (IV-V sec. d.C.), Casale Messano (IV sec. d.C.), tra Fosso Maggiore e Fosso Tre Ponti (V-VI sec. d.C.); queste ultime due già note (Frederiksen & Ward Perkins 1957: 106), non erano documentate per la fase tarda (Potter 1985: 156).

Alla lista vanno probabilmente aggiunti altri due siti. Nel 1946 in località Regolelli, a poche centinaia di metri dalle mura meridionali di *Falerii*, venne recuperata una statua acefala di togato, per la quale si propose una datazione, che non è stato possibile verificare, al IV sec. d.C. (*Notiziario* 1960: 443; Sommella Mura 1969: 36). La statua deve probabilmente far parte dell'arredo scultoreo di una ricca villa suburbana, cui appartengono evidentemente anche gli avanzi di 'fabbricato romano' registrati dalla *Carta Archeologica* (Gamurrini *et alii* 1972: 167 no.98; tav. IV no.98). Il rinvenimento di sigillata africana D, poco a Nord del sito protostorico e medievale della Torre, potrebbe indicare la sporadica frequentazione di una villa già individuata nelle vicinanze (Potter 1985: 136 fig. 35 e 1992: 644 fig. 4), di cui non era segnalata una fase tardoantica.

Tra Nepi e Baccano (*mansio ad Vacanas*), oltre alle ville di Casale dell'Umiltà e di Monte Gelato (Potter 1985: 156; Marazzi, Potter & King 1989, Potter 1992: 653-666), altre due ville presentano ora una frequentazione tardoimperiale. Quella di Grotta Arnaro (Frederiksen & Ward Perkins 1957: 79, fig. 3), con sigillata africana D di metà IV-metà V sec. d.C., non registrata

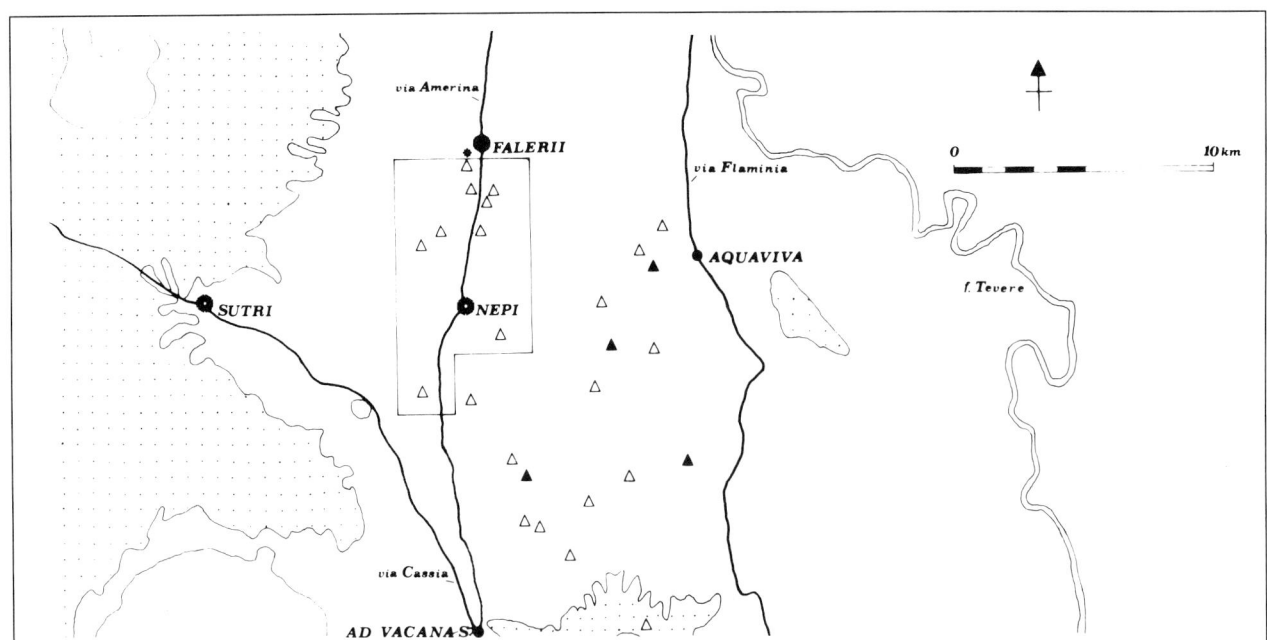

Fig. 2. Siti tardoantichi (IV-VI sec. d.C.) nell'Agro Falisco meridionale (nel riquadro le nuove attestazioni):

△ *Villa/fattoria* ▲ *Villa/fattoria con frequentazione altomedievale* ✶ *Catacomba* ✸ *Centro urbano* ● *Stazione stradale*

in precedenza e quella di S. Marcello, con sigillata africana D dello stesso periodo.

Tranne quelle di Monte la Macina (1,5 Km), Grotta Arnaro e Monte Gelato (2-2,5 Km), le ville-fattorie elencate sono situate a non più di 1 Km dalla via Amerina. I restanti siti noti sono per la maggior parte localizzati nelle aree interne a oltre 5 Km dall'Amerina e oltre 3 dalla Flaminia.

Il quadro, per alcuni versi nuovo, che emerge dalla ricerca permette alcune considerazioni di carattere generale. La tesi che l'insediamento rurale in età tardoantica abbia sfruttato esclusivamente zone interne, lontane dalla viabilità principale, insicura per gli eventi bellici (Potter 1975: 222-224 e 1985: 161; Wickham 1979: 82-84 per i siti altomedievali), va precisata ed attenuata. Se buona parte del popolamento è realmente concentrata in zone remote, la via Amerina, fondamentale arteria interregionale per comunicazioni e commerci (tra Roma e l'Umbria, più latamente tra il Tirreno e l'Adriatico), quanto meno non scoraggiava la continuità insediativa nelle sue vicinanze ancora nel V sec. d.C. Gli insediamenti lungo la via sembrano abbandonati nel corso del VI sec. d.C., evidentemente in relazione con gli eventi bellici (guerra greco-gotica e invasione longobarda); non diversamente accade nelle aree interne, dove tuttavia alcuni siti sembrano attardarsi alla prima metà del VII sec. d.C. In questo leggero scarto cronologico si può vedere l'indizio di una (maggiore) resistenza del tessuto insediativo tradizionale nelle zone remote (Christie 1987: 459) e forse la traccia di una quasi impercettibile continuità insediativa fino alle fasi d'incastellamento di IX e XI-XII sec. d.C. Esemplare in questo senso è il sito di Monte Gelato, dove indagini di scavo hanno documentato un'occupazione stabile fino al XI sec. d.C. (Marazzi, Potter & King 1989; Potter 1992: 662).

Bibliografia

Baglione, M.P. 1986. 'Il Tevere e i Falisci', *Archeologia Laziale*, 7, 124-142.

Brunetti Nardi, G. 1980 (a cura di). *Repertorio degli scavi e delle scoperte archeologiche nell'Etruria Meridionale III*, (1971-1975), Roma.

Bullough, D.A. 1966. 'La via Flaminia nella storia dell'Umbria (600-1100)', *Atti del III Convegno di Studi Umbri*, Perugia, 211-233.

Cangi, F. 1993. 'Paesaggi D'Etruria e di Puglia, *Storia di Roma*, 3, *L'Età Tardoantica*, II, *I luoghi e le culture*, Roma, 229-254.

Christie, N.J. 1987. 'Forum Ware, the Duchy of Rome, and incastellamento: problems of interpretation', *Archeologia Medievale*, 14, 451-466.

Cifani, G. 1992. 'Una tegola dipinta dall'area falisca. Un contributo alla pittura etrusca tardo orientalizzante', *Archeologia Classica*, 44, 263-271.

Cifani, G. 1994. 'La Necropoli della Tenuta Franca', in *Archeologia Uomo Territorio*, 13, 35-50.

Colonna, G. 1973. 'Ricerche sull'Etruria interna volsiniese', *Studi Etruschi*, 41, 45-72.

Colonna, G. 1988. 'I Latini e gli altri popoli del Lazio', *Italia omnium terrarum alumna*, Milano, 411-528.

Colonna, G. 1990a. 'Corchiano, Narce e il problema di Fescennium', *Civiltà dei Falisci*, (Atti del Convegno), Firenze, 111-140.

Colonna, G. 1993. 'Ceramisti e donne padrone di bottega nell'Etruria arcaica', in Meiser, G. (ed.) *Indogermanica et Italica. Festschrift für Helmut Rix zum 65 Geburtstag*, Innsbruck 1993, 61-68.

Cristofani, M. 1988. 'Etruschi nell'Agro Falisco', *Papers of the British School at Rome*, 56, 13-24.

Di Gennaro, F. 1988a. 'Il popolamento dell'Etruria Meridionale e le caratteristiche degli insediamenti tra l'età del bronzo e l'età del ferro', in *Etruria Meridionale. Conoscenza, conservazione e fruizione*, Roma, 59-82.

Di Gennaro, F.1988b. 'Primi risultati degli scavi della necropoli di Crustumerium. Tre complessi funerari della fase IV A', *Archeologia Laziale*, 9, 113-123.

Di Stefano Manzella, I. 1977. 'I nomi attribuiti alle due Falerii dalla tradizione letteraria antica e dalle epigrafi', *Rendiconti della Pontificia Accademia di Archeologia*, 49, 151-162.

Di Stefano Manzella,I. 1981. 'I. Regio VII-Etruria. Falerii Novi', *Supplementa Italica*, I, Roma, 101-176.

Duchesne, L. 1892. 'Le sedi episcopali nell'antico ducato di Roma', *Archivio della Società di Storia Patria*, 15, 475-503.

Fiocchi Nicolai, V. 1988. *I cimiteri paleocristiani del Lazio. I. Etruria Meridionale*, Città del Vaticano.

Fiorelli, G. 1879. 'Castel S. Elia', *Notizie degli Scavi di Antichità*, 261-262.

Frederiksen, M.W. & Ward Perkins J.B. 1957. 'The ancient road system of the Central and Northern Ager Faliscus', *Papers of the British School at Rome*, 25, 67-208.

Gamurrini, G.F., Cozza, A., Pasqui A. & Mengarelli R. 1972. *Carta Archeologica d'Italia (1881-1897). Materiali per l'Etruria e la Sabina*, (Forma Italiae, Serie II, Documenti I), Firenze.

Judson, S. & Hemphill, P. 1981. 'Sizes of settlement in Southern Etruria. 6th-5th centuries B.C.', *Studi Etruschi*, 49, 193-202.

La Rocca, C. 1992. 'Public buildings and urban change in northern Italy in the early mediaeval period', Rich, J. (ed.) *The City in Late Antiquity*, London-New York, 161-180.

Le Louet, E. 1880. 'Scoperta del cimitero dei SS. Gratiliano e Felicissima', *Bullettino di Archeologia Cristiana*, 5, 69-71.

Marazzi, F., Potter, T.W. & King, A. 1989. 'Mola di Monte Gelato (Mazzano Romano-VT): notizie preliminari sulle campagne di scavo 1986-1988 e considerazioni sulle origini dell'incastellamento in Etruria Meridionale alla luce dei nuovi dati archeologici', *Archeologia Medievale*, 16, 103-119.

Morselli, C. 1980. *Sutrium*, (Forma Italiae, Regio VII), Firenze.

Munzi, M. 1994. 'Nuovi dati sulla via Amerina e note prosopografiche sugli Egnatii di Falerii Novi', *Archeologia, Uomo, Territorio*, 13, 51-63.

Pasqui, A. 1903. 'Fabbrica di Roma. Nuova scoperta dentro alla città di S. Maria di Falleri e attorno alla sua necropoli', *Notizie degli Scavi di Antichità*, 14-19.

Pasquinucci, M. 1990. 'Allevamento transumante nell'Italia centro-meridionale', in Maggi, R., Nisbet R. & Barker G. (a cura di), *Archeologia della pastorizia nell'Europa meridionale I = Rivista di Studi Liguri*, 56: 165-177.

Peroni, R. 1989. *Protostoria dell' Italia continentale. La penisola italiana nell'età del bronzo e del ferro.* (Popoli e Civiltà dell'Italia Antica 9). Roma.

Petitti, P. 1990. 'La preistoria del territorio falisco. Cenni introduttivi. L'età del bronzo', *La Civiltà dei Falisci*, Firenze, 53-59.

Polidori, G. 1977. 'Ager Nepesinus', *Studi Etruschi*, 45, 296-297.

Potter, T.W. 1975. 'Recenti ricerche in Etruria Meridionale: problemi della transizione dal tardo antico all'alto medioevo', *Archeologia Medievale*, 2, 215-236.

Potter, T.W. 1976. *A Faliscan town in South Etruria. Excavations at Narce 1966-71*, London.

Potter, T.W. 1985. *Storia del paesaggio dell'Etruria Meridionale. Archeologia e trasformazioni del territorio*, Roma 1985.

Potter, T.W. 1991. 'Power, politics and territory in southern Etruria', in Herring, E., Whitehouse R. & Wilkins J. (eds.), *Papers of the*

Fourth Conference of Italian Archaeology, The Archaeology of Power, 2.2, London, 174–184.

Potter, T.W. 1992. 'Reflection of twenty-five years' fieldwork in the Ager Faliscus. Aproaches to landscape archaeology', Bernardi M. (a cura di) *Archeologia del paesaggio*, Firenze, 637–666.

Potter, T.W. & Whitehouse, D.B. 1984. 'Il castello di Ponte Nepesino e il confine settentrionale del ducato di Roma', *Archeologia Medievale*, 11, 63–147.

Quilici, L. 1983. 'La rete stradale del ducato di Spoleto nell'alto medioevo', *Atti del 9°Congresso Internazionale di Studi sull'Alto Medioevo*, 1, Spoleto, 399–420.

Quilici, L. 1989. 'Le antiche vie dell'Etruria', *Atti del II Convegno Internazionale Etrusco*, Firenze, 451–506.

Raspi Serra, J. 1974a. *Le diocesi dell'Alto Lazio. Corpus della scultura altomedievale*, Spoleto.

Raspi Serra J. 1974b. 'Insediamenti e viabilità in epoca paleocristiana nell'Alto Lazio', *Atti del III Congresso di Archeologia Cristiana. Antichità Altoadriatiche*, Trieste, 391–405.

Rellini, U. 1920. 'Cavernette e ripari preistorici nell'Agro Falisco', *Monumenti Antichi dei Lincei*, 26, 6–179.

Rendeli, M. 1991. 'Sulla nascita delle comunità urbane in Etruria Meridionale', *Annali Istituto Orientale di Napoli*, 13, 9–45.

Rizzo, D. 1985. 'Nepi (Viterbo)', *Studi Etruschi* 51, 401–402.

Sommella Mura, A. 1969 (a cura di). *Repertorio degli scavi e delle scoperte archeologiche nell'Etruria Meridionale (1939–1965)*, Roma.

Stefani, E. 1910. 'Nepi – Scoperte di antichità nel territorio nepesino', *Notizie degli Scavi di Antichità*, 199–222.

Stefani, E. 1918. 'Nepi – Antico sepolcro della necropoli nepesina', *Notizie degli Scavi di Antichità*, 16–19.

Wickham, C.J. 1979. 'Historical and topographical notes on early mediaeval South Etruria (part 2)', *Papers of the British School at Rome*, 34, 66–95.

Wickham, C. 1981. *Early Mediaeval Italy. Central Power and Local Society 400–1000*, London.

Zifferero, A. 1991. 'Forme di possesso della terra e tumuli orientalizzanti nell'Italia centrale tirrenica', in Herring, E., Whitehouse, R. & Wilkins, J. (eds.) *Papers of the Fourth Conference of Italian Archaeology. The Archaeology of Power*, 1, London, 107–134.

41

Ricognizioni nell'Ager Faliscus Meridionale

A. CAMILLI, L. CARTA, T. CONTI, A. DE LAURENZI & M. DE SIMONE

Sommario: *La relazione riguarda un progetto di ricognizione intensiva su larga area nell'Agro Falisco meridionale, e precisamente nel territorio della tavoletta I.G.M. 143 I SE – Nepi. I risultati presentati hanno carattere preliminare. In età orientalizzante è evidente una occupazione piuttosto accentrata nell'area urbana a cui il territorio fa riferimento, quella di Narce-Fescennium; In età arcaica si assiste ad un considerevole incremento dell'occupazione del territorio, apparentemente a scapito dell'area urbana, che tuttavia viene munita delle ben note fortificazioni. La conquista del territorio da parte di Roma è da porsi in età piuttosto antica, contemporaneamente alla presa di Veio e Capena anziché a quella di Falerii. Per tutto il IV ed il III secolo a.C. la scarsa occupazione farebbe propendere verso un utilizzo dell'area ad* Ager Publicus*; con l'instaurarsi dell' 'economia della villa' la densa occupazione del territorio rimane costante, con scarsa riduzione delle attestazioni nei secoli tardi. Pesantemente colpito dalle guerre greco-gotiche, il territorio ha una discreta ripresa nel medioevo, specie grazie alla fondazione della* Domusculta Capracorum.

INTRODUZIONE (AC)

La relazione interessa un progetto di ricognizione, curato dal settore 'Area Falisca' del Gruppo Archeologico Romano, di una porzione dell'Ager Faliscus meridionale ai confini con i territori Veiente e Capenate, con particolare attenzione ai comuni di Nepi (VT), Mazzano Romano (Roma) e Calcata (VT) (Fig.1.1). Si tratta di una zona con orografia piuttosto costante che presenta pianori tufacei separati da profonde depressioni create dall'azione di corsi d'acqua nella parte orientale ed alture meno ripide, dovute alla minore presenza degli alvei fluviali, nella zona occidentale. L'area è stata scelta sulla base di un *site-catchment*, impostato sul centro antico attualmente denominato Narce, come già definito dalle ricostruzioni statistiche proposte nel 1976 da Potter (1976: 25–28, fig.8), riviste nel 1981 da Judson ed Hemphill (1981), e da quella, peraltro piuttosto generica, recentemente proposta dallo Stoddart (1990). Va comunque specificato che questa definizione deve essere considerata funzionale esclusivamente per il periodo prcedente alla conquista romana; per le età successive i limiti imposti alla ricerca hanno valore solo come area campione, non rispecchiando più alcuna divisione politico-amministrativa, presunta o accertata.

La stima è stata corretta sulla base di nuovi dati topografici acquisiti recentemente e riguardanti le città dell'Etruria Tiberina. Gli originali e ben noti calcoli, basati sui poligoni calibrati di Thiessen, infatti, non consideravano una serie di piccoli centri abitati. Questi, infatti, dovevano essere dotati, per posizione, conformazione e durata di occupazione, di un *territorium*, se non indipendente in senso politico, certo dotato di un determinato grado di autonomia economica. Fra questi è probabilmente da inserire il moderno centro di Faleria. L'estensione molto maggiore, recentemente osservata (cfr., in questa stessa sede, il contributo di chi scrive e di B. Vitali Rosati), dell'abitato antico di Capena, porta inoltre a correggere le stime e ad estendere di molto, nel calcolo, il territorio di quest'ultima, escludendo ogni possibile contatto dell'area di influenza di Narce con le pendici del Monte Soratte. Il campione di territorio in oggetto, da localizzarsi nella tavoletta dell'Istituto Geografico Militare Foglio 143 Primo Sud Est, è ancora in fase di copertura e di studio: l'area attualmente già indagata è evidenziata nella Figura 1.2.

Le considerazioni storiche presentate, quindi, sono da considerarsi preliminari. Va, inoltre, sottolineato che i dati esposti sono esclusivamente quelli derivati dal nostro intervento sul territorio, fatta eccezione per alcuni siti particolari dei quali è stato necessario tenere conto.

Nel corso delle indagini sinora svolte le presenze rinvenute sono state circa 300, tra le quali 238 quelle configurabili come siti ben definiti cronologicamente e qualificabili.

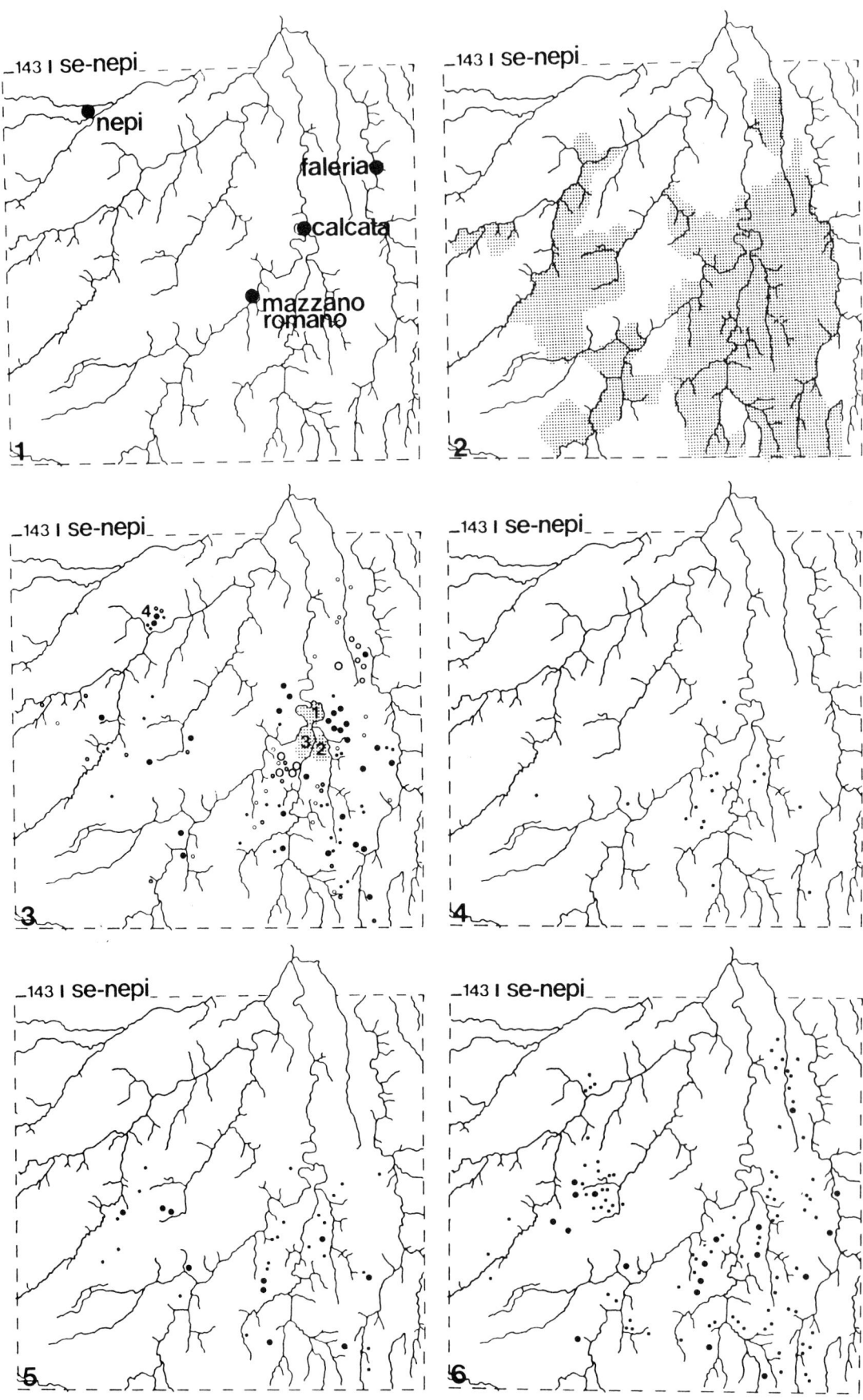

Fig. 1. Siti preromani e republicani (VII-I sec. a.C.)

DAL VII AL IV SECOLO A.C. (ADL)

Nella esposizione diacronica dei dati iniziamo dall'età orientalizzante, cioé ad uno stadio nel quale il processo formativo della città è già compiuto. I materiali di epoca preistorica e protostorica, rinvenuti nel corso della ricerca di superficie sono in fase di studio da parte del Dottor Vincenzo D'Ercole della Soprintendenza Archeologica per l'Etruria Meridionale. Nella carta di fase sono messi in evidenza i siti individuati, riferibili al periodo compreso tra l'età, appunto, orientalizzante e la fase finale della guerra romano-veiente del 396 a.C.

Nel settimo secolo la quasi totalità delle presenze è tuttavia riscontrabile solo nell'area dell'abitato e nelle sue immediate vicinanze. Questo stesso abitato è incentrato sulle tre colline contigue di Narce (Fig.1.3.1), Monte li Santi (Fig.1.3.3) e Pizzo Piede (Fig.1.3.2), e forse comprendeva, come già evidenziato dal Colonna (1990), alcuni nuclei minori urbanisticamente indipendenti su alture vicine (ad esempio quella dove sorge attualmente il paese di Calcata e la vicina quota 210). E' interessante a questo proposito notare, a conferma di quanti vogliono identificare il centro antico di Narce con l'*oppidum* falisco di *Fescennium*, come l'altura di Calcata Vecchia venga chiamata dagli anziani del luogo *'Vascena'*. E' nel corso del sesto secolo che assistiamo ad un aumento delle presenze su tutto il territorio, e contemporaneamente ad un calo quantitativo dei materiali raccolti sull'abitato; il grafico di Fig.2 evidenzia questo mutato rapporto dei materiali rinvenuti sulle colline di Narce, Pizzo Piede e sulle quattro zone campione definite sull'altura di Monte li Santi, precisando che i numeri sull'asse delle ordinate indicano la quantità dei frammenti raccolti. Ciò potrebbe fare ipotizzare un cambiamento della funzione del centro in rapporto alla campagna, in chiave economico-amministrativa e politica, anche se tale fatto non va letto come un declino dell'abitato. Infatti sembra da ascrivere a questa fase una certa monumentalizzazione del centro, riscontrabile soprattutto nella costruzione di consistenti strutture difensive. Le mura in opera quadrata, in diatoni ed ortostati, sono attualmente visibili sull'ultimo terrazzamento dell'altura di Narce e, a tratti, su quasi tutto il perimetro di Monte li Santi.

In generale possiamo osservare un'intensa occupazione dell'area, laddove i siti di maggiore consistenza risultano incentrati nelle zone prossime al centro urbano, mentre risultano di densità e classe gerarchica minore i siti nelle aree periferiche; fa eccezione, in quest'ottica, il nucleo di presenze nella zona di Grotta Arnaro (Fig.1.3.4), che potrebbe, però, essere letto come un *pagus* a protezione di uno dei pochi valichi funzionali del Fosso del Cerreto, evidente confine naturale, e della tagliata ad esso inerente.

Durante gli scontri tra Roma e Veio della seconda metà del quinto secolo avanti Cristo, i Falisci sono parte integrante della coalizione anti-romana; a più riprese, specialmente nel 437–435 e nel 402–397, il territorio falisco subisce devastazioni (Livio V, 8, 4).

Nel 396 cade Veio; Capena capitola l'anno successivo. Non abbiamo fonti, però, che ci attestino una effettiva conquista del territorio Falisco da parte dei Romani. Tuttavia, una notizia geograficamente significativa di uno scontro tra Camillo ed i Falisci e Capenati alleati *in agro Nepesino* poco prima della caduta di Veio, ci è fornita dallo stesso Livio che fa riferimento più volte a distruzioni e saccheggi avvenuti durante la guerra (Liv.

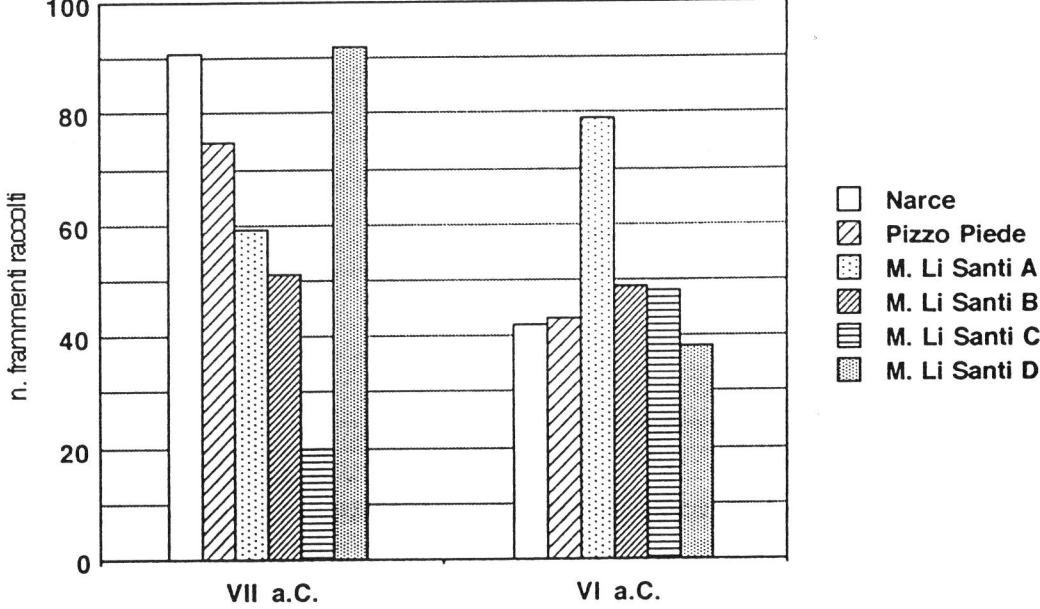

Fig. 2. Frammenti raccolti ai siti di Narce, Pizzo Piede e Monte li Santi

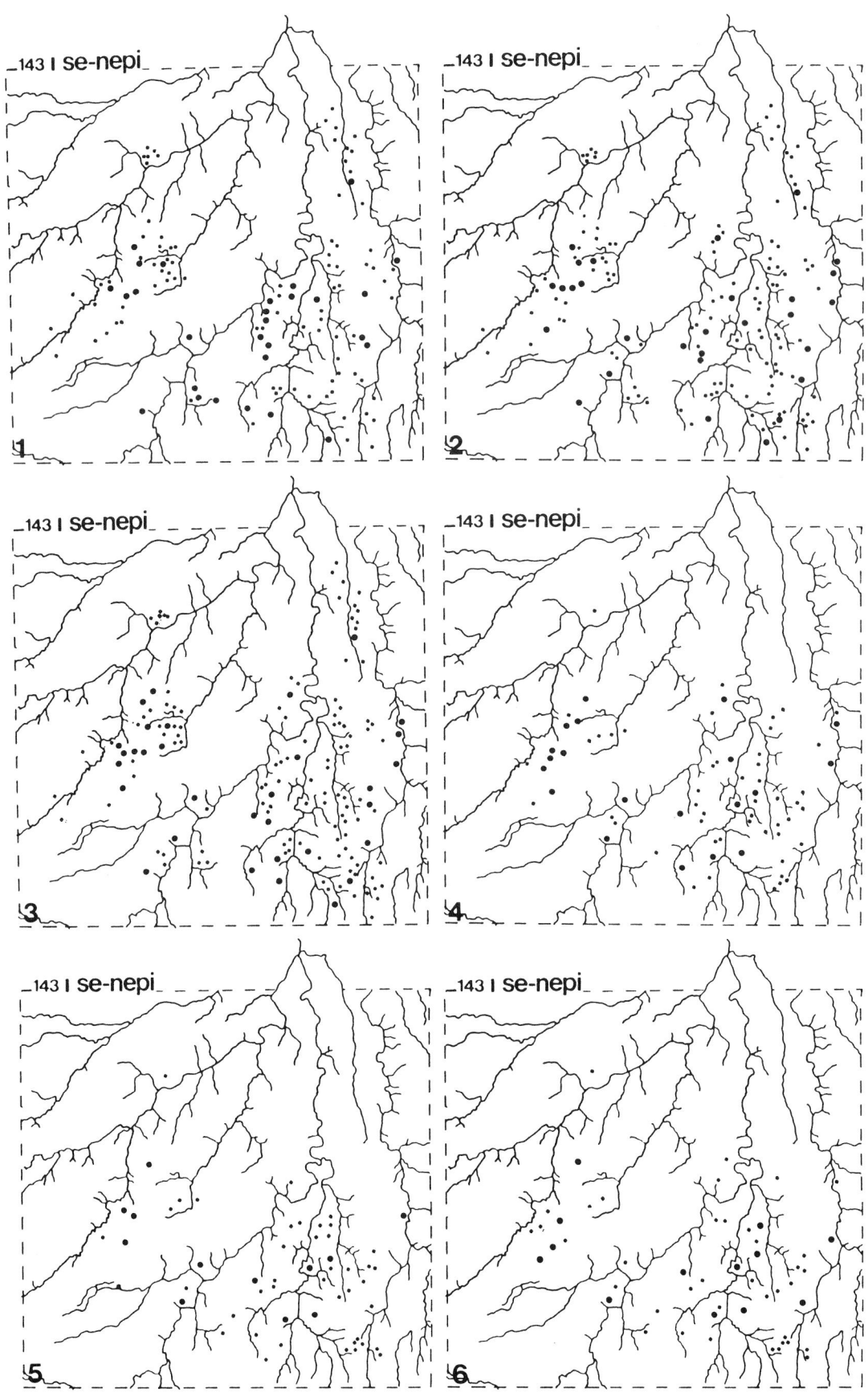

Fig. 3. Siti romani (I-V sec. d.C.)

V.12.5-6;V.13.12;V.14.7;24.2-3). Sono, invece, note assegnazioni di pochi anni successive ai disertori Falisci, Veienti e Capenati (Livio VI.4.4).

Osservando la carta di fase (Fig.1.4) appare chiaro l'effetto delle devastazioni; la pressocchè completa assenza di testimonianze abitative in questo periodo consente interessanti osservazioni sulle fasi più antiche della romanizzazione del territorio. I dati portano a pensare che l'area non sia stata soggetta alle assegnazioni, che probabilmente si verificarono in altre zone e presumibilmente nei territori capenate meridionale e veiente (Liverani 1984: 38). Si potrebbe quindi pensare ad una funzione di questa zona come *Ager Publicus* a disposizione dei nuovi cittadini, ed inoltre come fascia cuscinetto per *Falerii* ancora non sottomessa.

Dal III al I secolo a.C. (MDS)

Nel terzo secolo avanti Cristo (Fig.1.5) lo scarso insediamento, seppure in leggera ripresa, porterebbe a pensare che l'utilizzo di quest'area sia ancora ad *Ager Publicus*. Infatti questo territorio, evidentemente spopolato, potrebbe ben essere uno di quelli utilizzati per il pagamento dei *trientabula* nel 210 a.C., localizzabili, sulla base di Livio (XXXI.13.1-9), entro 50 miglia da Roma, nell'*ager publicus* Veiente per il Toynbee (1981, I:175,386; II:280-281). La pressocchè completa assenza di grandi insediamenti, contro una certa crescita di piccole presenze, porterebbe, infatti, a supporre un'occupazione di tipo spontaneo o quanto meno di basso livello.

Nel II secolo a.C. (Fig.1.6) la situazione cambia drasticamente. Parallelamente a quanto sembra accadere nell'Ager Veientanus, la nascita del sistema produttivo della villa non comporta la sparizione di entità minori come piccole fattorie e casali (fatto che sembrerebbe invece essere accaduto nell'Ager Cosanus; Celuzza & Regoli 1982: 57): sono proprio queste stesse, invece, ad avere un grande incremento in tale periodo. Si fa presente che la differenziazione in quattro classi gerarchiche delle attestazioni, cioé presenza, casa/capanna, villa di medie e grandi dimensioni, è ispirata alla divisione proposta dalla Celuzza e dalla Regoli. Per presenza si è intesa una semplice attestazione di ceramica databile. Per casa/capanna si sottintende una attestazione di piccole dimensioni ma con fasi cronologiche e funzioni ben definite dai frammenti ceramici raccolti, comunque senza traccia di materiali fittili e/o architettonici di lusso. Per villa di medie dimensioni ci si riferisce ad un complesso abitativo più articolato che abbia restituito anche materiali di lusso. La distinzione, infine, tra questo tipo di impianto e la grande villa, è costituita fondamentalmente dall'estensione maggiore dell'area di raccolta. Concorrono ovviamente a questa differenziazione, oltre a quanto sopra esposto, tutta una serie di dati e notizie raccolte sul sito in oggetto.

Nella zona occidentale sono inoltre localizzabili alcune aree di fitta presenza abitativa, favorite da un'orografia meno accentuata. Queste potrebbero, forse, rapportarsi a produzioni intensive e specializzate in relazione ai mercati dell'Urbe, con i quali l'area era collegata tramite la *Via Amerina*.

Nella zona orientale la disposizione stessa dei siti, la coesistenza in brevi spazi di strutture produttive di grandi e piccole dimensioni, in un rapporto costante di circa 1 a 5, testimonierebbe, come ipotizzato anche per aree vicine, uno sfruttamento del territorio mediante colonato. La situazione sembrerebbe perdurare costante per tutto il I secolo a.C. (Fig.3.1), ed è importante notare come i disordini avvenuti nella prima metà di questo stesso secolo non sembrano avere avuto effetto sul territorio.

L'età imperiale (TC)

La continuità è assicurata per i primi due secoli dell'impero (Figg.3.1; 3.2), per i quali si osserva, anzi, un leggero ulteriore incremento. E' da notare come, tuttavia, questo non sia assolutamente paragonabile alla crescita dell'occupazione del territorio in età augustea, situazione che sembra essersi verificata nella maggior parte dell'area interessata dal fenomeno dello sfruttamento a villa schiavistica.

Le numerose ville attestate in tutto il territorio hanno restituito, inoltre, diversi frammenti di anfore che, se pure ancora in fase di studio, consentono interessanti osservazioni sull'economia della zona. Il poligono di frequenza (Fig.4) mostra le produzioni di funzioni identificabili nello spazio compreso tra il II secolo a.C. ed il VI secolo d.C. E' evidentemente preponderante l'importazione di anfore vinarie in rapporto alle anfore olearie ed a quelle da conserva. Questo potrebbe indicare come non vi fosse grande necessità di importare olio, fatto che si può quindi direttamente collegare all'ipotesi di una produzione locale di questo prodotto. La scarsissima presenza di anfore olearie betiche del tipo Dressel 20, in generale strettamente inerenti a contesti legati all'amministrazione statale è un dato significativo, se pure ancora preliminare per azzardare ipotesi più precise di lavoro.

Una certa contrazione dei siti è ben visibile nella carta di fase relativa al III secolo d.C. (Fig.3.3). Questa crisi, tuttavia, sembra essere di tono ben minore di quanto normalmente asserito. La riduzione delle ville di piccole dimensioni è ben lungi dalla completa sparizione ed il rapporto tra grandi e piccoli siti, seppure in leggero calo, mantiene una certa correlazione.

Nel corso del quarto secolo (Fig.3.4) la contrazione è ancora più evidente ed ha maggiore effetto nelle zone più intensamente occupate nei secoli precedenti, come se fossero cessati i motivi economici per uno sfruttamento così intensivo, per di più di un'area tanto vicina alla *Via Amerina*.

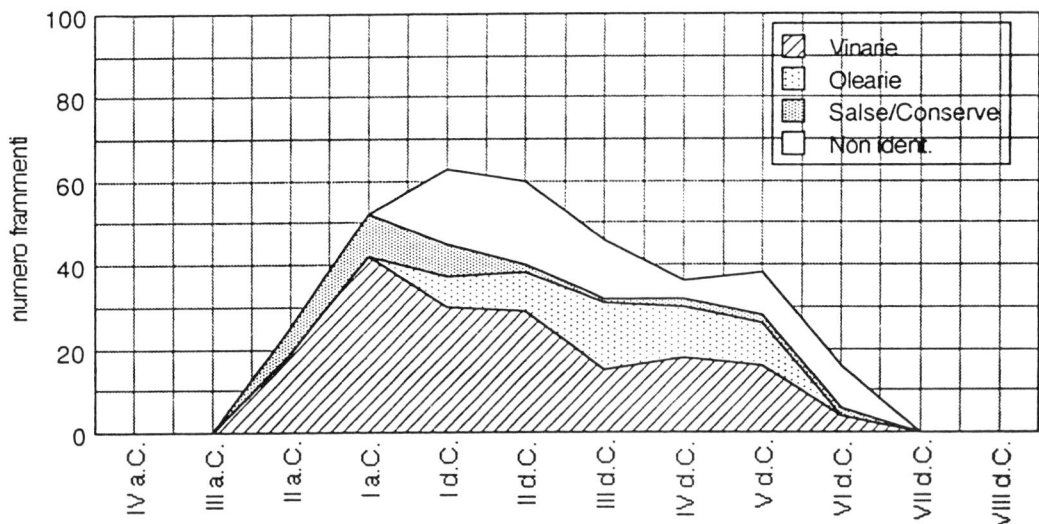

Fig. 4. Poligono di frequenza delle anfore d'importazione

Nel V secolo d.C. (Fig.3.5) lo spopolamento, seppure costante, non assume dimensioni drammatiche, segno evidente di come la zona fosse divenuta allora piuttosto periferica rispetto alle due grandi arterie di comunicazione (Amerina e Flaminia) che le sono a tutt'oggi tangenti.

Ben più chiaro è il calo delle presenze nei due secoli successivi (Fig.5.1), quando spariscono completamente le ville di grandi dimensioni e le attestazioni rinvenute si riducono, per un'area indagata di circa 50 Km², ad appena 17, concentrate in maniera particolare nei luoghi più interni (Potter 1975: 224). Il maggiore spopolamento, infatti, sembra avvenire proprio nelle zone pianeggianti che per giunta sono molto vicine al tracciato della *Via Amerina*. E' fortemente presumibile, quindi, che tutti i grandi spostamenti di truppe relativi alle guerre greco-gotiche, avvenissero sulle direttrici delle grandi arterie già considerate, con conseguenze facilmente immaginabili per il territorio circostante.

IL MEDIOEVO (LC)

Per quanto riguarda l'occupazione del territorio in età medievale, un esame esaustivo e completo non può prescindere dai dati dei fondamentali scavi della British School at Rome nell'importante sito della Mola di Monte Gelato (Potter & King 1988; Marazzi, Potter & King 1989; Potter 1991) (Fig.5.2.2). In attesa della pubblicazione

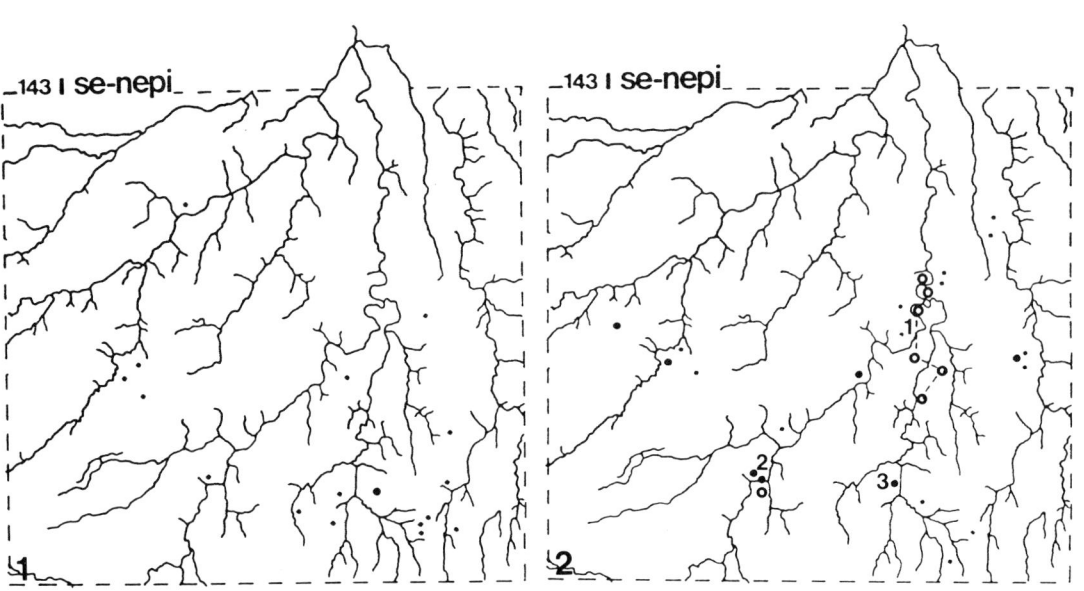

Fig. 5. Siti altomedievali e medievali

dei risultati finali della ricerca, tralasciamo una trattazione esaustiva dell'argomento. E' interessante segnalare, comunque, alcuni dati significativi relativi alla storia degli insediamenti fortificati di questa fase.

E' stata identificata una serie di torri a vista (Fig.5.2.1), alcune delle quali già note, collegate ad una linea N/S di presumibile comunicazione. Non si ha alcuna notizia di queste stesse strutture che dovrebbero riferirsi all'XI-XII secolo.

Inoltre è stato identificato un complesso di un certo rilievo in località La Rocchetta, su quota 187 di Monte Cinghiale (Fig.5.2.3). Si tratta di un sito emblematico per la continuità di vita a cui è stato soggetto. Esso si sviluppa su un piccolo pianoro tufaceo di forma allungata, interamente fortificato in età arcaica con murature in opera quadrata (Fig.6), assimilabile al noto e vicino abitato di Monte Santangelo. Tutto intorno allo stesso pianoro sono evidenti numerose tombe a camera scavate nella parete tufacea, successivamente reimpiegate come abitazioni. Infatti la rioccupazione di siti fortificati di epoca arcaica nel medioevo in analoghe condizioni di instabilità sociale, è un fenomeno ben attestato in gran parte dell'Etruria. In età romana la valletta sottostante viene occupata da una villa frequentata ininterrottamente, stando ai materiali di superficie raccolti, fino all'epoca tardo-antica. Il pianoro de La Rocchetta viene rioccupato nell'alto medioevo, come testimoniano alcuni frammenti di Forum Ware e di depurata acroma decorata a pettine, recuperati nella terra di riporto di uno scavo clandestino di un silos. L'abitato medievale doveva estendersi nelle propaggini settentrionali dello stesso pianoro, dove rimangono numerose tracce di riutilizzo delle cisterne preromane e delle fortificazioni arcaiche. Alcuni edifici dovettero essere realizzati con i materiali di spoglio delle vicine ville, tra i quali ad esempio una cornice modanata ora crollata, una base ed un rocchio di colonna che sono pertinenti ad un piccolo edificio, forse una cappella rurale. Sulle propaggini meridionali dell'altura una piccola necropoli di tombe a fossa del tipo a loggetta con copertura a lastroni di tufo displuviati è purtoppo oggetto di continui scavi clandestini. Il sito, del quale sarebbe auspicabile un'indagine di scavo, continua ad essere occupato fino al XII secolo, come testimonia il rinvenimento di frammenti di ceramica a vetrina sparsa. Si tratta, in effetti, di un incastellamento atipico, in quanto riutilizza le strutture difensive di età arcaica, senza la realizzazione di un vero e proprio *castrum*. La situazione presente su Monte Cinghale, quindi, non ha i connotati di una semplice rioccupazione, considerato il largo spettro cronologico della ceramica raccolta ed il gran numero di abitazioni in grotta.

Bibliografia

Celuzza, M.G. & Regoli, E. 1982. 'La Valle d'Oro nel territorio di Cosa', *Dialoghi di Archeologia,* IV, 31–62.

Colonna, G. 1990. 'Corchiano, Narce e il problema di Fescennium', *La Civiltà dei Falisci, Atti del XV Convegno di Studi Etruschi e Italici (Civita Castellana-Forte Sangallo Maggio 1987)*, Firenze, 111–140.

Judson, S. & Hemphill, S. 1981. 'Sizes of settlement in Southern Etruria, 6th-5th centuries B.C.', *Studi Etruschi,* 49, 193–202.

Liverani, P. 1984. 'L'Ager Veientanus in età repubblicana', *Papers of the British School at Rome,* 54, 56–48.

Marazzi, F., Potter, T.W. & King, A. 1989. 'Mola di Monte Gelato (Mazzano Romano – VT): Notizie preliminari sulle campagne di scavo 1986–1988 e considerazioni sulle origini dell'incastellamento in Etruria Meridionale alla luce dei nuovi dati archeologici', *Archeologia Medievale*, XVI, 103–119.

Potter, T.W. 1975. 'Recenti ricerche in Etruria Meridionale: problemi di transizione dal tardoantico all'altomedioevo', *Archeologia Medievale,* II, 215–236.

Potter, T.W. 1976. *A Faliscan Town in South Etruria. Excavations at Narce 1966-1971*, London.

Potter, T.W. 1991. 'Power, politics and territory in Southern Etruria', in E. Herring, R. Whitehouse & J. Wilkins (eds.), *Papers of the Fourth Conference of Italian Archaeology, The Archaeology of Power*, 2.2, London, 174–184.

Potter, T.W. & King, A. 1988. 'Scavi a Mola di Monte Gelato presso Mazzano Romano, Etruria Meridionale. Primo rapporto preliminare', *Archeologia Medievale*, XV, 253–311.

Stoddart, S. 1990. 'The political landscape in Etruria', *Accordia Research Papers,* I, 39–51.

Fig. 6. La Rocchetta – muratura in opera quadrata di età arcaica

42

Nuove Ricerche nell'Agro Capenate

A. CAMILLI & B. VITALI ROSATI

Sommario: *La relazione riguarda le prime ricognizioni effettuate per la redazione del volume della* Forma Italiae *relativo alla tavoletta IGM 144 IV SO, Rignano Flaminio. Si presenta la sintesi storico-topografica desumibile dai dati fino ad ora raccolti, mettendo in rilievo alcuni momenti storici di particolare importanza, quali lo sviluppo del territorio in età arcaica, la precoce romanizzazione, il lungo perdurare dell'economia della villa, dovuto alla vicinanza con Roma e con il Tevere, e la diffusa occupazione del territorio in età altomedievale e medievale. Vengono presentati anche i dati relativi alla raccolta di superficie per aree effettuata sull'altura della città di Capena, per la quale si propone una estensione della superficie abitata.*

1. Le nuove ricerche sull'agro capenate muovono dal progetto di realizzazione del volume della *Forma Italiae* della tavoletta 144 IV SO (Rignano Flaminio). L'area, prossima al Tevere, delimitata a nord dal Monte Soratte e compresa tra le antiche vie Flaminia e Tiberina, costituisce la porzione settentrionale del territorio di pertinenza dell'antico centro di Capena. Il progetto intende giungere ad una copertura intensiva dell'intera area con i soli limiti geografici imposti dalla tavoletta IGM. Intendiamo proporre una lettura diacronica del territorio ponendo attenzione ad alcuni momenti storici di particolare importanza. Il punto di partenza della ricerca è stato la localizzazione su base cartografica dei dati editi; fondamentale base per l'esame del territorio sono infatti i risultati del South Etruria Survey editi dal Jones agli inizi degli anni 60 (1962; 1963), e di quelli conservati presso l'archivio della Soprintendenza Archeologica per l'Etruria Meridionale. Tra questi, oltre ai dati relativi alla normale attività di tutela svolta dai funzionari, spiccano soprattutto quelli raccolti dai redattori della Carta Archeologica d'Italia (Gamurrini *et al.* 1972), e attualmente conosciuti solo in parte. E' doveroso un ringraziamento particolare al soprintendente prof. G. Schichilone e ai funzionari di zona C. Sforzini e G. Gazzetti.

E' stato effettuato il ricontrollo e la rilocalizzazione dei dati topografici raccolti; avendo constatato come a distanza di trent'anni dalle ultime esplorazioni sistematiche, il territorio fosse stato largamente compromesso e modificato, si è ritenuto necessario compiere l'autopsia dei materiali conservati presso i magazzini della Scuola Britannica di Roma, cosa che è stata possibile grazie alla cortesia della dott. A. Claridge. Il confronto dei dati ottenuti dalle nuove ricognizioni con i materiali d'archivio ha consentito da un lato di chiarire meglio la cronologia di frequentazione di alcuni siti, dall'altro di datare presenze ormai completamente obliterate. Si propongono alcuni esempi significativi del procedimento empirico attraverso il quale si è operata questa ridefinizione (Fig.1). Il grafico n. 1 ad esempio illustra la cronologia delle attestazioni dei materiali raccolti sul sito di una grande villa sulle pendici occidentali del Monte Soratte (Jones 1963: 127, n. 311). In questo caso le due cronologie comparate consentono di definire meglio l'arco cronologico di frequentazione del sito, che sembra ridursi consistentemente solo in età tardoantica. Per quanto riguarda il secondo esempio (Fig. 4.2), il ricontrollo della segnalazione del Jones (1962: 183, nn. 211, 212) ha reso possibile l'unificazione di due presenze ritenute distinte e la conferma del vuoto di attestazioni per il IV secolo d.C. La villa, di dimensioni ragguardevoli, è localizzata sul leggero pendio in località Monte Petrolo, ed ha restituito anche molti frammenti di marmi pregiati, tra i quali uno con un'iscrizione funeraria, molto frammentaria. Sulle pendici meridionali del Monte Soratte una presenza che sembrava di piccole dimensioni (Fig. 4.3 – Jones 1963: 127, n. 372), in seguito a profonde arature ha restituito materiali relativi ad un grande complesso di età romana con terme e strutture produttive, tra cui i blocchi in travertino dell'ara e delle *pilae* di un *trapetum* e frammenti di macine. L'analisi comparata dei materiali delle due raccolte effettuate sulla

403

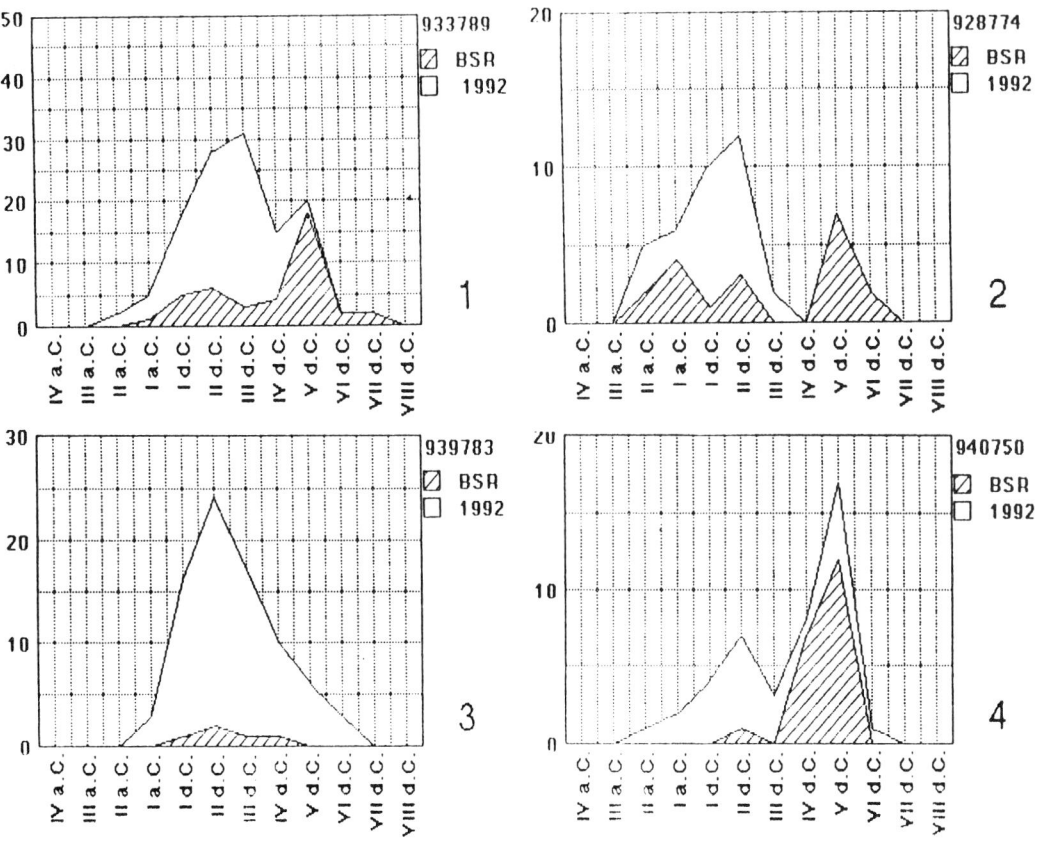

Fig. 1. Confronto dei dati raccolti da vecchie e da nuove ricognizioni.

grande villa in loc. M. Puledro (Fig. 1.4 – Jones 1962: 175, n. 177), impostata su di un importante asse viario di collegamento con la via Flaminia, consente l'estensione di ben cinque secoli dell'arco cronologico noto, che ben si adatta alla posizione privilegiata del sito.

La ricognizione intensiva del territorio, è ancora incompleta: sottolineiamo come la copertura di alcune zone anziché di altre non sia frutto di una scelta di campionatura ma sia assolutamente casuale; è possibile tuttavia fare alcune osservazioni relative all'evoluzione storica dell'area presa in esame, sulla base dei dati raccolti nelle ricognizioni sistematiche, con l'integrazione dei dati d'archivio.

Il territorio ha una morfologia piuttosto varia; dall'evidenza orografica del Monte Soratte, che domina tutta l'area, si passa ad una fascia di basse colline, a volte dal dolce andamento, a volte profondamente intaccate dai corsi d'acqua, che hanno creato vere e proprie forre nel banco tufaceo.

Si presentano le carte di fase con una scansione piuttosto ampia, partendo da una unica carta del periodo precedente alla conquista romana, per i secoli dal VII al V a.C., per poi seguire l'evoluzione dell'occupazione secolo per secolo, dato il maggiore dettaglio consentito dalla analisi ceramologica dei reperti di età romana.

Non vengono presentati i dati relativi all'occupazione preistorica e protostorica.

Uno dei risultati più interessanti è quello che riguarda l'occupazione del territorio nell'età precedente alla conquista romana (Fig. 2); anche se per questo periodo i dati provenienti dalle ricognizioni non sono utilizzabili molto spesso altro che per definire una generica presenza sul territorio, è importante portare alla conoscenza questa porzione di Ager Capenas, che fino ad ora è sempre stata considerata pressocché disabitata. Infatti le ricognizioni della Scuola Britannica di Roma edite dal Jones (1962; 1963) ormai trenta anni fa, indicavano un territorio completamente spopolato, privo di attestazioni rurali, cosa che contrasta singolarmente da un lato con la vivacità economica di Capena, almeno tra la fine dell'VIII e la metà del VI secolo a.C., dall'altro con la situazione delle campagne in questo stesso periodo nei territori circostanti l'agro capenate, come appunto l'agro falisco e veientano (Potter 1985: 90). Si può notare, in effetti, come la maggior parte delle attestazioni rinvenute fino ad ora, siano dovute probabilmente all'approfondirsi dei lavori agricoli che, se pure consentono di conoscere meglio la situazione del territorio diacronicamente, sono anche latori della distruzione irreversibile dei siti archeologici.

La maggior parte delle testimonianze di questo periodo sono affiorate insieme a presenze di età romana; i materiali ceramici purtroppo sono assai spesso poco qualificanti per esprimere altro che una generica pertinenza all'età arcaica. E' molto comune il rinvenimento di tegole e frammenti ceramici d'impasto, ma è assai difficile che siano riconducibili ad una forma determinata. Alcuni siti, che hanno restituito principalmente ceramica d'impasto, e che costituiscono dei punti chiave nell'interpretazione del territorio, verranno analizzati in seguito.

Una considerazione importante a margine della frequente associazione nel rinvenimento di materiale ceramico d'impasto e materiale di età romana, repubblicana e imperiale, è che questo è probabilmente indice di una discreta continuità di frequentazione dei siti rurali nel territorio. Infatti altrove si è notato come le ville romane, che a partire dal III sec. a.C. cominciano a costellare la campagna, non rioccupano le sedi degli insediamenti rurali arcaici. Il fenomeno è stato interpretato come una frattura netta nella dinamica degli insediamenti (Quilici Gigli 1985: 64-65). Quindi per il territorio in esame potrebbe essere testimoniata una notevole continuità di vita, almeno nei modi dell'occupazione del territorio.

La città di Capena si impianta, tra la fine del IX e l'VIII sec. a.C., sull'altura del 'Castellaccio' la quale si affaccia su un piccolo affluente del Tevere, il fosso di S. Martino (l'antico *Capenas* – Sil. It., *Pun.* XIII, 83, 6) come tutti i centri di questa zona che si pongono sempre a qualche chilometro di distanza dal Tevere. Per Capena forse ebbe una qualche importanza nella decisione della fondazione della città il 'Lago Vecchio' (Colonna 1986: 92), ormai prosciugato, intorno al quale tenderà a svilupparsi il centro abitato. Infatti l'altura del 'Castellaccio' ha una superficie abitabile di ca. 4,6 ettari (secondo i calcoli di Judson Hemphill 1981), area che risulta piuttosto piccola, rispetto ad altri centri vicini, come ad esempio Narce. L'estrema esiguità della superficie abitata e gli scarsi dati relativi al territorio fino ad ora conosciuti per l'età orientalizzante ed arcaica, non si accordano con l'importanza di Capena nell' ambito dell'Italia centrale. Già il Jones (1962: 132-134, fig. 2) aveva comunicato il rinvenimento di siti arcaici sulle colline di M. dell'Albuccio, M. Perazzeto, M. Aquila e M. Cornazzano (IGM 144 III NO Castelnuovo di Porto). Ricognizioni più recenti hanno confermato questi dati, ai quali si è potuto aggiungere il rinvenimento di altre concentrazioni di materiale ceramico attribuibili a questa fase della frequentazione di Capena. Così dal colle delle Saliere fino a M. Cornazzano si ottiene un'alternanza di piccoli nuclei di necropoli e di abitato, i quali sono molto probabilmente da identificare con parti della stessa città di Capena. Sull'altura del 'Castellaccio' quindi c'era solo una parte dell'abitato, più cospicua e ben difendibile, affiancata da una serie di altri insediamenti aperti, disposti ad anello intorno al 'Lago Vecchio'. Una disposizione simile non è sconosciuta nel mondo antico: un esempio analogo è costituito dalla città latina di *Gabii* (Guaitoli 1981) e permette di restituire maggiore consistenza ad una città chiamata tante volte in causa nelle vicende culturali dell'Italia centro meridionale (cfr. da ultimo Colonna 1988: 521-522; 1991). Sul 'Castellaccio' è stata effettuata una raccolta di superficie, impostata per aree (Fig.15). Quelle meno danneggiate dai lavori agricoli e che

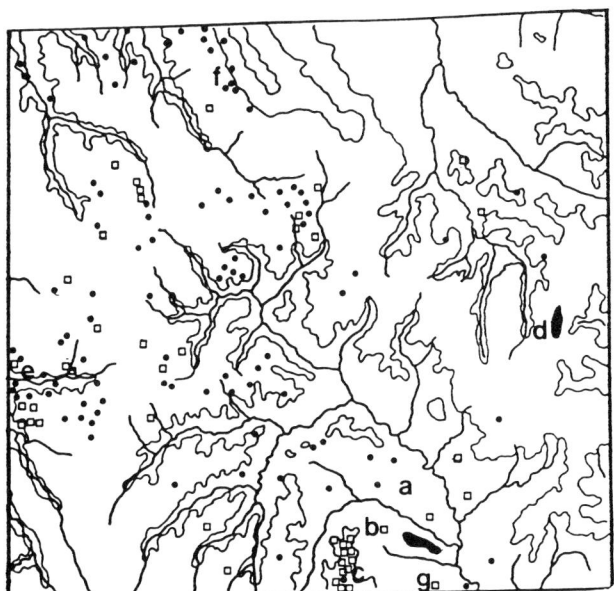

Fig. 2. Rinvenimenti e siti di epoca preromana.

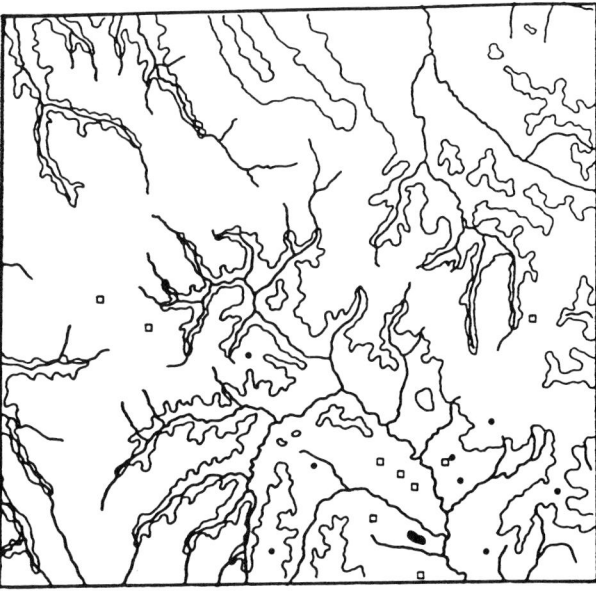

Fig. 3. Rinvenimenti e siti del IV secolo a.C.

probabilmente non furono mai scavate in passato, sono le zone contrassegnate con le lettere A e F; qui è stata rinvenuta la maggiore concentrazione di materiale ceramico compreso tra la tarda età del Ferro e l'età arcaica, anche se tutto il colle mostra tracce di una densa frequentazione per questo periodo, almeno fino al IV sec. a.C., quando si nota una marcata diminuzione dei materiali ceramici, anche se sempre diffusi su tutta l'area. Le aree A e F in seguito saranno interessate in misura molto minore da occupazioni di tipo abitativo. E' da segnalare inoltre che in queste zone l'erosione ha riportato in luce strutture in opera quadrata di tufo.

I nuclei più consistenti delle necropoli di Capena sono quelli delle Saliere (Fig.2.b), la più antica, riferibile alla fase di formazione della città nella tarda età del Ferro (Stefani 1958) e di S. Martino (Fig.2.a), la più estesa e l'unica geograficamente indipendente dalla città (Paribeni 1906). I numerosi nuclei, indagati agli inizi del secolo dallo Stefani (1958: 4, n. 1; Archivio Vecchio V.G., cart. 'Leprignano-Capena', senza inventario), disposti tra M. dell'Albuccio e M. Perazzeto identificano la necropoli 'Le Macchie' (Fig.2.c) e sono tuttora inediti. Tutte queste necropoli hanno la caratteristica comune di essere utilizzate continuativamente fino alla avanzata età romana, coerentemente a quanto si riscontra nell'agro falisco.

L'impressione che si ricava dall'analisi del territorio, per la parte indagata fino ad ora, è che esso si articoli attraverso un discreto insediamento sparso a carattere rurale. Si nota chiaramente come quasi sempre nelle vicinanze degli insediamenti minori (fattorie?) si rinvengano tombe isolate. L'articolarsi del popolamento in una fitta rete di fattorie sembra la caratteristica di questo territorio, come già notato, anche per l'agro veientano e falisco.

Unica necropoli isolata di una certa entità è quella di Monteverde (Fig.2.d), l'abitato relativo alla quale è ancora da identificare. Sulla base delle descrizioni dei pezzi rinvenuti in un intervento di recupero effettuato dalla Soprintendenza Archeologica per l'Etruria Meridionale (Brunetti Nardi 1981: 93-94) si può genericamente ricavare che le tombe siano state utilizzate dall'età arcaica fino almeno alla metà del III sec. a.C., secolo per il quale soccorrono i dati provenienti dall'analisi della ceramica a vernice nera (Schippa 1980).

Nell'analisi del territorio due gruppi di siti sembrano particolarmente significative: il complesso di presenze localizzato intorno a Torre Busson (Fig.2.e) relative sia ad abitato che a sepolcri, doveva fare riferimento al sito principale, che occupa il piccolo pianoro di forma triangolare, con pareti tufacee a picco ed accessibile solo da est, tramite una stretta sella. Intorno all'altura si aprono numerose tombe a camera scavate nel tufo. Già il Pasqui (Gamurrini et al. 1972: 312, n. 62) considerava questo sito come un villaggio preromano con la sua necropoli. La ricognizione sul posto, oltre ad aver evidenziato le altre presenze, ha potuto accertare l'esistenza di una cospicua quantità di ceramica di impasto, ascrivibile per i pochi frammenti riconoscibili al VII secolo a.C., dilavata dal sovrastante pianora nella valletta occidentale. Il complesso di siti di Torre Busson insieme a quello prospiciente in loc. Campo Maggiore, potrebbero avere funzione di controllo sulla via di fondovalle che conduceva da Capena a Narce.

L'altro gruppo di presenze significative si trovano sulle pendici occidentali del Monte Soratte (Fig.2.f); di queste soltanto due erano state precedentemente individuate (Jones 1963: 127, nn. 374-375). Forse a causa di lavori agricoli più profondi, sono apparse in superficie estese concentrazioni di tegole e materiale ceramico d'impasto, le quali costellano il pendio, seguendo la 'via dei Torreciani'. In questo caso non sono visibili le aree sepolcrali, riferite a questo denso nucleo di attestazioni. Non sono state rinvenute tracce di opere di fortificazione delle zone di abitato, ma è evidente che la loro posizione, per quanto aperta, è protetta dalla collocazione dominante la campagna circostante. La 'via dei Torreciani' è già stata riconosciuta come asse della viabilità di età arcaica (Quilici Gigli 1986: 75-76), che si dirige verso l'abitato di M. Ramiano e da qui al traghetto sul Tevere posto di fronte a Campo Rampone (IGM 144 IV NO, Stimigliano). Ad eccezione di questo nucleo di abitato, la maggior parte dei siti individuati per questa fase, sarà rioccupata, dopo la cesura del IV secolo a.C., da impianti rurali romani.

Il Monte Soratte, che si staglia a quota molto elevata sulle colline circostanti, risulta indicato come sede di un culto ad Apollo, anche di recente è stata resa nota una nuova iscrizione proveniente da lavori edilizi intorno alla chiesa di S. Silvestro sul Monte Soratte dedicata a Soranus Apollo (Di Stefano Manzella 1992). E' possibile che proprio dalla ipostasi etrusca del dio, Suri, derivi il toponimo attestato già dall'antichità (Colonna 1984-1985: 76). Al dio era sacra una grotta dai vapori pestilenziali, probabilmente una delle grotte dette i 'Meri'; nelle stesse grotte, il rinvenimento di un vaso a fiasca eneolitico sembra testimoniare già in questo periodo una frequentazione a scopo cultuale (Fugazzola Delpino 1990: 26).

Anche se la copertura del territorio non è stata ancora completata è tuttavia significativo come sia i dati editi che le recenti indagini registrino scarse presenze relative al IV sec. a.C. (Fig. 3); gli effetti della guerra tra Roma e Veio e la conseguente conquista del territorio capenate descritta da Livio sembrerebbero quindi ben visibili. Per quanto riguarda la città di Capena la raccolta di superficie effettuata sull'abitato rivela una forte contrazione della superficie frequentata; la capitolazione della città, che le fonti letterarie riportano come incruenta, ne deve comunque aver modificato l'assetto urbano.

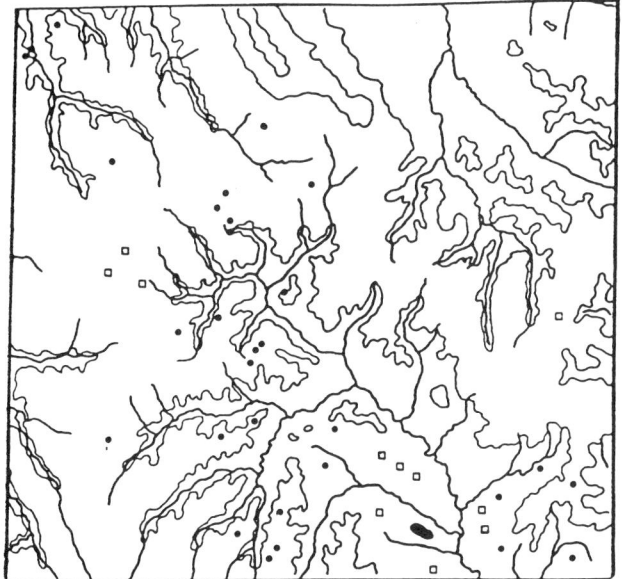

Fig. 4. Rinvenimenti e siti del III secolo a.C.

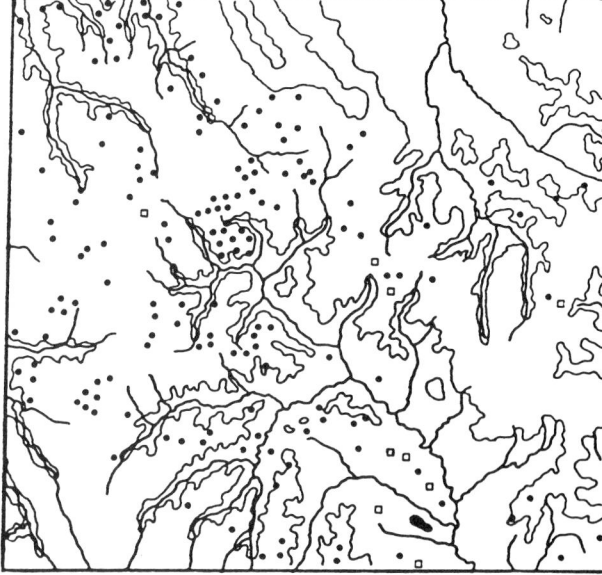

Fig. 5. Rinvenimenti e siti del II secolo a.C.

2. La situazione nel III secolo a.C. (Fig. 4) mostra una leggera ripresa; con lo sviluppo dell'economia della villa, l'occupazione del suolo, nel II secolo (Fig. 5) si fa più intensa: in questa zona sembrano convivere sia le ville di grandi dimensioni che le piccole proprietà. La maggior parte delle ville di grandi dimensioni che vengono realizzate in questo periodo hanno una frequentazione molto lunga: restituiscono infatti grandi quantità di materiale ceramico che permette di definire l'occupazione continuativa di questi siti fino alla fine delle importazioni della sigillata africana, come sembra accadere anche nell'area del Farfa Survey (Coccia & Barker 1989).

Anche se il numero totale delle ville testimoniate tra il II e il I secc. a.C. rimane pressoché invariato se non in leggero incremento, tuttavia si rileva, per il I secolo a.C. (Fig. 6), una sostanziale diminuzione di quantità nei materiali raccolti, forse effetto di una qualche ristrutturazione del territorio avvenuta nel corso della prima metà del secolo.

La notizia, riferita da Cicerone (*Ad fam.* 9. 17.2), dell'esistenza nel territorio di Capena di *ager publicus*, oggetto di misurazioni per ordine di Cesare si riferisce sicuramente a quella che sarà poco dopo la *Colonia Iulia Felix Lucus Feroniae* con la relativa centuriazione, e quindi probabilmente non ha riflessi sul territorio in oggetto, ma si riferisce ai campi della piana tiberina.

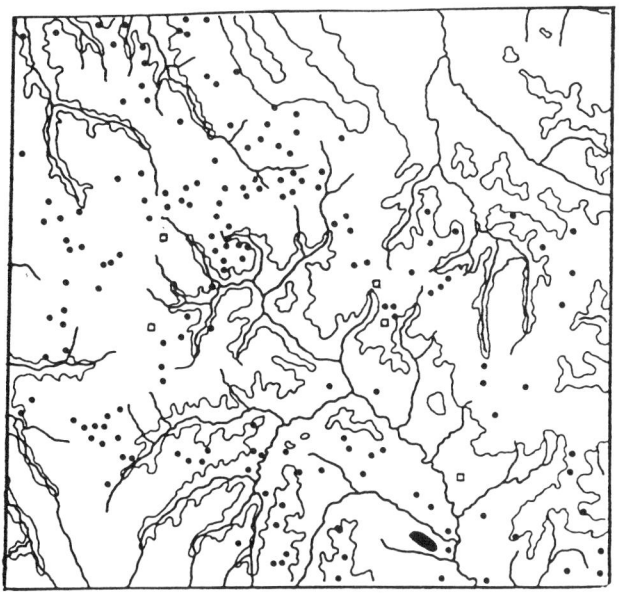

Fig. 6. Rinvenimenti e siti del I secolo a.C.

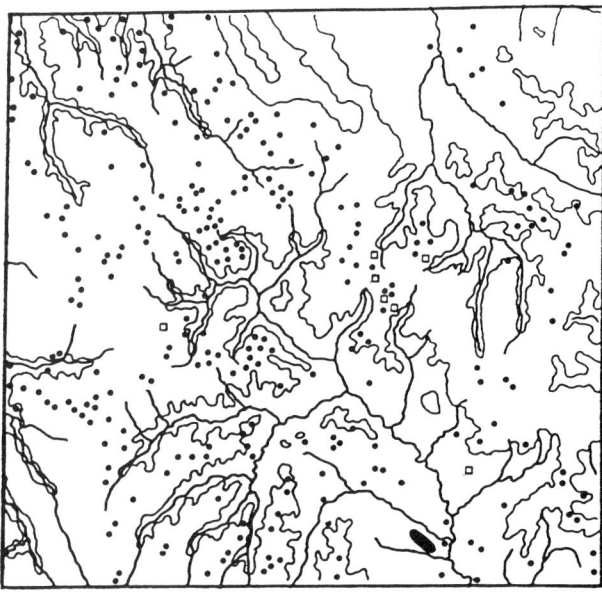

Fig. 7. Rinvenimenti e siti del I secolo d.C.

Nel I secolo d.C. (Fig.7) il territorio incrementa considerevolmente la sua occupazione; il sistema della villa schiavistica è quindi ben documentato, ma sembra più articolato, con presenza di fattorie dipendenti dai siti maggiori, indizio forse dell'impiego di coloni. L'uso del colonato in zona, infatti, ben concorda con le parole, riferite da Columella (*r. r.* I, 7, 3), di Lucio Volusio Saturnino, console nel 3 d.C. e patrono della vicina *Lucus Feroniae*, il quale suggerisce di preferire l'uso del colonato di origine locale (Manacorda 1982: 68).

Il quadro che emerge dalle evidenze registrate è molto vario: le ville con parte residenziale hanno restituito numerosi indizi di grande prosperità; sono molte le indicazioni della presenza di edifici termali e di uso di materiali edilizi di lusso, quali marmi pregiati, mosaici in pasta vitrea, vetri da finestra. Per quanto riguarda le parti produttive sono stati rinvenuti diversi torchi presumibilmente per produzione olearia: la presenza infatti di anfore olearie di importazione su tutto il territorio sembra piuttosto ridotta. Anche le fornaci per la produzione dei laterizi sono ben documentate, generalmente in prossimità dei fossi, vicino alle grandi ville.

E' interessante a questo proposito presentare i risultati dell'analisi dei materiali ceramici relativi ad un'estesa presenza, rinvenuta lungo il tracciato della via Flaminia antica: la grande quantità di frammenti raccolti (Fig.8.a) testimoniano una frequentazione continuativa piuttosto lunga, anche se di tono minore nell'avanzata età imperiale. Già dal II secolo d.C. il numero dei frammenti di ceramiche fini tende a diminuire (Fig.8.b), ma è ancora attestato; quello che risulta piuttosto inconsueto è la quasi completa assenza di terra sigillata africana attestata solo nella produzione A, in un sito che pure continua la sua frequentazione a discreto livello almeno fino al III secolo d.C.

Per quanto riguarda il II secolo (Fig.9), un indizio di crisi per alcune zone di Etruria è stato riscontrato già nei suoi primi decenni (Celuzza Regoli 1982); anche per l'agro capenate, come per il veientano, questo sembra accadere molto limitatamente; la storia del territorio capenate fin dall'età repubblicana è in effetti fortemente influenzata dalla vicinanza di Roma, collegata con agevoli vie di comunicazione quali la Flaminia e il Tevere. In età imperiale la mancanza si segnali di crisi nella qualità e nella quantità dei siti rurali ne testimonia il ruolo privilegiato di fornitori del mercato urbano. Contemporaneamente questo vi riversa prodotti di importazione assai rari nel testo d'Italia. A questo proposito è interessante notare come l'interscambio tramite il Tevere portasse nel territorio merci particolari in misura maggiore che in altre zone d'Etruria; la quantità di siti con presenza di sigillate orientali, ad esempio, è molto alta; 17 ville di dimensioni medio-grandi hanno restituito frammenti di questa classe ceramica di importazione.

La diminuzione di presenze nel III secolo si fa più sensibile (Fig. 10): ha tuttavia effetto per lo più sui siti di minore entità; come già detto la maggior parte delle grandi ville continua ad essere frequentata fino all'età tardoantica. La contrazione delle presenze continua, seppure in misura minore, anche nel IV secolo (Fig.11). A questa fase appartiene tuttavia la nota ed estesa catacomba dei Santi Martiri nei pressi di Rignano Flaminio (Fig.11.a; Fiocchi Nicolai 1988: 391); a questa, utilizzata tra la metà del IV e i primi decenni del V secolo, facevano certamente riferimento gli insediamenti rurali del territorio circostante, attirati dalla sepoltura privilegiata per la presenza delle deposizioni martiriali.

L'osservazione della carta di fase relativa al V secolo d.C. (Fig. 12) mostra chiaramente come numerose siano le testimonianze appartenenti a questa fase. E' da sottolineare tuttavia come molte di queste attestazioni siano da riferire ai materiali degli strati di abbandono, che per primi vengono intaccati dai lavori agricoli. E' comunque interessante osservare come le distruzioni avvenute lungo l'asse della via Flaminia, che come

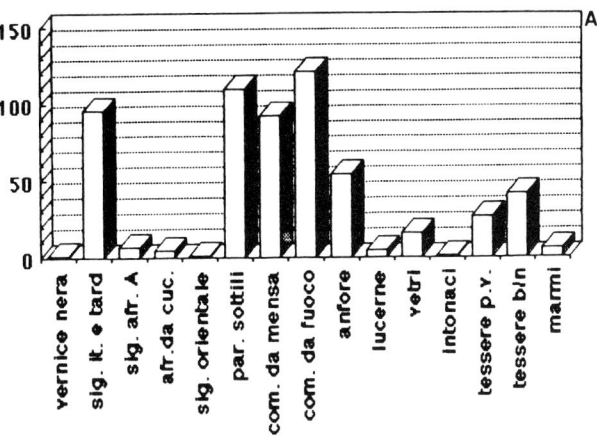

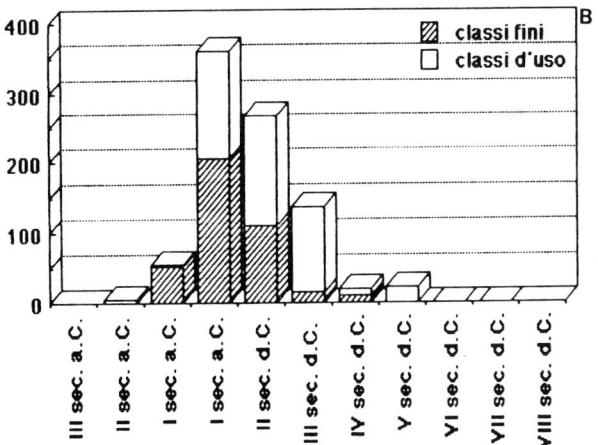

Fig. 8. L'analisi dei materiali ceramici a un sito lungo la via Flaminia.

Fig. 9. Rinvenimenti e siti del II secolo d.C.

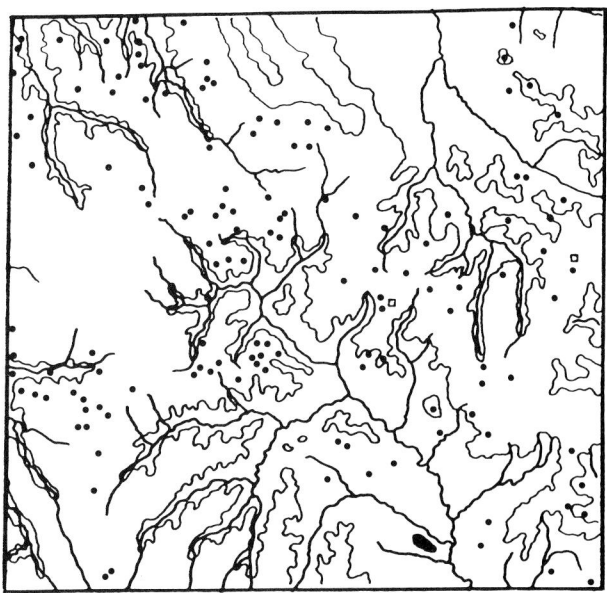

Fig. 10. Rinvenimenti e siti del III secolo d.C.

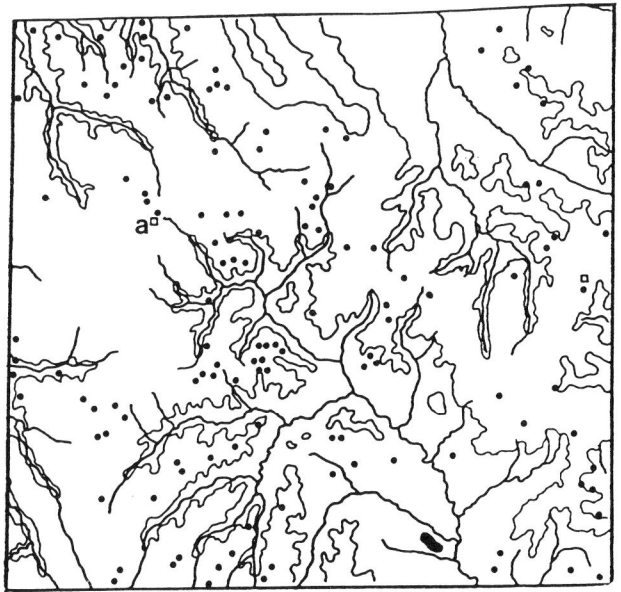

Fig. 11. Rinvenimenti e siti del IV secolo d.C.

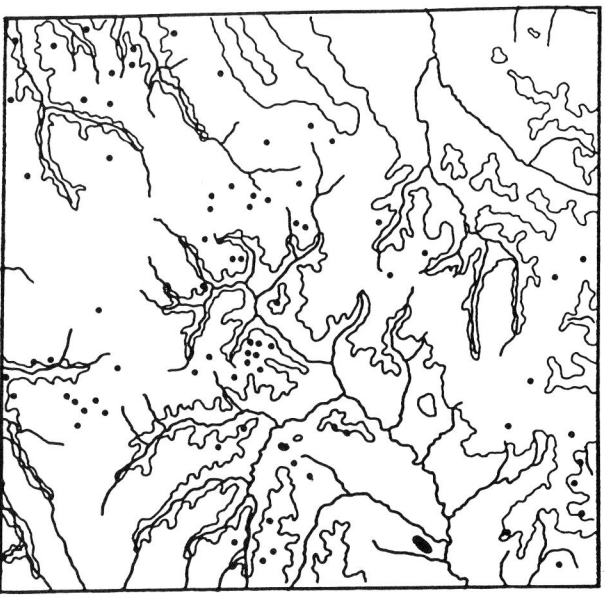

Fig. 12. Rinvenimenti e siti del V secolo d.C.

riferisce lo storico Jordanes (*Getica*, XXX) cominciano nel 410 con il passaggio dei Visigoti, non sembrano lasciare effetti duraturi sul territorio, dato che molti di questi siti hanno restituito materiali databili nell'arco di tutto il V secolo; alcuni insediamenti aperti nascono addirittura in questa fase. Il processo di abbandono che comunque comincia a definirsi marcatamente è ben evidente nella carta di fase dei due secoli successivi (Fig. 13). Nonostante ciò sono relativamente numerosi i siti che hanno restituito forme tarde di terra sigillata chiara D e ceramica di uso comune tardoantica; questo porterebbe a ridimensionare gli effetti sia delle guerre greco-gotiche che degli scontri del 592-593 tra Longobardi e Bizantini.

La vivacità economica di questo territorio, dovuta come già detto alla favorevole posizione tra il Tevere e la via Flaminia, già sottolineata per le età precedenti, è ben testimoniata nell'alto e nel basso medioevo (Fig. 14). E' quindi assai probabile che quest'area sia coinvolta nella ristrutturazione agraria operata dal papato che ha come manifestazione più nota la realizzazione delle *domuscultae*, una delle quali, quella di *Capracorum*, si trova a poca distanza dal limite occidentale dell'area esaminata (Marazzi 1991). Si nota il discreto numero di siti aperti che dovevano essere collegati con questa ristrutturazione; la maggior parte di questi, tra l'altro, ha restituito frammenti di Forum Ware. Un sito particolarmente significativo a questo proposito, in quanto 'aperto' e

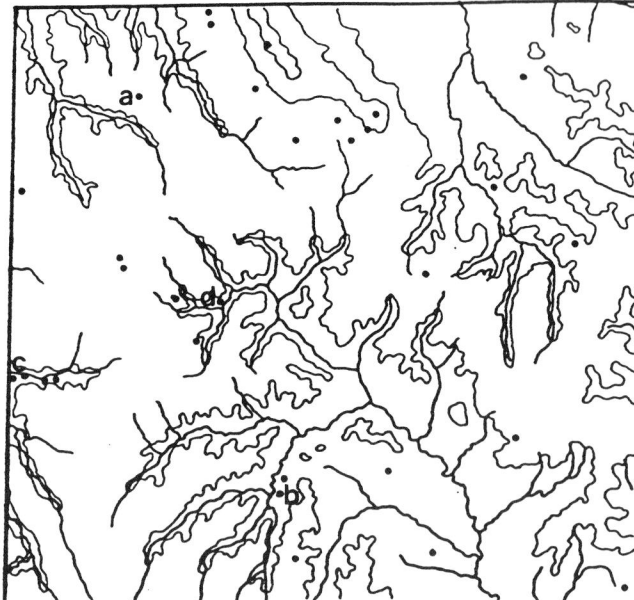

Fig. 13. Rinvenimenti e siti dei VI-VII secoli d.C.

Fig. 14. Rinvenimenti e siti de epoca medievale.

situato a poche centinaia di metri dalla spartacque occidentale della via Flaminia ha restituito frammenti di materiale ceramico che dimostrano la sua frequentazione in età tardoantica e altomedievale. I siti aperti sono spesso in relazione con siti fortificati che, con il X e XI secolo si trasformano in veri e propri castelli. E' interessante soffermarsi su due esempi di incastellamento piuttosto evidenti e ben noti dalle fonti documentarie medievali, di uno dei quali si propone la localizzazione. Il castello di Orciano (Fig. 14.b), il cui ricordo resta ben evidente nella toponamastica circostante il sito, è ben localizzabile sulla sommità di q. 187 del fosso di Montelarco, posto a controllo dell'asse viario di Vallelunga. I ruderi localizzati sulla castellina tufacea che sovrasta la strada non sono gli unici resti dell'abitato legato al *castrum*, noto già dalle fonti nel X secolo come *fundus*. Immediatamente a monte, infatti, sui resti di una grande villa romana con strutture in opera laterizia, insistono, affioranti sul terreno, strutture più tarde. Tra i materiali raccolti sono stati rinvenuti frammenti di Forum Ware e ceramica depurata acroma medievale. E' d'altra parte assai probabile che il castello non si esaurisse con la ben munita rocca, ma occupasse anche il vicino pianoro, considerata l'importanza del centro che sembra avesse cinque chiese nell'XI secolo (Conti 1980).

Una simile funzione di controllo di un asse viario di fondovalle aveva anche il castello di Morolo, noto già dal 996, identificato nell'attuale toponimo di Torre Busson e sito fortificato già dall'età arcaica (Fig.14.c). Questo è situato su un pianoretto di forma triangolare con pareti tufacee a picco, accessibile solo da est tramite una stretta sella. Dell'intero complesso sono attualmente visibili l'alta torre in blocchi squadrati, databile tra la fine del 1100 e il 1200, posta a difesa del lato più facilmente accessibile. Strutture relative ad un palazzotto rinascimentale che inglobò l'intero complesso sono visibili per un'altezza di due piani. Sicuramente collegata con questo complesso è una fornace di laterizi rinvenuta nella vallata sottostante. Tralasciando un esame più dettagliato del sito, in quanto gia indagato negli anni 60 dall'Istituto Danese di Roma (Stiesdal 1962), la recente raccolta dei materiali di superficie mostra una frequentazione ininterrotta dal VII secolo avanti Cristo all'età tardoantica e al medioevo; sono stati rinvenuti infatti frammenti di terra sigillata chiara D, forme di rozza terracotta tardoantica, ceramica a vetrina pesante e sparsa e ceramica acroma depurata. La presenza nelle immediate vicinanze di una grande villa frequentata almeno fino al V secolo è evidente esempio di un graduale spostamento dell'occupazione verso l'altura maggiormente difendibile. Questi abitati hanno stretti legami con gli importanti centri benedettini quali il monastero di S. Silvestro sul Monte Soratte e il monastero di Sant'Andrea in Flumine, i quali sono in realtà i veri punti focali a cui fa riferimento tutta la storia dell'occupazione del territorio collinense in questo periodo. Altri siti notevoli dei quali è necessario fare menzione, sono la chiesa di Sant'Abbondio presso Rignano, sorta su un tempio pagano (Gamurrini *et al.* 1972: 326), e il *Castrum Civitucolae*, sull'altura dell'antica città di Capena, che in quanto centro urbano a continuità di vita richiede un esame più dettagliato.

A conclusione di questo excursus si ritiene interessante presentare i dati che si evincono dalla raccolta di materiali di superficie effettuata per aree sull'altura di Capena, che indica come l'occupazione si differenzi nell'arco dei secoli (Fig. 15). I materiali dell'età del Ferro sono diffusi su gran parte del pianoro, con una maggiore concentrazione nell'area occidentale, che sembra essere

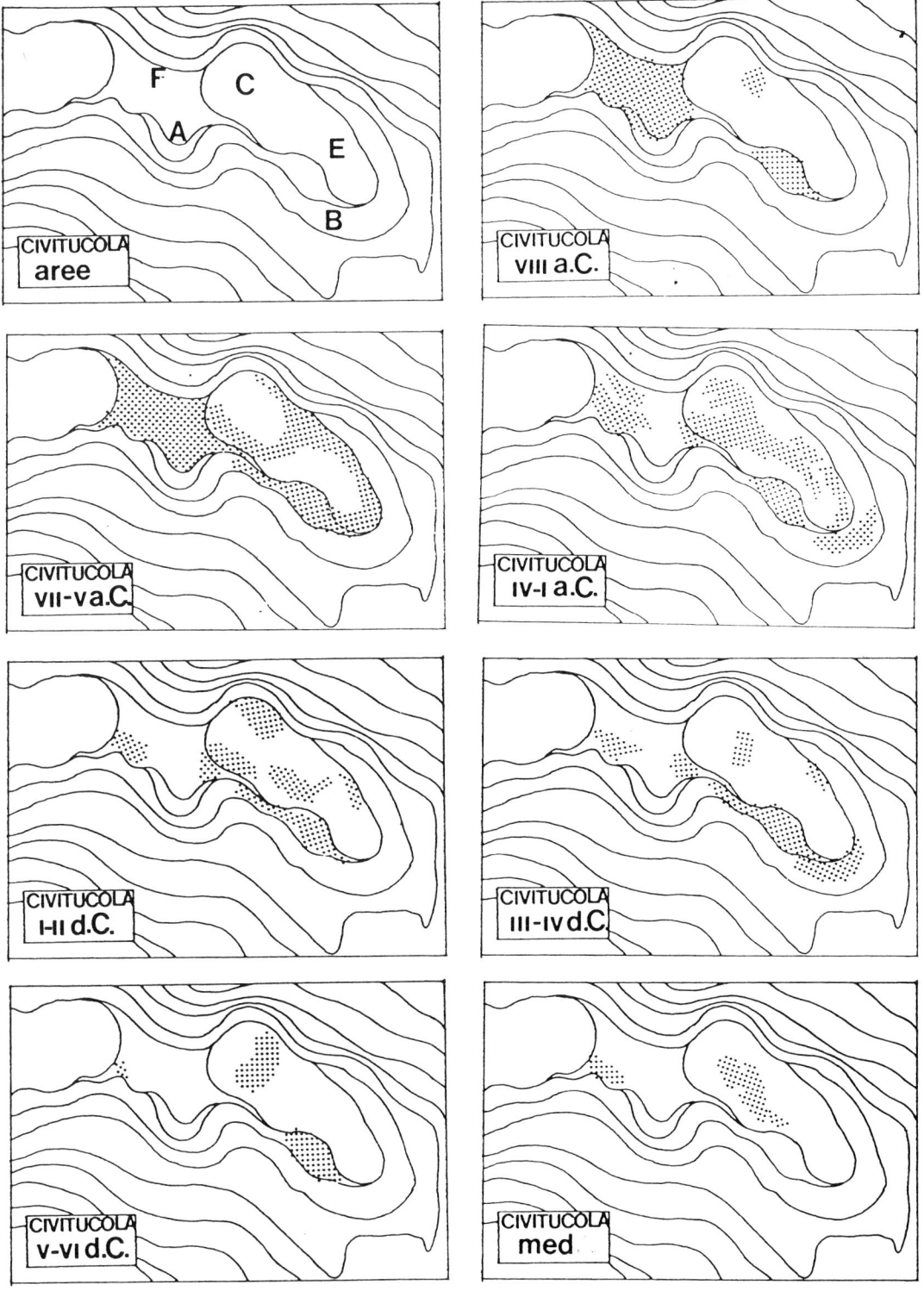

Fig. 15. La sequenza insediativa all'altura di Civitucola, Capena

stata interessata in misura molto minore da occupazioni abitative nel periodo successivo alla conquista romana. La maggiore diffusione dei materiali, come già notato, è comunque ascrivibile al VI secolo avanti Cristo, mentre nel V secolo i materiali seppure in misura ridotta sono ancora diffusi su tutta l'altura. La conquista romana della città del 395 è rispecchiata da una drastica riduzione delle attestazioni in tutta l'area; anche il III secolo sembra essere scarsamente documentato, mentre una ripresa si può porre a partire dal II secolo. A questa fase è probabilmente da riferire una risistemazione del centro urbano, come sembra testimoniare il rudere del Castellaccio, struttura probabilmente pubblica con paramento in opera incerta. La minore quantità di materiali di I secolo avanti Cristo è un fenomeno che, come già detto, interessa anche molti insediamenti nel territorio. Un quadro interessante nell'esame della fase di età repubblicana di Capena si può evincere dall'esame dei frammenti di ceramica a vernice nera provenienti dalla raccolta (a cura dell'amico E. A. Stanco al quale vanno i nostri ringraziamenti). Questi, per la fascia cronologica compresa tra il IV ed il III secolo a.C. sono poco rappresentati ed attribuibili quasi esclusivamente ad officine locali, falische e lucoferoniensi, con una modesta importazione da Roma. Ad una probabile fornace attiva nel III secolo sono da riferire anche frammenti di produzione locale e numerosi anelli distanziatori. Nel II e I secolo si pongono la maggior parte dei materiali, sia di produzione locale e di area tiberina, che di importazione: sono ben rappresentate le produzioni di tipo B-oide campane, quelle siciliane in campana C e quelle napoletane in campana A, segno della rinnovata capacità economica del territorio.

Per i secoli dal I al IV d.C. i materiali ceramici diminuiscono progressivamente, anche se ai primi tre secoli dell'età imperiale sono riferibili le numerose iscrizioni onorarie rinvenute in passato sull'altura. Per quanto riguarda l'arco cronologico compreso tra il V secolo e il medioevo la raccolta di superficie testimonia una continuità di occupazione dell'altura anche se ristretta principalmente alla sommità; sono stati rinvenuti infatti frammenti di Forum Ware, databili tra la fine del IX e l'XI secolo (Camilli & Vitali Rosati c.s.) e di ceramiche depurate acrome. La prima menzione di Capena, nei documenti medievali, risale al 1081, mentre risulta abitato per l'ultima volta nel 1236.

Bibliografia

Brunetti Nardi, G. 1981. *Repertorio degli scavi e delle scoperte archeologiche nell'Etruria Meridionale III (1971-1975)*, Roma.

Camilli, A. & Vitali Rosati, B. c.s. 'La ceramica a vetrina pesante da ricognizione di superficie nel territorio capenate', *Ceramiche di età medievale e moderna a Roma e nel Lazio*, I° Convegno di Studi (Roma, marzo 1993).

Celuzza, M.G. & Regoli, E. 1982. 'La Valle d'Oro nel territorio di Cosa', *Dialoghi di Archeologia*, 4.1, 31–62.

Coccia, S. & Barker, G. 1989. 'La ricognizione archeologica e la sua documentazione: recenti esperienze di ricerca della British School at Rome', *La Cartografia Archeologica. Problemi e prospettive, Atti del Convegno Internazionale* (Pisa, 21–22 marzo 1988), Pisa, 39–52.

Colonna, G. 1984-85. 'Novità sui culti di Pyrgi', *Rendiconti della Pontificia Accademia di Archeologia*, LVII, 57–88.

Colonna, G. 1986. 'Il Tevere e gli Etruschi', Il Tevere e le altre vie d'acqua del Lazio antico, *Archeologia Laziale*, VII, 90–97.

Colonna, G. 1988. 'I Latini e gli altri popoli del Lazio', in *Italia omnium terrarum alumna* (a cura di G. Pugliese Caratelli), Milano.

Colonna, G. 1991. 'Le civiltà anelleniche', *Storia della Campania I, L'evo antico* (a cura di G. Pugliese Caratelli), Napoli, 25–68.

Conti, S. 1980. *Sedi umane abbandonate nel patrimonio di S. Pietro*, Firenze.

Di Stefano Manzella, I. 1992. 'Nuova dedica a Soranus Apollo e altre iscrizioni dal Soratte', *Melanges de l'École Française de Rome*, 104, 1, 159–167.

Fiocchi Nicolai, V. 1988. *I cimiteri paleocristiani del Lazio, I. Etruria Meridionale*, Città del Vaticano.

Fugazzola Delpino, M.A. 1990. 'Cenni introduttivi sul Neolitico del territorio falisco', in *La Civiltà dei Falisci, Atti del XV Convegno di Studi Etrusco e Italici*, (Civita Castellana, 28–30 maggio 1987), Firenze, 23–52.

Gamurrini, G., Cozza, A., Pasqui, A. & Mengarelli, R. 1972. *Carta Archeologica d'Italia (1881-1887). Materiali per l'Etruria e la Sabina (Forma Italiae S. II. 1)*, Firenze.

Guaitoli, G. 1981. 'Gabii: osservazioni sulle fasi di sviluppo dell'abitato', *Quaderni dell'Istituto Topografia antica dell'Università di Roma* IX, 23–54.

Jones, G.D.B. 1962. 'Capena and the Ager Capenas', *Papers of the British School at Rome*, 30, 116–209.

Jones, G.D.B. 1963. 'Capena and the Ager Capenas II', *Papers of the British School at Rome*, 31, 100–158.

Judson Hemphill, 1981. 'Sizes of settlement on Southern Etruria, 6th-5th centuries B.C.', *Studi Etruschi*, XLIX, 193–202.

Manacorda, D. 1982. 'Il frantoio della villa dei Volusii a Lucus Feroniae', in *I Volusii Saturnini. Una famiglia romana della prima età imperiale* (Archeologia: materiali e problemi VI), 55–75.

Marazzi, F. 1991. 'Il conflitto fra Leone III Isaurico e il papato fra il 725 e il 733, e il 'definitivo' inizio del medioevo a Roma: un'ipotesi in discussione', *Papers of the British School at Rome*, 59, 231–257.

Paribeni, R. 1906. 'Necropoli dell'Agro Capenate', *Monumenti Antichi dei Lincei*, XVI, 277–490.

Potter, T.W. 1985. *Storia del Paesaggio dell'Etruria Meridionale*, Roma.

Quilici Gigli, S. 1985. 'Considerazioni sul popolamento della campagna romana dall'età mediorepubblicana all'inizio di quella imperiale', *Bollettino dell'Unione Storia e Arte*, LXXVIII, 3–4, luglio-dicembre 1985, 63 ss.

Quilici Gigli, G. 1986. 'Scali e traghetti sul Tevere in epoca arcaica', in *Il Tevere e le altre vie d'acqua del Lazio antico, Archeologia Laziale*, VII, 71–89.

Schippa, F. 1980. *Officine ceramiche falische*, Bari.

Stefani, E. 1958. 'Capena, scoperte archeologiche nell'agro capenate. Ricerche archeologiche nella contrada "Le Saliere"', *Monumenti Antichi dei Lincei*, XLIV, 191–196.

Stiesdal, H. 1962. 'Three deserted medieval villages in the Roman Campagna', *Analecta Romana Istituti Danici*, II, 63–100.

43

Notizie Preliminari sulle Ricognizioni a Capena e nel Territorio

Rita Turchetti, con Fabio Bartolini

(Centro Regionale per la Documentazione dei Beni Culturali e Ambientali del Lazio)

Sommario: *Il Centro Regionale per la Documentazione dei Beni Culturali ed Ambientali della Regione Lazio ha condotto ricognizioni sistematiche nel territorio del Comune di Capena, finalizzate alla catalogazione delle presenze archeologiche conservate. Si presentano in questa sede i risultati preliminari delle ricerche effettuate nella città antica, con particolare riguardo al cosiddetto Castellaccio, e nel territorio circostante la depressione del 'Lago Vecchio'.*

Secondo quanto previsto dal Piano di Censimento e Catalogazione dei Beni Culturali ed Ambientali della Regione Lazio (delibera Consiglio Regionale 642 del 1979) gli archeologi del Centro Regionale di Documentazione hanno condotto, dopo una ricerca bibliografica e d'archivio, ricognizioni sistematiche nel Comune di Capena (1986-90), effettuate in differenti condizioni climatiche ed agricole del terreno. Le indagini hanno consentito di redigere una carta archeologica, sulla più valida base allora disponibile (Aereofotogrammetrico della Soc. Aerofoto consult. 1987, scala 1:10000, con dettagli a scala 1:5000 per l'area della città antica), in cui le presenze sono state indicate secondo estensione e densità reali. Le ricognizioni, condotte insieme alle colleghe F. Fei, M.P. Moscetta ed A. Toro, hanno interessato tutto il territorio comunale con la sola esclusione delle zone boscate, di quelle urbanizzate, della necropoli di S.Martino (comune di Civitella San Paolo) e dell'area di *Lucus Feroniae*, oggetto di studi da parte della Soprintendenza Archeologica per l'Etruria Meridionale (con la quale si è collaborato durante la ricerca).

Tale scelta metodologica è motivata da due considerazioni, la prima è la consapevolezza della parzialità dei dati forniti dalla ricognizione, seppure accurata, rispetto a quanto realmente esistente sul territorio. La seconda è legata alla necessità di avere il maggior numero di indicazioni possibili, poichè l'indagine non è finalizzate solo alla tutela e alla valorizzazione del patrimonio, ma anche alla programmazione regionale (Piano Regolatore, Piani Territoriali Paesistici, progetti stradali, etc.). Bisogna inoltre precisare che tale ricerca si è potuta giovare dell'apporto di altri settori disciplinari, secondo una peculiarità, per alcuni versi unica, di questa struttura regionale. In particolare si è collaborato con l'architetto F. Bartolini per il rilievo e lo studio del cosiddetto Castellaccio e con i colleghi botanici per un'intervento sul medesimo monumento e più in generale per il censimento delle emergenze vegetazionali presenti nella città antica e nelle necropoli, al fine di poter suggerire indicazioni (la zona è di proprietà dell'Università Agraria, vincolata in base alla legge 1089) non solo per la conservazione delle presenze archeologiche ma anche dell'ambiente. In questa sede si presentano, seppure a livello preliminare, alcuni risultati della ricerca riguardanti l'area urbana con particolare riguardo al cosiddetto Castellaccio, ed il territorio circostante la depressione nota come 'Lago Vecchio' (fig. 1).

Area Urbana (r.t.)

Oggetto di una ricognizione particolare è stata l'area occupata dall'abitato capenate, situata tra il fosso di Vallelunga a nord ed il Lago Vecchio ed il suo emissario a sud (fig. 1). Dalla confluenza dei due nasce il fosso di S.Martino (poi Gramiccia), identificato con l'antico *Capenas* ricordato da Silio Italico (13, 83, 6); proprio nella ricchezza delle acque va ricercato uno dei motivi generatori della formazione della città, a cui si deve aggiungere la nota fertilità del terreno (Cic., *Flacc.*, 71).

Le ricerche, rese più difficili dalla scarsa visibilità offerta dal terreno, per lo più incolto e destinato a pascolo, sono state condotte soprattutto nella parte orientale ed in quella centrale del pianoro, ove in occasione di fatti stagionali e di rarissime arature è stato

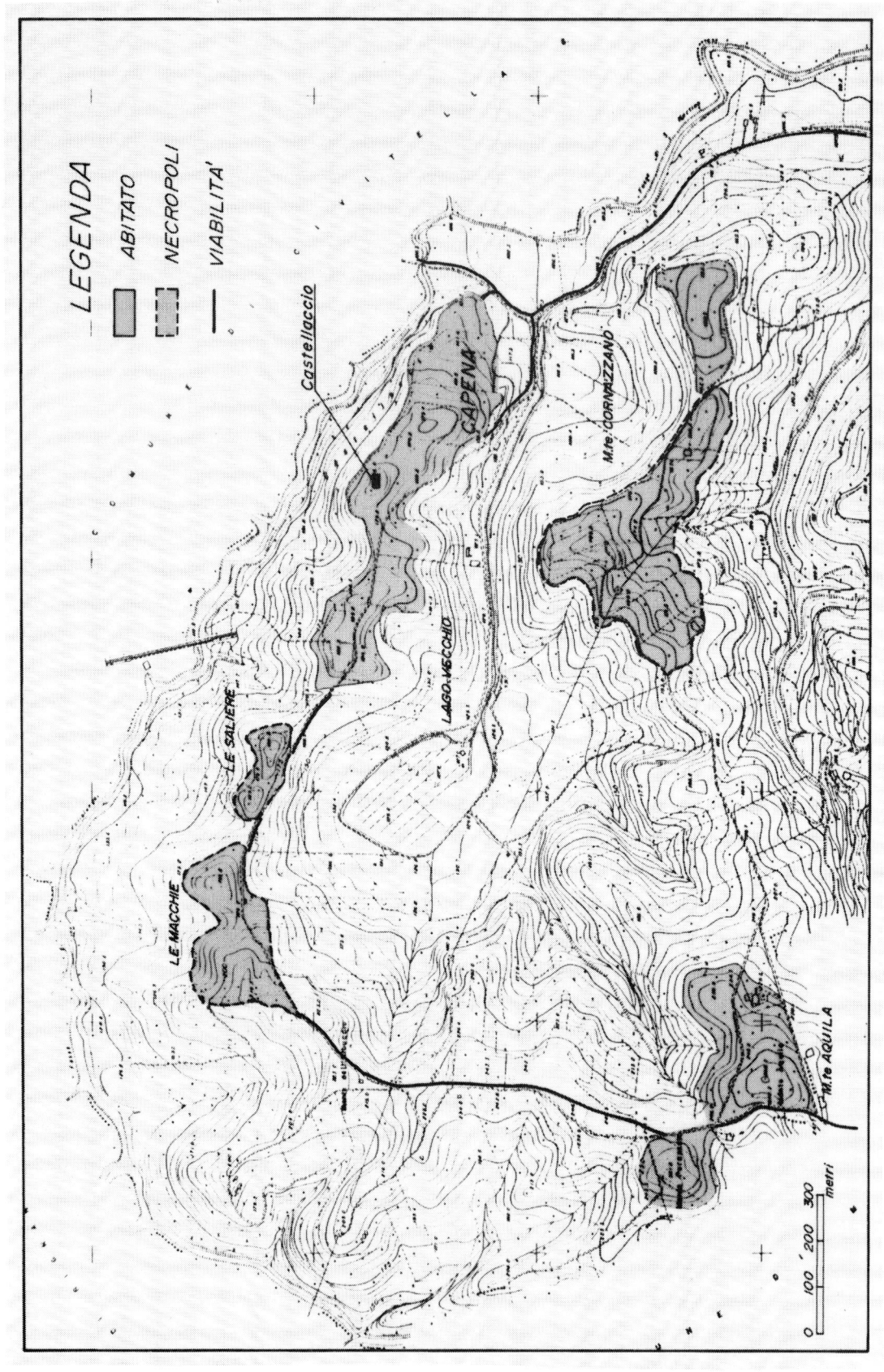

Fig. 1. *Carta archeologica.*

possibile effettuare accurate ricognizioni. Rispetto ai risultati degli studi precedenti (in particolare Jones 1962) è possibile evidenziare quanto segue: sulla sommità del colle del c.d. Castellaccio ed a ovest di questo sono stati rinvenuti materiali ceramici che testimoniano la fase più antica di occupazione del sito, databile con sicurezza a partire dall'età del Ferro. Tale datazione non deve essere considerata assoluta, poiché è possibile che esistano fasi di frequentazione più antiche, elemento questo che verrà o meno confermato dallo studio dei reperti in corso.

Per quanto riguarda i periodi orientalizzante ed arcaico i rinvenimenti di superficie documentano un'occupazione a carattere diffuso anche nella parte orientale del pianoro, definendo il perimetro della città in quello indicato dal circuito murario. Scavi clandestini ad est del c.d. Castellaccio hanno messo in luce pozzi e cunicoli (cfr. Ashby 1924: 162 n.174; Conti 1932: 28), facenti parte del sistema di approvvigionamento idrico e di smaltimento delle acque della città. Alcuni di questi sono riferibili con probabilità proprio alla fase arcaica, come sembrano testimoniare i materiali recuperati (frammenti ceramici abbandonati dai clandestini), che ne costituivano il riempimento.

A questa stessa fase sono da riferire gli abitati gravitanti sul bacino lacustre, e dislocati su monte Aquila e su monte Cornazzano (fig.1). In particolare quello su monte Aquila sembra più esteso di quanto indicato in passato (Jones 1962: 133–134); sul versante settentrionale rimane parte di un muro in opera quadrata di tufo, visibile per circa m. 4, mentre in un taglio relativo ad una strada moderna (a sud) è visibile parte di una fornace. Probabilmente sono da attribuire a questo stesso abitato i resti di abitazioni arcaiche, la fornace con relativa cisterna, un imponente muro in opera quadrata di tufo ed un tratto di strada basolata scavati dalla Soprintendenza Archeologica per l'Etruria Meridionale su monte Perazzeto (comune di Morlupo, probabilmente gli stessi visti da Ashby 1924: 155; Gazzetti 1992: 63–64). Nell'area sono anche tombe a camera, scavate in epoche diverse.

Questo abitato insieme a quello di Monte Cornazzano, di cui attualmente sono visibili solo pochi materiali ceramici, assumono particolare significato se posti in relazione con la limitata estensione di Capena, più volte rilevata (Judson & Hemphill 1981: 193 ss.); la loro occupazione sembra durare sino al I sec. a.C.

Alcune precisazioni riguardanti l'area urbana sono possibili anche per l'epoca romana. I dati di superficie sembrano indicare per la tarda età repubblicana e la prima età imperiale una concentrazione dell'abitato, da connettere probabilmente ad una più intensa occupazione del territorio, come testimoniano i risultati delle ricognizioni effettuate (per i problemi connessi alle assegnazioni di terre ai veterani cfr. Muzzioli 1985: 53–58). La situazione per la piena epoca imperiale sembra variare, data la quantità di materiali ceramici a cui si debbono aggiungere i reperti lapidei provenienti dagli scavi passati. A questa fase si può riferire anche un ambiente absidato in laterizio, con tracce di rivestimento in marmo, scavato e reinterrato dai clandestini.

L'epoca tardo antica e medioevale è documentata da strutture quali quelle scoperte negli scavi degli anni '30 (Conti 1932: 31–33), in parte riportate alla luce recentemente e da ceramica (in particolare quella c.d. a vetrina pesante).

FORTIFICAZIONI (R.T.)

E' stato verificato quanto ancora conservato delle mura di difesa, in opera quadrata di tufo (dim. med. dei blocchi m .1,30×0,42×0,50), segnalate in precedenza (Dennis 1848: 132; Ashby 1924: 160–163; Jones 1962: 134 ss). Attualmente sono visibili due tratti nella zona settentrionale (uno dei quali recentemente divelto), alcuni blocchi fuori posto sul versante meridionale ed un tratto sul versante sud-est, tagliato da una cava di caolino. Proprio questo taglio evidenzia in sezione la tecnica costruttiva di questo tratto di fortificazioni, con blocchi disposti di testa e di taglio. Porte erano sicuramente ad ovest (Ashby 1924: 160; Conti 1932: 26; Sommella Mura 1969: 24) a sud e ad est (Jones 1962: 139–40). Quanto rilevato sembra ascrivibile ad un unico sistema difensivo attribuibile alla fase precedente la conquista romana (VI-V sec.a.C.). Tagli artificiali, rilevati sul lato orientale del pianoro, e su parte del pendio settentrionale, oggi coperto da fitta macchia, ma ancora caratterizzato da un andamento quasi verticale, potrebbero essere forse riferiti ad un sistema difensivo più antico.

VIABILITÀ (R.T.)

Per quanto riguarda la viabilità interna questa è caratterizzata da un asse est-ovest, parallelo all'andamento del pianoro; tale asse è ricalcato in buona parte dall'attuale via campestre. Una via costeggiava il lato sud ed una il lato nord della parte orientale (area del c.d. foro), giungendo in prossimità del c.d. Castellaccio. La prima, portata alla luce durante gli scavi degli anni '30 (Conti 1932: 26) presenta basoli di calcare e margini in blocchi di tufo. La seconda, ancora ben visibile in recenti foto aeree, è stata in parte divelta da lavori agricoli per l'impianto di un vigneto, basoli sono ancora conservati ai margini del campo. Dalla porta sud, oltrepassato il fosso di Gramiccia una strada conduceva in direzione sud-est verso *Lucus Feroniae*, mentre in direzione nord-est si raggiungeva Fiano (Jones 1962: 201 ss.). Sul lato opposto, dalla porta occidentale, usciva una via di collegamento con la Flaminia e con Veio.

IL CASTELLACCIO (R.T., F.B.)

L'unica emergenza di rilievo conservata nella città è il

cosiddetto Castellaccio, ovvero un edificio di epoca romana, situato in posizione dominante (m. 186 slm.) all'interno dell'area urbana. La sua struttura è sempre stata visibile nei secoli scorsi ed ha subito nel tempo riusi ed utilizzi impropri, sino all'abbandono ed al degrado attuali. A tutt'oggi l'interpretazione della sua funzione non è chiara e varie sono state le ipotesi formulate: dalla 'basilica dei Capenati' (Galletti 1756: 3 ss; Guattani 1828: 29-33, fig.1), ad una torre (Gell 1846: 148-151), un sepolcro (Nibby 1848: 375-381), una villa romana (Dennis 1848: 124-135), un edificio medioevale (Tomassetti 1979: 378-385), una conserva d'acqua (Ashby 1924: 161-162, fig.2) ed infine un edificio pubblico (Jones 1962: 137 ss). Proprio questa difficoltà interpretativa, unita alla mancanza di un rilievo dettagliato delle strutture visibili, peraltro molto deteriorate, ha motivato questo approfondimento della ricerca.

Del monumento, costruito in opera incerta con scapoli piuttosto regolari di calcare locale, sono visibili tre lati: nord, ovest e sud. Il lato ovest è quello più conservato, all'esterno il livello attuale del terreno consente una migliore lettura rispetto agli altri due lati che risultano in parte interrati. In particolare quello nord è stato portato alla luce solo di recente (inverno 1987), a seguito di scavi clandestini, condotti con l'ausilio di mezzi meccanici, che hanno lasciato tracce inconfondibili sulla parete scoperta (fig. 5).

La pianta dell'edificio (m. 14,60 di largh. max. e m. 15,30 di lungh. max.) risulta articolata all'interno in due ambienti di dimensioni diverse (fig. 2). Rispetto a quanto noto da studi e da documentazione precedenti, si è riscontrato il crollo di buona parte del muro interno che, sino agli anni '40, era conservato per una lunghezza di circa m. 10,90 (Tale lunghezza è ricavata da appunti inediti dello Ashby conservati nell'Archivio della British School at Rome).

All'esterno, sui lati sud ed ovest è ancora visibile il basamento dell'edificio, emergente dal livello attuale del terreno per circa m. 2,50 di altezza sul lato occidentale e per circa m. 0,50 (in media) su quello meridionale. Superiormente sono inseriti blocchi di

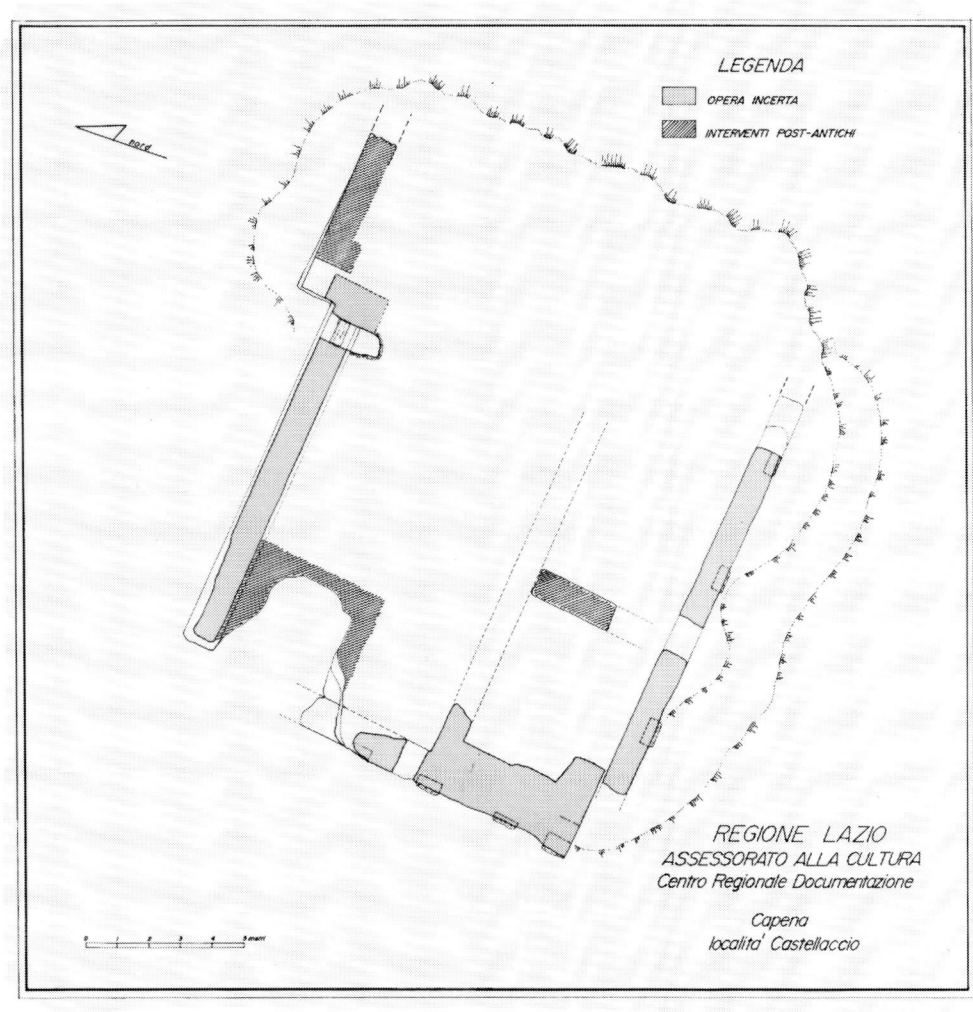

Fig. 2. Pianta del cosidetto Castellaccio alla quota di calpestio 'attuale'.

Fig. 3. Il monumento nella prima metà dell'800 (da Guattani 1828, tav.4) visto da sud. Le frecce indicano la lesione che ha provocato il crollo dell'angolo sud-ovest.

travertino (dim. cm. 80 × 35 × 50 in media), quattro sul lato ovest, di cui uno crollato di recente e tre sul lato sud, posti a distanze irregolari. Lo stato di conservazione di questi blocchi, notevolmente erosi e con tracce di scalpellature, non consente di comprenderne la forma e di determinarne le dimensioni originali. Sono inseriti ad una quota che corrisponde all'interno con il livello del pavimento, come riscontrabile nell'angolo sud-ovest, dove il crollo di parte del lato meridionale (cfr. fig. 3 e Jones 1962: tav.XXVI b) rende visibile la fondazione e l'alzato del muro in corrispondenza di uno dei blocchi.

L'altezza del basamento è rilevabile solo sul lato ovest, come mostrano le tracce visibili della sottostante fondazione. Non sono conservate indicazioni sul tipo di rivestimento utilizzato, tuttavia è forse possibile pensare ad una fodera di lastre inserite fra la base e i blocchi di travertino, o, più probabilmente, ad un rivestimento di intonaco e stucco (per un confronto, Guaitoli 1971). Sembra improbabile l'interpretazione del Jones che individua questi elementi come basi di ipotetiche lesene che, fra l'altro, non sarebbero poste a distanza regolare.

Per quanto riguarda l'alzato dell'edificio, il lato ovest, che è quello più conservato (lung. max m.9,30, alt. max. dal basamento m. 8,00, per un totale di m. 10,50 dal livello attuale del terreno), mostra tracce di cortina unicamente sopra il primo ed il terzo blocco di travertino (da sud). La forte erosione della parete rende visibile il conglomerato cementizio (fig. 4), costituito, come verificabile in più punti del monumento, essenzialmente da grosse scaglie di calcare cementate con poca malta. E' da notare, inoltre, che questo lato dell'edificio non è più solidale con gli altri due (fig. 2). Tale situazione, determinatasi almeno in parte dopo la metà dell'800 (fig. 3), consente di leggere nell'angolo sud-ovest un intervento, forse un irrigidimento della struttura; si tratta di un ripensamento in fase costruttiva che ha portato il muro da uno spessore originario di m. 1,15 a m. 2,90. Il lato meridionale (lung. max m. 15,30 spess. m. 0,90) emerge dall'attuale livello del terreno per un'altezza che non supera i 2 metri; anche in questo caso la cortina muraria risulta piuttosto deteriorata (fig. 4), è inoltre visibile una rottura situata a circa metà del muro.

Il lato nord (lung. m. 11,48 spess. m. 0,90 altezza max. m. 4,00) presenta caratteristiche costruttive diverse, non c'è traccia di basamento ma solo di fondazione e di parte dell'alzato del muro, il cui piano di spiccato corrisponde naturalmente a quello dei blocchi di travertino. La fondazione, realizzata in conglomerato di scaglie di calcare e malta (spess. m. 1,10), appare gettata a cavo

Fig. 4. Il monumento nei primi anni del '900 (foto P. Mackey da Ashby 1924) da sud-est.

Fig. 5. Il lato nord dopo lo scavo dei clandestini (1987). Sono riconoscibili la fondazione e l'alzato del muro, nonchè le inconfondibili tracce lasciate dalla ruspa. La freccia indica quanto resta dell'ingresso.

libero nell'affiorante banco di argilla, di cui conserva l'andamento (fig. 5).

All'estremità orientale del muro sono conservati resti di un ingresso (figg. 2 e 5), elemento questo che unito alle caratteristiche precedentemente descritte fa supporre un'articolazione diversa dell'edificio su questo lato. Proprio sul lato orientale andrebbe comunque cercato l'accesso al monumento, che probabilmente avveniva attraverso una scala (fig. 4). Sull'angolo sud-est scavi recenti hanno portato alla luce due piccole vasche rivestite di cocciopesto.

Lo spazio interno, come già detto, risulta diviso in senso est-ovest da un muro che attualmente è conservato per soli m. 1,70 di lunghezza (figg. 4 e 6). Il materiale proveniente dal crollo di gran parte di questo costituisce l'attuale piano di calpestio ed ha aumentato il dislivello esistente fra esterno ed interno dell'edificio. Anche in questo caso, delle murature perimetrali, risulta più conservata quella occidentale, che costituisce il lato di fondo degli ambienti. Questa seppure degradata, mostra ancora tracce della cortina e di un'apertura ricavata in età post-antica nel vano meridionale, mentre dell'altro rimane solo una piccola porzione di muro ormai distaccata e ruotata rispetto alla struttura principale.

Resta problematica, in questa fase della ricerca, l'interpretazione della destinazione originaria del monumento; non è, infatti, completo lo studio delle strutture ed i possibili confronti con edifici analoghi. A ciò si aggiunga che una definizione planimetrica del monumento sarebbe possibile solo attraverso saggi di scavo. Certo, il luogo occupato e le caratteristiche del manufatto fanno propendere per un edificio di tipo 'pubblico', la cui costruzione si può genericamente far risalire ad un periodo compreso fra la fine del II sec. a.C. e gli inizi del I sec. a.C. Gli elementi in nostro possesso, in particolare le caratteristiche strutturali del muro nord, consentono comunque di proporre una articolazione planimetrica riconducibile con probabilità ad un tempio a tre celee o ad *alii*. Se tale ipotesi si dimostresse fondate si potrebbe pensare ad una dedica a Cerere, il cui culto è testimoniato da tre basi dedicati a sue sacerdotesse, rinvenute nei pressi dell'edificio (*CIL* XI, 3933; Mancini 1953: 2055). L'assenza di tracce di rivestimento e gli scarsi elementi forniti dalla decorazione architettonica conservata non aggiungono altre indicazioni utili alla definizione del monumento.

Sul luogo sono stati rinvenuti unicamente un frammento di rocchio di colonna in travertino scanalato (diam. cm. 40, rocchi di colonne di analogo diametro sono sparsi nell'attuale abitato di Capena) e parte di un architrave in marmo, decorato superiormente con kyma lesbico trilobato (trafugato subito dopo il rinvenimento). Bisogna però ricordare le notizie relative alla scoperta di materiali architettonici avvenute in passato, di cui non è possibile stabilire provenienze certe, data la genericità delle descrizioni. E' questo il caso dell'architrave con l'iscrizione di Annio Architetto (*CIL* XI, 3945 conservata nei Musei Vaticani) e degli altri materiali descritti dal Galletti. Lo stesso problema si pone per quanto rinvenuto negli scavi del 1859 i cui documenti consentono solo una generica localizzazione delle scoperte (Archivio di Stato in Roma, Ministero dei Lavori Pubblici, b. 400 f. 3, analoga documentazione è conservata nell'archivio del monastero di S.Paolo). Da questi apprendiamo che furono fatte ricerche: "...sulla posizione della città di Capena...si è scoperto vicino al Castellaccio un residuo di travertino fino color bianco...più alcuni pezzi di travertino come sopra e molti frammenti di ornato, ed un pavimento di mosaico di diversi colori...", altri frammenti architettonici, tra cui capitelli, cornici, etc. si rinvennero poco distanti dall'edificio (cfr. Henzen 1864).

Lacunosa è, infine, anche la documentazione relativa agli scavi degli anni '30 (Conti 1932; Mancini 1953; per gli scavi precedenti cfr. Paribeni 1906a, 1906b; Stefani 1958); le immagini fotografiche relative testimoniano solo saggi di scavo all'esterno dell'edificio in esame (a sud e ad est), ma non conosciamo l'entità delle scoperte.

Il monumento in epoca post antica ha subito diverse trasformazioni, di cui restano tracce sui lati nord, ovest ed all'interno. Sul lato ovest è conservata parte di una struttura a pianta rettangolare (m. 4,30 × 3,70 spess. 0,80 ca. alt. max. 4,00), costruita con materiale di recupero (marmi, travertini etc.) utilizzato a fasce alternate, che sul lato nord fodera e si appoggia alla struttura antica (fig. 5). Analoga soluzione doveva essere stata adottata sul lato occidentale non più conservato. Un muro, costruito anch'esso con materiale di recupero, prolunga il lato nord di m. 4,00. Infine all'interno dell'edificio, l'ambiente meridionale risulta diviso in direzione nord-sud da un muro in opera mista (laterizio e tufelli) conservato per soli m. 2,5 (spess. m. 0,75).

Questi interventi, non riferibili a restauri (non risultano infatti tracce di restauri sulle murature antiche attualmente visibili) ma a trasformazioni dell'edificio, sono generalmente attribuiti alla chiesa di S.Giovanni, in uso sino al XIV sec. (Tomassetti 1979: 383–384) e ricordata da vari studiosi. In particolare il Galletti (1756: 53) descrive un ambiente absidato a lato del quale era un campanile 'per metà diroccato'. Vorremmo far notare che tale descrizione sembra trovare un riscontro più puntuale con i resti di un edificio absidato, individuato sempre negli scavi degli anni '30 (Conti 1932: 31–33) ed interpretato come tempio di Augusto, ma evidentemente riferibile ad una costruzione di epoca tarda, all'esterno ed all'interno della quale si rinvennero molte sepolture.

Tutti i dati raccolti sull'edificio vengono utilizzati per l'analisi dello stato di conservazione e per eventuali proposte di salvaguardia e valorizzazione, secondo le finalità e la metodologia adottate dal C.R.D.. Infatti alcune delle cause del degrado sono state individuate grazie all'esame della documentazione raccolta. Ad esempio il progressivo disassamento delle murature, in particolare del lato sud, ha fra le sue cause il dislivello esistente fra l'interno e l'esterno dell'edificio; tale dislivello è aumentato con il crollo della parete interna, già segnalato, avvenuto in epoca recente. A ciò si aggiunga che i tre lati conservati dell'edificio non sono più solidali fra loro.

Sono stati analizzati inoltre i danni causati dalla vegetazione infestante, in parte eliminata su indicazione dei colleghi botanici. Un esempio di difficile soluzione è visibile sul lato ovest, interessato dalla presenza di una grossa *Hedera helix* che se da un lato, con il proprio apparato radicale, spacca il conglomerato cementizio (fig. 5), dall'altro contribuisce, sulla sommità del muro, al mantenimento della coesione. A questi danni si aggiungano quelli prodotti dai già ricordati scavi clandestini.

Appare evidente a questo punto come sia indispensabile provvedere alla conservazione dell'edificio, elaborando un progetto in collaborazione con la Soprintendenza competente e con l'Università Agraria, proprietaria del terreno.

Fig. 6. Interno dell'edificio, lato di fondo.

Bibliografia

Ashby, T. 1924. 'La via Tiberina e i territori di Capena e del Soratte nel periodo romano', *Memorie della Pontificia Accademia,* I,2, 129–175.

Conti, V. 1932. *Notizie storiche sulla ubicazione di Capena,* Foligno.

Dennis, G. 1883. *The Cities and Cemeteries of Etruria*, 1, London (3ed.).

Galletti, P.L. 1756. *Capena municipio de' Romani. Discorso intorno al sito del medesimo con varie notizie del castello diruto di Civitucola posto nella provincia del Patrimonio*, Roma.

Gamurrini, G.F., Cozza, A., Pasqui, A. & Mengarelli, R. 1972. *Carta Archeologica d'Italia (1881-1897). Materiali per l'Etruria e la Sabina.* Forma Italiae, s.2, 1, Firenze.

Gazzetti, G. 1992. *Il territorio capenate*, Roma.

Gell, W. 1846. *The Topography of Rome and its Vicinity*, London.

Guaitoli, M. 1971. 'Un tempio di età repubblicana a Formia', *Quaderni dell'Istituto di Topografia Antica dell'Università di Roma*, VI, 1-12.

Guattani, G.A. 1828. *Monumenti Sabini*, 2, Roma.

Henzen, W. 1864. 'Scavi Capenati', *Bullettino dell'Instituto di Corrispondenza Archeologica*, XXXVI, 143-150.

Jones, G.D.B. 1962. 'Capena and the Ager Capenas, I', *Papers of the British School at Rome*, 30, 116-207.

Judson, P. & Hemphill. P. 1981. 'Sizes of settlement in southern Etruria, 6th-5th centuries B.C.' *Studi Etruschi*, XLIX, 193-202.

Mancini, G. 1953. 'Capena. Iscrizioni onorarie di età imperiale rinvenute in località Civitucola', *Notizie degli Scavi di Antichità*, 18-28.

Muzzioli, M.P. 1985. 'Capena e Lucus Feroniae', in *Misurare la Terra: Centuriazione e Coloni nel mondo Romano. Città, agricoltura, commercio: Materiali da Roma e dal Suburbio*, Modena.

Paribeni, R. 1906a. 'Leprignano. Scavi nella necropoli capenate', *Notizie degli Scavi di Antichità*, 178 ss.

Paribeni, R. 1906b. 'Necropoli del territorio capenate', *Monumenti Antichi dell'Accademia dei Lincei*, XVI, 277-490.

Paribeni, R. 1907. 'Leprignano. Iscrizioni latine', *Notizie degli Scavi di Antichità*, 675 ss.

Sommella Mura, A. 1969. *Repertorio degli scavi e delle scoperte archeologiche nell'Etruria Meridionale (1939-1965)*, I, Roma.

Stefani, E. 1958. 'Capena. Scoperte archeologiche nell'agro capenate. Ricerche archeologiche nella contrada "le Saliere"', *Monumenti Antichi dell'Accademia dei Lincei*, XLIV, 1-204.

Tomassetti, G. 1979. *La campagna romana antica, medioevale e moderna. Via Cassia e Clodia, Flaminia e Tiberina, Labicana e Prenestina*, III, (nuova ed. a cura di L. Chiumenti & F. Bilancia), Firenze.

44

La Necropoli della Via Amerina a *Falerii Novi*

L. Caretta, G. Innocenti, A. Prisco & P. Rossi

Sommario: *Il Gruppo Archeologico Romano in collaborazione con la Soprintendenza Archeologica per l'Etruria Meridionale, sta conducendo dal 1983 un progetto di scavo e valorizzazione di una delle necropoli di* Falerii Novi, *situata lungo la via Amerina. L'importante asse viario, databile ad un periodo immediatamente successivo al 241 a.C., anno della distruzione di* Falerii Veteres *(Civita Castellana), funge da perno dell'intero complesso archeologico, procedendo fino alla città di* Falerii Novi *di cui costituiva il cardine massimo. Nel tratto indagato la strada corre entro profonde ed ampie tagliate con il basolato in parte ancora conservato, su due ponti, uno dei quali ancora integro e transitabile. Nel corso dello scavo finalizzato alla scoperta della strada, sono stati condotti due saggi stratigrafici che hanno evidenziato una fase costruttiva non anteriore al I secolo a.C. e vari livelli di interro dal I secolo a.C. al IV secolo d.C. La necropoli si è sviluppata sfruttando intensivamente tutte le superfici disponibili delle tagliate e degli ampi spazi laterali alla strada. Le tombe esaminate sono fino ad ora 58 ma il numero delle sepolture è in realtà di gran lunga superiore. I tipi individuati e proposti in questo preliminare di tipologia sono 5: tombe a portico, tombe a camera, monumenti funerari, sepolcri ad ara o dado, colombari. Se ne propone una sequenza cronologica, basata su confronti architettonici, dati topografici e ceramologici di scavo e confronti storico-artistici per quelle che conservano l'originaria decorazione affrescata.*

Introduzione (L.C.)

Dagli anni '70 il Gruppo Archeologico ha effettuato anche una serie di ricognizioni non sistematiche; alcuni dei dati raccolti in tali occasioni sono inseriti nel contributo di G. Cifani e M. Munzi, al quale si rimanda per una esauriente silloge storico bibliografica dell'area; Un progetto di ricognizione sistematica intensiva su larga area partito dall'Agro Falisco Meridionale e in via di estensione è in corso dal 1987 e viene presentato nel contributo di A. Camilli, L. Carta, T. Conti, A. De Laurenzi, M. De Simone.

L'area oggetto dell'intervento di scavo, compresa nei territori dei Comuni di Civita Castellana, Fabrica di Roma, Nepi, Castel Sant'Elia, in Provincia di Viterbo, è delimitata (Fig.1) a sud dalla SS.311 che al km 10.300 interseca la via Amerina e, a nord, dalla Q.208 presso cui l'antico tracciato viario esce dall'ultima grande tagliata puntando direttamente su *Falerii Novi*. Perno dell'intero complesso è proprio la strada romana (Frederiksen & Ward Perkins 1957; Gamurrini *et al.* 1972; Radke 1981; De Lucia Brolli 1987 e 1991) che, perfettamente riconoscibile nel percorso, ricalcato dalla Via Comunale dei Tre Ponti e dalla Strada Vicinale di Fàlleri, ha conservato per lunghi tratti il lastricato a poligoni basaltici, le crepidini, i muri di contenimento della massicciata, quattro ponti che scavalcano Fosso dei Tre Ponti, Fosso Maggiore, Rio Calello, Rio Purgatorio (il primo viene presentato in questa stessa sede con uno studio di V. Antonelli).

Il complesso archeologico qui presentato risulta distinto in due settori dal Fosso Maggiore, che più ad est confluisce nel Fiume Treia, sotto Falerii Veteres (attuale Civita Castellana). Il settore meridionale è denominato Tre Ponti, mentre quello settentrionale è detto Cavo degli Zucchi (Fig.1), (Gamurrini *et al.* 1972: 416). Quest'ultimo comprende un tratto della via Amerina in buono stato di conservazione (Fig.1.B), attualmente riportato alla luce per una lunghezza complessiva di circa m.45, a partire dalla spalletta del

---

* Ci sembra quanto mai doveroso ricordare la figura e l'opera di Ludovico Magrini, fondatore dei Gruppi Archeologici d'Italia e del Gruppo Archeologico Romano, alla cui memoria vogliamo dedicare il nostro lavoro.

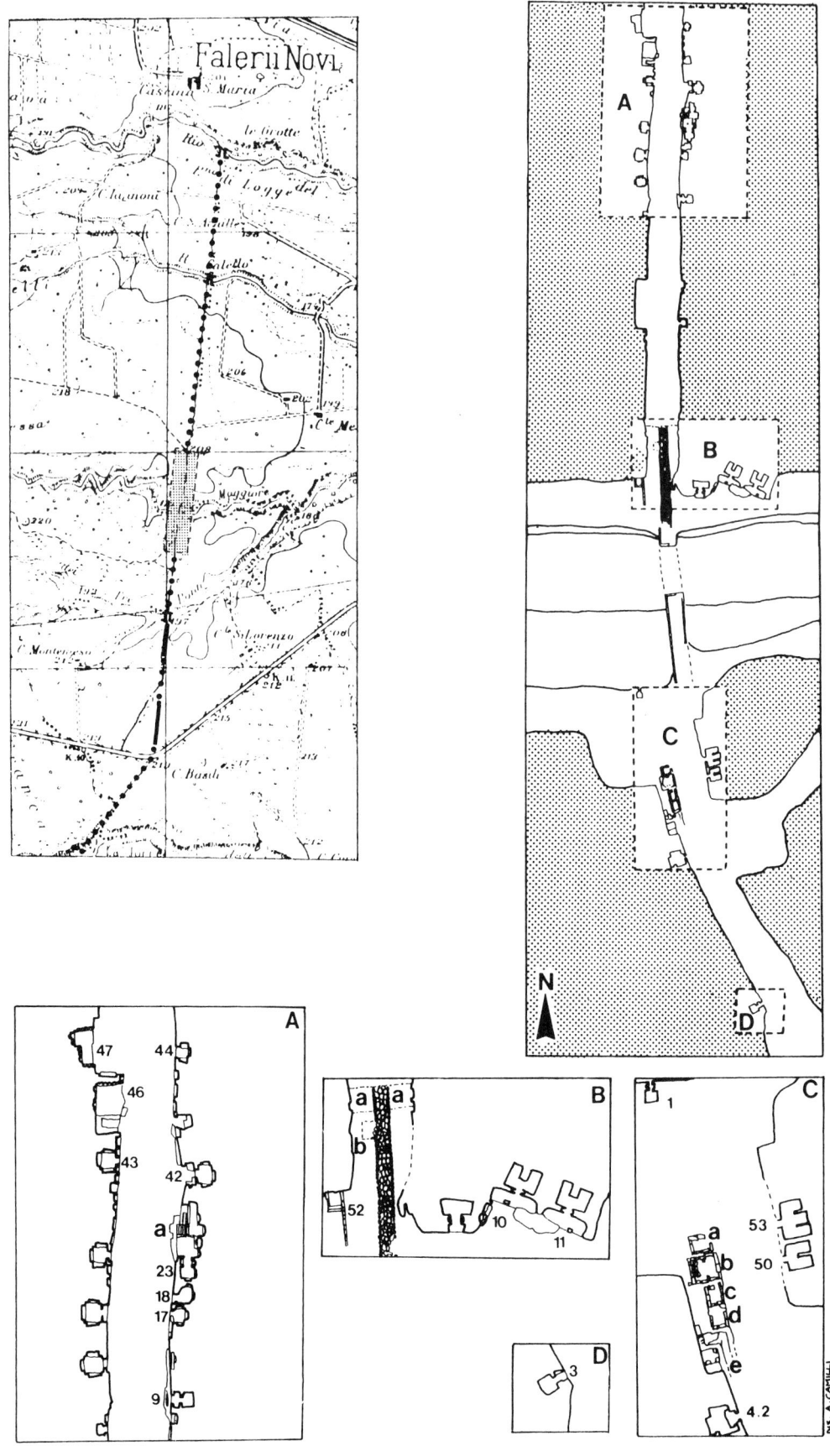

Fig. 1. Falerii Novi: *piante generali della necropoli*.

ponte sul Fosso Maggiore. La larghezza della massicciata, profondamente segnata dai solchi lasciati dalle ruote dei carri, è costantemente di m.2,40-2,45, mentre sembrerebbe variabile l'ampiezza delle crepidini, ancora non completamente scoperte e delimitate da una fila di blocchetti di basalto. Nel corso dell'intervento di scavo finalizzato alla scoperta della strada sono stati condotti due saggi stratigrafici (Fig.1.B) allo scopo di raccogliere nuovi dati sulle fasi di costruzione, utilizzo ed abbandono del basolato atualmente visibile.

Come è noto, il tracciato della via Amerina a nord di Nepi viene generalmente datato nell'ambito del terzo quarto del III secolo a.C., in un periodo immediatamente successivo al 241 a.C., anno della caduta di *Falerii Veteres*, quando Roma costruisce la nuova *Falerii* di cui l'Amerina viene a costituire il cardine massimo (Loreto 1989; Di Stefano Manzella 1979). A tutt'oggi non risulta siano state eseguite altre indagini stratigrafiche sulla via Amerina oltre quelle qui presentate e quelle che si riferiscono al probabile bivio Cassia-Amerina presso la *mansio ad Vacanas* (Gazzetti 1985: 44-45).

Il primo saggio stratigrafico nel Cavo degli Zucchi (Fig.1.B.b) è stato effettuato in corrispondenza di una 'piazzola' realizzata nella crepidine occidentale, a circa m.30 dal ponte (Munzi, c.s.). Gli strati più antichi relativi alla fase di costruzione ed in particolare al piano di posa dei basoli, hanno restituito materiali ceramici non anteriori al I secolo a.C. mentre una fase di obliterazione limitata alla 'piazzola' sembrerebbe databile a non prima del IV secolo d.C.

Il secondo saggio è stato effettuato su di un'area di maggiori dimensioni, adiacente alla 'piazzola' (Fig.1.B.a) e trasversale rispetto alla via anche se, per motivi pratici, non coincide con i limiti della tagliata che misura m.12 di larghezza. Sulle crepidini sono stati individuati due strati, simili per formazione e composizione, caratterizzati da un'accentuata pendenza verso il basolato che in più punti ne risultava coperto. La cronologia, sulla base degli scarsi materiali rinvenuti, è riferibile ad una fase tardo repubblicana e ad un'altra fase di III-IV secolo d.C. Lungo l'asse della strada sono stati, infine, rinvenuti almeno quattro strati di interro successivi, contenenti frammenti ceramici databili tra il I a.C. e la fine del II secolo d.C. Sono previste delle verifiche stratigrafiche sul restante tratto di m.200 circa, fino alla fine della tagliata.

La necropoli si è sviluppata sfruttando intensivamente le pareti delle tagliate e le ampie fasce laterali al lastricato stradale, corrispondenti ai marciapiedi. Il nucleo più cospicuo è infatti situato a cavallo del Fosso Maggiore dove le tagliate raggiungono dimensioni inconsuete. L'intero complesso è ben noto nella letteratura archeologica a partire dalla fine del secolo scorso (Gamurrini *et al.* 1972: 416-420) ma non vi erano mai state condotte indagini approfondite.

L'intervento ha riguardato due diversi indirizzi: lo scavo di settori apparentemente mai esplorati, la ripulitura e la documentazione di quelle tombe già saccheggiate e anche variamente utilizzate in tempi recenti come ricoveri per animali e persone. Le tombe sono state indicate con numeri o con lettere seguendo l'ordine di lavoro fino ad arrivare alle 58 indagate che costituiscono un terzo del totale attualmente visibile. Il numero delle deposizioni è in realtà di gran lunga superiore essendo attestato un utilizzo intensivo delle tombe a camera con sepolture ad incinerazione e ad inumazione, spesso coesistenti senza evidenti discriminanti.

Nell'effettuare lo studio della tipologia tombale riferibile all'intero complesso preso in esame sono stati individuati, sulla base di una schedatura minuziosa, cinque tipi principali che si presentano di seguito nell'ambito di tre specifici contributi relativi alle tombe a portico, alle tombe a camera, ai monumenti funerari costruiti ed ai colombari. Inoltre, loculi, arcosoli, fosse, nicchie sono osservabili lungo tutto lo svolgimento della necropoli ad occupare ogni superficie disponibile.

Al riguardo è esplicativa un'area ben delineata del Cavo degli Zucchi, denominata settore C (Figg.1.A.a; 5), dove compaiono diversi esempi gli uni vicini agli altri, senza soluzione di continuità e con varie cronologie.

In sede di conclusioni, gli elementi sino ad ora emersi evidenziano una prima fase di utilizzo della necropoli immediatamente successiva alla fondazione di *Falerii Novi* ma precedente l'attuale lastricato stradale con le tombe a portico 10 e 11 (Figg.1.B; 2). Analoghe alle altre due tombe a portico, 50 e 53 (Figg.1.C; 2) che sembrerebbero però collocabili in una fase cronologica posteriore, forse nell'ambito del II secolo a.C. Lo scavo di queste due ultime, già ampiamente compromesse, è tutt'ora in corso.

La seconda più consistente fase di sviluppo della necropoli coincide con l'età augustea. Sono infatti riconducibili ad essa il monumento a fregio dorico, i monumenti ad ara o a dado del settore Tre Ponti (Figg.1.C.a-b-c-d), le più antiche tombe dipinte (Figg.1.A.9; 1.D.3). La situazione pare mantenersi costante tra il I ed il II secolo d.C. mentre una fase di III secolo è testimoniata allo stato attuale delle ricerche solo a livello di riutilizzo di tombe preesistenti.

Infine di particolare importanza, per quanto probabilmente non pertinente all'uso funerario del sito, è l'attestazione di materiali tardoantichi da collegarsi con il persistente uso della via Amerina.

Le tombe a portico (P.R.)

Notevoli esempi di monumentalità, prosecuzione di una tradizione ben presente nelle necropoli rupestri dell'Etruria propria, sono offerti da due coppie di tombe a portico (Figg.1.B.10-11;C.50-53) riconoscibili al tipo 'di Falleri' (Colonna 1990: 133-135).

I due gruppi hanno diverso orientamento. A sud del

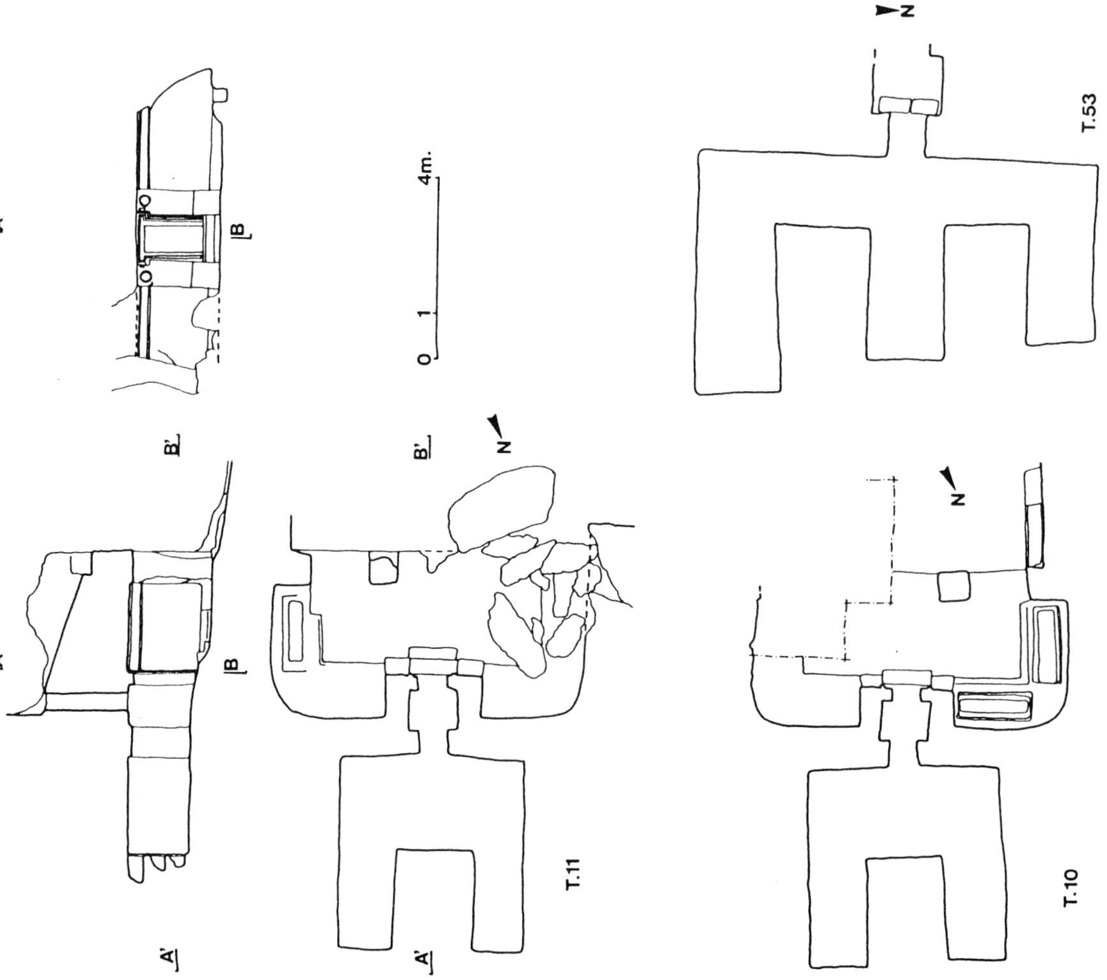

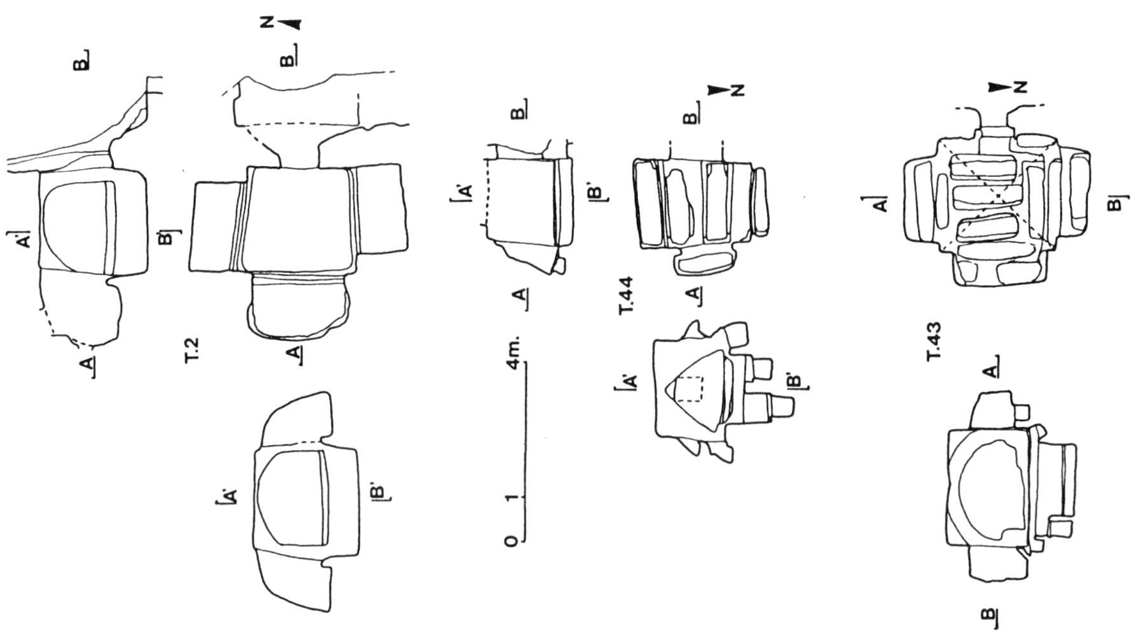

Fig. 3. Falerii Novi: *piante e elevazioni delle tombe T.2, T.44 e T.43.*

Fig. 2. Falerii Novi: *piante e elevazioni delle tombe T.11 e T.10.*

Fosso Maggiore le TT.50 e 53 risultano ortogonali all'asse della via Amerina, nell'area dove la tagliata assume la maggiore ampiezza, mentre a nord le TT.10 ed 11 occupano un ripiano del costone lungo il fosso, lateralmente rispetto alla strada (Frederiksen & Ward Perkins 1957: 104-107). Le tombe presentano una facciata a tre archi poggianti su pilastri rozzamente squadrati, originariamente sormontata da una cornice a blocchi di tufo alloggiati entro un profondo incasso; alcuni sono tuttora visibili nella loro originaria collocazione, sui massi di crollo delle facciate delle TT.10 e 53. La cornice costituiva il lato anteriore di una vasta terrazza probabilmente destinata ad un uso connesso con il culto. Nel caso della T.11 (Fig.2) la parete posteriore è tagliata a doppio spiovente (Gamurrini *et al.* 1972: 213, fig.143): ciò doveva conferire al monumento l'aspetto di una casa d'abitazione o di un oikos, ben visibile da chi transitava sull'Amerina verso *Falerii Novi*.

La T.53 (Fig.2), pur avendo la fronte completamente franata, ha conservato l'angolo SE della terrazza con le pareti lavorate a falsa opera quadrata: in una fase di utilizzo posteriore vi è stata ricavata una nicchia per urna cineraria.

Il vestibolo, a pianta rettangolare e soffitto piano, presenta nelle TT.10 ed 11 ampie banchine con fosse (Fig.2) lungo le pareti caratterizzate da un profilo curvilineo; nelle TT.50 e 53 sono stati ricavati loculi ed arcosoli. Caratteristica peculiare del vestibolo delle TT.10 ed 11 è la presenza di una cornice con cavetto e gola rovescia, scolpita lungo la parete di fondo e sui lati brevi.

Dal vestibolo l'accesso al vano della caditoia avviene mediante uno o più gradini, attraverso una porta con stipiti ed architrave sottolineati da un cornice terminante in tabula ansata, nel cui campo doveva trovarsi il *titulus* funerario dipinto. Tracce di colore rosso sono state, comunque, riscontrate solo nell'intradosso della porta della T.11. Accanto ai gradini si osservano (TT.10, 11) due parallelepipedi, probabilmente rappresentanti dei sedili sormontati, nella T.11, da due scudi rotondi scolpiti ai lati della tabula ansata. Sempre nella T.11 è presente un dettaglio di difficile interpretazione, ma probabilmente collegato con la presenza degli scudi: si tratta di un elemento curvilineo parzialmente eraso, posto tra lo scudo sinistro e l'architrave.

La camera funeraria è caratterizzata da un massiccio setto quadrangolare sporgente dalla parete di fondo, ai lati del quale si aprono due anditi che conferiscono alla pianta una tipica forma ad 'U'; la T.53 presenta due setti paralleli che suddividono la camera in tre anditi (Fig.2). Sulle pareti sono ricavati loculi e nicchie; queste ultime non sembrano però riferibili a sepolture ad incinerazione, fatta eccezione per la T.53.

La T.50 presenta in relazione con i loculi del setto centrale, estese tracce di colore rosso, sia direttamente a contatto del tufo sia su di una sottile scialbatura. Il cattivo stato di conservazione non consente, purtroppo, di formulare ipotesi, benchè siano attestati esempi inediti di iscrizioni funerarie con simili caratteristiche dalle necropoli dell'agro falisco.

Gli scarsi ma significativi materiali ceramici rinvenuti presso i due complessi indicano una frequentazione iniziata già a metà del III secolo a.C. (TT.10, 11) e proseguita fino alla metà del II secolo a.C. con successive riutilizzazioni in età tardo repubblicana ed augustea (TT.10, 53). Dal vestibolo della T.10 provengono inoltre materiali databili nell'arco dell'intero I secolo d.C. ma a questo proposito va rilevata la presenza di sepolture minori, esterne al vestibolo stesso.

Le tombe a camera (a.p.)

Le numerose tombe a camera della necropoli (Frederiksen & Ward Perkins 1957: 104-107) sono state distinte in cinque gruppi in base alle loro caratteristiche tipologiche:

Il Gruppo A (TT.2, 43, 44) (Fig.3), comprende tombe a camera a pianta quadrangolare con sepolture entro loculi semplici, arcosoli, nicchie e fosse nel pavimento. Il soffitto è generalmente piano, solo nella T.43 è a crociera. L'esame dei materiali rinvenuti suggerisce una prima utilizzazione del tipo durante l'età augustea con una successiva fase di II secolo d.C. a cui segue un riutilizzo databile al V secolo.

Il Gruppo B (TT.3, 9) (Fig.4), presenta un piccolo vestibolo con banchine laterali, camera a pianta quadrangolare decorata con pitture, letti con cuscini a sezione triangolare, soffitto piano. I materiali rinvenuti sembrano indicare una prima fase di I secolo d.C. con successivi riutilizzi nel IV e V secolo.

Al Gruppo C è ascrivibile la T.4 (Fig.4) con camera a pianta trapezoidale decorata con pitture, banchina lungo le pareti, soffitto piano. I materiali attestano una utilizzazione nell'ambito del I secolo d.C. con successive fasi di riutilizzo nel II e V secolo.

Il Gruppo D (T.23) (Fig.5) presenta camera a pianta quadrangolare con loculi ed arcosoli alle pareti, soffitto piano e vano con caditoia. Sulla base dei materiali rinvenuti sembrerebbe databile all'eta' augustea.

Il Gruppo E (T.18) (Fig.4) presenta camera a pianta irregolare, soffitto piano e numerose sepolture in loculi e fosse. Il materiale rinvenuto è tutto riferibile ad una fase di riutilizzo relativa al V secolo d.C.

Oltre ai tipi sopra descritti si notano altre tombe aventi caratteristiche date dalla commistione di elementi presenti nei tipi principali, che non sono state inserite in questo preliminare di tipologia.

Per quanto riguarda la presenza di numerosi esempi di pittura funeraria, è necessario premettere che lo stato di conservazione degli stessi non consente una lettura puntuale degli schemi decorativi anche nel caso delle cinque tombe più significative (TT.2, 3, 4, 9, 44). Comunque, sulla base delle osservazioni preliminari

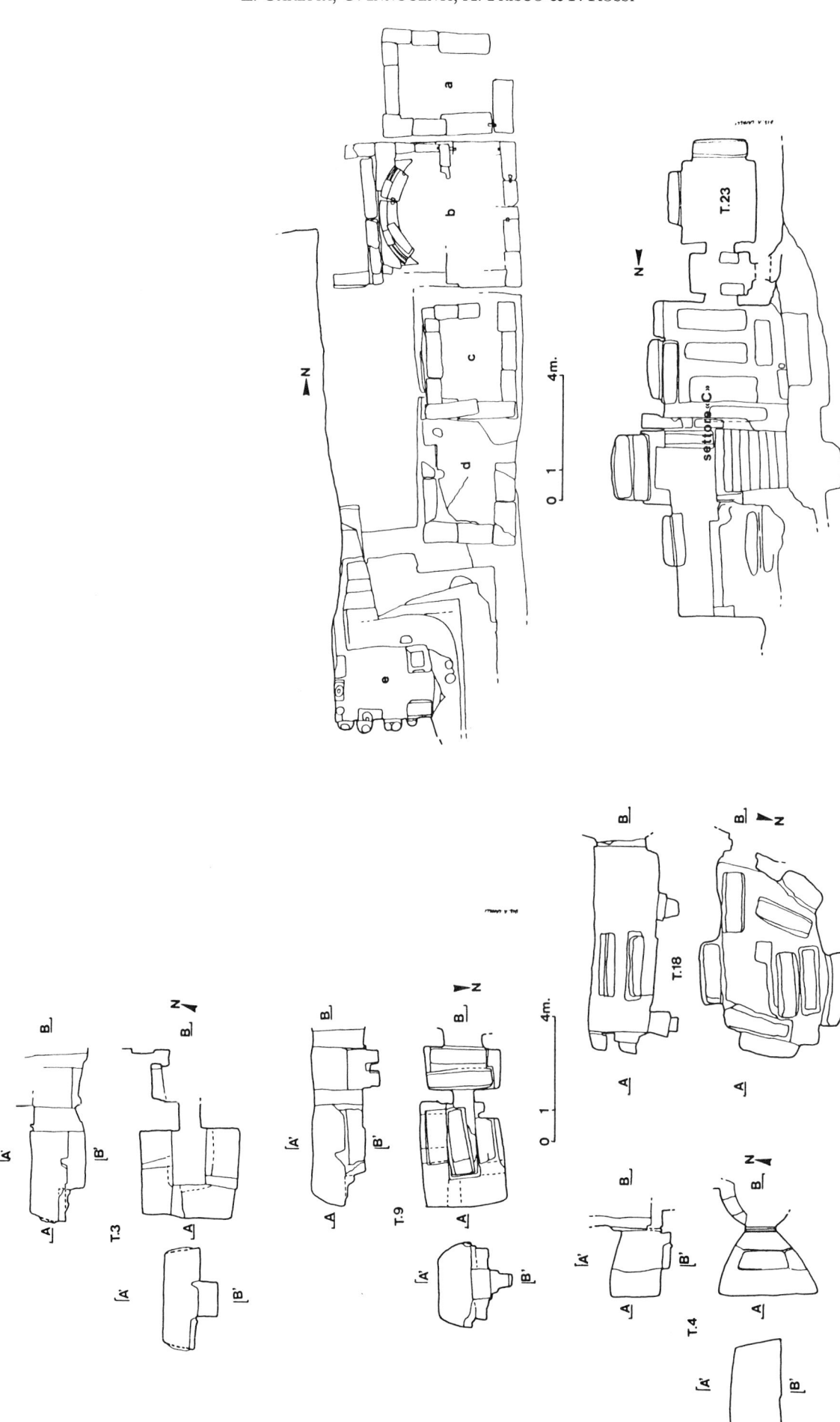

Fig. 5. Falerii Novi: tombe nei settori Tre Ponti e Cavo degli Zucchi.

Fig. 4. Falerii Novi: piante e elevazioni delle tombe T.3, T.9, T.4 e T.18.

Fig. 6. Falerii Novi: *T.4 pittura di una figura femminile alata.*

effettuate sembra di poter proporre tre serie cronologiche:

Le TT.3 e 9 potrebbero richiamare schemi di un tardo secondo stile o terzo iniziale di età giulio claudia. La T.9 (Frederiksen & Ward Perkins 1957: 104) presenta le pareti scandite da fascioni di colore rosso mentre gli elementi decorativi, privi di spunti prospettici, sono ridotti a motivi vegetali e ad una composizione di due brocche collocate al centro di un riquadro sulla parete sinistra della camera; l'intonaco dipinto del soffitto è ampiamente lacunoso.

Potrebbe rivelarsi interessante il confronto con l'ipogeo gentilizio di Montefiore presso Roma (Laidlaw 1964: 33–42), nel quale la scansione pittorica delle pareti e dei letti funerari, inquadrati da grandi campiture di colore bianco bordate di rosso e la raffigurazione di un'anfora su uno dei pilastri sembrano trattare temi molto simili, seppure in forma più grandiosa, a quelli della T.9. L'ipogeo di Montefiore è datato dalla Barbet (1985: 81–85) all'età augustea, collegandolo al più tardo secondo stile, il quale anticipa motivi delle pitture tarde.

Alla seconda serie, ascrivibile al periodo neroniano-flavio, appartengono le tombe 2 e 4. In particolare la T.2 presenta una sintassi decorativa più libera rispetto alle precedenti, come si può osservare nel soffitto, suddiviso in riquadri racchiudenti un elemento floreale quasi a ricordare un cassettonato. Nella T.4, invece, la partizione dei pannelli delimitati da cornici a motivi fitomorfi estremamente stilizzati (Fig.7), è associata ad una figura femminile alata resa con marcato senso pittorico (Fig.6) secondo un tardo terzo stile o quarto iniziale, forse riconducibile al periodo flavio.

Simili tematiche pittoriche sono presenti a Roma già nella tomba di Gaio Cestio, data sempre dalla Barbet (1985: 104–105) fra il 18 ed il 12 a.C. L'ambiente periferico in cui si trovano le tombe in oggetto potrebbe spiegare questo attardamento stilistico, esplicato in forme tecnicamente più povere.

La T.44 sembrerebbe invece riconducibile al periodo

Fig. 7. Falerii Novi: *T.4 motivi fitomorfi stilizzati*

traianeo adrianeo. 'E infatti tipico di quest'epoca un maggiore rigorismo che predilige severe partizioni geometriche cui si sovrappongono festoni e circoli.

TOMBE COSTRUITE E COLOMBARI (G.I.)

Nel settore dei Tre Ponti (Fig.1.C.b) è situato un monumento funerario a fregio dorico (Caretta 1986: 148) che, fatto oggetto di ripetuti e devastanti scavi clandestini e restaurato nel 1989 con fondi della regione Lazio per il Progetto Etruschi, non ha restituito materiali ceramici ad esso sicuramente attribuibili. Determinante è stata l'analisi degli elementi architettonici superstiti, che ha consentito di inserire la struttura nel secondo gruppo della classificazione proposta dal Torelli (1968: 36–38) comprendente esempi databili tra l'età del primo triumvirato e l'età augustea, con particolare sviluppo in quest'ultima fase. Il rinvenimento di questo monumento funerario ha dato l'avvio ad una ricerca di analoghi tipi presenti in area falisca. La ricerca ha già fornito i primi interessanti risultati (Caretta 1986: 149, n.1G), tanto più che la presenza di tali monumenti funerari non era stata rilevata nel territorio falisco (Torelli 1968: tav.B).

Di quattro monumenti (Fig.1.B.52; C.a-c-d; 5) riconducibili al genere ad ara o a dado (Torelli 1968: 36–38) diffuso in ambiente italico dalla fine del II e durante tutto il I secolo a.C., tre sono localizzati nel settore dei Tre Ponti, ed uno nel Cavo degli Zucchi. Quest'ultimo (Fig.1.B.52) è quello che sembra di più rispondere alle caratteristiche di questa classe, soprattutto per la presenza di una cornice modanata alla base, parzialmente obliterata da un riempimento che sembra costituire l'intera crepidine occidentale della via Amerina.

Il proseguimento dello scavo potrà chiarire il rapporto cronologico intercorrente tra il lastricato stradale, la crepidine e il monumento stesso che ha restituito materiali riconducibili a due fasi cronologiche principali.

La prima è riferibile all'utilizzo della struttura intorno alla metà del I secolo a.C.; la seconda, collocabile in età augustea, è forse attribuibile ad un'opera di bonifica dell'area esterna al monumento, fatta utilizzando in parte materiali più antichi provenienti da sepolture disturbate dell'area, databili tra la fine del II e gli inizi del I secolo a.C. Diversamente i monumenti nel settore dei Tre Ponti, ai lati del sepolcro a fregio dorico, risultano privi della cornice di base e di più rozza fattura (Fig. 5.a-c-d). La pianta è sempre quadrangolare e le strutture sono realizzate con blocchi squadrati di tufo.

Malgrado gli scavi clandestini è stato possibile recuperare materiale di contesto. Infatti, nella struttura meridionale (Fig. 5.d) è stata rinvenuta, entro un pozzetto ricavato nella terra di riempimento, una sepoltura ad incinerazione con relativo corredo databile all'età augustea.

Nell'area retrostante è stato inoltre effettuato un rinvenimento di particolare interesse. Si tratta del deposito dei resti di un rogo funebre, contenente un migliaio circa di frammenti di osso lavorato riferibili al rivestimento di un letto. Recentemente sono state ultimate le fasi di pulizia e assemblaggio dei frammenti curate dal settore restauro del Gruppo Archeologico Romano coordinato da A. Mazzoleni. Lo studio delle ipotesi ricostruttive è ancora in corso, come pure l'analisi stilistica e la ricerca dei confronti utili ad una precisa collocazione cronologica dei reperti che rientrano tra quelle produzioni dell'area centro italica diffuse tra il II a.C. e i primi decenni del I secolo d.C. (Talamo 1987–88: 19).

Nell'area davanti alla stessa struttura è stata rinvenuta un'iscrizione su tre blocchi frammentari di peperino (Munzi & Noviello 1989), tolti dalla loro collocazione originaria e disposti ancora integri su due file sovrapposte. La lettura proposta è la seguente:

[L(ucius) A]burius L(ucii) L(ibertus) Pelops
[Ci?]ncia C(aii) L(iberta) Flora
[A]buria [-] L(iberta) Glycera
L(ucius) Veturius L(ucii) L(ibertus) Antigonus

Interessante la presenza del gentilizio Veturius legato al culto in *Falerii Novi* di Silvanus Veturianus, poichè suggerirebbe una relazione di patronato tra il liberto citato e questa famiglia. L'iscrizione, che presenta i caratteri rubricati, può essere datata al periodo giulio claudio e più preferibilmente augusteo.

Fanno parte della necropoli anche tre colombari. Il primo (Fig.1.C.e; 5.e), situato ai Tre Ponti, consta di un piccolo vano quadrangolare privo della copertura e della parete orientale. Vi sono state rinvenute quindici sepolture ad incinerazione collocate entro nicchie sulle pareti e in alloggiamenti di varia forma scavati nel pavimento. I materiali recuperati sono databili alla prima metà del I secolo d.C.

Il secondo colombario (Fig.1.A. 46), situato nel Cavo degli Zucchi (Gamurrini *et al.* 1972: 214, fig.145), è collocato in un vano di più ampie dimensioni occupato in parte da una struttura destinata forse allo svolgimento di cerimonie connesse con il culto. Detta struttura è delimitata da banchine continue tagliate nel banco tufaceo e ha restituito materiali riferibili ad un contesto intatto, databile alla prima metà del I secolo d.C. Inoltre il colombario presenta sulla parete ovest chiare tracce di un riutilizzo d'epoca non precisabile, rappresentato da una rozza serie di gradini non riconducibili all'originaria funzione del monumento.

A poca distanza da questo, si trova un terzo e più grande colombario (Fig.1.A. 47), a pianta quadrangolare irregolare con numerose nicchie per cinerari e fosse sul pavimento (Gamurrini *et al.* 1972: 214 fig.145), che sarà oggetto d'indagine nelle prossime campagne di scavo.

Bibliografia

Barbet, A. 1985. *La peinture murale romaines styles decoratifs pompeiens*, Paris.

Caretta, L. 1986. 'Via Amerina, complesso funerario romano con sepolcro a fregio dorico', *Archeologia nella Tuscia II, Atti degli incontri di studio organizzati a Viterbo (1984),(Quaderni del Centro di Studio per l'Archeologia Etrusco-Italica*, 13), 145–153.

Colonna, G. 1990. 'Corchiano, Narce e il problema di Fescennium, in *La Civilta' dei Falisci, Atti del XV Convegno di Studi Etruschi ed Italici (Civita Castellana – Forte Sangallo, 1987)*, Firenze, 111–140.

De Lucia Brolli, M.A. 1987. 'La via Amerina', *Antiqua* 5–6, 27–41.

De Lucia Brolli, M.A. 1991. *L'Agro Falisco*, Roma.

Di Stefano Manzella, I. 1979. *Falerii Novi negli scavi degli anni 1821–1830*, Roma.

Frederiksen, M. & Ward Perkins, J.B. 1957. 'The ancient road systems of the Central and Northern Ager Faliscus', *Papers of the British School at Rome*, XXV, 67–209.

Gamurrini, G.F., Cozza, A., Pasqui, A. & Mengarelli, R. 1972. *Carta Archeologica d'Italia (1881–1897), Materiali per l'Etruria e la Sabina*, Firenze.

Gazzetti, G. 1985. 'La Valle di Baccano in età romana', *Bollettino d'Arte*, 29, 39–50.

Laidlaw, A. 1964. 'The Tomb of Montefiore, a new Roman tomb painted in the Second Style', *Archaeology*, 17,1, 33–42.

Loreto, L. 1989. 'Il conflitto romano-falisco del 241–240 a.C. e la politica romana degli anni successivi', *Melanges de l'École Française de Rome, Antiquité*, 74, 717–737.

Munzi, M. c.s. 'Nuovi dati sulla via Amerina e note prosopografiche su Falerii Novi', *Ricognizioni Archeologiche*, 6.

Munzi, M. & Noviello, C. 1989. 'Iscrizioni inedite dalla via Amerina', *Ricognizioni Archeologiche*, 5: 38–50.

Radke, G. 1981. *Viae Publicae Romanae*, Bologna.

Talamo, E. 1987–88. 'Un letto funerario da una tomba dell'Esquilino', *Bullettino della Commissione Archeologica Comunale di Roma*, XCII, 17–102.

Torelli, M. 1968. 'Monumenti funerari romani con fregio dorico', *Dialoghi di Archeologia*, II.1, 32–54.

45

Reconstructing a Gateway City: The Place of Nepi in the Study of South-Eastern Etruria

CATHARINE EDWARDS[1], CAROLINE MALONE[2] & SIMON STODDART[1]

([1]Department of Classics and Ancient History, [2]Department of Archaeology, University of Bristol)

Summary: *This paper provides the archaeological and historical setting of the gateway town of Nepi in south-eastern Etruria. The preliminary results of an interdisciplinary study are presented. These include excavation within the city and study of the Roman inscriptions. The present study is a component part of a wider programme to link knowledge of the rural landscape to the less well known urban centre.*

INTRODUCTION

The study of Nepi and its territory is a field project within a wider plan coordinated from the University of Bristol to enhance the information recovered by the well-known South Etruria survey of the British School at Rome. The Nepi project is contributing to the relatively little understood urban component of a relatively well known rural landscape (Potter 1979). This work represents a collaboration of ancient historians, architectural historians and archaeologists to reconstruct the development of a local city, which may have been an independent state, and its incorporation within the expanding imperial organisation of Rome. Nepi occupied a buffer or gateway position in both these processes (Fig. 3). At the time of first state formation it was placed between the large Etruscan city of Veii to the south and the largest Faliscan centre of *Falerii Veteres* to the north. At the time of the expansion of Rome, it was at the frontier of Roman political activity in its role as a colony located immediately to the south of the politically rearranged landscape of the northern Faliscan territory.

The current fieldwork is attempting to redress the balance of research. In common with much information for first millennium BC central Italy, previous work at Nepi has concentrated on excavating and analysing the impressive tombs and gravegoods (Stefani 1910; 1918; 1930; Bendinelli 1921). It is these that fill the local and national museums and, although products of death rituals, represent our best knowledge of contemporary life. By contrast, the Nepi project is principally a study of evidence for settlement life during the first millennium BC and the first five hundred years AD. The end result will necessarily be an integration of death rituals and domestic/public life. This will set the trajectory of Nepi within the wider context of central Italian state formation.

A preliminary step of integration has already been taken in this direction by the presentation here of the re-analysis of the Roman inscriptions of Nepi (some of which are funerary). Further work will be needed to integrate the domestic and public structure of the city with clues given by public inscriptions. Much work has already been undertaken on the road structure of the city, including the re-analysis of the major surviving gateway (Rustico 1986–87), and the settlement organisation, most importantly by the Soprintendenza Archeologica per l'Etruria Meridionale. It is, though, clear that these different strands of evidence can be worked together both to provide a fresh synthesis and to suggest new lines of research and excavation.

The broader project to enhance the South Etruria Survey has already led to the computerisation of the original paper records held in the British School at Rome and the linkage of that information to the artefacts stored in the same building. Work is now in progress, in collaboration with Italian colleagues, to enhance the coverage of the survey by integrating information found during other fieldwork. Further work will add the environmental background to the area in digitised form and relate these different levels of information to one another in a Geographical Information System (Harrison & Stoddart, n.d.). These procedures should allow both a greater clarity in presentation and a wider range of interpretative tools.

THE GEOGRAPHICAL CONTEXT

The Treia valley region is a large volcanic plateau landscape heavily dissected by the action of the Treia and its tributaries (Alvarez 1972). The major processes, after the deposition of the the last major ash flow tuffs (*Tufo Giallo di Sacrofano*) are attributable to fluvial erosion and deposition. The effect on the topography has been of considerable importance for the human exploitation of the area. The interbedding of permeable and impermeable deposits has led to numerous springs, essential for human settlement; fertile soils have developed on the products of volcanic activity. Surface drainage has had a differential effect on the landscape. The east-west streams have generally formed shallow valleys, whereas the north-south streams have cut deep canyons (of c. 100 m) that effectively divide the terrain. The stratigraphy revealed by these deep canyons contains the raw materials for building construction and pottery manufacture. Numerous pedestals for potential settlement have been formed. Isolation and defence have been maximised, although deposits of *Tufo Giallo di Sacrofano* do allow access by means of trails at restricted points to and from the gorges. These are the significant topographical constraints on local settlement which affected Nepi as much as other locations.

The town of Nepi (fig. 1) occupies one of these tuff outcrops around 48 km to the north of Rome in what was known to the ancient Romans as the *Ager Faliscus*. The old town sits on a tuff promontory, 225 m above sea level (approx. 1200 m long and varying in width from 50 to 350 m) which on the western side adjoins a volcanic plain sloping towards the south east (in recent years the town has spread extensively westwards). To the north and south of the spur are two gorges (of the Fosso del Cerro and the Fosso della Massa) which merge at the eastern end of the spur and go on to join the river Treia, a tributary of the Tiber.

THE PREHISTORIC BACKGROUND

Understanding of the early prehistory (pre-Bronze Age) of the *Ager Faliscus* is somewhat fragmentary. The cause of this has been much discussed. One reason may be attributed to the recovery strategies of some of the most extensive work (di Gennaro & Stoddart 1982), but this can only partly explain what must have been a relatively low demography of the region prior to the Bronze Age. Considerable flint collections are known to have been collected from the Nepi area, especially the Massa locality, in the period before 1918 by the local enthusiasts, Giannelli and De Maris (Rellini 1920: 113). Furthermore, in the 1970s, Neolithic pottery was recovered from the same Massa locality in an open site near Grotta Arnaro

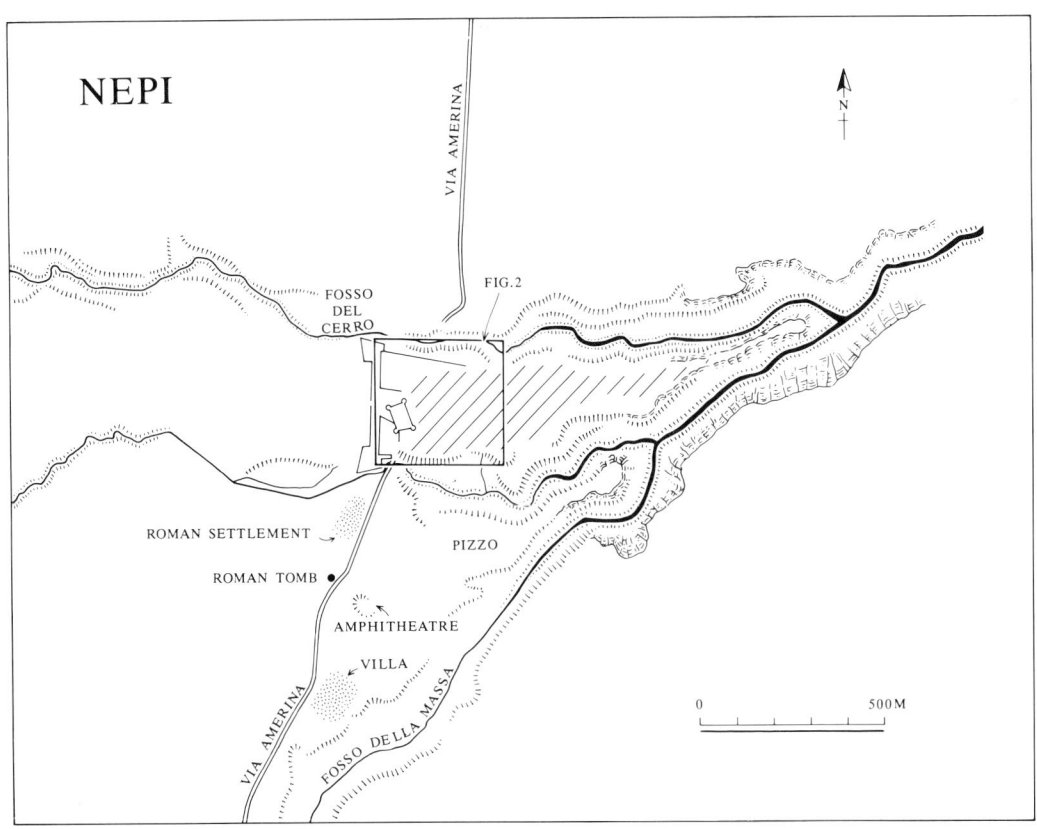

Fig. 1. The local topography of Nepi.

(Selmi 1976: 55). These finds clearly indicate human occupation, but the level of publication does not allow clarification of any details.

Most current models of state formation in central Italy emphasise the chronological depth of the processes of development, accompanied by a progressive concentration of population into larger settlements between the Final Bronze Age and the First Iron Age (Peroni & di Gennaro 1986; Spivey & Stoddart 1990; Barker & Stoddart 1994). The major question for the Faliscan territory is whether the region conforms to this Etruscan model of state formation or whether it already differs in some respects. Furthermore, the effect of the concentration of population in the later Etruscan centre of Veii to the south needs to be measured. Did this mobilisation of manpower affect the continuity of settlement occupation in the Faliscan area during the ninth century BC, the century of most rapid reorganisation? What were the precise mechanisms that caused the displacement of large populations?

The only thoroughly excavated settlement of Narce (Potter 1976) appears to confirm the chronological depth of the process but cannot provide incontrovertible evidence for the mechanisms involved. The earlier small-scale excavation of the site (Peroni & Fugazzola 1969) was differently interpreted at the crucial phase of transition between the tenth and eighth centuries (emphasising discontinuity rather than continuity). The lack of other relevant excavations and the fragile nature of surface materials precludes greater certainty in the rest of the area. Some authors even envisage a major break, at an earlier date, between the Middle Bronze Age and the Final Bronze Age that involved a considerable re-organisation of the settlement patterns from riverine to defended positions (Pettiti 1990).

The evidence from the territory of Nepi is beginning to create an independent testing ground of these various interpretations. Material from Porciano (Selmi 1976: 58) suggests a pattern of low population levels into the early Bronze Age. However, population had definitely increased by the end of the Bronze Age. The occupation of the naturally defended position of Torre dell'Isola has been re-dated to the Bronzo Finale (di Gennaro pers. comm.) and at least two other sites originally located during the British School at Rome surveys can be now dated to the Bronzo Finale (di Gennaro & Stoddart 1982, Appendix A, 57 and 60). The situation at Nepi itself in the Bronze Age is still unclear, although under active investigation by the current fieldwork. Some pottery diagnostic to the Bronze Age has been recovered from below the tuff spur, but this cannot be more accurately dated at present.

The situation at Nepi is much more clear from the eighth century BC onwards. Stratified deposits of material from the period 750–700 BC have been discovered in a section from the southern edge of the town. Further excavation near the Vescovado (Bishop's Palace) has revealed a continuous sequence of occupation from at least 625 BC into the Roman period. The combined current evidence suggests that Nepi was not occupied in the crucial period of 900–750 BC, the phase of major settlement nucleation in South Etruria. At this time, small sites may have been drained of manpower and even abandoned, attracted or coerced towards the growing centres of power such as Veii. A few Late Bronze Age sites, located on large, often volcanic, plateaux appear to have generated a monopoly of power and territorial control for a hundred and fifty years, under the new guise of Villanovan centres, before the rural territory was again repopulated (or recolonised) in the late eighth century BC.

STATE FORMATION

Two questions are traditionally formulated for the Faliscan area. To what extent were the Faliscans culturally, linguistically and ethnically distinct from the Etruscans? How many independent political components constituted the Faliscan territory? The ancient authors leave generous room for interpretation (Camporeale 1991). Many modern authors stress the linguistic link to Latin (Colonna 1988). Some modern authors interpret the term Falisci as connected with *Falerii Veteres*, in the same way as Veientes would be connected with Veii (Pallottino 1990: 11). This leaves Narce and Nepi in an intriguing buffer position between Veii to the south and *Falerii Veteres* to the north (Fig. 3). This must have been a fluid frontier, where Nepi was at times independent, at other times subject to one or other political authority. Most accounts of the Faliscan territory have focused on the more solid material provided by *Falerii* and Narce, to the detriment of Nepi.

The situation in the Narce complex is thus relatively well known. The Narce complex has been much researched, initially through its cemeteries (Pasqui 1902; Dohan 1942; Davison 1972) and more recently through settlement excavation (Peroni & Fugazzola 1969; Potter 1976). Surface survey of the component plateaux of the complex (Narce, Monte li Santi and Pizzo Piede) and modern excavation in the valley below have reconstructed an intricate shift in settlement density between the component parts. The overall position of Narce was highly strategic in the early to mid first millennium, located directly between the principal centres of *Falerii* and Veii, whereas Nepi is somewhat further to the west. The recent and important observation by Cristofani (1988) about the prominence of inscriptions in the Etruscan language from this Faliscan centre is therefore most apposite, particularly in contrast to their relative rarity from Nepi (Rix 1991: 19–21). Narce clearly had an important mediating role between Veii and *Falerii*, as measured by the major recorded products of cemeteries: inscriptions and imports.

Before the current project, the situation at Nepi was known exclusively from cemeteries. In addition, Nepi is largely neglected by the ancient authors (in preference to *Falerii*) (Camporeale 1991) and therefore the study of state formation and organisation has to be undertaken almost entirely through the study of non-literary material culture. The name of the town is given various different forms by ancient authors (*CIL* XI, p. 481). These include *Nepet*, *Nepete*, *Nepe* and *Nepeta*. Some claim the name derives from the serpent Nepa (and the town's coat of arms includes a serpent).

The recent excavations near the Vescovado (fig. 2) appear to be located within the ancient city but not at its focal point, even though they adjoin the medieval and modern cathedral. It is very difficult to characterise the nature of early public architecture without comparative evidence. However, the structures and associated material, although including some tentative evidence of ritual decoration, appear to be more domestic in character. If this interpretation is correct, they demonstrate the wealth of Nepi from the late seventh century BC. Imported pottery was not exclusively reserved for the rituals of death, but was employed in urban life. Finds include a fragment of gold jewellery and imitation Corinthian pottery from the beginning of the sequence and Attic Red Figure and a fine gem stone from later in the sequence.

The orientation of the excavated structures suggests substantial continuity in the organisation of city life right up to the incorporation of the town in the political organisation of Rome. An Archaic drainage system underlies the later Republican (?) domestic building and rests on precisely the same alignment. The main addition to the area in the Roman period was the insertion of a well in the early Imperial period, again in precise alignment with both the local drainage system and the more substantial building structures. The archaeological evidence suggests that the Romans worked through rather than against the preceding organisation of the city.

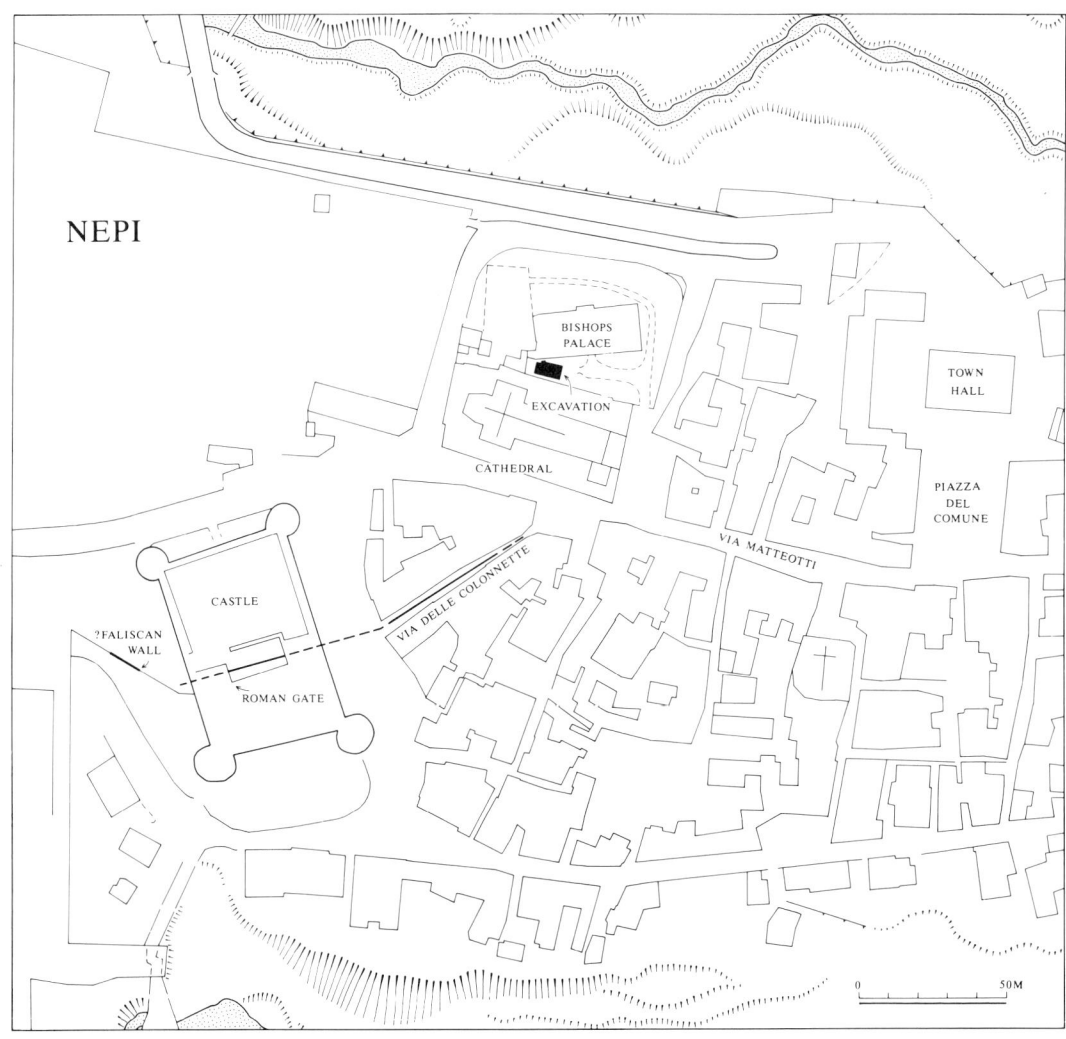

Fig. 2. The location of the excavation.

Nepi as a COLONIA LATINA

A major factor in the success of the Romans and their Latin allies against neighbouring communities such as the Etruscans was the practice of establishing new communities, known as *coloniae Latinae*, in the areas from which defeated enemies had been expelled. These were self-governing communities peopled by Romans and Latins. Their inhabitants, though not Roman citizens, had privileges under Roman law. Nepi seems to have had a *colonia Latina* in 383 BC (according to Livy, 6.21.4, or 373 according to Velleius Paterculus, 1.14.2). The nearby settlement of Sutri seems to have received a *colonia Latina* at around the same time. Livy notes the strategic importance of these two communities which he refers to as *loca opposita Etruriae et velut claustra inde portaeque* – "The two places commanded Etruria, serving as both barrier and gateway" (6.9.4; cf. 9.32.1).

It was probably at this time that the portion of the *Via Amerina* from Rome to Nepi (via Veii) was constructed, possibly following the course of an earlier road. The portion of the road leading northwards from Nepi to *Falerii Novi* most likely dates from 150 or so years later, as the latter town was founded in 241 BC to accommodate the inhabitants of the destroyed city of *Falerii Veteres* (Frederiksen & Ward-Perkins 1957: 90–91, 130–131, 187–188; Salmon 1982: 171–174). The *Via Amerina* was subsequently extended, joining the *Flaminia* at Luceoli.

Wiseman (1970) and Harris (1971) see the *Via Amerina* as a road intended to serve local traffic in contrast to roads such as the *Cassia* and the *Flaminia* which were intended to facilitate the long-distance transport of armies and supplies (and tended to by-pass small local centres) (Potter 1979: 102–109). The possible implications of the nature of traffic on the *Via Amerina* for the history of Nepi will be discussed below.

After the Latin War of 338–340 (a rebellion by Latin allies and others, successfully suppressed by the Romans), Latin colonies owed allegiance exclusively to Rome. New developments in some communities (such as the orthogonal town plan in Norba) seem to date from this time (Salmon 1982). There has not so far been evidence of changes datable to this period in Nepi. Livy makes brief reference to Nepi under the year 297 BC (14.3), though Harris considers this may be an attempt to fill a gap in the records (1971: 67).

The next mention of Nepi in historical sources relates to the Second Punic war. According to Livy, of the thirty Latin colonies in existence in 209 BC, twelve (including Nepi) protested to the Roman senate that they were unable to furnish the men and money required of them (Livy 27.9.7ff.). When the war was over, those towns who had withheld support were punished by a decision of the senate in 204 BC which required them to provide double the number of soldiers previously required of them (Livy 29.15). Harris (1971) provides the background for this period.

Nepi as a Roman MUNICIPIUM

Shortly after the Social War 91–87 BC (when allied communities in Italy fought to obtain the privileges of Roman citizens) Nepi, like many of the other urban centres in Italy south of the Po which did not already have Roman citizenship, acquired the status of a *municipium* (see Harris 1971: 230–250, for a detailed discussion of enfranchisement in Etruria). The approximate date of this development may be deduced from the type of local government structure evidenced by the inscriptions associated with the town (*quattuorviri* are very commonly to be found in *municipia* established immediately after the Social War).

CIL XI lists 53 inscriptions from Nepi, many of which are small fragments (3196–3242, 7540–7545). Three of these are to be found in the Portico of the Duomo, seven in the portico of the Palazzo del Comune and six in the Museo Civico (located in the Palazzo del Comune). A further two are to be found in the church of San Biagio and quite a number (mainly small fragments) in the church of Sant'Elia.

Three of the inscriptions from Nepi are dedications to members of the imperial family. 3200 is a dedication to Augustus, dated 12 BC, by the *magistri augustales* (discussed below). 3201 is a dedication to the emperor Septimius Severus, dated 194 BC, by the people of Nepi. 3202 is dedicated to Galerius Maximinus Daia (Caesar 305–310 AD) from *res republica Nepesinorum*.

Another late inscription (3203) commemorates one Flavius Eusebius, *v(ir) c(larissimus)*, who, Bormann suggests, may be the consul of AD 359. It is perhaps no coincidence that this inscription was kept in the church of San Eusebio on the road from Nepi to Ronciglione. Another inscription (3204), probably third century (though Groag suggests fourth (Groag & Stein 1933, I: 1587)), was set up to commemorate a woman called Velia Pumidia Maximilla by her husband, Aurelius Propinquus, who describes himself as *v(ir) c(larissimus)*, indicating membership of a senatorial family, if not necessarily (by this date) membership of the senate itself. *CIL* XI, 7570 (last seen in the nearby town of Ronciglione), a funerary inscription set up by sons to honour their father, Aurelius Propinquus, also entitled *v.c.*, most probably refers to the same man. Unusually, Aurelius Propinquus is praised by his sons for having augmented the family property through hard work and military service (*labore militiae industriaeque merito aucta re familiari*). There is as yet no firm evidence for Roman senators originating from Nepi.

Several inscriptions refer to decurions of Nepi (these include 3203, 3206, 3211, 3220). A number of inscriptions were set up by or in honour of local magistrates (including 3207, 3211, 3212, 3215, 3217). These mainly appear to date from the first and second centuries AD. According to a transcription of 3211 made in the sixteenth century (the inscription has suffered considerable erosion since then), Cn. Corellius Frontinus held the offices of *quattuorvir*, aedile, *quattuorvir i(ure) d(icundo)* and *q(uaestor) alimentorum* as well as being a *pontifex*. The inscription commemorates both the erection of a statue to him by his wife and the provision of *sportulae* (gifts of food or money) for the local *decuriones* and *augustales* and an *epulum* (feast) for the people in his honour by the *plebs* of Nepi, with money gathered in a collection. L. Sulpicius Clemens, commemorated by his son and daughter in *CIL* XI, 3215, also held a number of local magistracies. He is described as *quattuorvir i(ure) d(icundo), quattuorvir a.p., quaestor arcae r(ei) p(ublicae) Nepesinor(um), mag(ister) iuven(tutis), sevir [eq]uitum, praetor iuventutis*. Bormann interprets *a.p.* as an abbreviation for *aedilicia potestate* (*CIL* XI, p.481). It is interesting to note that M. Apisius Sabinus, who in the late second or early third century set up a funerary inscription for his wife Herenia Iusta (CIL XI, 3212), was a *duumvir* at Veii as well as a *quattuorvir* at Nepi.

A minor official, P. Tettius Certus, is commemorated in an inscription set up by his son (7541). The deceased, who is alleged to have lived to the age of 97, is described as *scrib(a) lib(rarius)* of the plebeian aedile (*aed. pl.*). 3207 attests a centurion of the pretorian guard, Quintus Petronius Urbanus. The occurrence of the name Pertinax suggests it is of relatively late date.

Two inscriptions refer to *pontifices* (besides 3211, described above, 3218 which is very fragmentary). The priests known as *augustales*, established by the emperor Augustus to take charge of the cult of the *genius Augusti* appear on several inscriptions (3206, 3211, 3213, 3214 and possibly also the fragmentary texts 3219 and 3220). Nestor, the *augustalis* commemorated in 3214, is described as having provided games (*ludi*) and as having provided an *epulum* for the citizens of Nepi for the second time (on the occasion of the dedication of a statue of his patron) – an interesting illustration of the devotion that might be publicly displayed by an ex-slave towards the memory of a man who had freed him. Two other inscriptions (3206 and 3211) list the *augustales* alongside the *decuriones* and *plebs* as recipients of benefactions.

CIL XI, 3200, dated to the first seven months of 12

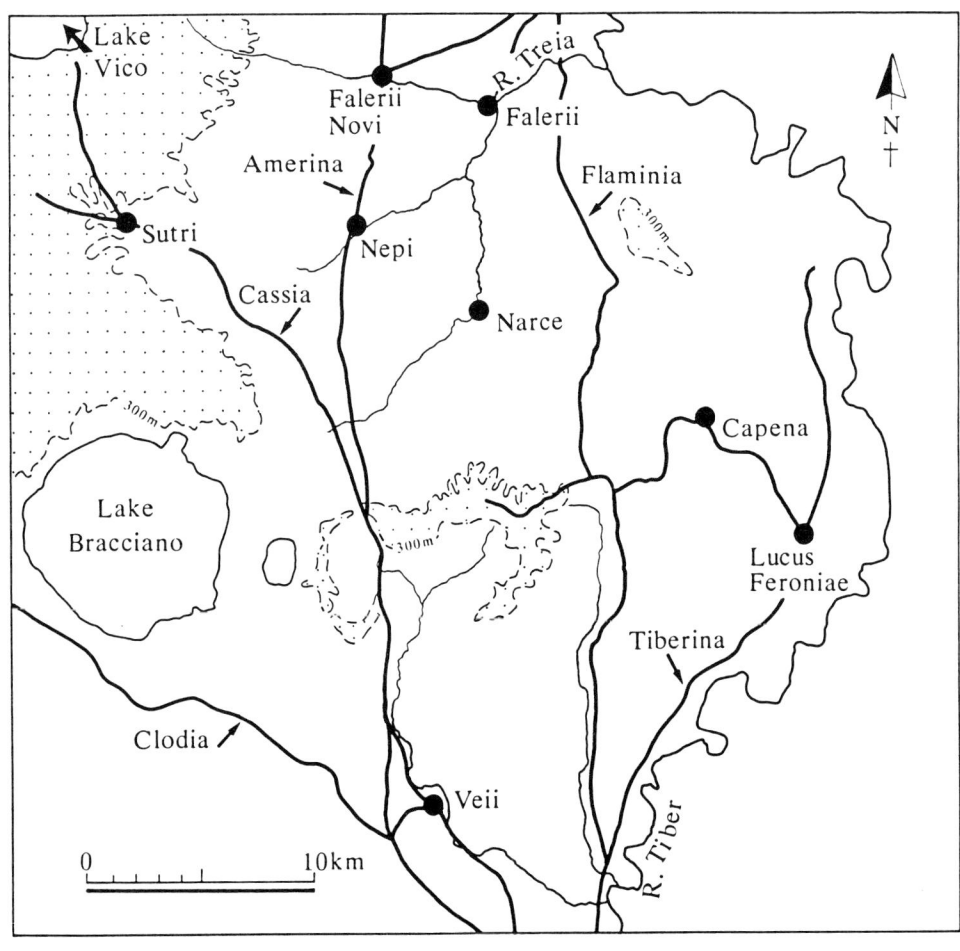

Fig. 3. South-eastern Etruria.

BC, refers not to *augustales* but to *magistri augustales* a term which appears on only a small number of inscriptions, almost all of which come from Italy, and which may indicate a different institution (Duthoy 1978: 1254–1309). Duthoy notes that of the 31 inscriptions recorded as referring to *magistri augustales* at least five come from South Etruria (1978: 1287). The Nepi inscription (3200) was set up in honour of Augustus by four men who constituted the first group of *magistri augustales* to be appointed in the town, Philippus, a freedman of Augustus, M. Aebutius Secundus, M. Gallius Anchiaius and P. Fidustius Antigonus.

It seems very likely that one of these, P. Fidustius Antigonus, should be identified with the P. Fidustius Antigonus whose name is inscribed on a white marble statue base (dimensions 0.65 × 0.45 × 0.45 m) now to be found in the local museum of Nepi. This inscription appears to be unpublished. It is tempting to suppose that there may also have been a connection between this individual and the woman Fidustia L.f. (daughter of Lucius) who commemorates her son Q.Veturius Pexsus in another inscription from Nepi (3205). This latter inscription seems, from the lettering used, to be first century in date, so that Fidustia might plausibly be a niece or granddaughter of L.Fidustius Antigonus. If Antigonus was (as most *augustales* were) a freedman, these inscriptions might be seen as attesting a family's rise from freed to equestrian status over three or four generations.

Q.Veturius Pexsus is described in 3205 (Devijver 1977, 859; 1987, 1170, V, 86) as *lupercus fabianus* (member of a college of priests) (Daremberg and Saglio 1877–1919), *ex collegio virtutis* (member of a veterans' association), *trib(unus) mil(itum)* for two years (a military rank held by equestrians) and *praefectus fabrum* (master of the carpenters) (Dobson 1966). The expression *ex collegio virtutis* is closely paralleled in two inscriptions from Gaul construed as part of the same text (*CIL* 4371, 4372; *AE* 1954, 104), commemorating men of similar standing (Christol & Demougin 1982: 141–153). *CIL* XI, 3205 also records the cost of the funerary monument as 20,000 HS. This is two fifths of Veturius's likely annual salary as a *tribunus militum* (Duncan-Jones 1965: 201, 242).

Another possible equestrian in Nepi may be traced in the very fragmentary 3216, restored to read *[Tre]boniu[s] Valens, [tr(ibunus) mil(itum)] a populo, [IIIIvir]i(ure) d(icundo)* (Devijver 1977: 792, T, 39).

Amongst the *augustales* or *magistri augustales* attested in inscriptions from Nepi are two imperial freedmen, Philippus Augusti libertus (3200) and M.Ulpius Thallus (3206). The latter inscription, on a statue base, was apparently set up by Thallus' wife and daughter to mark his generosity in providing an *epulum* (feast) for the decurions, *augustales* and *plebs* of Nepi, together with their wives and children. Another imperial freedman, Alypus, is mentioned in 7542. For an illuminating discussion of the position of imperial freedmen in *municipia* see Purcell (1983: 161ff).

Several local cults are attested in inscriptions. Two refer to the cult of Diana: 3198 is a dedication to *Diana compotens*, while 3210 was set up in honour of L.Aurelius Victor by the *iuvenes Nepessini Dianenses*. According to one local tradition, the temple of Diana may have been located near the site of the church of Santa Croce (Ranghiasci 1845: 39). This is now in ruins and accessible only with difficulty. The facade includes two Corinthian pilaster capitals which are probably antique. Another tradition places the temple on the site of the Basilica Sant'Elia in the nearby town of Castel Sant'Elia (Angelucci 1913). There seems no conclusive evidence in favour of either of these locations, though temples to Diana were quite often located outside the towns with which they were associated.

Another two inscriptions refer to the cult of Ceres. *CIL* XI, 3196 commemorates a sacrifice offered to *Ceres Augusta mater* on 18th April, AD 18 by L.Bennius Primus *magister pagi* and Bennia Primigenia, *magistra* (it is not clear which *pagus* is referred to). 3197 is a dedication made with public money to *Ceres frugifer*, fruit-bearing Ceres. Frederiksen and Ward-Perkins argue that these inscriptions should be linked with a shrine of Ceres on the Via Augusta towards Sutri (1957: 191).

An inscription which is reported to have been brought to Nepi in the late nineteenth century from a location close to Mount Soracte is probably not especially relevant to a study of the cults of Nepi but is interesting on its own account. *CIL* XI, 3199 is a large statue base of white marble commemorating the setting up of five altars in honour of the goddess Feronia by Hermeros, an expert marble worker (*magister ab marmoribus*) and slave of the emperor Claudius (the fourth line includes one of the new letters invented by that emperor).

According to local tradition a pagan temple, indeed the Capitolium, is said to have stood on the site of the present duomo. G.Ranghiasci, whose history of Nepi was published anonymously in 1845, refers to an inscription said to have been visible on the façade of the cathedral before it was severely damaged by French troops in 1798. According to his sources the first part of the text was as follows:

> D O M
> HEC VETUSTA BASILICA
> IN HAC ILLUSTRE PENTAPOLI
> IDOLOROM CULTUI PRIMITUS ERECTA
> VIX ORTA FIDE REGNANTE PETRO
> PTHOLOMEI ANTIOCHENI ET ROMANI NEPESINI
> PRIMORUM EPISCOPORUM OPERA

The inscription apparently went on to record that the site had now been converted into a place for the worship of the true God. The tradition linking the site of the Duomo with a pagan temple is also related by G.M.

Angelucci whose book *Sul Campo della Vittoria* (1913) celebrates the triumph of Christianity over paganism in the region of Nepi.

Certainly there seems to have been a bishop in Nepi from at least AD 419 (according to the *Liber Pontificalis*). Fiocchi Nicholai (1980) is dubious about the eleventh-century account of the martyrdom of Tolomeus and Romanus which attributes to them the foundation of the episcopate of Nepi in the time of the apostles (Bedini 1953: 12ff.). The oldest parts of the present structure he dates to the second half of the twelfth century or later. He does, however, see the tradition which links the site to a pagan place of cult as reinforced by a number of considerations, such as the apparent course of the *via Amerina*. The road, according to Frederiksen and Ward-Perkins, would have passed through this part of the town (suggesting that this area might have included the most important buildings) (1957: 90). He also notes the large number of inscriptions and pieces of ancient statuary which have come to light through road works and other excavations in this part of the town in the last century or so. For instance, *CIL* XI, 3200 & 3235 (the former an inscription in honour of the emperor Augustus set up by the first *magistri Augustales* in Nepi, the latter a private funerary inscription) were found when a drain was dug in the road running between the Piazza del Duomo and the Piazza del Comune (Fiorelli 1885: 396).

This road, now known as via Giacomo Matteotti (Fig. 2) (and before that as Via Vittorio Emanuele), was for a long time known as Via del Foro. There are other factors, too, which suggest that the *forum* in Roman Nepi was to be found in this part of the town. It is rumoured that three antique columns of fluted marble are still to be seen, apparently in their original position, in the cellar of no.53 Via Matteotti (these are perhaps to be identified with the columns referred to by Ranghiasci 1845: 48).

It seems likely from excavations recently conducted by the Soprintendenza (the results of which have not yet been published) that there was also a market area beside the *via Amerina* on the plain to the south west of the town. Potter suggests that the *forum* and *basilica* may have been located in this area in Roman times (1979: 116).

Other features of interest include the remains of an amphitheatre, now very much overgrown, about 200 m to the south of the town on the eastern side of the *via Amerina*, already noted by Pasqui (Gamurrini *et al.* 1972) and Ranghiasci (1845: 61). According to Pasqui (Gamurrini *et al.* 1972: 250), the elliptical arena measures 69 m by 41 m. He also notes extensive fragments of ancient building materials in the surrounding fields.

The core of a very substantial Roman mausoleum survives on the opposite side of the *via Amerina*. Ranghiasci plausibly suggests this monument may have commemorated the builder of the amphitheatre, since its position would make it hard to overlook for those returning from the games (1845: 61). A number of other Roman tombs have also been observed along roads leading towards Nepi. To the south of the town, on the eastern side of the *Via Amerina*, are to be seen the remains of Roman baths (Frederiksen & Ward-Perkins 1957: 87). Several fairly luxurious villas (Frederiksen & Ward-Perkins 1957, 181, two buildings about 3km north-west of Nepi) – though the idea that one to the south of the town belonged to the emperor Claudius is not especially plausible.

Numerous fragments of ancient statuary have been found in and around Nepi. A few of these are to be seen in the Museo Civico (these include part of a very large Hellenistic-style nude male torso), while some are now in museums in Rome (for instance, an Egyptian statue of basalt found in 1839, now in the Vatican collection). These finds are listed by Tomassetti (1979: 181–183).

NEPI AND SUTRI

These two towns are bracketed together by Livy. There are many similarities between their histories. Sutri is about 50 km from Rome and, like Nepi, is built on a tuff spur with gorges on either side. Both have been in continuous occupation since Etruscan times and earlier. Duncan (1958) and Potter (1979: 94–95) provide detailed discussion on Sutri. For a comparison of Nepi with other towns in south eastern Etruria see Nagle (1979).

Sutri was located on the *via Cassia*, and was the first major town on that road (which by-passed Veii) after Rome. The *Cassia* postdates the *Amerina* and, as was noted above, seems to have been designed for long distance traffic. Roman travellers heading for north-east Italy and beyond would very likely have stopped overnight at Sutri (Potter 1979: 115). Like Nepi, Sutri seems to have become a *municipium* after the Social War. Unlike Nepi, Sutri was raised to the status of a Roman colony, perhaps under the triumvirs (cf. *CIL* XI, 3254) (the *Liber Coloniarum* 217, 15–16, lists Nepi, too, as a colony but is not reliable). Strabo, writing in the time of the emperor Augustus, lists Sutri together with the larger towns of Etruria, such as Arezzo and Perugia, while Nepi is listed among the smaller centres (5.2.9). Pliny, likewise, writing a few decades later, places Sutri among the more substantial towns and Nepi among the smaller (*Nat. Hist.* 3.50–52). A number of Roman senators such as L.Pontius Aquila (Wiseman 1971: 253), P.Vergilius Pontianus (Wiseman 1971: 272) came from Sutri.

CIL lists 43 inscriptions from Sutri (3243–3280, 7546–7551), slightly less than from Nepi, though this does not seem significant. Three more (not listed in *CIL*) are published by Duncan (1958: 72–73). The most spectacular remnant of Roman Sutri is the amphitheatre carved from tuff, whose elliptical arena measures 50 m by 40 m; there are also remains of a Mithraeum (Duncan 1958: 70-72).

The fragments of ancient statuary currently visible in Sutri seem rather more numerous than those in Nepi (though this is hardly conclusive). The crypt of the Duomo in Sutri includes some impressive antique marble columns and capitals, reused, while two large Corinthian pillars are to be seen in the nave. While the survival of this larger volume of antique evidence from Sutri may be accidental, it seems to fit with the documentary evidence and is perhaps a reflection of Sutri's important location in Roman times as a stopping place on the *via Cassia*.

NEPI AFTER THE FALL OF ROME

Nepi's defensive virtues seem to have brought the town renewed importance for a period during the wars of the sixth century AD. For some time, the *via Flaminia*, the principal road from Rome to Ravenna, was blocked by the Lombards in the area around Spoleto and the *via Amerina* was used as an alternative route by the Byzantines. Nepi was of great strategic importance for control of this route and the historian Procopius (*Gothic Wars*, 4.35) refers to the town as a *phrourion* or guardpost. Bullough (1968) provides detail on the background to this period and Penteriani Iacoangeli and Penteriani (1986) information on Nepi.

CONCLUSION

The above account is in one narrow dimension merely the local history of a small town north of Rome. In another dimension it is illustrative of the varied strategies of state formation and imperial incorporation which have implications for the study of central Italy in particular, and comparative studies in general. Nepi was most probably occupied in the Bronze Age, but was profoundly affected by the political impact of the rapidly nucleating centre of Veii in the ninth century BC. This appears to have caused the reduction or even abandonment of Nepi as a centre of habitation until the late eighth century. From this phase onwards, there appears to have been a distinct continuity of settlement organisation and political continuity that was little affected by the take-over of Rome. Nepi played a key role in the extension of Roman power in central Italy, adopting new structures of local government devised by Rome. In more peaceful times, despite the town's proximity to the city of Rome, the inhabitants of Nepi seemed to have pursued ambitions on a local level rather than in the context of the wider empire. Nepi seems to have remained a prosperous, if small, town until at least the third century AD, while during the disturbances of the sixth century, its strategic position once again came to the fore.

ACKNOWLEDGEMENTS

This paper is based on the paper delivered at the Conference by SS and CM, the directors of the Nepi project, combined with the epigraphic and ancient historical evidence analysed by CE. The Nepi project, organised in collaboration with Francesco di Gennaro, Alessandro Guidi and other Italian colleagues, is funded by the following bodies: the the British Academy, the British School at Rome, Cassa Rurale ed Artigiana di Ronciglione, the Royal Archaeological Institute and the Society of Antiquaries. The Project would like to thank the Comune of Nepi (and in particular the then mayor, Pietro Soldatelli) for the invitation to research the origins of the town of Nepi. The project is grateful to the Soprintendenza alle Antichità per l'Etruria Meridionale (especially il Prof. G. Scichilone, la Dott.ssa D. Rizzo e la Dott.ssa De Lucia) for permission to excavate and scientific collaboration; also to the Bishop of Nepi and Civita Castellana for permission to excavate on their land. Further, the project extends thanks to the Direttore Generale and all the personnel of the Cassa rurale ed artigiana di Ronciglione, as well as to the Comunità dei Servi di Maria (and especially Padre Pietro Tollo) and the ristorante Crudelia for board and lodging.

The following individuals merit particular thanks: Piero Brunetti, Primo Concordia, Massimo Concordia, Francesco De Fazio, Luigi Fabrizi, Roberto Ginocchi, Pietro Gregori, Daniele Soldatelli and many others. Finally, Catharine Edwards would like to thank Mary Beard, Joyce Reynolds and Thomas Wiedemann for their invaluable assistance and advice in compiling the report on Roman Nepi.

Bibliography

Alvarez, W. 1972. 'The Treia valley north of Rome: volcanic stratigraphy, topographic evolution and geological influences on human settlement', *Geologia Romana* 11, 153-176.

Angelucci, G.M. 1913. *Sul Campo della Vittoria*, Rome.

Barker, G. & Stoddart, S. 1994. 'The Bronze Age of Central Italy, c. 2000-1000 BC', in Mathers, C. & Stoddart, S.K.F. (eds.), *Development and Decline in the Mediterranean Bronze Age*, Sheffield, John Collis Publications, 145-165.

Bedini, B. 1953. *I santi Tolomeo, Romano e campagni martiri*, Grottaferrata.

Bendinelli, G. 1921. 'Tomba a camera con seppellettile, rinvenuta in località Forano', *Notizie degli Scavi di Antichità* 1921, 356-358.

Bullough, D.A. 1968. *Italy and her Invaders*, Nottingham.

Camporeale, G. 1991. 'L'ethnos dei falisci secondo gli scrittori antichi', *Archeologia Classica* 52, 209-219.

Carver, M. & Stoddart, S. 1990. *Settlement and economy in South Etruria*. Unpublished preliminary Research Design.

Christol, M. & Demougin, S. 1982. 'La carriere d'un notable Narbonnais, au debut du 1er siecle après J-C', *Zeitschrift fur Papyrologie und Epigraphik* 49, 141-153.

Colonna, G. 1988. 'I latini e gli altri popoli del Lazio', in Pugliese Caratelli, G. (ed.) *Italia Omnium terrarum alumna. La civiltà dei Veneti, Reti, Liguri, Celti, Piceni, Umbri, Latini, Campani e Iapigi*, Milano, 411-528.

Cristofani, M. 1988. 'Etruschi nell'Agro Falisco', *Papers of the British School at Rome,* 56, 13–24.

Davison, J.M. 1972. *Seven Italic Tomb Groups from Narce,* Florence.

Devijver, H. 1977. *Prosopographia militiarum equestrium quae fuerunt ab Augusto ad Gallienum.* Pars Seconda. Litterae L – V, Universitaire Pers Leuven – Wetteren.

Devijver, H. 1987. *Prosopographia militiarum equestrium quae fuerunt ab Augusto ad Gallienum.* Pars Quarta. Supplementum 1. Universitaire Pers Leuven – Wetteren.

Di Gennaro, F. & Stoddart, S.K.F. 1982. 'A review of the evidence for prehistoric activity in part of south Etruria', *Papers of the British School at Rome,* 50, 1–21.

Dobson, B. 1966. 'The *praefectus fabrum* in the early principate', in *Britain and Rome: Essays in Honour of E. Birley on his Sixtieth Birthday.* Kendal, 61–84.

Dohan, E.H. 1942. *Italic Tomb Groups in the University Museum.* Philadelphia.

Duncan, G.C. 1958. 'Sutri (Sutrium): notes on southern Etruria 3', *Papers of the British School at Rome,* 13, 63–134.

Duncan-Jones, R. 1965. 'An epigraphic survey of costs in Roman Italy', *Papers of the British School at Rome,* 33, 189–306.

Duthoy, R. 1978. 'Les Augustales', *Aufstieg und Niedergang der römischen Welt* 2 (16) (2), 1254–1309.

Fiocchi Nicholai, V. 1980. 'Richerche sulle origini della cattedrale di Nepi', *Archeologia Laziale* 3, 223–227.

Fiorelli, G. 1885. 'Notizie degli Scavi di antichità comunicate dal socio G. Fiorelli al presidente. X. Nepi', *Notizie degli Scavi di Antichità,* 1885, 396.

Frederiksen, M. & Ward-Perkins, J.B. 1957. 'The ancient road systems of the central and northern Ager Faliscus', *Papers of the British School at Rome,* 25, 67–208.

Gamurrini, G.F., Cozza, A., Pasqui, A. & Mengarelli, R. 1972. *Carta archeologica d'Italia (1881–1897) materiali per l'Etruria e la Sabina.* (Forma Italiae serie II, Documenti 1), Florence.

Groag, E. & Stein, A. 1933. *Prosopographia Imperii Romani. Saec. I. II. III.* (2nd edition), Berlin and Leipzig.

Harris, W.V. 1971. *Rome in Etruria and Umbria.* Oxford.

Harrison, A. & Stoddart, S., n.d. *The South Etruria Enhancement Project.* Computer Applications and Quantitative Methods in Archaeology 1993, Staffordshire University.

Nagle, D.B. 1979. 'Towards a sociology of southeastern Etruria', *Athenaeum (Pavia)* 57, 411–441.

Pallottino, M. 1990. 'Presentazione del tema del convegno', in *Civiltà dei Falisci,* Firenze, 9–14.

Pasqui, A. 1902. 'Mazzano Romano. Scavi del principe del Drago nel territorio di questo comune', *Notizie degli Scavi di Antichità,* 1902, 321–55, 593–627.

Penteriani Iacoangeli, M.P. & Penteriani, U. 1986. *Nepi e il suo territorio nell'alto Medioevo (476–1311),* Rome.

Peroni, R. & Di Gennaro, F. 1986. 'Aspetti regionali dello sviluppo dell'insediamento protostorico nell'Italia centro-meridionale alla luce dei dati archeologici e ambientali', *Dialoghi di Archeologia,* 4 (2), 193–200.

Peroni, R. & Fugazzola, M. 1969. 'Ricerche preistoriche a Narce', *Bollettino di Paletnologia Italiana,* 78, 79–145.

Petitti, P. 1990. 'La preistoria del territorio "falisco". Cenni introduttivi. L'età del bronzo', in *Civiltà dei Falisci,* Firenze, 53–59.

Potter, T. 1976. *A Faliscan Town in South Etruria. Excavations at Narce. 1966–71,* London.

Potter, T. 1979. *The Changing Landscape of South Etruria,* London.

Purcell, N. 1983. 'The *apparitores*: a study in social mobility', *Papers of the British School at Rome,* 51, 125–173.

Ranghiasci, G. 1845. *Memorie o siano relazioni istoriche sull'origine, nome, fasti o progressi dell'antichissima città di Nepi,* Todi.

Raspi Serra, J. 1974. *Le diocesi dell'Alto Lazio. Bagnoregio – Bomarzo – Castro – Civita Castellana – Nepi – Orte – Sutri – Tuscania.* (Corpus della Scultura Altomedievale 8), Spoleto.

Rellini, U. 1920. 'Cavernette e ripari preistorici nell'Agro Falisco', *Monumenti Antichi,* 26, 5–180.

Rix, H. (ed.) 1991. *Etruskische Texte. Editio Minor. Bande II. Texte,* Tubingen.

Rustico, L. 1986–7. 'Rinvenimenti antichi nel sottoterraneo del castello di Nepi', *Archeologia Classica* 38–40, 70–81.

Salmon, E.T. 1982. *The Making of Roman Italy,* London.

Selmi, R. 1976. 'Presenze preistoriche nel bacino idrografico del treia', *Atti del II Convegno dei Gruppi Archeologici. Lazio,* Roma, 55–59.

Spivey, N. & Stoddart, S.K.F. 1990. *Etruscan Italy,* London.

Stefani, E. 1910. 'Scoperte di antichità nel territorio nepesino', *Notizie degli Scavi di Antichità,* 1910, 199–222.

Stefani, E. 1918. 'Antico sepolcro della necropoli nepesina', *Notizie degli Scavi di Antichità,* 1918, 16–19.

Stefani, E. 1930. 'Nepi. Scoperte varie avvenute nel territorio Nepesino', *Notizie degli Scavi di Antichità,* 1930, 520–529.

Tomassetti, G. 1979. *La campagna romana,* new edition, vol.III, Firenze.

Wiseman, T.P. 1970. 'Roman republican road-building', *Papers of the British School at Rome,* 38, 122–152.

Wiseman, T.P. 1971. *New Men in the Roman Senate. 139 BC – AD 14,* Oxford.

46

I Possedimenti del Monastero di S. Paolo f.l.m. (Roma) in Etruria Meridionale: Indagine Preliminare

LORENZA DE MARIA, FRANCESCA FEI, ROSSANA MARTORELLI & ANGELA TORO
(Centro Regionale per la Documentazione dei Beni Culturali e Ambientali del Lazio, Roma)

Sommario: *La presente ricerca è volta all'individuazione dei possedimenti del monastero di S. Paolo fuori le mura (Roma) fino al 1300 d.C. I dati scaturiscono principalmente dai documenti conservati nell'archivio dell'abbazia ed interessano, finora, solo l'area dell'Etruria Meridionale a nord di Roma. Numerose fonti archeologiche e documentarie confermano la progressiva formazione del* patrimonium *fra l'VIII e il XIV secolo. La verifica sul campo solo in rari casi ha ricondotto al riconoscimento delle sopravvivenze monumentali, più spesso i resti appaiono inglobati o nascosti dalle trasformazioni edilizie successive.*

METODOLOGIA E FINALITÀ DELLA RICERCA (R.M.)

Dal 1989 il Centro Regionale di Documentazione del Lazio, nell'ambito dell'attività di censimento e catalogazione dei BB. CC. AA., aveva esteso la sua sfera d'azione al territorio del c.d. 'Comprensorio del Lago di Bracciano', incluso in antico nella diocesi di *Forum Clodii/Manturianum,* equivalente agli attuali comuni di Bracciano, Anguillara Sabazia, Trevignano Romano, Manziana, Canale Monterano e in parte Oriolo Romano.

In un primo tempo l'indagine era stata mirata alla chiesa di San Liberato, situata nei pressi di Bracciano, sorta sulle rovine di una presunta villa romana e dedicata al culto dei santi Marco, Marciano e Liberato (vedi Atti Bracciano 1994, in particolare, per le vicende storico-archeologiche del sito, De Maria 1994; cfr. Christie, Gibson & Ward-Perkins 1991). L'edificio, che risale ad un'epoca ancora imprecisata, certamente esisteva nel IX secolo e dal X fu affidato dal papa Agapito II (946–955) ai Benedettini del Monastero di S. Paolo f.l.m., come attesta la bolla di Gregorio VII (1081) (Trifone 1908: 283).

In quell'occasione, constatando la scarsità di studi in proposito, si ritenne di notevole interesse per la conoscenza dell'assetto territoriale del primo medioevo avviare un censimento dei possessi fondiari che il Monastero di S. Paolo aveva in Etruria Meridionale. Inoltre, poichè presso la Biblioteca della British School at Rome giace inedito un elaborato di I. Adams, che prende in considerazione tali proprietà a partire dal 1300, si pensò di circoscrivere l'indagine entro un arco cronologico compreso fra le origini del patrimonio ed il 1300 (cfr. D'Amato 1988: 213–214).

Nel Museo Lapidario annesso alla basilica sono conservate due importanti testimonianze monumentali che attestano l'esistenza almeno fin dal VII secolo di un patrimonio fondiario di pertinenza dei monaci benedettini di S. Paolo. Nel settore III è un'epigrafe con il testo di una lettera di Gregorio Magno (590–604), datata al 25 gennaio 604, indirizzata a Felice *subdiaconus et rector Patrimonii Appiae,* nella quale si assegnano alla basilica i proventi ricavati dalla massa ad *Aquas Salvias* (Margarini 1650: 243). Sulla parete contigua è affissa una colonna, in origine impiegata nell'arco trionfale, su cui è inciso un decreto di un *Leo episcopus,* presumibilmente Leone III (775–816), per mezzo del quale le *oblationes* deposte dai fedeli sull'altare di S. Paolo venivano destinate al monastero (Margarini 1650: 384).

La ricerca è stata condotta in diverse fasi. In primo luogo si è intrapreso lo spoglio dei testi conservati presso l'Archivio del monastero stesso. In particolare, il *Codex Diplomaticus Paulinus* – che contiene bolle papali dall'epoca di Gregorio VII, atti di vendite, donazioni e concessioni in enfiteusi di terreni fra privati e monaci di S. Paolo (vedi Trifone 1908) – ha fornito una notevole quantità di dati, integrati poi da notizie desunte da documenti raccolti nel *Bullarium Casinense* (Margarini 1650–1670) e nel Codice Vaticano Latino 3927 (riportati dal Galletti). La rilettura di tali testi, peraltro editi dal Trifone (1908), unitamente al censimento bibliografico, ha permesso di individuare ed ubicare numerosi toponimi, ricostruendo così una mappa di siti, che anche solo allo stadio preliminare a cui è giunta la ricerca si presenta assai nutrita. I centri appaiono dislocati prevalentemente in rapporto alle grandi arterie di comunicazione – vie Clodia, Cassia, Tiberina e Flaminia – disseminati nelle campagne e collegati mediante diverticoli al sistema viario principale.

Si è poi proceduto alla ricognizione *in loco*, per verificare l'eventuale stato di sopravvivenza delle emergenze monumentali ed archeologiche, note da documenti e da studi precedenti. Sono emerse subito notevoli difficoltà, dovute alle trasformazioni edilizie succedutesi nei secoli, che hanno inglobato le strutture più antiche. Talvolta i resti sono del tutto distrutti o parzialmente emergenti, ma coperti dalla vegetazione. In questa prima fase è stato possibile effettuare dei sopralluoghi solo nelle seguenti località: Monterano (comune di Canale Monterano), San Liberato (comune di Bracciano); Campagnano; Capena, Castellaccio, San Leone e Montecanino (comune di Capena); Castelnuovo di Porto, Vaccareccia (comune di Castelnuovo di Porto); Cesano; Civitella S. Paolo, Pian del Monumento e Prosciano (comune di Civitella S. Paolo); Formello; Morlupo; Riano.

Pertanto, ci si propone in questa sede di esporre in sintesi i dati finora acquisiti, di cui una raccolta completa è depositata presso il Centro Regionale di Documentazione. Trattandosi del primo bilancio – solo preliminare – di un'indagine in corso, è certamente prematuro trarre delle conclusioni; si tenterà invece di suggerire ipotesi di lavoro da verificare nel corso della ricerca allo scopo di ricostruire il panorama dell'organizzazione ecclesiastica delle campagne attorno a Roma nell'alto medioevo e di individuare l'ingerenza del potere monastico anche sull'evoluzione topografica e monumentale dell'epoca.

Note introduttive (L.D.M.)

Il tentativo della presente ricerca di contribuire in qualche modo alla ricostruzione dell'assetto topografico dell'Etruria Meridionale nei secoli dell'alto medioevo non può prescindere da alcune note di carattere generale. Le difficoltà nel reperire fonti che forniscano dati attendibili e storicamente validi per questo arco cronologico non sono poche: in questo caso il silenzio della letteratura antica è praticamente assoluto fino al pontificato di Gregorio Magno. A quest'epoca si riferisce infatti un'iscrizione, datata all'anno 604, conservata nella Galleria Lapidaria del Monastero di S. Paolo, che testimonia la prima donazione di beni all'abbazia (Margarini 1650: II, 1; 1654: XVIII, n. 243; ICVR II, 4760; Silvagni 1943, tav. XII, 1). Si deve attendere però il secolo XI per avere informazioni più precise sulle proprietà dei monaci confermate nella famosa bolla di papa Gregorio VII del 1081 (Trifone 1908: 278). Tale documento menziona, in realtà, ben sei bolle precedenti relative ad un periodo compreso fra i secoli IX e XI, dei papi Pasquale I (817–824), Leone IV (847–855), Marino II (942–946), Agapito II (946–955), Silvestro II (999–1003) e Leone IX (1049–1055).

Non è un caso che i primi elementi concreti sui possedimenti territoriali di una certa rilevanza siano riferibili al secolo X: l'incertezza amministrativa determinatasi al crollo dell'impero carolingio e il conseguente accentrarsi del particolarismo locale furono le cause principali dell'avvio di quella grande opera di ristrutturazione dell'assetto fondiario del 'principato territoriale di S. Pietro' meglio noto come 'incastellamento' (cfr. Arnaldi 1991: 33 ss). Ed è sempre all'inizio del X secolo che molti fra i principali monasteri di Roma e del suburbio furono riformati dai monaci Cluniacensi al fine di renderli funzionali alle trasformazioni politico-sociali in atto: l'abbazia di S. Paolo fu riformata nel 937 (Mabillon 1739: III, 405) da Oddone di Cluny e i monaci ne assunsero *in toto* la custodia e l'amministrazione (Trifone 1908: 271).

I rapporti dei grandi monasteri di tipo basilicale, come S. Paolo, con la campagna e la loro posizione in tale ambito risultarono, come si è detto, dal crescente indebolimento dell'organizzazione imperiale da una parte e dall'espansione del cristianesimo, della vita religiosa e delle forme di culto dall'altra, non senza soddisfare anche finalità di ordine economico e sociale (Leccisotti 1957; Bosl 1982; Penco 1983; Picasso 1987: 3 ss; Prinz 1987).

Osservando la dislocazione dei grandi patrimoni monastici nei pressi di Roma, si deve rilevare che, quasi come una cintura di protezione, si era venuta a formare una sorta di anello di 'terre di S. Benedetto' e fra esse alcune signorie feudali: S. Paolo, Farfa, Subiaco, ma anche S. Martino al Cimino, Casamari, S. Vincenzo al Volturno, Montecassino ed altre minori (Toubert 1973: II, 1103–1126). Tra esse alcune sorsero in riferimento a tracciati stradali di rilievo: Farfa, ad esempio, si inserì al margine di uno degli assi portanti dei territori dell'Italia centrale, assumendo un ruolo di notevole importanza nelle vicende storiche legate ai rapporti intercorrenti fra i Longobardi, prima, i Franchi in seguito e il Papato (Whitehouse 1984; Pani Ermini 1985: 34, ivi ampia bibliografia).

Riguardo alla formazione dei grandi possedimenti abbaziali di S. Paolo in Etruria Meridionale, possiamo desumere un buon numero di notizie dalla già menzionata bolla di Gregorio VII, che ci informa circa le varie donazioni papali che andarono ad arricchire il *patrimonium* del monastero e di altri numerosi possessi dei quali non viene indicata la provenienza. Gregorio VII ed i suoi predecessori più vicini cercarono di dar vita ad uno stato monastico-feudale abbastanza potente e in grado di fronteggiare quello dell'abbazia di Farfa, tradizionalmente più legata alle volontà degli imperatori (Silvestrelli 1970: I, 224).

A questo scopo, dunque, furono donati al monastero di S. Paolo molti feudi che, come Fiano, Formello,

I Possedimenti del Monastero di S. Paolo f.l.m. in Etruria Meridionale

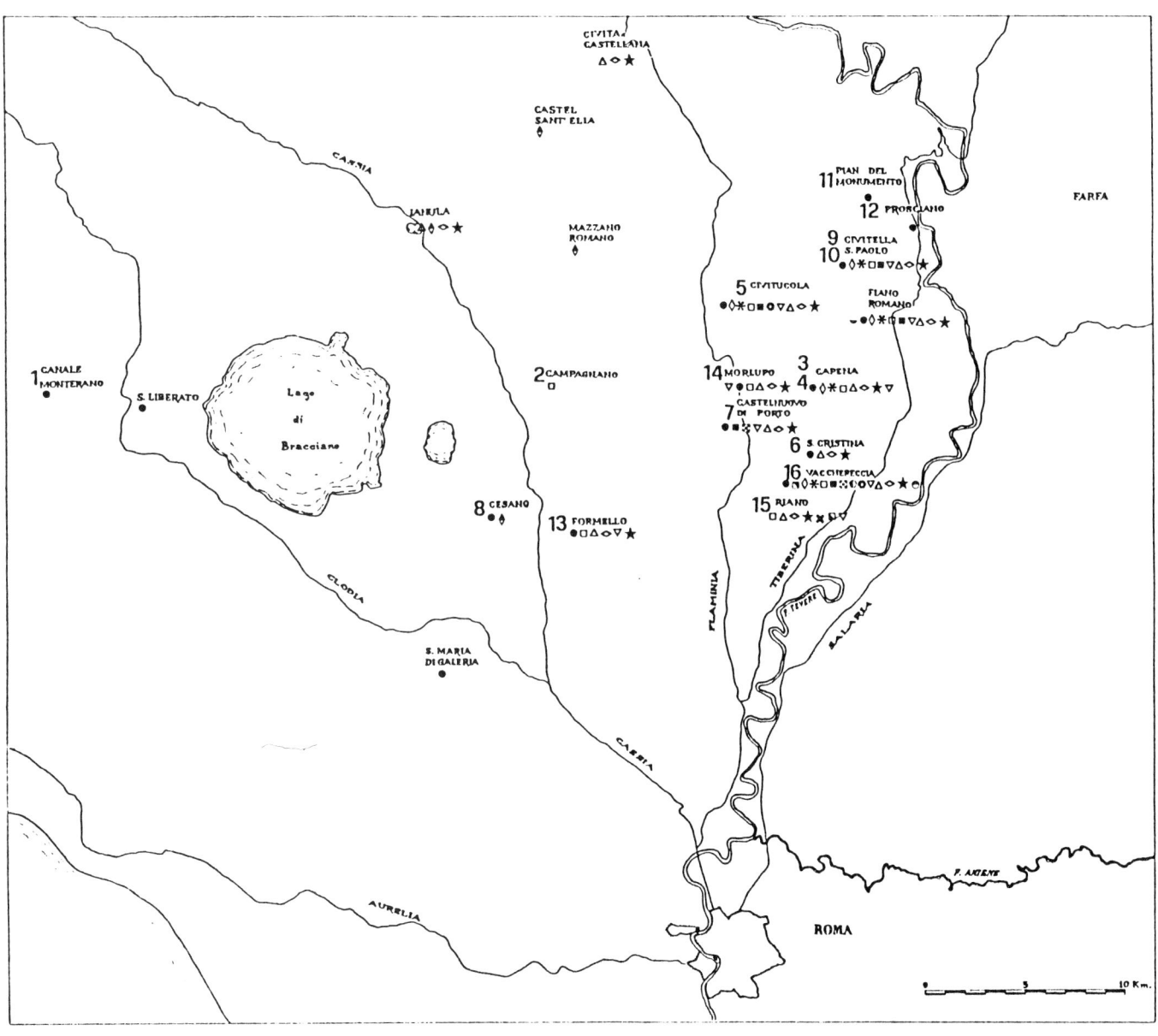

LEGENDA

- A - (1014) Diploma dell'imperatore Enrico III (MARGARINI 1650, II, pp. 113-114)
- B - (1072-1081) Donazione di Rogata di Cencio (MARGARINI 1650, II, p. 18)
- C - (1081) Bolla di Gregorio VII (MARGARINI 1650, II, p. 107)
- D - (1099-1118) Restituzione di Stefano, figlio di Teobaldo di Cencio (TRIFONE 1908, p. 207)
- E - (1099-1118) Concessione in enfiteusi di Anastasio, priore di S. Paolo, a Cencio e Stefano di Teobaldo (TRIFONE 1908, p. 287)
- F - (1130) Bolla dell'antipapa Anacleto II (MARGARINI, Codex, p. 18)
- G - (1139) Istanza di Azzo, abate di S. Paolo (GALLETTI 1756, pp. 65-66)
- H - (1139-1143) Istanza di Teobaldo, priore di S. Paolo (TRIFONE 1908, p. 289)
- I - (1158-1193) Rinuncia di Cencio di Stefano di Teobaldo (TRIFONE 1908, p. 290)
- L - (1158-1193) Concessione in enfiteusi di Maccabeo, abate di S. Paolo (TRIFONE 1908, pp. 290-291)
- M - (1186-1189) Diploma dell'imperatore Enrico VI (MARGARINI 1650, II, p. 217)
- N - (1203) Bolla di Innocenzo III (MARGARINI 1650, I, p. 25)
- O - (1212) Bolla di Innocenzo III (MARGARINI, Codex, p. 57)
- P - (1218) Bolla di Onorio III (TRIFONE 1908, pp. 294-300)
- Q - (1236) Bolla di Gregorio IX (MARGARINI 1650, I, p. 35)
- R - (1259) Vendita da parte delle famiglie de Veczosis e de Pezutis (TRIFONE 1908, pp. 302-303)
- S - (1241-1259) Istanza di Berardo, economo di S. Paolo (TRIFONE 1908, p. 303)
- T - (1282) Bolla di Martino IV (MARGARINI, Codex, p. 140)

Fig. 1. Localizzazione dei possedimenti del Monastero di S. Paolo f.l.m. noti da fonti documentarie. (Provincia di Roma, Assessorato alla Programmazione).

Morlupo, Capena (*Castrum Lepronianum*), Civitella S. Paolo, Castellaccio, Vaccareccia ed in seguito anche Campagnano, Riano e Castelnuovo di Porto, erano situati sulla riva destra del Tevere a nord di Roma, una zona dominata da Farfa sulla sponda opposta del fiume e dove quest'ultima tentava di estendere le sue mire espansionistiche (La Cronaca di Farfa riferisce di donazioni ricevute e di acquisti compiuti nell'XI secolo nel territorio di Nazzano, Fiano e Formello, cfr. Silvestrelli 1970: I, 224; Vetromile 1983: 211 ss.). Un siffatto tentativo di creare un grande stato feudale riuscì solo in parte: arginare l'espansione di Farfa non fu sufficiente per contrapporre un'adeguata ed efficace resistenza ai numerosi attacchi degli imperatori ed alle pesanti conseguenze che questi produssero su Roma e sul Papato (cfr. Silvestrelli 1970: I, 225).

A partire dalla fine dell'XI secolo si assiste ad una prima inversione di tendenza e ad una progressiva diminuzione dei possedimenti. A quest'epoca risale l'usurpazione da parte di Stefano di Teobaldo dei castelli di Fiano, Capena, Vaccareccia e Castellaccio che furono trasformati in enfiteusi da Pasquale II (Trifone 1908: 286). Soltanto nel 1203, sotto il pontificato di Innocenzo III, alcuni domini (tra cui Fiano, Capena, Civitella, Castellaccio e Castelnuovo di Porto) tornarono in possesso del monastero (Margarini 1650: I, 26).

Con il passare del tempo e il susseguirsi degli eventi, il *patrimonium* di S. Paolo visse alterne vicende per giungere al XVII secolo, quando rimasero all'abbazia i soli castelli di Nazzano, Capena e Civitella S. Paolo, unica proprietà ancora oggi conservata dai monaci Benedettini che ne stanno, peraltro attualmente, trattando la vendita.

Sopravvivenze archeologiche e monumentali (A.T.)

In questa sezione sono brevemente descritte le sopravvivenze archeologiche e monumentali riscontrate direttamente, nel territorio dell'Etruria Meridionale, relativamente ai secoli VIII-XIII. Di ogni sito – contrassegnato da un numero corrispondente alla localizzazione sulla cartografia – sono citati rispettivamente: toponimo moderno, comune, provincia di appartenenza, lettera alfabetica corrispondente alla fonte documentaria che lo menziona (fig.1), citazione relativa e dati emersi dai sopralluoghi nel territorio. Nella stessa cartografia sono ugualmente evidenziati – ma senza numero – siti relativi a possedimenti del Monastero di S. Paolo noti dai documenti di archivio, nei quali, però, non è stata ancora effettuata verifica diretta.

1 – Monterano
Canale Monterano (Roma)
C (1081) "... *medietatem civitatis Manturiane et totius territorii eius...*"

Attualmente nel paese, che fu abbandonato nel corso del secolo XVIII, relativamente alla fase benedettina, sopravvivono in stato assai rovinoso resti di strutture abitative e una chiesa a tre navate con tracce di decorazione affrescata, forse la S. Maria *in Manturiano* ricordata dal *Liber Pontificalis* nella vita di Stefano V (885-891). Nel territorio *civitatis Manturiane*, al km. 19 dell'odierna via Settevene – Palo, è la chiesa di S. Liberato, dedicata ai santi Marco, Marciano e Liberato. In base ai documenti ma soprattutto all'analisi delle tecniche costruttive, l'edificio può risalire al IX secolo per la struttura originaria. Alla fase benedettina (sec. X-XII?) si attribuiscono alcuni interventi di ampliamento della chiesa primitiva: le aggiunte della navatella nord e successivamente del catino absidale, nonché della torre campanaria. Inoltre si arricchisce anche la suppellettile architettonica e scultorea, della quale si conservano due mensole e un frammento di pluteo.

2 – Campagnano (Roma)
F (1130) "...*In Castello praeterea Campaniani...*"
All'interno della parrocchiale di S. Giovanni sono visibili alcuni bassorilievi (fig.2) di provenienza incerta, riutilizzati nella costruzione di tre altari, databili nel IX secolo (Raspi Serra 1974: 124-126; figg. 151-155). In un vicolo che inizia da via S. Giovanni è visibile – murata in una casa – una figura a rilievo nel tufo, denominata 'il Tifo', attribuita dalla Raspi Serra ai secoli VIII-IX (1974: 127; fig. 156), assegnata invece da V. Cavallo al secolo XIII (1992: 42). La chiesetta della Pietà, costruita direttamente sulla roccia, presenta un impianto originario in blocchi di tufo con abside a cordoni e archetti risalente ai secoli XII-XIII e rimaneggiamenti dei secoli XV-XVI. Sotto l'edificio è visibile un ambiente a volta sostenuta da una colonna con capitello a foglie d'acqua.

Fig. 2. Campagnano – Chiesa di S. Giovanni: altare.

3 – Capena (Roma)

C (1081)	"...*castrum vero Lepronianum* ..."
D (1099–1118)	"...*castrum quod vocatur Liprinianum*..."
E (1099–1118)	"...*castrum ... Lipriniani*..."
F (1130)	"... *Liprignanum*..."
M (1188)	"... *alia quoque castra... Liprinianum*..."
N (1203)	"... *castrum Lepriniani*..."
P (1218)	*Idem*
Q (1236)	*Idem*

Nel centro storico non si conservano strutture pertinenti ai secoli VIII-XIII. Il Palazzo dei Monaci, che mostra attualmente un impianto costruttivo risalente alla fine del 1500, insiste parzialmente sulle strutture del *castrum* medievale citato dalle fonti documentarie. Al centro del paese moderno, nel giardino pubblico, è visibile una fontana costituita da un piedistallo d'epoca recente sul quale poggia una vasca circolare decorata esternamente da protomi umane scolpite in corrispondenza dei punti cardinali. Iscrizioni corrono sui profili esterno e inferiore del bordo, nonché tra le protomi. I caratteri delle iscrizioni stesse e della decorazione sembrerebbero orientare verso un'esecuzione della vasca nel medioevo avanzato. Tra i reperti archeologici di una collezione privata è un frammento marmoreo di pilastrino o transenna, decorato da bassorilievo formato da un intreccio di nastro vimineo a tre capi che forma girali annodati tra loro. Ad un'estremità del pezzo è scolpito, entro un girale, un volatile che becca un grappolo d'uva. La datazione è assegnabile al IX secolo. Il frammento proviene dalla località Bombelli – vicina alla chiesa di S. Leone – dove era riutilizzato come gradino di una casa.

4 – Chiesa di S. Leone
Capena (Roma)

N (1203)	"...*ecclesia S.Leonis de Lepriniano* ..."
P (1218)	*Idem*
Q (1236)	*Idem*

La chiesa all'interno del cimitero presenta alcuni elementi strutturali e decorativi della costruzione originaria, datata presumibilmente al IX secolo: appartengono a questo periodo i due archi di luce differente tra le navate, i muri perimetrali della navata maggiore conclusa dall'abside semicircolare, le transenne delle finestre e i fregi del portale. Inoltre l'iconostasi della navata maggiore, che adotta motivi ornamentali altomedioevali, fu allestita e restaurata nel 1520, utilizzando le sculture di un precedente cancello del IX secolo. La navatella sinistra e gli affreschi che decorano le pareti di fondo delle navate e della controfacciata sono invece relativi al secolo XV.

5 – Castellaccio
Capena (Roma)

C (1081)	"... *tertiam partem civitatis Scapitinate*..."
D (1099–1118)	"... *Civitatucolas ... Strictilianam* ... "
E (1099–1118)	"... *Strictiniana* ..."
F (1130)	"... *medietatem Civitatis Stertiliane* ..."
G (1139)	"...*Strictiniani*..."
L (1158 – 1193)	"... *VI partem castri quod dicitur Civitas Strictiniana* ..."
M (1188)	"... *Civitellam Strictinianam* ..."
N (1203)	"... *Civitatem Stertinianam cum ecclesia Sancti Ioannis et lacu* ..."
P (1218)	*Idem*
Q (1236)	*Idem*

La struttura principale emergente sull'altura di Civitucola, sito dell'antica città di Capena, è il cosiddetto Castellaccio; l'edificio romano, costruito in opera incerta e genericamente datato tra la metà del II e gli inizi del I secolo a.C., presenta fasi di riutilizzazione in età post-antica che indicano continuità di vita fino a tutto il Medioevo. (Per una puntuale analisi delle strutture e dell'abitato di Capena antica cfr. Bartolini & Turchetti in questi stessi Atti e da ultimo Turchetti, c.s.).

6 – Monte Canino
Capena (Roma)

C (1081)	"... *duas ecclesias in Colina iuxta Vaccariciam ... S.Christina* ..."
N (1203)	"... *Castrum Bacchariciae cum ecclesia Sanctae Christinae* ..."
P (1218)	"... *Castrum Bacchariciae cum ecclesia Sancte Christine* ..."
Q (1236)	"... *Castrum Bacchariciae cum ecclesia Sanctae Christinae* ..."

La chiesa di S. Giustina è stata identificata da Jones (1962: 161–163), da Wickham (1979: 70–72) e da Fiocchi Nicolai (1988: 355) con un edificio di culto rinvenuto durante scavi effettuati nel 1934 sul Monte Canino (Pallottino 1937: 7–28), a circa un km. a NE di Vaccareccia. Tale edificio fu datato dallo studioso tra i secoli V e VII, ma il rinvenimento di un capitello altomedievale ne assicura la frequentazione almeno fino al IX secolo (Fiocchi Nicolai 1988: 355). Durante alcune ricognizioni sul sito, effettuate nel 1986 e nel 1989 nell'ambito di una precedente ricerca in corso di pubblicazione, sono stati riscontrati alcuni resti delle strutture messe in luce durante lo scavo del 1934. Inoltre sulla superficie erano visibili: frammenti di blocchi lavorati di travertino, un frammento di *torcular*, un basolo, frammenti di tegole e di laterizi. Il toponimo di S. Cristina è attualmente rimasto al ponte sul fosso Cento Valli situato a circa km.1,5 a NE del sito.

7 – Castelnuovo di Porto (Roma)

C (1081)	"... *medietatem Castelli Novi* ..."
G (1139)	"... *de Castello Novo* ..."
H (1139–1143)	*Idem*
M (1188)	"... *Castellum Novum* ..."
N (1203)	*Idem*
P (1218)	*Idem*
Q (1236)	*Idem*

Il paese odierno non conserva strutture o reperti relativi al periodo esaminato, ad eccezione del campanile duecentesco – fortemente restaurato – della chiesa di S. Maria Assunta, ricostruita nel XVIII secolo su un precedente impianto romanico (Panepuccia & Clementi 1990: 36 ss; Gallavotti Cavallero 1992: 103.).

8 – Cesano (Roma)

C (1081)	"... *Massam Cesanam*..."
O (1212)	"...*ecclesiam...Sancte Marie...in fundo Cesano* ..."

Attualmente nel paese non sono presenti sopravvivenze archeologiche e monumentali relative ai secoli VIII-XIII.

9 – Civitella San Paolo (Roma)

C (1081)	"... *Civitatem vero de Colonis* ..."
D (1099–1118)	"... *Civitatem de Colonis* ..."
E (1099–1118)	"... *Civitella* ..."
F (1130)	"... *Civitella de Colonis* ..."
G (1139)	"...*Civitellam*..."
M (1188)	"... *Civitellam de Collinis* ..."
N (1203)	"... *Civitatem Colorum* ..."
P (1218)	*Idem*
Q (1236)	*Idem*

Il Palazzo dei monaci costituisce l'ultimo possedimento dell'abbazia di S.Paolo nell'area esaminata. L'impianto costruttivo visibile, attribuibile al secolo XV, ha inglobato strutture preesistenti. Nel cortile interno, oltre a reperti archeologici lapidei ascrivibili ad epoche diverse, provenienti dalle località Prosciano, Miciano, Monte Tello e S. Martino, è conservato un resto di pilastrino pertinente a Civitella stessa o al territorio circostante, decorato da un intreccio vimineo con cerchi annodati, databile al IX secolo.

10 – Chiesa di S. Lorenzo
Civitella S. Paolo (Roma)

N(1203)	"... *ecclesiam Sancti Laurentii extra castrum Civitellae* ..."
P (1218)	*Idem*
Q(1236)	*Idem*

La chiesa del cimitero insiste su strutture romane pertinenti ad una grande villa che si estendeva probabilmente in tutta l'area occupata dal cimitero stesso (Gazzetti 1992: 70). L'edificio presenta fasi costruttive risalenti ad epoche diverse, ancora da studiare.

11 – Piano del Monumento
Civitella San Paolo (Roma)

C (1081)	"...*Monumentum*"

La *Massa Monumentum*, citata tra i beni del Monastero di S.Paolo nella bolla di Gregorio VII, fu posta in relazione dal Tomassetti con il tempio sul quale – secondo l'autore – insisterebbe la chiesa di S.Antimo a Nazzano (1884: 375). La Muzzioli (1980: 165) identifica il toponimo esaminato con la località Piano del Monumento a Nord della strada Fiano-Nazzano (km.9), dove furono rinvenuti reperti archeologici pertinenti ad una o più tombe monumentali sequestrati nel 1911.

12 – Prosciano
Civitella San Paolo (Roma)

C (1081)	"...*Priscianum*..."

La località *Priscianum*, dove esisteva una *massa* di proprietà del Monastero di S. Paolo all'epoca di Gregorio VII, è stata identificata con il toponimo Prosciano che non compare nella cartografia I.G.M. ma è presente in una carta del territorio di Civitella (XIX sec.) nell'Archivio di Stato di Roma. In tale località (toponimo I.G.M. "Monte Carboncello") in un terreno dei monaci di S.Paolo, nel 1863 furono rinvenuti resti di strutture murarie antiche e reperti archeologici trasportati nel Palazzo di Civitella (Muzzioli 1980: 163-164).

13 – Formello (Roma)

C (1081)	"...*Castrum quoque Formelli*..."
F (1130)	"...*Castellum insuper Formelli*..."
M (1188)	"...*Formellum*..."
N (1203)	"...*Castrum Formelli* ..."
P (1218)	*Idem*
Q (1236)	*Idem*

Attualmente nel paese non sono state rilevate persistenze monumentali relative al periodo esaminato, tranne i campanili delle chiese di S.Lorenzo e S.Angelo, che, sebbene fortemente rimaneggiati, sembrano pertinenti – come impianto originario – al periodo romanico. Il Palazzo Chigi – in corso di restauro – che presenta fasi costruttive relative ai secc. XV e XVII, insiste probabilmente sulle strutture del *castrum* medievale.

14 – Morlupo (Roma)

C (1081)	"...*Castrum Morilupo*..."
F (1130)	"...*Morlupum*..."
M (1188)	*Idem*
N (1203)	"...*Castrum quod vocatur Morlupum*..."
P (1218)	*Idem*
Q (1236)	*Idem*

All'interno della parrocchiale di S.Giovanni è conservata

una lastra di travertino con iscrizione sepolcrale. Tale epigrafe ricorda la costruzione di una chiesa ad opera del duca Giovanni di Leone, vissuto negli ultimi decenni del IX secolo (Muzzioli 1980: 163-164, 229).

15 – Riano (Roma)

F (1130)	"...*Castrum Regiani*..."
M (1188)	"...*Raijanum*..."
N (1203)	"... *Castrum Raiani*..."
P (1218)	*Idem*
Q (1236)	*Idem*
R (1259)	*Idem*
T (1282)	"...*Castri Reiani*..."

Attualmente nel paese non sono state rilevate persistenze monumentali relative al periodo esaminato. Tuttavia la presenza nel Castello Baronale, oggi sede del Comune, di muri diversi per forma e spessore da quelli del restante edificio fa supporre che il castello quattrocentesco, fortemente rimaneggiato nei secoli successivi, abbia inglobato un torrione a pianta rettangolare di età medievale.

16 – Vacchereccia

Castelnuovo di Porto (Roma)

B (1072-1081)	"...*Castrum nomine Baccaricie*..."
C (1081)	"...*Castellum Vaccaricie*..."
D (1099-1118)	"... *Castrum quod vocatur Baccaricie*..."
E (1099-1118)	"... *Castrum ... Baccaricie*..."
F (1130)	"...*Castrum Vaccaricie*..."
G (1139)	"...*de Castro Baccaricie*..."
I (1158 – 1193)	"...*de castro Baccaricie*..."
H (1139-1143)	"...*Baccaricia*..."
L (1158-1193)	"...*de Castro Baccaricie*..."
M (1188)	"...*Vaccariciam*..."
N (1203)	"...*Castrum Baccaricie*..."
P (1218)	"...*Castrum Vaccaricie*..."
Q (1236)	"...*Castrum Baccaricie*..."
S (1241-1259)	"...*quartam partem Castelli Baccaricie*..."

Il sito, frequentato dal periodo etrusco al medioevo, è localizzabile sulla cima della collina sovrastante a NO l'omonimo fontanile (per alcune precisazioni sui documenti d'archivio relativi al castello di Vacchereccia cfr. Carbonetti & Venditelli 1982). Intorno al 1761 il Galletti (1776:83) ricorda le rovine del Castello di Vacchereccia e il rinvenimento in esse di una iscrizione, poi collocata nel Monastero di S. Paolo, che cita Giovanni nipote di Alberico III e pronipote di Giovanni XIX, ivi sepolto nel 1030. Il Tomassetti, dopo aver localizzato il sito tra Monte Sette Monti e Monte Palombo, afferma di avervi visto ruderi, frammenti antichi ed una colonna scanalata. Negli anni '60 l'apertura di una cava di tufo, ancora oggi visibile presso il fontanile di Vacchereccia, ha distrutto le strutture medievali viste in ultimo dal Jones (1962: 151-154). Il sito è stato successivamente ricognito dal Wickham (1979: 66-69), che vi ha rinvenuto frammenti di ceramica medievale.

NOTE CONCLUSIVE (F.F.)

I dati d'archivio raccolti nel corso della ricerca, uniti a quelli scaturiti dalle ricognizioni territoriali, permettono, più che un bilancio, una serie di considerazioni sulla consistenza e l'importanza del *patrimonium* del Monastero di S.Paolo nei primi secoli della sua formazione e sulla sua attuale sopravvivenza. Seppur limitata geograficamente ad una porzione di territorio che certamente non rispecchia l'intera estensione della proprietà fondiaria, la ricerca ha evidenziato una dislocazione dei possedimenti più antichi in un'area storicamente molto significativa quale è quella della media valle del Tevere.

L'antico 'agro falisco-capenate' ed i territori ad esso limitrofi, favoriti dalla presenza del fiume e dalla nota fertilità del suolo, hanno visto sorgere già in epoca protostorica dei nuclei abitativi sulle colline prospicienti la vallata tiberina, che anche dopo la romanizzazione dell'area hanno continuato in molti casi a sopravvivere, mentre la campagna circostante si costellava di numerose ville rustiche, legate allo sfruttamento agricolo del territorio, che risultano ancora attive in età tardoantica (Gazzetti 1992: 6-11). La viabilità, rappresentata da percorsi importanti come quelli della Clodia, Cassia, Flaminia e Tiberina, ha certamente facilitato i collegamenti di questi nuclei fra loro e con Roma.

E' in un contesto così favorevole che si sviluppa una proprietà fondiaria che ha attirato l'interesse della Chiesa e dei privati già dalla sua prima formazione.

Come è noto, il *patrimonium Sancti Petri* viene istituzionalizzato solo dopo la donazione di Sutri dell'VIII secolo (Pietri 1975), ma all'interno del territorio su cui estende i suoi possedimenti esso deve prendere atto dell'esistenza di altri nuclei patrimoniali sorti precedentemente. La proprietà del Monastero di S.Paolo in questo ambito rappresenta, rispetto ad altre simili, un fenomeno anomalo, essendo stata creata non per il sostentamento di un ordine religioso o di una comunità di fedeli, ma per proteggere ed assicurare una cura perenne alla tomba dell'Apostolo (D'Amato 1988: 207-209).

Le carte del Monastero si sono rivelate delle vere e proprie miniere d'informazioni di ordine storico, topografico e toponomastico, utilissime per una ricerca archeologica. Basti solo pensare alla quantità di toponimi citati in riferimento all'ubicazione delle *res*, dei beni immobili fatti oggetto di transazioni, per rendersi conto di quale strumento indispensabile per le ricognizioni territoriali siano questi atti registrati al momento di acquisti, vendite e concessioni, al di là della loro evidente utilità per una ricostruzione storica di tipo documentario del patrimonio stesso.

I documenti riguardanti l'Etruria Meridionale si riferiscono all'epoca posteriore al Mille, quando il territorio mostra un notevole incremento demografico con il definitivo stabilizzarsi degli abitati ed un significativo popolamento della campagna, dovuto alla ripresa della coltivazione della terra (Schneider 1980: 235). Tutto questo è facilmente riscontrabile nel formulario relativo alle proprietà.

Già nella bolla di Gregorio VII del 1081 si parla di *castra* e di *castella*, segno evidente dell'avvenuta trasformazione di alcuni nuclei abitativi in centri caratterizzati dalla presenza di circuiti murari o da opere naturali di difesa. Infatti in alcuni casi viene specificato, riguardo alle proprietà, la loro posizione "*intus vel foris*" o "*extra castrum*". Del *castellum Baccariciae* fanno parte *munitiones*, mentre del *castrum Reiani* vengono ricordati "*turrim et domos et palacia et munitiones*", costruzioni caratteristiche di borghi fortificati, che attirano entro le mura una popolazione prima sparsa e organizzano intorno a loro le terre con sorprendente rigidità e precisione amministrativa. In un caso viene menzionato un *burgus*, termine che da luogo di mercato, qual era in età carolingia, assume più tardi il significato di sinonimo di *castellum* (Castagnetti 1982: 225-247).

Nelle campagne l'incentivazione allo sfruttamento agricolo, soprattutto sulla spinta della politica papale, trova testimonianza nelle chiese, variamente documentate nel territorio, che erano al centro di *massae* o di altri aggregati comunque impiantati con scopo agricolo. A questo ambito appartengono i *casalia*, aziende agricole fortificate, e i *fundi*, semplici fattorie o singoli appezzamenti di terreno (Quilici & Quilici Gigli 1984: 45). Sono importanti tali definizioni di toponimi perchè, accanto ai pochi resti monumentali, testimoniano ciò che rimane del primo costituirsi degli insediamenti feudali e delineano una fisionomia paesaggistico-architettonica del territorio che durerà fino al nostro secolo (Martorelli 1994; Fei 1994), unica testimonianza, a volte, di nuclei o di edifici dei quali tramandano almeno il nome.

Significativo è il caso di Capena: l'odierna città sorge in epoca medievale, con il nome di Leprignano, a circa km.2 dall'abitato più antico e, dovendo citare ambedue le località, il redattore degli atti menziona toponimi oggi scomparsi, ma che ci segnalano la diversità di origine dei due siti. Il termine Leprignano deriva da una storpiatura di *fundus Aproniani*, proprietà quindi pertinente inizialmente al territorio e solo in seguito definita *castrum*, mentre il nucleo abitativo più antico non più esistente resta comunque segnalato con il toponimo *Civitucola*, oggi sostituito da 'Castellaccio': il dato toponimico conferma dunque quello archeologico, poiché è proprio dal sito del Castellaccio che provengono le testimonianze archeologiche delle fasi più antiche di abitazione della zona.

La chiesa di S. Leone, appartenente anch'essa al territorio capenate, è menzionata separatamente come proprietà distinta e comprendente 'sue pertinenze', quali saranno state *massae* e *fundi*, di cui gli edifici religiosi sono in campagna i centri amministrativi, oltreché, naturalmente, di 'cura delle anime'.

Sulla base di quanto riportato nelle schede riguardanti le sopravvivenze monumentali ed archeologiche riferibili all'epoca anteriore al XIV secolo, è possibile proporre una sorta di suddivisione tipologica di quanto rimane delle testimonianze più antiche. Abbiamo visto che strutture murarie risalenti probabilmente alla fase del primo Medioevo, quando già appartenevano al *patrimonium* del Monastero, si rilevano oggi in pochi dei centri menzionati dai documenti.

Le murature della chiesa di S. Liberato di Bracciano, la cui datazione è confortata da alcuni rilievi scultorei cronologicamente risalenti a circa l'anno Mille, sono la sopravvivenza archeologica di un possedimento attestato già in una bolla di Agapito II nel X secolo e menzionato nella bolla di Gregorio VII (1081) non direttamente, ma come facente parte del territorio della *civitas Manturana* acquisita dal monastero in quegli anni (De Maria 1994).

Le strutture della chiesa della Pietà di Campagnano e forse di S. Lorenzo di Civitella S. Paolo testimoniano la fase di vita di questi edifici ascrivibile all'epoca dei documenti che li segnalano nell'ambito del *patrimonium*.

Un discorso a parte merita Monterano, il cui abbandono ha involontariamente permesso una sorta di autoconservazione di strutture del primo Medioevo, quando, come già detto, una parte della *civitas* entra a fare parte dei possedimenti del monastero. Abbiamo visto come murature più antiche siano inglobate in contesti più recenti: il Palazzo dei Monaci di Capena insiste su strutture preesistenti, così come sono riscontrabili fasi anteriori al XIV secolo per i campanili di Castelnuovo e di Formello.

Riguardo alle emergenze archeologiche, abbiamo in molti casi rilievi scultorei come unica sopravvivenza di fasi di vita contemporanee all'acquisizione dell'edificio da parte del monastero. I più significativi, sia per la qualità di esecuzione che per la ricchezza di motivi adottati, sono quelli della chiesa di S. Leone di Capena, vero campionario di decorazioni altomedioevali diffusissime in tutto il Lazio, la cui datazione alla metà del IX secolo conforta il dato architettonico e quello documentario (Fei, c.s.).

A questo ambito cronologico sono da riferirsi anche il capitello rinvenuto nel corso degli scavi eseguiti dal Pallottino nell'area della chiesa di S. Cristina (1937: 12, fig.5), una delle proprietà del monastero che più frequentemente ritorna negli atti; il frammento di transenna ritrovato non lontano da S. Leone e che ora fa parte della collezione Oddone e, infine, il pilastrino che si conserva nel Palazzo dei Monaci di Civitella, di provenienza sconosciuta ma comunque pertinente ad un territorio registrato come proprietà fin dai primi documenti.

A questi dobbiamo aggiungere il c.d. 'Tifo' di Campagnano e la vasca di fontana di Capena che, seppur risalenti cronologicamente ad una fase posteriore al Mille, si riferiscono ad un periodo di sicura appartenenza dei due *castra* al Monastero.

In ultimo ricordiamo l'iscrizione di Morlupo come unica testimonianza altomedioevale di un luogo di culto esistente nel *castrum Morilupi*.

Concludendo, ci sembra che la ricerca condotta possa suscitare l'interesse di tutti coloro che si accingono ad affrontare lo studio del territorio, non solo dell'Etruria Meridionale, ma di tutto il Lazio, laddove si estendevano le proprietà del monastero, dato che l'evoluzione territoriale ha risentito senza dubbio delle alterne vicende del suo popolamento, ma è altresì vero che la frequentazione di un sito è spesso determinata da chi lo gestisce.

APPENDICE

ISCRIZIONE DI MORLUPO (L.D.M.)

Allo stato attuale della ricerca sembra che l'unica testimonianza altomedioevale superstite a Morlupo, relativa al IX secolo, sia una lastra iscritta affissa all'interno della chiesa parrocchiale di S. Giovanni Battista (fig.3). L'iscrizione, nel corso degli anni, ha subito vari spostamenti: stando al testo, che sarà analizzato in seguito, doveva originariamente trovarsi a copertura di una tomba in un edificio di culto fatto costruire da un certo *Iohannis*, personaggio cui l'iscrizione è dedicata, che Tomassetti identificava probabilmente con uno dei Conti Tuscolani, mentre Mariani e Antonazzi con Giovanni, figlio di Leone, consigliere particolare e maestro delle milizie di papa Giovanni VIII (Tomassetti 1979: III, 376; Antonazzi 1980: 329, n. 1; Mariani 1980: 77; vd. pure Clementi *et alii* 1988: 21). Secondo Antonazzi, Giovanni fece costruire proprio la primitiva chiesa dedicata a S. Giovanni Battista, di tale edificio, però, si sa solo che era di dimensioni molto ridotte, absidato e preceduto da una scalinata (1980: 329, n. 4; cfr. Mariani 1980: 80–81).

Tomassetti ricorda che l'epigrafe fu ritrovata durante il restauro dell'altare della chiesa conventuale delle Suore Domenicane, adiacente alla parrocchiale, spostata in seguito nella piazzetta posteriore alla chiesa; all'epoca dello studioso "giaceva capovolta nella scala della cantina del convento" (1979: III, 376. A parere di Antonazzi 1980: 329, n. 2, la lapide tornò alla luce durante i lavori di ricostruzione della chiesa del 1593). In conseguenza al relativamente recente trasferimento delle suore in altra sede e alla ristrutturazione totale dello stabile, l'iscrizione ha trovato una più opportuna sistemazione, come si è detto, nella chiesa di S.Giovanni Battista. Si tratta di una lastra in travertino di cm. 68 x 137 x 16, con lettere di alt. cm. 3/6, in pessimo stato di conservazione, su cui resta inciso, seppure assai corroso, un testo epigrafico diviso su nove linee di scrittura; caratteri e *ductus* appaiono piuttosto irregolari. Tra le lettere, diverse per tipologia e modulo, si notino la particolare resa 'arrotondata' delle X, quella minuscola delle Q, mentre, a parere della Gray, le S, così come sono incise nel testo, compaiono frequentemente su monete e oggetti merovingi, ma sono piuttosto rare in epoca più tarda (1948: 120).

Da osservare, inoltre, la quasi totale assenza di abbreviazioni, fenomeno anche questo curioso per la fine del IX secolo; sembra infine quasi superfluo rilevare gli innumerevoli 'errori', riflesso evidente del progressivo, inarrestabile involgarimento della lingua latina.

Il testo, edito in passato da Tomassetti (1979: III, 376), Grossi Gondi (1918: 162), dalla Gray (1948: 120) e recentemente riconsiderato in uno studio più generale (Clementi *et alii* 1988: 21), non presenta grosse difficoltà interpretative, tuttavia si propone qualche piccola variazione di lettura:

Fig. 3. Morlupo – Chiesa di S. Giovanni Battista: iscrizione.

(signum crucis)   Ihc (sic) requiescit in pace
             Io(h)annis Comi filius
3   de Leo dux qui ista(m) eccle=
    sia(m) edificabit qui defu=
    ntus fuit in mense Iulio die
6   XVI temporibus Dom(i)no Ioh(annis)
    VIIII papa indictione prima ego Pe=
    turnia nobilissima fe(m)ina
9   magno sic mio amore fieri rogabit

Alla l.2 la Gray restituiva *Com(a)*, ma ad una attenta lettura sembra di poter leggere una I finale. Così pure, all'inizio della l.6, concordando con Grossi Gondi e Clementi, leggiamo *XVI* e non *XXVI* come proposto dalla studiosa.

Qualche osservazione particolare merita il numerale da far seguire a *Ioh(annis)* (l.7) : alcuni fra i precedenti editori hanno concordemente fornito la restituzione VIII, individuando appunto in Giovanni VIII il papa durante il cui pontificato fu deposto Giovanni figlio di Leone. Tale attribuzione aveva generato tuttavia qualche perplessità in Gray, la quale notava che Giovanni VIII era morto nel Dicembre 882, e che la prima indizione, citata nel testo, comprendeva il periodo che dal Settembre 882 andava allo stesso mese dell'883. La conseguente conclusione è che il mese di Luglio, cui si fa riferimento nell'iscrizione, doveva essere quello dell'883, sette mesi dopo la morte del pontefice. A riprova di ciò, un'analisi puntuale e ravvicinata del pezzo ha rilevato la presenza di quattro tratti verticali dopo il numerale V, che portano ad interpretare di conseguenza Giovanni IX e non VIII, come tradizionalmente si è fatto in passato. Giovanni IX fu eletto papa nell'Aprile dell'898 e regnò fino al 900 e, poiché la prima indizione in quel periodo cadeva tra l'897 e l'898, la data della morte di Giovanni (16 Luglio) sembrerebbe corrispondere perfettamente ai primi mesi del suo pontificato.

Se la lettura proposta è corretta, tale interpretazione indurrebbe a spostarne la datazione entro un ambito cronologico relativamente breve – quindici anni – il che, comunque, non comporterebbe nessun cambiamento: resta infatti il ricordo di un personaggio di spicco dell'epoca che, alla fine del IX secolo, fece edificare una chiesa a Morlupo, di cui oggi rimane, come unica testimonianza monumentale, l'iscrizione considerata. (L'incertezza sulla datazione è stata rilevata in anni più recenti da Clementi *et alii* 1988: 21, ivi bibliografia).

RINGRAZIAMENTI

Alla cortese disponibilità di Don Stefano Baiocchi si deve l'autorizzazione a consultare l'Archivio della Basilica di San Paolo f.l.m. Un vivo ringraziamento va al dott. L. Oddone per la segnalazione relativa al frammento di pilastrino, di cui è proprietario, proveniente dalla località Bombelli (Capena).

Bibliografia

Antonazzi, G. 1980. 'Caterina Paluzzi e la sua autobiografia (1573–1645)', in *Archivio italiano per la storia della pietà*, n.s. 8, Roma.
Arnaldi, G. 1991. 'Mito e realtà del secolo X romano e papale', in *Il secolo di ferro: mito e realtà del secolo X (XXXVIII Settimana di Studio del Centro Italiano di Studi sull'Alto Medioevo)*, Spoleto, 33 ss.
Bosl, K. 1982. 'Cultura cittadina e cultura rurale tra mondo antico e medioevo a confronto nella cristianizzazione delle campagne', in *Cristianizzazione ed organizzazione ecclesiastica delle campagne nell'alto medioevo: espansione e resistenza (XXVIII Settimana di Studio del Centro Italiano di Studi sull'Alto Medioevo)*, Spoleto, 19 ss.
Carbonetti Vendittelli, C. 1982. 'Precisazioni sui primi documenti riguardanti il castello di Vaccareccia nel territorio collinense', *Archivio della Società Romana di Storia Patria*, 105, 145–155.
Castagnetti, A. 1982. *L'organizzazione del territorio rurale nel Medioevo. Circoscrizioni ecclesiastiche e civili nella "Langobardia" e nella "Romania"*, Bologna.
Cavallo, D. 1992. *Antiche strade. Lazio. Via Cassia I. Via Cimina*, Roma.
Christie, N., Gibson, S. & Ward-Perkins J.B. 1991. 'San Liberato. A medieval church near Bracciano', in N. Christie (ed.), *Three South Etrurian Churches* (Archaeological Monographs of the British School at Rome, 4), London, 313–352.
Clementi, R., Farina, G., Mauro, M. & Vetromile, E. 1988. *Architettura in provincia: Morlupo. Un centro storico della campagna*, Roma.
D'Amato, C. 1988. 'Il monastero e il suo stato monastico', in *San Paolo fuori le mura a Roma* (a cura di C. Pietrangeli), Roma, 207 ss.
De Maria, L. 1994. 'Alle origini del cristianesimo nel territorio braccianese: considerazioni storico-topografiche sugli edifici di S. Liberato a Bracciano e di S. Stefano ad Anguillara Sabazia', in *Atti del Convegno "Antichità tardoromane e medievali nel territorio di Bracciano"* (Bracciano, giugno 1991), Viterbo, 39–63.
Fei, F. 1994. 'Sculture altomedioevali nelle chiese di S. Liberato di Bracciano e S. Stefano di Anguillara Sabazia', in *Atti del Convegno "Antichità tardoromane e medievali nel territorio di Bracciano"* (Bracciano, giugno 1991), Viterbo, 125–161.
Fei, F. c.s. 'Le sculture altomedievali' in *Capena e il suo territorio*.
Fiocchi Nicolai, V. 1988. *I cimiteri paleocristiani del Lazio, I, Etruria meridionale*, Roma.
Gallavotti Cavallero, D. 1992. 'Guida breve ai monumenti di età medioevale e moderna, in *Il territorio capenate*, Roma, 102–115.
Galletti, P. 1776. *Del Primicerio della Santa Sede Apostolica e di altri uffiziali maggiori del sacro Palagio Lateranense*, Roma.
Gazzetti, G. 1992. *Il territorio capenate*, Roma.
Gray, N. 1948. 'The palaeography of Latin inscriptions in the eighth, ninth and tenth centuries in Italy', *Papers of the British School at Rome*, 16, 38 ss.
Grossi Gondi, F. 1918. 'Excursus sulla paleografia medievale del secolo IX', in *Dissertazioni Pontificia Accademia Romana di Archeologia*, serie II, 13, 147 ss.
ICVR = *Inscriptiones Christianae Urbis Romae. Septimo saeculo antiquiores*, Città del Vaticano, 10 voll. 1922–1992.
Jones, G.D.B. 1962. 'Capena and the Ager Capenas (Part I)', *Papers of the British School at Rome*, 30, 116–207.
Leccisotti, T. 1957. 'Aspetti e problemi del monachesimo in Italia', in *Il monachesimo nell'altomedioevo e la formazione della civiltà occidentale (IV Settimana di Studio del Centro Italiano di Studi sull'Alto medioevo)*, Spoleto, 311 ss.
Mabillon, J. 1736–1745. *Annales ordinis S. Benedicti,* 6 voll., Lucae.
Margarini, C. *Codex Diplomaticus paulinus*, ms. n. 366 (Archivio del Monastero di S. Paolo f.l.m.).
Margarini, C. 1650. *Bullarium Casinense*, 2 voll., Venezia.
Margarini, C. 1654. *Inscriptiones antiquae basilicae S. Pauli ad viam Ostiensem, Romae.*
Mariani, S. 1980. *Morlupo. Notizie storiche e documenti*, Palermo.
Martorelli, R. 1994. 'Strutture murarie altomedioevali nelle chiese di S. Stefano (Anguillara Sabazia) e S. Liberato (Bracciano)', *Atti del Convegno Antichità tardoromane e medievali nel territorio di Bracciano*, (Bracciano, giugno 1991), Viterbo, 65–96.
Muzzioli, M. P. 1980. *Cures Sabini. Formae Italiae*, IV, 2, Firenze.
Pallottino, M. 1937. 'Capena. Resti di costruzioni romane e medievali in località "Montecanino"', *Notizie degli Scavi di Antichità*, XIII, 7–28.
Panepuccia, C. & Clementi, R. 1990. *Castelnuovo di Porto. Città e territorio*, Roma.

Pani Ermini, L. 1985. 'L'abbazia di Farfa', in *La Sabina medievale*, Roma.

Penco, G. 1983. *Storia del monachesimo in Italia. Dalle origini alla fine del medioevo*, Milano.

Picasso, G. 1987. 'Il monachesimo nell'alto medioevo', in *Dall'eremo al cenobio. La civiltà monastica in Italia dalle origini all'età di Dante*, Milano, 3 ss.

Pietri, Ch. 1975. *Roma christiana*, 2 voll., Roma.

Prinz, F. 1987. 'La presenza del monachesimo nella vita economica e sociale', in *Dall'eremo al cenobio. La civiltà monastica in Italia dalle origini all'età di Dante*, Milano, 241 ss.

Quilici, L. & Quilici Gigli S. 1984. *Il patrimonio archeologico e monumentale della XI Comunità montana del Lazio*, Roma.

Raspi Serra, J. 1974. *Corpus della scultura altomedievale*, VIII, *Le diocesi dell'Alto Lazio. Bagnoregio, Bomarzo, Castro, Civita Castellana, Nepi, Orte, Sutri, Tuscania*, Spoleto.

Schneider, F. 1980. *Le origini dei comuni rurali in Italia*, Firenze.

Silvagni, A. 1943. *Monumenta epigraphica christiana saeculo XIII antiquiora*, Città del Vaticano.

Silvestrelli, G. 1940. *Città, castelli e terre della regione romana*, Roma (riprod. anastatica Roma 1970).

Tomassetti, G. 1884. 'Della Campagna Romana', *Archivio della Società Romana di Storia Patria*, VII, 353 ss.

Tomassetti, G. 1884. *La campagna romana antica, medioevale e moderna*, (nuova edizione a cura di L. Chiumenti & F. Bilancia, Firenze 1979).

Toubert, P. 1973 *Les structures du Latium médiéval*, 2 voll., Roma.

Trifone, B. 1908. 'Le carte del monastero di S. Paolo di Roma dal secc. XI al XV', *Archivio della Società Romana di Storia Patria*, 31, 256 ss.

Turchetti, R., c.s. 'I risultati delle ricognizioni: il catalogo delle presenze archeologiche. I. Capena', in *Capena e il suo territorio*.

Vetromile, E. 1983. 'Nazzano', *Storia della città*, 26–27, 211 ss.

Whitehouse, D. 1984. 'Farfa abbey: the eighth and ninth centuries', *Arte Medievale*, 2, 245 ss.

Wickham, C. 1979. 'Historical and topographical notes on early mediaeval south Etruria: part II', *Papers of the British School at Rome*, 47, 66–95.

PART 5

Urbanism

L'Area Sud Occidentale del Palatino dai Primi Insediamenti all'Età Medio Rebubblicana

P. Pensabene, O. Colazingari, L. Borrello, P. Battistelli & S. Falzone
(Dipartimento di Scienze dell'Antichità dell'Università di Roma 'La Sapienza')

Sommario: *Questa comunicazione intende presentare i risultati delle più recenti ricerche nell'area sud occidentale del Palatino, svolte dal Dipartimento di Archeologia dell'Università degli Studi di Roma 'La Sapienza', e dirette dal Prof. Pensabene. L'intervento prevede una introduzione storico-topografica e contributi relativi ai saggi di scavo che hanno permesso di puntualizzare le conoscenze sulle più antiche fasi di occupazione del sito (età del Ferro), di ampliare il quadro sullo sviluppo urbanistico del colle in età arcaica, nonchè di definire l'organizzazione architettonica dell'area occidentale del santuario della* Magna Mater.

I. L'angolo sud ovest del Palatino, tra il tempio della *Magna Mater* e la c.d. Casa di Livia, a partire dal 1977, è stato oggetto d'indagine archeologica (vedi Pensabene 1978; 1979; 1980; 1981; 1983; 1985; 1988; 1990; 1993), nell' ambito di un progetto comune di ricerca tra il Dipartimento di Scienze dell'Antichità dell'Università di Roma e la Soprintendenza Archeologica di Roma (fig.1). Nel corso delle ultime campagne di scavo le ricerche si sono concentrate sullo studio delle fasi più antiche permettendo di puntualizzare meglio alcuni elementi dell'assetto urbanistico del colle e delle consistenze monumentali della zona in parte già note dagli scavi precedenti (Vaglieri 1907; Puglisi 1951: 1 ss.; Romanelli 1963: 214).

In particolare sulla base degli interventi Vaglieri, Puglisi e Romanelli il Gjerstad (Gjerstad 1960: 78–104; 1966: 452–488) aveva ipotizzato che, dopo l'abbandono delle capanne alla fine del terzo periodo laziale, la zona avesse subito una trasformazione con la costruzione di un terrazzamento relativo, tra l'altro, ad un tempio del VI secolo a.C. Tale terrazzamento e gli edifici vicini, secondo l'ipotesi di Gjerstad, vennero distrutti in seguito all'incendio gallico e con i resti di questi fu creata una nuova terrazza nel IV sec. a.C. Una nuova ristrutturazione e innalzamento dell'area si ebbe, sempre secondo il Gjerstad, alla fine del III sec. a.C., con la costruzione del tempio della *Magna Mater*. Queste osservazioni consentono una migliore comprensione dei resti murari in opera quadrata intorno all'angolo sud-ovest del Palatino, già indagati dal Säflund (1932), e che alla luce dei nostri scavi si sono definitivamente chiariti nel loro complesso come muri di sostruzione dei santuari della Vittoria e della *Magna Mater*"Inoltre, il raggiungimento del suolo vergine da noi operato in vari punti ha ampliato le nostre conoscenze sull'estensione dell'area occupata dalle capanne. Infatti nel lato sud occidentale è stato messo in luce un fondo di capanna (fig.1a) tipologicamente affine a quelli già noti, lo stesso più a sud all'estremità ovest della *via tecta*, mentre in tutta l'area indagata ed in particolar modo nella zona nord orientale, sono stati rinvenuti consistenti quantitativi di materiali dell'età del ferro in stratigrafie di età arcaica.

Tali ritrovamenti possono dunque fare ipotizzare un più esteso abitato che occupava probabilmente tutta l'area sud occidentale del colle senza escludere una continuità dell'insediamento verso est. Gli interventi succedutisi nel corso del VI secolo portarono ad una complessiva ristrutturazione e monumentalizzazione dell'area con la totale obliterazione delle strutture preesistenti. In questo periodo le pendici vennero sostruite mediante muri in blocchi di cappellaccio, già identificati da Säflund (1932: 7–10, 138 s.) e la parte superiore del colle venne ampliata con la creazione di un terrazzamento di cui rimangono tracce a ovest e a sud del tempio della *Magna Mater*. Avanziamo l'ipotesi che il lato orientale del terrazzamento dovesse passare ad est del vestibolo della cd. Casa di Livia sulla base delle diverse quote a cui è stato rinvenuto il banco tufaceo nelle trincee eseguite da Carettoni (1953: 126 ss.; 1957: 80–91). Venne regolarizzata contestualmente la viabilità di accesso al colle dal Velabro. Questo percorso, che andava a incrociare il tratto terminale delle *Scalae Caci* (fig. 2f), è riconoscibile nei muri di sponda, in blocchi di cappellaccio, inglobati nelle fondazioni

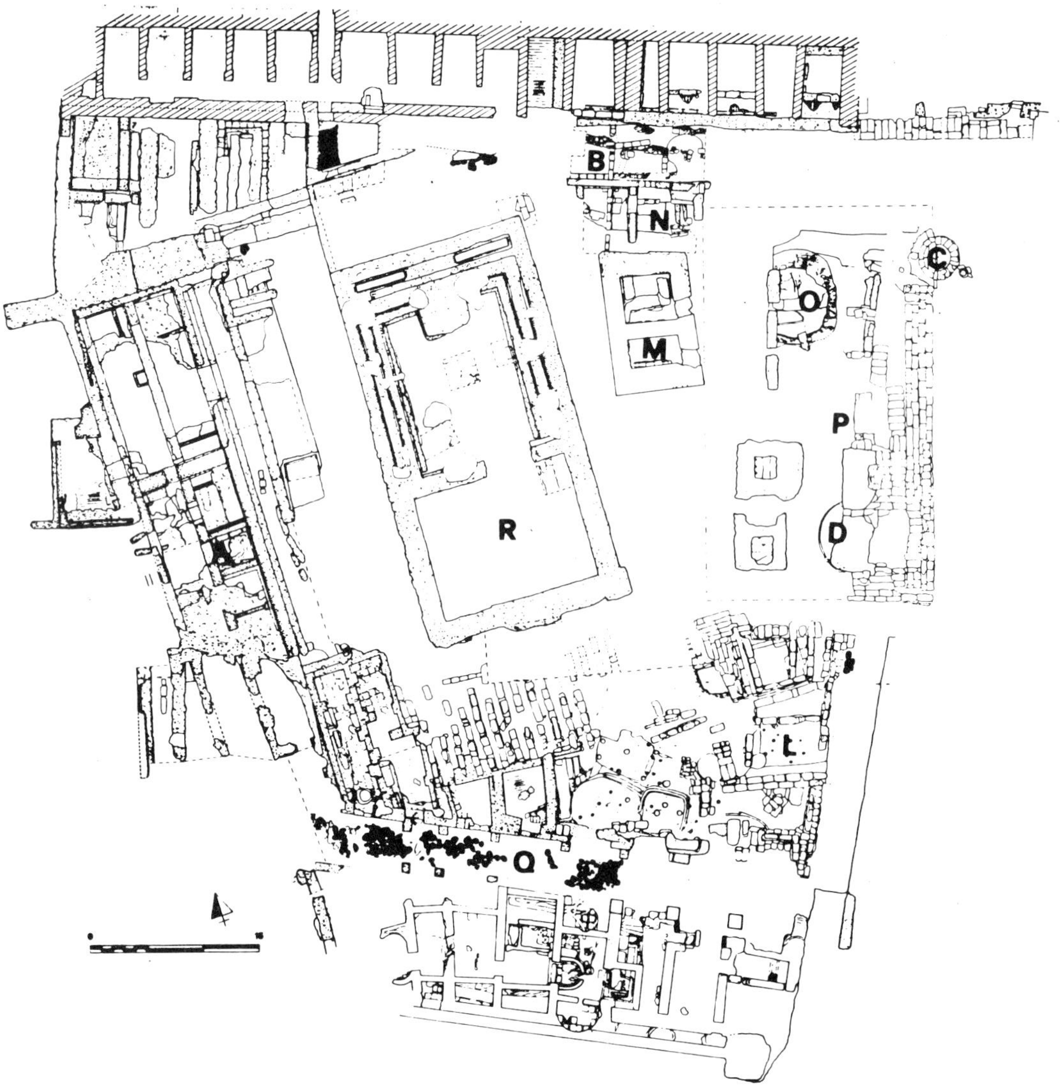

Fig. 1. Area sud-ovest del Palatino: pianta.

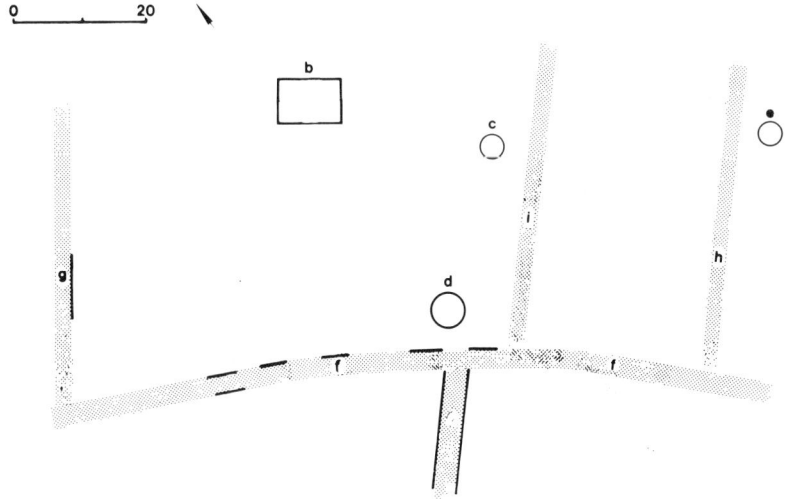

Fig. 2. Area sud-ovest del Palatino, pianta della sistemazione viaria e delle cisterne di età arcaica.

dei templi della *Magna Mater* e della Vittoria. Si può inoltre ipotizzare la presenza di un diverticolo coincidente con la sponda occidentale del terrazzamento (fig. 2g), mentre lungo il lato orientale una viabilità Nord-Sud potrebbe essere dimostrata dalla persistenza degli allineamenti delle case repubblicane al di sotto della *Domus Tiberiana* (fig. 2h) (cfr. Krause 1985: 17).

A questa sistemazione vanno connesse vaste opere di drenaggio e di raccolta delle acque (fig. 2). Altro aspetto caratterizzante la ristrutturazione urbanistica di età arcaica è la costruzione di edifici di culto, la cui presenza era già stata ipotizzata da Gjerstad sulla base dei cospicui ritrovamenti di decorazione architettonica fittile (1960: 82). Le nostre ricerche ci hanno permesso di arricchire le informazioni su questa fase. In particolare sono stati identificati, nell'angolo tra la strada arcaica già citata e la sommità delle *Scalae Caci* (fig. 1l), i resti di un piccolo podio rettangolare in blocchi di cappellaccio. Tale sacello potrebbe essere relativo ad un antico culto dei gemelli, legato quindi alla successiva edificazione, nel IV secolo a.C., della *Casa Romuli*, che le fonti collocano ad *Supercilium Scalarum Caci*. A circa m. 40 a nord di quest'ultimo edificio, al di sotto del c.d. *Auguratorium*, è stata rinvenuta una struttura rettangolare di cui si conservano parte del lato meridionale, formato da un muro di sei filari di blocchi di cappellaccio e le tracce di un filare perpendicolare (fig. 1m). Pur in mancanza di indicatori archeologici certi, non sembra di potersi escludere anche per questa struttura una destinazione cultuale, data la persistenza di orientamento degli edifici sacri posteriori che le si sovrappongono, ovvero il possibile sacello della Vittoria Virgo (Pensabene 1990: 47–50) e il c.d. *Auguratorium*. Tra la fine del VI secolo e gli inizi del V assistiamo ad una ripresa dell'attività edilizia con la costruzione di un edificio di culto (fig.1n) che comporta l'obliterazione di una cisterna a vasca quadrata. In questa fase sembra inquadrabile, allo stato attuale delle ricerche, la struttura di forma circolare (fig. 1o) rinvenuta al di sotto del podio del tempio della Vittoria, sulla cui destinazione alcune ipotesi sono forse possibili in base ad un elemento fittile modanato rinvenuto all'interno della struttura, in precedenza interpretato come base di colonna (fig. 7) (Pensabene 1993: 35–36, fig.17) e per il quale si può prendere in considerazione anche l'ipotesi che si tratti di una vera di pozzo (Durante & Gervasini 1987: 321 ss., fig. 215).

Una imponente fase di sistemazione del colle dovette verificarsi sullo scorcio del IV secolo a.C. quando si eressero nuovi muri di contenimento, in blocchi di Grotta Oscura e di Fidene, che ebbero lo scopo di consolidare sia le pendici sia i terrazzamenti che sulla sommità allargavano e regolarizzavano i margini naturali del colle (fig. 9, p1, p2). Contemporanea o di poco posteriore a questo intervento è la costruzione del grande tempio della Vittoria nel 294 a.C. (fig. 1p).

Il tempio, di cui rimane il basamento in blocchi di Grotta Oscura, è stato ricostruito come periptero sine postico (Pensabene, c.s., a). Alla edificazione del tempio della Vittoria è da connettere la costruzione di una grande piazza antistante il tempio che causò lo spostamento più a sud della strada precedente: in questo nuovo assetto viario è riconoscibile il *clivus Victoriae* (fig. 1q). Nello stesso ambito sono da collocare i resti di un edificio rettangolare posto a sud-est del precedente podio di età arcaica (fig. 8l). La posizione di questo sacello, in asse col tempio della Vittoria e presso il tempio della *Magna Mater* ha consentito la proposta di riconoscere in esso la *Casa Romuli*, menzionata dalle fonti e dai Cataloghi Regionari in questa posizione. L'altro grande intervento edilizio che modificò ulteriormente l'assetto topografico della zona è costituito dalla costruzione (tra il 204 e il 191 a.C.) del tempio della *Magna Mater*. La creazione della platea relativa all'area sulla quale si svolgevano i *Ludi Megalenses* determinò una riduzione dello spazio antistante il tempio della Vittoria, nonchè il rialzamento delle mura perimetrali della *Casa Romuli*, all'interno delle quali venne inoltre eretto un *sema*. In seguito all'incendio del 111 a.C. il tempio della *Magna Mater* fu ricostruito e in tale occasione tutta la zona fu monumentalizzata secondo la moda architettonica di influsso ellenistico che vide nel Lazio, proprio alla fine del II secolo a.C., numerosi santuari inseriti in grandiosi impianti e la sistemazione architettonica delle alture su cui sorgevano.

Le linee generali di sviluppo fin qui esposte sembrano mostrare come quest'area, delimitata ad est dalle fabbriche della casa di Augusto e a nord dalla *Domus Tiberiana*, in base ai dati finora emersi dalle indagini, a partire dal VI secolo ebbe esclusivamente funzioni pubbliche e cultuali: va infatti sottolineata la mancanza di strutture di edilizia privata fin dall'età arcaica e per tutta l'età imperiale. Ogni intervento urbanistico inoltre, pur modificando di volta in volta l'assetto generale dell'area, sembra aver previsto una conservazione dei luoghi di culto più antichi. Possiamo quindi affermare che la zona oggetto del nostro studio si riferisce ad un unico *templum*, ovvero ad un'area inaugurata collegata alla memoria di leggende e riferimenti antichissimi, relativi al culto delle origini. Pensiamo al fatto che proprio qui venne eretto il tempio della *Magna Mater*, identificata anche con la madre dei gemelli *Rhea Silvia*. E non dimentichiamo che Augusto, per rafforzare la sua immagine di nuovo 'fondatore' della città e dello stato, scelse di erigere la sua dimora proprio qui, nei pressi del luogo dove la leggenda collocava la casa di Romolo il 'primo fondatore'. *(P.Pensabene)*

II. All'interno della sistemazione urbanistica di VI e V secolo assume particolare rilievo la creazione di un vasto impianto di raccolta e distribuzione delle acque realizzato mediante un sistema di cisterne, anche sotterranee, collegate tra loro da una rete di gallerie (fig.2). Già note da scavi precedenti sono la cisterna di fronte alla casa di Livia (fig. 2c), la cisterna scoperta in cima alle *Scalae Caci* (Vaglieri 1907: 271 ss; 537 s.) (fig. 2d) e quella al di sotto della Casa di Livia (Gjerstad 1960: 98–102) (fig. 2e). Intorno alla metà del VI sec. a.C. è da collocare la struttura rettangolare rinvenuta nelle ultime campagne di scavo nell'area compresa tra il c.d. *Auguratorium* e la *Domus Tiberiana* (Pensabene 1993: 23) (figg. 2b; 3b; 4). Della struttura rimangono due muri perpendicolari tra loro, conservati rispettivamente per una lunghezza di m 5 e m 9, formati da blocchi di cappellaccio e di tufo.

Nell'area compresa tra l'*Auguratorium* e la *domus Tiberiana*, ad una quota di poco sottostante l'attuale piano di calpestio corrispondente al livello creato da P. Rosa nel 1870 in occasione degli interventi di scavo nella zona, è stato individuato il podio di un edificio di culto (figg. 1n; 3n; 4) il cui impianto sembra potersi assegnare ai primi anni del V secolo a.C. (Pensabene 1993: 23–25). L'edificio si colloca in un'area posta a Nord delle strutture arcaiche già identificate (v. premessa) (fig. 1 l, m) e ad ovest della cisterna a *tholos* davanti alla Casa di Livia (fig. 1c). Questa collocazione fa sì che l'edificio obliteri e riutilizzi parzialmente come fondazione la cisterna a vasca quadrata: sembra inoltre che i cunicoli b1 e b2 (fig.3) relativi alla cisterna siano stati in seguito riutilizzati per le pratiche rituali svolte nel tempio. Non è possibile stabilire con esattezza allo stato attuale delle conoscenze, quale fosse la viabilità di accesso all'edificio. La sistemazione individuata per l'età arcaica, con una viabilità est-ovest perpendicolare all'asse delle *Scalae Caci* (fig. 2f) ed una presumibile percorribilità nord-sud lungo le pendici occidentali del colle (fig. 2g) e nell'area al di sotto della Casa di Livia (fig. 2h), non fa escludere la presenza di percorsi tangenti l'area del tempio: in particolare il tratto compreso tra la Casa di Livia e la cisterna a tholos (fig. 2e) (Carettoni 1953: 146) che costituiva una via d'accesso sul lato orientale ai santuari della *Magna Mater* e della Vittoria, riprendeva probabilmente un assetto viario più antico. Dell'edificio rimane solo parte del podio orientato NO-SE e accessibile da SE. Tale podio è costituito da un terrapieno delimitato lungo il lato posteriore NO da un muro (fig. 3a) formato da quattro filari di blocchi di cappellaccio, di m 0,30 × 0,70, posti su assise di uguale altezza (fig. 4m). I muri laterali del podio non sono stati rinvenuti in quanto obliterati a nord dalla *domus Tiberiana* e a sud dalle fondazioni del cd. *Auguratorium* che ne mantiene su questo lato l'orientamento. Un piccolo saggio ha

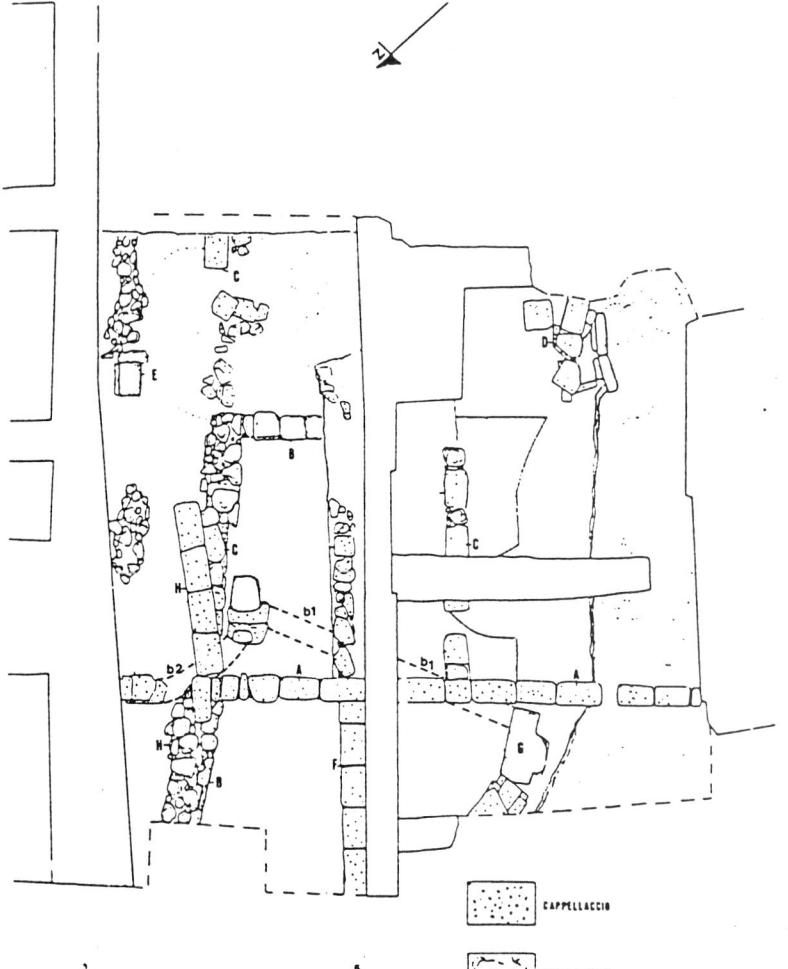

Fig. 3. Area sud-ovest del Palatino, pianta della cisterna (b) e del tempio (n).

permesso inoltre l'individuazione di parte del muro perimetrale sud-est, posto a m 14,50 dal muro posteriore del podio. Se ipotizziamo che gli edifici più tardi restituiscano l'allineamento dei muri laterali del tempio la larghezza dell'edificio dovrebbe risultare di ca. m 14. La cella dell'edificio è individuata in fondazione da due setti murari (fig. 3b, c) paralleli di blocchi e conci di tufo rosso e cappellaccio posti ad una distanza di m 5, la lunghezza conservata della cella è di m 7,50. In base ai dati in nostro possesso si possono dunque ricostruire con una certa attendibilità le dimensioni del podio che risulta avere un rapporto di 1:1 tra larghezza e lunghezza. Per quanto riguarda l'articolazione interna della *pars postica*, sulla quale si sono concentrate le nostre ricerche, pur ipotizzando una tripartizione, non è possibile ancora stabilire se si trattasse di un tempio a tre celle o a cella unica tra *alae*.

Il podio mostra, nel terrapieno e nei filari interni, evidenti tracce di ulteriori interventi, inquadrabili nella prima metà del IV sec a. C. Di particolare importanza, in questa fase, la costruzione, all'interno del podio, di due stipi (fig. 3d, e) formate da lastroni e blocchi di cappellaccio, il cui contenuto è stato asportato da fosse di spoliazione successive. Nella prima metà del III secolo a.C., in occasione della distruzione dell'edificio dovuta alla costruzione del tempio della Vittoria, vennero costruite due *favissae* nelle quali doveva essere deposta la suppellettile relativa al culto. All'esterno dell'edificio, lungo il lato ovest, venne realizzata una stipe a vasca quadrangolare (fig. 3f) all'interno della quale fu praticata una fossa rettangolare coperta da lastre di cappellaccio (fig. 3g). Lungo il lato nord venne inoltre praticata una fossa di forma quasi circolare, delimitata da scheggioni di tufo e da alcuni dei blocchi di fondazione della cella (fig. 3h), all'interno della quale vennero depositate le tegole di copertura del tetto.

La pianta dell'edificio sembra mostrare strette analogie con coevi edifici di Roma e del Lazio: in particolare, ad esempio, il tempio delle Stimmate a Velletri (Colonna 1984: 401-404) e il tempio arcaico di S. Omobono (Ioppolo 1989: 31-33). Non conosciamo la divinità alla quale era dedicato il tempio: i graffiti rinvenuti sul materale votivo sembrano riferirsi esclusivamente all'offerente. Un'analisi preliminare delle fonti attribuisce alla zona la presenza di luoghi di culto dall'età arcaica tra cui la *Curia Saliorum*, il tempio di *Juno Sospita*, il V sacello degli Argei, l'*Auguratorium* e un antico culto della Vittoria. *(L. Borrello – O. Colazingari)*

III. Nello spazio compreso tra le cisterne già note dalla storia degli studi e le strutture arcaiche identificate recentemente ad est del tempio della *Magna Mater*, è stata rinvenuta un'altra struttura (fig. 1o), presumibilmente arcaica, obliterata dalle fondazioni della cella

Fig. 4. Area sud-ovest del Palatino, tempio (n) e cisterna (b).

Fig. 5. Area sud-ovest del Palatino, pianta della struttura 'arcaica' rinvenuta sotto al podio del Tempio della Vittoria.

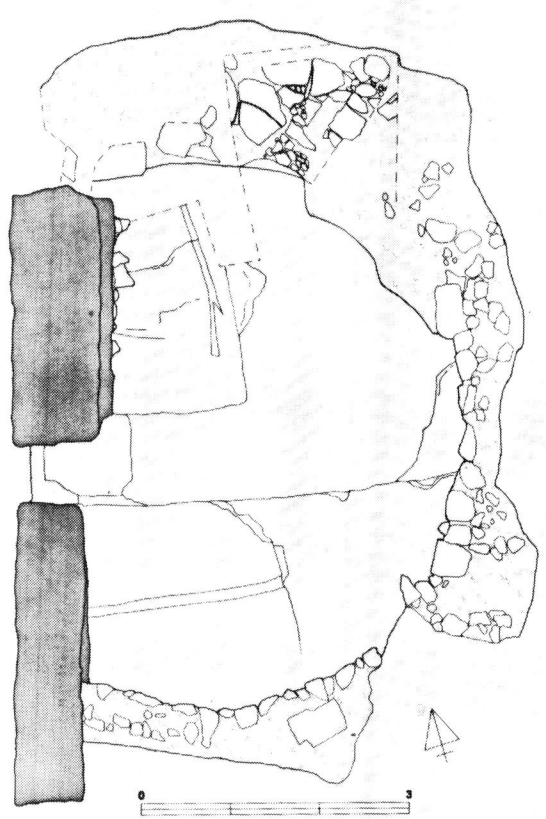

del tempio della Vittoria, ad essa sovrapposto. Essa si presenta di forma circolare (apparentemente di m 8 di diametro e conservata per circa m 3 di profondità) ed è scavata nel banco di cappellaccio e di argille naturali insistendo su cunicoli o gallerie preesistenti (probabilmente per il drenaggio delle acque), già crollati e riempiti, ricavati originariamente nei medesimi depositi naturali (di cui solo in piccola parte si possono seguire i tracciati originari, a causa degli interventi successivi nell'area) (fig. 5). L'alzato della struttura stessa, intaccato parzialmente nel tratto più alto da fosse di spoliazione, è costituito da due filari di blocchi irregolari di cappellaccio al di sopra dei quali si conserva una muratura costituita da scheggioni del medesimo materiale e da blocchetti di tufo granulare; entrambi i tipi di muratura foderano il taglio nei depositi argillosi, e poggiano direttamente sul banco di cappellaccio (fig. 6). Non si è conservata integra la parete in corrispondenza dei tagli preesistenti nella roccia, a causa di crolli successivi, ma è presumibile che tali vuoti siano stati tamponati con lo stesso tipo di opera muraria conservata in situ. Il fondo roccioso della struttura appare articolato in piani tuttora di difficile definizione, individuati da tagli almeno in parte corrispondenti a quelli esaminati in parete precedentemente. Subito a contatto del fondo è stato rinvenuto un primo strato di crollo dovuto al dissesto della parete nord-orientale della struttura, probabilmente avvenuto per cause naturali (legate forse alla presenza alle spalle di uno dei cunicoli crollati). Tra il crollo ed il pavimento non è stato individuato alcun deposito archeologico (battuto di frequentazione o accumuli di abbandono) a contatto con quest'ultimo, tanto da far supporre che la struttura non giacesse in disuso e non fosse priva di manutenzione al momento del primo crollo, anche se ciò rende piuttosto difficile la comprensione della funzione originaria svolta dalla stessa.

Quanto alla datazione della struttura, non abbiamo sicuri termini di cronologia assoluta, mentre si nota un'analogia piuttosto stretta con alcune murature delle fondazioni della terza e quarta fase delle 'case arcaiche' lungo la via Sacra (scavi Boni), databili alla fine del VI-inizio V secolo a.C. (Gjerstad 1953: 127 ss., figg. 131, 136-138); inoltre sono stati rinvenuti scarsi resti ceramici nella fossa di fondazione della struttura tra i blocchetti e l'argilla, in un piccolo tratto della muratura indagato, che forniscono una datazione non anteriore al VI sec. a.C. per la costruzione della stessa. In seguito al primo crollo della struttura è stata individuata una sequenza articolata di azioni di riempimento intenzionale della medesima con terra di riporto, intervallati da eventi di crolli successivi, anch'essi probabilmente di origine artificiale. Una prima analisi dei materiali contenuti nei diversi lembi del riempimento ha mostrato che esso fu un evento unitario in tutta l'area della struttura, protrattosi per un periodo piuttosto breve (mancando superfici significative o tracce di esposizioni prolungate agli agenti atmosferici), situabile non oltre la metà del IV sec.a.C., probabilmente in connessione con le trasformazioni urbanistiche successive all'incendio gallico (Pensabene 1993: 19-22, 27).

Nell'ambito dei reperti si segnala una notevole quantità di laterizi, di ceramica di impasto dell'età del ferro, tra cui alcuni frammenti della fase laziale II A (Falzone, c.s.), d'impasto rosso-bruno e chiaro-sabbioso, insieme a bucchero, ceramica depurata, a vernice nera e fine di importazione, tra cui alcuni frammenti graffiti (prevalentemente con lettere alfabetiche); sono stati inoltre rinvenuti frammenti di bronzo, tra cui una figurina a sagoma umana ritagliata su lamina, elemento piuttosto ricorrente nei depositi votivi romani e laziali associato spesso tra i vari materiali a piattelli votivi con incavo ('focaccine'), di cui un esemplare frammentario è presente nel suddetto riempimento (cfr. Sommella Mura 1976: tav.XVII,10, 19; Albertoni 1990: 73, n.3.6.61-78; Ferrea 1981: 148 ss, C61 e 66; Micozzi 1990: 238-239, n.9.6.45-46).

La provenienza di parte del materiale da contesti sacri è attestata altresì dal rinvenimento nelle medesime stratigrafie di numerosi frammenti fittili relativi forse al rivestimento della base di una colonna tuscanica in impasto chiaro sabbioso (databile alla fine del VI sec.) (fig. 7), a cui si uniscono altri frammenti di decorazione architettonica fittile del medesimo periodo (cfr. Battistelli 1990: 92, n.4.1.9, tav.VIII; 93, n.4.1.17; Pensabene 1993: 35-36, fig.17).

Ancora incerti appaiono i rapporti funzionali della struttura sia con l'edificio di culto in opera quadrata verso ovest poichè l'area tra i due non è stata indagata completamente, sia con le cisterne ed i relativi cunicoli di drenaggio verso est poichè, come suddetto, si sono sovrapposte le fondazioni del tempio della Vittoria. (S. Falzone)

Fig. 6. Area sud-ovest del Palatino, struttura 'arcaica' rinvenuta sotto al podio del Tempio della Vittoria.

IV. Nell'area antistante il podio del tempio della Vittoria è presente un insieme di strutture realizzate in opera

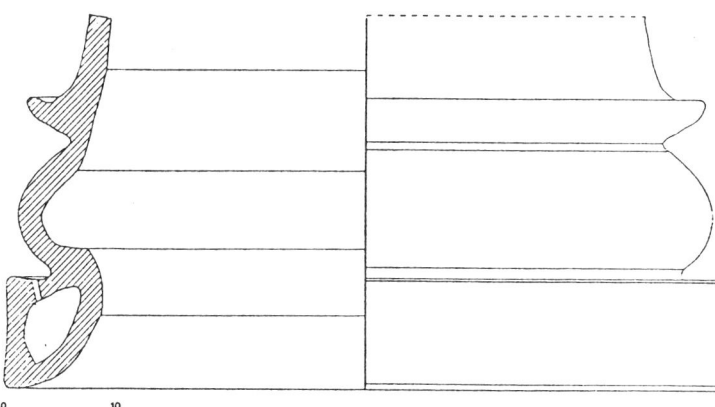

Fig. 7. *Area sud-ovest del Palatino, disegno ricostruttivo del profilo del rivestimento fittile della base di colonna, rinvenuta nella struttura 'arcaica' al di sotto del podio del tempio della Vittoria.*

quadrata di tufo messe in luce negli scavi del Vaglieri e recentemente rianalizzate (Vaglieri 1907: 186 ss.; Saflund 1932: 11 ss., tav. 4; Pensabene 1990: 87 ss.; Pensabene, c.s. b; 1993: 25-27). E'stato possibile individuare una prima fase costituita da un muro con andamento est-ovest, spesso originariamente tre filari e poggiato direttamente sulla superficie naturale del colle (di cui resta solo un breve tratto: fig. 8, 11); esso sembra interpretabile come la base della fronte di un grande terrazzamento approntato nell'area antistante il tempio, per colmare il dislivello tra quest'ultimo e il *clivus victoriae* (a sud). Alla base del muro è stata rinvenuta una fossa rettangolare tagliata nella roccia (simile ad altre individuate dal Vaglieri nell'area adiacente ad est, sotto le c.d. *Scalae Caci*), chiusa da un lastrone in tufo di Monteverde; attorno a questa fossa furono eretti i muri di una recinzione addossata contro il terrazzamento (si conservano solo i lati est e sud: Fig. 8 12, 13). E' probabile che alla fossa (risalente forse all'età protostorica), al momento del suo rinvenimento nel corso dei lavori per il terrazzamento della Vittoria, sia stato attribuito un significato sacro, anche per la sua posizione quasi in asse col tempio e che essa sia stata monumentalizzata all'interno di un'area di rispetto.

Le fonti letterarie segnalano la presenza, in questa zona, della *Casa Romuli*, sacello ancora esistente nell'avanzata età imperiale (Solin., 1, 17; Dion. Hal., I, 79; Varro, l.l., V; 54; Cass. Dio, LII, 16, 5-6; Prop., IV, 1, 9; Ios., *ant. Iud.*, XIX, 75-76; Curiosum e Notitia: Valentini-Zucchetti 1940: 128-132, 177-178); l'ipotesi di una identificazione del piccolo monumento qui esaminato con la *Casa Romuli* acquista fondamento anche dalla considerazione che questo spazio, contrariamente alle aree immediatamente adiacenti, fu costantemente rispettato nelle successive trasformazioni del santuario. Infatti, quando la costruzione del tempio di Cibele (204-191 a.C.) determinò un riassetto generale della zona e in particolare, la totale eliminazione del terrazzamento relativo al tempio della Vittoria, l'area sacra attorno alla fossa rettangolare fu estesa in direzione nord e separata dalla vasca relativa al culto di Cibele da un muro (fig. 9, 14), mentre sui lati est ed ovest altri muri la separavano rispettivamente dal tratto terminale del *clivus victoriae* e dalla platea del nuovo tempio (fig. 9, 15, 16). Il piano di calpestio in questa fase era notevolmente più alto rispetto al livello della roccia

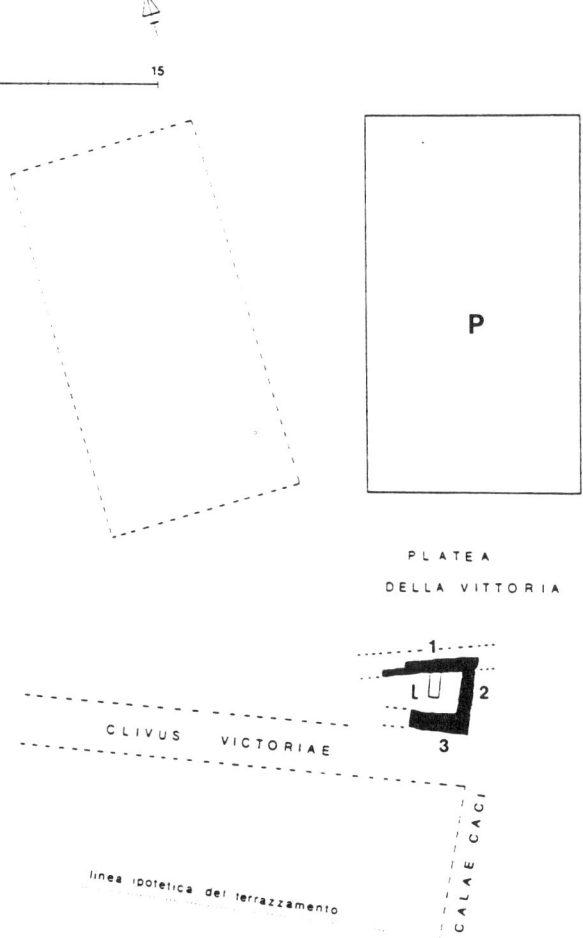

Fig. 8. *Area sud-ovest del Palatino, pianta della struttura rettangolare in opera quadrata (11 - 13) e del tempio della Vittoria (p).*

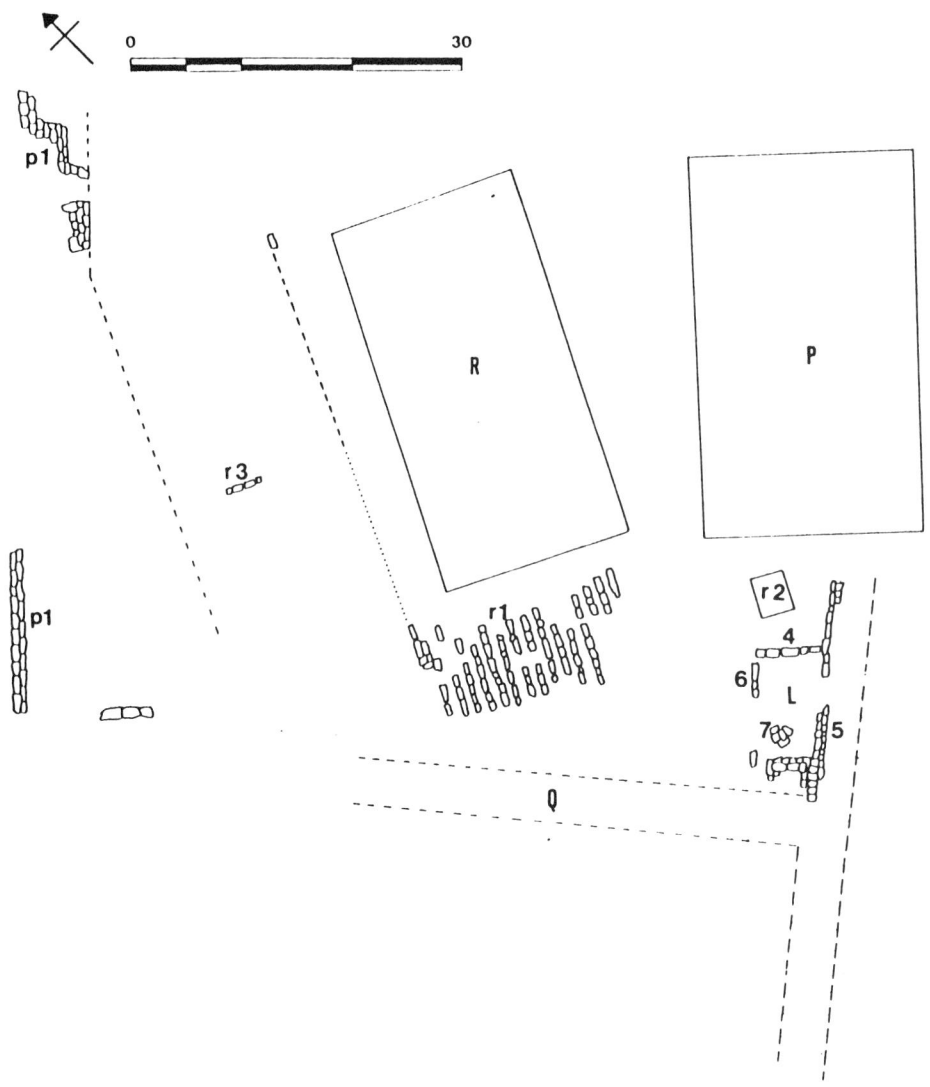

Fig. 9. Area sud-ovest del Palatino, pianta del tempio della Magna Mater *(I fase) e strutture circostanti.*

naturale e la posizione della fossa sacra era evidenziata da un *sema*, di cui si conservano tuttora le massicce fondazioni in opera quadrata di tufo (fig. 9, 17). Alla connessione archeologica tra la costruzione del tempio della Vittoria e la creazione (o si trattò del rifacimento di un sacello più antico?) della *Casa Romuli* fa riscontro una connessione di carattere ideologico: la sede del culto della Vittoria viene collocata nell'area sud-ovest del Palatino, in diretta relazione con i luoghi delle origini mitiche della città rappresentati non solo dalla Casa Romuli, ma anche dal *Lupercal* e dalla *Roma Quadrata*. *(P. Pensabene)*

V. Negli anni 204–191 a.C. l'area sud-occidentale del Palatino fu interessata da una profonda trasformazione in seguito alla costruzione del santuario dedicato alla *Magna Mater* Cibele (Liv., XXIX, 14, 13; XXIX, 37, 1–2). Lo scavo degli ultimi anni ha consentito di controllare e in gran parte di confermare quanto già proposto dal Romanelli in merito al tempio (Romanelli 1963: 221–240) e di portare alla luce ciò che resta dei vari settori del santuario.

Della costruzione originaria si conservano, oltre a resti di sostruzioni poste sul lato occidentale di cui si tratterà oltre, le fondazioni, in filari paralleli di opera quadrata di tufo, di un'ampia gradinata frontale (fig. 9, r1) ed una vasca con funzione rituale anch'essa in opera quadrata (fig. 9, r2), posta a sud-est. Di fronte alla gradinata vi era un'area pavimentata con lastre di tufo, delimitata a sud dal percorso del *clivus victoriae*. La gradinata e la platea venivano presumibilmente utilizzate anche per lo svolgimento delle rappresentazioni sceniche nel corso dei *Ludi Megalenses*. L'edificio templare di prima fase non è conservato; da impronte di blocchi visibili in elevato sul fianco occidentale del podio cementizio (risalente alla fase successiva) si può ipotizzare che, come le altre strutture coeve conservate, anch'esso fosse realizzato in opera quadrata. Il tempio di Cibele e tutte le strutture ad esso collegate furono costruiti con un orientamento (nord/sud) notevolmente divergente rispetto a quello (nord-est/sud-ovest) delle strutture arcaiche, del tempio della Vittoria, del *clivus victoriae* e delle sostruzioni in opera quadrata già edificate lungo le pendici sud-occidentali del colle (Säflund 1932: 3 ss.; fig. 9, p1). Tale orientamento permarrà invariato nel corso delle successive ristrutturazioni e verrà assunto da tutte le costruzioni, anche aggiunte in epoca successiva, inerenti il santuario, mentre le costruzioni da esso indipendenti, anche limitrofe (come ad esempio la *Domus Tiberiana*) riprenderanno l'orientamento 'antico'. Il santuario di Cibele pertanto appare caratterizzato da un orientamento unitario, costante ed esclusivo. Il santuario della *Magna Mater* fu costruito immediatamente ad ovest del tempio della Vittoria, ed alcuni annessi del nuovo tempio (gradinata frontale, vasca rituale, platea antistante) determinarono una drastica riduzione dello spazio precedentemente dedicato alla Vittoria (totale smantellamento della preesistente area terrazzata e conseguente modifica apportata alla *Casa Romuli*). Questa sovrapposizione forzata indica presumibilmente che ad ovest del tempio della Vittoria non doveva esservi uno spazio adeguato ad accogliere il nuovo santuario. All'epoca della creazione del tempio della Vittoria era già stato effettuato un grande intervento di sostruzione delle pendici sud-occidentali del Palatino, realizzato con una poderosa struttura in opera quadrata di tufo, tuttora parzialmente conservata alla base del colle (fig. 9, p1). Recentemente sono state rinvenute tracce di strutture di sostruzione (anch'esse in opera quadrata di tufo) costruite a monte, nell'area ad ovest del tempio di Cibele e con esso orientate: dunque coeve al tempio e più recenti rispetto alle sostruzioni parzialmente conservate a valle (fig. 10, r3). Da questi dati è possibile ipotizzare che lo spazio ad ovest del tempio della Vittoria, all'epoca in cui si stabilì di inserirvi il santuario di Cibele, non dovesse presentarsi come un terrazzamento ampio e ben sostruito, quale sarebbe stato se la massiccia muratura in opera quadrata, di cui si conservano resti a valle, si fosse elevata fino alla quota del piano superiore del colle. Al contrario, lo spazio doveva essere limitato, tanto che si rese necessario approntare nuove opere di sostruzione (presumibilmente raccordate con quelle preesistenti); queste ultime tuttavia sembra che non abbiano determinato una disponibilità di spazio tale da consentire che il nuovo edificio non interferisse sul vecchio.

La grande ricostruzione della fine del II sec. a.C. ha lasciato tracce archeologiche molto più consistenti; essa è caratterizzata dall'impiego del calcestruzzo nelle nuove costruzioni (tra esse il tempio, che fu totalmente ricostruito), mentre alcune delle strutture in opera quadrata del periodo precedente furono riadattate e riutilizzate. Lo spazio sulla fronte del tempio fu ampliato (probabilmente anche per esigenze connesse con la celebrazione dei *Ludi*), realizzando due livelli sovrapposti: un quartiere inferiore costituito dal *clivus victoriae* (coperto a volta e trasformato in *via tecta*) e da una serie di vani voltati affacciati ai due lati di esso (camere di sostruzione utilizzate come taberne a destinazione commerciale o artigianale), e un piano superiore, fondato sul quartiere sottostante, che costituiva un'ampia platea di fronte all'edificio sacro, assai più estesa rispetto a quella della fase precedente, in quanto non più delimitata dal percorso della strada. Inoltre la vasca sacra che nella fase precedente si trovava nell'area frontale fu obliterata, e ne fu costruita una nuova in un ampio spazio adiacente al fianco occidentale del tempio, delimitato da muri di recinzione continui e chiusi (un unico punto di accesso individuato nell'angolo nord-est). In estrema sintesi, questa ristrutturazione sembra mirare contemporaneamente ad un ampliamento degli spazi e ad una più marcata distinzione tra differenti settori, ciascuno caratterizzato in base ad una specifica funzione (quartiere di accesso con la *via tecta* e le taberne; tempio; platea per le manifestazioni sacre e le rappresentazioni sceniche; recinto occidentale racchiudente la vasca rituale). *(P. Battistelli)*

Bibliografia

Albertoni, M. 1990. 'Il deposito votivo presso il Clivo Capitolino – Materiali arcaici', *La grande Roma dei Tarquini*, Catalogo della mostra, Roma, 73–75.

Battistelli, P. 1990. 'Materiali dell'area sud ovest del Palatino', *La grande Roma dei Tarquini*, Catalogo della mostra, Roma, 91–95.

Carettoni, G. 1953. 'Roma – Palatino. Saggi per uno studio topografico della casa di Livia', *Notizie degli Scavi di Antichità*, 126 ss.

Carettoni, G. 1957. 'Roma – Palatino. Casa di Livia', *Notizie degli Scavi di Antichità*, 80 ss.

Cassieri, N. 1990. 'Circeii', *La grande Roma dei Tarquini*, Catalogo della mostra, Roma, 218.

Colonna, G. 1984. 'I templi del Lazio fino al V secolo compreso', *QuadAEI*, 8, 396–411.

Durante, G. & Gervasini, L. 1987. 'Marzabotto', *La formazione della città in Emilia Romagna*, Catalogo della mostra, Bologna, 316–325.

Falzone, S. c.s. 'Palatino – Tempio della Vittoria: testimonianze della prima età del Ferro', *Bollettino di Archeologia*.

Ferrea, L. 1981. 'Figurine di lamina di bronzo ritagliata', *Enea nel Lazio*, Catalogo della mostra, Roma, 148–149.

Gatti, S. 1990. 'Anagnia – La stipe votiva di S. Cecilia', *La grande Roma dei Tarquini*, Catalogo della mostra, Roma, 225–229.

Gjerstad, E. 1953. *Early Rome. I*, Lund.

Gjerstad, E. 1960. *Early Rome. III*, Lund.

Krause, C. 1985. *Domus Tiberiana – Nuove ricerche studi di restauro*, Zurigo.

Ioppolo, G. 1989. 'Il tempio arcaico', *Il viver quotidiano in Roma arcaica*, Catalogo della mostra, Roma, 34–36.

Marella Vianello, M. 1947. In *Antichità* I, parte III, 1 ss.

Micozzi, M. 1990. 'Satricum – La stipe votiva', *La grande Roma dei Tarquini*, Catalogo della mostra, Roma, 234–240.

Pensabene, P. 1978. 'Saggi di scavo sul tempio della Magna Mater del Palatino', *QuadAEI*, 1, 67–71.

Pensebene, P. 1979. '"Auguratorium" e tempio della Magna Mater', *QuadAEI*, 2, 67–74.

Pensabene, P. 1980. 'La zona sud-occidentale del Palatino', *QuadAEI*, 4, 65–81.

Pensabene, P. 1981. 'Nuove acquisizioni nella zona sud-occidentale del Palatino', *QuadAEI*, 5, 101–118.

Pensabene, P. 1983 'Quinta campagna di scavo nell'area sud-ovest del Palatino', *QuadAEI,* 7, 65-75.

Pensabene, P. 1985. 'Area sud-occidentale del Palatino', *Roma Archeologia nel centro*, I, Roma, 179-212.

Pensabene, P. 1988 'Scavi nell'area del tempio della Vittoria e del santuario della Magna Mater sul Palatino', *QuadAEI,* 16, 54-67.

Pensabene, P. 1990. 'L'area sud occidentale del Palatino', *La grande Roma dei Tarquini*, Catalogo della mostra, Roma, 86-90.

Pensabene, P. 1993. 'Campagne di scavo 1988-1991 nell'area sud-ovest del Palatino', *QuadAEI*, 21, 19-37.

Pensabene, P. c.s., a. 'Il tempio della Vittoria sul Palatino', *Bollettino di Archeologia*.

Pensabene, P. c.s., b. 'Casa Romuli sul Palatino', *Rendiconti della Pontificia Accademia*.

Romanelli, P. 1963. 'Lo scavo al tempio della Magna Mater e nelle sue adiacenze', *Monumenti Antichi dei Lincei*, XLVI, cc. 201-330.

Säflund, G. 1932. *Le mura di Roma repubblicana*, Lund.

Sommella Mura, A. 1976. 'Campidoglio - La favissa', in *Civiltà del Lazio Primitivo*, Catalogo della mostra, Roma, 145-146.

Vaglieri, D. 1907. In *Notizie degli Scavi di Antichità*, 185-205; 264-282; 444-460; 529-542.

Valentini, R. & Zucchetti, G. 1940. *Codice topografico della città di Roma*, I, Roma.

Virgili, P. 1989. 'I depositi votivi del tempio arcaico', *Il viver quotidiano in Roma arcaica*, Catalogo della mostra, Roma, 52-53.

48

Mediolanum dall'*Oppidum* Celtico alla Città Romana

Anna Ceresa Mori
(Soprintendenza Archeologica della Lombardia)

Sommario: *I risultati degli scavi effettuati negli ultimi dieci anni consentono di tracciare un quadro delle origini della città, dell'abitato celtico e della sua trasformazione in* colonia latina e poi in municipium civium romanorum, *mettendo in discussione le precedenti interpretazioni che volevano la città fondata* ex nihilo *secondo schemi programmatici ortogonali. I nuovi dati rendono ora più consistenti le ipotesi sull'esistenza nel sito di un abitato golasecchiano della fine del V secolo a.C. e dell*'oppidum *celtico del IV-III secolo a.C. ricordato dalle fonti storiche. L'analisi della stratigrafia archeologica di Milano mostra la presenza di vasti interventi di ristrutturazione nel periodo della romanizzazione, che hanno cancellato i resti degli insediamenti precedenti, lasciandone solo sporadiche tracce. Esse sono però sufficienti per ipotizzare un'evoluzione della città da centro protourbano nel periodo Golasecca IIIA, con la funzione di tramite tra l'Etruria e i paesi transalpini, ad* oppidum *celtico in cui l'avvio del processo di urbanizzazione sembra da porsi attorno alla metà del II secolo a.C. Allo stato attuale della ricerca, l'impianto urbanistico appare non ortogonale e condizionato dagli assi di accesso extraurbani e dai corsi d'acqua. Esso può essere interpretato come il risultato di un intervento di regolarizzazione dell'organizzazione spaziale dell*'oppidum, *voluto dalla classe dirigente locale sotto la spinta della penetrazione culturale romana.*

Introduzione

Negli ultimi dieci anni a Milano il salto di qualità effettuato nel campo dell'attività di tutela archeologica condotta dalla Soprintendenza, per quanto riguarda sia le modalità operative, sia la scelta degli obiettivi, sia le tecniche di scavo stratigrafico, ha permesso il recupero di una notevole quantità di dati, solo in parte pubblicati. Tanto questi ultimi, quanto l'analisi preliminare dei dati degli scavi non ancora editi, consentono ora di comprendere meglio il significato dei vecchi ritrovamenti e di tracciare un quadro delle origini della città, dell'abitato celtico e della sua trasformazione in *colonia latina* e poi in *municipium civium romanorum*. Il modello di sviluppo che ne risulta, anche se certamente ancora da verificare per molti aspetti, comporta la revisione di alcune tesi finora universalmente accettate sull'urbanistica di *Mediolanum* e può costituire una valida ipotesi di partenza per le future ricerche (Ceresa Mori 1990–91, 1992).

Fino al 1980, l'esistenza di un insediamento pre-romano sul sito era ritenuta del tutto ipotetica ed indimostrabile. L'attenzione degli studiosi era diretta prevalentemente ad indagare la città romana nei suoi principali monumenti. Nel 1914 De Marchi, esaminando l'andamento del reticolo viario attorno a piazza S. Sepolcro, avanzò l'ipotesi che in esso si dovesse riconoscere, sia pure alterato e deformato da successive ristrutturazioni, l'impianto ortogonale "dell'antica città romana, cresciuta accanto alla più antica e probabilmente irregolare città gallica". Al problema urbanistico sono stati dedicati numerosi contributi, i più significativi dei quali mi sembra possano essere sintetizzati come segue.

Il Mirabella Roberti (1973–74), rifacendosi all'ipotesi del De Marchi, ripresa poi dal Calderini (1953: 477–523), ha individuato nell'impianto urbanistico della città romana due 'piani regolatori': una zona centrale, una sorta di centro direzionale, articolata su assi ortogonali attorno alla piazza del Foro, in cui si incrociano il *cardo maximus* e il *decumanus maximus* (deviato però di 5° verso nord rispetto al reticolato urbano), e un secondo impianto ortogonale tra questo e le mura, con un orientamento NS, divergente rispetto al primo (fig.1). Questo secondo impianto, che sarebbe più antico, e coordinato agli assi centuriali del territorio, è messo dall'autore in relazione con la concessione dello *ius Latii* nell'89 a.C.

Il primo studioso che ha formulato ipotesi sull'insediamento insubre è Arslan (1982), che propone una sua

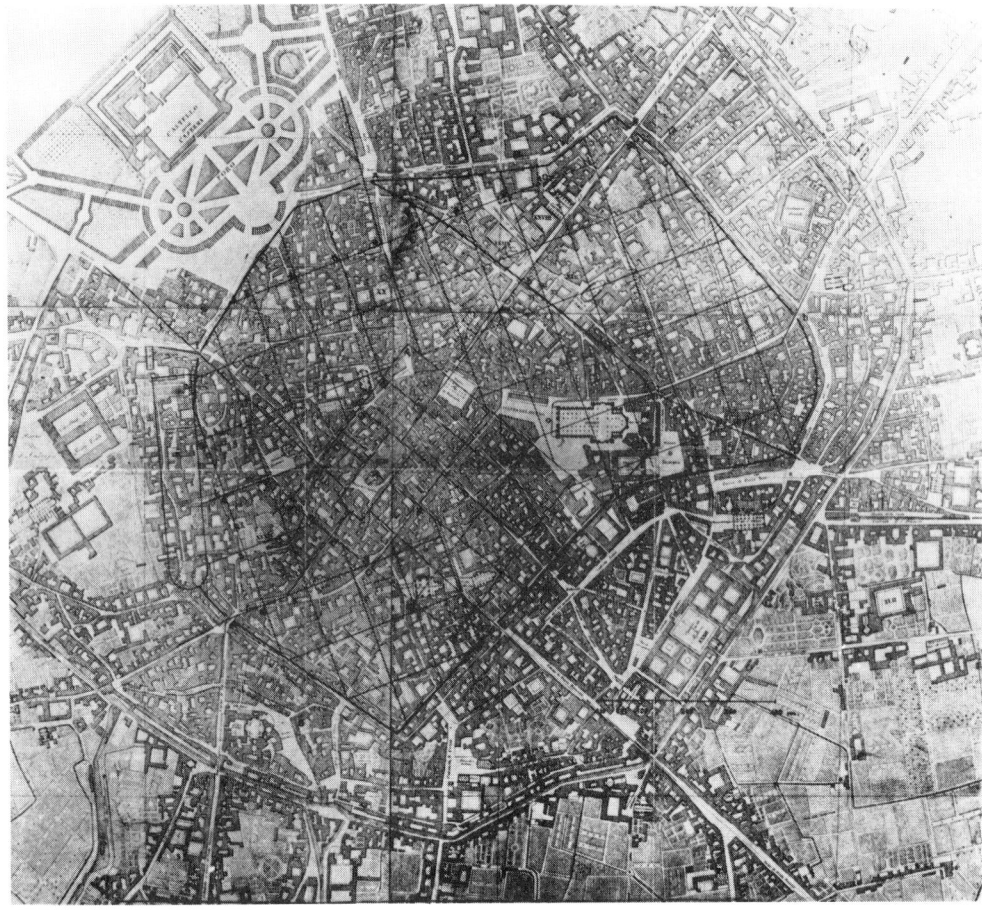

Fig. 1. Ipotesi ricostruttiva del tessuto viario di Mediolanum di M. Mirabella Roberti (1973-74).

collocazione nell'area delimitata dalla curva di livello 121, corrispondente ad una zona che suppone originariamente più elevata, compresa tra piazza Scala, il Duomo, piazza S. Sepolcro e l'inizio della via Dante (cfr. De Marinis 1984: 31). La città romana con impianto ortogonale sarebbe sorta come nuovo insediamento sviluppatosi accanto al nucleo preromano, lasciato al margine NE, o come ampliamento di tale nucleo, realizzato nell'area compresa tra le vie per Vercelli e per Como, tra la metà del II secolo a.C. e l'89 a.C. Nell'articolo viene giustamente sottolineata l'importanza degli assi stradali extraurbani che si incontrano nel settore NE. L'autore, che accetta in gran parte l'ipotesi del Mirabella Roberti, ritiene che la città romana sia stata realizzata su terreno libero, "evitando per quanto possibile la ristrutturazione radicale di aree già urbanizzate, anche se in modo primitivo".

Tocchetti Pollini (1984), riprendendo l'ipotesi del Mirabella Roberti, ritiene più antico l'impianto del Foro, da porsi in connessione con la costituzione della colonia di diritto latino, nell'89 a.C., nello stesso periodo in cui vengono realizzati edifici pubblici monumentali. Per l'impianto urbano NS il *terminus post quem*, secondo lo studioso, è l'età augustea.

L'analisi puntuale dei dati urbanistici forniti dai nuovi scavi, correlati con i vecchi ritrovamenti e con la cartografia antica, porta la Caporusso (1992) alla conclusione che l'alto numero di anomalie rispetto allo schema urbanistico NS ipotizzato dal Mirabella Roberti, riscontrato nel settore est della città, fa pensare ad "un piano regolatore molto fluido, che adotta lo schema canonico ad assi incrociati nel nucleo circostante il Foro, mentre per il resto sembra adeguarsi ad uno schema a raggiera di strade extraurbane di origine preistorica e protostorica". L'autrice riconosce nelle zone nord-ovest e sud-ovest nuclei orientati secondo il piano NS e li collega alla concessione del diritto latino nell'89 a.C.

Gli autori del capitolo conclusivo del volume dedicato agli scavi per la Metropolitana Milanese linea 3 (Arslan & Caporusso 1991: 351–358), ipotizzano nella fase preromana una serie di nuclei insediativi distinti, con diversi orientamenti, divisi "da cerniere costituite proprio dagli assi stradali fondamentali", che solo nel periodo romano sarebbero stati unificati. Tale interpretazione, che rifiuta l'ipotesi di un oppidum celtico fortificato, sostenuta da altri autori, si fonda essenzialmente sull'argomento 'ex silentio' dato dall'estrema frammentarietà dei dati di scavo relativi ai periodi più antichi. Viene anche formulata una nuova ipotesi sul *decumanus maximus*, tradizionalmente fatto coincidere con l'asse stradale che collegava la via per *Vercellae* e *Novaria* con quella verso *Laus* e *Roma*. L'assenza di prove archeologiche e cartografiche della sua continuità tra piazza S. Sepolcro e piazza Missori porta gli autori a respingere questa identificazione e a ritenere che la direttrice viaria verso *Laus* e *Roma*, in relazione con la centuriazione del territorio a sud di *Mediolanum*, sia da riferirsi ad epoca posteriore alla pianificazione urbanistica della città.

Come si vede, nel dibattito sull'ipotesi del Mirabella Roberti, appare prevalente la tendenza degli studiosi a collegare la pianificazione urbanistica di *Mediolanum* al periodo in cui l'ingresso della città nell'orbita romana viene sancito sul piano giuridico.

A livello generale, negli studi sulla romanizzazione nella Cisalpina, è ricorrente l'opinione che sia poco plausibile l'esistenza, sul sito delle colonie romane, di insediamenti preromani a carattere protourbano. I principali supporti a questa teoria sono argomenti 'ex silentio', come la scarsità dei ritrovamenti e il mancato rinvenimento di cerchie murarie, il noto passo di Polibio (II, 17, 9-11), in cui i centri della Transpadana sono definiti "villaggi privi di mura", e quelli analoghi di Strabone (V,1,6) e Livio (32,31, 2; 33,36,8) (Gabba 1984: 207-209; Tozzi 1986: 351; Scagliarini Corlaita 1991: 160, n.2). Sul fronte opposto, gli studiosi di protostoria hanno invece privilegiato un diverso punto di vista, che tiene conto del fatto che la scarsità dei ritrovamenti relativi alla tarda età del Ferro è spiegabile in centri come Milano, Brescia, Bergamo, dove la continuità dell'occupazione ha causato gravi lacune nella stratigrafia archeologica (Kruta 1980: 199-200; Frey 1986: 333-337; De Marinis 1990: 37; Tizzoni 1986: 351-353). Polibio, nella descrizione delle vicende belliche del 222 a.C., parlando della caduta di *Acerrae* e della protezione trovata dall'armata gallica a *Mediolanum*, dà una conferma indiretta del carattere urbano e fortificato di questi insediamenti.

L'ARCHEOLOGIA

Le due sezioni ideali della stratigrafia di *Mediolanum*, quella lungo il *cardo maximus* e quella lungo il *decumanus maximus* (figg.2-3), tracciate sulla base dei risultati degli scavi degli ultimi dieci anni (cfr. Appendice), mi sembra possano aiutare a chiarire alcuni dei punti controversi sull'evoluzione di questo centro. Il maggiore interro si trova all'interno delle mura romane, dove l'insediamento ha avuto vita più lunga, ed è quindi dovuto in parte all'accumularsi del deposito archeologico. Una notevole percentuale della stratigrafia è stata distrutta dalle cantine, che raggiungono una profondità di circa m.3,50 dal piano stradale, ma nella zona centrale della città, sotto il piano delle cantine, è ancora conservata una notevole parte di stratigrafia, da uno a due metri.

Nella sezione lungo il cardo (fig.3b), l'abbassamento di quota del terreno sterile che si può osservare a partire da via Valpetrosa, a sud della curva di livello 121, sembra confermare l'esistenza di un'area originariamente sopraelevata all'interno di tale curva (Arslan 1982: 183-191). E' anche interessante notare che il salto di quota a sud della isoipsa 121 è stato colmato nel periodo repubblicano; l'ipotesi che tale avvallamento possa essere identificato con il fossato difensivo dell'insediamento golasecchiano (ipotesi del Prof. M. Torelli) è suggestiva, ma un po' prematura, in assenza di altre verifiche sul terreno.

Nella parte centrale della città, quella press'a poco corrispondente all'impianto detto 'del Foro', si nota inoltre un accrescimento di terreno nel I-II secolo d.C., probabilmente riferibile ad interventi di livellamento e di reinterro a scopo di bonifica dei terreni umidi.

In questa sezione è interessante notare la presenza di strati riferibili al II-I secolo a.C. anche all'esterno delle cortine difensive repubblicana e massimianea, fatto dovuto alla presenza di tracce di insediamenti extra-murani già in epoca tardorepubblicana e primo-imperiale sia a NE sia a SW della città, in connessione con importanti direttrici viarie (Arslan & Caporusso 1991: 354).

Per la sezione NE-SW (fig.3a) è stata adottata per comodità come linea di sezione l'asse stradale corrispondente alle vie S.Maria alla Porta, S. Maria Fulcorina e del Bollo, identificato come *decumanus maximus* dal Mirabella Roberti, anche se sembrano valide le obiezioni recentemente sollevate contro tale identificazione. 'E interessante notare la pendenza degli strati, che mostra come la città si trovi su un piano inclinato da NNW a SSE. Il dislivello di quota nella zona tra corso di Porta Romana e via Lamarmora corrisponde al terrapieno delle mura medievali.

I livelli pertinenti al periodo più antico dell'insediamento, il Golasecca III A (fine V secolo a.C.), sono indicati in un unico punto. Contesti primari riferibili a questo periodo sono stati rinvenuti solo in due zone, Palazzo Reale (Iorio 1987: 132-137) e via Moneta (Ceresa Mori *et al.* 1987: 137-141), oltre ai resti di necropoli rinvenuti nel secolo scorso nel cortile dell'ospedale di S. Antonino (De Marinis 1981: 168-170), mentre relativamente numerosi sono i rinvenimenti di materiale residuo del periodo Golasecca III A. Si tratta di rinvenimenti fortuiti effettuati nel secolo scorso in via Meravigli e via Broletto angolo piazza Cordusio (De Marinis 1981: 167-171; 1984: 28-33) e di materiali residui rinvenuti recentemente negli scavi di via Moneta (Ceresa Mori & White c.s.), della Biblioteca Ambrosiana e di via Valpetrosa (Ceresa Mori 1992; 1990-91: 248-251; Ceresa Mori *et al.* 1990). L'area interessata dai rinvenimenti ha la forma di un triangolo con i vertici corrispondenti a via Meravigli, Palazzo Reale e via Valpetrosa (fig.6). Se si accetta l'ipotesi che essa fosse tutta occupata dall'insediamento, si deve concludere che

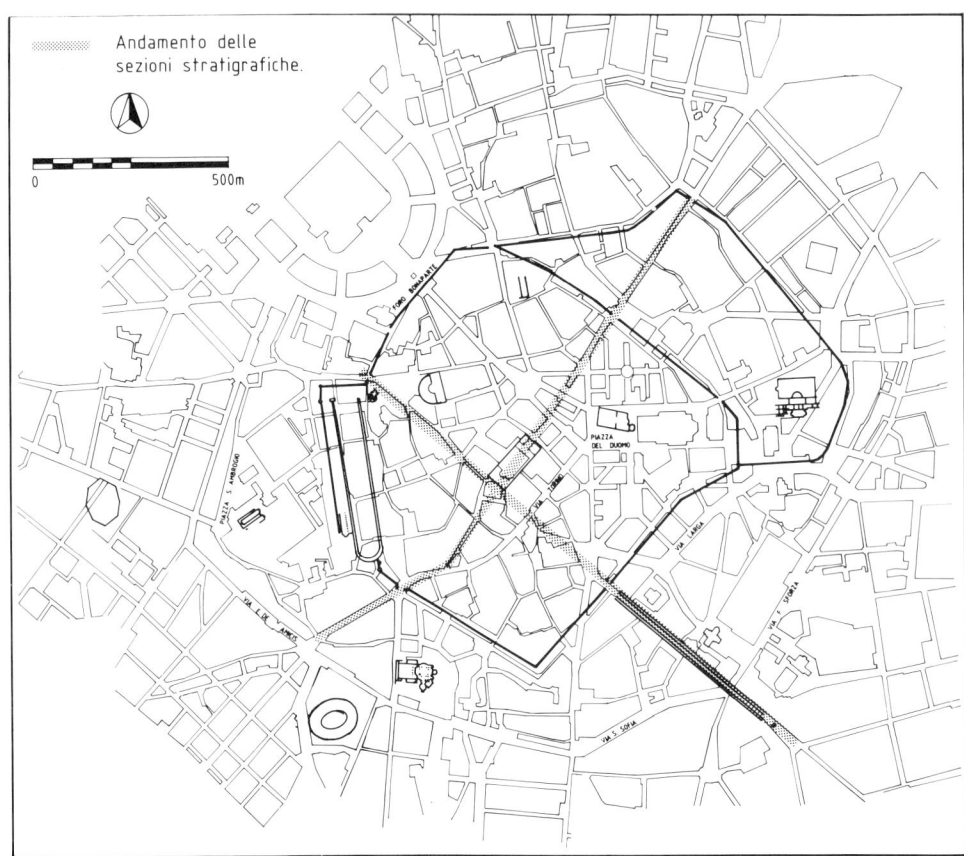

Fig.2. Tracciato delle due sezioni ideali della stratigrafia di Mediolanum *(disegno N. White).*

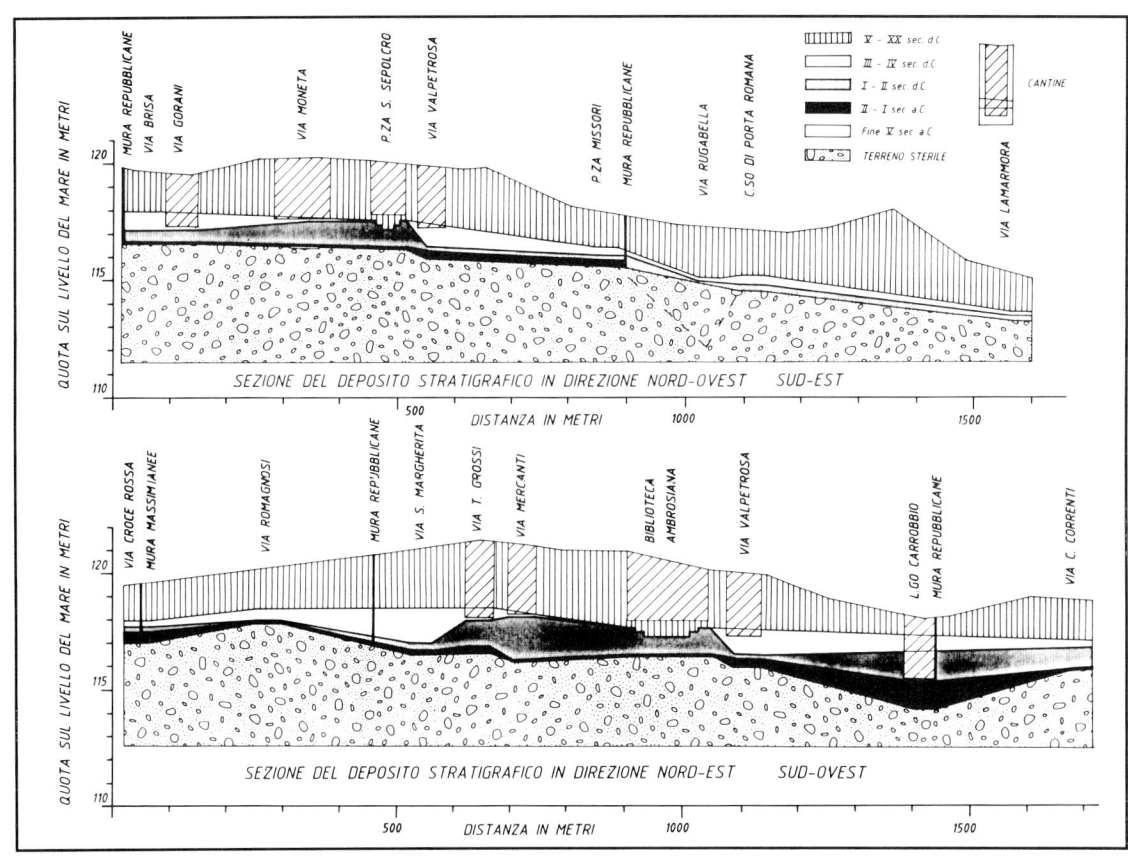

Fig.3a. Sezione stratigrafica NW-SE   *Fig.3b. Sezione stratigrafica NE-SW (disegno N. White).*

doveva trattarsi di un abitato a carattere protourbano dell'estensione di circa 12 ettari.

Nella sezione si può notare come la quota dei rinvenimenti golasecchiani coincida press'a poco con quella dei livelli del periodo della romanizzazione (II-I secolo a.C.): questo spiega la mancanza dei contesti primari, che si sono conservati eccezionalmente dove sono stati risparmiati dalle ristrutturazioni urbanistiche del periodo repubblicano. In entrambe le sezioni si nota la totale assenza dei livelli del IV-III secolo a.C. Se già quelli più antichi, della fine del V, si sono conservati solo sporadicamente, a maggior ragione si deve ritenere che quelli del periodo più recente, cioè dell'*oppidum* celtico, siano stati completamente distrutti dalle ristrutturazioni del II-I secolo a.C. Scarsi sono i materiali ralativi a questi secoli, venuti in luce in passato solo in via Rastrelli (De Marinis 1984: 31) e recentemente in via Moneta.

Gli scavi di via Moneta (1987-1991), hanno evidenziato la presenza di un livello di insediamento golasecchiano ed hanno permesso il recupero di materiali residui riferibili al La Tène B e C (IV-III secolo a.C.), tra cui sono da segnalare un bicchiere a portauovo decorato a occhi di dado del La Tène B1, ciotole con bande di grafite sotto l'orlo e lungo la gola, ceramica dipinta decorata con motivi geometrici a risparmio, per la quale finora non si sono trovati confronti (Tizzoni 1990-91: 260), due dracme insubri coniate a Milano (inizio e seconda metà del III secolo a.C.) (Arslan 1991: 78-79), ciotole ad orlo ingrossato con iscrizioni in caratteri nordetruschi (fig.4), una fibula ad arco serpeggiante, un elemento in bronzo con decorazioni di corallo, un frammento di kantharos St. Valentin (fine V-inizio IV secolo a.C.; Ceresa Mori 1992: 251 fig.3; cfr. Maggiani 1992: 93, nn.619, 620, tav.G; Moreno 1964: 203, tav.XLVI, 2).

Un fossato difensivo celtico, con sezione a V e buchi di palo sul lato nord, che risulta essere stato abbandonato attorno alla metà del II secolo a.C., aveva orientamento analogo a quello della strada romana lastricata della fase successiva, corrispondente all'attuale via Moneta (Ceresa More & White 1991: 114-115).

Nel periodo romano l'area era occupata da un isolato di abitazioni che subisce ristrutturazioni fino al IV secolo. Di particolare interesse sono le tecniche edilizie, documentate anche in vari altri scavi effettuati a Milano, che caratterizzano le fasi del periodo della romanizzazione tra la fine del II secolo a.C. e l'inizio dell'epoca imperiale romana. La presenza di costruzioni in legno, di cui restavano solo le tracce in negativo, o di muri realizzati con tecnica a pannelli in torchis e legno, poggianti su travi di legno orizzontali su muretti in ciottoli, i focolari in argilla e laterizi, la fondazioni a strati alternati di ghiaia e limo sono elementi che pongono *Mediolanum* in stretto collegamento con numerosi siti dell'Europa centrosettentrionale. Significativi sono anche gli indizi che si possono ricavare sulle planimetrie delle abitazioni, caratterizzate da una lunga persistenza nel tempo, con limitate trasformazioni. L'analisi dei frammentari dati di scavo permette di ipotizzare per gli edifici una pianta rettangolare con cortile retrostante. Confronti puntuali, sia per le tecniche edilizie, sia per la tipologia, sono riscontrabili, per citare l'esempio più recente, nel *vicus* svizzero di Lousonna Vidy (Berti & Castella 1992, sul Magdalensberg (Piccottini 1993: 203-205) e in Gallia (Desbat 1991: 147-160).

Lo scavo sotto la Biblioteca Ambrosiana ha confermato la presenza del lastricato della piazza in marmo di Verona. Sono venuti in luce, sul lato ovest, la canaletta per lo scolo delle acque meteoriche e parte dei gradini di accesso alle *tabernae*. Per realizzare la pavimentazione, probabilmente all'inizio dell'epoca imperiale, venne raso al suolo un quartiere di abitazioni in legno di cui restavano solo tracce in negativo date dai buchi di palo e solchi per travi, e qualche focolare. L'orientamento degli edifici sembra essere lo stesso del reticolato viario romano della zona (Ceresa Mori 1995).

Tra il materiale dello scavo sono da segnalare una fibula in bronzo con anima in cotto, del tipo definito nel secolo scorso 'simulacro di fibula', probabilmente di uso votivo (fig.5), e materiale ceramico del Golasecca III A, ceramica etrusco-padana e un frammento di kylix attica a figure rosse del pittore di Vienna 155, della prima metà del IV secolo a.C.

Lo scavo di via Valpetrosa, ancora in corso, ha restituito ceramica e fibule del periodo Golasecca III A. Particolarmente interessante è inoltre un'ansa di anfora rodia con bollo Ἐπὶ Ἀρχιβίου δαλίου (traduzione: 'Sotto il mandato di Archibios, nel mese di Dalios'), che si data attorno alla seconda metà del II secolo a.C. (Grace 1952: 524-525, 529; Mertens 1955: 89-93).

Discussione

In sintesi, le nuove conoscenze fornite da questi scavi, per quanto riguarda l'età del Ferro, indicano con ogni probabilità la presenza di un insediamento protourbano riferibile al periodo Golasecca III A (fine del V secolo a.C.). Allo scavo di via Moneta dobbiamo inoltre i primi dati noti a Milano sul La Tène C1 (IV-III secolo a.C.). La dracma insubre 'naturalistica' coniata a Milano, che costituisce un caso isolato a nord del Po, è databile all'inizio del III secolo a.C. Oltre ai materiali inquadrabili nella facies culturale della regione dei laghi e del Canton Ticino, è da segnalare un nuovo tipo di ceramica con decorazione geometrica a risparmio, caratterizzata da olle e bicchieri ovoidali, in cui la tecnica di lavorazione di tradizione golasecchiana si unisce a nuove forme e ad un'originale sintassi decorativa.

Il ritrovamento a Milano di frammenti di ceramica attica ed etrusco padana, collegandosi ad altre importazioni documentate a Lodivecchio, Cuggiono, Gola-

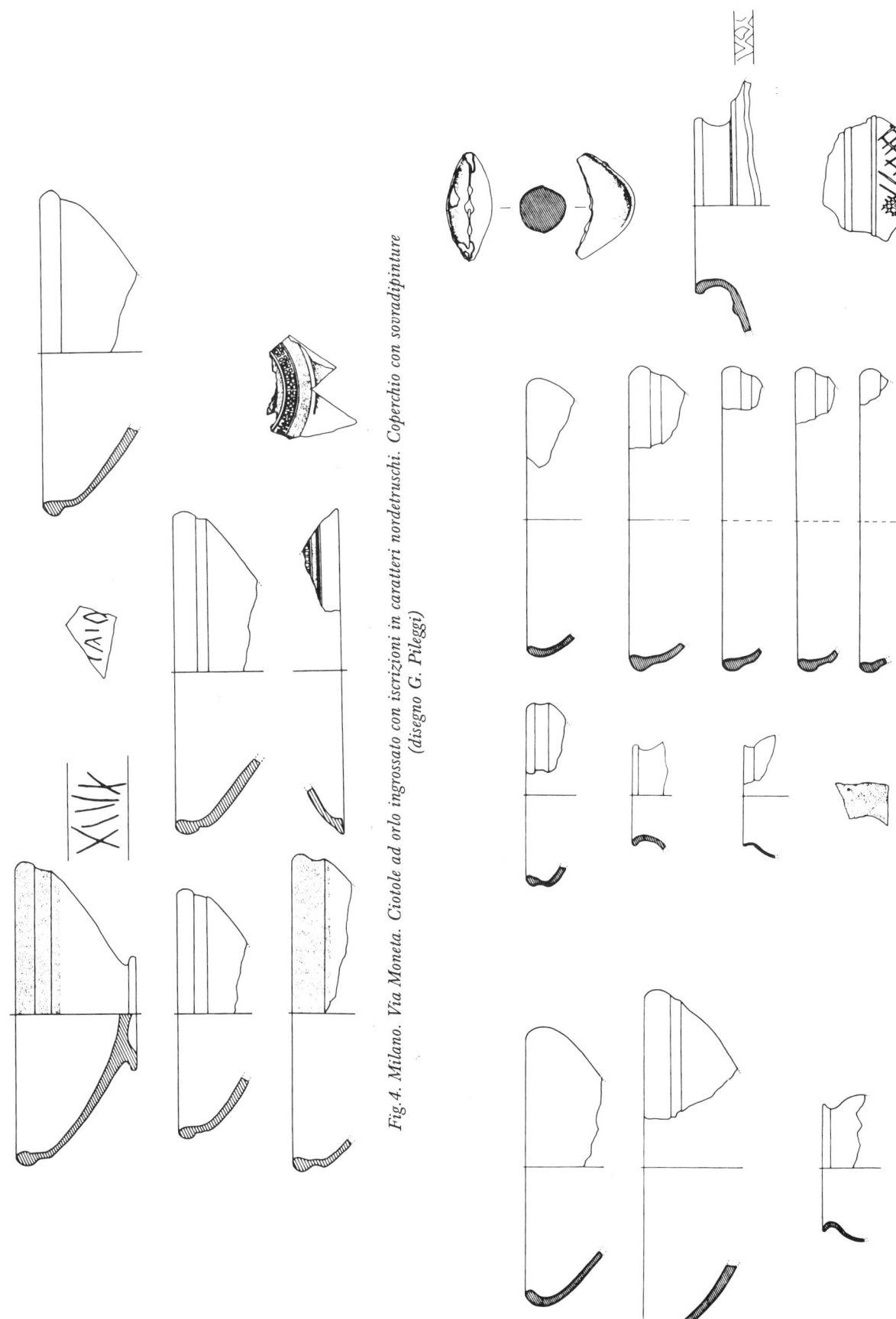

Fig. 4. Milano. Via Moneta. Ciotole ad orlo ingrossato con iscrizioni in caratteri nordetruschi. Coperchio con sovradipinture (disegno G. Pileggi)

Fig. 5. Milano. Biblioteca Ambrosiana. Frammenti di ciotole, ollette, urne golasecchiane e 'simulacro di fibula' (disegno G. Pileggi).

secca, Gravellona Toce e presso Biella, suggerisce l'esistenza di una corrente di traffico alternativa a quella tra l'Etruria Padana, Mantova, Brescia, Bergamo, Como e i paesi d'oltralpe, che, attraverso il lodigiano e Milano, raggiungeva le regioni a nord delle Alpi (De Marinis 1990: 18-22; Tizzoni 1990-91: 262). Il passaggio dal Golasecca III A2 al Golasecca III A3 segna il declino dell'abitato protostorico di Como, al quale sembra subentrare quello di Milano. La crescita dell'insediamento si inquadra nel processo di sviluppo comune ad altri centri lombardi a carattere protourbano, sorti in connessione con lo sviluppo degli scambi culturali e commerciali con l'Etruria (De Marinis 1986: 25-35).

Per quanto riguarda l'*oppidum* celtico nel IV-III secolo a.C., la scarsità delle attestazioni, sulla base della situazione stratigrafica che ho illustrato all'inizio, non autorizza ad escluderne l'esistenza, riducendolo ad una serie di "nuclei distinti dispersi su vaste aree" (Arslan & Caporusso 1991: 353), quindi con caratteri molto diversi da quelli di un *oppidum* fortificato. Oltre al passo di Polibio, che tra l'altro ricorda come a *Mediolanum* nel III secolo a.C. si trovava il tempio dove erano custodite le insegne auree inamovibili (Pol. II, 32,6), bisogna tenere presente che la definizione di villaggio data dallo storico deve essere valutata tenendo conto dei parametri di giudizio di un romano, abituato ad una realtà urbana di tipo mediterraneo (Cracco Ruggini 1990: 17).

Anche per il II secolo a.C. i dati sono piuttosto scarsi, ma le tracce di costruzioni in legno rinvenute in numerosi scavi in varie zone della città, con materiali riferibili alla fine II-inizio I secolo a.C., e il fossato di via Moneta, datato alla prima metà del II secolo e abbandonato poco dopo, attestano una notevole attività edilizia in questo periodo, e l'attuazione di ristrutturazioni urbanistiche. L'importazione di ceramica a vernice nera da Volterra (Frontini 1991: 29) e di anfore rodie (Arslan & Caporusso 1991: 353) anche se in piccole quantità, e la stessa ottima qualità della ceramica celtica rinvenuta, testimoniano la vitalità dell'economia dell'abitato in questo periodo.

I dati di scavo sembrano confermare l'opinione di numerosi studiosi, secondo cui la metà del II secolo a.C. segna un'accelerazione nel processo di romanizzazione, inteso come lenta e graduale diffusione di oggetti e modelli culturali. Dopo le vittorie romane, i foedera stipulati con gli Insubri comportarono condizioni non troppo gravose, come il pagamento di tributi e la fornitura di contingenti di soldati, senza confische di terre "per non compromettere la capacità economica e la preminenza sociale delle elites dominanti, che dalle eventuali confische sarebbero state danneggiate" (Gabba 1984: 215; 1986: 37-39; 1990: 76; Baldacci 1972: 105-107). Il processo di penetrazione culturale e commerciale fu agevolato, secondo Gabba, dalla partecipazione alle operazioni militari romane di truppe insubri che, ritornando nei luoghi d'origine, portavano nuove idee e modelli, dai contatti commerciali con le vicine colonie romane e dallo stabilirsi a nord del Po di ricche famiglie romane di proprietari terrieri. Gabba avanza l'ipotesi che già nella seconda metà del II secolo a.C. "vi sia stato anche nell'area insubre un lento ma inesorabile adeguamento delle istituzioni politiche locali ai modelli romani" (1986: 37). La romanizzazione, come osserva Torelli, "altro non è se non la formazione di un blocco storico omogeneo tra centro e periferia, fra aristocrazie coloniali e aristocrazie indigene filo-romane, di cui la forma urbana rappresenta l'aspetto tangibile di un raggiunto consenso e la trasposizione in chiave urbanistica di valori politici comuni" (Torelli & Gros 1988: 156).

L'attività edilizia che sembra caratterizzare l'*oppidum* della seconda metà del II secolo a.C. può essere appunto interpretata come il risultato dell'impulso verso l'urbanizzazione dato dal miglioramento dell'economia e dai contatti con le vicine colonie. La superficie interessata dai ritrovamenti di ceramica celtica, che raggiungono il perimetro delle mura repubblicane (fig.6), a mio parere è un indizio del fatto che l'*oppidum* del II secolo aveva un'estensione press'a poco uguale a quella della città romana del I secolo d.C., cioè di circa 80 ettari, che si può avvicinare a quella di *oppida* gallici come Alesia (97 ettari) (Tizzoni 1986: 351-352).

Per quanto riguarda il dibattito sul problema urbanistico, una risposta agli interrogativi irrisolti viene dall'analisi dei risultati degli ultimi scavi. E' però anche indispensabile liberare il campo dai pregiudizi romanocentrici, di stampo retorico e legati a presupposti ideologici ormai superati, che a mio avviso hanno molto condizionato gli studi su *Mediolanum* fino agli anni '80. Ciò anche a causa di carenze tecniche e metodologiche nella ricerca sul terreno, che non permettevano di riconoscere le tracce dell'abitato preromano. La tendenza a forzare i dati per incasellare ad ogni costo il reticolato stradale urbano di Mediolanum in due schemi ortogonali è stata determinata a mio avviso dall'immagine preconcetta di questo centro come di una colonia latina fondata *ex nihilo*. L'assenza di un impianto ortogonale in centri dove esisteva un insediamento di antica origine è un fenomeno frequente, documentato, ad esempio in Spagna ad *Ampurias*, in Gallia a *Glanum* e in numerosi centri della Narbonese (Torelli & Gros 1988: 263-271), nella Transpadana a Vicenza.

Nel dibattito tra gli opposti fronti dei 'teorici dei piani programmatici ortogonali' che inquadrano in rigide tipologie gli schemi di molte città, e dei 'partigiani del dubbio metodico' che ritengono determinanti le verifiche archeologiche sul terreno, la posizione di coloro che tendono a sottolineare i limiti di uno studio basato su criteri formali, rivalutando il peso dei fattori politico-sociali nelle scelte riguardanti l'organizzazione spaziale di una città, sembra la più logica (Gros 1985-87; Torelli & Gros 1988: 269-271, passim; Santoro Bianchi 1985: 375-392; Février 1990: 183-185).

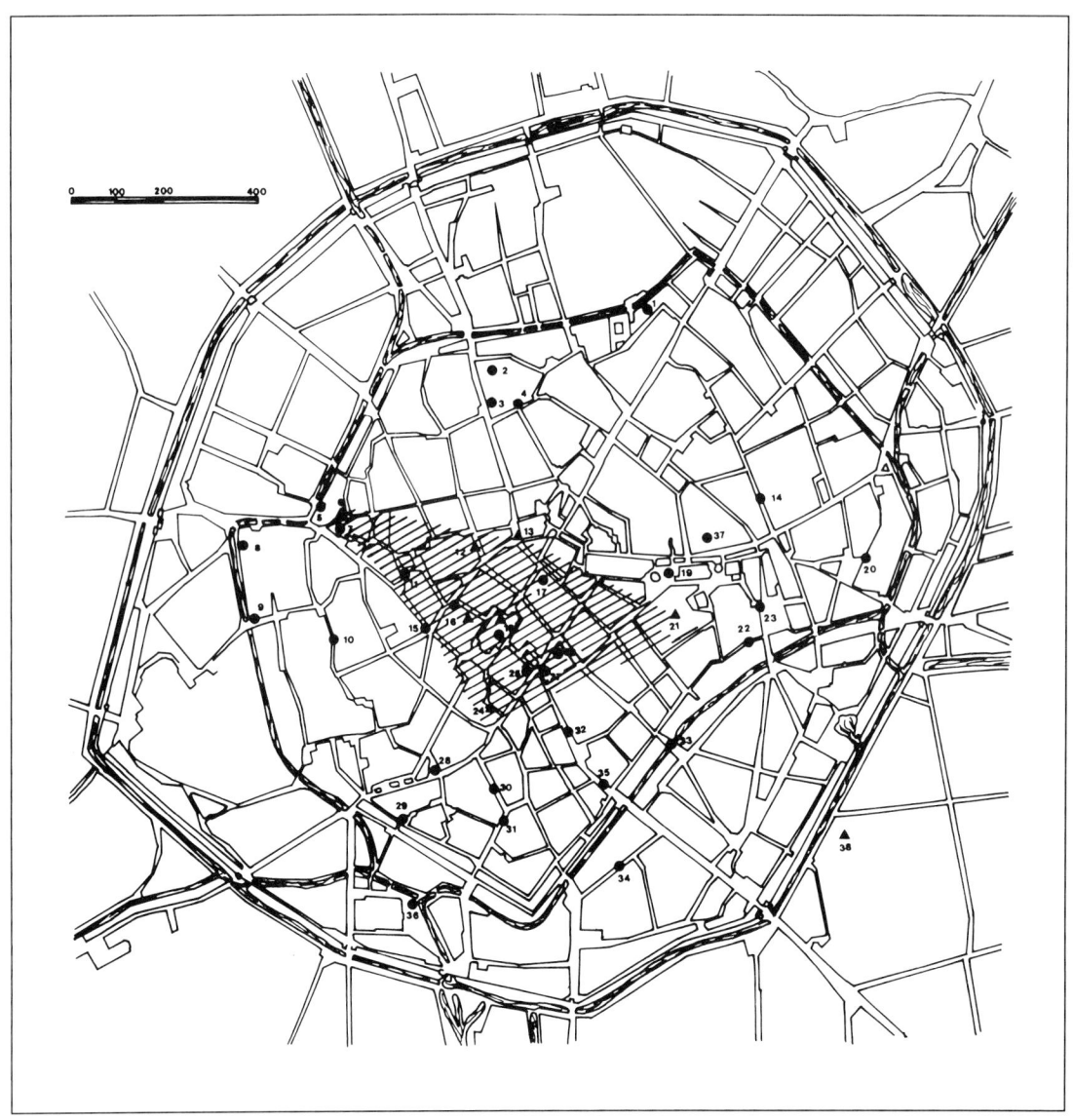

*Fig.6. Milano. Carta di distribuzione dei ritrovamento del periodo Golasecca III (▲) e della tarda età del Ferro (●).
A tratteggio l'area del presunto insediamento golasecchiano.*

*1. Via Monte di Pietà. 2. Via del Lauro. 3. Via Broletto. 4.Via dei Bossi. 5. Via S.Giovanni sul Muro. 6.Via Meravigli. 7. Via S.Maria alla Porta. 8. Monastero Maggiore. 9.Via S.Valeria. 10. Via Morigi. 11. Piazza Affari. 12. Via S.Maria Segreta. 13. Piazza Cordusio. 14. Via S.Paolo. 15. Via S.Maria Fulcorina. 16. Via Moneta. 17. Via Orefici angolo via Cantù. 18. Biblioteca Ambrosiana. 19. Piazza Duomo. 20. C.Europa. 21. Palazzo Reale. 22. Via delle Ore. 23. Piazza Fontana. 24. Via Valpetrosa. 25. Via delle Asole. 26. Via Speronari e S.Satiro. 27. Via Falcone. 28. S.Giorgio al Palazzo. 29. Via S.Vito. 30. Via dei Piatti. 31. Via Olmetto. 32. Via Unione. 33. Bottonuto. 34. Via Rugabella. 35. Piazza Missori. 36. Piazza Vetra. 37. Via S.Raffaele. 38. Ospedale di S.Antonino.
(disegno G.Pileggi).*

Nel caso di *Mediolanum* i risultati degli scavi, in accordo con le notizie storiche, mostrano che non si può parlare di pianificazione programmatica su un terreno libero, ma di progressiva trasformazione di un abitato di antica origine in città romana. L'analisi dei rinvenimenti mostra un numero di anomalie talmente alto rispetto agli schemi ortogonali proposti, da rendere inattendibile l'ipotesi di partenza. Le interpretazioni filologiche risultano del tutto inadeguate a comprendere la complessa genesi dell'impianto urbanistico della città.

Senza voler proporre soluzioni definitive, si presenta qui, come spunto di riflessione, un tentativo di ricostruzione del tessuto urbano della zona centrale della città romana, che tiene conto dei risultati degli ultimi scavi (fig.7) (Ceresa Mori 1992: 29–32). Come si può vedere, nella zona attorno alla piazza del Foro il *cardo*

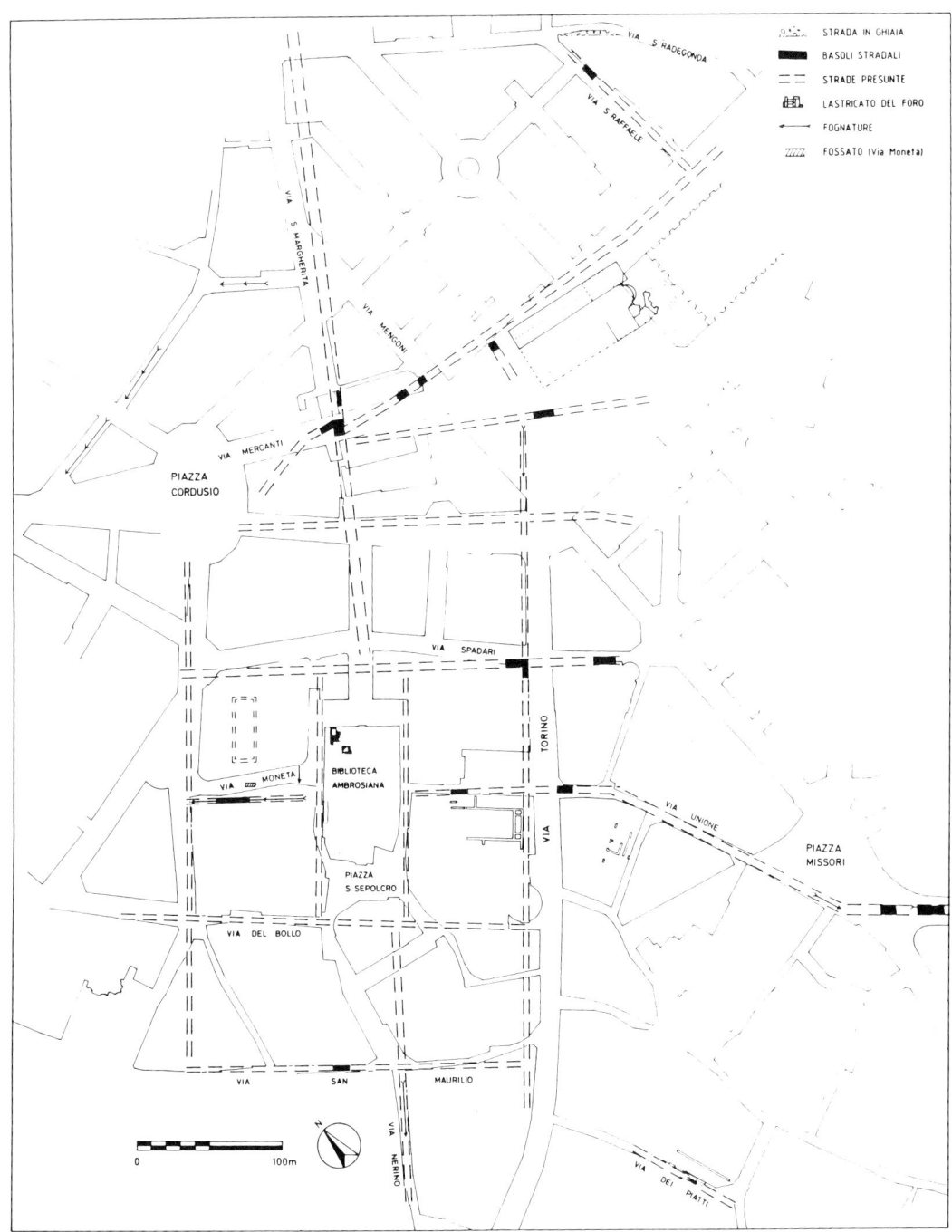

Fig. 7. Planimetria della zona centrale di Milano con ipotesi ricostruttiva del tessuto viario romano (disegno N. White).

maximus e l'asse considerato dal Mirabella Roberti come il *decumanus maximus* non sono ortogonali tra loro, le dimensioni degli isolati non sono costanti. Il *cardo maximus* taglia obliquamente la piazza del Foro e l'isolato compreso tra il decumano minore, corrispondente all'attuale via Orefici, e il *cardo maximus* ha la forma di un trangolo irregolare (Caporusso 1992: fig.5) dovuta allo sbocco in questo punto di un'importante arteria extraurbana, diretta verso Bergamo e Brescia, che nell'area a NW del Foro veniva a convergere con quella verso Monza, cioè il *cardo maximus*, e con quella verso Como, corrispondente alle attuali vie Broletto, Mercato e corso Garibaldi. Tale arteria proseguiva lungo il lato nord di piazza Duomo e in corrispondenza dell'attuale corso Vittorio Emanuele. Come si è detto sopra, i dati archeologici e la cartografia antica non documentano la continuità dell'asse stradale NE-SW tra piazza S. Sepolcro e piazza Missori. Nell'area a NE del Foro, il ritrovamento di due assi stradali convergenti, uno dei quali aveva lo stesso andamento dell'attuale via S. Raffaele, conferma che l'assetto stradale che si può osservare nella cartografia sei-settecentesca di Milano, prima delle grandi trasformazioni della seconda metà ottocento, conserva più di quanto non si fosse creduto l'originario tracciato stradale romano (Caporusso 1992: 50).

Numerosi rinvenimenti nella zona permettono di ricostruire alcuni allineamenti stradali, che corrispondono alle contrade della cartografia sette-ottocentesca. Sono stati messi in luce nel secolo scorso tratti di fognature e basolati romani in corrispondenza delle vie Bassano Porrone (Poggi 1911: 17-19), S. Protaso (Ceresa Mori 1986a: 274), S. Prospero (ATS, cart.21) e in piazza Cordusio angolo via Orefici (ATS, cart.21). Recentemente basolati relativi all'asse stradale verso Bergamo e Brescia, corrispondente all'attuale corso Vittorio Emanuele, sono venuti in luce nell'area di via Mercanti (ATS cart.100, relaz.1960), del Palazzo dei Giureconsulti (Ceresa Mori 1986b: 150) e in via Mengoni (Howes 1991: 229-235).

Un tratto di basolato in direzione NS, venuto in luce in piazza Duomo davanti ai portici nord della piazza (ATS cart.5b, 17-1-1964), è un interessante documento dell'orientamento degli assi stradali nell'area della basilica di S. Tecla che, come già aveva osservato il De Capitani d'Arzago (1952: 100, 110) doveva probabilmente seguire un più antico allineamento, attestato da preesistenti edifici romani venuti in luce nell'area durante gli scavi effettuati in piazza Duomo per un rifugio antiaereo nel 1943. Tale allineamento era determinato dalla direttrice verso Bergamo e Brescia.

La distribuzione degli spazi a *Mediolanum* doveva essere quindi molto condizionata dalle strade extraurbane e dai corsi d'acqua (Caporusso 1990: 94-96). Il settore nordorientale sembra essere stato interessato da percorsi che collegavano l'asse stradale verso Bergamo e Brescia con quello verso Monza.

Lo stretto rapporto tra i miglioramenti di status delle colonie e le ristrutturazioni urbanistiche con costruzioni di edifici pubblici è stato messo in rilievo da vari studiosi (Torelli & Gros 1988: 257-260; Scagliarini 1991: 160-170) e, nel caso di Milano, il potenziamento delle strutture urbane nel corso del I secolo a.C., è stato posto in connessione con la concessione dello *ius Latii* con la *Lex pompeia de Transpadanis* nell'89 a.C. e della cittadinanza romana nel 49 a.C. (Gabba 1984: 222; Cassola 1991; Bandelli 1992). L'esistenza a Milano di edifici pubblici monumentali nella I metà del I secolo a.C. (Rossignani 1986: 219-231) e gli interventi di ristrutturazione, attestati dagli scavi nello stesso periodo, trovano inoltre riscontro nelle notizie storiche ed epigrafiche che ricordano interventi nel campo dell'edilizia pubblica e dell'urbanistica dei municipi da parte dei magistrati locali (Sommella 1988: 121, 151).

La regolarizzazione dell'impianto urbano con la creazione di un razionale sistema fognario e stradale, la realizzazione della piazza del foro e della grande arteria di collegamento con Roma, corrispondente all'attuale corso di Porta Romana, sono le tappe del lento e graduale processo di trasformazione dell'*oppidum* celtico, che si può cogliere in modo altrettanto chiaro nelle tecniche edilizie e nella cultura materiale documentate dagli scavi.

Appendice

Method used for Constructing the Stratigraphical Sections

Nicholas White

The two stratigraphical sections represent a cross-section of the archaeological deposits in Milan. The information used to compile the drawings was taken from excavations carried out in the period from 1985 to 1992, which are indicated by the place names above each section. The dark vertical lines indicate the position of the republican walls and in the case of the lower diagram, on the left hand side, the walls belonging to the late third century expansion of the city. Before considering the information from the individual excavations it was decided to divide the chronological sequence into five main phases, which represent the principal periods of activity: the pre-Roman settlement (V – III centuries BC), the Republican city (II – I centuries BC), the early imperial period (I – II centuries AD), the later imperial period (III – IV centuries AD) and the post-roman deposits (V – XX centuries AD). Information was then recovered from each individual site on the basis of these chronological divisions. The levels used to compile the sections were taken primarily from well-dated floor levels or, where possible, a preference was given to road surfaces. In the case of varying levels on the site, within the same chronological phase, an average level was considered acceptable in that the variation never exceeded 0.30 m. However, in the case of the Forum (P.za S.Sepolcro – Biblioteca Ambrosiana) we have indicated both the level of the Forum and of the surrounding steps thus showing how it lay at a lower level than the adjacent streets. The depth of the cellars are shown, where they exist, to give an indication of the stratigraphy destroyed. The vertical scale used is forty times larger than the horizontal scale in order to accentuate the vertical stratigraphy.

Bibliografia
ATS *Archivio Topografico della Soprintendenza Archeologica della Lombardia.*
Arslan, E.A. 1982. 'Urbanistica di Milano romana. Dall'insediamento insubre alla capitale dell'impero', in *Aufstieg und Niedergang der Römischer Welt*, II, Berlin-New York, 179–210.
Arslan, E.A. 1990. 'Le monnayage celtique de la plaine du Po (IV-I siècles avant J.C.)', *Etudes Celtiques*, XXVII, 71–95.
Arslan, E.A. & Caporusso, D. 1991. 'I rinvenimenti archeologici degli scavi MM3 nel contesto storico di Milano', in *Scavi MM3. Ricerche di archeologia urbana a Milano durante la costruzione della linea 3*

della Metropolitana Milanese, 1982-1990, a cura di D. Caporusso, I, Milano, 351-358.
Baldacci, P. 1972. 'Le principali correnti del commercio di anfore romane nella Cisalpina. Importazioni ed esportazioni alimentari nella pianura Padana centrale dal III sec. a.C. al II d.C.', in *I problemi della ceramica romana di Ravenna, della valle Padana e dell'alto Adriatico* (Atti del convegno, Ravenna 1969), Bologna, 103-117.
Bandelli, G. 1992. 'Classi dirigenti e la loro promozione politica (II-I secolo a.C.)', *Dialoghi di Archeologia*, 10, 31-45.
Berti, S. & Castella, C.M. 1992. 'Architecture de terre et de bois à Lousonna-Vidy', *Archaologie der Schweiz*, 15, 4, 172-179.
Calderini, A. 1953. 'Milano archeologica', in *Storia di Milano* I, 1953, 465-719.
Caporusso, D. 1990. 'La situazione idrografica di Milano romana', in *Milano capitale dell'impero romano*, (Catalogo della mostra), Milano, 94-96.
Caporusso, D. 1992. 'Alcuni elementi per la topografia di Milano in età romana', in *Felix temporis reparatio*, (Atti del convegno archeologico internazionale: *Milano capitale dell'impero romano*, Milano marzo 1990), a cura di G.Sena Chiesa & E.A.Arslan, Milano, 45-53.
Cassola, F. 1991. 'La colonizzazione della Transpadana', in *Die Stadt in Oberitalien und in den nordwestlichen Provinzen des Römischen Reiches*, (Deutsch-Italienisches Kolloquium in italienischen Kulturinstitut Köln), Mainz am Rhein, 17-44.
Ceresa Mori, A. 1986a. 'Rinvenimenti archeologici a Milano nei disegni inediti della Consulta del Museo Archeologico', in *Scritti in ricordo di Graziella Massari Gaballo e Umberto Tocchetti Pollini*, Milano, 265-276.
Ceresa Mori, A. 1986b. 'Milano. Via Mercanti 2', *Notiziario della Soprintendenza Archeologica della Lombardia*, 150.
Ceresa Mori, A. 1990-91. 'La tarda età del Ferro a Milano alla luce dei recenti rinvenimenti', *Sibrium* 21, 247-258.
Ceresa Mori, A. 1992. 'La zona del foro e l'urbanistica di Mediolanum alla luce dei recenti scavi', in *Felix temporis reparatio*, (Atti del convegno archeologico internazionale: *Milano capitale dell'impero romano*, Milano marzo 1990), a cura di G. Sena Chiesa e E.A. Arslan, Milano, 27-43.
Ceresa Mori, A. 1995. 'Il foro romano di *Mediolanum*' XXV Settimana di Studi Aquileiesi, (Aquileia 24-28 aprile 1994, in stampa).
Ceresa Mori, A. et al. 1987. 'Milano.Via Moneta', *Notiziario della Soprintendenza Archeologica della Lombardia*, 11-22.
Ceresa Mori, A. et al. 1990. 'Milano. Indagini nella zona del Foro. Biblioteca Ambrosiana', *Notiziario della Soprintendenza Archeologica della Lombardia*, 173-185.
Ceresa Mori, A. & White, N., 1991. 'Via Moneta', *Notiziario della Soprintendenza Archeologica della Lombardia*, 114-115.
Cracco Ruggini, L. 1990. 'Milano da "metropoli" degli Insubri a capitale d'impero: una vicenda di mille anni', in *Milano capitale dell'impero romano*, (Catalogo della mostra), Milano, 17-23.
De Capitani d'Arzago, A. 1952. *La "Chiesa Maggiore" di Milano. S.Tecla*, (Ricerche della Commissione per la Forma Urbis Mediolani, 6), Milano.
De Marchi, A. 1914. 'A proposito della *forma urbis Mediolani*', in *Rendiconti del Reale Istituto Lombardo di Scienze e Lettere*, sez. II, XLVII, 417-430.
De Marinis, R. 1981. 'Il periodo Golasecca III A in Lombardia', *Studi Archeologici*, I, Bergamo, 43-284
De Marinis, R. 1984. 'La città in Lombardia. La sua nascita e la sua evoluzione. Protostoria degli insediamenti urbani in Lombardia', in *Archeologia urbana in Lombardia*, Modena, 22-33.
De Marinis, R. 1986. 'L'abitato protostorico di Como', in *Como fra Etruschi e Celti. La città preromana e il suo ruolo commerciale*, (Catalogo della mostra), Como, 25-38.
De Marinis, R. 1990. 'La preistoria e la protostoria', in *Storia di Lodi*, I, 9-32.
Desbat, A. 1991. 'La construction en terre à l'époque romaine' in *Matières à faire*, (Actes des séminaires publics d'archéologie. Centre Régional de Documantation Archéologique, La Citadelle, Besançon).

Février, P.A. 1990. 'Approches récents du fait urbain dans les Gaules', in *Villes et agglomérations urbaines antiques du sud-ouest de la Guale. Histoire et Archéologie*, (Deuxième colloque Aquitaine. Bordeaux 13-15 septembre), 177-190.
Frey, O.H. 1986. 'Sviluppo urbano celtico in Italia del Nord', in *Atti del 2 Convegno archeologico regionale. La Lombardia tra protostoria e romanità*, (Como 1984), Como, 333-337.
Frontini, P. 1991. 'Ceramica a vernice nera', in *Scavi MM3. Ricerche di archeologia urbana a Milano durante la costruzione della linea 3 della Metropolitana Milanese, 1982-1990*, a cura di D.Caporusso, 3,1, Milano, 23-39.
Gabba, E. 1984. 'Ticinum: dalle origini alla fine del III secolo d.C.', in *Storia di Pavia, I, L'età antica*, Pavia, 205-241.
Gabba, E. 1986. 'I Romani nell'Insubria: trasformazione, adeguamento e sopravvivenza delle strutture socioeconomiche galliche', in *Atti dal 2 Convegno archeologico regionale. La Lombardia tra protostoria e romanità*, (Como 1984), 33-44.
Gabba, E. 1990. 'La conquista della Gallia Cisalpina', in *Storia di Roma*, II. Torino.
Grace, V. 1952. 'Timbres amphoriques trouvées à Delos', *Bulletin de Correspondance Héllénique*, LXXVI, 514-533.
Gros, P. 1985-87. 'Remarques sur les fondations urbaines de Narbonnaise et de Cisalpine au début de l'empire', *Quaderni del Centro Studi Lunensi*, 10-12, 73-95.
Howes, B. 1991. 'Lo scavo di via Mengoni', in *Scavi MM3. Ricerche di archeologia urbana a Milano durante la costruzione della linea 3 della Metropolitana Milanese, 1982-1990*, a cura di D.Caporusso, Milano, 229-235.
Jorio, S. 1987. 'Milano. Palazzo Reale. Scavo nell'angolo SW del cortile principale', *Notiziario della Soprintendenza Archeologica della Lombardia*, 132-137.
Maggiani, A. 1992. 'Ceramica attica', in I. Damiani, A. Maggiani, E. Pellegrini, A. Saltini & A. Serges, *L'età del Ferro nel reggiano. I materiali delle collezioni dei Civici Musei di Reggio Emilia*, Reggio Emilia, 84-106.
Mertens, D. 1955. 'Marques d'Amphores', in D. Mertens, F. De Visscher, F. De Ruyt, S., De Laet, J. & Mertens, J. *Les fouilles d'Alba Fucens (Italie centrale) de 1951 à 1953 (3ᵉ partie)*, *L'Antiquité Classique* XXIV, 82-93.
Mirabella Roberti, M. 1973-74. 'Due piani regolatori nella Milano romana', *Atti CeSDIR*, V, Milano, 305-321.
Moreno, P. 1964. 'Ceramica di Saint Valentin al Museo Nazionale di Atene', *Archeologia Classica*, XVI, 200-212.
Piccottini, G. 1993. 'Tipologie e tecniche sul Magdalensberg', *Quaderni di Archeologia del Veneto*, IX, 196-205.
Poggi, F. 1911. *Le fognature di Milano*, Milano.
Rossignani, M.P. 1986. 'Monumenti pubblici e privati di età repubblicana nei centri urbani della Lombardia', in *Atti del 2 Convegno archeologico regionale. La Lombardia tra protostoria e romanità*, (Como 1984), Como, 215-239.
Santoro Bianchi, S. 1985. 'Alcune riflessioni su scuole e tipologie urbanistiche nell'Italia centrosettentrionale', *Caesarodunum*, 20, 1985, 375-392.
Scagliarini Corlaita, D. 1991. 'Impianti urbani e monumentalizzazione nelle città romane dell'Italia settentrionale', in *Die Stadt in Oberitalien und in den nordwestlichen Provinzen der römischen Reiches* (Köln 1989), Mainz, 159-178.
Sommella, P. 1988. *Italia antica. L'urbanistica romana. Guide allo studio della civiltà romana*, Roma.
Tizzoni, M. 1986. 'Alcune osservazioni su Milano preromana' in *S.Maria alla Porta: uno scavo nel centro storico di Milano*, a cura di A. Ceresa Mori, con la collaborazione di M. Tizzoni, *Studi Archeologici*, 5, Bergamo, 351-352.
Tizzoni, M. 1990-91. 'Prime osservazioni sui materiali preromani provenienti dagli scavi di via Moneta e della Biblioteca Ambrosiana in Milano', *Sibrium*, 21, 259-263.
Tocchetti Pollini 1984. 'Le città in età romana. L'inizio del fenomeno urbano e le sue trasformazioni', in *Archeologia urbana in Lombardia*, Modena, 34-47.
Torelli, M. 1990. 'Il modello urbano e l'immagine della città', in *Civiltà*

dei Romani. La città il territorio, l'impero. I, a cura di S. Settis, Milano, 43–93.

Torelli, M. & Gros, P. 1988. *Storia dell'urbanistica. Il mondo romano*, Bari.

Tozzi, P. 1986. Intervento, in *Atti 2 Convegno archeologico regionale. La Lombardia tra protostoria e romanità* (Como 1984), Como, 351.

49

Staties/Statonia

GILDA BARTOLONI
(Università di Roma 'La Sapienza')

Sommario: *Il rinvenimento alla fine del secolo scorso di ghiande missili di piombo iscritte (*Staties*) aveva considerato risolto il problema della localizzazione dell'antica* Statonia *e della* praefectura Statoniensis. *La* praefectura, *insieme alla* Saturniensis *dedotta dai Romani nel territorio vulcente dopo il 280 a.C., doveva occupare l'entroterra meridionale dell'agro vulcente. Le fonti antiche ricordano un* lacus *nell'*ager Statoniensis, *già individuato dal Cluver nel Lago di Mezzano. Il riesame paleografico e dei dati di scavo delle diverse ghiande offre lo spunto di riconsiderare il problema dell'identificazione del sito e di tentare un quadro sul popolamento del territorio vulcente nei periodi immediatamente precedente e successivo alla conquista romana.*

"Oltre Manciano, nella discesa verso il Fiora alcune tombe e nicchie funerarie nei dirupi e frammenti di ceramica nei pendii indicano il sito di una città etrusca. Non potei svolgere qui alcuna ricerca, poiché il sole ara all'orizzonte quando vi passai, e non ho più avuto occasione di tornare sul posto, però mi sembrò che la città dovesse trovarsi sull'altura circondata da dirupi, ora crestata dalle rovine di un castello. Non abbiamo possibilità di determinare quale fosse il suo nome... Il Fiora presenta qui gli stessi caratteri che a Vulci, un corso d'acqua impetuoso sovrastato da alti dirupi ricoperti a metà dalla vegetazione. Le rocce sono della stessa formazione, tufo rosso o bianco, ricoperto da uno strato di travertino bianco..." (Dennis 1883; Kennet 1991: 66). Così G. Dennis descrive la località denominata Poggio Buco nei pressi di Pitigliano ("Le piatte distese intorno a Pitigliano sono piene di tombe, specialmente verso ovest, dove per miglia la pianura ne è tutta crivellata" – Kennet 1991: 23), da lui visitata nel 1843 e ricorda gli scavi 'piuttosto promettenti' (ma evidentemente di poca entità se altrove dichiara che "non sono mai fatti degli scavi, ma il caso di tanto in tanto porta tombe alla luce") effettuati 'di recente' da Carlo Campanari (Colonna 1986: 7). A questi ultimi si deve il rinvenimento di una tomba a dado e di una con elementi architettonici interni, che rimandano a rapporti con i centri dell'Etruria meridionale.

Bisogna attendere la fine del secolo, gli anni 1894–1896, perché si abbiano nello stesso sito ricerche più estese, ma non direi però ancora di carattere sistematico. L'interesse principale dello scavatore, infatti, il pittore Riccardo Mancinelli, è quello di vendere al migliore offerente gli oggetti venuti in luce negli scavi (Bartoloni 1992). Il rinvenimento in questi scavi, resi noti da G.Pellegrini (1896, 1898) – il quale purtroppo non risulta abbia sovrinteso a nessuna delle campagne di scavo (cf. Zanini 1991) – di una ghianda missile (fig.1) con l'iscrizione *Staties* (e non *Statnes* come lesse Pellegrini 1889) sembra rispondere all'interrogativo posto dal Dennis ("non abbiamo possibilità di determinare quale fosse il suo nome") sull'identificazione della città ubicata sull'altura circondata da dirupi del Dennis, cioè sul pianoro denominato Le Sparne dell'Abbadia, presso il vocabolo Poggio Buco (o Poggio Bucato), nome indubbiamente derivato dalle numerose tombe ivi scavate. Le rovine del castello, descritte da Dennis, sembrano piuttosto appartenere ad una antica badia con convento o ritiro dei monaci, fatta distruggere dai Medici nel 1604 (Pellegrini 1989: 17). Da qui il nome Sparne dell'Abbadia del Fiume, usato da R.Mancinelli nel

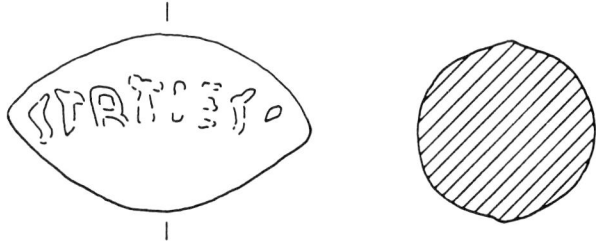

Fig. 1. Ghianda missile plumbea con iscrizione – STATIES.

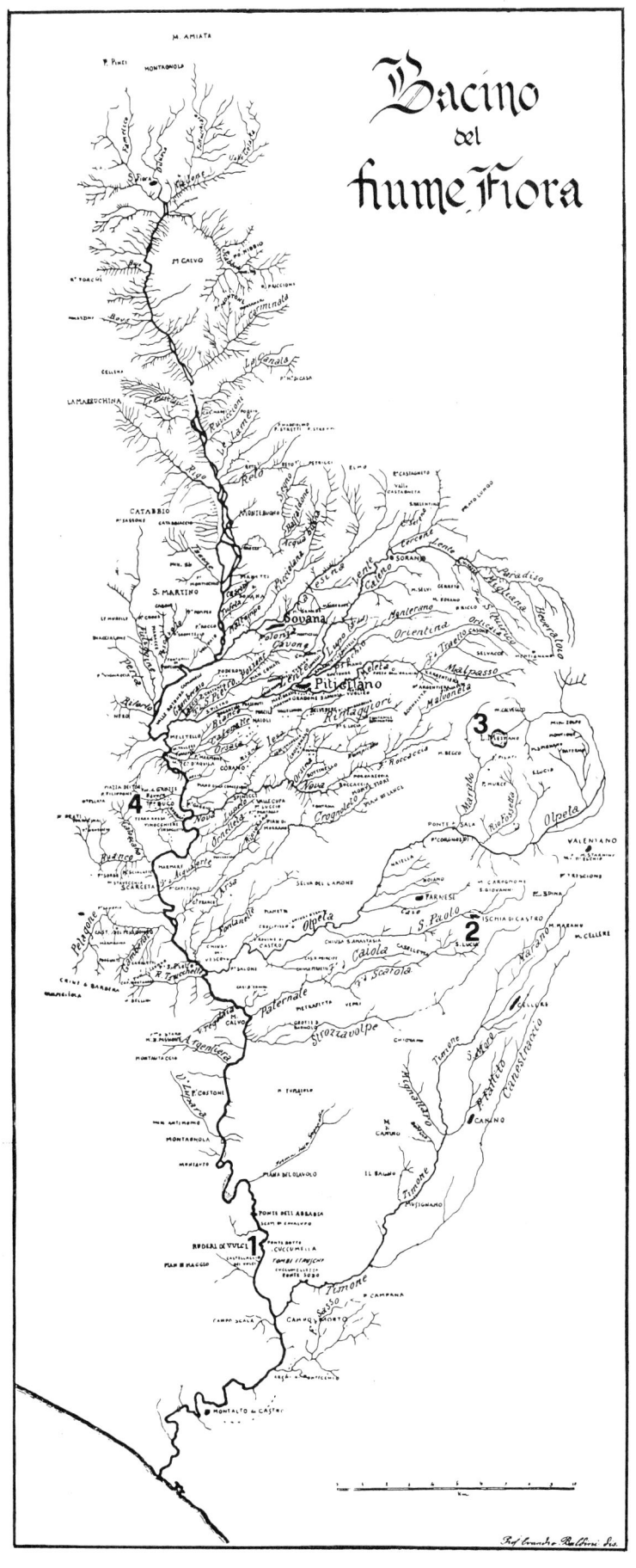

Fig. 2. Il bacino del fiume Fiora: 1 = Vulci; 2 = Castro; 3 = Lago di Mezzano; 4 = Poggio Buco

catalogare gli oggetti da lui recuperati (Archivio Sopr. Arch. per la Toscana = SAT A e F 1895-97; cfr. Matteucig 1951: 11, n.26). Mancinelli e Pellegrini riconobbero infatti nella iscrizione sulla ghianda missile l'indicazione del nome della città: *Statonia* la piccola città, una delle *policnai sucnai* di Strabone (V, 226) localizzata presso un lago (*Statoniensis* appunto, riconosciuto nel lago di Mezzano), da cui prese il nome la prefettura romana (Pellegrini 1898: 430-431).

Tale identificazione ebbe pieno successo nella letteratura archeologica fino agli anni settanta del nostro secolo (ad. es. Milani 1912: 75, 266; Matteucig 1951 e 1969: 437-440; Pallottino 1968: 188; Scullard 1969: 129; Harris 1971: 151), allorchè osservazioni di Colonna sul luogo di rinvenimento e sull'analisi dell'epigrafe (1974; 1975: 166) fece preferire la vecchia ipotesi di Cluverio in base alla quale *Statonia* sarebbe da identificare con Castro (fig.2): da una parte la notizia del rinvenimento della ghianda ai piedi della rupe doveva denotare come nemico della città colpita il possessore del proiettile, dall'altra il caso obliquo in cui si presentava l'iscrizione sembrava indicare il marchio di un fabbricante piuttosto che un'indicazione topografica.

Nuovi dati sul luogo di rinvenimento e un riesame dell'iscrizione ripropongono la questione in altri termini.

Dai carteggi conservati all'Archivio di Stato di Roma e l'Archivio della Soprintendenza Archeologica per la Toscana risulta che la ghianda missile iscritta sia stata trovata non come asserito da Pellegrini sotto la rupe ma bensí tra i resti del c.d. tempio insieme ad altro materiale architettonico e votivo (Archivio SAT a9 n.80 lettera dell'11.8.1905; cfr. Pellegrini 1898: 441). Inoltre un riesame dei contesti di rinvenimento delle altre ghiande con identico stampo iscritto (almeno sei), per cui è accertata solo la provenienza da Poggio Buco e dintorni, indica come collocazione preferenziale l'area delle necropoli (Mazzolai 1960: 16; Matteucig 1969; Cao di San Marco 1971: 355). Raveggi nel 1931 pubblicando un esemplare donato al Museo Archeologico di Firenze (inv.89213, ora disperso) ne indica precisamente la provenienza da una tomba (1931: 194; cfr. Mazzolai 1960: 16). Tra il materiale più tardo della necropoli di Poggio Buco sono del resto frequenti le ghiande missili, anche non iscritte (Bartoloni 1972: 218).

Una più precisa lettura dell'iscrizione etrusca: *Staties* e non *Statnes* (Colonna 1975: 166); *Staties* e non *Statiesi*, dovuto alla cattiva lettura (per lo più non autottica) del trattino finale, dà maggior peso ad una recente interpretazione di A.Maggiani (1988: 132) sia sulla cronologia di tale tipo di manufatti che sull'interpretazione dei nomi iscritti: il confronto con analoghi esemplari greco-romani, porterebbe a identificarli con quelli dei capi dell'armata proprietaria dei proiettili.

Già Poggi (1884: 16-19), notando il parallelismo tra manufatti romani ("di cui tanta copia è nelle collezioni archeologiche") divise quest'ultime in quattro categorie:

1) nomi topografici ed etnici; 2) le 'note consolari' che ne determinarono la data; 3) il nome delle legioni che le usarono, nonchè dei rispettivi primipili, tribuni o generali; 4) motti diretti contro i nemici contro i quali era lanciato il proiettile. Alla terza categoria risulta appartenere l'iscrizione impressa sul gruppo di ghiande plumbee in esame: proiettili di tal tipo con indicato il nome del proprietario dell'officina non sembrano attestate nè in ambiente greco nè in ambiente romano. Interessante è l'origine osca del nome Statie (campano con nome etruschizzato? - Morandi 1978: 575): l'iscrizione in caso obliquo indicherebbe `appartenente a *Statie*'. Nelle ghiande missili con iscrizioni latine il nome del primipilo (Poggi 1884: 17 ss; Buonamici 1932: 400 ss) è generalmente in caso nominativo.

Dai contesti di rinvenimento (necropoli e area sacra) sembrerebbe di poter dedurre un certo vanto dei frombolieri ad appartenere a questo manipolo, tanto da fregiarsi di tale 'segno'.

L'uso dei proiettili da fionda in piombo, comune in Grecia dal IV secolo a.C., viene considerato introdotto nell'esercito romano in seguito all'impiego di truppe ausiliarie achee nel 189 a.C. (Daremberg & Saglio, II,2,1261). Tuttavia tale ipotesi non sembra essere avallata dal dato paleografico delle numerose ghiande missili recanti iscrizioni in etrusco. L'esame dei caratteri dell'iscrizione in esame ad esempio rimanda a tipi grafici della fine del IV-III sec. a.C. (Maggiani 1988: 132; 1990).

Non sembrerebbe del tutto assurdo in tal caso riconoscere nel titolare delle ghiande una sorta di capitano di ventura osco-campano, chiamato da genti dell'Etruria centrale (vulcenti ?) ad aiutarli nel frenare la travolgente espansione romana e in tale funzione aver assunto un ruolo importante per coloro che lo avevano ingaggiato. Si potrebbe anche trattare però di uno di quei 'principotti etruschi' (di famiglia di origine forse campana) che, secondo il racconto liviano (Livio X,36 ss.), quando Marco Fabio alla fine del IV secolo a.C. penetrò nell'interno dell'Etruria, usavano la servitù di campagna come milizia d'accatto (cfr. Cristofani 1977).

Indubbio appare il collegamento *Staties-Statonia*. Si potrebbe perciò ipotizzare che Statonia debba il nome a un tale eroe 'salvatore'.

Nonostante l'opinabilità di tali ipotesi appaiono tuttavia in più casi attestati gentilizi e nomi di eroi eponimi connessi con nomi di città etrusche. Si possono ricordare ad esempio *curtun-curtuna, tarkunus-tarkuna, fuflun-fufluna, vatlmi-vatluna* (Pallottino 1979: 721-723). La connessione *Statie-Statonia* potrebbe essere così spiegata: dal morfema Stat con l'aggiunta della desinenza di appartenenza -na avremo *Statu-na*, la città di *Statie*. Il collegamento con un episodio storico così tardo non trova controindicazioni nelle notizie riportatici dalle fonti letterarie (Seneca, Plinio, Strabone), che sembrerebbero da riferire a un momento tardo-repubblicano (Rendeli 1991): difficilmente si può risalire ad una fase molto

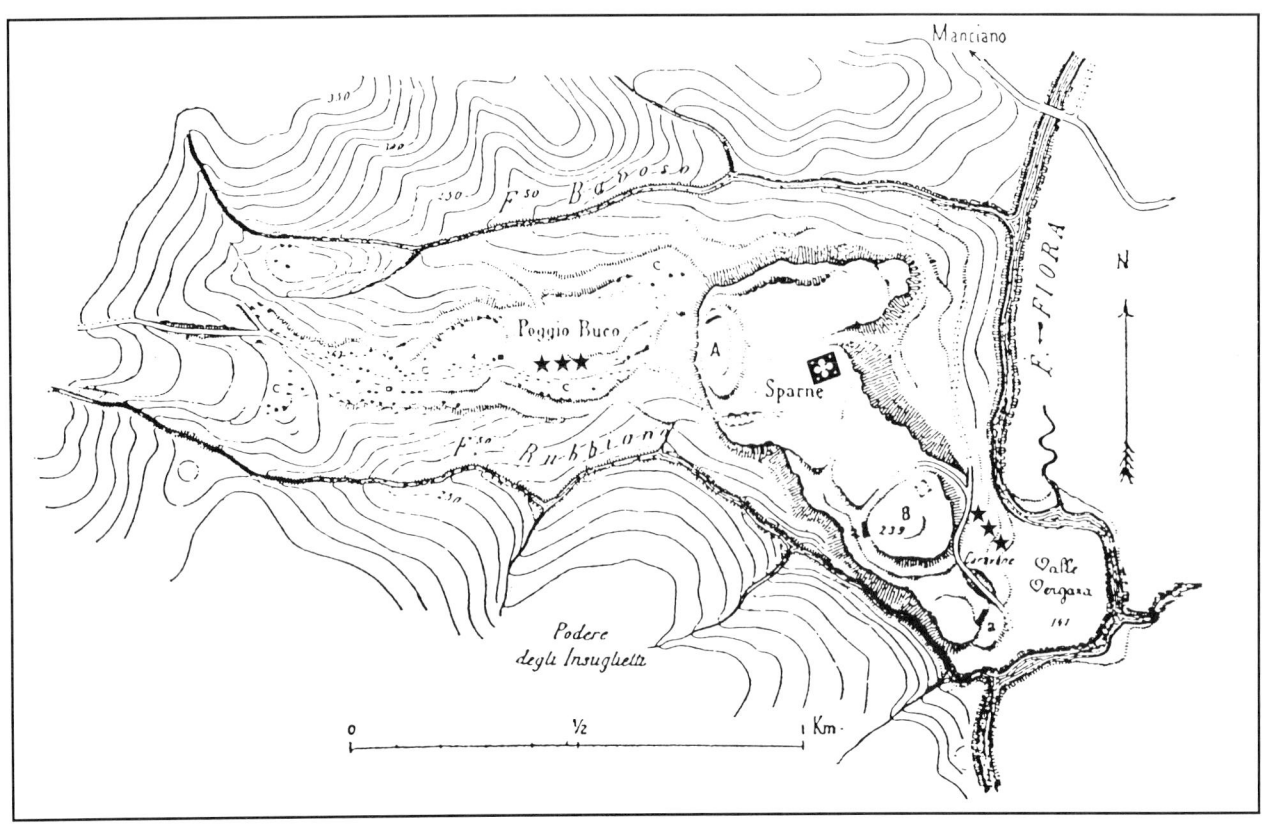

Fig. 3. Il pianoro delle Sparne e la contigua necropoli di Poggio Buco: vengono indicate le evidenze di età ellenistica.

più antica della completa ristrutturazione del territorio vulcente avvenuta con la conquista romana del 280 a.C.

Queste nuove acquisizioni (la provenienza delle ghiande e la nuova lettura dell'epigrafe) quindi inducono a mio avviso a rivedere l'ipotesi sull'ubicazione di Statonia. Oltre Poggio Buco e Castro si è pensato a Pitigliano (Dennis), a Farnese (Mannert), a Marsiliana (Pauly), tutti centri del territorio vulcente, "in quel tratto cioè di paese che ha come suo centro nel piccolo lago di Mezzano, nel quale da Cluverio in poi sono tutti d'accordo nel riconoscere lo *Statoniensis lacus*, menzionato da Seneca (N.Q. III,23) e da Plinio (N.H. XXXVI,49)" (Pellegrini 1898: 431). E' recentissima la proposta, ancora da verificare però, di ubicare *Statonia*, più all'interno nei dintorni di Viterbo, contraddicendo quindi la comune opinione che vede questo centro antico legato all'area vulcente (Stanco 1985, e ricerca in corso).

La scelta di Castro rispetto a Poggio Buco era stata motivata anche da altri fattori (Gazzetti 1985: 78–79): innanzitutto la maggior consistenza e ricchezza delle suppellettili funerarie in età arcaica, che non corrisponde però ad una eguale differenza in età ellenistica, quindi una occupazione capillare del territorio circostante che ben si addirebbero alla *praefectura Statonienses*, che insieme alla *Saturniensis* dedotta dai Romani nel territorio vulcente dopo il 280 a.C., doveva occupare l'entroterra meridionale dell'agro vulcente (Stanco 1985: 79–80; Rossini & Sperandio 1985: 80–84).

La carenza di ricerche intensive nell'area circostante Poggio Buco non permette però già per l'età arcaica di comprendere appieno il ruolo di questo centro, a cui la presenza di una fortificazione, di un edificio ad indubbio carattere pubblico, di tre strade d'accesso e di altre opere quali cuniculi o tagliate attribuisce un certo rilievo (Bartoloni 1992): non si può quindi parlare con certezza di assenza di forme di organizzazione e sfruttamento del territorio intorno a Poggio Buco (cfr. Rendeli 1991). Già da una ricerca bibliografica si evincono diversi dati sul territorio immediatamente circostante in età ellenistica: ad esempio l'insediamento di Piazza dei Tori, abitato nel VII-VI secolo appare rioccupato nel III-II sec. a.C. (Pellegrini 1989: 144) o bronzetti come quello di Afrodite che si allaccia il sandalo, rinvenuto tra Poggio Buco e Scarceta (Minto 1912: 209 ss), indicano il gusto delle gentes ivi residenti. Altri materiali ellenistici, non si sa però da che tipo di contesto, sono stati recuperati presso il ponte romano circa 1 km a Nord delle Sparne (Mazzolai 1960: 6). Già dagli scavi Mancinelli si conosceva la rioccupazione della periferica necropoli degli Insuglietti in epoca repubblicana (Pellegrini 1898: 445). Il confine della prefettura, poi, non è detto dovesse seguire il corso del Fiora, come sembrerebbe evincersi da una recente proposta (Rossini & Sperandio 1985). I grandi corsi d'acqua che furono spesso visti come confine tra i diversi territori delle città etrusche (Colonna 1986), non sembrano mai aver avuto questo ruolo in ambito romano. Si veda già in età arcaica il rapporto tra Roma e le altre città latine e il Tevere (Bartoloni 1986).

L'acquisizione da parte della Soprintendenza dei materiali della collezione Vaselli, con una piccola percentuale di materiali di età medio e tardorepubblicana (teste votive di terracotta, specchi di bronzo, ceramica a vernice nera, ceramica acroma ecc. – Archivio fotografico SAT nn.45930-36; ringrazio Silvia Goggioli per la possibilità di prendere in esame questa documentazione inedita), ripropongono il problema dell'entità del sito Le Sparne-Poggio Buco, nei periodi immediatamente precedenti e successivi alla conquista romana. Pellegrini (1898: 439 ss) nella relazione degli scavi Mancinelli elenca i numerosi oggetti pertinenti ad un deposito votivo rinvenuti nei pressi del citato edificio arcaico insieme ai più famosi fregi, che testimoniano un attività di questo luogo di culto per almeno tre secoli ed una notevole frequentazione. Le tombe rinvenute nella necropoli di Poggio Buco ("nella proporzione del dieci per cento" rispetto a quelle del periodo arcaico – 1898: 434, n.1; 1899), soprattutto nell'area centrale della necropoli, indicano una indiscussa ripresa di vita nell'abitato relativo (1898: 445 ss) (fig.4). Tra i materiali del deposito votivo, oltre la già citata ghianda plumbea, degni di nota appaiono alcuni vasi iscritti, statue e statuine di terracotta riproducenti figure ammantate (1898, fig.5), teste velate (forse cfr. Donati & Michelucci 1981: 219, n.532), membra umane tutte fittili, ceramica a vernice nera, monete ecc., purtroppo materiale non più rintracciato, ma dalla desrizione inquadrabile mella serie omogenea di depositi votivi attribuiti all'espandersi di Roma nella penisola (Comella 1981): indicative le teste di offerenti velate testimonianti il rito romano. Tra i materiali della necropoli specchi e vasi di bronzo, oreficerie, pietre preziose incise, paste vitree, ecc. (Pellegrini 1898: 445-446. Mancinelli ha proposto la vendita al Museo Archeologico di Firenze di almeno cinque corredi – Archivio SAT A9 1899, n.377/142 – cfr. Bartoloni 1972).

Nessuno degli oggetti recuperati o descritti nelle relazioni di scavo ottocentesche rimanda con sicurezza ad una rioccupazione prima della conquista romana dell'inizio del III secolo a.C.: secondo Livio alla fine del IV secolo l'interno dell'Etruria apparve ai Romani particolarmente incolto. Il tipo di materiale inoltre rimanda a quella koinè italica provocata dalla colonizzazione romana.

Tale rioccupazione capillare del territorio diviso in *praefecturae* trova riscontro in una contrazione dell'area abitata nel pianoro di Vulci (Guaitoli 1985: 58). Il periodo meglio rappresentato appare proprio il III secolo e l'inizio del II secolo a.C., sembrerebbe cioè prima del nuovo intervento romano nel territorio, che provocò la deduzione della *colonia* di *Saturnia*.

Pur riconoscendo non assolutamente risolutive queste annotazioni per l'identificazione del sito di Statonia, appare chiaro che l'area Sparne-Poggio Buco sia di nuovo abitata dai primi decenni del III secolo a.C. (ma il sito è escluso in Carandini 1985) e in maniera sembrerebbe più consistente che a Castro, da dove per ora si conoscono un corredo di fine IV secolo a.C. e un piccolo gruppo di corredi di II-I sec. a.C. (Gazzetti 1985: figg. 72-74; Rendeli 1991).

Inoltre l'importanza strategica del sito, pur non potendo provare la sua posizione nel tracciato della via Clodia, inequivocabile secondo Lopes Pegna (il rudere di ponte romano sul Fiora presso le Sparne rappresenterebbe l'indizio più sicuro del tracciato della via – Lopez Pegna 1953: 403 ss), dubbia secondo Radke (1981: 307 ss), per la sua centralità nel corso del fiume Fiora, grande arteria dell'Etruria centrale non può essere scemata in età romana. L'altura tufacea da cui si domina un vasto orizzonte che spazia dal Monte Amiata ai rilievi che delimitano il lago di Bolsena, può essere considerato un avamposto prima voluto da Vulci, poi da Roma, a controllo delle direttrici verso l'Etruria interna.

Bibliografia

Agostiniani, L. 1991. 'Per la storia dell'etruscologia ottocentesca: la figura scientifiva di Vittorio Poggi', in *Miscellanea etrusca e italica in onore di Massimo Pallottino*, (*Archeologia Classica* XLIII), 499-509.

Bartoloni, G. 1972. *Le tombe da Poggio Buco nel Museo Archeologico di Firenze*, Firenze.

Bartoloni, G. 1986. 'I Latini e il Tevere', in *Il Tevere e le altre vie d'acqua del Lazio antico* (*QuadAEI* 12), Roma, 98-110.

Bartoloni, G. 1992. 'Palazzo o tempio? A proposito dell'edificio arcaico di Poggio Buco', in *AION Archeologia e storia antica*, XIII, 9-33.

Buffa, M. 1935. *Nuova raccolta di iscrizioni etrusche*, Firenze.

Buonamici, G. 1935. *Epigrafia Etrusca*, Firenze.

Cao di San Marco, B. 1971. In *Rivista di Epigrafia Etrusca*, XXXIX, nn. 31-32.

Carandini, A. (a cura di), 1985. *La romanizzazione dell'Etruria: il territorio di Vulci*, Milano.

Colonna, G. 1974. 'La cultura dell'Etruria meridionale interna con particolare riferimento alle necropoli rupestri', in *Atti dell'VIII convegno nazionale di Studi Etruschi e Italici. Aspetti dell'Etruria interna*, Firenze, 253 ss.

Colonna, G. 1975. 'A proposito del Morfema etrusco – si', in *Archaeologica. Studi in onore di A.Neppi Modona*, Firenze, 165-171.

Colonna, G. 1977. 'La presenza di Vulci nelle valli del Fiora e dell'Albegna prima del IV sec.a.C.', in *Atti del X Convegno di Studi Etruschi e Italici: La civiltà arcaica di Vulci e la sua espansione*, Firenze, 189-214.

Colonna, G. (a cura di) 1986. G.Dennis, E.C.Hamilton Gray, *Città e necropoli d'Etruria. Tuscania, Grotte di Castro (VT)*.

Colonna, G. 1986. 'Il Tevere e gli Etruschi', in *Il Tevere e le altre vie d'acqua del Lazio antico* (*QuadAEI* 12), 90-97.

Comella, A. 1981. 'Tipologia e diffusione dei complessi votivi in Italia in età medio- e tardo repubblicana. Contributo allo storia dell'artigianato antico', *Mélanges de l'École Française de Rome, Antiquité*, XCIII, 717-803.

Cristofani, M. 1977. 'Problemi poleografici dell'agro cosano e caletrano in età arcaica', *Atti del X Convegno di Studi Etruschi e Italici: La civiltà arcaica di Vulci e la sua espansione*, Firenze, 255 ss.

Daremberg, Ch. & Saglio, E. 1877. *Dictionnaire des antiquitès grecques et romaines*, Paris.

Dennis, G. 1883. *The Cities and Cemeteries of Etruria*, London.

Donati, L. & Michelucci, M. 1981. *La Collezione Ciacci nel Museo Archeologico di Grosseto*, Roma.

Gazzetti, G. 1985. 'Statonia. La città e il suo territorio', in Carandini 1985, 78–79.

Guattitoli, M. 1985. 'Vulci. La città prima della conquista', in Carandini 1985, 57–58.

Harris, W.V. 1971. *Rome in Etruria and Umbria*, Oxford.

Kennet, D. (a cura di), 1991. G. Dennis, *Città e necropoli d'Etruria, Sovana-Saturnia-Pitigliano-Sorano, Grotte di Castro(VT)*.

Lopez Pegna, M. 1953. 'Itinera Etruriae – II', *Studi Etruschi*, XXII, 139 ss.

Maggiani, A., Pellegrini, E. 1985. *La media valle del Fiora dalla Preistoria alla Romanizzazione*, Pitigliano.

Maggiani, A. 1988. 'Glandes Plumbaee', in *Il patrimonio disperso*, Piombino, 132.

Maggiani, A. 1990. 'Alfabeti etruschi in età ellenistica', in *La scrittura nell'Etruria antica. Annali della Fondazione per il Museo "Claudio Faina"*, IV, 177–217.

Matteucig, G. 1951. *Poggio Buco. The Necropolis of Statonia*, Berkeley.

Matteucig, G. 1969. 'Statonia Revisited', in *Hommages à Marcel Renard* III, Bruxelles, 431–440.

Mazzolai, A. 1960. 'Appunti per la cronologia delle tombe di Poggio Buco', *Bollettino della Società Storica Maremmana* II, 3–26.

Milani, A. 1912. *Storia e guida ragionata del R. Museo Etrusco di Firenze*, I, Firenze, 75 e 266.

Minto, A. 1912. 'Di un gruppetto in bronzo rappresentante Aphrodite che si slaccia il sandalo', *Bollettino d'Arte*, 209–216.

Mornadi, A. 1978. 'Le iscrizioni medioadriatiche', in *PCIA* VI, 561–583

Pallottino, M. 1979. 'Nomi etruschi di città', *Saggi di Antichità* II, Roma, 710–726.

Pallottino, M. 1978. *Thesaurus Linguae Etruscae. I. Indice lessicale*, Roma.

Pellegrini, E. 1989. *La necropoli di Poggio Buco. Nuovi dati per lo studio di un centro dell'Etruria interna nei periodi orientalizzante ed arcaico*, Firenze.

Pellegrini, G. 1896. 'Pitigliano. Necropoli e pago etrusco di Poggio Buco nel comune di Pitigliano in provincia di Grosseto', *Notizie degli Scavi di Antichità*, 266–279.

Pellegrini, G. 1898. 'Pitigliano -Risultato degli scavi del 1896–97 a Poggio Buco, dove supponesi Statonia, e nuovi trovamenti di antichità in altre parti del territorio pitiglianese', *Notizie degli Scavi di Antichità*, 429–449.

Pellegrini, G. 1899. 'Di un'antica città scoperta in Etruria', *Atene e Roma* II, coll.5–13.

Poggi, V. 1884. *Appunti di Epigrafia Etrusca*, Genova.

Radke, G. 1981. *Viae Publicae Romanae*, Bologna.

Raveggi, M. 1931. 'Pitigliano (Statonia). Ritrovamento di una seconda ghianda missile di piombo iscritta presso Poggio Buco', *Notizie degli Scavi di Antichità*, 194–195.

Rendili, M. 1991. *Città e territorio nell'Etruria meridionale*, tesi di dottorato, Roma.

Rittatore Vonwiller, F. & Lotti, T. 1941. 'Castro e il suo territorio', *Studi Etruschi*, XV, 299 ss.

Rossini, F. & Sperandio, A. 1985. 'Statonia. Il popolamento', in Carandini 1985, 80–84.

Scullard, H.H. 1969. *Le città etrusche e Roma*, Milano.

Stanco, E. 1985. 'Statonia. L'organizzazione della prefettura', in Carandini A. (a cura di), *La romanizzazione dell'Etruria: il territorio di Vulci*, Milano, 79–80.

Ward Perkins, J.B. 1970. 'Città e pagus. Considerazioni sull'organizzazione primitiva della città nell'Italia centrale', in *La città etrusca e italica preromana*, Bologna, 293–298.

Zanini, A. 1993. 'Evidenze della fine dell'età del bronzo sull'Acropoli A delle Sparne – Poggio Buco, Pitigliano (GR). Nota preliminare', *Preistoria e Protostoria in Etruria – Atti del I Incontro di Studi – Saturnia (Manciano) – Farnese 17–19 maggio 1991*, Milano, 363–372.

50

Modelli d'Insediamento della Romanizzazione nell'*Ager Gallicus* e *Picenus*

Mario Luni
(Istituto di Archeologia e Storia dell'Arte Antica dell'Università di Urbino)

Sommario: *Le recenti ricerche archeologiche permettono di meglio comprendere il modello d'insediamento della romanizzazione nell'ager Gallicus e Picenus, dove le prime colonie vengono fondate nell'area di precedenti insediamenti indigeni sorti in luoghi di particolare significato, quali ad esempio i terrazzi presso le foci dei fiumi adriatici. La portuosità naturale di questi siti ha determinato già in età preromana il sorgere di insediamenti costieri, poi occupati tra III e II secolo a.C. con fondazioni di colonie romane. Questo è il caso di* Sena Gallica *(Senigallia) e* Castrum Novum *(presso Giulianova) tra 290 e 284 a.C., di* Ariminum *(Rimini) nel 268 a.C., di* Pisaurum *(Pesaro) e* Potentia *(presso Porto Recanati) nel 184 a.C. Queste città vengono realizzate secondo un preciso schema programmatico. Lo stesso progetto politico-militare romano era finalizzato alla presa di possesso dei luoghi di maggiore significato strategico – in precedenza abitati – con la fondazione di colonie sulla sommità di alture nei pressi della costa: così si è verificato a* Hatria *(Atri) tra 290 e 284, a* Firmum *(Fermo) nel 264 a.C., a* Aesis *(Iesi) nel 247 a.C. e ad* Auximum *(Osimo) nel 157 a.C.*

Per restare entro i limiti prefissati verranno presentati in sintesi i primi risultati della ricerca in corso sulla origine e sulle fasi di vita di una serie di città romane della regione medioadriatica, con l'intento di chiarire la tipologia dei modelli di insediamento nel territorio. Va premesso inoltre che qui si può fare riferimento alla fase urbana solo ad iniziare dal III secolo a.C., ossia da quando – dopo la battaglia del Sentino (295 a.C.) – i Romani hanno preso gradualmente possesso dell'*ager Gallicus* e di quello *Picenus*.

Sulla base di documentazione archeologica si è potuto di recente ulteriormente constatare che le prime colonie si insediano nell'area di precedenti abitati indigeni sorti in luoghi di particolare significato, quali ad esempio i terrazzi presso le foci dei fiumi adriatici. La portuosità naturale di questi siti assume un valore spesso emblematico in questo contesto, tale da avere determinato già in età preromana il sorgere di insediamenti costieri quali avamposti in pianura di vicini abitati d'altura, caratterizzati da uno sviluppo di tipo protourbano.

Seguendo le varie fasi della romanizzazione dell'*ager Gallicus* e *Picenus*, ed in particolare la successione delle deduzioni coloniali di III-II secolo a.C., si può ora osservare con maggiore fondamento rispetto al passato che il programma politico-militare romano era finalizzato alla presa di possesso dei luoghi di maggiore significato strategico – in genere in precedenza abitati -, con la fondazione di colonie lungo la costa presso foci fluviali e talvolta su alture a breve distanza: *Sena Gallica*, *Hatria* e *Castrum Novum* (290–284 a.C.), *Ariminum* (268 a.C.), *Firmum* (264 a.C.), *Aesis* (247 a.C.), *Pisaurum* e *Potentia* (184 a.C.), *Auximum* (157 a.C.).

Sena Gallica (Senigallia)

La colonia è stata fondata nel 290–288 o nel 284 su un terrazzo naturale, di neppure dieci metri di altezza, in connessione con la foce del *Sena* (Misa) e in un contesto di laguna costiera (Ortolani & Alfieri 1953). Peculiare è il significato strategico del nuovo centro, che viene ubicato nel punto in cui sbocca a mare la vallata la cui testata inizia in un punto assai prossimo al luogo della battaglia del Sentino (Fig. 1). *Sena Gallica* si pone a presidio dell'*ager Gallicus* meridionale, come centro di sbocco vallivo al termine della via naturale di penetrazione seguita dai Romani dalla vallata del Tevere a quella del *Sena* sul versante adriatico, attraverso la gola di Scheggia (Luni 1989).

Già Alfieri ha ipotizzato, in corrispondenza del terrazzo su cui agli inizi del III secolo a.C. è stata fondata la prima colonia medio-adriatica, la preesistenza di un centro senonico ed anche pre-gallico in relazione col commercio marittimo paleo-greco e greco. La proposta si è basata su una serie di indizi ed anche sull'esame delle fonti letterarie, ma ha suscitato un certo dibattito (Zuffa 1979) a causa della mancanza di documentazione archeologica.

Nel corso di lavori eseguiti in anni recenti nel centro storico di Senigallia, che è ubicato nello stesso sito della città romana, sono venuti in luce a circa tre metri di profondità alcuni antichi materiali significativi, in un contesto archeologico non ben definito (Stefanini 1991). È qui segnalato il recupero di frammenti di ceramica tra cui l'"ansa di un'anfora rodia con bollo, frammenti di vasellame a vernice nera e il piede di una *kylix* con iscrizione arcaica graffita". Sembra che altri frammenti

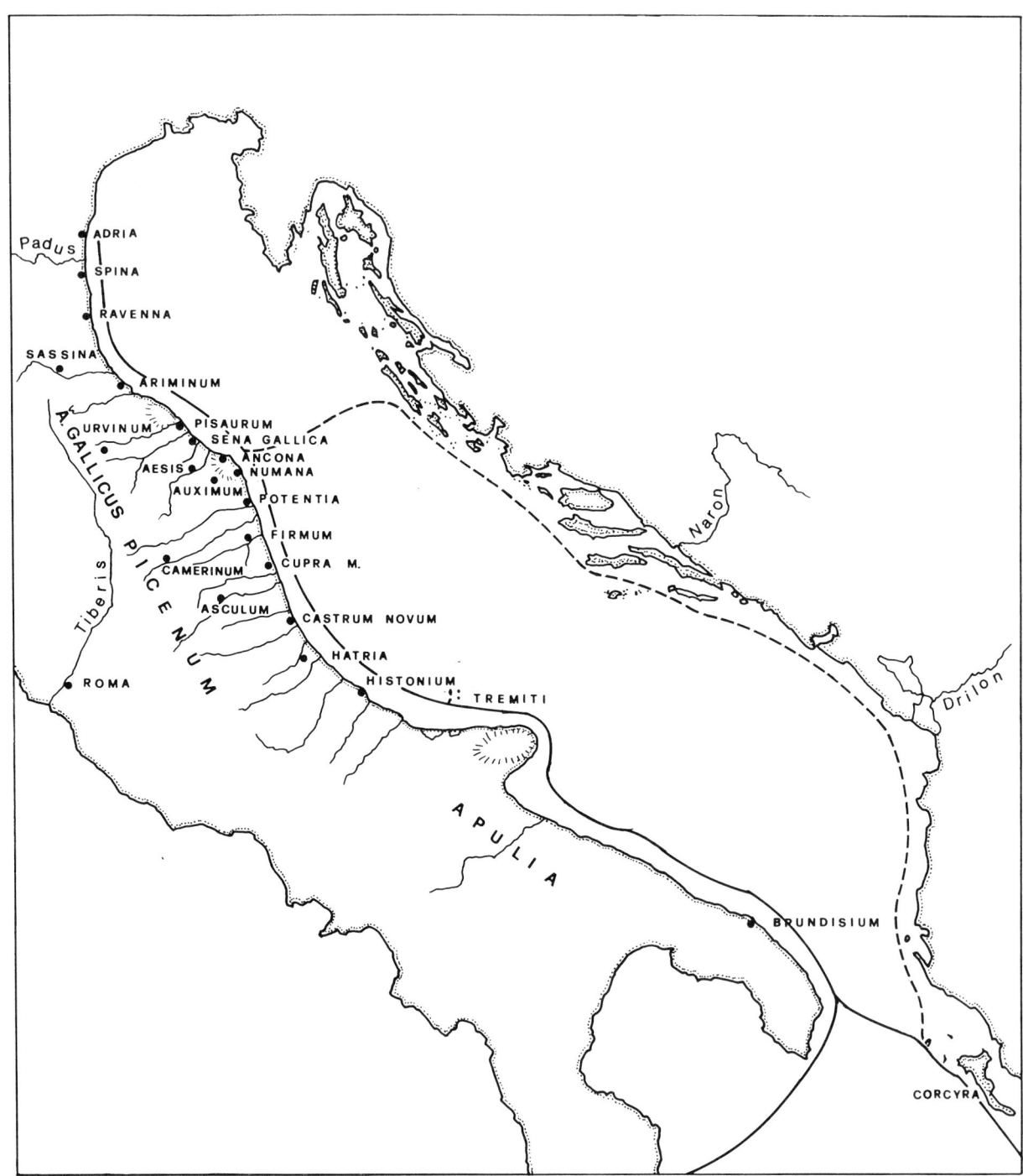

Fig. 1. Le città romane segnalate nella carta sono state impiantate nell'ager Gallicus e Picenus tra III e II secolo a.C. nel sito di insediamenti protostorici sorti su terrazzi alle foci di fiumi, lungo la rotta padana, o in luoghi di altura di particolare significato strategico (dis. G. Barozzi).

ceramici a vernice nera, forse attici, provengano da un altro vicino scavo in profondità. In mancanza di ulteriori dati si può solo prendere atto del ritrovamento di documentazione riferibile ad età preromana, rinvenuta ad una profondità tale che la presenza dell'acqua e di strutture in riferimento alla fase di vita di epoca romana non ha reso possibile raccogliere altre utili indicazioni.

Si viene a riproporre anche a Senigallia una situazione simile a quella riscontrata quindici anni fa in scavi condotti a più di tre metri di profondità nel centro storico di Rimini, dove tra numerose analoghe difficoltà sono state rinvenute tracce sicure di epoca preromana (Maioli 1980), delle quali si riferirà tra breve. Anche per Senigallia va constata per ora la scoperta di significativi indizi riferibili, se non al popolamento, almeno alla assai probabile frequentazione preromana del terrazzo alla foce del *Sena*, in un contesto di coeva portuosità naturale. Nella stessa area venne impiantata la colonia secondo un preciso schema programmatico e con isolati a pianta rettangolare (un *actus* per due).

Altre due colonie vengono fondate negli stessi anni alla estremità meridionale del Piceno, *Hatria* (Atri) e *Castrum Novum* (presso Giulianova), con la precisa funzione di controllo militare sulla regione allora occupata (Sommella 1988; Gros & Torelli 1988). Nel primo caso si tratta di un centro d'altura a circa dieci chilometri dal mare, impiantato sul sito di un precedente abitato indigeno, in riferimento col quale sono state rinvenute ceramica protostorica e due necropoli con materiali di VI-V secolo a.C. (Azzena 1977; Gros & Torelli 1988).

In scavi nell'area del mercato coperto e della Cattedrale è stata recuperata ceramica d'impasto e buccheroide, oltre a frammenti a figure rosse di vasi apuli e di *skyphoi* a vernice nera con decorazioni sovradipinte (fabbriche di Gnathia). Si tratta di tracce significative dell'insediamento preromano, sul terrazzo sommitale del colle su cui poi è stata edificata la città romana secondo un impianto urbanistico a maglia regolare, con gli isolati di due *actus* per tre. Questo "addensamento abitativo con caratteristiche di stabilità" era probabilmente collegato con il vicino approdo sulla foce del fiume *Macrinos*, attivo già prima della romanizzazione del territorio.

Poco si conosce di *Castrum Novum* (nel sito di S. Maria a Mare), sulla foce del fiume Tordino, fornita di uno scalo forse già in età preromana (Schmiedt 1978), come sembra confermare il ritrovamento in tombe di ceramica almeno di IV secolo a.C. (comunicazione di A. Staffa, della Sopr. Archeologica dell'Abruzzo).

Ariminum (Rimini)

La colonia romana è fondata nel 268 nella parte settentrionale dell'*ager Gallicus*, quale avamposto contro i Galli della pianura Padana. Si tratta di un centro strategico fondamentale nel contesto della penetrazione della romanizzazione verso Nord, che costituisce una tappa importante per circa mezzo secolo, almeno fino alla guerra annibalica.

Non è un caso se attorno al 220 a.C. la via *Flaminia* viene aperta da *Roma* lungo la valle del Tevere, e, dopo il favorevole valico della Scheggia (m 632), lungo quella del Metauro fino a raggiungere la costa adriatica nella zona dove poi sorse *Fanum Fortunae* (Fano) e di seguito fino ad *Ariminum* (Luni 1988). Si è trattato di una precisa scelta strategica e funzionale, determinata dal tracciato naturale più agevole, frequentato già in età preistorica. La via consolare, infatti, non può essere sorta *ex-novo* in pochi anni ed ha di certo utilizzato il percorso di una antica pista preromana.

Con la fondazione di *Ariminum* questo tracciato preistorico costituisce il percorso naturale più breve da *Roma*, anche rispetto a quello più a Sud attraverso il *Sentinus*, il *Sena* e lungo la costa adriatica. La pista preromana dovrebbe avere assunto un qualche ruolo nel quadro degli avvenimenti connessi alla romanizzazione della pianura Padana e alla distribuzione viritana di terre attuata nel 232 con la *lex Flaminia* (*de agro Gallico Piceno viritim dividundo*). Determinanti per la ristrutturazione del percorso menzionato in via consolare sono state probabilmente le vittoriose campagne militari condotte con base ad *Ariminum* contro i Galli nel 225-224 e la decisiva vittoria di *Clastidium* del 222, con la conseguente deduzione coloniale di *Placentia* e *Cremona*.

La nuova colonia si è insediata su un terrazzo del Quaternario, sopraelevato di neppure dieci metri sul livello del mare, in corrispondenza dell'antica foce dell'*Ariminus* (Marecchia) ed in parallelo con la coeva linea di costa. Ci si trova di fronte ad una situazione simile a quella che caratterizzava il sito di *Sena Gallica* ed anche in questo caso la scelta della ubicazione del centro di sbocco vallivo tiene conto in particolare modo della portuosità naturale della foce fluviale e della fondamentale via costiera.

Già Zuffa (1962, 1979) aveva proposto l'esistenza di un centro di foce in epoca preromana sul terrazzo fluviale su cui sarà fondata la colonia, popolato dai vicini insediamenti d'altura sulle colline di Covignano (Scarpellini 1981; Ortalli 1987). Numerosi frammenti di ceramica attica, apula e campana, datati tra il VI e il III secolo a.C., sono stati recuperati negli anni '60 e '70 dagli scarichi di terreno nel vecchio alveo del Marecchia e collegati con l'attività edilizia nel centro storico di Rimini (Riccioni 1970, 1987; Zuffa 1978).

In qualche caso sono stati effettuati scavi fortuiti e talvolta anche sistematici; essi sono stati condotti a diversi metri di profondità, spesso in condizioni difficili a causa della presenza dell'acqua, risultando così complicata la lettura degli strati in connessione col vergine. Tra i materiali più antichi messi in luce ne sono segnalati alcuni riferibili all'VIII secolo. Nell'area dell'ex

Vescovado è stato rinvenuto in due diversi punti uno spesso strato 'a vespaio' di frammenti ceramici sia di fabbricazione locale che di importazione dall'Attica, dalla Magna Grecia, dal Lazio e dall'Etruria, datati dalla seconda metà del V al II secolo a.C. (Riccioni 1987).

Più significativo lo scavo nell'area del Mercato coperto, che ha messo in luce due spessi strati sovrapposti, costituiti da terreno antropico nerastro. Nella giacitura superiore sono stati rinvenuti "cocci apuli, campani, laziali ed etruschi", datati fra IV e III secolo a.C., mentre nello strato più in profondità sono stati recuperati solo frammenti di vasi attici a figure rosse e a vernice nera riferibili fra gli ultimi decenni del V e gli inizi del IV secolo a.C.

Anche nei sondaggi più recenti, eseguiti negli anni 1977-79 presso l'ex Convento di S. Francesco, sono stati evidenziati in almeno tre siti diversi 2-3 strati antropici di età preromana, ad una profondità che varia dai tre ai quattro metri (Maioli 1987a, 1987b). Significativa in questo caso è la scoperta, nella giacitura più profonda, di pochi resti di un insediamento databile al IV-III secolo a.C., che risultano assai compromessi dagli scavi di epoca romana e successivi. Si tratta di alcuni brevi tratti di muri "a secco in sassi di fiume, con resti di un piano pavimentale", costruiti in immediata sovrapposizione al terreno vergine. Al centro di una di queste strutture era presente "uno scasso ottenuto in opera", per l'alloggiamento di "un palo verticale con funzioni strutturali". Sul pavimento sono stati rinvenuti numerosissimi frammenti di "incannicciato di argilla, cotta e lisciata esternamente". Murature dello stesso tipo, quasi totalmente distrutte da edifici romani, erano state localizzate presso l'ex Hotel Commercio.

Nello strato relativo a una abitazione è stato trovato un frammento di *kylix* a v.n., databile alla seconda metà del IV a.C., nel contesto di materiali di V-IV secolo. Al di sopra dei resti di muri a secco lo strato antropico è caratterizzato da frammenti di ceramica di impasto, di una *kylix* attica riferibile al 480-460, di altra ceramica a v.n. La categoria di cocci più numerosa è riconducibile a "*skyphoi* del tipo del cigno rosso", databile tra la fine del IV e l'inizio del III secolo.

In definitiva, l'area di questi ritrovamenti si presenta assai ampia ed è stato notato che l'estensione dell'abitato preromano si dovrebbe sviluppare sotto tutta la parte centrale della città romana. La colonia di *Ariminum* viene ubicata sullo stesso fondamentale terrazzo fluviale; è caratterizzata da un impianto urbanistico a maglia regolare, con isolati a pianta rettangolare, e determina la repentina monumentalizzazione secondo un progetto prestabilito del sito dell'insediamento protostorico, il quale mostra di avere raggiunto almeno tra IV e III secolo una fase di sviluppo di tipo protourbano. Per quanto riguarda il ritrovamento di muri a secco di abitazioni di insediamenti protostorici in area medioadriatica, si riferirà più avanti.

FIRMUM (FERMO)

Questo centro d'altura è situato a breve distanza dalla costa, presso le vicine foci fluviali del Tenna e dell'Ete Vivo. È stato osservato che la *colonia* del 264 fu sovrapposta ad un insediamento preesistente (Polverini 1987), tenendo conto anche di un passo di Velleio (I 14,8: *At inizio belli Punici Firmum et Castrum colonis occupata*).

L'origine in età protostorica di *Firmum* era stata sostenuta dal Napoletani (1907), anche sulla base dei resti di una 'cerchia preromana' di mura e di monetazione 'arcaica'. Sebbene questi due elementi siano da riferire in modo piuttosto attendibile al primo impianto della colonia latina, la documentazione archeologica preromana segnalata nei pressi della città confermerebbe l'esistenza di un abitato coevo (Pasquinucci & Parise 1987).

La presenza di estese necropoli dell'età del Ferro nella collina fermana e nelle vicinanze lascia presupporre l'ubicazione sul pianoro sommitale dell'altura di un consistente insediamento (Annibaldi 1965; Lollini 1976). Si tratta di un sepolcreto villanoviano (IX sec. a.C.), di uno datato fra VIII e VII e di altri resti che attestano continuità di vita nel VI secolo e oltre.

In questo caso la colonia si insedia sull'alto di una collina d'importanza strategica al centro del Piceno, con funzione di controllo della fondamentale via costiera e delle foci dei due fiumi vicini. Si può osservare che qui si ripropone la stessa situazione già riscontrata nelle precedenti fondazioni di città romane medioadriatiche, ubicate nel sito di un preesistente abitato piceno che probabilmente aveva raggiunto una fase di sviluppo di tipo protourbano.

AESIS (IESI)

La colonia è stata fondata nel 247 a.C. su un terrazzo naturale sulla sommità di un colle alto poco più di 90 metri s.l.m. Esso è situato sulla sinistra del fiume *Aesis* (Esino), a circa quindici chilometri dalla costa, e domina l'ampia vallata fino alla foce. Si tratta di un centro d'altura, posto in posizione strategica a Nord di *Ancona*, a controllo di un significativo incrocio stradale tra la via che risaliva la valle verso i passi appenninici e quella interna di collegamento tra *Salaria* e *Flaminia*. L'antica esistenza di questo diverticolo tra le due strade consolari passava per *Aesis*, come è attestato da una iscrizione della seconda metà del I secolo a.C. rinvenuta non lontano dalla città (Alfieri, Gasperini & Paci 1985; Luni 1984-86). A Iesi è stata anche individuata documentazione circa l'esistenza di una officina di ceramiche a vernice nera attiva dal III secolo a.C. fino alla metà del I (Brecciaroli Taborelli 1983; Megna 1990).

Va osservato che nella medio-bassa vallata dell'Esino sono state scoperte testimonianze consistenti relative alla civiltà picena di VI e V secolo, come ad esempio a Pianello di Castelbellino e a Mergo. Alcune analoghe attestazioni sono documentate sulla vicina collina di S. Maria degli Aroli, dove, in un'area di necropoli, è stata rinvenuta una *kylix* attica a figure rosse.

Nella stessa Iesi è stata raccolta di recente nel centro storico documentazione archeologica riferibile alla frequentazione della sommità dell'altura in età pre-romana. Nel corso di lavori di ripulitura di una grande 'cisterna' romana sono stati rinvenuti numerosi frammenti di ceramica di impasto grossolano in uno strato antropico di terra assai nera immediatamente al di sopra del terreno vergine. In attesa dello studio del significativo materiale non si può che registrare l'esistenza di tracce di frequentazione (o di popolamento) in età preromana dell'area su cui nel 247 si è insediata la colonia di *Aesis*, con un impianto urbanistico regolare e con isolati a pianta rettangolare.

Inizia a configurarsi qui una situazione analoga a quella riconosciuta con scavi nel 1982–83 a *Sassina* (Sarsina) (Ortalli 1987), dove su buona parte dell'alto terrazzo dominante la valle del Savio sono stati rinvenuti materiali archeologici e livelli di occupazione riferibili almeno al IV secolo a.C. La città romana è stata costruita nell'area di un insediamento stabile d'altura protostorico, in un luogo naturalmente difeso, che alle soglie della romanizzazione si stava strutturando con "una serie ravvicinata di edifici", in un contesto "piuttosto primitivo" di tipo protourbano.

Pisaurum (Pesaro)

Lo scavo eseguito nel 1977 nel centro storico di Pesaro ha potuto accertare che la zona su cui nel 184 a.C. è stata insediata la colonia di *Pisaurum* era stata almeno in parte occupata nei secoli precedenti da un abitato protostorico, per altro già ipotizzato dall'Olivieri (Luni 1982, 1984). Si tratta di un terrazzo sopraelevato di circa dieci metri s.l.m., presso l'antica foce del *Pisaurus* (Foglia) e in relazione con la via costiera, che ha utilizzato nel luogo un probabile favorevole guado.

Sono stati qui messi in luce i resti di almeno due abitazioni parzialmente in muratura, con le fondazioni ed il primo spiccato costruiti a secco con grossi ciottoli di arenaria. Le pareti in origine erano costituite da una intelaiatura in pali di legno e incannicciato, ricoperta da argilla sui due lati; al di sopra poggiava il tetto, costituito da tegoloni e coppi. Si può osservare che si tratta di un tipo di solida abitazione che trova ormai confronti in strutture coeve rinvenute in scavi sia nelle Marche che nella vicina Romagna, realizzate nell'area medioadriatica nell'età del Ferro finale.

Resti di muratura di case di questo tipo, ad esempio, sono segnalati nel riminese a Covignano, a Riccione, a Monte Faggeto nella valle del Conca (Zuffa 1969; Scarpellini 1981) e a Verucchio (Gentili 1985). In quest'ultimo caso è stata rinvenuta una abitazione, datata al V secolo a.C. sulla base dei frammenti ceramici rinvenuti sul piano pavimentale. Altri esempi sono noti a S. Martino di Gattara, Casola Valsenio, Monte Bibele e Marzabotto (Von Eles Masi 1981; Vitali l991). Si tratta di strutture costruite con la tecnica del palancato che, ad esempio, trovano diffusione anche in centri etruschi già prima del 500 a.C. (Östenberg 1975). In merito alle situazioni emblematiche di Rimini e Sarsina si è riferito sopra.

Scarse sono le notizie sugli abitati 'piceni' (Lollini 1976), tra i quali quello di Montalto di Cessapalombo, del IV secolo a.C. – con bassi muretti perimetrali a secco, con elevato in strutture lignee e con copertura di tegoloni e coppi – ed i coevi 'capannoni' di Belmonte. Vanno aggiunti i resti dell'insediamento indigeno sul colle dei Cappuccini in Ancona, dove è stato rinvenuto un tratto di muretto di pietre a secco e parti di 'intonaco' in uno strato di V secolo, contenente anche frammenti di ceramica attica (Lollini 1956; Luni 1992).

Significativa in questo contesto si presenta la recente scoperta a Matelica, erede del municipio romano di *Matilica*, di parte di un'abitazione protostorica con muri a secco, che ha restituito in strato anche frammenti di ceramica attica a figure rosse (Virzì 1986; Luni *et al.* l991). Da tutti questi esempi sopra mostrati si può in definitiva constatare l'esistenza nell'età del Ferro finale nella regione medioadriatica di solide abitazioni stanziali, che sono state realizzate in un contesto di abitato che ha raggiunto alle soglie della romanizzazione uno stadio di vita di tipo protourbano. La documentazione che si è resa disponibile in anni recenti è ancora modesta e frammentaria, ma assai indicativa e in ogni caso tale da lasciare intravedere ulteriori sviluppi in merito alla conoscenza del processo di urbanizzazione in atto nella regione nel Piceno IV B-VI (fine VI-inizi III secolo a.C.).

Tornando ai resti dell'abitato preromano scoperti a Pesaro, si può per giunta osservare che sono stati qui rinvenuti numerosi frammenti di ceramica d'impasto classificabili nell'ambito del Piceno IV B-V (fine VI – inizi IV sec. a.C.), oltre ad un gran numero di altri di ceramica attica a figure nere, a f.r. e a vernice nera (Luni l991). Materiale analogo è stato trovato in uno strato antropico, in immediata sovrapposizione al terreno vergine, anche in un'area ad una certa distanza da quella che ha restituito i tratti delle due abitazioni menzionate.

L'insediamento preromano di Pesaro – sebbene finora sia stato riconosciuto su un'estensione limitata rispetto a quella della città romana che si è ad esso sovrapposta – costituisce un esempio peculiare di abitato stabile, in gran parte in muratura, sorto in ambiente piceno nell'età del Ferro finale. Esso è ubicato proprio in un'area in cui è anche attestata l'esistenza della scrittura (vd. le coeve iscrizioni di Novilara), oltre alla presenza di un 'luco sacro' che con probabilità ha origini preromane.

Questo centro indigeno di foce – avamposto costiero

dell'abitato piceno d'altura di Novilara – è ubicato sul tratto terminale del *Pisaurus*, allora frequentato come porto-canale dai naviganti greci lungo la rotta padana. Nel pesarese, in definitiva, tra V e IV secolo la cultura picena mostra di avere raggiunto un notevole livello di sviluppo, in qualche modo favorito dal prolungato contatto con la più evoluta civiltà greca, tramite gli approdi commerciali in Adriatico.

Nel 184 a.C. la colonia romana di *Pisaurum* viene ubicata sullo stesso terrazzo su cui era sorto l'abitato indigeno ed è costituita secondo un piano programmatico caratterizzato da una maglia regolare di isolati a pianta rettangolare (Luni 1984).

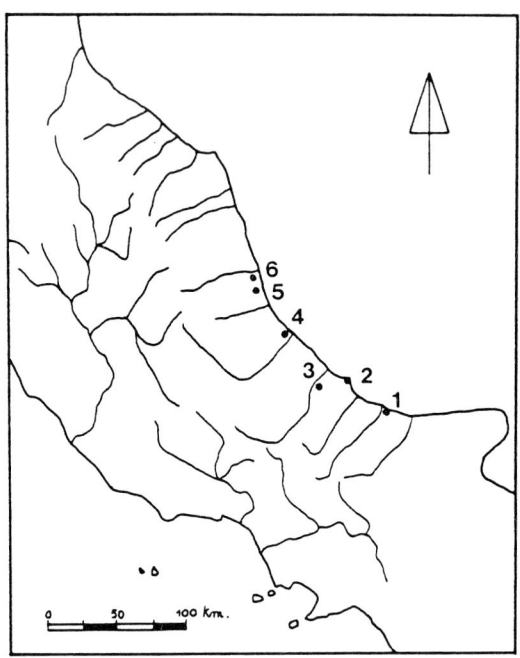

Fig. 2. Carta geografica dell'Italia centrale con l'indicazione dei siti menzionati nel testo.

1) Campomarino (CB); 2) Punta Aderci (Vasto – CH);
3) Fonte Tasca (Archi – CH); 4) Colle del Telegrafo (Pescara);
5) Fortellezza (Tortoreto – TE); 6) Martinsicuro (TE).
(dis. V. Scarci, Sopr. Arch. Chieti).

POTENTIA (PRESSO PORTO RECANATI)

La colonia romana è stata fondata nel 184 a.C. su un terrazzo naturale sulla sponda sinistra dell'antica foce del fiume Potenza (*Flosis*). Il pianoro risulta sopraelevato di alcuni metri s.l.m. e presenta le stesse caratteristiche di quello utilizzato nello stesso anno per la fondazione della colonia di *Pisaurum*, più a Nord. Ambedue rientrano nel programma strategico di potenziamento della difesa della costa medioadriatica e di rilancio della romanizzazione dell'*ager Gallicus* e di quello *Picenus* dopo la guerra annibalica.

La riscoperta archeologica della città è dovuta soprattutto a recenti scavi che hanno consentito di riconoscere le linee generali nel piano programmatico che caratterizzava l'impianto urbanistico ad assi perpendicolari del centro di nuova fondazione (Percossi 1985, 1990, 1991; Moscatelli 1987). In recenti saggi in profondità si è verificata la scoperta di uno strato antropico presente immediatamente al di sopra del terreno vergine. La Percossi riferisce che si tratta del più antico livello di occupazione finora rinvenuto, di colore nero, ricco di cenere e carbone e con frammenti di ceramica d'impasto.

In attesa dello studio dei materiali recuperati e di nuovi dati di scavo si può solo prendere atto della prima significativa attestazione di uno strato di frequentazione preromana nel terrazzo su cui nel 184 a.C. si è insediata la colonia di *Potentia*. Va anche rilevato che qui si ripropone lo stesso modello delle fondazioni coloniali in connessione con foci di fiumi medioadriatici prese in esame in precedenza, quali quelle attuate più a Nord sull'*Ariminus*, sul *Pisaurus* e sul *Sena*. In questi tre casi è stata accertata in età protostorica la presenza di un insediamento presso la laguna costiera o la foce, utilizzata come porto-canale nel contesto della frequentazione della rotta costiera da parte di naviganti greci dediti a commerci sul delta del Po (Luni 1981).

Va aggiunto che sulla vicina collina di Montarice, prospiciente l'antica foce del Potenza, sono stati rinvenuti frammenti di ceramica d'impasto e di vasellame tornito riferibili ad epoca protostorica; tra questi si segnala il recupero di alcuni pezzi di ceramica attica sia a f.n. che a f.r. (Luni & Marchegiani 1992). I materiali raccolti sulle pendici del colle attestano la continuità di vita nel luogo dall'età del Bronzo alla successiva età del Ferro. In particolare l'insediamento preromano di Montarice viene ad inserirsi in un ambito territoriale abitato in un arco di tempo compreso tra la metà del VI e il V secolo a.C. Necropoli picene di vaste proporzioni sono state inoltre individuate sia a Recanati che a Porto Recanati.

Si può probabilmente constatare qui verso la fine dell'età del Ferro un rapporto di dipendenza tra l'abitato sul colle di Montarice e l'avamposto sull'antica foce del Potenza, così come si è verificato tra l'insediamento sulle colline di Novilara e quello alla foce del *Pisaurus* ed ancora tra l'abitato sul colle di Coviganno e quello costiero sull'*Ariminus*.

Il ritrovamento in profondità dello strato di frequentazione preromano alla foce del *Flosis*, in corrispondenza della probabile laguna costiera, richiama in qualche modo quello segnalato a *Ravenna*, dove in due pozzi stratigrafici sono stati rinvenuti materiali locali e d'importazione riferibili all'insediamento preromano, costituitosi verso la fine del V ed in vita fino al III secolo a.C. (Bermond Montanari 1987, 1990). Esso era disposto lungo la rotta costiera e in relazione con gli altri porti adriatici sopra menzionati.

Auximum (Osimo)

È l'ultima colonia (157 a.C.) fondata lungo la costa medioadriatica nel II secolo a.C. È ubicata nell'immediato entroterra, in relazione con l'importante porto di *Numana*, in posizione dominante (m 265) e lungo assi di traffico che risalgono la vallata del *Misco* (Musone) e del *Flosis* (Potenza), dove si attesta una serie ininterrotta di stanziamenti preromani dalla costa ai valichi appenninici (Luni 1992).

Materiali protostorici rinvenuti in diverse località del territorio osimano sembrerebbero indiziare la preesistenza di un popolamento sparso che gravitava sul centro protourbano già nell'età del Ferro finale e di tracciati viari preromani. La presenza di ceramica attica di V secolo attestata nel sito dell'abitato piceno e nell'adiacente necropoli (Gentili 1990), nonché nell'insediamento suburbano di Monte S. Pietro, documenta il ruolo assunto dal centro d'altura preromano in relazione al controllo della fascia costiera prospicente e del flusso commerciale che dallo scalo di *Numana* risaliva la vallata.

Tra i materiali del sepolcreto piceno attorno a Osimo si segnala un gruppo di frammenti di vasellame a vernice nera riferito alla classe della ceramica protocampana e campana, da collocarsi nell'arco di tempo che intercorre tra la metà del IV e la metà del III sec. a.C. (Gentili 1990). Coppette tipologicamente analoghe sono state rinvenute in città nei lavori di ampliamento del mercato coperto e stanno a documentare le ultime fasi della vita dell'abitato protostorico, che giunge alle soglie della romanizzazione.

I materiali relativi alla presenza romana sulla sommità del colle vengono a sovrapporsi direttamente agli ultimi livelli dell'insediamento piceno. In vari punti della città, infatti, sono stati raccolti in strato frammenti di ceramica a vernice nera 'campana', databili tra la metà del III e gli inizi del I sec. a.C. Della colonia sono conservati alcuni tratti di mura in opera quadrata e sono riconoscibili i due assi viari principali, ortogonali tra loro (Luni & Marchegiani 1993).

La stessa circostanza è constata anche a Urbino (*Urvinum Mataurense*), dove in recenti scavi sulla sommità del colle su cui si è insediato l'*oppidum* romano cinto da mura in opera quadrata sono stati rinvenuti in diversi punti livelli di occupazione protostorica. In genere in strati di terra nera sono stati messi in luce numerosi frammenti di ceramica d'impasto e 'campana', riferibili almeno al periodo tra il IV e III secolo a.C. (Luni 1993).

Ankon (Ancona)

Un caso a sé è costituito da *Ankon*, insediamento siracusano impiantato nel IV secolo a.C. (Braccesi 1977). Questa fondazione è stata determinata dalla caratteristica forma a gomito del promontorio formato dalla estrema punta settentrionale del colle Guasco che, all'epoca, si proiettava in mare costituendo il più importante porto naturale medioadriatico occidentale.

Il significativo paleonimo *Ankon* si è conservato fino ai nostri giorni e sembra risalire alla prima frequentazione greca del sito, con esplicito riferimento alla coeva morfologia della costa, che si piega a formare il menzionato braccio ricurvo: di qui la designazione dell'abitato nel luogo (Luni 1992). Lo stesso nome è attestato sul rovescio di monete di bronzo datate agli inizi del III secolo a.C., sulle quali è rappresentato anche un braccio piegato a gomito (Panvini Rosati 1974). Sul diritto è presente una testa femminile coronata di mirto, messa in riferimento a strutture sul colle Guasco attribuite al tempio di Venere, sulla cui fase originaria si discute se risalga al periodo dello stanziamento siracusano (fine IV sec. a.C.) oppure alla prima metà del III a.C.

Assai indicativa è la segnalazione sul colle dei Cappuccini di resti di un insediamento indigeno esistito dal IX agli inizi del V secolo (Piceno I-IV: Lollini 1956, 1976). Sono stati qui recuperati frammenti di ceramica attica ed è stato anche rinvenuto un tratto di muretto di pietre a secco e parti di 'intonaco'. Ci aspetteremmo di trovare in sovrapposizione anche tracce del popolamento siracusano, ma purtroppo nessuna testimonianza archeologica indicativa, almeno di IV secolo, è stata rinvenuta nel luogo né nel colle Guasco, sebbene siano stati eseguiti numerosi scavi in profondità in vari siti (Lollini 1978; Traina & Massei 1984). Oggetti provenienti dal Mediterraneo orientale (Mercando 1986) sono stati recuperati nella necropoli ellenistico-romana (III-I sec. a.C.), della quale sono attestati significativi tratti.

Resti di abitato preromano sono venuti in luce nel 1982 sul vicino colle del Montagnolo, immediatamente a sud-ovest del promontorio. Esso è situato in prossimità della costa e domina l'ampia insenatura formata dalle estreme propaggini settentrionali del massiccio del Conero. Nel corso di scavi, in due aree vicine, sono stati rinvenuti materiali piceni di V-IV secolo a.C., assieme a frammenti ceramici di importazione. È stata avanzata l'ipotesi che qui sia sorta la città siracusana (Lollini 1976; Landolfi 1987). Ai fini della presente ricerca, la Ancona romana si è sviluppata sul promontorio formato dal colle Guasco, in un contesto di continuità (eccetto che per il IV secolo) con l'insediamento indigeno, formato da abitazioni simili a quelle rinvenute a Pesaro e giunto ad uno stadio protourbano.

Conclusioni

Il prolungato contatto con la più evoluta cultura greca tramite gli scali lungo la costa, frequentati da naviganti in relazione con gli empori padani, deve avere favorito il processo di acculturazione delle genti del Piceno e dell'*ager Gallicus*. Va aggiunto che esse si sono dimostrate assai ricettive all'utilizzazione di vasellame pregiato di importazione da mensa.

Fig. 3. Frammenti di ceramica figulina dipinta a motivi geometrici lineari da Punta Aderci (Vasto – CH). (fot. M. Vitale, Sopr. Arch. Chieti).

In merito alle abitazioni indigene di V-IV sec. a.C. disponiamo solo di dati frammentari, in parte ancora inediti e dovuti a ritrovamenti recenti. Si comincia tuttavia a delineare il tipo di casa in uso, per lo più costruita con materiale di lunga durata. Si tratta di abitazioni semplici ma solide, e non già di capanne, disposte a breve distanza tra loro. Talvolta si è notato, come nel caso di Rimini, che questo tipo di insediamento verso l'età del Ferro finale ha raggiunto anche una certa estensione, sebbene in un contesto di disposizione casuale.

Il duraturo contatto con la cultura greca deve avere esercitato un certo influsso sulla acquisizione della tecnica di costruzione sopra descritta ed anche determinato poli di aggregazione di una certa consistenza, soprattutto nei siti di commercializzazione dei prodotti di scambio ed in particolare su terrazzi alle foci di fiumi. La documentazione fornita dallo scavo di necropoli e abitati nella regione medioadriatica ci mostra che la quantità di materiale di importazione è assai rilevante, in genere pervenuto attraverso la via commerciale più agevole, ossia tramite la rotta costiera che si collegava con la Grecia e con l'Italia meridionale.

Va rilevato che merita credito il riconoscimento della rotta frequentata dai commercianti greci lungo la costa occidentale dell'Adriatico fino al Gargano e più a Sud verso la Magna Grecia e la Grecia (Alfieri 1975; Braccesi 1977; Luni 1981). In relazione con questo percorso sono da segnalare circa venti foci fluviali, tutte sedi di potenziali scali, oltre ad alcune insenature naturali.

La presenza siracusana in *Ankon* non può che sottintendere la normale frequentazione della rotta occidentale perché sarebbe impensabile che le imbarcazioni provenienti dalla Sicilia si siano sottoposte al gravoso doppio attraversamento dell'Adriatico in mare aperto, con tutte le conseguenti difficoltà della navigazione non a vista e senza strumenti, per percorrere la rotta orientale, forse più comoda ma di maggior durata. Inoltre, la presenza consistente nel Piceno alla fine del V e nel IV secolo di ceramica apula, lucana e attica, spesso del tipo presente anche a Spina, confermerebbe questi contatti prolungati (Lollini 1976; Landolfi 1985; Luni 1992).

L'importazione nella regione medio ed altoadriatica di materiali provenienti dall'Attica e dalla Grecia Orientale attesta la frequentazione commerciale della stessa rotta anche nel VI-V sec. a.C. (Landolfi 1987; AA.VV. 1991; Luni 1992). Va aggiunto che la presenza in Italia meridionale di materiali che ci riportano al mondo piceno e il ritrovamento nella regione medioadriatica dei caratteristici vasi dipinti della Daunia confermano l'esistenza di contatti duraturi tra le due aree, probabilmente per mare. In merito alla recente scoperta di ceramiche iapigie sulla costa abruzzese della prima età del Ferro o del Bronzo finale, si veda la nota in appendice. È segnalata anche ceramica micenea (III B) nell'area medioadriatica (Luni 1992).

In conclusione la fondazione delle più antiche colonie romane nella regione menzionata è avvenuta nei siti di precedenti centri indigeni, sorti lungo la costa in connessione con foci di fiumi oppure ubicati in punti strategici dell'immediato entroterra. Essi hanno in genere raggiunto una fase di sviluppo di tipo protourbano. Le città romane che sono state costruite sulla stessa area, sono state realizzate secondo un preciso schema programmatico, come si è notato negli esempi emblematici sopra riportati.

Appendice

L'Abitato di Punta Aderci presso Vasto (CH) e le Ceramiche Dipinte Iapigie sulla Costa Abruzzese

Alessandro Usai

Negli anni 1991 e 1992 la Soprintendenza Archeologica dell'Abruzzo ha condotto ricerche preliminari nel sito costiero di Punta Aderci, due chilometri ad Ovest dell'insenatura di Punta Penna e dell'attuale porto di Vasto (Fig. 2: 2).

Il sito è costituito da due rilievi di dura breccia cementata, affacciati sul mare ai due lati della foce del torrente Apricino; il rilievo orientale è assai pronunciato e forma un piccolo promontorio quasi conico, mentre quello occidentale raccorda in leggera pendenza il letto del torrente col pianoro retrostante alla costa. L'erosione marina e l'apporto di detriti hanno provocato nel corso dei millenni l'arretramento del fronte roccioso dei due rilievi e l'avanzamento della spiaggia fra loro compresa, e quindi la scomparsa di quella che in epoca protostorica doveva essere una marcata insenatura.

Nel sito di Punta Aderci sono stati finora individuati resti di quattro abitazioni. Il primo, un fondo di capanna o scarico di rifiuti, si trova a mezza costa sul ripido pendio del promontorio orientale ed è stato sezionato dall'erosione marina ed atmosferica; tra i reperti recuperati sono indicativi due frammentini decorati a nastri campiti con fine punteggiato (più uno simile sporadico raccolto nelle vicinanze), un frammento di collo con bordo a tacche e un frammentino appartenente forse ad un manico nastriforme con apici revoluti. Tali elementi sono riferibili alla fase appenninica della media età del Bronzo (XIV sec. a. C.). Sul pendio circostante sono stati raccolti numerosi cocci sporadici d'impasto e figulini ed alcuni frammenti di scorie di ferro, la cui pertinenza contestuale deve essere ancora ben valutata.

Sul rilievo occidentale di Punta Aderci sono stati individuati tre fondi di capanna, riconoscibili in superficie dopo l'aratura per il terriccio grigiastro e per l'abbondanza di reperti. Questi ultimi fondi di capanna misurano circa m. 4/6 x 8/10; pertanto, malgrado la dispersione del sedimento provocata dall'aratro, sembrerebbero riferibili a case allungate, probabilmente incavate nel suolo o costruite in elevato con tronchi e rami.

Il materiale raccolto sistematicamente nei tre fondi di capanna descritti è poco caratteristico; sono frequenti le ciotole carenate con anse a maniglia orizzontale, mentre gli unici ornamenti sono cordoni plastici lisci e digitati; notevoli anche una grossa ansa a ponte intera con leggero cordone in rilievo sul dorso (capanna 2) e un peso da telaio piramidale (capanna 4). Vi sono anche alcuni frammenti di grossi fornelli fittili e pezzi d'intonaco d'argilla concotta con tracce d'impressioni di rami.

Gli elementi più importanti sono tre frammenti figulini dipinti in bruno con motivi lineari (Fig. 3), raccolti entro i fondi di capanna 2 e 3, che rientrano nella classe iapigia protogeometrica del Bronzo finale (XI-X sec. a. C.) o tutt'al più in quella geometrica della prima età del Ferro (IX-VIII sec. a. C.).

Il rinvenimento di ceramica d'importazione dalla Puglia non è ormai un fatto isolato nei siti costieri molisani ed abruzzesi della fase di passaggio tra età del Bronzo ed età del Ferro. Esemplari simili, sempre in numero piuttosto ridotto, sono infatti venuti in luce negli abitati di Campomarino (CB) (Faustoferri 1991), di Fonte Tasca presso Archi (CH) (Radmilli 1979, 1980, 1981), del Colle del Telegrafo di Pescara (Mori, Tozzi, 1970), della Fortellezza di Tortoreto Alto (TE) (D'Ercole, com. pers.), di Martinsicuro (TE) (Arias 1965) (Fig. 2). Tranne Fonte Tasca, distante circa 15 chilometri dal mare, tutti i siti menzionati sono posti su alture costiere, per lo più connesse con foci fluviali e con le principali vie di penetrazione interna (Biferno, Sangro, Pescara, Tronto).

L'occupazione del sito di Punta Aderci nell'età del Bronzo e forse agli inizi dell'età del Ferro sembra pertanto direttamente connessa con l'approdo, forse in funzione più della pesca che degli scambi marittimi. Per quest'ultimo aspetto poteva eventualmente essere avvantaggiato un abitato protostorico ipotizzabile sul vicino promontorio di Punta Penna, sede di importanti centri di età italica, romana e medievale, in posizione di controllo sulla sottostante insenatura che costituisce ancor oggi il miglior approdo naturale della costa abruzzese meridionale.

Nonostante le carenze delle ricerche svolte negli insediamenti dell'età del Bronzo lungo la fascia costiera adriatica, i rinvenimenti di Punta Aderci, pur nella ridotta consistenza dell'abitato, confermano l'importanza della regione nello svolgimento di traffici terrestri e marittimi, dei quali la migliore testimonianza a noi pervenuta è rappresentata dalla ceramica figulina dipinta iapigia.

Bibliografia

AA.VV. 1991. *La ceramica attica figurata nelle Marche*, Castelferretti.

Alfieri, N. 1975. In AA.VV., *Introduzione alle antichità adriatiche*, Chieti, 83-90.

Annibaldi, G. 1965. 'Fermo', in *E.A.A.*, III, 625.

Arias, C. 1965. 'Resti di un villaggio piceno a Martinsicuro (Teramo)', *Atti della Società Toscana di Scienze Naturali*, S.A., 72, 287-298.

Bacchielli, L. 1985. 'Domus Veneris quam dorica sustinet Ancon', *Archeologia Classica*, XXXVII, 106-137.

Bermond Montanari, G. 1981. In *La Romagna tra VI e IV secolo*, Bologna, 12.

Bermond Montanari, G. 1987. 'Ravenna', in AA.VV., *La formazione della città in Emilia Romagna*, Bologna, 377-382.

Bermond Montanari, G. 1990. 'Demografia del territorio nella pre-protostoria e la prima fase insediativa a Ravenna', in AA.VV., *Storia di Ravenna*, I, 31-47.

Braccesi, L. 1977. *Grecità adriatica*, Bologna.

Brecciaroli Taborelli, L. 1983. 'Saggio di applicazione della tipologia Morel. L'officina di Aesis', *Opus*, II, 1, 291-295.

Faustoferri, A. 1991. 'I rapporti con l'Apulia: la ceramica di argilla depurata', in AA.VV., *Samnium, Archeologia del Molise*, Roma, 72-75.

Gentili, G.V. 1985. 'Testimonianze villanoviane e estruscoidi a Verucchio', in AA.VV., *La formazione della città in Emilia Romagna*, Bologna, 207-218.

Gentili, G.V. 1990. *Osimo nell'antichità*, Bologna.

Gros, P. & Torelli, M. 1988. *Storia dell'urbanistica. Il mondo romano*, Bari, 138-139.

Landolfi, M. 1985. 'Presenze galliche nel Piceno a Sud del fiume Esino', in AA.VV., *Celti ed Etruschi nell'Italia centro settentrionale dal V secolo a.C. alla romanizzazione*, Bologna, 443-468.

Landolfi, M. 1987. 'I traffici con la Grecia e la ceramica attica come elemento del processo di maturazione urbana della civiltà picena', in AA.VV., *La formazione della città in Emilia Romagna*, II, Bologna, 187-199.

Lollini, D.G. 1956. 'L'abitato preistorico e protostorico di Ancona', *Bollettino Palentologia Italiana*, LXV, 237-262.

Lollini, D. 1976. 'La civiltà picena', in AA.VV., *Popoli e civiltà dell'Italia antica*, V, Roma.

Luni, M. 1981. 'Nuove tracce della frequentazione greca in Adriatico occidentale e riconoscimento dello scalo marittimo greco di S. Marina di Focara', *Rendiconti della Accademia dei Lincei*, XXXVI, 45-76.

Luni, M. 1982-1983. 'Resti di abitato preromano a Pesaro', *Studia Oliveriana*, n.s. II-III, 7-18.

Luni, M. 1984. 'Topografia storica di Pisaurum e del territorio', in AA.VV., *Pesaro nell'antichità*, Venezia, 108-180.

Luni, M. 1984-1986. 'Nuovi documenti sulla Flaminia dall'Appennino alla costa adriatica', *Atti e Memorie della Deputazione Storia Patria - Marche*, 89-91, 169-180.

Luni, M. 1988. 'Intervento di Augusto nel tratto di Flaminia sul versante adriatico', *Rendiconti della Accademia dei Lincei*, XLIII, 235-247.

Luni, M. 1991. 'Pesaro', in AA.VV., *La ceramica attica figurata nelle Marche*, Ancona, 68-70.

Luni, M. 1992. 'Ceramica attica nelle Marche settentrionali e direttrici commerciali', in AA.VV., *La civiltà picena nelle Marche*, Ripatransone, 331-363.

Luni, M. 1993. 'Le origini di Urvinum Mataurense. Dall'insediamento protostorico all'oppidum romano', in *Studi in onore di P. Zampetti*, Ancona (in stampa).

Luni, M., Biocco, E. & Marchegiani, P. 1991. 'Matelica', in *Bibliografia Topografica della Colonizzazione Greca in Italia*, Pisa-Roma, 485–491.

Luni, M. & Marchegiani, P. 1992. 'Montarice', in *Bibliografia Topografica della Colonizzazione Greca in Italia*, Pisa-Roma, 252–257.

Luni, M. & Marchegiani, P. 1993. 'Osimo', in *Bibliografia Topografica della Colonizzazione Greca in Italia*, Pisa-Roma, (in stampa).

Maioli, M.G. 1980. 'Per la storia di Rimini nel V e nel IV secolo a.C., in AA.VV., *Analisi di Rimini antica. Storia e archeologia per un museo*, Rimini, 83–85.

Maioli, M.G. 1987a. 'Resti di insediamento presso l'ex convento di S. Francesco', in AA.VV., *La formazione della città in Emilia Romagna*, Bologna, II, 404–408.

Maioli, M.G. 1987b. 'Resti di un insediamento preromano a Rimini: lo scavo dell'ex convento di S. Francesco. Relazione preliminare', in AA.VV., *Celti ed Etruschi nell'Italia centro-settentrionale dal V secolo a.C. alla romanizzazione*, Bologna, 381–392.

Massei, L. 1976. 'Presenza siceliota alla foce del Po', *Archeologia Classica*, 69–80.

Megna, A.M. 1990. 'Ipotesi per una ricostruzione del piano programmatico di Aesis', in AA.VV., *Le Marche. Archeologia storia territorio*, Fano, 41–95.

Mercando, L. 1986. 'L'ellenismo nel Piceno', in AA.VV., *Hellenismus in Mittelitalien*, Göttingen, 160–218.

Mori, G. & Tozzi, C. 1970. 'Resti di un insediamento piceno al Colle del Telegrafo a Pescara', *Atti della Società Toscana di Scienze Naturali*, S.A., 77, 217–230.

Moscatelli, V. 1987. 'Materiali per la topografia storica di Potentia', in *Miscellanea in onore di F. Allevi*, Agugliano, 429–438.

Napolitani, G. 1907. *Fermo nel Piceno*, Roma.

Ortalli, J. 1987. 'Le statue in marmo (di Covignano)', in AA.VV., *La formazione della città in Emilia Romagna*, Bologna, 306–309.

Ortalli, J. 1987. 'Sarsina', in AA.VV., *La formazione della città in Emilia Romagna*, Bologna, 392–396.

Ortolani, M. & Alfieri, N. 1953. 'Sena Gallica', *Rendiconti della Accademia dei Lincei*, VIII, 152–180.

Östenberg, C.E. 1975. *Case etrusche di Acquarossa*, Roma, 16.

Panvini Rosati, F. 1974. 'Monetazione preromana sulla costa italiana', *Rivista Italiana di Numismatica*, XII, 86.

Percossi, E. 1985. 'Insediamenti nel territorio di Recanati', *Picus*, V, 99–135.

Percossi, E. 1990. 'Porto Recanati (Mc)', *Bollettino Archeologico*, III, 51–55.

Percossi, E. 1991. 'Porto Recanati: area archeologica di Potentia', in M. Luni (a cura di), *Scavi e ricerche nelle Marche*, Urbino, 58–59.

Polverini, L., Parise, N.F., Agostini, S. & Pasquinucci, M. 1987. *Firmun Picenum*, I, Pisa.

Radmilli, A. M 1977. *Storia dell'Abruzzo dalle origini all'età del Bronzo*, Pisa.

Radmilli, A. M. 1979. 'Fonte Tasca', *R.S.P.*, XXXIV, 324–325.

Radmilli, A. M. 1980. 'Fonte Tasca', *R.S.P.*, XXXV, 390–391.

Radmilli, A. M. 1981. 'Archi', *R.S.P.*, XXXVI, 340–341.

Riccioni, G. 1970. 'Antefatti della colonizzazione di Ariminum alla luce delle nuove scoperte', in AA.VV, *La città etrusca e italica preromana*, Bologna, 263–273.

Riccioni, G. 1987. 'Rimini. Gli antefatti protostorici', in AA.VV, *La formazione della città in Emilia Romagna*, Bologna, 397–404.

Scarpellini, D. 1981. In AA.VV., *La Romagna fra VI e IV secolo*, Bologna, 295–296, 328, 340.

Schmiedt, G. 1978. 'I porti italiani nell'alto medioevo', in AA.VV., *La navigazione mediterranea nell'alto medioevo*, Spoleto, 212–220.

Sommella, P. 1988. *L'Italia antica. L'urbanistica romana*, Roma, 72–73.

Stefanini, S. 1991. 'La città romana di Sena Gallica', in AA.VV., *Archeologia delle valli marchigiane. Misa Nevola e Cesano*, Perugia, 141–159.

Traina, G. & Massei, L. 1984. 'Ancona', in *Bibliografia Topografica della Colonizzazione Greca in Italia*, Pisa-Roma, 232–242.

Virzì, R. 1986. 'Recenti scoperte nelle province di Ancona e Macerata', in *Le strade nelle Marche. Il problema nel tempo*, (Atti Conv. Fano-Fabriano-Pesaro-Ancona, 1984), Urbino, 353–354.

Vitali, D. 1991. 'Monte Bibele', in *L'alma mater e l'antico. Scavi dell'Istituto di Archeologia*, Bologna, 22–31.

Von Eles Masi, P. 1981. In *La Romagna tra VI e IV secolo a.C.*, Bologna.

Zuffa, M. 1962. 'Nuove scoperte di archeologia e storia riminese', *S.R.*, XIII, 85–132.

Zuffa, M. 1969. 'Nuovi dati per la protostoria della Romagna orientale', in *Atti Memorie della Deputazione Storia Patria-Romagna*, XX, 99–124.

Zuffa, M. 1970. 'Abitati e santuari suburbani di Rimini dalla protostoria alla romanità', in AA.VV., *La città etrusca e italica preromana*, Bologna, 299–315.

Zuffa, M. 1978. 'La tutela, la ricerca e l'organizzazione archeologica a Rimini dal 1800 ad oggi', in AA.VV., *Storia di Rimini dal 1800 ai nostri giorni*, III, Rimini, 171–264.

Zuffa, M. 1979. In *I Galli e l'Italia. Catalogo della mostra*, Roma, 154–155, n. 21.

51

La Nascita della Città in Abruzzo: Tradizioni, Insediamenti e Nuovi Modelli (IV–I sec. a.C.)

ADELE CAMPANELLI

(Soprintendenza Archeologica dell'Abruzzo)

Sommario: *Nuovi dati sull'organizzazione urbana di centri la cui data di inizio tradizionale viene posta dopo la guerra sociale invitano a ripensare al fenomeno dell'urbanizzazione nella regione dell'Abruzzo, analizzando i dati archeologici nel complesso del panorama generale sopratutto nei casi di* Superaequum, Marruvium, Lucus Angitiae, Corfinium *e* Teate Marrucinorum. *Tracce di abitazioni con pavimenti databili al II sec. a.C. emergono dagli scavi nei centri urbani in coordinamento con strade e santuari riferibili ad epoche anche più antiche e in alcuni casi con cinte urbane 'poligonali'.*

INTRODUZIONE

Recenti acquisizioni archeologiche relative a scavi condotti nel sito di alcune città romane d'Abruzzo contribuiscono alla rilettura del processo di urbanizzazione delle aree medioitaliche in diretta connessione col fenomeno della municipalizzazione post-guerra sociale. E' stato autorevolmente affermato (La Regina 1970: 191) che il lento processo di inurbamento prese le mosse anche in area abruzzese dalle trasformazioni economiche che nell'ambito del II secolo a.C. videro il formarsi di nuovi ceti abbienti, sia con i profitti dei cambiamenti nell'organizzazione dell'agricoltura italica tradizionale, sia in conseguenza della grande espansione del commercio italico in Oriente e in Occidente (Gabba 1972: 74).

Inoltre la sempre più profonda integrazione tra i Romani ed alleati favorita dai contatti diretti durante le campagne di guerra, da alleanze matrimoniali e, non da ultimo, dalla presenza sul territorio delle colonie latine strutturate ad immagine di Roma, dovette portare senza dubbio alla diffusione e alla penetrazione della cultura urbana in Abruzzo. Prova di questa permeabilità agli influssi romani, non solo nelle aree dove la presenza diretta è sicuramente all'origine del fenomeno, è la diffusione delle imitazioni dell'artigianato artistico ceramico, fittile, della moneta romana, delle tecniche costruttive e delle pratiche funerarie.

E' probabile, come da più parti del resto acclarato, che nell'organizzazione che seguì la guerra sociale vennero municipalizzate entità già in corso di urbanizzazione la cui definitiva sistemazione urbanistica trovò forma compiuta in età giulio-claudia.

Siano essi originati da *vici* preminenti sull'*hinterland* paganico o da santuari tribali attorno ai quali si era sviluppato un abitato organizzato sembra, sulla base delle acquisizioni archeologiche degli ultimi dieci anni, di poter affermare che nessuno dei siti municipalizzati dopo la guerra sociale esaminato qui di seguito manchi di tracce di precedenti impianti. Anche se non è possibile definire città questi embrioni urbani perché non ne sono chiari tutti gli elementi qualificanti (quali soprattutto le mura), tuttavia è perseguibile un'ipotesi di lavoro che interpreti alcuni dati omogenei emersi per lo più in scavi di emergenza.

Inoltre la revisione tuttora in corso, di monumenti e materiali archeologici da tempo scavati, ha condotto alla formulazione di una prospettiva storica che tenta di inquadrare in un più equilibrato rapporto le entità urbane, riconosciute anche dalle fonti, con il fiorire dei grandi santuari federali, testimonianza di un'esperienza architettonica e costruttiva di notevole impegno e del tutto analoga alle zone limitrofe campane e latine cui non si disconosce la realtà di città già nel III e II secolo a.C.

Lungi dal negare il protrarsi, documentato fino all'età imperiale, delle strutture amministrative legate all'organizzazione paganico-vicana, profondamente radicate nella realtà economica abruzzese, anche in presenza di nuclei urbani preminenti, si tenta in questa sede di documentare l'esistenza di forme embrionali di città prima dell'organizzazione municipale.

MARRUVIUM

Uno dei siti sul quale è stata già affermata la probabilità

di un preesistente insediamento è *Marruvium* (Letta 1988: 225), il principale centro dei Marsi. L'assetto definitivo, cui non fu certamente estraneo il console del 33 d.C. *Octavius Laenas*, discendente di un quattuorviro locale attivo nel I secolo a.C., ricordato per aver costruito le strade, venne comunque raggiunto dopo la metà del I secolo d.C. Tuttavia il nome, legato alla formazione di leggende in età anteriore alla guerra sociale, è certamente preromano, e sarei propensa a credere connesso con il sito della futura città romana. L'esistenza di *Marruvium* per lo meno nella II metà del II secolo a.C., è documentata dalla dedica di spoglie provenienti dalla presa di Cartagine da parte di Scipione Emiliano ai Marsi, rifacimento adrianeo di un originale del II secolo a.C. (Letta & d'Amato 1975: 71).

Inoltre solo una preesistenza di qualche entità urbana giustificherebbe la scelta di posizionare il *municipium* in posizione decentrata rispetto alla via Valeria sulla riva del lago Fucino.

A questi vanno aggiunti altri dati archeologici come la dislocazione delle aree sepolcrali utilizzate dal IV secolo all'età romana a N dell'attuale sito di San Benedetto dei Marsi sul tracciato della Valeria, probabilmente in relazione ad un ponte sul Giovenco, e lungo la viabilità circumlacuale, e la presenza nella maggior parte dei saggi di scavo di ceramica d'impasto, di aes rude nonchè di un triente della serie fusa con i tipi dell'*oinochoe* al D/ e il corno dell'abbondanza al R/, combinazione inedita nel panorama delle emissioni del III secolo a.C..

Tralasciando il problema della localizzazione e della diffusione delle emissioni di aes grave di zecche dell'Italia Centrale, questo dato va posto in relazione con il rinvenimento in un'area prossima all'incrocio della via lungo il lago con la viabilità proveniente da NE della dedica del III secolo a.C. agli dei Novensides (Letta 1988: 230).

E' in quest'area, a cui è rimasto il toponimo di Civita, che probabilmente si sviluppò un abitato coordinato con l'incrocio della viabilità territoriale, orientamento poi ripreso nella fase municipale. In quest'ottica vanno forse letti i lacerti di pavimenti e muri da poco emersi e non ancora indagati a N in via Piave. In una trincea per la posa in opera di infrastrutture moderne sono venuti alla luce due ambienti pavimentati con un mosaico col motivo cd. a canestro ed intersezioni di tessere irregolari di pietre policrome e l'altra con un pavimento in elementi fittili romboidali di varie gradazioni di rosso: lontana imitazione del diffuso motivo di orgine ellenistica dei cubi prospettici (Campanelli 1995). Potendo porre, anche se in via del tutto provvisoria, questo complesso tra la fine del II e l'inizio del I secolo a.C., avremmo in realtà la documentazione di una domus coordinata all'impianto post-guerra sociale che va a raccordarsi ai due complessi rinvenuti durante gli scavi degli anni '80 (Sommella 1985: 371), l'uno in loc. Civita con pavimenti in signino rosso con inserzione di tesserine bianche formanti losanghe e battuti bianchi con *crustae* policrome, l'altro identificabile come portico con fascia mosaicata e campo in cocciopisto con inserzione di tesserine romboidali disposte su file parallele, di epoca leggermente successiva, tutti e due inquadrabili nell'ambito della *civitas foederata* anteriore il 90 a.C. o subito dopo.

L'urbanizzazione raggiunse il suo apice nella prima metà del I secolo d.C. con la programmazione di vie e infrastrutture idriche, dovute abbiamo visto ad Ottavio Laena e con la costruzione dei grandi monumenti pubblici, teatro, anfiteatro, basilica, tempio dell'area forense, oltre alle notevoli *domus* con affreschi e pavimenti in mosaici policromi emersi un po' dovunque nell'ambito della città antica.

AMITERNUM E PELTUINUM

Nel comprensorio sabino *Amiternum* fu la città principale conquistata nel 293 a.C. e dal 290 a.C. *civitas sine suffragio*. Purtroppo ancora oggi non abbiamo documentazione della fase di istituzione della *praefectura* anche se l'esistenza di una classe locale ricca nel II secolo a.C. sembra non discutibile (Segenni 1985: 78). Più a S i territori a destra e a sinistra dell'Aterno venivano amministrati da altre due *praefecturae*: *Aveia* e *Peltuinum*. Per *Aveia* è già stata ipotizzata e in qualche modo documentata l'esistenza del centro murato (organizzato in isolati regolari sulla base del rapporto 2:3) già nel II secolo a.C., in virtù della precoce romanizzazione avvenuta in concomitanza con le assegnazioni viritarie (La Torre 1985: 169).

Peltuinum invece conserva scarse tracce dell'impianto urbano precedente la guerra sociale, che doveva sorgere lungo un percorso di antica tradizione pastorale poi utilizzato come tracciato della via Claudia Nova, in connessione con un santuario di Apollo, di cui si è rinvenuta un'epigrafe con dedica APELLUNE riutilizzata in una taberna ancora in uso nel IV secolo d.C. (Sommella 1995: 284) e resti consistenti dell'area sacra precedente la fase augustea (scavi Campanelli 1994).

CORFINIUM

In area peligna è *Corfinium* il centro di più antica tradizione insediativa. Ai margini del pianoro occupato poi dalla città del I secolo, la necropoli fittamente utilizzata ha restituito sepolture dal V secolo a.C. sino all'età romana (Van Wonterghem 1974: 643; scavi D'Ercole 1994).

Il cambiamento delle tradizioni insediamentali e l'ipotetico formarsi dell'entità urbana scelta come capitale dagli Italici e ricordata, insieme a *Sulmo*, da Strabone come città in mezzo ad una popolazione che abitava in villaggi, dovette avvenire durante il II secolo a.C. La lenta opera di romanizzazione cominciata nel IV secolo a.C. è documentabile con l'uso di suppellettile di imitazione della vernice nera rinvenuta nelle numerosissime tombe a grotticella tipiche dell'area peligna nell'età ellenistica.

La città nata probabilmente nel V secolo a.C., come molti centri in analoghe situazioni topografiche, da un insediamento *inter amnas* posto su un'arce fortificata naturalmente e rafforzata da opere poligonali dovette espandersi, probabilmente nel II secolo a.C., lungo le due direttrici divergenti della via di Pratola e via Poppedio, su antichi percorsi ripresi nel secondo caso dal tracciato della via Valeria che entrava in città nell'odierno sito della Madonna di Loreto. La porta d'accesso ha lasciato nel classico ideogramma a zampa di gallina una prova indiretta. I due orientamenti sono del resto ben visibili anche all'interno del borgo medievale dove il teatro (datato ai primi anni del I secolo d.C.) segue l'orientamento della via Valeria mentre la spina del borgo è sull'asse della via di Pratola che cambia direzione verso S in corrispondenza del presunto sito di un'altra porta. Su questo tracciato extraurbano è la necropoli più frequentata della *Corfinium* italica, ellenistica e romana. Gli scavi della città romana in corso hanno finora documentato le fasi più propriamente imperiali e in un saggio appena intrapreso è stato individuato, nell'area del presunto foro, un ambiente adiacente ad un'area pavimentata a grosse lastre con muri in opera incerta e pavimenti in mosaico col motivo cd. a canestro. Relativo alla fase del II sec. a.C. è il santuario di S. Ippilito, in corso di scavo, dedicato ad Ercole.

Superaequum

L'unico centro in cui è invece possibile a tutt'oggi leggere un rifacimento integrale della pianificazione urbana pur in presenza di un precedente indigeno è *Superaequum*. Recenti scavi programmati sulla base di una lunga serie di ritrovamenti casuali hanno consentito di delineare meglio il quadro topografico di *Superaequum, municipium* peligno della Valle Subequana (Van Wonterghem 1984: 75).

La città romana fu organizzata in una pianura intervalliva delimitata a N e a S da due corsi d'acqua: il Rio S. Marino e il Rio S. Agata, conosciuta col toponimo di Macrano, ai piedi dell' attuale centro di Castelvecchio Subequo. Il sito già noto nel XVII secolo ha restituito una notevole quantità di documenti epigrafici e di materiale archeologico ascrivibile, per la maggior parte, al periodo giulio-claudio (Buonocore 1989: 116).

Il sistema insediamentale della Valle Subequana, caratterizzato dai siti fortificati attestati sulle quote più alte intorno ai 1000 metri nelle età del bronzo e del ferro, dovette, già nell'ambito del V secolo a.C. essere attratto nel fondovalle da motivi anche di ordine commerciale sviluppando una serie di agglomerati urbani intorno a santuari e sorgenti ed in connessione con la rete viaria di collegamento con Roma e con la Valle dell'Aterno. La rete distributiva dell'organizzazione paganico-vicana che ha la sua più antica attestazione in quest'area nel II secolo a.C. è più o meno coincidente con la distribuzione dei comuni attuali (Mattiocco 1984: 9).

Certamente la fase augustea rappresentò il momento in cui *Superaequum* ebbe il maggior impulso edilizio. Ciò è documentato da varie epigrafi che si riferiscono a opere edilizie compiute nella prima età imperiale come la lastricatura di una strada ad opera dei cinque liberti addetti alla *cura viarum* del *municipium*, dal famoso testo di Q. Ottavio Sagitta (Buonocore 1989: 112) che parla di *sacrae basilicae, forum et viam ad templum Romae et Augusti* degli anni precedenti il 14 d.C. e sempre in età augustea l'iscrizione del magistrato Tito Pompullio Lappa che fece costruire per disposizione testamentaria un mercato coperto destinato alle vendite all'asta e agli appalti (Van Wonterghem 1984: 83).

Le fonti epigrafiche concordano con le evidenze archeologiche emerse in questi ultimi anni quando sono stati individuati resti consistenti di costruzioni pubbliche realizzate in opera reticolata e finemente decorati da intonaci dipinti e pavimenti mosaicati, tra le quali una *porticus* con almeno due fasi costruttive. Lo scavo degli strati profondi inglobati nelle fondazioni ha restituito, coperti da uno strato contenente frammenti di ceramica a vernice nera e d'impasto dell'età del ferro, muri a grossi ciottoli non legati da malta con andamento diverso dalle strutture di età romana. Dell'alzato in mattoni crudi si sono rinvenute labili tracce in corso di scavo.

La ricerca archeologica del 1990 ha individuato un ambiente di vaste dimensioni pavimentato con un mosaico col motivo delle stelle di otto rombi. In posizione eccentrica, racchiuso entro un motivo a treccia policroma a due capi, è un emblema in opus sectile realizzato con piastrelle in marmo giallo antico legate da listelli di cipollino, come bordo esterno del tappeto musivo e bordura dell'emblema è il motivo delle pelte nere.

Sigillate dal mosaico, ma visibili nel taglio operato nei lavori edili che hanno originato il rinvenimento, sono leggibili alcune buche con materiale eneolitico.

Parzialmente inglobati nel muro di fondo del portico sono state rinvenute tracce di un muro in ciottoli della fase arcaica, coordinato ortogonalmente al muro già rinvenuto nel 1984. A N e a S del muro di fondo del portico sono stati scavati due gruppi rispettivamente di sei e quattro ollette del tipo in uso nel IV e III secolo a.C. Gli elementi archeologici sembrerebbero definire dunque un'area pubblica costruita nel corso del I secolo d.C. caratterizzata da un'ampia aula monumentale aperta su un portico. Alle spalle, ma in connessione, era un altro edificio che raccordava quote diverse e doveva funzionare come portico.

Inoltre è stata individuata una frequentazione della valletta di Macrano documentabile sin dalle fasi eneolitiche (III millennio) (D'Ercole 1988: 408). In una fase successiva coincidente con l'età del bronzo e del ferro, quando la vocazione insediamentale preferì i siti di fondovalle, i muri a ciottoli con alzato in mattoni crudi documentano un'organizzazione degli spazi di cui non conosciamo ancora il disegno complessivo. Le tombe della loc. Il Passatore (VI-V secolo a.C.) marcano il confine tra la città dei vivi e quella dei morti.

In connessione con questo abitato va posto, almeno a partire dal II secolo a.C., un santuario di *Hercules Victor* localizzato vicino ad una copiosa sorgente sul luogo della chiesa medioevale di S. Agata. Qui più che altrove si ha la sensazione che la struttura paganica non abbia prodotto un centro preminente rispetto agli altri, anche se l'occupazione di Macrano iniziata nel V secolo a.C. con la decadenza del centro fortificato di Forca Caruso, sembra costituire la continuità abitativa di un gruppo egemone assai numeroso (ca. 300 sepolture individuate in un arco dall'VIII al V secolo a.C.) che controllando il valico prima e poi la conca, mantiene la sua sfera di influenza sull'intera Valle Subequana.

Teate

Lo scavo che da anni la Soprintendenza conduce sulle pendici dell'acropoli dove in età giulio-claudia fu eretto l'anfiteatro (Campanelli 1984), ha consentito la reinterpretazione di uno strano edificio ancora in vista nel secolo scorso ed identificato fantasiosamente con il *ludus gladiatorum* in relazione con la vicinanza al teatro, ancora spesso confuso con l'anfiteatro (De Chiara 1887). In realtà ciò che rimane di quell'edificio è il livello di fondazioni in calcestruzzo azzerato volontariamente nel momento in cui venne trasformata la pendice collinare per adattarla al complesso terrazzato di età tardo-repubblicana di cui restan tracce della *porticus* ad 'L'. La presenza del deposito votivo delle terrecotte architettoniche, rinvenuto nel 1965 nell'area, chiarisce la funzione del sito.

La difficoltosa interpretazione dei resti di fondazione totalmente privi di stratigrafie archeologiche asportate durante il grande stravolgimento che la Civitella ha subito soprattutto nel secolo scorso quando è stata trasformata in Piazza d'Armi, non può non tener conto della destinazione cultuale. In realtà è possibile l'identificazione con l'impianto di un complesso templare di almeno tre edifici di diversa dimensione di cui si conservano due frontoni leggibili quasi interamente (Campanelli 1994: 146). Le terrecotte architettoniche del deposito votivo della Civitella sono databili al momento di strutturazione dell'area sacra avvenuto in occasione del progetto di gusto ellenistico nell'ambito della I metà del II sec. a.C.

I più stretti confronti dei materiali di rivestimento fittile di Chieti sono con quelli di Luni, Cosa, Ardea e Roma. Il complesso, ora in corso di studio delinea un quadro di rapporti culturali soprattutto con Roma e con gli ambienti coloniali già molto attivo nel II secolo a.C. Frammenti di elementi decorativi del tutto analoghi e in alcuni casi anche della stessa matrice sono stati rinvenuti negli sterri eseguiti agli inizi del secolo nell'area intorno ai cd. Tempietti, identificata come zona forense.

Questo dato va posto in relazione con le strutture in opera quadrata visibili sotto l'impianto templare giulio-claudio. La fondazione, in alcuni casi emergente di queste mura in opera quadrata, è della stessa tecnica di quelle presenti sulla Civitella nel cd. edificio De Chiara per le quali possiamo dunque immaginare un alzato analogo.

Anche in questo caso va considerato il dato indiretto della localizzazione delle aree necropolari rinvenute in località S. Anna e Villa Comunale; nella via Orientale e nelle vicinanze della porta medioevale (zona Mater Domini) di uscita dalla città verso l'entroterra, in direzione della Majella, tutte utilizzate tra il IV secolo e l'età tardorepubblicana.

I villaggi protostorici documentati sin dagli inizi del primo millennio a.C. (D'Ercole 1990: 73) localizzati sulle alture devono aver dato luogo, in un momento non ancora precisato, ad un unico insediamento avente come fulcro la valle, poi occupata dal foro, sede di un santuario connesso con un pozzo sacro e l'acropoli della Civitella. La similitudine tra i materiali rinvenuti nei due siti fa pensare che i due complessi sacri abbiano avuto una fase di rivestimento architettonica del tutto analoga durante il II secolo a.C.

Prende forma dunque un insediamento abitato sicuramente nel III-II secolo a.C. caratterizzato dal passaggio della viabilità di crinale di tradizione indigena su cui si attestano due complessi cultuali di notevole impegno costruttivo e significato culturale quali le strutture in opera quadrata connesse con i cd. tempietti e il complesso sacro sull'Acropoli terrazzato in età tardo-repubblicana. I limiti dell'area abitata sono definiti dalla presenza delle necropoli coeve.

La committenza di questi complessi decorativi fa parte di una comunità fortemente radicata nell'esperienza ellenistica recepita solo formalmente a livello artistico locale. Le scelte artistiche e ideologiche riflettono il gusto eclettico delle classi emergenti profondamente influenzate dalla cultura urbana. In un'ipotesi suggestiva si potrebbe immaginare che tra i Marrucini coinvolti nelle operazioni di evergetismo di età repubblicana vi fossero gli *Asinii*, in prima linea come i *Vettii Scatones* e i *Poppaedi Silones,* Marsi nella rivolta del 90 a.C. D'altra parte, come acutamente osservato (Torelli 1982: 199), la precoce apparizione della *gens Asinia* nel senato romano non può avere un'origine legata unicamente alla strategia politica.

Il pendant topografico di *Teate*, a controllo dei territori della riva opposta dell'*Aternum* in area Vestina doveva essere *Pinna* che ora comincia a restituire le tracce dei più antichi edifici repubblicani.

INTERAMNIA

Meno controversa sembra essere l'esistenza di un insediamento protourbano precedente la *Interamnia* romana. Le fonti individuano chiaramente le fasi amministrative del *conciliabulum*, del *municipium* e della *colonia*. Era già stato notato che l'impianto urbano con isolati di 270 × 200 piedi romani delimitato ad O da una cinta muraria in opera quadrata, era per analogia con altri centri, ipotizzabile nell'ambito del II secolo a.C. (Migliorati 1976: 255).

Recenti interventi d'urgenza hanno riportato alla luce ambienti con mura in opera incerta, pavimenti in cocciopesto con motivo a crocette, in signino rosso con inserimento di scaglie bianche disposte su assi trasversali e di un interessante tipo a piccoli sassolini con fascia perimetrale mosaicata. Inoltre coordinata con questi resti di abitazioni è stata rinvenuta una strada glareata (Staffa 1990: 20). Dunque, questo da poco emerso, sembra essere l'aspetto del primo impianto urbano di *Interamnia* nel momento in cui era definita *conciliabulum*, leggermente divergente dagli orientamenti della città dell'età imperiale.

DISCUSSIONE

Il quadro che si è delineato sulla base di esempi selezionati in connessione con la nuova acquisizione di dati archeologici se non desta particolari problemi nei casi delle *praefecturae* vestine (per non parlare delle colonie latine di cui infatti non è stata fatta menzione) e di Teramo chiarisce forse in parte quel rapporto tra insediamenti e municipalità dei centri che si mantennero nella condizione di *civitates foederatae* fino al 90 a.C.

L'assenza di un'ingerenza diretta di Roma crea non pochi problemi nella comprensione dei momenti di inizio del processo di urbanizzazione e dell'autorità che la presiedette nonchè dei modelli utilizzabili per la pianificazione urbanistica.

Tuttavia non va sottaciuto il notevole grado di organizzazione amministrativa, di esperienza architettonica e abilità edificatoria documentato nei santuari maggiori dell'area medio-italica, nè la penetrazione di prodotti artigianali o di imitazione diffusi senza particolari differenze in tutte le aree dove era posizionato un centro urbano di rilievo (*Marruvium, Corfinium, Teate, Interamnia*), fatti che hanno un loro preciso parallelo nella circolazione monetaria (Campanelli & Catalli 1983).

E' anche da immaginare che la presenza delle colonie latine abbia favorito il processo di romanizzazione anche nei suoi aspetti insediamentali favorendo il passaggio da situazioni abitative come quella documentata a *Superaequum* a nuclei protourbani organizzati sugli assi di attraversamento tradizionali, nonchè la diffusione degli schemi programmatici.

Il recepimento di modelli culturali e dei modi di vita romani sembrerebbe poter avere come possibile fossile-guida l'associazione di muri in opera incerta con i cd. *scutulata pavimenta* dei tipi noti a Roma e a Pompei già alla metà del II secolo a.C.

L'aggancio cronologico locale è a tutt'oggi puntualizzato nel pavimento rinvenuto nei giardini dell'Arcivescovado di Atri sovrapposto ad un altro in signino con motivo a torri e arco voltato coerente quest'ultimo con la fondazione coloniale del 289 a.C. (Azzena 1987: 51). Il secondo pavimento è caratterizzato da un bordo di mosaico a canestro con *crustae* marmoree e campitura interna a ciottoli di fiume spaccati e levigati e tessere irregolari di vario colore. Termine *postquem* di datazione del complesso riutilizzato come fornace in età rinascimentale è il riempimento contenuto tra i due pavimenti costituito da uno scarico omogeneo di forme di vernice nera, probabilmente pertinenti allo scarico di una fornace, databile tra il III-II secolo a.C..

Se queste *domus* caratterizzate da pavimenti in signino decorato, battuti con *crustae* marmoree, *scutulata* e muri in opera incerta, potessero essere considerate le case dei ceti emergenti italici in possesso di notevoli fortune economiche e di una cultura fortemente ellenizzata che non è più plausibile immaginare residenti nelle case di terra di tradizione sannita, avremmo la possibilità di riequilibrare un quadro storico costituito da santuari, necropoli, artigianato artistico e nuclei urbani con una continuità insediativa che nell'evoluzione completa possiamo immaginare esemplificata da *Antinum* dove alla cinta volsca (del V secolo a.C.) seguì il *municipium* senza soluzione di continuità o di *Lucus Angitiae* la cui cinta muraria molto simile a quella primitiva di Alba e forse coeva doveva racchiudere una città organizzata sulle terrazze, ancora riconoscibili, intorno al tempio e al bosco sacro di Angitia ben prima dell'istituzione municipale (Campanelli 1995: 360).

Questa tendenza all'urbanismo frutto non del potere romano ma di scelte programmatiche autonome influenzate dalla cultura urbana, seleziona i siti emergenti nell'*hinterland* paganico già abitati o frequentati per motivi diversi: da quelli cultuali a quelli più specificamente economici.

I dati acquisiti nel corso delle ricerche archeologiche degli ultimi dieci anni – in parte qui presentati – incrociati con la ricognizione delle aree centuriate contribuiscono alla definizione dell'inizio del ruolo delle città d'Abruzzo nel corso dei secoli, puntualizzando le fasi cronologiche e i modi di occupazione di un territorio la cui vocazione insediamentale tradizionale in abitati sparsi ha prodotto in precise condizioni economiche e storiche città del tenore de L'Aquila nell'età di Federico II.

Ringraziamenti

Questo lavoro è il frutto di molti anni di ricerche sulle città abruzzesi originate nella stragrande maggioranza dei casi da lavori d'urgenza. Ringrazio tutti i collaboratori della Soprintendenza Archeologica dell'Abruzzo: Umberto De Luca, Lucio Frati, Gino Galliani, Marcello Iannicca, Giuseppe Mancini, Lucio Patullo, Vincenzo Scarci, Silvia Serano, Vincenzo Torrieri e Mauro Vitale che hanno contribuito agli scavi, nonchè agli allievi e al prof. Paolo Sommella che hanno attivamente partecipato alle campagne di scavo di molte delle località citate nel testo. Un ringraziamento del tutto personale va al mio compagno di vita arch. Claudio Finarelli per la disponibilità e l'interesse con cui sostiene le mie ricerche.

Bibliografia

Azzena, G. 1987. *Atri. Forma e Urbanistica*. Roma.
Buonocore, M. 1989. *Superaequum*, in *Supplementa Italica*, n.s., Roma.
Campanelli, A. 1984. 'L'anfiteatro di Chieti: nuovi dati sull'urbanistica della città romana', *Quaderni dell'Istituto di Archeologia dell'Università di Chieti*, 3, 1982/83, 163 ss.
Campanelli, A. 1994. 'Le terrecotte architettoniche della Civitella di Chieti: le lastre a matrice', *Ostraka*, 111-1, 123 ss.
Campanelli, A. 1995. 'Dagli insediamenti sparsi alle città', in *Il Lago Fucino e il suo Emissario*, Pescara.
De Chiara, C. 1885. *Origini e monumenti della città di Chieti*, Chieti.
D'Ercole, V. 1988. 'Scavi e scoperte: Abruzzo', *Studi Etruschi*, LIV, 1986, 408 ss.
D'Ercole, V. 1990. 'La preistoria dal quinto al primo millenio avanti Cristo', in *Chieti e la sua provincia*, Chieti, 69 ss.
Gabba, E. 1972. 'Urbanizzazione e rinnovamenti urbanistici nell'Italia centro-meridionale del I secolo a.C.', *Studi Classici e Orientali*, XXI, 73 ss.
La Regina, A. 1970. 'Note sulla formazione dei centri urbani in area sabellica', in *Atti del Convegno di Studi sulla Città etrusca e italica preromana*, Imola, 191 ss.
La Torre, F. 1985. 'Il processo di urbanizzazione nel territorio vestino: il caso di Aveia', *Archeologia Classica* XXXVII, 154 ss.
Letta, C. 1988. '"Oppida", "vici" e "pagi" in area Marsa. L'influenza dell'ambiente naturale sulla continuità delle forme di insediamento', *Geografia e storiografia nel mondo classico*, Contributi dell'Istituto di Storia Antica, XIV, Milano, 217 ss.
Letta, C. & D'Amato, S. 1975. *Epigrafia della Regione dei Marsi*, Milano.
Mattiocco, E. 1984. 'Superaequum in piano Macrano', *Rassegna di Studi sul Territorio*, n. 7 ss.
Migliorati, L. 1976. 'Municipes et Colonii. Note di urbanistica teramana', *Archeologia Classica*, XXVIII, 242 ss.
Segenni, S. 1985. *Amiternum e il suo territorio in età romana*, Pisa.
Sommella, P. 1985. 'Centri storici e archeologia urbana in Italia. Novità dall'area mesoadriatica', in *Arqueología de las ciudades modernas superpuestas a las antiguas*, Madrid, 359 ss.
Sommella, P. 1995. 'Il culto di Apollo a Peltrinum città dei Vestini', *Mélanges Raymond Chevallier*, Caesarodunum, XXIX, 279 ss.
Staffa, A.R. 1990. 'Teramo: nuovi dati per la ricostruzione dell'assetto antico della città', *Xenia*, 19, 20 ss.
Torelli, M. 1982. 'Ascesa al Senato e rapporti con i territori d'origine: Regio IV', *Tituli*, 5, 165 ss.
Van Wonterghem, F. 1974. 'Note sulla topografia e l'urbanistica di Corfinio', *Bullettin de l'Institut historique Belge de Rome*, Miscellanea Charles Verlinden, XLIV, 641 ss.
Van Wonterghem, F. 1984. *Superaequum, Corfinium, Sulmo, Forma Italiae, Regio IV*, I, Firenze.

52

Incastellamento Urbano a Roma: Il Caso degli Orsini

Francesca Bosman

Sommario: *Il fenomeno dell'incastellamento non va ristretto esclusivamente al suo significato ormai classico di edificazione di centri fortificati accentrati sul territorio da parte dell'autorità locale, per motivi sia strategici che economici che sociali. Il termine può infatti comprendere un più vasto ventaglio di possibilità, tra cui è il cosidetto incastellamento urbano. Prendiamo qui il caso di Roma: all'interno delle mura si creano a partire dall'XI secolo, per poi raggiungere il massimo sviluppo nel XIII secolo, gruppi di potere nobiliare. Ognuna di queste famiglie, attraverso permute, compravendite e successive costruzioni ex novo, si creò dei quartieri 'privati', in posizione più o meno strategica rispetto alla topografia urbana, controllando le arterie della viabilità della città. Furono proprio le rovine degli edifici classici ad esser ristrutturate, sopraelevate da parte delle famiglie della nobiltà romana, con il risultato di vere e proprie fortezze, isole all'interno della topografia urbana. Si esamina qui in questo studio in particolare lo sviluppo del patrimonio della famiglia Orsini a Roma.*

Introduzione

Magister Gregorius, pellegrino inglese che visitò Roma nel XIII secolo, iniziando la sua descrizione della città, l'apostrofò così: "*Vehemencius igitur admirandam censeo tocius urbis inspectionem, ubi tanta seges turrium, tot aedificia palatiorum, quot nulli hominum contigit enumerare*"[1].

La stessa immagine della città emerge dalla lettura degli Statuti del 1363, dove si nota una chiara preoccupazione da parte delle autorità per la presenza di torri e fortilitia costruite dalla nobiltà romana a partire dal XII secolo, edifici che potevano facilitare la guerriglia cittadina. Nell'art.63 Lib.II dello Statuto si proibiva di gettare pietre dall'alto di torri o case più alte di sette metri e mezzo, cioè cinque palarie del senato Romano, pena la confisca dell'edificio stesso. E ancora nell'articolo 201 Lib.II si ingiungeva a tutti i baroni romani di non ospitare "*homicidas, exbanditos aut infames personas in domibus seu fortillitiis eorum*", sotto la pena di mille marchi d'argento[2].

È importante puntualizzare che torri e fortezze cittadine non vanno viste come singoli edifici disseminati nel tessuto urbano, ma come elementi facenti parte di veri e propri complessi nobiliari, progettati e organizzati per imporre e garantire il potere della famiglia proprietaria del complesso, all'interno delle mura cittadine, con tutte le implicazioni socio/economiche che tale potere comportava. Tale fenomeno era chiaramente collegato alle vicende politiche romane del XII-XIII secolo, per cui la formazione di consorterie nobiliari legate a famiglie baronali portò ad inevitabili suddivisioni e spartizioni topografiche della città stessa. Il valore politico che la torre aveva anche da un punto di vista simbolico, per la famiglia a cui apparteneva, si intravede chiaramente anche dalla lettura delle cronache duecentesche: sono indicativi per questo caso i provvedimenti presi nel 1258 dal senatore di Roma Brancaleone degli Andalò, che per limitare l'"*insolentiam et superbiam nobilium Romanorum...dirui fecit eorundem nobilium turres circiter centum et quadraginta et solo tenus complanari*"[3].

Si esaminerà in questa sede l'esempio costituito dalle fortificazioni urbane della famiglia baronale degli Orsini. È mia intenzione analizzare se vi sia stata una strategia in tutti gli acquisti e costruzioni di immobili attribuibili agli Orsini, all'interno delle mura, avvenuti tra la fine del XII e la fine del XIII secolo, e se la famiglia dimostrò di avere un progetto urbanistico nel costruire un vero e proprio sistema urbano di fortificazioni che fosse in grado di svolgere funzioni di controllo sia strategico-militare che economico.

Il patrimonio Orsini

Il patrimonio Orsini dentro Roma era costituito da quattro nuclei principali:

1) le case presso la chiesa di S.Angelo in Pescheria, nell'attuale ghetto;

2) le case strette intorno alla torre Pertundata nell'area della chiesa seicentesca di S.Carlo ai Catinari;

3) gli edifici costruiti sulle rovine del Teatro di Pompeo, che nel medioevo era definito *Trullum*, intorno alla torre detta Arpacasa;

4) il complesso di Monte Giordano nel rione Ponte.

Il nucleo di S.Angelo in Pescheria venne acquistato per la maggior parte nel 1271: il 16 marzo di quest'anno Giacomo di Napoleone e Matteo Orso Orsini comprarono da Giovanni Cintii 18 domus, una casa di cinque palarie, i ruderi di alcune torri poste ai piedi dell'edificio detto "v*asca et tino*", una torre detta Baroncina, ed alcuni casalina. Tutti situati tra la chiesa di S.Salvatore dei Baroncini e la Maxima, nella regione di S.Angelo [4]. La chiesa di S.Salvatore dei Baroncini, demolita nel 1657 da Alessandro VII, era situata nell'attuale via del portico d'Ottavia, presso la piazza Giudea[5], mentre con Maxima si volevano indicare i resti ancora visibili nel XIII secolo, sempre in via del Portico d'Ottavia, delle *porticus Maximae*, portici di età classica, che attraversando tutto il Campo Marzio, collegavano il teatro di Marcello con il ponte Elio, all'altezza del mausoleo di Adriano[6]. Il nucleo Orsini di S.Angelo in Pescheria va dunque localizzato lungo questa strada (fig.1); le demolizioni del 1885 di un intero isolato proprio in quest'area[7], ed il restauro delle facciate degli edifici attuali, rendono difficile l'identificazione dei singoli elementi del complesso, se si eccettuano i resti di una torre in laterizi ancora ben riconoscibile confinante con la chiesa di S.Angelo che potrebbe essere collegata ad una delle torri Orsini[8].

Il secondo nucleo comprendeva invece gli edifici costruiti sulle sostruzioni del teatro di Pompeo, ancora ben visibile nel XII secolo, e definito nel Medioevo trullum. Dalla metà del XII secolo al 1296, attraverso vari atti di vendita[9] gli Orsini acquistarono dalle famiglie degli Stinchi, dei Catellini e dei Cintii la parte del *trullum* confinante con la chiesa di S.Barbara e S.Maria (tuttora esistenti, la prima in via dei Giubbonari e la seconda in via di Grottapinta), la chiesa di S.Martino (oggi demolita ma riconoscibile nella pianta cinquecentesca del Bufalini[10] in via dei Giubbonari) e la piazza di Campo de' Fiori. Ricostruendo dunque i limiti topografici del complesso, risulta che gli Orsini si impossessarono di tutta la metà meridionale della cavea del teatro

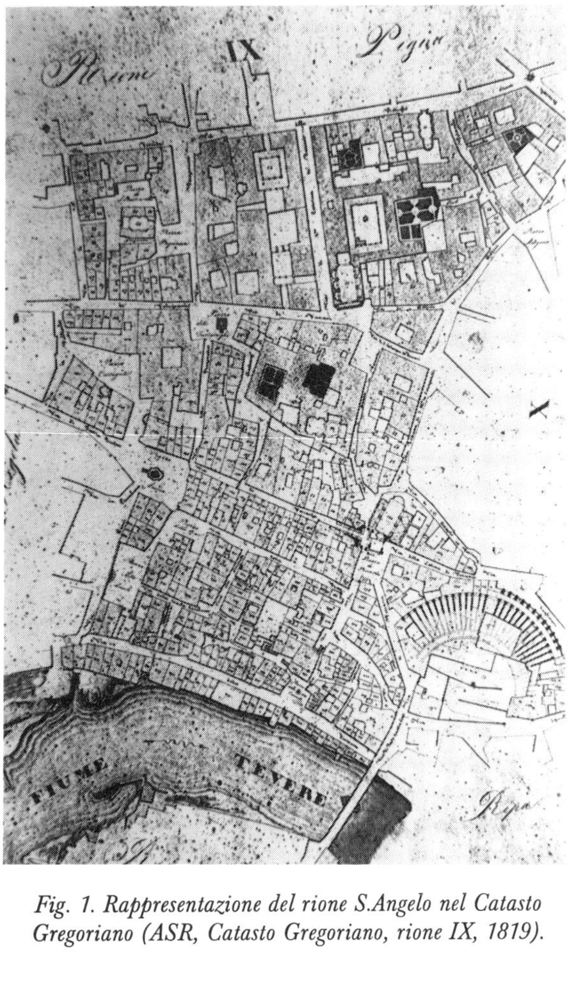

Fig. 1. Rappresentazione del rione S.Angelo nel Catasto Gregoriano (ASR, Catasto Gregoriano, rione IX, 1819).

Fig. 2. Particolare della pianta di Roma di G. Braun, S. Novellanus, F. Hogenberg del 1575. Evidenziata la torre Pertundata.

pompeiano area attualmente compresa tra le odierne vie dei Giubbonari, Campo di Fiori, piazza dei Satiri e via dei Chiavari, e vi edificarono sopra un complesso di edifici costituito da una torre maggiore detta Arpacasa, con la facciata principale che dava su Campo di Fiori, una torre minore detta *Arpacasella*, un *palatium columpnatum*, varie case, orti, criptae e casalina. Insediate sulle sostruzioni del Trullo, ed interne al complesso erano le due chiese di S.Barbara e S.Maria[11].

Il terzo nucleo, confinante con quello del *Trullum*, era costituito dagli edifici che verso la metà del XIII secolo erano appartenuti alla famiglia Mannetti. Tra il 1276 ed il 1294 gli Orsini a tappe successive acquistarono l'intero complesso[12]; esso constava di una torre principale detta *Pertundata*, del *palatium* ad essa collegato, di un forno, una loggia e varie domus. Il tutto era circondato da un muro merlato. Negli atti di vendita questi immobili sono detti in regione *Caccabariorum*, l'area dell'attuale via Arenula, e presso la chiesa di S.Benedetto detta appunto "*de turre Pertundata*", demolita nel XVII sec. ma ben riconoscibile nelle piante cinquecentesche di Roma, accanto alla chiesa seicentesca di S.Carlo ai Catinari[13]. Possiamo di conseguenza ipotizzare che il complesso della *Pertundata* era localizzato nell'area ove ora sorge S.Carlo ai Catinari, per la cui costruzione, agli inizi del 1600, fu demolita, come ci testimoniano i documenti, un'intera "*isola Orsini*"[14]. L'unico documento che forse ci illustra la torre prima della sua demolizione, è una pianta prospettica di Roma del 1575 (fig.2) dove l'edificio in questione sembra completamente circondato da case[15].

Una volta compiuta l'acquisizione dei due complessi dell'*Arpacasa* e della *Pertundata*, gli Orsini collegarono con una cortina muraria intervallata da torri, i due complessi confinanti della *Pertundata* che il cronista medievale Saba Malaspina definisce: "*quondam fortericiam in Campo Flore...quae Arpacata vulgari eloquio vocabatur ...turrificatam circulariter*"[16] e dell'*Arpacasa*, costituendo così una vera e propria fortezza.

Queste considerazioni si basano essenzialmente sul rinvenimento di tre torri medievali, inglobate oggi nei palazzi moderni, equidistanti tra loro, costituite da una cortina in blocchetti di tufo, che dovevano appunto costituire il recinto perimetrale di questo complesso[17]. Un documento del 1296 inoltre, descrivendo gli edifici che componevano il complesso, cita anche un "*ipsorum circuitu cum introitibus et exitibus earum*", che lascia chiaramente intendere la presenza di un perimetro che isolava il complesso dagli edifici circostanti[18]. Nelle immediate vicinanze, ma esterne al circuito, della fortezza principale, sempre proprietà Orsini, erano le due torri de Mafferonis e Bovesca, definite dai documenti "*in regione Arenula*", ma non meglio localizzate topograficamente[19]. Le piante cinquecentesche e seicentesche di Roma (fig.3 e 4) ci mostrano la fortezza del *Trullum* ormai decurtata di tutta la zona della *Pertundata*, conseguenza sia delle alienazioni fatte dagli Orsini a partire dalla seconda metà del XIV sec. di porzioni del complesso[20], sia della costruzione della chiesa di S.Carlo ai Catinari, i cui lavori iniziarono verso la fine del 1500.

L'ultimo nucleo era il gruppo di edifici costruiti sull'altura di Monte Giordano[21]. Il Monte definito nel XIII secolo *mons Johannis Roncionis*, probabilmente dal suo primo possessore, era un rialzo artificiale del terreno, sotto il quale Lanciani volle localizzare le rovine del teatro di Statilio Tauro. Ancora nessuno scavo ha potuto confermare questa ipotesi. Anche in questo caso gli Orsini acquistarono successivamente i singoli edifici del complesso, che poi circondarono e forificarono con una cortina muraria. Un documento del 1262, che riporta

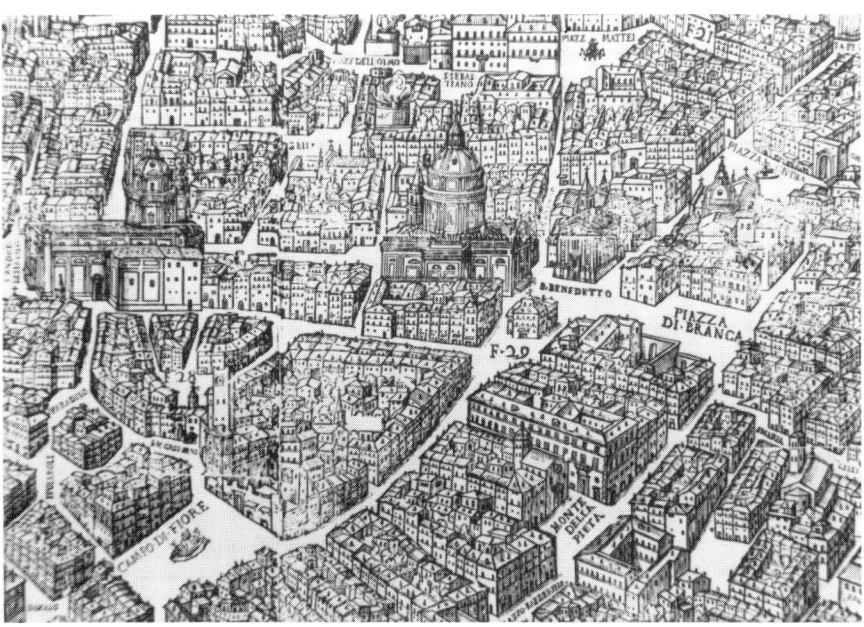

*Fig. 3. Particolare della pianta di Roma di G.Maggi del 1774. Al centro il complesso dell'*Arpacasa.

Fig. 4. Particolare della pianta di Roma di S. Du Perac del 1577. Evidenziati il complesso di Campo di Fiori e di Monte Giordano.

la divisione dei beni tra due rami della famiglia, ed uno del 1267[22], ci consentono di individuare i singoli elementi del complesso di Monte Giordano: del nucleo vero e proprio facevano parte: "*domibus terrineis cum inclaustro...iuxta pedem turris maioris ipsius Montis et in logia existente in dicto Monte Johannis Ronzonis.*" Al complesso va aggiunta la chiesa di S.Maria detta appunto de Monte, citata sulle fonti per la prima volta nella bolla pontificia di Alessandro III, del 1178[23].

Nel già citato documento del 1262 vengono anche elencate le spese sostenute dagli Orsini per la "*defensionem turricelle et domorum, postquam mons qui dicitur Iohannis Roncionis pervenit ad dominum Napuleonem domini Mathei Rubei, fratres et nepotes ipsius*". Come è riportato sul documento questi beni passarono nel patrimonio della famiglia poichè "*clerici de Sancto Celso, nulla propter hoc soluta pecunia vel promossa, concesserunt dicto domino Napuleone..*". È difficile capire se già nel 1262 si intendesse per defensionem una cinta muraria lignea che inglobasse tutto il monte. In un documento del 1273 citando i beni Orsini in quest'area si parla di "*fines seu ripas Montis Iohannis Roncioni*", suggerendo l'idea di un luogo comunque ben circoscritto ed isolato dagli edifici circostanti. Solo in un atto del 1334, comunque, vengono chiaramente nominate delle "*domos infra muros Montis*"[24]. La rappresentazione più antica del Monte, contenuta in un codice del 1420[25], che comunque sembra riprendere un prototipo trecentesco, ce lo mostra con una cinta muraria merlata, intervallata da torri, all'interno della quale si intravede un palazzo a tetto spiovente. Anche nelle miniature di Pietro del Massaio del 1469 (fig.5) e di

Fig. 5. Particolare della miniatura di Pietro del Massaio del 1469.

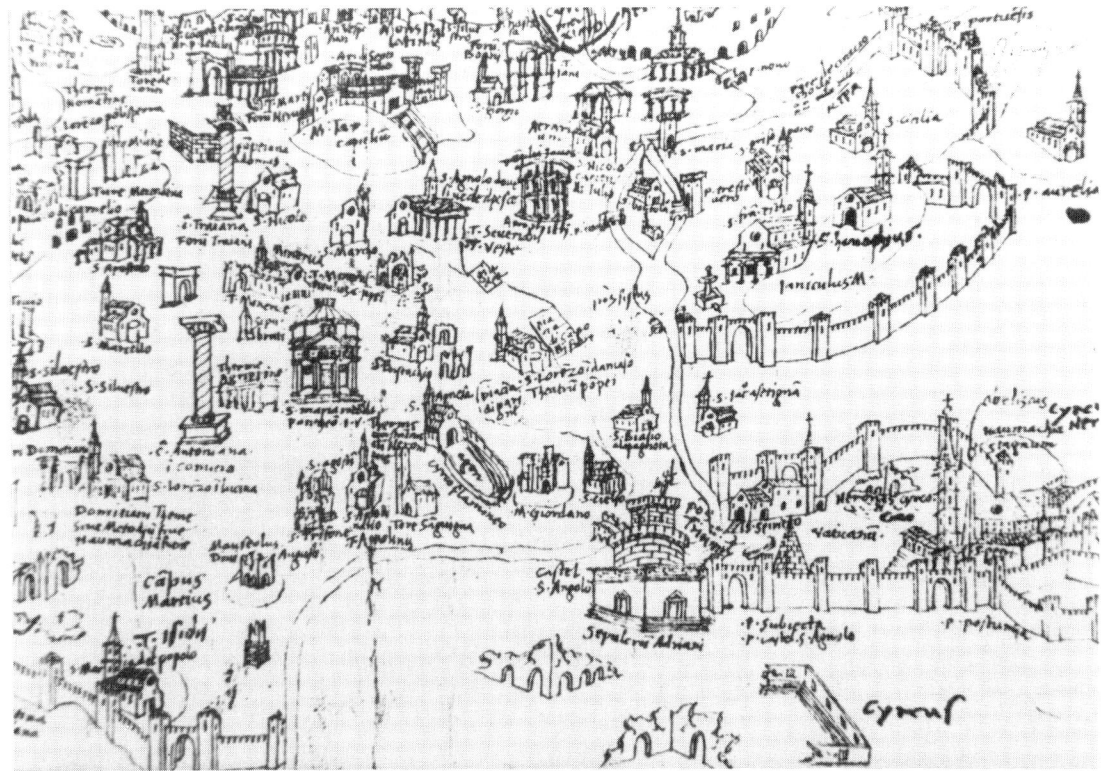

Fig. 6. Disegno di Alessandro Strozzi (1474).

Alessandro Strozzi del 1474 (fig.6), il complesso ha tutto l'aspetto di una fortezza.

Le piante successive del Tempesta e del Maggi del XVI e XVII secolo (fig.7), lo rappresentano invece già trasformato da fortezza in dimora signorile, con l'ampia scalinata d'accesso[26]. Il singolo complesso di Monte Giordano venne poi completamente circondato da edifici che gli Orsini acquistarono nel corso del XIII secolo, con il chiaro intento di proteggere ma anche di creare una area urbana in funzione degli interessi economici legati al complesso principale. Gravitavano infatti intorno al Monte, nel rione Ponte, sempre di proprietà Orsini, circa 15 domus, la torre detta del Campo con loggia e palazzo annessi, la torre detta *"Merulata olim Nicolai Johannis Lombardi"*, la *turris Amatiscorum*, la *turris Nova*, la *turris que vocatur Faiolum*[27].

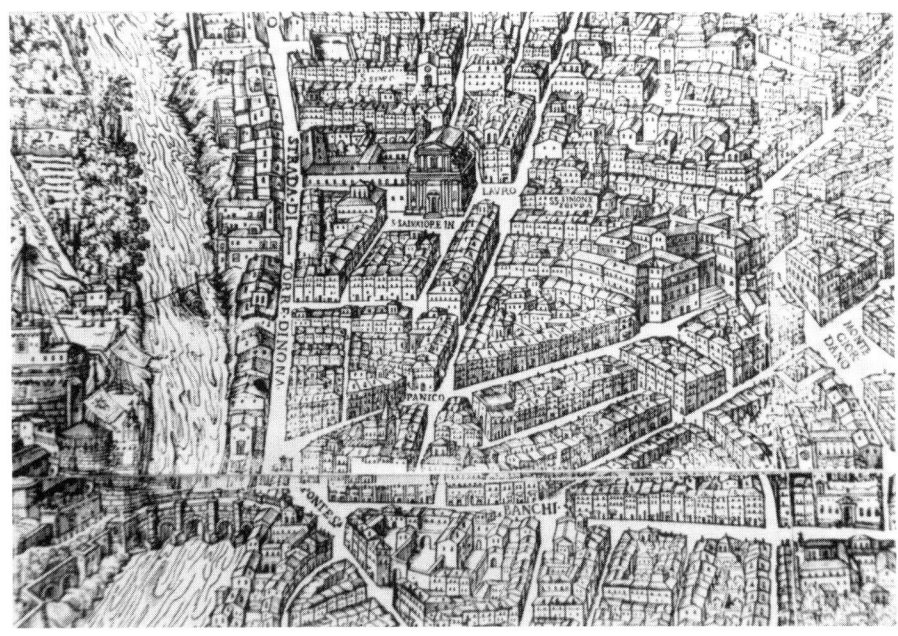

Fig. 7. Il Monte Giordano rappresentato nella pianta di Roma di G.Maggi del 1774.

Strettamente collegati al Monte, erano poi gli edifici medievali identificati dal Quilici tra il lungotevere di Tor di Nona e via della Rondinella, poco distanti da questo. Si tratta essenzialmente di una torre in laterizi, di un edificio in tufelli ad essa appoggiato, e della scomparsa torre di Nona, demolita dopo il 1675 per la costruzione del teatro omonimo, che, come ha chiaramente dimostrato lo stesso Quilici, era stata costruita a difesa del molo qui esistente, costruito in epoca classica, in corrispondenza della posterula *Dimitia* delle mura Aureliane[28]. Il molo e la relativa posterula risultano utilizzati ancora nel Medioevo: un documento del 1395 contenente la donazione di Tor di Nona da parte di Iohannes Iacobelli Ursini alla Società del Salvatore ad Sancta Sanctorum, la definisce come "*meam turrim cum omnibus accasamentis et pertinentiis etiam in portu fluminis existentibus retro dictam turrim quae turris vulgariter nuncupatur Torre della Nona*"[29]. La torre ed il suo porticciolo comunicavano direttamente con il complesso di Monte Giordano attraverso le vie dette oggi della Rondinella e dei Marchigiani.

Il possesso di un punto di approdo sul Tevere rappresentava nel XIII secolo un importante elemento sia politico che economico; il fiume unitamente alle grandi vie consolari ancora in uso nel Medioevo, costituiva un'importante via di comunicazione tra Roma e la campagna circostante, della quale i principali possessori erano le grandi famiglie baronali ed il papato. Essi perseguivano infatti un'attenta politica che mirava al controllo delle strade che portavano a Roma, e conseguentemente dei punti di approdo lungo il Tevere[30]. È noto infatti come la città avesse allora un ruolo preminentemente parassitario in relazione ai prodotti che provenivano da queste terre. Come è testimoniato dalle cronache trecentesche, l'afflusso di grano in città era direttamente ed oculatamente regolato proprio dai baroni romani, in grado anche di creare e risolvere le carestie a seconda dei loro intenti politici. Non è solo un caso che prima nel XIII secolo, e poi nel XIV secolo, sia Brancaleone degli Andalò che Cola di Rienzo, avessero previsto tra i provvedimenti contro la grande nobiltà romana, anche lo stretto controllo da parte del Comune, di tutte le strade consolari, dei porti lungo la costa e degli approdi lungo il Tevere[31]. Il molo di Tor di Nona poteva garantire agli Orsini, attraverso il corso del fiume, l'afflusso di quei prodotti che, provenienti dalle loro terre in Sabina, giungevano così direttamente nei magazzini del complesso di Monte Giordano, dove probabilmente avveniva lo stoccaggio[32].

Non va peraltro dimenticato che il papa Niccolò III al secolo Giovanni di Matteo Rosso Orsini, come narra Giovanni Villani "tolse alla Chiesa castello Santangiolo e diello a messer Orso suo nipote", che effettivamente in un atto del 1278 è definito dal pontefice "*senatoris Urbis gerens officium, castrum S.Angeli et fortellitias...intus et extra Urbem*"[33]. La fortezza di Castel S.Angelo veniva così a trovarsi proprio davanti al molo e alla Torre di Nona, sull'altra sponda del Tevere. Solo nel 1335 il castello fu restituito dagli Orsini alla Chiesa[34].

Il processo d'incastellamento urbano

A questo punto comparando i quattro complessi appena descritti emerge chiaramente come gli Orsini avessero seguito uno stesso criterio per la costituzione dei loro patrimoni urbani, sfruttando essenzialmente come base resti di edifici romani come la cavea del teatro di Pompeo con i portici antistanti, il portico di Ottavia, le *porticus Maximae* e l'altura artificiale di Monte Giordano. Tutti e quattro i complessi avevano come punto centrale di riferimento, anche nella documentazione di allora, una torre principale, attorno alla quale si stringevano palazzi con logge, case cedute a diversi affittuari, edifici di servizio come forni, cripte e magazzini, spazi aperti come orti e casalina. I singoli complessi, ad eccezione di quello di S.Angelo in Pescheria (l'eccezione potrebbe però dipendere anche da lacune documentarie), vennero poi recintati da cortine murarie di difesa.

Comunque, il sistema difensivo dei quattro nuclei era ancora più complesso. Gli Orsini si preoccuparono di rafforzare la sicurezza ed il controllo delle loro fortezze urbane anche con altri espedienti. Da un lato provvidero all'acquisto di singole torri, esterne ai quattro nuclei principali, ma collocate nelle immediate vicinanze, dall'altro perseguirono invece un'attenta politica di alleanze con le famiglie confinanti. Ne sono testimonianza i matrimoni che legarono alcuni degli Orsini con membri della famiglia Savelli, installata nel teatro di Marcello, confinante con le case Orsini di S.Angelo in Pescheria, e con la famiglia Tartari, installata nella contrada del Satro che occupava la metà settentrionale del *Trullum*; per fare solo alcuni esempi, Margherita Orsini nipote del cardinale Francesco Orsini sposò Cintius Tartari, mentre Napoleone figlio di Matteo Rosso Orsini prese in moglie Marsilia sorella del cardinale Giacomo Savelli, alla quale, nel suo testamento del 1279, il fratello lasciò in usufrutto la terza parte di tutti i suoi beni urbani, tra cui la fortezza Savelli costruita sulle rovine del teatro di Marcello, direttamente confinante con le case Orsini di S.Angelo[35]. I legami di buon vicinato sono riscontrabili anche dalla lettura di alcuni contratti in cui gli Orsini si scelsero come *testes, fide iussores* e *procuratores* membri della nobiltà ad essi confinante, come i Tartari, i Boccamazza (le cui case erano situate intorno alla chiesa di S.Nicola dei Calcararii, presso l'attuale piazza Argentina), i Cenci (il cui palazzo presso l'attuale via Arenula confinava con le case Orsini del rione S.Angelo)[36].

Ma vediamo, collocando all'interno del tessuto urbano tutti e quattro i complessi sopra descritti, se sia possibile individuare un preciso progetto perseguito dalla famiglia nell'acquisto e nella costruzione di queste fortificazioni. Partendo da sud abbiamo il primo nucleo presso il portico di Ottavia, tra la sponda del Tevere ed il teatro di Marcello. Seguono poi il secondo ed il terzo complesso (*Pertundata* e *Arpacasa*), nell'area del teatro di Pompeo e dei portici antistanti, l'altura di Monte Giordano con la sua estrema propaggine di Tor di Nona costruita sul molo romano antistante la *posterula Dimitia* delle mura Aureliane, e per ultimo la fortezza di Castel S.Angelo che la famiglia ricevette in donazione da Niccolò III, costruita sul mausoleo di Adriano. Tutti questi monumenti classici si trovavano lungo una delle principali arterie della viabilità antica del Campo Marzio. Si trattava della cosidetta via Triumphalis, che dal circo Flaminio si dirigeva al santuario del Tarentum e da qui al ponte Neroniano. In seguito con la costruzione del mausoleo di Adriano, la strada fu deviata verso il ponte Elio, e da qui allo stesso mausoleo. Sappiamo che le porticus *Maximae* fiancheggiavano tutto il suo percorso[37]. La strada rimase in uso per tutto il Medioevo, mantenendo anche in quest'epoca una grande importanza per il traffico interno della città. Nell'itinerario di Einsielden dell'VIII-IX secolo, è ricordata come il tragitto percorso dalla moltitudine dei pellegrini che da S.Pietro si dirigevano verso S.Paolo fuori porta Ostiense[38]. La costruzione di numerose chiese lungo questo tratto testimoniata dal catalogo delle chiese di Cencio Camerario del 1192, e da quello dell'anonimo di Torino del XIV secolo, e la sua rappresentazione nella pianta di Roma di fra Paolino da Venezia del 1320, ne testimonia l'uso almeno fino al XIV secolo[39]. Negli statuti dei maestri delle strade di Roma del 1452, essa viene espressamente citata tra le vie cittadine che dovevano essere pulite ogni sabato, come la "*via dallo canale de Ponte in sino ad Sancto Angilo Pescivendolo*". Nel XV secolo ancora, la strada è ricordata sia nel Diario di Jacopo da Volterra, in un passo in cui è descritta una passeggiata del pontefice Sisto IV, sia in un epigramma del Brandolin, dedicato allo stesso papa[40]. Nei due brani è chiaramente messo in risalto il traffico commerciale esistente sulla via, per la presenza di botteghe e banchi, tanto da meritarsi il nome di via "*mercatoria*"[41].

Tutti e 4 i nuclei Orsini erano collocati lungo questa arteria viaria, in modo da poterne controllare l'intero percorso da S.Angelo in Pescheria a sud, fino alla sua estremità settentrionale costituita da Castel S.Angelo. Topograficamente gli Orsini avevano costruito i loro complessi sia in corrispondenza delle due estremità della strada, sia nel punto centrale del suo percorso, che coincide più o meno con l'attuale piazza di Campo di Fiori, dove sorgeva il complesso del Trullo (fig.8). Essi si assicurarono così due punti importanti sul Tevere: uno a sud di fronte l'isola Tiberina, presso S.Angelo in Pescheria, nodo commerciale importante, dove sin dai primi secoli del Medioevo si teneva il mercato cittadino

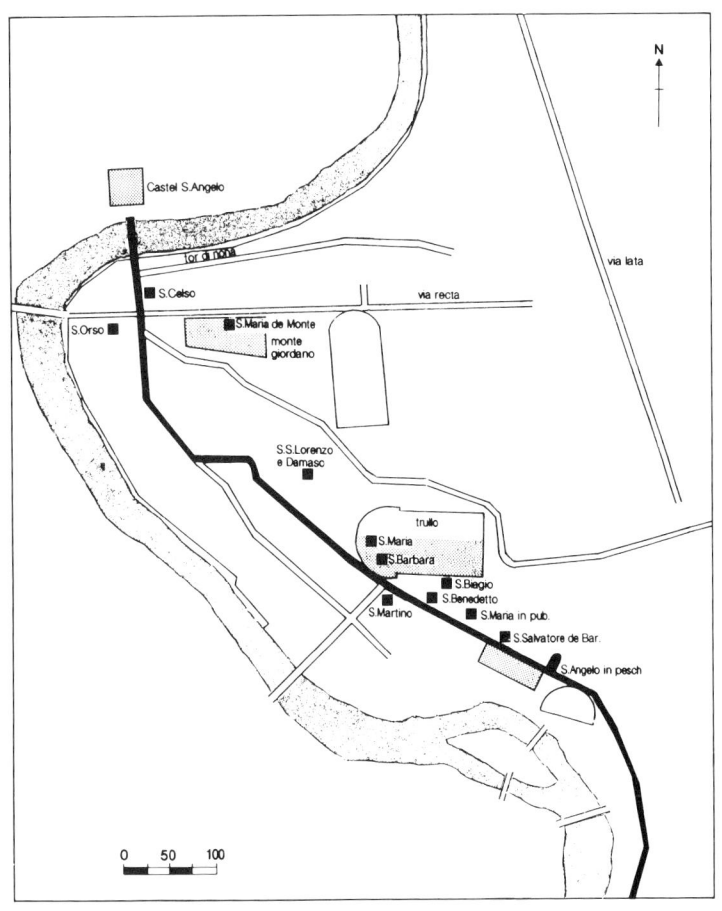

Fig. 8. Ricostruzione della viabilità medievale del Campo Marzio.

del pesce, che arrivava direttamente dal più importante porto di Ripa grande, sulla sponda destra del Tevere presso l'attuale Porta Portese[42]; e l'altro verso nord presso il molo di Tor di Nona, il cui nome derivando da Torre dell'Annona suggerisce anche un punto di riscossione di tasse e pedaggi. Il così detto ripatico, pedaggio pagato da chiunque facesse sbarcare della merce lungo i punti di approdo del Tevere, se nell'altomedioevo fu una prerogativa papale, a partire dal XIII secolo circa divenne di competenza comunale. Esistono comunque numerosi casi, nei quali il Comune, non essendo in grado di gestire questo traffico navale, appaltava il diritto di risossione dei pedaggi a singoli privati, che il più delle volte risultavano essere membri della nobiltà romana[43]. Il molo era anche ben protetto, sulla sponda opposta del Tevere, da Castel S.Angelo, che dal pontificato di Niccolò III (1277–1280) fino alla fine del XIV secolo rimase possesso Orsini. Impadronirsi di Castel S.Angelo, e quindi dell'antistante ponte, equivaleva inoltre ad avere il controllo di un importante accesso alla basilica di S.Pietro, meta continua dei pellegrini che vi si riversavano da ogni parte del mondo occidentale. La fortezza di Monte Giordano inoltre, era situata in un punto strategicamente importante, essendo in grado di controllare anche parte del tracciato della via Recta, strada perpendicolare alla nostra, che proveniva dall'area nord del Campo Marzio, staccandosi dalla via Lata.

La costruzione di sistemi di fortificazioni, le alleanze con le famiglie confinanti, il controllo di punti di approdo lungo il Tevere, e di un'intera strada che attraversava una zona di Roma già fittamente abitata e importante da un punto di vista commerciale, furono gli elementi che garantirono agli Orsini la riuscita di una ben precisa politica di occupazione del suolo urbano che fosse in grado di tutelare sia i loro interessi dentro le mura, che quelli legati ai possessi terrieri del distretto.

Note
Abbreviazioni utilizzate nel testo:
ASC   Archivio Storico Capitolino
ASR   Archivio di Stato di Roma
ASRSP   Archivio della Società Romana di Storia Patria
ASV   Archivio Segreto Vaticano
BAV   Biblioteca Apostolica Vaticana
MEFRA   Melanges dell'École Française de Rome, Antiquité
MEFRM   Melanges dell'École Française de Rome, Moyen Age-Temps Modernes

1. Valentini Zucchetti, *Codice topografico della città di Roma*, Roma 1940–1953, Vol.II, 143.
2. C. Rota, *Statuti della città di Roma*, Roma 1880, 114–115, 192. Per il problema degli edifici superiori alle cinque palariae cfr. E. Hubert, *Espace urbain et habitat à Rome*, Rome 1990, 230–231.
3. In *Chronica Maiora Matthaei Parisiensis*, ed. London 1880, 709. Sul valore simbolico assunto dalle torri per le famiglie nobili romane nel medioevo cfr. M. Vendittelli, 'Note sulla famiglia e sulla torre degli Amateschi in Roma nel secolo XIII', *ASRSP*, 105, 1982, 157–174; idem, 'La famiglia Curtabraga. Contributo alla storia della nobiltà romana del Duecento', *MEFRM*, 101, 1989/1, 177–272; A.M. Cusanno, *Le fortificazioni medievali a Roma. La torre dei Conti e la torre delle Milizie*, Roma 1991.
4. In *ASC*, Arch.Orsini, II A I 53, regesto in C. De Cupis, *Regesto degli Orsini*, Sulmona 1903, vol.I, 65, e in G.Marchetti Longhi, 'Theatrum et Crypta Balbi, Turris Pertundata et Balneum Cintiis', *Rendiconti Pont. Acc. Rom. Arch.* XVI, 1940, 285–287. Per la torre Baroncina cfr. F. Tomassetti, *Le torri medievali di Roma*, Roma 1990, 69–72; A. Katermaa Ottela, *Le casetorri medievali di Roma*, Helsinki 1981.
5. Per questa chiesa cfr. M.Armellini, *Le chiese di Roma*, Roma 1982, 571.
6. Per i *porticus Maxima* e per la topografia classica di questa zona di Roma cfr. R. Lanciani, 'L'itinerario di Einsiedeln e l'Ordo di Benedetto Canonico', *Monumenti dei Lincei*, I, 1891, 437–552; S.B. Platner & T. Ashby, *A Topographical Dictionary of Ancient Rome*, Rome 1929, 40, 423; F. Castagnoli, 'Il Campo Marzio nell'antichità', *Mem.Acc.Lincei*, I, 1948, 148–151; F. Coarelli, Il Campo Marzio occidentale. Storia e topografia', *MEFRA*, 1977/2, 807–846; L. Quilici, 'Il Campo Marzio occidentale', *Analecta Romana*, X, 1983, suppl., 59–85; E. La Rocca, *La riva a mezzaluna*, Roma 1984, 66; idem, 'Via di S.Paolo alla Regola. Scavo e recupero di edifici antichi e medievali', *Notizie degli Scavi di Antichità*, serie VIII, XL-XLI, 1986-87, 175–418.
7. Riguardo alle demolizioni in questa zona cfr. F. Castagnoli, C. Cecchelli, G. Giovannoni & M. Zocca, *Topografia ed urbanistica di Roma*, Roma 1958, 584.
8. V. Livi in L. Pani Ermini & E. De Minicis (a cura), *Archeologia del Medioevo a Roma*, Taranto 1988, 51–66.
9. In *ASC*, Arch. Orsini, II A I 2, 25; II A II 29, 36, 46, 48, regesti in C. De Cupis 1903, cit.vol.I, 29, 79, 81, 82, 85, 87–90.
10. Per la pianta di Roma del Bufalini cfr.A.P. Frutaz, *Le piante di Roma*, Roma 1962, tav.202.
11. Per un'analisi più dettagliata del complesso del *Trullum* cfr. F. Bosman, 'Una torre medievale in via Monte della Farina: ricerche topografiche e analisi della struttura', *Archeologia Medievale*, XVII, 1990, 633–660.
12. In *ASC*, Arch.Orsini, II A II 6,42, regesti in De Cupis 1903 cit.vol.I, 64,84.
13. La chiesa è ben individuabile nelle piante di Roma cinquecentesche di L. Bufalini, S. Du Perac, A. Tempesta, ed in quella settecentesca di G. Maggi (in Frutaz 1962, cit. tav. 202, 250, 266, 315).
14. *ASV*, Segr. del Tribunale del Vicariato, b.45, foglio 98; F.P. Valle, *Stato generale o libro de' stabili del collegio dei santi Biagio e Carlo in Roma*, manoscritto 1742, foglio 32r.
15. Si tratta della pianta di Roma di G. Braun, S. Novellanus, F. Hogenberg del 1575, in Frutaz 1962, cit., II, tav.235.
16. Saba Malaspina, *Rerum Sicularum Historia*, in L.A. Muratori, *RIS*, VIII, 864, Roma 1724.
17. Per la ricostruzione topografica della fortezza Orsini edificata dall'unione del complesso dell'*Arpacasa* con quello della *Pertundata* cfr. F. Bosman 1990 cit.
18. In *ASC*, Arch.Orsini, II A II 48, regesto in De Cupis 1903, cit., I, 87–90.
19. La torre de Mafferonis venne acquistata dagli Orsini il 29/9/1249 (ASC, Arch. Orsini II A I 33, regesto De Cupis 1903, cit., I, 56) mentre il 29/11/1244, acquistano la torre Bovesca da un certo Bobo *filius quondam Fordivoglie Guttifredi Bobonis* (in ASC, Arch.Orsini II A I 27, regesto in De Cupis 1903, 54). Brevi cenni storici sulle due torri sono in Katermaa Ottela 1981, cit.; Tomassetti 1990, 89–90, 253–254.
20. Per le successive alienazioni di porzioni del complesso fatte dagli Orsini alle famiglie confinanti, a partire dalla prima metà del XIV secolo cfr. Bosman 1990, cit.
21. F. Asso, 'Note sull'origine dell'altura detta Monte Giordano', *Quaderni dell'Istituto di Storia dell'Architettura dell'Universita' di Roma* I, 1953, 12–53; P. Pecchiai, *Palazzo Taverna a Monte Giordano*, Roma 1963; R. Krautheimer, *Roma. Profilo di una città, 312–1308*, Roma 1980, 375; Tomassetti 1990, cit., 343–348.

22. Il documento del 1262, è in *ASCV*, regesto in P. Savignoni, 'L'archivio storico del comune di Viterbo', *ASRSP*, 18, 1895, 300-302; ringrazio S. Carocci per avermi permesso di leggere la sua trascrizione del documento, ancora in corso di stampa. L'atto del 1267 è in *BAV*, Arch. Capitolo S.Pietro, caps.61, fasc.225. Di S. Carocci si veda il recente contributo *Baroni di Roma. Dominazioni signorili e lignaggi aristocratici nel Duecento e nel primo Tercento*, Roma 1993.
23. C.Hulsen, *Le chiese di Roma nel Medioevo*, 1927, 350; P.F. Kehr, *Italia pontificia*, 1907, vol.II, 180.
24. 1273, 9 febbraio, in *BAV*, Arch. Capitolo S.Pietro, caps.61, fasc.225; 1334, 20 maggio, in G. Caetani, *Regesta chartarum. Regesto delle pergamene dell'archivio Caetani*, 1925-30, vol.2, 87-93.
25. La miniatura è rappresentata in F. Asso, 1953, cit.
26. In Frutaz 1962, cit. tav.157 (Pietro del Massaio), 159 (A. Strozzi), 271 (A. Tempesta), 314 (G. Maggi).
27. Queste notizie provengono dall'analisi dei due documenti del 1262 e 1267 citati in n.22. Per le singole torri cfr.Tomassetti 1990, cit.; Katermaa Ottela 1981, cit.; per la torre del Campo: M.T. Russo, 'La torre del Campo a Monte Giordano', *Strenna dei Romanisti*, 26, 1965, 374-382. Che i possessi Orsini fossero molto numerosi nel rione Ponte, proprio davanti alla basilica di S.Pietro, sull'altra sponda del Tevere, emerge dalla lettura del *Chronicon fratris Francisci Pipini*, (in L. Muratori *RIS*, vol.IX, 724), dove il cronista parlando della politica nepotistica del pontefice Niccolò III, al secolo appunto Giangaetano Orsini, descrive i lavori fatti in S.Pietro, giustificandoli in questo modo: "*summis sumptibus construxit palatia et pomerium quae sunt circa Sanctum Petrum ex pecunia collecta de decima proventum universarum Ecclesiarum...ut ibi celebritas Curiae Romanae esset in vestibulis aedium propinquorum eius*".
28. L.Quilici, 'Un vicolo ed una torre medievali a Tor di Nona e loro implicazioni nella topografia del Campo Marzio', *Bull. Comm. Arch. Com. di Roma*, 86, 1978-79, 141-151; P. Adinolfi, *Il canale di Ponte e le sue circostanti parti*, Roma 1860, 8-20; C. Corvisieri, 'Delle posterule Tiberine tra la porta Flaminia ed il ponte Gianicolense', *ASRSP*, I, 1878, 79-122; D. Marchetti, 'Di un antico molo per lo sbarco dei marmi, riconosciuto sulla riva sinistra del Tevere', *Bull. Comm. Arch. Com. di Roma*, 1891, 45-60; A. Cametti, 'La torre di Nona e la contrada circostante dal medioevo al secolo XVII', *ASRSP*, 1916, 411-466.
29. 1395, 1 settembre, in *ASC*, Arch.Orsini II A IX 44.
30. Per il problema della navigabilità del Tevere nel basso medioevo, L.Palermo, *Il porto di Roma nel XIV e XV secolo: strutture socio-economiche e statuti*, Roma 1979; Idem, *Il mercato del grano a Roma tra Medioevo e Rinascimento*, Roma 1980. Per l'aspetto più generale del Tevere come via di comunicazione cfr. T. Leggio, 'Le principali vie di comunicazione nella Sabina Tiberina tra X e XII secolo', *Il Territorio*, 1985, 3-19 e 1986, 102-108.
31. Per le vicende politiche romane di Brancaleone degli Andalò e di Cola di Rienzo: E. Duprè Theseider, *Roma dal comune di popolo alla signoria pontificia (1252-1377)*, Roma 1952. Per l'intervento di Cola di Rienzo sui punti di approdo del Tevere cfr. Anonimo Romano,*Cronica*, ed. G. Porta, 1981, 113-114.
32. Il problema dello stoccaggio nei magazzini urbani dei prodotti provenienti dai possessi nobiliari del distretto è ripreso in H. Broise,J.C. Maire Vigueur, 'Strutture famigliari,spazio domestico e architettura civile a Roma alla fine del Medioevo', in *Storia dell'Arte Italiana*, XII, 1983, 99-160. In Sabina gli Orsini avevano possessi nelle località Foglia, Grapignano, Poggio Sommavilla, tutte e tre situate lungo il corso del Tevere. Ringrazio F.Allegrezza che mi ha permesso di consultare la carta di distribuzione dei possessi Orsini da lei fatta in occasione della sua tesi di dottorato all'Università degli Studi di Firenze a.a.1991, dal titolo *Gli Orsini dal XIII al XV secolo. Tratti di una stirpe tra affermazioni territoriali e dinamiche familiari*.
33. G.Villani, *Cronica*, Lib.VII, c.LIV; 1278, *ASC*, Arch.Orsini II A II 13, regesto in De Cupis 1903 cit., II, 71-72.
34. P. Pagliucchi, *I castellani del Castel S.Angelo di Roma*, Roma 1906, 23-27, ed il testamento di Napoleone di Orso Orsini, in *ASC*, Arch.Orsini II A IV 17, regesto De Cupis 1903 cit., 176-177.
35. Per le vicende della famiglia dei Tartari cfr. P. Sfligiotti, 'Note sulla famiglia romana dei Tartari e sulle proprietà nel Satro (secoli XIII-inizi XV)', *ASRSP*, 114, 1991, 57-76; il testamento del cardinale Giacomo Savelli è in A. Paravicini Bagliani, *I testamenti dei cardinali del Duecento*, Roma 1980, 197-206.
36. Per gli atti in questione cfr.1249, 29 settembre, vendita della torre dei Mafferonis, 1271, 16 marzo, vendita di case nel rione S.Angelo in *ASC*, Arch. Orsini II A I 53; 1275, 4 maggio divisione di beni extra muros tra membri Orsini in Arch.Orsini II A II 5; 1291, 25 maggio, testamento di Elena vedova di Iacopo di Napoleone Orsini in P. Savignoni art.cit., 29-30; 1292, 3 ottobre, vendita di case nel *Trullum* in Arch. Orsini, II A II 36; 1311, 2 giugno,divisione di beni tra due membri Orsini in Arch. Orsini II A III 13. Per la famiglia dei Cenci: C. Fraschetti, *I Cenci. Storia e documenti dalle origini al secolo XVIII*, Roma 1935; M. Bevilacqua, *Il Monte dei Cenci. Una famiglia romana e il suo insediamento urbano tra Medioevo ed età moderna*, Roma 1988; per i Boccamazza cfr. Paravicini Bagliani 1980, cit., 353-382; G.Marchetti Longhi, 'Ricordi medievali nell'area sacra di piazza Argentina', *Capitolium* 1929, 10-18; Idem, 'Le contrade medievali della zona in circo Flaminio: il Calcarario', *ASRSP*, XLII, 1910, 401-536; A. Salimei, 'Note di topografia romana', *ASRSP*, LIII-LV, 1930-32, 397-404.
37. Cfr.nota 6.
38. Valentini Zucchetti 1940-1953, cit., II, 169-175.
39. Valentini Zucchetti 1940-1953, cit., III, 197-318. La pianta di Fra Paolino da Venezia è in Frutaz 1962, cit., II, tav.143.
40. In E. Re, 'I maestri di strada', *ASRSP*, 43, 1920, 5-102; per il diario di Jacopo da Volterra cfr. Muratori, *RIS*, t.XXIII, 141; gli epigrammi del Brandolin sono riportati in E. Muntz, *Les arts à la cour des Papes*, Roma 1882.
41. U. Gnoli, *Topografia e toponomastica di Roma medievale e moderna*, Roma 1939, 107-108.
42. In R. Krautheimer 1980, cit., 315; C.Benocci, *Il rione S.Angelo*, 1980, 22.
43. Sul problema dei dazi e gabelle per le merci che arrivavano a Roma dal Tevere cfr. M.L. Lombardo, *La dogana di Ripa e Ripetta nel sistema dell'ordinamento tributario a Roma dal medioevo al secolo XV*, Roma 1978.

PART 6

Technology and Trade

53

Aspetti della Metallurgia nell'Italia Continentale tra XVI e XI Secolo a.C.: Produzione e Relazioni Interregionali tra Area Centrale Tirrenica e Area Settentrionale

ENRICO PELLEGRINI

(Museo Nazionale Preistorico Etnografico L. Pigorini, Roma)

Sommario: *Vengono illustrati i dati preliminari di una ricerca sulla produzione metallurgica dell'Italia centrale tirrenica (valli del Fiora e dell'Albegna) nei secoli XVI-XI. Nell'ambito del programma finora svolto, per il quale si è fatto uso di osservazioni metallografiche condotte con la tecnica della Microscopia Ottica ed Elettronica a scansione con analisi localizzata mediante microsonde EDS e WDS, si è data particolare importanza all'esame dei contatti con alcune aree dell'Italia settentrionale, già segnalati da vari studiosi (palette con innesto a cannone e pani a piccone), e ora riproposti da nuovi materiali (spade, fibule, asce) e dalla revisione della documentazione edita (pani a barra e ad ascia).*

La ricerca, della quale si presentano in questa sede i dati preliminari, è finalizzata ad approfondire le conoscenze relative alla metallurgia del rame in Italia durante l'età pre- e protostorica e ad evidenziare le possibili relazioni intercorse tra i vari centri di produzione nell'ambito del complesso ciclo metallurgico 'estrazione-raffinazione-prodotto' (Casagrande *et al.* 1993). Nell'attuale fase, lo studio si è concentrato nella zona compresa tra i bacini dei fiumi Ombrone e Fiora, da sempre ricca di testimonianze relative alla metallurgia (Peroni 1971: 175–243; Bietti Sestieri 1981; Cocchi-Genick & Grifoni 1989), ma che un'intensa attività di ricerca e di studio ha recentemente posto di nuovo all'attenzione degli studiosi (fig. 1).

Si tratta di un'area con elevate potenzialità agricole e d'allevamento (Sestini 1981; Ciacci 1981) inserita tra le due maggiori zone metallifere dell'Italia continentale, le Colline Metallifere a nord, e i Monti della Tolfa a sud, caratterizzata essa stessa dalla presenza di numerosi giacimenti (Giardino 1984; Zifferero 1991), anche se di

Fig. 1. Valli del Fiora e dell'Albegna con la localizzazione dei siti citati nel testo:
1- lago di Mezzano;
2- Pitigliano;
3- Scarceta;
4- Piano di Tallone;
5- 'tra Manciano e Samprugnano';
* massiccio dell'Amiata;
▲ miniera di Antimonio nei pressi di Manciano, loc. La Campigliola.

511

piccola entità, che devono aver favorito lo sviluppo di una precoce attività metallurgica. Già a partire dall'Eneolitico e, ancor più, nella successiva età del bronzo antico, l'area in esame mostra una rilevante presenza di manufatti metallici, sia isolati che in ripostigli, principalmente asce (Cocchi-Genik & Grifoni 1989: 134, 141; Peroni 1971). Nella successiva fase del Bronzo medio anche questa regione, come il resto della penisola, mostra una netta flessione nell'attestazione di oggetti metallici che si accompagna ad una completa assenza di ripostigli, situazione tanto più impressionante se confrontata con il periodo precedente.

Se l'attività di ricerca sul territorio ha potuto individuare diversi nuovi insediamenti (Negroni Catacchio & Miari 1991-92), le presenze relative agli oggetti metallici sono per ora, tranne che per un'ascia tipo Canterano dal lago di Mezzano (Franco 1982: 174, M1-21) riferibile alla facies di Grotta Nuova (Carancini 1991-92: 239), del tutto nulle.

Ad un nuovo assetto socio-economico dell'intera area in esame deve quindi attribuirsi l'intensa attestazione dell'attività metallurgica che riprende a manifestarsi a partire dal Bronzo recente (Peroni 1989). La documentazione mostra ora una maggiore articolazione: sono infatti attestati non solo manufatti singoli e ripostigli, ma anche evidenze relative alle attività fusorie. Inoltre, a partire da questa fase, l'insieme dei dati archeologici e delle analisi metallografiche indica, nell'ambito della produzione metallurgica, la presenza di un'organizzazione complessa e l'esistenza di collegamenti ad ampio raggio, specialmente con l'area dell'Italia nord-orientale, fatto questo già puntualizzato da tempo (Bietti Sestieri 1973, 1981; Negroni Catacchio 1983), ma che i nuovi dati prospettano ora in maniera più complessa e articolata (Fugazzola Delpino 1992: 296).

Analizzando in dettaglio la documentazione, estremamente interessante si presenta quella di Mezzano riferibile al Bronzo recente. Oltre alla presenza di un'ascia ad alette estese (Carancini 1979: 179, n. 18; 183) recenti indagini hanno consentito il rinvenimento di un gruppo di oggetti metallici particolarmente importante nell'ambito della problematica qui affrontata. Si tratta di due splendidi esemplari di spade a codolo, in ottimo stato di conservazione, che rientrano, anche se con caratteristiche del tutto particolari, nel tipo Arco e nel tipo Canegrate, la diffusione del quale appariva finora limitata all'area settentrionale (Pellegrini 1993).

Al tipo Arco (fig. 2) rimandano il lungo codolo con apice a mazzuolo sfaccettato, a sezione ottagonale, che si collega alla base mediante un raccordo campanulato, con due chiodi al di sotto, e la foggia generale slanciata con espansione accentuata verso la punta; caratteristica del tipo Pépinville è invece la base della lama, più stretta di quest'ultima, alla quale si raccorda mediante un accenno di spalla (Bianco Peroni 1970: 33). Per quanto riguarda invece il tipo Canegrate (Bianco Peroni 1970: 39, n.88), l'esemplare di Mezzano (fig. 3) ne costituisce il solo altro esempio noto (ma a differenza dell'esemplare di Canegrate, in questo di Mezzano la base della lama, lateralmente munita di dentellatura, è più stretta di quest'ultima e vi si si raccorda mediante un accenno di spalla). Occorre comunque sottolineare che questo tipo era stato definito essenzialmente in base alle affinità con i 'pugnali Peschiera' (Bianco Peroni 1970: 39 e n.1) e che per ora mancano ulteriori dati di riferimento.

Relativamente all'attestazione di attività fusorie, devono essere segnalate le recenti acquisizioni dagli insediamenti di Pitigliano e Scarceta, queste ultime attribuibili alla fase terminale del periodo (XII secolo a. C.).

Dall'insediamento di Pitigliano proviene un frammento di valva di forma di fusione per ascia ad alette in tufite (Pellegrini 1985: 47–48). Il frammento comprende la metà inferiore della valva con la lama e una parte delle alette. Lo scarso sviluppo della lama rispetto alle alette ne rende plausibile la pertinenza alla classe delle asce ad alette estese. In quest'ambito, alcuni elementi quali la rigidità dei margini della lama ed il carattere massiccio del prodotto finito, in termini di impiego del metallo, favoriscono un'attribuzione nell'ambito del XIII secolo. A questa stessa cronologia conduce anche il confronto con un'ascia rinvenuta a Mezzano (Carancini 1979: 179, fig. 2, n. 18 e p. 183).

Particolarmente importante per la ricchezza della documentazione appare il complesso di bronzi e forme di fusione dall'insediamento di Scarceta (Soffredi 1973; Poggiani Keller 1988). Ad un primo nucleo rinvenuto nel 1972 nella 'capanna XIII' (Soffredi 1973) costituito da sei forme di fusione per punta di freccia, arpione, paletta rettangolare, ascia ad alette e lesine, si è aggiunto l'ulteriore rinvenimento da questa stessa area di altre tre forme di fusione frammentarie, oltre a scorie di fusione di bronzo e un frammento di ugello in terracotta, elementi questi che portano ad identificare l'area della 'capanna XIII' come una vera e propria 'officina metallurgica' (Poggiani Keller 1993).

La presenza di una struttura 'specializzata' non appare del resto isolata a Scarceta. Nell'area della 'grande capanna ovale' degli scavi di Poggiani Keller sono infatti attestate tracce di lavorazione del ferro e la presenza di manufatti metallici sia interi che frammentati: lesine, punte di freccia, fibule ad arco di violino foliato con o senza noduli, ad arco semplice, frammenti di falci oltre che oggetti in ambra e pasta vitrea (Poggiani Keller 1993).

La cronologia della maggior parte di questi manufatti si inserisce abbastanza agevolmente nell'ambito del XII secolo a. C. Ad un tipo riferibile a questo orizzonte si può attribuire la forma di fusione per ascia ad alette, che presenta ancora un forte sviluppo del tallone (Pellegrini 1985). A questo stesso orizzonte sembra riportare anche la forma di fusione per paletta accostabile ad altri esemplari con innesto a codolo piuttosto che a

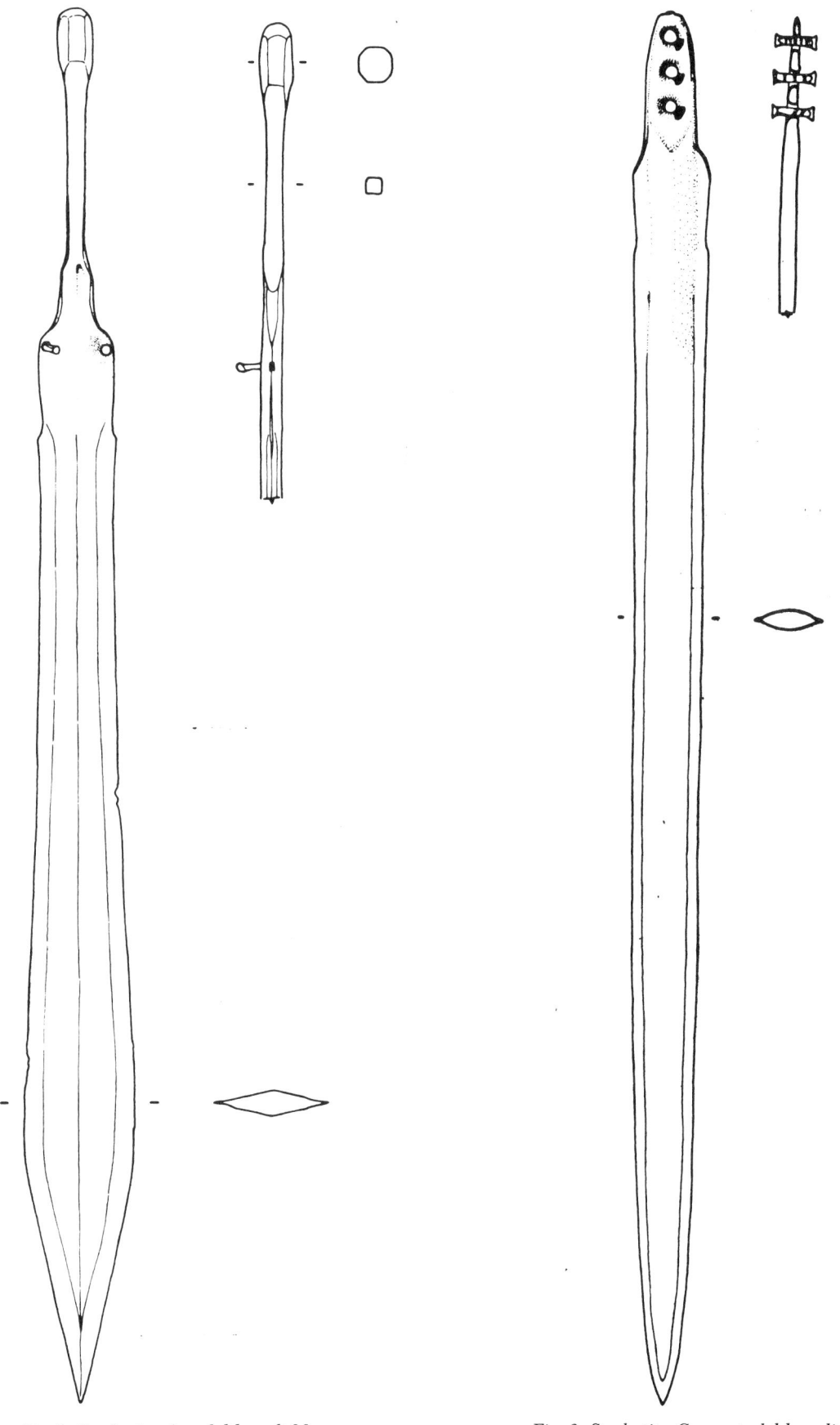

Fig. 2. Spada tipo Arco dal lago di Mezzano.

Fig. 3. Spada tipo Canegrate dal lago di Mezzano.

quelli con innesto a cannone 'tipo Manciano/Samprugnano' dell'età del Bronzo finale. In ultimo, sempre al XII secolo riporta la presenza di un frammento di fibula ad arco di violino foliato con noduli che rappresenta un importante elemento di collegamento, oltre che con l'area settentrionale e adriatica, anche con il vicino insediamento di Mezzano dove è attestato un esemplare appartenente a questo stesso tipo (per il tipo e la cronologia, cfr. Peroni 1980: 13; 1989: 83-84).

A questo stesso orizzonte, secondo quanto è emerso da un recente studio, deve essere attribuita anche una parte degli oggetti che costituiscono il ripostiglio di Piano di Tallone (Pellegrini 1992a). Si tratta del nucleo costituito dal coltello tipo Matrei, varietà A (fig. 4.6) e dai pani in forma di ascia (fig. 4.1-5), un tipo caratteristico dell'arco alpino in un arco cronologico che va dal Bronzo antico fino al Bronzo recente (cfr. Mayer 1977: 66-71).

Per completare il quadro relativo al XII secolo occorre infine ricordare un'ascia ad alette pertinente al tipo Pertosa, Varietà A (fig. 5) proveniente, ancora una volta, da Mezzano, e una fibula ad arco di violino rialzato ritorto dalla grotta sepolcrale dei Sassi Neri presso Capalbio (Grosseto) (Negroni Catacchio 1981: 352, fig. 91.A).

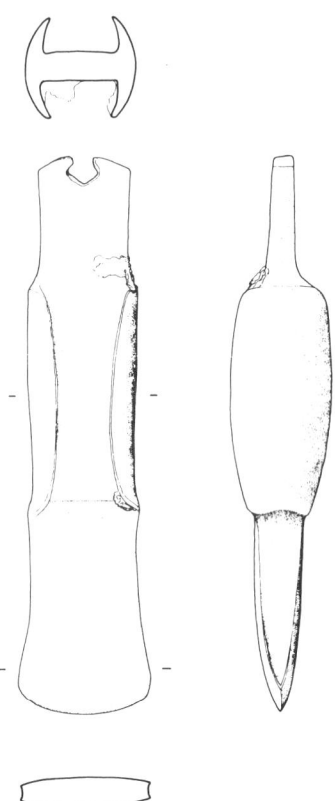

Fig. 5. Ascia ad alette dal lago di Mezzano.

Anche per quanto riguarda l'orizzonte più antico del Bronzo finale, i legami con l'area settentrionale risultano molto stretti. Il rinvenimento più importante della zona in esame, il ripostiglio denominato 'tra Manciano e Samprugnano' (Pellegrini 1992a, 1992b; cfr. Peroni 1989: 88) mostra, infatti, tipi propri dell'area nord-orientale. Il ripostiglio si caratterizza per la presenza di numerosi frammenti di pani metallici di un tipo particolare denominato, per la caratteristica forma, 'a piccone', e di palette con innesto a cannone. I 'pani a piccone' sono distribuiti in un'area che comprende Svizzera, Savoia, Francia, Croazia, Veneto, Romagna, Marche (fig. 6A) (Pellegrini 1992b; cfr. Borgna 1992: 27-33). Una distribuzione analoga, cioè orientata verso il nord e la costa adriatica, si osserva anche per l'altra classe, le cosiddette 'palette con innesto a cannone', fino ad ora attestate in contesti in cui sono presenti anche i 'pani a piccone' (fig. 6B). Particolarmente importante appare la presenza a Frattesina di Fratta Polesine di entrambe le classi di oggetti e di una forma di fusione per le palette (Bellintani & Peretto 1972: tav.II.10-11).

Con la trama di collegamenti evidenziati a livello tipologico si accorda una prima serie di analisi chimiche in assorbimento atomico (tab.I e II) e metallografiche effettuate su una parte degli oggetti provenienti dall'area in esame e su materiali dai ripostigli dell'area settentrionale di Madriolo, caratterizzato dalla presenza di

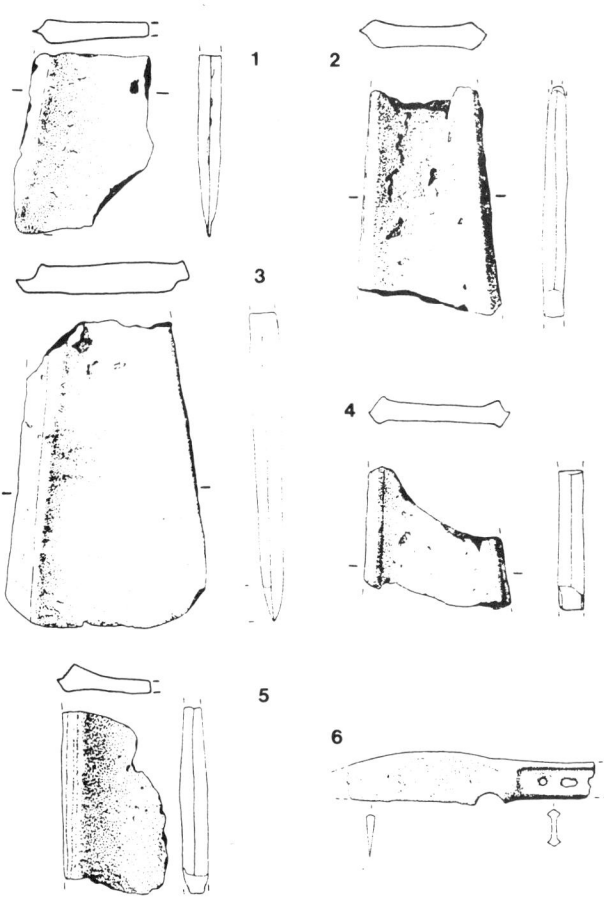

Fig. 4.1-5. Pani ad ascia dal ripostiglio di Piano di Tallone.
4.6. Coltello tipo Matrei, Varietà A.

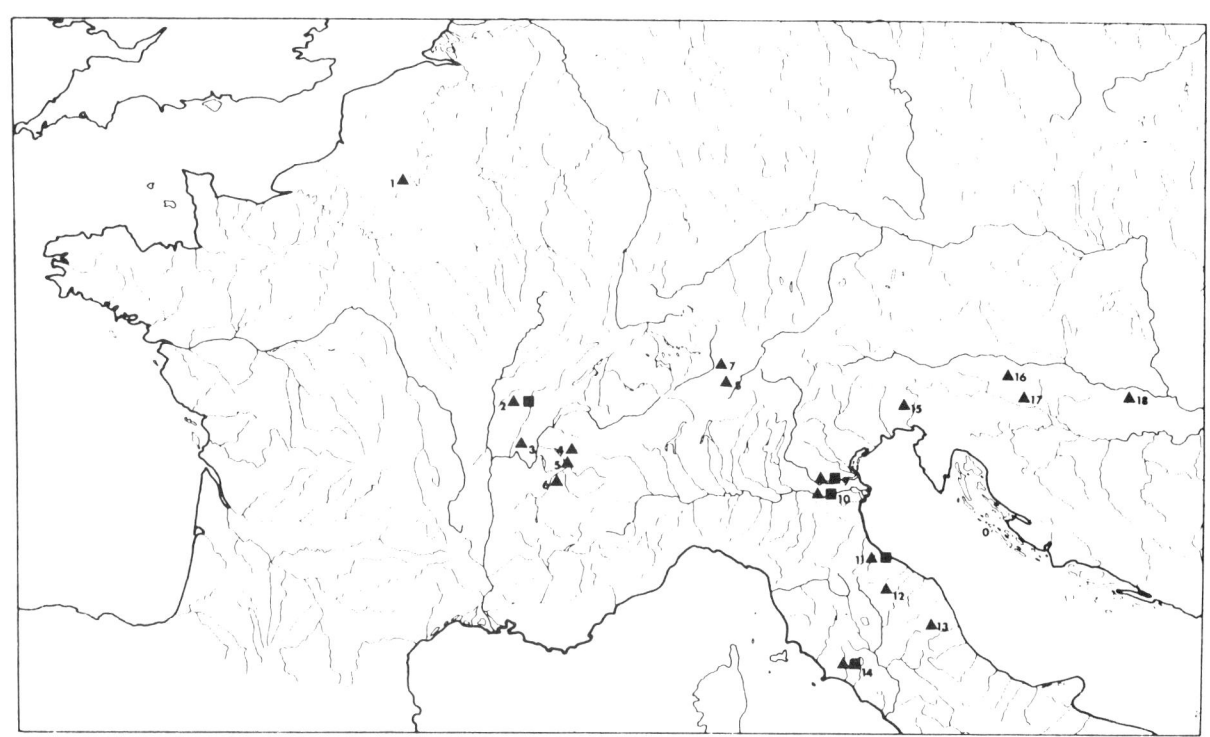

Fig. 6. Carta di distribuzione dei siti con pani a piccone (A, ▲) e palette con innesto a cannone (B, ■):
1- Caix; 2- Larnaud; 3- Laigneu; 4- Thenèsol; 5- Albertville; 6- Goncelin; 7- Schiers; 8- Filisur; 9- Montagnana; 10- Frattesina;
11- Poggio Berni; 12- Chiuse del Frontone; 13- Marsia; 14- 'tra Manciano e Samprugnano'; 15- Madriolo; 16- Miljana;
17- Ivanec Bistranski; 18- Kapelna

'pani a piccone', e di Casalecchio (Rimini), collegato all'Italia centrale per più aspetti ma, in particolare, per la presenza di una forma di fusione per ascia ad alette come a Manciano/Samprugnano. Comune ai due ripostigli, oltre alla forma di fusione, è la presenza di grandi quantità di ossidi di ferro sulla superficie di alcuni oggetti (sulla probabile lavorazione del ferro durante la tarda età del Bronzo cfr. Delpino 1988; tracce di lavorazione del ferro sono presenti anche a Scarceta):

In base ai dati acquisiti (cfr. Casagrande *et al.* c.s), si può osservare anche in questo caso il ricorrere di alcune situazioni che mettono in evidenza stretti legami tra l'area centrale tirrenica (in particolare i rinvenimenti di Piano di Tallone e Manciano/Samprugnano) e l'area centro-settentrionale, anche se ciascun gruppo mantiene caratteristiche proprie. In particolare, i collegamenti possono essere confermati dalla presenza, in piccole quantità, dei seguenti elementi chimici:

Tab.I. Analisi degli oggetti del lago di Mezzano eseguiti in assorbimento atomico

Campioni	Cu (ppm)	Sn (ppm)	Pb (ppm)	Fe (ppm)	Ni (ppm)	Co (ppm)	AS (ppm)	SB (ppm)
Ascia n.3	678	64.0	5.0	-	-	0.15	8.4	<0.3
Ascia n.7	485	32.9	3.1	4.1	-	0.17	6.4	<0.3
Spada n.8	495	36.9	2.0	1.3	-	0.24	4.7	<0.3
Spada n.9	609	56.0	3.0	2.0	1	<0.05	2.7	<0.3

Tab.II. Percentuale in peso degli elementi nelle leghe originali

Campioni	Cu (%)	Sn (%)	Pb (%)	Fe (%)	Ni (%)	Co (%)	As (%)	SB (%)
Ascia n.3	89.2	8.4	0.7	-	-	0.002	1.1	<0.03
Ascia n.7	85.4	5.8	0.5	0.7	-	0.003	1.1	<0.05
Spada n.8	91.7	6.8	0.4	0.2	-	0.04	0.9	<0.04
Spada n.9	84.1	8.6	0.4	0.3	0.1	<0.01	0.4	-

- piombo (Piano di Tallone; Casalecchio; Madriolo);
- ferro e cobalto (Manciano/Samprugnano e Madriolo);
- nichel (Manciano/Samprugnano; Madriolo)
- antimonio (Manciano/Samprugnano; lago di Mezzano; Casalecchio).

L'esistenza di antimonio nei materiali dell'area in esame può derivare dallo sfruttamento dei giacimenti di *stibina*, nella zona di Manciano. In particolare questa ipotesi appare confermata dall'alta percentuale di questo minerale evidenziato dall'analisi della forma di fusione in metallo per ascia ad alette del ripostiglio 'tra Manciano e Samprugnano'.

La presenza di nichel, cobalto e antimonio sembra essere prerogativa dei campioni di Madriolo e Manciano/Samprugnano, mentre il fatto che essi compaiano solo in traccia indica l'uso di minerali più o meno complessi e non un processo di alligazione voluto. I collegamenti tra questi due centri risultano tanto più stretti se si considera che i dati di Frattesina per le analoghe classi di materiali (pani a piccone e palette con innesto a cannone) presentano un situazione del tutto diversa. Questi stessi elementi sono presenti in traccia anche nei campioni del lago di Mezzano; anche in questo caso l'ipotesi di uno stretto collegamento tra questi due siti appare altamente probabile.

Tra gli altri dati evidenziati dalle analisi microstrutturali possono essere sottolineati i seguenti:

- relativamente alle palette con innesto a cannone provenienti da Manciano/Samprugnano, almeno un campione presenta una matrice di solo Cu, mentre negli altri essa è normalmente di lega Cu-Sn;

- anche per quanto riguarda i pani a piccone sono presenti campioni di solo Cu insieme ad altri di bronzo; nel caso di campioni ricchi in ossido di piombo e con assenza di ferro appare plausibile l'utilizzo intenzionale di galena (PbS).

Particolarmente interessante appaiono infine i risultati delle analisi metallografiche eseguite sulle spade di Mezzano. La microstruttura dell'esemplare tipo Arco ha evidenziato la presenza di grani equiassici con geminati di origine termica e la completa assenza di segni distintivi della rilavorazione della lama; la spada tipo Canegrate ha mostrato invece la presenza di una struttura dendritica, tipica dei getti "grezzi di fusione" (Garagnani, Spinedi & Baffetti 1993). Entrambi i manufatti potrebbero rientrare quindi in una sfera rituale, ed essere considerate come offerte votive anche se non si può escludere che si tratti più semplicemente di oggetti non finiti.

Nel tentativo di riassumere in un quadro organico le osservazioni fin qui svolte, possiamo osservare che se nelle prime fasi dell'età del Bronzo antico le fogge metalliche nell'area in esame presentano, come appare dagli studi di Carancini, una distribuzione limitata ad un ambito geografico ristretto, già sullo scorcio di questa fase è possibile cogliere un collegamento tra l'area tirrenica e quella centrale e orientale dell'Italia settentrionale che andrà progressivamente intensificandosi spingendosi fino alla Campania (Carancini 1991-92: 237, 239), ma che caratterizzerà in maniera del tutto particolare questa zona. Tali relazioni non si limitano al solo ambito metallurgico ma investono anche il repertorio vascolare. Per l'orizzonte antico del Bronzo medio si hanno esempi in questo senso dal lago di Mezzano (D'Erme, Pellegrini & Petitti 1991-92: 692) e, più a sud, dal lago di Bracciano (Fugazzola Delpino 1982: 132, 140–141; Capoferri 1988: 182); successivamente anche da Scarceta.

Nell'ambito di una più generale scarsezza di oggetti metallici riferibili al Bronzo medio, l'ascia di Mezzano attesta, in qualche modo, una continuità della fiorente attività metallurgica della fase precedente che avrà nella tarda età del bronzo i suoi esiti più importanti. Di rilevante importanza appare inoltre la presenza di un'ascia ad alette mediane dal vicino territorio di Orvieto, di tipologia prettamente padana (Carancini 1991-92: fig. 4.11).

Relativamente alla produzione vascolare, i contatti tra le due aree appaiono ora meno puntuali, tuttavia è interessante notare la presenza di frammenti ceramici di 'tipologia appenninica' in alcuni insediamenti del Veneto, in una zona che durante il Bronzo finale presenterà stretti legami con l'area in esame (Fasani & Salzani 1975; Leonardi 1973: tav.68A, 1).

Con la tarda età del bronzo la quantità e qualità dei dati disponibili consentono osservazioni più puntuali. Un'attività metallurgica effettuata *in loco*, ipotizzabile già per le fasi più antiche (Carancini 1991-92: 250–252), è ora attestata da una serie organica di elementi: aree di lavorazione, forme di fusione, ripostigli. Inoltre, l'alto contenuto in rame evidenziato dall'analisi metallografiche di alcune panelle consente di assimilare i campioni esaminati a residui di operazioni fusorie e quindi, comunque, non estrattive. Questo dato, anche se per ora effettuato su un limitato numero di campioni è della massima importanza in quanto offre una base di riscontro oggettivo all'ipotesi di un'articolazione del complesso ciclo che sottintende l'attività metallurgica. Appare molto probabile infatti che le località in cui si estraeva il minerale e in cui si svolgeva la prima lavorazione fossero distinte da quelle delle officine in cui si producevano gli oggetti finiti e, possibilmente, gestite da gruppi differenti. Quali effettivamente fossero le zone di approvvigionamento allo stato attuale dello studio, e in mancanza di ricerche specifiche, è impossibile dire, tuttavia, come già accennato, appare altamente probabile lo sfruttamento di risorse locali, in particolare quelle di antimonio.

Anche i contatti evidenziati con l'area settentrionale restano alquanto problematici. Infatti, se le 'affinità tipologiche' evidenziate possono trovare veicolo nella koinè metallurgica che si afferma proprio a partire dal XIII secolo tra Italia, Europa ed Egeo (Bietti Sestieri 1976-77: 202; Peroni 1985), occorre ricercare le motivazioni che sono alla base del massiccio inserimento della zona in esame in questo circuito. Un contributo in questa direzione potrebbe essere fornita, se confermata da altri dati, dall'esame di un campione proveniente dalla Sardegna (in studio da parte della d.ssa Lo Schiavo alla quale vanno i nostri ringraziamenti) nel quale sono state riscontrate inclusioni di antimonio, elemento assai raramente presente nei metalli di origine sarda.

Se del tutto ipotetici rimangono per ora la direzione e i ruoli dei collegamenti intravisti è forse possibile, per un breve arco cronologico, individuare i percorsi attraverso cui essi si svolgevano partendo dall'esame della distribuzione dei 'pani a piccone' (l'ampiezza di tali contatti e la presenza nell'arco alpino di cospicui giacimenti di rame e galena, rende difficile limitarne le motivazioni in una generica 'ricerca dei metalli' a senso unico nord-sud. Sembra invece più ragionevole ipotizzare un interscambio di materie prime (rame-antimonio) o anche un intervento dell'area settentrionale nel vivace e stimolante 'mercato tirrenico'. In quest'ottica risulterebbe funzionale l'inserimento di Casalecchio).

Abbiamo visto che per quanto riguarda i ripostigli italiani, questi pani, insieme alle palette con innesto a cannone, gravitano principalmente verso l'area adriatica. Anche nel ripostiglio 'tra Manciano e Samprugnano', il solo noto al di qua dell'Appennino, sono presenti elementi riconducibili all'area adriatica: si tratta di due tipi di spilloni a rotella di cui uno, in particolare, attestato solo in questo ripostiglio e nella necropoli di Pianello (Peroni 1980: 34, isoida 39).

L'ipotesi di una rotta commerciale, in cui confluiscono anche elementi dell'Europa centrale, che, in stretto collegamento con la via dell'ambra, dal *Caput Adriae* si sviluppa lungo l'Adriatico fino all'area egea è ormai ampiamente documentata (Harding 1984: 229-266; Vagnetti 1986: 213, n.45). Da quanto è stato precedentemente detto, e ponendo in risalto il ruolo che potrebbe aver avuto il mare Adriatico nell'ambito degli scambi commerciali tra Europa centrale e Italia settentrionale da un lato e mondo egeo dall'altro, si potrebbe pertanto ipotizzare che la produzione dei 'pani a piccone', originariamente localizzata nell'area delle Alpi (cfr. Borgna 1992), sia poi confluita in un più ampio circuito commerciale in cui la redistribuzione lungo il settore adriatico potrebbe essere stata svolta dall'insediamento di Frattesina, situato nella valle del Po, la cui importanza durante l'età del Bronzo finale come centro di produzione e di commercio è ormai pienamente attestata.

Un ulteriore apporto in favore di questa ipotesi potrebbe essere rappresentato da una particolare varietà di 'pane a piccone', caratterizzata dallo spessore sottile (fig. 7), presente nel ripostiglio marchigiano di Marsia, e che ha precisi riscontri tra il materiale di Madriolo, in quello del ripostiglio 'tra Manciano e Samprugnano' e, soprattutto, con un frammento tipologicamente analogo dal ripostiglio cipriota di Enkòmi (Matthaus 1985: 41-45, tav. 126.15).

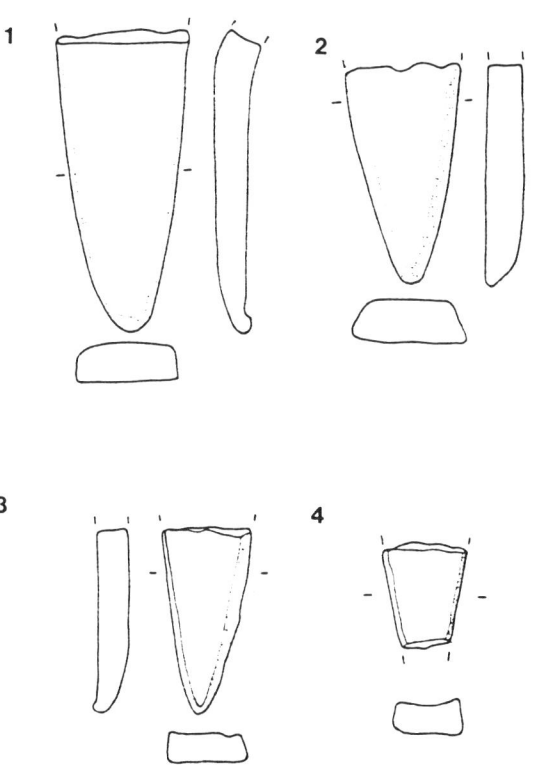

Fig. 7. Pani a piccone del tipo 'sottile'; 15- Enkòmi; 16- Marsia; 17- Madriolo; 18- 'tra Manciano e Samprugnano'.

Ringraziamenti

La ricerca è condotta nell'ambito del Progetto Finalizzato CNR 'Chimica Fine II' (Metodologie di Salvaguardia dei Beni Culturali e del Patrimonio Edilizio) e sviluppata, per quanto riguarda le indagini analitico-strutturali, con l'Istituto di Metallurgia dell'Università di Bologna. Desidero esprimere un particolare ringraziamento al dott. Gian Luca Garagnani per i consigli e i suggerimenti forniti nel corso del lavoro e ricordare il prof. Paolo Spinedi, recentemente scomparso; si ringrazia inoltre la dott.ssa Adriana Baffetti per la collaborazione relativa alle indagini analitico-strutturali. Il progetto di ricerca relativo all'insediamento del lago di Mezzano è diretto dalla d.ssa P. Petitti della Soprintendenza Archeologica all'Etruria Meridionale che ringrazio vivamente per l'invito a studiare il materiale metallico. Inoltre devo offrire particolari ringraziamenti al prof. Raffaele De Marinis e alla d.ssa Patrizia Frontini per aver agevolato e permesso l'esame della spada di Canegrate; alla d.ssa Poggiani Keller per le notizie relative ai recenti rinvenimenti di Scarceta, ancora in fase di studio; alla d.ssa A.M. Sestieri per aver permesso di prendere in considerazione, in via preliminare, i dati relativi alle analisi delle campioni da Frattesina; al prof. Carancini per la cortesia e liberalità con le quali ha messo a disposizione informazioni relative a studi ancora in fase di elaborazione.

Bibliografia

AA.VV. 1993. *Vulcano e Mezzano. Insediamento e produzioni artigianali nella media valle del Fiora nell'età del bronzo,* Valentano.

Bellintani, G.F. & Peretto, R. 1972. 'Il ripostiglio di Frattesina ed altri manufatti enei raccolti in superficie. Notizie preliminari', *Padusa,* VIII, 32-49.

Bernabò Brea, L. & Cavalier, M. 1980. *Melïgunìs Lipára,* IV, Palermo.

Bianco Peroni, V. 1970. *Le spade nell'Italia continentale,* (*Prähistorische Bronzefunde,* IV,1), München.

Bianco Peroni, V. 1974. 'Altre spade dall'Italia continentale, Beiträge zu italienischen und griechischen Bronzefunde', H. Müller-Karpe ed., *Prähistorische Bronzefunde* XX,1, München, 1-26.

Bietti Sestieri, A. 1973. 'The metal industry of continental Italy, 13th to the 11th century BC and its connections with the Aegean', *Proceedings of Prehistoric Society,* 39, 383-424.

Bietti Sestieri, A. 1976-77. 'Contributo allo studio delle forme di scambio della tarda età del bronzo nell'Italia continentale', *Dialoghi di Archeologia,* IX-X, 201-41.

Bietti Sestieri, A. 1981. 'Produzione e scambio nell'Italia protostorica. Alcune ipotesi sul ruolo dell'industria metallurgica nell'Etruria mineraria alla fine dell'età del Bronzo', in *L'Etruria mineraria, Atti del XII Convegno di Studi Etruschi e Italici,* Firenze, 223-264.

Borgna, E. 1992. *Il ripostiglio di Madriolo presso Cividale e i pani a piccone del Friuli-Venezia Giulia,* Roma.

Bouzek,J. 1985. *The Aegean, Anatolia and Europe: Cultural Interrelations in the Second Millennium B.C.,* Göteborg.

Capoferri, B. 1988. *Cronologia dell'età del bronzo media e recente nell'area transpadana centro-orientale,* Brescia.

Carancini, G.L. 1975. 'Gli spilloni nell'Italia continentale', *Prähistorische Bronzefunde,* XIII,2, München.

Carancini, G.L. 1979. 'Alcuni aspetti della metallurgia nel Lazio nel corso dell'età del Bronzo', *Archeologia Laziale,* II, 177-84.

Carancini, G.L. 1991/92. 'L'Italia centro-meridionale', in *L'età del Bronzo in Italia nei secoli dal XVI al XIV a. C.,* (Atti del Congresso Viareggio 1989, *Rassegna di Archeologia,* 10), 235-54

Casagrande, A., Garagnani, G.L., Poli, G. & Spinedi, P. 1992. 'Considerazioni sulla metallurgia del rame nell'antichità: studio delle inclusioni in pani, panelle e lingotti', in *Archeometallurgia, ricerche e prospettive, Atti del Colloquio Internazionale di Archeometallurgia,* Bologna-Dozza Imolese, 1988, Bologna, 149-157.

Casagrande, A., Garagnani, G.L., Landi, E., Pellegrini, E. & Spinedi, P., 1993. 'Indagini analitico-strutturali su reperti metallici di età protostorica dell'Italia continentale: dati e considerazioni preliminari su un programma di ricerca pilota', *Studi Etruschi,* LVIII, 316-331.

Casagrande, A., Garagnani, G.L, Pellegrini, E. & Spinedi, P., c.s. 'Microstructural and analytical characterization of Bronze Age copper ingots and some metallic artefacts', *Second Southern-European Conference on Archaeometry,* 19-21 April 1991, PACT, c.s.

Ciacci, A. 1981. 'L'ambiente naturale', in *Gli Etruschi in Maremma,* M. Cristofani (ed.), Milano, 9-27.

Cocchi Genick, D. & Grifoni Cremonesi, R. 1989. *L'età del Rame in Toscana,* Viareggio.

Delpino, F. 1988. 'Prime testimonianze dell'uso del ferro in Italia', *Pact,* 21, 47-68.

De Marinis, R. 1984. 'Tre nuove spade della tarda età del Bronzo', *Notiziario della Soprintendenza Archeologica della Lombardia,* 46-47.

D'Erme, L., Pellegrini, E. & Petitti, P. 1991-92. 'L'insediamento sommerso del lago di Mezzano', in *L'età del Bronzo in Italia nei secoli dal XVI al XIV a. C.,* (Atti del Congresso Viareggio 1989, *Rassegna di Archeologia,* 10), 692-93.

Fasani, L. & Salzani, L. 1975 'Nuovo insediamento dell'età del Bronzo in località "Fondo Paviani" presso Legnago (Verona)', *Bollettino del Museo Civico di Storia Naturale di Verona,* II, 259-81.

Franco, M.C. 1982. *L'insediamento preistorico del Lago di Mezzano,* Roma.

Fugazzola Delpino, M.A 1982. 'Rapporto preliminare sulle ricerche condotte dalla Soprintendenza Archeologica dell'Etruria Meridionale nei bacini lacustri dell'apparato vulcanico sabatino', *Archeologia Subacquea,* (suppl. 4 del Bollettino d'Arte), 123-49.

Fugazzola Delpino, M.A. 1992. 'Note di topografia preistorica', *Bullettino di Paletnologia Italiana,* 83, n.s. I, 279-322.

Garagnani, G.L., Spinedi, P. & Baffetti, A. 1993. 'Caratterizzazione microstrutturale ed analisi chimiche dei reperti metallici', in AA.VV. 1993, 87-95.

Giardino, C. 1984. 'Insediamenti e sfruttamento minerario del territorio durante la media e tarda età del Bronzo: ipotesi e considerazioni', *Nuovo Bollettino Archeologico Sardo,* 123-141.

Gustin, M. 1979. *Notranjska. K zacetkom zelezne dobe na severnem jadranu,* Ljubljana.

Harding, A.F. 1984. *The Mycenaeans and Europe,* London.

Leonardi, G. 1973. *Materiali preistorici e protostorici dal Museo di Chiampo, Vicenza,* Venezia.

Mayer, E.F. 1977. 'Die Äxte und Beile in Österreich', *Prähistorische Bronzefunde,* IX, 9, München.

Matthäus, H. 1985. *Metalgefässe und Gefässuntersetzer der Bronzezeit der geometrischen und archaischen Periode aus Cypern, Prähistorische Bronzefunde,* II.8, München.

Montelius, O. 1895-1912. *La civilisation primitive en Italie depuis l'introduction des metaux,* Stockolm.

Negroni Catacchio, N. 1981. 'Sassi Neri (Capalbio, Grosseto)', *Sorgenti della Nova. Una comunità protostorica e il suo territorio nell'Etruria meridionale,* N. Negroni Catacchio (ed.), Roma.

Negroni Catacchio, N. 1983. 'Rapporti tra l'area alto-adriatica e quella medio tirrenica durante il Bronzo finale', *Padusa,* XIX, 65-78.

Negroni Catacchio, N. & Miari, M. 1991/92. 'L'area tra Fiora e Albegna: nuovi dati su paesaggio e popolamento', in *L'età del Bronzo in Italia nei secoli dal XVI al XIV a. C.,* Atti del Congresso Viareggio 1989, *Rassegna di Archeologia,* 10, 393-402.

Pellegrini, E. 1985. 'Forma di fusione per ascia ad alette', in Aranguren, B., Pellegrini, E. & Perazzi, P., *L'insediamento protostorico di Pitigliano, campagne di scavo 1982-83,* Pitigliano, 47-49.

Pellegrini, E. 1989. 'Un ripostiglio inedito del Bronzo finale dalle collezioni del Museo L. Pigorini', *Studi Etruschi,* LV, 3-20.

Pellegrini, E. 1992a. 'Nuovi dati su due ripostigli dell'età del bronzo finale del Grossetano: Piano di Tallone e "tra Manciano e Samprugnano"', *Bullettino di Paletnologia Italiana,* 83, n.s. I, 341-360.

Pellegrini, E. 1992b. 'Aspetti regionali e relazioni interregionali nella produzione metallurgica del bronzo finale nell'Italia continentale: i ripostigli con pani a piccone', in *Archeometallurgia, ricerche e prospettive, Atti del Colloquio Internazionale di Archeometallurgia,* (Bologna-Dozza Imolese, 1988), Bologna, 589-603.

Pellegrini, E. 1993. 'Aspetti della metallurgia nel comprensorio del lago di Mezzano e nella media valle del Fiora dal Bronzo antico all'XI sec. a.C.', in AA.VV. 1993, 73-85.

Peroni, R. 1971. *L'età del Bronzo nella penisola italiana, vol. I, L'antica età del Bronzo,* Firenze.

Peroni, R. (ed.) 1980. *Il Bronzo finale in Italia,* Bari.

Peroni, R. 1985. 'Presenze micenee e forme socio-economiche nell'Italia protostorica', *Magna Grecia e Mondo Miceneo, Atti del XXII Convegno di Studi sulla Magna Grecia,* Taranto, 211-84.

Peroni, R. 1989. *Protostoria dell'Italia continentale. La penisola italiana nelle età del Bronzo e del Ferro,* Roma.

Poggiani Keller, R. 1988. 'L'insediamento della media e tarda età del bronzo di Scarceta (Manciano-GR)', *Museo di Preistoria e*

Protostoria della valle del fiume Fiora, N. Negroni Catacchio (ed.), Manciano.

Poggiani Keller, R. 1993. 'Anticipazioni sul complesso dei manufatti di bronzo e sull'attività metallurgica in situ nelle fasi tarda età del Bronzo dell'insediamento di Scarceta', in AA.VV. 1993, 105–124.

Salzani, L. 1989. 'Gazzo Veronese, necropoli del Turbine', *Quaderni di Archeologia del Veneto*, V, 167–170.

Sestini, A. 1981. 'Introduzione all'Etruria mineraria: il quadro naturale e ambientale', in *L'Etruria mineraria, Atti del XII Convegno di Studi Etruschi e Italici*, Firenze, 3–21.

Soffredi, A. 1973. 'II e III Campagna di scavo nell'abitato preistostorico di Scarceta (Manciano), Anni 1971-72', *Atti della XIV Riunione Scientifica dell'Istituto Italiano di Preistoria e Protostoria*, Firenze, 28–43.

Vagnetti, L. 1982. 'Quindici anni di studi e ricerche tra il mondo egeo e l'Italia protostorica', in Vagnetti, L. (ed.), *Magna Grecia e mondo miceneo. Nuovi documenti*, Taranto, 9–40.

Vagnetti, L. 1986. 'Cypriot elements beyond the Aegean in the Bronze Age', *Acts of the International Archaeological Symposium*, Nicosia, 201-214.

Vinski Gasparini, K. 1973. *Kultura polja sa žarama u sjevernoi Hrvatskoj*, Zadar.

von Eles Masi, P. 1986. *Le fibule nell'Italia continentale*, (*Prähistorische Bronzefunde*, XIV,5), München.

Zifferero, A. 1991. 'Miniere e metallurgia estrattiva in Etruria meridionale: per una lettura critica di alcuni dati archeologici e minerari', *Studi Etruschi,* LVII, 201-241.

54

La Ricostruzione Grafica di Alcune Strutture Residenziali e di Servizio in Etruria: Problemi e Metodi

N. Negroni Catacchio & M. Miari

(Istituto di Archeologia, Università degli Studi di Milano)

Sommario: *Vengono presentate in questa sede alcune ipotesi di ricostruzione grafica relative ai principali modelli abitativi dell'Etruria protostorica, con particolare riguardo alle strutture degli abitati del Bronzo Finale di Sorgenti della Nova e di Sovana. La ricostruzione grafica delle abitazioni e delle strutture di servizio rinvenute negli insediamenti protostorici non esaurisce le sue finalità nella semplice visualizzazione ed evidenziazione dei risultati delle ricerche, ma consente, attraverso un'analisi minuta dei dati di scavo, di gettare nuova luce sui criteri di suddivisione dello spazio, sia interno che esterno alle singole unità residenziali, sulla reale consistenza dei nuclei abitativi e sull'organizzazione delle zone comuni destinate a particolari funzioni produttive e domestiche. Supporto indispensabile per la ricostruzione grafica sono stati sia i dati di carattere 'etnografico', in particolare quelli desumibili dallo studio delle capanne utilizzate dei pastori come ricovero stagionale di persone ed animali, sia quelli di carattere archeologico, ovvero le rappresentazioni di abitazioni, quali le urne a capanna dell'età del Ferro e alcune tombe ceretane. Per le strutture di servizio, particolare attenzione è stata prestata al legame esistente con le unità residenziali, distinguendo tra attività e funzioni proprie ad ogni nucleo abitativo e ambienti utilizzati in comune. Dall'analisi delle caratteristiche tecnico-funzionali è infatti emersa l'esistenza di un alto livello di specializzazione nella destinazione delle singole strutture, soprattutto per quanto riguarda forni, focolari e aree di cottura.*

Ci è sembrato interessante presentare in questa sede le ricostruzioni grafiche di alcune abitazioni e strutture di servizio rinvenute negli scavi dell'abitato del Bronzo Finale di Sorgenti della Nova (Viterbo) e negli strati, sempre del Bronzo Finale, dell'abitato poi etrusco di Sovana (Grosseto).

L'esigenza di usare le ricostruzioni grafiche come strumenti di lavoro deriva dalla complessità degli attuali metodi di scavo, che tendono a suddividere i numerosi dati che si raccolgono in 'unità di informazione' già pronte per essere elaborate, rendendo estremamente frazionati i risultati della ricerca. Il momento della sintesi conclusiva assume di conseguenza una particolare rilevanza, poichè deve rendere di nuovo unitaria una informazione parcellizzata, organizzandola in una costruzione organica e ben strutturata, che entri a far parte delle conoscenze acquisite. In molti casi le parole sono insufficienti, solo l'immagine corrispondente all'ipotesi finale puo renderla immediatamente comprensibile; ma c'è di più, ed è questo il risultato più interessante del lavoro di ricostruzione grafica su cui ci siamo impegnati: poichè nella ricostruzione, supponiamo di una capanna, ogni singolo elemento deve essere rappresentato, ma anche giustificato, si è necessariamente costretti ad analizzare e a combinare in modo unitario, logico e congruente tutti i dati a disposizione, quelli emersi dal proprio o da altri scavi, quelli iconografici, quelli che, per analogia, possono essere ricercati nel contesto etnografico o, come in alcuni casi è avvenuto, nella simulazione dell'archeologia sperimentale.

La ricostruzione grafica si pone quindi non solo come un supporto che rende più chiara e comprensibile l'ipotesi conclusiva, ma soprattutto come uno strumento di approfondimento e meditazione di non trascurabile portata.

1. Le abitazioni (NNC)

Nella ricostruzione della capanne protostoriche, abbiamo utilizzato due gruppi ben distinti di fonti: da una parte quelle di carattere 'etnografico', cioè tutta una serie di informazioni ricavate dallo studio delle capanne costruite fino a non molti anni fa da pastori, contadini e carbonai come ricovero per persone e animali; noi stessi le abbiamo rilevate gli anni scorsi in Maremma, supportandone l'analisi con alcuni studi generali sull'argomento; l'altro gruppo di dati, che si può definire 'archeologico' e iconografico è costituto dalle rappresentazioni di abitazioni contemporanee o vicine nel tempo all'epoca di cui ci si occupa (cfr. Cataldi *et al.* 1962; Sorgenti Nova 1981 e 1995; Bartoloni *et al.* 1987; Catalogo Manciano 1988: 199–231). Nel caso in esame rientrano in questo gruppo le urne a capanna dell'età del Ferro, alcune tombe a camera, specie ceretane, di epoca orientalizzante e pochi altri oggetti distribuiti nello stesso arco di tempo. Naturalmente è quest'ultimo insieme di dati a fornire il contributo determinante alla ricostruzione dell'aspetto esteriore dell'abitazione, mentre il primo fornisce utili indicazioni per quanto riguarda i particolari costruttivi e l'adozione di soluzioni tecniche o più propriamente architettoniche.

Sorgenti della Nova

In questo grande insediamento si sono riscontrati alcuni modelli di abitazioni che si ripetono con poche varianti in punti diversi della rupe su cui sorge l'abitato. Ad essi corrispondono probabilmente alcune differenti categorie sociali, secondo una ipotesi interpretativa altrove proposta (Sorgenti Nova 1995) e sulla quale non è possibile in questa sede tornare.

Le abitazioni a pianta ellittica

Presentano alcune specifiche tecniche costruttive: la presenza di una canaletta perimetrale che ospita i buchi dei pali relativi alle pareti, le quali non hanno tuttavia la funzione di reggere il tetto; l'esistenza di una o due serie di pali interni portanti; la quasi assoluta mancanza di resti di rivestimenti di argilla per le pareti, per le quali si è quindi supposta una copertura con materiali vegetali.

1. L'abitazione 2 del settore III (fig. 1)
Quanto rimane delle tracce sul terreno, probabile frutto di successivi rifacimenti, rivela sostanzialmente l'esistenza di una canaletta perimetrale esterna che, secondo l'ipotesi qui proposta, ospitava la parete dell'abitazione; una seconda canaletta, qui considerata interna per analogia con gli elementi della capanna più avanti illustrata, serviva a suddividere gli spazi interni, mentre due serie di buchi ospitavano i pali longitudinali che costituivano il sistema portante.

Nella ricostruzione grafica si è innanzi tutto completata la pianta della capanna, integrandola nei tratti mancanti: si è individuato l'asse maggiore dell'ellissi e lo si è utilizzato come asse di simmetria della struttura. In tal modo la capanna risulta suddivisa in tre navate, mentre una robusta parete, ipotizzabile per la presenza di quattro grossi buchi di palo, isolava dal resto la parte posteriore, cui si accedeva probabilmente attraverso una porta. Si è poi ricostruito l'alzato, mettendo in evidenza la veduta laterale esterna, la sezione trasversale e l'assonometria generale. Data la scarsità di rivestimenti d'argilla, si è ipotizzato un rivestimento delle pareti simile a quello delle capanne attuali, costituito da un doppio strato: quello inferiore composto da cannette di palude, legate una a fianco dell'altra a creare lunghe strisce accostate e quello superiore formato da ciuffi di paglia inseriti capovolti.

Il tetto dell'abitazione era sostenuto da coppie di grossi pali, su cui doveva appoggiare una capriata. Sfruttando come punti di appoggio le pareti perimetrali della capanna, veniva realizzata un'intelaiatura con travi, poi unite tra loro con traverse orizzontali, realizzando così una struttura su cui veniva adagiato il rivestimento del tetto. Usando invece come punto di appoggio le travi centrali, si otteneva la sopraelevazione dal tetto e l'apertura delle due finestre sommitali per la fuoriuscita del fumo, simili a quelle delle urne a capanna. Sul modello delle medesime urne è stata ricostruita anche la pendenza. E' importante sottolineare come le tracce delle strutture sopravvissute permettano di ricostruire in questo caso un modello assai simile a quello dei cinerari in questione. L'unica differenza sostanziale sembra costituita dal rivestimento, per il quale si è ipotizzata una struttura vegetale simile a quella delle

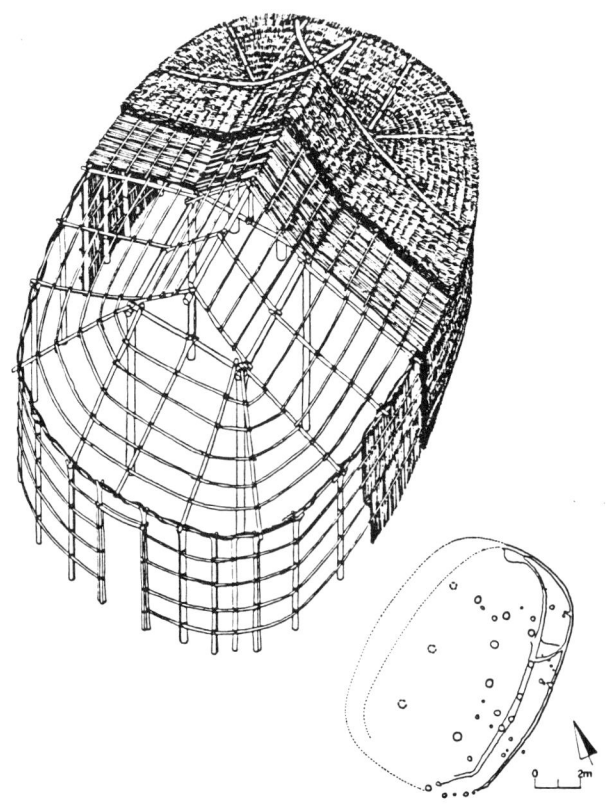

Fig. 1. Sorgenti della Nova (VT). Abitazione a pianta ellittica n.2 del settore III. Ipotesi di ricostruzione: assonometria.

pareti. E' infine possibile ipotizzare che anche nella situazione reale, come nelle urne a capanna, il rivestimento era trattenuto da una serie di pali impostati alla sua base, che si incrociavano sporgendo sul colmo.

I dati relativi all'altezza sono stati ipotizzati analizzando le proporzioni desunte dall'insieme delle fonti citate e dai particolari strutturali della abitazione stessa: profondità e diametro dei buchi di palo e loro reciproca distanza; ne risulta all'interno un'altezza di poco superiore ai due metri lungo le pareti, di circa 3 metri lungo i pali centrali e di 4 metri al centro. Naturalmente queste misure saranno maggiori all'esterno, dove la copertura delle pareti e del tetto doveva assumere un certo spessore.

2. L'abitazione del settore Vc (figg.2–3a)

Questa abitazione si discosta in parte dalla precedente: presenta infatti dimensioni maggiori, almeno nella lunghezza e una diversa distribuzione interna dei buchi di palo rimasti. La porzione superstite è piuttosto esigua e rende la ricostruzione meno certa che nel caso precedente. Si è comunque dovuta scartare l'ipotesi delle tre navate, come nell'esempio sopra illustrato, poichè in questo caso è stata individuata una sola serie di pali allineati lungo l'asse maggiore. Su queste basi l'abitazione risulta più lunga e in proporzione più stretta di quella precedente: più simile alle capanne dei pastori che alle urne a capanna.

La tecnica costruttiva delle pareti è simile a quella sopra descritta, con pali allineati all'interno di una canaletta che termina nell'area dell'ingresso; la parete corrispondente alla facciata risulta impostata non su canaletta, ma su buchi di palo. Il rivestimento proposto è simile al precedente. La copertura è costituita da un tetto a doppio spiovente, piùttosto alto, sorretto dalla serie di pali centrali. In questo caso, mancando i pali laterali di appoggio, non si può creare il rialzo centrale e, di conseguenza, neppure le due aperture sommitali. Resta attuabile invece l'ipotesi della serie di piccoli pali incrociantisi alla sommità, la cui funzione era quella di trattenere il rivestimento. E' interessante notare che la porta non è costruita al centro della facciata, ma al lato del palo centrale portante, sul quale si appoggia, come in genere avviene nelle capanne attuali con struttura analoga.

Nella ricostruzione grafica si è completato il perimetro

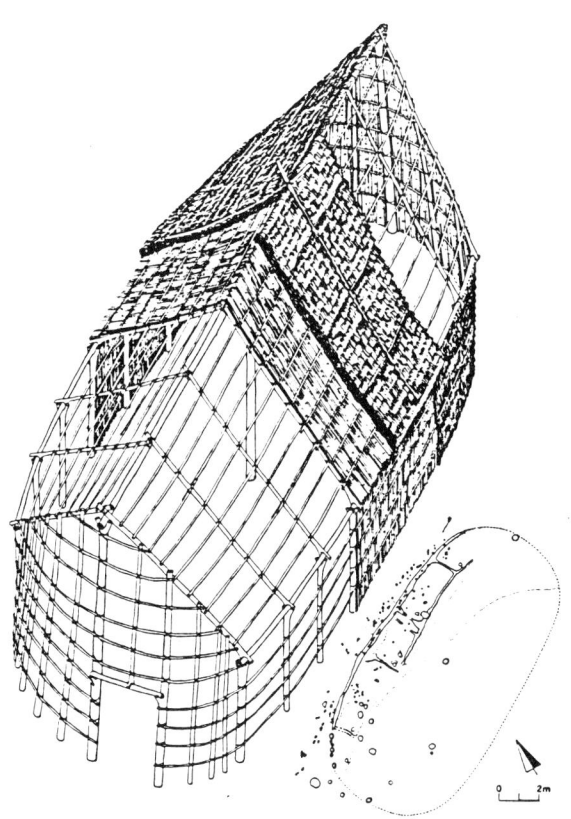

Fig. 2. Abitazione a pianta ellittica del settore Vc. Ipotesi di ricostruzione: assonometria.

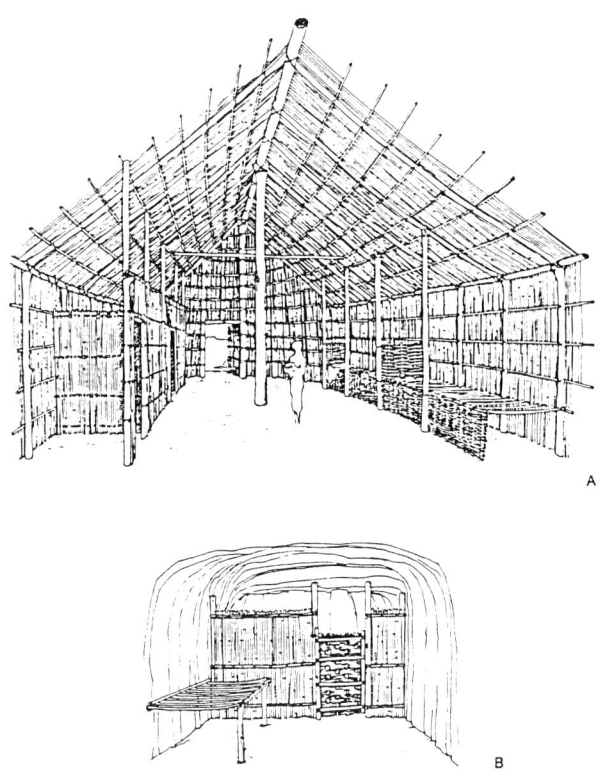

Fig. 3. A: Abitazione a pianta ellittica del settore Vc. Ricostruzione dell'interno. B: Grotta 13 del settore III. Ipotesi di ricostruzione dell'interno.

della pianta e integrato un terzo buco di palo lungo la linea mediana, in un'area intaccata da successivi interventi medievali. Si sono ricostruiti la sezione trasversale, la veduta laterale esterna e l'assonometria.

L'abitazione misura in pianta m 14 x 7 circa. L'altezza all'interno, calcolata secondo i criteri sopra illustrati, supera di poco i 2 metri lungo le pareti e raggiunge i 5 al culmine dei pali centrali. Appaiono chiare alcune suddivisioni interne appoggiate al lato maggiore conservato. Queste tracce residue sul terreno hanno anche permesso di ipotizzare l'aspetto dell'interno, che risulta essere un grande ambiente ai cui lati sono costruiti piccole stanze separate da leggere pareti, usate probabilmente per dormire, oppure robusti ripiani o sedili, che potevano fungere anche da letti, come suggeriscono i confronti attuali e i letti di pietra collocati uno di seguito all'altro nelle tombe etrusche. Qui si sono associate entrambe le ipotesi, suggerendo la coesistenza di ambienti per dormire e di piani attrezzati per le necessita della vita quotidiana.

Le capanne a base incassata

1. Le capanne 1 e 2 del settore I (figg.4-5)

Anche in questo caso la situazione risulta complessa e la ricostruzione problematica: le capanne si aprono sul pianoro sommitale della rupe, quasi privo di terra e sottoposto a continua erosione. Numerosi buchi di pali sono distribuiti su tutta l'area, addensandosi nella parte verso valle. Essi diventano più rari invece proprio attorno alle capanne, soprattutto intorno alla Cap.2, che ne è quasi totalmente priva. Poichè tuttavia la roccia è costituita da una serie di bassi strati sovrapposti che si sono venuti nel tempo via via sfaldando, sembra possibile che almeno in parte i buchi siano andati persi.

Le capanne hanno basi subcircolare e subellittica profondamente infossate; la 1 misura m 4 (compreso il portichetto) per 4.50 circa, per una profondità massima di m 1.30; presenta un ingresso a corridoio con gradini; la 2 misura m 3.30 × 3.50, con una profondita massima di cm 70 circa; ha un ingresso semplice, con un gradino che ospita due buchi di palo.

Si propongono di entrambe due ipotesi ricostruttive: la prima fa riferimento alla 'capanna cilindro-conica' della tradizione locale ed etnografica: in questo caso le pareti, distinte dal tetto e costruite con la tecnica sopra illustrata, sono formate da una serie di pali di non grandi dimensioni, terminanti, come al solito, con una forcella. Alcuni di questi pali, se non tutti, data la scarsità dei buchi corrispondenti, dovevano essere infilati nella roccia. Con una corda vegetale, più volte ripassata, i pali venivano legati tra loro.

Sulla parte sommitale i leganti formavano una

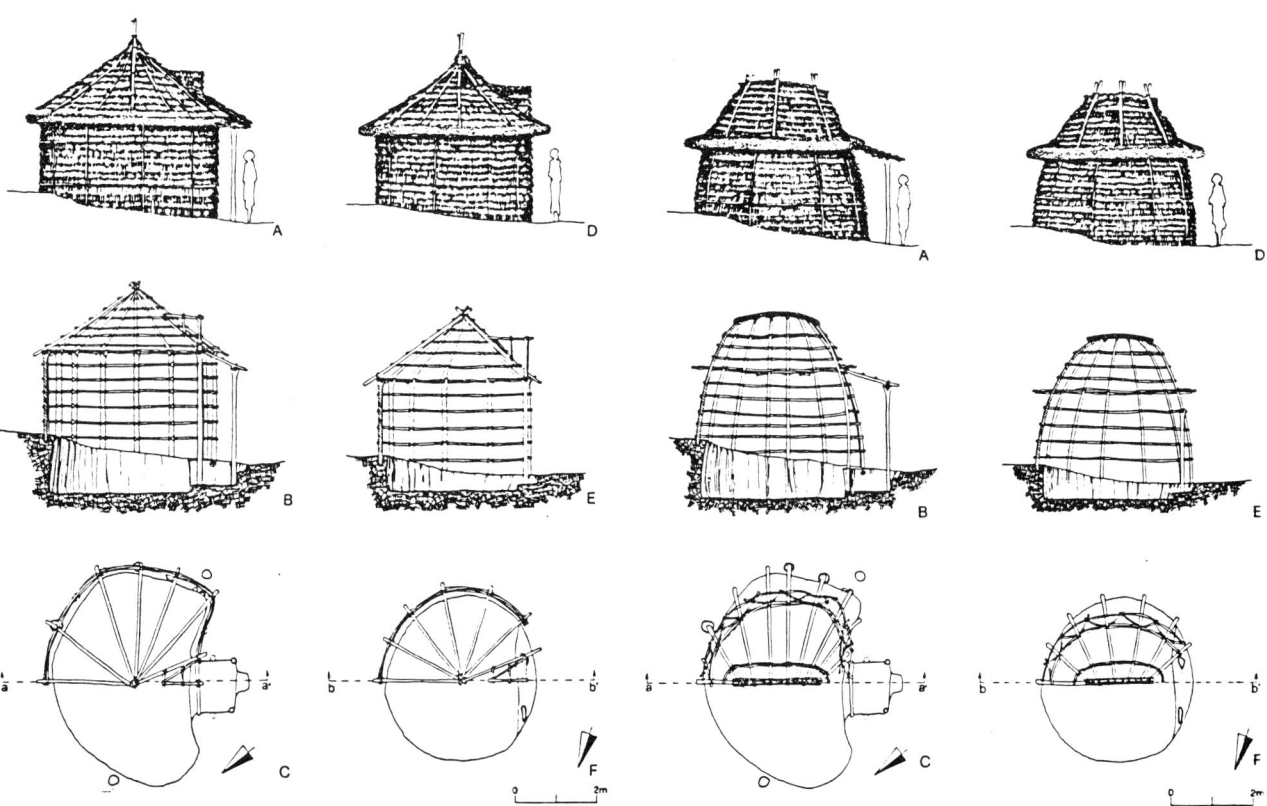

Fig. 4. Capanne 1 (A-B-C) e 2 (D-E-F) del settore I. Prima ipotesi di ricostruzione. A,D: prospetto laterale; B,E: sezioni; C,F: piante.

Fig. 5. Capanne 1 (A-B-C) e 2 (D-E-F) del settore I. Seconda ipotesi di ricostruzione. A,D: prospetto laterale; B,E: sezioni; C,F: piante.

'treccia', sulla quale, oltre che sui pali delle pareti, si appoggiavano i pali del tetto che si univano sulla cima ed erano ancora legati con corde vegetali. I grandi buchi presenti accanto al perimetro della Cap.1 potevano ospitare alcuni pali appoggiati obliquamente alla parete come contrafforte e denominati, nella Valle del Fiora, 'toccaterra'. Sui pali perimetrali corrispondenti all'ingresso poteva essere impostata la struttura relativa alla finestra sommitale, come nelle urne a capanna, mentre le tracce presenti nell'ingresso della Cap.1 permettono di ricostruire un piccolo portico, simile, anche se di minori dimensioni, a quello della capanna del Sett. Ve.

Nella ricostruzione grafica sono stati aggiunti alcuni buchi di palo perimetrali: l'altezza interna della Cap. 1 risulta di circa 3 metri lungo il perimetro e supera i 4 al centro, mentre quella della Cap. 2 va da poco più di 2 metri a circa m 3.50; l'altezza massima complessiva del portichetto è di circa m2.50.

Nell'insieme questa ricostruzione non è troppo dissimile dall'urna a capanna da Vulci-Osteria, che rappresenta evidentemente una abitazione a base infossata.

La seconda ipotesi ricostruttiva fa invece riferimento alle urne a capanna a pianta subcircolare con pareti e tetto ricurvi. In questo caso tra le pareti e il tetto non esiste alcuna soluzione di continuità: i pali perimetrali, scelti in un legno flessibile, si riuniscono alla cima legandosi ad un fascio di verghe collocate sulla sommità. Esempi di questa tecnica costruttiva, definita, sulla base del tipo di volta, 'a botte discontinua', sono presenti anche tra i primitivi attuali. Il displuvio del tetto era ricavato ancora con rami flessibili intrecciati alla parete e collocato, nella capanna 1, all'altezza del portichetto.

Per la ricostruzione grafica si è usata la medesima planimetria delle ricostruzioni precedenti, ma, almeno nel caso della Cap.1 si sono maggiormente utilizzati i buchi perimetrali rinvenuti. L'altezza complessiva della Cap.1 risulterebbe di quasi 4 metri, mentre la Cap.2 sarebbe alta circa m 3.50. Particolarmente significative appaiono le assonometrie.

Le abitazioni in grotta

Si è detto nelle parti precedenti che le grotte potevano assumere funzione differenziata. Di alcune tuttavia la destinazione ad uso abitativo sembra fuori di dubbio, soprattutto se si analizzano le ipotesi ricostruttive. Si sono prese in considerazione in questa sede le tracce rinvenute all'interno della grotta 13 nel settore III.

1. La grotta 13 del settore III (fig. 3b)

L'analisi delle tracce in pianta porta a ricostruire per l'ingresso un sistema del tutto identico a quello delle capanne e un interno sorprendentemente simile a quelli precedentemente analizzati. I buchi di palo e gli altri incavi che corrono a una certa distanza dalla parete a destra dell'ingresso suggeriscono l'esistenza di una struttura leggera, qui ipotizzata come un grande ripiano, forse con funzione di letto, simile a quelli della abitazione del Sett. Vc e della capanna del Sett. Ve. Tuttavia è possibile anche l'esistenza di un piccolo ambiente chiuso da pareti lignee, simile a quello ricostruita nella abitazione del Vc. Lo spazio a destra invece, sembra libero da arredi interni e destinato forse alla mensa e alle attività domestiche. La pianta suggerisce anche l'esistenza di una parete lignea, un robusto divisorio dotato di porta, che isola un ambiente più interno, largo circa m 1.5 e lungo m 4. I buchi di palo sul fondo, secondo il modello interpretativo qui proposto, indicano l'esistenza di ripiani simili a quelli delle parte anteriore, in questo caso quasi sicuramente considerabili come letti.

Sovana

Le abitazioni a pianta ellittica (figg.6–7)

Negli scavi recenti di Sovana, ai limiti dell'area ovest del pianoro sommitale, sono state rinvenute due serie di buchi di palo pertinenti a due abitazioni a pianta ellittica in gran parte distrutte dal taglio di una cava di epoca ellenistica.

Nonostante l'esiguità della parte rimasta, peraltro abbastanza significativa, sulla base dell'esperienza di Sorgenti della Nova e dei numerosi confronti tipologici da altri siti dell'Etruria, è stato possibile ricostruire graficamente con buona approssimazione almeno l'abitazione più occidentale, che, nella sua pianta a tre

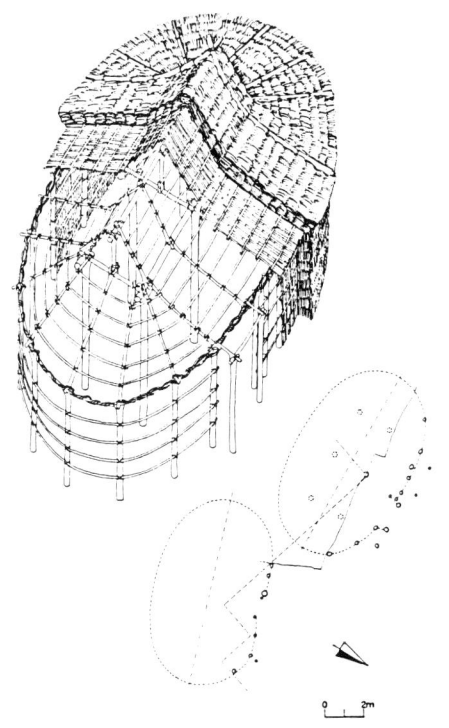

Fig. 6. Sovana (GR). Abitazioni a pianta ellittica 1 e 2. Ipotesi di ricostruzione delle piante e assonometria della Abitazione 1.

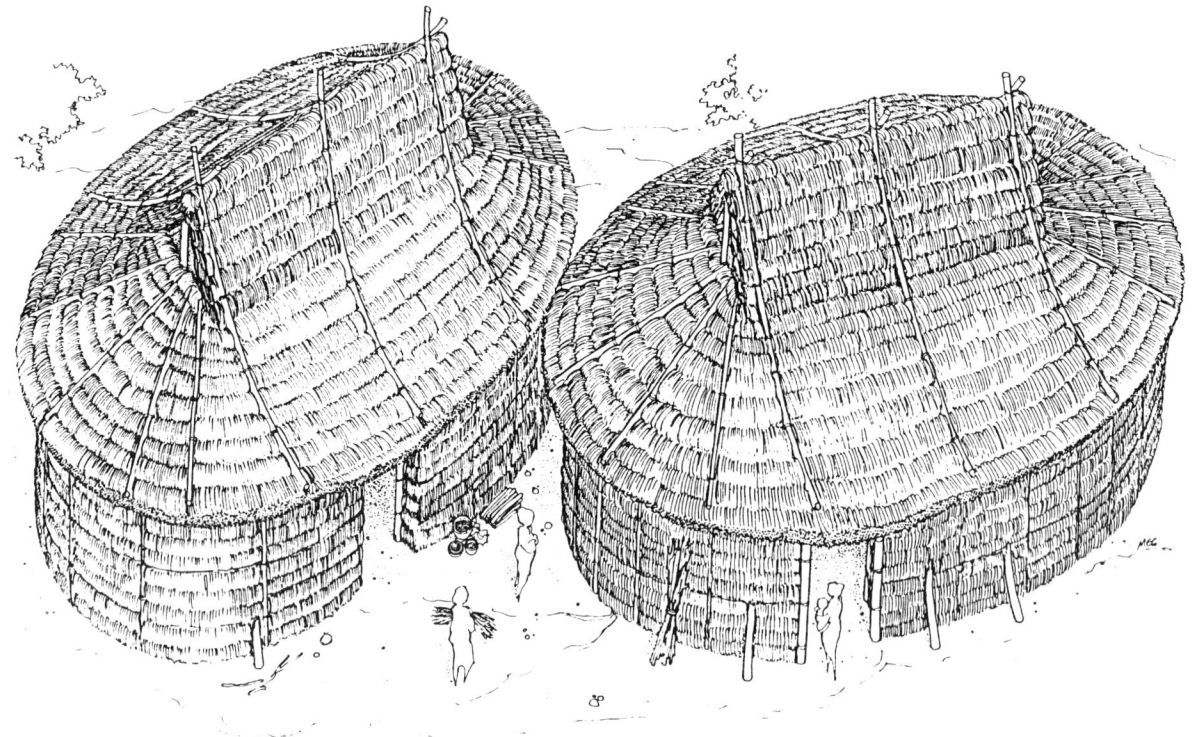

Fig. 7. Sovana (GR). Abitazioni a pianta ellittica: ipotesi di ricostruzione.

navate, appare del tutto simile a quella del Sett.III di Sorgenti della Nova: presenta infatti la stessa lunghezza (10 metri) e una larghezza di poco inferiore (m 6); gli stessi elementi strutturali, compresa la sopraelevazione centrale del tetto e le due finestre laterali. Anche per queste capanne si è proposta una copertura vegetale, poichè non sono stati rinvenuti frammenti di argilla pertinenti ai rivestimenti delle pareti, ma occorre ricordare che a Sovana il pianoro sommitale è stato ristrutturato fino al tardo medioevo e quindi i resti protostorici sono assai scarsi. Anche la reciproca collocazione spaziale delle due abitazioni, assai vicine e l'una quasi di fila all'altra è molto simile a quella di Sorgenti della Nova. Vi sono tuttavia anche importanti elementi di differenziazione: in particolare i pali perimetrali, anche in questo caso non portanti, non sono collegati da alcuna canaletta e gli ingressi si aprono sul lato lungo invece che su quello corto: entrambe questa caratteristiche trovano numerosi confronti in Etruria.

2. LE STRUTTURE DI SERVIZIO: FORNI, CUCINE, FOCOLARI E VANI DI IMMAGAZZINAMENTO (MM)

La ricostruzione grafica delle strutture di servizio rinvenute nell'insediamento di Sorgenti della Nova ha consentito di gettare nuova luce sull'organizzazione delle zone comuni destinate a particolari funzioni produttive e domestiche e sul legame esistente con le singole unità residenziali.

Dall'analisi delle caratteristiche tecnico-funzionali è infatti emersa l'esistenza di un alto livello di specializzazione nella destinazione delle singole strutture, sia per quanto riguarda quelle adibite alla cottura e preparazione degli alimenti, sia per gli ambienti di immagazzinamento e conservazione delle derrate. Anche sulla base di precisi confronti istituibili con gli abitati coevi, in particolare per alcuni tipi di strutture quali i forni in cotto, è infatti innegabile l'esistenza in Etruria di un preciso rapporto tra modalità costruttive e destinazione d'uso già nel corso delle fasi finali dell'età del Bronzo, con significativi precedenti che verranno di volta in volta individuati. La funzionalità di tali modelli sembra poi confermata dal perdurare di alcune tipologie fino ad epoca etrusco-arcaica.

Le strutture di servizio sono state, pertanto, prese in esame sotto il duplice profilo delle modalità costruttive e della loro specifica destinazione d'uso, sia che essa fosse connessa con l'utilizzazione del fuoco, come per forni, focolari e vani destinati alla cottura dei cibi, sia che servissero per l'immagazzinamento e la conservazione delle derrate.

Sul versante rivolto a nord della rupe di Sorgenti della Nova sono stati rinvenuti, nel settore III e III distrutto, due forni in cotto (Sorgenti Nova 1981: 436-442; Miari 1995), simili per forma e tecnica costruttiva ed entrambi alloggiati all'interno di due nicchie appositamente scavate nella parete rocciosa, vicino ad altri vani a destinazione probabilmente abitativa. L'ottimo stato di conservazione del primo forno, oggi restaurato ed esposto, ha consentito la ricostruzione grafica del secondo (fig.8; 9A). Entrambi i forni, alti non più di cm 70, hanno pavimento in cotto alto cm 10, pareti e volta a cupola in cotto, spesse cm 20, sulla cui sommità si apre un foro circolare di sfiato (diametro cm 20), mentre l'apertura frontale è ampia cm 30. Le due strutture differiscono solo nella pianta, subcircolare in un caso (diametro interno cm 85), subellittica (misure interne cm 110 × 65) nell'altro, ma possiedono la stessa ampiezza di superficie interna (50–60 cm quadrati) e un uguale volume complessivo (50 cm cubi circa).

L'insieme delle caratteristiche tecnico-strutturali inserisce i due forni di Sorgenti della Nova nel tipo di forno in cotto ben attestato in Italia fin dal principio dell'età del Bronzo (cfr. Miari 1995). Si tratta di un tipo di struttura altamente specializzata, alla cui precisione tecnico-costruttiva corrisponde una funzione altrettanto specifica, conservatasi fino ad epoca etrusca, come testimoniano i forni del centro arcaico di Acquarossa (Oestemberg 1975; Scheffer 1981. Cfr. Cassano *et al.* 1987).

Per quanto riguarda l'uso cui erano destinate tali strutture, le interpretazioni correnti propendono a considerarli ora forni domestici da cucina, ora fornaci per ceramica, sussistendo il dubbio che sia già possibile individuare per tali epoche differenze tecnico-costruttive tra le strutture utilizzate per cuocere il cibo e quelle adibite alla cottura dei manufatti ceramici. In realtà il tipo del forno in cotto mal si inquadra nelle caratteristiche richieste per cuocere la ceramica. La presenza di una cupola fissa esclude infatti la cottura secondo il metodo del focolare all'aperto (Cuomo 1971–72: 371–373), né vi è modo di separare i vasi dal combustibile, come avviene invece nelle fornaci verticali.

Viceversa, le fornaci di epoca pre-protostorica rinvenute in Italia sono riconducibili ai tipi del focolare all'aperto o della fornace verticale (Miari 1995): si tratta cioè di strutture a base incassata nel terreno, con pareti rivestite internamente di argilla cotta, talvolta di pietre, spesso prive di tracce di copertura permanente. Quanto alle loro dimensioni, hanno un'ampiezza maggiore dei forni: il diametro superiore delle fosse è raramente inferiore a mq 1.5, di contro all'ampiezza dei forni in cotto che oscilla mediamente tra mq 0.5 e 1.5.

La copresenza a *Cures Sabini* sia di un forno in cotto databile alla fine dell'VIII sec. a.C., sia di una rudimentale fornace per ceramica dell'VIII–VII sec. a.C. (Guidi *et al.* 1985; Alfonsetti & Guidi 1988) sembrerebbe confermare inoltre la specializzazione funzionale dei due tipi di strutture, anche se non si escludono casi di uso a fini artigianali dei forni in cotto, come a S. Maria di Ripalta (Nava & Pennacchioni 1981).

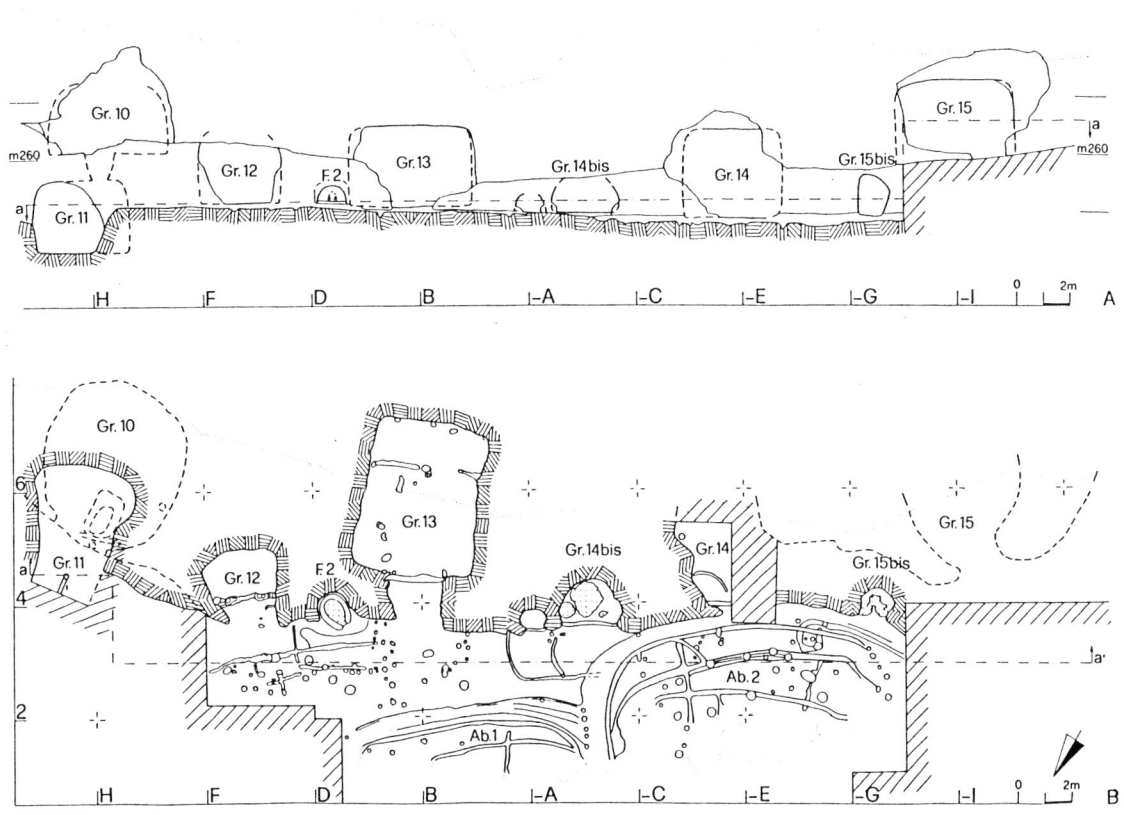

Fig. 8. Sorgenti della Nova (VT): pianta (B) e alzato (A) del settore III. Il forno è indicato con F2.

Sotto il profilo tecnico-funzionale la più importante caratteristica dei forni in cotto rimane comunque quella che potevano essere utilizzati indifferentemente per cuocere a diretto contatto col combustibile, inserendo all'interno la brace, oppure mediante irraggiamento indiretto, preriscaldando con la brace il forno e poi togliendola al momento della cottura o ancora riscaldandolo dall'esterno e tutt'attorno e cuocendo per conduzione. Diversi erano pertanto i cibi che vi potevano essere cotti: la tecnica del preriscaldamento del forno o della cottura per conduzione, confermata a Sorgenti della Nova dal rinvenimento, nel Sett. III, di un ampio strato di ceneri e carboni nell'interstizio tra la parete rocciosa della nicchia e il forno stesso, doveva essere sfruttata per la cottura di pane o focacce, come esemplificato anche da testimonianze iconografiche antiche (Scheffer 1981: 106-107; 1987). Agevole doveva essere poi all'interno dei forni la tostatura dei semi e dei cereali, la cottura diretta dei cibi in vasi posti direttamente sulla brace o l'affumicamento di carni o pesce, utilizzando legna umida (Coles 1981: 43).

I forni in cotto non sono l'unico esempio nell'abitato di Sorgenti della Nova di strutture adibite esclusivamente alla cottura degli alimenti. Sempre nel settore III la grotta 10 (fig.8), del diametro di m 5.5 circa, era destinata ad assolvere alle funzione di un grande focolare.

Al suo interno sono stati infatti rinvenuti tre successivi livelli di focolari realizzati su altrettanti piani di preparazione in cui erano visibili le tracce di numerosi buchi di palo. Nel terreno attorno ai focolari, ricco di carboni e cenere, erano frequentissimi i resti ossei animali. Secondo la ricostruzione proposta (fig.9B), alcuni buchi di palo dovevano probabilmente sorreggere strutture lignee accessorie per sostenere graticole e spiedi per arrostire i cibi, grazie al contatto diretto delle carni con la fonte di calore, nonchè pentole la bollitura dei cibi.

Fig. 9. Sorgenti della Nova (VT): ipotesi di ricostruzione. A. Il settore III dalla grotta 12 alla grotta 14 bis; B. La grotta 10; C. L'interno della capanna del settore Ve con il focolare.

Nella ricostruzione si scorge poi, nel pavimento della grotta 10 in prossimità dell'ingresso, un pozzetto artificialmente scavato nella roccia, a pianta subrettangolare, ampio m 1.5 × 1 alla sommità e m 1 × 0.5 alla base e profondo circa m 1. La sua posizione, dentro la grotta destinata ad uso di cucina e il rinvenimento al suo interno di un vaso, caduto poi col crollo del diaframma divisorio di roccia nella sottostante grotta 11, fanno ipotizzare che si trattasse di silos per il grano o altre derrate alimentari. La forma del pozzetto, lunga e stretta, particolarmente idonea per conservare i cibi in un luogo asciutto, permetteva di mantenere stabile la temperatura interna (Brandt 1988). Il silos ha una capienza di circa un metro cubo, di poco inferiore alla capacità dei pozzetti comunemente attestati per l'immagazzinamento delle derrate (Coles 1981: 33–37), ma comunque sufficiente per il sostentamento di un nucleo familiare di 5-6 persone (cfr. Kramer 1980 e Ampolo 1980).

Di particolare interesse risulta, sempre nel Sett.III di Sorgenti della Nova, anche l'organizzazione spaziale degli impianti di servizio, che vede le strutture di deposito sempre strettamente collegate a quelle adibite all'uso di cucina. Tale è infatti la disposizione di altri due vani scavati artificialmente nella roccia: la grotta 12, che si apre accanto al forno in cotto e la piccola nicchia scavata accanto alla grotta 14bis (fig.8).

La Gr.12 ha pianta rettangolare, è ampia m 2.7 × 1.6 ed alta m 2.2: la sua superficie complessiva non raggiunge pertanto i 5 mq (di contro ai 26 mq della vicina grotta 13, a destinazione abitativa), mentre la sua potenziale capienza come magazzino si aggira intorno ai 9 metri cubi. Nella ricostruzione proposta (fig.9A) il magazzino presenta un semplice cancello d'ingresso chiuso da un portello mobile, mentre il forno risulta accessibile dal lato della Gr.13, mediante un cancello ligneo, di cui restano nel tufo le tracce dei buchi di palo in cui erano infisse sia le parti fisse sia quelle mobili dell'ingresso. Altre canalette e buchi di palo, ancora visibili nella roccia (fig.8), fanno però supporre che, in una sistemazione precedente dell'area, il forno e la Gr.12 costituissero un sistema unitario, chiuso da una più ampia recinzione.

Ancora più piccola, meno di 1 mq, la nicchia che doveva servire da piccolo magazzino per la struttura denominata Gr.14bis, con cui costituiva un complesso unitario recintato da una palizzata lignea ed accessibile dalla parte dell'abitazione ellittica n.2 (fig.8). La presenza di una canaletta attorniata da buchi di palo in prossimità della parete di roccia fa pensare ad un cancello di separazione tra le due piccole nicchie, mentre le canalette poste all'ingresso delle due strutture dovevano alloggiare un sistema di chiusura costituita da tavole lignee poste orizzontalmente (fig.9A).

Il pavimento della grotta 14bis, di forma semicircolare e con una superficie di mq 3, era costituito da un piano di concotto esteso a tutta la superficie interna, impostato su un vespaio di ciottoli e cocci. Analogo piano di concotto aveva anche la grotta 15 bis (fig.8), di forma subcircolare e superficie di circa mq 1 ed entrambe le strutture avevano le pareti chiuse a formare un riparo solo verso monte e il fronte d'ingresso completamente aperto. Carboni, ceneri e resti ossei animali erano ugualmente diffusi su tutto il piano e nelle aree antistanti, ad indicare che le nicchie dovevano essere utilizzate come ampi focolari. La mancanza di un soffitto chiuso doveva servire ad agevolare la fuoriuscita del fumo, mentre la parete a monte costituiva un riparo dai fenomeni atmosferici.

Anche per questo tipo di strutture si deve pertanto ipotizzare che fossero destinate alla cottura dei cibi, probabilmente non mediante arrostimento come nella grotta 10, ma grazie all'ausilio di fornelli, pentole da fuoco o altro. Nella Gr. 14bis la piccola rientranza lungo la parete occidentale poteva essere utilizzata a guisa di piano d'appoggio.

Una conferma di questa interpretazione viene dall'abitato etrusco di Acquarossa ove, accanto alla grotta cucina della zona J, simile alla grotta 10 di Sorgenti della Nova, è stata rinvenuta una nicchia semicircolare alta un metro, delle dimensioni giuste per contenervi un fornello, mentre una seconda nicchia, nella zona L, conteneva ancora i frammenti di un fornello e di un vaso utilizzato per cuocere il cibo (Oestemberg 1975; Scheffer 1981, 1986).

Essendo così marcata la specializzazione degli ambienti destinati alla cottura degli alimenti è d'obbligo chiedersi quale fosse la funzione dei focolari trovati all'interno delle abitazioni.

Il termine focolare è di per se stesso estremamente generico e viene utilizzato per indicare tipi di strutture diversissime tra loro, come una semplice lente di ceneri e carboni o un'ampia fossa dalle pareti rivestite di argilla cotta, differenze cui corrispondono poi diverse finalità d'uso. La prima distinzione da farsi, fondamentale sotto il profilo tecnico-costruttivo, è quella che separa i *focolari su piano* dai *focolari a base incassata*. Ciascuna delle due categorie è poi ulteriormente divisibile, sulla base dei materiali impiegati per la loro costruzione e del grado di specializzazione tecnica, rispettivamente in: focolari senza base di preparazione e focolari con base di preparazione in pietre o concotto; focolari in fossa semplice e focolari in fossa con pareti rivestite di argilla o pietre (cfr. Gascò 1985 e Miari1995).

Nella prima categoria rientrano di norma tutti i focolari di uso domestico, non legati a particolari attività produttive e/o artigianali, quali la cottura della ceramica o la lavorazione dei metalli. Tra essi, il focolare *senza base di preparazione* è uno dei tipi più frequenti a Sorgenti della Nova. Limitato spesso a una semplice lente di terreno carbonioso e di cenere, di forma generalmente subcircolare, la cui superficie non supera 1 metro quadrato di ampiezza, il tipo si riscontra esclusivamente all'interno delle abitazioni (cfr. Sorgenti Nova 1995; Miari 1995, ove doveva svolgere funzioni di riscaldamento e illuminazione e, mediante l'ausilio di fornelli fittili, di cottura di semplici cibi.

Nella proposta di ricostruzione della zona centrale del settore III (fig.9A), completata sulla base dei dati di scavo, si scorge, ai limiti del corridoio di accesso della grotta 13 e in posizione favorevole per la fuoriuscita del fumo, il focolare sormontato da un fornello. Il rinvenimento, in prossimità dell'ingresso, di una grossa macina con relativo macinello sembra convalidare l'uso abitativo dell'ambiente ipogeo.

Focolari con base di preparazione si ritrovano, oltre che nelle grotte e nicchie cucina già viste, in cui la presenza di un piano in concotto su cui accendere il fuoco e di un vespaio sottostante indicano l'alto grado di funzionalità di questi focolari destinati alla cottura dei cibi, anche all'interno di strutture per cui non è ipotizzabile una funzione di servizio. In questi casi l'esistenza di un piano di concotto impostato direttamente (senza vespaio di cocci e pietre) sulla roccia di base sembra indicare piuttosto che si trattava di un focolare fisso, costruito intenzionalmente al momento della fondazione della struttura e strettamente collegato ad essa. Immutata doveva essere, comunque, la loro funzione all'interno dell'abitazione ove poteva servire per illuminare, riscaldare o reggere un contenitore ceramico per la cottura dei cibi (fig.9C).

Dalle ipotesi di ricostruzione elaborate per le strutture di servizio di Sorgenti della Nova, sulla base di un'analisi puntuale dei dati di scavo, emerge pertanto l'esistenza sia di un elevato grado di specializzazione tecnico-funzionale sia di articolate forme di organizzazione spaziale delle aree destinate a particolari funzioni produttive e domestiche. L'analisi delle strutture destinate alla cottura degli alimenti mostra infatti la presenza, in un unico settore dell'abitato, di almeno tre tipi di strutture, il forno in cotto, la grotta cucina e le nicchie focolare, ciascuna delle quali particolarmente idonea per un tipo di cottura dei cibi, quale la tostatura, l'arrostimento o la lessatura. I focolari interni alle abitazioni dovevano invece svolgere per lo più funzioni di riscaldamento e illuminazione.

Quanto all'organizzazione spaziale dell'abitato, la connessione delle strutture di cucina con i vani per l'immagazzinamento delle derrate era sottolineata da recinti e palizzate lignee che suddividevano le aree attrezzate esterne, ne articolavano gli spazi e ne delimitavano le zone.

Ringraziamenti

Tutte le ricostruzioni qui presentate sono state effettuate in collaborazione con Ercole Negroni e sono state rese graficamente da Elena Gonano.

Bibliografia

Alfonsetti, D. & Guidi, A. 1988. 'Cures Sabini', in *Problematiche*, 41-52.

Ampolo, C. 1980. 'Le condizioni materiali della produzione. Agricoltura e paesaggio agrario', in *La formazione della città nel Lazio*, Atti del Convegno, Roma 1977 = *Dialoghi di Archeologia*, ns, 2, 15-46.

Bartoloni, G., Buranelli, F., D'Atri, V. & De Santis, A. 1987. *Le urne a capanna rinvenute in Italia*, Roma.

Brandt, J.R. 1988. 'Ficana. Alcune osservazioni su capanne e fosse', in *Problematiche*, 12-28.

Cassano, S.M., Cazzella, A., Manfredini, A. & Moscoloni, M. 1987. *Coppa Nevigata e il suo territorio. Testimonianze archeologiche dal VII al II millennio a.C.*, Roma.

Cataldi, G., Farneti, R., Larco, R., Pellegrino, F. & Tamburini, P. 1982. 'Tipologie primitive. 1. I tipi "radice"', in *Quaderni di Studio sulle tipologie e sulla architettura delle origini*, L'Alinea ed., Firenze.

Catalogo Manciano 1988 = *Il Museo di Preistoria e Protostoria della valle del fiume Fiora. Catalogo del Museo di Manciano* (a cura di N. Negroni Catacchio), Manciano.

Chapelot, J. & Fossier, R. 1985. *The Village and House in the Middle Ages*, London.

Coles, J. 1981. *Archeologia sperimentale*, Milano.

Cuomo Di Caprio, N. 1971-72. 'Proposta di classificazioni delle fornaci per ceramica e laterizi nell'area italiana dalla preistoria a tutta l'epoca romana', *Sibrium*, XI, 371-461.

Gascò, J. 1985. *Les installation du Quotidien. Structures domestiques en Languedoc du Mésolithique à l'Age du Bronze d'apres l'étude des abris de Font-Juvenal et du Roc-de-Dourgne dans l'Aude*, in Document d'Archéologie Française 1, Paris.

Guidi, A. *et al.* 1985. 'Cures Sabini', *Archeologia Laziale*, VII, Roma, 77-92.

Kramer, C. 1980. 'Estimating prehistoric populations: an ethnoarchaeological approach', in *L'archéologie de l'Iraq du début de l'époque Neolithique a 393 avant notre ère. Perspectives et limites de l'interpretation anthropologique des documents = Colloques Internationaux du Centre National de la Recherche Scientifique*, 580, (Paris Juin 1978), 315-334.

Miari, M. 1995. 'Tipologia delle strutture di servizio', in *Sorgenti Nova*.

Modi, C. 1988. 'Architettura spontanea: le capanne, in *Catalogo Manciano*, 207-230.

Nava, M.L. & Pennacchioni, G. 1981. *L'insediamento protostorico di S. Maria di Ripalta (Cerignola). Prima campagna di scavi*, Cerignola.

Oestemberg, C.E. 1975. *Case etrusche di Acquarossa*, Roma.

Problematiche 1988 = *Problematiche di scavo delle strutture abitative dell'età del Ferro, Quaderni della Soprintendenza Archeologica del Lazio 1*, Roma.

Scheffer, C. 1981. *Acquarossa, Vol.II:1, Cooking and Cooking Stands in Italy 1400-400 B.C.*, (Acta Inst.Rom.R.Sueciae, 4, 38:2:1), Stockholm.

Scheffer, C. 1986. 'La vita quotidiana nell'ambiente domestico', in *Architettura etrusca nel Viterbese. Ricerche svedesi a San Giovenale e Acquarossa 1956-1986*, Roma, 109-128.

Scheffer, C. 1987. 'Forni e fornelli etruschi di età arcaica', in *L'alimentazione nel mondo antico. Gli Etruschi*, (Catalogo della mostra, Ministero per i Beni Culturali e Ambientali), Roma, 97-105.

Sorgenti Nova 1981 = *Sorgenti della Nova. Una comunità protostorica e il suo territorio nell'Etruria meridionale* (a cura di N. Negroni Catacchio), CNR, Roma.

Sorgenti Nova 1995. = *Sorgenti della Nova. L'abitato del Bronzo Finale*, (a cura di N. Negroni Catacchio), Firenze.

55

Industry and Technology at Borgo Le Ferriere-*Satricum*, 700–300 BC

A. J. Nijboer

(Department of Archaeology, University of Groningen)

Summary: *Our knowledge of the production of artifacts in Latium Vetus from the 7th-3rd centuries BC is mainly based on the study of the products and their mode of manufacture and only rarely on the means of production like the raw materials and kilns. The excavations of the settlement at* Satricum *have furnished data on kilns and debris of industrial activity, revealing continuous pottery- and iron manufacture during this period. In particular, the production of iron artifacts in the Orientalizing period heightens the economic importance of* Satricum *since iron was regarded highly valuable in this period. Iron in tombs like the Tomba Bernardini and the wealthy tombs at Castel di Decima indicates the importance of this new metal for tools. As well as data on local manufacture, the excavations produced weights which yield information about the mechanism by which metals could be traded at set rates from the 7th century BC onwards. These weights represent pre-monetary fixed metallic units relating the value of copper to the value of silver. These units should not, however, be viewed seperately. They are part of trade and there is no trade without surplus of production. Therefore it is interesting that the oldest known Italian fixed metallic monetary units have been found at the manufacturing community working at* Satricum.

INTRODUCTION

In past years extensive research has been carried out at Borgo Le Ferriere-*Satricum* by the University of Groningen (the Netherlands). The site Borgo Le Ferriere-*Satricum* (from now on referred to as *Satricum*) is situated in South Lazio, approx. 60 km. south-east of Rome. The excavations have been published thoroughly (cf. in particular Maaskant-Kleibrink 1987, 1992; Beijer 1991b). Dr. Beijer concluded his paper with the remark that "with regard to the economic causes of the wealth of the families at *Satricum*, the excavations of 1989 furnished new data. In a layer of the same phase as the rectangular timber building from the seventh century BC, hundreds of iron slags have been found. Technical details about provenance and manufacture are not yet available, but the mere fact of the abundant presence of iron in the settlement has important implications for the understanding of the origins of the economic level, and consequently for the rise of the aristocratic class in the settlement at Borgo Le Ferriere" (1991b: 36). During the 1991 excavations further evidence was found for advanced industry from the seventh century BC onwards. This paper will present this evidence and moreover will discuss the analysis of the debris of the industrial activity, beginning with the presentation of the excavated artifacts being kilns, wasters and slags.

The discussed material covers pottery- and iron manufacture. Due to the quantity of debris excavated, the production must have been considerable: this is important if one tries to reconstruct the economy and development of proto-urban or urban centres in antiquity. Urban centres can be defined as a religious and political nucleus as well as an economic centre (Starr 1977: 98). At *Satricum* religion, politics and economy appear to go hand in hand. The many temples excavated and the enormous content of the votive deposits or 'treasuries', make it possible to state that the religious importance of *Satricum* from an early period onwards is beyond doubt. With regard to the the political organisation, archaeology hardly yields direct information. As in other Latin centres of the seventh century BC, the social stratification at *Satricum*, exemplified in the so-called princely tombs, was advanced enough to assume that some of the factors shaping a political organisation were present. The ruling class of Latium Vetus appears to have been strong enough by the second half of the seventh century to impose the use of fixed metallic units. However, the units themselves seem to have been imported from regions to the south of *Satricum*. The designation of this fixed metallic monetary unit is the most important stage in the early history of money (Crawford 1985: 19). A weight found in a seventh century context at *Satricum* clearly presents itself as a

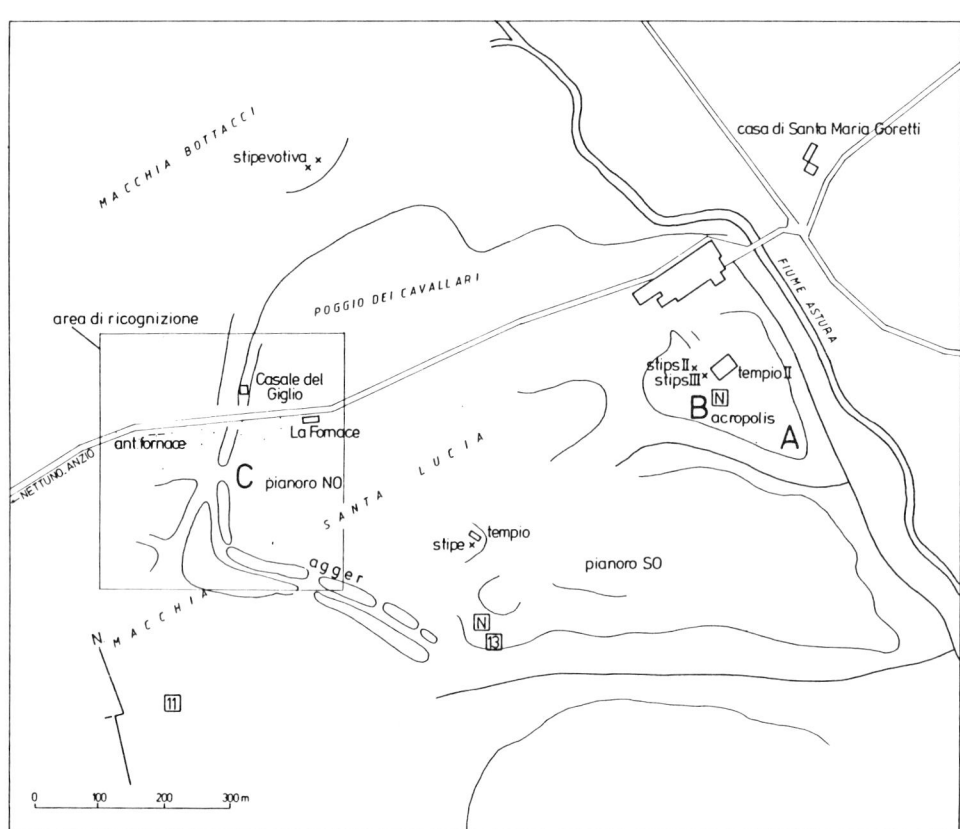

Fig. 1. Map of Borgo Le Ferriere/<Satricum>; A, B, and C indicate the position of the pottery kilns.

unit and, moreover, one that closely corresponds with the weight of the theoretically calculated Roman-Oscan pound, being about 273 gr. (see below).

Finally, it must be emphasised that this paper will not discuss other aspects of the economy such as agriculture or public works which would have been as important as the production of pottery and iron. Agriculture in particular remained the solid base on which the presented development could ensue (at *Satricum* it seems that the economic significance of the sanctuary prevailed – Attema *et al.*, this volume).

The pottery kilns

The oldest pottery kiln (kiln A in fig. 1) was built in the seventh century BC on the outskirts of the acropolis in square C27. Of this kiln only part of the combustion chamber was preserved thus making it difficult to classify it more precisely than being of round shape with a *praefurnium* attached (fig.2). It belongs to the first category in the classification made by Cuomo di Caprio (1972). The kiln was made by digging a hole into undisturbed soil in which the support of the raised oven floor was placed. This support was made of local tufa blocks of which many large, burned fragments were found inside the combustion chamber. It is possible that the raised oven floor was also made of tufa slabs. Due to the firing of the undisturbed soil, the contours of the kiln could

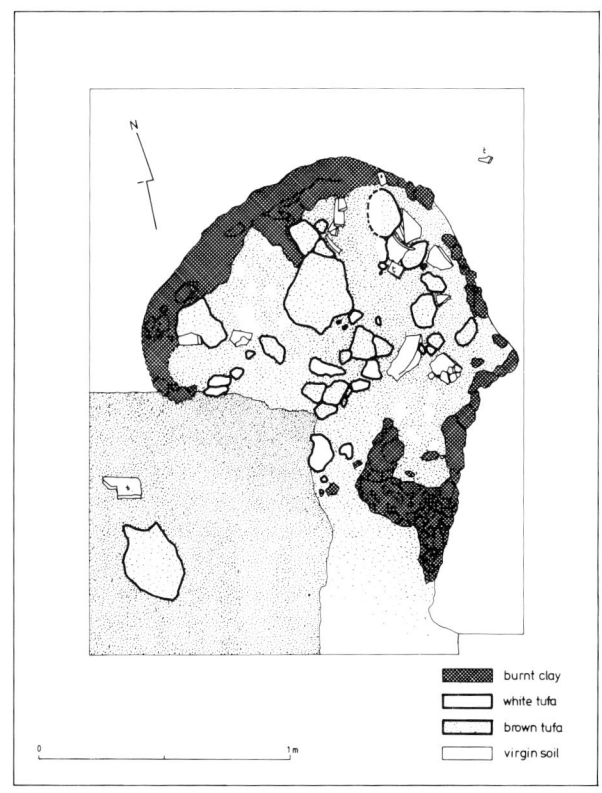

Fig. 2. Plan of kiln A.

be calculated measuring 140 cm. (width) by 165 cm. (length; height preserved for about 30 cm).

In between the tufa and the grumi of the kiln, pottery was found which had been exposed to too high a temperature. This included bowls, jars and cooking stands, many of which were decorated with plastic cord decoration (fig.3). All pottery found in the kiln was locally made. Parallels of similar pottery have been excavated elsewhere, including *Lavinium* (Gastagnoli 1975:14–19).

The kiln and its contents are dated to the late seventh century BC, as confirmed by the pottery associated with the many wasters found in a trench excavated near the kiln, on the slope of the acropolis. The wasters were shapeless and their forms could not be identified (though an Etrusco-Corinthian bowl was found among the associated pottery).

The fabric of the pottery artifacts inside the kiln was consistent in colour, clay matrix and tempering material. This consistency made it easier to investigate the provenance of the clay and the tempering material, both of which are locally easily available. One of the local clays utilised was quarried from the marine terraces, which were created by changes in the sea level during the Early Holocene to Wurmian Age (Sevink 1984: 104). The marine terrace at Le Ferriere contains quartz, subrounded fragments of flint and to some extent local volcanic minerals; these minerals are mixed with the clay in varying quantities. Samples of these deposits were fired and thin-sectioned. These thin sections were compared with ones made from the pottery samples from the kiln. The thin-sections of the clays and pottery show considerable conformity especially when taken into account the possible different processing techniques used in antiquity. For example, the thin-section of a clay sample from the marine terrace contained *c.* 30% quartz, 1–2% plagioclase, 2–3% chert and some biotite while a thin-section of an impasto bowl excavated in the kiln, contained the above plus grog and volcanic rockfragments indicating that they were mixed with other non-plastic inclusions. The processing of the clay with crushed volcanic rockfragments accounts for the presence in the clay-matrix of augite, volcanic glass fragments and some garnet.

Making statements about provenance studies of pottery, relating local clays with excavated pottery is precarious since similar clays occur elsewhere in Latium. However, in view of the presence at *Satricum* of kilns, wasters, suitable clays and identical mineral compositions of both clays/tempering materials and pottery it must be concluded that archaeology cannot submit more evidence for the use of local resources and local pottery production.

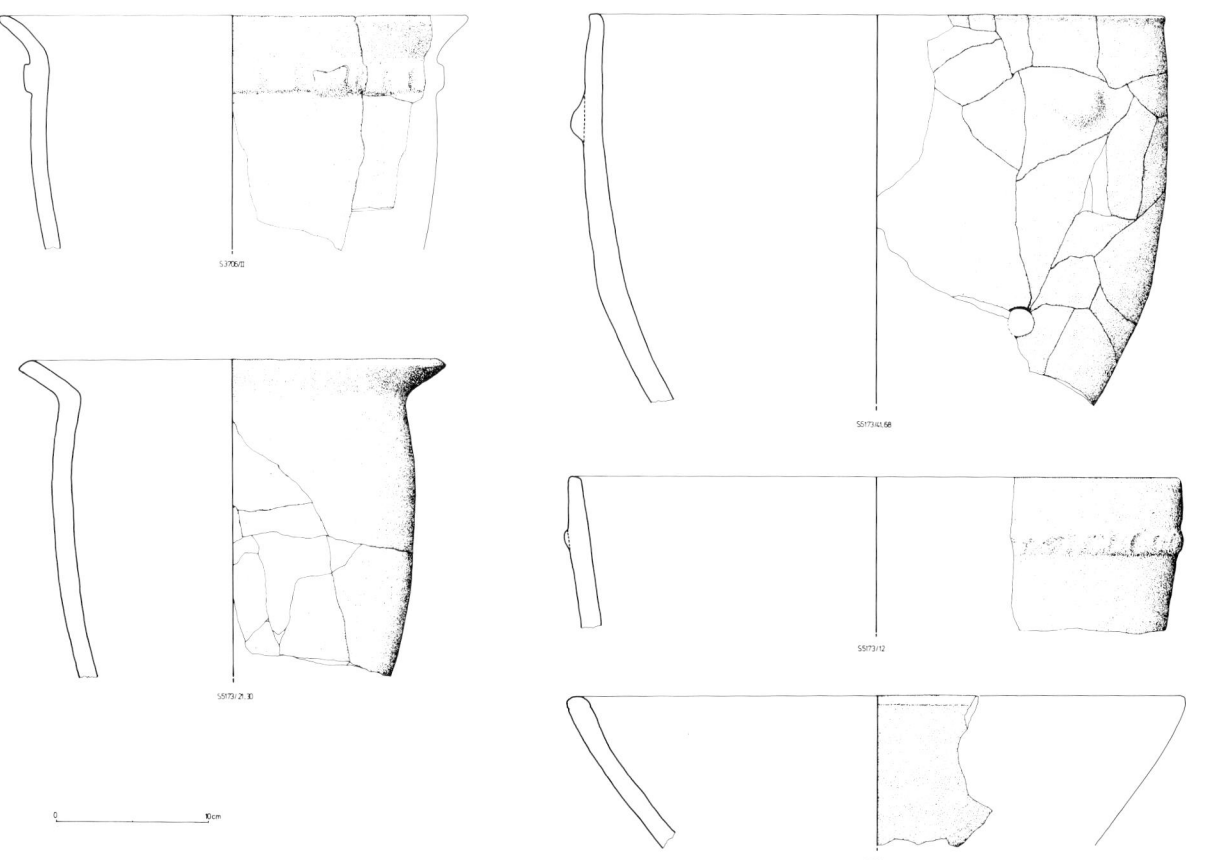

Fig. 3. Pottery found in kiln A.

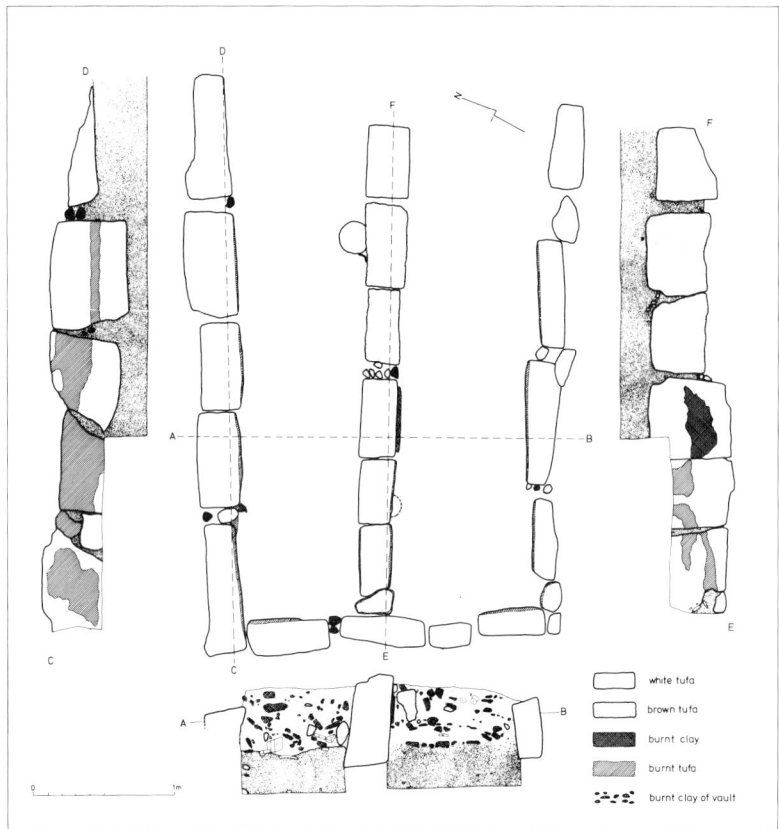

Fig. 4. Plan and section of kiln B.

After establishing the type of pottery produced at *Satricum* in the seventh century, similar pottery found in the settlement can now be investigated. Amongst this there were many sherds from the huts which were excavated in the last century. Our excavations have yielded sherds of a holmos from the destruction layer of a seventh century timber building (Beijer 1991b), which shows remarkable resemblance to the pottery found in the kiln. The quartz and tempering material of the holmos is smaller in size but this could be due to the processing of the unfired clay. However, the similarities of colour, clay matrix and minerals between the locally produced pottery and the holmos, make it likely that the stand was also produced at *Satricum*. Thus it can be concluded that as well as the coarse ware found in the kiln, more advanced products like the holmos were produced locally.

The seventh century pottery was manufactured both for the local market and for trade in Latium Vetus. Beijer (1991: 63–86) has shown that the local pottery was partly of an advanced technology; the amphorae are made of a fairly depurated clay on a vast potter's wheel from the early seventh century BC onwards.

The second kiln excavated was of a more advanced type and was rectangular of shape, dating from the sixth century BC (kiln B in fig.1). The kiln was found along the edge on the south side of the acropolis and is about 3.7m long, 2.7m wide and its height was preserved up to 55 cm (fig.4). Again only the combustion chamber with *praefurnium* was preserved. It is classified as kiln-type IIc since it has two parallel main corridors and arches supporting the raised oven floor (Cuomo di Caprio 1979: 75–80). Similar kilns of the same date are found in Laurentina Acqua Acetosa (Bedini 1981: 254–7; 1990: 173) and in Southern Italy (Cuomo di Caprio 1979: 83–6) – however, none of these are dated before the sixth century BC. The combustion chamber was filled with debris from the kiln structure, pottery and wasters from the sixth century. The blocks of tufa which formed the sub-structure of the kiln were dug into a layer containing seventh century wares.

The debris of the kiln structure was identified as fragments from arches and brick-like material all of which are tempered with organic matter like grass. Of the brick-like material more than 100 kg was excavated. The bricks were probably used for building the arches and the upper structure of the kiln.

The pottery inside the kiln consisted of wasters and both white and red firing storage jars, plain jars, bowls and tegulae (fig.5). Among the white fired tiles there are several decorated with a black oblique stripe (fig.6), for which a parallel, though with a red stripe, was found in Rome on the Forum Boarium (Gjerstad 1960: fig. 272). Fig.6 shows well-fired tegulae as wasters on which

INDUSTRY AND TECHNOLOGY AT BORGO LE FERRIERE-*SATRICUM*, 700–300 BC

Fig. 6. *White-firing tegulae with decoration found in kiln B.*

Fig. 5. *Pottery found in kiln B.*

the decoration flows over the surface of the tegulae. It was evident from the wasters that white and red firing clays were used in the earthenware manufacture. The fabric and mineral-content of the white-firing tiles and pottery was similar to the fabric and mineral-content of the temple decoration dated *c.* 500 BC. The material used for the production of these tiles was probably a primary clay, a weathered tufa, which occurs at several places in and around *Satricum*. The associated minerals of the tufas and weathered tufas are quartz, biotite, augite, olivine, rock fragments, leucite, volcanic glass and occasionally chert and garnet. These minerals were found to be the same as identified in the thin-sections of the temple decoration (Kars *et al.* 1987: 60; McDonnell et al. 1990: 1–23).

Several weathered tufas in and around the site were augered, although none of them rendered a white colour when fired. The colours of the fired augered clays range from buff to red with colour changes occuring with increased temperatures. The missing white firing clay might be due to intensive agricultural activities in the area which must have affected the primary clay deposits or to the processing techniques used in antiquity.

Evidence from the soil-survey has shown that potters working at *Satricum* could and obviously did utilise the various clays and tempers available locally; the main sources being from the marine terraces and the weathered tufas. It is concluded that the bulk of the terracottas and pottery excavated was produced from local clays and temper. The registered differences, for example in the several decoration systems of the temple, are likely to be due to different processing techniques of the clays or to the use of different clay deposits in the area, as the minerals found in the terracotta-systems occur locally. Some scholars ascribe the provenance of the various fabrics of the temple decoration to areas either north of Rome, Campania or the Alban Hills (Kars *et al* 1987: 62–63; Knoop 1987). This view is not shared because local resources are not taken into consideration. It seems highly unlikely that in the sixth century BC the materials used for the terracotta decorations of the temples were imported from other regions when the tufa blocks used for the construction of the same temples were quarried locally. The more so if we consider that for covering the first temple with the required 1400 tiles, 16 to 17.000 kg. clay was needed (Rendelli 1990: 139). This figure does not even include the imbrices nor the architectural decoration.

The last of the three production sites of local pottery was situated about one kilometer to the west of the acropolis, near the *agger* and to the south of the road to Antium (kiln C on fig.1). The actual kiln was excavated during the last century revealing fifth to fourth century BC votive terracotta objects such as a head, an uterus and feet (della Seta 1918: 320; Gastagnoli 1963: 515). Associated with the terracottas, a mould for forming a foot was found. Two areas with concentrations of kiln material were recently surveyed which indicates that there could have been at least two kilns in this area. The pottery and blocks of tufa found during the survey suggests that this area was also inhabited.

The recently surveyed fragments of the raised oven floor imply that the kilns were fairly large. The presence of raised oven floors with ventilation holes indicates that the kilns had separate combustion- and firing chambers. The survey also yielded wasters of tiles, imbrices and other pottery of the fifth to fourth century BC. Therefore, as well as votive terracottas, domestic pottery and roofing material were being produced. Thin-sections of the ceramics recovered from this area contain a variety of minerals which occur locally. The clay matrix of ceramics from the pottery deposits near the *agger* corresponds to the clay of the marine terraces, a deposit of which was identified adjacent to the kilns (Attema *et al.* 1992).

IRON PRODUCTION

At *Satricum* pottery production was not the only industry. The economic significance of this settlement was enhanced by the production of iron artifacts. Large quantities of iron slags were recovered. The slags can be dated from the seventh to third century BC. The presence of slags in the settlement was noted in a variety of contexts ranging from huts to votive deposits. A concentration of slags was found in square E19, east of the temple. The pottery associated was impasto rosso, black burnished impasto and bucchero. Irregularly-shaped and plano-convex iron slags are also found occasionally in the seventh century BC settlement, suggesting that the production of iron artifacts was carried out on a larger scale than can be estimated by the deposits of slags in E19. Moreover, slags could have been dumped on the slope of the acropolis in a similar way as the wasters of the seventh century pottery were. During the fifth and fourth centuries BC it appears that slags were placed together with pottery or iron artifacts in the votive deposit where irregularly-shaped slags and plano-convex slags with the kiln-lining still attached have been excavated. The presence of slags in votive contexts is well documented. There are several examples of votive deposits containing amongst other materials, slags and iron artifacts like the deposit at Amelia (Monacci 1988: 83) and the deposit forming the foundation platform of the Vesta temple on the Forum Romanum (Boni 1900: 172–183). The presence of metal artefacts and slags at several sanctuaries in Italy indicates the need for further research. It could be that their presence reflects the activity of the dedicant or that they were paid as a revenue or tithe to the deity (Grottanelli 1988: 243–55).

The above-mentioned slags are the earliest evidence for the production of iron artifacts in Latium Vetus and have been identified as bloomery slags. Three slags from *Satricum* were analysed by prof. Dr. H-G. Bachmann. The result (in weight percent) of the X-ray Fluorescence analysis is tabulated below:

	S4982	S4906/A	S4906/B
Al_2O_3	7.7	8.4	5.5
SiO_2	27.1	46.5	23.8
P_2O_5	0.6	0.3	0.7
K_2O	1.4	2.0	1.3
CaO	1.0	1.0	0.7
TiO_2	0.2	0.3	0.1
MnO	1.6	0.7	0.7
Fe_2O_3	60.1	40.4	66.5
Sum	**99.7**	**99.6**	**99.3**

The high iron content is similar to that of the slags encountered in Populonia (Minto 1943: 36–38). This high percentage arrives either from the use of primary ores with a high iron content or for a poor recovery. Several of the slags have the furnace lining still attached and therefore have a high silica and low iron content due to the reaction of molten slag with the furnace lining. The furnaces for the production of iron artifacts have not yet been discovered on or around the acropolis.

The development of iron technology falls into three stages (Snodgrass 1980: 336–337):

(i) the production of iron ornaments;

(ii) the introduction of iron tools with sharp cutting edges but in a smaller quantity than similar Cu-alloy tools;

(iii) the prevalence of iron tools over Cu-alloy tools.

In order to study this development at *Satricum*, research is presently underway to estimate the output of the iron workshop. The major difficulty is that most of the iron artifacts were excavated in the last century and have not yet been published. The research undertaken so far on early iron objects from Latium Vetus does not include the iron artifacts excavated at *Satricum* and yet the number of iron objects from the site is imposing. For example, the iron objects from the tombs dating from *c.* 750 to 600 BC, include knives, daggers, lances, swords, spears and even jewellery. However, the majority of the iron objects are excavated in stips I dating from 725–540 BC – these include daggers, swords, knives, axes, sickles, spears, shafts, pins, bars, nails, horse-bits, rings, fibulae and bracelets. The iron jewellery is especially interesting to study since the presence of iron ornaments is considered to indicate the introduction of iron. Hartmann (1985: 285–289) for instance, who has examined the iron artifacts from the ninth and eighth centuries BC in Southern Etruria, sets great store by the eighth century ornaments from Veii, Tarquinia and Rome. He suggests a South-North spread of iron technology, introduced by the Greeks and exemplified in the excavations at Pithekoussai (a.o. Klein 1972: 34–39). It is important to note that after the demonstrated iron production on Ischia from the middle of the eighth century onwards, iron production commences at, for example, Acquarossa and *Satricum*. At Acquarossa (near Viterbo) iron and copper-alloy artifacts were excavated in zone K indicating that both iron and copper were processed (Ostenberg 1983: 84–96). This processing of metals at Acquarossa took place in a settlement consisting of huts which is similar to the situation at *Satricum*. Both settlements display comparable stages of urbanisation, with huts being replaced by houses with stone foundations (courtyard houses). This implies that the manufacture at a site of metal artifacts was one of the factors that triggered the 'urbanisation process'.

It is possible to describe in detail one type of iron object, the axe, of which seven of different sizes were found in the votive deposit, stips I. In 1991, the excavation of the area south of the temple yielded three more examples, found with a Cu-alloy bracelet, a bowl, a fibula, a piece of raw, unworked iron and a lead weight (fig.7); the associated pottery was bucchero, a black burnished carinated bowl and an amphora decorated with a double spiral. This concentration of objects has been dated to the second half of the seventh century BC. Most of the objects were found next to, or on top of each other and no material of earlier date was found. The objects were excavated in the north-west corner of square B18 in an area of ca. $2m^2$, 50 cm. below the surface of the soil and were miraculously preserved in between plough furrows. The three iron axes and the seven axes of the same type from the votive deposit, make a total of ten socketed iron axes from *Satricum*. These axes can be compared with similar iron axes from Latium Vetus of the same period which are: three from Caracupa, two from the tomba Bernardini and one from Velletri. Due to the number of axes from *Satricum* and the iron production demonstrated by the iron slags and the piece of raw iron, it is assumed that iron socketed axes were produced here from the second half of the seventh century onwards. In this respect one has to be aware that the production of iron axes signifies the use of more advanced technology than for example the production of ornaments and knives.

Due to the fact that at *Satricum* iron tools are in the majority by at least the mid-seventh century BC, the third or final stage in iron technology can be ascribed to that period. Moreover, it is significant that the tools excavated in stips I are made of iron and not of Cu-alloy as if there was no transition period between the use of Cu-alloy tools and their replacement with iron.

The lead-weights found at *Satricum* are worth noting,

Fig. 7. Metal finds from south of the temple.

since they constitute the mechanism by which metals could be traded at set rates. The first weight described is dated to the second half of the seventh century BC and is certainly a unit of weight due to the single embossed iron mark. It weighs approx. 267 g. but has been slightly damaged in antiquity (it had also lost some weight due to corrosion). Taking this into consideration, the closest parallel to this weight is the much discussed Roman-Oscan pound of about 273 g. This is the average weight of the first substantially issued Roman coin, the libral As/ 'Prow' series of the third century BC. More than a century ago, Mommsen considered that these coins were issued at a standard of approx. 10 ounces while Haeberlin was convinced that the Romans originally adopted the Oscan pound of approx. 273 g. More recently, scholars have either denied the existence of this weight unit (Thomsen 1957: vol.II; 22–33) or have taken a more pragmatic view stating that varying weights for the pound were in use in Italy (Crawford 1985: 15–16). This last view is confirmed by the second weight found at Le Ferriere in Stips I, dated to between 725–540 BC. This weight has a gravity of *c.* 340 g. which is close to the weight Haeberlin (1910: 82–83) called the Italian pound and other scholars the Roman-Attic, 'Campanian' Mina or pound, at *c.* 341 g. (cf. Pink 1938: 11).

Discussion is further complicated due to the few number of weights actually known. Occasionally reference is made to weights in publications without specifications of their actual gravity. Further study leading to the publication of known weights is needed. This would be especially important as it appears that different standards were in use at *Satricum* (Nijboer 1994).

On the subject of fixed metallic monetary units, it is suggested that such a unit must have existed in Rome from the mid-sixth century onwards (Crawford 1985: 21). The Roman-Oscan pound has traditionally been recognised as a fixed metallic monetary unit, relating the value of Cu-alloy to the value of silver (Haeberlin 1909: 35–36). Modern scientists agree on relating the value of 10 ounces Cu-alloy (being 273 gr.) to 2 scruples of silver (being 6,6 gr.) (Burnett 1989: 34; Crawford 1985: 40). Whatever the relation between Cu-alloy and silver might have been in the second half of the seventh century BC, this unit was in use at *Satricum* at a very early date, 50 to 100 years before the proposed fixed metallic monetary unit for Rome was introduced.

CONCLUSIONS

The picture of the pottery production at *Satricum* shows continuous local manufacture from the seventh until the fourth century BC. This is exemplified by the presence of kilns and associated pottery. *Lavinium*, another centre with religious importance in Latium Vetus, shows similar evidence. The kilns there date from the eighth to the third century BC (Fenelli 1984: 341-343). In Southern Italy there were several Greek colonies with the same continuity of pottery production, illustrated by kilns excavated at these sites (for example towns like Locri, Gela and Naxos). It is striking that once the production was established in these towns it continued, becoming a reason for their importance as economic centres.

The importance of the settlement at *Satricum* is further enhanced by the production of iron artifacts from the middle of the seventh century onwards. In view of the slags found in stips II, this production is likely to have continued into the fourth century BC.

The two weight standards should be viewed in conjunction with the production of pottery and iron. Research has shown that exchange between different cultures in the Orientalizing period increased rapidly. Therefore it is not surprising that in this period these cultures used fixed metallic units as a pre-monetary system in order to be able to trade. This view is supported by the evidence presented in this paper. The oldest known, fixed metallic monetary units of Italy can now be located at the manufacturing community working at *Satricum*.

Bibliography

Attema, P.A.J., Bouma, J.W., Nijboer, A.J. & Olde Dubbelink, R. 1992. 'Il Sito di Borgo le Ferriere <Satricum> nel secoli V e IV A.C.', *Archeologia Laziale*, 20, 75-86.

Bedini, A. 1981. 'Edifici di Abitazione di epoca arcaica in località Acqua Acetosa-Laurentina', *Archeologia Laziale*, 3, 253-257.

Bedini, A. 1990. 'Laurentina-Acqua Acetosa', in *La Grande Roma dei Tarquini*, (Convegno, Palazzo delle Esposizione, giugno- settembre 1990), Roma, 171-177.

Beijer, A.J. 1991a. 'Un centro di produzione di vasi d'impasto a Borgo Le Ferriere ('Satricum') nel periodo dell'orientilizzante', *Papers of the Netherlands Institute in Rome*, 50, 63-86.

Beijer, A.J. 1991b. 'Impasto pottery and social status in Latium Vetus in the Orientalising period (725-575 BC): an example from Borgo Le Ferriere ('Satricum')', in Herring, E., Whitehouse, R. & Wilkins, J. (eds.), *Papers of the Fourth Conference of Italian Archaeology, London, The Archaeology of Power, Part 2*, 21-39.

Boni, G. 1900. 'Nuove scoperte della città e nel suburbio regione VIII. Le recenti esplorazioni nel sacrario di Vesta', *Notizie degli Scavi di Antichità*, 159-191.

Burnett, A.M. 1989. 'The beginnings of Roman coinage', *Annali*, 36, 33-64.

Crawford, M. 1985. *Coinage and Money under the Roman Republic*, London.

Cuomo di Caprio, N. 1971-72. 'Proposta di classificazione delle fornaci per ceramica e laterizi in area italiana', *Sibrium*, XI, 371-464.

Cuomo di Caprio, N.1979. 'Pottery- and tile-kilns in South Italy and Sicily', in McWhirr, A. (ed.), *Roman Brick and Tile*, BAR Int. Series 68, Oxford, 73-97.

Della Seta, A. 1918. *Museo della Villa Giulia*, Roma.

Fenelli, M. 1984. 'Lavinium', *Archeologia Laziale*, 6, 325-344.

Gastagnoli, F. 1963. 'Satrico', *L'Universo*, 43, 504-518.

Gastagnoli, F. 1975. *Lavinium II, Le Tredici Are*, Roma.

Gjerstad, E. 1960. *Early Rome III*, (Svenska Institutet i Rom, Skrifter 40, XVII:3), Lund.

Grottanelli, C. 1988. 'Of Gods and Metals. On the economy of Phoenician sanctuaries', *Scienza dell'Antichità*, 2, 243-255.

Haeberlin, J.E.J. 1909. *Die metrologischen Grundlagen der altesten Mittelitalischen Munzsysteme*, Berlin.

Haeberlin, J.E.J. 1910. *Aes Grave*, Frankfurt a. Main.

Hartmann, N. 1985. 'The use of iron in 9th and 8th century Etruria', *Papers of Italian Archaeology IV*, Part iii, BAR International Series 245, Oxford, 285-294.

Kamermans, H. 1980. *Verslag Fysisch Geografisch Onderzoek Omgeving Le Ferriere*, Groningen.

Kars, H., Moltzer, J.G. & Knoop, R.R. 1987. 'Petrography of archaic antefixes from Satricum', *Babesch*, 62, 57-65.

Klein, J. 1972. 'A Greek Metalworking Quarter, Excavations on Ischia', *Expedition*, Vol.14, No.2, 34-39.

Knoop, R.R. 1987. *Antefixa-Satricana. Sixth century architectural terracottas from the Sanctuary of Mater Matuta at Satricum (Le Ferriere)*, Assen.

Maaskant-Kleibrink, M. 1987. *Settlement Excavations at Borgo Le Ferriere-<Satricum>*, Vol.I, Groningen.

Maaskant-Kleibrink, M. 1992. *Settlement Excavations at Borgo Le Ferriere-<Satricum>*, Vol.II, Groningen.

McDonnell, R.D. & Kars, H. 1990. 'A petrological and geochemical study of Late Archaic statuary from Satricum', *Natuurwetenschappelijke Afdeling ROB*, Intern Rapport 90/6, Amersfoort, 1-23.

Minto, A. 1943. *Populonia*, Pistoia.

Monacchi, D. 1988. 'Nota sulla stipa votiva di Grotta Bella (Terni)', *Studi Etruschi*, 54, 75-99.

Nijboer, A.J. 1994. 'A pair of early fixed metallic monetary units from Borgo Le Ferriere (Satricum)', *Numismatic Chronicle*, 1-16.

Ostenberg, C.E. 1983. 'Acquarossa, Periodi preistorici e protostorici', *Notizie degli Scavi di Antichità*, ser.8, Vol.37, 79-97.

Pink, K. 1938. *Römische und Byzantinische Gewichte in österreichischen Sammlungen*, (Sonderschriften des Österreichischen Archäologischen Institutes in Wien, XII), Wien.

Rendelli, M. 1990. 'Materie prime, tecniche e tipi edilizi', in *La Grande Roma dei Tarquini*, (Convegno, Palazzo delle Espozione, giugno-settembre 1990), Roma, 138-139.

Sevink, J., Remmerzwaal, A. & Spaargaren, O.C. 1984. *The Soils of Southern Lazio and Adjacent Campania*, Publicatie van het Fysisch Geografischen Bodemkundig Laboratorium van de Universiteit van Amsterdam, Nr. 38, Amsterdam.

Snodgrass, A.M. 1980. 'Iron and early metallurgy in the Mediterranean', in Wertime, T.A. & Muhly, J.D. (eds.), *The Coming of the Age of Iron*, New Haven, 335-375.

Starr, C.G. 1977. *The Economic and Social Growth of Early Greece 800-500 B.C.*, New York.

Thomsen, R. 1957. *Early Roman Coinage*, 3 Vols., Kopenhaven.

56

Archeologia delle Miniere: Note sul Rapporto tra Insediamenti e Mineralizzazioni in Italia Centrale

ANDREA ZIFFERERO

(Musei Civici di Allumiere e Tolfa, Roma)

Sommario: *L'analisi dei bacini minerari, da un punto di vista archeominerario ed archeometallurgico, implica approcci differenziati, che prevedono indagini archeologiche ed archeometriche, funzionali alla ricostruzione di un quadro storico. La relazione illustra i risultati e le ipotesi emerse nel corso di un progetto di ricognizione topografica, attuato nel Lazio settentrionale, includente il bacino minerario dei Monti della Tolfa. Particolare attenzione viene rivolta a mettere in luce le tendenze del popolamento, ripartito in periodi, in relazione al sistema socio-economico di riferimento e allo sfruttamento delle risorse minerarie.*

Le ricerche nei settori dell'archeologia mineraria e della metallurgia estrattiva sono oggetto di rinnovata attenzione da parte degli studiosi: le indagini sulle miniere e sui luoghi di lavorazione dei minerali stanno, infatti, arricchendo il quadro delle conoscenze relative agli aspetti tecnologici e socio-economici di molte comunità dell'Italia antica, medievale e moderna (Cuomo di Caprio & Simoni 1989; Antonacci Sanpaolo 1992).

L'avvio di procedimenti d'indagine correlati alle varie fasi di estrazione dei minerali, di produzione e smercio del metallo, hanno messo in evidenza la necessità di sviluppare tecniche di analisi archeometrica più specifiche, finalizzate alla documentazione dei prodotti semilavorati e finiti: accanto alle ricerche di laboratorio, tuttavia, emerge in modo sempre più evidente il ruolo insostituibile della ricerca archeologica e d'archivio, per inserire i dati archeometrici all'interno di una cornice storica (esemplare, in questo senso, Rothenberg & Blanco Freijeiro 1981).

Lo scavo e la documentazione delle miniere, la ricognizione sistematica delle emergenze archeologiche localizzate nei comprensori minerari, possono portare a quadri ricostruttivi di ampio respiro, funzionali a registrare l'approccio antropico nei confronti delle mineralizzazioni, in una prospettiva diacronica.

La valutazione dei giacimenti minerari come una delle potenziali risorse da attivare all'interno di un territorio, in rapporto all'assetto socio-economico del periodo di riferimento, rappresenta un'acquisizione fondamentale nel processo legato all'interpretazione dei dati archeologici (Cambi 1986): in questo modo si può giungere a definire con chiarezza la possibilità che in determinati periodi non sia stato conveniente, per ragioni derivanti dall'assetto socio-economico dei comprensori, coltivare i giacimenti o svolgere attività di metallurgia estrattiva.

Le iniziative promosse in Toscana nel trascorso decennio hanno contribuito a mutare in profondità le cognizioni circa lo sfruttamento dei giacimenti nella regione: in particolare, è significativo rilevare come si sia riusciti a ricondurre e a mantenere la ricerca su un piano storico-archeologico, nel quale sono stati messi a fuoco i caratteri socio-economici, topografici ed ambientali inerenti le comunità legate al controllo e alla coltivazione delle miniere (Francovich *et al.* 1989; Corretti 1991).

Il progresso delle indagini ha fatto luce, proprio in Toscana, su episodi di coltivazione di giacimenti minerari rispetto a periodi, per i quali i dati erano inesistenti o le aspettative potenzialmente negative: nel caso del periodo romano, nonostante le fonti sembrino indicare una stasi nell'attività mineraria (Plinio, *N.H.* III, 20, 138; XXXIII, 21, 78), le indagini di superficie condotte tra l'isola d'Elba e la fascia costiera compresa tra Cecina ed il golfo di Follonica hanno permesso di accertare che la siderurgia era basata sul sistema produttivo della *villa*; il periodo medievale, inoltre, si è rivelato senza dubbio il più ricco di nuove evidenze (Francovich *et al.* 1989).

Le analisi sugli altri comprensori minerari dell'Italia centrale non sono assolutamente paragonabili, per qualità e quantità dei dati, alla situazione toscana. Da una parte, infatti, le ricerche incentrate sulle miniere sono da avviare o sono state appena avviate; dall'altra, il periodo privilegiato è senza dubbio quello preromano, con una grave lacuna per ciò che concerne soprattutto il Medioevo: ciò è particolarmente evidente per i giacimenti laziali (cfr. Negroni Catacchio 1988; Fortini 1988).

In questa sede si discutono alcune ipotesi derivate da un'indagine archeomineraria, inserita all'interno di un progetto di ricerca di superficie, in corso nel Lazio settentrionale, a cura della Soprintendenza Archeologica per l'Etruria Meridionale, in collaborazione con il Gruppo Archeologico Romano ed i Musei Civici di Allumiere e Tolfa: i primi risultati sugli aspetti archeominerari ed archeometallurgici sono stati editi di recente o sono, tuttora, in corso di pubblicazione (Zifferero 1991; 1992; c.s.).

Il comprensorio sondato è quello dei Monti della Tolfa (fig.1): il bacino minerario è stato inserito integralmente nel progetto di ricognizione topografica, proprio per valutare il diverso grado d'incidenza dell'impatto antropico nei confronti delle mineralizzazioni (tipologie insediative in rapporto alla geomorfologia della zona; assetto e distribuzione degli impianti di lavorazione dei minerali), e con i quadri socio-economici, noti o presunti, riferibili ai periodi di occupazione del settore, dalla protostoria al basso Medioevo (cfr. Gazzetti & Zifferero 1990).

Se gli studi precedenti hanno, comunque, stabilito un rapporto tra insediamenti ed aree mineralizzate, in base alla *site catchment analysis*, a partire dall'età del bronzo finale (Giardino 1984), la situazione relativa ai periodi successivi è largamente insufficiente: gli unici elementi di rilievo sono quelli prodotti dagli studiosi locali che, tuttavia, sono spesso discutibili nella metodologia di approccio (cfr. Brunori & Mela 1990): in ogni caso, con l'eccezione del periodo medievale, sono scarsissime o del tutto inesistenti le tracce di

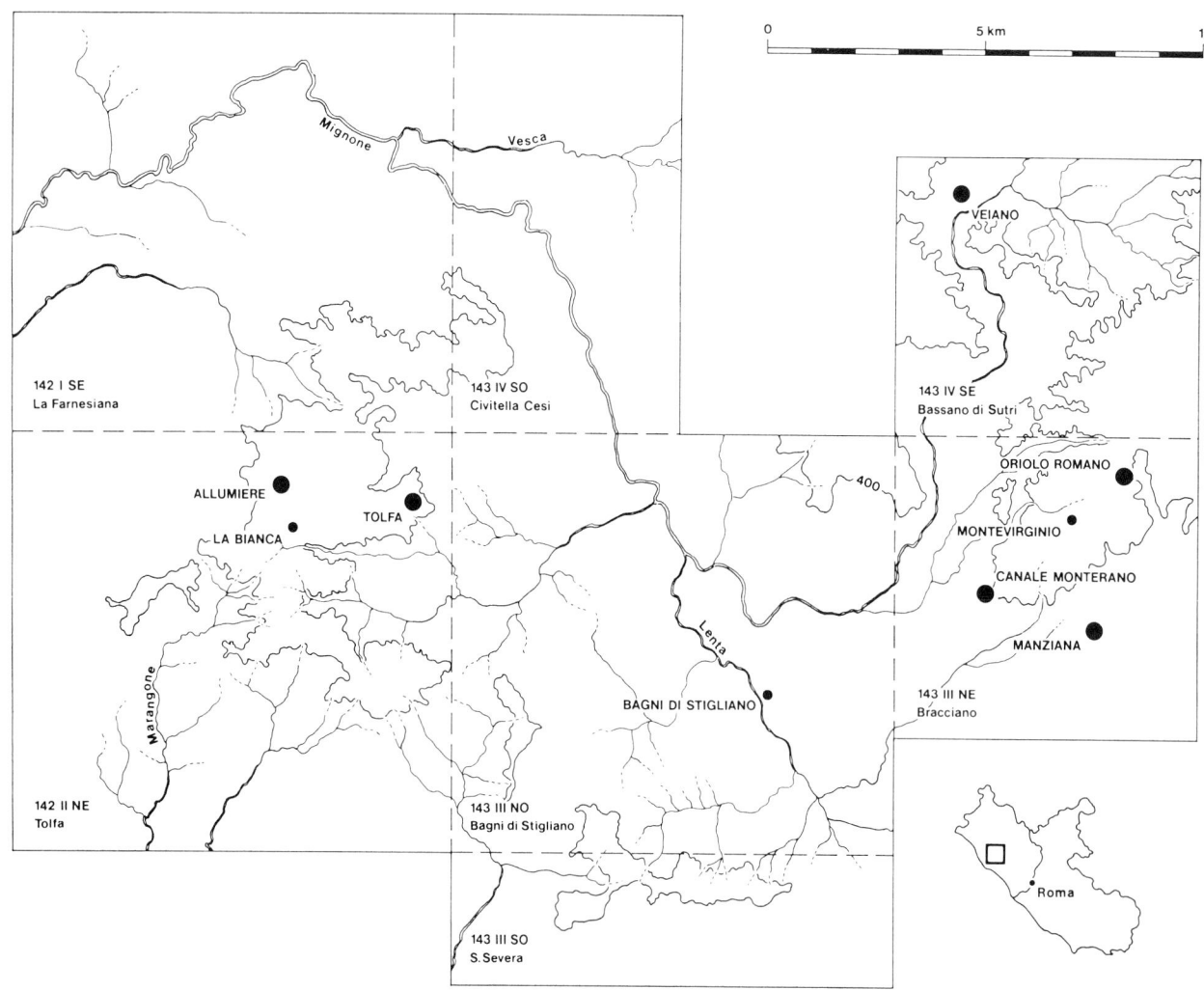

Fig. 1. Lo spazio campionato dal progetto Monti della Tolfa – valle del Mignone, con l'indicazione delle relative tavolette IGMI; in evidenza, i centri attualmente abitati.

metallurgia estrattiva; pari scarsità di dati si deve registrare per le tracce di attività mineraria più antica desumibili dalle miniere, obliterate dalle successive lavorazioni di età moderna.

Dal punto di vista mineralogico, la conoscenza del bacino tolfetano è stata perfezionata a partire dal dopoguerra con studi specifici, miranti a definire entità e dislocazione dei giacimenti (bibliografia essenziale in Contoli *et al.* 1980).

Nella cartografia acclusa, comprendente il settore occidentale del campione disegnato per il progetto (costituito dalle tavolette IGMI 142 I SE, La Farnesiana, 142 II NE, Tolfa e di parte della 143 IV SO, Civitella Cesi e della 143 III NO, Bagni di Stigliano), il comprensorio è presentato con la definizione del bacino metallifero meridionale, compreso tra il Poggio della Stella e la Roccaccia, mineralizzato a solfuri piombo-argentiferi e ferriferi, e del bacino alunitifero, gravitante a nord di M.Urbano, del quale si è preferito registrare l'estensione topografica delle coltivazioni, protratte dalla seconda metà del XV agli anni del secondo conflitto mondiale (figg.2–8).

L'analisi del popolamento, suddivisa in periodi, effettuata sulla base del rapporto tra insediamenti ed aree mineralizzate, permette le seguenti osservazioni:

Età del Bronzo Finale (fig.2)

Nel bacino minerario gli insediamenti privilegiano le fasce superiori ai 400 m s.l.m., e sono a diretto contatto con il bacino alunitifero; è interessante osservare come ad un sito indagato in modo sistematico, sull'Elceto (Toti 1976: 29 ss.) (fig.2:13), corrisponda un gruppo di presenze situate in corrispondenza di miniere di alunite (miniera Provvidenza in località Trincere: fig.2:11; Cave vecchie: fig.2:12) (Di Gennaro 1986: 77 ss.). La situazione ripropone quella dei giacimenti cinabriferi dell'Amiata, dove l'attività estrattiva ripresa nel secolo scorso, ha portato in luce utensili e tracce di estrazione protostorica (Zifferero 1991: 207 ss.).

Nel caso dei Monti della Tolfa, la presenza dell'alunite, associata al cinabro, può aver costituito uno dei principali elementi di sviluppo delle comunità. Per esse è stata recentemente ipotizzata da R.Peroni (1989: 298 ss.), una configurazione gentilizio-clientelare di tipo preurbano: i mezzi di produzione sono ancora in possesso delle comunità, nelle quali, tuttavia, è già avvenuta un'articolazione in senso verticale.

A questo proposito, un valore particolare assume la presenza della ceramica micenea nell'area tolfetana-allumierasca e nel bacino idrografico del Mignone, che è stata ricondotta alla pratica di scambi, anche se non organizzati e sistematici, o comunque di contatti con i *traders* egei (Bietti Sestieri 1988): ipotizzando che tali contatti siano avvenuti per via marina, acquista importanza il fatto che il toponimo *Pyrgoi*, come ha sottolineato Pugliese Carratelli (1962), sia attestato soltanto in territorio pilio, tra la Trifilia e la Messenia.

Non altrettanto evidente è il rapporto tra insediamenti e bacino metallifero, dove le uniche tracce di frequentazione, limitate, peraltro, a sepolture, sono testimoniate a Poggio Ombricolo (fig.2:17); gli scarsi indizi circa la presenza di masselli in rame o oggetti in ferro in contesti della zona potrebbero indicare uno sviluppo precoce della siderurgia alla fine dell'età del bronzo, come del resto si evince dai dati provenienti dalla valle del Fiora, ma sono insufficienti per documentare un'attività di metallurgia estrattiva da minerale locale (Toti 1986: 42 ss.; Delpino 1991).

Età del Ferro – antica e media età orientalizzante (fig.3)

Le trasformazioni profonde che avvengono nell'assetto delle comunità protostoriche medio-tirreniche e che portano, secondo Peroni (1989: 426 ss.), alla formazione di una società gentilizio-clientelare di tipo protourbano, investono in pieno il bacino minerario tolfetano, inducendo, in sostanza, il collasso del sistema insediativo montano e quindi, verosimilmente, l'abbandono delle presunte attività estrattive.

Per quanto attiene alla coltivazione e allo scambio dei minerali metalliferi, è probabile che l'attivazione del bacino minerario toscano abbia introdotto un ulteriore elemento destabilizzante per una ripresa delle coltivazioni minerarie sui Monti della Tolfa: purtroppo anche le indicazioni sullo sfruttamento dei depositi di ematite elbana sono estremamente scarse: secondo Fedeli (1983: 177 ss.), sarebbe possibile ritenerli produttivi a partire dalla seconda fase villanoviana, se non già dalla fine della prima fase.

La stratificazione sociale e le capacità di articolazione terrestre e di mobilità marina delle comunità villanoviane meridionali sono così sviluppate, ormai, da poter avviare un processo di scambio continuato con le comunità dell'Etruria mineraria, secondo un'ipotesi sempre più accreditata (cfr. Bartoloni 1987: 40 s.).

La frequentazione delle coste tirreniche da parte dei coloni euboici introduce una nota di complessità nel quadro: la dinamicità della società villanoviana meridionale è tale da favorire, fin dai primi rapporti, finalizzati probabilmente all'acquisizione di minerale di ferro, la formazione di scambi privilegiati con i greci, fungendo sostanzialmente da *relais* con i centri dell'Etruria mineraria, che controllano i giacimenti (Gras 1981: 320 ss.).

Come ho già sostenuto in altra sede, penso sia possibile individuare nelle sabbie ferrifere della costa medio-tirrenica uno dei catalizzatori principali (se non il primario), dei contatti iniziali tra prospettori minerari euboici ed *aristoi* villanoviani meridionali: è, infatti, interessante osservare (e probabilmente non si tratta di

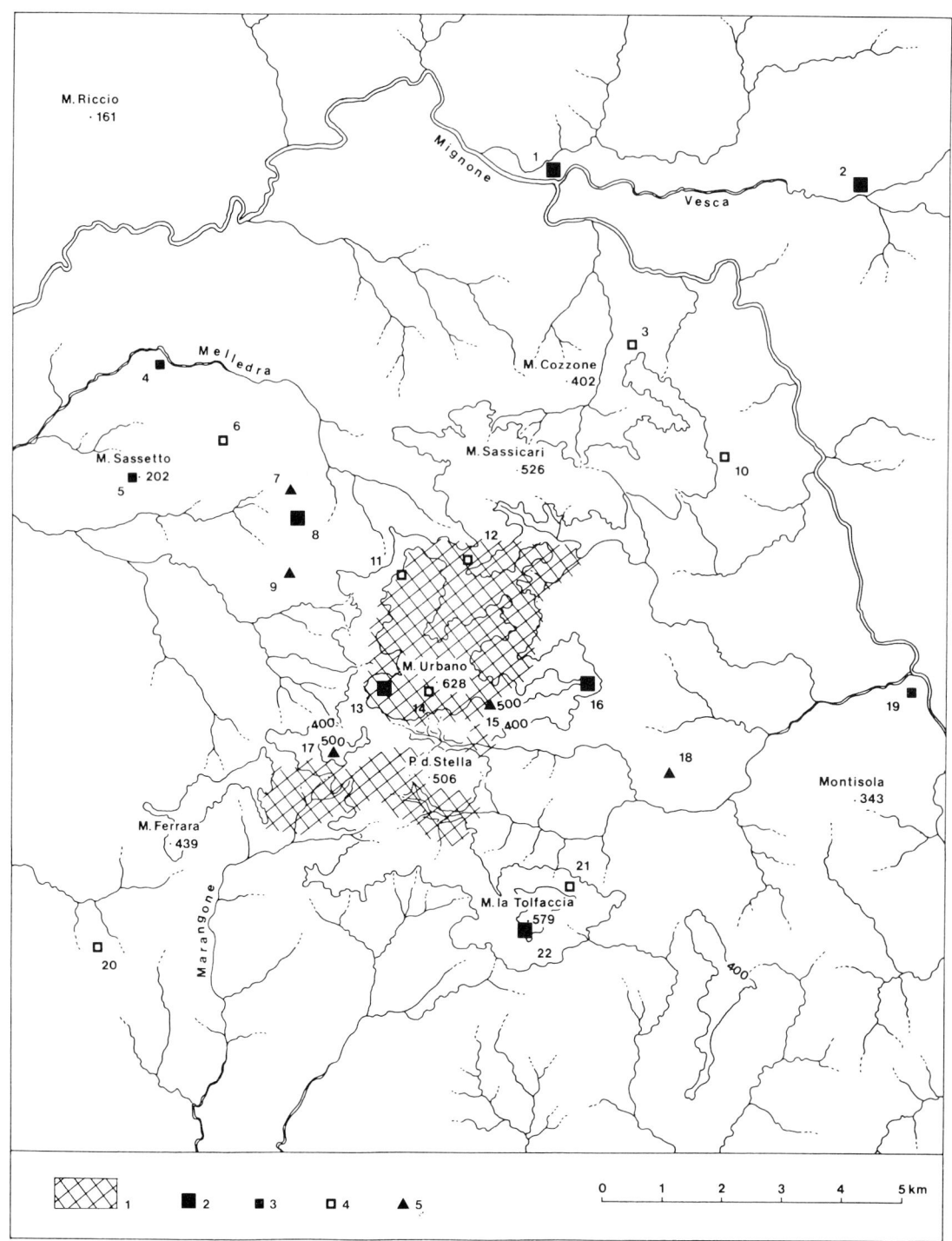

Fig. 2. Il settore del campione durante l'età del bronzo finale.
1 = estensione delle mineralizzazioni e dell'area di estrazione dell'alunite (a nord) e dei minerali metalliferi (a sud); 2 = insediamento con superficie superiore ai 3 ha; 3 = insediamento con superficie inferiore ai 3 ha; 4 = presenza; 5 = area sepolcrale.

Topografia di riferimento nel testo:
1 = Luni sul Mignone (Blera); 2 = S. Giovenale (Blera); 3 = Costa Grande (Tolfa); 4 = Uliveto di Cencelle (Tarquinia); 5 = Monte Sassetto (Allumiere); 6 = Ripa della Fonte (Allumiere); 7 = Forchetta di Palano (Allumiere); 8 = Monte Rovello (Allumiere); 9 = Poggio della Pozza (Allumiere); 10 = Coste del Marano (Tolfa); 11 = Miniera Provvidenza, Le Trincere (Allumiere); 12 = Cave Vecchie (Allumiere); 13 = Elceto (Allumiere); 14 = Monte Urbano (Allumiere); 15 = Cava Gangalandi (Allumiere); 16 = Tolfa; 17 = Poggio Ombricolo (Allumiere); 18 = Poggio della Capanna (Tolfa); 19 = Rota (Tolfa); 20 = Campanile di S. Giovanni (Civitavecchia); 21 = Granciare (Allumiere); 22 = La Tolfaccia (Allumiere).
I toponimi sono quelli utilizzati in Di Gennaro 1986.

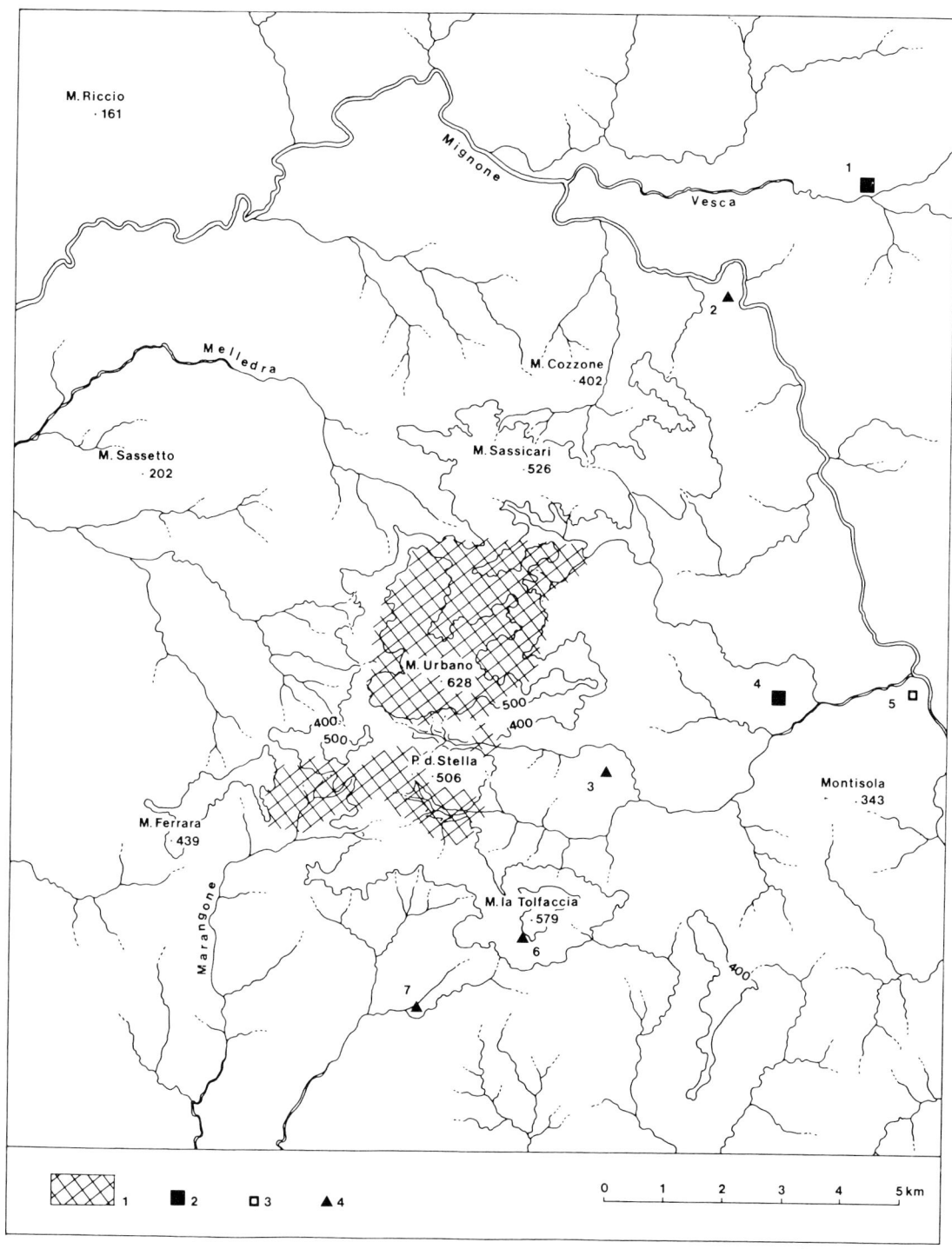

Fig. 3. Il settore del campione tra l'età del ferro e la media età orientalizzante.
1 = estensione delle mineralizzazioni e dell'area di estrazione dell'alunite (a nord) e dei minerali metalliferi (a sud); 2 = insediamento con superficie superiore ai 3 ha; 3 = presenza; 4 = necropoli o tomba isolata.

Topografia di riferimento nel testo:
1 = S. Giovenale (Blera); 2 = Lampregnana (Tolfa); 3 = Fontana del Papa (Tolfa); 4 = Pian Conserva (Tolfa); 5 = Rota (Tolfa); 6 = La Fontanaccia (Allumiere); 7 = Colle di Mezzo (Allumiere).

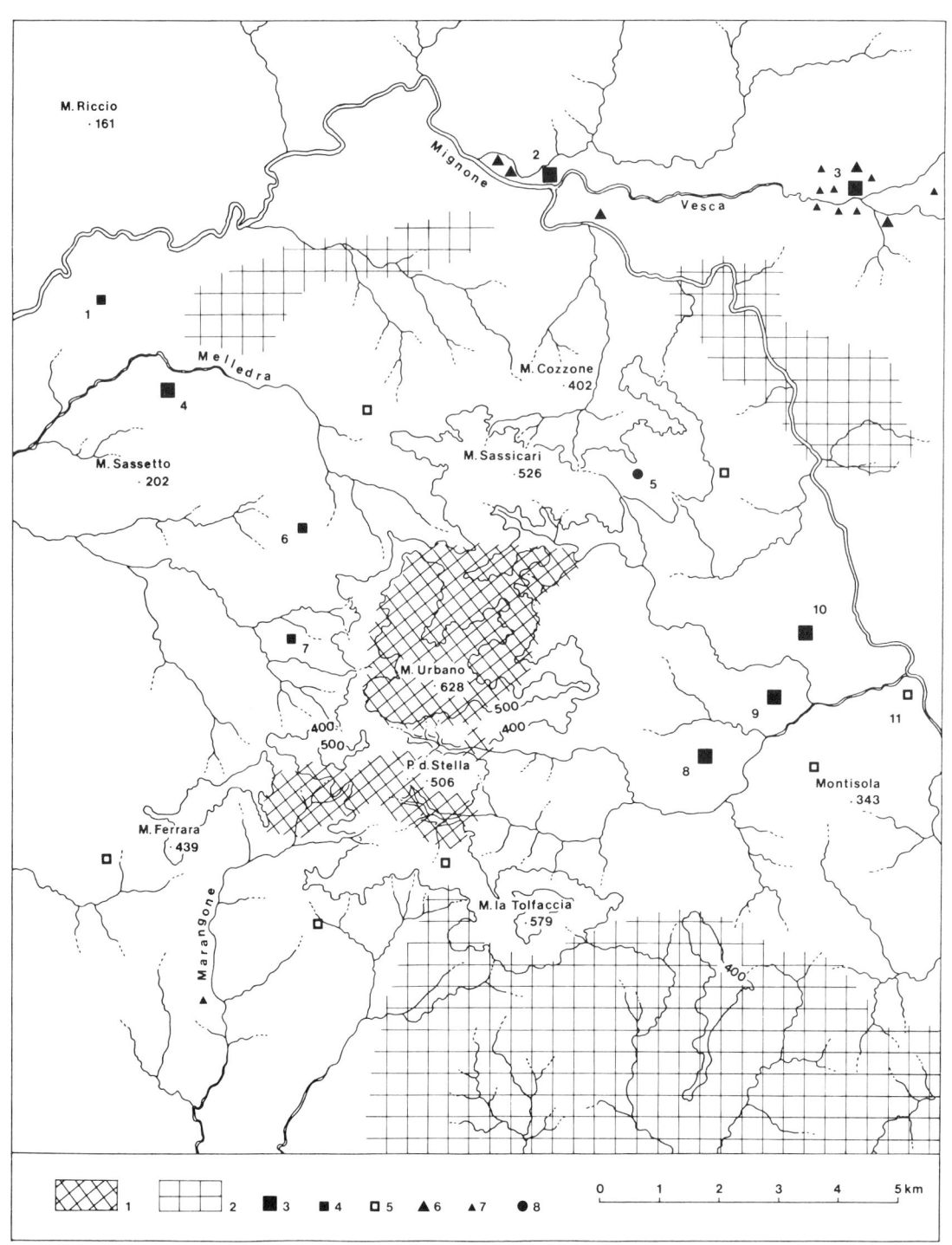

Fig. 4. Il settore del campione tra la tarda età orientalizzante e l'età classica.
1 = estensione delle mineralizzazioni e dell'area di estrazione dell'alunite (a nord) e dei minerali metalliferi (a sud); 2 = area con densità accentuata di siti aperti; 3 = abitato di pianoro con superficie superiore ai 3 ha; 4 = sito aperto o area insediativa di cui è accertata l'estensione; 5 = presenza; 6 = necropoli 7 = tomba isolata; 8 = area sacra.

Topografia di riferimento nel testo:
1 = Poggio Camposicuro (Tarquinia); 2 = Luni sul Mignone (Blera); 3 = S. Giovenale (Blera); 4 = Centocelle (Tarquinia); 5 = Grasceta dei Cavallari (Tolfa); 6 = Monte Rovello (Allumiere); 7 = Monte Pietroso (Allumiere); 8 = Pian dei Santi (Tolfa); 9 = Pian Conserva (Tolfa); 10 = Pian Cisterna (Tolfa); 11 = Rota (Tolfa).

un fattore legato al caso), come la presenza della frazione pesante (costituita principalmente da magnetite, associata a titanite ed ilmenite) nelle sabbie del litorale, nell'arco costiero compreso tra il Monte Argentario e l'area anziate, coincida con l'attestazione documentata della ceramica euboica o d'imitazione (Zifferero c.s.).

Al di là del fatto che le stesse sabbie siano state utilizzate o meno nella siderurgia, queste considerazioni potrebbero contribuire a fornire un ulteriore apporto nella definizione delle ragioni che hanno spinto gli euboici a frequentare le coste medio-tirreniche nell'VIII secolo a.C.; un parere positivo, in questo senso, ha espresso Sperl (1989), sottolineando l'esistenza di sabbie ferrifere, ricche di titanite, nell'isola d'Ischia.

Nel comprensorio minerario tolfetano, i segni relativi alla ripresa del popolamento, peraltro scarsissimi intorno alla metà-seconda metà dell'VIII secolo a.C. (fig.3:3–6), sembrano prefigurare le tendenze del popolamento successivo, incentrato sulla fascia pedemontana inferiore ai 400 m e sul bacino idrografico del Mignone.

L'assetto socio-economico è chiaramente quello aristocratico, basato sull'emergenza dei nuclei gentilizi che esercitano un controllo, rivendicando quindi un possesso, sulla terra circostante i principali abitati su pianoro tufaceo della zona (fig.3:1 e 4), attraverso un sistema a maglie molto larghe, incentrato anche su forme di sepoltura poste a distanza dai centri abitati (fig.3:2).

TARDA ETÀ ORIENTALIZZANTE – ETÀ CLASSICA (fig.4)

Tra la seconda metà del VII ed il IV secolo a.C. si sviluppa un sistema di popolamento intensivo, che porta, oltre all'incremento degli abitati su pianoro tufaceo, anche all'attivazione dei siti aperti, indirizzati verso le zone a più spiccata vocazione agricola (il periodo e i caratteri degli insediamenti sono illustrati in Zifferero 1990a). I settori a maggiore densità di occupazione sono quelli di fondovalle, gravitanti sul bacino idrografico del Mignone, e quelli pedemontani, particolarmente in corrispondenza degli altopiani digradanti verso la costa tirrenica.

E' la fase in cui è più evidente la pertinenza del comprensorio in esame al territorio controllato da Cerveteri, sia pure con un carattere di marginalità: esso si configura, a tutti gli effetti, come una zona di frontiera tra il territorio cerite e quello tarquiniese. I dati sull'eventuale attività mineraria e/o metallurgico-estrattiva, sono, di fatto, irrilevanti: nel bacino alunitifero ed in quello metallifero non vi sono, almeno al momento attuale, elementi indicanti una frequentazione etrusca finalizzata a tale scopo.

ETÀ REPUBBLICANA (fig.5)

L'età repubblicana rappresenta, per certi versi, un'ulteriore e progressiva specializzazione del processo di popolamento rurale avviato nel periodo etrusco: il sistema è naturalmente quello della *villa*, che comprende nel proprio ambito il settore produttivo: i pochi casi indagati di *villae* attivate nel periodo medio-repubblicano indicano un elevato grado di specializzazione nella produzione agricola e della ceramica (Munzi 1990; Camilli 1992).

Molti abitati etruschi su pianoro tufaceo, con l'inserimento nell'orbita amministrativa romana, all'inizio del III secolo a.C., vengono abbandonati o sopravvivono con la superficie parcellizzata da varie proprietà fondiarie.

Nel settore pedemontano il sistema di bonifica etrusco, avviato con opere di terrazzamento dei pendii, adattati alla presumibile conduzione di colture intensive, viene ripristinato e ampliato dagli agricoltori romani, come si può dedurre dai numerosi siti identificati (Zifferero 1990a, tabella 1). Esistono, per questo periodo, attestazioni di presenze insediative nell'area mineraria, ma non sono collegate con attività di estrazione dell'alunite o metallurgico-estrattive (Brunori 1985: 21 s.).

ETÀ IMPERIALE (fig.6)

Dopo una sostanziale tenuta del sistema insediativo nella prima età imperiale, con una predilezione per le zone più fertili dei fondovalle e dell'area pedemontana, si verifica una flessione nel popolamento intorno alla metà del III secolo d.C. (Gazzetti 1990). I settori di maggiore frequentazione restano, comunque, quelli del periodo repubblicano: egualmente carenti o non significative sono le tracce di attività minerarie o metallurgico-estrattive (Brunori 1984: 29 s.); l'assetto economico della zona sembra, anzi, indirizzato verso la produzione agricola e l'allevamento (Incitti 1990).

ALTO MEDIOEVO (fig.7)

Al forte decremento degli insediamenti fanno riscontro alcune presenze significative, che indicano una sopravvivenza molto ristretta del sistema della *villa* in conseguenza della guerra greco-gotica (Benelli & Nardi 1990; Vitali Rosati *et al.* 1992).

Nel comprensorio, comunque, le scarse attestazioni di *Forum ware* indizierebbero la vitalità di alcuni poli (Coccia & Nardi 1992): tra essi, l'abbazia di S.Arcangelo presso M.Piantangeli (fig.7:6), la cui posizione strategica, in prossimità dei guadi del medio corso del Mignone, sembra prefigurare l'attività di allevamento degli ovini o, comunque, di controllo degli itinerari di transumanza, recentemente attribuita all'ignota abbazia di S.Maria del Mignone, probabilmente da localizzarsi lungo il basso corso del fiume (Tron *et al.* 1984; Leggio 1990: 103 s.).

In base alle attestazioni delle fonti, tra i principali centri abitati prima del mille c'è quello di Centocelle (o

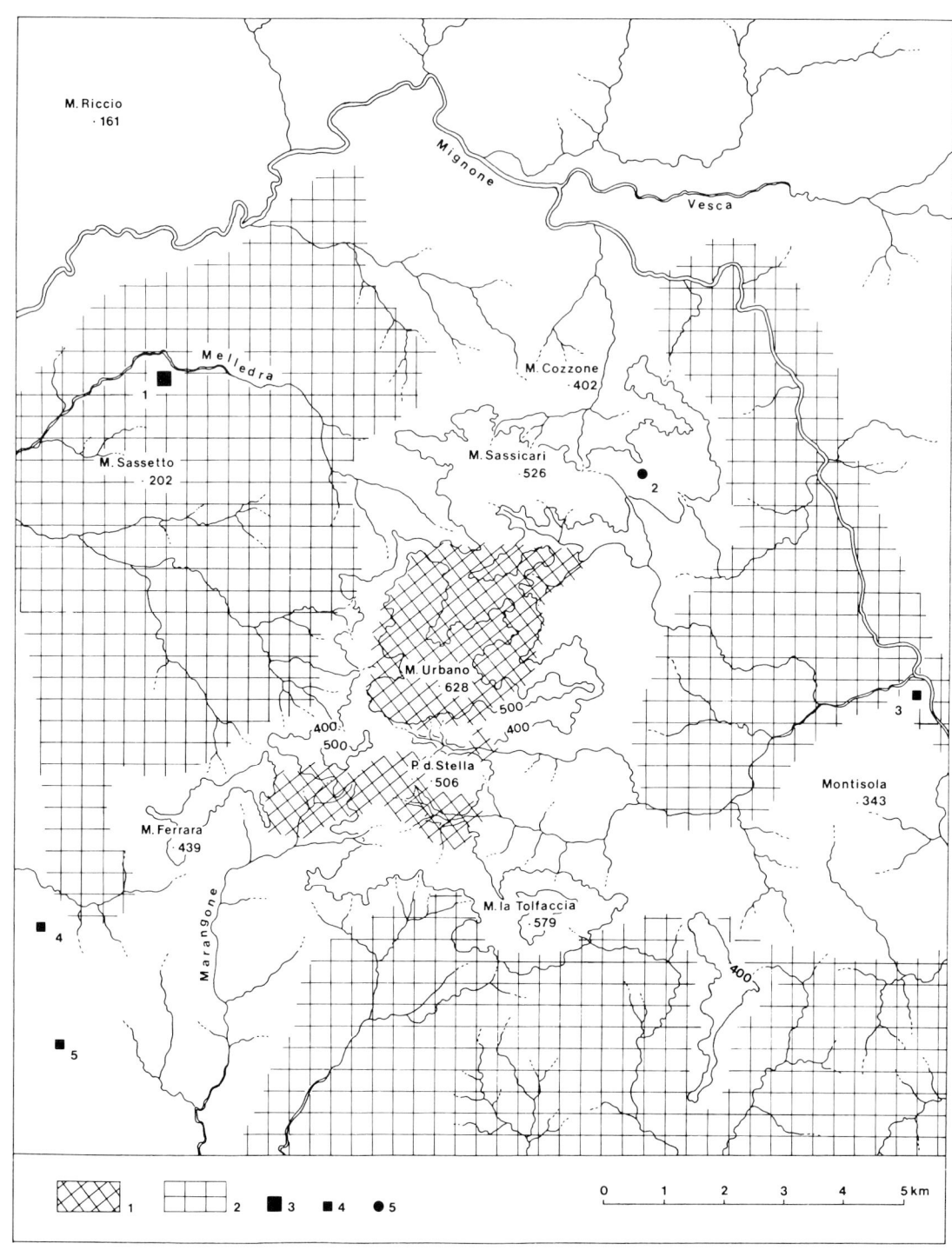

Fig. 5. Il settore del campione in età repubblicana.
1 = estensione delle mineralizzazioni e dell'area di estrazione dell'alunite (a nord) e dei minerali metalliferi (a sud); 2 = area con densità accentuata di siti aperti; 3 = abitato di pianoro con superficie superiore ai 3 ha; 4 = villa o area insediativa di cui è accertata l'estensione; 5 = area sacra.

Topografia di riferimento nel testo:
1 = Centocelle (Tarquinia); 2 = Grasceta dei Cavallari (Tolfa); 3 = Rota (Tolfa); 4 = Aquae Tauri (La Ficoncella) (Civitavecchia); 5 = Terme Taurine (Bagni di Traiano) (Civitavecchia).

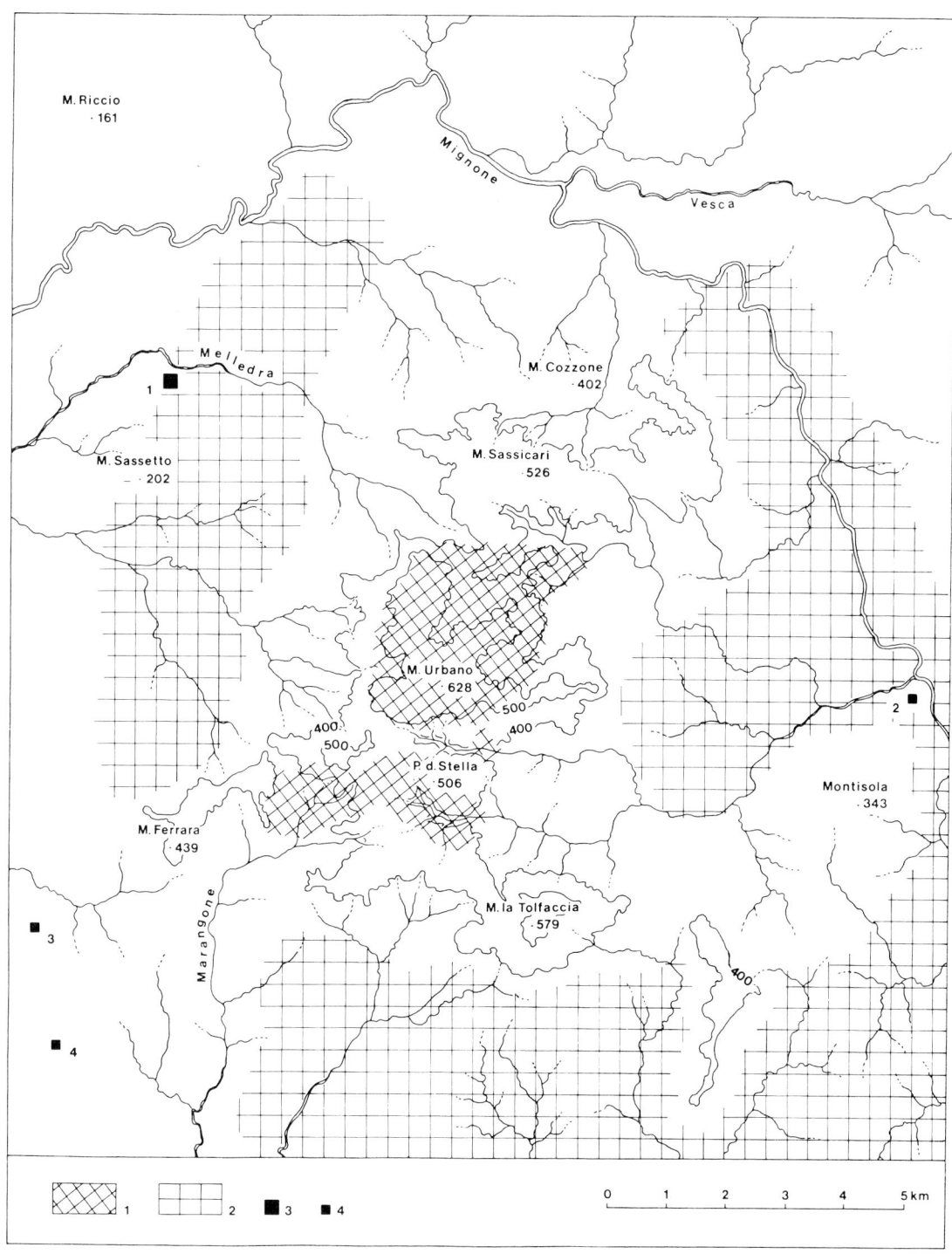

Fig. 6. Il settore del campione in età imperiale.
1 = estensione delle mineralizzazioni e dell'area di estrazione dell'alunite (a nord) e dei minerali metalliferi (a sud);
2 = area con densità accentuata di siti aperti; 3 = abitato di pianoro con superficie superiore ai 3 ha;
4 = villa o area insediativa di cui è accertata l'estensione.

Topografia di riferimento nel testo:
1 = Centocelle (Tarquinia); 2 = Rota (Tolfa); 3 = Aquae Tauri (La Ficoncella) (Civitavecchia);
4 = Terme Taurine (Bagni di Traiano) (Civitavecchia).

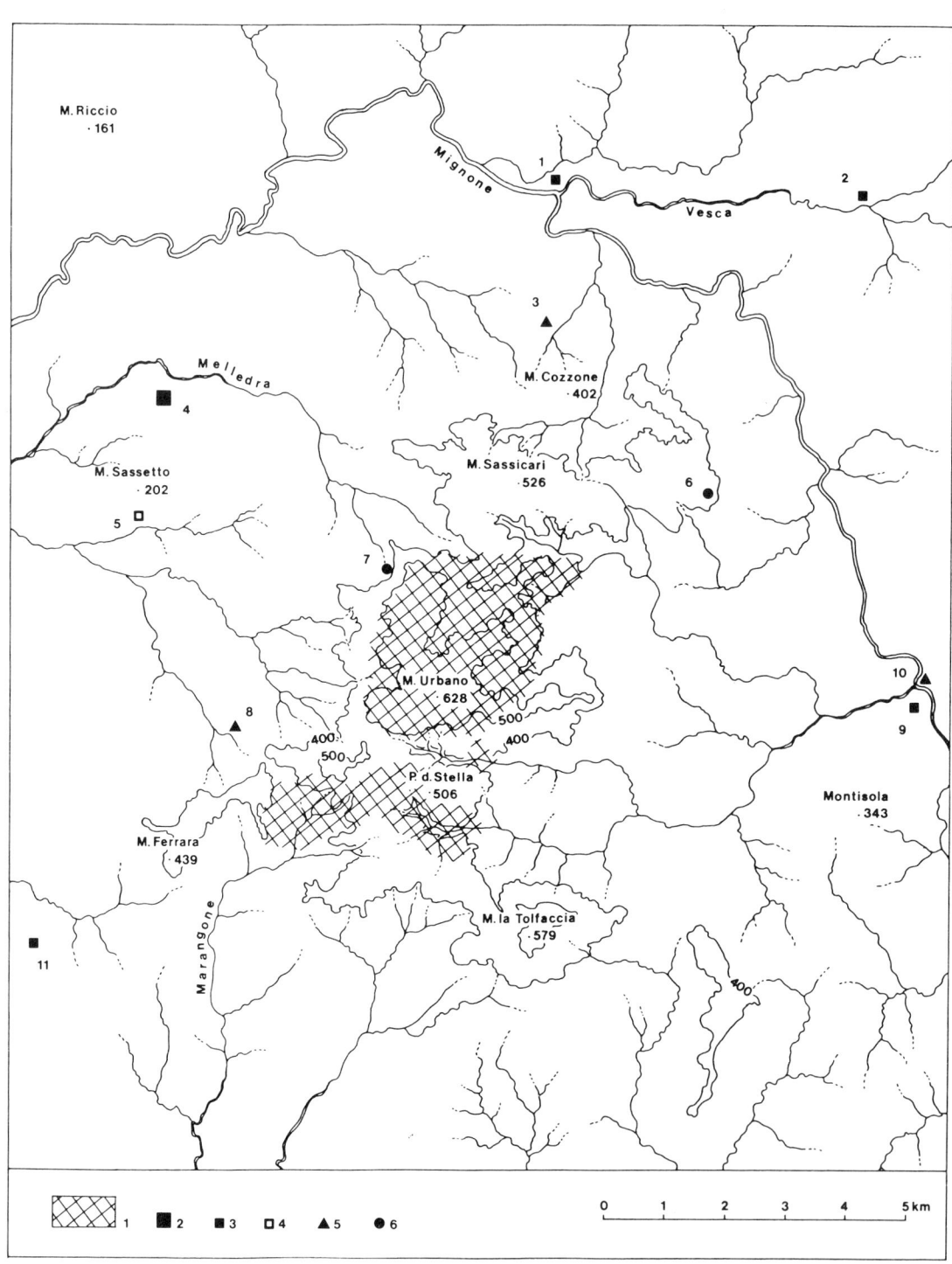

Fig. 7. Il settore del campione in età alto-medievale.
1 = estensione delle mineralizzazioni e dell'area di estrazione dell'alunite (a nord) e dei minerali metalliferi (a sud);
2 = centro abitato; 3 = centro minore; 4 = presenza; 5 = area sepolcrale; 6 = centro monastico.

Topografia di riferimento nel testo:
1 = Luni sul Mignone (Blera); 2 = S. Giovenale (Blera); 3 = Poggio Finocchio (Tolfa); 4 = Centocelle (Tarquinia); 5 = Caprareccia (Allumiere); 6 = Monte Piantangeli (Tolfa); 7 = Eremo della Trinità (Allumiere); 8 = Vaccareccia (Allumiere); 9 = Rota (Tolfa); 10 = Castellina di S. Pietrino (Tolfa); 11 = Aquae Tauri (La Ficoncella) (Civitavecchia).

Cencelle) (fig.7:4), che controllava l'accesso ai Monti della Tolfa e alla media valle del Mignone e l'insediamento monastico della Trinità (fig.7:7) (Nardi 1991; Brunori 1987).

Il secondo, frequentato da monaci agostiniani per la sua prossimità ad una sorgente d'acqua, si trova in sostanza a diretto contatto con alcune aree di estrazione dell'alunite (per la topografia delle cave cfr. Pompei 1933): queste sono sicuramente successive alle prime cave attivate nella seconda metà del XV secolo, ma hanno la denominazione significativa di Cava della Trinità e Cava dei Romani, una circostanza che potrebbe rimandare ad episodi di coltivazione avviati in una fase precedente la tradizionale scoperta dei depositi alunitiferi.

Sarebbe suggestiva l'ipotesi di una limitata attività estrattiva e di preparazione dell'allume promossa dal centro monastico, dal quale, tra l'altro, proviene un presunto crogiolo di fusione, verosimilmente bassomedievale (conservato nel Museo Civico di Allumiere: Brunori 1987: tav.4), che farebbe pensare ad una configurazione produttiva del sito: ciò, del resto, sarebbe in linea con quanto si va mettendo in luce in alcune regioni italiane (Francovich *et al.* 1989: 59 s.).

Basso Medioevo (fig.8)

Il basso medioevo è senza dubbio il periodo più ricco di attestazioni: secondo la tradizione storiografica, si chiude con la scoperta dei giacimenti di alunite, avvenuta ad opera di Giovanni da Castro intorno al 1460; lo sfruttamento delle mineralizzazioni metallifere sarebbe stata avviata soltanto in seguito all'apertura delle cave di allume (Di Carlo *et al.* 1984).

Esistono, tuttavia, alcuni indizi che permettono di anticipare l'inizio delle coltivazioni dei solfuri piombo-argentiferi e degli idrossidi ferriferi a partire almeno dal XIII secolo, grazie alla menzione nelle fonti documentarie del *castrum Ferrarie*, identificato nelle emergenze visibili in località Roccaccia (fig.8:14), nel cuore del bacino metallifero (Brunori 1984).

La scoperta e lo scavo di un edificio ecclesiastico, a cura dell'Associazione Archeologica A.Klitsche de La Grange di Allumiere, ha confermato l'articolazione dell'insediamento, del quale erano visibili in precedenza soltanto resti di una torre (Tron 1982: 82). All'interno di esso, è stato anche raccolto materiale semilavorato che fa presupporre un'attività metallurgico-estrattiva del piombo e siderurgica, in parallelo con quanto è stato documentato in altri siti medievali della Toscana (Francovich *et al.* 1989).

Una situazione analoga nel rapporto con l'area mineralizzata è quella intuibile per Poggio Ombricolo (fig.8:13), dove l'ipotesi di identificare il luogo con il castello di *Montelumbricum* (Tron 1982: 63 s.), troverebbe una conferma nei materiali ceramici da esso provenienti, attribuiti alla tarda età del ferro, che invece indicano chiaramente un'occupazione multifase dall'età del bronzo finale al Medioevo (Toti 1986: 78).

Questa forma di insediamento incastellato, a diretto contatto con le miniere, rappresenta una conferma per l'ipotesi di un controllo dei giacimenti minerari da parte di consorterie signorili, i cui interessi economici erano legati allo smercio e/o alla lavorazione dei minerali (Francovich *et al.* 1989).

La subordinazione suggerita dalle fonti documentarie, all'inizio del XV secolo, del *castrum Ferrarie* a *Tulfa nova* (fig.8:16), sede di un popoloso insediamento tra la fine del XII e la prima metà del XV secolo (Nardi 1992), può acquisire ulteriore significato con il recente ritrovamento di materiale semilavorato che indica un'attività siderurgica, proprio a *Tulfa nova* (Zifferero 1992).

La coltivazione e la lavorazione dei minerali metalliferi avrebbe, perciò, costituito uno dei principali motivi di sviluppo del comprensorio, e non è da escludere che eventuali conflitti di interessi in merito al commercio dei minerali o del metallo abbiano determinato l'abbandono e la distruzione di *Tulfa nova*, poco dopo la metà del XV secolo.

Le fonti qualificano, infatti, gli eredi di Giovanni da Castro, che nel frattempo hanno mantenuto i diritti di partecipazione agli appalti minerari, come promotori, alla fine del XV secolo, della costruzione (su licenza pontificia) di un impianto siderurgico presso i resti della chiesa di S.Severella, identificata ora con certezza lungo il corso del Melledra, in località La Farnesiana (fig.8:4) (Nardi & Zifferero 1990: 470); è un indizio della trasformazione del sistema socio-economico facente capo al bacino minerario, anche in senso topografico.

Un altro centro presso il quale le ricerche hanno evidenziato un'attività siderurgica è Centocelle (fig.8:3), abbandonato a partire dall'inizio del XV secolo: per la maggiore distanza dal bacino minerario, è possibile che il minerale vi arrivasse anche per canali commerciali diversi, e in questo senso non è da sottovalutare l'ipotesi di una provenienza elbana, considerando la dipendenza dell'abitato in questione da Corneto, riscontrabile dall'inizio del XIV secolo (Zifferero 1992).

Del resto, è verosimile anche un flusso di minerale elbano verso i suddetti centri siderurgici del comprensorio tolfetano, per arricchire il tenore metallico del ferro, in considerazione del fatto che vi si riducevano le limoniti derivate dai cappellacci di alterazione dei solfuri locali (analogamente a quanto si è messo in luce a Rocca S.Silvestro, nel campigliese: Francovich *et al.* 1989): dati oggettivi sul commercio della vena di ferro elbana nel Lazio, supportati dalle fonti documentarie, sono disponibili a partire dal XII secolo (Zifferero 1990b: 73; 1991: 224 ss.).

Per quanto attiene alla coltivazione dell'alunite, qualche elemento di novità può essere costituito dall'attestazione di ceramica precedente l'inizio della

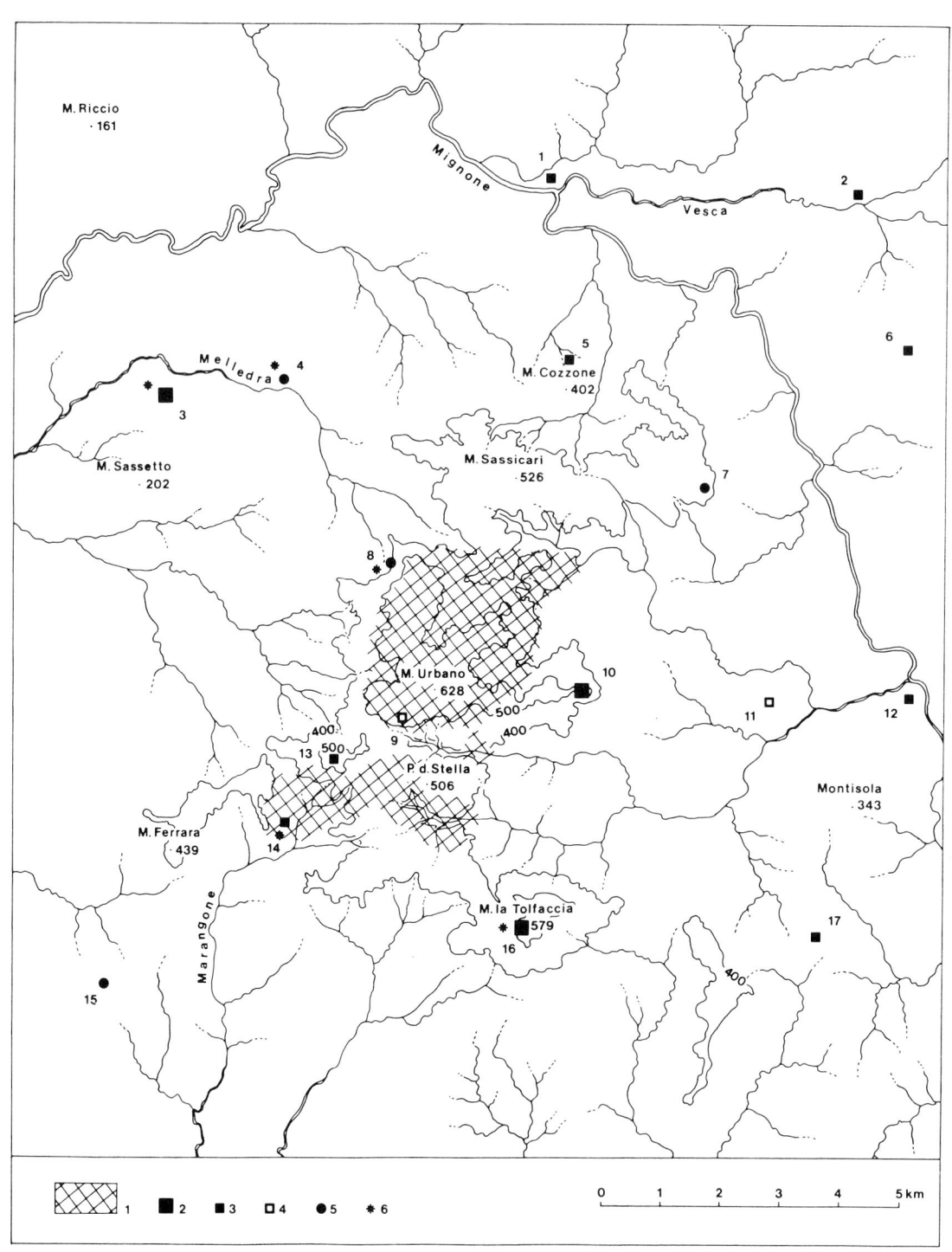

Fig. 8. Il settore del campione in età basso-medievale.
1 = estensione delle mineralizzazioni e dell'area di estrazione dell'alunite (a nord) e dei minerali metalliferi (a sud); 2 = centro abitato; 3 = centro minore; 4 = presenza; 5 = centro monastico; 6 = attività di metallurgia estrattiva.

Topografia di riferimento nel testo:
1 = Luni sul Mignone (Blera); 2 = S. Giovenale (Blera); 3 = Centocelle (Tarquinia); 4 = S. Severella (La Farnesiana) (Allumiere); 5 = Castellaccio di M.Cocozzone (Tolfa); 6 = Monte Monastero (Blera); 7 = Monte Piantangeli (Tolfa); 8 = Eremo della Trinità (Allumiere); 9 = La Bianca (Allumiere); 10 = Tolfa; 11 = Pian Conserva (Tolfa); 12 = Rota (Tolfa); 13 = Montelumbricum *? (Poggio Ombricolo) (Allumiere); 14 =* Castrum Ferrarie *(La Roccaccia) (Allumiere); 15 = S. Egidio (Civitavecchia); 16 =* Tulfa nova *(Allumiere); 17 = Monte Castagno (Tolfa).*

seconda metà del XV secolo, proveniente proprio dall'area che è ritenuta uno dei primi luoghi di estrazione da parte di Giovanni da Castro: si tratta di un gruppo di reperti in maiolica arcaica di produzione alto-laziale, cortesemente attribuiti da M.Ricci ad un arco cronologico compreso tra il tardo XIV e l'inizio del XV secolo, rinvenuti in una situazione stratigrafica purtroppo non documentata a sufficienza, in località La Bianca (fig. 8:9) (Brunori 1985: 40 ss., tavv. 1 e 3).

Ciò fa ipotizzare una frequentazione medievale della zona in una fase anteriore l'impianto della *lumiera* della Bianca (avvenuto, secondo le fonti documentarie, all'inizio del XVI secolo): considerando il contatto con uno dei settori più ricchi di mineralizzazioni alunitifere del bacino, è possibile che tale frequentazione fosse in qualche modo collegata ad attività estrattive, probabilmente condotte su piccola scala.

Conclusioni

In conclusione, è possibile avanzare le seguenti considerazioni e ipotesi:

a) le tendenze del popolamento, documentate nel bacino minerario tolfetano, presuppongono la presenza di un sito a breve distanza dai giacimento minerari, come una delle condizioni necessarie per lo sviluppo delle attività estrattive;

b) i periodi nei quali si sono verificate queste condizioni sono l'età del bronzo finale, in cui è probabile che sia stata effettuata un'attività di ricerca e di estrazione dell'alunite e del cinabro, ed il Medioevo, in una fase sicuramente precedente la tradizionale scoperta dei giacimenti alunitiferi, limitatamente ai minerali metalliferi;

c) forme di controllo dei giacimenti minerari sono presumibili per l'età del bronzo finale e per il Medioevo: queste vennero attuate attraverso un sistema di insediamenti che, senza dubbio, facevano parte di un territorio strutturato ed organizzato con finalità produttive;

d) sembra possibile escludere, al momento, che il sistema socio-economico ricostruibile nei periodi etrusco e romano si sia accresciuto in funzione di un'attività mineraria e/o metallurgico-estrattiva, in considerazione delle tendenze espresse dal popolamento, distribuito in fasce a vocazione rurale abbastanza spiccata.

e) i risultati dell'indagine mi pare confermino la prospettiva metodologica di partenza, di considerare i giacimenti minerari una risorsa da attivare in presenza di condizioni particolarmente favorevoli, influenzate dall'assetto socio-economico delle comunità promotrici dell'attività mineraria e/o metallurgico-estrattiva.

Bibliografia

Antonacci Sanpaolo, E. (a cura di) 1992. *Archeometallurgia: ricerche e prospettive* (Atti del convegno), Bologna.

Bartoloni, G. 1987. 'Le comunità dell'Italia centrale tirrenica e la colonizzazione greca in Campania', in Cristofani M. (a cura di), *Etruria e Lazio arcaico*, Roma, 37–53.

Benelli, E. & Nardi, S. 1990. 'Sepolture alto-medievali dalla Vaccareccia (Allumiere)', in Gazzetti & Zifferero 1990, 467–470.

Bietti Sestieri, A.M. 1988. 'The "mycenaean connection" and its impact on the central Mediterranean societies', *Dialoghi di Archeologia* 1, 23–51.

Brunori, E. 1984. 'Ritrovato l'antico "Castrum Ferrarie"', *Notiziario del Museo Civico di Allumiere* 6, 13–42.

Brunori, E. 1985. 'Quando la lumiera era alla Bianca', *Notiziario del Museo Civico di Allumiere* 7, 7–48.

Brunori, E. (a cura di) 1987. *La chiesa della SS. Trinità nella tradizione eremitica agostiniana: salvaguardia e recupero* (catalogo della mostra), Civitavecchia.

Brunori, E. & Mela, A. 1990. 'Le risorse minerarie nell'antico territorio di Caere', in Maffei & Nastasi 1990, 220–232.

Cambi, F. 1986. 'L'archeologia di uno spazio geografico: il progetto topografico ager Cosanus – valle dell'Albegna', *Archeologia Medievale*, XIII, 527–544.

Camilli, A. 1992. 'Nuove scoperte archeologiche nei Monti della Tolfa. 1: la villa di Freddara', in Herring *et al.* 1992, 99–103.

Coccia, S. & Nardi, S. 1992. 'La valle del Mignone e i Monti della Tolfa', in Paroli L. (a cura di), *La ceramica invetriata tardoantica e altomedievale in Italia* (atti del convegno), Firenze, 471–474.

Contoli, L., Lombardi, G. & Spada, F. 1980. *Piano per un parco naturale nel territorio di Allumiere e Tolfa*, Roma.

Corretti, A. 1991. *Metallurgia medievale all'isola d'Elba*, Firenze.

Cuomo di Caprio, N. & Simoni, C. (a cura di) 1989. *Dal basso fuoco all'altoforno* (atti del convegno), *Sibrium* 20.

Delpino, F. 1991. 'Siderurgia e protostoria italiana', *Studi Etruschi* 56, 3–9.

Di Carlo M., Di Giulio, N., Franceschini, P., Moretti, C. & Torreti, F. 1984. *La società dell'allume. Cultura materiale, economia e territorio in un piccolo borgo*, Roma.

Di Gennaro, F. 1986. *Forme di insediamento tra Tevere e Fiora dal bronzo finale al principio dell'età del ferro*, Firenze.

Fedeli, F. 1983. *Populonia. Storia e territorio*, Firenze.

Fortini, P. 1988. 'Nuovi insediamenti preromani nell'area laziale del Parco Nazionale d'Abruzzo e del pre-Parco', in *Il territorio del Parco Nazionale d'Abruzzo nell'antichità* (atti del convegno), Civitella Alfedena, 51–63.

Francovich, R., Cucini, C., Mannoni, T. & Cucchiara, A. 1989. 'Le strutture produttive del ferro negli insediamenti medievali della Toscana', in Cuomo di Caprio & Simoni 1989, 57–76.

Gazzetti, G. 1990. 'Storia del territorio in età romana', in Maffei & Nastasi 1990, 101–103.

Gazzetti, G. & Zifferero, A. (a cura di) 1990. 'Progetto Monti della Tolfa – Valle del Mignone: secondo rapporto di attività (1985–1989)', *Archeologia Medievale*, XVII, 435–476.

Giardino, C. 1984. 'Insediamenti e sfruttamento minerario del territorio durante la media e la tarda età del bronzo nel Lazio: ipotesi e considerazioni', *Nuovo Bullettino Archeologico Sardo* 1, 123–141.

Gras, M. 1981. 'L'Etrurie minière et la reprise des echanges entre l'orient et l'occident: quelques observations', in *L'Etruria Mineraria* (Atti del XII Convegno di Studi Etruschi e Italici), Firenze, 315–332.

Herring, E., Whitehouse, R. & Wilkins, J. (a cura di) 1992. *Papers of the Fourth Conference of Italian Archaeology 4. New Developments in Italian Archaeology: Part 2*, London.

Incitti, M. 1990. 'Alcuni aspetti economici dell'area dei Monti della Tolfa in età romana: note preliminari', in Maffei & Nastasi 1990, 113–118.

Leggio, T. 1990. 'Il castello di Rascino nel Medioevo', *Il Territorio* 2–3, 92–111.

Maffei, A. & Nastasi, F. (a cura di) 1990. *Caere e il suo territorio. Da Agylla a Centumcellae*, Roma.

Munzi, M. 1990. 'La villa rustica di Pian Conserva (Tolfa)', in Gazzetti & Zifferero 1990, 451–453.

Nardi, S. 1991. 'Cencelle. La cinta difensiva medievale', in *Storia della città* 53, 15–22.

Nardi, S. (a cura di) 1992. 'Indagini nella rocca di "Tulfa nova" (Allumiere): rapporto preliminare di attività (1990-1991)', *Archeologia Medievale,* XIX, 437–452.

Nardi, S. & Zifferero, A. 1990. 'Ricognizioni nell'area della Farnesiana (Allumiere)', in Gazzetti & Zifferero 1990, 470.

Negroni Catacchio N. 1988. 'Inquadramento storico e culturale', in *Il Museo di Preistoria e Protostoria della valle del fiume Fiora,* Manciano, 33–83.

Peroni, R. 1989. *Protostoria dell'Italia continentale. La penisola italiana nelle età del bronzo e del ferro,* Roma.

Pompei, A. 1933. 'I giacimenti minerari della Tolfa in provincia di Roma', in *Relazione sul Servizio Minerario nell'anno 1931* (a cura del Ministero delle Corporazioni), 57, 277–304.

Pugliese Carratelli, G. 1962. 'Achei nell'Etruria e nel Lazio?', *Parola del Passato* 82, 5–25.

Rothenberg, B. & Blanco Freijeiro, A. 1981. *Studies in Ancient Mining and Metallurgy in South-West Spain,* London.

Sperl, G. 1989. 'Il sentiero europeo del ferro', in Cuomo di Caprio & Simoni 1989, 17–22.

Toti, O. 1976. 'Le presenze protovillanoviane nel territorio tolfetano', *Notiziario del Museo Civico di Allumiere* 5, 25–40.

Toti, O. 1986. 'La «Civilta' Protovillanoviana» dei Monti della Tolfa', in *La «Civilta' Protovillanoviana» dei Monti della Tolfa. Societa' ed economia tra XI e IX secolo a.C.,* Civitavecchia, 11–85.

Tron, F. 1982. *I Monti della Tolfa nel Medioevo,* Roma.

Tron, F., Berretti, R., Gorra, M., Pieri, E. & D'Aloia, F. 1984. *L'abbazia di Piantangeli,* Roma.

Vitali Rosati, B., Rinaldoni, C. & Felici, F. 1992. 'Nuove scoperte archeologiche nei Monti della Tolfa. 3: la villa di Poggio Smerdarolo – Piana di Rio Fiume', in Herring *et al.* 1992, 111–117.

Zifferero, A. 1990a. 'Città e campagna in Etruria meridionale: indagine nell'entroterra di Caere', in Maffei & Nastasi 1990, 60–70.

Zifferero, A. 1990b. 'Insediamenti ed economia: appunti sulle risorse minerarie dei Monti della Tolfa', in Maffei & Nastasi 1990, 71–75.

Zifferero, A. 1991. 'Miniere e metallurgia estrattiva in Etruria meridionale: per una lettura critica di alcuni dati archeologici e minerari', *Studi Etruschi* 57, 201–241.

Zifferero, A. 1992. 'Giacimenti minerari e insediamenti nel Lazio settentrionale: recenti acquisizioni e prospettive di ricerca', in Antonacci Sanpaolo 1992, 81–103.

Zifferero, A. c.s. 'Giacimenti di alunite e popolamento di età preromana sui Monti della Tolfa', *Notiziario del Museo Civico di Allumiere* 9, in corso di stampa.

57

The Supply of Building Materials to the City of Rome

JANET DELAINE
(Department of Archaeology, University of Reading)

Summary: *This paper presents the first results of a new investigation into the supply of building materials for the city of Rome, which forms part of a broader on-going study of the Roman building industry. Stress is laid on the importance of the local geology and topography for determining the conditions of extraction and the ease of transport to Rome, and a number of specific cases are discussed. Ethnographic models from the 19th century are used to estimate the man-power requirements for pozzolana extraction, and this is placed in the context of a single building project – the Baths of Caracalla – in order to indicate the scale of operations. Quantitative assessment is also used to answer questions concerning the routes used to transport travertine in the imperial period. The supply of brick and lime are discussed, with particular reference to the possible role of Terracina and the origins of lime-burning as an agricultural operation. The final section examines the role played by the production and transport of building materials to Rome in the rural economy, placing rural landowners in the main entrepreneurial roles but suggesting the possiblities of more widespread economic benefits through the use of contract labour.*

INTRODUCTION

The supply of materials is a critical factor in the success of any construction project, and the building programmes of Republican and imperial Rome can have been no exception. Indeed, the role played in the development of a specifically Roman architecture by the obvious limitations and the gradually emerging potentialities of the local building materials is all too familiar. The study of this aspect of the building industry in Rome, however, has focused largely on chronological developments, on the ever widening search for better stones for ashlar construction – the tufas of Fidenae, Grotta Oscura, Monteverde and Anio, Gabine stone and peperino, travertine – and on the gradual evolution of that quasi-magical material, Roman concrete, with its requirements of pozzolana and lime and its brick facing (Lanciani 1897: 32–42; Frank 1924; Blake 1947: 21–44). I am referring here to the ordinary bulk building materials of Rome, and have no intention on this occasion of addressing the rather different case of imported luxury marbles.

My concern in this paper, however, is not with the development of architecture but with the process of building, and thus with the organisation of building supplies rather than merely with the sources of building materials. Apart from the obvious consideration that without the materials there can be no building, the production of bulk building materials is also critical for the economics of construction, accounting very roughly for between one third and one half of the total labour expended on a building excluding any transport requirements (cf. Scavizzi 1983: 5–56 for 17th century Italy, and Clarke 1992: 101 for 18th century London). This raises a quite different set of questions to those usually asked: not where are the quarries, but why are they there? Not, where are the materials used, but how did they get there? How were they produced, by whom, and for whose benefit? In addition, instead of looking at the effects of their use in Rome, we need to look at the relationship of their production to the surrounding area. Even to begin to address these points for all the building materials of Rome would require a volume to itself, and in this short paper I can do little more than sketch the general lines of my inquiries and outline a few specific cases – mainly from my research on the Baths of Caracalla (DeLaine 1992) and Hadrianic Ostia (DeLaine 1996) – which serve to show the potential of this approach.

As a final preliminary, a few words are necessary to define the factors which affect the viability of a source of building materials. Fitchen has summarised the essential considerations affecting a builder's choice of material:

"...the location of its source, the reliability and sufficiency of its supply, the feasibility of its procurement, the methods and routes of its transportation to the building site, its quality, and its cost." (Fitchen 1986: 49)

All of these considerations hinge ultimately on the combination of local geology and topology. Only with the cost of materials do other factors such as competition, subsidies, monopolies, and profit come into play, but even in this case it is the geology and location of the source which determine the basic cost structure, based on the manpower required for production – itself dependent on the conditions of procurement – and the cost of transport. While the reasons behind the original decision to exploit any particular potential source of building materials can only be guessed at, the essential prerequisites for exploitation lay in the physical situation.

QUESTIONS OF EXTRACTION

Such considerations allow for a re-evaluation of the major building materials of Rome, starting with the geology of complex and important volcanic deposits emanating from the Sabatini volcanoes to the north of Rome and the Latial volcanoes (Colli Albani) to the south (fig. 1). Rome itself lies at the extreme edge of the deposits coming from the Latial volcanoes, deposits which include the lithoidal tufas to which the Monteverde and Anio tufas belong, and the major pozzolanas (fig. 2). Below the pozzolanas are the more coarse and friable tufas of the Sabatini volcanoes, including those from Grotta Oscura and Fidenae. Not all these deposits are uniform within themselves, and the bed of lithoidal tufa is both relatively thin and variable in thickness. On the whole the important deposits from the Latial volcanoes are absent north and west of the city, while to the south and east they are covered by a further pozzolana deposit of far less value for making concrete, and by a tongue of lava which provides the basalt used in paving the roads of Rome. On the right bank of the Tiber there is no pozzolana and the Latial lithoidal tufas appear only at Monteverde; the Monte della Creta and the valleys south and west of the Vatican, however, abound in the

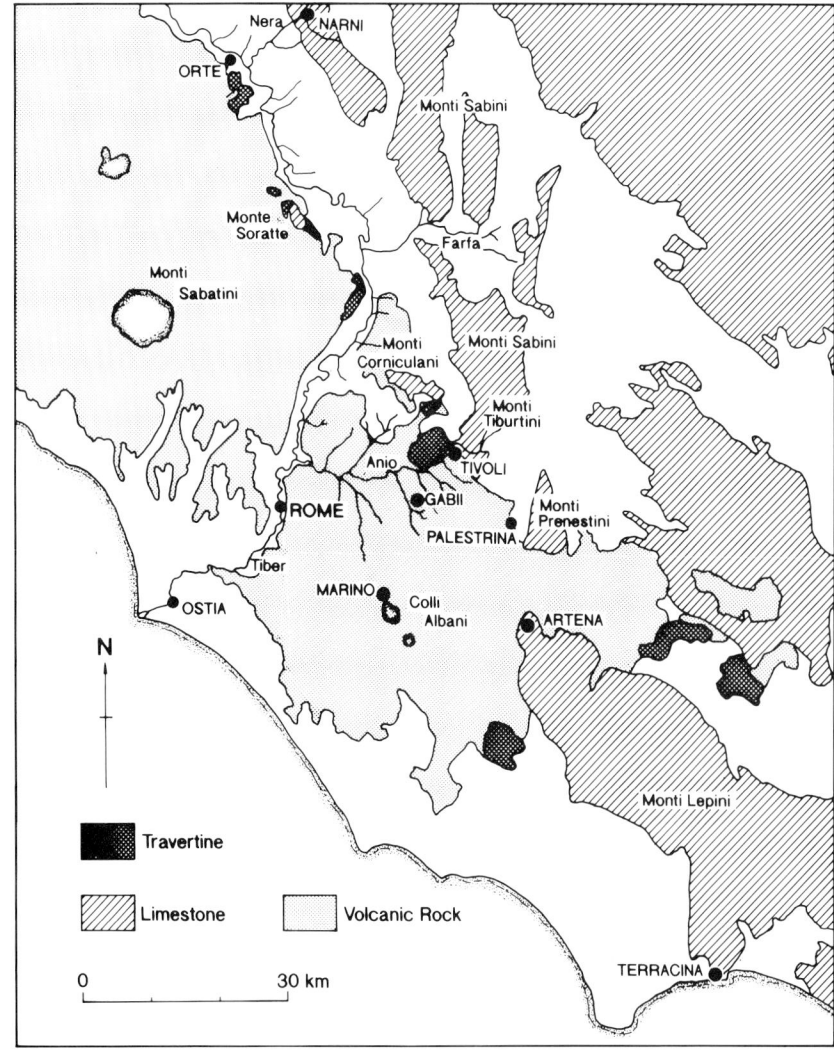

Fig. 1. Volcanic and limestone areas around Rome.

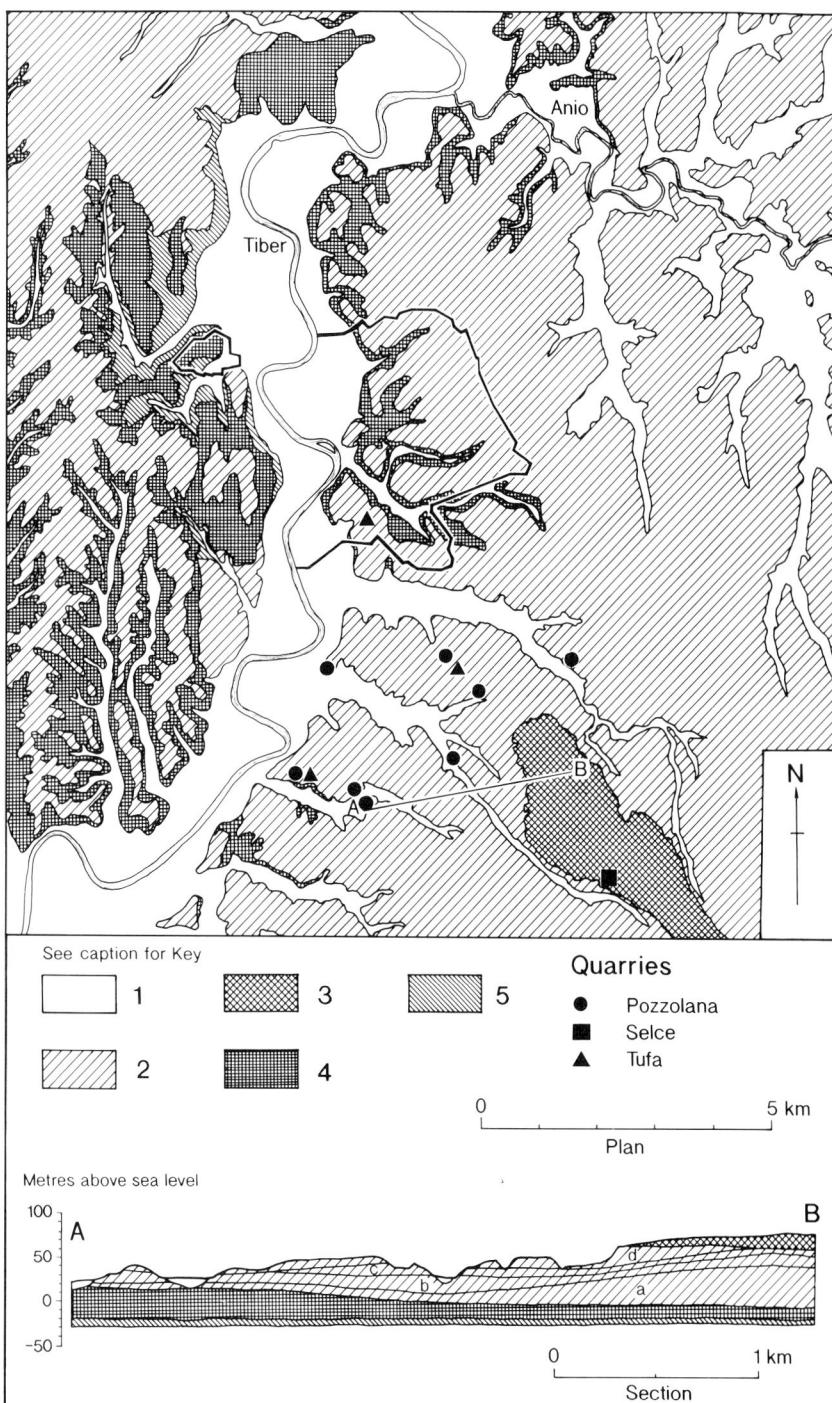

Fig. 2. Geology of Rome. Simplified map and section (after Sciotti 1982, figs. 1 & 2)

Key:
1. Recent alluvial deposits;
2. Main volcanic (pyroclastic) deposits –
   (a) tufas ('tufi antichi')
   (b) red and black pozzolanas,
   (c) tufa ('tufo lionato')
   (d) grey pozzolana;
3. Basaltic lava from Latial volcanoes;
4. Fluvio-lacustrine sediments (Sicilian formation);
5. Blue marine clays (Pliocene).

clays of the Pleistocene and Pliocene deposits (Ventriglia 1971; Sciotti 1982).

Rome thus stands at a geological interface which both provides a wide variety of possible materials and makes many of them easily accessible, an essential element in the ease of procurement. Without heavy mechanised earth-moving equipment, open-cast quarrying is only feasible where there is no deep overburden to remove, while for deeper beds the desired stratum needs to be accessible from the side in a natural cut. Here the topography of Rome and its surroundings come into play, the valleys of the Anio and the Tiber and those of their tributaries such as the Marrana della Caffarella or the Fosso di Tor Carbone, Fosso delle Tre Fontane, and Fosso di Pozzo Pantaleo creating natural points of access to lower lying strata. This can easily be seen in the geological section (fig. 2). It comes as no surprise then to find that many of the quarries usually identified as being worked by the Romans, such as the pozzolana near San Paolo fuori-le-Mura, or the tufas and pozzolanas from Grotta Perfetta or Tre Fontane lie precisely in such positions. Good beds exposed in such natural cuts were often exploited by tunnelling in from the sides, leaving the land above intact but causing untold problems for modern developers (Sciotti 1982); one of the best preserved and most accessible examples is at the Fosse Ardeatine.

One of the greatest hindrances to identifying the Roman quarries is of course the continuing exploitation of these materials in later periods, but this has its compensations. Until the advent of mechanisation this century the methods used in quarrying appear to have been little different from those used by the Romans, and the logistics, if not the economics, should have been much the same as well. Thus, for example, data on the operation of pozzolana quarries in the 1880s provide a possible ethnographic model for the Roman period (DeMarchi 1894). Each quarry was operated by a small number of men working at the face, each producing about 10 cubic metres per 12–hour day, controlled by an overseer and supervised by an administrator. The material was either loaded at the face into carts by independent carters, or, where the face was tunnelled far into the hill-side, was removed to the quarry entrance by the quarrymen using wagons on rails and loaded into carts there. In the Roman period the removal from the face, without rails or wheelbarrows, must have been more labour intensive, and the economic difference this produced is reflected in 18th century duty on pozzolana which was much lower where there was no access for carts to the quarry face (Scavizzi 1983: 30–31). It is easy to show that if the material had to be moved by manpower only 50 m from the quarry face this would roughly quadruple the amount of labour required, so that only two and half cubic metres could be produced for each man-day of labour, or two cubic metres if we include the overseer and administrator. Thus for the quarter of a million cubic metres of pozzolana needed to build the Baths of Caracalla (DeLaine 1992: 318), roughly a hundred men would have had to work for 300 days each year for the four years of the main construction period.

Questions of Transport

From the actual quarrying let us move to the methods and routes of transportation. For the materials we have been discussing so far, the transport must have been by land, most likely by ox-cart or, where large blocks were not required, by pack animals. To judge by the size of normal loads suggested by the Prices Edict of Diocletian (17.3–5) and the Theodosian code (8.5.30), which are compatible with figures from other pre-industrial technologies (Cotterell and Kaminga 1990: 194, Table 8.1; White 1984: 129), the amount of traffic generated by this on some of Rome's major highways was potentially very large. If all the quarter of a million cubic metres of pozzolana needed for the Baths of Caracalla was brought by ox-cart from the quarries near San Paolo over the first four years of construction, and assuming a maximum load per cart of 1500 *librae* or almost half a tonne, one cart must have left the quarry every minute for 12 hours of every day for 300 days of the year. Photographs taken during the building boom of the Risorgimento showing long lines of ox-carts heading back to the selce quarries on the via Appia suggest that the hypothetical figures for imperial Rome are not as unlikely as they sound; I leave it to the reader to work out the implications for keeping the roads clean. On the other hand, it is more likely that several sources of pozzolana using different routes were employed, especially when we take into account the needs of other building projects in that period. Since the carts could make 2 to 3 return trips a day, between 250 and 350 carts – and men – would have been needed to transport the pozzolana, that is two to three times as many as were needed to produce it.

If we move further away from Rome (fig. 3), the problems of transport increase; each cart bringing stone from the Gabine quarries would have taken 12 hours to reach the city along the Via Prenestina, those from the peperino quarries near Marino almost two days. It is not surprising, then, that many of the famous quarries

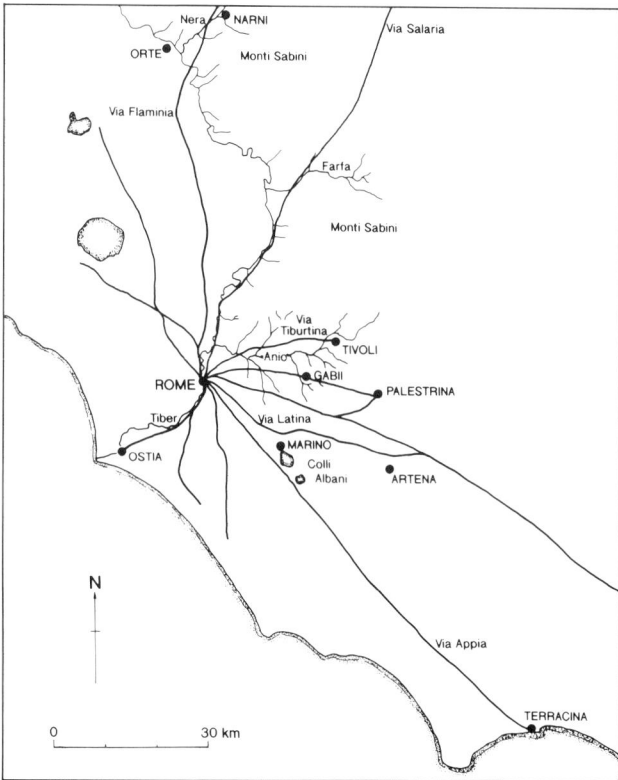

Fig. 3. Principal roads supplying Rome.

which produced stone for ashlar construction are located with easy access to water: Fidenae; Grotta Oscura where the Tiber lies close to the west side of its flood-plain; the impressive Anio quarries at Tor Cervara; and of course the travertine quarries below Tivoli. For the latter two we have confirmation from Strabo (V.3.7) that the Anio was the preferred transport route in the later Republic, as I believe it must have been during the empire. All the same, it has been argued that after the widening of the Via Tiburtina in 30 BC, road transport was preferred (Mari 1983: 366–67, following Lanciani 1885: 35).

The implications of this are worth considering. If we accept Lanciani's figure of 5.5 million cubic metres of travertine extracted from the quarries (1897: 35–36) and divide this over 400 years – the period of greatest exploitation – each of 300 days, then even allowing for 15% waste from the quarrying one cart carrying half a tonne of travertine must have left the quarry every 3.5 minutes. Each of these carts would have taken three days to make the round trip to Rome, needing at least 550 carts altogether in constant operation over a 12-hour day. These are very crude averages, and at times of large building projects the figure must have been higher. We can check the order of magnitude using the Colosseum. Dividing the 100,000 cubic metres estimated by Cozzo (1928: 212) over 10 years of 300 days would have meant 1 cart carrying half a tonne leaving every 4 minutes, and since the greatest use of travertine was in the earlier stages of construction the time period was probably shorter and the frequency of departures correspondingly higher. In addition, this cannot have been the only travertine in use in these years, and the possibility of stockpiling close to Rome would only serve to redistribute the transport requirements, not reduce them. In addition we have to allow for other traffic trying to use the Via Tiburtina between Rome and Tivoli at the same time, the households of the Roman aristocracy moving to their summer villas among them. When the travertine was once again being worked on a large scale in the Renaissance for the building of St Peter's in Rome, the pope gave the banks of the Anio from Ponte Lucano to the confluence of the Tiber to the Reverenda Fabbrica specifically to facilitate the transport of the travertine, and the Anio was made navigable for barges loaded with stone (Cascioli 1923: 12). It is hard to imagine the Romans doing otherwise, even if some travertine for small projects, for use outside of Rome or for other areas less accessible by water did in fact travel by road.

The Question of Brick and Lime

If we now turn to the two major manufactured materials used in construction – brick and lime – geology, topography, and transport routes once more play their part, with the additional requirement of ready sources

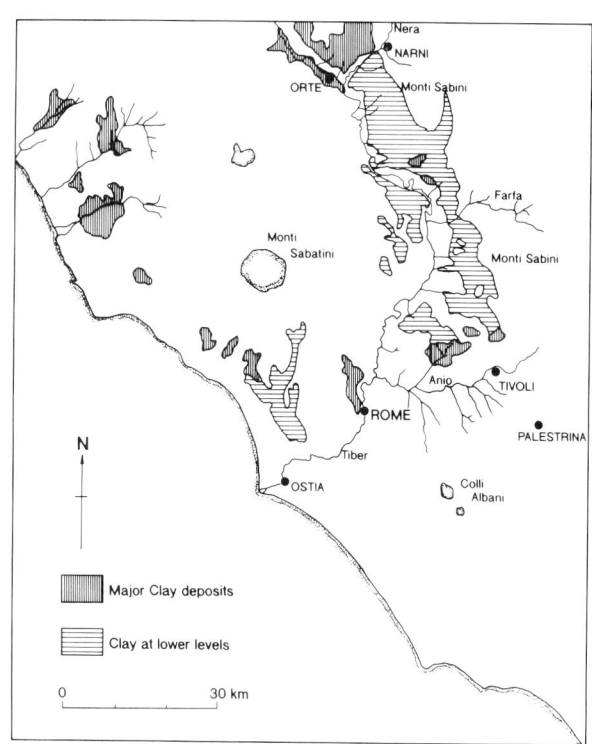

Fig. 4. Clay deposits around Rome.

of fuel. Despite the fact that only a few brick-kilns have been discovered in and around Rome (Petracca & Vigna 1985) and very few brick-producing areas are mentioned in the literary sources (the main exception being the famous Vatican *figlinae*), many of the sources of brick have been identified by the Finnish epigraphers from the place names recorded on the brickstamps (Steinby 1978: 1507–1509). Virtually all are either around Rome itself, higher up the valley of the Tiber as far as the large clay deposits around Orte and Narni, or in the lower valleys of the Sabina (fig. 4). The latter were identified by Huotari using the toponyms recorded in the early medieval Farfa registers, and it can be argued that all the brickfields supplying the Baths of Caracalla came from imperial domains in this general area (DeLaine 1992: 178), part of which was after all known as the *fundus caesariensis* (Giorgi & Balzani 1879–1914: II.29; III.196; IV.22). One possible reason for the development of such sources of production away from the immediate environs of Rome lies at least in part in the problems of supplying the city with fuel; easier by far to make the bricks in the hilly Sabine region where fuel could be obtained from natural woodland or farmed coppice than to add to the large quantities of fuel which had to be transported to Rome for other purposes.

Identifying the precise sources of the lime used in construction in Rome is rather more difficult and the whole question of supplying Rome with lime has been much neglected. The recently excavated lime-kiln of

Augustan date near *Lucus Feroniae* discussed in this volume by Sergio Fontana provides the first well-documented example of a kiln which may have served Rome, and sets it in the wider context, underlining the difficulties in supplying Rome with lime, since all the main limestone areas lie a considerable distance from the city. From Pliny (*HN,* XXXVI.53) we know that the preferred lime for building came from quarried stone, *saxum album* according to Vitruvius (*de arch.* II.5.1) or *candissimum* according to Cato (*Agr.* XXXVIII.2), and this should be the hard limestone of the mountains around Rome, occurring at Monte Soratte, in the Sabina, the Monti Cornicolani, Tiburtini, and Prenestini, continuing until they meet the sea at Terracina (fig. 1). Even more than with brick, the kilns have voracious appetites for fuel which could be easily supplied from these mountainous regions. The actual kilns, however, are likely once more to be located at the interface where the slopes come down to the waterways or to the roads of the plains. To Fontana's example at Lucus Feroniae we can add the evidence for lime-working identified by Quilici (1982: 124–184) near Artena, a good candidate in my opinion for supplying the dense settlements of the Colli Albani but rather less convincing in relation to Rome itself due to the absence of an obvious transport route other than the long journey by road. Elsewhere Quilici has argued more persuasively for the movement of limestone for construction from the Sabina down the Tiber with the strong possibility of an associated lime industry (Quilici 1986: 211), to which could be added the limestone quarries of Monte Soratte which Vitruvius mentions as a source of building stone but which could also have produced lime. The most interesting case is Terracina, at the one point where the limestone mountains come down to the sea. According to the Theodosian code (14.6.3 and cf. Symmachus, *Rel.* 40.3), Terracina was supplying Portus and possibly Rome with lime and – significantly – firewood in the late empire "according to ancient usage". If we use the relation between the cost of land and water transport established by Duncan-Jones (1982: 366–69) based on the Prices Edict, it would in fact cost only half as much to bring lime from Terracina to Rome by water as it would to bring it from Tivoli by road, and not much more than to bring it from Monte Soratte or Tivoli using the Tiber and Anio respectively.

This question of supplying lime to Rome can also be placed in a wider economic context, as has been done for the supply of pozzolana to the Baths of Caracalla and for the travertine needed for the Colosseum. Similar calculations for lime production suggest that would be possible to build the Baths of Caracalla from the lime produced by only 35 lime-kilns of 60 cu. m capacity under constant production, that is firing ten times each year for the main four-year construction period (DeLaine 1992: 335–36). Such a kiln would be larger than that described by Cato (*Agr.* XXXVIII.1), but rather smaller than those at *Lucus Feroniae* discussed by Fontana. The total number of men employed would be in the order of 300, although more might be needed in the winter months to gather fuel – there are too many variables in this to tell. On a very rough estimate, only 7 kilns operating under these conditions would have been needed each year for twenty years for the entire Hadrianic rebuilding of Ostia, although there were of course other large demands from the capital itself. Altogether at any one time perhaps no more than 100 lime kilns in full operation would have been needed to supply the demands of Rome and its ports. This is a surprisingly small number. The demand for lime for agricultural purposes (Dix 1982: 341–42), however, is likely to have been much higher, and there is nothing in Cato's account to suggest that any – let alone all – the lime from his kilns was intended for building.

THE PRODUCTION OF BUILDING MATERIALS AND THE RURAL LANSDSCAPE

The relation between the production of lime for agriculture and the production for construction is of particular importance in understanding the the case of Terracina. The town was founded as a colony with areas of rich agricultural land, that to the north preserving vestiges of centuriation dating possibly to the early second century B.C. as well as a reasonable number of villas both in the plain and on the lower slopes of the surrounding hills (Lugli 1926; Longo 1985). The conditions are ideal for the development of lime burning for agricultural purposes within the context of villa economies, as demonstrated by Cato's near contemporary description of a lime-kiln as forming a natural part of any estate with access to the raw materials, a development which was then extended to cover lime for construction. It may be no coincidence that at least two Republican consular families (the Aemilii Lepidi and the Sulpicii Galbae) whose members were involved in major construction works at the Emporium in Rome also had property at Terracina. Indeed, the same M. Aemilius Lepidus who as aedile in 193 BC built the Porticus Aemilia at the Emporium outside the Porta Trigemina (Livy XXXV.10.12) used his office when censor in 179 BC to have improvements made to the harbour of Terracina (Livy XL..51.2), reputedly to serve his own estates although they presumably also advantaged the whole region, the products of which included the famous Caecuban wine. We can only assume that the primary destination was Rome, and it would not be surprising if lime was included among other agricultural products.

For Terracina the relation between the production of building materials for the capital and the rural landscape is admittedly hypothetical, but we are on much more secure ground when we look at the areas around the Anio tufa quarries and the travertine quarries below Tivoli, the material for both of which is conveniently collected in the *Forma Italiae* series (Quilici 1974; Mari 1983, 1991). This is not the place to discuss problems of site identification or detailed chronology, but to draw attention in both cases to the sites of all definite villas, known tombs and concentrations of material datable roughly to the late Republican and imperial periods (Quilici 1974: fig. 18; Mari 1983: figs 14–15, 1991: fig. 11); the point is that both areas are densely inhabited. In the case of the Anio tufa quarries, villas have been found right up to the boundaries of the quarry area, including one with walls built over quarry refuse (Quilici 1974: 73–77) and it is worth remembering that these quarries were also continued in galleries allowing the land above to remain in use. The same kind of result is found in the probable brick- and lime-producing area of the Sabina covered by the Farfa survey (Moreland 1986, 1987 and cf. Reggiani 1985: fig. 49); the locus classicus for intense rural settlement in Rome's hinterland is of course the South Etruria survey (Potter 1979: 120–137) of which the Ager Capenas around the possible lime-producing areas of Soracte and Lucus Feroniae forms an important part (Jones 1962, 1963). It is just such areas of dense rural settlement in reasonable proximity to Rome, including high concentrations of villas and thus of medium to large-scale landowners, that are likely to have on call the necessary labour for extraction and, as far as land transport was used, the ideal conditions for rearing and maintaining the necessary draught or pack animals. In terms of the quarrying operations reliant on land transport, the need for a large number of transport animals is likely to have been of greater economic importance than the need for simple labour; note the 3:1 proportions of transport to labour for the pozzolana for the Baths of Caracalla, as likewise for some of the generic tufas.

Finally I would like to raise the question, "Cui bono?" In terms of absolute quantities of materials in ashlar construction, the most important are the good tufas and travertine; in concrete construction, the poorer tufas are most important, followed by the pozzolana which provides the bulk as well as the hydraulic properties of the mortar. The greater the volume of material used, the closer to Rome, on the whole, it is found. The materials which need proportionally more manpower to produce – bricks and lime – are also needed in smaller quantities, and are often produced at sites further from Rome but potentially close to suitable waterways. For lime production at least the absolute quantities are relatively small and the whole operation could be managed as part of estate production. The same it seems to me is true for brick, where the quantities are equally small and the manpower requirements similar to those for lime. All the brick for the Baths of Caracalla could have been produced by 30 or so officinae operating a single reasonably large kiln fired 7 to 8 times a year over 4 years (DeLaine 1992: 336), and for the Hadrianic rebuilding of Ostia 8 to 10 kilns operating over twenty years would have been ample even taking the roof tiles into account. Recent work has tended to stress the economic importance of brick production for the senatorial order (Steinby 1982), but the figures derived from the actual buildings suggest that this may be exaggerated.

What is more important perhaps is the role of materials production *and* transport in the overall rural economy. Steinby's interpretation of the brickstamp as a *locatio-conductio* contract underlines the entrepreneurial role played by the owner of the natural resource (Steinby 1993). If we extend this to all of the lime production and presumably to the volcanic products as well, then it is as usual the rural landowner – imperial, senatorial or lesser being – who benefits in the first instance, since the resultant product is at his disposal. The advantages held by the larger landowners at the higher levels of society would consist partly in the ability to provide labour and transport, and partly through established contacts with large contractors in the capital, but the involvement of quite little people is not necessarily excluded – the owner of a single ox-cart used for transport, for example. Where the production is contracted out, the benefits are spread more widely; since the producers must have been paid, it was presumably at least partly in cash (cf. Howgego 1992: 25–27), and this may have been one small but not insignificant way in which the monetary system was sustained in these sometimes peripheral regions.

In the introduction to this paper I stressed that my concern was with the organisation of building supplies for the city of Rome rather than just with their sources. The value of identifying the specific sources lies in establishing the physical conditions of extraction and the probable routes used for transport, although general suggestions concerning the sources of supply based on a careful study of the geology and topography of the area around Rome can be instructive. But it is only by taking a quantitative approach – however crude – to the questions of production and transport that it is possible to place the building materials of Rome where they belong, in the wider economic context.

Acknowledgements

This paper forms part of a larger study on the building industry of imperial Rome which arose out of the author's doctoral thesis on the Baths of Caracalla. Thanks are due to Dott.ssa I. Jacopi of the Soprintendenza Archeologica di Roma and Dott.ssa A. Gallina Zevi of the Soprintendenza di Ostia for permission to carry out the detailed surveys of the Baths of Caracalla and the Insula of the Paintings at Ostia respectively, which form the basis of the quantitative analyses. Research into the geology of Rome was facilitated by the kindness of Prof. M. Sciotti and his colleagues at the Facoltà di Ingegneria, Università di Roma. Ray Laurence, Hugh Petter, and Clayton Fant were invaluable companions on several field trips. Steve Allen kindly drew the maps. The author would also like to express her gratitude to the Craven Committee, the Meyerstein Foundation, and St John's College, Oxford for grants allowing her to study in Rome, and to the British School at Rome for its long-standing support of this research.

Bibliography

Blake, M.E. 1947. *Ancient Roman Construction in Italy from the Prehistoric Period to Augustus*, Washington.

Cascioli, G. 1923. *Bibliografia di Tivoli, Studi e Fonti per la Storia della Regione Tiburtina*, Tivoli.

Clarke, L. 1992. *Building Capitalism. Historical Change and the Labour Process in the Production of the Built Environment*, London.

Cotterell, B. & Kamminga, J. 1990. *Mechanics of Pre-Industrial Technology*, Cambridge.

Cozzo, G. 1928. *Ingegneria romana*, Rome.

DeLaine, J. 1992. *Design and Construction in Imperial Roman Architecture: The Baths of Caracalla in Rome*, unpublished PhD thesis, University of Adelaide.

DeLaine, G. 1996. 'The Insula of the Paintings. A model for the economics of construction in Hadrianic Ostia', in A. Zevi & A. Claridge (eds.), *Roman Ostia Revisited: Archaeological and Historical Papers in Memory of Russell Meiggs*, forthcoming.

DeMarchi, L. 1894. 'Le cave di pozzolana nei dintorni di Roma', in *Studio sulle condizioni di sicurezza delle miniere e delle cave in Italia*, Rome, 1-25.

Dix, B. 1982. 'The manufacture of lime and its uses in the western Roman provinces', *Oxford Journal of Archaeology*, 1, 331-345.

Duncan-Jones, R. 1982. *The Economy of the Roman Empire*, 2nd ed., Cambridge.

Fitchen, J. 1986. *Building Construction before Mechanization*, Cambridge, Mass.

Frank, T. 1924. *Roman Buildings of the Republic: An Attempt to date them from their Materials*, (Papers and Monographs of the American Academy in Rome III).

Giorgi, I. & Balzani, U. 1879-1914. *Il Regesto di Farfa*, Rome.

Howgego, C. 1992. 'The supply and use of money in the Roman world', *Journal of Roman Studies*, LXXXII, 1-31.

Jones, G.D.B. 1962. 'Capena and the Ager Capenas: Part I', *Papers of the British School at Rome*, 30, 116-207.

Jones, G.D.B. 1963. 'Capena and the Ager Capenas: Part II', *Papers of the British School at Rome*, 31, 100-158.

Lanciani, R. 1885. 'Relazione sui ritrovamenti di antichità, 13 dicembre 1885, via Tiburtina', Cod. Vat. Lat. 13047, via Tiburtina, ff. 34-37.

Lanciani, R. 1897. *The Ruins and Excavations of Ancient Rome*, Boston and New York.

Longo, P. 1985. Resti di divisioni agrarie nel territorio dell'odierno Lazio. Tarracina', in *Misurare la terra: Centuriazione e coloni nel mondo romano. Città, agricoltura, commercio: materiali da Roma e suburbio*, Modena, 40-44.

Lugli, G. 1926. *Forma Italiae I.i. Ager Pomptinus Pars Prima: Anxur-Terracina*, Rome.

Mari, Z. 1983. *Forma Italiae I.xvii. Tibur, Pars Tertia*, Florence.

Mari, Z. 1991. *Forma Italiae 35. Tibur, Pars Quarta*, Florence.

Moreland, J. 1986. 'Ricognizione nei dintorni di Farfa', *Archeologia Medievale*, XIII, 333-343.

Moreland, J. 1987. 'The Farfa survey: a second interim report', *Archeologia Medievale*, XIV, 409-418.

Potter, T.W. 1979. *The Changing Landscape of South Etruria*, London.

Quilici, L. 1974. *Forma Italiae I.x. Collatia*, Rome.

Quilici, L. 1982. *La Città di Artena* (Latium Vetus, IV), Rome.

Quilici, L. 1986. 'Il Tevere e l'Aniene come vie d'acqua a monte di Roma in età imperiale', in *Il Tevere e le altre vie d'acqua del Lazio antico* (Quaderni del Centro di Studio per l'Archeologia etrusco-italica, 12), Rome.

Reggiani, A.M. 1985. 'La villa rustica nell'agro Sabino', in *Misurare la terra: Centuriazione e coloni nel mondo romano. Città, agricoltura, commercio: materiali da Roma e suburbio*, Modena, 61-65.

Scavizzi, C.P. 1983. *Edilizia nei secoli XVII e XVIII a Roma*, Quaderni 6, Rome.

Sciotti, M. 1982. 'Engineering geological problems due to old underground quarries in the urban area of Rome, Italy', *Proceedings of the 4th International Congress, International Association of Engineering Geology*, I, Delhi, 211-225.

Steinby, M. 1978. 'Ziegelstempel von Rom und Umgebung', *Reale Encyclopaedia* Suppl. XV, cols 1489-1531.

Steinby, M. 1982. 'I senatori e l'industria laterizia urbana', *Tituli 4: Epigrafia e Ordine Senatorio I*, 227-237.

Steinby, M. 1993. 'L'organizzazione produttiva dei laterizi: un modello interpretativo per l'instrumentum in genere?', in W.V. Harris (ed.), *The Inscribed Economy*, (Journal of Roman Archaeology Suppl. no. 6), 139-144.

Ventriglia, U. 1971. *La geologia della città di Roma*, Rome.

White, K.D. 1984. *Greek and Roman Technology*, London.

58

Un Impianto per la Produzione di Calce presso *Lucus Feroniae*

Sergio Fontana

Sommario: *Nel 1987 uno scavo di emergenza, promosso dalla Soprintendenza Archeologica dell'Etruria Meridionale, nei dintorni di* Lucus Feroniae *ha portato alla luce strutture pertinenti ad un vasto impianto di età augustea per la produzione di calce. Sono stati rinvenuti tre grandi forni oltre a una serie di ambienti annessi usati probabilmente per l'alloggio dei lavoranti. Le caratteristiche strutturali e l'ampiezza dell'impianto fanno ritenere probabile una produzione di calce su larga scala protrattasi forse per alcuni decenni. Il sito dista dal centro di* Lucus Feroniae *1,2 km ed è posto nelle immediate vicinanze del Tevere. Appare probabile che parte della produzione di calce venisse trasportata per via fluviale per rifornire i cantieri di Roma.*

Oggetto di questa ricerca è un grande impianto di epoca augustea per la produzione di calce che è stato scavato nel 1987 nelle immediate vicinanze di *Lucus Feroniae*. Le strutture rinvenute permettono di fare alcune considerazioni sull'importanza economica e i modi di produzione della calce tra il I sec. a.C. e il I sec. d.C., quando, alla grande mole dei programmi architettonici portati a termine a Roma e nelle città dell'Italia centrale, fece riscontro una sempre maggiore specializzazione produttiva nella fabbricazione dei materiali edilizi (Torelli 1980).

I resti dell'impianto sono stati rinvenuti nella località detta in vocabolo 'Prato la Corte' nella zona delle 'Cese'. Nella cartina alla fig.1 è stato evidenziato il posizionamento del sito rispetto alla principali emergenze archeologiche della zona: la *colonia* romana di *Lucus*

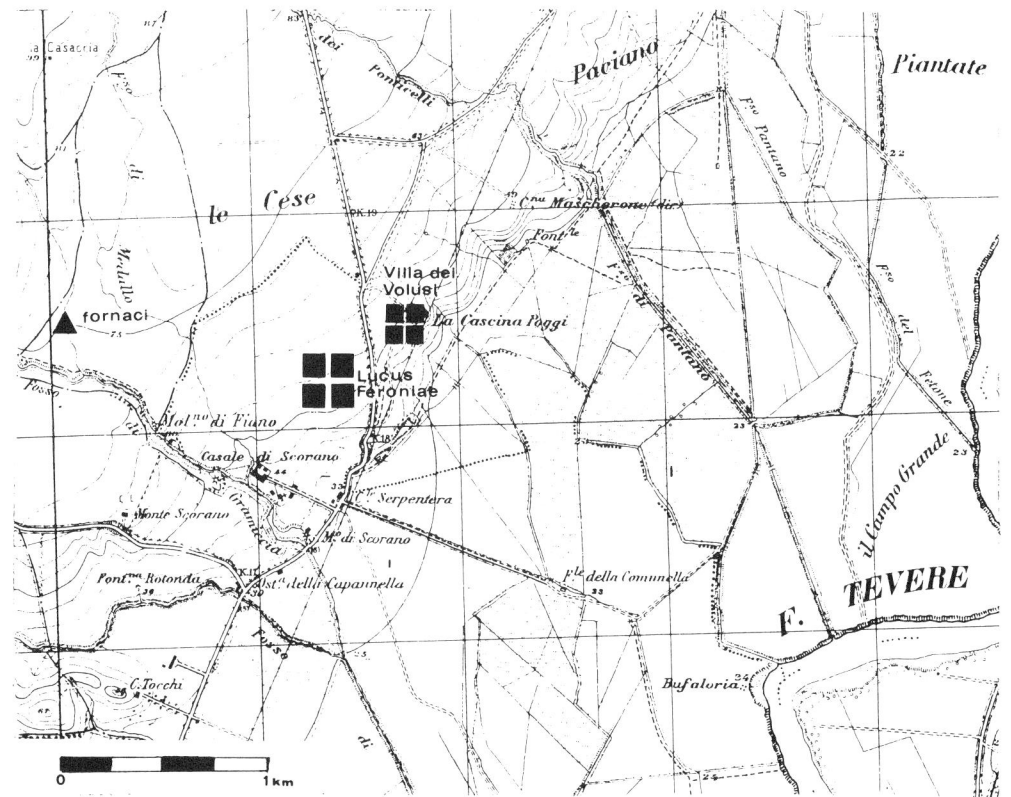

Fig. 1. Posizionamento del sito.

Feroniae, da cui dista 1,2 km, e la grande villa dei Volusi Saturnini.

A partire dai primi anni 80' la zona delle 'Cese' è stata oggetto di vari scavi di emergenza conseguenti alla lottizzazione del territorio per la costruzione dell'area industriale di Fiano Romano. Immediatamente a contatto con le strutture di cui ci occuperemo sono stati scoperti, a partire dal 1982, i resti di una vasta villa (fig.2) (Gazzetti 1992: 44-46). Questo insediamento si è ampliato successivamente all'abbandono dei forni per la produzione di calce obliterando parte dell'area occupata dalle strutture produttive. Circa 40 metri a sud dell'impianto è stato individuato un tratto della strada lastricata che collegava *Lucus Feroniae* a Capena. Da tale via si dipartiva un piccolo diverticolo che costeggia sul lato est le strutture produttive. Questo viottolo lastricato era probabilmente interno alla villa.

LE STRUTTURE PRODUTTIVE

L'intervento archeologico sul sito si è svolto in due indagini di salvataggio conseguenti alla costruzione di un capannone industriale e all'allargamento di una strada interpoderale. Gli scavi, seguiti al blocco dei lavori, si sono svolti nella primavera del 1987 sotto la guida del Dott. Gianfranco Gazzetti, ispettore della Soprintendenza Archeologica dell'Etruria Meridionale.

Le indagini hanno permesso di rinvenire tre forni per la produzione della calce (fig.3, nn.1-3), alcuni vani connessi con le calcare, e ancora ambienti costruiti dopo

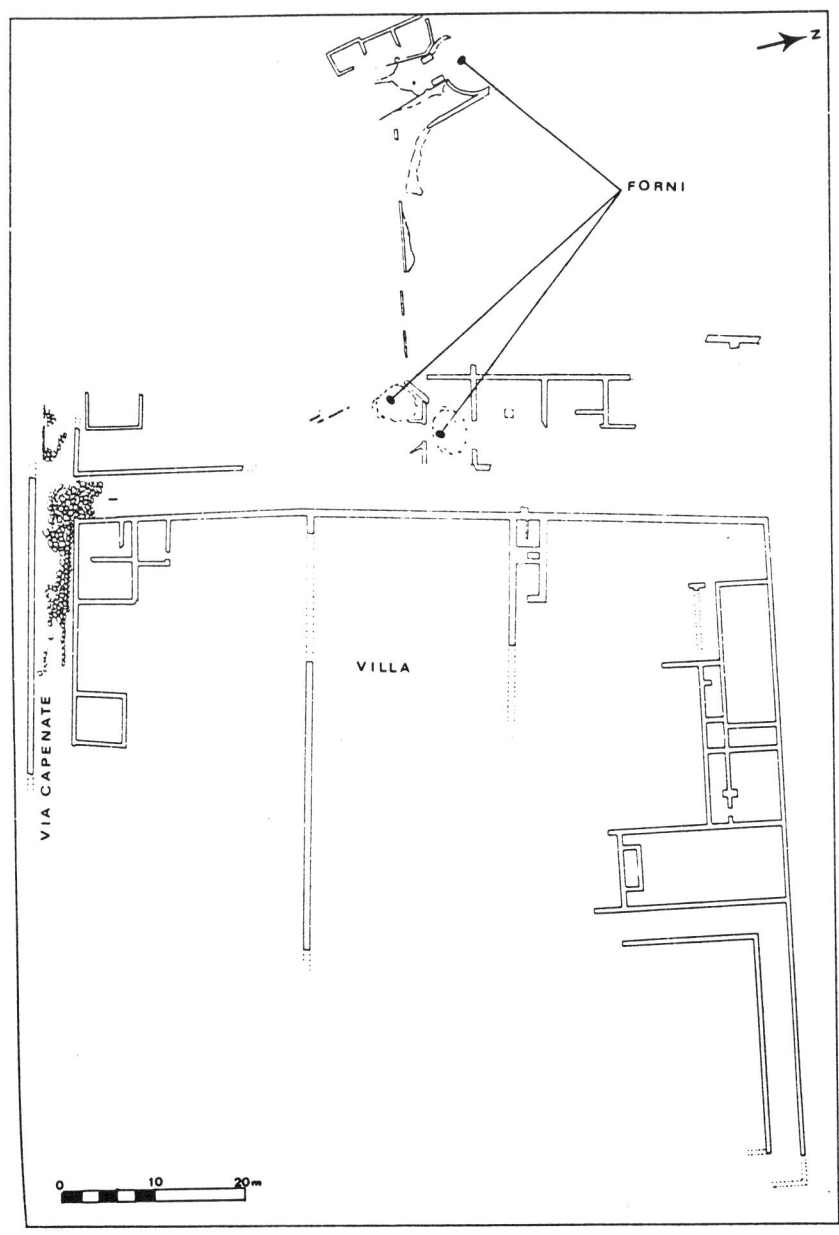

Fig. 2. L'impianto produttivo e le strutture limitrofe.

la fine dell'utilizzo dell'impianto che devono essere messi in relazione con un ampliamento della parte periferica della villa attigua.

Nella zona occidentale dello scavo si trova il forno di maggiori dimensioni (fig.3.1), una struttura in parte interrata, originariamente con pianta ellittica. Il *praefurnium* si apre in direzione sud su un'area posta allo stesso livello del forno (settore A). A sud est della calcara vi sono tre vani quadrangolari certamente accessori all'attività produttia (ambienti B, C, D). Le strutture murarie sono prive di fondazione, costruite da un conglomerato di pietre e malta senza cortina. L'intensa attività agricola, in età moderna, ha ridotto l'altezza dei muri degli ambienti a 30–40cm.

Il forno e il settore A hanno un livello di calpestio di 120 cm, più basso rispetto a quello dei vani. Quest'area fu dunque ricavata scavando il paleosuolo argilloso, su cui le strutture poggiano, e il sottostante banco lapideo. Il lato orientale del settore A è delimitato da un muro costruito controterra e contraffortato con un elemento in tufo.

Particolarmente ben conservato è il *praefurnium* che appare delimitato da due pilastri parallelepipedi in muratura. Su questi doveva originariamente poggiare una copertura a volta ove veniva scaricato parte del grande peso delle pietre da calcinare. Durante lo scavo sono venute alla luce tra i pilastri alcune pietre refrattarie sbozzate. È probabile che esse fossero parte della copertura crollata dopo l'ultimo utilizzo del forno. Dai pilastri si dipartiva il muro, approsimativamente ellittico,

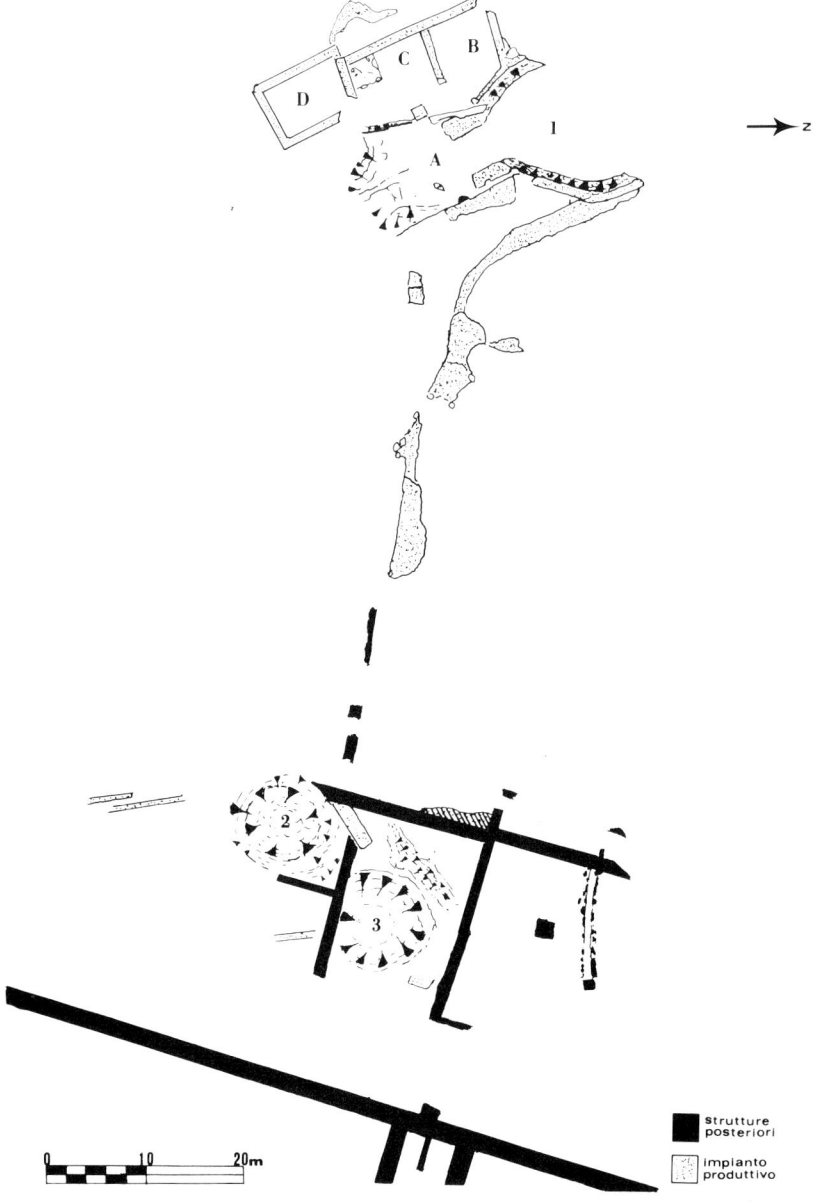

Fig. 3. L'impianto produttivo.

Fig. 4. Veduta dell'area orientale dello scavo.

Fig. 5. Focolare nell'ambiente C.

che rivestiva la fornace. Questa struttura è conservata per un'altezza massima di 160 cm, di cui circa 40 in elevato. Un profondo scasso, effettuato prima dell'intervento della Soprintendenza, ha distrutto la metà settentrionale del bacino della fornace; dacché risulta complesso riconoscerne con esattezza le dimensioni originarie: appossimando la forma del bacino ad un'ellisse esso avrebbe dovuto avere un asse maggiore di circa 7,5 metri ed uno minore di circa 5 metri.

A poca distanza dal *praefurnium* si è conservato un pilastrino in pietra grigia, alto 70 cm., con un'evidente traccia di usura nella parte superiore. Sul pilastrino dovette scorrere un elemento oblungo usato forse per muovere la paratia che regolava l'afflusso dell'aria all'interno della camera di combustione o per scaricare la calce viva dopo il processo di cottura.

La grande fornace venne realizzata successivamente agli ambienti B e C. Per impiantare la calcara l'angolo settentrionale dell'ambiente B venne tagliato e le dimensioni del vano furono ridotte con la costruzione di un piccolo muro obliquo. Un unico muro delimita ad occidente gli ambienti B e C mostrando la contemporaneità di questi due vani. Addossato all'angolo nord dell'ambiente C è stato rinvenuto un piccolo focolare quadrangolare probabilmente usato per la cottura dei cibi (fig.5).

Il lato meridionale dell'ambiente C si affaccia direttamente sull'area antistante il *praefurnium*; un blocco squadrato di travertino, posto al limite del vano prospicente al settore A, potrebbe essere servito come base di un piedritto, forse ligneo, per sostenere la copertura. Si sarebbe così venuta a creare un'ampia apertura di comunicazione tra l'ambiente C e il vestibolo del forno. I vani avevano molto probabilmente un tetto di tegole e coppi che sono stati rinvenuti in grande quantità nello scavo degli strati di distruzione.

A sud dell'ambiente C, un altro vano rettangolare (D), di dimensioni minori, venne costruito su uno strato spesso e compatto formato di argille e materiali calacarei concotti che dovevano costituire il rifiuto della produzione di calce; tale formazione si estendeva a sud del settore A per una superficie di circa 250 metri quadrati.

Dal lato orientale della grande fornace si diparte un massiccio muro che, con un andamento irregolare, prosegue per circa 20 metri in direzione est verso gli altri due forni.

Nella zona orientale dell'area indagata le due calcare rinvenute (fig.3.2 e 3) risultano completamente scavate nel banco di travertino; esse sono di dimensioni notevolmente minori avendo entrambe un diametro di circa 3,5 m e una profondità di 2 m. In questa area si sovrappossero ai forni tre vani rettangolari con diverso orientamento rispetto alle strutture dell'impianto produttivo. Tali ambienti sono da riconnettersi a strutture periferiche della villa che si estese in questa zona, probabilmente nel corso della prima età imperiale, dopo che i forni 2 e 3 erano stati abbandonati e colmati. Le parti in elevato, e i *praefurnia*, delle due calcare furono distrutte per la costruzione di queste strutture. Soltanto un breve tratto di muratura, che lambisce a nord-est la fornace 2, può certamente riconnettersi alle strutture originarie dell'impianto produttivo.

Per forma e dimensioni le calcare 2 e 3 appaiono molto simili a quelle rinvenute a Iversheim in Renania, caratterizzate anch'esse da una camera di combustione scavata nel terreno ad un livello di alcuni metri più basso rispetto al *praefurnium* (Solter 1970).

I materiali ceramici rinvenuti nei riempimenti dei forni e nelle stratigrafie degli ambienti annessi, pur essendo ancora in corso di studio, offrono utili elementi per definire la cronologia del complesso. Le forme ed i bolli dei frammenti di Terra Sigillata Italica negli strati di abbandono non sono posteriori all'età tiberiano-claudia, pur trattondosi di tipi già prodotti durante il regno di Augusto. Nei riempimenti delle calcare 2 e 3 sono stati rinvenuti alcuni frammenti di anfora Dressel 2-4. La produzione di questo contenitore iniziò attorno al 10 d.C., ciò indica la posterità rispetto a questa data, delle colmata delle fornaci.

Tenendo presente i materiali residui, in depositi posteriori, non vi sono elementi che attestino una frequentazione dell'area prima della seconda metà del I sec. a.C. Possiamo dunque considerare molto probabile un pieno utilizzo dell'impianto nel corso dell'età augustea.

Dopo l'abbandono il vestibolo della grande calcara venne colmato con terra e pietrame; i frammenti ceramici rinvenuti sembrano indicare una datazione dello strato al II sec. d.C. In tale riempimento furono ricavate due sepolture databili, in base ad una lucerna di corredo, al IV sec. d.C. Altre tombe di età tarda, coperte da tegole, furono scoperte alcune decine di metri più a sud. Queste tombe costituiscono una propagine della vasta necropoli che si sviluppò in età imperiale lungo la via Capenate (Gazzetti 1992: 39).

Attualmente tutte le strutture sono state ricoperte ed i ritrovamenti sono conservati presso il museo di *Lucus Feroniae*.

Funzionamento e produttività del complesso

Nel grafico alla fig.6 abbiamo schematizzato i probabili movimenti degli operai nell'area occidentale dell'impianto produttivo. Dobbiamo supporre una circolazione di uomini, regolata dai tempi dei massacranti turni lavorativi, tra gli ambienti annessi ed i luoghi di lavoro. L'ambiente C, che si apre direttamente sul vestibolo della grande fornace, doveva ospitare, nei momenti di pausa, gli uomini che sorvegliavano il funzionamento della calcara durante i lunghi processi di cottura. La piccola cucina, posta in questo ambiente, costituisce una testimonianza della vita quotidiana di questi operai (fig.5). Gli ambienti B e D potevano essere utilizzati come dormitori. Una parte considerevole del lavoro, necessario al funzionamento della calcara, consisteva nel trasportare verso il forno le pietre e il legname e nel portar via la calce prodotta; appare molto probabile che questo traffico si svolgesse in direzione sud, verso la via Capenate distante poche decine di metri.

Il fuoco veniva alimentato attraverso il *praefurnium* dal quale entrava anche l'aria necessaria alla combustione. Il caricamento delle pietre da calcinare doveva

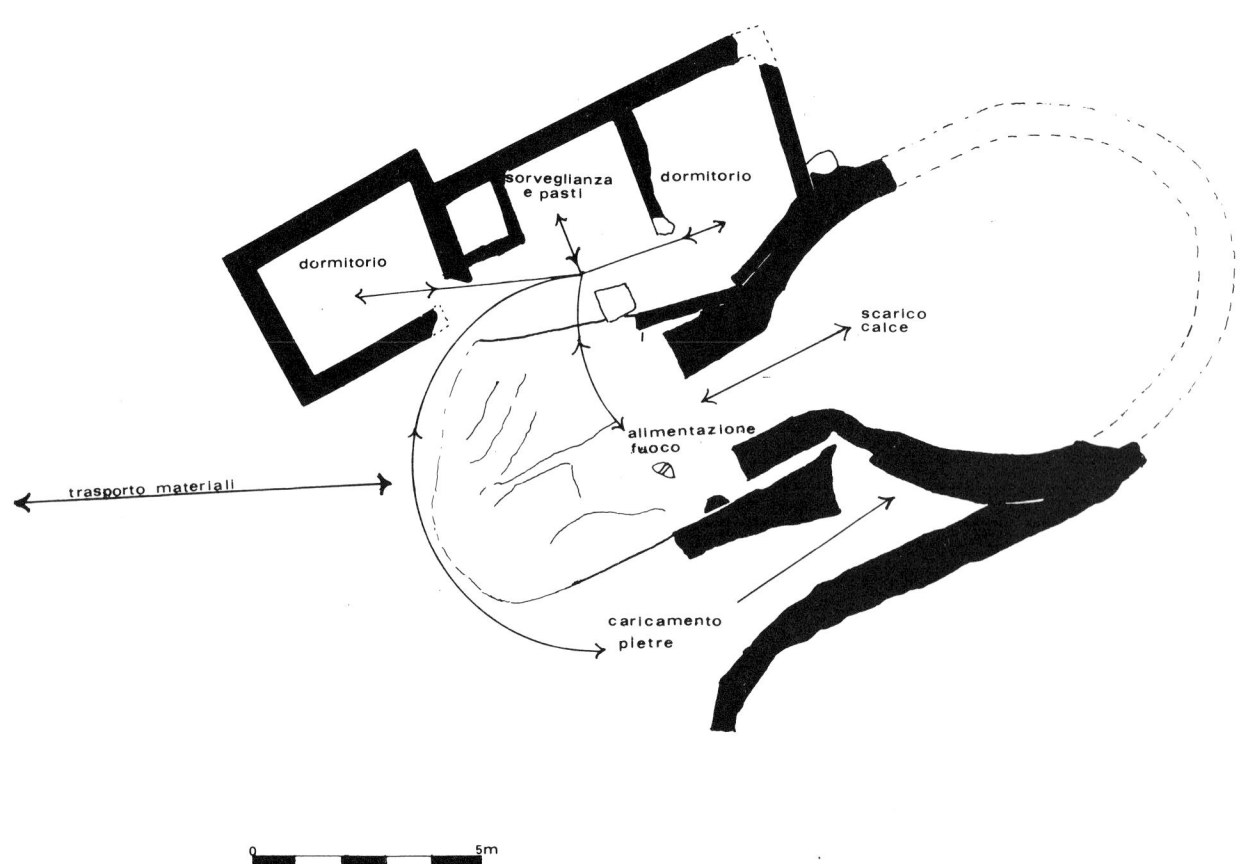

Fig. 6. Ricostruzione ipotetica dei percorsi e delle azioni dei lavoranti nell'area del grande forno.

avvenire dall'alto, forse dal lato est con l'ausilio di un piano inclinato. Al termine del procedimento di cottura i materiali calcinati venivano recuperati attraverso il *praefurnium* dopo aver fatto crollare la volta posticcia che aveva sostenuto il carico. Durante lo scavo sono stati rinvenuti, ai lati del vestibolo del forno, ampi mucchi di pietre calcinate da riferirsi all'ultima attività della calcara.

La presenza di ambienti annessi al grande forno potrebbe indicare la volontà di predisporre delle strutture produttive da utilizzarsi continativamente per un periodo di tempo relativamente lungo. Le altre calcare conosciute di epoca romana non hanno vani di alloggio o di servizio chiaramente connessi con l'attività dei forni ad eccezione del grande impianto di Iversheim che produsse calce per molti decenni tra il II e il III sec. d.C. (Solter 1970: 15).

Per il precario stato di conservazione dei forni, esiste un'indubbia difficoltà nel cercare di valutare la capacità produttiva totale dell'impianto. In base a confronti con simili strutture antiche e moderne (Adam 1984: 72-73; Dix 1982: 335-336; Jackson & Dix 1973: 130-131; Solter 1970: 39-40) e a calcoli sulle dimensioni conservate possiamo ritenere che le tre calcare, funzionando contemporaneamente, potessero produrre ogni mese un quantitativo tra i 200 e i 300 metri cubi di calce.

Con il materiale prodotto i cantieri riforniti dall'impianto avrebbero potuto costruire mensilmente alcune migliaia di metri cubi di muratura cementizia.

La pietra e il legname sono ovviamente le materie prime per la produzione di calce. Adatti alla calcinazione sono i vari tipi di roccia calcarea (Dix 1982: 331-332) e il travertino al cui utilizzo si riferisce esplicitamente Palladio (*op. agr.* I,X,3). Il sito qui esaminato sorge su un formazione travertinosa (Carta Geologica d'Italia, foglio 144) anche se nella zona vi sono numerosi affiorementi calcarei (Jones 1963: 137, fig.13).

Dopo essere stata estratta in blocchi la pietra doveva essere frantumata in scaglie per facilitare il processo di calcinazione; a tale operazione era destinata una parte considerevole del lavoro umano. La cottura della pietra necessitava di grandi quantità di legna da ardere: per ogni metro cubo di prodotto dovevano essere necessari, a seconda dell'essenza utilizzata, da 1,7 a 3,3 m^3 di legname (DeLaine 1992: 173).

Il territorio di *Lucus Feroniae* si presenta attualmente completamente privo delle aree boschive che pure dovevano originariamente sussistere come testimonia il toponimo del centro. L'assenza di vegetazione silvestre poteva riscontrarsi già nella prima età moderna come mostra la carta di Eufrosino della Volpaia del 1547 (Frutaz 1972: II, tav.XIII,1a). L'area in età romana conobbe un forte sfruttamento agricolo, e l'intensa distribuzione delle ville sul territorio (Jones 1962: 191-207) non appare compatibile con ampie distese boschive. L'approvigionamento per i forni poteva venire dalle pendici orientali del Soratte o dalla riva sabina del Tevere. Per esigenze economiche appare però più probabile che siano stati sfruttati i limitati appezzamenti boschivi nelle immediate vicinanze dell'impianto contribuendo così alla deforestazione dell'area.

LA DESTINAZIONE DEL PRODOTTO: I CANTIERI DI *LUCUS FERONIAE* E L'APPROVIGIONAMENTO DI ROMA

Determinare la destinazione della calce prodotta costituisce un punto fondamentale nell'interpretazione di questa evidenza archeologica. Per svolgere tale ricerca occorrerà in primo luogo considerare la domanda di calce che poteva venire dalle aree limitrofe all'impianto.

A *Lucus Feroniae*, in età augustea, è epigraficamente attestata l'edificazione di vari monumenti, spesso ad opera dei Volusi Saturnini: appare molto probabile che risalgano a questa epoca anche le numerose strutture abitative in opera reticolata poste attorno al foro (Torelli 1973-74: 747-750; Gazzetti 1992: 26-32). Nello stesso periodo la grande villa dei Volusi, situata a poca distanza dalla città, venne notevolmente ampliata (Moretti & Sgubini Moretti 1970: 16-23). Un'ulteriore testimonianza di questa intensa attività edilizia può venire dall'epitaffio, rinvenuto in Roma, di Epigono Volusiano *exactor operis* in *Lucus Feroniae* (*CIL* VI, 37422). Il ruolo di questo personaggio, proveniente dalla *familia* dei Volusi, era dunque quello di sovraintendere ad una grande impresa architettonica nella colonia o nel territorio limitrofo (Torelli 1973-74). Il sepolcro, presso la necropoli Salaria, da cui proviene l'iscrizione, può essere datato all'età di Augusto.

I cantieri della zona sicuramente ebbero bisogno di un'ingente produzione di calce nel periodo augusteo ma, accanto all'ipotesi di un utilizzo in ambito locale, va anche tenuta presente la possibilità che parte del prodotto venisse trasportata a Roma. La grande attività edilizia della città dovette certamente essere sostenuta da impianti, in grado di produrre calce su larga scala, posti nelle zone calcaree meno distanti e meglio collegate. Il fabisogno di calce doveva essere enorme: ancora dopo la metà del IV sec. d.C., quando l'attività edilizia era assai ridotta, la prefettura urbana necessitava di un'approvigionamento annuo di 3000 carri (*Codex Theod.* 14.6.3); la stessa fonte ci informa anche sul fatto che i curiali della Tuscia dovevano fornire 900 carri di calce.

Ad eccezione di Terracina, ricordata in una relazione di Simmaco (*rel.* 40.3) e nel Codice Teodosiano (14.6.3), mancano nelle fonti antiche riferimenti precisi ai luoghi di produzione della calce usata a Roma.

L'ipotesi che le calcare di *Lucus Feroniae* abbiano fornito calce a Roma appare plausibile per varie ragioni. Nella fig.7 sono state evidenziate le aree con formazioni calcaree e travertinose del territorio intorno a Roma. Come si noterà vi è una certa distanza tra l'Urbe, sorta su una formazione vulcanica, e le zone segnalate. In particolare il nostro sito si colloca sulla prima area utile a questa produzione che si incontra risalendo la valle del Tevere. Sul fiume, nel tratto prospiciente *Lucus Feroniae*, dovevano esistere vari approdi (Quilici 1986: 205-206), uno dei quali è stato recentemente individuato in località 'Baciletti', 3,5km a nord-est del centro antico (Camilli 1991). La posizione dell'impianto produttivo risulterebbe dunque assai favorevole per il trasporto del prodotto per via fluviale.

Starbone (V, 3.7) fornisce un'interessante testimonianza di come gran parte dei materiali da costruzione usati a Roma giungessero attraverso il Tevere e l'Aniene. Inoltre, la documentazione archeologica ha consentito di evidenziare la provenienza dall'area tiberina di altri materiali da costruzione come i prodotti laterizi bollati da figline umbre ampiamente attestati in città (Quilici 1986: 213).

Dal punto di vista giuridico la produzione di calce rientrava nelle attività rustiche (*Vep. dig.* 32.55.3). La comercializzazione di questo materiale non subì generalmente limitazioni diverse da quelle relative ai

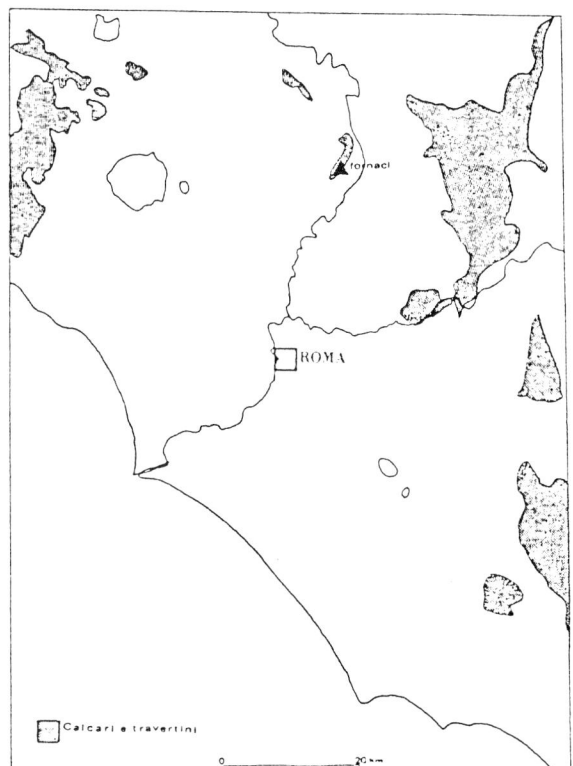

Fig. 7. Le aree geologicamente favorevoli alla produzione di calce nei dintorni di Roma
(Carta Geologica d'Italia al 500'000, foglio 2).

prodotti agricoli. Già Catone sembra alludere alla possibilità di vendere questo prodotto (*agr.* 16; 38,4); inoltre una inscrizione rinvenuta presso Capua attesta, nella prima età imperiale, l'esistenza della figura del *Negotians Calcararius* (*CIL*, X.3947). In età romana, con la grande diffusione della muratura cementizia, la produzione di calce potè dunque divenire un'attività specializzata volta essenzialmente al profitto oltre che all'autoconsumo.

'E probabile che i forni di *Lucus Feroniae* fossero sotto il controllo dei Volusi Saturnini o di loro liberti; tale supposizione è suggerita dall'importanza economica e politica che questa famiglia rivestì nella zona e dall'intensa attività edilizia da loro promossa in età augustea.

Ringraziamenti

Desidero ringraziare in modo particolare Gianfranco Gazzetti per avermi permesso di partecipare allo scavo e di studiare il sito, e per molti utili suggerimenti. Ringrazio inoltre: Mauro Incitti, Janet DeLaine, Barbara Vitali Rosati, Andrea Camilli e Luisa Musso per gli aiuti e le preziose informazioni fornitemi.

Bibliografia

Adam, J.P. 1984. *La Costruction Romaine. Materiaux et Techniques*, Paris.

Camilli, A. 1991. *L'agro capenate centrale e settentrionale*, tesi di laurea non pubblicata, Università di Roma.

DeLaine, J. 1992. *Design and Construction in Imperial Roman Architecture: the Baths of Caracalla in Rome*, tesi di PhD non pubblicata, University of Adelaide.

Dix, B. 1982. 'The manufacture of lime and its uses in the Western Roman provinces', *Oxford Journal of Archaeology*, 1, 331–338.

Frutaz, A.P. 1972. *Le carte del Lazio*, Istituto di Studi Romani, Roma.

Gazzetti, G. 1992. *Il territorio capenate*, Roma.

Jackson, D. & Dix, B. 1973. 'A Roman lime-kiln at Weekley, Northants.', *Britannia*, 4, 128–140.

Jones, G.D.B. 1962, 1963. 'Capena and the Ager Capenas', *Papers of the British School at Rome*, 30, 106–207; 31, 100–158.

Moretti, M. & Sgubini Moretti, A.M. 1979. *La villa dei Volusi a Lucus Feroniae*, Roma.

Quilici, L. 1986. 'Il Tevere e l'Aniene come vie d'acqua a monte di Roma in età imperiale', *Archeologia Laziale*, 7,2, 198–214.

Saguì, L. 1986. 'Crypta Balbi (Roma). Lo scavo nell'esedra del monumento romano', *Archeologia Medievale*, xiii, 345–355.

Solter, W. 1970. *Romische Kalkbrenner im Rheinland*, Dusseldorf.

Torelli, M. 1973–74. 'Feronia e Lucus Feroniae in due iscrizioni latine', *Archeologia Classica*, xxv-xxvi, 741–750.

Torelli, M. 1980. 'Innovazioni nelle tecniche edilizie romane tra il I sec. a.C. e il I sec. d.C.', *Atti del Convegno: tecnologia, economia e società nel mondo romano*, Como.

Vitali Rosati, B. 1991. *L'agro capenate settentrionale*, tesi di laurea non pubblicata, Università di Roma.

La Sigillata Adriatica in Abruzzo

GINA MARTELLA
(Dipartimento di Archeologia, Università di Chieti)

Sommario: *Quando si parla di Terra Sigillata Italica, la mente corre subito alla sigillata aretina, puteolana o dell'agro romano. Poco rilievo invece viene dato alla sigillata prodotta nelle fabbriche considerate 'minori' ma che hanno avuto allo stesso modo ampia diffusione ed utilizzo. Uno di questi tipi di sigillata è quella detta 'adriatica', nome che gli fu dato dallo Stenico, poichè proveniente dalla costa adriatica. L'interesse per la sigillata adriatica nasce dallo studio che ho effetuato sulla sigillata rinvenuta a* Iuvanum *in occasione del II Convegno di Studi tenutosi a Chieti: in quell'occasione ho osservato che vi erano vari elementi che non rientravano in classi definite, ma che potevano essere prettamente autoctone. In questa sede offro una discussione sulla sigillata 'adriatica' nell'Abruzzo.*

Quando si parla di terra sigillata italica, il primo pensiero è rivolto alla sigillata aretina o puteolana. Poco rilievo, invece, viene dato alla produzione delle fabbriche considerate minori, ma che hanno avuto allo stesso modo ampia diffusione ed utilizzo.

Il motivo per cui i centri minori sono poco trattati è da ricercare nella mancanza di dati che possano portare ad un ampliamento della carta di diffusione delle produzioni locali. E' chiaro che la produzione aretina, per l'alta qualità dei prodotti, venisse esportata largamente, come è assodato che ci fosse una certa mobilità di produttori all'interno della penisola italiana per la creazione di nuove botteghe. I modelli aretini così richiesti si prestavano facilmente ad essere imitati in tutto anche da artigiani che nulla avevano a che fare con la zona di Arezzo, ma che riuscivano a far entrare nelle case anche dei meno abbienti questi oggetti che, essendo di produzione locale, avevano un prezzo minore.

Per ciò che riguarda la sigillata italica, e soprattutto i centri di produzione, viene sempre citato un passo di Plinio il Vecchio (*Nat. hist.*, XXXV, 160–161) che riporta la notizia dell'esistenza di alcune botteghe tralasciando altre come quelle di Pozzuoli che pure hanno prodotto vasi di ottima qualità e di larga diffusione:

> "*Maior quoque pars hominum terrenis utitur vasis. Sarnia etiamnunc in esculentis laudantur.. Retinent hanc nobilitatem et Arretium in Italia, et calicum tantum Surrentum, Hasta, Pollentia, in Hispania Saguntum, in Asia Pergamum. Habent et trallis ibi opera sua et in Italia Mutina: quoniam et sic gentes nobilitantur. Haec quoque per maria terrasque ultro citroque portantur, insignibus rotae officinis...*"

Se Plinio sia attendibile come fonte o no, non sta a me giudicarlo, ma credo che sia importante anche solo il fatto che alcune notizie ci siano.

Il quadro che si ha oggi dei centri di produzione di sigillata italica vede Arezzo come città dominante, seguita da Pozzuoli e da altri centri del nord Italia quali Ravenna, Aquileia, Cremona che producono sì terra sigillata italica, ma di un tipo un pò diverso sia per forme che per decorazioni, mentre c'è un vuoto nelle regioni centro-meridionali, se si esclude l'agro romano (Fig.1).

Il mio intento non è quello di fornire una serie affascinante di nuove acquisizioni a livello di rinvenimento di matrici o di scarichi di officine, ma quello di suscitare studi e seguenti pubblicazioni da parte di chi ha avuto ed ha la possibilità di svolgere scavi nel centro-sud. Infatti il problema che si pone allo studioso non è la mancanza di scavi sistematici, ma la penuria di dati che non permettono un ampliamento delle conoscenze.

Il mio interesse per i centri di produzione minori di sigillata, nasce dallo studio che ho effettuato sulla sigillata rinvenuta a *Iuvanum* in occasione del II Convegno di studi tenutosi a Chieti in 1992. *Iuvanum* è un *municipium* situato in Abruzzo, nella provincia di Chieti, in fase di scavo dal 1980 da parte della Prof. E. Fabbricotti e della Soprintendenza Archeologica di Chieti.

Il mio studio sul materiale di *Iuvanum* era partito dall' analisi dei bolli di sigillata italica per poter avere un' idea chiara delle provenienze che si pensavano scontate, senza nessun problema di attribuzione. Invece, di problemi ce ne sono stati e molti. Lo studio inizialmente si è rivolto ai bolli, piuttosto numerosi, per lo più pertinenti a forme lisce. La gran parte non trova riscontro

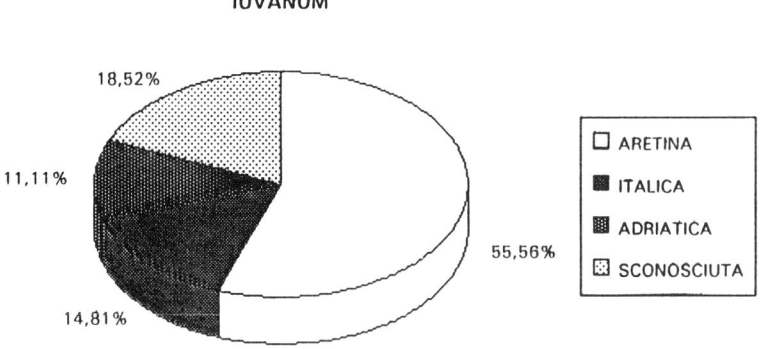

Fig. 1. Carta della diffusione della Sigillata Padana, tratta da Pucci.

nell'Oxè & Comfort (1968) per quanto riguarda la grafia, benchè il *figulus* sia ben identificabile, non solo, ma in riferimento alle provenienze, la maggioranza è composta da bolli aretini, ma un'alta percentuale riguarda bolli sconosciuti, per i quali non è stato possibile riconoscere il *figulus*. I restanti provengono dall' area padana e dall' agro romano.

Per quanto riguarda questi bolli sconosciuti non ho potuto fare a meno di pensare che possano provenire da fabbriche non ancora scoperte ed indagate anche se continuo a cercare nel materiale già edito. Non è certo semplice districarsi fra possibili fabbriche sconosciute e magari delle filiali di figline già esistenti ma ancora da scoprire, poichè, facilmente, si è tratti in inganno.

Il materiale che presenterò in questa occasione è stato per lo più rinvenuto nella campagna di scavo del 1992 ed è completamente inedito.

Appartengono ad anni precedenti il 1992 due bolli in *planta pedis*; la caratteristica che li accomuna è l'argilla tendente all'arancio e l'ingubbiatura arancio rossastra di qualità scadente e poco resistente:

N° c. provv. 010 Iuvanum 1991 Q AB2 sett. AB2a str. II – Tav. I,1
Frammento di fondo con bollo in *planta pedis* di un ceramista che si firma *T CL CT* non identificabile, anche se è possibile determinare la presenza di prenome e gentilizio. Argilla arancio rosata, abbastanza depurata, polverosa al tatto, con frattura netta ed ingubbiatura bruno arancio.

N° c. provv. 872 Iuvanum 1981 Q AB2 str. II – Tav. I, 2
Frammento di fondo con bollo in *planta pedis* non ben identificabile poichè si è conservata solo la lettera N. Non compare nell'Oxè & Comfort 1968. Argilla arancio rosata, abbastanza depurata, con frattura netta ed ingubbiatura bruno arancio.

Per ciò che riguarda i bolli del 1992, due non compaiono nell'Oxè & Comfort (1968) e sono una novità assoluta. Il frammento riporta le lettere Æ poco leggibili sul fondo dello stesso appartenente ad una piccola coppa; in un primo momento ho pensato ad una variante della fornace di *Ateius* di Arezzo, ma la mia ipotesi è stata completamente messa da parte, in ogni caso, probabilmente, proviene da Arezzo o da qualcuna delle città ospitanti centri produttivi di un certo livello poichè argilla ed ingubbiatura sono di buona qualità.

Una curiosità caratterizza ulteriormente questo oggetto: una parola graffita nella faccia inferiore del fondo della coppetta di difficile interpretazione che rientra in un filone già noto a *Iuvanum* in altri tre esemplari già pubblicati (Martella c.s.) ed in uno inedito ed ancora più particolare poichè il ceramista è *Philo* di Arezzo e sulla faccia opposta presenta graffito il nome del *figulus* ma non con il *Ph* bensì con la *F*.

Avevo già ipotizzato che questi graffiti potessero essere delle attestazioni di proprietà ma, per quanto riguarda il frammento del ceramista *Philo*, ritengo che sia una riproposta della firma effettuata, forse, da un proprietario che non sapeva con quali lettere si scrivesse il nome del produttore, ma in questo caso ci si muove nel campo delle ipotesi.

Tornando al frammento di fondo della coppetta con le lettere Æ, la parola graffita nella faccia inferiore è BROCI, per la quale ho dei problemi di interpretazione non ancora risolti.

N° c. provv. 018 Iuvanum 1992 Vano X str. III, tg. II – Tav. I,3
Frammento di fondo con bollo centrale riportante le lettere Æ. Non compare nell'Oxè & Comfort 1968. Sulla faccia inferiore compare una parola graffita. Argilla rosata, ben depurata, polverosa al tatto, con frattura netta ed ingubbiatura bruno rossastra.

N° c. provv. 025 Iuvanum 1992 Q B III, humus – Tav. I, 4
Frammento di fondo di piatto con bollo rettangolare, centrale del ceramista aretino *Philo*. Sulla faccia inferiore del fondo compare graffito il nome del ceramista ma scritto con la lettera *F* invece del *PH*. Argilla rosata, ben depurata, polverosa al tatto, con frattura netta ed ingubbiatura bruno rossastra.
Cfr: Oxè & Comfort 1968: 334, n. 1314. Non vi compare nella stessa forma.
Datazione: I sec. a. C.

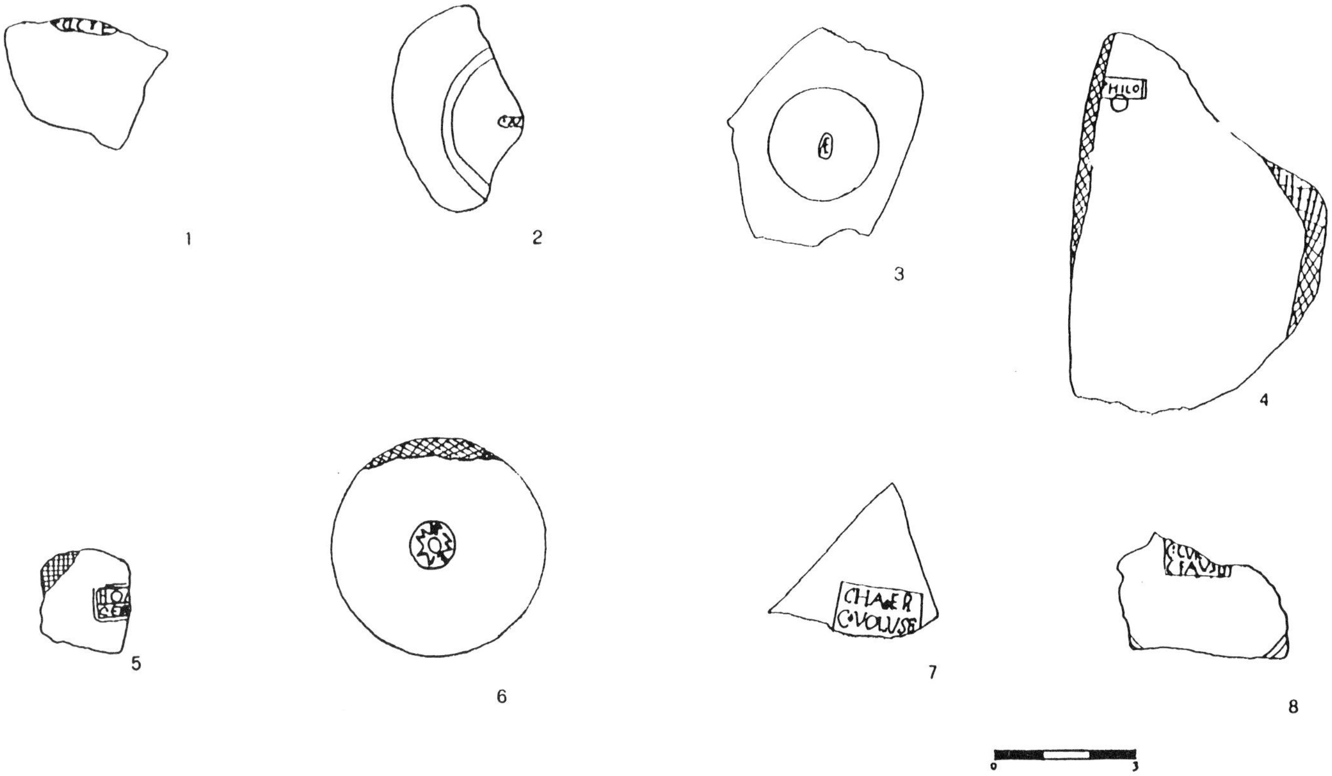

LA SIGILLATA ADRIATICA IN ABRUZZO

Tav. I. Bolli da Iuvanum.

Tav. II. Bolli da Iuvanum.

Il secondo frammento di bollo che non compare nell'Oxè & Comfort 1968 e nei repertori di scavo è rettangolare, doppio ma mutilo della seconda parte.

N° c. provv. 023 Iuvanum Vano X str. III, tg. II – Tav. I,5
Frammento di fondo con bollo centrale, rettangolare, doppio di un ceramista sconosciuto, ma di probabile derivazione aretina, si conservano solo le lettere *HO/C.E*. Argilla rosata, ben depurata, polverosa al tatto, con frattura netta ed ingubbiatura bruno rossastra. Lungh. cm 2; largh. cm 2,3; spess. cm 0,5.

Quattro sono i bolli dei quali è possibile rintracciare il *figulus* ma che sono delle varianti che non compaiono nell'Oxè & Comfort 1968. Il primo è circolare, centrale e conserva le lettere *MEMMIT*; con ogni probabilità si tratta di *Memmius* di Arezzo che in genere ricorre in *planta pedis* o in forma rettangolare, nel nostro caso in più c'è la lettera *T* che certamente non è il prenome del produttore, ma, forse, l'iniziale del prenome di uno schiavo o liberto.
L'altro frammento è una variante delle firme del ceramista *VOLUSENUS* di Arezzo. Nell'Oxè & Comfort non compare il nome *C HAER* che può essere un lavorante della bottega di *Volusenus*. La seconda parte del bollo trova confronto solo con uno simile di *Phylades C. Volusi* (Oxè & Comfort 1968: 559, n.2486).
Il penultimo, proviene probabilmente da Roma, ed è del ceramista *C. CURTIUS*. Il nome *Faustus* è del suo lavorante. In questa forma non compare nell'Oxè & Comfort. L'ultimo è, forse, una variante della firma di *NAEVIUS* di Pozzuoli ed è anch'esso rettangolare e centrale.

N° c. provv. 021 Iuvanum 1992 Vano X str. III, tg. II – tav. I.6
Frammento di fondo con bollo circolare, centrale, pertinente ad una coppetta del ceramista aretino *Memmius*, piuttosto diffuso in Italia ed all'estero. Di norma i bolli sono rettangolari oppure in *planta pedis*. Argilla rosata, ben depurata, polverosa al tatto, con frattura netta ed ingubbiatura bruno rossastra.
Cfr: Oxè & Comfort 1968: 258–264, nn. 984–1009.
Datazione: II sec. d.C.

N° c. provv. 022 Iuvanum 1992 Q B III, humus – Tav. I,7
Frammento di fondo con bollo rettangolare, centrale, doppio del ceramista aretino *Volusenus*. Argilla rosata, ben depurata, polverosa al tatto. con frattura netta ed ingubbiatura bruno rossastra. Lungh. cm 3; largh. cm 3,5; spess. cm 0,5.
Cfr: Oxè & Comfort 1968: 555–560, nn. 2468–2491.
Datazione: I sec. a.C.

N° c. provv. 024 Iuvanum 1992 Q B III, humus – Tav. I,8
Frammento di fondo con bollo rettangolare, centrale doppio del ceramista romano *Curtius Rufus* di Roma; in questa forma non compare nell'Oxè & Comfort. Argilla rosata, ben depurata, polverosa al tatto, con frattura netta ed ingubbiatura bruno rossastra.
Cfr: Oxè & Comfort 1968: 178, n. 573.
Datazione: I sec. a.C.

N° c. provv. 019 Iuvanum 1992 Q CIII, humus – Tav. II, 1
Frammento di fondo con bollo rettangolare, centrale probabilmente di *Naevius* di Pozzuoli; chiude la firma un rametto ornato da foglioline. Sotto questa forma non è stato possibile rintracciarlo. Argilla rosata, ben depurata, polverosa al tatto, con frattura netta ed ingubbiatura bruno rossastra.

Gli ultimi bolli sono due belle firme di *Ateius* e di *C.MR* che compare per la seconda volta a *Iuvanum*.

N° c. provv. 017 Iuvanum 1992 Vano X str. III, tg. II – Tav. II,2
Frammento di fondo con bollo rettangolare, centrale, probabilmente di un piatto del ceramista aretino *Ateius*, piuttosto noto sia in Italia che all'estero. Argilla rosata, ben depurata, con frattura netta ed ingubbiatura bruno rossastra. Lungh. cm 9,7; largh. cm 5,8; spess. cm 0,6.
Cfr: Oxè & Comfort 1968: 42–90, nn. 140–186.
Datazione: I sec. a. C.

N° c. provv. 020 Iuvanum 1992 Q C III, humus – Tav. II, 3
Frammento di fondo con bollo in *planta pedis* di *C.MR* di Arezzo già rinvenuto in una variante a *Iuvanum*. Argilla rosata, ben depurata, polverosa al tatto, con frattura netta ed ingubbiatura bruno rossastra. Lungh. cm 0,9; largh. cm 1,8; spess. cm 0,5.
Cfr: Oxè & Comfort 1968: 255, n. 979; Martella, c.s.
Datazione: I sec. d.C.

Come si può notare, sono solo due i bolli di chiara derivazione, gli altri pongono tutti dei problemi di attribuzione e, soprattutto, propongono nuovi nomi di aiutanti di produttori di oggetti in sigillata. Ciò mi sembra piuttosto eccezionale, poiché *Iuvanum* è stato sì un centro florido ma non avrei mai pensato che potesse restituire dei materiali in così gran numero e di tale importanza. Tutto ciò fa ben sperare per le prossime campagne di scavo dei prossimi anni.
Molto stupita mi aveva lasciato anche la presenza di molto materiale presente e proveniente dal Nord Italia che non riguarda solo la sigillata, ma anche altre classi ceramiche. Certo, la sigillata padana ha avuto una diffusione piuttosto vasta, come è possibile notare dalla mappa delle presenze dell'Oxè & Comfort nella quale non ancora compare Iuvanum che può esservi inserita a pieno titolo (Fig. 2).
Il motivo di una tale espansione è da ricercare nella buona qualità dei manufatti che si presentano come una sorte di evoluzione della sigillata aretina. La forma più diffusa è certamente rappresentata dal tipo *Sariusschalen*, una coppa biansata caratterizzata da una forte rientranza posta sopra la parte ottenuta a matrice e che presenta il labbro volto verso l'interno. Questa forma è piuttosto frequente lungo tutta la costa adriatica da Aquileia, attraverso Bologna, Rimini, le Marche, l'Abruzzo e la Puglia.
Un bell'esemplare è stato studiato e pubblicato da Stenico (1971: 145–155) ed è proprio quello proveniente da Ordona, caratterizzato da una decorazione composta

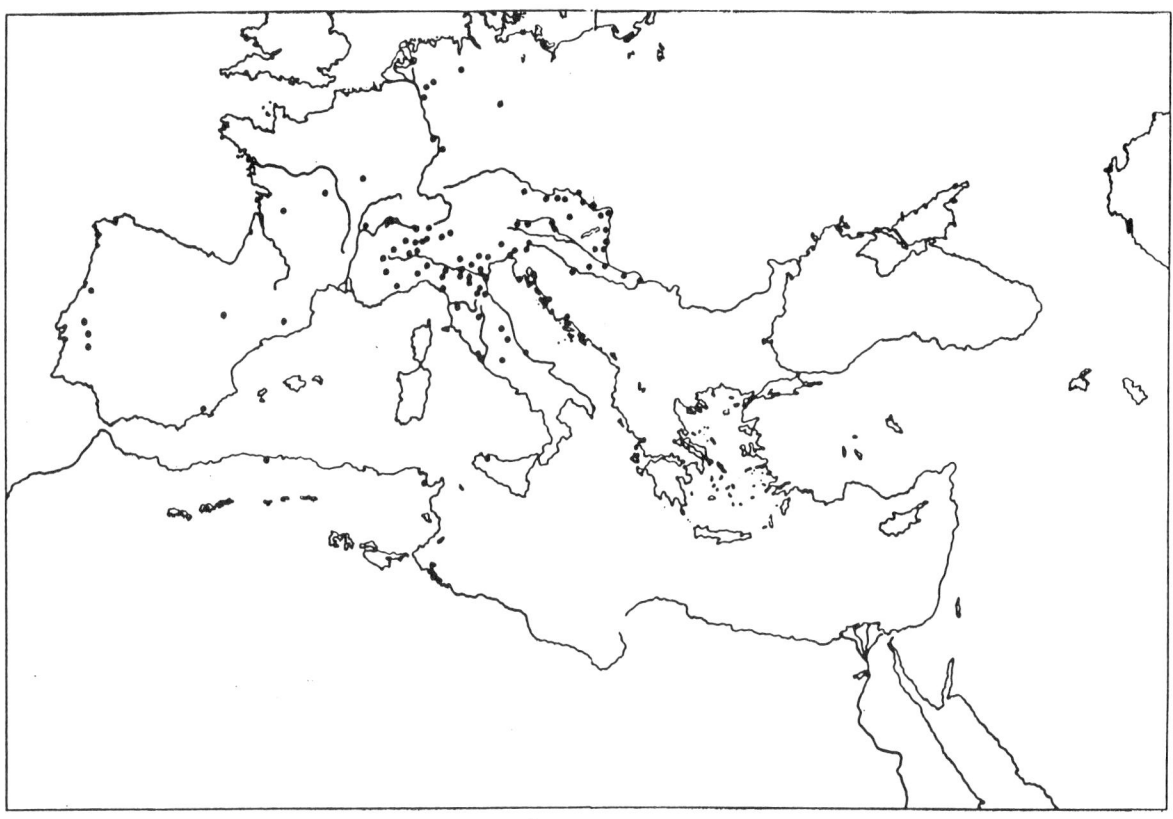

Fig. 2. Grafico che illustra la provenienza della Terra Sigillata rinvenuta a Iuvanum, in base ai bolli editi.

da una serie di triangoli isosceli ai cui vertici si trovano degli elementi vegetali racchiusi da una decorazione a forma di lira tra i quali sono presenti due busti con volti dai tratti negroidi. La decorazione si conclude con un serto di vite continuo. Stenico afferma che il serto di vite non è peculiare nella sigillata Nord italica, mentre lo sono quelle che sono definite 'vesciche piumate' come in molti frammenti presenti nel Museo di Bologna di chiara derivazione bargatea (Fava 1962: 45–75, tav.3) o anche altri elementi vegetali, soprattutto quelli composti da duplici o triplici linee che si intersecano formando rombi o triangoli ai vertici dei quali si trovano delle foglie composte (Fava 1962: tav.5, 7, 8). Molto diffusi sono anche i bicchieri tipo Aco, sempre di produzione Nord italica.

In genere la sigillata padana, pur conservando un'argilla ben depurata, in frattura appare di un colore tendente all'arancio e la vernice si presenta più bruna dell'aretina pur essendo di buona qualità. Stenico (1971: 152–153) definisce di qualità eccellente alcuni frammenti provenienti da Corfinio; per essere più precisi, i frammenti sono tre ed appartengono tutti alla stessa coppa e sono decorati da foglie di vite con tralci, un nodo ed una infruttescenza globulare; io ne ho tratto notizia dall'articolo di Stenico, ma non ho avuto modo di vederli dal vivo e sono dello stesso stile della matrice, sempre proveniente da Corfinio (Fig.3). Infatti anche qui è presente un serto di vite e predominano elementi vegetali anche se ormai di maniera.

Questi rinvenimenti sono molto importanti per la conoscenza dell'evoluzione della sigillata, infatti, sia nel Nord Italia, sia a Corfinio sono proprio gli elementi vegetali ad essere riportati con maggior frequenza anche se non raggiungono i livelli dell'aretina che contemporaneamente vive un periodo splendido.

Fig. 3. Matrice proveniente da Corfinio.

Se a Corfinio sono stati rinvenuti altri frammenti simili non posso dirlo come anche non so se siano stati riportati alla luce dei punti di fuoco che si possano collegare alla produzione di terra sigillata poiché gli scavi sono ancora in corso da parte della Soprintendenza Archeologica di Chieti. Comunque, è da rilevare la presenza a Vittorito, un paese nei pressi di Corfinio, di un sarcofago, attualmente inglobato nel muro della Chiesa di S. Michele Arcangelo, nella cui iscrizione compare il nome di *Lucius Sarius Felix* che dal Wonterghem (1984: 199–200, n.601) è associato ad un *Sarius Felix* del quale compaiono alcuni bolli su sigillata di Corfinio, come anche a Pentima (Fig.4).

L.SARIO.L.FIL.FELICI.DECVRIONI.CORFINIENSIVM

IVVENI.INC.QUI.VIXIT.ANNIS.XXX.MENSIBVS.VI.DIEBVS.X

L.SARIVS.FELIX.PATER.ET.PONTIA.IVSTINA.MATER.FILIO

PIISSIMO.ET.L.SARIVS.IVSTINVS.FRATER.ET.SARIA.FELICV

LA.SOROR.POSVERVNT

L D D D

Fig. 4. Trascrizione dell'epigrafe del sarcofago inglobato nella chiesa di S. Michele Arcangelo a Vittorito (CH) - trascrizione effettuata dalla Dott.ssa Delia Golini.

Il collegamento è piuttosto seducente, soprattutto se si pensa che i bolli di *Sarius Felix* sono stati rinvenuti anche a Rimini ed Aquileia (Oxè & Comfort 1968: 399, n.1660), ma un problema è che il *Sarius Felix* dell'epigrafe funeraria è appartenente alla tribù *Sergia*, quindi non poteva provenire da Arezzo, per cui un'ipotesi di collegamento fra i due sembra improbabile, anche se non è da escludere che *Sarius Felix* avesse avuto contatti con Arezzo, oppure avesse assoldato degli schiavi provenienti da fabbriche aretine, ma tutto ciò è pura supposizione. Resta il fatto che Corfinio produceva sigillata ed anche di buona qualità e sicuramente la esportava, come dimostrano i bolli. Stenico (1971: 155) conia la definizione di 'sigillata adriatica' in relazione al rinvenimento di un frammento di matrice ad Ordona che sembra seguire lo stesso filone di quella di Corfinio, cioè di terra sigillata prodotta non in ambito aretino. La matrice di Ordona è piuttosto importante se si pensa che ad essa è seguito il rinvenimento, nel 1976, di una fabbrica di terra sigillata la cui esistenza era stata già ipotizzata nel 1966 (Fig.5).

E *Iuvanum*? Ho già detto che la sigillata rinvenuta proviene da molte località, anche sconosciute, ma per il momento non è possibile parlare di produzione di sigillata a *Iuvanum* anche se qualche tentativo, secondo me, è stato fatto.

Nei primi anni ottanta, nella zona a Sud-Est del foro fu riportato alla luce un ambiente piuttosto singolare che venne denominato Ambiente F (Fig.6). Per quello che riguarda i problemi strutturali, rimando all'intervento della Dott. ssa Natalina Ciacio (1990: 101–104), pubblicato negli Atti del I Convegno su *Iuvanum,* mentre è interessante puntare l'attenzione sul rinvenimento in detto ambiente di un forno ceramico nell'angolo N-W. La presenza di un forno era stata già ipotizzata durante il rinvenimento di blocchi di argilla cruda di colore sia rosso mattone che verde e di una quantità incredibile di ceramica comune di varie forme nonché terra sigillata, pareti sottili grigie e vetro in abbondanza. Il forno è di forma circolare e si è conservata solo la camera di combustione al di sotto del piano di calpestio; da notare la presenza al centro di essa di una piccola olpe tenuta da pietre contenente carboni ed argilla rossa che è stata rinvenuta anche tutt'intorno.

L'ipotesi che era stata fatta, era quella di un umidificatore che rendesse l'atmosfera riducente durante la cottura, oppure che l'olpe contenesse degli ingredienti che in fusione potessero essere aggiunti all'argilla depurata per verniciare i vasi. Inoltre, sempre nell'angolo N-W, si rinvenne un piano di lavoro in bipedali simile ad un altro allineamento, rinvenuto in anni precedenti, in un altro ambiente adiacente.

La fornace doveva avere una buona produzione che pare spaziasse a varie forme di ceramica comune e, forse, anche al vetro, come ha ipotizzato la Dott.ssa Daniela Della Valle (c.s.), produzione testimoniata anche dal rinvenimento di molte scorie di vetro, di ferro, di stagno fuso e piombo. Non solo, ma doveva essere anche una bottega piuttosto fornita a giudicare dalla quantità di ceramica rinvenuta e da una probabile vetrina piena di oggetti in vetro dei quali è stato possibile ricostruire solo una coppa.

Fra tutto il materiale rinvenuto, mi ha incuriosito un frammento di coppa, che sembra un tentativo mal riuscito di riprodurre un oggetto in aretina: il ceramista non è riuscito nella cottura ed anche nella verniciatura,

Fig. 5. Matrice rinvenuta ad Ordona, tratta da Stenico.

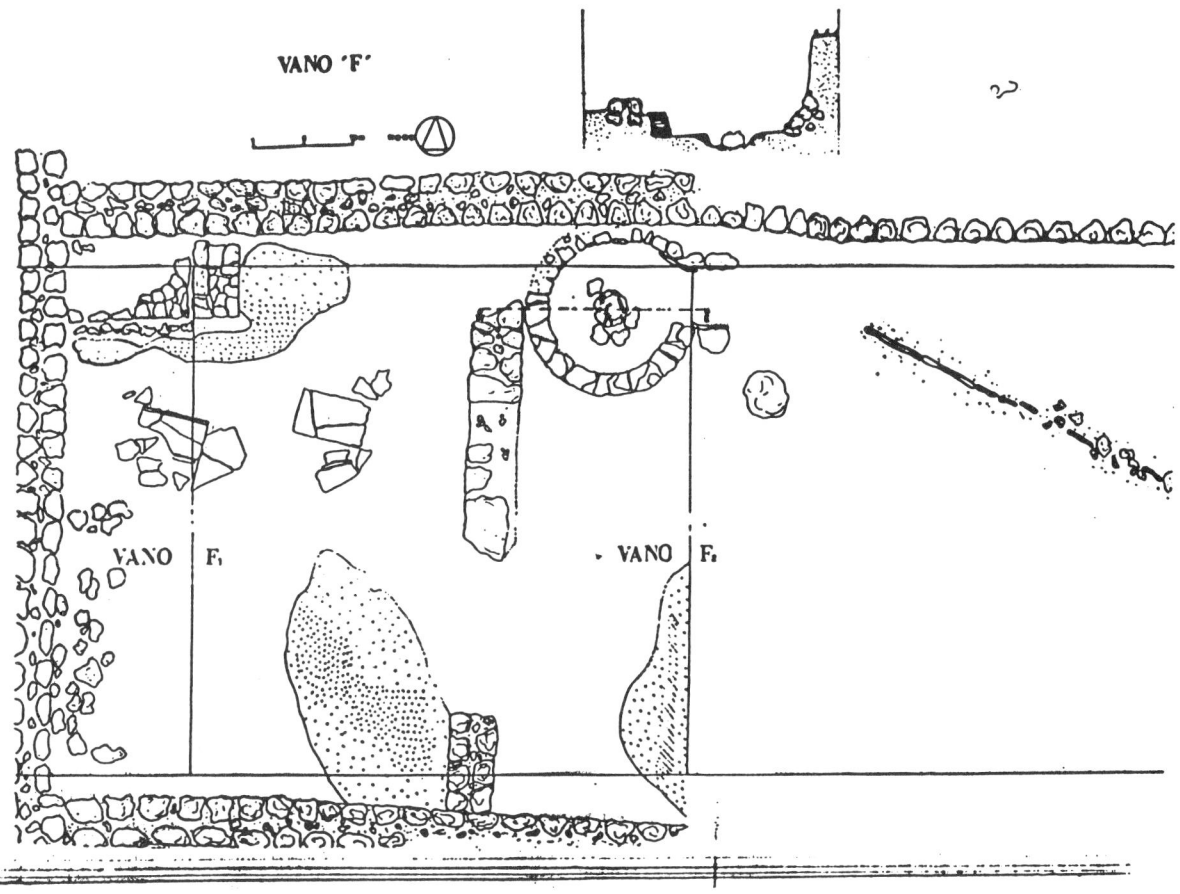

Fig. 6. Pianta dell'ambiente F a Iuvanum.

come si può notare dalla goccia colata in malo modo; a me sembra proprio un tentativo locale, soprattutto poiché di frammenti con ingubbiatura quasi inesistente color marrone rossastro ve ne sono molti altri, anche se non è possibile assegnarli con certezza a questa fornace locale (Fig.7).

Un altro oggetto del quale non ho trovato ancora confronti nella sigillata è una coppetta che al momento del rinvenimento era completamente sigillata, ma che in seguito ha perduto tutta l'ingubbiatura della quale restano solo poche tracce (Fig.8). Interessanti sono le impressioni che io ho ritenuto fossero imitazioni del

Fig. 7. Frammento di coppa rinvenuto nella bottega che ospitava la fornace.

Fig. 8. Coppetta sigillata decorata ad impressioni.

vetro, supportata in ciò anche da un frammento di coppa in vetro rinvenuto proprio nella fornace. L'argilla non è molto depurata e l'ingubbiatura scomparsa così repentinamente mi fanno pensare ad un prodotto di scarsa qualità.

Il rinvenimento di una fornace all'interno di uno scavo provoca sempre in tutti i partecipanti la speranza che la ceramica venuta alla luce venisse prodotta proprio lì e si fa a gara per cercare elementi di supporto alle proprie teorie. L'ipotesi di un tentativo di produzione di sigillata non mi sembra proprio da escludere, ma sottolineo che è solo un tentativo, per il momento, ed anche poco riuscito. A livello di datazione, la fornace si può assegnare al I sec. d.C. ed ha funzionato fino a parte del II sec. d.C., dato ottenuto sulla base di monete rinvenute sotto il crollo della tettoia.

Bibliografia

Ciacio, N. 1990. 'Iuvanum', *Atti del I Convegno di Studi*, Chieti, 101-104.

Della Valle, D. c.s. 'I vetri, Iuvanum', *Atti del II Convegno di Studi*, Chieti 1992.

Fava, S. 1962. 'Una ignota produzione di sigillata padana nel Museo di Bologna', *RCRF Acta* IV, 45-75.

Martella, G. c.s. 'La terra sigillata italica, Iuvanum', *Atti del II Convegno di Studi*, Chieti 1992 (in corso di stampa).

Mertens, J. 1979. 'Rapport sommaire sur les travaux des campagnes de 1976-77', in *Ordona* VI, Bruxelles.

Oxè, A. & Comfort, H. 1968. *Corpus Vasorum Arretinorum*, Bonn.

Stenico, A. 1971. 'Terra sigillata nord italica e terra sigillata adriatica a Herdonia', in *Ordona* III, Bruxelles-Rome, 145-155.

Vanderhoeven, M. 1976. 'La terre sigillée lisse', in *Ordona* V, Bruxelles, 79-182.

Vanderhoeven, M. 1979. 'La terre sigillée á relief', in *Ordona* VI, Bruxelles, 83-104.

Van Wonterghem, F. 1984. *Superaequum, Corfinium, Sulmo, Forma Italiae*, Firenze.

60

La Ceramica a Pareti Sottili Grigie

Oliva Menozzi
(Dipartimento di Archeologia, Università di Chieti)

Sommario: *Questo contributo prende in esame la produzione e diffusione della ceramica a Pareti sottili grigie in Italia. Non esistono studi specifici sull'argomento ed i materiali risultano prevalentemente inediti. La ceramica a Pareti sottili grigie, che è sempre stata inclusa nella ceramica a Pareti sottili, è però una importante classe ceramica a se stante con caratteristiche omogenee proprie che la contradistinguono. Si tratta di ceramica fine da mensa, diffusa nel bacino Mediterraneo tra il I sec. a.C ed il II d.C., che è spesso stata messa in relazione per le sue caratteristiche tipologiche e per il suo repertorio decorativo con altre classi di materiali come la Terra Sigillata Italica, il vetro, i recipienti metallici. Generalmente la ceramica a Pareti sottili grigie è considerata tipica della Valle Padana e dell'area nord Adriatica. Alla luce dei nuovi rinvenimenti però non si può più affermare che questa ceramica ebbe una distribuzione prevalentemente locale, ma è possibile ampliare i confini della sua distribuzione.*

Il mio interesse per la ceramica a Pareti sottili grigie è nato durante l'analisi di materiali inediti provenienti da siti archeologici presenti in Abruzzo. Lo studio si è poi esteso ai rinvenimenti di ceramica a Pareti sottili grigie in tutto l'ambito italiano per cercare di capire i problemi connessi con la sua produzione e diffusione. Non esistono studi specifici su questo argomento. Sino ad ora questo materiale è stato incluso nella categoria della ceramica a Pareti sottili e non si è mai operata una distinzione tra questi tipi di ceramica. In realtà le Pareti sottili grigie, sia per caratteristiche tipologiche che tecniche, rappresentano una vera e propria classe ceramica distinta ed omogenea.

In passato questa classe ceramica è stata definita da studiosi come il Greene (1979: 10) o lo Zuffa (1962: 109) Terra Sigillata Nigra o Terra Sigillata Buccheroide. La Marabini Moevs (1973: 211–227) definisce tale tipo di ceramica 'produzione Alpina' e nel suo studio la mette in relazione con precedenti classi ceramiche, come il Bucchero, la Ceramica a Vernice nera, la Ceramica di La Tène e la Terra Nigra Belga. L'unica trattazione specifica sull'argomento è stata effettuata dalla Dott.sa Maioli (1972: 106–124; 1973: 59–77), sulla ceramica a Pareti sottili grigie proveniente dall'area Ravennate, contribuendo così a stabilirne con più precisione la cronologia.

Nella sua evoluzione tipologica e nel repertorio decorativo questo tipo di ceramica si ispira a svariate classi di materiali, dalla Terra Sigillata Italica, al Vetro, ai recipienti metallici. Si tratta di ceramica raffinata e principalmente da mensa, caratterizzata da forme in genere di piccole dimensioni e sottile spessore delle pareti. Il caratteristico colore grigio dell'argilla è il risultato di un processo di cottura in atmosfera riducente, con una riduzione cioè quasi totale dell'ossigeno presente nel forno. Le superfici dei recipienti in questo materiale si presentano ricoperte da un sottilissimo strato di colore, costituito da argilla molto diluita, che con la cottura assume varie tonalità dal grigio al nero e rende le superfici lisce ed omogenee. A volte questa ingubbiatura può mancare del tutto e le superfici sono solo polite. Cronologicamente questo tipo di ceramica si diffuse tra il I sec. a.C. ed il II sec. d.C., con attardamenti, specie in nord Europa, sino al III sec. d.C.

I contesti di rinvenimento di tale tipo di ceramica, come si può vedere nella Fig. 1, comprendono sia ambienti a carattere abitativo, che pubblici, come ad esempio *tabernae* e locali di servizio, che funerari.

Per comodità di consultazione si è preferito organizzare lo studio delle forme e delle decorazioni della ceramica a Pareti sottili grigie in un catalogo apparte (vedi *infra*) in cui sono descritte le caratteristiche principali delle varianti tipologiche e delle decorazioni più attestate, con indicazione dei siti di provenienza e della cronologia.

In generale nello studio delle forme si possono individuare due tipi fondamentali. Il TIPO I, che potremmo definire bicchiere, è caratterizzato da un diametro della bocca di misura sempre inferiore all'altezza del recipiente; mentre il TIPO II, che comprende coppe e coppette, presenta un diametro della bocca generalmente superiore alla sua altezza. Questi due tipi fondamentali presentano poi numerosissime varianti, dettate da differenze cronologiche e gusti locali.

Da un punto di vista cronologico, i bicchieri alti ed affusolati, TIPO I A (Tav. I), rappresentano la variante più antica, già prodotta all'inizio del I sec. a.C. in officine ceramiche dell'area Padana occidentale, con una distribuzione prevalentemente locale (Ricci 1984: 348). Dopo il primo quarto del I sec a.C. cominciano ad affermarsi nuove officine ceramiche, come ad esempio quelle di Ravenna (Ricci 1984: 349) ed Aquileia (Buora 1987: 6–9), le forme tendono generalmente a divenire più basse e ad arrotondarsi, si affermano infatti le varianti B, C e D del TIPO I (Tav.I e II) e l'area di diffusione di tale ceramica inizia ad ampliarsi. L'età tardo repubblicana ed Augustea segnano invece l'affermazione del TIPO II, che non sostituisce del tutto il TIPO I, si continuano infatti a fabbricare le varianti C ed F, ma viene senz'altro prodotto ed esportato in quantità superiori. La Fig. 2 evidenzia infatti che i rinvenimenti di ceramica a Pareti sottili grigie effettuati sin'ora sono per la maggior parte costituiti da varianti del TIPO II.

Vari sono i tipi di decorazione riscontrati. Accanto ad esemplari lisci, o decorati semplicemente a rotella, si trovano decorazioni ad incisione (Tav.V,B), databili tra l'ultimo quarto del I sec.a.C. e il primo quarto del I sec. d.C.

I motivi decorativi eseguiti alla barbotine sono molteplici e ampiamente attestati. Si riscontrano ad esempio semplici mammillonature (Tav.V,C,22–23), punti a rilievo (Tav.V,C,24), piccole foglie (Tav.V,C,37–39), che creano anche festoni o decorazioni geometriche, già attestate a partire dall'età augustea (Tav.V,C,25–34,37–44). Sempre con la tecnica della barbotine sono eseguite le bacellature (Tav.V,C,35–36) di evidente imitazione di forme vitree e databili a partire dall'età claudia. Altro tipo di decorazione alla barbotine ampiamente attestato è caratterizzato da elementi vegetali (Tav.VI,C,1–22), diffusi soprattutto dall'età flavia e per tutto il I sec. d.C. Particolarmente diffuso dall'età neroniana è la decorazione con scaglie a nervature verticali, eseguite alla barbotine poco rilevate e spesso associate a rotellature (Tav.VI,C,17–20). Tra le decorazioni meno diffuse per questo tipo di ceramica troviamo invece le impressioni (Tav.V,C), che si affermano intorno alla metà del I sec.a.C., e la sabbiatura, attestata sin da età augustea, ma più popolare in età claudia.

In base alle Figg. 3 e 4, in cui sono evidenziate le percentuali d'incidenza dei vari tipi di decorazione nelle due forme principali, si può notare che molto numerosi sono i materiali privi di decorazione, soprattutto nella forme di TIPO I, mentre le decorazioni più attestate sono la barbotine e le rotellature.

Fin'ora la ceramica a Pareti sottili grigie è stata considerata prodotto tipico della Valle Padana e dell'area Nord-Adriatica, con una distribuzione quasi esclusivamente locale. Ciò è dovuto anche al fatto che attualmente gli unici materiali di tal genere pubblicati e le uniche fornaci conosciute di questa ceramica sono stati rinvenuti in queste aree. I centri di produzione che si conoscono infatti, in base a rinvenimenti di forni o scarti di lavorazione, sono localizzati in area Ravennate (Ricci 1984: 348–349), a Bologna (Bergamini 1980, no.304) ed Aquileia (Buora 1987: 6–9).

Alla luce dei nuovi rinvenimenti però è possibile ampliare i confini della diffusione di questa classe ceramica. Non sembra azzardato infatti affermare che questo tipo di ceramica si diffuse, specie durante il I ed il II sec. d.C., in tutto il mondo romano. I siti in Italia, oltre l'area Nord-Adriatica, in cui è stata rinvenuta ceramica a Pareti sottili grigie, sono infatti numerosissimi. Rinvenimenti di tali materiali si segnalano ad esempio in vari siti, editi e non, delle Marche (Mercando 1981: 410–413) e dell'Abruzzo (vedi Menozzi 1992), a Luni (Cavalieri Manasse 1973: 332–354), Cosa (Marabini 1973: 211–227), Sutri (Duncan 1964: 88), Ornavasso (Bianchetti 1895, tavv.XXII-XXIII, nos.2–5, 7 9, 22), Orvieto (Hayes 1976: 80), Ventimiglia (Lamboglia 1939: 211–212; 1947: 172–175), Ardea (Andren 1961: 49), Pollenzo (Mosca 1962: 39–70; 1968: 336–349), Rimini (Riccioni 1970: 325), nell'area del Garda (Granier 1965: 253–300).

Questo tipo di ceramica inoltre non si rinviene solo in siti italiani, ma in tutto il bacino Mediterraneo. Ad esempio sono numerosi i rinvenimenti di questa ceramica nella Pannonia, come nella necropoli di Emona (Plesnicar-Gec 1972, tavv.XXII, XXVII. XLC, XCV, CVII, etc.), in cui sono stati rinvenuti numerosi esemplari di recipienti in ceramica a Pareti sottili grigie, sia di tipo I che II. Non si tratta certo di rinvenimento sporadico nella zona poichè altre coppette di questo materiale si rinvengono in vari siti della ex Iugoslavia (Bonis 1942, tavv.XIX,46–48; XX,40–72; XXI,1–15; Griffiths 1987–88: 119–128). Anche in Grecia si segnalano rinvenimenti a Corinto (Hayes 1973, tav.89, no.185), ed Atene (Robinson 1959: F26). Una grande quantità di ceramica a Pareti sottili grigie è stata rinvenuta in recenti scavi a Knossos (Sacket 1992: 166–168), a Creta, che sino a poco tempo fa era ritenuta un'area con scarsa presenza di tali materiali. Poco numerosi i rinvenimenti in Asia e Africa, come ad esempio Caesarea in Palestina (Hayes 1976: 31) e Sidi Khrebish Bengazi (Kenrick 1985: 307–319), ma scavi e segnalazioni future potrebbero far aumentare il numero di siti.

Più numerose le segnalazioni in Europa centrale, come ad esempio Cavaillon (Dumoulin 1965: 19), Glanum (Rolland 1946: 26), Magdalensberg (Egger 1955: 34; 1956: 48; 1958: 89–90; 1959: 89; 1961: 111–112), Vindonissa (Ettlinger & Simonett 1952: 54–56,

La Ceramica a Pareti Sottili Grigie

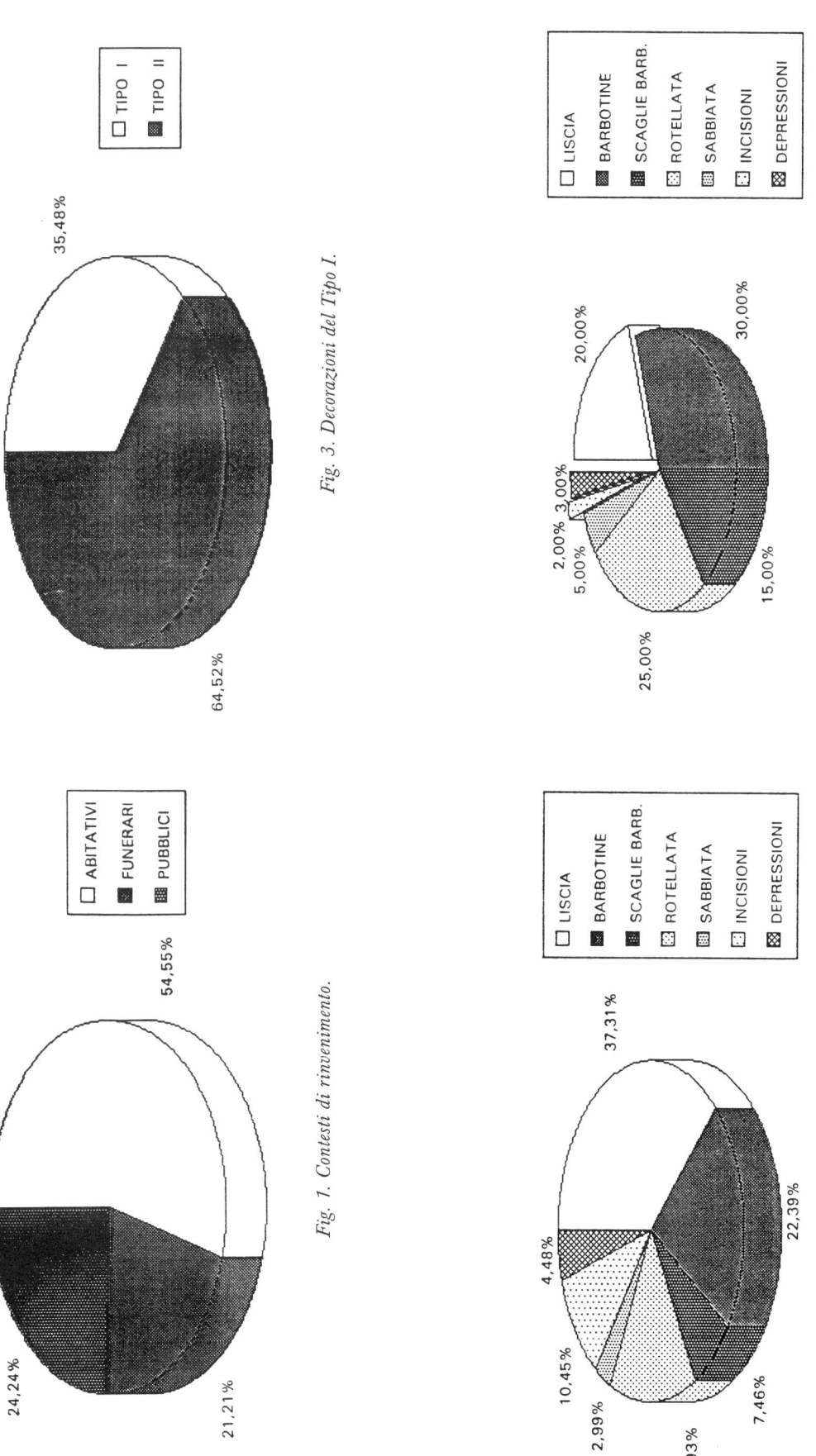

Fig. 1. Contesti di rinvenimento.

Fig. 2. Tipologia delle forme.

Fig. 3. Decorazioni del Tipo I.

Fig. 4. Decorazioni del Tipo II.

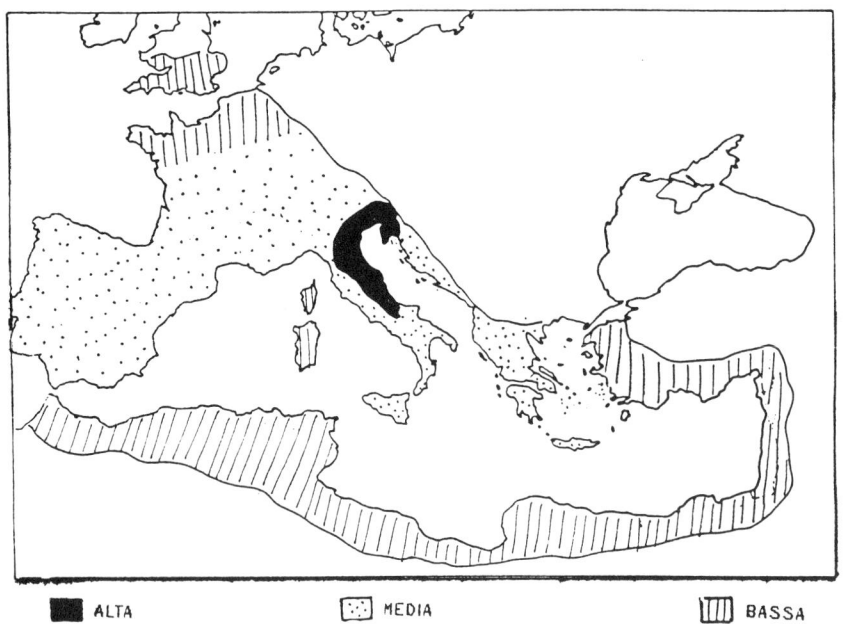

Fig. 5. Mappa di diffusione della ceramica a Pareti sottili grigie.

nos.265-286), e nel Ticino (Ulrich 1914, pl.LII,2a; LXXIII,1-5; LXXXIV,7-11). Particolarmente importanti per stabilire l'esatta cronologia di tali materiali, sono i rinvenimenti effettuati in siti posti sul *limes*, che hanno avuto un periodo di vita limitato e ben documentato cronologicamente, come ad esempio ad Haltern (Loeschcke 1909: 101-322). Numerosissimi rinvenimenti sono stati effettuati nella penisola Iberica, in siti quali Maiorca, Ibiza in cui il materiale è tipologicamente vario, Ampurias ed altri siti spagnoli, nonchè portoghesi quali Belo e Lisbona (Mayet 1975). Segnalazioni di rinvenimenti di ceramica a Pareti sottili grigie si hanno prò anche in Nord Europa, come ad esempio in Britannia (Gillam 1957: 49-50).

In base ai numerosissimi nuovi siti segnalati, con presenza di tale tipo di ceramica, si può dedurre che in realtà non ci si trova di fronte ad una produzione locale di minima diffusione, ma ad una ceramica presente in tutto il Mediterraneo. Come si evince dalle Figg. 5 e 6 sulla diffusione di tale tipo di ceramica, l'area in cui essa è più ampiamente attestata è quella centro-nord Adriatica, in cui è da individuare anche l'area di origine, ma già dalla metà del I sec. a.C. essa viene esportata e probabilmente anche localmente imitata in tutto il bacino Mediterraneo, soprattutto in centro Europa, Pannonia e Grecia e probabilmente questi dati sono destinati a cambiare con nuovi rinvenimenti e segnalazioni.

La mancanza quindi di attestazioni di tale materiale sin'ora in aree al di fuori della zona Padana, non era dovuta alla sua mancata diffusione, come erroneamente si riteneva, bensì alla scarsità di dati pubblicati relativi a questa ceramica.

Catalogo delle Forme

In questo catalogo sono presentate le due forme principali, con le varianti tipologiche, mentre numerosissime sono le sottovarianti, dovute spesso a differenze minime ed impercettibili dettate da gusti locali e da cronologie diverse, per cui se ne presentano solo gli esemplari più attestati e soprattutto interamente, o quasi,

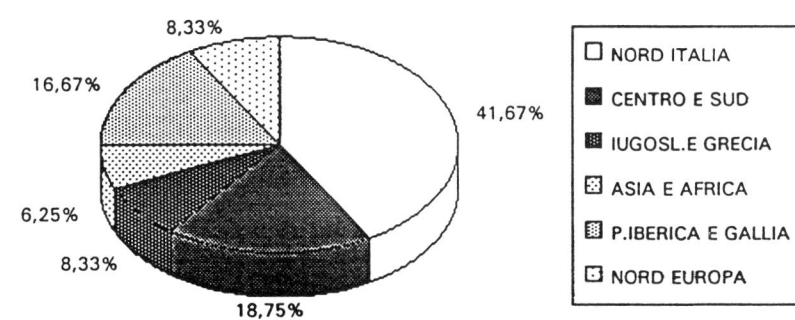

Fig. 6. Aree di diffusione.

ricostruibili. Il catalogo è organizzato in base alle tavole allegate e presenta la descrizione della forma, delle varianti e l'elenco delle attestazioni per ogni variante, con indicazione della cronologia e della località di provenienza.

Forma Tipo I (Tav.I e II)

Si tratta di bicchieri e urnette, con un diametro della bocca sempre di misura inferiore all'altezza del corpo del recipiente, o, in rari casi (Tav.II,variante F,3), uguale. La forma è attestata, con le sue varianti, già all'inizio del I sec. a.C. e viene ampiamente prodotta per tutto il secolo. Con la fine della Repubblica e la prima età imperiale viene prodotta in minor quantità, poichè sostituita, anche se non del tutto, dalla forma di TIPO II. La variante più antica è quella caratterizzata da bicchieri alti ed affusolati (variante A), sostituita con il passare del tempo da forme più basse e capienti (varianti B e C), mentre le varianti più attestate con l'età augustea sono quelle a corpo più piccolo, quasi come veri e propri bicchieri (varianti E e F).

Variante A (Tav.I,A,1-8) – Bicchieri alti ed affusolati, prodotti nel I sec.a.C. in officine ceramiche della Val Padana e di Aquileia, e diffusi soprattutto in Nord Italia, Francia e Penisola Iberica. Le sottovarianti locali più attestate presentano generalmente orlo estroflesso, pareti verticali e fondo piatto, a volte con piccolo piede modanato (Tav.I,A,1).

1 – Ornavasso (Graue 1974: 165, tav.40-44), metà I sec. a.C.
2 – Ampurias (Almagro 1953, fig.288,I), I sec. a.C.
3 – Ornavasso (Graue 1974, tav.6.5), seconda metà I sec. a.C.
4 – Porto Recanati (Mercando 1974, tomba 219, n°3, fig.278), fine I sec. a.C. – inizio I sec. d.C.
5 – Cavaillon (Dumoulin 1965, fig.21), età tardo-repubblicana.
6 – Ibiza (Mayet 1975, tav.II,n°8), I sec. a.C.
7 – Ornavasso (Graue 1974, tav.36.6), I sec. a.C.
8 – Cavaillon (Dumoulin 1965, fig.21,0), seconda metà del I sec. a.C.

Variante B (Tav.I,B,1-8) – Bicchieri e urnette caratterizzati da pareti verticali, orlo piccolo e verticale o lievemente estroflesso, fondo piatto, altezza variabile dai 9 ai 12 cm e diametro della bocca dai 6 ai 9 cm. Le misure inoltre possono anche variare in base alle officine ceramiche di provenienza. Si trovano diffusi, in base alle segnalazioni attuali, in Nord Italia, Penisola Iberica, Francia, Austria, Pannonia e Grecia. Cronologicamente si diffondono soprattutto tra la seconda metà del I sec. a.C. e la prima metà del I sec. d.C.

1 – Ibiza (Mayet 1975, tav.X, n°74), età augustea.
2 – Maiorca (Mayet 1975, tav.X, n°72), seconda metà del I sec. a.C.
3 – Cosa (Marabini 1973, forma XI), terzo quarto del I sec. a.C.
4 – Emona (Petru 1972, tav.CXII, tomba 4, n°8), metà I sec. d.C.
5 – Magdalensberg (Schindler Kaudelka 1975, tav.18, 93a), tra il 20 ed il 30 d.C.
6 – Aquileia (Ricci 1984: 258, tav.LXXXII,7), metà I sec. d.C.
7 – Corinto (Hayes 1973, tav.89, n°185), età claudio-neroniana.
8 – Ibiza (Mayet 1975, tav.VII, 58), di cronologia incerta.

Variante C (Tav.I,C,1-10) – Bicchieri ed urnette a corpo globulare, con orlo verticale o estroflesso, spesso variamente sagomato, pareti emisferiche, fondo piatto o con piccolo piede modanato. Essi sono ampiamente attestati in Italia ed Europa centrale e si diffondono soprattutto dalla fine del I sec. a.C. per tutto il I sec. d.C.

1-2 – Ravenna (Maioli 1973: 71-72, figg.31-32), età claudio-neroniana.
3-4 – Ravenna (Maioli 1972: 119, n°11-12), tra la fine del I sec.a.C. alla metà I sec. d.C.
5 – Ornavasso (Bianchetti 1895: 186, tomba 165, tav.XX,10), età augustea.
6 – Ibiza (Mayet 1975, tav.XXVI, 195), età augustea.
7-8 – Sutri (Duncan 1964: 88, fig.7, nn°17,18), tra il 60 ed il 70 d.C.
9 – Torino (Greene 1979: 78-79, fig.33-4), di cronologia incerta.
10 – Ventimiglia (Lamboglia 1950: 123, nn°45-50, fig.97), tra il 29 ed il 90 d.C.

Variante D (Tav.II,D,1-5) – Bicchieri biansati, con orli estroflessi ed a volte modanati, pareti verticali, o carenate o globulari, fondo piatto o, più spesso, piccolo piede modanato. Si diffondono soprattutto in Nord Italia e nella Penisola Iberica nel I sec. d.C. e agli inizi del II sec. d.C.

1 – Cordova (Mayet 1975, tav.III, n°23), I sec. d.C.
2 – Ibiza (Mayet 1975: 58, tav. XXVI, n°200), di cronologia incerta.
3 – Ibiza (Mayet 1975: 33, tav.VIII, n°60), di cronologia incerta.
4 – Cosa (Marabini 1973: 78, 271, tavv.10,61, n°113), età tiberio-claudia.
5 – Pieve del Finale (Pallares 1965: 19, fig.7, n°10), II sec. d.C.

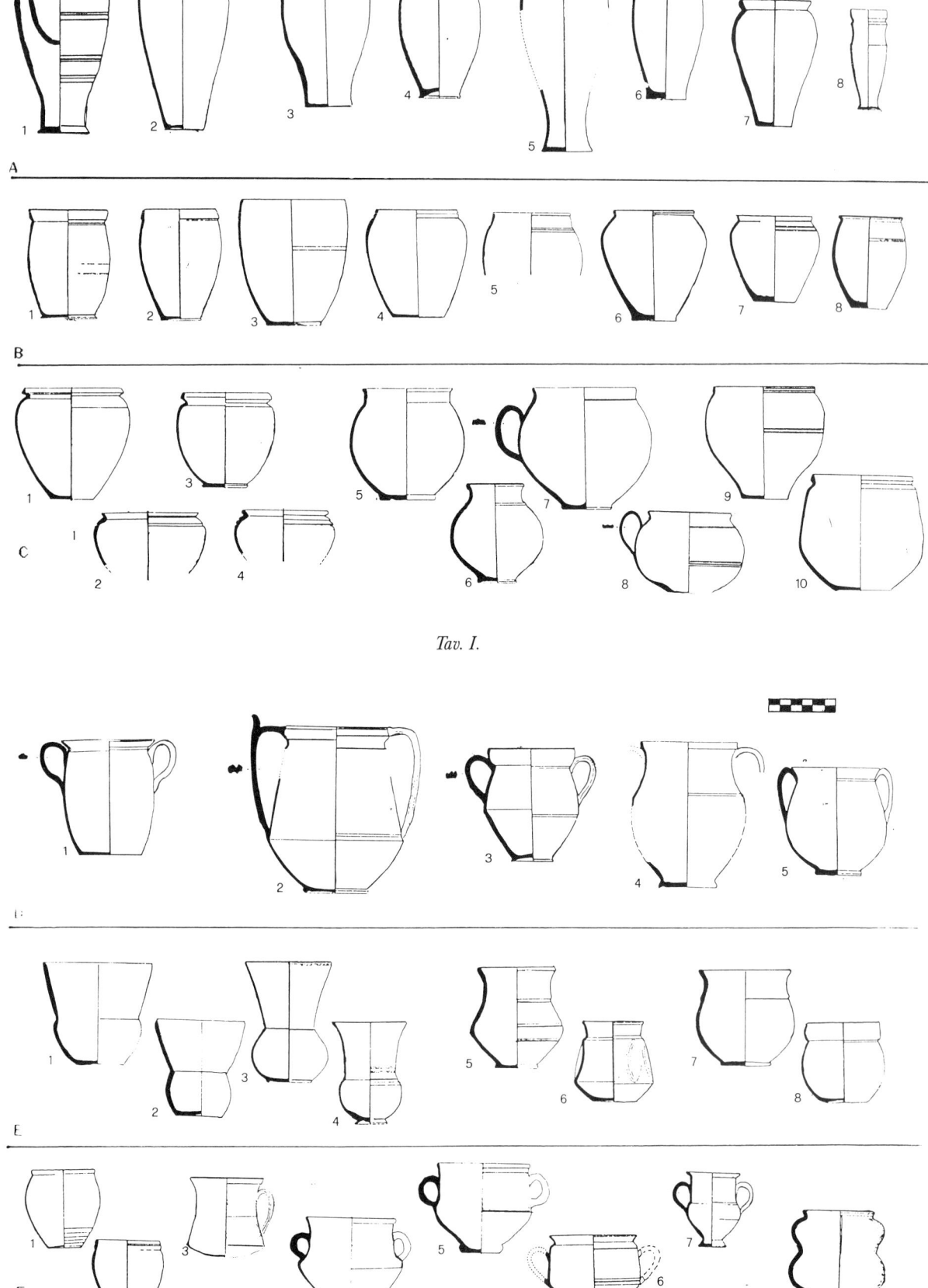

Tav. I.

Tav. II.

Variante E (Tav.II,E,1-8) – Bicchieri di piccole dimensioni, varianti da cm 7,5 a cm 11 in altezza e con diametro della bocca oscillante tra 6 e 10 cm. Sono caratterizzati da un labbro abbastanza alto, generalmente distinto dal corpo, corpo globulare o carenato, fondo piatto o con piccolo piede modanato. Si diffondono, soprattutto tra la seconda metà del I sec. a.C. e l'età augustea, in Nord Italia e nella Penisola Iberica.

1-2 – Gabi (Vegas 1968: 29, figg.10,80), dopo il 70 a.C.
3-4 – Maiorca (Mayet 1975: 40, tav. XII, nn°89,92), fine I sec. a.C. inizio I sec. d.C.
5 – Ornavasso (Graue 1974: 99, tav.69.3), età augustea.
6 – Maiorca (Mayet 1975: 38, tav.XI, n°83), seconda metà del I sec. a.C.
7 – Ornavasso (Graue 1974: 94, tav.41.6), età augustea.
8 – Ibiza (Mayet 1975: 38, tav.VI, n°31), età augustea.

Variante F (Tav.II,F,1-8) – Bicchieri di piccole dimensioni, varianti dai 5 ai 9 cm in altezza e con diametro della bocca oscillante tra i 4 ed i 6 cm. Presentano in genere orlo di piccole dimensioni, verticale o lievemente estroflesso, pareti variamente sagomate, con o senza anse, fondo piatto (figg.1-2), o convesso (fig.3), o piccolo piede sagomato o modanato (figg.4-7). Si diffondono in tutto il bacino Mediterraneo, soprattutto tra l'età augustea e la metà del I sec. d.C.

1 – Magdalensberg (Schindler Kaudelka 1975, tav.15, 77a), età augustea.
2 – Aquileia (Ricci 1984: 259, tav.LXXXII, n°14), età augustea.
3 – *Iuvanum* (Menozzi 1992, forma 2), intorno alla metà del I sec. d.C.
4-5 – Slovenia (Plesnicar-Gec 1983-84: 457, fig.5), di cronologia incerta.
6 – Ibiza (Mayet 1975: 60, tav.XXVIII, n°214), di cronologia incerta.
7 – Cesarea di Palestina (Hayes 1976: 31, n°147), di cronologia incerta.
8 – Bologna (Bergamini 1980, tav.XVI, n°287), da età tardorepubblicana a età giulio-claudia.

Forma Tipo II (Tav. III e IV)

Si tratta di coppette con il diametro della bocca di misura sempre superiore all'altezza del corpo. Se ne individuano in questa sede tre varianti principali, costituite da coppette emisferiche, carenate ed a labbro distinto. Questo tipo si diffonde a partire dall'età augustea in tutto il bacino Mediterraneo, sino a sorpassare e quasi a sostituire il Tipo I. Data l'enorme diffusione di tale tipo e la probabile fabbricazione in numerosi centri esistono numerosissime sottovarianti, tra cui si è cercato di riportare nel seguente catalogo le più attestate e più ricostruibili.

Variante A (Tav.III, A, 1-36) – Coppette a pareti verticali o emisferiche. Le sottovarianti possono avere sia un piccolo orlo verticale, semplice o modanato (figg.1-26), che orlo poco più grande, estroflesso o variamente sagomato. Le pareti emisferiche o verticali, si presentano lisce o con una o più solcature o modanature. Il fondo può presentarsi piatto, o con piccolo o più alto piede modanato. Numerosi sono anche gli esemplari di coppette di tale tipo ansate.

1 – Ravenna (Maioli 1972: 120, n°19), I sec. d.C.
2-3 – Ravenna (Maioli 1972: 119, nn°1-2), seconda metà del I sec. a.C.
4 – Magdalensberg (Schindler Kaudelka 1975, tav.16, forma 80a-b), dalla metà del I sec. d.C. fino ad età adrianea.
5 – Budrio (Silvestri 1971: 39, fig.12), di cronologia incerta.
6-7 – Maiorca (Mayet 1975: 62, tav.XXIX, n°220), età tiberio-claudia.
8 – Torino (Greene 1979: 78, fig.33.2), età augusteo-tiberiana.
9 – Ravenna (Maioli 1972: 122, n°44), I sec. d.C.
10 – Ornavasso (Greene 1979: 99, fig.24.5), I sec. d.C.
11-12– Mahon ed Ibiza (Mayet 1975: 67, tav.XXXIII, figg.256,258), età augusteo-tiberiana.
13 – Cosa (Marabini 1973, pl.45, n°419).
14 – Sidi Khrebish Bengazi (Kenrick 1985, fig.59, n°475), di cronologia incerta.
15 – Emona (Petru 1972, tav.XVII, tomba 121, n°27), prima metà del I sec. d.C.
16-17– Ravenna (Maioli 1972: 119, 121, nn°7,26), dalla metà del I sec. d.C.
18 – Emona (Plesnicar-Gec 1972, tomba 105, tav.27, n°6), età augusteo-tiberiana.
19 – Ornavasso (Graue 1974: 251, tav.57, n°4), età augustea.
20 – Ravenna (Maioli 1973: 67, n°21), seconda metà del I sec. d.C.
21 – Aquileia (Ricci 1984: 298-299, tav.XCVI, 4), I sec. d.C.
22 – Ravenna (Maioli 1972: 121, n°31), seconda metà del I sec. d.C.
23 – Ampurias (Almagro 1955: 35, fig.13, nn°2, 2a), dalla metà del I sec. d.C.
24-26–Ravenna (Maioli 1972: 121, nn°32-34), seconda metà del I sec. d.C.
27 – Orvieto (Hayes 1976: 80, fig.9,n°142), di cronologia incerta.
28 – Maiorca (Mayet 1975: 64, tav.XXIX, n°230), di cronologia incerta.

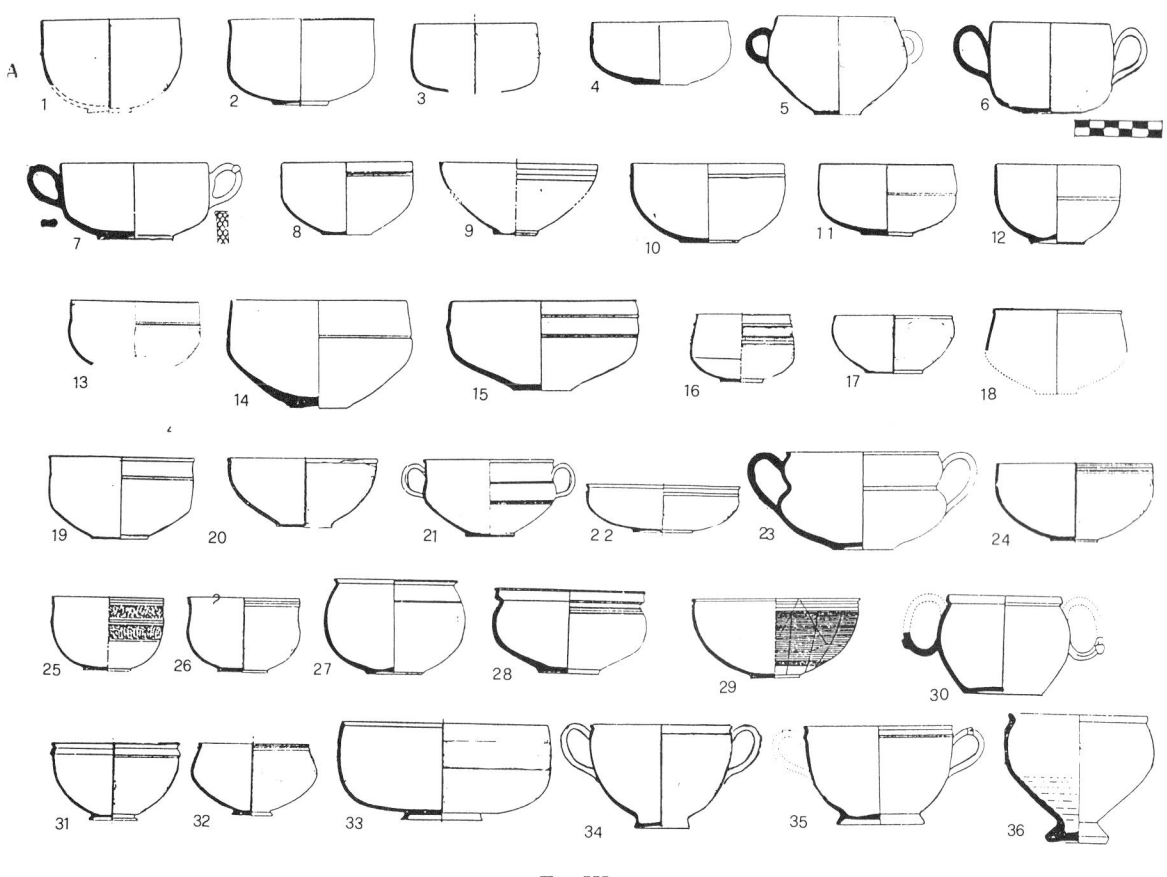

Tav. III.

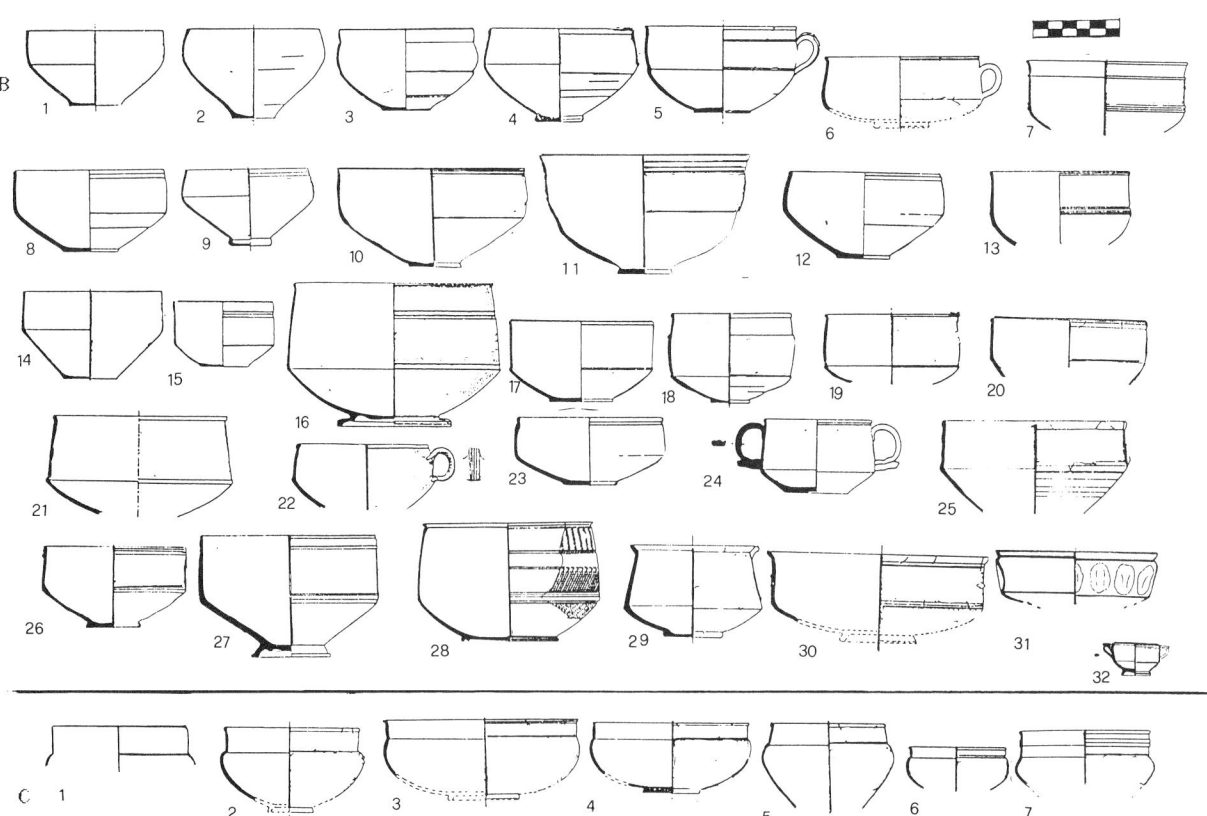

Tav. IV.

29 - Ravenna (Maioli 1972: 121,fig.30), metà del I sec. d.C.
30 - Ibiza (Mayet 1975: 34, tav.XIII, n°64), età augustea.
31-33- Ravenna (Maioli 1972: 120-122, nn°17,35,38), seconda metà del I sec. d.C.
34-35- Cosa (Marabini 1973, forma XLI), età augustea.
36 - Sidi Khrebish Bengazi (Kenrick 1985, fig.59, n°466), di cronologia incerta.

Variante B (Tav.IV,B,1-32) – Coppette carenate, ampiamente attestate e diffuse in tutto il bacino Mediterraneo soprattutto nel I sec. d.C. Le sottovarianti presentano sia orlo verticale, semplice o sottolineato da una o più solcature o modanature, che piccolo orlo estroflesso. Le parti sono carenate, con la carenatura liscia o segnata da uno o più solchi. Il fondo è generalmente piatto o con piede modanato. Numerosissime sono le sottovarianti di questo tipo.

1-2 - Ravenna (Maioli 1972: 122, nn°46,49), fine del I sec. inizi del II sec. d.C.
3 - Emona (Pleniscar-Gec 1972, tav.XCIX, tomba 373, n°18), I sec. d.C.
4 - Ravenna (Maioli 1972: 122, n°48), fine I sec. inizi II sec. d.C.
5 - Ravenna (Maioli 1972: 122, n°45), I sec. d.C.
6 - Ravenna (Maioli 1972: 120, n°21), metà I sec. d.C.
7 - Ravenna (Maioli 1972: 119, n°4), età augustea.
8 - Ornavasso (Graue 1974: 100, fig.23.9), età augusteo-tiberiana.
9 - Ravenna (Maioli 1972: 122, n°47), fine I sec. d.C.-inizi II sec. d.C.
10 - *Iuvanum* (Menozzi 1992, forma 3, variante C), età neroniana.
11 - Aquileia (Maselli Scotti 1984: 276, fig.7), I sec. d.C.
12 - Ornavasso (Graue 1974: 100, fig.23.8), I sec. d.C.-inizi II sec. d.C.
13 - Vindonissa (Greene 1979, fig 5, n°13),40-70 d.C.
14 - Ravenna (Maioli 1972: 122, n°50), fine I sec. d.C.-inizi II sec. d.C.
15 - *Iuvanum* (Menozzi 1992, forma 3, variante E), I sec. d.C.
16 - Villa Potenza (Mercando 1971: 410, fig.12, n°4), da età tiberiana a tutto il I sec. d.C.
17 - *Iuvanum* (Menozzi 1992, forma 3, variante E), I sec. d.C.
18-19- Ravenna (Maioli 1972: 119, nn°3,5), età augustea.
20 - *Iuvanum* (Menozzi 1992, forma 3, variante D), da età tiberiana a tutto il I sec. d.C.
21 - Ravenna (Maioli 1972: 119, n°6), prima metà del I sec. d.C.
22 - Villa Potenza (Mercando 1971: 410, nn°1-2), I sec. d.C.
23 - Ornavasso (Graue 1974: 100, fig.23.7), età augusteo-tiberiana.
24 - Lisbona (Mayet 1975, tav.XXVII, n°218), I sec. d.C.
25 - Ravenna (Maioli 1972: 120, n°16), seconda metà del I sec. a.C.
26 - *Iuvanum* (Menozzi 1992, forma 3, variante C), seconda metà I sec. d.C.
27 - Emona (Petru 1972, tomba 803, tav.LIII, n°19), I sec. d.C.
28 - Luni (Cavalieri Manasse 1973, tav.60, n°10), I sec. d.C.
29-30- Ravenna (Maioli 1972: 120-121, nn°24,27), seconda metà del I sec. d.C.
31 - Ravenna (Maioli 1972: 119, n°10), età augustea.
32 - Provenienza indeterminata (Hayes 1976, fig.9, n°141), I sec. d.C.

Variante C (Tav.IV,C,1-7) – Ciotole a labbro distinto, caratterizzate da alto labbro verticale, distinto dalle pareti, pareti emisferiche, fondo con piccolo piede modanato. La forma è molto diffusa in area Adriatica, ed ampiamente attestata nel Ravennate. Cronologicamente questa forma ebbe il periodo di massima diffusione nella seconda metà del I sec. d.C., mentre le prime attestazioni sono di età augustea.

1 - *Iuvanum* (Menozzi 1992, forma 4, variante A), seconda metà del I sec. d.C.
2-3 - Ravenna (Maioli 1972: 120, nn°20-21), seconda metà del I sec. d.C.
4 - *Iuvanum* (Menozzi 1992, forma 4, variante B), seconda metà del I sec. d.C.
5 - Ravenna (Maioli 1972: 120, n°15), seconda metà del I sec. d.C.
6 - Ravenna (Maioli 1972: 119, n°8), età augustea.
7 - Ravenna (Maioli 1972: 121, n°25), seconda metà del I sec. d.C.

Catalogo delle Decorazioni

Le principali decorazioni attestate nella ceramica a pareti sottili grigie sono riportate nelle Tavole V e VI e catalogate in base al tipo di decorazione, con specificata la loro cronologia e provenienza. I quattro principali tipi di decorazione attestati sono: A- rotellatura, B- incisioni, C- impressioni, D- decorazioni alla barbotine.

Rotellature (Tav.V,A, 1-15)

Questo tipo di decorazione è abbastanza diffuso nella ceramica a Pareti sottili grigie ed è ampiamente attestato in numerosissimi siti in tutto il bacino Mediterraneo. Cronologicamente la sua diffusione inizia con l'età augustea, divenendo il tipo di decorazione più diffusa con il I e II sec. d.C. I vari tipi di decorazione a rotella

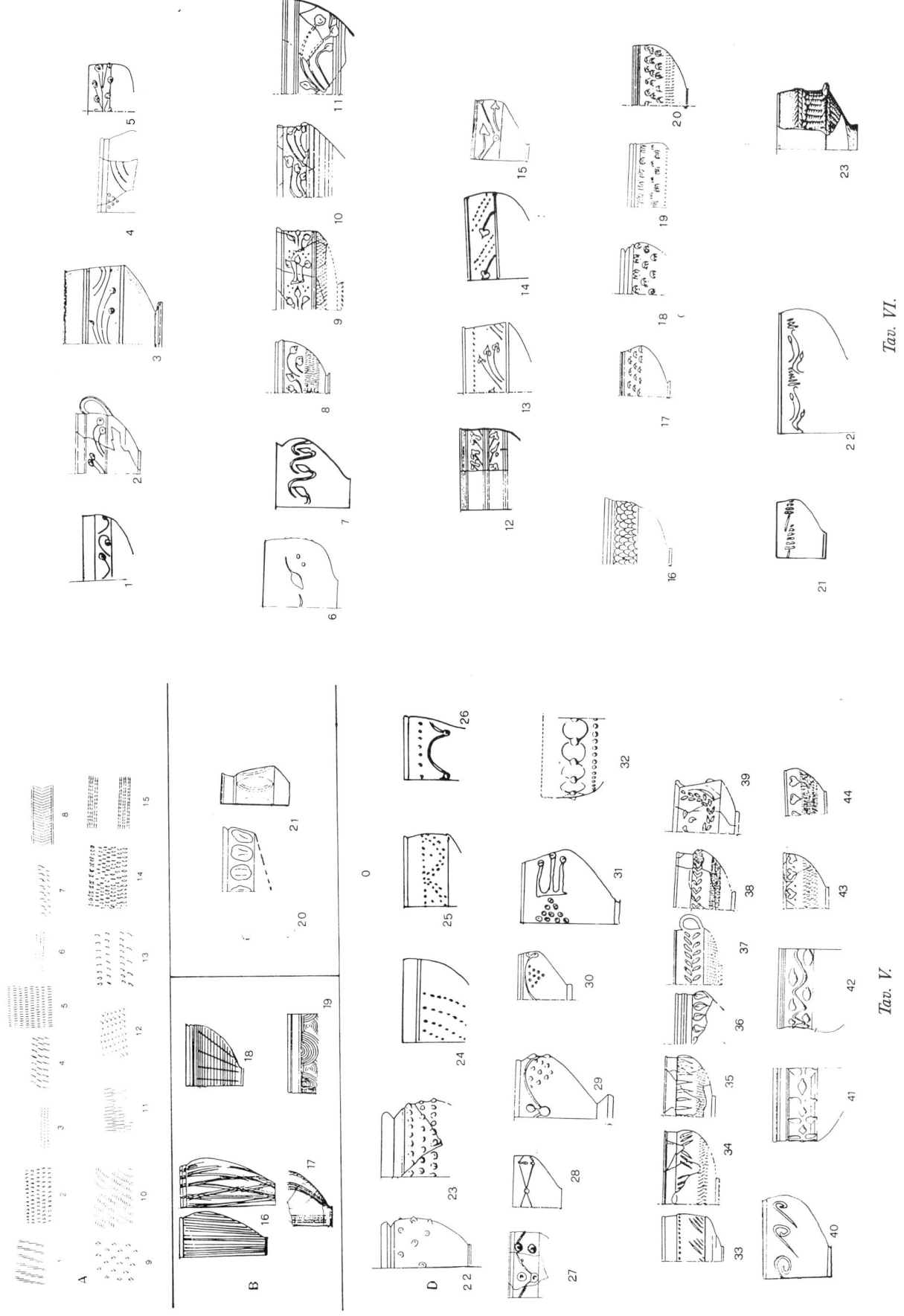

riportate sono tratte dalla catalogazione delle decorazioni della ceramica a Pareti sottili, effettuata da Ricci, nell'Atlante delle forme ceramiche (1984: 316-318, tav.CII, figg.1-16). Nella ceramica a Pareti sottili grigie si trovano spesso associati vari tipi di decorazione a rotella, oppure le rotellature con altri tipi di decorazione, come barbotine o impressioni.

Incisioni (Tav.V,B, 16-19)

Sono costituite da fitte incisioni, che creano vari tipi di decorazione. Più attestate sono le incisioni costituite da linee verticali o orizzontali (figg.16-18) su tutto il corpo del recipiente. Più rara è invece la decorazione ad incisione rinvenuta a Creta, consistente in fitti cerchi concentrici di varie dimensioni. Le decorazioni ad incisione, non molto diffuse nella ceramica a Pareti sottili grigie, sono attestate dall'ultimo quarto del I sec. a.C. al primo quarto del I sec. d.C.

Tav.V,B.
16 – Ravenna (Maioli 1972: 121-122, nn°36,41).
17 – Bologna (Bergamini 1980, tav.XVI, n°288).
18 – *Iuvanum* (Menozzi 1992, decorazione su forma 1, variante A).
19 – Creta (Sackett 1992: 167, tav.165, n°18).

Impressioni (Tav.V,C, 20-21)

Sono poco diffuse nella ceramica a pareti sottili grigie e cronologicamente attestate dalla metà del I sec. d.C. Due sono le varianti impiegate per questo tipo di ceramica, le impressioni di forma minore, o ditate (fig.20), e quelle di misura maggiore, poste a coprire tutta la superficie del vaso (fig.21).

Tav.V,C.
20 – Ravenna (Maioli 1972: 119, n°10).
21 – Maiorca (Mayet 1975, tav.XI, n°83).

Barbotine (Tav.V,D, 22-44, Tav.VI, 1-22)

La barbotine è senz'altro il tipo di decorazione più attestata in questo tipo di ceramica, specie durante il I sec. d.C. I motivi decorativi sono vari, dalle semplici mammillonature e puntini a rilievo (figg.22-24), di età claudio-neroniana, ai festoni tipici d'età augustea (figg.25-26), ai motivi geometrici e stilizzati (figg.27-31,40-42), attestati dalla seconda metà del I sec. d.C., alle bacellature (figg.35-36), attestate a partire dall'età di Claudio. Tra le decorazioni alla barbotine più antiche, attestate a Ravenna, compaiono i piccoli triangoli formati da linee decrescenti poste obliquamente (Tav.V, fig.33) e le rosette (Tav.VI, fig.5), databili alla prima metà del I sec. d.C. Dalla seconda metà del I sec. d.C. si afferma inoltre una decorazione caratterizzata da piccole foglie disposte in vario modo (figg.34,36-39). Tra i temi vegetali sono molto diffusi i petali formati da mammillature e da sottili steli (Tav.VI, figg.1-4), attestati dalla metà del I sec. d.C. Tipiche dell'età flavia sono le foglie d'acqua lanceolate, disposte variamente (Tav.VI, figg.6-11). I petali cuoriformi invece (Tav.VI, figg.12-15) si diffondono intorno alla metà del I sec. d.C. La decorazione a barbotine più ampiamente attestata è costituita da piatte scaglie con nervature verticali (Tav.VI, figg.17-20), inquadrabile cronologicamente dall'età tiberiana a tutto il I sec. d.C., ed in special modo in età neroniana e flavia, e spesso associata a rotellature. Meno attestate invece sono le scaglie più rilevate (Tav.VI, fig.16) e le foglie di felce, o palmette, (Tav.VI, figg.21-22), databili alla seconda metà del I sec. d.C. Un singolare e raro tipo di decorazione si trova su una coppa carenata proveniente da Bologna (Tav.VI, fig.23) e riproduce la lavorazione intrecciata del vimini, delimitata da un motivo a treccia, databile intorno alla metà del I sec. d.C.

Tav,V,D.
22 – Ravenna (Maioli 1973: 71-72, figg.31-32).
23 – Sidi Khrebish Bengazi (Kenrick 1985, fig.59, n°467).
24 – Bologna (Bergamini 1980, tav.XLVII, n°1087).
25-26 – Ravenna (Maioli 1972: 119, nn°5,8).
27 – *Iuvanum* (Menozzi 1992, decorazione su forma 3, variante D).
28 – Ravenna (Maioli 1972: 122, n°49).
29 – Sidi Khrebish Bengazi (Kenrick 1985, fig.59, n°466).
30 – Ravenna (Maioli 1972: 122, n°47).
31 – Budrio (Silvestri 1971: 39, fig.12).
32 – Creta (Sackett 1992: 167, tav.164, n°9).
33-34 – Ravenna (Maioli 1972: 119-120, nn°3,20).
35 – *Iuvanum* (Menozzi 1992, decorazione su forma 4, variante B).
36-39 – Ravenna (Maioli 1972: 120-121, nn°15, 23, 25, 27).
40 – Emona (Plesnicar-Gec 1983-84: 461, fig.8).
41-42 – Creta (Sackett 1992: 167, tav.164, nn°10-12).
43-44 – Ravenna (Maioli 1972: 120-121, nn°22, 26).

Tav.VI,D.
1 – Bologna (Bergamini 1980, tav.XVI, n°284).
2-3 – Porto Recanati (Mercando 1971: 410-411, fig.12.1-2).
4 – *Iuvanum* (Menozzi 1992, decorazione su forma 3, variante D).
5 – Ravenna (Maioli 1972: 119, n°2).
6 – Cosa (Marabini 1973, pl.45, nn°420-421).
7 – Emona (Plesnicar-Gec 1983-84: 461, fig.8).
8-11 – Ravenna (Maioli 1972: 120-121, nn°16, 17, 24, 28).
12 – Luni (Chiaramonte Trere 1977, tav.245, n°23).
13 – Ravenna (Maioli 1972: 119, n°6).
14 – Emona (Plesnicar-Gec 1983-84: 461, fig.7).

15-16- Aquileia (Miotti 1987: 276-277, figg.7-8).
17-18- Ravenna (Maioli 1972: 119, 121, nn°11, 34, 35).
19-20- *Iuvanum* (Menozzi 1992, decorazione forma 3, variante C).
21-22- Emona (Plesnicar-Gec 1983-84: 457, fig.5).
23 -Bologna (Bergamini 1980, tav.XVI, n°286).

Bibliografia

Almagro, M. 1953. *Las Necropolis de Ampurias, I*, (Monografias Ampunitanas, 3), Barcellona.
Almagro, M. 1955. *Las Necropolis de Ampurias, II*, (Monografias Ampunitanas, 3), Barcellona.
Andrén, A. 1961. *Scavi e scoperte sulla necropoli di Ardea*, Opuscula Romana, III.
Bergamini, M. 1980. *Centuriatio di Bologna*, Roma.
Bianchetti, E. 1895. *I sepolcreti di Ornavasso*, Atti della Società di Archeologia e Belle Arti per la Provincia di Torino, IV.
Bonis, E. 1942. *Die kaiserzeitliche Keramik von Pannonien*, (Diss. Pann. Ser., II, 420).
Buora, M. 1987. 'Scarti di fabbrica di fornaci Aquileiensi', *Aquileia Chiama*, XXXIV.
Cavalieri Manasse, G. 1973. 'La ceramica a pareti sottili', in *Scavi di Luni I*, Roma.
Chiaramonte Trere, C. 1977. 'La ceramica a pareti sottili', in *Scavi di Luni II*, Roma.
Dumoulin, A. 1965. 'Puits et fosses de la colline Saint Jacques à Cavaillon', *Gallia*, 23.
Duncan, G. 1964. 'A Roman Pottery near Sutri', *Papers of the British School at Rome*, 32, n.s.19.
Egger, R. 1955, 1956, 1958, 1959, 1961. 'Die Ausgrabungen auf dem Magdalensberg', *Carinthia* I, 145; I, 146; I, 148; I, 149; I, 151.
Ettlinger, E. & Simonett, C. 1952. *Romische Keramik aus dem Schutthugel von Vindonissa*, Basel.
Granier, J. 1965. 'Trouvailles fortuites et "glanes" archeologiques sur le litoral Gardois', *Rivista di Studi Liguri*, XXXI.
Graue, J. 1974. *Die Gräberfelder von Ornavasso*, Hamburg.
Greene, K. 1979. *The Pre-flavian Fine Wares. Reports on the Excavation at Usk 1965-1976*, Cardiff.
Gillam, J. 1957. *Types of Roman Coarse Pottery Vessels in Northern Britain*, Newcastle.
Griffiths, K. 1987-88. 'The Roman pottery from Nadin-Gradina, Dalmatia, Yugoslavia', *Rei Cretariae Romanae Fautores Acta*, XXIX-XXX.
Hayes, J.W. 1973. 'Roman Pottery from the South Stoà at Corinth', *Hesperia*, 42.
Hayes, J.W. 1976. *Roman Pottery in the Royal Ontario Museum*, Toronto.
Kenrick, C. 1985. *Excavations at Sidi Khrebish Bengazi (Berenice), III, Part I*, Tripoli.
Lamboglia, N. 1939. 'Nuovi scavi nella necropoli di Albintimilium', *Rivista Ingauna e Intemelia*, 4.
Lamboglia, N. 1947. 'Gli scavi della zona paleocristiana di S.Calogero (Albenga)', *Rivista di Studi Liguri*, XIII, 1947.
Lamboglia, N. 1950. *Gli scavi di Albintimilium e la cronologia della ceramica romana*, Bordighera.
Loeschcke, S. 1909. 'Keramikfunde in Haltern', *Altertumskommission für Westfalen, Mitteilungen*, V.
Maioli, M.G. 1972. 'Vasi a pareti sottili grigie del Ravennate', *Rei Cretariae Romanae Fautores Acta*, XIV-XV.
Maioli, M.G. 1973. 'Ceramica a pareti sottili del Ravennate', *Studi Romana*, XXIV.
Marabini Moevs, M. 1973. 'The Roman thin walled pottery from Cosa (1948-1954)', *MAAR*, XXXII.
Maselli Scotti, F. 1984. 'La ceramica ad Aquileia. Il vasellame da mensa', *Antichità Altoadriatiche*, XXIV, Udine.
Mayet, F. 1975. *Les ceramiques à parois fines dans la péninsule Ibérique*, Paris.
Menozzi, O. 1992, c.s. 'La ceramica a pareti sottili grigie a Iuvanum', *Iuvanum: II Convegno di Studi*, Marzo-Aprile 1992.
Mercando, L. 1971. 'Villa Potenza', *Notizie degli Scavi di Antichità*, XXV.
Mercando, L. 1974. 'La necropoli di Porto Recanati', *Notizie degli Scavi di Antichità*, XXVIII.
Miotti, T. 1987. 'I sette castra di Paolo Diacono', *Castelli del Friuli VII*, Pordenone.
Mosca, E. 1962. 'Scavi del luglio 1960 e 1961, nella necropoli di Pollenzo', *Bollettino della Società di Studi Storici, Archeologici ed Architettonici della Provincia di Cuneo*.
Mosca, E. 1968. 'Note archeologiche Pollentine', *Rivista di Studi Liguri*, XXIV.
Pallarés, F. 1965. 'La necropoli romana della Pieve del Finale', *Rivista Ingauna e Intemelia*, n.s.XX,nn.1-3.
Petru, S. 1972. *Emonske Nekropole*, Ljubljana.
Plesnicar-Gec, L. 1972. *Severno Emonsku Grobisce. The Northern Nekropolis of Emona*, Ljubljana.
Plesnicar-Gec, L. 1983-84. 'Thin walled pottery from Slovenia', *Rei Cretariae Romanae Fautores Acta*, XXV-XXVI.
Ricci, A. 1984. 'Ceramica a pareti sottili', *Enciclopedia dell'Arte Antica - Atlante delle Forme Ceramiche II*, Roma.
Riccioni, G. 1970. 'Un complesso edilizio di età romana scoperto a Rimini nell'area dell'ex vescovado, Relazione topografica preliminare', *Atti Mem. Bologna*, XX.
Robinson, H. 1959. *The Athenian Agora, V. Pottery of the Roman Period. Chronology*, Princeton.
Rolland, M. 1946. *Fouilles de Glanum*, (Gallia, I suppl.).
Sackett, L. 1992. *Knossos from Greek City to Roman Colony. Excavation at the Unexplored Mansion II*, Oxford.
Schindler Kaudelka, E. 1975. *Die dunnwandige Gebrauchskeramik vom Magdalensberg*, Klagenfurt.
Silvestri, E. 1971. 'Budrio. Accertamenti archeologici nel territorio centuriato', *Notizie degli Scavi di Antichità*, XXV, I.
Ulrich, R. 1914. 'Die Gräberfelder in der Umgebung von Bellinzona', in K.T. Tessin, *Katalog des Schweiz Laudesmuseums*, Zurich.
Vegas, M. 1968. 'Römische Keramik von Gabii', *Bonner Jahrbucher*, 168.
Zuffa, M. 1962. 'Nuove scoperte di archeologia e storia Riminese', *Studi Romana*, XIII.

61

La Ceramica Comune nei Siti dell'Italia Settentrionale dall'Età Tardo Antica al Medioevo: Variazioni Tipologiche e Funzionali del Corredo Domestico

L. MAFFEIS, M. M. NEGRO PONZI MANCINI

(Università di Torino)

Sommario: *Il lavoro di analisi condotto sulla ceramica di Trino-S.Michele (Vercelli, Italia) ha permesso la classificazione sistematica della ceramica comune di un sito occupato dall'età romana al medioevo, considerando contestualmente la composizione mineralogica, la tecnologia di produzione e le varianti morfologiche di ciascuna fase. La correlazione dei tipi forma/impasto, con dimensioni diverse in età romana e nel medioevo e la distinzione tra vasellame da fuoco e vasellame per conservazione e consumo del cibo, ha permesso confronti tra i recipienti e i cibi cucinati in basi ai risultati delle analisi archeozoologiche e palinologiche nei diversi siti, in periodi caratterizzati da clima e organizzazione economica diversi, compresi alcuni scavi di riferimento della Francia meridionale. Inoltre, il confronto tra la ceramica comune rinvenuta negli scavi e quella rappresentata nelle rare fonti iconografiche coeve permette di collegare le variazioni del corredo ceramico dell'area padana e alpina altomedievale e medievale alle variazioni d'uso di presentazione in tavola e di consumo del cibo.*

1. INTRODUZIONE

L'aumento in anni recenti di scavi sistematici in siti con fasi sia tardo antiche che altomedievali ha messo costantemente in evidenza un'ampia varietà di forme e di impasti ceramici nel periodo più antico e una forte riduzione nel periodo più recente, fino ad una dominante prevalenza di forme chiuse con rare forme forme aperte polifunzionali, i c.d. bacini-coperchio. Le forme ceramiche altomedievali conservano fino al VI secolo tipologie e tecniche di produzione precedenti, anche se parzialmente modificate; le tipologie medievali a forma chiusa appaiono nell'alto medioevo e sono quasi esclusive dal X al XII secolo, quando inizia, con tempi diversi nelle diverse aree, una nuova diversificazione delle tipologie ceramiche domestiche.

La brusca diminuzione di varietà formale del corredo domestico altomedievale è stata posta in relazione con la caduta di distribuzione commerciale ad ampio raggio delle produzioni accentrate tardo antiche (ceramiche fini) e con variazioni di scelta e consumo del cibo (scomparsa delle forme da tavola per uso individuale, modifiche delle regole sociali di organizzazione del pasto). Le osservazioni, però, sono state basate in prevalenza sulla scomparsa di determinate tipologie legate al commercio mediterraneo e sul confronto tra siti diversi, ciascuno dei quali caratterizzato in genere soltanto da alcune fasi e spesso anche da situazioni socio-economiche diverse. Le tipologie di vasellame funzionale destinato alla preparazione e al consumo del cibo sono invece strettamente dipendenti dalle risorse disponibili per le diverse classi sociali in ciascuna area e in ciascun periodo e quindi dal tipo di alimentazione da esse derivato: la persistenza tipologica delle forme ceramiche e delle caratteristiche produttive è quindi strettamente collegata alle caratteristiche ambientali ed alla continuità di risorse commerciali dei diversi siti, suscettibili di variazioni secondo fattori sia climatici che politici.

Nel sito di S.Michele di Trino, localizzato nella pianura piemontese sulla sponda sinistra del Po, è stata accertata una continuità di insediamento, realizzata con alternanza di fasi differenziate nella planimetria e nelle funzioni, che ha permesso un'analisi sistematica del materiale ceramico d'uso comune dall'età romana al XIII secolo (Negro Ponzi *et al.* 1989; Negro Ponzi 1992; Joris 1992). Ricerche geologiche, palinologiche e zooarcheologiche, affiancate sistematicamente allo scavo (Negro Ponzi *et al.* 1991) hanno permesso di definire per questo sito un quadro diacronico dettagliato, tipico dell'area padana occidentale per forma di insediamento ed organizzazione economica, con una lenta evoluzione di produzioni ceramiche locali, nelle quali si può tentare un'analisi del rapporto dei fattori sociali e alimentari con la caratterizzazione del materiale d'uso comune e dell'impatto delle fasi critiche ambientali e politiche sull'evoluzione tipologica ceramica.

2. Clima e ambiente

I dati palinologici e ambientali indicano per la pianura padana orientale, e ora anche per quella occidentale, episodi ripetuti di piogge ed esondazioni tra il II sec.a.C. e I sec.d.C. Nell'ultimo periodo preromano e nel primo periodo imperiale, il clima dell'area prealpina era relativamente umido, non particolarmente favorevole allo sviluppo della cerealicoltura. Nel tardo antico invece le fasce di pianura lungo il corso dei fiumi presentano un clima caratterizzato da ambiente caldo e talora umido, caratterizzato nell'area piemontese e ligure da querceto misto, con frassino, carpino e ontano (Castiglioni *et al.* 1992: 355-356): un paesaggio non di fitta foresta, ma di bosco alternato a radure e prati. A partire dal tardo IV-V secolo e fino al VII, la zona alpina, estesa sia alla pianura padana che alla bassa valle del Rodano, presenta un clima umido e freddo, caratterizzato da piogge e da straripamento frequente dei fiumi, a cui seguì tra VIII e XII secolo un periodo di *optimum* climatico, il c.d. WMP ('Warm Medieval Period'), nel quale si sviluppa e si afferma un nuovo modello economico (Duby 1978: 3-38). Tra IX e X secolo l'area alpina è caratterizzata da un equilibrio diffuso tra attività agricola, allevamento per consumo alimentare e sfruttamento del bosco, con importanza variabile tra le diverse componenti, ma senza che in nessun caso una di esse prevalesse nettamente sulle altre (Montanari 1979: 19-21). Nell'alto medioevo la cerealicoltura appare basata su specie diverse e affiancata dall'orto e dalla vigna; dopo il Mille, invece, si afferma progressivamente una prevalenza dell'agricoltura, e in particolare della coltura dei cereali, che con l'estensione delle terre coltivate e l'introduzione di nuove specie (i grani primaverili accanto a quelli invernali), nuovi strumenti e nuovi metodi (forme perfezionate di rotazione) passa da coltura di sussistenza a coltura dominante e fonte principale di alimentazione (Montanari 1980: 79-97). La riduzione progressiva delle terre disponibili per il pascolo coincide con una riduzione progressiva dell'allevamento e quindi con mutamenti delle risorse disponibili e una caratterizzazione crescente del regime alimentare secondo le diverse condizioni sociali ed economiche. Nello stesso tempo la scarsa resa agricola, insufficiente ai bisogni accresciuti di una popolazione in forte aumento, amplifica gli effetti delle annate anomale e moltiplica gli episodi di carestia. A partire dal XIV-XV secolo le fonti documentano l'inizio di un diverso ciclo, caratterizzato insieme da un nuovo peggioramento climatico (la c.d. `piccola età glaciale') e da nuovi sviluppi tecnologici e produttivi (Slicher Van Bath 1966: 399-425).

Sia i dati delle fonti (come l'inventario della corte regia di Annapes dell'inizio IX secolo in Francia o il polittico di S.Giulia di Brescia, nel Nord Italia, degli inizi del X secolo) che le analisi paleobotaniche disponibili segnalano nell'alto medioevo la dominanza della segale (Montanari 1979: 109-127), non come ripiego dovuto al peggioramento del clima, e alla diminuzione della popolazione rurale, come si è a lungo pensato, ma come continuazione di una tradizione forse ininterrotta nell'area (Castelletti 1974-1975; Castelletti 1976). Alla segale si affiancavano il frumento e, in percentuale variabile tra la Padania orientale e occidentale, l'orzo; in Francia appare importante anche la presenza della spelta, poco diffusa in Italia (Nada Patrone 1981: 72), come ormai il farro, che era stato invece importante in età romana; in Lombardia e Piemonte (novarese e vercellese) era largamente coltivato il panico, mentre il miglio era diffuso in tutta l'area padana (Nada Patrone 1981: 67-68). Tutti i cereali erano consumati prevalentemente come farina per polente semiliquide, il *pulmentum*, il cibo di base delle classi dipendenti, direttamente derivato da un cibo analogo di età romana, la *puls* (Muffatti Musselli 1988). A questi grani 'minuti' erano associati i legumi (Montanari 1979: 150-165), coltivati in campo come colture primaverili e consumati sia freschi con erbe aromatiche e salse, secondo l'uso già diffuso in età romana, sia ridotti a farina: in particolare era usata la farina di fave, mescolata a quella di frumento (Nada Patrone 1981: 129-130). A S. Michele di Trino la fava è attestata nella fase di X-XI secolo (Nisbet, in Negro Ponzi *et al.* 1989) insieme al pisello, poco utilizzato nell'alto medioevo, ma diffuso invece in seguito; altrove erano usati anche ceci, vecce e fagioli. Un'importanza particolare avevano nell'alimentazione del medioevo anche gli ortaggi (Montanari 1979: 309-371) che non erano soggetti a prelievo da parte dei proprietari, a differenza dei cereali e dei legumi; normalmente gli ortaggi erano coltivati presso le abitazioni in orti accuratamente concimati, mentre era invece coltivata nei campi la rapa, che per la facile coltivazione e conservazione era un cibo importante per i ceti poveri nei mesi invernali, come le castagne, per lo più usate in farina, ma anche bollite, fritte o arrostite. Il castagneto, sfruttato sia per il legname che per la raccolta dei frutti, era diffuso prevalentemente sui rilievi, ed è infatti scarsamente rappresentato a Trino, mentre nella pianura continuava a prevalere il querceto, associato all'allevamento dei suini allo stato brado.

Il vasellame domestico, nel quadro di questo tipo di alimentazione, era utilizzato sia per la cottura dei cibi (paioli per i *pulmenta*, vasi da fuoco per le carni e le verdure) che per la conservazione, non solo di lardo e strutto, condimenti quasi esclusivi nell'area padana, ma anche per composti preparati in anticipo e conservati per l'inverno e per salse con erbe aromatiche e spezie, che accompagnavano la carne lessata o in umido. L'uso di abbondanti quantità di spezie era già diffuso in età romana, e nell'alto Medioevo è specificamente attestato, ad esempio, in un testo di dietetica della prima metà del VI secolo (Anthimus, in ed. Teubner 1877: 7-22), che ricorda una salsa speziata con vino, da aggiungere alla carne cotta in agrodolce, in aceto e miele, con ortaggi e radici; lo stesso trattato ricorda come cibi diffusi cereali, legumi, frutta e il latte con i suoi derivati. La persistenza della tradizione romana appare con chiarezza dal confronto delle fonti romane, come il manuale di Apicio, con quelle altomedievali e con i ricettari medievali, attestati dalla fine XIII-XIV secolo (Flandrin & Redon 1981), che conservano ingredienti e tecniche di cottura sostanzialmente immutati dall'antichità.

3. Vasellame da tavola
nelle fonti archeologiche

La ricerca considera alcuni complessi di vasellame domestico particolarmente rappresentativi del materiale altomedievale e medievale di area padana, derivati dall'esame di un'ampia serie di siti dell'Italia settentrionale con fasi comprese tra il V-VI e l'XI-XII secolo e con caratteristiche insediative simili a quelle di S.Michele di Trino: per il tardo antico Zignago e Savignone in Liguria, Terno d'Isola, Lomello, Monte Barro e Manerba in Lombardia – oltre ai siti urbani di Castelseprio e di Brescia, Via A.Mario – e per il Medioevo i castelli di Manzano (Piemonte), Filattiera (Lunigiana), Piadena (Lombardia) e Rocca di Rivoli (Veneto); sono inoltre stati selezionati, dopo un analogo esame, alcuni siti di confronto dell'area francese sud-occidentale: in particolare un sito altomedievale (Hyères-sur-Amby in Delfinato, nella fase del VI-VIII secolo) e tre siti medievali, due dei quali (Colletières e Huez nel Delfinato, XI secolo) di carattere produttivo non fortificato e uno coevo con caratteristiche di fortificazione (Cucuron in Provenza). In tutti i casi si tratta di siti con esigenze funzionali e generali simili, dove quindi le possibili variazioni diacroniche di alimentazione dovevano dipendere da differenze climatiche o di organizzazione produttiva intervenute tra le differenti fasi.

I dati disponibili in base alle analisi polliniche e ai ritrovamenti di resti vegetali, semi e ossa animali, indicano che in tutti i siti la componente dell'allevamento, è sempre presente accanto a quella agricola nell'alimentazione degli abitanti tra il VI e il XII secolo e che essa era normalmente rappresentata da animali giovani, allevati e macellati per il consumo alimentare, anche se con percentuali diverse delle specie nei differenti siti. In Liguria nel sito di Zignago (XI-XII secolo) sono prevalenti i suini, come nei consumi privilegiati urbani attestati nella stessa epoca nel palazzo vescovile di S.Maria di Castello a Genova (Cartledge 1978a,b) o anche nel castello di Manzano in Piemonte (Bedini 1992: 237-9), ma a Pertice nel VI-VII secolo erano presenti in quota significativa accanto ai suini anche i bovini (Castiglioni *et al.* 1992: 339-354), come a S. Stefano Belbo e a Trino in Piemonte – e nelle fasi medievali della stessa Trino e di Lomello (Lombardia) – mentre risultano quasi assenti alla stessa data a Zignago (Biasotti & Isetti 1981) e presenti in quota minima a Filattiera (Biasotti & Giovinazzo 1982). In alcuni casi, come a Filattiera, è stata confermata dagli scavi l'importanza dell'allevamento degli animali da cortile (Biasotti & Giovinazzo 1982: 361), attestati dalle fonti sia tra i cibi di ambiente rurale che sulla tavola delle classi privilegiate. Questo dato concorda pienamente con gli studi sull'alimentazione contadina nell'alto medioevo, che hanno sottolineato anche il ruolo della caccia e della pesca nell'alimentazione rurale e l'importanza dello sfruttamento delle risorse collettive (Montanari 1979). Nello stesso tempo è stata confermata dalle analisi paleobotaniche la continuità nell'Italia settentrionale e nell'arco alpino, durante l'alto medioevo, delle polente e cibi semiliquidi a base di differenti cereali, integrati nell'alto medioevo da verdure e carne bollita in pezzi (Ferro, in Negro Ponzi *et al.* 1989), con ampio uso di aromi e spezie: il corredo domestico altomedievale dei siti citati, pur caratterizzato da una apparente semplificazione tipologica, era quindi in realtà ancora funzionale a tecniche di cottura accurate e tradizionali e ad un tipo di alimentazione sostanzialmente analogo nelle aree rurali a quello dei periodi precedenti.

Il recipiente ceramico dominante è costantemente l'olla, con o senza tracce di fumigazione, quindi utilizzato sia come vaso da fuoco che come contenitore, però con varianti di forma e di impasto tra i diversi siti.

Nei siti tardo antichi il vasellame da fuoco è normalmente formato da olle a fondo piano, con impasto grossolano. In Liguria le olle hanno corpo globulare con orlo estroflesso più o meno arrotondato (fig.1:27-29) (Savignone: Fossati, Bazzurro, Pizzolo 1976: 316) o corpo ovoidale con pareti sottili, ma sempre con orlo espanso e estroflesso (fig.2:1-6) (Zignago, fase altomedievale: Cabona Ferrando, Gardini & Mannoni 1978: 353-361); a Savignone le olle erano associate con un tipo anomalo di ciotole con orlo inflesso e rivestimento interno, in impasto grezzo vacuolato, a Zignago con ceramiche da tavola e anfore di tradizione tardo antica. In Lombardia, ad esempio a Lomello, a questa data la ceramica a impasto grossolano è associata con olle e ciotole in impasto depurato ed eventualmente con abbondante pietra ollare (Blake, Maccabruni & Mannoni 1987: 163, fig.4, 164-5); a Terno d'Isola, insediamento produttivo di V-VI secolo, olle con bordo sagomato (fig.2:20-22) accompagnano piccole pentole a tesa orizzontale e coperchi con orlo rientrante e prese a tacche (Fortunati Zuccalà, Vitali & Zonca 1986 : 78-82), mentre a Monte Barro (prima metà del VI secolo) olle a fondo piano con orlo estroflesso (in impasto duro e depurato come a Trino-S.Michele), coperchi e catini-coperchio sono associati a varie forme invetriate: olle e ollette con bordo sia estroflesso che rientrante (fig.2:13, 14), ciotole

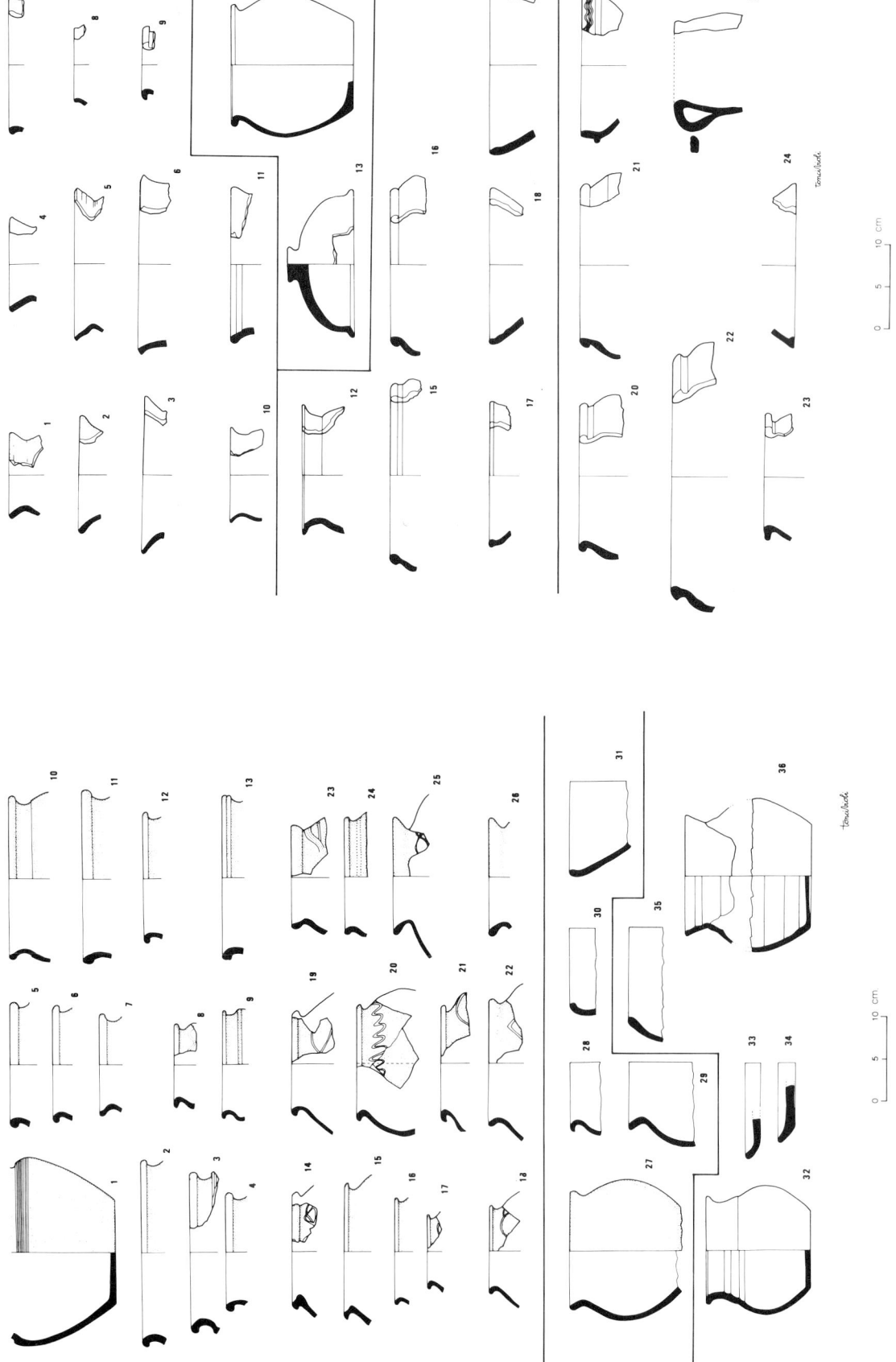

Fig. 2. Italia settentrionale, ceramica comune. Zignago: fase altomedievale: 1-8; fase medievale: 9-11; Monte Barro, prima metà VI sec.: 13-14; Manerba, V-VII sec.: 12, 15-19; Terno d'Isola, V-VII sec.: 20-24.

Fig. 1. Italia settentrionale, ceramica comune. Trino, V-VI sec.: 1-4 olle da fuoco, 5-13 olle per conservazione; X-XI sec.: 14-23; XII-XII sec.: 24-26; Savignone, V-VI sec.: 27-31; Filattiera: 32-37.

a bordo diritto, vasi a listello, un orcio con ansa a nastro (Nobile 1991: 64–76); a Manerba, dove sono rappresentate fasi dal IV all'VIII secolo, è attestata ceramica funzionale sia grezza che in impasto depurato: la ceramica grezza, lavorata a tornio lento, con orlo semplicemente estroflesso o arrotondato su imboccatura rientrante e pareti spesso decorate, è associata a ceramica sigillata (ciotole con orlo a tesa decorata e un'olla) di IV-V secolo e invetriata della stessa data; la ceramica in impasto depurato presenta forme diverse di olle, bacili, brocche e vasetti con ansa e orlo a listello (fig.2:12–19) (Carver, Massa, Brogiolo et al. 1982: 269–275).

A Trino (Joris 1992) nei contesti di tardo V-VI secolo le forme da fuoco sono olle con due ordini di grandezza (fig.1:1–4), accompagnate da olle più piccole, ma di varie dimensioni per la conservazione degli alimenti (fig.1:5–13) e scarsi recipienti per liquidi. Scompare in questa fase il vasellame fine da mensa che era ancora presente tra tardo IV e V secolo. Nelle fasi medioevali le olle sono prevalentemente da fuoco, e di dimensioni più piccole di quelle altomedievali (fig.1: 14–22); solo a partire dal XII secolo appaiono nuovamente recipienti non da fuoco: olle da conservazione e una produzione in impasto depurato da tavola o polifunzionale (fig.1: 24:26).

Nel Medioevo in Liguria le olle sono ancora in impasto grossolano foggiato a tornio lento, con orlo sia estroflesso che rientrante, ma associate con boccali trilobati con ansa a nastro, in impasto depurato (fig.1: 32,37) (Filattiera, XII secolo; Cabona, Mannoni, Pizzolo et al. 1982: 346, tav.I; 348, tav.II); nel basso medioevo, le olle, basse e con orlo estroflesso, sono realizzate sia in impasto tenero con foggiatura a mano che in impasto duro con foggiatura a tornio e associate con testelli, boccali e piccole anfore in impasto depurato (fig.2:9–11) (Zignago: Cabona Ferrando, Gardini, Mannoni 1978: 354–355, tav.XII). In Lombardia, a Piadena, le olle, attestate dalla fine IX agli inizi del XII secolo, sono globulari, con impasto grossolano, orlo rettangolare estroflesso e decorazioni a pettine (Brogiolo & Gelichi 1986: 300); dal X secolo compaiono pentole ovoidi con orlo arrotondato o tagliato e prese sopraelevate (ibid. tav.VIII): le stesse forme sono attestate nelle fasi di X-XI e XIV secolo a Brescia, via A.Mario, dove le pentole hanno pareti rigate, ma sono presenti anche pentole medio-piccole con pareti lisce (ibid. 307, 309, tavv.VIII-IX). Le olle e pentole sono ovunque associate con catini-coperchio e, a Brescia, con tegami tronco-conici. In Piemonte, a Trino, le olle di X-XI secolo sono ovoidi a base piana e presentano orlo estroflesso arrotondato, in alcuni casi con incasso interno per coperchio o con orlo arrondato su breve collo contratto; solo nella fase di XII-XIII secolo compaiono vasi per liquidi, in impasto molto depurato (Joris 1992), con largo orlo estroflesso, mentre a Manzano (fase della prima metà del XIII secolo) le olle con orlo estroflesso, spesso su collo molto corto, talvolta decorate con scanalature o a rotella (Micheletto & Cortelazzo 1988: tav.LII; 1990: fig.21) sono associate solo con catini-coperchio e con rara pietra ollare, molto abbondante invece a Trino-S.Michele e a Piadena; manca completamente a Trino e Manzano l'invetriata, presente invece in coevi siti francesi.

Nei siti francesi le olle altomedievali sono globulari, con collo corto e orlo estroflesso arrotondato (Hyères-sur-Amby): le più antiche (VI-VII secolo) ancora cotte in atmosfera ossidante, hanno decorazioni a rotella e sono associate con mortai e piccole ciotole; in seguito nell'VIII-IX secolo dominano olle cotte in atmosfera riducente, con impasto piuttosto grossolano, ma ben tornito, senza collo, con bordo estroflesso o a fascia pendente e decorazioni a scanalature orizzontali o oblique oppure a linee incise ondulate (fig.3: 1–5) (CNRS 1978: tav.VIII-IX). L'alimentazione risulta mista anche in questi siti, basata sui cereali (sono state rinvenute macine per grani 'grossi') ma integrata dall'allevamento degli ovocaprini, con quote minori di suini e bovini (Porte 1983: 82). Il corredo domestico altomedievale con olle, corrispondeva quindi anche nella Francia meridionale ad un'alimentazione ricca sia di cereali che di carne. Il tipo medievale è attestato, tra altri siti, a Charavines (prima metà dell'XI secolo; Colardelle 1980; Colardelle & Verdel 1993): olle sia per cottura che per conservazione, in impasti fini e ben torniti con pareti sottili, con forma globulare, fondo bombato segnato da spigolo di passaggio alla parete, collo poco marcato e bordo estroflesso o a fascia; la spalla è talvolta decorata a rotella, il fondo è spesso segnato con motivi impressi a rilievo con stampi di legno (fig.3: 6,7,9) (ibid. figg. 31–32; per i marchi Reynaud, Colardelle et al. 1975: 252–254; Faure Boucharlat et al. 1978: 429–440). Il corredo domestico comprendeva anche brocche di forma e impasto simile, ma con beccuccio e e ansa a nastro (fig.3: 8) e sia le olle che le brocche possono presentare vetrina esterna a tono giallo o verde (Faure Boucharlat et al. 1978: 437). Le condizioni eccezionali di conservazione del sito, ricoperto dalle acque poco tempo dopo il suo abbandono, hanno permesso la conservazione di piatti in legno tornito del diametro di 30–44 cm, con piede a disco o ad anello e pareti svasate (fig.3: 10–12), alcuni con marchio interno simile a quelli stampati sul fondo delle olle (fig.3: 13). Sono attestate anche ciotole emisferiche, più piccole, lavorate a coltello e sgorbia in modo più rustico (fig.3: 14) ancora simili a scodelle di tradizione alpina protostorica (Colardelle 1980: figg.41–42). Sono attestati cucchiai in legno sia per cucina con lungo manico diritto (fig.3: 15), in bosso o frassino che per cibo con manico leggermente ricurvo (fig.3: 16). Le analisi paleobotaniche hanno individuato grande abbondanza di segale, come a Trino, con avena e frumento, poco miglio, poco orzo e pochi legumi, soprattutto fave e piselli, abbondanti frutti spontanei e grani d'uva (A.V. 1988: 41, n.129). L'alimentazione

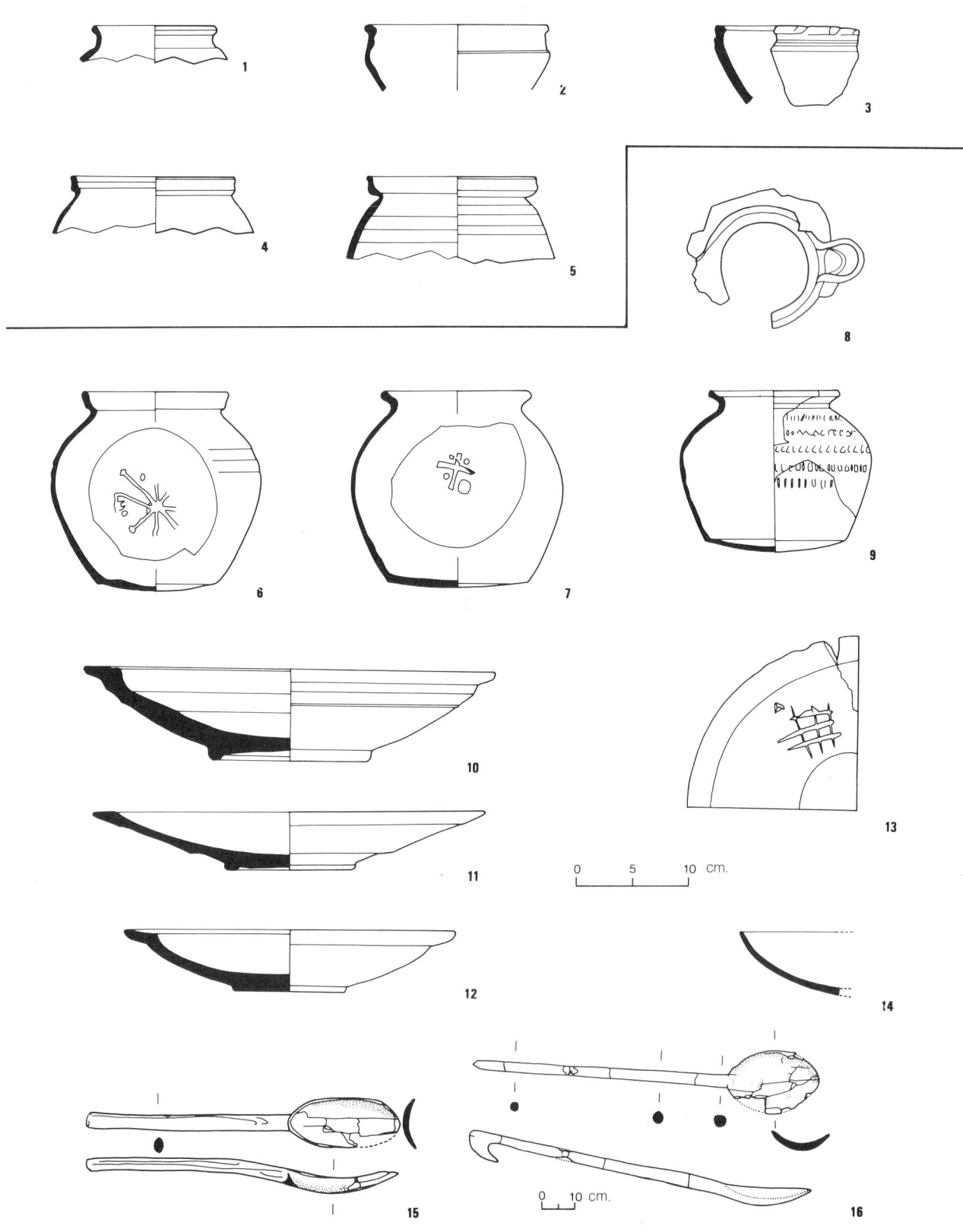

Fig. 3. Francia meridionale, ceramica comune. Hieres-Sur-Amby, VI-VIII sec.: 1-5; Colletieres, XI sec.: 8-16.

comprendeva importanti quote di carne, in larga maggioranza (70 %) suini (Colardelle 1980: 209–211, ann.III; Colardelle & Verdel 1993), attestati nello stesso periodo con analogo corredo domestico di olle e brocche anche a Cucuron in Provenza, ma anche caprovini, bovini e scarsi animali selvatici: cervo, capriolo, cinghiale, lepre, che sembrano invece avere avuto un ruolo alimentare più importante nel Nord Italia fino dall'alto medioevo (Montanari 1980b), tanto che il cervo poteva essere tenuto anche allo stato domestico (Montanari 1985: 633).

Il tipo ceramico dominante in tutti i siti considerati, sia nord-italiani che sud-francesi, appare costantemente l'olla con corpo espanso e il collo o la bocca ristretta, associata, nei siti e nelle fasi di più evidente derivazione tardo antica, con forme aperte a ciotola o a bacile a listello, del diametro prevalente di 14/20 cm.; il diametro di imboccatura delle olle varia nel periodo tardo antico tra 10 e 20 cm. (ad esempio a Castelseprio); nel periodo altomedievale e medievale sembra di poco maggiore, però ad esempio a Cucuron varia tra 8 e 11 cm (Fixot & Pelletier 1983: figg.6–9); tipo presente anche a Trino che poteva corrispondere ad usi particolari.

La forma dell'olla appare però inadatta alla cottura delle polente e e dei cibi semi-solidi che richiedevano rimescolamento; inoltre le dimensioni delle olle più piccole sembrano insufficienti per la cottura della quantità di cibo necessaria per una famiglia, composta mediamente almeno di 6-8 persone. In età romana esisteva infatti per la cottura della *puls* un recipiente specifico, il *caccabus*, e uno studio recente ha proposto di identificarlo in un piccolo calderone in bronzo a pareti diritte o leggermente concave, con diametro della bocca di circa 16–20 cm., conosciuto dal I al III-IV sec.d.C. anche in varianti in argilla (Muffatti Musselli 1988: 279–281; Salza Prina Ricotti 1987: 160, n.65). Sembra probabile che anche in età tardo antica e altomedievale la cottura delle minestre e polente avvenisse in paioli o recipienti analoghi in metallo – non conservati negli scavi perchè accuratamente riutilizzati come rottame quando venivano scartati, data la scarsità del metallo nell'alto medioevo – mentre le olle potevano essere riservate, nelle diverse varianti di forma, alla cottura di piccole quantità di cibi particolari o per riscaldare i cibi da aggiungere alla preparazione base di cereali: carni spezzettate, verdure e salse. Forme di paiolo o calderone da fuoco sono infatti attestate archeologicamente in siti medievali dal ritrovamento di catene di sospensione e compaiono in iconografie nord-italiane (fig.4:2, Magnani 1934: tav.XXXVII, f.198 v., Mille circa; cf. par.4). Le differenze di forme e di impasti delle olle potevano quindi corrispondere non tanto a generiche variazioni produttive, ma piuttosto a prodotti di diversa qualità e costo, per funzioni diverse. Dal raffronto sistematico delle forme e degli impasti nei livelli altomedievali e medievali di S.Michele di Trino è chiaramente apparso che esistevano correlazioni tra la tipologia e la tecnica di produzione dei vasi: alcune varianti di olle erano costantemente associate con impasti più depurati e cotti a temperatura più alta, e quindi meno porosi, mentre altre, cotte a temperatura inferiore, mostrano prevalentemente tracce di fumigazione: queste olle erano certamente utilizzate sul fuoco, mentre le olle non fumigate dovevano avere funzione prevalente di vasi da dispensa o di contenitori di liquidi. In tutti i siti presi in esame è stata riscontrata nelle olle notevole varietà diacronica di forma degli orli e una serie variabile di rapporti tra imboccature e diametri: se le varianti corrispondevano a richieste funzionali specifiche, il corredo domestico doveva avere una varietà d'impiego maggiore di quanto la predominanza delle sole forme chiuse sembri suggerire. Inoltre, la scomparsa dall'alto medioevo delle scodelle e delle piccole forme aperte nel corredo domestico in ceramica, mentre appaiono diffusi i catini-coperchio e sono attestate alcune forme aperte di diametro maggiore, sembra derivare dalla restrizione dell'uso della terracotta alle sole forme e agli usi nei quali essa era indispensabile (è da notare che nell'alto medioevo è attestato l'uso sul fuoco di ciotole coperchio a Brescia e di catini a Ventimiglia: Olcese 1989), mentre il vasellame destinato alla consumazione dei cibi, realizzato in età romana in ceramica e in particolare in ceramica fine, venne progressivamente realizzato in materiali diversi, soprattutto legno e metallo. Documenti medievali ricordano, anche per l'area piemontese, il lavoro di tornitura di vasellame in legno come attività economica collegata allo sfruttamento del bosco (Comba 1988: 112–116) così come fonti storiche e ritrovamenti archeologici attestano l'esistenza di oggetti in metallo prezioso appartenenti a ceti privilegiati o a tesori ecclesiastici.

4. VASELLAME DA TAVOLA NELLE FONTI ICONOGRAFICHE

Un particolare interesse per l'uso del vasellame da mensa rivestono in questo senso le fonti iconografiche, e in particolare le miniature dal VI all'XI secolo, con scene di banchetti e tavole imbandite. Scene di riunione intorno ad una mensa, spesso con significato rituale, sono presenti in numerosi codici tardo antichi, del V-VI secolo: in essi appare sulla tavola vasellame individuale, raffinato e variato, con forme sia in terracotta che in vetro e metallo. Nei secoli successivi l'attività dei miniatori appare saltuaria e legata soprattutto a codici di uso ecclesiastico: le illustrazioni appaiono prevalentemente derivate da modelli più antichi e non sono quindi significative degli usi contemporanei; contemporaneamente i materiali di uso quotidiano sono particolarmente scarsi dall'VIII al X secolo anche tra i reperti archeologici. Di rilevante interesse appaiono perciò, sia per la data che per la esecuzione in area piemontese culturalmente coincidenti con i materiali di Trino, le miniature di un Sacramentario eseguito per il vescovo di Ivrea Warmondo intorno all'anno 1000, probabilmente nello stesso *scriptorium* di Ivrea. Il codice presenta gruppi di miniature diverse: alcune, di carattere ufficiale, come la consacrazione dell'imperatore Ottone III e soggetti sacri, derivati dalla tradizione iconografica religiosa ufficiale, altre, come scene del Vangelo e scene di martirio dei santi, con elaborazione delle iconografie tradizionali e dettagli di vestiario, strumenti e oggetti d'uso derivati da modelli coevi e altre ancora, di soggetto non tradizionale, come una serie di illustrazioni del rituale funerario, immediatamente derivate dall'esperienza diretta del miniatore.

Per quanto riguarda il vasellame domestico e da tavola, esso è rappresentato con chiarezza, soprattutto in due scene relative alle Nozze di Cana (fig.4:1) e all'Ultima cena. Nelle Nozze di Cana, scena quindi di banchetto importante e festivo (Magnani 1934, tav.X, f.27), Cristo tocca con una bacchetta alcune idrie poste a terra, basse, con corpo globulare, gola marcata e ampia imboccatura svasata, simili a forme di olle rinvenute in diversi scavi coevi; la tavola rettangolare in legno è coperta da una tovaglia, sulla quale sono posati pani spezzati, tre coltelli con lunga lama appuntita, due coppe profonde su alto piede sagomato e un calice con orlo estroflesso lavorato, forse perlinato, affiancato da un piccolo oggetto non immediatamente identificabile : mancano del tutto sia piatti che bicchieri individuali. E' da notare anche il bicchiere a cono molto alto, forse con piccola base, tenuto in mano dal personaggio dietro il Cristo, l'*architriclinarius* che assaggia il vino e segnala il carattere ufficiale del banchetto. Nell'Ultima Cena, una scena di cena semplice, strettamente centrata, con taglio straordinariamente moderno, sui soli personaggi e con ambiente individuato solo da una lucerna a più becchi su una colonna (Magnani 1934, tav.XIV, f.50 V.), Cristo e gli Apostoli sono raccolti intorno ad una tavola ovale sulla quale compaiono pani spezzati, numerosi coltelli, tre larghe coppe su alto piede sagomato e lo stesso piccolo attrezzo già notato nella tavola precedente; le coppe contengono pesci, che hanno in questo contesto un chiaro significato simbolico. Anche su questa tavola mancano del tutto piatti o scodelle individuali, come in una scena di mensa signorile in una nota miniatura del Codice *De Universo* di Rabano Mauro (A.V. 1959: 27), databile all'XI secolo (fig.5: 1): due personaggi sono seduti ad una tavola coperta da una ricca tovaglia e uno di essi taglia con un coltello un cibo consistente, forse un pezzo di carne, tenendolo fermo entro un'ampia coppa con piede a nodo con una pinza, o un attrezzo a due rebbi, mentre il secondo porta alla bocca un identico attrezzo e ha un secondo coltello davanti a sè. L'oggetto a due punte ha un manico allungato, con un piccolo pomolo superiore: la forma generale sembra simile agli oggetti non identificati del codice di Warmondo e anche le dimensioni, leggermente più piccole del coltello, sembrano corrispondere. Questo tipo di utensile sembra però eccezionale nelle rappresentazioni di banchetto dell'XI e XII secolo e doveva corrispondere, come il vestiario dei personaggi e il tipo dei mobili riccamente intagliati, ad una condizione privilegiata. Anche in questo caso, tuttavia, sul tavolo sono posati soltanto diversi pani, il cibo è contenuto in un unico oggetto da portata e mancano sia piatti che bicchieri individuali, anche se i personaggi sembrano avere posate personali.

Il tipo dell'ampia coppa compare in miniature dell'XI secolo come piatto di portata principale anche in altre aree europee. In un manoscritto francese della seconda metà dell'XI secolo con scene della "Vita e miracoli di S.Mauro" (Troyes), ad esempio, è rappresentato lo stesso tipo di allestimento di mensa, con coltelli e pani poggiati sulla tovaglia e cibi entro coppe con piede, secondo usi e tipologie di vasellame che sembrano largamente diffuse; analogamente in un manoscritto con episodi della vita di Saint Aubin d'Angers (Bibliothèque Nationale di Parigi, fine dell'XI secolo) la tavola di un banchetto di nozze è apparecchiata solo con due grandi coppe baccellate a due colori, mentre un personaggio beve in una coppa con piede (Lat.1390, Fol.1 v: A.V.,1988, fig.11). Bicchieri a coppa sono presenti anche nel codice di Warmondo, nella scena delle Marie al Sepolcro (Magnani 1934, tav.XIX, f.66 v.) e in una miniatura illustrativa delle preghiere per i defunti, di iconografia originale e, come si è ricordato, probabilmente locale (Ibid. tav.XXXVI in basso, f.195 v.).

Una rappresentazione delle Nozze di Cana, contenuta in un Evangeliario del monastero di S.Benedetto in Polirone, eseguito verso la fine dell'XI secolo, permette anch'essa un'interessante confronto con l'analoga più antica scena del Sacramentario di Warmondo. La miniatura non rappresenta in questo caso il momento del miracolo, ma genericamente quello del banchetto: i personaggi, raccolti come quelli del codice di Warmondo su un solo lato di una tavola rettangolare, hanno davanti a sé diversi pani, tre coltelli, quattro coppe su basso piede conico e un calice, ma quattro servi si affacendano portando altre basse coppe emisferiche appoggiate sul palmo di una sola mano e altri tre versano vino in grandi hydrie poggiate a terra da contenitori diversi: una piccola anfora portata sotto il braccio, una grande anfora appoggiata sulla spalla e una brocchetta a corpo globulare con un solo manico, tenuta per il collo cilindrico. Il vasellame da tavola è ancora quello altomedievale, ma la forma delle hydrie, grandi, con corpo ovoide e riccamente decorato, è nettamente diversa da quella del Sacramentario. Anche le coppe e il calice hanno forma diversa e più bassa, con orlo evidenziato e in due casi corpo riccamente decorato, che potrebbe indicare vasi in metallo o, meno probabilmente, in vetro. Vasi in metallo o vetro con orlo

Fig. 4. Sacramentario di Warmondo, Arch. Cap.Ivrea (Mille circa).
1: Nozze di Cana.   2: Rituale per i defunti.

Fig. 5.1: Hrabanus Maurus, De Universo (Montecassino) (XI sec.).

Fig. 5.2: Sacramentario di Warmondo, Arch.Cap.Ivrea: Adorazione dei Magi.

estroflesso e una coppa con pareti riccamente decorate, probabilmente in metallo, compaiono in affreschi nella navata maggiore di S.Calocero a Civate, che rappresentano il miracolo della manna e quello delle acque amare e sono datati poco prima della metà dell'XI secolo; nella stessa scena compare anche un calice cilindrico decorato che sembra in vetro: vetri di forma simile con pitture a smalto venivano prodotti all'epoca nel mediterraneo orientale, ed è possibile che siano qui riflessi oggetti di importazione o influssi bizantini nella formazione del pittore.

Coppe su piede ritornano ancora più volte in miniature del XII secolo. Per l'area che qui interessa si può citare una pagina di una Bibbia Atlantica della Biblioteca Ambrosiana (Storia di Milano 1954, III: p.756), probabilmente eseguita a Milano, ma anche scene coeve a pittura in un eccezionale complesso di pannelli per soffitto della chiesa di S.Martino a Zillis, in Svizzera, datati al 1130 (Murbach & Heman 1967: 12), dove, in pannelli rappresentanti l'Ultima Cena, compaiono ancora le grandi coppe su piede con pani e coltelli, ma anche, accanto a coppe leggermente diverse e con orlo lavorato, calici con coperchio (fig.6: 1), anch'essi, come le coppe, ancora non individuali (ibid: O-V 136, O-VII 137); in un'altro pannello, con nascita di Gesù, una coppa bassa (fig.6: 2), portata da una donna assistente, contiene un cibo liquido che viene raccolto da Maria con un cucchiaio che sembra fatto in legno (ibid: C-VII 61) e una grande coppa simile è usata anche per nutrire o abbeverare un animale fantastico (ibid: J-IX 17).

Fig. 6. Zillis, Chiesa di S.Martino (XII sec.).

1: Ultima Cena.   2: Natività di Gesù.

Il tipo di vasellame da tavola rimase quindi sostanzialmente invariato dal X-XI secolo fino alla metà del XII secolo: in affreschi del XIII a Mantova (S.Maria del Gradaro: Toesca 1987:fig.99) e a Brescia (S.Maria di Mitra della Nave: Storia di Brescia 1963: 801) sono infatti rappresentati sulle tavole calici con piede posti davanti a ciascun commensale, bicchieri e piccole coppe individuali e taglieri o piatti rotondi per la presentazione dei cibi.

Le coppe larghe sono utilizzate in una scena di Adorazione dei Magi del manoscritto di Warmondo (fig.5:2), insieme con un vaso a listello, anche come contenitori per presentare i doni (Magnani 1934: tav.IX, f.26 v.); lo stesso tipo di scena compare ancora nel Codice Magno, manoscritto della liturgia piacentina datato intorno al 1130 (Quintavalle 1963: 87–88), dove i Re recano le offerte in recipienti a coppa con piccolo piede (Velli 1984: 745) e in un pannello con Adorazione dei Magi del coevo soffitto di Zillis, dove i Re offrono i doni in grandi coppe con piccolo piede portate sulle due mani velate dal mantello (Murbach & Heman 1967: E-III 71, E-IV 72). Recipienti emisferici con piede sono rappresentati a Zillis anche nella scena della Lavanda dei piedi e come contenitore di porpora da filare nell'Annunciazione (*ibid*: O IV 135, B VIII 55) e compaiono ancora fino alla metà del XIV secolo,
integrati con altre forme in scene sia sacre che profane.

Resta da osservare che nessun contesto archeologico medievale ha finora restituito forme ceramiche a piede del tipo descritto, che doveva essere invece per la frequenza e varietà di rappresentazioni molto diffuso. Inoltre, le coppe contengono, nella grande maggioranza delle scene citate, dei pesci per esigenze di simbologia cristiana, ma comunque cibi apparentemente solidi e mancano sulle tavole scodelle adatte a cibi liquidi. Cibi predominanti nell'area alpina erano invece, come si è ricordato, le zuppe, le polente e le minestre, mentre la carne, anche se con eccezioni per pollame e pesci, era considerata cibo tipico delle classi privilegiate : anche il vasellame che la conteneva, in metallo o altro materiale pregiato, era perciò probabilmente proprio delle classi più agiate, mentre i *pulmenta* della tavola comune dovevano essere portati in tavola in vasellame diverso, come le olle in impasto depurato o forse anche alcune forme dei c.d. catini-coperchio, muniti di listello per una salda presa e forse anche per appoggio su sostegni circolari e così le bevande, alle quali potevano essere destinate, ad esempio, le olle con impasto poco poroso cotto ad alta temperatura e orlo molto estroflesso, attestate a Trino dal XII secolo. Forme a scodella, frequenti nell'area padana nel IV-VI secolo in ceramica invetriata e in imitazione sigillata, sono ancora rappresentate, in ceramica depurata con ingobbio a fasce, nel VII-prima metà dell'VIII secolo nel sito di Classe (Fiumi & Prati 1983: fig.6), ma dovettero essere sostituite nel Nord-Italia nel primo medio evo, e forse già prima nelle aree di cultura germanica, da ciotole o piatti in legno, non più disposti in vista sul tavolo, ma portati con il cibo e sgomberati immediatamente dopo l'uso.

Bibliografia

Fonti:

Anthimus, *De observatione ciborum, epistula ad Theudoricum regem Francorum*. Iterum edidit Valentinus Rose, Teubner, Lipsia, 1877.

AA.VV. 1959. *La vita medievale italiana nella miniatura*, Roma.

AA.VV. 1987. *L'alimentazione nel mondo antico, I Romani, età imperiale*, Ministero per i Beni culturali e ambientali, Roma.

Andreolli, B., Fumagalli, V. & Montanari, M. (a cura di), 1985. *Le campagne italiane prima e dopo il Mille*, Bologna.

Bedini, E. 1992. 'Osservazioni preliminari sui resti faunistici', in E. Bedini, E. Micheletto, 'Indagine archeologica al castello di Manzano (Comune di Cherasco – Prov. di CN). Secondo rapporto preliminare (1990-1991)', *Archeologia Medievale*, XIX, 223-242.

Biasotti, M. Giovinazzo, R. 1982. 'I reperti faunistici di Filattiera', *Archeologia Medievale*, IX, 358-362.

Biasotti, M., Isetti, P. 1981. 'L'alimentazione dall'osteologia animale in Liguria', *Archeologia Medievale*, VIII, 239-246.

Bierbrauer, V. 1990. 'La ceramica grezza di Invillino Ibligo, Friuli e i suoi paralleli nell'arco Alpino centrale e orientale', *Archeologia Medievale*, XVI, 57-58.

Blake, H. & Maccabruni, C. 1985. 'Lo scavo a Villa Maria di Lomello (Pavia)', *Archeologia Medievale*, XII, 189-212.

Blake, H., Maccabruni, C. & Mannoni, T. *et al.* 1987. 'Dallo scavo a Villa Maria di Lomello (Pavia), 1984: la buca tardo antica', *Archeologia Medievale*, XIV, 157-187.

Bonora, E., Falcetti, C., Ferretti, F., Fossati, A. Imperiale, G., Mannoni, T., Murialdo, G. & Vicino, G. 1988. 'Il "Castrum" tardo antico di S.Antonino di Perti, Finale Ligure (Savona): fasi stratigrafiche e reperti dell'area D. Seconde notizie preliminari sulle campagne di scavo 1982-1987', *Archeologia Medievale*, XV, 335-396.

Brogiolo, G.P. & Castelletti, L. 1991. *Archeologia a Monte Barro I. Il Grande edificio e le torri*. Lecco.

Brogiolo, G.P. & Gelichi, S. 1986. 'La ceramica grezza medievale nella pianura padana', in *La ceramica medievale nel Mediterraneo occidentale, Atti del III Congresso Internazionale*, (Siena 1984), Firenze, 293-316.

Brogiolo, G.P. & Lusuardi Siena, S. 1980. 'Nuove indagini archeologiche a Castelseprio', in *Atti del 6 Congresso Internazionale di Studi sull'Alto Medioevo*, (Milano 1978), Spoleto, 475-515.

Cabona, D., Conti, G. & Pizzolo, O. 1985. 'Scavo dell'area ovest del villaggio abbandonato di Monte Zignago: Zignago 3', *Archeologia Medievale*, XII, 213-243.

Cabona, D., Mannoni, T. & Pizzolo, O. 1982. 'Gli scavi del complesso medievale di Filattiera in Lunigiana', *Archeologia Medievale*, IX, 331-364.

Cabona Ferrando, I., Gardini, A. & Mannoni, T. 1978. 'Zignago 1: gli insediamenti e il territorio', *Archeologia Medievale*, V, 273-372.

Cartledge, J. 1978a. 'Le ossa animali dell'area sud del chiostro di S.Silvestro a Genova, 1977', *Archeologia Medievale*, V, 437-451.

Cartledge, J. 1978b. 'The animal bones from the cloister of S. Silvestro, Genoa' in *Papers in Italian Archaeology, I* (eds. H. Blake, T. Potter, D. Whitehouse), BAR International Series 41, ii, Oxford, 358-363.

Carver, M.O.H., Massa, S. & Brogiolo, G.P., 'Sequenza insediativa romana e altomedievale alla Pieve di Manerba (BS)', *Archeologia Medievale*, IX, 237-296.

Castelletti, L. 1974-1975. 'Segale (Secale Cereale L.) subfossile a Lomello', in *Atti del Centro Studi e Documentazione Impero Romano*, 6, 55-71.

Castelletti, L. 1976. 'Resti vegetali macroscopici da Refondou presso Savignone', *Archeologia Medievale*, III, 326-328.

Castelletti, L. & Somaini, A. 1988. 'Indagini paleobotaniche', in Castelletti, L., Brogiolo, G.P., Nobile, I. 'Scavi di Monte Barro. Comune di Galbiate, Como (1986-7)', *Archeologia Medievale*, XV, 238-247.

Castiglioni, E., Cupelli, G., Falcetti, C., Ferretti, F., Fossati, A., Giovinazzo, R., Murialdo, G., Mannoni, T., Palazzi, P., Panizza, M., Parodi, L., Ricci, R. & Vicino, G. 1992. 'Il "castrum" tardo-antico di S.Antonino di Perti, Finale Ligure (Savona): terze notizie preliminari sulle campagne di scavo 1982-1991', *Archeologia Medievale*, XIX, 279-368.

C.A.T.H.M.A. Association 1986. 'La ceramique du Haut Moyen Age en France Méridionale: éléments comparatifs et essai de comparation', in *La ceramica medievale nel Mediterraneo occidentale, Atti del III Congresso Internazionale*, (Siena 1984), Firenze, 27-50.

Chronique des Fouilles Medievales, 1981. 'Hyères-sur-Amby (Isère). Larina', *Archéologie Médiévale*, XI, 265-266.

Colardelle, M. 1983. 'L'habitat immergé de Colletières', *Dossier Histoire et Archéologia*, 78, 83-84.

Colardelle, R. & M. 1980. 'L'habitat médiéval immergé de Colletières a Charavines (Isère). Premier bilan des fouilles', *Archéologie Médiévale*, X, 167-269.

Colardelle, M & Verdel, E. (a cura di) 1993. *Les habitats du lac de Paladru (Isère) dans leur environment. La formation d'un terroir au XIème siècle*, Paris.

Comba, R. 1988. *Contadini, signori e mercanti nel Piemonte medievale*, Bari.

Des Burgondes à Bayard. Mille Ans de Moyen Age (Mostra 1981: Grenoble, Lyon, Valence, Paris, Chambery, Annecy, Bourg-en-Bresse, 1981-1984).

Duby, G. 1978. *Le origini dell'economia europea*, (ed.it.), Roma-Bari.

Fiumi, F. & Prati, L. 1983. 'Note sulla ceramica comune', in *Ravenna e il porto di Classe*, Bologna, 118-126.

Fixot, M. & Pelletier, J.P. 1983. 'Une forme originale de fortification médiévale provencale: le Castelas de Cucuron (Vaucluse)', *Archéologie Médiévale*, XIII, 89-115.

Flandrin, J.L. & Redon, O. 1981. 'Les livres de cuisine italiens des XIV et XV siècles', *Archeologia Medievale*, VIII, 393-408.

Fortunati Zuccalà, Vitali, M.G. & Zonca, A. 1986. 'Terno d'Isola (Bergamo). Presso la chiesa di S.Vittore', *Notiziario 1985 della Soprintendenza Archeologica della Lombardia*, 78-82.

Fossati, S. Bazzurro, S. & Pizzolo, O. 1976. 'Campagna di scavo nel villaggio tardo antico di Savignone (Genova)', *Archeologia Medievale*, III, 308-325.

Fossati, S. & Mannoni, T. 1981. 'Gli strumenti della cucina e della mensa in base ai reperti archeologici', *Archeologia Medievale*, VIII, 409-419.

Gelichi, S. 1983. 'Ceramica grezza altomedievale', in A.V. *Ravenna e il Porto di Classe*, Bologna, 127-129.

Ginatempo, M. 1984. 'Per la storia degli ecosistemi e dell'alimentazione medievali: recenti studi di archeozoologia in Italia', *Archeologia Medievale*, XI, 35-61.

Joris, C. 1992. *La ceramica comune altomedievale e medievale in Piemonte. Aspetti tipologici e funzionali dei materiali di Trino Vercellese*, tesi di Laurea in lettere, Università di Torino, a.a. 1991-2, inedita.

Magnani, L. 1934. *Le miniature del Sacramentario d'Ivrea e di altri codici Warmondiani*, Città del Vaticano.

Maffeis, L. 1991. *Alimentazione nel Medioevo: vasellame da tavola e da cucina nelle fonti archeologiche e in quelle iconografiche*, tesi di laurea in Lettere, Università di Torino, a.a. 1991-2, inedita.

Mannoni, T. 1970. 'La ceramica d'uso comune in Liguria prima del XIX secolo', *Atti del III Convegno Internazionale della Ceramica*, Albisola, 295-335.

Mannoni, T. 1983. 'Insediamenti poveri nella Liguria di età romana e bizantina', *Rivista di Studi Liguri*, XLIX, 254-264.

Massa, S. & Portulano, B. 1990. 'Brescia, Santa Giulia, scavo 1987 (Ortaglia settore Y 2). Dati preliminari sulla ceramica comune: V-VII sec.', *Archeologia Medievale*, XVII, 111–120.

Micheletto, E., Cerrato, N. & Cortelazzo, M. 1990. 'Indagine archeologica al castello di Manzano (comune di Cherasco – Cn). Rapporto preliminare (1986–1989)', *Archeologia Medievale*, XVII, 235–266.

Montanari, M. 1975. 'Cereali e legumi nell'alto medioevo. Italia del nord, sec. IX-X', *Rivista Storica Italiana*, 439–492.

Montanari, M. 1979. *L'alimentazione contadina nell'alto medioevo*, Napoli.

Montanari, M. 1980a. 'Mutamenti economico-sociali e trasformazione del regime alimentare dei ceti rurali nel passaggio dall'alto al pieno medioevo. Considerazioni sull'Italia padana', in A.V., *Medioevo rurale*, Bologna, 79–97.

Montanari, M. 1980b. 'Il ruolo della caccia nell'economia e nell'alimentazione dei ceti rurali dell'Italia del Nord. Evoluzione dall'alto al basso medioevo', in *La Chasse au Moyen Age. Actes du Colloque de Noce (1979), Centre d'Études Médiévales de Nice. Publications de la Faculté de Lettres et des Sciences Humaines de Nice*, 20, 331–345.

Montanari, M. 1981. 'Storia, alimentazione e storia dell'alimentazione. Le fonti scritte altomedievali', *Archeologia Medievale*, VIII, 25–37.

Montanari, M. 1985. 'Gli animali e l'alimentazione umana', in *L'uomo di fronte al mondo animale, Settimane di Studio del Centro Italiano di Studi sull'Alto Medioevo*, XXXI, (Spoleto 1983), Spoleto, 619–671.

Muffatti Musselli, G. 1988. 'Per una storia dell'alimentazione povera in epoca romana: la "puls" nelle fonti letterarie, archeologiche, paleobotaniche', *Rivista Archeologica dell'Antica provincia e Diocesi di Como*, 170, 269–290

Murbach, E. & Heman, P. 1967. *Zillis, images de l'univers roman*, Zurich.

Negro Ponzi Mancini, M.M. *et al.* 1989. *S.Michele di Trino. Un villaggio, un castello, una pieve tra età romana e altomedioevo*, (Studi Trinesi 8), Casale Monferrato.

Negro Ponzi Mancini, M.M. *et al.*, 1991. 'L'insediamento romano e altomedievale di S.Michele a Trino (Vercelli). Notizie preliminari sulle campagne 1984–1990', *Archeologia Medievale*, XVII, 381–428.

Negro Ponzi Mancini, M.M. 1992. 'L'insediamento fortificato altomedievale di S.Michele a Trino (Vercelli, Italia)', *Papers of the Fourth Conference of Italian Archaeology 4, New Developments in Italian Archaeology* 2, 193–211.

Nobile, I. 1991. 'Cermica grezza', in Brogiolo & Castelletti, 63–77.

Olcese, G. 1989. 'La ceramica comune di Albintimilium: notizie preliminari sull'indagine archeologica e archeometrica', *Rivista di Studi Liguri*, LV, 149–228.

Panazza, G. & Brogiolo, G.P. 1988. *Ricerche su Brescia altomedievale. I. Gli studi fino al 1978. Lo scavo di via A.Mario*, Brescia.

Porcher, J. 1959. *La miniatura francese*, Milano.

Porte, P. 1983. 'La camp de Larina, forteresse mérovingienne (Hiéres-sur-Amby/Isère)', *Dossiers Histoire et Archéologie*, 78, 79–82.

Quintavalle, C.A. 1963. *La miniatura a Piacenza*, Venezia.

Reynaud, J.F., Colardelle, M., Bailly-Maitre, M.C., Boucharlat, E., Clermont, M., Mandy, B. & Manipoud, B. 1975. 'Etude d'une ceramique régionale: les vases à fond marqué du XI siècle dans la region Rhone-Alpes', *Archéologie Médiévale*, V, 243–286.

Salza Prina Ricotti, E. 1987. 'Alimentazione, cibi, tavola e cucine nell'età imperiale', in A.V., *L'alimentazione nel mondo antico. I romani, età imperiale*, Roma, 71–130.

Slicher Van Bath, B.H. 1966. 'Les climats et les récoltes en haut moyen age', in *Agricoltura a mondo rurale in Occidente nell'alto medioevo*, (Spoleto 1965), Spoleto, 399–425.

Storia di Mantova, Le Arti, I, 1960, Istituto Carlo d'Arco per la Storia di Mantova.

Storia di Milano 1954, Milano, Fondazione Treccani degli Alfieri per la storia di Milano.

Velli, A.M. 1984. 'La miniatura a Piacenza dal IX al XIII secolo', in *Storia di Piacenza, dal vescovo conte alla signoria*, vol.2, 727–754.

Zastrow, O. 1983. *Gli affreschi romanici nella provincia di Como*, Lecco.

62

Produzione e Distribuzione dei Denari Svevi e Angioini nel Regno di Sicilia alla Luce dei Rinvenimenti

Lucia Travaini

(Fitzwilliam Museum, Cambridge)

Sommario: *Le fonti documentarie testimoniano che la monetazione nel Regno di Sicilia sotto gli Hohenstaufen e sotto Carlo I di Angiò era coniata da due zecche principali, specificamente Brindisi (che produceva i denari per la penisola) e Messina (che riforniva la Sicilia e la Calabria); inoltre, Manfredonia fu attiva come zecca dal 1263 al 1266. I tipi impressi nelle due zecche principali erano diversi, ma i numismatici sono finora riusciti a stabilire poche attribuzioni relative alle zecche. Alcuni denari possono mostrare una S per 'Sicilia' o una A per 'Apulia', ma per la maggior parte non recano segni di zecca e sono stati classificati solamente come 'Messina o Brindisi'. Recenti ritrovamenti, provenienti sia da scavi che da tesoretti, possono ora consentire attribuzioni più precise. Pare chiaro che alcuni tipi compaiono solo in Sicilia e Calabria ed altri solo nel sud d'Italia, senza effettiva sovrapposizione fra di loro. Questa netta differenziazione dei rinvenimenti è una valida base per attribuire i tipi a Messina o a Brindisi, e per impostare alcune considerazioni generali sulla distribuzione della moneta nel regno svevo e angioino.*

Premessa

Produzione e distribuzione della moneta costituiscono un capitolo importante nell'organizzazione amministrativa del Regno di Sicilia nel XIII secolo: nuovi contributi su questo tema sono emersi da recenti indagini numismatiche, inizialmente volte a perfezionare l'attribuzione di zecca dei denari emessi in Sicilia e in Italia meridionale dai sovrani svevi Enrico VI (1194–97), Federico II (1197–1250), Corrado IV, I di Sicilia (1250–54), Corradino (1254–58), Manfredi (1258–66), e da Carlo I d'Angiò (1266–85). Oltre che contribuire alle attribuzioni di zecca, la distribuzione dei rinvenimenti nello spazio e nel tempo, pur basata su dati ancora parziali e quindi modificabili, offre un contributo concreto al dibattito sulla storia monetaria del Regno, suggerendo ipotesi sul movimento e sulla durata dei denari nella circolazione, sulle *renovationes monetae* attuate con le *collectae* nonchè sul movimento di uomini e cose nel Regno: questioni di non lieve peso, che non si possono qui trattare con completezza. Il nostro scopo è quello di fornire nuovi dati, e proporre semmai alcune ipotesi di lavoro per ulteriori approfondimenti.

I rinvenimenti di denari dei suddetti sovrani, con una lista di tutti i tipi finora noti, sono già stati in parte esaminati in Travaini (1993) che include anche vari tipi di denari mancanti nel libro di Spahr (1976), finora riferimento principale per questi materiali. All'articolo suddetto si rimanda per gli aspetti più specificamente numismatici, mentre in questa sede si affronteranno in particolare i problemi relativi all'interpretazione della distribuzione dei tipi nelle due parti del Regno.[1]

I denari del Regno

Quando l'imperatore Enrico VI prese il Regno di Sicilia nel 1194, riorganizzò il sistema monetario. La monetazione normanna nel Regno era costituita da tarì d'oro, diversi nominali di basso argento, e da monete di rame; la produzione era centralizzata nelle zecche di Messina (tarì e monete di rame per la Sicilia), Palermo (tarì e monete argentee per tutto il Regno), Salerno (monete di rame per la parte settentrionale e tarì di oro basso), Amalfi (tarì di oro basso). Enrico VI continuò a far emettere tarì siciliani, ma abolì le monete di rame e sospese i tarì continentali, e fece dei denari di mistura la principale moneta per l'uso interno in tutto il Regno.

Come in età normanna, il Regno era amministrativamente diviso in due parti principali, dette Capitanerie, a loro volta divise in Giustizierati: una parte, corrispondente al territorio dell'antica contea di Sicilia e Calabria, comprendeva l'isola e la Calabria fino alla *porta Roseti*, mentre l'altra parte corrispondeva al territorio del ducato di Puglia, con Gaeta e Capua, fino al fiume Tronto.

Ciascuna parte del Regno era servita da una zecca: Palermo, e poi Messina, per la parte siciliana; Brindisi, e brevemente Manfredonia, per la parte settentrionale. Questo assetto fu spezzato con il Vespro nel 1282, quando la Sicilia passò sotto il dominio aragonese.

La monetazione dei denari fu studiata per la prima volta in modo globale da Blancard (1864) che pubblicò un documento noto come il formulario di Marsiglia, una lista di denari emessi dal 1221 fino ai successori di Federico II, compilata dal legato pontificio nel Regno intorno al 1285: la sua importanza sta nel fatto che per ogni emissione elencata viene indicato il titolo di fino.

Winkelmann (1880) offrì ulteriori commenti sul tema, e Sambon (1896) diede la classificazione generale di tutto il materiale noto, basandosi sul contenuto di fino di ciascun tipo, ottenuto mediante analisi distruttive, e datandolo secondo i dati offerti dalle fonti (esaminati più avanti). La classificazione di Sambon è ancora grosso modo quella seguita attualmente, da Spahr, ed ancora da chi scrive: è notevole che, nonostante la ricchezza dei materiali e delle fonti scritte, queste serie non siano state analizzate più recentemente per verificare la classificazione e i dati di Sambon. Se comunque esiste una classificazione generale, ben pochi tentativi sono stati compiuti per stabilire le attribuzioni di zecca (Travaini 1993).

Almeno 114 tipi di denari sono noti per Enrico VI, Federico II, Corrado I, Corradino, Manfredi, e Carlo I d'Angiò. Questi tipi sono generalmente ben noti, ma finora ben pochi di essi erano stati attribuiti ad una zecca o all'altra. I tipi battuti in Sicilia e a Brindisi erano sempre differenti uno dall'altro, ma solo una piccola parte presenta un elemento valido per l'attribuzione di zecca: A o AP per Apulia; S o SICIL per Sicilia. Per sei tipi di Carlo I d'Angiò si conoscono gli ordini di zecca per le emissioni del 1276, 1277 e 1278, che contengono anche i disegni (Minieri Riccio 1878). Ma per la maggior parte degli altri tipi vi era incertezza di attribuzione, indicata con 'Messina o Brindisi' oppure 'Brindisi?' o 'Messina?' se vi era qualche elemento per ritenere una zecca più probabile dell'altra. Anche le attribuzioni a Manfredonia erano per lo più incerte.

I denari prodotti contemporaneamente dalle due zecche avevano lo stesso peso e contenuto argenteo, ed in teoria potevano circolare su tutto il territorio, e non solo nella parte dove erano stati distribuiti. In pratica, tuttavia, è più probabile che ciascun tipo avesse circolato prevalentemente nella rispettiva parte di distribuzione. Su questo si era già basato Sambon attribuendo a Brindisi un tipo di Federico II rinvenuto in un ripostiglio trovato a Suio, senza però continuare simile procedimento per altri tipi.

Proprio i rinvenimenti isolati ed i ripostigli sono la chiave per l'attribuzione di zecca: analizzando la distribuzione dei denari in 11 ripostigli ed in vari rinvenimenti è emerso un quadro assai preciso: su 114 tipi, 81 hanno un dato di provenienza da ripostiglio o da scavo, o da entrambi (Tabella 1, aggiornata rispetto a quella in Travaini (1993), con l'aggiunta dei dati dagli scavi di Otranto). Di questi 81 tipi, solo due risultano presenti su entrambe le parti: un tipo di Federico II probabilmente del 1243, rinvenuto sia a Monte Iato in Sicilia che a Ordona in Puglia (Tabella 1, n. 36), ed un tipo di Carlo I, con leggenda APVL, e quindi verosimilmente di Brindisi, rinvenuto nel ripostiglio di Vibo Valentia (n. 84). Tutti gli altri tipi, invece, sono stati rinvenuti ciascuno in una sola delle due parti del Regno, indicando in linea generale che i denari prodotti in Sicilia, e distribuiti in Sicilia e Calabria, difficilmente raggiungevano l'altra parte del Regno, e così i denari prodotti a Brindisi o Manfredonia. Ulteriori rinvenimenti potranno perfezionare, e modificare, il quadro delle attribuzioni, ma i dati a nostra disposizione, basati spesso sulla testimonianza parallela di ripostigli e ritrovamenti isolati, sembrano costituire un buon campione. E' questo il primo studio in questa direzione, ed offre una testimonianza inedita di un aspetto dell'organizzazione del Regno: produzione – relativamente all'individuazione della zecca –, distribuzione e circolazione dei denari.

I RINVENIMENTI: RIPOSTIGLI

I ripostigli di denari svevi e angioini di cui ho trovato notizia sono 12, dei quali 11 provenienti dal territorio del Regno, ed uno proveniente da Tiro in Terra Santa (cfr. Appendice 1 e fig.1). Per molti di essi si hanno solo notizie incerte, così come incerta è la provenienza e la stessa composizione. Si possono notare tuttavia alcune caratteristiche: sette ripostigli provengono dalla parte siciliana del Regno, quattro dalla parte continentale; in tutti i casi, quali che siano le condizioni del ritrovamento e la dimensione del ripostiglio, si nota una presenza di denari provenienti da una sola delle due zecche del Regno: la ricorrenza delle presenze in un gruppo o nell'altro ha permesso di attribuire ad una zecca o all'altra gran parte dei tipi finora non attribuiti, e di stabilire l'area di provenienza per ripostigli come quelli di 'Marks' o di 'Cambridge', privi di ogni dato ad essa relativo.

Il fenomeno di 'zecca unica' si osserva, come è più logico, nei ripostigli contenenti uno o pochi tipi, con breve escursione cronologica, come è il caso dei ripostigli di Siracusa (un solo tipo), Sicilia ante 1982 (due tipi), Monte Iato (due tipi), Suio (un tipo), 'vicino Napoli' (due tipi), Sicilia ca. 1970 (un tipo), Vibo Valentia (10 tipi, concentrati tra 1250 e 1278; qui è l'unica eccezione tra tutti i ripostigli esaminati: un denaro APVL di Carlo I, n. 84 nella Tabella). Il fenomeno di 'unica zecca' si osserva tuttavia anche in ripostigli 'di risparmio' a più ampia escursione cronologica, accumulati probabilmente in momenti successivi, come quelli di 'Marks' (parte continentale del Regno, 129 denari da Federico II, 1197–1250, a Carlo II d'Angiò, 1285–1309), di 'Cambridge' (parte siciliana, 34

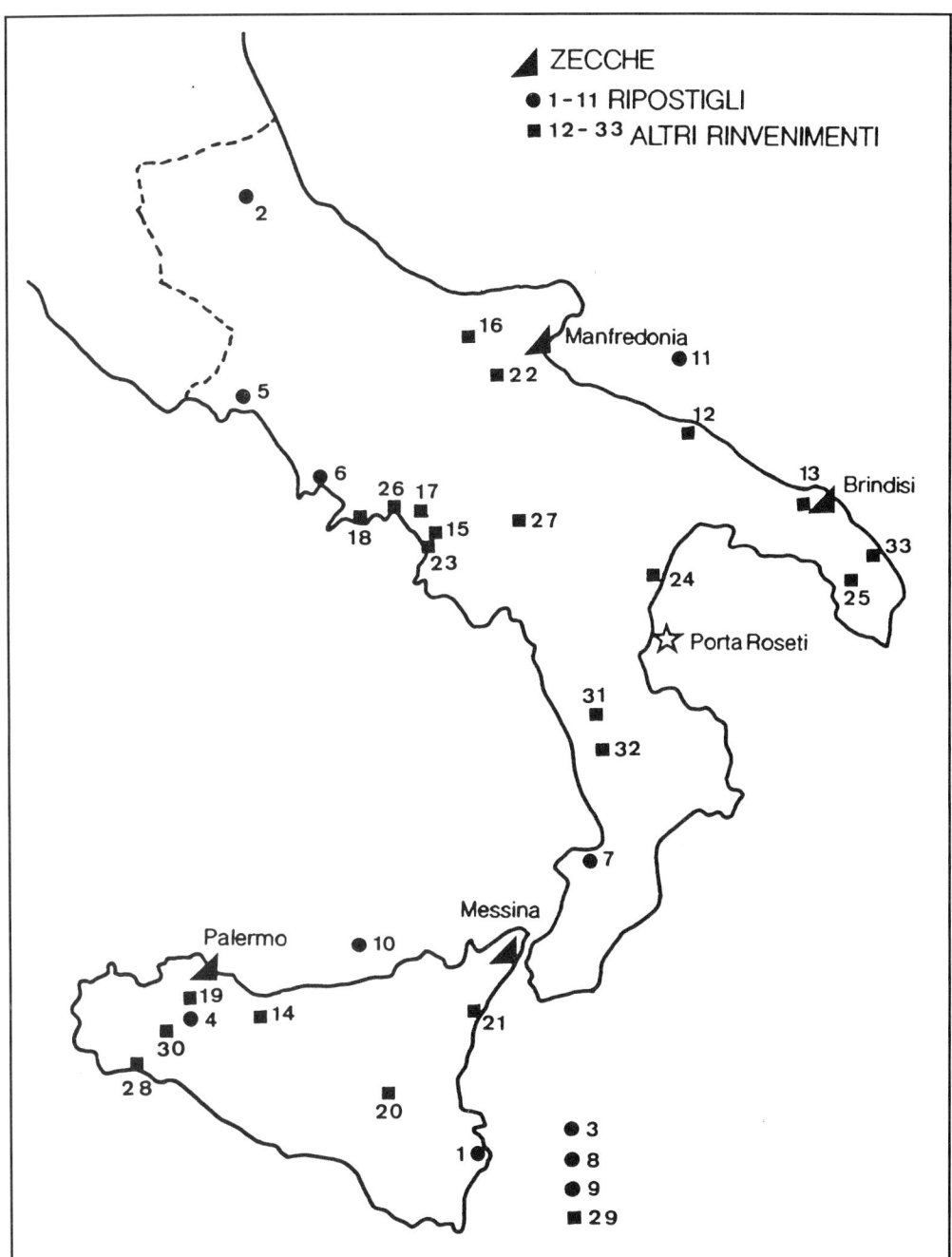

Fig. 1. Distribuzione (ripostigli e altri rinvenimenti) dei denari svevi e angioni nel Regno di Sicilia.
Ripostigli: 1. Siracusa; 2. Collecorvino; 3. Sicilia; 4. Monte Iato; 5. Suio; 6. 'vicino Napoli'; 7. Vibo Valentia; 8. Sicilia; 9. 'Cambridge'; 10. Sicilia settentrionale; 11. 'Marks'. Altri rinvenimenti: 12. Bari; 13. Brindisi; 14. Brucato; 15. Capaccio Vecchia; 16. Castel Fiorentino; 17. Eboli; 18. Minori; 19. Monte Iato; 20. Morgantina; 21. Naxos; 22. Ordona; 23. Paestum; 24. Policoro; 25. 'Salento'; 26. Salerno; 27. Satriano; 28. Selinunte; 29. Sicilia; 30. Entella; 31. Orsomarso; 32. San Sosti; 33. Otranto.

denari da Enrico VI a Carlo I), e di Sicilia settentrionale (61 denari da Enrico VI a Federico III d'Aragona, oltre a tre denari di Genova).

Al contrario, il ripostiglio di Tiro in Terra Santa, con escursione cronologica da Enrico VI a Carlo I, mostra denari di entrambe le zecche, e conferma a suo modo che i denari delle due zecche avevano di volta in volta lo stesso valore e potevano eventualmente circolare su tutto il territorio del Regno, anche se ciò non pare avvenisse.

RITROVAMENTI ISOLATI E DA SCAVO

I dati sui rinvenimenti vengono da 22 siti, e non possono

certo considerarsi completi (cfr. Appendice 2). Alcuni siti hanno fornito materiale abbondante, come Ordona, Otranto e Brucato. Da ciascuno dei siti i denari da Enrico VI a Carlo I appartengono a tipi ritrovati finora solo sulla relativa area di appartenenza; unica eccezione il tipo n. 36, di cui un esemplare fu rinvenuto a Monte Iato ed a Ordona.

La Tabella 1 mostra l'elenco di 114 tipi di denari da Enrico VI a Carlo I d'Angiò, con i dati di provenienza sintetizzati in due colonne: la prima indica le provenienze da Sicilia e Calabria, la seconda dalle altre provincie continentali; il numero si riferisce al totale dei pezzi rinvenuti (^ = ripostigli; * = rinvenimenti isolati; il punto interrogativo indica incertezza sul tipo di rinvenimento ma non sull'area di provenienza; per esempio, 23^^^ indica un totale di 23 esemplari da tre ripostigli, e 7**** indica 7 esemplari da quattro siti diversi):

Tabella 1

N.	Sicilia e Calabria		Italia meridionale	
	^	*	^	*
Enrico VI (1194-7)				
1-2	-	-	-	-
3	19+^	-	-	-
4	55^^	2**	-	-
5	-	-	-	-
6		1?	-	-
7	-	-	15+^	3**
8	23^^^	4*	-	-
9		1?	-	-
Federico II (1197-1250)				
10	-	-	-	2*
11	27^^	2*	-	-
12	-	-	-	-
13		4?	-	-
14		1?	-	-
15	49^^	4*	-	-
16	-	2*	-	-
17		1?	-	-
18	-	-	-	-
(1220-37)				
19	-	2*	-	-
20		2?	-	-
21	1^	-	-	-
22	7^	1*	-	-
23	-	-	n^	1*
24	-	-	-	-
25		1?	-	-
26	-	1*	-	-
27	1^	2*	-	-
28	-	-	-	1*
29	1^	-	-	-
30	-	-	-	1*

(Tabella 1)

N.	Sicilia e Calabria		Italia meridionale	
	^	*	^	*
(1238-50)				
31	-	-	2^	8****
32-4	-	-	-	-
35	-	-	1^	6*****
36	-	1*	-	1*
37	-	-	-	8**
38	-	-	-	-
39	2^	-	-	-
40	-	-	-	7****
41	5^	1*	-	-
42-4	-	-	-	-
45	-	-	3^	4**
46	-	-	2^	-
47	-	-	-	5**
48	-	-	3+n^^	1*
49	-	-	-	n?
Corrado I (1250-54)				
50	-	-	19^	7****
51	-	-	-	-
52	7^^	-	-	-
53	1^	-	-	-
54	-	-	8^	13*****
55	-	-	-	-
Corradino (1254-58)				
56	-	-	6^	1*
57	2^	-	-	-
58-63	-	-	-	-
64	-	-	9^	4**
Manfredi (1258-66)				
65	-	-	8^	4****
66	-	-	3^	-
67	-	-	1^	-
68	-	-	21^	1*
69	4^^	2**	-	-
70	1^	1*	-	-
71	-	-	5^	3***
72	-	2*	-	-
73	-	-	7^	-
74-6	-	-	-	-
77	-	-	1^	-
78	2^^	7*	-	-
79	-	-	-	4***
80	-	-	4^	-
81	4^	5*	-	-
82	4^^	9*	-	-
83	-	-	-	-
Carlo I (1266-85)				
84	1^	-	-	-
85	-	1*	-	-
86	3^^	-	-	-
87	-	-	-	-
88	-	-	3^	1*
89	-	-	1^	-

(Tabella 1)

N.	Sicilia e Calabria		Italia meridionale	
	^	*	^	*
90	-	-	4^	1*
91	-	-	-	-
92	-	-	-	2**
93-4	-	-	-	-
95	4^^	-	-	-
96	-	-	-	-
97	-	-	2^	2*
98	-	-	-	1*
99	-	-	-	-
100	-	-	1^	5***
101	1^	-	-	-
102	-	2*	-	-
103	-	-	1^	5***
104	11^	1*	-	-
105	-	-	4^	-
106	-	-	4^	-
107	4^^	-	-	-
108	-	-	-	-
109	3^^	-	-	-
110	-	-	3^	1*
111	3^^	-	-	-
112	7+^^^	-	-	-
113	-	-	-	-
114	-	-	1^	-

Osservazioni sulla classificazione e sulla distribuzione dei denari da Enrico VI a Carlo I d'Angiò

Enrico VI (1194-97)

Appena preso il potere nel Regno (incoronato a Palermo nel Natale 1194), Enrico VI abolì le monete di rame e riorganizzò la produzione della moneta di basso argento, che già i normanni avevano prodotto, in varie denominazioni; chiuse la zecca di Salerno e aprì la zecca di Brindisi destinata alla produzione dei denari per la parte continentale del Regno. A Brindisi sembra attribuibile un solo tipo, a nome di Enrico e Costanza, recante AP per Apulia (Tabella 1, n. 7): è questo l'unico suo tipo rinvenuto in quella parte del Regno. Per gli altri tipi di denari di Enrico si hanno provenienze siciliane e calabresi. Si credeva comunemente che Enrico avesse anche chiuso la zecca di Palermo, ma è invece ormai accettato che la zecca della capitale avesse continuato ad operare ancora fino almeno ai primi anni di Federico II. A Messina fu certamente interrotta la produzione di monete di rame, ma non sappiamo quando vi si cominciarono a produrre i denari; nell'impossibilità di precisare, i denari siciliani sono stati attribuiti come Messina/Palermo.

Federico II (1197-1250)

La classificazione dei denari di Federico II da noi utilizzata è ancora sostanzialmente quella di Sambon, e qui bisogna fare alcune precisazioni. Sambon si servì essenzialmente di due fonti: il già menzionato formulario di Marsiglia, che descrive sei diversi gruppi di emissioni di denari, di qualità progressivamente ridotta, inquadrati in un ambito cronologico che va dal 1221 (*quando imperator venit in Regnum*) fino ai successori di Federico (*post dominum imperatorem alii domini*, Winkelmann 1880-I: doc. 1002 pp. 763-5), e la cronaca di Riccardo di San Germano, che ricorda varie emissioni dal 1221 al 1242. Sambon organizzò poi i risultati delle sue analisi distruttive secondo i dati delle fonti. A proposito della testimonianza di Riccardo di San Germano, Sambon fece una distinzione tra emissioni per le quali la cronaca riporta l'abolizione dei denari precedenti (*veteres cassati sunt*, nel 1221, 1225, 1236, 1239), ed emissioni in cui tale abolizione non è indicata (1242), ed interpretò le prime come emissioni con peggioramento di titolo (Sambon 1896: 212; Travaini 1993). Questo dovrà essere verificato, eventualmente con analisi non distruttive effettuate su ampia campionatura: i denari imperiali del 1221, ad esempio, non sembrano avere un fino peggiore dei precedenti di Enrico; l'abolizione dei denari *veteres* si riferiva probabilmete a tutti i tipi di denari 'vecchi' che circolavano nel Regno, con particolare riferimento a quelli stranieri, come fu poi ribadito dagli ordini del 1222.

La prima parte del regno di Federico fu caratterizzata da grande instabilità; la zecca di Brindisi restò chiusa probabilmente da 1197 al 1215 circa. Di questo periodo, solo un tipo (Tabella 1, n. 10) proviene dalla parte settentrionale del regno (Ordona), forse battuto a Brindisi nel primo anno di regno di Federico. Tutti gli altri denari anteriori al 1221 hanno invece una provenienza siciliana, inclusi tre tipi a nome di Federico e Costanza d'Aragona (Tabella 1, nn. 15-17): sembra dunque che la maggior parte dei denari di quel periodo fosse stata prodotta a Messina/Palermo.

Federico fu incoronato imperatore a Roma il 22 novembre 1220. Dopo l'incoronazione vi furono probabilmente alcune emissioni celebrative, piuttosto rare, con il nuovo titolo imperiale, tutte siciliane (Tabella 1, nn. 19-21). Solo nel settembre 1221 Federico riorganizzò la produzione monetaria: chiuse allora la zecca di Palermo, e fece battere a Brindisi e Messina i nuovi denari *imperiales* (nn. 22-23). Pagano Balduino, già capo della zecca di Messina, ebbe l'incarico di organizzare la riapertura della zecca di Brindisi, e nell'aprile 1221 ebbe dall'imperatore il privilegio del *locum* di Viareggio in Toscana, che era stato distrutto da Federico Barbarossa e non più riedificato (Huillard-Bréholles, II/1: 169-71). Tale privilegio fu ritenuto una prova che Brindisi dovette aver funzionato già qualche tempo prima del 1221, ma è probabile che esso fosse semplicemente un segno di stima imperiale verso il fedele zecchiere, ed insieme un modo per legarlo più saldamente agli obblighi di fedeltà e segretezza propri dell'incarico, ma ancor più cogenti in vista del particolare uso della moneta che Federico stava per introdurre: emissione e distribuzione forzosa della moneta per nutrire le casse imperiali.

I denari del settembre 1221, dunque, furono distribuiti 'contro la volontà del popolo al cambio di 16 per tarì' (come risulta dal formulario di Marsiglia), mentre il valore effettivo avrebbe dovuto dare 23 denari e 1/4 per tarì. Questa imposizione generò malcontento, al quale si accompagnavano anche accuse di 'falsa moneta' per l'imperatore (dovute al cambio imposto piuttosto che al contenuto argenteo in se stesso). Federico, che aveva ormai posto sotto controllo l'amministrazione del suo stato, il 10 settembre mise a tacere ogni protesta ed impose con vigore in tutto il Regno il monopolio di circolazione dei suoi denari imperiali: ...*non faciam aliquem mercatum pro alio argento vel alia moneta quam pro denariis novis Brundisii* [e di Messina per l'altra parte del Regno].

Non possiamo dire esattamente fino a che punto il monopolio fosse rispettato, ma sembra che in generale lo fosse: da quel momento i denari imperiali sono attestati nei ritrovamenti delle due parti del Regno. I dati, come si è detto, sono provvisori, ma sembra di poter affermare che il controllo statale ed il sistema della distribuzione forzata dei denari capillarmente in tutto il Regno non lasciassero molto spazio ad altra moneta per gli scambi più comuni.

Nuovi denari furono emessi nel 1225 (*et veteres cassati sunt*), in occasione delle nozze di Federico con Isabella, figlia di Giovanni di Brienne re di Gerusalemme (nn. 26-27). Altra distribuzione forzata di denari nuovi fu imposta nel 1228, per finanziare la crociata (nn. 28-29). Nessun'altra emissione è ricordata dalle fonti fino al 1236, ma non si può escludere che denari fossero stati emessi comunque (ed in tal caso si dovrebbe rivedere la datazione proposta da Sambon per alcuni tipi). Nel 1231 iniziò la coniazione degli augustali d'oro a Brindisi e Messina; l'organizzazione di una *sicla auri* a Brindisi iniziò nel 1229 (Travaini 1994, 156).

Nel 1236 è ricordata l'emissione di nuovi denari, per finanziare la guerra in Lombardia; e poco dopo, nel luglio 1238, Federico, all'assedio di Brescia, avendo bisogno urgente di denaro ad ogni costo, ordinò una nuova emissione, per la quale inviò nel Regno tutti i dettagli, ivi inclusa la descrizione del tipo. Nella stessa lettera Federico ordinò anche di rimuovere dall'ufficio alcuni zecchieri 'infedeli, che avevano rivelato ai mercanti il vero valore dei denari emessi', e di sostituirli con zecchieri 'di fiducia, che non abbiano altri interessi che non il bene dello stato': in questa occasione Federico concesse notevoli privilegi ai monetieri (Winkelmann 1880: 637; Travaini 1988: 44). I nuovi denari furono battuti a Brindisi nel gennaio 1239 (probabilmente il tipo n. 31). Nessun tipo è stato finora attribuito a Messina per quell'anno; il 6 maggio 1240 gli zecchieri di Messina ricevettero l'ordine di inviare tutto il denaro raccolto in seguito alla nuova emissione, ma non è possibile sapere se si trattasse dei denari del 1239 o di altri ancora (Sambon 1896: 357; Sambon *c*.1916: 100).

Nel 1242 vi fu una nuova emissione, ricordata da Riccardo di San Germano, ma senza dire se vi fosse stata abolizione dei denari vecchi. Sambon attribuì al periodo 1242-1249 un gran numero di tipi, suggerendo una emissione all'anno; le attribuzioni di zecca sono state ora precisate grazie ai rinvenimenti: apparentemente sembra che la zecca di Brindisi avesse svolto un ruolo di maggiore importanza che non Messina. Nell'aprile 1248, subito dopo la sconfitta di Vittoria (Parma), è documentata una nuova emissione di denari, apparentemente allo stesso titolo argenteo dei precedenti (Sambon 1896: 362; Winkelmann 1880: 707, 711-12). Sambon poi attribuì due tipi di denari molto sviliti (nn. 48-49) al 1249, secondo la testimonianza del ripostiglio 'vicino Napoli', composto unicamente da questi due tipi e da un tipo di Corrado I.

Oltre ai denari, si conoscono mezzi denari, e, probabilmente, quarti di denaro, ma l'intero sistema deve essere meglio investigato. Dei 40 tipi di denari di Federico II elencati in Travaini 1993, sette mancano in Spahr (1976).

Corrado I (1250-54) e Corradino (1254-58)

A Federico successe il figlio Corrado, che morì il 21 maggio 1254, lasciando il regno al figlio Corradino. Manfredi resse il regno in suo nome fino al 1258. Secondo il formulario di Marsiglia tutti i denari dei successori di Federico avevano un fino di 1,96%, e furono imposti a 24 per tarì.

E' stato affermato che la zecca di Brindisi fosse stata inattiva tra 1250 e 1256, in quanto ribelle agli svevi (Sambon c.1916: 114; Spahr 1976: 207). Tuttavia, la distribuzione dei denari dei due Corradi (nn. 50-64) nei rinvenimenti sembra seguire le linee precedenti, con tipi diversi per le due parti, tanto da far supporre che la zecca di Brindisi avesse continuato ad operare normalmente, e del resto fin dall'inizio del 1253 il Regno risultava pacificato e sotto controllo (Cuozzo 1989: 775-776). Non si può escludere tuttavia che le monete fossero in casi particolari prodotte nella sola Messina e distribuite poi anche in Italia meridionale.

Manfredi (1258-66)

Manfredi fu incoronato re di Sicilia a Palermo il 10 agosto 1258, diffusa la notizia falsa della morte di Corradino. Fondò la città di Manfredonia, e vi trasferì la zecca di Brindisi. Dei 19 tipi di Manfredi (nn.65-83) molte attribuzioni di zecca sono state corrette: alcuni tipi con M centrale attribuiti a Manfredonia devono essere attribuiti a Messina, e viceversa, in base ai rinvenimenti (la M centrale stava evidentemente per Manfredi, e non per la zecca). Solo due tipi sembrano attribuibili a Brindisi per l'indicazione A e AP, tradizionale di quella zecca; per gli altri tipi 'continentali' non è invece possibile allo stato attuale distinguere tra denari di Brindisi e di Manfredonia. Benchè secondo il formulario di Marsiglia i suoi denari fossero della stessa lega dei precedenti, la loro qualità appare molto deteriorata.

Carlo I d'Angiò (1266-85)

Carlo d'Angiò fu coronato a Roma il 6 gennaio 1266 e il 6 febbraio sconfisse ed uccise Manfredi alla battaglia di Benevento. Carlo conservò le strutture amministrative dello stato svevo; nel maggio 1266 reiterò il monopolio di circolazione dei suoi denari nel Regno; le zecche per i denari, chiusa quella di Manfredonia, continuarono ad essere Brindisi e Messina (Barletta fu attiva per brevissimo tempo nei primi anni) e la nuova zecca di Napoli, aperta nel 1278, produsse per lui solo i nuovi carlini d'oro e d'argento.

Carlo deluse subito i sudditi del Regno che avevano sperato in un alleggerimento della pressione fiscale: già nel dicembre del 1266 Carlo riscosse la sua prima 'colletta' (*generalis subventio*), e suscitò persino la diretta reazione pontificia (Galasso 1992: 17, 53-55). La 'colletta', che ancora con Federico aveva un carattere straordinario, divenne un mezzo ordinario di finanziamento dello stato, accanto agli introiti della secrezia (imposte sui consumi, traffici e prodotti particolari), dei beni della corona, e delle operazioni mercantili; lo scontento popolare è descritto in numerose fonti relative al Vespro. I suoi denari sono di cattiva qualità e sono stati spesso definiti di rame. Il loro valore era divenuto così basso che non si produssero più mezzi denari; per alcuni tipi si conoscono dei cosiddetti 'multipli' che non sono stati però ancora ben indagati.

Dei denari di Carlo I, alcuni tipi sono attribuibili grazie all'indicazione APVL per Brindisi e SICIL per Messina (n. 84, APVL, rinvenuto nel ripostiglio di Vibo Valentia, e nn. 85-86). Per le emissioni del 1276, 1277 e 1278 sono conservate le istruzioni di zecca per entrambe le zecche, contenenti anche i disegni dei tipi, che corrispondono agli esemplari giunti fino a noi (nn. 106-111; Minieri Riccio 1878: 118-9, 140-1). Per gli altri tipi l'attribuzione di zecca si è resa possibile grazie ai rinvenimenti (Travaini 1993: con quattro tipi assenti in Spahr).

Con il Vespro (30 marzo 1282) l'unità del Regno di Sicilia si spezzò e la Sicilia, e per alcuni anni anche la Calabria (fino alla pace di Caltabellotta nel 1302), passò sotto il governo aragonese, ed ebbe una monetazione propria. Nella parte angioina del Regno venne allora l'impegno a migliorare la moneta e ad abolire l'imposta monetaria (1283); di fatto la produzione di denari a Brindisi fu interrotta per alcuni anni. La circolazione minuta in Italia meridionale subì alcune trasformazioni, illustrate più avanti.

AMMINISTRAZIONE FINANZIARIA E DISTRIBUZIONE DEI DENARI NEL REGNO (1194-1285)

L'esame globale dei rinvenimenti di denari del Regno dai ripostigli e dai ritrovamenti isolati, presentati alla Tabella 1, permette di rilevare vari aspetti della circolazione monetaria, anche in relazione ai rinvenimenti di denari stranieri, e pone anche molti quesiti.

La tabella evidenzia chiaramente come i denari svevi di Enrico VI e Federico fino al 1221 circa siano presenti quasi unicamente in Sicilia. Ciò conferma quanto già noto sul grande uso di denari stranieri nella parte settentrionale del Regno tra 1180 e 1220: a causa dello scarso controllo statale i denari stranieri, prevalentemente provisini e lucchesi, non venivano cambiati in moneta locale, ma circolavano localmente. Federico II ne abolì la circolazione nel 1221-22.

I DENARI STRANIERI NEL REGNO

I denari lucchesi *enrici* e quelli di Genova (1139-1339) ebbero una certa diffusione in Sicilia (D'Angelo 1984: 41), ma la loro cronologia non è precisa a causa dei tipi immobilizzati. In Italia meridionale, dove la documentazione è più abbondante, i ritrovamenti di denari lucchesi, provisini, angevini e altri (il cui uso è attestato anche nelle fonti scritte: Martin 1986) confermano come la circolazione fosse dominata da monete straniere prima delle nuove disposizioni di Federico II nel 1221-22. Per quanto la datazione di tali denari non sia strettamente precisabile, si suggerisce in via di ipotesi un termine ante-1222 per la loro circolazione: i provisini di Champagne trovati isolatamente a Otranto, Ordona e Salerno, e nel ripostiglio di Montescaglioso in Basilicata (Curtotti 1989) sono tutti di Thibault II (1125-52) o di Enrico I o II (1152-97), mentre assente è il tipo attribuito a Thibaut IV (1201-53) e datato post 1224 (Dumas & Barrandon 1982: 58, 95); questa considerazione, unitamente all'esistenza del forte monopolio di circolazione imposto da Federico, sembra smentire l'ipotesi di una datazione fino alla metà del XIII secolo per i provisini dei rinvenimenti sud-italiani (Abulafia 1991: 355). Del resto, imitazioni di provisini furono prodotte a Roma dal 1180 circa, ma non se trovano nel territorio del Regno nel XIII secolo, ad esclusione dell'area di Gaeta: un provisino del Senato romano trovato a Bari appartiene al XIV secolo. Anche per i denari angevini ai tipi immobilizzati di Fulk, trovati isolatamente a

Satriano e a Otranto, la datazione va dal XII agli inizi del XIII secolo. Anche per i lucchesi *enrici* si può supporre una circolazione nel Regno ante 1222. Per quanto vi fosse sempre un certo spazio all'ingresso di denari stranieri, si deve tener conto dell'ipotesi che il monopolio imposto nel 1222 riuscisse a limitarne fortemente l'uso.

Più difficilmente databili sono un denaro di Valence da Bari (1157-1276) e due denari di Melgueil, da Salerno e da Otranto (XII-XIII secolo). Al XIII secolo appartiene un denaro dei vescovi di Maguelonne da Castel Fiorentino; un denaro di Siena (post 1250-66) da Ordona. Denari di Ancona, databili al XIII secolo, sono stati rinvenuti isolatamente a Ordona e Castel Fiorentino, da dove pure è un denaro di Ravenna (post 1231): la loro penetrazione è legata alle relazioni commerciali tra la Puglia e i centri adriatici, ma non si può definirli 'moneta locale' se vigeva un regime di stretto monopolio della moneta.

I denari del Regno

Stranieri o locali, i denari nei rinvenimenti del Regno non sono numerosi, fino al 1238 circa. Unificando i dati, ancora parziali, dei rinvenimenti relativi al XIII secolo con quelli del periodo X-XII secolo, si osserva il seguente andamento, che, si ripete, dovrà essere verificato sulla base di dati più ampi: numerosi rinvenimenti nel X e prima metà XI secolo, anche in aree rurali, con progressiva riduzione tra XI e XII secolo; relativamente poche monete per il XII secolo e primi tre decenni del XIII secolo, e per lo più limitate alle aree urbane. Il numero di monete rinvenute cresce apparentemente solo dal 1239, e quindi in ritardo rispetto a quanto rilevato ad esempio per l'Italia settentrionale o per l'Inghilterra (Travaini 1995; Spufford 1988: 379-386).

A partire da un tipo datato 1238-39 i denari federiciani si presentano molto numerosi tra i ritrovamenti isolati, soprattutto nella parte settentrionale del Regno. L'abbondanza dei ritrovamenti si può spiegare in primo luogo con l'aumento effettivo della quantità di moneta coniata, e il diminuito valore intrinseco dei denari, un accresciuto uso di moneta negli scambi, e quindi la maggior facilità nel perderla: seppur apparentemente con ritardo, la monetizzazione dell'economia rurale si sviluppò anche nel contesto feudale del Regno, dove si venne a creare tra l'altro una rete di fiere e mercati che implicavano l'uso di moneta. Non è un caso che proprio la bolla della scomunica del 1239 accusasse Federico di essere un falsario, viot i; suoi denari.

Nonostante la maggiore quantità di moneta in uso, il rapporto tra zecca di origine e luogo di rinvenimento rimane lo stesso, confermando la 'sedentarietà' di questi denari tra 1238 e 1282 (le attribuzioni di zecca proposte sulla base dei rinvenimenti potranno essere perfezionate o modificate grazie a nuovi materiali, ma in linea generale il quadro non dovrebbe subire grosse alterazioni). E' noto che la moneta minuta circola solo localmente, ma tutto il Regno era in teoria area di circolazione per i denari di Brindisi e di Messina. Come spiegare dunque la 'sedentarietà' dei denari del periodo 1238-1282?

Si è da più parti posto l'accento sulle scarse relazioni tra le province del Regno, sulle cattive vie di comunicazione, sull'autonomia di molti paesi (De Rosa 1986; Tucci 1990). Questo tuttavia non mi sembra poter spiegare completamente il fenomeno. Vi sono alcuni elementi infatti che indicano come subito prima e subito dopo quel periodo vi fosse stato un certo movimento di moneta minuta tra le due parti del Regno.

I dati sui rinvenimenti nel Regno di Sicilia in età normanna, peraltro molto scarsi, non sono direttamente paragonabili con quelli dell'età sveva, poichè la monetazione normanna era trimetallica, ed inoltre Ruggero II nel 1140, pur riorganizzando unitariamente il sistema monetario, lasciò molti dei particolarismi locali. Qualche affinità con il sistema dei denari svevi si riscontra per le monete di rame, che erano prodotte a Salerno per la parte settentrionale del Regno, e a Messina per Sicilia e Calabria: gli unici dati a nostra disposizione indicano una discreta presenza a Salerno di follari di Messina di tutti i sovrani normanni (Foresio 1893: tav. VI.172-4, 163; tav. VIII.246-9; tav. X.346-7, 362; Peduto 1993: 222).

Per quanto riguarda il periodo successivo al 1282, si può segnalare che a Brucato in Sicilia, oltre a 64 denari aragonesi di Messina del periodo 1285-1336, sono stati rinvenuti 14 denari angioini di Napoli, di Carlo II (1285-1309) e di Roberto (1309-43), la cui presenza indica una netta viariazione rispetto al periodo precedente (Bresc-Bautier 1984: 474). Se questi dati attestano un certo movimento di moneta minuta tra le due parti del Regno in età normanna e dopo il Vespro, si può supporre che una delle cause della 'sedentarietà' dei denari del Regno tra 1238 e 1282 sia da cercare nel sistema delle continue *renovationes*: dopo il Vespro le *renovationes* annuali ebbero fine, il controllo sul circolante si allentò, ed i denari restarono di conseguenza in circolazione più a lungo.

Considerando che dal 1238-39 si verificarono emissioni e distribuzioni di denari a scadenza quasi annuale, con abolizione dei vecchi denari ad ogni nuova emissione, la 'sedentarietà regionale' dei denari sarebbe attribuibile al fatto che questi denari restavano in circolazione per un tempo molto breve, appena un anno circa, e poi venivano *cassati*, cioè aboliti; questa continua *renovatio monetae* limitava fortemente le occasioni di movimento verso le altre regioni.

Il fenomeno della *renovatio monetae* è noto e in alcuni casi ben documentato in tutta l'Europa medievale in vari periodi (Suchodolski 1961; Blackburn 1986). Nessun caso tuttavia è paragonabile al Regno di Sicilia per il tipo di documentazione raccolto: un territorio così vasto, diviso amministrativamente in due parti, ciascuna servita da una sola zecca, che presenta una linea di demarcazione così netta tra aree di circolazione dei prodotti di ciascuna zecca.

Come avveniva una *renovatio*? Per ogni 'terra' di ciascun Giustizierato veniva fissata la quantità di denari da distribuire, in cambio di altra moneta, ad un corso certamente assai vantaggioso per il re: un sistema che poco più tardi fu introdotto in Francia da Filippo il Bello (Spufford 1988: 302).

Quale moneta era data in cambio della nuova? Generalmente è stato affermato (ad esempio, Barone 1926: 128) che per la nuova moneta si dava 'buona moneta d'oro e d'argento'. La documentazione sulle collette indica certamente i proventi in once, tarì e grani, ma questi erano la moneta di conto; sembra lecito supporre che non tutti pagassero in moneta d'oro o di 'buon argento'. E' verosimile che almeno in parte i denari vecchi venissero dati in cambio di quelli nuovi: la distribuzione poteva così rappresentare il momento del rinnovamento della moneta. Somme irrisorie come '14 grani' imposti alla *terra Sansonecti*, o 'un tarì e due grani' imposti alla *terra Philippi de Venafro* nella cedola per l'imposta in Terra d'Otranto nel 1276, furono pagate verosimilmente in denari vecchi (Barone 1926).

Noi non sappiamo fino a che punto ci fosse l'obbligo di cambiare la moneta in quella nuova, oltre al quantitativo previsto nella *cedula taxationis*; nessuna legge sembra aver impedito il semplice possesso di vecchia moneta, e così si spiega la presenza di denari di vari sovrani nei ripostigli di risparmio come quelli di 'Marks', 'Cambridge' e Sicilia settentrionale; è possibile inoltre che, in mancanza di moneta corrente, vecchi denari potessero essere usati, al valore di metallo, per qualche modesta transazione. I vecchi denari, dunque, potevano essere in parte utilizzati o rimessi in uso in momenti di minore controllo sul circolante, come potè essere avvenuto in Sicilia dopo il 1282: si spiegherebbero in tal modo anche i dati dagli scavi di Brucato dove i denari svevi e di Carlo I sono stati rinvenuti sempre associati con monete posteriori, senza per questo doversi trattare sempre di circolazione continuata (Bresc-Bautier 1984: 477).

Probabilmente non era sempre facile per il sovrano riscuotere moneta aurea: lo prova emblematicamente il fatto che perfino le 'once d'oro' dovute nel 1270 e nel 1280 come tributo dalla Tunisia erano in effetti pagate più in argento di 'monete di miliaresi' che in doppie d'oro, come il re avrebbe voluto (Galasso 1992: 64; Travaini 1992). Nel 1280 Carlo I d'Angiò accettava al valore di metallo pesato in pagamento per le imposte monete ufficialmente non circolanti nel Regno, come vari denari tornesi 'nel caso non si potesse riscuotere *aurum tarenorum carolenses et augustales*'(Mazzoleni 1969: 29-30; Travaini 1984: 361).

Se dunque i denari svevi e angioini tra 1221-39 e 1282 circa restavano nella parte del Regno dove erano stati prodotti e distribuiti, come è emerso dall'esame dei ritrovamenti, ciò può essere giustificato dalla loro breve circolazione dovuta alle distribuzioni forzose annuali, anche se dovranno essere approfondite le indagini sul movimento di uomini e cose all'interno del Regno.

Questa situazione monetaria portava un'altra conseguenza: i vecchi denari residui aboliti dalla circolazione corrente, ma non restituiti, conservavano un valore come metallo monetato a peso, che pur sempre conteneva una percentuale di argento. E' probabile che questi denari fossero in parte esportati dal Regno come metallo: già Federico II si era reso conto di questo, e nel 1222 proibì espressamente la vendita di *argentum vel bolzonem alicui qui extra Regnum portare voluerit*, e la ribadì nel 1238 (*bulzonalia de Regno nullatenus extrahantur*) (Sambon 1896: 339-40, 355; Garufi 1898: 136; Travaini 1988: 51). Non è escluso che il ripostiglio di Tiro rappresentasse un gruzzolo di tali denari fuori corso. E' vero comunque che ritrovamenti isolati di denari svevi e angioini in Terra Santa non sono rari e fanno presupporre una certa circolazione, specialmente nel XIII secolo, quando il controllo sul circolante era divenuto meno efficace (Metcalf 1986: 82).

La documentazione numismatica viene a confermare, con l'efficienza delle *renovationes*, l'efficienza dell'intero sistema fiscale, amara per i regnicoli, e non ultima causa del Vespro. Dopo il Vespro la Sicilia conobbe la nuova monetazione aragonese, mentre la parte angioina del Regno vide il forte afflusso dei denari tornesi della Grecia franca, documentati diffusamente in tutta l'Italia meridionale inclusa la Calabria in ritrovamenti isolati (Ordona, Otranto, Salerno, Capaccio Vecchia, Castel Fiorentino, Scribla), e ripostigli (Vibo Valentia, Policoro), e finora non in Sicilia (Travaini 1991).

Conclusioni

I rinvenimenti qui considerati sono solo un campione, ma i dati ci sembrano indicativi ed omogenei per delineare il seguente quadro della produzione, distribuzione e circolazione dei denari nel Regno di Sicilia.

Il sistema di produzione e distribuzione dei denari creato da Enrico VI per le due parti del Regno non ebbe piena attuazione in Italia meridionale, dove la circolazione dei denari stranieri continuò, e si accentuò dopo la sua morte, fino al 1220. Negli anni 1197-1220 i denari di Federico II furono prodotti e circolanti quasi unicamente in Sicilia. Nel 1221-1222 Federico riorganizzò il sistema di produzione e distribuzione dei denari, ed impose il monopolio di circolazione; dal 1239 le *renovationes* divennero sempre più frequenti, rendendo la circolazione dei denari estremamente breve, ostacolando di fatto i movimenti verso l'altra parte del

Regno. Dopo il 1282 il sistema si alterò, il Regno fu diviso, il controllo allentato e le *renovationes* sospese. Si aprì allora, nella parte angioina, un nuovo spazio a denari stranieri, mentre i denari locali restavano in circolazione più a lungo, e giungevano più lontano. Gli Aragonesi in Sicilia crearono una loro moneta, ma il disordine pare confermato da una disposizione del 12 dicembre 1315 in cui il re proibiva la circolazione di *denarios veteres alterius cunei quam cunei siclae* (Bresc-Bautier 1984: 477).

Note
1. Per l'individuazione dei tipi si segue la numerazione di Travaini 1993 – così in Tabella 1 – al quale si rimanda per la descrizione dei tipi e le illustrazioni, e per la tavola delle concordanze con Spahr.

APPENDICE 1

Ripostigli

(Il numero del tipo indicato si riferisce alla numerazione di Travaini 1993, al quale si rimanda per la descrizione e per la tavola delle concordanze con Spahr).

1. *Siracusa* 1889: oltre 19 denari di Enrico VI e Costanza, tipo 3-6 (*NSc* 1889, 92).
2. *Collecorvino* (Pescara, Abruzzo) 1867: 15 denari di Enrico e Costanza tipo 7, un denaro di Federico II tipo 35: il materiale pubblicato come 'ripostiglio' è molto eterogeneo ed il cosiddetto ripostiglio è quindi molto incerto (Cherubini 1868).
3. *Sicilia* ante 1982: 94 denari dei qualli 46 di Enrico VI tipo 4, e 48 di Federico II con Costanza d'Aragona, tipo 15. Occultato 1209? (Pancari 1982).
4. *Monte Iato* (Palermo) 1984: 27 denari, di cui: 3 di Enrico e Federico tipo 8; 18 di Federico tipo 11; 6 non identificati (Isler 1984). Occultato 1198?
5. *Suio* (presso Gaeta) c. 1900: 'un gruzzolo copiosissimo composto unicamente di questi denari' tipo 23 (Sambon c.1916: 92). Occultato 1221?
6. *Vicino Napoli*, XIX secolo: 'copioso ripostiglio in cui si trovarono solo monete di questo tipo [48-49] miste a denari della prima emissione di Corrado' (Sambon c.1916: 105). Occultato c. 1252.
7. *Vibo Valentia* (Catanzaro) 1970/2: 23 denari come segue: un denaro tornese di Chiarenza di Guillaume de Villehardouin (c.1250-77), 1 denaro di Manfredi tipo 82; 21 di Carlo I dei tipi 84, 86, 101, 104, 107, 109, 111, 112 (Arslan 1981). Occultato dopo il 1278.
8. *Sicilia* c.1970: sul mercato di Palermo, composto unicamente di denari di Carlo I tipo 112 (D'Angelo 1992).
9. *'Cambridge'*, 1956 (provenienza siciliana dedotta dai tipi di monete; al Fitzwilliam Museum): 34 denari, di cui: due di Enrico e Federico tipo 8; due di Federico II tipi 15, 27; cinque di Corrado I tipi 52, 53; uno di Corradino, tipo 57; 11 di Manfredi tipi 69, 78, 81, 82; 13 di Carlo I tipi 86, 95, 107, 109, 111, 112 (Travaini 1993). Occultato dopo il 1278.
10. *Sicilia settentrionale* 1978: disperso nel commercio, era originariamente composto da oltre 100 denari dei quali 64 identificati: otto di Enrico e Costanza tipo 4; 18 di Enrico e Federico tipo 8; 25 di Federico II tipi 11, 21, 22, 29, 39, 41; tre di Corrado I tipo 52; tre di Manfredi tipi 69, 70, 78; tre di Carlo I tipo 95; uno di Federico III d'Aragona (1296-1337); tre denari di Genova (*Coin Hoards* 5, 1979: 128).
11. *'Marks von Marsfeld'* 1857, disperso (provenienza dalla parte settentrionale del Regno dedotta dai tipi di denari): 210 monete di cui 132 identificate (ma tre intrusive); i 131 denari svevi e angioini sono i seguenti: 10 di Federico II tipi 31, 45, 48; 27 di Corrado I tipi 50, 54; 15 di Corradino tipi 56, 64; 50 di Manfredi tipi 65, 66, 67, 68, 71, 73, 77, 80; 24 di Carlo I tipi 88, 89, 90, 97, 100, 103, 105, 106, 110, 114; tre di Carlo II zecca di Napoli (Marks von Marsfeld 1858; Travaini 1993).
12. *Tiro, Israele* 1967: disperso, conteneva una quantità imprecisata di denari di Enrico VI tipo 4, Federico II tipi 27, 31, 40, 42, 49, Corado I tipo 54, Corradino tipo 57, Manfredi tipo 82, Carlo I tipo 97 (Du Quesne Bird & Metcalf 1979-81).

APPENDICE 2

Ritrovamenti isolati e da scavi

Bari, scavi nel castello: Federico II tipi 35, 40; Corrado I tipo 54; Corradino tipo 64. Denari di Lucca, Valence. Un provisino romano del XIV secolo (Di Capua 1983).
Brindisi/a, nel Museo, da ritrovamenti locali: Federico II tipi 40, 45; Corrado I tipi 92, 103 (Travaglini 1976-7).
Brindisi/b, da vari scavi urbani: Corrado I tipo 54; Manfredi tipo 71. Un denaro di Ancona del XV secolo per un errore è stato indicato come XI secolo (Cocchiaro, Marinazzo & Travaglini 1990).
Brucato (Palermo), scavi: Federico II tipo 39; Manfredi tipo 72; Carlo I tipi 85, 102, 104 (tutti di zecca siciliana); 6? di Carlo II della zecca di Napoli (Bresc-Bautier 1984).
Capaccio Vecchia (Salerno) scavi: Federico II tipi 7, 31. Denari tornesi della Grecia franca (Travaini 1984).
Castel Fiorentino (Foggia), scavi: Manfredi tipo 65. Denari di Maguelonne, Ancona, Ravenna (Rovelli & Gourdin 1987).
Eboli (Salerno), presso 'zona Pirchio, località S. Antonio': Federico II tipi 35, 40 (Catalli 1971-2).
Entella (Palermo), scavi: Federico II tipi 22, 26 (Canzanella e altri 1990).
Minori (Salerno), scavi nell'area della villa romana: Carlo I tipo 110. Un denaro di Pavia di Federico II (Libero Mangieri 1985-8).
Monte Iato (Palermo), da diverse campagne di scavo: Enrico VI tipi 4, 8; Federico II tipi 11, 19/a, 27, 36, 41 (Bloesch 1972; Bloesch e Isler 1975 e 1976; Isler 1987).
Morgantina (Aidone, Enna) scavi: Federico II tipi 15/a, 16 (Buttrey e altri, 1989).
Naxos (Taormina, Messina) scavi: Manfredi tipo 69 (Guzzetta 1980-81).
Ordona (Foggia), da varie campagne di scavo: Federico II tipi 10, 31, 35, 36, 37, 40, 45, 47, 48; Corrado I tipi 50, 54; Corradino tipo 64; Manfredi tipi 65, 71, 79; Carlo I tipi 98, 100. Denari di Venezia (XI-XII sec.), di Champagne, tornesi della Grecia franca (De Boe, 1965; Scheers e Bex, 1974; Scheers e van Heesch 1988).
Orsomarso (local. Castello di Raione, Cosenza), in superficie:

un denaro di Enrico VI tipo 4 (Tocci 1989: 110).

Otranto (Lecce) scavi: Enrico VI e Costanza tipo 7/a; Federico II tipi 28/a, 31, 35/a, 47; Manfredi tipi 68, 71, 79; Carlo I tipi 90, 92, 100, 103. Denari di Melgueil, Champagne, Anjou (a nome di Fulk), di Lucca *enrici*, di Pavia un denaro non precisato, diversi denari tornesi della Grecia franca (Travaglini 1992).

Paestum (Salerno) scavi nel santuario di Afrodite in località Santa Venera: Federico II tipo 23; Corrado I tipi 50, 54; Manfredi tipi 65, 69 (Buttrey 1993).

Policoro (Matera), scavi nell'area dell'acropoli di Eraclea: Federico II tipo 31. Un gruzzolo di 8 denari tornesi della Grecia franca da una tomba (Hunsel 1973).

'Salento' (Lecce), vari ritrovamenti nella regione: Federico II tipo 37; Corrado I, 54; Carlo I, 103 (Travaglini 1982).

Salerno/a, scavi nel castello: Corrado I tipo 49; Corradino tipo 55. Un denaro di Melgueil, un tornese di Chiarenza (Libero Mangieri 1986).

Salerno/b, scavi nella chiesa di S. Salvatore de Fondaco: denari di Corrado I tipo 49; Manfredi tipo 65; Carlo I tipi 88, 97 e 100, non descritti in dettaglio ed identificati grazie ai disegni nella tavola (Peduto 1991).

San Sosti (Cosenza), in superficie: un denaro di Enrico VI tipo 4 (Tocci 1989: 111).

Satriano (Potenza) scavi: Federico II tipi 30, 35 (Kent 1970).

Selinunte (Trapani) scavi: Manfredi tipi 69, 70, 72, 78, 81, 82: Selinunte/a (Trasselli 1972); Selinunte/b (Tusa Cutroni 1958-9); Selinunte/c (Tusa Cutroni 1968; cfr. Travaini 1993: 134).

Sicilia, non precisabile: Federico II tipi 11, 17, 19 (D'Angelo 1979).

Bibliografia

Arslan, E.A. 1981. *Vibo Valentia 1970/2, Ripostigli monetari in Italia-Schede anagrafiche*, Milano.

Barone, N. 1926. 'La cedola per l'imposta ordinata da re Carlo I d'Angiò nel 1276 per la circolazione della nuova moneta di denari in terra d'Otranto', in *Studi di storia napoletana in onore di Michelangelo Schipa*, 127-139.

De Boe, G. 1965. 'Les monnaies (1962-63)', in *Ordona I, Les campagnes de 1962 et 1963*, ed. J. Mertens (Etudes de Philologie, d'Archèologie et d'Histoire Anciennes-Institut historique Belge de Rome, VIII), Bruxelles- Rome, 80-87.

Blackburn, M. 1986. 'The Welbourn (Lincs.) hoard 1980-82 of Aethelred II coins', *British Numismatic Journal* 55, 79-83.

Blancard, L. 1864. 'Des monnaies frappées en Sicile, au XIIIe siècle, par les suzerains de Provence', *Revue Numismatique* n.s. IX, 212-230, 294-231.

Bloesch, H. 1972. 'Münzen vom Monte Iato', *Schweizer Münzblätter*, 86, 33-37.

Bloesch, H. & Isler, H.P. 1975. 'Monte Iato: La quinta campagna di scavo', *Sicilia Archeologica*, 28-29, 29-38.

Bloesch, H. & Isler, H.P. 1976. 'Monte Iato: La sesta campagna di scavo', *Sicilia Archeologica*, 32, 9-23.

Bresc, H. 1986. *Un monde Médieterranéen: Economie et société en Sicile 1300-1450*, 2 volls (Bibliothèque de l'École Française d'Athènes et de Rome, 262), Rome.

Bresc-Bautier, G. 1984. 'Les monnaies', in *Brucato. Histoire et archéologie d'un habitat médiéval en Sicile*, ed. J.-M. Pesez, (Collection de l'Ecole Française de Rome, 78), vol. II, Roma, 473-496.

Buttrey, T. ed altri. 1989. *Morgantina Studies. II. Results of the excavations conducted at Morgantina by Princeton University, the University of Illinois, and the University of Virginia, The coins*, Princeton N.J.

Buttrey, T. 1993. 'The coins', in *The Sanctuary of Santa Venera at Paestum, I*, J. G. Pedley & M. Torelli (eds.) (Archeologia Perusina, 11), 251-259.

Cagiati, M. 1915. 'Le monete del re Manfredi nel Reame delle Due Sicilie', *Atti e Memorie dell'Istituto Italiano di Numismatica*, II, 229-256.

Cagiati, M. 1913, 1916. *Le monete del Reame delle Due Sicilie da Carlo I d'Angio' a Vittorio Emanuele II*, Napoli.

Canzanella, M.G. e altri, 1990. 'Entella. Relazione preliminare della campagna di scavo 1988', *Annali della Scuola Normale Superiore di Pisa. Classe di Lettere e Filosofia*, ser, 3, 20, 2-3, 429-552.

Catalli, F. 1971-72. 'Vita dei Medaglieri. Soprintendenza alle antichità delle provincie di Salerno, Avellino e Benevento', *Annali dell'Istituto Italiano di Numismatica*, 18-19, p. 314.

Cherubini, G. 1868. 'Rispostiglio di monete dei bassi tempi', *Periodico di Numismatica e Sfragistica*, I, 88-95.

Cocchiaro, A., Marinazzo, A. & Travaglini, A. 1990. 'Monete dagli scavi di Brindisi (1984-88)', *Annali dell'Istituto Italiano di Numismatica*, 37, 81-133.

Cuozzo, E. 1989. 'L'unificazione normanna e il regno normanno-svevo', in *Storia del Mezzogiorno II, Il medioevo*, 2, Napoli, 593-785.

Curtotti, A. 1970. 'Il tesoro di Montescaglioso (Matera)', *Bollettino Storico della Basilicata* 5, 181-191.

D'Angelo, F. 1979. 'Denari bucati di Federico II di Sicilia', *Archeologia Medievale*, VI, 367-370.

D'Angelo, F. 1984. *Aspetti della vita materiale in epoca normanna in Sicilia*, Palermo.

D'Angelo, F. 1992. 'Un denaro inedito di Carlo I d'Angiò', in *Studi sulla Sicilia Occidentale in onore di Vincenzo Tusa*, Padova, 39-40.

Dell'Erba, L. 1929. 'La monetazione sveva nell'Italia meridionale ed in Sicilia', *Bollettino del Circolo Numismatico Napoletano*, 7-100.

Di Capua, M. 1983. 'Vita dei Medaglieri. Rinvenimenti monetali nel Castello di Bari', *Annali dell'Istituto Italiano di Numismatica*, 30, 181-194.

Du Quesne Bird, N. & Metcalf, D. 1979-81. 'The Tyre hoard and other finds from the time of the Crusades', *Hamburger Beiträge zur Numismatik*, 33/35, 55-61.

Foresio, G. 1891-93. *Le monete delle zecche di Salerno*, 2 voll., Salerno (rist. an. Salerno 1988).

Galasso, G. 1992. 'Il regno di Napoli. Il Mezzogiorno angioino e aragonese (1266-1494)', *Storia d'Italia* diretta da Giuseppe Galasso, vol. XV, I, Torino.

Garufi, C.A. 1898. 'Monete e conii nella storia del diritto siculo dagli arabi ai Martini', *Archivio Storico Siciliano*, n.s. 23, 7-171.

Grierson, P. 1992. 'The Coinages of Norman Apulia and Sicily in their International Setting', *Anglo-Norman Studies* XV, 117-132.

Guzzetta, G. 1980-1. 'Rinvenimenti monetali da Marina di Recanati (Naxos)', *Annali dell'Istituto Italiano di Numismatica*, 27-28, 259-286.

Hänsel, B., 1973, 'Policoro (Matera). Scavi eseguiti nell'area dell'acropoli di Eraclea negli anni 1965-1967', *Notizie degli Scavi di Antichità*, 415-491.

Huillard-Broholles, J.L.A. 1852-61. *Historia Diplomatica Friderici II*, Paris.

Isler, H.P. 1984. 'Monte Iato. Quattordicesima campagna di scavo', *Sicilia Archeologica*, 56, 5-23.

Isler, H.P. 1987. 'Monte Iato: La diciassettesima campagna di scavo', *Sicilia Archeologica*, 65, 11-24.

Kent, J.P.C.,1970. in D. Whitehouse, 'Excavations at Satriano: a deserted medieval settlement in Basilicata', *Papers of the British School at Rome*, 38, 188-219.

Libero Mangieri, G. 1985-8. 'La villa romana di Minori: il dato numismatico', *Apollo, Bollettino dei Musei provinciali del Salernitano*, VI, 165-194.

Libero Mangieri, G. 1986. 'Gruzzoli di monete medievali e moderne rinvenuti nel castello di Salerno', *Bollettino di Numismatica*, 6-7, 205-230.

Marks von Marksfeld, J. 1858. *Vierzig Münzen der Normannen, Hohenstaufen und Anjou in Sizilien und Neapel von 1166 bis 1309*, Milano.

Matzke, M. 1993. 'Der denar von Lucca als Kreuzfahrermünze', *Schweizerische Münzblatter*, 43, 36–44.

Mazzarese Fardella, E. 1966. *Aspetti dell'organizzazione amministrativa dello stato normanno e svevo*, Milano.

Mazzoleni, J. (ed.) 1969. *I registri della Cancelleria Angioina*, vol. XXII, Napoli.

Metcalf, D.M. 1986. 'Ritrovamenti di monete del regno di Sicilia negli stati crociati d'Oriente', *Bollettino di Numismatica*, 6–7, 81–84.

Minieri Riccio, C. 1878. *Saggio di Codice Diplomatico*, I, Napoli.

Pancari, G. 1982. 'Sul denaro di Costanza d'Altavilla con Federico II e di un tipo di denaro inedito della minorità di Federico', *La Numismatica*, (aprile), 95–97.

Peduto, P. 1991. 'Il gruzzolo del S. Salvatore de Fondaco a Salerno: follari, tarì, denari del secolo XI', *Rassegna Storica Salernitana*, n.s. 8, 33–71.

Peduto, P. 1993. 'Considerazioni su di un nuovo catalogo delle emissioni della zecca di Salerno', *Rassegna Storica Salernitana*, n.s. X.1, 217–225.

Rovelli, A. & Gourdin, P. 1987. 'Le monete', in *Fiorentino, campagne di scavo 1984-1985*, a cura di M.S.Calò Mariani, Galatina, 47–48.

Runciman, S. 1976. *I Vespri siciliani*, trad. ital. Milano.

Sambon, A. 1896. 'Les deniers Siciliens de billon', *Annuaire de la Sociète de Numismatique*, Paris, 209–232, 333–365.

Sambon, A. c. 1916. *Normanni, Svevi, Angioini* (s.l.s.d.).

Scheers, S. & Bex, Fl, 1974. 'Les monnaies trouvées durant les campagnes de 1964 à 1968', in *Ordona IV. Rapports et Etudes*, ed. J. Mertens (Etudes cit., XV), Bruxelles-Rome, 105–137.

Scheers, S. & van Heesch, J. 1988. 'Les monnaies trouvées durant les campagnes de 1972 à 1986', in *Ordona VIII. Rapports et Etudes*, ed. J. Mertens, Centre Belge de Recherches archeologiques en Italie centrale et meridionale, (Etudes cit., XXV), Bruxelles – Rome, 229–293.

Spahr, R. 1976. *Le monete siciliane dai bizantini a Carlo I d'Angiò (582-1282)*, Zurich-Graz.

Spufford, P. 1988. *Money and its Use in Medieval Europe*, Cambridge.

Suchodolski, S. 1961. '*Renovatio monetae* in Poland in the 12th century', *Polish Numismatic News* (Supplemento a Wiadomosci Numismaticzne, V), 57–75.

Tocci, O. 1980. *La Calabria nord-occidenatle dai Goti ai Normanni. Insediamenti e vie di comunicazione*, Cosenza.

Trasselli, C. 1972. 'Selinunte medievale', *Sicilia Archeologica*, V, 17, 45–53.

Travaglini, A. 1976-7. 'Vita dei Medaglieri. Museo Provinciale di Brindisi', *Annali dell'Istituto Italiano di Numismatica*, 23–24, 259–272.

Travaglini, A. 1982. *Inventario dei rinvenimenti monetali del Salento. Problemi di circolazione*, Roma.

Travaglini, A. 1992. 'Le monete', in *Excavations at Otranto, volume II: The Finds*, ed. F. D'Andria & D. Whitehouse, Galatina, 241–278.

Travaini, L. 1984. 'Le monete di Capaccio Vecchia: Campagne di scavo 1974, 1975, 1976, 1977, 1978', in A. Buko e altri, *Caputaquis Medievale, II, Ricerche 1974-1989*, Salerno, 357–374.

Travaini, L. 1988. 'Mint organisation in Italy between the XIIth and XIVth centuries: a survey', in *Later Medieval Mints: Organisation, Administration, Techniques*, The 8th Oxford Symposium on Coinage and Monetary History, ed. N.J. Mayhew & P. Spufford, (BAR, int. ser. 389), Oxford, 39–60.

Travaini, L. 1991. 'I denari tornesi nella circolazione monetaria dell'Italia meridionale tra XIII e XV secolo, in *Ermanno A. Arslan Studia Dicata*, Glaux 7, Milano, III, 711–726.

Travaini, L. 1992. 'Miliarenses e grossi argentei: una identificazione errata?', *Bullettino dell'Istituto Storico Italiano per il Medioevo*, 98, 383–94.

Travaini, L. 1993. 'Hohenstaufen and Angevin denari of Sicily and Southern Italy: their mint attributions', *Numismatic Chronicle* 153, 91–135.

Travaini, L. 1994. 'Zecche e monete nello stato federiciano', in *Federico II e il mondo mediterraneo*, Palermo, 146–164.

Travaini, L. 1995. *La monetazione nell'Italia normanna*, (Istituto Storico Italiano per il Medio Evo, Nuovi Studi Storici 28), Roma.

Tucci, U. 1990. 'Le comunicazioni terrestri e marittime', in *Le Italie del tardo medioevo*, a cura di S. gensini, Pisa, 121–141.

Tusa Cutroni, A. 1958-9, e 1968. 'Vita dei Medaglieri. Soprintendenza alle Antichità per le Province di Palermo e di Trapani', *Annali dell'Istituto Italiano di Numismatica*, 5–6, 306–318, e 15, 190–225.

Winkelmann, E. (ed.) 1880. *Acta Imperii Inedita*, Innsbruck, I, 763–765, no. 1002.